WHO'S WHO IN IRELAND

THE INFLUENTIAL IRISH

lack Blackshaw Blake Blaney Blood Bodley Bohan Boland Bolger Bolton Boorman Bouchier-Hayes Bourke Bowe Bow
Breslin Brett Brighton Britton Brophy Brosnan Brough Brown Browne Brunker Bruton Buckely Budd Buggy Bulb
Callanan Cally Callery Campbell Canavan Canny Carberry Carey Carney Carson Casari Cashman Cassells Cass
Clune Coady Cody Coen Coffey Cogan Coghlan Coleman Colgan Collier Collins Colton Comyn Concannon Con
osgrave Costelloe Costigan Coughlan Coulson Coulter Coveney Cowen Cowley Cowman Coyle Craig Crawford Cree
cy Dalgarno Daly Danaher Dardis Avern Davis Davison De Blacam De Bri De Bromhead De Bruin De Brún De Burgh
en Dobson Doherty Donleavy Donlon Donnelly Donoghue Donovan Dooley Doorley Dorgan Douglas Downer Dow
Megan Empey English Ennis Enright Erwin Evans Fahey Faithfull Fallon Fanning Farrell Fay Feeney Fegan Fehilly F
bon Fitzpatrick Flanagan Flannery Flavin Fleming Fleming Flood Flynn Foley Forde Fox Foyle French Friday Friel Fu
igan Gilmore Gilsenan Gleeson Glynn Goan Godsil Goggin Good Goodman Gordan Gorman Goulding Graham Gra
rafin Hanahoe Hanley Hanlon Hardiman Harding Haren Harney Harrington Harris Harvey Haslett Hastings Haug
Heneghan Hennessy, Henry Heraty Herbst Hession Hewson Hickey Higgins Hilditch Hill Hillery Hinfelaar Hobbs Ho
nd Hynes Inchiquin Ioakimides Irwin Jackson Jennings Jewell Johnson Jones Jordan Jorgensen Joyce Juncosa Kane Kavan
Keohane Kerins Kerr Kett Keyes Kiberd Kielty Kiely Kierans Kiernan, Kilcullen Kilduf Kilkenny Killeen Killian Kilroy K
Leyden Lillingston Linehan Liston Lloyd Weber Logan Logue Looney Loughrey Luke Lundberg Lynch Lyons Lysaght L
ier Maguire Maher Mallaghan Mallin Malone Maloney Manahan Mannion Mansergh Mansfield Mara Marren Ma
Carthy Mc Clarty Mc Clean Mc Closkey Mc Colgan Mc Cormack Mc Coubrey Mc Coy Mc Cracken Mc Creery Mc Cre
Mc Gann Mc Garry Mc Geady Mc Geary Mc Gee Mc Ginley Mc Gonagle Mc Govern Mc Gowan Mc Grattan Mc Guck
hlin Mc Manus Mc Namara Mc Nicholas Mc Redmond Mc Sharry Mc Verry Mc Williams McAlinden McGuckian McMa
gue Moore Moran Moriarty Morrice Morris Morrissey Morrisson Mortell Mountjoy Moylan Moynes Mulcahy Muld
e Nash Nathan Naughton Neill Nellis Nelson Newman Ní Bhraináin Ní Bhraonáin Ní Chulleanáin Ni Dhomhnaill Ní R
bhghaill Ó Fiannachta Ó Gallchóir Ó Hailpín Ó Muircheartaigh Ó Neachtain Ó Seireadáin Ó Snodaigh O'Buach
uiv O'Donnell O'Donoghue O'Donovan O'Driscoll O'Duinn O'Dwyer O'Faolain O'Gara O'Hagan O'Halloran O'H
dan O'Rorke O'Rourke O'Shea O'Suilleabhain O'Sullivan O'Toole O'Herlihy Oliver Orde Ormonde Osborne Owens O
Ponsonby Powell Power Prasifka Pratt Prendergast Prenderville Preston Prior Proud Purcell Puri Pye Queally Quigley Q
he Rochford Rogers Rohan Rolfe Ronan Rooney Rosney Ross Rosse Rothwell Russell Ryall Ryan Sargent Saunders Scan
dan Sherry Shipsey Shortall Shovlin Sinnott Sisk Sligo Smith Smithwick Smullen Smurfit Smyth Somers Sparks Spil
tton Taylor Teehan Teeling Telford Territt Tighe Timmins Todd Toib Í N Treacy Trethowan Trevor Trimble Tubridy Tu
Whelan Whelehan Whitaker White Whyte Williams Woods Woodworth Wrixon Zotto Abbott Abercorn Abrahams Ache
deley Bailey Baker Ballagh Ballintine Ballyedmond Banville Bardwell Barrett Barrington Barry Bartels Barton Bates
Bohan Boland Bolger Bolton Boorman Bouchier-Hayes Bourke Bowe Bowler Bowman Boyce Boyd Boylan Boyle Brads
Brough Brown Browne Brunker Bruton Buckely Budd Buggy Bulbulia Bunnburdon Burke Burns Burnside Burrows Bu
Carberry Carey Carney Carson Casari Cashman Cassells Cassidy Cavanagh Cawley Chadwick Chawke Chesneau Ch
Colgan Collier Collins Colton Comyn Concannon Condell Connell Connelly Connolly Conroy Considine Conway Co
ney Cowen Cowley Cowman Coyle Craig Crawford Creedon Cronin Crookshank Crosbie Cross Crowley Crown Cro
De Blacam De Bri De Bromhead De Bruin De Brún De Burgh De Paor De Rossa De Valera De Vere-White Deane Dele
noghue Donovan Dooley Doorley Dorgan Douglas Downer Downey Doyle Drew Drumm Drury Duffy Duggan Da
hey Faithfull Fallon Fanning Farrell Fay Feeney Fegan Fehilly Fenn Fennelly Fenner Ferran Ferris Fewer Fiacc Filan
leming Flood Flynn Foley Forde Fox Foyle French Friday Friel Fuller Furness Gaffney Gageby Gallagher Galvin Gal
il Goggin Good Goodman Gordan Gorman Goulding Graham Gratzer Gray Greene Greenslade Greevy Gregory G
ng Haren Harney Harrington Harris Harvey Haslett Hastings Haughey Haughton Haverty Hayes Healy Heaney He
n Hewson Hickey Higgins Hilditch Hill Hillery Hinfelaar Hobbs Hoctor Hogan Holland Hollywood Holman Hooper
s Jewell Johnson Jones Jordan Jorgensen Joyce Juncosa Kane Kavanagh Kean Keane Kearney Kearns Keating Keaveney Ke
Kierans Kiernan, Kilcullen Kilduf Kilkenny Killeen Killian Kilroy King Kinsella Kitt Knuttle Kürten, Lally Lanigan La
Logan Logue Looney Loughrey Luke Lundberg Lynch Lyons Lysaght Mac Cann Mac Conghaill Mac Entee Mac Mena
loney Manahan Mannion Mansergh Mansfield Mara Marren Marren Marrinan Quinn Marshall Martin Maughan Ma
n Mc Cormack Mc Coubrey Mc Coy Mc Cracken Mc Creery Mc Creevy Mc Cullough Mc Dolald Mc Donagh Mc Do
Gee Mc Ginley Mc Gonagle Mc Govern Mc Gowan Mc Grattan Mc Guckian Mc Guinness Mc Guire Mc Hugh Mc Kee
c Redmond Mc Sharry Mc Verry Mc Williams McAlinden McGuckian McManus Meade Meagher Mealy Mee Miller Mi
is Morrissey Morrisson Mortell Mountjoy Moylan Moynes Mulcahy Muldoon Mulhern Mullen Mulligan Mullin
on Newman Ní Bhraináin Ní Bhraonáin Ní Chulleanáin Ni Dhomhnaill Ní Riain Ni Shuilleabháin Nickerson Nolan No
uircheartaigh Ó Neachtain Ó Seireadáin Ó Snodaigh O'Buachalla O'Cuinneagáin O'Dea O'Donoghue O'Driscoll O'F
Duinn O'Dwyer O'Faolain O'Gara O'Hagan O'Halloran O'Hara O'Hare O'Higgins O'Kane O'Kelly O'Loan O'Ma
ivan O'Toole O'Herlihy Oliver Orde Ormonde Osborne Owens Oxx Paisley Parker Parkhill Parlon Parsons Patterson
nderville Preston Prior Proud Purcell Puri Pye Queally Quigley Quin Quinlan Quinlivan Quinn Quirk Rabbitte Rapple
ney Ross Rosse Rothwell Russell Ryall Ryan Sargent Saunders Scanlon Schmidt Scott Scott-Lennon Née Fitzpatrick
ligo Smith Smithwick Smullen Smurfit Smyth Somers Sparks Spillane Spring Stafford Stagg Standún Stapleton

WHO'S WHO IN IRELAND

THE INFLUENTIAL IRISH

EDITED BY ANGELA A. PHELAN

© Madison Publications Limited 2006

British Library Cataloguing in Publication Data
ACIP catalogue record for this book is available from the British Library

ISBN   0-9518728-3-4   978-0-9518728-3-3

First published in 2006
by
Madison Publications Limited
Adelaide Hall, 3 Adelaide Street,
Dun Laoghaire, Co. Dublin, Ireland

Publisher: Kevin Kelly
Editor: Angela Phelan
Production: Kevin Gurry
Design: First Impression

Printed and bound by
MCC Graphics

CONTENTS

IRELAND

CONTENTS

IRISH AMERICA

ACKNOWLEDGEMENTS

Tom Cullen

Rachel O'Kane

Bernie O'Sullivan

Brendan Herlihy

FOREWORD

What a difference little over half a decade makes. Ireland is virtually unrecognizable as the same country since the last edition of this book was published in 1999; Any attempt to provide a definitive listing of Ireland's most influential people right now is like trying to catch hold of quicksilver. Everything is changing by the nano second and influential people are emerging in just about every walk of life all the time. However amidst all this change the one constant remains the people of Ireland, its richest resource. Their genius, their capacities, their energy and their great qualities of eternal optimism is made manifest within these pages. This is not another Rich List, rather it is a list of the richness of Ireland, and the multitalented men and women who influence it and make it what it is today, one of the most successful economies in the world.

Nowhere has this change been more evident than in the world of property development,where home grown Irish men are now successfully spreading their empires all over the world. The IT sector has continued to expand with many of the early pioneers are now successful international venture capitalists. And while Irish Medical Services are held in low esteem by the general public, the country now boasts a number of world experts in their particular specialty and a pioneering medical entrepreneur, James Sheehan, also an internationally acclaimed engineer and orthopedic surgeon.

One of the changes reflected here is the increasing influence of women in every walk of life. We have a wonderful woman as President of Ireland, and until recently a formidable Tánaiste (deputy Prime Minister). The Hon Mrs Susan Denham is one of three women who sit on the Supreme Court. There are women Ombudsmen, one of the country's top telecom company's has a woman chief executive; a young woman manages one of the country's race tracks; there are female leading academics, a university president, barristers, medical consultants and a host of supremely successful businesswomen. A number of pioneering women have shattered the glass ceiling in the Civil Service to become Secretaries General of top Government departments.

Another significant change from the last edition is the number of people recording legal separations, divorces, 2nd and 3rd marriages and same sex partnerships.

The rich tapestry that is contemporary, colourful Ireland stitches together John Banville an international literary award winner, Louis le Brocquy, internationally acclaimed painter and at ninety the oldest person in the book, Cecilia Ahern, best selling author and at 24 the youngest woman, author and entry in the book, her father, Taoiseach Bertie Ahern, who has presided over the Celtic Tiger economy, magnificent sportspeople like Cork hurler Sean Óg Ó hAlpín, genius racehorse trainer Aidan O'Brien and champion jockeys Ruby Walsh and Nina Carbery.

In the international world of science, Tipperary born scientist Louis Ronan's biotechnology company was the first worldwide to develop a rapid test screening system for BSE while influential clerics Fr Alex Reid and Rev Harold Good OBE , indefatigable workers to bring peace witnessed that, beyond any shadow of doubt, the arms of the IRA have now been decommissioned. Roman Catholic priests, brothers, Jack and Aengus Finucane have spent a life time toiling for the Third World's disadvantaged since they set up the worldwide charity Concern. They are among a rich vein of committed men and women, who at a time of unprecedented wealth in Ireland still concentrate on the less well off here at home and abroad and make a very significant difference.

Of course people of Irish origin have long wielded influence abroad. This is manifest from the extraordinary success of the Irish in the United States, where some 45 million now claim Irish ancestry. Of note are the Irish born, internationally recognized surgeons like Dr Patrick Boland of Memorial Sloan Kettering, scientists like John O Ryan of Macrovision, California, Supreme Court Judge, Jennifer Anderson, Hollywood actors Colin Farrell and Pierce Brosnan, Academy Award winning make up artist Michèle Burke and Wall Street's top boardrooms boasts Irish and Irish American CEO's. These too have been chronicled.

All data for this book was either obtained from the individuals or from material in the public domain.

My sincerest thanks for his major contribution go to my editorial assistant Ciarán MacGonigal whose energy, commitment and good humour never wavered. I greatly appreciate the welcome I got in the top boardrooms throughout Ireland and US where Captains and Kings of Industry were so generous with their time. Thank you also to the leading academics, sportsmen and women and members of the Clergy. In addition thanks goes to the many top medical consultants, 'legal eagles', politicians, bankers, diplomats and civil servants for their enthusiasm and contributions. Finally thank you to publisher Kevin Kelly for commissioning me to work on such an exciting project and to his PA Colette O'Brien for her endless cooperation. Part of the excitement of contemporary Ireland means a book like this is never finished, it is but a snapshot in time and will always have to be a work in progress.

Angela Phelan

14 October 2006

ABBOTT, The Hon. Mr Justice, Henry; HIGH COURT JUDGE
b 1947, Mullingar, Westmeath; *m* Pauline Heffernan; 1*s* 3*d*; *edu.* St. Mary's, Mullingar; Franciscan College, Gormanstown, Co. Westmeath; University College Dublin; King's Inns; BA (Economics); Barrister at Law; Judge of the High Court; Called to the Bar 1972; General Election unsuccessful candidate (FF Longford/Westmeath) 1977; Member Westmeath Co. Council (Mullingar/Lough Owel) 1979-2000; Member 25th Dáil (FF Longford/Westmeath) 1987-'89; Member Joint Oireachtas committee on Women's Rights 1987-'89; Member VEC Westmeath; Director Midlands Region Tourism Organization 1985; Member Midlands Regional Development Organization 1980-'81; PRO World Youth Coarse Angling Championships Midlands 1987; Member Midlands Angling Organization; Dáil Select Committee Judicial Separation and Family Law Reform Act 1989; called to the Inner Bar 1992; Senior Counsel; appointed to the High Court 2002; Judge of the High Court 2002 to date. Recreations: GAA, coarse angling. Contact: High Court, Dublin 7. **T** 01 888 6000 www.courts.ie

> Has been an important advocate/judge for family law, women's rights and the law concerning children; has delivered some important judgements relating to the public's right to know and in matters relating to judicial separation.

ABERCORN K.G., His Grace, Duke of, James, Hamilton; PEER, LANDOWNER, BOARD MEMBER
b 1934; *m* Anastasia, Alexandra née Phillips (*qv*); 2*s*.1*d*; *edu.* Eton College; Royal Agricultural School, Cirencester; Duke, (*cr.*1868), Knight of the Garter, Lord Lieutenant, Lord Steward of HM's Household; joined army Lt. Grenadier Guards 1952; MP Fermanagh & South Tyrone (Unionist) 1964-'70; director Northern Bank 1970-'97; Chairman Laganside Development Corporation 1989-'96; Director Northern Ireland Development Board 1982-'87; Council of Europe 1968-'70; European Economic and Social Committee 1973-'78; President Royal UK Beneficent Association 1979 to date; Patron Royal Ulster Agricultural Association 1990-'96; President Buildings Society Association 1986-'92; Trustee Winston Churchill Memorial Hons Trust 1991-2001; Col Irish Guards 2000; High Sheriff, Co. Tyrone 1970; LL.B (QUB) 1997; Lord Lieutenant Co. Tyrone 1987; Knight of the Garter 1999; Lord Steward HM's Household 2001 to date; Member of the Board of Governors and Guardians The National Gallery of Ireland 2003 to date. Clubs: Brooks, London. Recreations: shooting, skiing. Contact: Barons Court, Omagh, Northern Ireland BT78 4EZ. **T** 028 8166 1470 **F** 028 8166 2231

> The only Irish resident Duke, a great landowner and a Northern Ireland grandee: although the position is much reduced from 19th century days, he remains a powerful background figure; very much an establishment figure in royal household terms and in certain Irish social circles; appointed by the Irish government to the board of the National Gallery.

ABERCORN, Her Grace, Duchess of, Anastasia Alexandra, 'Sacha' née Phillips; HEAD, PUSHKIN PRIZE FOUNDATION
b 1946, Arizona, USA; *m* James Hamilton, Duke of Abercorn KG (*qv*); 2*s*.1*d*; *edu.* D. Litt (*hc*) 2003; founded the Pushkin Prize in honour of her ancestor, the great Russian writer, Alexander Pushkin, in 1987. As an all-Ireland writing project this has been a great success in the context of bridging the sectarian and political educational divide in Ireland: the Pushkin project has been integrated in elements of cross-border peace and reconciliation and other pieces of social engineering in Northern Ireland. Has restored the interior of the Abercorn family seat at Barons Court, and utilises the building complex for a wide range of social, cultural and inter-personal development courses. Contact: Pushkin Prize Office, Barons Court, Omagh, Northern Ireland BT78 4EZ. **T** 028 8166 1470 **F** 028 8166 2231

> A widely respected cultural ambassador; has also secured the future of the family home and contributes in many ways to the life of the Province; like her husband she is a professional courtier at the royal court in London; she enjoys the company of artists, horsemen, clergy and writers.

ABRAHAMS, Declan; MASTER BESPOKE TAILOR
b 1958, London; *m* Tania Keane; 2*d*; *edu.* Terenure College, Dublin; Sandford Park School, Ranelagh, Dublin; Managing Director, Abrahams Bespoke Tailors; Responsible for developing family tailoring business into one of the major specialist menswear retailers in Dublin; Has introduced many of the now famous international brands to Ireland including Cerruti, Faconnable, Zegna; also developed with Italian partners own ready-to-wear suit brand, now one of the top selling suit collections. Clubs:

Merrion Cricket Club, Edmondstown Golf Club, ex-Wanderers Rugby Club. Recreations: cricket, rugby, golf, aviation. Contact: 17 Sth Anne Street, Dublin. **T** 01 677 0167 **F** 01 6770000 email dec@menswear.ie

A discreet bespoke tailor for the country's discerning, sartorially elegant and very private businessmen; impeccable, restrained yet opulent sense of style.

ACHESON, Carrie, née Barlow; COMPANY DIRECTOR
b 1934, Tipperary; *m* Hugh Acheson; 1*s*; *edu*. Presentation Convent, Clonmel; Mercy Convent, Carlow; London School of Business Studies; Company Director; TD (FF South Tipperary) 1981-'82; former Mayor of Clonmel; former Alderman Clonmel Borough Council; served on Tipperary South Riding Co. Council 1974-'81; Member: I.M.I.; Director Irish Shipping Ltd. 1980-'81. Clubs: Clonmel GAA. Recreations: GAA. Contact: Western Lodge, Clonmel, Co. Tipperary. **T** 052 25560

Member of the well-known Barlow family of Clonmel and sister of former Senator Treas Honan; now the voice of the National Ploughing Association at the annual ploughing championships; bright, articulate and very fashion conscious, famous for her chapeaux.

Gerry Adams

ADAMS, Gerard, 'Gerry'; PUBLIC REPRESENTATIVE/PRESIDENT SINN FEIN
b 1948, Belfast; *m* Colette McArdle; 1*s*; *edu*. St Finian's Primary School, Belfast; St. Mary's Christian Brothers School, Belfast; M.P.; President Sinn Féin; Member of Parliament (Belfast West) 1997 to date; joined the Republican movement 1964; interned 1971; rearrested; released 1976; Member Northern Ireland Assembly 1982; leader of Sinn Féin 1983 to date; Elected Westminster MP (Provisional SF, West Belfast) 1983; Hume-Adams Agreement which played a key part in the adoption of the peace strategy by the Republican movement 1993; Elected to NI Forum 1996; Thorr Award Switzerland 1996. *Publ. Falls Memories*, autobiography 1982; *Politics of Irish Freedom* 1988; *Pathway to Peace*; *Cage Eleven*, autobiography 1990; *The Street and Other Stories* 1992; *Selected writings* 1994; *Before The Dawn*, autobiography 1996; *An Irish Voice, the Quest For Peace* 1997; *An Irish Journal* 2001; Contact: Sinn Féin, 55 Falls Road, Belfast BT12. 4PD; Teach Seosamh MacGiolla Buí, 51/53 Falls Road, Belfast BT12 4PD. **T** 049 9022 3000 **F** 048 9022 5553

Took the constitutional path to peace in 1996 and caused a split in Sinn Féin as a result; along with John Hume, successive Taoisigh, British prime ministers and US president Bill Clinton, he has been a central figure in the evolution of the peace process in Northern Ireland which resulted in the final decommissioning of arms by the IRA in September 2005; a razor sharp intellect, highly articulate, a superb TV performer, Adams is seen by many, especially in the US, as the acceptable face of Sinn Féin/ IRA; cynics argue that he's moved the motto from tiocfaidh ár lá to tiocfaidh Armani, a reflection on his sartorial elegance.

AGAR, David; COMMERICAL PROPERTY CONSULTANT, ACQUISITION & DEVELOPMENT
b 1960, Dublin; *m* 1st Gina (*decd*); 2*s* ; 2nd Rachel Brown; 1*d*; *edu*. St. Andrew's College, Booterstown, Dublin; Commercial Property Consultant, Acquisition and Development; Recreations: golf, travel, flying. Contact: Suite One, The Mall, Beacon Court, Sandyford, Dublin 18. **T** 01 213 7777 **F** 01 213 7778 email agar@iol.ie www.agar.ie

The Dublin estate agent has developed a good market share in the highly competitive auctioneering business; one of the newer property boys, well known for his high profile involvement in the Tiger Trust Charity which he set up in memory of his late, first wife Gina.

AGNEW, David; MUSICIAN
b 1960, Dublin; *m* Adele King (Twink) (*qv*); separated; 2*d*; *p* Ruth Hickey; 1*s*; *edu*. University College Dublin; College of Music, Dublin; Trinity College, London; B.Sc. M.Sc. Botany LTCL; Musician/Oboeist; Heinz Holliger, Maurice Bourgue International Master Classes, London, Paris, Avignon, Cologne; joined RTE Concert Orchestra 1982. Publ: *Music of The Night* 1989; *The Way I Feel* 1992; *Celtic Moods* 1996; *A Celtic Christmas* 1997; *Pure Moods* 1998; Celtic Music Series licensed in US 2000; *Hearts Quest* 2001; recorded with The Chieftains, Phil Coulter, Frank Patterson; The Original *Riverdance, Lord of The Dance*; Contact: RTE Symphony Orchestra, Montrose, Dublin 4. **T** 01 208 3111 email oboeking.com

The gifted musician has finally emerged from the shadow of his high-profile, estranged wife Adele King, 'Twink'; is recognized in his own right as the finest classical oboeist in Ireland;

AHERN, Bertie; PUBLIC REPRESENTATIVE/ TAOISEACH
b 1951, Dublin; *m* Miriam Kelly; separated; 2*d*; *edu.* St. Patrick's National School; St. Aidan's CBS, Whitehall, Dublin; College of Commerce, Rathmines, Dublin; University College Dublin; Taoiseach; Dublin District Milk Board 1969-'74; Accountant Mater Hospital 1974-'77; elected to Dail (FF Dublin Finglas) 1977 and re-elected to date; Assistant Chief Whip 1980-'81; Party Spokesman on Youth 1991; Minister of State at the Department of the Taoiseach and Defence March-December 1982 and Government Chief Whip; Minister for Labour 1987; former Member of Dublin County Council; Lord Mayor of Dublin 1986-'87; Director of Election for Brian Lenihan's Presidential campaign 1990. Leader of the FF Party 1994; Leader of the Opposition 1994-'97; Taoiseach and leader of Fianna Fáil 1997 to date; President European Council January-June 2004; Former member Board of Governors, IMF, World Bank, EIB (Chairman, 1991-'92), 1991-'94; Recipient, Grand Cross of the Order of Merit with Star and Sash, (Germany) 1993; The Stara Planina (Bulgaria) 2005. Recreations: sports, reading, gardening. Contact: Office of the Taoiseach, Government Buildings, Upper Merrion Street, Dublin 2. **T** 01 662 4888 **F** 01 6764048 email taoiseach@taoiseach.gov.ie web www.taoiseach.gov.ie

Bertie Ahern

The truest blue Dub, Ahern is also very proud of his South West Cork roots where both his parents hailed from and where he spent many happy summers; achieved his long held ambition when he became the youngest Taoiseach in Irish history in 1997; his political legacy will include Social Partnership, the Good Friday Agreement, the ongoing fuelling of the Celtic Tiger economic miracle, which has transformed Ireland into one of the most dynamic economies in the world. perhaps history will record as his greatest achievement the delivery of the ultimate, glittering prize – peace in our land – with the IRA finally laying down arms in September 2005; a widely respected and admired leader of Fianna Fáil; makes much of his man-in-the-street approach which disguises the steely determination of his political stance – what you see is much less than what you get; still haunted by his mentor the late CJ Haughey's alleged assessment of him as 'the most skilful, the most devious and most cunning of them all'; proving that he is more than a local politician, his achievements as EU President in 2004 saw him receive unanimous respect and kudos from all of the major world leaders.

Takes great pleasure and pride from the achievements of his two daughters, Georgina, married to Nicky Byrne (qv) of pop group Westlife, and Cecelia (qv) now an international best-selling author. He stands on the brink of political greatness as he approaches the next general election when he will attempt to return Fianna Fáil as the main political party in the next government; has stated his intention to retire from active politics by age 60 (2011) and to pursue leisure activities including golf, more reading and even more gardening; however the cognoscenti predict he will pass the torch, or, in FF parlance, an cliabh solais, to his successor much sooner.

AHERN, Cecelia; AUTHOR
b 1982, Dublin; single; *edu.* Pobailscoil Neasáin, Baldoyle, Dublin; Griffith College, Dublin, Degree in Journalism and Media Communications; Author; *PS I Love You* was the highest-selling début book of 2004, reaching number one in Ireland and the UK, and also a bestseller in Europe and the US; second book *Where Rainbows End*, released the same year, achieved the same success; third book *If You Could See Me Now* due in November 2005; books have been sold in over 50 countries; seven figure Disney contract for latest book 2005; nominated for IMPAC award 2005. Contact: Marianne Gunne O'Connor, Morrisson Chambers, Suite 17, 32 Nassau Street, Dublin 2 **T** 01 677 9100 **F** 01 677 9101 email mgoclitagency@eircom.net web www.ceceliaahern.ie

Cecelia Ahern

At the tender age of 23, Bertie Ahern's (*qv*) younger daughter is an international best-selling novelist; very low profile, has her mother Miriam's good looks and remains very close to her only sister Georgina and to both parents; no sooner finished her journalism degree than her first novel was snapped up by Rupert Murdoch's HarperCollins for a seven-figure sum; it was announced at Cannes Film Festival 2006 that two time Oscar winner Hilary Swank will play the lead in movie version of PS I Love You which will be

directed by Richard LaGravanese and Wendy Finerman will be produce; proving she
was no one-hit wonder, her next two chick lit novels have also hit the number one spot
in several countries; now no big deal to see the Fifth Avenue New York windows of
Barnes and Noble devoted to the young Dublin author, who takes it all in her stride.

Dee Ahearn

AHEARN, Dee; MARKETING EXECUTIVE TREASURY HOLDINGS
b 1968, Tipperary; single; *p* Ciaran O'Donnell; 1*d*; *edu.* Convent of Mercy, Cahir,
Co. Tipperary; College for Distributive Trades, Leicester Square, London; Director Sales and
Marketing, Treasury Holdings; 8 years group marketing director the Gunne Group; Member Board of
Directors Gunne Residential; Member of Management Executive CB Richard Ellis Gunne;
Chairperson Make A Wish Foundation Ireland. Recreations: cars, shopping. Contact: Treasury
Holdings, 35, Barrow Street, Dublin 4. M 087 261 5944 email dahearn@treasuryholdings.ie

The energetic and elegant Treasury marketing executive is well respected in property
circles.

Dermot Ahern

AHERN, Dermot Chris; PUBLIC REPRESENTATIVE
b 1955, Drogheda, Co Louth; *m* Maeve Coleman; 2*d*; *edu.* Marist College Dundalk, University College
Dublin; Incorporated Law Society of Ireland 1973-'76; Bachelor of Civil Laws; Minister, Foreign
Affairs; Local Authority Councillor 1979-1991; elected to Dáil Éireann (FF) 1987 to date; Assistant
Government Chief Whip 1988-'91; Minister for State at Dept. of Taoiseach and Defence 1991-'92.
Minister for Social, Community and Family Affairs 1997-2002; Minister for Communications,
Marine and Natural Resources 2002-'04; Minister for Foreign Affairs 2004 to date. Recreations: all
sport, including wind surfing, swimming and golf. Contact: Dept. of Foreign Affairs, Iveagh House,
Dublin 2. **T** 01 478 0822 web www.foreignaffairs.gov.ie

Hard-working, highly ambitious, articulate minister who draws heavily on his legal
training to ensure that he achieves political correctness; sees himself as a serious
challenger for the top job when his namesake moves on to smell the roses – at least they
share one thing in common, their Cork roots; unlikely to become an eco warrior in
North County Dublin following his almost comic tree-climbing experiences in that area
in 1997; a civil servant's dream – a dull if safe pair of hands at the helm of Foreign
Affairs at a sensitive time.

AHERN, Michael; PUBLIC REPRESENTATIVE
b 1949, Dungourney, Co. Cork; *m* Margaret Monahan; 3*d*; edu. Dungourney NS, Co. Cork; Rockwell
College, Cashel, Co. Tipperary; University College Dublin; BA (Economics, Politics, Psychology);
Kimmage Manor, Dublin (Theology); Minister of State, Department of Enterprise, Trade and
Employment (FF); Secondary school teacher 1970-'72; Accountancy student, Coopers/Lybrand, Cork
1973-'77; Financial Controller, building construction firm, Cork 1977-'81; Principal of Registered
Audit & Accountancy Practice 1981-2000; First elected to the Dáil (FF Cork East) 1982; has retained
his seat to date; Minister of State at the Dept. of Enterprise, Trade and Employment with special
responsibility for Trade and Commerce 2002 to date. Contact: Dept. Trade and Employment, 23,
Kildare Street, Dublin 2. **T** 01 631 2121 **F** 01 631 2827

Son of the legendary Senator Liam Ahern (of 'bags of guns fame') and grand-nephew
of the late TD John Dineen; steeped in Fianna Fáil tradition, low profile, quietly spoken
Junior Minister.

AHERN, Noel; PUBLIC REPRESENTATIVE
b 1944, Dublin; *m* Helen Marnane; 2*s* 1*d*; *edu.* O'Connell School, CBS, Dublin; University College
Dublin; College of Commerce, Rathmines, Dublin (DPA, MCIT); Junior Minister Environment,
Heritage, Local Government and also Community, Rural and Gaeltacht Affairs; member of the
Cabinet Committee on Social Inclusion; first elected to the Dáil in 1992; Party Spokesperson on the
Environment with special responsibility for Housing 1994-'97; chairperson Oireachtas All-Party Dáil
Committee on Social Community & Family Affairs 1997-02; member Dublin City Council 1985-02;
former Chairperson of Housing and Traffic Committees and Chairperson of the North West Area
Committee 2001-'02; former Branch officer and member of National Executive of the Transport
Salaries Staffs Association; Minister of State at the Department of Environment and Local
Government, with responsibility for Housing and Urban Renewal, and at the Department of
Community, Rural and Gaeltacht Affairs with responsibility for Drugs Strategy and Community

Affairs 2002 to date. Contact: Department of Environment, Heritage and Local Government, Custom House, Dublin 1. **T** 01 8882591 **F** 01 878 6676 web www.environ.ie

> Quietly-spoken junior minister who does not possess the ease and charm of his legendary brother, Bertie Ahern (*qv*); unlikely to put a foot wrong and fiercely loyal to the same brother; despite influence at the top, unlikely to get 'the full car' ie. a seat at the Cabinet table.

Noel Ahern

AIKEN, James, 'Jim'; CONCERT PROMOTER
b 1932, Armagh; *m* Anne; 1*s* 4*d*; *edu*. St. Patrick's College, Armagh; Concert Promoter; Director, Aiken Promotions; Promoting music and events in Ireland for over 40 years. Recreations: horse racing, Gaelic football. Contact: Aiken Promotions, Vicar St, 58-59 Thomas St, Dublin 8. **T** 01 454 6656 **F** 01 454 6787 email jg@aikenpromotions.com

> One of the giants of show business in Ireland for nearly half a century; highly respected in a world populated with enormous egos; no mean feat.

AIKEN, Peter, Kevin; CONCERT PROMOTER
b 1961, Belfast; *m* Mary O'Shea; 2*s* 1*d*; *edu*. St Patrick's College, Armagh; Rathmore Grammar School, Belfast; University Of Ulster; qualified accountant; Managing Director Aiken Promotions; Concert Promoter 1983 to date. Clubs: Carryduff GAA Club. Recreations: sport. Contact: Aiken Promotions, Vicar St, 58-59, Thomas St, Dublin 8. **T** 01 454 6656 **F** 01 454 6787 email peter@aikenpromotions.com

Peter Aiken

> Followed in father Jim Aiken's (*qv*) footsteps, big shoes to fill; now one of top two concert promoters in Ireland; highly regarded; puts in the hours; good company, great raconteur, amusing; excellent relationship with top promoters in the UK and US; owns Vicar Street with Harry Crosbie (*qv*).

AIKINS, Kingsley; PRESIDENT AND CEO, AMERICAN IRELAND FUND AND THE IRELAND FUNDS
b 1951, Dublin, Ireland; *m* Claire Mc Donough;1*s* 2*bd*; *edu* The High School, Dublin, Trinity College Dublin, (economics); post-graduate Diploma, International Marketing; has studied and worked extensively in France and Spain; for five years he was the Sydney, Australia based representative of the Irish Trade Board and the Industrial Development Authority (IDA) of Ireland; ran his own marketing consultancy company; was also a founding director of The Australian Ireland Fund and for two years served as Executive Director responsible for the growth of the Fund in Australia and establishing The Ireland Fund of New Zealand; moved to Boston to take over as Executive Director of The American Ireland Fund, January, 1993 - 95; (The Fund was set up in 1976 and since then the Worldwide Ireland Funds have raised over $300 million for projects of Peace, Culture, Community Development and Education throughout the island of Ireland); appointed Chief Executive of the Worldwide Ireland Funds now active in 11 countries including Ireland, June 1995 - 2000; appointed President and CEO of The American Ireland Fund and The Ireland Funds, June 2000; was also responsible for the successful five-year 'Hope and History Campaign' to raise $100 million. Member, Institutes of Marketing, Export and Linguistics. Recreations: golf, swimming, cycling, music. Contact, 5, Foster Place, Dublin 2. **T** 01 662 7878 **F** 01 662 78 79 email KAikins@ irelfunds.org web www. irelfunds.org/ireland

> This personable Irishman has not only been a wonderful helmsman for the American Ireland Funds and the Ireland Fund, he has also been an outstanding ambassador for Ireland throughout the world; charming, pragmatic, a wonderful raconteur, has established the AIF and The Ireland Funds as one of the top philanthropic organizations in the world; highly respected and extremely popular on both sides of the Atlantic.

AKRAM, Yasmine; ACTOR
b 1981, Drogheda Co. Louth; single; *edu*. St. Oliver's Community College, Drogheda, Co. Louth; Royal Academy of Dramatic Art (RADA), London; BA Acting Degree; Actor; Drogheda Youth Theatre 1994; Calipo Theatre Company Primary School Drama Theatre 1996/'97/'99/2000/'02/'03; appeared in company productions; Film/TV; from 1999-2002 *Podge & Rodge, The Lounge, My Name Is Not Down* (Dept. of Education); *Planet Love* (music video); 2005 Bank of Ireland Millennial Scholar

Yasmine Akram

ship to RADA. Contact: 27, Parkway, Grangerath, Dublin Road, Drogheda Co. Louth.
email yasmineakram@yahoo.co.uk

This young actor is gifted and has terrific stage presence, clarity and articulation; her
interest in gender and race issues show in her acting preferences, but overall will make a
wonderful Shakespearian actor in a grand declamatory style.

ALDERDICE, Rt. Hon. LORD, John; PSYCHIATRIST, LIFE PEER
b 1955, Northern Ireland; *m* Joan Hill; 2*s* 1*d*; *edu.* Ballymena Academy; Queen's University of Belfast
and graduated MB, BCh, BAO (1978); MRC. Psych (1983); Fellow of the Royal College of
Psychiatrists (FRC.Psych) 1997; Honorary Fellow of the Royal College of Physicians of Ireland
(1997); Honorary Fellow of the Royal College of Psychiatrists and of the British Psychoanalytical
Society (2001); Psychiatrist/ Psychoanalyst; joined the Alliance Party in 1978; elected Party Leader
1987; elected to Belfast City Council 1989; elected to the new Northern Ireland Forum1996; led the
Alliance delegation there and in the multi-party talks chaired by US Senator George Mitchell; raised
to the peerage 1996; took his seat on the Liberal Democrat benches in the House of Lords 1996; was
one of the negotiators of the Belfast Agreement signed on Good Friday 1998; elected Executive
Member, Federation of European Liberal, Democrat and Reform Parties 1987; Treasurer 1995; Vice
President, ELDR 1999 to 2003; elected a Vice-President of Liberal International, the world-wide
federation of some 90 liberal political parties 1992; Deputy President 2000; President Liberal
International 2005; elected member Northern Ireland Assembly (Belfast East) 1998; resigned as
Leader of the Alliance Party 1998; appointed Speaker New Assembly 1998; retired 2004;
Commissioner Independent Monitoring Commission, 2004 to date; to avoid a conflict of interest he
took the decision to resign as Speaker with effect from the end of February 2004 ; involved in national
and international religious and professional organizations; helped to found a number of Northern
Ireland charities and professional organizations; elder in the Presbyterian Church in Ireland. Contact:
Independent Monitoring Commission, PO Box 709, Belfast BT2 8YB. **T** 048 9072 6117 F 048 9072
6082 email imc@independentmonitoringcommission.org
www.independentmonitoringcommission.org

A brave North of Ireland liberal who has been heroic in his attempts to restore decency
and tolerance to public life in Northern Ireland; takes a consistently strong
constitutional approach to public governance.

ALLEN, Bert; HOTELIER
b 1935, Wexford; single; *p* 1st Anne Hudson; 2*s*; *p* 2nd Geraldine Fitzgerald; 3*s* 3*d*;
edu. Newtown School, Waterford; Farmer, Meat Processor and Exporter; established Slaney Meats in
the 1970s, now Slaney Food Group; has a number of hotels in Ireland and Scotland, including the
Bewley's Hotel franchise with the flagship property strategically located in Ballsbridge, Dublin 4;
Bewley's Hotel Dublin Airport 2006; Developing upmarket apartments on site of former Killiney
Court Hotel due for completion 2006. Contact: Slaney Food Group, Ryland, Bunclody, Co. Wexford.
T 054 77155

The former cattle trader is a major landowner in Co Wexford and holds a sizeable
property portfolio at home and abroad; from his early involvement in the Granville
Hotel, Waterford and the Talbot Hotel in Wexford he has emerged as one of the major
hoteliers in Ireland; a hard nosed, tough, commercial businessman, he has diversified
into a range of business activities including the Darina Allen (*qv*) ice creams with his
cousin-in-law.

ALLEN, Colm; SENIOR COUNSEL
b 1951, Dublin; *m* Amanda Grieve; 2 *s*; *edu.* Marian College, Ballsbridge, Dublin 4; University College
Dublin; King's Inns; BCL; Barrister at Law; Senior Counsel; called to the Irish Bar 1978; Inner Bar
1992; practises on the Dublin circuit; member of the Bar England, Wales. Chairman, The Rehab.
Group. Clubs: St. Stephen's Green, Fitzwilliam Tennis Club, Rathsallagh Golf Club. Recreations:
wine, food. Contact: The Law Library, 1 Arran Square, Arran Quay Dublin 7. **T** 01 817 4978
email allen@iol.ie

One of the most formidable S.C.'s in the Law Library, with a phenomenal mind and
forensic attack; to the fore of the Planning Tribunal; gregarious, wonderful raconteur,
loves to sing at parties, larger than life; with strong Fianna Fáil connections.

ALLEN, née O'Connell, Darina; COOK/TEACHER/AUTHOR/TV PERSONALITY
b 1948, Laois; *m* Timothy Allen; 2*s* 2*d*. *edu*. Dominican Convent, Wickow; College of Catering, Cathal Brugha Street, Dublin; Dip.Hotel and Catering Mgmt; Cook Ballymaloe House Cork 1968; Owner/Principal Ballymaloe Cookery School 1981 to date; *Publ*. regular columns in *The Irish Tmes* and *Image*; four *Simply Delicious Cookbooks, Ballymaloe Cookery Course*, and cookery series for RTE; Certified teacher; Certified Culinary Professional and Food Professional; International Association of Culinary Professionals; Board member Bórd Iascaigh Mhara; member IACP and Euro Toque Guild of Food Writers. Recreations: gardening, reading, walking, tennis. Contact: Ballymaloe Cookery School, Shanagarry, Midleton, Co. Cork. **T** 021 464 6785 **F** 021 464 6909 email enquiries@ballymaloe-cookery-school.ie

> The gregarious Co. Laois-born cook achieved national recognition through her Simply Delicious TV series and cookery books; has fitted in well as successor to her famous mother-in-law Myrtle Allen (*qv*) by establishing the Ballymaloe Cookery School internationally; her star plummeted when she employed a professional public relations consultant to downplay her husband's conviction for downloading pornography; however she has re-established her reputation and she and the school have recovered their popularity.

ALLEN, Elizabeth, 'Liz'; CRIME FICTION WRITER
b 1969, Dublin; *m* Andrew Hanlon (*qv*); 1*s* 2*d*; *edu*. Stanhope Convent, Stoneybatter, Dublin; Queen's University Belfast; Crime Fiction Writer; freelanced from the age of fourteen for the *Evening Herald*; correspondent, *Evening Herald* Tallaght edition, 1986-'88; freelance journalist, 1988-'92; freelance journalist, *Irish Independent*, specialising in investigative pieces, 1992-'96; was prosecuted under the Official Secrets Act for investigation of the Brinks Allied Robbery 1995; crime correspondent, *The Sunday Tribune* 1996; crime correspondent, *Sunday Independent* 1996-01; successful crime fiction writer. Recreations: horse riding, travel. Contact: Darley Anderson Agency, Estelle House, 11, Eustace Road, London SW6 1JB **T** 0044 207 385 6652 **F** 0044 207 386 5571 email enquiries@darelyanderson.com web www.darleyanderson.com

> Took over the mantle of crime correspondent at the Sunday Independent from her murdered colleague Veronica Guerin; the beautiful blonde was highly regarded professionally; left the Sunday Independent in controversial circumstances and subsequently won a major law suit against the newspaper; now a successful crime author with two bestsellers under her belt.

ALLEN, née Hill, Myrtle; COOK
b 1924, Waterford; *m* Ivan (*decd*); 2*s* 4*d*; *edu*. Newtown School, Waterford; Fresham Heights, Surrey, UK; Trinity College Dublin, LL.D, (*hc*) University College Cork LL.D (*hc*); Cook; vice president Macra na Feirme; moved to Ballymaloe with husband Ivan 1948; operated mixed farm; retired from Association 1964; opened hotel and restaurant in Ballymaloe House 1964; *Publ. The Ballymaloe Cookbook; Myrtle Allen's Cooking at Ballymaloe House; Good Food in Cork*. Contact: Ballymaloe House, Shanagarry, Co. Cork. **T** 021 465 2531 email info@Ballymaloe.ie

> Doyenne of Irish cuisine; pioneered the concept of Ireland as the food basket of Europe by promoting her home-grown organic vegetables, free-range meat and poultry products; her influence extended far beyond the south-west coast of Ireland where she first sourced quality fish and shell fish for her famous Yeats room at Ballymaloe House near Midleton in Co. Cork; she internationalized her concept by opening La Ferme Irlandaise in Paris which became a shop window for Irish cuisine and the emerging Irish farmhouse cheese industry; with her late husband Ivan she developed a hugely successful Irish country house hotel whose trade mark was wholesome, delicious Irish food served in an informal setting, with her grandchildren as background extras.

ALLEN, Rachel Sheila née O'Neill; COOK
b 1971, Dublin; *m* Isaac Allen; 2*s*; *edu*. Alexandra College, Milltown Dublin; 12 Week Cookery Course at Ballymaloe 1990; Cook; food writer *Sunday Tribune* magazine September 2005; teacher Ballymaloe Cookery School; 13-part TV series *Rachel's Favourite Food* (BBC, UTV & in Australia, Africa and Italy); *Rachel's Favourite Food for Friends* 2005; regular appearances on *Saturday Kitchen* with Anthony Worrell Thompson; *Publ. Rachel's Favourite Food Cookery Book* 2004; *Rachel's Favourite Food for Friends* 2005; food writer for *Image* 2002 to date; writer for BBC *Good Food Magazine*. Recreations: "skiing once a year, don't get much time for much else" Contact: Ballymaloe Cookery School,

Shanagarry, Co. Cork. **T** 021 464 6785 **F** 021 464 6909 email rachandzac@yahoo.co.uk

Third generation of the Ballymaloe Allen family (husband Issac is Myrtle's grandson; keeps the Allen flag flying high and even further afield through her internationally acclaimed TV series; her culinary skills, easy manner and great beauty combine to make her a true latter day domestic goddess.

Barry Andrews

ANDREWS, Barry; PUBLIC REPRESENTATIVE

b 1967, Dublin; single: *edu.* Blackrock College, Dublin; University College Dublin; King's Inns; Masters in Modern History; Public Representative; Barrister at Law; Secondary school teacher at Ballyfermot SC 1991-'92, English and economics: Sutton Park 1992-'96, history: Bruce College 1996-'97, history; Barrister at Law 1997 to date; Board member Southside Partnership; Board of Governors Royal Irish Academy of Music; elected to Dún Laoghaire-Rathdown Council (Blackrock Ward); elected to Dáil Éireann (FF Dún Laoghaire) 2002; member of the Joint Oireachtas Committees on Education & Science and European Affairs; appointed Chairman Ógra Fianna Fáil by An Taoiseach, 2005 to date. Contact: 20, Monkstown Farm, Dún Laoghaire, Co. Dublin. T 01 618 3856 F 01 618 4599 web www.barryandrews.com

Bright, articulate, good public performer; destined for greater things in politics.

ANDREWS, David; CHAIRMAN IRISH RED CROSS

b 1936; *m* Annette Cusack; 2*s* 3 *d*; *edu.* Coláiste Mhuire, Parnell Square, Dublin; St Joseph's College, Roscrea; University College Dublin, BCL; King's Inns, BL; Chairman Irish Red Cross; Chairman AIG Insurance (Ireland); elected FF Deputy for Dún Laoghaire 1965; Parliamentary Secretary to the Taoiseach, Jack Lynch; Minister for Defence and Chief Whip 1970-'73; Minister of State, Foreign Affairs and Justice 1977-'80; Minister for Foreign Affairs 1992-'93; Minister for Defence & the Marine 1993-'94; Fianna Fáil Spokesman on Tourism & Trade 1995-'97; Minister for Defence June-October 1997; Minister for Foreign Affairs 1997-2001; Chairman Irish Red Cross; Chairman AIG Insurance. Recreations: fishing, walking. Contact: International Red Cross, 16, Merrion Square, Dublin 2. **T** 01 676 5135 **F** 01 661 4461 info@redcross.ie

Son of the legendary Todd Andrews, former chief of Bórd na Móna, CIE and RTÉ; brother of former TD and MEP, Niall Andrews: the eloquent, laid-back barrister was highly regarded by the mandarins in Iveagh House; with his international background was an ideal choice as the chairman of the Irish Red Cross.

ARNOLD, Dr, Bruce, OBE; JOURNALIST, BIOGRAPHER, ART CRITIC

b 1936, UK; *m* Mavis Cleave; 2*s* 1*d*; *edu.* Kingham High School; Trinity College Dublin; Journalist, Biographer, Art Critic; freelance journalist working throughout the 1960s with *The Irish Times, Sunday Press, Sunday Independent, Hibernia* and editor, *The Dubliner*; Correspondent, *The Guardian* 1962-'68; Political Commentator and Parliamentary Correspondent, *Irish Independent* 1972-'80s; London Editor *Irish Independent* 1986-'87; Literary Editor and Political Commentator *Irish Independent* 1987 to date; *Publ. A Concise History of Irish Art; Orpen, Mirror to an Age; What Kind of Country; Margaret Thatcher, A Study In Power; Biography of Jack Lynch; Swift: An Illustrated Life; Art Atlas of Britain and Ireland; The Scandal of Ulysses; Mainie Jellett and the Modern Movement in Ireland*; novels: *A Singer at the Wedding; The Song of the Nightingale; The Muted Swan; Running to Paradise*; three films: *The Scandal of Ulysses, Images of Joyce; To Make It Live, Mainie Jellett*; also *A Passionate Man*, an opera based on the life of Jonathan Swift; former chairman and board member of the National College of Art and Design, member of the Board of Governors and Guardians of the National Gallery of Ireland. Contact: *Irish Independent*, 27 -32, Talbot Street, Dublin 1. T 01 705 5500 email b.arnold@unison.independent.ie

Tough and analytical, brings a tautness to all the topics on which he writes; a frequently controversial media figure, his avid interest in public life inevitably brings him into public conflict with government and the Irish establishment; a witty and sartorially elegant man

ARNOLD, Hugo; JOURNALIST/AUTHOR/CONSULTANT

b 1962, Dublin; *m* Susan Bruce Smith 1*s* 1*d*; *edu.* New University of Ulster; Writer; *Publ. Simple Suppers* 1996; *Outdoor Feasts* 1998; *Henry Harris at Harvey Nicholas* 1998; *Buying the Best* 2000 and the *Avoca Café Cookbook* 2000; *Avoca Café Cookbook 2* 2003; *Wagamama: the Cookbook* 2003;

Wagamama: Ways with Noodles due 2006 and *Avoca @Home* due 2007; Contact: 8 Vesey Place, Dún Laoghaire, Co Dublin. **T** 01 284 4344 **F** 01 284 4382

> Takes a robust approach to the art of cooking; explains his menu ideas clearly and succinctly; a calm confident food writer.

AUNGIER, Grace Mary; CHIEF EXECUTIVE, PERIODICAL PUBLISHERS ASSOCIATION OF IRELAND
b 1960, Dublin; *m* Dr Jean-Paul Mosnier; 2*s*; *edu.* Dominican College, Santa Sabina, Sutton, Co Dublin; University College Dublin; BA; H.Dip.Ed; Chief Executive Periodical Publishers Association of Ireland; Advertising Director Image Publications; Major Accounts Manager *Sunday Tribune*; Chief Executive, Periodical Publishers Association of Ireland, 2000 to date. Clubs: Lansdowne Lawn Tennis Club. Recreations: tennis, swimming, golf, reading. Contact: 18 Upper Grand Canal Street, Ballsbridge, Dublin 4. **T** 01 667 55 79 email aungierg@eircom.net

> Highly motivated, personable woman at the helm of the periodical circulation monitoring body where she has introduced interesting training schemes and made some welcome changes.

Grace Aungier

AUSTIN, Pat; INVESTMENT BANKER
b New York; single; 1*s* 1*d*; *edu.* Valley Forge Military Academy; State University of New York; Hofstra University; Federal Law Enforcement Training Centre; B.A. Political Science; Investment Banker; Criminal Investigator Degree; Series 7 and Series 63 Investment; Commissioned 2nd Lieutenant, US Army; Chairman, Montaigne Investments (Ireland); Chairman, Broadworks Communications; Chairman, Blackrock Publishing Ltd, Chairman, Eden Recruitment; Chairman, Montaigne Ventures Ltd. Clubs: The Kildare Golf and Country Club; St James Club. Recreations: scuba diving, classical music, cigars. Contact: 8-10 Rockhill, Blackrock, Co. Dublin. Contact: Merrion Square, Dublin 2. **T** 01 212 1224 **F** 01 212 1272 email pat@investeurope.net

> Created a stir in marketing circles with his full-on New York charm when he arrived in Dublin a few years ago to work in the wine business prior to becoming an investment banker.

AYLWARD, Liam, Gerard; PUBLIC REPRESENTATIVE
b 1952, Kilkenny; *m* Kathleen Noonan; 2*s* 2*d*; *edu.* St. Kieran's College, Kilkenny; City & Guilds, England, Laboratory Technician; Public Representative; member Kilkenny County Council 1974-'92; member of the Council of Europe 1987-'92; elected to Dáil Éireann (FF) 1977 to date; Minister of State at Dept. of Energy 1988-1989; Minister of State at Dept. of Education 1992-'94; Minister of State at Dept. of Agriculture and Food 2002-'04; MEP 2004 to date. Contact: Aghaviller, Hugginstown, Co Kilkenny. **T** 056 68703 www.europarl.eu.int

> Son of former Senator Bob Aylward, a major figure in Kilkenny GAA circles; had a baptism of fire in the political cauldron of Carlow/Kilkenny where the Aylward/Gibbons political dynasties were in permanent conflict, with Aylward being aligned to the Haughey faction and the Gibbons clan closely associated with the Jack Lynch side of Fianna Fáil; a traditional, hardworking FF TD who continuously delivers for his constituents, he was a reluctant candidate in the 2004 European elections when he took a seat for FF in the Leinster constituency.

AYLWARD, Seán; CIVIL SERVANT
b 1955, Dublin; *m* Agnes; *edu.* St. Vincent's CBS, Glasnevin, Dublin; Institute of Public Administration, Diploma in Public Administration 1977; University College Dublin, BA (English & Economics) 1980; Trinity College Dublin M.Sc. (Public Management) 2000; Career Civil Servant 1973 to date; Secretary General, Dept of Justice, Equality & Law Reform; Private Secretary to the Taoiseach 1980s; Director General Irish Prison Service 1999-2004. Recreations: Irish history. Contacts: 94 St. Stephens Green, Dublin 2. **T** 01 602 8316. **F.**01 661 6612 email sfaylward@justice.ie

> Archetypical civil servant; meticulous on detail, tough in negotiations, which serves him well in his current position.

BACIK, Ivana, Catherine; REID PROFESSOR, CRIMINAL LAW
b 1968, London; *p* Alan Saul; *edu.* Alexandra College, Dublin 6; Trinity College Dublin 1985-'89; London School of Economics 1990-'91; Inns of Court School of Law, London 1991-'92; LL.B., LL.M., BL, F.T.C.D; Barrister at Law; Reid Professor of Criminal Law, Criminology and Penology, Trinity College Dublin 1996 to date; fellow Trinity College Dublin 2005; lecturer in Law, Trinity College Dublin 1995-'96; editor, *Irish Criminal Law Journal* 1997-2003; practising Barrister, Law Library, Dublin 1996 to date; called to the Irish Bar July 1994; member, King's Inns, Dublin 1994 to date; called to the Bar of England and Wales, Middle Temple, London 1992; member, Middle Temple Inn of Court, London 1991 to date; assistant lecturer in Law, National College of Industrial Relations Dublin 1993-'95; lecturer (part-time), 'Women and the Law' course, Centre for Women's Studies, Trinity College Dublin 1994-'95; part-time Seminar Teacher (Legal Process and Land Law), Law School, University of Kent, Canterbury, Kent 1992-'93; part-time Lecturer in Law, Business School, University of North London 1992-'93; pupil barrister, Chambers of David Turner-Samuels QC, Cloisters, London 1993-'93; pupil barrister, Chambers of Joseph Boothby, 3 Temple Gardens, London 1992-'93; president, Students' Union, Trinity College Dublin 1989-'90; Member Democracy Commission 2003 to date; TASC (Think Tank for Action on Social Change) 2002 to date; Friends of the Earth (Ireland) 2004 to date; Corn Exchange Theatre Company 2004 to date; Burren Law School, Ballyvaughan, Co. Clare May 2001; Burren Law School Committee 1998 to date; Irish Penal Reform Trust 2001-'03; Irish Family Planning Association 1999-2005; Well Woman Centre 1995-'97; Irish Council for Civil Liberties 1996-'99; Hon. Sec. Trinity College Dublin Law Alumni Association 1996-2004; TCD Law Alumni Association Executive 2004 to date; Steering Committee member, Irish Women Lawyers Association 2001-03; Amnesty International; American Society of Criminology; British Society of Criminology; stood for election as Labour Party candidate in European Parliament elections, Dublin constituency 2004; involved in different civil liberties/human rights/women's rights campaigns; regular contributor to legal, political and social debates in different media, newspapers, radio and television); Publ. extensive professional publications from 1995 to date. Recreations: theatre, film, cycling, swimming, travel and languages. Contact: Law School, Trinity College, Dublin 2. **T** 01 608 2299 **F** 01 677 0449 email icbacik@tcd.ie

Ivana Bacik

Brave, articulate and focussed without losing humanity; displays excellent qualities without giving ground in her argument; in the tradition of the Reid Professorships of recent years could be Uachtarán na hÉireann two elections away; watch this space!

BADDELEY, David, John; MANAGING DIRECTOR, VOLVO MOTORS
b 1961, Bridgewater, England; *m* Jan; 1*s* 2*d*; *edu.* Lymm Grammar School near Manchester; 8 O Levels; 4 A Levels; Degree in Accountancy; BA (Hons); qualified as an Accountant with Chartered Institute of Management Accountants 1987; Managing Director Volvo Car, Ireland; accountant for timber importer Mallinson-Denny; Fisons Pharmaceuticals; joined Volvo 1988; held various roles in the UK and Europe including Product & Marketing Manager for Volvo Car Finance and latterly as Training Manager for Ireland & UK; Managing Director Volvo Car Ireland 2005 to date. Recreations: keen inland waterways boater. Contact: c/o Volvo Car Ireland, Killakee House, The Square, Tallaght, Dublin 24. **T** 01 462 1122 **F** 01 462 1137 email dbaddeley@volvocars.com

David Baddeley

Started his life in the world of business as an accountant; has spent much of his career getting away from those early roles; once described as a radical realist, he is a person who is enthusiastic for change but tempers this with a pragmatic view of what is achievable.

BAILEY, Michael 'Mick'; MANAGING DIRECTOR, BOVALE DEVELOPMENTS LTD
b 1953, Co. Roscommon; *m* Teresa ; 1*s* 4*d*; *edu.* Ballintubber National School, Co. Roscommon; Founder and Managing Director, Bovale Developments Ltd; has built up one of the largest construction/property development companies in the country. Contact: Bovale Developments Ltd, St. Patrick's House, South Circular Road, Dublin 8. **T** 01 453 7598 **F** 01 453 7615

The legendary Bailey brothers Mick and Tom hit the national headlines through their involvement in the Flood Tribunal; as witness, the late James Gogarty testified to asking Mick Bailey if a receipt would be provided for the money they were about to hand over to Ray Burke. the infamous reply was: "Will we, fuck!"; one of the largest-scale house builders and owners of building land in the greater Dublin area, he is also among the wealthiest, while retaining his personable West of Ireland roots; created a tax settlement record in Ireland in 2006 paying the revenue commissioners €22 million; utterly gregarious, extraordinarily popular in the business and bloodstock worlds, a permanent feature in the Ballybrit Suite at the Galway races; renowned for his rendition of 'The West's Awake' at Cheltenham and other race meetings.

BAKER, Jane Catherine; FASHION CONSULTANT
b Dublin; single; *edu.* St. Joseph's, Stanhope Street, Dublin; Fashion Consultant; Manager Chez Marcel Switzers; joined Regine 1985; opened first Fran & Jane shop in Cork 2002; Fran & Jane shops in Blackrock 2003, Clarendon Street, Dublin 2004, Clonmel, Co. Tipperary 2005; sales and marketing director, Regine; partner with Fran Nolan (*qv*) Fran and Jane shops. Recreations: walking, reading, fundraising (Next Step charity), watching TV. Contact: Regine Ltd, Unit 14, Fashion City, Ballymount Road Upper, Ballymount, Dublin 24. **T** 01 408 0853 **F** 01 4295528 email info@regine.ie

Jane Baker

> Gregarious, innovative and hardworking; has an innate sense of style; indefatigable worker for Next Step charity.

BALLAGH, Robert; ARTIST/DESIGNER
b 1943; *m* Elizabeth Cabrini; 1*s* 1*d*; *edu.* Blackrock College, Dublin; Bolton St. College of Technology, Dublin (Architecture 3 years); Artist/Designer; designed stamps for An Post; designed banknotes for the Central Bank of Ireland; created stage designs for Oscar Wilde's *Salome*, Samuel Beckett's *Endgame* and *Riverdance*; designed the setting for the opening ceremony of the Special Olympics Dublin 2003; is represented in the National Gallery of Ireland, the Ulster Museum, Dublin City Gallery, The Hugh Lane, The Albrecht Dürer House, Nuremberg; Career retrospectives in Lund, Sweden 1983; Moscow 1989; Publ. *Dublin: a book of photographs by R. Ballagh* 1981; *Robert Ballagh, a biography* by Ciarán Carty 1986; *Portrait of Michael Farrell and other works by Robert Ballagh*, Brian O'Doherty 2004. Clubs: Aosdána; Fellow of the World Academy of Art Science. Recreations: walking, swimming. Contact: 3 Temple Cottages, Broadstone, Dublin 2. **T** 01 830 5339

Robert Ballagh

> Bright, friendly and a polemicist; has seen himself elevated to a Living Old Master which has not dented his appetite for controversy both artistic and political; an approachable and pragmatic exponent of his art, life and politics.

BALLANTINE, Sarah, Pamela; TV PRESENTER/REPORTER
b 1958, Belfast; *divorced*; *edu.* Richmond Lodge School, Belfast; Evendine Court, Malveryn; College of Business Studies Belfast; Business Studies, National Broadcasting School London; 9 O Levels; London Chamber of Commerce Secretary; National Broadcasting Diploma; Presenter/reporter *UTV Live at 5.30*; Presenter/reporter *RPM Motor Sport*; Downtown Radio and part-time presenter; part-time newsreader, presenter BBC Radio Ulster; UTV continuity announcer and newsreader 1984. Recreation: cycling, gym, swimming, reading, television, cinema, dining out, helping charitable organisations. Contact: UTV, Havelock House, Belfast BT 7 1EB. **T** 028 90 26 2000 **F** 028 90 26 28 email p.ballintine@ utvplc.com

Pamela Ballantine

> For many years a very popular face on UTV.

BALLYEDMOND, The Lord; Edward Haughey; CHAIRMAN, NORBROOK LABORATORIES
b 1944, Ireland; *m* Mary, The Lady Ballyedmond; 2*s* 1*d*; *edu.* Christian Brothers School, Dundalk; LLD (*hc*) DBA (*hc*) FRCSI (*hc*) OBE, JP; Chairman/CEO Norbrook Laboratories Ltd; Chairman/ Managing Director Ballyedmond Castle Farm Ltd (largest research farm for animal medicines in Europe); Chairman/ Managing Director Corby Castle Estate, Cumbria (3,000-acre agricultural and sporting estate); Chairman and Managing Director Haughey Air (public transport helicopter company certified by CAA) Chairman and Managing Director Haughey Airports Ltd (owners of Carlisle Airport); Director, Bombardier Shorts plc; Member House of Lords; former Irish Senator (Taoiseach's nominee); Member Forum for Peace and Reconciliation; Member of the Parliamentary Committee on Foreign Affairs; Member of the British-Irish Inter- Parliamentary Body; Chairman Irish Aviation Authority; Honorary Consul Chile; Member Board University College Dublin Foundation; Director Armagh Observatory; Trustee Dublin City University 1995 to date; Trustee Royal College of Veterinary Surgeons, London 2001 to date; Chairman Pharmacy Development Board of Royal College of Surgeons in Ireland; Member Board of the Institute for British-Irish Studies. Clubs: Savage Club, London; Reform Club, Belfast; Kildare Street Club and University Club, Dublin. Recreations: Shooting. Contact: Ballyedmond Castle, Rostrevor, Co. Down. **T** 028 302 69824 **F** 028 3026 9951 email chairman@norbrook.co.uk

The Northern businessman was unique in holding political seats in both An Seanad and – a life-long ambition – in the House of Lords; a highly successful entrepreneur, a global player in the veterinary pharmaceutical world; with his elegant, solicitor wife Mary, entertains beautifully at his castles in Rostrevor, London and Wales.

John Banville

BANVILLE, John; MAN BOOKER PRIZE WINNER; AUTHOR, CRITIC, DRAMATIST, LITERARY EDITOR.
b 1945, Wexford; *m* Janet Dunham; separated; 2*s* 2*d*; *p* Patricia Quinn; *edu.* Christian Brothers; Sub-editor *The Irish Press*; Literary Editor *The Irish Times* 1988-'99; Chief Literary Critic *The Irish Times* 1999 to date; *Publ.* short stories; *Long Lankin* 1970; Novels: *Nightspawn* 1971; *Birchwood* 1973; *Doctor Copernicus* 1976; *Kepler* 1981; *The Newton Letter* 1982; *Mefisto* 1986; *The Book of Evidence* 1989 (also produced as a stage play); *Ghosts* 1993; *Athena* 1995; *The Untouchable* 1997; *The Sea* 2005; (nominated for the Man Booker Prize 2005).Winner Man Booker Prize, 2006. Contact: The Irish Times, 10 – 16 D'Olier Street, Dublin 2. **T** 01 675 8000

A quiet, retiring but emphatic writer with great style and verve; uncanny in his observations on the human condition.

BARDWELL, Leland; WRITER
b 1926, India; *edu.* Alexandra College, Dublin; *Publ; The Mad Cyclist* 1970; *Girl on a Bicycle* 1977; *That London Winter* 1981; *The House* 1984; *There We Have Been* 1989; *The Fly and the Bed Bug* 1984; *Dostoevsky's Grave* 1991; Short stories: *Coll; Different Kinds of Love* 1987; *No Regrets* 1984. Contact: Pier House, Balliaful, Co. Sligo. T 071 916 3788

Writes and lives on the edge of the Irish experience, but has a particular if understated capacity to evoke atmosphere.

BARRETT, Gerry; PROPERTY DEVELOPER/HOTELIER
b Galway; *m* Catherine; 1*s* 2*d*; edu. St Joseph's Patrician College, Nuns Island, Galway; University College Galway; BA; H.Dip. Ed; Founder & Group Chairman of Edward Holdings; Managing Director of Edward Holdings Ltd; Managing Director of Monogram Hotels Ltd. Clubs: Galway Corinthians RFC. Contact: Kitty Hall, Edward Square, Galway. **T** 091 865400 **F** 091 865444 email info@edwardholdings.com

The former school teacher has hit the world of property development running with the acquisition of several trophy sites and properties in Dublin and the west of Ireland; his Dublin 4 development Edward Square sold out in days; successful bidder (?100 million) for the Great Southern Hotels in Eyre Square and Corrib Galway and also in Killarney (August 2006); extremely intelligent and switched on, totally focussed at all times.

BARRETT, Richard; TREASURY HOLDINGS
b 1952, Ballina, Co. Mayo; single; *edu.* Quay National School, Ballina, Co. Mayo; Castleknock College Dublin; Trinity College Dublin; King's Inns; Barrister at Law; established Treasury Holdings with John Ronan (*qv*) 1989; Awards: Castleknock College Past Pupil of the Year jointly with school-friend and business partner Johnny Ronan (*qv*) 2005. Contact: Treasury Holdings Group, The Warehouse, 35 Barrow Street, Grand Canal Docks, Dublin 4 **T** 01 618 9300 **F** 01 618 8389 email info@treasuryholdings.ie

Extremely low profile, sharp commercial intellect, sartorially elegant; with business partner Johnny Ronan (*qv*) blazed the trail nationally and internationally for Irish property developers through their company Treasury Holdings.

BARRETT, Roy; STOCKBROKER
b 1963; *m* Susie Lynch; 1*s* 1*d*; *edu.* Blackrock College, Dublin; University College Dublin, BCL, MBS; Stockbroker; Equity Analyst with Warburg Securities 1987-'89; Banker with Paribas 1989-'90;

Director International Equities, NCB Group Ltd 1990-'95; Head of Equities, Goodbody Stockbrokers 1995-'97; Managing Director, Goodbody Stockbrokers 1997 to date; Director, Irish Stock Exchange, Tilman Asset Management. Recreations: soccer, horse racing. Contact: Goodbody Stockbrokers, Ballsbridge Court, Dublin 4. **T** 01 667 0400 **F** 627 7111 web www.goodbody.ie

Succeeded to the top spot in one of the country's leading stockbrokers at a very young age: the business world awaits his next move.

BARRINGTON, Colm; INVESTMENT BANKER

b 1946; *m* Maryrose; 2*s* 1*d*; *edu.* Gonzaga College, Dublin; University College Dublin MA.; Institute of Public Administration, Diploma in Public Administration; Investment Banker; Aer Lingus 1969-'73; Omni Hotels Corporation 1973-'79; GPA Group 1979-'92; GE Capital Aviation Services 1993-'94; Managing Director, Babcock & Brown Ltd.1994 - to date. Clubs: Royal Irish Yacht Club; Bray Sailing Club, Druids Glen Golf Club, Powerscourt Golf Club. Recreations: Yacht Racing, Olympic Sailing Development. Contact: Babcock & Brown, West Pier, Dún Laoghaire, Co.Dublin **T** 01 231 1900 **F** 01 231 1901 email colm.barrington@babcock&brown.com

Dynamic business executive who led the successful bid for take over of Eircom 2006; won a landmark case against the Bank of Ireland on his GPA share loan for the aborted IPO of that company; renowned yachtsman who has participated in the Round Ireland race on many occasions.

BARRINGTON, Kathleen; BUSINESS JOURNALIST

b 1960, Dublin; *m* Niall Murphy; 1*s* 1*d*; *edu.* Holy Child, Killiney, Co.Dublin; University College Dublin; BA 1st.Class Hons; University of Göttingen, Germany (Scholarship); Columnist *The Sunday Business Post*; Business Correspondent (*SBP*) 1990-'95; Markets Editor (*SBP*) 1995-'98; Business Correspondent, *Irish Independent* 1998-2001; Business Editor (*SBP*) 2001- '02; Awards: Business Journalist of the Year, ESB National Media Awards 2003. Recreations: skiing, walking, Pilates. Contact: 29, St. Catherine's Park, Glenageary, Co. Dublin. **T** 01 280 7455 email kathleen.barrington@gmail.com

Well respected journalist throughout the business world.

Kathleen Barrington

BARRY, Frederick, John; CHIEF EXECUTIVE NATIONAL ROADS AUTHORITY (NRA)

b 1951; *m* Elaine; 2*s* 1*d*; *edu.* Franciscan College, Gormanstown, Co. Meath; University College Dublin; B.Eng. (Civil); Trinity College Dublin; Mgt. Dip. King's Inns; Barrister at Law; Fellow of the Institution of Ireland; Chief Executive National Roads Authority; formerly Managing Director of a number of companies including Jacobs Engineering Group (Jacobs Ireland, UK, Northern California). Clubs: Royal St George Yacht Club, Regent Bridge Club, Glen of the Downs Golf Club. Contact: National Roads Authority, St. Martin's House, Waterloo Road, Dublin 4. **T** 01 660 2511

Low profile businessman who faces major challenges in delivering on the necessary improvements to service Ireland's increasing infra-structural needs.

BARRY, Gerald; COMPOSER

b 1952; *edu.* University College Dublin; M.A.; B.Mus; Amsterdam Muzieklyceum; Cologne Musik Hochshule; Vienna Musikhochshule; studied composition with Stockhausen, Kagel, Schat and Cerha, organ with Gerard Gillen and Piet Kee; recipient of State scholarships from Ireland, Australia, Germany and Holland; many of his works have been commissioned by the BBC, including *Chevaux-de-Frise*, *Hard D* for Orkest de Volharding and *The Conquest of Ireland*; his opera *The Intelligence Park*, commissioned by the London Institute of Contemporary Arts, was premiered at the Almeida Festival 1990, his second opera *The Triumph of Beauty and Deceit* was written for Channel 4; work was commissioned for Frankfurt Radio Symphony Orchestra 1997. Contact: Oxford University Press, 70 Baker Street, London, W1M 1DJ. **T** 0044 171 616 5900

His most recent opera and CD releases have placed him centrally in the world of contemporary Irish music. His opera, The Bitter Tears of Petra von Kant, produced in 2005 in London by the English National Opera, is an example of his current status as a composer of importance.

BARRY, Gerald, Joseph 'Gerry'; BROADCASTER
b 1947, Dublin; single; *edu.* Belvedere College, Dublin 1; University College Dublin; BA Economics and Politics; Broadcaster; Reporter, then Deputy Editor to Editor in RTÉ News Features 1970-'83; Political Correspondent and Deputy Editor for *The Sunday Tribune* 1983-'93; Editor/Presenter RTÉ Radio 1's *This Week* show to date; *Publ.* consultant/contributor to *Magill Book of Politics*; consulting editor of *Modern Irish Lives.* Recreations: music, sport, election literature. Contact: RTE, Radio center, Montrose, Donnybrook, Dublin 4 **T** 01 208 3111 email barryg@rte.ie

> Incisive, experienced political journalist, now one of the elder statesmen in RTÉ; well regarded in political circles.

BARRY, Oliver; ENTREPRENEUR
b 1940, Co Cork; *m* Noleen Walshe; 2*s*; 1 *decd*; *edu.* Banteer National School; St Colman's College Fermoy; Entrepreneur; worked in the family wholesale fruit and veg. business and with the Agricultural Institute/An Foras Talúntais; changed career to become one of the most successful showband managers and impresarios; launched Siamsa Cois Laoi in the 1970s to raise funds for Páirc Uí Caoimh; member of the RTÉ Authority 1982-'85; late 1980s won, with James Stafford and Terry Wogan, franchise for Century Radio, the first independent national radio service; closed down in 1991; featured in the Mahon Tribunal because of the involvement of then Communications Minister Ray Burke who had issued the station's licence; successfully developed Hollystown Golf Course. Contact: Hollystown Golf, Hollystown, Dublin 15. T 01 820 7444 **F** 01 820 7447 email info@hollytown.com www.hollystown.com

> As one of Ireland's top impresarios brought world famous performers to Irish venues including Frank Sinatra, Michael Jackson and James Last; pioneered first pay-and-play golf course in Ireland at Hollystown, Co Dublin; great company, a loyal friend, Fianna Fáil activist and backbone of Cork GAA supporters.

BARRY, Peter; CHAIRMAN BARRY'S TEA
b 1928, Cork; *m* Margaret O'Mullane; 4*s* 2*d*; *edu.* Model School, Cork; Christian Brothers College, Cork; Chairman Barry's Tea; Member of Dáil Éireann (FG Cork South) 1969; Deputy Leader of Fine Gael 1979; Minister for Transport & Power 1973-'76; Minister for Education 1976-'77; Minister for the Environment 1981-'82; Minister for Foreign Affairs 1982-'87; Anglo Irish Agreement 1985; First Joint Chairman Anglo-Irish Inter-Governmental Conference 1985; Tánaiste 1987; Contested leadership of Fine Gael and lost to John Bruton 1987; retired from politics at General Election 1997 and was succeeded by his daughter Deirdre Clune (*qv*) who held his seat; Chairman Barry's Tea 1998-2005; Former Chairman National Gallery of Ireland Foundation. Recreations: greyhounds, fine wine, food. Contact: Kinsale Road, Cork **T** 021 491 5000 **F** 021 431 3606 email info@barrystea.ie www.barrystea.com

> Warm, personable, political heavyweight; now one of the biggest collectors of Michael Collins memorabilia; one of Cork's merchant princes; became a major and highly respected figure in the political world, especially through his work in Foreign Affairs; many say he inherited Jack Lynch's mantle as being the most respected figure in Cork politics after the 'Real Taoiseach' left the political stage.

Sebastian Barry

BARRY, Sebastian; WRITER, POET, DRAMATIST
b 1955, Dublin; *m* Alison Deegan; 2*s* 1*d*; *edu.* Catholic University School; Trinity College Dublin (read English & Latin); Writer, Poet, Dramatist; lived in England, France, Greece and Switzerland 1977-'85; Honorary Fellow in Writing at the University of Iowa 1984; Elected to Aosdána 1989; Ansbacher writer-in-residence The Abbey Theatre 1990; Member of the Abbey Board 1990-'91; Writer Fellow at Trinity College, Dublin 1995-'96; Novels: *Macker's Garden* 1982; *Strappado Square* 1983; *Time Out Of Mind* 1983; a novel for younger readers, *Elsewhere, the Adventures of Belemus* 1985; *The Engine By Owl Light* 1987; *The Water Colourist* 1983; *The Rhetorical Town* 1985; *Fanny Hawke Goes To The Mainland Forever* 1989; *The Whereabouts of Eneas McNulty* 1998, translated into seven languages; Plays: *The Pentagonal Dream*; *Boss Grady's Boys* 1988; *Prayers of Sherkin* 1990; *White Woman Street* 1992; *The Steward of Christendom* 1995, which won the Christopher Ewart-Biggs Memorial Prize, the Ireland/America Literary Prize, the Critics' Circle Award for Best New Play, The Writers' Guild Award (Best Fringe Play); also won the Lloyds Private Banking Playwright of the Year award in the same year; *The Only True History of Lizzie Finn* 1995; *Our Lady of Sligo* 1998, joint winner of the Peggy *Ramsay Play Award; Annie Dunne 2002; Whistling Psyche 2004; A Long Long Way* 2005 (short listed for Man Booker Prize 2005). Recreations: fly fishing, old houses, tennis. Contact:

The Agency, 24 Pottery Lane, Holland Park, London w11 4lz. **T** 0044 71 727 1346 **F** 020 7727 9037
email info@theagency.co.uk

Son of architect Frank Barry and actor Joan O'Hara; a graceful and erudite stage
writer, with well-delineated imagery.

BARRY, Susannah, Elizabeth; COMPANY DIRECTOR/RECRUITMENT
SPECIALIST
b 1974, Dublin; single; *edu.* Loreto College, St. Stephen's Green, Dublin 2; University
College Dublin; BA Hons in Spanish and Economics; DIT Mountjoy Square, Dublin,
International Marketing and Spanish, Postgraduate Diploma 1995-'96; Director and
founder of Hunter Marshall, top tier recruitment consultancy specialising in financial
services, sales, marketing, shared services recruitment for home and international
markets. Contact: 7, D'Olier Street, Dublin 2. **T** 01 6170200 **F** 01 6170201
email susannah.barry@huntermarshal,com

Dynamic and focused, thrives on challenges and success.

BARRY, Tony; MANAGING DIRECTOR, BARRY'S TEA
b 1962, Cork; *m* Karen Duffy; 2*s* 1*d*; *edu.* Christian Brothers College, Cork; University
College Cork; B. Comm; Chartered Accountant; Managing Director Barry's Tea;
joined the family firm started by his great grand uncle James J. Barry in 1901;
subsequently run by his grandfather Anthony Barry and expanded by his father Peter
Barry (*qv*); Barry's Tea and Bank of Scotland (Ireland) joined forces to buy Northern
Foods, owned by Batchelors, for about €95 million December 2003; deal involved
setting up of a joint venture vehicle, Maiden Acquisition Company, through which the
two parties made their investment. Contact: Kinsale Road, Cork. **T** 021 491 5000
F 021 431 3606 email info@barrystea.ie web wwwbarrystea.ie

Susannah Barry

Fourth generation Barry to head up the Cork-based tea company; has taken the
business route rather than the political road like his father and grandfather
diversifying the company into media – TV Channel 6.

BARTELS, Adriann, Gerben; RESORT MANAGER
b 1965, Kenya, East Africa; *m* Catherine 2*s*; *edu.* Clongowes Wood College, Co Kildare; DIT College
of Catering, Cathal Brugha Street, Dublin; H (Dip) in Hotel Management; Trinity College Dublin
B.Sc.; Resort Manager; Front Office Manager Penny Hill Park Hotel 1989-'90; Assistant Manager
Sheen Falls Lodge 1990-'94; Train Manager The Royal Scotsman Train 1994-'96; General Manager
Sheen Falls Lodge 1996 – '06; Resort Manager The Marlbrook, Clonmel, Co. Tipperary (due to open
2008) 2006 – todate;. Awards: 'Hotel Manager of the Year' in 2003 (Irish Hotel & Catering Institute).
Clubs: Ring of Kerry Golf Club. Recreations: golf, art, diving, poker, travel, clay pigeon shooting.
Contact: Adrian Bartels, Kenmare, Co Kerry. M 087 219 4352 email adriannbartels@vodafone.ie.

Adriann Bartels

Highly respected hotelier who made Sheen Falls one of the best hotels in the country
with a national and international A-list clientele.

BARTON, Bernard; SENIOR COUNSEL
b 1951, Dublin; *m* Anne Marie; 2*s* 2*d*; *edu.* Glenstal Abbey, Murroe, Co Limerick; University College
Dublin; Kings Inns; Bachelor of Civil Law (Hons), Barrister-at-Law 1977; Barrister at Law, Senior
Counsel; entered practice 1978, Called to the Inner Bar 1988, Barrister-at-Law New South Wales
Australia 1993; Publ: author of many articles in Law Periodicals; consultant to *The Irish Text Book on
The Motor Insurers Bureau* by Richard Lyons B.L. and Kathleen Noctor B.L; Senior Counsel to
Transfusion Positive representing victims of Hepatitis C; Clubs: Member Kings Inns Dublin, Royal
Irish Yacht Club, Kildare Street & University Club, Powerscourt Golf Club, Grand Prior Military and
Hospitaller Order of St. Lazarus of Jerusalem; Recreations: game shooting, game fishing, hill
walking, sailing, travel, golfing, family interests, and charitable work through the St. Lazarus
organisation; Contact: Law library, Four Courts, Dublin 7. **T** 01 8174364
email abarton@eircom.net

One of the most prominent and busiest Round Hall silks, with an extensive civil law
practice; destined for the Bench; an urbane, witty and effective lawyer; the eldest son

of James T. Barton, former Chairman of the Industrial Credit Corporation, and Managing Director of Ever Ready Garages Group; a brother of Philip Barton, Partner Deloitte and Touche and Dr. John Barton, Consultant Cardiac Physician Portiunucla Hospital, Ballinasloe, Co. Galway; has a particular interest in family history and the origins of the Irish State.

BATES, Ray; FORMER MANAGING DIRECTOR, THE NATIONAL LOTTERY
b 1947, Dublin; *m* Mary Elliott; 1*s* 1*d*; edu. O'Connell's Christian Brothers School; Trinity College Dublin; B.Sc. (Comp), M.Econ.Sc.; Managing Director An Post The National Lottery; Civil Servant Dept. of Agriculture, Finance and Public Service 1965-'80; Head of Division OECD (Paris) 1980-'83; Department of Finance and Social Welfare 1987-'89; Systems Manager, involved in setting up Lotto, National Lottery 1987-'89; Chief Executive National Lottery 1989 - 2006. Recreations: music, theatre, bridge; Contact: The National Lottery, Lower Abbey Street, Dublin 1. **T** 01 836 4444

Has been efficient and successful in the promotion and development of the Lottery; has made millions for the State coffers through Lottery and Lotto outlets.

BEGG, David; GENERAL SECRETARY, IRISH CONGRESS OF TRADE UNIONS
b 1950, Dublin; *m* Marie Boland; 2*s* 1*d*; *edu*; Kevin Street College of Technology, Dublin; General Secretary Irish Congress of Trade Unions; Technologist ESB 1971-'79; Deputy General Secretary ESB Officers Association 1979-'83; General Secretary ESB Officers Association 1983-'85; General Secretary Postal and Telecommunications Union 1990; General Secretary Communications Union 1985-'90; General Secretary Irish Congress of Trade Unions 2002 to date. Recreations: reading, film, theatre, gardening. Contact: ICTU Head Office, 31-32 Parnell Square, Dublin 1. **T** 01 889 7777 **F** 01 887 2012 email congress@ictu.ie web www.ictu.ie

David Begg

Regarded as a very skillful strategist, well able to turn the minds of government and other employers to the facts of life as the unions see them; his power and influence – not to mention the prestige of his position - is very considerable indeed.

BEHAN, John; SCULPTOR
b 1938, Dublin; *m* 1st. Constance Short; *div.*; 1*s* 2*d*; *edu*. North Strand VEC, Dublin; Bolton Street Technical School, metalwork; NCAD, Kildare Street, Dublin 2; evening classes Ealing Art College, London 1960-61; Royal Academy College, Oslo, 1968 winter term; Sculptor; qualified as an art metalwork apprentice in1960 after seven-year apprenticeship; first exhibited sculpture in the Irish Exhibition of Living Art in 1960 and in all the major shows in Ireland since then, including the Royal Hibernian Academy, Independent Artists, Group '65, Project '67, New Artists Group and the Western Artists Group; JNF Group tour to Israel 1999; Founder member of the Project Arts Centre in 1967; in 1970 along with Peter O'Brien began casting bronze statuary resulting in the start-up of the Dublin Art Foundry; participated in Graphic Art shows in India, Switzerland and the USA during 1960s and 1970s; Member of the Arts Council 1973-'78. Clubs: United Arts Club Dublin. Recreations: reading and travel. Contact; 13 Court Lane, Wood Quay, Galway. **T** 091 521135

John Behan

The maker of so many iconic Irish images that one forgets he forged them as a young sculptor; his work is now highly collected, and is regularly used in Official State Presentation Pieces; a friendly, unassuming man committed to his art.

BENNETT, Mary; COMPANY DIRECTOR
b 1938; *m* Eddie; 1*s* 2*d*; *edu*. Convent of Mercy, New Ross, Co Wexford; Convent of Mercy, Gort, Co Galway; Company Director; Director Ireland West Tourism; Chairperson Galway City & Co Enterprise Board; Director Galway Chamber of Commerce; Past President Chamber of Commerce of Ireland; Former Director Aer Lingus; Former Director Irish Tourist Board; Former Director Irish Goods Council; President of ISPCC; Director National Breast Cancer Institute; Director of Eunalele Ireland; Past World President of Skal International; Proprietor Treasure Chest, Galway to date. Recreations: tourism, travel. Contact: Treasure Chest, William Street/Castle Street, Galway. **T** 091 563862 **F** 091 567757 email marybennett@eircom.net

A major figure in the tourism industry in the West of Ireland and one of its best ambassadors; an extremely bright and successful business woman.

BENTON, Seán, Brian; CHAIRMAN, OFFICE OF PUBLIC WORKS
b 1949, Dublin; *m* Marie; *2s 1d*; *edu*. Drimnagh Castle CBC; Trinity College Dublin; M.Sc (Strategic Management); Chairman Office of Public Works; Director of Finance, Department of Health 1992-95; Commissioner, Office of Public Works 1996-02; Chairman, Office of Public Works 2002 to date; director, Our Lady's Hospice, Harold's Cross, Dublin; board member, Campus Stadium Ireland Development Ltd, Barretstown Gang Camp, National Gallery of Ireland, Dublin. Clubs: Beech Park Golf Club, Rathcoole, Dublin. Recreations: sport, reading, voluntary work in healthcare. Contact: Office of Public Works, 51 St. Stephen's Green, Dublin. **T** 01 647 6000 **F** 01 661 0747 email info@opw.ie web www.opw.ie

Seán Benton

> An able and astute Chairman of the OPW; is steering it through a period of great change in its public service remit; urbane, witty, smart and charming, knows which buttons to push to get a project moving; an impressive performer with a serious social conscience.

BERESFORD, Marcus, Rt. Hon. Lord Decies; SOLICITOR AND IRISH PEER
b 1948; *m* 1st Sarah Jane Gunnell; (*m. diss*); *m* 2nd. Edel Hendron; *2s; 2d; edu*. St. Columba's College, Dublin; Dublin University, M.Litt; Partner A & L Goodbody Solicitors; Marcus Hugh Tristam de la Poer Beresford, Solicitor and Irish peer; 7th Baron in the Kingdom of Ireland (cr.1812); Member, Editorial Board Irish Law Reports Monthly and Employment Law Reports; Former chairman A&L Goodbody; Fellow Chartered Institute of Arbitrators; voted Ireland's top commercial litigator by *Who's Who Legal 2005*; Trustee of the Alfred Beit Foundation Ltd; *Publ*. contributed to a variety of publications in Ireland and abroad on employment law and other topics; former editor of the International Bar Association's *Employment & Industrial Relations Law Journal*; retired chairman, Employment & Industrial Relations Law Committee of the International Bar Association. Recreations: horseracing, eventing. Contact: A&L Goodbody, International Financial Services Centre, North Wall Quay, Dublin 1. **T** 01 649 2000 **F** 01 649 2649 email law@algoodbody.ie

> A retiring man who hasn't let his peerage get in the way of his work; he remains extremely effective and hardworking.

BERGIN, Joan; DESIGNER
b 1943, Dublin; *edu*. Dominican Convent Cabra, Dublin; Sisters of Charity, King's Inns Street, Dublin; Swedish Arts Council Scholarship to study Furniture Design, Scandanavia; promoted Irish product design worldwide 1970s; established Bergin Designs 1978; interior design projects include Guinness pubs and boardrooms, houses for Noel Pearson and Daniel Day Lewis, night clubs include Lillies Bordello; Costume designer film credits include *My Left Foot, In the Name of the Father, Dancing at Lughnasa, The Honeymooners*; TV credits include *Sunday Night at the Olympia* (RTÉ), *Sweeney Todd* (HBO), *A Bright Shining Tie* (HBO); theatre credits include all the Noel Pearson musicals, works in all the major theatres; Fellow of the Chartered Society of Designers (UK); first woman Vice President 1990. Recreations: theatre, good food, Connemara. Contact: The Costume Mill, Capel Street, Dublin 1. **T** 01 874 8611 **F** 01 874 0495

> More than a costume designer, on set she's Mother Courage; great at mollifying tempestuous actresses; very popular, highly respected and much sought after.

BERKERY, Michael; GENERAL SECRETARY, IRISH FARMERS ASSOCIATION
b 1948, Toomevara, Co. Tipperary; *m* Mary Delaney; *1s 2d; edu*. Toomevara National School; Monmouthshire Agriculture College, South Wales; General Secretary Irish Farmers Association; Sec 1968-77; Executive Secretary IFA (Pigs Committee) 1977- 84; General Secretary Irish Farmers Association 1984 - to date; Chairman FBD Insurance; Recreations: travel, GAA. Contact: IFA, Irish Farm Center, Bluebell, Dublin 12. **T** 01 450 0266 web www.ifa.ie

> One of the most recognizable figures in Irish agriculture; has been a major player in Social Partnership which has contributed to the development of the miracle Irish economy; politically shrewd; from a well-known FG background but has developed very strong links with all political parties; good company, personable and an avid Tipperary hurling supporter.

Pauline Bewick

Maeve Binchy

BEWICK, Pauline; ARTIST

b 1935, Co. Kerry; *m* Patrick Melia; *2d*; *edu.* Douris National School, Kenmare; St Catherine's School, Bristol; National College of Art, Dublin; Artist; began artistic career singing and dancing in Dublin revues; worked as a set designer, Pike Theatre; Freelance artist, has exhibited in various groups and solo exhibitions in Ireland, UK, Germany, Italy, France, Belgium, Canada and USA; Retrospectives: Guinness Hop Store 1985, RHA Gallagher Gallery 1996; Noted book illustrator, tapestry designer and stained glass artist (Bewley's Cafes); *Publ. Pauline Bewick's Ireland; An Artist's Year*; Has written an illustrated Ireland and Artist's Year 1990, *The Yellow Man*, 1995, *The South Seas and a Box of Paints* 1996; subject of a biography by Dr. James White, *Pauline Bewick: Painting a Life*, and of a documentary, *A Painted Diary,* by David Shaw Smith; member, Board National College of Art and Design 2003 to date. Contact: Taylor Galleries, 16 Kildare Street, Dublin 2. **T** 01 676 6055.

A charming, hard-working artist whose only fault may be that she makes it all seem so easy, simple and light-hearted; her facility in word and image is enormous, and she remains eternally youthful and optimistic; kind and generous.

BINCHY, Maeve; AUTHOR

b 1940, Dalkey, Co. Dublin; *m* Gordon Snell; *edu.* Holy Child Convent, Killiney, Co. Dublin; University College Dublin; BA; Author; Teacher, History and Latin Dublin 1960-'68; Author; Journalist *The Irish Times* 1968-02; attended the first Merriman School, Ennis 1968; University College Dublin, D.Litt (*hc*) 1990; *Publ. Light a Penny Candle, Echoes, Firefly Summer, Silver Wedding, Circle of Friends,* (also a 1995 movie starring Minnie Driver and Chris O Donnell, dir. Pat O'Connor) *Evening Class, Tara Road,* (also a 2005 movie starring Andie McDowell; dir. Gilles MacKinnon; prod. Noel Pearson [*qv*]); *The Glass Lake, Nights of Rain and Stars.* Recreations: reading, travel, friends. Contact: Christine Green Authors' Agent, 6 Whitehorse Mews, Westminster Bridge Road, London SE1 7QD **T** 0044 020 7401 8844 **F** 00 44 020 7401 8860 email info@christinegreen.co.uk web www.christinegreen.co.uk

The grande dame of Irish novelists and original purveyor of chick lit in this country describes with great insight and humour inner turmoil and, in particular, the sensitivities of women without in any sense being a declamatory feminist; she remains largely unmoved by her huge popularity and just gets on with life and her writing.

BINCHY, William; REGIUS PROFESSOR OF LAWS TRINITY COLLEGE DUBLIN

b 1947, Dalkey, Co. Dublin; *m* Dr Alice O'Connor; *edu.* St Conleth's College, Dublin; University College Dublin; King's Inns; BA, BCL, LLM; Barrister-At-Law; Regius Professor of Laws, Trinity College Dublin; was special legal adviser on family law reform to the Dept. of Justice, preparing legislation on family maintenance, protection of the family home and domestic violence; as Research Counsellor to the Law Reform Commission advised on reform of law relating to the status of children; has represented Ireland at the Hague Conference on Private International Law in the areas of marriage and inter-country adoption; member the Irish Human Rights Commission; has actively contributed to public discussion of human rights issues, including those relating to divorce, abortion, Travellers and asylum seekers; participated in a programme held in Dar-es-Salaam on constitutionalism for the Tanzanian judiciary; co-organiser of a training programme for the magistracy of Botswana and organiser of the annual African workshop on constitutionalism for the Chief Justices and senior judiciary of African states, held in Trinity College Dublin, now in its tenth year; Visiting Fellow at Corpus Christi College, Cambridge, for the Michaelmas term of 2002; was a member of the Hederman Committee to Review the Offences Against the State Acts, reported May 2002; has authored and co-authored books on private international law, tort and family law. Areas of interest: African human rights law; family law; human rights, jurisprudence, medical law, private international law, tort. Contact: Room 01C, Law School, House 39 Trinity College, Dublin 2. **T** 01 608 2297 **F** 01 677 0449 email wbinchy@tcd.ie web www.tcd.ie/Law/WilliamBinchy.

Contrary to his public profile, a charming and deeply concerned academic anxious for the very best in a contemporary Irish society.

BIRD, Charlie; CHIEF REPORTER, RTÉ NEWS

b 1949; separated; *2d*; *edu.* University of Life; Chief Reporter, RTE News; Library Assistant, *The Irish Times,* 1971-'73; Researcher RTÉ Current Affairs, 1974-'80; Journalist, RTÉ News 1980; Chief Reporter RTÉ News; Special Correspondent RTÉ News to date; as RTÉ Correspondent has been involved in covering most of the major political stories in Ireland over the past 20 years; *Publ.* co-author with George Lee (*qv*) *Breaking the Bank, The Story of NIB*; Presenter/scriptwriter of two major RTÉ TV documentaries on President Mary Robinson; former Chairman, Dublin Broadcasting Branch NUJ; Journalist of the Year 1998 with George Lee(*qv*). Recreations: hill walking, reading and watching reports of politics. Contact: RTÉ, Donnybrook, Dublin 4. **T** 01 208 3111 **F** 01 208 2620 web www.rte.ie

Charlie Bird

> Politicians know they're in trouble when he appears on their doorstep, and, worse, they know there's no escape; his in-your-face style doesn't appeal to all; has broken a raft of major stories; has a tendency to become part of the plot; not keen when the spotlight turns on him, surprisingly.

BIRTHISTLE, Lorcan Gerard; CEO ST LUKE'S HOSPITAL, THE NATIONAL CANCER HOSPITAL

b 1962, Dublin; *m* Lucille; *edu.* Marian College, Ballsbridge, Dublin; National College of Ireland; Trinity College Dublin; BA; CEO St. Luke' Hospital, Rathgar, Dublin; Administrative and management posts in Mater Hospital, Jervis Street Hospital, Richmond Hospital, Dublin Dental Hospital, St Luke's Hospital. Recreations: golf, Arsenal FC. Contact: St Luke's Hospital, Highfield Road, Rathgar, Dublin 6. **T** 01 4065159 email ceo@slh.ie

BLACK, Frances, Patricia; SINGER/SONG WRITER

b 1961; *m* Brian Allen; 1*s* 1*d*; *edu.* Lead singer with Black Family 1986-'88; Arcady 1988-'91; commenced solo career 1993 to date; recordings include *The Black Family* 1986 (with family), *Time for Touching Home* 1989, *After the Ball* (Arcady) 1991, *Frances Black and Kieran Goss* 1992, *Talk To Me* 1994, *The Sky Road* 1995, *The Smile on your Face* 1997, *Don't Get Me Wrong* 1998; *The Best of Frances Black* 2000; *How High The Moon* 2003; Awards: Lord Mayor's Award 1997, IRMA Award Best Irish Female Artist 1995, IRMA Award Best Album by Irish Female 1997, National Entertainments Award Best Newcomer 1994, Irish World Awards Best Solo Artist 1995, Irish World Awards Best Album 1996; winner the solo award and the overall award Celtic Fusion Festival 2005; Recreations: walking, cinema, travel. Contact: Pat Egan Sounds Ltd., 2 Merchants Quay, Dublin 8. **T** 01 679 770. **F** 01 679 7495 web www.frances-black.net

> Hugely successful especially in the United States where she plays to sold-out houses; still willing to fight the good fight as she did for the Rossport Five in Dublin 2005; one of Ireland's most famous female singers continues to go from strength to strength.

BLACK, Mary; SINGER

b 1955; *m* Joe O'Reilly; 2*s* 1*d*; *edu.* St Louis Convent Rathmines; Singer; played first gig aged 14 with brother Terence's folk band; recorded first album with brother Shay and his band, General Humbert 1975; toured extensively with brothers and sister, recorded two albums under the title, *The Black Family* 1986; replaced Dolores Keane in De Danaan 1983-'86; released solo debut album *Mary Black* 1983 on Dara Records label (a company set up with husband/manager Joe O'Reilly); albums released include *No Frontiers* 1989 (double platinum), *Babes in the Wood* 1991, *The Holy Ground* 1993, *Circus* 1995, *Shine* 1997; collaborates with guitarist/producer Declan Sinnott. *Shine* 2001; *Song for Ireland (USA)* 2003; *Full Tide* 2005. Recreations: reading, walking. Contact: Dara Management, Unit 4, Great Ship Street, Dublin, Dublin 8. **T** 01 478 1891 **F** 01 47 2143 web www.mary-black.net

> From her earliest days in General Humbert and De Danann has had a huge loyal following; a consummate artist with a voice and range that just keeps getting better.

BLACKSHAW, Basil; ARTIST

b 1932, Glengormley, Co Antrim; *edu.* Methodist College Belfast; Belfast College of Art; received a scholarship to study in Paris 1951; Artist; participated at three ROSC Exhibitions: ROSC 1971 Dublin, ROSC 1980 in Cork and ROSC 1988 in the Guinness Hop Store in Dublin; Exhibited numerous times at the Arts Council Gallery, Belfast (1964, 1974, 1981 and 1983); enjoyed many successful shows with the Tom Caldwell Gallery in Belfast from 1973-1992; The Arts Council of Northern Ireland organized an major retrospective exhibition, which traveled to the Ormeau Baths Gallery Belfast, the RHA Gallagher Gallery, Dublin and the Crawford Municipal Gallery, Cork 1995; a selection of paintings from this exhibition also went on tour to several museums in the United States; Celebrated his 75th birthday with an exhibition of 38 new paintings at the Ulster Museum 2002; a major monologue on Blackshaw was edited and published by Eamon Mallie 2003; Member: honorary member of the Royal Hibernian Academy; Aosdana; Recreations: dog breeding and horse training. Contact: Solomon Gallery, Powerscourt Townhouse, South William Street, Dublin 2. **T** 01 679 4237 **F** 01 671 5262 email info@solomongallery.com

His work is represented in many public collections in Ireland, including those of the Ulster Museum, Trinity College Dublin, the Arts Council of Ireland, Bank of Ireland, AIB Bank, the Hugh Lane, Northern Bank, the Joyce Museum and the University of Ulster.

Rhona Blake

BLAKE, Rhona, Elizabeth; MANAGING DIRECTOR FLEISHMAN HILLIARD
b 1961, Dublin; *m* Charles Murless (*qv*); 2*s* 1*d*; *edu.* Convent of The Sacred Heart, Mount Anville, Dublin; University College Dublin; BA; PR Consultant; Managing Director and Partner Fleishman-Hillard; PR Consultant, Pembroke Public Relations 1985- 90; Founding Director/ Manager, Fleishman-Hillard Saunders 1990-05; served on board of Tote Ireland 1995- 98; Managing Director and Partner Fleishman-Hillard 2005 - to date; currently sits on AA Ireland Motoring Policy Committee. Recreations: retail, travel, politics, current affairs. Contact: 15 Fitzwilliam Quay, Dublin 4. **T** 01 618 8444 **F** 01 660 2244 email blaker@fleishmaneurope.com

Sharp commercial intellect, good lateral thinker, one of the best proponents of her business in this country, elegant and fun to boot.

BLANEY, Orlaith; MANAGING DIRECTOR MC CANN ERICKSON
b 1970, Co. Armagh; single; *edu.* Our Lady's College, Templeogue, Dublin; University College Dublin; Dublin Institute of Technology; B.Soc. Sc. (Hons); Postgraduate Diploma in Marketing Management; Managing Director Mc Cann Erickson 2002 to date; member Board, Unicef Ireland; Board, IAPI. Recreations: swimming, triathlons (completed Chicago Triathlon 2004/'05) Contact: Mc Cann Erickson, Hambleden House, 19-26 Lower Pembroke Street, Dublin, 2. **T** 01 676 6366 email Orlaith_blaney@europe.mccann.com

Having achieved the top slot in her company at a young age, now much is expected of her; ambitious, hardworking; her sporting competitiveness gives her an added edge in her work.

BLOOD, Baroness May; CHAIRPERSON, IMPACT TRADING, NORTHERN IRELAND
b Belfast 1938; *edu.* Donegall Road Primary School, Belfast; Linfield Road Secondary School, Belfast; Chairperson, Impact Trading, Northern Ireland; Cutter and Supervisor at Blackstaff Linen Mill Company 1952-'90; Manager Cairn Martin Wood Products 1991-'94; Information Officer for Great Shankill Partnership Company 1994; OBE 1995; Hon LL.D. University of Ulster; Life Peer in the title of Rt. Hon Baroness Blood of Blackwaterstown, Co.Armagh 1999; Hon. LL.D Queen's University Belfast 2000. Contact: 7 Black Mountain Place, Belfast or House of Lords, London SW1. web www.womenwagingpeace.net/content/members/blood.

An effective communicator in the social activist mode in the Shankill and greater Belfast area.

BODLEY, Seoirse; COMPOSER, CONDUCTOR
b 1933; separated; 2*s* 3*d*; *edu.* Coláiste Mhuire, Dublin; High School of Commerce; Royal Irish Academy; State Music School Stuttgart, D.Mus. LTCL; awarded Arts Council Prize in musical composition 1956; also University College Dublin Macauley Fellowship; Emeritus Professor of Music, University College Dublin; Compositions: *Ceol* (a choral symphony); *A Concert Mass Symphony No. 3, 4, and 5; Fraw Musica*, premiered Schlosskirche, Torgau 1996; *Pax Bellumque* (text Wilfred Owen and Thomas MacGreevy) premiered National Concert Hall, 1997; *News from Donabate* 1999; Orchestral work commissioned for National Youth Orchestra for Year 2000; work for Voice and Orchestra (for Bernadettte Greevy) 2000; *Piano Concerto 30*, 2000; composer song cycles and film scores; former Chairman, Association of Irish Composers; Chairman, Irish Folk Music Society; member, Aosdána. Recreations: canoeing, camping in North America. Contact: Music Department, University College Dublin, Belfield, Dublin 4. **T** 01 706 7777 web www.ucd.ie

A national treasure, his work in composition is of great importance in the canon of Irish music; regarded as the modern national style in many respects.

BOHAN, Edward 'Eddie'; PUBLIC REPRESENTATIVE, AUCTIONEER, PUBLICAN
b 1932, Longford; *m* Betty Lambert; 1*s* 3*d*; *edu.* Longford Secondary School; Public Representative (Senator since 1987) Auctioneer, Publican; Chairman, Bohan Property Consultants; started in the licensed premises business with Bohans, Meath Street, Dublin, 1960s; went on to own, buy and sell many pubs in Dublin and throughout the country; co-owner with Charlie Chawke (*qv*), Lord Lucan, Lucan Co. Dublin; The Oval, Middle Abbey Street, Dublin; member, Joint Committees on Finance and the Public Service: on Justice, Equality and Women's Rights 1997-2002; Seanad Spokesperson on Finance (with special responsibility for the Office for Public Works) 2002 to date; executive member, Dublin Licensed Vintners Association; former Underwriter, Lloyds. Recreations: racing. Contact: Seanad Eireann, Kildare Street, Dublin 2 . **T** 01 618 3391 **F** 01 6184171 email eddiebohan@oireachtas.ie

Charming and well connected, one of the most popular and influential members of the Upper House and the Fianna Fáil Party; a major power broker in the licensed vintners trade and in property in this country; one of the top auctioneers who has brokered many of the biggest licensed premises deals in the country for many years now.

BOLAND, Eavan, Ashling; POET, PROFESSOR
b 1944, Dublin; *m* Kevin Casey; 2*d*; *edu.* Sacred Heart Convent, New York; Holy Child Convent, Dublin; Trinity College Dublin; BA 1966; Trinity College Dublin; Litt. D (*hc*) 2004; Publ. Poetry: *New Territory* 1967; *War Horse* 1975; *In Her Own Image* 1980; *Night Feed* 1982; *The Journey* 1986; *Outside History* 1990; *In A Time Of Violence* 1994; *Object lessons* 1995; *Lost Land* 1998; *Making Of A Poem* 1999; *Code* 2000; *Translations; After Every War* 2004; Poet in Residence at the National Maternity Hospital during its 1994 centenary; Mabury Knapp Professor, Stanford University, California; Professor, Director, creative writing program, Stanford University, California. Recreations: computers. Contact: 4, Ailesbury Grove, Dundrum, Dublin 16. **T** 01 298 1073

A thoughtful and insightful poet who is clear, analytical and precise; as a personality not well known outside a small group in Ireland, but her reputation is world class and her sensibilities are well marked and fully rounded; a delightful, charming, gracious person close up, a good friend and a determined upholder of the nobility of the Bardic tradition.

Eavan Boland

BOLAND, Frank; MANAGING DIRECTOR, FRANK BOLAND LTD
b 1938; *m* Judy Lane (*decd.*); 3*s* 1*d*; *edu.* Christian Brothers School, Cork; Managing Director, Frank Boland Ltd 1960 to date; Chairman B&I Lines; Director, Beamish & Crawford; Cork Communications Ltd; former Director Aer Lingus; Vice-President Cork Chamber of Commerce; Chairman Cork Enterprise Board; Member Cork Harbour Commissioners. Clubs: Cork Golf Club, Royal Cork Yacht Club. Recreations: boating. Contact: Frank Boland Ltd., Mallow Road, Cork. **T** 021 303271

A popular and influential figure in the Cork commercial world.

BOLGER, Aisling; INSTALLATION ARTIST, SCULPTOR
b 1982, Kilkenny; single; *edu.* Ormond College, Kilkenny; Chelsea College of Art, London; University of the Arts, London BA (Fine Art, Sculpture); Slade School of Art, MA (Fine Art); NCAD; Ballyfermot College (Animation); Artist, Sculptor, Installation; Residency Art & Geography Centre, Catalonia, Spain 2001; *Under the Hawthorn*, team production of a film by the Young Irish Film Makers for Channel 4; trainee buyer on the Neil Jordan film *Breakfast on Pluto*. Recreations: sport, member of the Serpentine Long Distance Group, Battersea Park, London. Contact: 3, Prolouge, Callan, Co. Kilkenny. email fluffybolger@hotmail.com

This apparently quiet young artist has great skills in persuading others to do her will. A unique vision, and seen as such by her contemporaries in the art world, she remains determined, private and driven. An undoubted future awaits her in the gallery world and in inter-active art practice.

BOLGER, Dermot; AUTHOR, PUBLISHER
b 1959; *m* Bernadette Clifton; 2*s*; *edu.* St. Canice's School, Finglas, Dublin; Beneaven College, Finglas; Author, Publisher; factory hand Unidare, Finglas; library assistant Dublin County Council;

Dermot Bolger

Founder and General Editor, Raven Arts Press 1977-'92; Co-founder and Executive Editor, New Island Books 1992 to date; *Publ.* recipient of A.E. Memorial Award, The Macauley Fellowship and The Sunday Tribune Arts Award, among others, for his six novels, *Night Shift; The Woman's Daughter; The Journey Home; Emily's Shoes; A Second Life; Father's Music;* edited and devised the collaborative novels *Finbar's Hotel* and *Ladies Night at Finbar's Hotel;* received the Samuel Beckett Award, the BBC Stewart Parker Prize and two Edinburgh Fringe First Awards for his plays, which include *The Lament For Arthur Cleary; Blinded By the Light; In High Germany; The Holy Ground; One Last White Horse; April Bright* and *The Passion of Jerome;* author of six collections of poetry including *Taking My Letters Back – New & Selected Poems;* editor of various anthologies, including *The Picador Book of Contemporary Irish Fiction;* Executive Editor New Island Books; former Member of the Arts Council of Ireland; Member of Aosdána. Recreations: soccer, golf. Contact: New Island Books Ltd, 2, Brookside, Dundrum Road, Dublin 14. **T** 01 298 9937

Second to none as an admirer of football and its sidewinders; is a thoughtful and careful writer whilst remaining popular; not adverse to the sound byte.

BOLGER, James, Stephen 'Jim'; RACEHORSE TRAINER

b 1941; Co. Wexford; *m* Jackie Foley; 2*d*; *edu.* Oylegate N.S; CBS Enniscorthy; College of Commerce Rathmines, Dublin; Racehorse Trainer 1976 to date; races won to date: Yorkshire Oaks, Irish Oaks (twice), Moyglare Stud Stakes (twice), Cheveley Park, Phoenix Champion Stakes (twice), Prix de l'Abbaye, Prix de l'Opéra, Gold Seal Oaks, Oaks d'Italia, Irish Derby, King George VI & Queen Elizabeth Diamond Stakes, Ballymoss Stakes (twice), Heinz Phoenix Stakes (twice), Gallinule Stakes (twice), Pretty Polly Stakes (four times), Coronation Stakes, Nassau Stakes, Lowther Stakes, Premio Regina Elena, Tetrach (three times), Mulcahy Stakes (twice), Park Stakes, Royal Whip Stakes (twice), Brownstown Stakes, Desmond Stakes (four times), Musidora Stakes (twice), Athasi Stakes (twice), Lingfield Oaks Trial, Lancashire Oaks (twice), Railway Stakes (six times), Ballymacoy Stakes, Shernazar Curragh Stakes (three times), Mount Coote Stud Stakes, Anglesey Stakes (three times), Futurity Stakes (twice), Blandford, Derrinstown Derby Trial (twice), Phoenix Sprint Stakes (twice), Princess of Wales Stakes, International Stakes, Tattersalls Gold Cup, Leopardstown 1,000 Gns. Trial (four times); holds all-time Irish record for flat racing; recipient of two Texaco horseracing awards. Clubs: Wexford GAA Supporters Club. Recreations: hurling, football, racing. Contact: Glebe House, Coolcullen, Carlow. **T** 056 444 3150/58 **F** 056 444 3256 email jsb@iol.ie

A debonair, extremely bright man; one of Ireland's top trainers, not afraid to challenge the racing hierarchy; a keen Wexford GAA follower and committed Fianna Fáil supporter.

BOLTON, Ivan, Wesley; HEADMASTER

b 1949; *m* Hilda 1*s* 1*d*; *edu.* Hibernian Marine School, Clontarf, Dublin; Trinity College Dublin BA 1970; H.Dip.Ed (Hons) 1971; Teacher of History, Geography & English, Royal School Cavan 1971; Vice Principal 1973-'89; Headmaster 1989 to date; in 1985 established and ran the first network of microcomputers in Co. Cavan; continued the organisation of networking of computers in the school through to the mid-1990s with Apple Macintoshes, all this before Department of Education policies on networking in schools were developed. Clubs: St. Angelo MFC Enniskillen Co. Fermanagh. Recreations: model engineering, computers, photography. Contact: Royal School Cavan, Co. Cavan. **T** 049 436 1605 **F** 049 4361636 email; notlob@iol.ie

A pioneer in e-learning in the north midlands and border region; exceptional intellect, superb educator.

BOORMAN, John; FILM DIRECTOR

b 1933, Shepperton, England; *m* 1st Christel Kruse; (*m diss*); 1*s* 3*d*; *m* 2nd Isabella Weibrecht; 2*s* 1*d*; *edu.* Salesian College, London; dry cleaner and journalist writing film reviews for magazines and BBC radio 1950-1955; joined BBC as an assistant editor 1955-1965; first feature *Having A Wild Weekend* 1965; *Point Blank* 1967; *Hell In The Pacific* 1968; *Deliverance* 1972 (Oscar nomination); *Zardoz* 1974; *Exorcist II The Heretic* 1977; *Excalibur* 1981; *The Emerald Forest* 1985; *Hope and Glory* 1987 (Oscar nominations Best Picture, Best Screenplay, Best Director) *Where The Heart Is* 1990; *Beyond Rangoon* 1995; *Lumière et compagnie* 1996; *Lee Marvin, A Personal Portrait* 1998; *The General* 1998; *Tailor of Panama* 2001; *Country of My Skull* 2004; *Memories of Hadrian* 2006; Member of jury at the Cannes

Film Festival 1992; awarded the fellowship of the British Film Academy 2004; President of the Young Irish Film Makers, a youth-based film training organisation based in Kilkenny. Contact: ICM, 76 Oxford Street, London, W1D 1BS. **T** 00 44 (0)20 7636 6565 **F** 00 44 (0)20 7323 0101 email directors@icmlondon.co.uk

A cerebral, ambitious director who has hovered on the brink of greatness; a wonderful storyteller, something that invariably plays a major role in his direction; has refused to bow to trends; highly regarded among movie moguls and the number crunchers in Hollywood and New York.

BOUCHER-HAYES, Philip; JOURNALIST
b 1971; *m* Suzanne Campbell; *edu.* Newtown School, Waterford; UCD BA (History & Politics); Freelance radio reporting 1993-'96; Producer, Gay Byrne Radio Show 1996; Presenter Radio Ireland (Today FM) 1997; Reporter/ presenter *5-7 Live* RTÉ Radio 1 1998-2005; reporting from Kosovo, Israel-occupied Territories, Iraq, EU Accession States, US Presidential Elections, South East Asian tsunami affected countries. Recreations: walking the dog, travel. Contact: Radio Centre, RTÉ, Donnybrook, Dublin 4. **T** 01 208 3967 **F** 01 208 3027 email. pbh@rte.ie

His trenchant middle-class tones can annoy as much as they persuade; has the confidence to ask the question others pussyfoot around; seems to hold strong social and political views.

BOUCHIER-HAYES, Timothy; SOLICITOR
b 1953, Dublin; *m* Sinead Phelan; 2*d*; *edu.* St. Conleth's College, Dublin; UCD, BCL; Law Society; Solicitor; Partner, McCann FitzGerald, specialising in Construction and Projects; Fellow Chartered Institute of Arbitrators; awarded Special Prize by the Institution of Engineers of Ireland for Outstanding Contribution and Commitment To The Activities of The Institution 2003; Member Irish Amateur Fencing Federation (former Hon. Sec); holder of several national titles in fencing 1969-'84; represented Ireland at junior and senior world fencing championships 1969-'81. Clubs: Milltown Golf Club, Pembroke Fencing Club. Recreations: fencing, golf. Contact: McCann FitzGerald, 2 Harbourmaster Place, IFSC, Dublin 1. **T** 01 829 0000 **F** 01 829 0010 email tim.bouchierhayes@mccannfitzgerald.ie

Has been consulted by private developers and public authorities alike in relation to most of the major construction projects undertaken in Ireland over the past two decades; has extensive experience of dealing with developers, architects, engineers, surveyors and builders; recently has been advising on PPP projects.

BOURKE, Jonathan; 'Jay'; RESTAURANT AND NIGHTCLUB OWNER
b 1966, Dublin; *m* Sarah Harte; 1*s* 1*d*; *edu.* St.Columba's College, Dublin; Trinity College Dublin; BA Economics; Restaurant, Bar and Nightclub owner; opened Wolfman Jack's, Rathmines, Dublin 1989; his company Sherland Enterprises has a chain of restaurants and nightclubs with a turnover of €20million plus; employs more than 400 staff; restaurants include Eden Restaurant; GUBU; Rí Rá Nightclub; The Globe Bar; Grafton Guest House; The Market Bar; the Café Bar Deli restaurant chain; Odessa Restaurant; Odessa Club; Fish; Bewley's Grafton Street; The Savoy Theatre and Bodega Bar, Cork; The Roundy House, Cork; The Long Bar, London; Bellinter House, Navan, Co. Meath, a classical mansion designed by Richard Castle; *The Mentor* RTÉ series 2005 with Dr. Sarah Bolger. Clubs: Royal St. George Yacht Club. Recreations: reading, movies, theatre, sailing. Contact: Sherland Entertainment Ltd, 37, Drury Street, Dublin 2. **T** 01 677 4835/ 01 671 6678 **F** 01 677 45 85 email jonathan.bourke@hotmail.com

With business partner Eoin Foyle has created and run some of Ireland's most successful and innovative restaurants, bars and clubs; a trailblazer in his industry since the 1980s; able, shrewd and capable, he has driven forward his hospitality interests in Dublin, Cork and London; no slouch, no wonder he's been cited as an advice facilitator as seen on television.

BOWE, Mary, née Murphy; HOTEL PROPRIETOR
b 1936, Castlepollard, Co.Westmeath; *m* Raymond Bowe; 2*d*; *edu.* Loreto Abbey, Rathfarnham; Shannon College of Hotel Management; H.Dip Hotel and Catering

Mary Bowe

Management; Fellow Irish Hotel and Catering Institute; Member of Shannon College of H H Trust; Proprietor Marlfield House Hotel, Gorey, Co.Wexford; worked in the Savoy Hotel, London; Europaisher Hof, Heidelberg; Manager of Woodbrook Golf Club; opened Restaurant Esker Lodge in family home at Curracloe, Co.Wexford 1964; bought Marlfield House 1977; opened Marlfield House Hotel 1978; subsequently invited into the prestigious Relais et Chateau marketing consortium and Irish Blue Book. Clubs: RAC. Recreations: music, travel, interior design, work, gardening and art collecting. Contact: Marlfield House, Gorey, Co. Wexford. **T** 055 21124 **F** 055 21572 email info@marlfieldhouse.ie

> Doyenne of the country house hotel sector; a warm, friendly, engaging personality, who maintains meticulous standards; has a prodigious memory, can remember a once-off guest from 17 years ago; runs an immaculate glamorous hotel; a good friend, great listener and born to shop, she remains supreme in a class of her own.

BOWLER, Gillian; CHAIRPERSON IRISH LIFE & PERMANENT plc;
b 1952; *m* Harry Sydner; 1*sd*; *edu*. England; Founded Budget Travel 1975; Joint Managing Director, with Harry Sydner, Budget Travel (part sold to Granada plc, September 1987, remaining stake sold to Thomson Group 1996); awarded Doctor of Laws (*hc*)1989; Fellow Irish Management Institute 1990; Fellow Irish Marketing Institute, 1995; Honorary Fellow Sales Institute of Ireland, 2005; currently Chairperson Fáilte Ireland; Chairperson Irish Life & Permanent plc; non-executive director of several leading companies, Grafton Group plc and Voluntary Health Insurance; past president of the Institute of Directors; Recreations: modern art, country weekends, reading and cooking. Contact: Budget Travel, 134 Lower, Baggot Street, Dublin 2 **T** 01 661 3122 www.budgettravel.ie

> Glamorous travel innovator and darling of the media whose trade-mark continues to be the designer shades she wears as a headband year-round; a hard-nosed businesswoman who took on and beat a male-dominated industry to establish her company as one of the most profitable Irish travel companies with an annual turnover in excess of €200 million and a 42% market share; her commercial success and political savvy have been recognized by a string of quality directorships in the public and private sector.

BOWMAN, Dr John; HISTORIAN AND BROADCASTER
b 1942, Dublin; *m* Eimear Philbin; 2*s* (1 *decd.*); 1*d*; *edu*. Belvedere College Dublin; University College Dublin; Trinity College Dublin; Ph.D; Historian and Broadcaster; Joined Radio Éireann 1962; became the presenter and commentator on numerous current affairs programmes, as well as an analyst of political developments and interviewer of politicians on radio and later on television; presented current affairs programme *Today Tonight*; has chaired political programme *Questions and Answers* for a number of years; presents *Bowman Saturday 8.30.* on RTÉ radio, a weekly compilation of material from broadcasting archives at home and abroad; *Publ. De Valera and the Ulster Question 1917–1973* 1982, *Portraits: Belvedere College, Dublin, 1832- 1932* 1982, *Jonathan: Jonathan Philbin Bowman – Memories, Reflections, Tributes* 2002; former President, Irish Association for Cultural Economic and Social Relations 1993. Contact: RTÉ, Montrose, Donnybrook, Dublin 4. **T** 01 208 3111 **F** 01 208 2620 web www.rte.ie

> The well-known and respected historian is now one of the elder statesmen of the RTE scene; highly informed on current affairs; has an engaging interviewing style; brings a unique objectivity to all his work.

John Bowman

BOYCE, Most Reverend, Philip; BISHOP OF RAPHOE
b 1940; single; *edu*. Carmelite College, Castlemartyr, Co Cork; Teresianum, Rome (Pontifical Faculty of Theology); Doctorate in Theology with Specialisation in Spirtuality; Teacher of Spiritual and Dogmatic Theology, Teresianum, Rome; Member of the Congregation of Divine Worship and the Discipline of the Sacraments; *Publ. The Challenge of Sanctity: a study of Christian perfection in the writings of John Henry Newman* (Rome) 1974; *Spiritual Exodus of John H. Newman* (Thérèse of Lisieux) 1979; *The Virgin Mary in the Writings of JH Newman*, Ed. with Introduction; *Peter – Gracewing* 2001; also articles on spiritual & Carmelite themes. Recreation: reading, walking. Contact: Bishop's House, Letterkenny, Co Donegal. **T** 074 912 1208 **F** 074 912 4872 email raphoediocese@eircom.net

> A somewhat surprising choice for a rural northwestern diocese, he nevertheless brings a sense of great spirituality and compassion to his ministry; may yet end up in Armagh.

BOYD, Dermot, Gordon, Mahon; ARCHITECT
b 1967, Belfast; *edu.* Inchmarlo Preparatory School, Belfast; St Andrew's College, Dublin; Trinity
College Dublin, B.ArchSc; Dip.Arch, Dublin Institute of Technology; member of the Royal Institute
of Architects of Ireland MRIAI 1997; Architectural Students Association DIT, President 1988;
Architectural Association of Ireland President 1997; Council of the Royal Institute of Architects of
Ireland 1998; Editorial Board of Architecture Ireland 1999; private practice 1993 to date; Boyd Cody
Architects 2000 to date (with Peter Cody); Ahrends, Burton and Koralek 1987; Alberto Campo
Baeza 1988; Scott, Tallon, Walker 1990; John Pawson 1991-92; Shay Cleary 1993; McCullough
Mulvin 1994 to date; lecturer Dublin Institute of Technology 1996 to date; University of Strathclyde
Glasgow 1997; University College Dublin 1998, 2003, 2004; American Institute of Architects 2000;
Architectural Association of Ireland 2001, 2004; Architectural Association, London 2001; Queen's
University Belfast 2003, 2005; Trinity College Dublin 2004; Projects: Higgins Apartment, London
1993; Viva Shop Barcelona, 1995; Unlimited Shop Madrid 1996; Anne McDevitt Clinic, Dublin,
1996; Watson Loft, New York 1997; Watson Apartment, London 1997; Nectar Juice Bar, Ranelagh
1998; McDevitt House, own house 1999; Watson House, New York; Liston Shop, Canning House
2001; Daly House; Ballagh House; Monaghan County Offices; Dillon Malone/ Mulvin House 2002;
Lacey/McGrath House; Hogan/Shivnen House 2003; Sweeney House; Pratt House; Harty House
2004; Hiney House; Gleeson/Reihill House; Croke House 2005; *Awards:* First Prize, FIS
Collaboration 1996; RIAI Regional Award 1998; AAI Award Special Mention 1999; AAI Special
Award; RIAI Award Special Mention 2000; RIAI Award Special Mention 2001: First Prize
Monaghan County Offices Competition; RIAI Award Special Mention; AAI Award Special Mention
2002; RIAI Award, AAI Special Mention 2003; Opus Award Special Mention 2004; AAI Downes
Medal; AAI Award; RIAI Award; RIAI Award Special Mention 2005; work exhibited: Athlone
Riverside Competition 1993; 20/20 Chair Exhibition 1993; Tales from Two Cities 1994; FIS 1996;
Smithfield Competition 1998; RIAI Regional Awards 1998; AAI Awards 1999; RIAI Awards 2000;
RIAI Awards; Affordable Housing 2001; RIAI Awards 2002; RIAI Awards; AAI Awards 2003;
Practising Architecture – RHA, AAI Awards, RIAI Awards; Opus Awards 2004; Annual Exhibition
RHA; AAI Awards, RIAI Awards 2005. Recreations: the pursuit of love and pleasure; Contact: The
Studio, 15, Upper Baggot, Street, Dublin 4. **T** 01 667 7277 **F** 01 667 7278
email info@boydcodyarch.com www.boydcodyarch.com

> Higher profile recently than hitherto; has a sound and smart middle-class practice;
> willing to expand the boundaries of reconjugating Dublin redbrick.

BOYLAN; Ken, Brian, Patrick; MAKE-UP ARTIST;
b 1972; *p* Chris; *edu.* Newpark School, Newtownpark Avenue, Blackrock, Dublin; Inchicore
VEC, drama and stagecraft; Diploma in drama stagecraft; ITEC Diploma in Make Up; began
in the industry in Opera di Verona in Italy; returned to work in all major Irish magazines and
on TV with *Off the Rails*; became head make-up artist for Giorgio Armani for three years; left
to set up Boylan and Balfe: The Make-Up People with fellow make-up artist and friend Ellie
Balfe. Clubs: "If you mean nightclubs, I go to the following, Spirit, Spy, Pod and sometimes
Renards". Recreations: reading, tennis, eating out, theatre, fashion, music and clubbing.
Contact: The Square, Larch Hill, Santry, Dublin 9; M 087 2381212
email ken@boylandandbalfe.com

> A latter-day Svengali who can transform any look; always in demand, has developed a
> very successful A-list business throughout the country.

BOYLE, Consolata, Mary; COSTUME DESIGNER
b 1949, Dublin; *m* Donald Taylor Black; 1*d*; *edu.* Holy Child School, Killiney, Co. Dublin;
University College Dublin; BA Archaeology and History; West Surrey College of Art and
Design; Diploma in Textile Design; Freelance Costume Designer; trained as a designer Abbey
Theatre; Resident Designer Peacock Theatre; was initially sets and costume designer for Peacock,
Focus, Irish Theatre Company, Project Arts Centre, Eblana, Gate, Abbey, Gaiety, Field Day; Theatre
credits include *Translations,* Field Day, sets and costumes 1980; *Double Cross,* Field Day, dir. Jim
Sheridan, sets and costumes 1986; *Juno and the Paycock* , dir. Joe Dowling, Gate, Broadway and
World Tour 1986-'88; *Twelfth Night,* dir. Joe Dowling, Gate; *Drama at Inish,* dir. Garry Hynes, Abbey;
The Plough and the Stars, dir. Stephen Rea, Gaiety; Film credits since 1976 include *Anne Devlin, The
Irish RM (series III), The Courier, Troubles, December Bride, The Playboys, Into the West, The Snapper,
Widow's Peak, The Secret of Roan Inish, Mary Reilly, Moll Flanders, The Van, Trojan Eddie, The Serpent's
Kiss, This is my Father, Love and Rage, The Winslow Boy, Angela's Ashes, Nora, Endgame, The Actors,
The Lion in Winter, Asylum;* Golden Satellite Awards Nomination 1997 (*Moll Flanders*) IFTA Award
2000 (*Angela's Ashes*); Emmy Award 2004 (*The Lion in Winter*); Nomination Costume Designers'

Ken Boylan

Consolata Boyle

Guild 2005 (*The Lion in Winter*). Recreations: reading, music, walking.

The great Irish export in stage design terms; her work has been seen and appreciated worldwide.

BRADSHAW, Lar; MANAGEMENT CONSULTANT

b 1960; *m* Claire; 1*s* 1*d*; *edu.* Rosmini College, Drumcondra, Dublin; University College Dublin; IMD Switzerland; BA, MBA, MIIE; Chairman, Dublin Docklands Development Authority; Director Anglo Irish Bank; Chairman The WELL; recently retired Director of McKinsey Inc Worldwide; Formerly Managing Director McKinsey Ireland. Clubs: Glen of the Downs Golf Club. Recreations: music, gym, creative writing, golf, football: Contact: Dublin Docklands Development Authority, Custom House Quay, Docklands, Dublin 1. **T** 01 818 3300 **F** 01 818 3399 email info@dublindocklands.ie web www.ddda.ie

A man with an international reputation; a major influence in the development of the Dublin Docklands at a very critical time.

BRADY, Angela, Maria, ARCHITECT /PARTNER

b 1957; *m* Robin Mallalieu 1*s* 1*d*; *edu.* Holy Child Convent, Killiney, Co Dublin; Dublin School of Architecture, Bolton Street, Dublin; BArchSc Dipl Arch. FRIAI, RIBA, FRSA. ARB; Graduated from Dublin School of Architecture 1981; Post-graduate scholarship Kunstacademie Copenhagen 1981-'82; worked in Toronto then came to London 1982-'83; worked for commercial architectural practices 1983-'87 until set up partnership with husband Robin Mallalieu; Formed Brady Mallalieu Architects 1987; Award-winning architectural practice; Chair RIBA Women In Architecture 1999-2005; Coordinator www.diverscity-architects.com exhibition, travelling to 12 cities around the world; on English Heritage/CABE Urban Panel & Civic Trust National Panel; Runs workshops to promote architecture to the public. Recreations: art & design, Irish art, TV (ITV house building programme (www.buildingthedreams.co.uk); 10K charity marathon, Dublin. Contact: 90 Queens Drive London N4 2 HW. **T** 00 44 208 880 1544 **F** 0044 208 880 2687 web; www.bradymallalieu.com

A very able, inventive and imaginative architect who has a keen perspective on the urban landscape and its furniture.

BRADY, Conor; MEMBER, GARDA OMBUDSMAN'S COMMISSION

b 1949; *m* Ann Byron; 2*s*; *edu.* Cistercian College Roscrea, Co. Tipperary; University College Dublin; BA, MA; Newspaper consultant, *The Village* magazine; Editor Emeritus *The Irish Times*; edited the College Paper UCD; reporter *The Irish Times* 1969-'73; Editor *The Garda Review* 1974-'75; reporter/presenter RTÉ Radio News 1975-'76; Features Editor *The Irish Times* 1977-'79; editor *The Sunday Tribune* 1981-'82; deputy editor *The Irish Times* 1985-'86; editor *The Irish Times* 1986-2002; consultant editor *The Village* magazine 2004 to date; member, Executive, World Forum Newspaper Editors, (Chairman 1995-'99); chairman, Board of Counsellors European Journalism Centre, Maastricht 1994-'99; senior teaching fellow, The Michael Smurfit Graduate School of Business in Modern Media 2002 to date; member, Remembrance Committee for Victims of Violence in Ireland 2003 to date; member, The Garda Ombudsman's Commission 2005 - to date; Publ. *Guardians of the Peace; Up With The Times*, autobiography 2005; Clubs: Hibernian & Stephens Green Club, Dublin. Recreations: reading, travel, golf. Contact: Department of Justice, Equality and Law Reform, 94 St. Stephens Green, Dublin 2. **T** 01 6028202 **F** 01 6615461

As editor for 16 years he left an indelible stamp on The Irish Times; during his tenure at Ireland's paper of record, circulation grew from 80,000 to about 120,000; his going was clouded in the difficulties of marketing strategies and a severance package that was remarkable for a financially strapped newspaper; his 2005 autobiography has already made more than ripples with the chattering classes; a jolly man, son of a former Garda Commissioner, he and cousin Olivia O'Leary are important figures in their own right, not without their own Politics and politics.

BRADY, Cyprian, Francis; PUBLIC REPRESENTATIVE

b 1962, Dublin; *m* Valerie; 1*s* 1*d*; *edu.* St. Joseph's Christian Brothers School, Fairview, Dublin; Senator, Member Seanad Éireann; Dept. of Education 1981-'87; Dept. of Social Welfare 1987-'91;

Dept. of Finance 1991-'97; Dept. of the Taoiseach 1997-2002. Clubs: Westmanstown Golf Club. Recreations: golf. Contact: c/o St. Luke's, 161, Lr. Drumcondra Road. Dublin 9. **T** 01 837 41291 **F** 01 836 8227 email brady@oireachtas.ie

> The older and less well-known of the Drumcondra Brady Bunch; brother of former Dublin Lord Mayor Royston; loyal servant of An Taoiseach who has got his reward by being a nominated candidate for the next general election; but will he be on the final ticket ?; if he does getting into the Dáil could present a major challenge.

BRADY, Francis, Brian, 'Rory'; ATTORNEY GENERAL/BARRISTER AT LAW
b 1957, Dublin; *m* Siobhan; 2d; *edu.* Synge Street CBS; University College Dublin; King's Inns (Dublin); B.C.L, B.L; Attorney General/ Barrister at Law; called to the Bar 1979; Senior Counsel 1994; Chairman of the Bar Council 2000; Attorney General 2002 to date; *Publ.* various articles in legal publications. Clubs: Fitzwilliam LTC, New York Athletic Club, Kildare Street & University Clubs. Recreations: walking, swimming. Contact: Government Buildings, Upper Merrion Street, Dublin 2. **T** 01 661 6944 **F** 01 676 1806 email info @ag.irlgov.ie

> Popular and high earning Senior Counsel who kept his head and his friendships when he became 'The Attorney'; a crucial éminence grise advising Government in the underpinning of the IRA ceasefire/peace process; stylish and sociable silk; under fire as a result of the sex/rape legislation controversy 2006; but will still grace the Bench in the near future.

BRADY, Dr, Hugh, Redmond; PRESIDENT, UNIVERSITY COLLEGE, DUBLIN/ DOCTOR/ SCIENTIST
b 1959 Dublin; *m* Dr Yvonne O'Meara; 3s; *edu.* Newbridge College; University College Dublin; M.B., B.Ch, B.A.O., University College Dublin 1982; B.Sc. Pharmacology, University College Dublin 1984; M.R.C.P.I. Royal College of Physicians, Ireland 1985; F.R.C.P.I., Royal College of Physicians,Ireland 1991; Diplomate, American Board of Internal Medicine, USA 1992; Ph.D., Physiology, University College Dublin 1993; Diplomate, American Board of Nephrology, USA 1993; M.D., University College Dublin 1994; Summary of Publications and Patents: Total: 143; 78 peer-reviewed research publications, 35 review articles, 26 book chapters, 2 book editorships, 2 patents pending or awarded; Personal research interests: Pro-resolution pathways in inflammatory disease that can be harnessed for therapeutic gain; Application of novel genomic and bioinformatic approaches to the identification of novel therapeutic targets in diabetic nephropathy and other kidney diseases; President, University College Dublin 2004 to date; Pro-vice Chancellor, National University of Ireland 2000-03; Head of Department, Medicine & Therapeutics 1996-2003; Acting Director, Conway Institute of Biomedical and Biomolecular Research, UCD 1999-01; Professor of Medicine and Therapeutics, UCD and Mater Misericordiae Hospital 1999- 00; Associate Dean for Research, Faculty of Medicine, UCD 1995-99; Associate Professor of Medicine, Harvard Medical School 1995-'99; Assistant Professor of Medicine, Harvard Medical School 1991-94; Instructor in Medicine, Harvard Medical School 1989-'91; Chief, Renal Section, Medical Service, Brockton-West Roxbury Department of Veterans Affairs Medical Center, Boston, MA, USA 1993-'96; Attending Physician, Department of Medicine, Brigham & Women's Hospital, Boston, MA, USA 1990-'96; Clinical and Research Fellow, Brigham & Women's Hospital, Harvard Medical School, Boston, MA, USA 1987-'89; Clinical Fellow, University of Toronto, Ontario, Canada 1986-'87; Intern and Senior House Officer, St. Vincent's and St. Laurence's Hospital Dublin 1982-'86; Membership of Institutional, National and International Committees and Boards University College Dublin; Faculty of Medicine Executive 1999-2000; President's Research Committee 2001-03; Conway Institute, Board of Management 2002-03; Head of Department, Medicine & Therapeutics 2000-03; Board of Directors, Dublin Molecular Medicine Centre Mater Misericordiae University Hospital 2003-05; Medical Executive / Council 1998-00; Chairman, Mater College for Postgraduate Research and Education 1999-03; Board of Management 2000-03; *National*: Higher Education Authority 2001-04; Chairman, Health Research Board of Ireland 2003-03; President, Irish Nephrological Society 2001 - 03; Health Research Board of Ireland 1997-02; Expert Advisory Panel, Irish Medicines Board 1997-99; Irish Committee on Higher Medical Training 1997-03; *International*: Coordinating Committee European – Japanese Nephrology Forum 1997-2003; National Kidney Research Fund (UK), Grant Review Committee 1999-03; Scientific Programme Committee, ERA-EDTA/EKRA Congress, Copenhagen 2002; Scientific Programme Committee, American Society of Nephrology 2000-03; American Society of Nephrology Taskforce on Acute Renal Failure 2002-03. Clubs: Killiney Golf Club, East Clare Golf Club. Recreations: family, rugby,golf. Contact: President's Office, Tierney Building, University College Dublin, Belfield, Dublin 4. **T** 01 716 1618/1704 **F** 01 716 1170 email president@ucd.ie

Hugh Brady

A University President for the 21st century, an energetic and driven president of his college who has achieved enormous change in a very short space of time; he has brought his modernising hand to all around him; has more supporters than detractors and has altered the onward agenda for UCD.

BRADY, Paul; SINGER, SONGWRITER
b 1947, Strabane; *m* Mary Elliot; 1*s* 1*d*; *edu*. Sion Mills PES School; St. Columb's College, Derry; University College Dublin; Singer and Songwriter; began to perform in college 1965; left college to join The Johnstons; moved to London with The Johnstons 1969; moved to New York 1972; to Dublin 1974, joined Planxty; Duo with Andy Irvine 1976-'78; Albums: *Welcome Here Kind Stranger* 1983; *Back To The Centre* 1985; *Primitive Dance* 1987; *Trick Or Treat* 1991; *Spirits Colliding* 1995; wrote nearly 50 songs; Rykodisc remastered and re-released six of his previous albums 1998: *Hard Station; True For You; Back To The Centre; Primitive Dance; Trick Or Treat* and *Spirits Colliding*; Best-Of collection *Nobody Knows* 1999; *The Best Of Paul Brady (1970s-1990s); Oh What A World* 2000; formed own record label, PeeBee Music, released *The Missing Liberty Tapes* 2001; RTE television six-programme series *The Paul Brady Songbook* 2002; *The Havana Way* 2003; new album *Say What You Feel* 2005; Awards: Melody Maker Folk Album of the Year Award 1987; Stag/*Hot Press* Music Critics Award for Best Single 1981; Best Song 1982; Best Songwriter 1985; Best Songwriter and Best Male Vocalist 1986; National Entertainment Opel Award 1986; top of *Hot Press* Readers' Poll since 1980. Recreations: scuba diving, gardening, theatre, photography. Contact: Liz Devlin, 30, Glengara Park. Dún Laoghaire, Co. Dublin. **T** and **F** 01 236 0641

Continues to push out the boundaries not only of his own talent but of Irish contemporary music in the new millennium.

BRADY, His Grace, The Most Reverend, Sean; ARCHBISHOP OF ARMAGH
b 1939, Laragh, Co. Cavan; single; *edu*. Caulfield National School, Laragh; St Patrick's College, Cavan; St Patrick's College, Maynooth; Pontifical Irish College, Rome; BA (Ancient Classics); Licentiate in Theology (STL Lateran University Rome); Doctorate in Canon Law (DCL Lateran University, Rome); L.L.D, (*hc*) University of Ulster 2002; Archbishop of Armagh; Ordained priest 1964; ordained Coadjutor Archbishop of Armagh 1995; succeeded as Archbishop of Armagh 1996; installed as Archbishop of Armagh 1996; Professor, St Patrick's College, Cavan 1967-80; Vice-Rector Irish College, Rome 1980-87; PP, Castletara, Co. Cavan (Ballyhaise) 1993-94; Coadjutor Archbishop of Armagh 1995-96; Archbishop of Armagh and Primate of All Ireland 1996 to date; Chairman of Irish Episcopal Conference 1996 to date; Chairman of Standing Committee of Irish Episcopal Conference 1996 to date; Chairman of Episcopal Visitors to St Patrick's College, Maynooth 1996-2001; Member of the Holy See's Pontifical Commission for the Cultural Goods of the Church 2002 to date. Motto: *Jesum Christum Cognoscere* (To Know Jesus Christ: cf John 17:3). Contact: Ara Coeli, Armagh, BT61 7QY **T** 028 3752 2045 **F** 028 3752 6182 email admin@aracoeli.com.

Low profile, quiet, spiritual man with a high degree of humility; seen as a man of the people.

BRADY, Thomas, John; JOURNALIST
b 1951; *m* Mary Burns; 1*s* 1*d*; *edu*. Naas CBS; Journalist, *Leinster Leader* 1969-'72; reporter *Irish Press* 1972-'73; security correspondent *Irish Press* 1973-'85; deputy news editor *Irish Press* 1985-'87; news editor *Irish Press* 1985-'89; Security editor Independent News & Media 1989 to date. Clubs: Naas GAA. Recreations: horseracing, GAA, music, walking. Contact: 27/32 Talbot Street. Dublin 1. **T** 01 7055713 **F** 01 7055790 email tbrady@unison.independent.ie

Hard working, well respected, well connected security editor.

BRAIDEN née Egan, Olive, Carmel; CHAIRPERSON, ARTS COUNCIL OF IRELAND
b 1946, Ballymote, Co. Sligo; *m* Sean Braiden; 3*s* 2*d*; *edu*. Coláiste Muire, Ballymote, Sligo; UCD Social Science; Trinity College Dublin; M.Phil (Gender studies) 2003; Chairperson Arts Council of Ireland; joined Dublin Rape Crisis Centre as a volunteer 1983; appointed Director of the Centre 1990-2000; initiated counselling training programmes in Croatia and Bosnia in 1993 to date; planning for similar programmes with Kosovar refugees in Albania; initiated unique study on 'Legal Process and Victims of Rape' 1998 (funded by Grotius Programme); Member Amnesty, Children's

Rights Alliance, Ireland Action for Bosnia, Unifem – United Nations Women's Organisation; Board Member Well Woman Centres; Irish Court Services Transitional Board 1998; Independent Radio and Television Commission 1998; The Judicial Appointments Advisory Board 1999; Irish delegate to EU Commission Expert Committee on Crime Victims' Issues 1998; nominated 'European Women of the Year' 1993; unsuccessful candidate European Parliament election 1994; listed in the Expert Group on Child Abuse Guidelines Dept. of Health 1998; The National Steering Committee on Violence against Women Dept. of Justice 1998; appointed chair Crisis Pregnancy Agency; Chair of the PVG on Benchmarking for the Dept. of Justice; appointed Chair, The Arts Council of Ireland 2003 to date. Clubs: Royal Dublin Society, Friend of the Hugh Lane Gallery; Friend of the National Concert Hall. Recreations: current affairs, music (jazz), theatre, cinema, cooking, family, friends. Contact: The Arts Council, 70, Merrion Square, Dublin 2. **T** 01 618 0200 **F** 01 676 1302

Olive Braiden

> An unflappable, energetic and articulate woman with good Fianna Fáil political connections; not afraid to take difficult decisions; she faces many challenges in the Arts Council into the future.

BRANDON, née Orr, Cherry, Ann; ARTIST/FARMER

b 1931, Dublin; *m* Ernest Brandon; *decd*; 1*d*; *edu*. Merstham Grange, Surrey, England; The Hall, Monkstown, Co Dublin; Alexandra College, Dublin; Trained privately with artists in Ireland and abroad; Royal College of Art Examinations; Lecturer on the Holy Land; Private (Fashion) Artist and Designer primarily on international scene to date; designs for Giorgio Armani for the seasonal colour palettes in Ireland and in Italy; Board Member ISPCC; Royal Dublin Society; Member of Institute of Designers in Ireland. Clubs: The Royal Horticultural Society. Recreations: horse breeding, racing, gardening. Contact: Clonageera, Durrow, Co Laois. **T** 0502 36108 **F** 0502 36154

> A lively, vivacious and gracious artist; mixes the arts with civic works and equine interests; sees life as a great garden; no wonder Giorgio Armani relies on her vivid colour sense.

BRAYDEN, David, James; SENIOR LECTURER COLLEGE OF LIFE SCIENCES/ PRINICIPLE INVESTIGATOR CONWAY INSTITUTE

b 1963, Dublin; *m* Anne O'Loughlin; 2*d*; *edu*. Sandymount High School, Dublin; University College Dublin, B.Sc (1st Class Hons) Pharmacology; Cambridge, M.Sc Pharmacology 1985; Cambridge M. Phil 1987; Cambridge, Ph.D Pharmacology 1989; Research Assistant Cambridge University 1989; Post-doctoral Research Fellow Stanford University California 1989-'91; Senior Scientist and Project Manager Elan Corp. Dublin 1991-01; Current Chairman UK/Ireland Controlled Release Society; *Publ.* Editorial Board Member Journals, *Drug Discovery To Day; Advanced Drug Delivery Reviews; European J. Pharm. Society;* 2004 winner of best paper in Veterinary Controlled Release CRS; Consultant to Merrion Biopharma, TEVA Industries; two books; 46 peer-reviewed scientific papers, seven patents. Clubs: Glenageary Tennis Club (Captain 1996). Recreations: Tennis, walking Curracloe beach, Wexford, die-hard Liverpool FC fan. Contact: Room H 018, Veterinary Building, University College Dublin, Belfield, Dublin 4. **T** 01 716 6013 **F** 01 716 6023 email david.brayden@ucd.ie

BRAZIL, Tony; MANAGING DIRECTOR, LIMERICK TRAVEL

b 1943, Limerick; *m* Sheila McNamara; 3*s*; *edu*. St James Christian Brothers School; University College Dublin, B.Comm; Managing Director, Limerick Travel; Assistant Regional Manager, Shannonside Tourism 1966-69; Marketing Manager, Dan Ryan Rent-a-Car Ltd, 1969-71; Managing Director/Owner, Limerick Travel 1971 to date; Member, Marketing Institute; Honorary Spanish Consul (Clare/Limerick); President, Irish Travel Agents Association 1990-92 and 2000-03; Director, Bórd Fáilte 1974-88; Aer Rianta 1985-89; Member Board Hunt Museum 1997 to date. Recreations: reading, Rotary. Contact: Limerick Travel, Bedford House, Bedford Row, Limerick. **T** 061 204444 **F** 061 204455. web www.letsgotravel.ie

> Low profile, well connected and respected; has achieved great things with his business and works very hard for the wider interests of the South Western Region.

BREATHNACH, Paddy; FILM DIRECTOR
b 1964; single; *edu.* Scoil na Leanbh, An Rinn, Co. Pórt Láirge; Sallynoggin Community School;
University College Dublin; BA (Philosophy and Politics); Film Director; worked as director on
Exploring the Landscape series with Éamon de Buitléar; directed *A Stone of the Heart* 1991; founded
Treasure Films with Robert Walpole 1992; directed *The Road to America* 1993; *Ailsa* (producer Ed
Guiney) 1994; directed *WRH* six-part documentary for RTÉ; *A Long Way Home* 1995; other director
credits include *I Went Down* (producer Robert Walpole), produced *South Paw* (director Liam
McGrath) with Robert Walpole 1998, selected for Sundance Festival 1999; Awards: Euskal Media
Award, San Sebastian Film Festival (for *Ailsa*); New Director's Prize, Jury Prize, Best Screen Play
Award, Special from Fipresci Jury, San Sebastian Film Festival 1997, Silver Disc Award, Bogota; Best
Director Award, Thessaloniki Film Festival 1977, selected for World Cinema section at Sundance
Festival 1998 and premiered New York 1998 *(all for I Went Down);* Special Jury Prize, *Stone of the
Heart,* Cork 1991; Member Board of Directors. Dublin Film Festival. Contact: Treasure Films,
Shamrock Chambers, 1-2 Eustace Street, Dublin 2. **T** 01 670 9609 **F** 01 670 9612.

An engaging film maker who awaits his second wind; much expected of him.

BREHENY, Martin; GAA EDITOR, IRISH INDEPENDENT
b 1953; *m* Rosemary ; 1*s* 1*d*; *edu.* Coláiste Seosaimh, Glenamaddy, Co Galway; GAA Editor Irish
Independent; general reporter *Tuam Herald* 1976-'79; sports writer, Irish Press Group 1979-95;
sports writer *Ireland on Sunday* 1996-99; GAA Editor, *Irish Independent* since April 2005. Clubs:
Kilkerrin/Clonberne GAA Club (Galway); St. Jude's GAA Club, Templeogue, Dublin. Recreations:
'All sports, plus proving to people that sports writers are also interested in politics, drama, flying,
thinking and being honest'. Contact: 3, Knocklyon Road, Templeogue, Dublin 16. Irish Independent,
29-30 Talbot Street, Dublin 1 **T** 01 705 5000 email mbreheny@eircom.net

Brings honesty, commitment, passion and a real feel for rural Ireland, to his GAA
reportage.

BREEN, Sean, Macarius; PARISH PRIEST
b 1937; single; *edu*; St Patrick's College Cavan; University College Dublin; Maynooth College; BA
(Philosophy Politics & Ethics); Theology at Maynooth; A curate in various parishes in the
Archdiocese of Dublin County and City; entire career involved in parish work. Recreations: racing in
general, a general interest in all sports, especially international soccer matches. Contact: The
Presbytery, Chapel Street, Ballymore Eustace, Naas, Co Kildare. **T** 045 864114

Appropriately, Ireland's best known and loved racing priest has three race tracks in his
parish; an international celebrity in the racing world since he first began to bless the
Irish runners and riders and offer Mass for a successful day's punting each morning at
the Cheltenham Festival; always a sought-after tipster; 'The Breener' is not only one of
Ireland's best known clergymen, he is undoubtedly part of the fabric of the Irish racing
world.

BRENNAN, Barry; MANAGING DIRECTOR, JOHNTSON PRESS
b 1956, Galway; *m* Jackie; 1*s* 1*d*; *edu.* St. Jarlath's College, Tuam, Co. Galway; BA IMI GIT; (MGMT);
DIP Marketing; Group Marketing Director Independent News and Media Ireland plc; Adidas Ireland;
Wrangler (VF CORP), London & Brussels; Independent News & Media plc; Managing Director
Johnson Press 2006 – todate. Recreations: sport, travel, books, film. Contact: Johnston Press,
Leinster Leader, 14, South Main Street, Naas, Co. Kildare. T 045 897302
email brianbrennan@leinsterleader.ie web www.leinsterleader.ie

The former Galway Gaelic footballer gave a new marketing focus to IN&M during his
sojourn at Abbey Street; has moved on to more lucrative and convenient pastures.

BRENNAN, Brian; HOTEL PROPRIETOR AND PROPERTY DEVELOPER
b 1965; single; *edu*; Gorey CBS, Gorey, Co Wexford; Trainee Manager in Burlington Hotel Dublin; at
23 had progressed to Senior Assistant Manager; moved to Mont Clare Hotel as General Manager;
purchased the Arklow Bay Hotel, Co. Wicklow 1994; purchased Springhill Court Hotel, Kilkenny
1996; Bettystown Hotel, 2006; Clonmel Park Hotel, 2006; in recent years has built up a sustained
property portfolio in Ireland, Spain and New York. Recreations: all sports, GAA, soccer, golf, marathon
running, golf. Contact: Gorey Hill, Gorey, Co Wexford. M 086 2521458 email Brian@Arklowbay.com

Cut his teeth in the hospitality business in the well-known family pub, the 64 in Gorey; the progressive hotelier has, at a young age, built up an enviable reputation in the industry through hard work, innovative management and vision.

BRENNAN, Brian, Stephen; JOURNALIST
b 1945, Dublin; *m* Mary; 3*d; edu.* Drimnagh Castle Christian Brothers; University College Dublin; B.Sc; *Irish Independent* Investigative Team; *Irish Press*; *Sunday World* reporter; *Evening Press* sub-editor; *Sunday Independent* Deputy Editor; *Irish Independent* Associate Editor; *Irish Independent* Weekend Editor; member *Irish Independent* Investigative Team. Recreations: sport, theatre, conversation. Contact: *Irish Independent*, 27 – 32, Talbot Street, Dublin 1 **T** 01 705 5000 email brianbrennan@unison.independent.ie

An extremely hardworking journalist who built up the Irish Independent Weekend magazine into a successful, interesting, feature-packed read; highly respected, good sense of humour.

BRENNAN, Cecily; ARTIST
b 1955; Co Galway; *m*; 1*s; edu.* National College of Art & Design, Dublin 1st Class Honours; Artist; selected solo shows: Project Art Centre 1982; The Iceland Work, Taylor Galleries Dublin 1988; Douglas Hyde Gallery Dublin 1992; Bandaged Heart, Taylor Galleries Dublin 2001; Nuova Icona, Venice 2005; Balancing, Ormeau Baths Gallery, Belfast 2005; Melancholia, Oratomodi, San Ludovico, Venice, Italy; Selected Group Shows: Siar 50, IMMA; The Trouble with Talkies, group show ADI Projects London 2005; Artists for Amnesty IMMA 2004; Something Else, Turkey, Finland; Holy Show, Chester Beatty Gallery 2003. Recreations: film, food, literature. Contact: 13 Kenilworth Park, Harold's Cross, Dublin 6W. **T** 01 492 3808 **F** 01 492 3808 email cecilybrennan@eircom.net

An inventive and engaging painter whose continuing exploration of the hidden delights within the visual world continue to fascinate her as much as her audience; this artist's eye has long been central to her work; has held her palette with honour and dignity.

BRENNAN, Donald; FASHION DESIGNER
b 1965; single; *edu.* St. Thomas More School, Bedford, UK; University of Hertfordshire UK, BA (Hons) Business Studies; after graduation moved to France; marketing; moved into fashion sector; established Oakes fashion house with Niall Tyrrell (*qv*) 1996; second label Tyrell & Brennan launched Fashion Week Paris 2005; this newest label is now sold into five European countries and the US; plans to open a Paris office and extend into the Middle-Eastern markets. Recreations: painting, sculpting, cooking, reading, Latin American dancing. Contact: Oakes, 11, South William Street, Dublin 2. **T** 01 670 4178 F 01 677 0363 email oakes @eircom.net web www.oakes.ie

Known for his superb tailoring; with partner Niall Tyrell designs flattering fashion that attracts a sophisticated clientele.

BRENNAN, Eamonn, Noel; CHIEF EXECUTIVE, IRISH AVIATION AUTHORITY
b 1957; *m* Mary; 2*s* 1*d; edu.* St. Joseph's College, Galway, University College Galway; Institute of Chartered Accountants; Bachelor of Commerce; Fellow of the Institute of Chartered Accountants; Fellow of the Institute of Transport; Chief Executive, Irish Aviation Authority; Commercial Director IAA 1995-2003; Consultant & Financial Accountant in Asia & Europe 1989-95. Contact: Aviation House, Hawkins Street., Dublin 2. **T** 01 6718 655 **F** 01 679 2934 email Eamonn.Brennan@IAA.IE

With vast increase in air traffic and the fleets of privately own jets and helicopters, this position becomes pivotal for a safe, well run and well regulated industry.

BRENNAN, Francis; HOTELIER
b 1953, Dublin; single; *edu.* CUS Leeson Street, Dublin; Degree Hotel Management; Cathal Brugha Catering and Hotel Management College Dublin; Parknasilla Hotel,

Francis Brennan

Co. Kerry 1978-'80; Park Hotel, Kenmare 1980-'95. Recreations: work, travel. Contact: Park Hotel Kenmare, Co Kerry. **T** 064 41280 **F** 064 41402 email info@parkkenmare.com

> One of the country's most innovative hoteliers; only tolerates perfection; has created an oasis in Kenmare long recognised by bon viveurs from all over the world; led the spa posse with the award winning Samhas Spa which, though only a few years old, has received international acclaim.

BRENNAN, John Gerard; HOTELIER

b 1965; *m* Gwen; 1*s* 1*d*; *edu.* C.U.S Lesson Street Dublin; St Mary's Ballisodare, Sligo; Cornell School of Hospitality New York; Masters in Hotel Management from Francis Brennan; Managing Director, Park Hotel, Kenmare, Co. Kerry; joined the Sligo Park Hotel as a barman , 1982; Over the following 12 years progressed to Assistant Manager with responsibility for Leisure Development and Sales; joined his brother Francis in the Park Hotel Kenmare and quickly embarked on a redevelopment program 1994; researched the world's spa market and developed the deluxe destination spa SAMAS which opened in 2003; currently working with Sean Mulryan's Ballymore Homes on a spa development in Canary Wharf London; also developing a multimillion euro residential development on the grounds of the Park Hotel Kenmare, THE RETREATS., with interiors by Viscount David Linley 2006 – 2007; launch of AURASPAS a worldwide network of lifestyle destinations 2007; Clubs: Kenmare Golf Club, Kenmare Bay Sailing Club, The Wine Society; Recreations: golf, sailing. Contact: The Park Hotel, Kenmare, Co. Kerry. **T** 064 41200 **F** 064 41402 email info@parkkenmare.com web www.parkkenmare.com

> Undoubtedly the energy and inspiration behind SAMAS, recognized as one of the world's top spas which now offers its own range of products and treatments is indefatigable in his search for perfection and will go to the ends ot the earth in the pursuit of excellence (he went to Katmandu sourcing product for his spa); like his brother Francis (*qv*) has boundless energy, is easy going, enjoys life and is a wonderful ambassador for Kenmare, Kerry and Ireland.

John Brennan

BRENNAN, John, Joseph; HOTEL DIRECTOR

b 1962, Dublin; *m* Doris Reynolds; *edu.* St Michael's College, Ballsbridge, Dublin; Trinity College Dublin; Dublin College of Catering; MA, B.Sc (Hons), H Dip; Regional Vice President and General Manager of Four Seasons Hotel and Resorts; Spent 21 years in Four Seasons Hotels and Resorts in Malaysia, Hong Kong, London, Tokyo, Dallas, Philadelphia and Toronto; Regional Vice President and General Manager of Four Seasons Hotel and Resorts to date. Recreations: golf, reading. Contact: Four Seasons Hotel Dublin, Simmonscourt Road, Dublin 4. **T** 01 665 4800 **F** 01 6672195 email john.brennan@fourseasons.com www.fourseasons.com

> Brennan brings an international reputation and standards to the Irish hotel scene, managing the first Irish Four Seasons, a true five-star property, in Ballsbridge, Dublin; the son of the late Michael Brennan, the legendary hotelier who built up the Doyle Hotel group with the late PV Doyle, he has pursued an illustrious career with the Four Seasons Hotel chain all over the world; is credited with driving up hotel standards not only throughout the capital – resulting in Dublin becoming one of Europe's most attractive locations – but also throughout the country.

BRENNAN, Joseph 'Joe'; DIPLOMAT

b 1949, Dublin; single; *edu.* Gonzaga College, Dublin; University College Dublin; BA(Hons) History and Politics; College of Europe, Bruges; Diploma Higher European Studies; Diplomat; Deputy Chief of Protocol, Dept. of Foreign Affairs 1973 to date; Diplomat Dept. of Foreign Affairs: postings Belgium, Netherlands, France, Saudi Arabia, Italy; Deputy Secretary General to President Mary Robinson 1991-95; assigned to *L'Imaginaire Irlandaise*, France 1995-96; Cultural Division 1996-97; Deputy Chief of Protocol 1997 to date. Recreations: music, theatre, travel, people. Contact: Dept. of Foreign Affairs, Iveagh House, Dublin 2. **T** 01 408 2749

> A true diplomat and thoroughly civilized man who returns all telephone calls, a trait as rare as hen's teeth in public servants; the oracle on protocol; scion of a long-playing Irish political and business family, he's known all over the world in diplomatic and musical circles.

BRENNAN, Michael; HOTELIER

b 1964, Dublin; single; *edu.* St. Michael's College, Ballsbridge, Dublin; Dublin College of Catering, Cathal Brugha Street, Dublin; Trinity College Dublin; B.Sc. Mgmt; MA; General Manager Hotel Europe; worked in a number of Doyle Hotels including Berkeley Court, Westbury Hotel, Burlington Hotel. Clubs: Killarney Golf & Fishing Club. Recreations: golf, travel. Contact: Hotel Europe, Killarney, Co. Kerry. **T** 064 71350 email Michael.Brennan@liebherr.com www.killarneyhotels.ie

> Second son of the late Michael Brennan, one of Ireland's most respected hoteliers; also followed in the footsteps of elder brother John (*qv*); runs a tight ship at the Hotel Europe and has breathed new life into one of the most beautifully located hotels in the country.

BRENNAN, Niamh; PROFESSOR

b 1954, Dublin; *m* Michael McDowell (*qv*); 3*s*; *edu.*UCD B.Sc. 1976 (Microbiology), Warwick University Ph.D 1996; FCA, chartered accountant; Michael MacCormac Professor of Management at University College Dublin; Academic Director of the Institute of Directors Centre for Corporate Governance, UCD; KPMG Chartered Accountants 1976- 80; Lecturer UCD 1980- 97; Senior Lecturer UCD 1997- 99; Michael MacCormac Professor of Management, University College Dublin 1999 to date; Head of Dept. of Accounting UCD 2002 to date; Academic Director Institute of Directors Centre for Corporate Governance, UCD 2002 to date; Associate Dean of Research Faculty of Commerce, Graduate School of Business, UCD/Smurfit School of Business Studies 2004 to date; Non-executive director Ulster Bank; Health Services Executive; Former non-executive director of Lifetime Assurance (Bank of Ireland's Life Assurance subsidiary); Coillte, the State Forestry company; Co-Operation Ireland; Member audit committee of the Dept. of Agriculture and Food; Chaired Commission on Financial Management and Control Systems in the Health Services; Publ. Has published widely in the areas of Financial Reporting, Corporate Governance and Forensic Accounting: Brennan, N. and Hennessy, J., *Forensic Accounting* 2001; Pierce, A. and Brennan, N., *Principles and Practice of Group Accounts: A European Perspective* 2003; Brennan, N. and McDermott, M., *Alternative Perspectives on Independence of Directors, Corporate Governance: An International Review* 2004; Contact: Room Q208 Accountancy, University College Dublin, Belfield, Dublin 4. **T** 01 716 4707 **F** 01 1716 4765 email niamh.brennan@ucd.ie

> Built up a impressive array of directorships in the State and private sectors; bright, able and astute; A straight-from-the-hip performer; has the capacity to rub people up the wrong way; extremely well respected in the business and academic worlds; with husband Michael Mc Dowell (*qv*) makes an extremely dynamic duo.

BRENNAN, Nicky; PRESIDENT GAA

b 1950, Kilkenny; *m* Mairéad; 5*c*; *edu.* Conahy N.S.; St. Kieran's College, Kilkenny; President, GAA; trained as accountant Avonmore Co-op; head IT Glanbia plc; won 4 All-Ireland Senior Hurling Medals with Kilkenny; former chairman Kilkenny GAA Board and Leinster Provisional Council; former Manager Kilkenny hurling team. elected President GAA 2006 – todate; Recreations: GAA. Contact: Croke Park, St. Joseph's Avenue, Off Clonliffe Road, Dublin 3. **T** 01 819 2323 **F** 01 819 2324 email info@gaa.ie web www.gaa.ie Dublin 3.

> From a prosperous farming family in North Kilkenny, bright, articulate and has a managerial approach to his GAA involvement; faces a difficult challenge following in the footsteps of his predecessor Sean Kelly (*qv*), the darling of the media for promoting the opening up of Croke Park to other sports; will carve out his own niche at the top of Ireland's largest sporting organization in his own inimitable, businesslike way.

BRENNAN, Séamus; PUBLIC REPRESENTATIVE

b 1948, Galway; *m* Ann O'Shaughnessy; 2*s* 4*d*; *edu.* St. Joseph's School, Galway; University College Galway, B.Comm, BA; University College Dublin, M.Comm; qualified as an accountant; General Secretary, Fianna Fáil 1973-80; Senator (Taoiseach's nominee) 1977-81; Minister for Trade and Marketing 1987-89; Minister for Tourism and Transport 1989 -91; Minister for Tourism, Transport and Communications 1991-'92; Minister for Education 1992-93; Minister for Commerce and Technology 1993-94; Fianna Fáil spokesperson on Transport, Energy and

Séamus Brennan

Communications; 1995 -97; Government Chief Whip 1997- 02; Minister of State to An Taoiseach and at the Department of Defence; Minister for Transport 2002 – 04; Minister for Social and Family Affairs 2004 to date. Clubs: Grange Golf Club; David Lloyd Riverview. Recreations: golf, tennis. Contact: 9, Braemor Road Churchtown, Dublin 14. (constituency office). **T** 01 662 4888 web www.welfare.ie

At the coal face of Irish politics for 30 years; good media performer; ambitious politician whose career has noticeably slowed down in recent times.

BRENNAN, Stephen Denis Patrick; ACTOR

b 1955; *m* Martina Stanley; *sep*; *p*; 1*s* 3*d*; *edu.* Terenure College Dublin; Actor; began his acting career in the Gate Theatre, Dublin, with *The Barretts of Wimpole Street* in 1971; to date has played more than 50 leading roles including Brian Friel's *Living Quarters*, Tom Murphy's *The Morning after Optimism*, Brian Moore's *The Emperor of Ice Cream*, Tom Kilroy's *Talbot's Box* which transferred to the Royal Court, London; *Joseph and His Amazing Technicolor Dreamcoat* 1974; *Jesus Christ Superstar* 1975; Abbey Theatre Company 1976-83; title role in *Hamlet*, with Royal National Theatre, London 1984; starred in many Gate Theatre productions including *Private Lives, Waiting for Godot, Tartuffe, Cyrano de Bergerac*; TV includes *El Cid, Ballykissangel*; films include *Eat the Peach; Beckett on Film* directed by Robin Lefevre; Member Irish Actors Equity; The Theatrical Cavaliers Cricket Club. Recreations: painting, gardening songwriting, interior decorating, drinking, women. Contact: Aude Powell, Brunskill Management, Suite 8A, 169, Queensgate, London SW7. **T** 0044 171 581 3388.

Able, charming and can play right across the range of roles; thinks deeply about his roles and has been fortunate with many of them; having been a glamorous juve he now plays major leading roles with élan.

BRESLIN, Cathal; PIANIST

b 1978, Derry; single; *edu.* Royal College of Music, London; BMus (1st Class Hons) 2001; Royal Northern College of Music, Manchester 2003; PPRNCM (professional performance); PG Dip with distinction 2002; Master of Music (Distinction) 2002; CCEA Language School, Spanish, Madrid 2003-'04; CCEA Language School Madrid, Chinese Mandarin; Current Doctoral Studies (Doctor of Musical Arts, University of Ann Arbor, University of Michigan; Pianist; Recent concerts; Mozart Concerto Ulster Orchestra 2005; Tour of Valencia Province, Spain 2005; NCH Rising Star Recital 2005; performances in Athens, Hong Kong 2004; only featured Irish artist at Mozart Concerto, European Broadcasting Union's Mozart Anniversary Year Project 2006; Awards: AXA Dublin International Piano Competition Special Awards 2003; First Prize 'Carlet' Spain; Second Prize 'Grand Konserteum' Greece; Bank of Ireland Millennial Scholarship 2005; Fulbright Scholarship 2005. Contact: 35 Troy Park, Derry BT48 7RL. **T** 028 71 351040 **M** 078 55 4444 25 email cbreslinpianist@yahoo.co.uk

One of the new generation of rising stars. Talented, organised, polite; his high level of musicality has ensured that his progress is rapid and deservedly so.

BRETT, James, 'Jim'; MANAGING DIRECTOR BRETT GROUP

b 1952; *m* Frances Minogue; 2 *s*; *edu.* Windgap National School; Christian Brothers School, Callan, Co Kilkenny; University College Dublin, B.Ag.Sc.; Radio Producer/Presenter, RTÉ 1975-80; Assistant Editor, *The Farmer* 1979-81; Director, Brett Group, Kilkenny-based family agribusiness 1980, Managing Director since 1989; Fianna Fáil supporter, member of Kilkenny County Council since 1985; Board member and former Chairman, Radio Kilkenny; Member and former Chairman, South East Regional Authority; Member EU Committee of the Regions, The Society of Feed Technologists, A.S.A. Clubs: Mount Juliet Golf and County, Callan Golf Club. Recreations: reading, tennis. Contact: Brett Brothers Ltd., Callan, Co. Kilkenny. **T** 056 25140 **F** 056 25353

The former Fianna Fáil County Councillor may revise his Dáil ambitions with a vacancy looming in the constituency; an astute businessman, he has grown and developed the family agri-provender business in a very competitive sector.

Malcolm Brighton

BRIGHTON, Malcolm; MANAGING DIRECTOR, CONAI DESIGNS

b 1951, London, England; *m* Caroline; 2*d*; *edu.* Horley County Secondary, Sussex, England;

Managing Director and Director, Conai Designs; Franchisee, Habitat Ireland and Northern Ireland which operates three stores, in Dublin, Galway and Belfast; Retail Management Trainee, Grants of Croydon 1968-72; Merchandise Manager, Debenhams 1972 -77; Merchandise Buyer, Habitat UK 1977-84; Vice President of Buying and Merchandising, Conran's USA/NYC 1984-86; Merchandise and Buying Director, Habitat UK 1986-90; Logistics Director, Habitat Group 1990- 92; Buying, Merchandise, Logistics & Franchise Director, Habitat UK 1992- 96; Deputy Chief Executive of Habitat Group, based in Paris 1996 – 98; Deputy Chief Executive in charge of buying and design, Habitat Group 1998-02; Bought franchise rights for Ireland 2002 to date. Recreations: golf, fishing, travel. cultures of other countries, wine. Contact: Habitat, 6-10 Suffolk Street, Dublin 2. **T** 01 677 1433

> Bright, innovative with an excellent eye for design; has built his Habitat franchise into a major player in the furniture and furnishings business in Ireland.

BRITTON, Brian, Vincent; HOTELIER
b 1950, Rossnowlagh, Co. Donegal; *div.*; *2s 1d*; *edu.* Franciscan College, Gormanstown, Co Meath; Trinity College Dublin; FCA, BBS; Peat Marwick Mitchell, Zambia 1975-77; deputy chief executive, Goodman International Ltd; Managing Director Britton Consultants Ltd; Sandhouse Hotel Ltd 1991 to date; Contact: Sandhouse Hotel, Rossnowlagh, Co. Donegal. **T** 042 932 2994 **F** 042 932 2995 email bbritton@eircom.net

> Bright, charming, highly articulate accountant; for many years the acceptable face of the meat industry in Ireland; keen sportsman; former president of the Irish Surfing Association.

BRITTON, David A; DIRECTOR, JAMES ADAM & COMPANY
b 1963, Rossnowlagh, Co. Donegal; *m* Karen Reihill; *1s 1d*; *edu.* Sligo Grammar School; Trinity College Dublin, BBS, ACA; trained Stokes Kennedy Crowley; joined family hotel business in Co. Donegal Sandhouse Hotel 1988-90; joined Adam & Sons 1990-92; established The Frederick Gallery, Dublin with wife Karen 1992-05; Director James Adam & Co 2005 to date. Clubs: RIAC. Recreations: weekend gardener, wine, food. Contact: James Adam & Co., St Stephen's Green, Dublin 2. **T** 01 676 0261 **F** 01 662 4725 email d.britton@adams.ie

> Well informed and connected which ensured the success of his Frederick Gallery; has taken a career change in recent times and should be a good acquisition.

David Britton

BROPHY, Michael; MANAGING DIRECTOR, SUNDAY WORLD
b 1949, Dublin; *m* Eileen Noonan; *1s 1d*; *edu.* Marian College, Ballsbridge, Dublin; Dublin Institute of Technology; Night Editor, *Irish Independent* 1980; Editor, *Evening Herald* 1985; Editor and Director of Independent Star Limited 1990; Managing Director, *Sunday World* and Terenure Printers 1995 to date. Clubs: DLSP Rugby Club, David Lloyd Riverview Fitness; Roundwood Golf Club. Recreations: rugby, golf. Contact: *Sunday World*, Independent House, 27-32 Talbot Street, Dublin 1. **T** 01 884 8901

> Despite increased competition manages to keep Ireland's first red-top Sunday performing well.

Michael Brophy

BROSNAN, Denis; CHAIRMAN, HORSE RACING IRELAND
b 1944, Tralee; *m* Joan McNamara; *2s 2d*; *edu.* St Brendan's College, Killarney; University College Cork, M.Sc; Chairman, Horse Racing Ireland; worked as a detergent salesman before joining Golden Vale as Production Manager; General Manager, North Kerry Milk Products 1972; prime mover in the co-operative movement among Kerry farmers; formed Kerry Co-operative 1974: within three years turnover had trebled; masterminded the flotation of Kerry Co-Op, now Kerry Group 1986; acquired Beatreme Foods and moved into the US market, acquired for £250 million; DCA Foods Industries 1994; acquired Dalgety plc for £394 million; Chairman, Irish Horseracing Authority 1994 to date; has announced his decision to stand down as Chairman HRI at the end of 2006; Next Generation Clubs UK with John Magnier (*qv*), JP Mc Manus (*qv*), Michael Tabor, Billie Jean King. Recreations: GAA sports, soccer, racing, golf. Contact: Horse Racing Ireland, Thoroughbred County House, Kill, Co. Kildare. **T** 045 842 800 **F** 045 842 801 email dbrosnan@hri.ie

> Having spent over 30 years with the Kerry Group, mainly as Chief Executive and

Denis Brosnan

latterly as Chairman, developing it into a major global food corporation, Brosnan retains his deep interest in the bloodstock industry and racing through his chairmanship of HRI (Horse Racing Ireland) and his own stud in Croom, Co. Limerick. Surprised many in the food industry with his rapid exit from the boardroom of his beloved Kerry Group plc; maintains an impressive property portfolio; also involved with the 'Three Wise Men' – JP Mc Manus (*qv*), John Magnier (*qv*), Dermot Desmond (*qv*) – in the rapidly expanding Barchester Nursing Home Group in the UK which is expected to do an IPO in the near future.

BROUGH, David, Joseph; UNIVERSITY CHAPLAIN
b 1967, Dublin; single; *edu*. Árdscoil La Salle, Raheny, Dublin; Holy Cross College, Clonliffe, Dublin. Dip Phil.; St.Patrick's NUI Maynooth, Co. Kildare (BA, BD); Roman Catholic Chaplain, University College Dublin; Deacon, Westminster Cathedral London 1991; Curate St. Kevin's Parish, Kilnamanagh, Dublin 1992-'97; Chaplain/Student Advisor UCD 1997 to date; Director of Accord Counselling Centre, Dún Laoghaire; Promoter of Annual UCD Arts Fashion Show, Treasurer UCD Comedy Society. Recreations: travel, history, reading, autobiography, Radio D.J. Contact: Apt 1, St. Stephen's, UCD Belfield, Dublin 4. **T** 01 260 5582 **F** 01 716 8543 email david.brough@ucd.ie

Well respected and liked by students and faculty; empathises with their everyday issues; very active on campus.

BROWN, Terence, Peter, McCord; PROFESSOR AND DEAN OF ARTS AND HUMANITIES
b 1944, Loping China; *m* Suzanne; 1*s* 1*d*; *edu*. Sullivan Upper School Holywood, Co. Down; Magee University College, Derry; Trinity College Dublin (MA, Ph.D); Professor of Anglo Irish Literature Trinity College Dublin; Professor and Dean of Arts and Humanities; Trinity College Dublin 1968 to date; *Publ. Louis Mac Niece: Sceptical Vision; Northern Voices; Poets from Ulster; Ireland A Social and Cultural History 1922-2002; Ireland's Literature: Selected Essays; The Life of W. B. Yeats: A Critical Biography.* Recreations: reading, walking, music. Contact: Arts Department, Trinity College, Dublin 2. **T** 01 606 1400 web www.tcd.ie

A thoughtful and hardworking Professor whose published critiques on Irish writing and on Irish Northern sensitivities are landmarks of academic excellence. His insights given time and space will outlast those written by some of his contemporaries.

BROWNE, Daniel 'Dan'; CHIEF EXECUTIVE, DAWN MEATS
b 1937, Co. Cork; *m* Kay McGoldrick; 2*s* 2*d*; *edu*. Douglas National School, Cork; Colaiste Chriost Ri; University College Cork; University College Dublin; B.Ag. Sc; M.Ag. Sc. Managing Director Dawn Meats; An Foras Taluntais (Teagasc) Moorpark, Co Cork 1962 – 1973; International Meat Processors meat factory, Midleton 1973 – 1980; Dawn Meats 1980 to date; served on a number of State boards; Contact: Dawn Meats, Grannagh, Waterford. **T** 051-309200 web www.dawnmeats.com

The former researcher for An Foras Taluntais (now Teagasc) has become a most successful businessman running the Dawn Meats Group, Ireland's biggest meat company; served as the chairman of Teagasc; well connected politically.

BROWNE, Mark, Edward; GENERAL MANAGER MONART SPA
b 1965, Enniscorthy, Co. Wexford; single; *edu*. CBS, Enniscorthy, County Wexford; Griffin Group In-house Management Programme; General Manager Monart Spa; Trainee Manager, Hotel Rosslare, Wexford 1983-88; Chef Placement, Hotel du Rond Point de Longchamp, Paris France 1988-89; Asst. Front Office Manager, Hyatt Regency Grand Cayman 1989-91; General Manager, Ferrycarrig Hotel, Wexford 1991-05; General Manager, Monart Destination Spa 2005 to date. Recreations: keeping fit, horses, arts and leisure. Contact: Monart Day Spa, The Still, Enniscorthy, Co. Wexford. **T** 086 8122 165 email mark.browne@griffingroup.ie web www.griffingroup.ie/monarthouse.html

Handsome ebullient and warm personality; for 14 years at the helm of the Ferrycarraig Hotel where even the most demanding diva was totally pampered; will well-suit the chic clientele at Ireland's first destination spa, Monart.

BROWNE, Tom; MANAGING DIRECTOR, ANGLO IRISH BANK IRELAND
b 1963, Limerick; *m* Diane McKee; 2*s*; *edu.*Ard Scoil Ris, Limerick; University of Limerick;
University College Dublin; BBS; MBS; Managing Director, Anglo Irish Bank (Ireland); joined Allied
Irish Bank 1979 - 90; joined Anglo Irish Bank 1990 – todate Clubs: Druids Glen Golf Club, Lahinch
Golf Club. Recreations: GAA, golf. Contact: Anglo Irish Bank, 18 -21, St. Stephen's Green, Dublin 2.
T 01 616 2000 email angloirishbank.ie web www.angloirishbank.ie

Tom Browne

> Gregarious, extremely popular, first class operator, well thought of in financial circles;
> an excellent golfer and played football Limerick from 1983 –97 and Railway cup from
> 1984 -90.

BROWNE, Vincent; BROADCASTER, COLUMNIST, PUBLISHER, JUNIOR COUNSEL
b 1944, Newcastlewest, Co. Limerick; *m* Jean Learmond; 2*d*; *edu.* National School, Broadford, Co.
Limerick; Ring, Co. Waterford; St Mary's Dromcollogher; Castleknock College, Dublin; University
College Dublin; King's Inns: BA; LLB; Broadcaster, Journalist, Publisher, Junior Counsel; Researcher
/reporter for RTÉ; Prague correspondent *The Irish Times*1968; editor *Nusight* magazine 1969-'70;
Northern news editor, The Irish Press Group 1970; founder/editor relaunched *The Sunday Tribune*
1983-94; weekly columnist with *The Irish Times* 1995 to date; relaunched *Magill* 1997; sold *Magill*
1998; radio programme *Tonight with Vincent Browne* 1996 to date; called to the Bar 1997;
publisher/editor *The Village* 2004 to date. Contact: The Village, 44, Westland Row, Dublin 2.
T 01 642 5050 email vbrowne@thevillagemagazine.ie

> Known, respected and some would say feared, for his probing questions which have
> left many of his interviewees in tatters; a man who divides opinion in Ireland like no
> other; a forensic journalist; a good face for radio where his programme 'Tonight with
> Vincent Browne' has been a major success.

BRUNKER, Linda; SCULPTOR
b 1966, Dublin; *separated*; *edu.* Mount Temple, Dublin; National College of Art & Design, Dublin;
Diploma in Fine Art, Sculpture 1988; Degree in Fine Art, Sculpture 1989; Sculptor; Full-time artist
since graduating from NCAD in 1988, specialising in sculpture; quickly became known for her
unique style of casting open filigree bronzes, a technique which she developed and for which she has
been critically acclaimed. Exhibited mostly in Ireland and USA; has had solo exhibitions at the
Solomon Gallery in Dublin; has completed large and public commissions in many countries, such as
'Continuum', St Helen's Hotel, Stillorgan, County Dublin, 'The Wishing Hand', Offices of the Dept.
of Education, Dublin, 'Voyager', at the Montage Resort, Laguna Beach, California and 'The People's
Council', City Hall, Laguna Beach, California; Maintains studios in Dublin and in California. Clubs:
Sculptors Society of Ireland, International Sculpture Center, USA. Recreations: opera, goat keeping,
ancient mystical studies. Contact: 20 Oakwood Park, Glasnevin North, Dublin 11. M 087 207 3848
The Solomon Gallery, Powerscourt Townhouse, South William Street, Dublin 2. **T** 01 679 4237
email brunker@iol.ie email info@solomongallery.com

Linda Brunker

> This NCAD-educated artist is a hit in the US particularly in New York and California;
> her work encompasses figurative imagery and abstraction in a rare fusion of style; her
> work is much sought after by collectors and galleries alike because of her exploration
> of the physical and spiritual world.

BRUTON, Alan Matthew; HAIRDRESSER
*b*1957; *m* Dolores Mc Evoy; M.Diss; 1s; *p* Sonja Mohlich (*qv*); *edu.* Engineering H.A. O'Neills; Hair
Stylist/ Salon Owner/ hairdresser David Marshall 1979- 84; started Reds 1984 to date; owner Reds,
Shelbourne Hotel, Dublin 2 – 2006; Reds Four Seasons Hotel, Dublin 4 2005 – todate. Clubs:
Shelbourne Club. Recreations: sailing, golf cooking. Contact Reds, Four Seasons, Simmonscourt
Road, Dublin 4. **T** 01 665 4000 M 086 835 7963 email salesredshairgrp.com

> A rare combination: first class businessman and top class hair stylist; ambitious, a keen
> intellect, stylish, good company; has one of the best clienteles in the country.

BRUTON, Richard Joseph; PUBLIC REPRESENTATIVE
b 1953, Dublin; *m* Susan Meehan; 2*s* 1*d*; *edu.* Belvedere College Dublin; Clongowes Wood College,
Co.Kildare; University College Dublin; BA, MA; Nuffield College Oxford M.Phil (Oxon) Economics;
Public Representative; Member of Dáil Éireann (FG Dublin North Central); Economist, Economic

and Social Research Institute 1973-'75 and 1981; Economist Cement Roadstone Holdings plc. 1978-81; Member Meath County Council 1979-82; Elected to Seanad Éireann, Agricultural Panel 1981-82; Member Joint Oireachtas Committee on Public Expenditure and Women's Rights 1982-87; Elected TD for Dublin North Central 1982; Spokesperson, Enterprise & Employment 1987-94; Member of Dublin City Council 1991-94, and 1999-2003; Minister of State, Dept of Industry 1986; Minister for Enterprise and Employment 1994-95; President European Industrial Council 1998; Director of Policy 2001-'02; TD Dublin North Central (FG) 2002 to date; Publ. (co-authored) *Irish Economy* 1975; *Irish Public Debt* 1979; (co-authored) *Drainage Policy in Ireland* 1982; Recreations: reading, running, swimming, tennis, and all kinds of sports. Contact: 210 Griffith Avenue, Drumcondra, Dublin 9. T 01 618 4063 F 01 618 4501 email richard.bruton@finegael.ie or richard.bruton@oireachtas.ie www.richardbruton.com

The younger brother of former Taoiseach John Bruton, 'Baby Bruton' possesses a very sharp intellect but is perceived to be more academic than political; was an effective if unspectacular minister in the Rainbow coalition of the 1990s.

BUCKELY, Joseph Anthony 'Joe'; COMPANY DIRECTOR
b 1950, Limerick; *m* Eleanor; 2*s* 1*d*; *edu.* Oatlands College, Dublin; Managing Director, First Impression, Designers Company. Clubs: Powerscourt Golf Club, The Marketing Society. Recreations: golf. Contact: First Impression Designers, 2 Main Street, Donnybrook, Dublin 4. T 01 203 3800 F 01 203 3850 email joe@firstimpression.ie

Founder of First Impression, Ireland's leading, award-winning and pioneering design company – the first major designer in Ireland to re-brand (from Corporate Graphics Ltd) and first to build a purpose-built design studio on the high street in one of Dublin's most prestigious locations; an astute and innovative businessman with a passionate interest in design and more than a keen interest in the property market.

BUCKLEY, Most Reverend, Dr John, Joseph; BISHOP OF CORK AND ROSS
b 1939, Inchigeela, Macroom, Co. Cork; single; *edu.* St. Finbarr's College, Farranferris, Cork; University College Cork; St. Patrick's College, Maynooth, Co. Kildare; BA, BD, HDipEd. DD; Bishop of Cork and Ross. Clubs: Road Bowling Club. Recreations: bowling. Contact: Cork & Ross Diocesan Offices, Redemption Road, Cork. T 012 430 171 F 021 430 1557 email secretary@corkandross.org

The 'Bowling Bishop' is one of the most popular and respected people in Co. Cork; a loyal Cork GAA fan, he was a handy hurler in his day, displaying his skills with many clubs; a real breath of fresh air and man of the people who maintains close links with his community.

BUCKLEY, Leslie; MANAGING DIRECTOR L.F. BUCKLEY & ASSOCIATES
b 1944, Cork; *m* Carmel Mackey; 2*s* 1*d*; *edu.* Presentation College, Cork; University College Cork, BSc, MSc; worked in various management positions with leading Irish companies, including the Jefferson Smurfit Group and Waterford Crystal; established own consultancy company, L.F. Buckley and Associates 1990; has been retained on various key appointments including the restructuring of Waterford Crystal and Aer Lingus; appointed Acting Chief Executive of Irish Steel which was successfully sold to a suitable partner 1994; carried out major review on Irish Rail 1996; appointed Acting CEO Esat Telecom Ltd 1996; appointed to the National Commission on Nursing by Minister of Health 1997; Director, Fexco, Rennicks, IMOS, National Utilities Ltd., Esat Telecommunications Ltd., Esat Digifone Ltd., Radio 2000, 98FM Classic Hits, Esat Telecom Group plc., Totalnet Ltd., Eunet Ireland Ltd., Cork Internet Services Ltd., Bridgecom Ltd., Bridgecom Group Ltd., Bridgecom Technologies Ltd., Bridgecom Networking Ltd., Bridgecom Munster Ltd. Recreations: marathon running, wind surfing hill walking, swimming. Contact: 5, Rocklands, Harbour Road, Dalkey, Co. Dublin. T 01 602 6390

Best known for his recent work with Denis O'Brien (*qv*); very bright and brings a clinical approach to his business activities.

BUCKLEY, Michael; COMPANY DIRECTOR
b 1944, Cork; *m* Anne Twomey; 1*s* 2*d*; *edu.* The Lough National School, Cork; St. Finbarr's Seminary, Farranferris, Cork; St. Patrick's College, Maynooth, Co. Kildare; BA; MA; Chairman

Joe Buckely

National Advisory Board, Industrial Strategy and Competitiveness 2005 to date; Civil Servant; Chef de Cabinet to President of the European Court of Auditors; Assistant Secretary Dept of Social Welfare; Dept. Finance; M.D. National City Brokers Stockbrokers; Head of Investment Banking Allied Irish Bank Group; MD Allied Irish Banks Capital Markets; Director M & T Bank Board (until 2006) New York State; CEO Allied Irish Bank 1999-2005; Director DCC plc 2005 - to date; Chairman, National Advisory Board, Industrial Strategy and Competitiveness 2005 to date; Chaired Buckley Review of Public Service Pay Scales; former Director Custom House Docks Developments. Clubs: Recreations: golf, sailing. Contact: DCC plc., DCC House, Brewery Road, Stillorgan, Co. Dublin **T** 01 279 9400 **F** 01 283 1017 email info@dcc.ie web www.dcc.ie

> The accident prone chief executive survived many scandals at the head of Ireland's largest bank; shy, articulate, keen intellect, good strategist, attributes which served him well, though his inability to engage with people conveyed the impression of aloofness; well connected with both the political and permanent governments (all owe him a debt of gratitude for the salary increases he recommended in his Buckley Report).

BUCKLEY, Tara; DIRECTOR GENERAL RGDATA
b 1961, Dublin; *m* Fergal Keane; 2*s* 1*d*; *edu.* Convent of the Sacred Heart, Mount Anville Dublin; Trinity College Dublin; B.Mod (History), HDipEd; Dublin City University Post-Graduate Diploma in Journalism; Director General RGDATA (retail grocers, dairy & allied traders association); Journalist *Sunday Tribune*; Journalist Irish Press Group; Political Correspondent *Evening Herald*; Public Relations Manager REHAB Group; General Manager Corporate Communications VHI. Recreations: sports, politics, arts, theatre. Contact: Rock House, Main Street, Blackrock, Co. Dublin. **T** 01 283 1244 **F** 01 283 2206 email tbuckley@rgdata.ie

> Extremely able, well informed and ambitious; always well prepared, knows her brief and represents her people extremely well.

Tara Buckley

BUDD, The Hon Justice Declan; JUDGE OF THE HIGH COURT
b 1943; *m* Ann Lawson; 1*s* 3*d*; *edu.* St. Stephen's School, Dublin; Radley; Trinity College Dublin, Classical Exhibition 1962; Foundation Scholarship, History and Political Science; Mod. 1964, LLB 1968; King's Inns BL; called to the Bar 1968; called to the Inner Bar 1981; appointed Judge of the High Court 1991; as a member of the Leinster Circuit had a broadly based practice; member of the Tribunal with the Railways Inspector concerning the Buttevant and Cherryville Rail Crash Inquiries; *Publ.* co-author (with Ross Hinds) *The Hist and Edmund Burke's Club*; former Irish squash and international and interprovincial hockey player. Contact: The Four Courts, Morgan Place, Dublin 7. **T** 01 825 5555

> A thoroughly decent, hard working, low key member of the judiciary and an excellent representative of the Dublin legal establishment.

BUGGY, Niall , Michael; ACTOR
b 1948, Dublin; *m* Mary; *edu.* St. Patrick's National School, Drumcondra, Dublin; Sandymount High School Dublin; Actor; Former Abbey Theatre actor; acting credits include *Borstal Boy*; *Death is for Heroes*; *I'm Gettin' Out of This Kip*; *It's Later Than You Think*; *One For The Grave*; *One Of Our Own*; *Swift*; *Tarry Flynn*; *The Actress and the Bishop*; *Three Sisters*; *The Gigli Concert*; *Uncle Vanya*; *Dead Funny*; *Give Me Your Answer Do*; *The Misanthrope*; *Juno and the Paycock*; *The Rivals*; *Love For Love*; *Travesties*; Film Credits include *Zardoz*; *That Time*; *Vicious Circle*; *Sweeney Todd*; *The Lonely Passion of Judith Hearne*; *Close My Eyes*; Television credits include *Upwardly Mobile*; *Father Ted*; *Red Roses For Me*; *The Butcher's Boy*. Contact; ICM, The Barracks, 76, Irishtown Road, Dublin 4. **T** 01 667 6455

> An amazingly effective leading, character actor with great stage and radio presence.

BULBULIA, Abdul; MEDICAL DOCTOR
b 1940, Johannesburg, South Africa; *m* Katherine; 2*s* 1*d*; *edu.* Primary and Secondary Education in South Africa; Graduated Royal College of Surgeons Ireland; Post-graduate training Ireland, England and Scotland 1965-73; LRCP.SI, DRCOG, LFOM; Medical Doctor; General Practice, Waterford 1973 to date; Fellow Royal Academy of Medicine; Ministerial appointee to The Irish Medical Council 1994-99 & 1999-04; Chair International Affairs Committee, Medical Council; Chairperson Arts Committee, Medical Council; Board Governors & Guardians National Gallery of Ireland; President

of Waterford Healing Arts Trust; Council Member of the Friends National Gallery; Irish Contemporary Arts Society; Benefactor R.H.A. (Royal Hibernian Academy); Member Selection Committee of the Haverty Trust (which purchases art works for public collections); Member of the Selection Committee of the Taylor Award (Royal Dublin Society); Council member of the Friends of the National Collection; Board of Garter Lane Arts Centre 1980-83; Founder Art in Health Movement in Ireland. Clubs: Dublin Zoological Society (life member), Kildare Street & University Clubs, Irish Georgian Society. Recreations: Irish Art. Contact: Woodstown House, Woodstown Upper, Co. Waterford. **T** 051.382333 **F** 051 382336 email akbulbulia@eircom.net

Highly respected doctor; extremely popular, passionate about art, artists and art practice; has undertaken some important commissions and innovative arts residencies in hospitals. These carry real meaning, unlike many others which are simply sinecures.

BULBULIA, Katharine; PROGRAMME MANAGER/POLITICAL ADVISOR

b 1943, Dublin; *m* Dr Abdul Bulbulia (*qv*); 2s 1d; *edu.* Roslyn Park, Sandymount, Dublin; Convent of the Sacred Heart of Mary, Ferrybank, Waterford; University College Dublin; BA; Programme Manager/Political advisor to the Tánaiste - 2006; member of the Seanad 1981-89; For a period was Deputy Leader of Government Party in Senate; Member of Waterford County and City Councils 1979-90; First woman ever elected to Waterford County Council; Executive Director of Waterford Chamber of Commerce 1991-97; Founder member and sponsor of the Irish Anti-Apartheid Movement; Founder member of Irish Chapter of AWEPA, a Europe-wide and African parliamentary association in solidarity with the democratic forces in South and Southern Africa and now committed to assisting the democracies in that region by way of capacity building and information exchange programmes. Contact: Upper Woodstown, Co. Waterford. **T** 051 382333 email akbulbulia@eircom.net

A quietly spoken effective political advisor; low profile, extremely able, well respected; works her own circuit and absolutely devoted to the cause of the PDs; will no doubt assume a new role in the Party in the near future.

BUNN, Michael, 'Mike'; PHOTOGRAPHER

b 1942; *p* Betty Wall; *edu.* St Oliver's and St. Xavier's, London; Camberwell Art School, figure drawing; busked in streets of Europe and travelled the world as ship's steward; worked in restaurant business in Spain; self-taught photographer, first major assignment was to sell Irish travel shots to Aer Lingus; moved into fashion photography and has featured in all major international magazines, a pioneer in Irish fashion photography; currently one of the leading Irish photographers; creative works include *Ireland, the Taste and the Country* (script and photographs); has illustrated many books; recipient, I.C.A.D. Awards: Satzenbrau Fashion Photography Award, *Sunday Independent* Arts Award. Recreations: fanatical fly fisher, country pursuits. Contact: The Cottage, Ballyrush, Castle Baldwin, Co. Sligo. **T** 071 916 5255

Extremely innovative, fashion photographer with an unerring 'eye'; kicked the whole fashion photography scene here up several notches.

BURDON, Andy; ARCHITECTURAL DIRECTOR

b 1958, Damascus, Syria; *m* Angela 1s 1d; *edu.* Rockwell College, Co. Tipperary, University College Dublin, BArch; Architecture Director BCDH Architects; Andy Burdon Architects 1997; Director Burdon Dunne Architects 2000-'04; Director BCDH Architects 2004 to date; Director of award-winning architectural practice; Competition winner Docklands landmark design, Premiated Irish World Pavilion Arts, University of Limerick; School of Film and Design UCD. Clubs: Rathgar Tennis Club. Recreations: tennis, sailing, outdoor pursuits, film, theatre. Contact: 89, Booterstown Avenue, Blackrock, Co. Dublin. **T** 01 215 8500 **F** 01 215 8501 email andy.burdon@bcdh.com

Director of the award winning architectural group that will produce Dublin's first skyscraper and change the skyline of Dublin irrevocably; many feel it's a long time coming.

Andy Burdon

BURKE, Garry; CEO, PEMBROKE GROUP LTD

b 1958, Galway; *m* Mary; 2s.1d. *edu.* Coláiste an Rísigh, Ennis, Co.Clare; University College Galway, B.Comm. FCA; CEO Pembroke Group Ltd.; Held various positions in the finance group and financial services team at GPA Group plc.; Deputy chief executive capital markets of GPA 1993; GE

Capital Aviation Services Managing Director Capital Markets; Pembroke Capital (equity participant) 1995: Pembroke is now owned jointly by Rolls Royce plc and GATX Corporation. Clubs: Limerick Golf and Country Club. Recreations: Director Gúna Nua Theatre Company. Contact: Shannon Airport House, Shannon, Co. Clare. **T** 061 70160 **F** 061 474 912

> A former GPA high flier who has not only maintained momentum but flown much higher and faster while remaining almost unknown to the wider world.

BURKE, Joseph, 'Joe'; MUSICIAN

b 1939, Loughrea, Co. Galway; *m* Ann Conroy Burke; *edu.* Kilnadeema National School; Musician; started as a farmer; moved to full-time career in music; gave first public performance November 1955; performing and recording for the last 50 years; record labels include Gael Linn, Outlet, Shanachie, Green Linnet Records, New Century Music; classical solo albums sold worldwide; performed at Carnegie Hall, New York, Royal Albert Hall, London, Unuesque Hall, Paris, American Musical Hall, San Francisco; has given workshops and masterclasses worldwide; Awards: All-Ireland Senior Accordion Championship 1959/1960; Traditional Musician of the Year RTÉ 1970; AIB Traditional Musician of the Year Award 1977; Hall of Fame Rostrevor 1990; Irish World (London) Lifetime Achievement Award 1997; Boston College Award 2000; has represented Ireland at Montmagny International Accordion Festival, Quebec, and has toured with various prestigious musicians. Recreations: music, history, Gaelic Games. Contact: Kilnadeema, Loughrea, Co. Galway. **T** 091 842419 email joeburkemusic@eircom.net web www.joeburkemusic.com

> The one-time farmer who went on to become a self trained traditional musician with an international following; is credited with starting a major revival of interest in the accordion.

BURNS, John; JOURNALIST

b 1965, Lancaster, UK; *m* Jacinta; 1*s* 2*d*; *edu.* Cistercian College, Roscrea, Co. Tipperary; College of Commerce, Rathmines, Dublin; Journalist and Criminologist; News Editor, *The Sunday Times*; *Irish Property News* 1986; Researcher, RTÉ including *Kenny Live* 1986-'93; Dublin Correspondent, *The Sunday Times* 1993-'95; North of Ireland 1995-'96; News Editor *The Sunday Times*, Ireland 1997 to date. Clubs: Rathmines Chess Club; Dublin Journalists Golf Society. Recreations: Chess, golf, fantasy football, reading. Contact: *The Sunday Times*, Bishop's Square, Redmond Hill, Dublin 2. **T** 01 479 2412 **F** 01 479 2421 email john.burns@sunday-times.ie

> Bright, ambitious and dogged follower of stories; extensive sources; has cultivated some serious hitters; likeable and affable; has interesting views on people which might surprise them.

BURNSIDE, David; PUBLIC REPRESENTATIVE

b 1951, Ballymoney, County Antrim; *m* Fiona; *edu.* Coleraine Academical Institution; Queen's University Belfast; (Politics and Ancient History); MP Ulster Unionist Party; became press officer of the Vanguard Unionist Progessive Party (VUPP) 1974-'77; Director public relations, Institute of Directors 1979-'84; Director public affairs British Airways 1984-'93; established his own public relations company, David Burnside Associates 1993; also acted as chairman New Century Holdings; unsuccessful in retaining the Westminster seat of South Antrim for the UUP in 2000 by-election; won the South Antrim constituency at the general election of June 2001; continued to voice criticism of his party leader, David Trimble; along with two fellow Westminster MPs, resigned from the party's group at Westminster from June 2003 until October 2003; returned as a member for the constituency of South Antrim to the Northern Ireland Assembly 2003 to date; Member of Commons Select Committee on Environment, Food and Rural Affairs 2001 to date. Contact: The House of Commons, London, SW1A 0AA **T** 00 44 020 7219 3000

> A relentless critic of David Trimble, the one time British Airways PR man uses all of his media savvy in his political career; an extremely sharp performer.

BURROWS, Rgt, Rev. Michael; BISHOP OF CASHEL AND OSSORY

b 1962; *m* Claire; 3*s* 1*d*; *edu.* Wesley College, Dublin; Trinity College Dublin; BA Mod (History and Political Science) M Litt; Bishop of Cashel and Ossery; ordained 1988; served his curacy at Douglas Union w. Frankfield (Cork); became Dean of Residence at Trinity College Dublin in 1991- 94 and Minor Canon at St Patrick's Cathedral, Dublin; In he moved back to Cork diocese to be Incumbent of

Bandon Union 1994 –'96; appointed Canon at Cork and Cloyne Cathedrals 1996 – 02; appointed Dean of Cork and Incumbent St Finbarr's Union, succeeding his brother-in-law, Michael Jackson, who had been appointed Bishop of Clogher 2002 – 06; appointed Bishop of Cashel and Ossory 2006 – todate; Contact: Knocknabooley, Stoneyford, Co. Kilkenny. **T** 056 772 8818 **F** 056 772 8928 email bishop@cashel.anglican.org

At General Synod 2005, he stated that he regularly gives Holy Communion to parishioners in long-standing homosexual relationships; claimed that it was possible for the church to exist with two integrities on the subject of sexuality; will have to be a great conciliator with all of his dispersed flock in what is a scattered and rural series of Dioceses; much of the welfare of the South Eastern Church of Ireland will be dependent on his work as a Pastoral Leader; time will tell how well the Electoral College made this particular choice of a City Dean to a Country Bishop with no particular track record to note thus far.

Richard Burrows

BURROWS, Richard; GOVERNOR, BANK OF IRELAND
b 1949; *m* Sherril Dix; 1*s* 3*d*; *edu.* Wesley College, Dublin; Governor Bank of Ireland; Assistant to Managing Director, Edward Dillon & Company Ltd 1970-'72; General Manager, Fitzgerald & Company 1972; Managing Director Old Bushmills Distillery Company 1972; General Manager, Irish Distillers Ltd 1976; Managing Director Irish Distillers Group plc 1978; Chairman, /joint Chief Executive Pernod Ricard 1991- 05; former President, IBEC (The Irish Business and Employers Confederation); non executive chairman, Irish Distillers – todate; non executive director Pernod Ricard, todate; Governor Bank of Ireland 2005 to date; member, Trilateral Commission, (European Group); Dublin Member, Institute of Chartered Accountants. Recreations: rugby, sailing. Contact: Bank of Ireland HQ, Baggot Street, Dublin 2. **T** 01 661 5933 **F** 01 661 5671 email richard.burrows@boimail.com www. bankofireland.ie

An international businessman with a number of prestigious directorships; a former president of IBEC, son of the late George Burrows; a keen yachtsman.

BURTON, Joan; PUBLIC REPRESENTATIVE
b 1949, Dublin; *m* Pat Carroll; 1*d*; *edu.* Stanhope St. Sisters of Charity, Dublin; University College Dublin, B.Comm; Chartered Accountant, Labour TD (Dublin West); Institute of Chartered Accountants in Ireland; Chartered Accountant Price Waterhouse 1970-76; Senior Lecturer in Accounting, DIT 1977-02; Lecturer University of Dar es Salaam, Tanzania, Irish Aid Programme/APSO 1983-1986; elected Dublin County Council, Mulhuddart Ward 1991; elected Dáil Éireann, Dublin West 1992; Labour Party spokesperson Finance 2005; Minister of State, Social Welfare 1992-94; Minister of State Development Co-operation 1995-97; Minister of State Dept of Justice 1995-97; Fingal County Council, Castleknock Ward 1999. Clubs: Fingal Walkers; Africa, former Hon.Sec. Irish Anti-Apartheid Movement. Recreations: films, books, walking, swimming, travel. Contacts: Dail Eireann, Kildare Street, Dublin 2. **T** 01 618 4006 **F** 01 618 4174 email joan.burton@oireachtas.ie www.joanburton.ie.

A bright, high profile politician, one of the stars of the Labour Party; always on top of her brief; has performed well as a minister when in government and in opposition is marking her minister very closely.

BUTLER, Daniel James 'Dan'; SECRETARY GENERAL, EQUESTRIAN FEDERATION OF IRELAND
b 1954, San Francisco; divorced; 1*s* 1*d*; *edu.* Advanced Management Programme, INSEAD, Fontainebleau, France 1992; Secretary general, Equestrian Federation of Ireland; System Management, University of Southern California, MS 1985; Public Administration, Oklahoma University, MA 1983; US Naval Academy BS Chemistry 1977; Secretary General, Equestrian Federation of Ireland; Equestrian Federation of Ireland, Director General 2002 to date; Xybernaut Corp. Managing Director (EMEA) Boeblingen, Germany 1998-02; Optym Professional Services, Inc. 1997- 98; Vice President, Operations (Palo Alto, CA) 1997- 98; Computing Devices International (division of Ceridian Corporation) 1983-97, Executive Director (Washington, DC) 1995-'97, Executive Director, International Programmes (Washington, DC) 1993-95, Managing Director CD PLUS S.A. (Paris, France) 1990-'93; European Director (London, UK) 1987-89; Senior Programme Manager/Department Manager (Washington, DC) 1983-86; member, Institute of Directors. Clubs: Royal Dublin Society. Recreations: music, theatre. Contact: Equestrian Federation

of Ireland, Kildare Paddocks, Kill, Co. Kildare. **T** 045 886678 **F** 045 878430
email danielbutler@horsesport.ie

>His impressive career to date and superb international training should enable him to
>bring a clear and much needed open management style to the Federation.

BUTLER, Jean; DANCER
b 1971, New York; *m* Cuan Hanly; *edu.* Birmingham University, UK, BA, Theatre Studies; Dancer;
attended dance classes from age four; trained in ballet and tap, won consecutive regional, national and
world championships; danced with The Chieftains, touring throughout America, Canada, Europe
and Japan; appeared on the new Chieftains album alongside Mick Jagger; performed for Princess
Diana at the royal premiere of *Far and Away*; represented Ireland at Expo '92 in Seville, Spain;
choreographed and starred in *Riverdance* during Eurovision 1994; enjoyed international acclaim with
Riverdance:The Show in Dublin, Belfast, Cork, London, New York, Los Angeles; Movies: *Brylcreem
Boys*; Publ. *Jean Butler's Masterdance Class* (DVD). Contact: The Agency, 47 Adelaide Road, Dublin 2.
T 01 661 8538 **F** 01 676 0052.

>The beautiful New Yorker changed Irish step dancing forever; left her mark on stages
>across the world and in the hearts of people everywhere; blazed a trail in Riverdance:
>The Show; no one ever really matched her afterwards.

BYRNE, Anthony; PIANIST, LECTURER IN PIANO
b 1958; Dublin; *m* Patricia Ferrins; 1*s* 1*d*; *edu.* University of Western Ontario, Canada; Julliard
School, New York, USA; Associate of the Royal College of Music ARCM; Concert Pianist and
Lecturer in Piano at the Royal Irish Academy of Music; one of Ireland's leading pianists; played in
many countries and is a frequent soloist with the National Symphony Orchestra and RTÉ Concert
Orchestra; recorded CDs of contemporary Irish piano music and has given first performances of
many new works; has broadcast on radio and television. Clubs: Royal Dublin Golf Club. Recreations:
golf, movies, chess, reading, computers. Contact: 190 Duncluce Road, Clontarf, Dublin 3.
T 01 833 5085 **M** 086 261 8706

>One of Ireland's leading pianists; played in many countries and is a frequent soloist
>with the National Symphony Orchestra and RTÉ Concert Orchestra.

BYRNE, Breffni; CHAIRMAN, NCB STOCKBROCKERS
b 1946, Dublin; *m* Jane; *edu.* University College Dublin B.Comm; FCA; Chartered Accountant;
Managing Partner of the Audit and Business Advisory practice of Arthur Andersen in Ireland;
Director of Risk Management for Andersen's audit practice in Scandinavia, the Middle East and
Africa; Chairman NCB Stockbrokers; non-executive director of Irish Life and Permanent 2004 to
date; Coillte Teoranta; Tedcastle Holdings Limited; also a number of other companies. Contact: NCB
Stockbrokers, 3, Georges Dock, IFSC, Dublin 1. **T** 01 611 5611 **F** 01 611 5998
email invfunds@ncb.ie

>One of the country's top auditors; is much sought after for as a board member.

BYRNE, Catherine; ACTOR
b 1954, Dublin; *m* John Olohan; 2*s*; *edu.* Holy Faith Convent, Glasnevin, Dublin; Actor; window and
interior design display artist, Arnotts; trained Abbey School of Acting; member Irish Theatre
Company, The Abbey Theatre Company; starred in numerous productions including *Yerma* (Peacock
Theatre); *Whistle in the Dark* (Abbey Theatre); *Da* (Abbey Theatre); *The Field* (Abbey Theatre);
Dancing at Lughnasa (Abbey Theatre, London and New York); *Wonderful Tennessee* (Abbey Theatre
and New York); *Give Me Your Answer Do* (Abbey Theatre and New York); *The Plough and the Stars*
(Gaiety Theatre); *Factory Girls* (Druid Theatre); *Choke My Heart* (Red Kettle); *A Month In The
Country* (Gate Theatre); *Molly Sweeney* (London and New York); television and film work includes
Fair City (RTÉ); *Kidnapped* (Disney); *Upwardly Mobile* (RTÉ); *Eat The Peach* (film); Awards: Harvey
Award for best actress. Recreations: film, music, sculpting in spare time. Contact: First Call
Management, 29 -30 Dame Street, Dublin 2. **T** 01 679 8401 **F** 01 679 8353

>Serious minded and literate exponent of her art; has played some very heavy and hard
>hitting roles on stage; has a terrific stage presence; wonderful exponent of Brian Friel's
>heroines; also well able for lighter roles with post-modern irony.

BYRNE, Claire; TV3 NEWS ANCHOR

b 1975; *m* Richard Johnson; separated; *edu.* Brigidine Convent, Mountrath, Co Laois; College of Commerce, Rathmines, Dublin; DIT Aungier Street, Dublin; Certificate in Journalism; Radio Journalist 1995-'97; Senior Broadcast Journalist BBC Radio 1997-'98; News Editor, Channel 103FM Jersey, Channel Islands 1998-'99; news anchor TV3 and reporter 1999-'01; news anchor ITN London, Channel 5 2001-'02; Ireland AM presenter 2002-'04; TV3 news anchor 2004 to date. Recreations: walking, reading. Contact: TV3 Television Network, Ballymount, Dublin 24 **T** 01 419 3442 web www.tv3.ie

Made the switch from the laid back sofa of breakfast TV to serious news anchor seamlessly; good appearance and delivery, a first class professional.

BYRNE, Clive, Richard; SCHOOL HEADMASTER

b 1956; *m* Patricia; 3*d*; *edu.* St. Vincent's CBS, Glasnevin; University College Dublin; BA, HdipEd, CTCT, DipEd Admin, M.Ed; Principal St. Mary's College, Rathmines, Dublin; taught in Mount Temple Comprehensive School; Principal Presentation Brothers College, Glasthule; Principal St. Mary's College, Rathmines since 1997; Clubs: President NAPD 2005-06, National Association of Principals & Deputy Principals, Clontarf Rugby Club, St. Mary's RFC. Recreations: sport, especially rugby, music, classical music, theatre, cooking. Contact: St. Mary's College, Rathmines, Dublin 6 **T** 01 406 2100 **F** 01 4972574 email CliveByrne@stmarys.ie

Clive Byrne

BYRNE, David, M; CHAIRMAN NATIONAL CONCERT HALL

b 1947, Monasterevan, Co. Kildare; *m* Geraldine Fortune; 2*s* 1*d*; *edu.* Monasterevan CBS; Dominican College, Newbridge, Co. Kildare; University College Dublin, BA; King's Inns Dublin, Barrister-at-Law; Founder Chairman Free Legal Advice Centre (FLAC) 1969-70; called to the Bar in 1970 and Inner Bar in 1985; Member Bar Council 1974-87 and Hon. Treasurer 1982-83; Member Executive Committee Irish Maritime Law Association 1974-92; Member National Committee of International Chamber of Commerce 1988-97; Member of Government Review Body on Social Welfare Law 1989; Member of ICC International Court of Arbitration, Paris 1990-97; Fellow Chartered Institute of Arbitrators; Extern examiner for arbitration and competition law, King's Inns 1995-'97; Member Barristers Professional Practices Committee 1995-'97; Member Constitution Review Group 1995'96; Attorney General 1997'99; appointed European Commissioner for Health and Consumer Protection July 1999-04; former Member of the Council of State 1997-99; returned to Senior Counsel 2004 to date; non-executive director Irish Life and Permanent 2004 to date. Chairman, National Concert Hall, 2006 – todate. Clubs: Royal Irish Yacht Club, Blainroe Golf Club. Recreations: golf, sailing. Contact: National Concert Hall, Earlsford Terrace, Dublin 2 **T** 01 417 0077 **F** 01 417 0078 email: info@nch.ie .www.nch.ie

Civilized, urbane and sartorially elegant; is one of Bertie Ahern's close coterie of lay advisors; had a slightly above-average career as a commissioner in Brussels; was possibly too moderate a force to achieve more than he did in the hurly burly of the Berlaymont.

BYRNE, Kieran; DIRECTOR, WATERFORD INSTITUTE OF TECHNOLOGY

b 1950, Cork; *m* Evelyn; 1*s* 1*d*; edu. University College Cork, BA, HDipEd, Masters in Education; PhD in University Strategic Management, IMHE; *Publ.* topics on History, Science and Technology; Education Policy Making and Planning; served as director of publications for ten years at European Association of Education for the *European Journal* (CARFAX, Oxford); president, European Association of Teacher Education, Brussels 1977-00; former president of the Educational Studies Association of Ireland; lecturer, Mary Immaculate College, Limerick 1977-'94; head of education, Mary Immaculate College, Limerick 1985-94; Dean of Education, University of Limerick 1994-01; Director, Waterford Institute of Technology 2001 to date. Contact: Waterford Institute of Technology, Waterford. **T** 051 302015 **F** 051 357735 email director@wit.ie

BYRNE, Nicholas, Bernard, Adam, James 'Nicky'; SINGER, WESTLIFE

b 1978, Dublin; *m* Georgina Ahern; *edu.* Pobailscoil Neasáin, Baldoyle, Dublin; selected for Leeds United FC (Youth Training Scheme); goalkeeper 1995; played for Irish Youth National teams; stayed at Leeds until 1997; formed Westlife with Shane Filan (*qv*), Kian Egan (*qv*), Mark Feehily (*qv*) and Bryan Mc Fadden 1998; Westlife have had 12 number one singles in England; *Publ.* four pop albums, one Greatest Hits album and one Swing Album to July 2005; successful all over the world especially

Scandinavia and South East Asia; have also had record-selling indoor arena tours and are one of the biggest pop acts to ever come out of Ireland. Recreations: soccer, supports Manchester United, travel, flying, 'walking our puppies with my wife'. Contact: Sony BMG Records, Embassy House, Ballsbridge, Dublin 4 **T** 01 647 3400 web www.westlife.com

> Favourite Westlife moment was meeting the Pope; known for his husky singing voice, which is featured in all of Westlife's music; with wife Georgina loves shopping especially for new home in London.

BYRNE, Pat; CHAIRMAN, NON EXECUTIVE, CITYJET
b 1954; *m* 1st Anne; (*m.dis*); 2d; *m* 2nd Jane; 1s; *edu*. Presentation Brothers, Bray, Co. Wicklow; banking; co-founder Savings & Investment; sold to Woodchester in the late 1980s; left Woodchester 1991; formed CityJet 1994; CityJet and Air France first formed alliance 1996; the two carriers commenced a code-sharing arrangement on Dublin-Paris CDG 1997; led to CityJet operating the route under a franchise agreement by which Air France buy out CityJet; resigned as Chief Executive 2000; executive Chairman 2000-'04; Non-executive chairman CityJet 2004 to date; Awards: Air Transport Users Committee of the Chambers of Commerce of Ireland Airline of the Year 1994; Best Executive and Best Economy Class Service on the London route 1994; Best Airline – Ireland/London and Ireland/Europe 1995; Best airline Ireland/London 1996; Best Airline Ireland/Europe 1997; Institute of Transport Management Best Short Haul Airline 2004; Director, Rainmaker. Recreations: flying light aircraft, running. Contact: CityJet Head Office, Swords Business Campus, Balheary Road, Swords, Co. Dublin **T** 01 870 0144 **F** 01 870 0135

> Put his money where his mouth was and started Cityjet; unlike most other short haul airlines, it continues to offer a decent service.

BYRON, Patricia Emer; CHIEF EXECUTIVE, PERSONAL INJURIES ASSESSMENT BOARD
b 1960, Dublin; *m* Robert Duffy; 2s; *edu*. Loreto Convent, Navan, Co. Meath; University College Dublin; B.A. AC 11; Chief Executive, Personal Injuries Assessment Board; Started career on graduate programme with Norwich Union Fire Society 1981-'83; Moved to consultancy focusing on Risk Management, Claims Management, Process Review and Reengineering for 15 years, predominantly working with General Insurance sector 1983-'98; first female President of the Insurance Institute of Dublin 1994; invited to join Hibernian Insurance Executive management team in advance of merger activities; led key project reviewing 'value for spend' on Legal, Medical, Motor engineering and other services 1998-2004; first female Chairperson, The Motor Insurers Bureau of Ireland, (body charged with administration of compensation to victims of uninsured driving.); final strand of implementation plan (IT) completed 2005; Appointed CEO, PIAB 2004. Clubs: Sandymount Lady's Golf Society, David Lloyd at Riverview, Dublin. Recreations: sports, running, watching rugby, cycling, reading, walking the beach in Kilmore Quay. Contact: Personal Injuries Assessment Board, PO Box 9732, Tallaght, Dublin 24. **T** 01 463 4551 **F** 01 463 4596 email Sorcha.Coady@piab.ie web www.piab.ie

> Led strategic review and change management process at The Motor Insurers Bureau of Ireland where the spend at start of process was €90m per annum on claims arising from uninsured driving, current spend in region of €60m 2001; though she has her work cut out for her now, should be well able to ensure greater compliance to correct standards.

CAFFREY, Oliver James; PROPERTY DEVELOPER

b 1950, Co Kildare; *m* Yona Shiryan (*qv*); 4*s* 1*d*; *edu*. De La Salle; Christian Brothers; UCD; 2 Goal Polo Handicap; Director International Adjustment Bureau Luxembourg; Princess Homes (Owner/Director); Princess Development (Owner/Director); Polo One Restaurant (Owner/Director); won all the major polo tournaments in Ireland, including the Freebooters Cup three consecutive times; several tournament cups in UK; played for Ireland in Palm Beach Florida. Clubs: Groucho Club London; A.I.P.C. Polo Clubs; Arts Club, Dover St. London; Marks Club, London; Harry's Bar, London. Recreations: polo, arts, theatre, travel, reading, antiques, sailing. Contact: Villa Vega, 2 Ave De Provence, Eze Sur Mer, 06360 France. **T** 00 33 49 3044019 **F** 00 33 493 044 019

A charming man about town, popular with everybody; always cheery and full of bonhomie; an enthusiast for life.

Yona Caffrey

CAFFREY, née SHIRYAN Yona; SCULPTOR / ARTIST

b 1951, Tel Aviv, Israel; *m* Oliver Caffrey (*qv*); 4*s* 1*d*; *edu*. The Selisberg Academy, Jerusalem; The Bat Yam Institute for Modern Art; poems in a literary magazine in Israel; short stories in Irish magazine; last exhibition, Walton Gallery, London 2003. Recreations: reading, writing, swimming, gardening, travel, photography, architecture. Contact: The Orchard, Furness, Naas, Co. Kildare. **T** 045 883 706 **F** 045 883 706 email yona@yonashiryan.com

A considerable force in her own right; calm, cool and assured, she is proud of her husband and her children and modest about her art; she may well be the velvet fist in the iron glove.

Mark Cagney

CAGNEY, Mark; BROADCASTER

b Cork; *m* 1st Ann Humphries (*decd.*); 2nd Audrey Byrne; 2*s* 2*d*; *edu*. Christian Brothers College Cork; Presenter Ireland AM; joined RTE 1977; part of the original line-up of 2FM (Radio 2); joined RTE in 1977; was part of the original line-up of 2FM, broadcasting on its first night on air. During his time with 2FM, Mark presented a variety of shows, from the seminal Night Train to the Drive Time show; won a Jacobs Award for radio, 1985; left 2FM to join Dennis O'Brien in applying for a radio license, which was to become 98FM, 1989; with 98FM for seven years, presenting the mid-morning programme and the late night talk show; joined TV3, presenter Ireland AM 1999 to date. Awards: IFTA, 02 TV Personality of the Year 2005. Contact: TV3, Ballymount Industrial Estate, Clondalkin, Dublin 22. **T** 01 419 3333 email mark.cagney@tv3.com web www.tv3.ie

Made the switch from the world of pop, rock and roll at 2FM to schmoozing celebrities on the sofa at Ireland AM; the Cork-born presenter is very intelligent, with a wide range of interests making him able to switch from thorny politicians to celebrity wannabees; easy style and warm personality makes him the perfect male to wake up to and a worthy recipient of the 02 TV Personality of the Year 2005.

CAHILL, Liam; DIRECTOR COMMUNICATIONS, LABOUR PARTY

b 1950, Waterford; *m* Patricia; 1*s* 1*d*; *edu*. Mount Sion CBS Waterford; University College Dublin; BCL; Director Communications, Labour Party; Officer Revenue Commissioners 1972-'77; Dept. Justice 1977-'79; senior Correspondent RTE (Economics & Politics); Spokesperson EU Presidency Ireland 1990; Head Public Affairs AIB 1991-'93; Programme manager David Andrews 1993-'95; Manager Media Relations Intel Corp. 1995-2000; Partner Keating and Associates 2000-'04; Principal Liam Cahill Consultancy 2004-'05; Director Communications 2005 to date. *Publ. Forgotten Revolution* 1990; *An Fear Rua: The GAA Unplugged* (internet site). Clubs: Dunsany GAA Club, Co. Meath. Recreations: reading, oil painting, hill walking, GAA. Contact: The Labour Party, 5th Floor, Leinster House 2000, Kildare Street, Dublin 2. **T** 01 618 3428 email liamcahill@oireachtais.ie

Quiet and reserved, very personable when you get to know him; a total professional; wide range of media experience.

CAIRNDUFF, Alice Maureen; JOURNALIST

b 1938, Rathkeale, Co. Limerick; *m* Ian Bruce Cairnduff (*decd*); 3*s*; *edu*. Our Lady's Priory, Haywards Heath, UK; Winkfield Place, Windsor, UK; University of Madrid, Spain; journalist-writer; columnist, *The Sunday Press*; book reviewer, *The Irish Independent*; freelance work with magazines and journals, Ireland, the UK, US, Spain; radio and television contributor; Member Irish Tourism Authority. *Publ.*

Who's Who in Ireland, The Influential 1000 (1984, 1991, 2000); *Exquisite Behaviour* 1995. Recreations: walking, theatre, reading, being with friends. Contact: Failte Ireland, Baggot, Street Bridge , Dublin 2. **T** 01 602 4000 **F** 01 855 6821

A popular Dublin hostess; able and shrewd; an active PD supporter.

CALLAGHAN, John; COMPANY DIRECTOR
b 1942, Dublin; *m* Maureen Gibney; 2s 1d; *edu.* St James' Christian Brothers School; College of Commerce, Rathmines; trainee accountant with Peter Kennedy & Co 1960-65; Company Director; chief accountant, Smith Motor Group 1966-70; manager, corporate finance, KPMG (formally Stokes Kennedy Crowley) 1970-74; partner 1974; personnel partner 1974-76; corporate finance partner 1976-83; managing partner 1984-91; international council member KPMG/ Peat Marwick 1984-2001; chief executive/director, Fyffes plc 1991-93; director, First Active 1993; chairman 1999-2003; non executive director, Glanbia, Vivas, Rabobank; investor, Fitzsimons Hotel, Temple Bar, Dublin; Director Fellow, Institute of Chartered Accountants, Institute of Bankers, Institute of directors (President 1996-97, 1977-98); member Institute of Taxation. Clubs: St. Stephen's Green. Recreations: golf, music. Contact: Vivas Health, Paramount Court, Corrig Road, Sandyford, Dublin 18. **T** 1850 717 717 email info@vivashealth.ie

Meteoric career rise to become one of the youngest managing partners of one of the big five accountancy firms; since leaving mainstream accountancy has moved around the boardrooms of several plcs.

CALLAN, Patricia; DIRECTOR, SMALL FIRMS ASSOCIATION
b 1974, Dublin; *m* Conor Nolan; *edu.* Loretto Convent, Mullingar; BA Mod (Economics) Trinity College Dublin; MA International Studies, University of Limerick; Dip. Employment Law, National College of Ireland; Director Small Firms Association; joined IBEC Mid West Region 1997; executive SFA 98 - 00; Appointed assistant director SFA 2000 – 06; Appointed Director SFA 2006. Contact: SFA, Confederation House, 84 -86 Lr. Baggot Street, Dublin 2. **T** 01 605 1602 **F** 01 638 1602 email patricia.callan@ibec.ie web www.sfa.ie

Patricia Callan

Low profile, home grown IBEC insider whose considerable ability was recognized from the beginning: emerged into the top spot when her predecessor Pat Delaney (*qv*) moved back to IBEC; brings a different management style to the influential SFA.

CALLANAN, Frank; BARRISTER/ WRITER
b 1956, Dublin; single; *edu.* Gonzaga College, Dublin; University College Dublin; College of Europe, Bruges, Belgium; Kings Inns; BA, MA, Ph.D., Barrister at Law; Barrister, Senior Counsel and Writer; called to the Bar 1979; called to the Inner Bar 1998; Works on the Eastern and Dublin Bar in General Practice; *Publ. The Parnell Split* 1991; *T. M. Healy* 1996; *The Literary and Historical Society 1955-2005* (editor) 2005. Clubs: Colony Rooms. Contact: P.O. Box 5939, Distillery Buildings, 145-151 Church Street, Dublin 7. **T** 01 817 4619 **F** 01 496 4032 email fcallanan@lawlibrary.ie

An able and adroit Senior Counsel; has undertaken some important political writings on Parnell and Tim Healy and more recently the history of the L&H (UCD), in which he played some notable part in his day.

CALLELY, Ivor; PUBLIC REPRESENTATIVE
b 1958, Dublin; *m* Jennifer Foley; 2s 1d; *edu.* St. Paul's College, Raheny, Dublin; Fairview College of Education; Diploma in Business Studies and Accounting; Public Representative, (FF Dublin South); elected to Dublin Corporation 1985; elected to Dáil Éireann 1989 to date; Chairman of the Eastern Health Board, Chairman of the Child Care Advisory Committee 1991; Fianna Fáil Assistant Whip 1993-1995; Policy Co-ordinator 1995-1997; Chairperson of the Oireachtas Joint Committee on Enterprise and Small Business 1997; Chairman of the Eastern Regional Health Authority 2000; appointed Minister of State at the Department of Heath and Children with special responsibility for services for older people 2002; appointed Minister of State at the Department of Transport with special responsibility for Traffic Management, Dublin Transport, Road Safety, Motor Insurance & Vehicle Standards, Road Haulage and the Irish Aviation Authority 2004; resigned ministry December 2005. Clubs: Clontarf Golf Club, Clontarf Lawn Tennis Club, Clontarf Yacht and Boat Club, Clontarf GAA Club, Clontarf Rugby Football Club. Contact: 191 Howth Road, Killester, Dublin 3.

T 01 833 4331 or 01 604 1311 F 01 833 4332 or 01 604 1404 www.ivorcallely.ie

Possibly the most elegant member of the House; one of the top vote catchers in the country who services his constituency meticulously from one election to the next; his mobile office – 'The Callely Caravan' – is a permanent feature, at different locations, throughout his constituency; his apparent lack of political judgement in the unseemly, very public wrangle with the Taoiseach over a number of issues does not augur well for a return from the back benches to which he was transferred with what now looks like undue haste.

CALLERY, Susan; ART GALLERIST

b 1964, Cork; partner James Thompson; 1*s* 2*d*; *edu.* Loretto Abbey, Rathfarnham, Dublin; Crawford Municipal School of Art, Cork; National College of Art and Design Dublin (B.Des ANCAD); Art Gallerist; opened the Greenlane Gallery, Dingle 1992; moved to Holyground, Dingle 2003. Recreations: horse riding, Irish art, boats, dogs. Contact: Greenlane Gallery, Dingle, Co. Kerry. T 066 91 52 018 F 066 915 2047 email info@greenlanegallery.com

A charming, able and astute gallerist who has her Kerry base but who also moves in the enemy's camp; a good stable of artists – some swear she could sell ice to the Eskimos; has the commercial acumen of her family.

CAMPBELL, Niall Paul; ACCOUNTANT

b 1972; *m* Catherine Burke; *edu.* St. Michaels CBS Dun Laoghaire, Co Dublin; Dublin City University; BA in Accounting & Finance 1992, MBS Accounting 1993; Accountant; Member of the Institute of Chartered Accountants; Partner KPMG (Previously Stokes Kennedy Crowley) 1993 to date; joined as trainee, progressed to Manager 1997, Director 1999, Partner 2001; Articles Publ. in *Accountancy Ireland*; *Irish Tax Review*; *Finance Dublin* and newspaper commentary; Clubs; Cuala GAA Club. Recreations: GAA, hill walking, cycling, soccer, music, travel. Contact: 1 Harbourmaster Place, IFSC, Dublin 1. T 01 410 1174 F 01 412 1174 email niall.campbell@kpmg.ie

Well-respected in business and accountancy circles.

CAMPBELL, Patrick; EXECUTIVE CHAIRMAN, CAMPBELL BEWLEY GROUP

b 1942; *m* Veronica Dolan; 3*s* 2*d*; *edu.* Marlborough Street National School; Belvedere College, Dublin; Marian College, Ballsbridge; College of Catering, Cathal Brugha Street, Dip. Hotel Mgmt; Management Trainee, Ashford Castle; Piccadilly Meridien (London), Hotel Opalen (Gothenburg) 1963-65; Executive Chairman, Campbell Bewley group; Founder Chief Executive, Campbell Bewley Group 1986-96; Campbell Bewley Group also acquired a number of contract catering companies in the UK between 1996 and 1999, acquired Rebecca's Restaurant and Catering chain in Boston, USA 1997; formed a strategic alliance with Aramark Corporation USA 2000; Operates as Java City USA; closed Bewley's Cafes Dublin 2004; Awards: Irish Distillers/*Irish Press* Business Person of the Year Award 1989-90. Recreations: walking, running, skiing, art, sports. Contact: Campbell Bewley Group Ltd., Northern Cross, Malahide Road, Dublin 17. T 01 816 0700 F 01 816 0681 email ccl@campbellcatering.ie

A renowned artist and sculptor, is one of the shrewdest of businessmen; transformed Campbell Catering into a major international player by first rescuing legendary Bewley's chain; developed the company into the market-leader; disengaged from the landmark Bewleys, Grafton Street in 2005; competes successfully with Starbucks in it's own backyard in the US.

Noelle Campbell Sharp

CAMPBELL SHARP, Noelle, Pia; GALLERY OWNER

b 1943, Dublin; *m* Neil Campbell-Sharp; separated; 1*d*; Director, Origin Gallery; Founder/Director Cill Rialaig Artists Retreat; Journalist/Editor *Irish Tatler*; Publisher; sold seven magazines to Robert Maxwell; lost heavily on value of shares on Maxwell's death and collapse of Maxwell Communications Media group; founded Cill Rialaig artist retreat in SW Kerry, where over 1200 artists and writers have been given free residencies; Former director/ council member Arts Council 2003. Recreations: the arts in general, Irish language revival, old and specialist motor cars, Napoleonic memorabilia. Contact: 83 Harcourt Street, Dublin 2. / Ballinskelligs, Co. Kerry T 01 478 5159 F 01 478 5826 email origingallery@eircom.net

Flamboyant, single minded, energetic commercial businesswoman; has the capacity to ruffle feathers in officialdom.

CANAVAN, Jennifer; DIRECTOR, TOM CANAVAN MOTORS
b 1976, Dublin; *m* Myles O'Donohgue; *edu.* Mount Sackville Secondary School, Chapelizod, Dublin; DIT Mountjoy Square, Diploma in Marketing; Director, Tom Canavan Motors; started in family business doing the basics, took a more involved interest in the business when father became ill; worked in GE Capital Woodchester; Permanent TSB; Ballsbridge Motors; currently Director Tom Canavan Motors. Recreations: golf, travel, reading, walking. Contact: Canavan Motors, East Wall Road, Dublin. **T** 01 836 4433 email jennifercanavan@tomcanavanmotors.ie, www.tomcanavanmorots.ie

The second generation of Canavans is involved in this highly successful auto dealership; bright, hardworking and ambitious.

CANAVAN, Margaret; CHAIRWOMAN, TOM CANAVAN MOTORS
b London, UK; *m* Tom Canavan (*decd*); 5*d*; *edu.* Cardinal Manning Secondary School, London; Business /introduction to Law, University College Dublin; *Irish Times* Course; Managing Director and Chairwoman, Tom Canavan Motors; Secretary/PA, Bill O'Herlihy Public Relations; Trinity College, Treasury section; housewife. Clubs: Kildare Hotel and Country Club, Straffan, Co. Kildare. Recreations: golf, reading, travel. Contact: Tom Canavan Motors, East Wall Road, Dublin. **T** 01 836 4433 www.tomcanavanmotors.ie

Despite not having much knowledge of the motor trade prior to the untimely death of husband Tom Canavan, has learned extremely quickly; surprised many by being hands-on; settled in at the helm of the company for the past seven years; maintains an extremely successful business and plans to expand on the existing site.

Margaret Canavan

CANNY, Barry J; RESTAURANTEUR, WINE MERCHANT
b 1955, Dublin; *m* Dee; 3*d*; *edu.* Oaklands College, Dublin; London School of Design; proprietor, Peploe's Wine Bistro, Dublin; worked in construction industry; proprietor Browns Hotel, Dublin; Clubs: The Groucho, London, Glen of the Downs Golf Club, Dun Laoghaire Golf Club. Recreations: motor racing, vintage cars, art. Contact: 16 St. Stephen's Green, Dublin 2. **T** 01 671 1496 **F** 01 671 1497 **E** drinkwine@peploes.com

Amiable entrepreneur who made a name for himself with his boutique hotel, Browns, which he subsequently sold, and smart brasserie Peploes; currently developing a wine production vineyard in France.

Barry Canny

CARBERRY, Derrick Noel; MAKE-UP ARTIST
b 1975; *p* Jay Molloy; *edu.* Edenderry Vocational School, Edenderry, Co. Offaly; Make-up artist; Computer technician, Intel, Dublin 1994-'99; Make-up artist Mac Cosmetics, Brown Thomas, Dublin 1999-05; Artistic director Brown Sugar, 2005 to date. Recreations: horses, socialising, keeping fit, cooking, travel. Contact: 18 Parkgate Place Apts, Parkgate Street, Dublin 8. **M** 086 8414582

The former head of Mac joined Brown Sugar and brought his high profile clientele with him; always in huge demand for society weddings and parties all over the country; the ladies claim he can make "any old bag" looked beautiful.

CARBERRY, Nina; CHAMPION LADY JOCKEY
b 1984, Dublin; *edu.* National School Rathoath, Co. Meath; Loreto Convent Navan; Jockey; started racing ponics aged 11, took jockey license age 16; a regular in the winners' enclosure with victories at Cheltenham Festival on Dabiroun in the Fred Winter Memorial, the first woman since Gee Armytage to triumph against the professional jockeys at the festival, March 2005; Punchestown Festival, May 2005; Galway Festival, on Dasher Reilly, July 2005; Champion leading lady jockey 2005; Awards: *Irish Times* Mitsubishi Electric Sportswoman of the Month March 2005. Recreations: hunting, running, swimming. Contact: Ballybin, Ashbourne, Co. Meath. **T** 01 825 6272 **M** 086 359 0521

Grand daughter of the legendary Dan Moore who trained L'Escargot, daughter of the equally famous Tommy, who won three Gold Cups and a Grand National winner in the 1970s and sister of champion jockey Paul; struck a decisive blow for the mighty Carberry racing dynasty at Cheltenham 2005 when she brought Dabiroun home at 20/1; seems set for an equally successful career.

CARBERRY, Paul; JOCKEY

b 1974; single; *edu.* National School, Ratoath; Dunshaughlin Community College; obtained jockey's licence aged 16; winner for Jim Bolger in that first year; top apprentice jockey; main trainer Noel Meade; won the Aintree Grand National Champion on Bobby Jo 1999; champion jockey, became the first man since Charlie Swan in 1996/97 to ride a century of winners 2002. Recreations: showjumping, hunting, hunter trials, water skiing. Contact: Ballybin, Ashbourne, Co. Meath. **T** 01 825 6272 **M** 086 816 9894

Having learnt his trade through hunting, show jumping and point-to-pointing in Ireland, is now a highly respected and stylish champion jockey; rode a century in 2002 but hugely disappointed the vast Irish following at Cheltenham 2005 when he failed to deliver on Harchibald; further disappointed his fans when he was arrested for a misdemeanor on board an Aer Lingus flight October 2005 and was subsequently found guilty.

CARBERRY, S.J. Patrick Joseph; EDITOR THE MESSENGER

b 1944, single; *edu.* Coláiste Mhuire, Parnell Square, Dublin; University College Dublin; University College Galway; Milltown Institute of Theology & Philosphy; BA (Hons); H.Dip in Ed (Hons); BD (Hons); Lic. Theol (Hons); Editor, Sacred Heart Messenger. Contact: 37 Lower Leeson Street, Dublin 2. **T** 01 676 7491 **F** 01 661 1606 email sales@messenger.ie ,www.messenger.ie

Has ensured that *The Messenger* retains its position as Ireland's largest selling magazine.

CAREY, DJ; BUSINESSMAN

b 1970, Kilkenny; *m* Christine (separated); 2*s* 1*d*; *p* Sarah Newman; *edu.* Gowran National School, Co. Wexford; St. Kieran's College, Kilkenny; Company Director; winner of record nine All Star Awards; five All Ireland Senior Hurling Medals; one All Ireland Under-21 and minor Hurling medals; eight Leinster Hurling medals; two All Ireland Colleges medals; three railway Cup medals; twice Texaco Hurler of the Year (1993 & 2000); former All Ireland Hand Ball champion; retired from hurling 2006; DJ Carey Coaching School. Clubs: Young Ireland's Gowran; Mount Juliet, Golf and Country Club; The Kildare Hotel and Country Club. Recreations: sport, golf. Contact: DJ Carey Enterprises, Demense, Gowran, Co. Kilkenny. **T** 056 772 6566 **F** 056 7726565 email info@djcarey@eircom.net web www.djcarey.com

A latter-day icon in the GAA world who has built a business profile around his sporting achievements; top class golfer, comfortable in the company of other sportsmen.

CAREY, Michael; CEO, JACOB FRUITFIELD GROUP

b 1962, Dublin; *m* Alison Cowzer; 2*d*; *edu.* St.Vincent's CBS, Glasnevin, Dublin; University College Dublin; B.Comm. MBS; Chief Executive-Majority Shareholder of Jacob Fruitfield Food Group; Brand Manager, Batchelors, Dublin; Marketing Manager, Biscuits, Yorkshire UK; Marketing Director, Cantrell & Cochrane, Ireland; Marketing Director, Irish Biscuits, Dublin; Managing Director Evian/Volvic (UK & Ireland), London; Marketing Director, Fox's Biscuits, Yorkshire, UK; Marketing Director, Kelloggs (UK/Ireland) Manchester; Awards: winner Ernst and Young Entrepreneur of the Year (Industry Section) 2005. Clubs: Powerscourt Golf Club. Recreations: golf, family/children, travel. Contact: Jacobs Fruitfield Food Group, Blessington Road, Tallaght, Dublin. **T** 01 404 3816 email michael.carey@jacobsfruitfield.com

Michael Carey

Low profile, commercially savvy, his achievements were recognized by winning The Ernst and Young Entrepreneur of the Year for the Industry Section 2005.

CAREY, Pat; PUBLIC REPRESENTATIVE

b 1947, Castlemaine, Co. Kerry; single; *edu*; Presentation Brothers College, Milltown, Co. Kerry; St. Patrick's Training College, Drumcondra, Dublin; University College Dublin; Trinity College Dublin; BA, H.Dip.Ed; Public Representative TD (FF Dublin North West) 1997 to date; member, Dublin City Council 1985-2002; member, Dublin City Vocational Education Committee 1988-91 (chairman 1988-91); chairman, Council of Technology, Bolton St. 1985-91; member, Council of College of Catering, Cathal Brugha Street, Dublin. 1985-91; member, Governing Body Dublin Institute of Technology 1985-94; co-chairman, TCD DIT Liaison Council 1988-91; chairman, School Committee of Coláiste Éoin and Colaiste Íde, Finglas 1985 to date; Plunkett College, Whitehall 1985-91; member, NCEA 1991-96; former chairman, Catholic Youth Council 1991-96; former primary school teacher, vice principal. Recreations: politics, local affairs, arts, culture. Contact: Constituency Office 2, Finglas Town Centre, Dublin 11.**T** 01 864 4118 **F** 01 864 4199 email pcarey@oireachtas.ie

Although he likes the rough and tumble of politics and particularly elections, he is regarded as a gentleman, which may explain why he didn't make the cut for major political appointment. But may yet go far.

CARNEY, Professor, Desmond Niall; CONSULTANT MEDICAL ONCOLOGIST

b 1947, Dublin; *m* Patricia; 3*s* 2*d*; *edu*. Belvedere College, Dublin; University College Dublin; Mater Misericordiae Hospital, Dublin; National Cancer Institute, USA; M.B., M.D., PhD., F.R.C.P.I. Consultant Medical Oncologist; Post Graduate Education Dublin 1971-'76; Clinical Scientist National Cancer Institute 1976-'84; Consultant Medical Oncologist Mater University Hospital 1984 to date; President International Association for Study of Lung Cancer (IASLC) 2000-'07; *Publ.* More than 300 peer reviewed publications including: *Nature*; *Science; PNAS; Lancet*; *New England Journal of Medicine*; Previous Chairman and board member Irish Cancer Society. Recreations: reading, sport, music. Contact: Mater University Hospital/ Mater Private Hospital, Eccles Street, Dublin 7. **T** 01 885 8610 **F** 01 830 6469 web www.mater.ie

Desmond Carney

Internationally trained, one of the most highly respected oncologists in the country; caring, kind, friendly and totally approachable, held in the highest esteem by his patients for whom he demands the very best treatment; an excellent media performer with relaxed style and a rare ability to demystify his speciality.

CARNEY, The Hon. Mr. Justice Paul; JUDGE OF THE HIGH COURT

b 1943; *m* Marjorie Young; 3*s* 1*d*; *edu*. Gonzaga College, King's Inns; Judge of the High Court; called to the Bar in Ireland 1966; called to the Bar of England and Wales 1969; called to the Inner Bar 1980; Appointed Judge of the High Court 1991; President of the Irish Association for the Protection of the Financial Interests of the European Community. Clubs: Kildare Street and University Club, Dublin. Contact: The High Court, Dublin 7. **T** 01 872 5555 **F** 01 872 1620

A civilised, serious man, conscious of his duties and responsibilities on the Bench; brings his natural common sense to bear upon proceedings; acted as election agent for Michael McDowell (*qv*).

CARROLL, Claudia; ACTOR/NOVELIST

b Dublin; single; *edu*. College of Music, Dublin; Gaiety School of Acting; University College Dublin; BA; Actor/Novelist; *Publ. He Loves Me Not, He Loves Me* 2004; *The Last of the Great Romantics* 2005; *Remind Me Again Why I Need A Man* 2006. Recreations: reading (especially Jane Austen), Abba; Contact; Marianne Gunne O'Connor, Morrisson Chambers, Suite 17, 32 Nassau Street, Dublin 2 **T** 01 677 9100 **F** 01 677 9101 email mgoclitagency@eircom.net

Has maintained a high profile through her work as a thesp, best known as Nicola Prendergast in *Fair City* and latterly as a best-selling novelist.

CARROLL, Liam; PROPERTY DEVELOPER

b Dundalk; *m* Roisín; 1 *s* 2 *d*; *edu*. Marist College Dundalk; Mechanical Engineer; High Court action brought against Zoe by The National Authority for Occupational Health and Safety due to poor safety standards on building site 1997; ordered to pay IP £100,000 to charity; paid IP£200 million for Dunloe Ewert in a head-to-head with Noel Smyth 2000; remerged as a significant power broker in the battle for Jury's Doyle 2005 when he sold his shares to the Doyle

Claudia Carroll

sisters for €49.9 million giving them control of the group. Recreations: golf. Contact: Zoe Developments, 765, South Circular Road, Dublin 8. **T** 01 679 5399

Low profile, better known as the owner of Zoe Developments; very private; shuns the social scene; no trappings of wealth; enjoys golf at a pay and play club; first to take advantage of Section 23 legislation; does wonderful work for charity; has now built up a big organization and owns substantial properties and sites particularly in the city center and greater Dublin area; emerged in July 2006 as the buyer of Dermot Desmond's (*qv*) 21.57 holding in Greencore for €170 million making the food firms future uncertain since pundits predict his main interest lies in Greencore's property portfolio.

CARROLL, Paul; MANAGING PARTNER A&L GOODBODY
b Dublin; *m* Fiona; 3*s* 1*d*; *edu*. Blackrock College, Dublin; Trinity College Dublin; Solicitor; apprenticed A&L Goodbody; opened A&L Goodbody London office 1988; Resident partner London 1990-1992, specialising in banking and tax-based finance transactions; Managing Partner A&L Goodbody 2001; a corporate finance specialist, has advised Irish and international clients on a wide range of significant transactions; advises particularly on mergers and acquisitions, both public and private, foreign investment, shipping and general corporate matters; Business Lawyer of the Year in Ireland (Chambers & Partners) 2002. Contact: A&L Goodbody International Financial Services Centre North Wall Quay Dublin 1. **T** 01 649 2000 **F** 01 649 2649email pcarroll@algoodbody.ie web www.algoodbody.ie

Led the Irish legal team advising on the acquisition of Eircom plc by Valentia Telecommunications Limited, one of the largest and most hotly contested takeovers in Irish business history.

CARSON, Paul; MEDICAL PRACTITIONER/NOVELIST
b 1949, Belfast; *m* Jean; 1*s* 1*d*; *edu*. St Macnissis College, Garron Tower, Co Antrim, N. Ireland; Trinity College Dublin; BA, MB, BCh, BAO; Medical practitioner /Novelist; Publ. five health books, two children's novels, five medical thrillers; numerous articles, reports in medical and national press; medical doctor 1975 to date; writer and novelist 1986 to date. Interests: childhood allergy; commercial fiction, medical thriller genre; Recreations: Staying alive. Contact: 1 Greygates, Mount Merrion, Co Dublin. **T** 01 288 9295 **F** 01 278 0248 email carfam@indigo.ie

Prolific and popular as a serious medical commentator and for his best selling medical thrillers.

CASARI, Giorgio; RESTAURATEUR, THE UNICORN
b 1959, Italy; *m* Noreen; 2*s* 1*d*; *edu*; Obligatory Schools in Italy; Intensive three years live-in Catering & Tourism Industry College in Stresa (Lake Maggiore); Co Owner with Jeff Stoke (*qv*) The Unicorn; three months public relations course in Milan; Six months Hotel Management course; five years of summer stage work around Europe to learn the three top European languages, French, English and German. Clubs: Merrion Hotel Fitness Center. Recreations: cars, travel, theatre, opera. Contact: Unicorn Restaurant, Merrion Row, Dublin 2. **T** 01 662 4757

If he didn't exist he'd have to be invented; with wife Noreen and business partner Jeff Stokes (*qv*) he invented the Unicorn, a Dublin landmark; that he has not only retained the old-timers but made it party central for the latest A-listers, is a tribute to innate good commercial sense as well as a love of food and people.

Giorgio Casari

CASEY, Karl; MANAGING DIRECTOR, KARL CASEY HAIRDRESSERS, WATERFORD
b 1944, Kilmacthomas, Co. Waterford; *m* Anne; 2*s* 1*d*; *edu*. St. Augustines College, Dungarvan, Co. Waterford; Hairdresser; MD Karl Casey Hairdressers; in business in Waterford for 38 years. Clubs: Waterford Castle Golf Club; Tramore Golf Club; Director/Sec. Waterford and Tramore Racecourse. Recreations: national hunt racing, golf. Contact: Waterford and Tramore Racecourse & Co. Ltd, Tramore, Co. Waterford. **T** 051 381 425

A leading Waterford business man; currently involved in the relocation of the Tramore racetrack to a new beachside location.

CASEY, Norah Colette; PUBLISHER

b 1960; *m* Richard Hannaford; 1*s*; *edu.* St. Joseph's Convent, Stanhope Street, Dublin; University of Wales; Ph.D.(eng); Registered General Nurse (RGN); Vale of Leven Hospital, Scotland; Certificate Burns & Plastic Surgery, Bangor, Lothian; NCTJ Certificate in journalism 1983; Harlow College 1987; Certificate in TV Studio Production, Ealing College, London 1990, RGN, CBPS, NCJ; Publisher; Editor Director, Scutari Projects, London 1989-95; M.D. Rcw publishing company, London 1995-98; Editor *The Irish Post* newspaper, London 1998-2001; CEO/Publisher, Smurfit Media UK 1999-2003; CEO Smurfit Communications 2001-2004; CEO Harmonia 2004 to date; Chair. Mayor of London's St. Patrick's Day Advisory Forum; Founder Member Women's Irish Network, London; Member International Women's Forum; Board Member Angels Quest; Board Member Music Network. Recreations: Good food and wine, travel, spending lots of time with son. Contact: Harmonia, Clanwilliam House, Clanwilliam Place, Dublin 2. **T** 01 2405 35 **F** 01661 9486 email ncasey@harmonia.ie

Norah Casey

Innovative, successful publisher in a male-dominated world; more than well able to hold her own.

CASEY, Patricia Rosarie; PROFESSOR OF PSYCHIATRY

b 1952; *m*; 2*s*; *edu.* Presentation Convent Fermoy; Loreto Convent Fermoy; University College Cork; MB, BCL, BAO (medical degree), FRCDI, FRC Psych (Postgraduate qualifications), MD; Professor of Psychiatry; qualified as doctor UCC 1976; Postgraduate training in Psychiatry Nottingham and Edinburgh 1979-85; Consultant Psychiatrist/Statuatory Lecturer UCC/Cork University Hospital 1985-92; Professor of Psychiatry/Consultant Psychiatrist Mater Misericordiae Hospital Dublin 1997 to date; editor of peer perceived international psychiatric journal *Quarterly Journal of Mental Health*; elected to Medical Council 1994-90 and chaired Fitness to Practice Committee; Publ. *From the Heart: Mental Health Questions Answered*. Recreations: classical music, writing. Contact: Dept of Psychiatry, Mater Misericordiae Hospital, Eccles St, Dublin 7. **T** 01 8032176 **F** 01 8309323 email: Profcasey@easclear.ie

Well-known media performer with firm views on a number of health matters.

CASEY, Pierse; INVESTMENT BANKER

b 1955, Dungarvan, Co. Waterford; *m* Judy Lynch; 2*s* 3*d*; *edu.* Christian Brothers College, Dungarvan; Clongowes Wood College, Co. Kildare; University College Dublin, B.Comm; FCA, FCMA; Investment Banker; accountant Craig Gardner, Dublin 1976-80; KMPG, Bermuda 1980-82; DCC, Dublin & London 1982-99; Director 1987-88; Chief Executive, Equity & Corporate Finance, London 1989; bought Omnilogic with Apax Partners 1993; set up Fayrewood; floated Fayrewood on AIM 1996; along with APAX acquired a number of small companies including British firm Interface Systems International and Paris-based Banque Magnetique; bought ComputerLinks 1997; set up Irish office of Apax Partners 1998; floated ComputerLinks on now disbanded Neuer Market, Frankfurt 1999; Director Alchemy Partners (London) 2001 to date; Fitzwilliam Capital; resigned from Fayrewood 2005. Clubs: RAC Club, London; Wentworth Golf Club; Moor Park Golf Club, London; Fitzwilliam LTC, Dublin; Doonbeg Golf Club; Druids Glen Golf Club. Recreations: golf, chess. Contact: 10, Fitzwilliam Square, Dublin 2. **T** 01 661 2671 **F** 01 661 3057

Very low profile, takes a forensic approach to acquisitions.

CASHMAN, Liam; BLOODSTOCK BREEDER

b 1937; *m* Catherine Beecher; 1*s* 1*d*; *edu.* Kilmagner National School; Salesian Agricultural College, Pallaskenry; Bloodstock Breeder; took over family stud farm 1971; Rathbarry Stud, founded in 1935; sister stud Glenview opened 1991; has bred By the Way, Earth Stopper, Danish Knight, Alpride, Savage, Unconditional Love, Casque Blue, Locombe Hill, Liprandi, Lagado, Bajan, Humberts Landing; stallions at stud include Acclamation, Barathea, Charmwood Forest, Rainbow, For Life, Royal Abjar, Tagula; Principal winners: Alpride, Savage, Unconditional Love, Casque Blue, Locombe Hill, Liprandi, Lagado, Bajan, Humbert's Landing, Blueberry Forest, Noah's Ark etc. Recreations: GAA, horse racing, farming. Contact: Rathbarry Stud, Fermoy, Co. Cork. **T** 025 36362 **F** 025 36602.

One of Ireland's longest established bloodstock breeders and trainers in the country, continues to expand to this day; now stands both flat and National Hunt stallions; a keen Cork hurling supporter.

Peter Cassells

CASSELLS, Peter; CONSULTANT

b 1949, Meath; *m* Paula Carey; *edu.* St. Patrick's Classical School, Navan; Institute of Public Administration, Dip Admin; Consultant: Public Servant (Ministry Of Social Security) 1969 – 73; Economic and Social Affairs Officer Irish Congress of Trade Unions 1973 – 82; Assistant General Secretary, ICTU 1982 –87; General Secretary, ICTU 1987 – 02; Lead Negotiator, Partnership Programmes,1987 – 02; Chairman, National Centre For Partnership and Performance 2002 – to date; Member, National Economic and Social Council 1982 – '02; Chairman, Industrial Development Board (FORFAS) 1997 – 04; Adjunct Professor , National College of Ireland 1997; Executive Committee, European Trade Union Confederation 1982 – 02; board member European Trade Union Confederation. A newcomer to electoral politics, he defeated , Peter Ward, Labour's 2002 General Election candidate in the Meath constituency for the party's nomination, garnering 70% of the vote; Executive Chair, Irish National Center for Partnership and Performance 2001 – 04; consultant on issues concerning organisational change, to a number of key Irish organisations, including the Electricity Supply Board and the Irish postal service; Government appointed chairman of the committee to resolve the Rossport /Shell Gas Field impasse 2006; Recreations: GAA, Manchester United fan, Irish Wheelchair Association. Contact: 14, Parnell Square, Dublin 1. **T** 01 814 6300

> Highly respected figure in trade union and business circles; one of the main architects of modern day social partnership which has underpinned the Celtic Tiger.

Constance Cassidy

CASSIDY, Constance; BARRISTER AT LAW

b 1960s, Dublin; *m* Edward Walsh (*qv*); 3*s* 4*d*; *edu.* Our Lady's Bower, Killashee, Naas, Co. Kildare; Trinity College Dublin; BA (Mod); Kings Inns; Barrister at Law; called to the Bar 1985; called to the Inner Bar 2001; expert in licensing law; Publ. definitive *Cassidy on the Licensing Acts* (three editions); licensing handbooks; articles in professional journals; lecturer to Licensed Vitners Assoc, Vintners Federation; Incor law Judiciary; with husband Edward Walsh bought Lissadell 2003; Irish Business Woman of the Year (*Irish Tatler*) 2001. Recreations: cooking, gardening, reading and chilling out. Contact: Law library, Four Courts, Dublin 7. **T** 01 817 4465 **F** 045 435 665 emailccassidy@eircom.net.

> Extremely stylish, the country's leading licensing lawyer; chateleine of a great house where she's brought great common sense to the whole project; proved the OPW advisors wrong by more than 90% when she and her husband bought (€3.75 million), refurbished (€1 million), and reopened the Great House with it's windows to the West for under €5 million, whereas the OPW advisors were suggesting €30 million plus; idea of bliss "to take a hot bath at the end of the day when the children are in bed."

CASSIDY, Donie; PUBLIC REPRESENTATIVE

b 1945, Castlepollard, Co. Westmeath; *m* Anne Geraghty; 4*s*; Public Representative, Buisnessman; Senator 1982-02; Elected to the Dail 2002; Leader of the Seanad 1997-02; chairman Enterprise Trade and Small Business Committee; chairman, Committee of Procedure and Privileges 1985-03; member of Westmeath County Council 1985-03 (chairman 1989/1990); Midland Health Board 1985-05; Member of Westmeath VEC 1979-2003; Chairman North West Meath Council 2000-03; Clubs: Founding member Delvin Golf Club (past president, past captain); former West Meath minor hurler 1962/1963; past player and vice president Castle Pollard Hurling Club; life member Mullingar Golf Club. Recreations: golf, hurling; Cassidy Hotel sponsors Westmeath hurling team 2000 to date. Contact: Castlepollard, Co Westmeath. **T** 01 618 3578 **F** 01 618 4172 (Constituency Office) 044 45442 email doniecassidy@oirechtas.ie

> Able, astute and very skilled in public matters; a shrewd and successful businessman; gave Mary O'Rourke her come-uppance when he took her seat at the last general election but could have his work cut out to retain it next time out.

CASSIDY, Neil; MANAGING DIRECTOR, CASSIDY WINES Ltd

b 1955, Cork; *m* Noreen; 1*s* 2*d*; *edu.* Templeogue College, Dublin; Bolton Street College of Technology, Dublin; B.Sc ARICS; Managing Director Cassidy Wines Ltd; Mulcahy McDonagh Surveyors 1977-81; IDA 1981-83; Cassidy Wines 1983 to date. Clubs: Milltown Golf Club; David Lloyd Riverview. Recreations: golf, tennis, skiing. Contact: Cassidy Wines Ltd. Magna Drive, Magna Business, City West Business Park, Dublin 24. **T** 01 466 8900 **F** 01 466 8932 email ncassidy@cassidywines.com

Son of Kevin Cassidy, the retired army officer who with great prescience founded Cassidy Wines and became one of Ireland's most successful wine merchants; is a bright, low key businessman; has already vastly expanded the original company.

Neil Cassidy

CASSIDY, Marie Therese; PROFESSOR/STATE PATHOLOGIST
b 1955, Scotland; *m* Philip O'Brien; *edu.* Elmwood Senior Secondary, Bothwell, Scotland; University of Glasgow; MB, ChB, MRC Path; Professor/ State Pathologist; Hospital Pathologist 1980-85; Consultant Forensic Pathologist 1995-97; Deputy State Pathologist 1998-2002; State Pathologist 2005 to date. Recreations: medico-legal study, reading. Contacts: Office of State Pathologist, Marino, Malahide, Dublin 5. **T** 01 853 4871 email mcassidy@statepthology.gov.ie

For many years deputy to John Harbison; not only hardworking but hugely overworked; despite the nature of her work has a sunny disposition; is widely respected.

CAVANAGH, Tom; CHAIRMAN CAVANAGH'S MOTOR GROUP
b 1931; *m* Marie O'Neill; 2*s* 2*d*; *edu.* Christian Brothers School, Fermoy; University College Cork; B. Comm; H. Dip; LL.D (*hc*); Chairman Cavanagh's Motor Group; teacher Vocational Education Committee, Cork 1952-53; joined family motor business in Fermoy; built business into one of the major family controlled motor trade firms in the South; former director Allied Irish Bank; former chairman, currently director, Conrad Hotel; patron Cheshire Homes, Cork; trustee, Multiple Sclerosis Society of Ireland; trustee, Fermoy Golf Club; chairman trustees of St. Colman's Cathedral, Cobh; founding chairman Irish Business Against Litter; member of board of trustees Glucksman Gallery, Cork 2003 to date; Board of University College Cork 1983 to date; UCC board member Fenton Gallery Cork. Recreations: voluntary community work, reading, travel, arts, theatre, anti-litter campaigns. Contact: Cavanagh of Fermoy, Ashe Quay, Fermoy, Co. Cork. **T** 025 31211 **F** 025 32345. email info@cavanaghsoffermoy.ie

A civic minded and cultured man; extremely successful; has tried to tidy up, not to say, clean up Ireland, particularly rural Ireland; embraces change when it's good, but not for it's own sake.

CAWLEY, Noel; MANAGING DIRECTOR IRISH DAIRY BOARD
b 1944, Sligo; *m* Anita; 2*d*; *edu*; St. Nathy's College, Ballaghaderreen, Co Roscommon; University College Galway B.Sc; University College Dublin PhD; University of California, Berkeley, Post Doctoral Fellowship; Fullbright Scholarship; Managing Director, Irish Dairy Board; Arthur Guinness UK, brewing and middle management responsibilities 1971-1974; Irish Dairy Board (formerly an Bord Bainne) 1974 to date, variety of roles covering research and development, commercial, marketing and general management; appointed executive director in 1976 and managing director in 1989; five Scientific Papers Ireland and USA; a member of five specialist groups set up by successive Ministers for Agriculture to draw up five-10 year plans for the development of agriculture and food since 1980, including the most recent in 2004; honorary life member of the RDS and a member of its council and management board. Recreations: horse racing, show jumping, GAA and golf, stud owner and horse breeder. Contact: Irish Dairy Board, Grattan House, Mount Street Lower, Dublin 2. **T** 01 661 9599 **F** 01 661 2778 email idb@idb.ie web www.idb.ie

Noel Cawley

The Sligo-born scientist has been chief executive of the Irish Dairy Board since 1989 in an era of major change in the industry; low profile, highly intelligent businessman; an equestrian who has been chairman of the Irish Horse Board for many years.

CAWLEY, Philip, Richard; DISC JOCKEY TODAY FM
b 1966, Dublin; single; 1*s* 1*d*; *edu.* Senior College Ballyfermot; Post Leaving Certificate Television and Media; Disk Jockey ToDay FM; 2 FM 1985-89; local radio 1989-96; Today FM 1997 to date. Clubs: Motorcycle Action Group. Recreations: cruising in my BMW, running in Brittas Bay, cycling, swimming, walking with the kids. Contact: Today FM, 124 Abbey Street, Dublin 1. **T** 01 804 9014 **F** 01 804 9099 email philip@todayfm.com

CHADWICK, Michael; EXECUTIVE CHAIRMAN GRAFTON GROUP PLC
b 1951, Dublin; *m*; 1*s*; *edu.* Trinity College Dublin, BA, MSc; appointed to the board of established family firm 1979; Executive Chairman 1985 to date; acquired Atlantic Homecare 1985; Opened first

Woodies DIY Superstore in Sandyford 1987; now 19 Woodies nationwide; renamed company Grafton Group plc; acquired Bradley UK 1996; P.P.S. Mortars UK; R.J. Johnson UK 1996; Plumbline, Edinburgh, Jackson, England 2003; joined board of Pochin plc (UK) 2005; Acquired main Irish rival Heiton 2004. Contact: Grafton Group plc, Heron House, Corrig Road, Sandyford Industrial Estate, Dublin 18. **T** 01 216 0600 **F** 01 295 4470 email info@graftonplc. web www.graftonplc.com

The first to spot the trend in DIY when Grafton opened it's first Woodies in Dublin; a low profile, courteous, conservative businessman; possesses an exceptionally shrewd business acumen and now employs 9,500 employees at over 450 locations in Ireland and the UK.

CHAWKE, Charlie; PUBLICIAN

b 1949, Adare, Co. Limerick; *m* Bernice; *2s 3d*; *edu.* Adare CBS, Co. Limerick; Publican; apprentice bar man Davy Byrnes, Dublin; barman in Eddie Bohan's (*qv*) pub; acquired Mc Govern's Bar, Wexford Street, Dublin in partnership 1972; acquired Bridge House, Crumlin Road, Dublin 1974; acquired The Goat Grill, Goatstown, Dublin 1982; acquired The Dropping Well, Milltown, Dublin 1994; acquired The Oval, Middle Abbey Street, Dublin (in partnership with Eddie Bohan) 1994; acquired The Lord Lucan, Newcastle Road, Lucan, Co. Dublin 1997; acquired father's pub Bill Chawkes, Adare, Co. Limerick 1998; acquired The Bank Bar, Dame Street, Dublin 2002; acquired The Orchard, Rathfarnham, Dublin 2005; Member of consortium bidding to take over Sunderland FC 2006. Clubs: Woodbrook Golf Club, Adare GAA, Comrades Hurling Club, Dublin. Recreations: golf, "drinking Heineken with friends in The Swan, Aungier Street". Contact: Dropping Well, Milltown, Dublin. **T** 01 496 9338 **F** 01 497 9882 email the dropwell@indigo.ie

Like many of the leading publicans is diversifying into hotel and property development; a major sports fanatic (an investor in Sunderland FC 2006) and a keen Limerick GAA supporter.

CHAWKE, Marie, Catherine; HOTELIER

Marie Chawke

b 1972, Limerick; *m* Pat Chawke (*qv*); *edu.* Drishane Convent, Millstreet, Co. Cork; Hotel Management College, Shannon, Co. Clare; First Class Dip. International Hotel Management; General Manager, Aghadoe Heights Hotel and Spa; sales and banqueting co-coordinator Royal Hospital Kilmainham, Dublin; General manager Randles Court Hotel, Killarney, Co. Kerry; General manager Hayfield Manor, Hotel, Cork; General Manager Aghadoe Heights Hotel Killarney, Co. Kerry. Clubs: Limerick and Kilmallock GAA. Recreations: golf, travel, GAA, skiing. Contact: Aghadoe Heights Hotel and Spa, Fossa, Killarney, Co. Kerry. **T** 064 31766 email marie.chawke@aghadoeheights.com www.aghadoeheights.com

Extremely savvy and switched on, her five-star experience is evident in the attention to detail and lavished on her guests; excellent staff is testimony to her good communications and motivational skills.

CHAWKE, Patrick Joseph; HOTELIER

b 1967; *m* Marie (*qv*); *edu.* St Peters College, Wexford; Galway Mayo Institute of Technology; H Dip Hotel and Business Management; Hotelier; assistant manager, Hilton Hotel, Dusseldorf 1989-90; assistant manager, Three Lakes Hotel, Killarney 1990-91; assistant manager, Great Southern Hotel, Rosslare 1991-92; deputy general manager, Great Southern Hotel, Killarney 1992-94; general manager, Corrib Great Southern Hotel, Galway 1994-97; general manager, Maryborough House Hotel, Cork 1997-2000; General Manager, Aghadoe Heights Hotel, Killarney. Clubs: Killarney Golf and Fishing Club, Killarney Athletic Club. Recreations: golf, skiing, reading. Contact: Aghadoe Heights Hotel and Spa, Fossa, Killarney, Co. Kerry. **T** 064 31766 email pat.chawkc@aghadoeheights.com web www.aghadoeheights.com

A top class, hands-on hotelier, runs a first class establishment that includes the best spa in Ireland; with wife Marie has seen this hotel go from strength to strength with a discerning national and international clientele.

CHESNEAU, Edmond; DESIGNER

b 1953; divorced; *p* Janet; *1d*; *edu.* Saint Ferdinand, Chartres, France; Cachan University Paris; BT in

Electro Technique; self-taught in design and leather goods industry (with some initial help from an ex-craftsman from Hermès); created the Chesneau Leather Product Line and its branding; opened flagship store in Dublin 2004. Clubs: Kilkenny Flying Club. Recreations: horse riding, flying, reading, diving, photography, walking, travel. Contact: Bennettsbridge, Co Kilkenny. **T** 056 772 7456 **F** 056 7727 329 email ches@indigo.ie

It's been a long and winding road for this French designer of luxury leather goods; while he always produced wonderful work, the business seemed to stop and stall; finally appears to have all his ducks in a row and with a wonderful store on Wicklow Street in Dublin, his stylish handbags and accessories are as much objects of desire as those directly across the street.

CHURCH, John Nicholas; CEO ARTHRITIS IRELAND
b 1964, Dublin; edu. Terenure College Dublin 6; UCD, Dublin 4; University of Louvain, Belgium; Kingston University, London; B.Sc, Degree in International Marketing, Diploma Direct Marketing; CEO Arthritis Ireland; Arthritis Ireland 2005-to date; Richmond Marketing 2000-2004; Coca Cola Company 1995-2000; Bank of Ireland 1988-1995. Clubs: Terenure College RFC, Old Wesley RFC, Castle Golf Club. Recreations: rugby, music. Contact: 1 Clanwilliam Square, Grand Canal Quay, Dublin 2. **T** 01 661 8188 **F** 01 661 8261 email jchurch@arthritisireland.ie

John Church

Brings a wealth of much needed marketing experience to the not for profit sector.

CLAFFEY, Una; POLITICAL ADVISOR
b 1947, Dublin; single; *edu.* Mercy Convent, Mourne Road, Drimnagh; Loreto High School Beaufort, Rathfarnham; University College Dublin BA; University D'Aix, Marseilles; primary school teacher 1970-71; studied community politics, Boston, Mass. 1971-74; organised Sec. Resources Protection Campaign, Dublin 1975-77; production assistant, RTE 1977-82; presenter/reporter, *Today Tonight* 1982-90; presenter *Morning Ireland* 1990-91; RTE political correspondent 1991-2000; political adviser to An Taoiseach (*qv*) 2000 to date; Publ. *The Women Who Won - Women Elected to Dail* 1992; Awards: Commendation 1977 AEJ Award for coverage of 50th Anniversary of VE Day in Moscow; French Government, Legion d'Honneur 2005; Chevalier de l'Ordre National du Merite French Republic. Recreations: food, travel, hurling, life. Contact: Department of An Taoiseach, Government Buildings, Merrion Square, Dublin 2. **T** 01 619 4020

The former TV correspondent plays a much lower profile role since joining Taoiseach Bertie Ahern's staff as political advisor; astute, highly influential.

CLANCY, Catherine Consilio; ASSISTANT COMMISSIONER AN GARDA SIOCHANA
b 1954, Portnoo, Donegal; single; *edu.* locally; Templemore Training Centre An Garda Siochana; Honours Degree Police Management; Diploma in Criminology; assistant commissioner, Northern Region An Garda Siochana; joined an Garda Siochana 1974; assigned to Pearse Street Garda Station Dublin 1975; promoted sergeant 1989; promoted inspector 1993; superintendent 1996; chief superintendent 1999; assistant commissioner Northern Region, Sligo 2003 to date; served in Pearse Street, Naas, The Technical Bureau of Investigation, Ballyshannon, Co. Donegal, Community Relations Unit, Donegal, Lucan, Letterkenny; semester lecturer in Criminology Penn State University, USA; member of Public Appointments Board for the Public Service. Recreations: music, brass bands, walking, the countryside. Contact: An Garda Siochana, Pearse Road, Sligo.

The first woman at this rank in the Garda Siochana; well-liked for her open manner and friendly disposition; brings a well-rounded and disciplined approach to her work; ambitious for herself and for all women in the force; tipped to be the first woman Commissioner.

CLANCY, Patrick, 'Paddy'; JOURNALIST
b 1943, Sligo; m Bernadette Hanna; 1s 2d; edu. Summerhill College, Sligo; Journalist; reporter *Sligo Champion* 1960-1964; *Donegal People* 1964-1965; *Irish Press* 1965-1967; *Brighton Evening Argus* 1967-1968; *Daily Telegraph* 1968-1974; *Daily Express* 1974-1979; founded Clancy News Service 1979-1982; founder/senior partner Irish International News Agency 1982-1989; editor News, Sport Century Radio 1989-1991; reporter later head of bureau *Irish Sun* 1992-2004; presenter *It Says In The Papers*, RTE Radio 1991 to date. Clubs: Shelbourne Club. Recreations: soccer. Contact: Rossnowlagh Road, Ballyshannon, Co Donegal.

Ireland's original 'Fleet Street' tabloid newshound; larger than life personality; great storyteller; an incredibly hard worker; great contacts; loyal friend.

CLANDILLION, Margaret; AVIATION FINANCE CONSULTANT
b 1960, Dublin; *m* John Mulcahy *(qv)*; 3*s*; *edu*. Santa Sabina Convent, Sutton; Trinity College Dublin, BA Legal; Blackhall Place (awarded first prize and AIB Award for company law); Aviation Finance Consultant; apprenticed to Mason Hayes and Curran; joined GPA general counsel 1985-93; co-founder, with Brian Goulding and Michael Dolan, Pembroke Group Ltd., specialists in aircraft ownership, leasing and the provision of financial services to aviation; the company has acquired, owned and managed a fleet of over 100 aircraft with a market value of over £2 billion 1993-01; joined the board of Aergo Capital, Denis O'Brien-owned aircraft leasing company 1999 to date. Clubs: Powerscourt Golf Club, Mount Juliet Golf Club, David Lloyd Riverview Fitness Club. Recreations: golf, reading, socialising. Contact: Aergo Capital, 16, Clanwilliam Terrace, Grand Canal Quay, Dublin 2. **T** 01 676 1077 **F** 01 661 5383

A dynamic aviation expert; now functioning as an international consultant to the worldwide aviation business; sold her interests in Pembroke Group to Rolls Royce; a major player in the very macho world of international aviation.

CLARKE, Darren Christopher; PROFESSIONAL GOLFER
b 1968, Dungannon, Co.Tyrone, Northern Ireland; *m* Heather Tosh; decd; 2*s*; *edu*. The Royal Down School, Dungannon, Co. Tyrone; Professional Golfer; turned Pro 1990; Alfred Dunhill Belgian Open 1993; Linde German Masters 1996; Benson & Hedges International Open 1998; Volvo Masters 1998; Compass Group English Open 1999; WGC-Andersen Consulting Match Play Championship 2000; Compass Group English Open 2000; Dimension Data Pro-Am (South African Tour) 2001; Chunichi Crowns (Japan Tour) 2001; Smurfit European Open 2001; Compass Group English Open 2002; WGC NEC Invitational 2003; Benmore Developments Northern Ireland Masters (Challenge Tour) 2003; Mitsui Sumitomo VISA Taiyeiho Masters 2004; Currently 17th in European Tour Order of Merit with €899,030; 45th in the US PGA Tour Money List with $1,456,921; 17th in the World Ranking; Finished: PGA European Tour 2nd in 1998 Volvo Order of Merit with £902,867; 8th in 1999 Volvo Order of Merit with €731,291; 2nd in 2000 Volvo Order of Merit with €2,717,965; 3rd in 2001 Volvo Order of Merit with €1,988,055; 22nd in 2002 Volvo Order of Merit with €848,023; 2nd in 2003 Volvo Order of Merit with €2,210,051; 8th in 2004 Volvo Order of Merit with €1,563,802; USPGA Tour: 28th in the US Money List with $2,009,819; European Ryder Cup team member: four consecutive appearances 1997, 1999, 2001 (2002) and 2004; represented Ireland in the World Cup from 1994-1996 and the Alfred Dunhill Cup from 1994-1999; represented GB & Ireland in the 2000 and 2002 Steve Ballesteros Trophy. Recreations: films, rugby, reading, cars, fishing. Contact: International Sports Management Ltd, Cherry Tree Farm, Cherry Tree Lane, Rostherne, Cheshire, WA14 3RZ England. **T** 0044 1565 832 100 **F** 0044 1565 832 200
web www.darrenclarke.com

Darren Clarke

The Dungannon man, who started swinging a club before he was 11 years old has enjoyed a consistently successful career; a driven, extremely hard worker, is well liked on the Tour; despite the tragic death of his wife in August 2006, still stepped up to the plate to represent Europe in the Ryder Cup 2006.

CLARKE, The Hon. Mr. Justice Frank; JUDGE OF THE HIGH COURT
b 1951, Dublin; *m* Jacqueline Hayden; 1*s* 1*d*; *edu*. Warrenmount National School; Drimnagh Castle Christian Brothers Schools; University College Dublin BA; Kings Inns BL. Barrister At Law; Judge of the High Court; called to the Bar 1973; Inner Bar 1985; professor, Kings Inns 1977-1985; vice-chairman, Employment Appeals Tribunal 1984-89; member Bar Council 1976-77 and 1989-04; treasurer 1984-87; judge High Court 2004 to date. Clubs: Kildare Street and University Club. Recreations: National Hunt Racing; music, theatre. Contact: High Court, Morgan Place Dublin 7. **T** 01 888 6505 **F** 01 872 5669 email highcourtcentral@courts.ie

A charming, witty, able advocate; his genial manner, particularly in court, may disguise his forensic mind; much is expected of his input into the judiciary.

CLARKE, Rt. Rev. Ken, Herbert; BISHOP of KILMORE, ELPHIN and ARDAGH
b 1949, Belfast: *m* Helen; 4*d*; *edu.* Sullivan Upper School, Hollywood, Co. Down; Trinity College, Dublin; BA (div. Test.); Bishop, Kilmore, Elphin and Ardagh; *Publ: Called to Minister?*; contributor to *Evangelicals in Ireland*; curate, Maghealin 1972-75; curate, Dundonald 1975-78; missionary, South American Mission Society 1978-82; incumbent of Crinken Chruch, Dublin 1982-86; rector, Coleraine 1986-2001; Bishop of Kilmore, Elphin and Ardagh 2001 to date: Recreations: walking, reading, golf, church growth, leadership. Contact: 48 Carrickfern, Cavan. **T** 049 437 2759 email bishop@kilmore.anglican.org

> Modern and effective, regarded as a good preacher; tricky enough post as his diocese is on the border.

CLARKE, Rachel; MANAGING DIRECTOR MJ CLARKE & SONS LTD
b Dublin; *edu.* Muckross Park College, Dublin; Managing Director, MJ Bell & Sons; secretary Bell Advertising 1990-93; Design and Place Dublin 1993-95; unit manger Bell Advertising 1995-98; managing director Bell 1998-2003; commercial director Oglivy Group 2003-04; travelled the world 2004-05; chief operating officer MCD 2005 –06; MD, MJ Clarke and Sons Ltd 2006 – to date. Clubs: David Lloyd Riverview; Recreations; horse riding, music, walking. Contact: Whitechurch Road, Rathfarnham, Dublin 14 **M** 087 2421588 **T** 01 4933386 email rclarke@mjclarkes.com

> Having risen to the top of the advertising world, this extremely bright woman undertook a new challenge at the helm of Denis Desmond's (*qv*) MCD; swapped the world of rock 'n roll for family construction company.

CLARKE, Most Revd. Richard, Lionel; BISHOP of MEATH and KILDARE
b 1949, Dublin; *m* Linda; 1*s* 1*d*; *edu.* Wesley College, Dublin; Trinity College, Dublin; King's College, London; M.A. B.D. Ph.D; Publ: *And Is It True?*; Bishop of Meath and Kildare; curate, Holywood, Co. Down 2000; curate, St. Bartholomew's Church, Dublin 1975-77; Dean of Residence Trinity College Dublin 1974-84; rector of Bandon, Co. Cork 1984-93; Dean of Cork 1993-96; Bishop of Meath and Kildare 1996 to date. Clubs: Kildare Street and University Club. Recreations: music, poetry, history. Contact: Bishop's House, Moyglare, Maynooth, Co. Kildare. **T** 01 628 9354 email bishop@meath.anglican.org

> The only modern Irish Bishop who had to deal with heresy in his own Diocese. A modernizer with effective administrative skills in a new Ireland.

CLARKE, Zoë, Sylvia; MAKE UP ARTIST/TUTOR
b 1967; single; *edu.* Glenlola Collegiate School, Bangor; University of London; BSc Anthropology; Make Up Artist; began in Mac Cosmetics, London; Make Up For Ever 1995; Freelance makeup artist and tutor; Publications: currently writing a make-up book. Recreations: film, walking, swimming, gym, reading, fashion, drama, dancing, music. Contact: 36 South Hill, Dartry, Dublin 6. **T** 01 4973672 **M** 087 2649480 email zoe@zoeclarke.com

> One of the original highly trained Mac make up artists in Ireland; in addition to being a brilliant artist is also an excellent teacher; great personality; her book, with all the tricks of her trade, is eagerly awaited.

CLAYTON, Adam; MUSICIAN
b 1960, Chinnor, Oxfordshire, UK; *p* Susie Smith; *edu.* St. Columba's College, Rathfarnham, Dublin; Mount Temple Comprehensive, Malahide, Dublin; musician, bassist, U2; joined Max Quad Band; joined Feedback; joined and initially managed U2, Bono (*qv*) Edge (*qv*) Larry Mullen (*qv*) before Paul McGuinness (*qv*) became the fifth member of the band. Best rock album, 'Sometimes You Can't Make It On Your Own', Grammy 2006; Song of the Year; Album of the Year 'How to Dismantle an Atomic Bomb' Grammy 2006; Best Rock Performance 'Sometimes You Can't Make It On Your Own', Grammy 2006; Contact: Principle Management, 30-32 Sir John Rogersons Quay, Dublin 2. **T** 01 677 7 330 **F** 01 677 7276

> Once the wild child of the band, now totally genial, self effacing and charming; regarded as one of the best bass players in the world.

Adam Clayton

Shay Cleary

CLEARY, James, Martin 'Shay'; ARCHITECT
b 1951; *m* Lulu, 2s 1d; *edu.* De La Salle College, Waterford; School of Architecture, University
College Dublin; Bachelor of Architecture (Hons); Fellow Royal Institute of the Architects of
Ireland (FRIAI); member Royal Institute of British Architects (RIBA); Principal/Managing
Director, Shay Cleary Architects; worked in Paris for Marcel Breuer and Candilis Josic and
Woods; in London for Neave Brown; design tutor at UCD School of Architecture 1977-96;
partner Grafton Architects 1977-80; partner Cleary & Hall Architects 1981-86; director
Group'91 Architects 1990-98; visiting professor to Princeton University Graduate School
1989; work has been published extensively both at home and abroad; Fellow of the Royal
Institute of Architects of Ireland 1998; past president of the Architectural Association of
Ireland 1980; Established SCA in 1987; projects include The Irish Museum of Modern Art;
Royal Hospital Kilmainham; New Galleries Royal Hospital Kilmainham; Arthouse Multi
Media Centre, Temple Bar; Project Arts Centre, Temple Bar; Cork County Hall; Cork
County Library Headquarters; Office Building Dawson Street; Santry Cross Gateway
Development; Alto Vetro Residential Tower Dublin; Office Tower Grand Canal Quay Dublin; The
Liffey Trust Dublin. Recreations: travel, reading. Contact: Mount Pleasant Business Centre, Upper
Mount Pleasant Avenue, Ranelagh, Dublin 6. **T** 01 4125090 **F** 01 4978087 email scleary@sca.ie

A brilliant architect who is now regarded as a modern master; his able intervention in
some heritage buildings has stood the test of recent times, and use; quiet and shy, he's
still a familiar figure among the older, smart crowd in Dublin on a Saturday.

CLIFFORD, His Grace Most Rev. Dermot; ARCHBISHOP OF CASHEL AND EMILY
b 1939; single; *edu;* Clogher National School; St Brendan's College, Killarney; Maynooth College,
Co. Kildare, BSc.; Irish College, Rome, BD, STL; University College Cork, HDipEd; London School
of Economics, MSc (Econ); Loughborough University of Technology, PhD; Archbishop, Cashel and
Emily; Dean of Studies, St. Brendan's College, Killarney 1964-72; Diocesan Secretary, Diocese of
Kerry 1974-1986; chaplain, St. Mary of the Angels Home for Special Children 1976-86; co-adjutor
Archbishop, Cashel and Emily 1986-1988; Archbishop of Cashel 1988 to date; Publ. *The Social Costs
and Rewards of Caring* 1990; articles in *The Furrow*; patron: GAA, St. Patrick's College, Thurles;
Tipperary Rural and Business Institute; trustee, Bothar. Recreations: reading, walking. Contact:
Archbishop's House, Thurles, Co. Tipperary. **T** 0504 21512 **F** 0504 22680.

Theologically conservative; his profile is enhanced by being patron of the GAA, a
position inherited from Dr Croke, first patron of the GAA.

CLOAKE, Mary; DIRECTOR, THE ARTS COUNCIL OF IRELAND
b 1962, Co. Wexford; single; *edu.* Trinity College Dublin; Dublin City University B.A. Mod; MA;
Director Arts Council of Ireland/An Chomhairle Ealaíon; Arts Council Staff 1987; arts officer
Dundalk Urban District Council 1990-93; regional development officer, Arts Council 1993-97;
development director Arts Council 1997- 99; assistant director Arts Council 2000-04; acting
director Arts Council 2004-05; director Arts Council 2005 to date; visiting faculty Notre Dame
University, Keough Institute, South Bend, Indiana 2005; appointed to Board of Culture Ireland 2005;
visiting faculty Magill University Journalism and Public Affairs faculty 2004; member of board
Rejoyce 100 2004. Recreations: all the arts; dining with friends. reading. Contact: The Arts Council,
70 Merrion Square, Dublin 2. **T** 01 618 0225 **F** 01 661 0349 email mary.c@artscouncil.ie

Plenty of charm, she is totally committed to the Arts; well liked and trusted by her
community.

CLUNE, Deirdre née Barry; PUBLIC REPRESENTATIVE
b 1959, Cork; *m* Conor Clune; 4s; *edu.* Ursuline Convent Blackrock, Co. Cork; University College
Cork BE; Trinity College Dublin; Dip Management Engineers; H.Dip. Environmental Engineering;
Lord Mayor, Cork; member Cork City Council; elected Dáil Éireann 1997-2002 (FG); failed to be
re-elected 2002; Lord Mayor Cork 2005-06. Contact: City Hall Cork. **T** 021 496 6222
F 021 431 4238 web www.corkcity.ie/citycouncil

Daughter of Peter Barry and granddaughter of the late Anthony Barry, the third
generation of the Barry family to be a Dáil Deputy and Lord Mayor of Cork; bright
and ambitious though not the most politically savvy; lost her seat in the 2002 General
Election but maintains a high profile in her native city.

COADY, Treasa née Ni Laoire; BOOK PUBLISHER

b 1951; *m* Jim Coady; *3d*; *edu.* Scoil Chaitrions, Eccles St., Dublin; qualified as an occupational therapist; Book Publisher; occupational therapist in clinical practice 1972-80; established Amach Faoin Aer Teo to publish books on environmental matters, with film-maker Eamon de Buitlear 1981; established Town House and Country House Ltd., 1986, list broadened to include fiction, biography, illustrated non-fiction and occasional children's books; has published over 150 books to date including the works of David Bellamy, Frank Mitchell, Mary Lavin, Deirdre Purcell, Julie Parsons, Fergus Linehan, Brian Kennedy, Helen Dillon, Ulick O'Connor, John Hume, Mike Murphy; member CLE Irish Bookpublishers Association. Recreations: choral singing, reading, yoga, family. Contact: Town House and Country House, Trinity House Charleston Road, Ranelagh, Dublin 6. **T** 01 497 2399 **F** 01 497 0927

> An important publisher whose imprint is better known than many larger publishers; always produces works of great quality and interest; a significant cultural player.

CODY, Brian; KILKENNY HURLING MANAGER

b 1954, Kilkenny; *m* Elsie; *2s*; *edu.* St. Patrick's NS, Kilkenny; St. Kieran's College, Kilkenny; St. Patrick's Training College, Drumcondra, Dublin; National School teacher/ Kilkenny hurling manager; teacher St. Patrick's National School, Kilkenny 1974 to date; manager Kilkenny senior hurling team 1998 to date; captained Kilkenny minor hurling team to an All Ireland title 1972; repeated that feat when he captained All Ireland senior team 1982. Awards: four All Ireland senior titles; three National League medals; two All Ireland Under-21 medals; two All Star awards; two All Ireland club medals with James Stephens; one All Ireland college medal. Clubs: James Stephens GAA Club 'The Village'. Recreations: hurling, hurling, hurling. Contact: St. Patrick's De La Salle National School, Kilkenny City.

> The most successful hurler on the playing pitch has transferred his star qualities to a managerial role with the Kilkenny senior hurlers who he led to their most recent All Ireland victory against Cork, September 2006; a man of few words, his laid-back style disguises his steely determination for himself and his team; has achieved just about every honour in the game but remains as driven as ever.

CODY, Patrick J; PUBLISHER

b 1953; *m* Maura Byrne; *1s 1d*; *edu.* Cost accountancy, one year; marketing, one year; Business Development Programme, Irish Management Institute, Dublin; Publisher; trainee accountant, Institute for Industrial Research and Standards 1973-75; marketing executive IIRS 1975-80; sales manager (publications) EOLAS 1980-83; sales and marketing manager 1983-85; managing deirector and co-founder, Kompass Ireland 1985 to date; co-founder Kompass Internet 1995 to date; member Marketing Institute of Ireland, Irish Direct Marketing Association (chairman 1995); Irish Internet Association (founding director 1997). Awards: Irish Direct Marketing Award, Supreme Award 1998. Clubs: St. Margaret's Golf and Country Club. Recreations: golf, travel. Contact: Kompass Ireland Information House, Parnell Court, Granby Row, Dublin 1. **T** 01 872 8800. **F** 01 873 3711 email info@kompass.ie

> Realised the possibilities of desktop publishing and online marketing, publishing and e-learning very early on; moved quickly to capitalise on it, stealing a march on many.

COEN, Rynal; DIRECTOR OF COEN HOLDING LTD

b 1934; *m* Dairin Mathews; *3s 3d*; *edu.* Blackrock College; Director, Coen Holdings ltd; joined family firm of builders' providers in County Galway; director (former chairman and managing director), Coen Holdings Ltd; director, various private companies; former chairman, Galway Hospice. Clubs: Lahinch Golf Club, Gort Golf Club, Portmarnock Golf Club, Gort, Galwegians RFC. Recreations: golf, rugby. Contact: Coen Holdings Ltd., Station Road, Gort, Co. Galway. **T** 091 631511 **F** 091 631513.

> The former Connaught interprovincial rugby player, one of the well known Gort business family, has diversified the builders providers to Galway and Tullamore; has served on the board of the ESB.

COFFEY, Eddie, EDITOR, THE NATIONALIST, CARLOW

b 1962, Galway; *p* Suzanne Pender; *3d*; *edu.* St. Raphael's College, Loughrea, Co Galway; College of

Commerce, Rathmines, Dublin; graduate of Journalism; Editor, *The Carlow Nationalist*; journalist, *The Roscommon Champion*; *The Longford Leader*; deputy editor, *The Longford Leader*; editor, *The Kildare Nationalist*; editor, *The Nationalist*, Carlow; Regional Journalist of the Year 1990. Clubs: Co. Carlow Golf Club. Recreations: GAA, hurling in particular; played hurling for Longford; won NHL DIV4 medal. Contact: 8 Lacken Rise, Tullow Road, Carlow. **T** 059 917 0113 **F** 059 913 0301 email coffeyspender@eircom.net

> Taken over from the legendary Liam D. Bergin and brings a wealth of provincial experience to *The Nationalist*.

COGAN, Patrick Joseph; FRANCISCAN PRIEST, CEO, RESPOND HOUSING ASSOCIATION
b 1945, Cork; single; *edu*: Colaiste Chriost Rí, Turners Cross, Cork; B.A. UCG, B.D. Antohianum College, Rome; S.T.L. Antohianum College, Rome; CEO Respond Housing Association; *Publ*: several papers on housing and community development in Ireland; several compilations of Hymns for congregational use; Franciscan priest, Ennis 1970-1978; Guardian, Franciscan Community, Waterford 1978-84; founder member and chief executive Respond Housing Association 1982 to date; has provided 3,500 dwellings; biggest housing association in Ireland; nearly 1,000 dwellings under construction; Respond organizes the only degree course in Housing Studies in Ireland in association with UCD; member Housing Finance Agency plc (third term); member Benchmarking Performance Verification Group for Local Authorities. Clubs: Waterford Golf Club. Recreations: golf, politics, theology, general knowledge, current affairs. Contact: Franciscan Friary, Waterford. **M** 087 236 0239 **F** 051 304006 email pat.cogan@respond.ie

> One of those who, inspired by St. Francis, has taken the ideal literally of housing the homeless poor; more effective than many of those who clamour on television for our attention; a real modern mendicant friar who lives his ministry.

COGHLAN, Paul; PUBLIC REPRESENTATIVE
b 1944, Killarney; *m* Peggy O'Shea; 2*s* 3*d*; *edu*. St. Brendan's College, Killarney; De La Salle College, Waterford; Senator (FG) elected Industrial and Commercial Panel; joined Provincial Bank of Ireland 1962; self-employed estate agent and insurance broker, property developer; elected to Seanad 1997 to date; currently FG spokesperson Enterprise, Trade and Employment in the Seanad; former member Kerry Co. Council; Killarney UDC; Dingle Harbour Commissioners; vice chairman Kerry Fisheries and Coastal Management Committee; trustee and former chairman Muckross House, Killarney; member and past president Killarney Chamber of Commerce; founding director Radio Kerry. Contact: Seanad Éireann, Kildare Street, Dublin 2. **T** 01 618 3000

> One of the most popular Senators in Seanad Éireann; has the capacity to cross party lines to garner votes in the very difficult Seanad elections; a shrewd businessman with major commercial interests in Killarney; content to remain a Senator thereby allowing Sean Kelly, the GAA President, a clear run in the next general election.

COLEMAN MORIARTY, Kate; CONSULTANT EYE & OCULOPLASTIC SURGEON
b 1961, Dublin; *m* Paul Moriarty (*qv*); separated; 1*s* 1*d*; *edu*. St. Mary's College, Arklow, Co. Wicklow; The High School, Rathgar, Dublin; Royal College of Surgeons in Ireland; MB BcH. BAO B. Sc NUI UCD, Vret University Amsterdam (Ph.D); FRCOplhx (London Royal College of Ophthalmology Fellowship); FRCS (Ed) Edinburgh, Royal College of Surgeons Fellowship; Consultant Eye & Ocuplastic Surgeon, Blackrock Clinic & Mount Carmel Hospital, Dublin; trained Eye & Ear Hospital Dublin, Mater Hospital Dublin; St. Michael's Hospital Dún Laoghaire (consultant), Blackrock Clinic and Mount Carmel; trustee Chester Beatty Library Dublin. Publ: medical journals; Robucam contributor; *The Art of Botulinum Toxin in Facial Rejuvenation* 2004. Clubs: Powerscourt Golf Club, Dún Laoghaire Golf Club, Royal St. George Yacht Club. Recreations: golf, sailing, tennis, gardening, art. Contact: Suite 22, Blackrock Clinic, Co. Dublin. **T** 01 288 3576 email kcoleman@indigo.ie

> Successful oculoplastic surgeon with special interest in Botulinum toxins (botox); voted Dublin's most glamorous doctor, excellent advertisement for her profession.

COLEMAN, Shane Austin; JOURNALIST
b 1969, Dublin; *m* Evelyn Conroy; 1*s*; *edu*; St. Mary's College Dundalk; Trinity College Dublin; Dublin City University; BA Economics & Politics, MA Journalism; Political Correspondent *Sunday Tribune*; business journalist *Irish Independent*; business editor *Sunday Tribune*; account director Drury

Shane Coleman

Communications; currently political correspondent *Sunday Tribune*. Recreations: travel, reading, history, sport, wine. Contact: The Sunday Tribune, 15 Lower Baggot Street, Dublin 2. **T** 01 631 4307 **F** 01 661 5302 email scoleman@tribune.ie

Has brought a new incisiveness to political reportage and analysis at The Trib.

COLEMAN, Terence; CHAIRMAN SCORPION GROUP
b 1943; *m* Anita; 1*s* 3*d*; *edu*. University College Dublin B.Comm; Chairman, Scorpion Group; client service executive, AC Nielson of Ireland; manager, North America, Irish Distillers; chief executive, The Process Company of the Jefferson Smurfit Group; founder and chairman, Scorpion Group. Clubs: Fitzwilliam LTC. Recreations: family pursuits, fly fishing, shooting, flying. Contact: Scorpion Group, Siemens Road, Northbank Industrial Estate, IRLAM, Manchester, M30 5BL. **T** 0044 161 777 9666.

Was a low profile businessman in the UK for many years; hit the headlines here when he paid over €6 million for the Lavery house in Sorrento Terrace, Dalkey in what was then a record price for a Dublin residential property.

COLGAN, Michael; THEATRE MANAGER/PRODUCER
b 1950; *m* Susan FitzGerald; separated; 1*s* 2*d*; *edu*. St James's Christian Brothers School, Dublin; Trinity College Dublin; BA; director at the Abbey Theatre 1974-77; company manager, Irish Theatre Company 1977-78; manager, Dublin Theatre Festival 1978-81; artistic director 1981-83; director, Gate Theatre 1984 to date; executive director Little Bird Films 1986-95; guest director, Parma Festival, Italy 1982; member, Irish Arts Council 1989-94; recipient *Sunday Independent* Arts Award 1985 and 1987; Awards: National Entertainment Award 1996 (Eamon Andrews Special Award for the Beckett Festival); board member, Gate Theatre, Dublin Theatre Festival, Millennium Festivals Limited; chairman, St. Patrick's Festival; member, Governing Authority DCU; founded Belacqua Film Company 1998. 75th birthday celebration of Harold Pinter at The Gate, days before he received the Nobel Prize for Literature 2005; Produced the Tony Award winning Faith Healer by Brian Friel, Booth Theater, Broadway 2006. Recreations: music, cinema, reading. Contact: Gate Theatre, Dublin 1. **T** 01 874 4368. **F** 01 874 5373

Great company and a wonderful raconteur; larger than life, the public face of successful Irish theatre; has achieved more with the tiny, historic Gate Theatre than many other theatre managers could dream of; has an uncanny ability to read what the Irish market wants to see; in his world, theatre is not only drama and commercial driven, it's also fun; perhaps that explains why he never has a shortage of sponsors.

COLLIER, Declan; MANAGING DIRECTOR DUBLIN AIRPORT plc
b 1955, Dublin; *m* Jan Winter; 1*d*; *edu*. Trinity College Dublin; BA Economics; MA, Economics; Chief Executive Dublin Airport Authority plc; joined Exxon Mobil/Esso 1985; managing director Esso Ireland; moved to Britain with responsibility for the European interests of the company 2002-05; CEO Dublin Airports Authority, with responsibility for Shannon and Cork airports 2005 to date; Aer Rianta International with investments in Birmingham, Hamburg and Dusseldorf as well as the Great Southern Hotels loss-making chain; also operates in 14 other venues in North America and the Middle East, oil fuel sales and the Shannon College of Hotel Management. Recreations: rugby, walking, cycling. Contact: Head Office, Dublin Airports Authority, Dublin Airport. **T** 01 814 1111 **F** 01 814 4120 email declan.collier@dublinairportauthority.com web www.dublinairportauthority.com

Modern business executive who faces a major challenge in developing the new terminal at Dublin airport to meet the growing unrest of the travelling public; will be kept more than busy in his current position.

COLLINS, Anthony E; SOLICITOR
b 1939, Dublin; *m* Mary Deasy (*qv*); 3*s* 1*d*; *edu*. Xaviers School, Donnybrook, Dublin; St. Gerards School, Bray; Downside Somerset (UK); Trinity College Dublin; BA; B.Comm; Incorporated Law Society; Solicitor; solicitor's apprentice, Eugene F. Collins 1959; partner 1964; senior partner 1978; director Grafton Group plc; deputy chairman 1995 to date; chairman Automobile Association (Ireland) 1978 to date; director Leinster Leader 1972; chairman 1988-2005. Publ. include various legal articles; Hon. Member, Canadian Bar Association; president, Incorporated Law Society of

Ireland 1984-1985. Clubs: President Strollers Club 1988-91, Three Rock Rovers Hockey Club (Club Captain 1995-96). Recreations: sport, music. Contact: Eugene F. Collins, Temple Chambers, 3 Burlington Road, Dublin 4. **T** 01 202 6400 **F** 01 667 5200 web www.efc.ie

> Impressive performer, manages a most successful legal practice; sought after as a company director bringing a wide range of experience to the boardroom.

COLLINS, Anthony M; SENIOR COUNSEL
b 1960, Connecticut, USA; *edu.* Blackrock College Dublin; Sandymount High, Dublin; Trinity College Dublin; Kings Inns, Dublin; BCL; BL; Barrister, Senior Counsel; legal advisor or 'Referendaire' to Judge O'Higgins and later Judge Murray in the Court of Justice, the European Communities, Luxembourg 1991-'97; returned to practice at the Irish Bar 1997; called to the Inner Bar 2003. Contact: The Law Library, Four Courts, Dublin 7. **T** 01 817 5000 **F** 01 817 5150

> Is amongst the foremost Irish experts and authors in European and Irish Administrative Law; regularly appears before the Court of Justice and in the Supreme Court.

COLLINS, Finghin James; CONCERT PIANIST
b 1977, Dublin; single; *edu.* Gonzaga College, SJ, Dublin; Royal Irish Academy of Music, Dublin; Dublin City University BA in music performance 1999; Geneva, Premier Prix avec Distinction 2002. *Publ;* Claves CD Mozart and Beethoven Concertos 2000; Lyric fm CD 104 *Impromtu* 2005; Claves Schumann planned for release 2006; first prize in Clara Haskil International Piano competition, Switzerland 1999; has appeared with some of the world's major orchestras and conductors: Chicago Symphony, Houston symphony, City of Birmingham Symphony etc; board member, National Concert Hall 2001-05. Recreations: travel, foreign languages, opera, gardening. Contact: 56 Mount Carmel Road, Goatstown, Dublin 14. **T** 01 298 5402 **F** 01 290 5402 email infofinghincollins.com web www.finghincollins.com

> A young man who already has a long career behind him; his 2006 CD release will undoubtedly bring him more fame and acclaim; the bigger break into the wider world awaits this talented young pianist.

COLLINS, Liam; JOURNALIST
b 1953, Dublin; *m* Helen; 1*s* 3*d*; *edu.* Oatlands CBS, Stillorgan, Co. Dublin; reporter *Sunday Independent*; *Westmeath Examiner*; *Longford News*; *Evening Herald*; *Sunday Independent*; broke AIB DIRT story 1998. Recreations: Ladies Gaelic football (daughters play); thrillers; ballad singing; old country pubs. Contact: *Sunday Independent*, 27 – 32, Independent House, Talbot Street, Dublin 1. **T** 01 7055695 **F** 01 705 5779 email lcollins@unison.independent.ie

> From a family steeped in 'ink'; gregarious, well connected.

COLLINS, Mary née Deasy; JUDGE DISTRICT COURT
b 1945, Cork; *m* 1st Edward Dillon (*decd.*); 2nd Anthony Collins (*qv*); 3*s* 1*d*; *edu.* St Aloyusious, Cork; St Louis Convent Monaghan; University College Dublin; B. Comm; H.Dip; Kings Inns; Barrister at Law; Judge ; Porter Morris; appointed 1996; Clubs: Milltown Golf Club, Powerscourt Golf Club; Recreations: golf, skiing, gardening, music. Contact: Four Courts, Dublin 7. **T** 01 888 6529 email mcollins@court.ie

> Highly intelligent woman who demonstrates a strong humanitarian and sensitive approach in the discharge of her judicial role; gregarious and always extremely elegant.

COLLINS, Sean M; VETERINARY SURGEON, STUD FARMER
b 1926; *m* Hanne Jorgensen; 3*s* 1*d*; *edu.* Blackrock College, Veterinary College of Ireland, MRCVS; Veterinary Practitioner; owner/manager, Corbally Stud, Kildare; one of the major independent stallion stations in Ireland, stallions include Desert Style, Paris House, Persian Bold and Priolo; President and Founder, Irish Equine Centre (Johnstown/Kildare); chairman Irish European Breeders Fund; member of Irish Turf Club; former chairman, Irish National Stud & Irish Thoroughbred Breeders Association. Clubs: Hermitage Golf Club, Luttrellstown Golf and Country Club. Recreations: fishing, golf. Contact: Corbally Stud, Celbridge, Co. Kildare. **T** 01 628 8081 **F** 01 627 3166

A retiring man, with Kerry roots, who created one of the major independent stallion stations in the country, which he sold some years ago.

COLLINS, Stephen; JOURNALIST
b 1951, Dublin; *m* Jean; 1*s* 2*d*; *edu.* Oatlands College, Mount Merrion, Dublin; University College Dublin; BA, MA; reporter *Irish Press* 1976-87; political correspondent *Sunday Press* 1987-95; political editor *Sunday Tribune* 1995 to date. Publ. *The Power Game: Ireland Under Fianna Fail* 2001, *The Cosgrave Legacy* 1996; *Spring and the Labour Story* 1993. Recreations: reading, history. Contact: Sunday Tribune, 15 Lower Baggot Street, Dublin 2. **T** 016183090 email scollins@tribune.ie

The other Collins brother; a highly respected observer of the Irish political scene; a good TV performer.

COLTON, Rt. Rev. William Paul; LORD BISHOP OF CORK, CLOYNE AND ROSS
b 1960, Derry; *m* Susan; 2*s*; *edu.* Ashton School, Cork; Lester B. Pearson College of the Pacific (United World Colleges), B.C. Canada; University College Cork; Trinity College Dublin; Irish School of Ecumenics (currently part time post-graduate student), Cardiff University, BCL, Dip. Th. M .Phil & in progress LL.M, Cardiff; Lord Bishop of Cork, Cloyne and Ross 1984; Deacon 1985; priest 1984-87; curate, Lisburn 1985-87; Bishop's chaplain 1987-90; vicar choral St. Anne's Cathedral, Belfast 1990-99; rector of Castleknock, Mulhuddart & Clonsilla 1997-99; canon, Christ Church Cathedral 1993-99; religious programmes RTÉ 1994-99; actors' union chaplain 1999; general synod; chairman board of St. Luke's Home, Cork; chairman, Secondary Education Committee 2004/05; participant in the European Consortium for Church and State Research 1992-97; member of the Central Committee, Conference of European Churches. Clubs: Kildare Street & University Club, Dublin, Manchester United Football Club, Garryduff Sports, Cork. Recreations: sport, reading, Manchester United, cinema, theatre, music, computers, travel. Contact: Cork, Cloyne and Ross Diocesan Office, St. Nicholas' House, 14, Cove Street, Cork. **T** 021 431 0773 **F** 021 496 8467 email bishop@cork.anglican.org

Rt. Rev. Paul Colton

This apparently amiable Bishop presides over a far flung diocese and is shaping up to succeed to one of the Primacies if John Neill gets the nod for Armagh; a follower of Man U. civilised and urbane, able, held in a high degree of admiration and liking in the Northern Anglican Province in Ireland; he may yet have a future beyond this Island's shores; certainly a Bishop to watch.

COMYN, Edward Frederick; BARRISTER AT LAW
b 1929; *m* Rosemary McGuire; 4*d*; *edu.* Belvedere College, Dublin; University College Dublin; King's Inns; Barrister At Law; called to the Bar 1952; called to the Inner Bar 1975; elected Bencher of King's Inns 1992. Clubs: Royal Irish Yacht Club. Recreations: fishing, reading, listening to music. Contact: The Law Library, Four Courts, Dublin 7. **T** 01 872 0622. **F** 01 872 0455

A gracious, suave and able Senior Counsel, has many admirers; able, astute and meticulous in all he does; very popular on the legal and social circuit in Dublin.

CONDELL, Catherine; STYLIST & FASHION SHOW PRODUCER
b 1957; *div.*; *edu.* Holy Faith, Dominick St. Dublin; Stylist; window dresser Hickey's fabrics 1975-79; Switzers 1979-83; Brown Thomas in-house stylist & show producer 1983-99; freelance stylist and fashion show producer 1999 to date. Career highlight: styling and producing three supermodel shows at the Point 1996, 2000, 2003. Recreations: movies, art, theatre. Contact: 8 Ardmore Avenue, NCR, Dublin 7. **T** & **F** 01 8383457 email catherinec@iol.ie

Catherine Condell

The country's leading fashion stylist; for many years worked exclusively for Brown Thomas; now a successful freelance consultant.

CONNELL, His Eminence, Desmond, Cardinal; RETIRED ARCHBISHOP OF DUBLIN AND PRIMATE OF IRELAND
b 1926, Dublin; single; *edu.* St. Peter's School, Phibsboro, Dublin; Belvedere College, Dublin; University College Dublin, BA, MA; Catholic University of Louvain, Ph.D; ordained at Clonliffe College Church 1951; assistant professor Metaphysics 1972; Retired Archbishop of Dublin;

appointed Dean, Dept. of Philosophy and Sociology 1983, re-elected 1986; granted title Monsignor 1984; served as chaplain to Poor Clares and Carmelites; awarded D.Litt (*hc*), National University of Ireland 1981; member Irish Hierarchy's Theological Commission; a noted linguist and recognised authority on the 17th century French priest/philosopher Nicolas Malebranche. Recreations: reading, walking, music. Contact: **T** 01 837 3732 **F** 01 836 9796.

A poor communicator; very spiritual academic who found it difficult to grasp the pace of change in Irish society.

CONNELLY, Alpha Margaret; CEO HUMAN RIGHTS COMMISSION
b 1947, Belfast; *edu.* Methodist College, Belfast; Trinity College Dublin; University College London; McGill University Canada, BA (Hons); LL.M.; D.C.L.;CEO Human Rights Commission; lecturer in law, University College Cardiff 1976-80; lecturer, Faculty of Law University College Dublin 1981-92; research counsellor to the Law Reform Commission 1992-96; legal advisor Dept of Foreign Affairs 1996-2002; chief executive of the Human Rights Commission 2002 to date; Publ. numerous publications in the fields of international and human rights; founder member of The Equality Studies Centre, University College Dublin. Clubs: Irish Donkey Society, Alpaca Association of Ireland. Recreations: people, places, wildlife. Contact: Human Rights Commission, 4th Floor, Jervis House, Jervis St. Dublin 1. **T** 01 858 9601 **F** 01 858 9609 email aconnelly@Ihrc.ie

Recognised world expert in public international law.

CONNOLLY, Geraldine Denise; SENIOR COUNSEL
b 1958, Bangor; *m* Patrick O'Reilly; *edu.* Sion Hill, Blackrock, Dublin; Kings Inns; Institute of Arbitration (Diploma in Arbitration); La Sorbonne Paris (Diploma in French); Barrister-at-law; Senior Counsel; fellow of the Chartered Institute of Arbitration; called to the Bar 1983; called to the Inner Bar 1996; Clubs: The Chelsea Arts Club London; Recreations: contemporary art, languages, film, travel; Contact: The Law Library, Four Courts, Dublin 7. **T** 01 8174941 **F** 8174901 email por246810@yahoo.ie

Very stylish, able and experienced silk specialising in personal injuries cases and labour and employment matters.

CONNOLLY, Michele; DIRECTOR, CORPORATE FINANCE KPMG
b 1972, Oxford, England; *m* Liam Lynch; *edu.* Beech Hill College, Monaghan; University of Ulster, Jordanstown, Northern Ireland BA (hons) accounting with computing, first in Degree Class, Honours List each year; Associate of the Institute of Chartered Accountants in Ireland, (first in Northern Ireland, fourth in all of Ireland in finals) 1996; Director KPMG Corporate Finance (currently responsible for KPMG's Project Finance Team, focusing on Public/Private Partnerships on Transport, Leisure, Health, Justice) 1998 to date; Price Waterhouse, Belfast 1992-97; FPM Chartered Accountants, Newry Co. Down, actively involved in several education related committees for ICAI 1997-98; regular conference speaker, Dublin Civic Connection, providing professional support to social/community based projects; Publ. regular contributor to industry magazines *Business and Finance*; *Project Finance International*; *International Project Finance Association*; *The Sunday Times*; *Accountancy Ireland*; *Project Management*. Recreations: hill walking, completed seven-day trek in Andes to raise funds for Concern 2004. Contact: Stokes Place, St. Stephens Green, Dublin 2. **T** 01 410 1546 **F** 01 412 1546 email michele.connolly@kpmg.ie

One of the bright and extremely impressive young professionals engaged in the popular Public Private Partnership (PPP) area.

CONSIDINE, Thomas; FORMER SECRETARY GENERAL DEPARTMENT FINANCE
b 1945, Co. Clare; *m. edu.* St. Flannans College, Ennis, Co. Clare; University College Dublin; BA (History & Economics); Former Secretary general, Department Finance; joined Civil Service Dept Post & Telegraphs 1963; moved to Dept. Education; appointed administrative officer Dept. Finance 1974; appointed principal officer Dept. Finance 1974-86; assistant secretary Dept Finance 1993-2000; secretary general 2000 –'06. Contact: Department Finance, Government Buildings, Upper Merrion Street, Dublin 2, Ireland. **T** 01 676 7571 **F** 01 678 9936 email webmaster@finance.irlgov.ie web www.finance.gov.ie

The invisible man has a very sharp intellect and exercised major influence in the permanent government; very personable and shy; unlike his predecessors did not take over top slot at Central Bank; an avid Clare GAA supporter.

CONROY, Michael, Robert; ARCHITECT
b 1974; *p* Dr Ruth Hamill; *edu*. St Colman's College, Claremorris, Co Mayo; University College Dublin, School of Architecture; (Arch Studies), B Arch, MRIAI; Architect; Horan Keogan Ryan Architects, Dublin 1997-2000; Axis Architecture 2000-02; Architect at Pask & Pask Architects, Dundee, Scotland 2002 to date. Clubs: Dundee City Swimming Club; Amnesty International. Recreations: road runner, hiking, reading. Contact: 21 Elizabeth Crescent, Newport on Tay, Fife DD68DY, Scotland. **T** 0044 1382540913 email bobtuse@hotmail.com

CONROY, Noel, GARDA COMMISSIONER
b 1943, Blacksod, Co. Mayo; *m* Mary; 1*s* 1*d*; Commissioner of An Garda Síochána, joined the Garda Síochána 1963; served in Finglas, Kevin Street, Cabra, Store Street, Santry, Central Detective Unit and at the Crime & Security Section at Garda Headquarters; graduated from executive programmes in policing in Europe, from the FBI Academy and the FBI National Executive Institute; most of his service has been in detective branch; deputy commissioner in charge of Operations 1996-2003 (had responsibility for all operational resources concerned with crime investigation, drugs enforcement, security matters and tactical planning); Garda Commissioner 2003 to date. Awards: 1981 Scott Medal for Bravery. Recreations: golf, reading. Contact: Garda HQ, Phoenix Park, Dublin email comstaff@iol.ie web www.garda.ie

Quiet man, extremely low profile commissioner, came up through the ranks with a distinguished record of achievement in the Force; at a time of great turmoil and change in the Force has yet to make a significant mark in the Commissioner's office.

CONWAY, Patrick; COMMERCIAL DIRECTOR, HEINEKEN IRELAND
b 1956, Tullamore, Co. Offaly; *m* Maura; 2*s*; *edu*. University College Dublin; B.Ag. Sc.; Commerical Director, Heineken Ireland; joined Elanco, Ireland; moved to company's UK head quarters; joined AH Robbins: Whitehall Laboratories; joined Heineken Ireland, marketing director 1991; appointed commercial director; Recreations GAA, playing the piano. Contact: Murphy's Brewery, Leitrim Street, Cork City. **T** 021 450 3711 **F** 021 450 3011 email info@heinekenireland.ie web www.heinekenireland.ie

Astute, gregarious and extremely popular executive; hard working and ambitious for himself and his company; well known as a top class entertainer on the piano.

COOKE, Barrie; PAINTER
b 1931, England; 3*d*; *edu*. Harvard University; BA; Painter; four retrospective exhibitions; mural Trinity College Dublin 1966; mural Bank of Ireland 5th Avenue New York 1968; mural O'Reilly Hall UCD 2000; mural St. Mollings Church Co. Carlow 2005. Clubs: Honorary Member Royal Hibernian Academy of Arts, Dublin. Recreations: angling. Contact: Kerlin Gallery, Dublin 2. **T** 01 670 9093

A quiet and humorous man, who stays away from the public gaze; a painter of inner vision; his themes of waterfalls, escarpments and especially fish in many forms are characteristic signature pieces; his mixed media pieces based on the Pike fish are iconic and rare.

Barrie Cooke

COOMBES, Ian Francis; HEADMASTER
b 1959; *m* Gynnis Trinder; 1*s* 2*d*; *edu*. Bandon Grammar School, Bandon, Co. Cork; BA History & Geography (hons), University College Cork; H. Dip.E (hons); M.Ed. (1st Hons), University College Cork; college scholar UCC 1978; Diocesan Youth Officer for West Cork 1980s; bursary to represent Ireland at the 52nd Council of European Geographers Seminar 1991; Comenius Programme involvement with Virgil Project and Quality Partnership of the Regions EU; Hon. Secretary of the Irish School Heads Association 2000; active in the European Studies Project Pilot Scheme 1989, which pioneered email as a communications medium between schools; Principal of Bandon Grammar School August 1999 to date. Clubs: Bandon Rugby Club, Bandon Tennis Club. Recreations: rugby, hill walking, shooting, cinema, photography, reading and local history. Contact: Richmount, Bandon, Co. Cork. **T** 023 41713 **F** 023 44404 email info@bandongrammer.ie

COONEY, Garret; SENIOR COUNSEL
b 1935, Longford; *m* Sheila; 3*s*; *edu.* Castleknock College, Dublin; UCD (BA), King's Inns (Barrister-at-law); Senior Counsel; Clubs: St. Mary's RFC, Ashbourne Golf Club, Milltown Golf Club (House Member); Recreations: reading history and biography, rugby, playing golf. Contact: Law Library, The Four Courts, Dublin 7;

> A top flight legal eagle who has appeared in many high profile cases in the higher courts over the last few decades; a formidable presence in the Round Hall and not taken lightly by his peers; a very busy all round practitioner, being briefed in many defamation proceedings involving press and broadcast media; has strong views and decries "the rapid growth of punitive bureaucracy and the consequential decline of the personal liberty of the Irish citizen".

COONEY, Marie Therèse née WHITE; DIRECTOR, TIPPERARY WATER
b 1952, Dublin; *m* Patrick Joseph Cooney (*qv*); 3*s* 2*d*; *edu.* Loretto Convent, Balbriggan Co. Dublin; studied French, Avignon, one year; Spanish, Seville one year; company director Tipperary Water; banking, Lombard & Ulster; Tipperary Water, PR & Marketing 1984 to date; Director Maynooth Foundation Board. Clubs: Royal Tara Golf Club, Ballinalee, Co. Meath, Erinvale Golf Club, South Africa. Contact: Ringlestown House, Kilmessan, Co. Meath. **T** 046 90 25 992 **F** 046 90 25 994 email mariecooney@gleesongroup.ie

> Able, extremely keen intellect, one of her company's greatest assets; a natural marketer, loyal, extremely popular.

COONEY, Patrick; MANAGING DIRECTOR GLEESON GROUP
b 1947, Drogheda, Co Louth; *m* Marie Therese White (*qv*); 3*s* 2*d*; *edu.* Christian Brothers, Drogheda; Institute of Certified Accountants, FACCA 1968; ACCA, Audit Senior with Deloitte, Plender, Griffith, London 1970-72; investigating accountant 1972-74; managing director, Gleeson Group 1974 to date. Clubs: St Stephen's Green Club. Recreations: shooting, collector antique guns. Contact: M &J Gleeson & Co, 15 Cherry Orchard Estate, Ballyfermot, Dublin 10. **T** 01 626 9787 **F** 01 626 0652.

> Has grown a relatively small company steadily and built it into a major player in the drinks industry; shrewd, affable businessman.

COOPER, Colm 'Gooch'; KERRY FOOTBALLER
b 1983, Killarney; single; *edu.* St. Brendan's College, Killarney; Institute of Technology Tralee; B.Management/Finance; Bank Official, Allied Irish Bank; Killarney/ Kerry Footballer; won All Ireland Senior Football 2004; four Munster medals; two All Star awards; a host of underage medals. Selected for the International Rules Competition 2005. Clubs: Dr Crokes, GAA Club, Killarney. Recreations: all sport, golf, socialising. Contact: AIB, 25 Main Street, Killarney, Co. Kerry. **T** 064 31922

> The bright young star crashed onto the national scene in 2003 and is one of the most naturally gifted Gaelic footballers of the modern era.

COOPER, Mathew Joseph 'Matt'; BROADCASTER, JOURNALIST, DOCUMENTARY MAKER
b 1966; *m* Aileen Hickie; 1*s* 3*d*; *edu.* North Monastery CBS, Fairhill, Cork; University College Cork; B.Comm; NIHE Dublin; graduate Diploma in Journalism; Presenter and Editor *The Last Word*, Today FM; columnist *Irish Examiner*; contributor to other newspaper titles; RTE *Primetime Investigates* documentary on tax avoidance 2005; joined *Business & Finance* magazine 1988; reporter *Sunday Business Post* 1989; assistant editor *SBP* 1992; business editor *Irish Independent* 1993; associate editor 1995; editor *The Sunday Tribune* 1996; Today FM 2002; presented *Marketplace* RTE 1991/92; *The Sunday Business Show* on Today Fm 2000-02; Journalist of the Year 1993, 2001; Business Journalist of the Year 1992, 1999; Young Journalist of the Year 1991. Clubs: Sunday's Well Rugby Club, Bishopstown, Cork GAA Club. Recreations: sport, cinema, books, food, music. Contact: Today FM, 124 Upper Abbey Street, Dublin 1. **T** 01 804 9000 email mcooper@todayfm.com

Matt Cooper

Has made the transition from print media to radio and television quite seamlessly; extremely highly regarded in business circles; well connected.

COOTE, John, Hugh; INTERIOR DESIGNER

b 1949 Australia; divorced; 1*s* 2*d*; *edu.* Stawell Technical School of Mines, Victoria, Australia; Royal Melbourne Institute of Technology, Melbourne, Australia; School of Interior Design; Head of Cootehill Design, New York 1972 to date; own business, works internationally on architectural and interior projects, specialising in construction and design of large scale houses and interiors; Publ. contributor to *Architectural Digest*, English *House and Gardens*, Australian *Vogue, Belle*, American *House and Garden*. Clubs: Kildare Street & University Club, Dublin. Recreations: reading, travel to exotic countries, architectural research. Contact: Bellamont Forrest, Cootehill, Co. Cavan. email john.coote@bigpond.com

John Coote

Internationally acclaimed interior decorator; his Irish home is a wonderful advertisement for his considerable talents; Bellamont Forrest is the most perfect Palladian Mansion in Ireland based on the principles of La Rotunda by Antonio Palladio; has restored the house to pristine glory.

CONCANNON, John; CEO IRELAND WEST TOURISM

b 1973, Mayo; *m* Mary; 1*d*; *edu.* St. Jarleths College, Tuam; UCD (B.Comm); MBS; DMP; Higher Dip in Marketing Practice (DMP), Marketing Institute of Ireland; CEO, Ireland West Tourism; marketing executive Dubarry Shoes Ballinasloe; Unilever brand manager, product group manager 1997; marketing manager ice cream division 1999-2000; CEO Ireland West Tourism 2004 to date. Recreations: spending time with family and friends, going to see live music (all genres from trad to rock to classical to jazz), playing the guitar (badly), reading, swimming, theatre, travel, just started to learn the drums. Contact: Ireland West Tourism, Aras Fáilte, Forster Sreet, Galway. **T** 091 537 700 **F** 091 537 733 email jconcannon @ Irelandwest .ie

A brilliant and innovative marketing man; expected to really push out the boat for the West of Ireland.

COPELAND, Louis: MASTER TAILOR

b 1949, Dublin; *m* Mary; 1*s* 1*d*; *edu.* St. Patrick's College, Drumcondra; Parnell Square Tailoring and Textiles; London City and Guilds for Tailoring; apprentice, tailor and cutter; Managing Director, Louis Copeland & Sons; began working in the family business 1962, now six shops in the Copeland Group: four in Dublin, one in Galway, and the first ever Hugo Boss shop Dundrum Shopping Centre; won retailer of the year for Great Britain and Ireland 1998; stockists of Europe's leading menswear brands; clothier to Ireland's soccer and rugby international teams. Clubs: David Lloyd/ WPO. Recreations: walking, gym, golf, work. Contact: 40, Capel Street, Dublin 1. **T** 01 872 1600 **F** 01 873 3609 email louis@louiscopeland.ie web www.louiscopeland.com

Carrying on a family tradition; is known for his own sartorial elegance and sense of style; dresses many of the country's A-team politicians, including Bertie Ahern (*qv*), businessmen and entertainers; a born showman and the best advertisement for his own business.

COPPEL, Andrew Maxwell; CHAIRMAN TOURISM IRELAND

b 1950, Belfast; *m* June; 1*s* 1*d*; *edu.* Belfast Royal Academy; Queen's University Belfast, FCA; CEO Racecourse Holdings Trust 1973; Queen's University Belfast (Law); chartered accountant Coopers & Lybrand 1977; Morgan Grenfell & Co. Ltd. 1986; group finance director Ratners Group plc. 1990; chairman and chief executive Sale Tierney plc. 1993-2003; group chief executive Queen's Moat Houses plc 2004 to date; chief executive Racecourse Holdings Trust; chairman of Tourism Ireland Ltd; vice president of Queen's University Association London. Clubs: Burhill Golf Club, St. George's Hill LTC, Claygate LTC. Recreations: tennis, golf, rugby. Contact: 23 Buckingham Gate, London, SW1E 6LB. **T** 0044 020 7963 9042 **F** 0044 020 7963 9044 email andrewcoppel@rht.net

The Belfast-born, former investment banker faces a major challenge promoting Ireland as a tourist destination at a time of rising prices here and unprecedented competition internationally.

CORR, Andrea Jane; SINGER/SONGWRITER
b 1974, Dundalk; single; *edu.* in Dundalk; Lead vocalist and tin whistle performer with Celtic rock
group The Corrs 1990 to date; spotted by Bill Whelan during a pub gig, met US Ambassador Jean
Kennedy Smith, invited to play in Boston; met David Foster while there; signed up by 143 Records
(Atlantic Group); toured with various other bands such as The Rolling Stones; released album
Forgiven Not Forgotten 1995; *Talk on Corners* went platinum/multiplatinum in 15 territories and gold
in countless others 1997; *MTV Unplugged* 1999; *In Blue* gave the band their first ever no. 1 single
Breathless 2000; *Best of* 2001; *Borrowed Heaven* 2004; *Home* album of much loved Irish classic songs
2005; have sold 35 million records worldwide. Awards: Brit Award, Best International Act 1999;
nominated Best Actress in a Feature Film, IFTA 2005; film work includes *The Commitments*; *Evita*; a
guest appearance on *Beverley Hills 90210* (TV); *The Boys and Girl From County Clare* 2004. Contact:
Barry Gaster, Glasthule Lodge, Glasthule, Co. Dublin. **T** 087 223 8572
web www.thecorrswebsite.com

> Ambitious for a career on the silver screen; public acclaim in this area is still awaited.

CORR, Caroline Georgine; MUSICIAN/ SONGWRITER
b 1973, Dundalk; *m* Frank Woods; 1*s* 1*d*; *edu.* in Dundalk; Vocalist and drummer/ bodhran/ piano
with The Corrs 1990 to date; a performace for then US Ambassador Jean Kennedy Smith led to a
mini tour in the US; led to signing with 143 Records ((Atlantic Records); released album *Forgiven Not
Forgotten* 1995; *Talk on Corners* went platinum/multiplatinum in 15 territories and gold in countless
others 1997; *MTV Unplugged* 1999; *In Blue* gave the band their first ever no. 1 single *Breathless* 2000;
Best of 2001; *Borrowed Heaven* 2004; *Home* album of much loved Irish classic songs 2005; have sold
35 million records worldwide. Awards: Brit Award, Best International Act, 1999; Honorary MBE
2005; film credits include *The Commitments*; guest appearance *Beverley Hills 90102* (TV). Contact:
Barry Gaster, Glasthule Lodge, Glasthule, Co. Dublin. **T** 087 223 8572
web www.the corrswebsite.com

> An able and talented musician and an articulate spokesperson for the breastfeeding
> movement in Ireland.

CORR, James Steven Ignatius 'Jim'; MUSICIAN/ SONGWRITER
b 1964, Dundalk; single; *p* Gayle Williamson; 1*s*; *edu.* Dundalk; Performs on keyboard and piano with
The Corrs 1990 to date; following a gig in Boston (US) band were signed with 143 Records (Atlantic
Records); have toured extensively; released album *Forgiven Not Forgotten* 1995; *Talk on Corners* went
platinum/multiplatinum in 15 territories and gold in countless others 1997; *MTV Unplugged* 1999; *In
Blue* gave the band their first ever no. 1 single *Breathless* 2000; *Best of* 2001; *Borrowed Heaven* 2004;
Home album of much loved Irish classic songs 2005; have sold 35 million records worldwide. Awards:
Brit Award, Best International Act, 1999; Honorary MBE 2005; film credits include *The
Commitments* and a guest appearance on *Beverly Hills 90210* (TV). Recreations: motor racing,
helicopters. Contact: Barry Gaster, Glasthule Lodge, Glasthule, Co. Dublin. **T** 087 223 8572
web www.the corrswebsite.com

> The oldest of The Corrs and the one who started it all; a talented musician, some say
> the most talented in the group; he is also involved in producing, mixing and editing;
> loves a joke; extremely popular.

CORR, Sharon Helga; MUSICIAN/SONGWRITER/SINGER
b 1970, Dundalk; *m* Gavin Bonnar; 1*s*; *edu.* Dundalk; Vocalist and violinist with The Corrs 1990 to
date; played in small gigs throughout Ireland, invited to Boston, signed up with 143 Records (part of
Atlantic Records); have toured extensively; released album *Forgiven Not Forgotten* 1995; *Talk on
Corners* went platinum/multiplatinum in 15 territories and gold in countless others 1997; *MTV
Unplugged* 1999; *In Blue* gave the band their first ever no. 1 single *Breathless* 2000; *Best of* 2001;
Borrowed Heaven 2004; *Home* album of much loved Irish classic songs 2005; have sold 35 million
records worldwide. Awards: Brit Award, Best International Act, 1999; Honorary MBE 2005; film
credits include *The Commitments* and a guest appearance on *Beverly Hills 90210* (TV). Contact: Barry
Gaster, Glasthule Lodge, Glasthule, Co. Dublin. **T** 087 223 8572 web www.the corrswebsite.com

> Lively public performer who transformed the traditional fiddle and made it relevant to
> modern rock.

CORRIGAN, Maria; PRINCIPAL PSYCHOLOGIST, ST. JOHN OF GODS/ COUNCILLOR
b 1968, Dublin; single; *edu.* Holy Faith Convent, The Coombe, Dublin; University College Dublin; BA; MA; Principal Psychologist St. John of Gods Menni Services; psychologist Tipperary SE Health Board 1994; St. John of Gods, Dublin 1994 to date; councillor (Fianna Fáil) Dun Laoghaire/ Rathdown 1999 to date; stood for Fianna Fáil (Dublin South) General Election 2002; member Psychological Association of Ireland; Recreations: walking, reading, travel, tennis. Contact. County Hall, Marine Road, Dun Laoire, Co. Dublin. **T** 01 294 2201 email corm@indigo.ie

> An extremely focussed, hardworking professional; polled extremely well in her first general election outing; expected to make a major break through in the next election.

COSGRAVE, Terence; EDITOR, CHECKOUT
b 1963; single; *edu.* Cistercian College, Roscrea; Christian Brothers Schools, Roscrea; Algonquin College, Ottawa, Ontario, Canada; Diploma in Journalism, Dublin City University, Ireland; Master's Degree (hons) Political Communications; Editor Checkout; journalist *Sunday Press* 1987; moved to Canada 1988; studied and worked for various journals; returned to Ireland 1996; *Medicine Weekly* 1997-98; editor *Checkout* (won 1st award for *Checkout* later that year) 2001; *Checkout* magazine was Ireland's Business Magazine of the Year 2001, 2003, 2004; 2002 was the runner up in the most influential publication in Ireland in the Retail and Food & Drink Area. Clubs; Meadowvale Tennis Club. Recreations: music, politics, history, tennis, golf, snooker. Contact: Adelaide Hall, 3 Adelaide St. Dún Laoghaire, Co. Dublin. **T** 01 230 0322 **F** 01 236 5900 email editor@checkout.ie

> Extremely well regarded in industry circles as a bright and innovative editor.

Terence Cosgrave

COSTELLOE, Joe: PUBLIC REPRESENTATIVE
b 1945, Sligo; *m* Emer Malone; *edu.* Geevagh, Sligo; Summerhill College, Sligo; Maynooth College; University College Dublin; BA; H.Dip.Ed; Public Representative Labour, Dublin Central; former secondary teacher; elected to Dáil Éireann 2002; elected to Seanad Éireann 1997-2002 (Leader Labour Group); member Dáil Éireann 1992-97; Labour rep on British Irish Parliamentary Body 1997 to date; chairperson Labour's Policy Development Commission 1995 to date; member Seanad Éireann 1989-92; member Dublin City Council 1991-2003; chair Central Area Committee 2000-01; chair Heritage Area Rejuvenation Project 2000-01; chair O'Connell Street Integrated Plan 2000-01; chair Dublin VEC 1993-00; Deputy Lord Mayor 1991-92; former president Association of Secondary Teachers. Contact: 66 Aughrim Street, Dublin 7. **T** 01 618 3896 **F** 01 618 4596 email joe.costelloe@oireachtas.ie

> The Sligo native built his political reputation on work for the Prisoner's Rights Organization; a good local deputy who has carved out a national profile for himself by highlighting a range of social issues.

COSTELLOE, Paul; DESIGNER
b 1945, Dublin; *m* Anne Cooper; 5s 2d; *edu.* Blackrock College Dublin; Chambre Syndical de la Haute Couture, Paris; Designer; worked in design in Paris, Milan and New York; set up own design and manufacturing company in Dungannon, Northern Ireland; retail department store in Brown Thomas, Dublin and leading department stores in the UK and throughout Europe; also designed a range of home furnishings, tableware for Wedgwood, cutlery, china, glass and silverware for Newbridge Silverware, crystal for Cavan, optical range for Cambridge; commissioned to design homeware range for Dunnes Stores 2005; designer British Airways uniform 1992-2004. Commissioned to design a collection for the Ryder Cup WAGS 2006; Awards: Fil D'Or Award France (three times), Designer of the Year UK (two nominations), Designer of the Year Ireland 1991. Recreations: painting, theatre, cinema, golf, snooker Contact: Paul Costelloe International Ltd., 27 Cheval Place, London, SW7 1EW. **T** 044 171 589 9484. **F** 0044 171 589 9481

> Flamboyant but definitely not a stereotypical fashion designer; in his trade mark denim jeans and white shirt always cuts a towering dash; talented, consummately stylish with no nonsense, tells it like it is, whether it's PC or not; a total breath of fresh air.

COSTIGAN John Francis; MANAGING DIRECTOR GAIETY THEATRE, DUBLIN
b 1952, Dublin; *m* Maria McDermottroe; 2d; *edu.* St. Michael's College, Ballsbridge, Dublin; Commerce of Commerce, Rathmines, Dublin; Managing Director Gaiety Theatre, Dublin; freelance

production 1973-83; head of production Abbey Theatre 1983-86; head of touring Abbey Theatre 1987-90; freelance production 1991-95; general manager Dominion Theatre 1994-95; managing director Gaiety Theatre 1996 to date. Clubs: Stephen's Green Club, Dublin. Contact: Gaiety Theatre, South King Street, Dublin 2. **T** 01 6771717 email johncostigan@gaietytheatre.com web www.gaietytheater.com

In less than a decade has supervised the modernization and the restoration of the Gaiety to former glory days; has developed a commercial edge for the much loved Dublin treasure without losing its integrity and has brought life back to South King Street.

Mary Coughlan

COUGHLAN, TD, Mary; PUBLIC REPRESENTATIVE
b 1965, Donegal Town; *m* David Charlton;1*s* 1*d*; *edu*. Ursuline Convent, Sligo; University College Dublin, B. Soc. Sc; Public Representative; Minister for Agriculture; former social worker; first elected 1987 and at each subsequent election; appointed Minister for Agriculture and Food 2004; Minister for Social and Family Affairs 2002-04; Minister of State at the Dept. of Arts, Culture, Gaeltacht and the Islands 2001-02; member Joint Committee on Tourism, Sport and Recreation; Member British-Irish Interparliamentary Body; spokesperson on Educational Reform 1995-'97; chairperson, Joint Committee on the Irish Language 1993-95; member of Donegal County Council 1986 to date; member of Co. Donegal Vocational Education Committee 1991-92; chairperson Board of Management, Abbey Vocational School, Donegal Town; member of Board of Management of the Tourism College, Killybegs; president Killybegs Coast and Cliff Rescue Service; member of Chomhcoiste na Gaelige, chairperson 1993-94; elected Honorary Secretary of Fianna Fáil 1995; Contact: Quay Street, Donegal Town. **T** 074 972 4270 **F** 01 661 1013

A daughter of the late Cathal Coughlan and niece of the late Clement Coughlan; ambitious, good personality; seems well suited as the first woman to don ministerial wellies at the Department of Agriculture.

COULSON, Paul; CHAIRMAN YEOMAN INTERNATIONAL GROUP plc
b 1952, Dublin; *m* Moya Wall; 2*s* 2*d*; *edu*. Gonzaga College, Dublin; Trinity College Dublin BBS; Chairman Yeoman International Group plc; Accountant with C&L now Price Waterhouse Cooper 1973-82; chief executive, Yeoman International Group plc 1982-89; chairman 1989 to date; Yeoman International Group plc; acquired UK leasing company CLF 1990; sued SG Warburg that had brokered the CLF deal and won a landmark case; controlling interest in Ardagh (Irish Glass Bottle) 1998; Ardagh acquired UK glass company Rockware, 1999; closed Irish Glass plant Ringsend 2002; took Ardagh private 2003; member Institute of Chartered Accountants in Ireland. Clubs: Fitzwilliam Lawn Tennis Club, Donnybrook Tennis Club, Portmarnock Golf Club. Recreations: golf, tennis Contact: Yeoman International Group plc, Yeoman House, Richview Office Park, Dublin 14. **T** 01 283 7388 **F** 01 283 7323

'The Cooler' is a hard-nosed, forensic businessman; very sharp intellect; maintains a very low profile and is not media friendly.

COULTER, Phil; MUSICIAN
b 1942, Derry; *m* 1st (*m. diss*); *m* 2nd Geraldine Brannigan; 2*s* 4*d*; *edu*. St.Colomb's Derry; Queen's University Belfast; Musician; moved to London 1964; With Bill Martin wrote winning Eurovision Song Contest *Puppet on a String* 1967; Co wrote *Congratulations* Eurovision runner up 1968; *All Kinds of Everything* sung by Dana, won the Eurovision Song Contest 1970; His composition *My Boy* a major hit with Richard Harris; *My Boy* an international hit with Elvis Presley 1972; during the 1970s co-wrote and co-produced *Remember, Shang A Lang, Summer Love Sensation, All of Me Loves All of You; Heart of Stone, Give it Me Now, The Bump, Fancy Pants, Julie Anne* for US Band Kenny; a massive number one *Forever and Ever* for SLIK featuring Midge Ure;. produced three ground breaking albums for Planxty, early 1970's; wrote and produced albums with the Furey Brothers: *Sweet Sixteen, The Old Man, Steal Away;* wrote *Scorn Not His Simplicity.* and *The Town I Loved So Well* now an worldwide anthem; *Classic Tranquility* 1984; *Sea of Tranquility;* visiting Professor Boston College 1997; major appearances include four sell out concerts at Carnegie Hall and an outdoor performance on Capitol Hill, Washington DC with the National Symphony Orchestra before an audience of 600,000; performed for three US Presidents at The White House; performed and toured with James Galway; recorded *Winter's Crossing;* produced *Romantic Themes and Celtic Dreams;. Healing Angel* a

collaboration with Roma Downey, Derry born star of the record breaking TV series *Touched By An Angel*; *Highland Cathedral* 1999; *Coulter and Company* TV Show, 2003, 2004, 2005; *You're A Star* (judge) 2003; silverware: 23 Platinum, 39 gold, 52 Silver Albums. Contact: 4 Seasons Music, Bray Co. Wicklow. **T** 01 286 9944 web www.philcoulter.com

> His remarkable body of work speaks volumes about the genius of this charismatic artist; extraordinarily creative and hardworking, a genial man who has a particular interest in up and coming young performers; outspoken and a breath of fresh air in a cut-throat industry.

COVENEY, Simon; MEMBER EUROPEAN PARLIMENT

b 1972, Cork; single; *edu.* Clongowes Wood College, Co. Kildare; University College Cork; BA (Economics & History); Gurteen Agricultural College; Royal Agricultural College, Cirencester, UK; BS Land Management & Agriculture; Member the European Parliament; worked Scotland (Land Management Advisor); farmer, Cork 1997-'98; led the Sail Chernobyl Project which involved sailing a boat 30,000 miles around the world and raised €650,000 for charity 1997-'98; elected TD FG Cork South 1998; TD 1998-'04; Fine Gael Spokesperson on Drugs and Youth Issues, Assistant Chief Whip and Secretary of Fine Gael Parliamentary Party 1998-'02; re-elected to the Dáil 2002; appointed Opposition Spokesperson and Shadow Minister for Communications, Marine and Natural Resources 2002-04; member of various Oireachtas Committees including Family, Social and Community Affairs, Education and Science, Communications, Marine and Natural Resources and the Strategic Management Initiative Committee; member European Parliament for Munster (Fine Gael)/European Peoples' Party and European Democrats (EPP-ED) 2004 to date; member The Committee on Foreign Affairs, The Committee on the Internal Market and Consumer Protection, The Committee on Fisheries; author of the European Parliament's annual report on Human Rights in the World 2004; report adopted by European Parliament April 2005; appointed co-ordinator for Human Rights for the EPP-ED Group 2005. Clubs: Royal Cork Yacht Club. Recreations: sailing, (Grade A Sailing Instructor & Qualified Life Guard), rugby (played for Ireland at college and captained school team), also played for Garryowen and Cork Constitution, hurling, gaelic football. Contact: 6a, Anglesea Street, Cork. **T** 021 431 3100 **F** 021 431 6696 email scoveney@europarl.eu.int web www.simoncoveney.ie

Simon Coveney

> A first class representative for Fine Gael; stood and won his late father Hugh's seat in Cork South; may seek to return to national politics; hoping to help raise the profile of Fine Gael in Munster.

COWAN, Brian; PUBLIC REPRESENTATIVE

b 1960; *m* Mary Molloy; 2 *d*; *edu.* Clara National School; Cistercian College, Roscrea; University College Dublin; Incorporated Law Society; Public Representative (FF) Minister for Finance; deputy leader Fianna Fáil; formed legal partnership, O'Donovan & Cowen; Elected to Dáil Éireann June 1984 in the Laois-Offaly by-election, caused by the death of his father, Bernard Cowen; Minister Finance 2004 to date; Minister for Foreign Affairs 2000-04; Minister for Health and Children 1997-2000: Minister for Transport, Energy and Communications 1993-94: Minister for Labour 1992-93; Opposition Spokesperson for Agriculture 1994-97 and for Health 1997-97; Member of Offaly County Council 1984-92: Offaly Vocational Education Committee 1989-92: British/Irish Interparliamentary Body and member of its sub-committee on Political and Security Matters 1991-92; he was a member of Fianna Fáil Party Commission to review the aims and structures of the party. Recreations: golf, reading. GAA Contact: Department of Finance, Government Buildings, Upper Merrion Street, Dublin 2. **T** 01 676 7571 **F** 01 6789936 email webmaster@finance.irlgov.ie

Brian Cowan

> Took his solicitor father Ber Cowan's seat; political heavyweight and deputy leader of Fianna Fáil; gregarious and personable, he is seen to be in pole position for the top job if offered or forced but won't fight for it; no obvious opponent at this time; politically shrewd, sharp legal brain; highly articulate, the Fianna Fail Rottweiler is feared by political opponents; a steely presence; doesn't suffer fools gladly; outgoing, enjoys life, golf, racing; socializes extensively; always counted on to sing a few songs.

COWLEY, Dr. Jerry; PUBLIC REPRESENTATIVE

b 1952, Galway; *m* Teresa; 3*s* 2*d*; *edu.* St. Muredach's College, Ballina; University College Galway; Kings Inns Dublin; MB.B.Ch.D.Ch.D.Obst.MRCGP.MICGP .LL. BL; Public Representative (Ind); medical doctor; general practitioner; barrister; co-founder and former chairperson National Federation of Group Water Schemes; director of the Irish Council for Social Housing; chairperson

St. Brendan's Village in Mulranny, a sheltered housing scheme; incorporated Irish Institute for Rural Health 1996. Awards: People of the Year 1998. Mayo Man of The Year 1999; NUI Alumnni Award Heathcare Medical Science 2000. Clubs: Cumann Bádoiri Acla, Mayo Sailing Club. Recreations: sailing. Contact: Mulranny, Co. Mayo. **T** 098 36287 (Office) **F** 098 36299
email jerry.cowley@oireachtas.ie

> Has proved that one issue can make a huge difference; an incredibly hard worker and extremely articulate, the Galway born medical doctor created national headlines when he made health his platform for the 2002 General Election and again by his support for the Rossport Five; easily elected; looks a safe bet to hold onto his seat at the next outing.

COWLEY, Martin; HOSPITAL CEO
b 1945; *m* Pat; 2*s* 2*d*; *edu.* Blackrock College, Dublin; College of Commerce, Rathmines (now DIT); Hospital CEO; chartered accountant; trainee accountant 1963-68; auditor KPMG 1969-73; financial controller Mater Hospital 1973-92; chief executive Mater Hospital Dublin 1992 to date. Clubs: Claremont, Railway Union Tennis Club. Recreations: tennis, toastmasters. Contact: Mater Misericordiæ Hospital, Eccles Street, Dublin 7. **T** 01 803 2203 email mcowley@mater.ie
web www.mater.ie

COWMAN, Steve; CHIEF EXECUTIVE, GREENSTAR WASTE MANAGEMENT
edu. University College Dublin; Sheffield University, England; Trinity College Dublin; B.Eng; M.Eng; M.M.Sc; Chief Executive, Greenstar; worked in Ireland, Europe, North America and Asia in the electronics industry; management positions include: technical development manager, Enterprise Ireland; engineering and development director, General Electric; general manager, Harris Corporation Power TVS Division; senior vice president of marketing and new product development, General Semiconductor; general manager, Vishay Intertechnology; president and European managing director, Volex Europe 1984-03; CEO Greenstar 2003 to date. Contact: Greenstar Head Office, Unit 6, Ballyogan Business Park, Ballyogan Road, Sandyford, Dublin 18. **T** 01 294 7900
web www.greenstar.ie

Brian Coyle

COYLE, Brian; CHAIRMAN OF AUCTION HOUSE
b 1934, Dublin; single; *edu.* Clontarf High School, Dublin; St. Fintan's College, Sutton, Dublin; University of Reading; qualified as a chartered surveyor; Chairman Adams Auction House; joined James Adam & Sons Auctioneers and Estate Agents, Dublin; lecturer in Fine Arts, University College Dublin; frequent lecturer in US and UK; president Board of Visitors, The National Museum of Ireland and National Botanic Gardens, Glasnevin; member of Executive Board of the National Museum of Ireland 2004 to date; former president Irish Auctioneers and Valuers Institute; F.I.A.V.I. Publ. international journals of fine arts and antiques; television appearances; organising seminars on fine art and antiques countrywide. Recreations: golf, bridge art, reading, conversation, food, wine, amateur dramatics. Contact: James Adam & Co, 26 St. Stephens Green, Dublin 2. **T** 01 676 0261 email b.coyle@jamesadam.ic web www.adams.ie

> This gregarious and knowledgeable man has long led the promotion of Irish Art in the Salesrooms; social and witty, is highly regarded and trusted by collectors and bridge players alike.

COYLE, John; COMPANY DIRECTOR
b 1946; *m* Sally Doyle; 3*s* 3*d*; *edu.* Colaiste Iognaid; Glenstal Abbey; University College Dublin, BA M. Econ Sc.; College d'Europe, Bruges, Dip. Hautes Études Européennes; management trainee, CIE 1969-70; work study operator, Battery Makers 1970-71; Company Director; financial controller, Renvyle House Hotel 1972-83; currently chairman Hygeia Chemicals Ltd.; Renvyle House Hotel; Steelforms Ltd.; Galway Airport; vice president Eurochambres; past president, Galway Chamber of Commerce, Chambers of Commerce of Ireland, Galway Civic Trust; Development Board University College Galway; chairman Galway Race committee. Clubs: Galway Co. Club, Galway Bay Sailing Club, Corofin Fishing Association, The Amicable Society. Recreations: sailing, shooting, walking, reading. Contact: Hygeia Chemicals Ltd., Carrowmoneash, Oranmore, Co. Galway. **T** 091 794722

> One of Galway's leading businessmen; inherited all of his father's entrepreneurial skills; friendly, bright intellect with a sharp commercial edge; involved in many community and business organizations in his native city.

CRAIG, Maurice James Waldron; ARCHITECTURAL HISTORIAN
b 1919, Belfast; widower, *m* Beatrice Hunt (*m.dis*); *m* Jeanne Edwards (*decd*); *p* Agnes Bernelle (*decd*); 1*s* 1*d*; *edu.* Castlepark Dalkey, Co. Dublin; Shrewsbury School, England; Magdalene College, Cambridge; Trinity College Dublin BA., Ph.D; Architectural Historian; Inspector of Ancient Monuments, London 1951-70; Honorary Fellow of Trinity College Dublin, Honorary Fellow of Royal Institute of Architects of Ireland; Cunningham Medallist Royal Irish Academy; publ. *The Volunteer Earl* 1948; *Dublin 1660-1860* 1952; *Irish Book Bindings to 1800* 1954; *Classic Irish Houses* 1976; *The Elephant and the Polish Question* 1993; *Mausolea Hiberniaca* 1999; *100 Poems by Landor* 1999; *Cats and their Poets* 2000. Recreations: ship modelling, book collecting. Contact: Bungalow 1, Abbeyfield, Alma Road, Monkstown, Co. Dublin. **T** 01 236 0637.

Maurice Craig

> Austere in purely aesthetic terms, a most delightful and engaging authority on more than just architecture. To stand in a field of cattle with attendant bull whilst he discourses upon and conjures up a long lost dwelling is to be a stoic, but so hugely memorable that even the beasts of the field are stilled by his stentorian "Be quiet Sir!"

CRAWFORD, Leo; CEO BWG GROUP
b 1959, Dublin; *m* Adrienne McCabe; 2*s*; *edu.* St. Joseph's CBS, Fairview, Dublin; BBS; Trinity College Dublin; FCMA; CEO, BWG Group; group finance director, Irish Distillers Group 1991-1996; CEO, BWG Group 1996 to date; chairman, SPAR 2005; member IBEC National Executive Council. Clubs: Sutton Lawn Tennis Club, Sutton Golf Club; St. Margaret's Golf Club. Recreations: tennis, golf, GAA, football, socialising, travel. Contact: Greenhills Road, Walkinstown, Dublin 12. **T** 01 409 0300 **F** 01 450 9127 email lcrawford@bwg.ie

> The very popular face of his company; conservative, highly able and shrewd; a sports fanatic.

CREEDON; John, Joseph; BROADCASTER & WRITER
b 1958, Cork; *m* Monica; 4*d*; *edu.* Sacred Heart College, Carrignavar, Co Cork; Started Arts Degree at University College Cork 1976 but did not finish; Diploma in Regional Studies (Hons) UCC 2004;a variety of Certs & Diplomas in Speech Craft, Gaeity; producer/presenter *John Creedon* RTE Radio 1; joined RTE Radio 1 in 1987; awarded a Jacobs Award for *Risin' Time* 1989; awards for comedy writing and two records with his character "Terence", hairdresser to the stars; adjudicator at the *Hot Press* Rock Awards, The Dublin Theatre Festival and the National Final of John Player Tops; A Fairplay for Airplay Award; presented live radio and TV simulcasts including The Dublin International Piano competition; Musician of the Future from the National Concert Hall; *Messiah* with the Academy of St. Martin in the Fields for Channel Four; wrote and presented TV documentary *City Life* and music series *Jazz*; presented *Winning Streak*; *Family Matters*; *Live @3*; *Review of the Week*; *The Health Show* and has been a guest on *Kenny Live*; *The Late Late Show* and *Nationwide*; wrote and presented *Campus Classics*; columnist with *The Examiner* and articles/features for *The Sunday Independent*, *The Irish Times* and *The Star*. Recreations: theatre, live music, travel, gardening, angling, natural history. Contact: John Creedon Show, RTE, Cork. **T** 021 480 5877 email CREEDON@RTE.ie

John Creedon

> Ultra bright and friendly with a warm personality that guarantees his radio programme a huge following; still retains many of the traditional values of his west Cork roots; a bridge between the old school RTE and new hipsters; Cork City soccer fanatic; a breath of fresh air.

CROOKSHANK, Anne Olivia; ART HISTORIAN
b 1927, Whiteabbey, Co. Antrim; single; *edu.* Convent of the Sacred Heart of Mary, Carlisle; BA (History) Trinity College, Dublin; MA Courtauld Institute of Art;Art Historian; *Publ.* with Knight of Glin *The Painters of Ireland* 1978; *Watercolours of Ireland* 1994; *Ireland's Painters* 2002; with Eoin O'Brien *Portrait of Irish Medicine*; *Irish Art 1600 to Present Day*, *Irish Sculpture From 1600 to Present Day*, *Mildred Anne Butler*; numerous catalogues, entries in magazines; worked in the Tate gallery 1952-54; assistant librarian Courtauld Institute of Art, London University; Keeper of Art, Belfast Museum and Art Gallery, later the Ulster Museum 1957-65; founded art history department, Trinity College Dublin 1966; later became a fellow and professor; retired 1987. Recreations: looking at paintings, sculpture, architecture, embroidery anywhere in the world. Contact: **T** 074 915 1137

> A force of nature in the world of art and academic scholarship; as a professor in

Trinity College she gave great leadership, and as a Fellow Emerita she still does; grown men tremble at her stentorian tones, but overall a kindly force for good in the arts.

CRONIN, Anthony; WRITER

b 1926, Wexford; *m* 1st Therese Campbell; (*m.diss*); 2*d*; *m* 2nd Anne Haverty (*qv*); *edu*. Blackrock College Dublin; University College Dublin; King Inns; Barrister At Law, Writer and Biographer; wrote for *The Bell*; literary critic *Time & Tide, Nimbus*; co-founded with Patrick Swift *The Literary Journal X*; columnist *The Irish Times* 1976-80 and 1983-87; cultural advisor to Charles Haughey 1980-92; a principal in the establishment of Aosdána, an organisation for creative artists 1983; member of the Board of Governors & Guardians The National Gallery of Ireland 2002 to date; Publ. include *The Life of Reilly*; *A Question of Modernity*; *Identity Papers*; *Reductionist Poems*; *The Irish Eye*, a selection of his writings 1985; *The End of the Modern World* 1989; *A Question of Modernity* 1992; *No Laughing Matter* 1989; *The Last Modernist* 1996; weekly columnist for poetry, *The Sunday Independent*. Recreations: literature, reading, cultural politics, racing (for many years racing correspondent of *The Sunday Tribune*). Contact: Aosdána, 70 Merrion Square Dublin 2. **T** 01 618 0200

A lively and intelligent writer with the reputation of being a debunker of myths and a hard hitting critic in his columns; as the cultural gauleiter for his political chief he strayed beyond the correct and was an over-enthusiastic advocate for his master's voice; remains however an important literary voice of the 1940s and 1950s, with an authentic sense of time and place.

CROSBIE, Alan; CHAIRMAN, THOMAS CROSBIE HOLDINGS

b 1954, Cork; *m* Mary McSweeney; 4*s* 1*d*; *edu*. Clongowes Wood College, Naas, Co. Kildare; Harvard Business School, OPM Programme; Chairman Thomas Crosbie Holdings; Chairman Examiner Publications; advertising sales Courier Mail, Brisbane, Australia 1980; commercial director, Examiner Publications (Cork) Ltd. 1981-1993; Irish National Dragon Champion 1992; *Publ. Don't Leave It To The Family*; president European Newspaper Publishers 1996-1998; chief executive, Examiner Publications, 1993-2002; director Press Association 2001 to date; chairman Examiner Publications; chairman Thomas Crosbie Holdings Ltd; executive chairman Thomas Crosbie Holdings 2002 to date; chairman Down Syndrome Society of Ireland 2003 to date. Contact: 97 South Mall, Cork. **T** 021 427 2214 **F** 0 21 427 4234 email alan.crosbie@tch.ie web www.tch.ie

Fifth generation Crosbie to manage the company; quiet spoken, personable, dynamic businessman; is actively involved in promoting awareness and fund raising in aid of Down Syndrome; a champion yachtsman also involved in sailing for the disabled.

CROSBIE, Henry 'Harry'; PROPERTY DEVELOPER

b 1946; *m* 1st Elizabeth Bethel (*decd.*); 1*s* 2*d*; *m* 2nd Rita Fox; *edu*. Rockwell College, Co. Tipperary; Mount Sackville, Dublin; Property Developer; worked in family haulage business, Henry A. Crosbie; formed own tanker haulage company; managing director, Henry Crosbie Tankers; moved into the entertainment business; purchased the Point Depot, Dublin; opened Vicar Street 1998; chairman, Spencer Dock Development Ltd; hosted own TV show, *Start Me Up* 1996-97; Recreations: rock music, walking, architecture, Georgian furniture. Contact: The Point Depot, East Link Bridge, North Wall Quay, Dublin 1. **T** 01 836 6777

One of the quiet men of the property world; not only talked the talk but also walked the walk with his vision for dockland living, he was light years ahead of everyone; energetic, imaginative and highly successful businessman; has changed little and remains an authentic rock and roller.

CROSBIE, Thomas Edward 'Ted'; DIRECTOR, THOMAS CROSBIE HOLDINGS

b 1931, Cork; *m* Gretchen Kelleher (*decd*); 3*s* 3*d*; *edu*. Christian Brothers College Cork; University College Cork, BSc (chemistry); post graduate studies, Sweden; Director, Thomas Crosbie Hldings; maintenance engineer, Cork Examiner 1953-63; production and projects director 1963-80; productions and projects director, Harvey Printers 1969-82; chairman, Cork Examiner 1976-79; chief executive 1983-93; executive chairman 1993-97; non-executive chairman 1997-2002. Clubs: Cork Golf Club, Royal Cork Yacht Club (former Admiral), Cork Scientific & Historical Society. Awards: Hall of Fame Print Awards 1977. Recreations: sailing (racing and cruising), reading, model engineering, opera. Contact:97 South Mall, Cork. **T** 021 427 2214 **F** 0 21 427 4234 email ted.crosbie@tch.ie web www.tch.ie

A gregarious, hard-nosed businessman; took the difficult decision to bring in outside management to gear up 'de paper' to meet the challenges of the millennium; as a result the company has diversified into other areas of the media world and has become highly profitable.

CROSS, Dorothy; ARTIST
b 1956, Cork; Leicester Polytechnic, England; San Francisco Art Institute, California; B.A; MFA; Artist; major exhibitions include: Ebb, Douglas Hyde Gallery Dublin 1988; Powerhouse Philadelphia 1991; Croquet, Frith Gallery London 1994; even, Arnolfini Gallery Briston UK 1996; Cry, San Antonio, Texas 1996; Istanbul Biennal, Turkey 1997; Ghost Ship, Dún Laoghaire which also won the Nissan Art Prize 1999; Liverpool Biennial, England 1999; Medusae by the artist and her brother Professor Tom Cross 2000; large-scale exhibition Irish Museum of Modern Art, Kilmainham, Dublin 2005; Publ. *Gone: Site Specific Works by Dorothy Cross* by Prof. Robin Lydenberg; *Dorothy Cross* Irish Museum of Modern Art; Frith and Kerlin Gallery Catalogues; represented by the Frith Gallery, London. Contact: The Kerlin Gallery, Annes Lane, South Anne Street, Dublin 2 **T** 01 670 90 93 **F** 01 670 996 email gallery@kerlin.ie

Is an inventive and skilled artist especially in her most recent exploration of multi-media work with the newest technologies and music; her work is included in the permanent collections of; Goldman Sachs, London; Irish Museum of Modern Art, Dublin; Tate Modern, London; Norton Collection USA; Art Pace Foundation Texas.

CROWLEY, Brian; PUBLIC REPRESENTATIVE
b 1964, Bandon, Co. Cork; single; *edu.* Hamilton High School, Bandon, Co. Cork; University College Cork; Dip. Law; M.E.P.; printer, auctioneer, local radio announcer, rock bank singer; Taoiseach's (Albert Reynolds) nominee to the Senate 1993; elected to the European Parliament for Munster 1994 to date; Legal Affairs Committee, Rules and Procedures Committee and Social Affairs Committee; President UEN Group in EU Parliament; leader Fianna Fáil Group in EU; member Council of State. Recreations: music. Contact: Maryborough Lodge, Marybough Hill, Douglas, Cork. **T** 021 489 6433 **F** 021 489 6401 email briancrowleymep@eircom.net web www.briancrowleymep.ie

Brian Crowley

The son of legendary West Cork's former Fianna Fail T.D., the late Flor Crowley, is an extraordinarily hard worker, extremely bright and articulate with oodles of charisma; due to an accident in 1980 is paralysed from the hips down and confined to a wheelchair; his popularity converts into the highest personal vote in the country, which he received at the EU elections; many would love to see him in the Dáil, rather than the Berlaymont, where undoubtedly he would progress to Taoiseach.

CROWLEY, Caroline; SOLICITOR
b 1961, Dublin; *m* Peter Chapman; 1*s*; *edu.* Holy Child Convent, Killiney, Co. Dublin; University College Dublin; Law Society of Ireland; BA (Hons); Solicitor, accredited mediator; partner, Hayes Solicitors; Hayes Solicitors 1990; partner Hayes solicitors 1999; former member Broadcasting Complaints Commission; involved in fundraising for Down Syndrome Ireland; trustee Oesophageal Cancer Fund. Clubs: Charlesland Golf Club, Contemporary Irish Art Society. Recreations: golf, art, languages (speaks French and Italian). Contact: Lavery House, Earlsfort Terrace, Dublin 2. **T** 01 662 4747 **F** 01 661 2163 email crowley@hayes-solicitors.ie

An extremely able, multi-lingual solicitor; focused with a sharp intellect; indefatigable supporter of Downs Syndrome Ireland.

CROWLEY, Carrie; BROADCASTER
b 1967, Waterford; single; broadcaster, primary schoolteacher; five years local radio presenting and producing a variety of programmes in South East; theatre, both amateur and professional 1988-91; co-presented (with Ronan Keating) The Eurovision Song Contest 1997; presenter *Snapshots* RTE Radio. Recreations: Irish language, hill walking, swimming, reading. Contact: RTE Radio Center, Montrose, Donnybrook, Dublin 4. **T** 01 208 3111 **F** 01 208 2620 web www.rte.ie

A good radio presence, but she hasn't made the great strides which seemed to be hers for the making a few years ago; if not quite dumbed down, her radio shows haven't advanced either, which is a loss to her listeners; still has time to regroup and reconnect with her mainly middle aged and middle brow audience.

CROWLEY, Frances Majella; HORSE TRAINER

b 1973, Co Kilkenny; *m* Pat Smullen; 1*d*; *edu.* St. Brigid's College, Callan; University College Dublin; B. Comm. (Hons); Veterinary College, Post. Grad. Equine Science; Horse Trainer; joined family training establishment; amateur champion rider 1994-95, 1995-96; obtained Trainers Licence 1998; has trained over 300 winners including Grade 1 winner *Premalee,* listed and group placed *Golden Rule, Moscow Express* (25 races including Galway Plate); Drinmore Novice Chase Grade 1; Danehill Dancer two-year-old stakes; first woman to train a Classic Winner in Ireland (*Saoire*: 1000 Guineas) 2005. Recreations: sleeping and eating out. Contact: Clifton Lodge, Ballysax, The Curragh, Co. Kildare. **T** 045 442 652 email cliftonlodgeracing@eircom.net

> Daughter of the legendary Joe Crowley, extremely talented trainer whose attention to detail is recognized as one of her great strengths; the first Irish woman to train a Classic winner in 2005; the one time champion amateur jockey is sister-in-law of leading trainer Aidan O'Brien (*qv*)

CROWLEY, Kieran James; DIRECTOR RYECOURT, LTD

b 1951, Cork; *m* Jacqui; 2*d*; *edu.* St Finbarr's College, Farranferris, Cork; BA, University College Cork; FCA, Fellow, Institute of Chartered Accountants in Ireland; Director, Ryecourt, Ltd; trained with Coopers and Lybrand (PWC); financial controller Nortel Ireland & Europe; consultant to Irish and foreign investment companies 1986 to date; chairman SFA (Small Firms Assoc) 1998-2004; director AIB; Dyno-Rod; member of IBEC National Economic Council. Clubs: Royal St George Yach Club, Rathsallagh Golf Club, Lahinch Golf Club. Recreations: hurling, rugby, sailing, golf. Contact: 12 York Road, Ringsend, Dublin 4. **M** 086 242 4026 email kcrowley@ryecourt.ie

> Astute, energetic businessman; achieved national prominence as chairman of the Small Firms Association when that sector underpinned the Celtic Tiger; great company with a sharp commercial intellect.

CROWLEY, Laurence; BUSINESSMAN

b 1937, Dublin; *m* Mella Boland; 1*s*; *edu.* Belvedere College, Dublin; University College Dublin, B.Comm; Fellow, Institute of Chartered Accountants; Partner KPMG Stokes Kennedy Crowley 1961-90; chairman, PJ Carroll & Company plc., 1990 to date; Director Bank of Ireland 1996-2005; Deputy Governor Bank of Ireland 1995-97; Governor, Bank of Ireland 2000-05; Director of Elan Corporation plc.; Chairman, Council of Gaisce, The President's Awards 2005 to date. Clubs: Portmarnock Golf Club. Recreations: golf, theatre. Contact: P.J. Carroll & Company Limited, Burton Hall Park, Sandyford, Dublin 18. **T** 01 205 2300 web www.pjcarroll.ie

> A somewhat aloof business man who was a highly successful receiver/ liquidator and moved on to boardrooms of many major companies including the ultimate prize, Governor of the Bank of Ireland, imitating his late brother Niall, for many years chairman AIB.

CROWLEY, Niall; CHIEF EXECUTIVE OFFICER, EQUALITY AUTHORITY

b 1956, Dublin; single; *edu.* Gonzaga College, Dublin; Trinity College Dublin; St. Patrick's College, Maynooth, Co. Kildare; BA, BAI; Chief Executive Officer, Equality Agency; Publ. *An Ambition For Equality*; Ove Arup and Partners1978-82; Construtora Integral Sofala, Mozambique 1982-86; Pavee Point 1987-99; Chief Executive, Equality Authority, 2005 to date. Contact: The Equality Authority. 2, Clonmel Street, Dublin 2. **T** 01 417 333 **F** 01 417 3331

> As the voice of equality for the State, this scion of commercial and accounting princes brings all the authority and self-confidence of his background and education to bear upon his pronouncements.

CROWLEY, Peter; FINANCIAL CONSULTANT

b 1962, Dublin; *m* Clodagh O'Brien; 1*d*; *edu.* Gonzaga College, Dublin; Trinity College, BA, BAI civil engineering FCA; Chief Executive, IBI; joined KPMG 1984; director KPMG Corporate Finance 1987-93; Director IBI Corporate Finance 1993-96; executive director SIGMA Communications Group 1996-99; chief executive IBI 1999 – '06; Chairman Dublin Theatre Festival; non-executive director Irish Continental group; SIGMA Communications Group. Clubs: Fitzwilliam LTC, Portmarnock Golf Club. Recreations: theatre, live music, sailing, golf, travel. Contact: 40, Mespil Road, Dublin 4. **T** 01 637 7800 email peter.crowley@ibicf.ie

Extremely popular and respected in the business community; has maintained the standards of excellence of his immediate predecessors in the highly competitive area of corporate finance; due to leave IBI at the end of 2006 to commence own financial consultancy.

CROWLEY, Philip; DEPUTY CHIEF MEDICAL OFFICER, HEALTH SERVICE EXECUTIVE. *b* 1960, Dublin; *m* Emma Curtis; 1*s* 1*d*; *edu.* Gonzaga College, Dublin; University College Dublin; MD, BAO, B.Ch; Deputy Chief Medical Officer, Dept. Health and Children; previously worked in Nicaragua 1989-94; worked in Newcastle on Tyne where he spearheaded a project to assess the mental health needs of asylum seekers in the NHS 1994-2002; was the first Director of the General Practice in Deprived Urban Areas initiative, having also practiced in a deprived area of Dublin's north inner city; held the position of Director of the College's GP Care in a Multicultural Society project for two years; has been national Non Consultant Health Doctor leader with the Irish Medical Organization; was the GP trainee representative on the ICGP Council; deputy Chief Medical Officer, Department Health and Children 2005 to date; *Publ. Primary Care: Learning From The Building Healthy Communities Programme,* Combat Poverty Agency 2005; *Mental Health Needs of Immigrants* publ. *Journal of Public Mental Health* 2005; *Putting the Public Back Into Public Health* (co wrote) *Journal of Edidemiology* 2005; *Evidence Briefing Suicide Prevention* 2004; *Primary Care Treatment Involving the Community – Is Community Development The Way Forward? Journal of Management Medicine* 2002. Clubs: Recreations: tennis, football, golf. Clubs: Clonmore Golf Club, Clonakilty, Co. Cork. Contact: Department of Health and Children, Hawkins House, Hawkins Street, Dublin 2. **T** 01 635 3000 email philip_crowley@health.irlgov.ie

One of the Crowley 'dynasty' (father Niall Crowley was managing partner of SKC (now KPMG) and chairman Allied Irish Banks); his equally successful siblings include Vincent (CEO INM) Peter (MD IBI) Niall (CEO Equality Authority), Maurice (GM AIB) Emma (leading Dublin solicitor); his career to date displays a deep concern for the underprivileged in society.

CROWN; John Paul; MEDICAL PROFESSOR, CONSULTANT ONCOLOGIST *b* 1956, Dublin; separated; 1*s* 2 *d*; *edu.* Synge Street CBS; Terenure College; University College Dublin; MB, BCL, BAO 1980, BSC 1982; MRCPI 1983; MBA 2000; Newman Clinical Research Professor UCD 2005; Professor; Consultant Medical Oncologist, St. Vincents/Lukes 1993 to date; assistant professor Memorial Sloan Kettering Cancer Centre 1991-93; clinical assistant physician Memorial Sloan Kettering 1989-91; fellow assistant physician Memorial Sloan Kettering 1987-91; fellow Mt. Sinai Hospital New York; registrar in oncology St. James' Dublin 1984-88; registrar in medicine Guys Hospital London 1984; SHO Federated Dublin Hospital 1982-84; postgraduate student UCD 1981; intern Mater Hospital 1982; co-chair Glo Celtic Oncology Group; founder inaugurate chair Irish Clinical Oncology Resident Group, current chairperson. Recreations: writing, politics, current affairs, travel. Contact: St. Vincent's Consultants, Herbert Avenue, Dublin 4. **T** 01 269 5033 **F** 01 283 7719 email johncrown@icorg.ie

A dedicated and driven internationally renowned oncologist; used to working in a top class environment before his return to Ireland; refuses to accept the medical status quo or generally accepted levels of mediocrity; unlike most of his peers is not afraid to buck the system.

CROZIER, William 'Bill'; ARTIST *b* 1930 Glasgow, Scotland; *m* Katharine Crouan; *edu.* Glasgow School of Art; Artist; moved to Paris to paint 1950; then to Dublin; worked as a scene painter in various theatres including The Theatre Royal, The Regal Rooms, The Capital, The Olympia, The Gaiety with his friend the writer Anthony Cronin (*qv*); first solo exhibition 1957; began teaching painting at Winchester School of Art, Hampshire UK 1970; acquired a house near Ballydehob, West Cork 1980s; began exhibiting with Arthur Tooth & Son, London 1958, 1960, 1961, 1968, 1970; Drian Galleries, London 1958, 1960, 1961, 1965, 1968, 1970; Flowers, Flowers East, and Flowers, Carberry West Cork, the 1970s and '80s; The Grafton Gallery, Dublin 1983; The Taylor Galleries, Dublin; Scottish Gallery, Edinburgh & London 1991, 1985, 1989, 1990; National Museum Gdansk, Poland 1990; major retrospective RHA Gallagher Gallery, Dublin and Crawford Gallery, Cork 1990; The West Cork Art Centre; The Graphic Studio Dublin, Skibbereen, West Cork 2003; honorary member Royal Hibernian Academy of Arts, Dublin. Recreations: horse racing, music, good food, wine, theatre, the singing of Cavan O'Connor, Barcelona. Contact: Taylor Galleries, 16 Kildare Street, Dublin. **T** 01 676 6055

An extraordinarily charming and amusing companion, with a wide ranging interest in all aspects of life from Cavan O'Connor's singing to good food and wine; his work is rooted in his observations of natural things; loves a story and tells good ones too.

CRYAN, Mary Geraldine; BUSINESS ADVISOR/CEO

b 1958, Dublin; *m* Jim Toomey; 1*s* 1*d*; *edu*. St. Anne's Milltown, Dublin; Nano Nagle College, Carrick on Suir, Co. Tipperary; University College Dublin; B.Comm; CEO Cryan Associates Company Director and Business Advisor; advisor to technology sector; former chairperson, Irish Software Association; chairperson Advisory Council for Science Technology and Innovation; chairperson Statistical Solutions; non executive director of several technology companies. Publ. *The New Pioneers, Building A Winning Company in the US Market; Guide To Selling And Distributing Software In The US.* Clubs: Dunlaoghaire Golf Club, Blackrock Tennis Club. Recreations: tennis, golf, current affairs, reading. Contact: **T** 01 288 4897 email; mgcryan@indigo.ie

The former chairperson of the Irish Software Association is recognized as a leading software expert; a focused businesswoman much in demand for government advisories and board directorships.

Mary Cryan

CULLEN, Martin; PUBLIC REPRESENTATIVE

b 1954, Waterford; *m* Dorthe; separated; 3*s* 1*d*; *edu*. Waterpark College, Waterford; Waterford Regional Technical College; Minister for Transport; Minister for the Environment, Heritage and Local Government 2002-04; Minister of State at the Department of Finance, with special responsibility for the Office of Public Works 1997-2002; member of Joint Committee on Women's Rights 1987-88; member of Public Accounts Committee March 1993-November 1993; member of Select Committee on Social Affairs 1993-1994; vice chairman of the Committee for Commercial State-Sponsored Bodies 1995-97; member of the Finance and General Affairs Committee 1995-97; first elected to Dail Éireann 1987; front bench spokesperson on a variety of portfolios including Enterprise and Employment 1993; Industry and Commerce 1988-89; Tourism, Transport and Communications 1987-'88; Seanad Éireann 1989-92; member, Waterford City Council 1991-97; mayor Waterford City Council 1993-94; former director, Waterford Economic Development Board and South-East Regional Tourism Organisation; former chief executive of the Federation of Transport Operators; Founding member, Waterford Round Table 1979. Contact: 8, Ballinakill Crescent, Waterford. **T** 051 844 860 **F** 051 876 943

A switcheroo from the PDs to Fianna Fáil ensured that Waterford City got it's first minister in the history of the state; articulate, accident prone, the e-voting debacle and Monica Leech appointment back-fired politically; despite a high national profile faces a major challenge at local level in the next election.

CULLEN, Michael; PROPERTY DEVELOPER

b 1963, Dublin; *m* Dolores Delaney; 1 *s; edu*. Terenure College; University College Dublin; B. Comm; Chairman and Chief Executive Beacon Medical Group; Director Des Cullen Cars; Competitor Ferrari 360 Challenge cars. Recreations: motor racing. Contact: The Mall, Beacon Court, Sandyford, Dublin 18. **M** 086 255 1338 web www.beaconhospital.ie

First turned his day job as a director of Des Cullen motors into a passion for motor racing Ferrari 360s internationally; most recently is a serious property developer with the Beacon Court Medical group – the private hospital and clinic in South Dublin; has ambitious plans to roll out seven more similar facilities nationwide.

CULLEN, Michael; PAINTER

b 1946, Kilcool, Co. Wicklow; *p* Biddy Mulcahy; 1*s* 2*d*; *edu*. Blackrock Academy, Lower Mount Street, Dublin; National College of Art, Dublin; Central College of Art, London (life drawing);Painter; *Publ.* Gandon Press profile update 2006; *Irish Arts Review,* 2004; *Drawing,* edited Jim Savage, Cork 2001. Recreations: history, reading, travel. Contact: 6, Henrietta Street, Dublin 1. **T** 01 872 4090 email jazz@indigo.ie

A painter of deep and passionate cerebral impulse, whose every mark on the canvas is restrained and represents a private language; communicates great feelings and emotions with an economy of painterly gesture rarely matched in Irish art; a very nice man who is beloved by his friends and has no enemies.

CULLEN, William 'Bill'; CHAIRMAN RENAULT IRELAND/ AUTHOR
b 1942; *m* Rita Campbell; separated; 2*d*; *p* Jackie Lavin; *edu.* St. Canice's School, Dublin; O'Connells
Christian Brothers School, Dublin; LL.D NUI (*hc*); Chairman Renault Ireland; Chairman The
Glencullen Group; Started selling fruit in Moore Street Dublin 1947; Joined Walden Motor
Company 1956; General Manager 1964-73; Managing Director, Fairlane Motor Company (Ford
Dealership) 1974-86; Acquired Smith Group from Waterford Glass 1986; Chairman and Chief
Executive, Renault Ireland Distributors 1986 to date; Chairman, Irish Youth Foundation; Owner,
Muckross Park Hotel, Killarney, Co. Kerry; Director, Aer Rianta (Irish Airports Authority); *Publ. It's
A Long Way From Penny Apples* 2002; *Golden Apples* 2005. Awards: Inaugural Princess Grace
Humanitarian Award 2004; Clubs: Kildare Hotel and Country Club, Killarney Golf and Fishing
Club. Recreations: golf, tennis, squash. Contact: Renault, Kylemore Road, Dublin 10. **T** 01 605 5500
F 01 626 4978 www.pennyapples.com

The ultimate rags to riches story of modern Ireland, as set out in his book *It's A Long
Way From Penny Apples*; hardworking, single-minded businessman who now enjoys
the fruits of his labour and a new career as an author and motivational speaker.

CULLINAN, Bernadette Maria 'Bernie'; CHAIRPERSON IRISH SOFTWARE ASSOCIATION
b 1958, Dublin; *m* Colin Meagher; 1*s* 1*d*; *edu.* Muckross Park, Donnybrook, Dublin; University
College Dublin; B.Comm; MBA; FCMA; Chairperson Irish Software Association; Accountant BM
Brown 1981-83; Cognotec 1983-86; Virgin Group (London and Australia) 1986-93; McIver Crotty
Consultants 1994-98; Novum 1998-2000; Performix Technologies 2000-05; Interim Chief Executive
Officer, Steeltrace 2005 to date. Recreations: swimming. Contact: IBEC, Confederation House,
84/86 Lower Baggot Street, Dublin 2. **T** 01 605 1500 **F** 01 638 1500
email Bernie@dramaticconcepts.com web www.ibec.ie

An extremely able executive who can expertly navigate the technology sector;
currently heading up the influential Irish Software Association.

CULLINANE, Stephen Joseph; SPORTS EDITOR TV 3
b 1971, Dublin; *m* Grainne Seoige (*qv*); *edu.* Oatlands College, Stillorgan, Dublin;
University College Dublin; University College Galway; BA (pure history); Diploma in Applied
Communications; TV3 Sports Editor; news and sports reporter, Irish Press Newspaper Group; news
and sports presenter, Radio Kerry; presenter, RTE *Ear To The Ground*; sports presenter, FM104;
sports presenter, Today FM; sports editor TV3. Recreations: sport, music, reading, travel. Contact:
TV3 Ireland, Westgate Business Park, Ballymount, Dublin 24. **T** 01 419 3358
email stephen.cullinane@tv3.ie.

Having cracked it in sports reporting at TV3, must, like his high profile wife, be
aiming from a move to a major network in the not too distant future.

CUMMINS, Adrian; CHIEF EXECUTIVE, HOSPITALITY IRELAND
b Galway; *edu.* University College Galway; GMIT; Institute of Languages and Business,
Galway; Chief Executive Hospitality Ireland; appointed CEO Irish Hospitality Institute in
September 2004 to date; elected director of Ireland West Tourism; founder member of
Galway East Tourism; special media adviser to Minister of State Noel Treacy; 13 years
experience in tourism and marketing, having previously worked as sales and marketing
manager for the Shannon Oaks Hotel & Country Club; has lectured in Japan on the role of
rural tourism in Ireland; a past winner of the National Sales and Marketing Awards. Contact:
8, Herbert Lane, Dublin 2. **T** 01 662 4790 **F** 01 662 4789 email chiefexecutive@ihi.ie

Adrian Cummins

CURRAN, Edmund; EDITOR-IN-CHIEF IMN NORTHERN IRELAND
b 1944; *m* 1st Romaine Carmichael (*m diss*); 2nd *m* Pauline Beckett; 2*s* 2*d*; *edu.* Royal School,
Dungannon; Queen's University, Belfast (B.Sc. Dip.Ed); reporter, features writer, leader
writer 1966-74; deputy editor, *Belfast Telegraph* 1974-88; Editor in Chief IMN Northern
Ireland; Editor, *Sunday Life* 1988-93; editor, *Belfast Telegraph* 1993-05; Editor-in-chief IMN's
newspaper titles in Northern Ireland 2005 to date; member, Guild of Editors Parliamentary & Legal
Committee; board member, Co-operation Ireland; advisory board member Salvation Army. Awards:
UK Regional Editor of the Year 1992. Clubs: Royal County Down, Belvoir Park Golf Club, Belfort
Boat Club Recreations: politics, sport. Contact: Belfast Telegraph, 124-144 Royal Avenue, Belfast
BT1 1EB, Northern Ireland. **T** 208 01232 264000.

CURRAN, Noel, Anthony; MANAGING DIRECTOR, RTE TELEVISION
b 1965, Dublin; *m* Eimear Quinn; *edu.* Patrician Brothers High School, Carrickmacross, Co Monaghan; NIHE, Glasnevin, Dublin; BA (Communication Studies); MD TV, RTE; Editor, current affairs, RTE; Director Andec Communications, independent production company; Producer/director RTE; News editor, *Business & Finance* magazine. Recreations: hiking, music, film. Contact: RTE Donnybrook, Dublin 4. **T** 01 208 3120

Bright, hardworking and innovative; efficient and well able to be the man for the job because of his current affairs and public affairs broadcasting; facing into some challenges but background and training should bring him through.

CURRAN, Richard; DEPUTY EDITOR SUNDAY BUSINESS POST
b 1968, Dublin; *m* Kathy Donaghy; *edu.* Patrician Brothers High School, Carrickmacross, Co. Monaghan; Trinity College Dublin; Dublin City University; BA Mod.; Masters in Journalism; Deputy Editor, *Sunday Business Post*; Business journalist with *Irish Independent*; Visiting lecturer in journalism Universidad Anahuac del Sur, Mexico City 1994; Business journalist *Business & Finance* magazine 1996; Assistant editor and business editor *The Sunday Tribune* 1996-99; Business correspondent RTE News 1999-2000; Business editor *Irish Independent* 2000 to 06; Deputy editor Sunday Business Post 2006 todate; part-time presenter on Today FM's *Last Word* and *Sunday Business Show. Publ.* Co-author *Ireland's Entrepreneurial Elite.* Recreations: running, hill-walking, reading, modern Irish history, Roman history. Contact: Sunday Business Post, 80, Harcourt Street, Dublin 2. **T** 01 602 6000 **F** 01 4786189 email rcurran@sbpost.ie web www.sbpost.ie

The former RTE business correspondent is a well informed economic journalist who has ensured that the business pages of Ireland's largest selling daily newspaper have retained their edge in a fiercely competitive climate.

CURTIN, Donal; CHIEF EXECUTIVE AN POST
b 1947, Cork; *m* Barbara; three children; *edu.* Ballinlough National School; Coláiste Chriost Rí; University College Cork; BE (Elect); Chief Executive An Post; commercial director ESB; several high level posts in ESB International (ESBI); business consultant 2002-03; chief executive of An Post 2003 to date; Contact: GPO, O' Connell Street, Dublin 1. **T** 01 705 7000 web www.anpost.ie

The Cork born engineer is popular in business circles with his easy personality and laid-back approach; this disguises a forensic approach to business; the former ESB executive has his work cut out in the difficult postal area.

Brendan Curtis

CURTIS, Brendan; GROUP OPERATIONS DIRECTOR CLARION HOTELS
b 1962, Wexford; *p* Martine Andel; *2s 2d; edu.* St. Peter's College Boarding School, Co. Wexford; graduated DIT Cathal Brugha Street, Dublin; Trinity College Dublin; Honours BSc in Management and Higher Diploma in Hotel and Catering Management; Group Operations Director, Clarion Hotels; started career Forte Hotels, Dublin International Hotel 1981-85; managed Actons Hotel Kinsale 1989-92; joined Clarion Hotels 2000; appointed group operations director for Clarion Hotels in Ireland 2005; general manager Forte Crest Dublin Airport Hotel 1992-98; regional manager for the group covering London, Heathrow and Gatwick 1998-2000; Clarion Dublin ISFC 2000-03; group operational director Clarion Hotels 2003 to date. Clubs: Rush Golf Club. Recreations: family man. Contact: Clarion Hotels Ireland, Clarion Hotel, Dublin IFSC, IFSC, Dublin 1. **T** 01 433 8929 **F** 01 433 8831 email bcurtis@clarionireland.com

Opened three new hotels in 2005 and took over the Dublin Holiday Inn; more hotels planned for next year, including Carton House in Maynooth.

CUSACK, Evelyn; METEOROLOGIST
b 1967; single; 1*d; edu.* Convent of Mercy, Moate, Co. Westmeath; University College Dublin; B.Sc (Physics Hons); M.Sc Physics; Meteorologist; Joined Met Éireann 1982; RTE Meteorology broadcaster 1988 to date; Lectures on weather related topics; Promotes physics in schools/universities with the Institute of Physics; Represents Met Éireann at International Conferences on Meteorology. Clubs: Irish Meteorogical Society. Contact: RTE, Montrose, Donnybrook, Dublin 4. **T** 01 208 0000 email evelyn.cusack@rte.ie

Professional metreologist who demystifies iso bars and low pressure troughs with great élan; with her no nonsense approach to weather forecasting is an excellent ambassador for Met Eireann.

Evelyn Cusack

DALGARNO, Conor; MANAGING DIRECTOR & IT COMPANY OWNER

b 1968, Dublin; *m* Joanna Nathan Ayres; 1*s*; *edu*. Trim CBS; Information Technology Consultant; owner of Silkweb Design & Omni Computer Needs; security consultant UK; president of Trim Chamber of Commerce. Clubs: Trim Veteran and Vintage Car Club. Recreations: photography, mountain biking, cooking, collecting models. Contact: Emmet Street, Trim, Co. Meath. **T** 046 948 1599 **F** 046 943 7615 email conor@dalgarno.ie

> An active and energetic Meath man; head of the Trim Chamber of Commerce; showcasing the Castle of Trim with his opera project; wants the best developments for his home town.

Conor Dalgarno

DALY, His Eminence, Cathal Brendan; CARDINAL AND RETIRED ARCHBISHOP

b 1917, Loughguile, County Antrim, Northern Ireland; single; *edu*. St. Patrick's National School, Loughguile; St. Malachy's College Belfast; Queen's University Belfast (MA); Institut Catholique de Paris (LPh); St.Patrick's College Maynooth, Co. Kildare (D.D); Archbishop Emeritus of the Metropolitan See of Armagh and Primate Emeritus of All Ireland; member of the Sacred College of Cardinals. Ordained Priest 1941; classics master, St. Malachy's College Belfast 1945-46; lecturer in scholastic philosophy, Queen's University Belfast 1946-63; reader in scholastic philosophy Queen's University Belfast 1963-67; Bishop of Ardagh & Clonmacnois 1967-82; Bishop of Down & Connor 1982-90; Archbishop of Armagh and Primate of All Ireland 1990-96; elevated to College of Cardinals 1991; Archbishop Emeritus 1996 to date; D.D.(*hc*) Queen's University Belfast; D.Litt (*hc*) Trinity College Dublin; LL.D (*hc*) NUI; LL.D.(*hc*) Notre Dame University, South Bend Indiana USA; LL.D.(*hc*) St. John's University, Jamaica, New York; DD (*hc*) Exeter University UK; LL.D.(*hc*) Sacred Heart University, Fairfield, Connecticut USA. *Publ. Morals, Law and Life* (1962); *National Law Morality Today* (1965); *Violence in Ireland and Christian Conscience*(1973); *Peace, The Work of Justice*(1979); *Morals and Law*(1991); *Tertullian the Puritan and His Influence*(1993); *Northern Ireland-Peace - Now is the Time*(1994); *Love begins at Home*(1995); *Moral Philosophy in Britain from Bradley to Wittgenstein* (1996); *Steps on my Pilgrim Journey* (1998); *The Minding of Planet Earth* (2004); contributor to: *Prospects for Metaphysics* (1961); *New Essays in Religious Language*(1969); *Intellect and Hope*(1968); *Understanding the Eucharist*(1969); chaired the working party which published the report *Violence in Ireland*(1976); 17 Pastoral Letters to his dioceses, 1983 -1996; published 16 Addresses on the Day of World Peace, 1982-2000. Contact: Ard Mhacha, 23 Rosetta Avenue, Belfast BT9 3HG. **T** 028 9064 2431 **F** 028 9049 2684 email daly@btinternet.com

DALY, Frank; CHAIRMAN, REVENUE COMMISSIONERS

b 1946, Abbeyside, Dungarvan, Co.Waterford; *m* Elaine; 2*s*; *edu*. Christian Brothers School, Dungarvan; University College Dublin; B. Comm; chairman Revenue Commissioners; joined Revenue Office 1963, served a number of postings including assistant secretary, and accountant general of revenue, Revenue Commissioner 1996; director for office of Chief Inspector of Taxes, and Direct Taxes Policy and their implementation 2001-2002; chairman Revenue Commissioners 2002 to date. Contact: The Revenue Commissioners, Office of the Chairman, Dublin Castle, Dublin 2. **T** 01 647 5000 **F** 01 671 1826 email info@revenue.ie

> Highly respected in corridors of power in Leinster House and among the mandarins; low profile, friendly and entertaining company; a big supporter of the Waterford hurling team who enjoys vacations in the Déise country.

Frank Daly

DALY, Francis 'Frank'; SOLICITOR

b 1943, Cork; *m* Patricia O'Connor; 2*s* 2*d*; *edu*. Glenstal Abbey, Murroe, Co. Limerick; University College Cork; Law Society of Ireland; B.C.L, solicitor; senior partner Ronan Daly Jermyn Solicitors, Cork; chairman Solicitors Disciplinary Tribunal; past president Law Society of Ireland 1996-97. Clubs: Cork Golf Club, Cork Constitution RFC, University College Cork RFC. Recreations: golf, rugby. Contact: 12, South Mall, Cork . **T** 021 480 2700 **F** 021 480 2790 email frank.daly@rdj.ie

> This merchant prince of Cork has become a major property player while presiding over one of the biggest, privately owned legal practices in the country.

DALY, Seán; GYNECOLOGIST

b 1963, Dublin; *m* Carmen Deegan; *edu*. Terenure Colllege; Trinity College Dublin; BA. MB. BAO, Bch. M.A. DCH. MRCOG FRCPI. MD; Master/CEO Coombe Women's Hospital, 1999-2005; Editor, *One Body*; 40 published articles. Clubs: Hermitage Golf Club; Carton Golf Club.

Recreations: golf, family. Contact: Coombe Women's Hospital, Cork Street, Dublin 8. **T** 01 408 5280

A dynamic young Master who set high standards for one of Ireland's oldest maternity hospitals; an impressive media performer.

DANAHER, J. Gerard 'Gerry'; SENIOR COUNSEL
b Co. Limerick; *m* Audrey Hanley; separated; 2*d*; *edu.* Rockwell College, Co. Tipperary; University College Cork (BA); Kings Inns; Barrister at Law; Senior Counsel; called to the Bar 1978; called to the Inner Bar 1998; in general practice Dublin Circuit; member of the Northern Ireland Bar; appointed Board Central Bank; chairman of the executive board of the National Library of Ireland 2005 to date. Contact: P.O.Box 4460 158/9 Church Street .Dublin 7. **T** 01 817 5038 email gdanaher@lawlibrary.ie

A lively and engaging barrister who enjoys political life and the company of politicians; highly sociable, his wit and ready repartee in court earns him friends and wins the match.

DARDIS, John Michael; SENATOR/JOURNALIST
b 1945, Dublin; *m* Beatrice Lane; 1*s* 2*d*; *edu.* Newbridge College; University College Dublin (B.Ag.Sc); arable editor, *Irish Farmer Journal* to 1989; candidate European elections (Leinster) 1989 and 1994; member Seanad Éireann 1989 to date; deputy leader Seanad Éireann 1997 to date; member of Kildare County Council 1991–2003; former party chairman; former agricultural journalist of the year. Clubs: Leinster Association of Rugby Referees (Life Member); Newbridge RFC (President); North Kildare Trout & Salmon Anglers; Rathsallagh Golf Club; member of Forum on Europe Steering Committee. Recreations: rugby, angling, golf, the Irish Times Crossword. Contact: Belmont House Newbridge, Co Kildare. **T** 045 431 665 **F** 045 434 794 email jdardis@eircom.net.

Sharp intellect and good communicator, well informed on economic and agri business matters; has failed to make the break through to the Dáil or European Parliament.

DAVERN, Michael; CHIEF EXECUTIVE, THE KILDARE HOTEL AND COUNTRY CLUB
b 1967, Cashel, Co. Tipperary; *m* Aideen; 1*d*; *edu.* Shannon College of Hotel Management 1988; Chief Executive The Kildare Hotel and Country Club; General Manager Sandy Lane Golf and Properties, Barbados; The Green Monkey and The Country Club, designed by Tom Fazio 2001–2005; General Manager Fancourt Hotel and Country Club Estate, South Africa 1997–2001; Kildare Hotel and Country Club opening team 1991–1997; Chief Executive Officer Kildare Hotel and Country Club 2005 to date. Contact: Kildare Hotel and Country Club, Straffan, Co. Kildare. **T** 01 601 7200 **F** 01 601 7299 email: resortsales@kclub.ie web www.kclub.com

Michael Davern

With an international reputation has returned to Kildare, where he started his career; with the Ryder Cup at the K Club this year, he holds one of the most challenging and envied hotel positions in the world; already his hand can be seen in the welcome changes at The K; has had plenty of experience dealing with VIPs and fragile egos.

DAVIS, Julian; PUBLIC RELATIONS CONSULTANT
b 1954; *m* Mary (*qv*); 2*s* 2*d*; *edu.* Kilkenny College, Mount Temple, Dublin; University of Limerick (BA, Physical Education and English); director Fleishman Hillard; presenter 'Lets Go'. Sports editor, RTE 1980-1986; Pembroke PR 1986-1990; director Fleishman-Hillard 1990-2005; Clubs: Luttrellstown Golf Club, Sutton Tennis Club. Recreations: golf, tennis, squash, cycling, skiing, Manchester City Fan, extreme sporting challenges- Four Peaks 2005. Contact: Fleishman Hillard, Fitzwilliam Quay, Dublin 4. **T** 01 618 8444 **F** 01 660-2244 email davisjv@fleishmaneurope.com

Julian Davis

Solid performer for his clients; highly respected and popular within the industry.

DAVIS, Mary; DIRECTOR, SPECIAL OLYMPICS IRELAND
b 1954, Mayo; *m* Julian David; (*qv*); 2*s* 2*d*; *edu.* Hons Leaving Cert; Leeds University Dip.Ed: University of Alberta, B.Ed (Hons); St. Patrick's College, Drumcondra, Dublin, Certificate Educational Admin; Director Special Olympics, Ireland; teacher Coolmine Community School; St. Michael's House, Head of P.E; Exec. Dir. Special Olympics Ireland 2003; CEO 2003 Special Olympics World Games. Recreations: golf, antiques, outdoor pursuits. Contact: Special Olympics Ireland, 4th Floor, Park House, North Circular Road, Dublin 7. **T** 01 869 1704 **F** 01 869 1686 email mary.davis@specialolympics.ie

Having made reality her dream of staging in Ireland the first Special Olympics outside the US, she became one of the most popular and high profile women in the country; at one point it even looked as if she might be a contender for the Áras in 2004; a total dynamo, now sits on some of the most prestigious boards in the country and many feel a political challenge could await.

DAWSON, Barbara; DIRECTOR DUBLIN CITY ART GALLERY (The Hugh Lane)
b 1957; *m* Paul McGowan; separated; 1*s* 1*d*; *edu.*Brigidine Convent, Tullow, Co. Carlow; University College, Dublin; Trinity College Dublin; BA; H.Dip.Ed.; Director Dublin City Art Gallery – The Hugh Lane Municipal Gallery of Modern Art; Research Assistant, later Administrator, National Gallery of Ireland; Exhibitions Organiser Hugh Lane Municipal Gallery of Modern Art 1988; Director Hugh Lane Municipal Gallery Modern Art 1991 to date; Publ. include; *Turner in the National Gallery of Ireland* as well as papers and articles for art reviews and magazines; Member Irish Art Historians Association; Clubs: David Lloyd Fitness Club, Shillelagh and District Hunt Club. Recreations: horse riding, skiing, theatre, opera. Contact: Charlemont House, Parnell Square North, Dublin 1. **T** 01 2225550 **F** 01 872 2182 email bdawson.hughlane@dublincity.ie web www.hughlane.ie

A smart, tough, sassy public official who works the system well; adores new art and the razzmatazz of arts publicity; stole a march on the other galleries by getting Francis Bacon's studio.

D'ARCY, Brian Fr; R.C.PRIEST, RECTOR, THE GRANN, ENISKILLEN
b 1945, Enniskillen; single; *edu.* St Michael's College, Enniskillen; UCD; Seminary at Mount Argus; post-graduate in CTU, Chicago; Franciscan School of Theology, San Francisco; qualifications in philosophy, theology, pastoral care, counselling, journalism and broadcasting; Rector/Superior St Gabriels, The Grann, Enniskillen; Media Chaplain. Editor, *The Cross Magazine* 1970-75; lecturer in communications & production editor, The Communications Center, Booterstown, full time, 1975–77, part time1977– 83; Rector/Vicar/Administrator Mount Argus parish/community 1977–83; Rector and Parish Priest, Mount Argus 1983 –89; Rector The Grann 1987– 86; Rector Crossgor 1996–98; Rector The Grann 2000 to date; columnist, *Dancing News* 1965–85; columnist *Sunday World* 1976 to date; broadcaster RTE & BBC (Ulster and London) 1978 to date. Publ. nine books on pastoral theology: *A Little Bit of Religion,* Vols 1, 2 &3; *A Little Bit of Hope*; *A Little Bit of Love; Reflections From the Heart,* Vols 1 & 2, *Life of Blessed Charles*; Recreations: sport, music, communications, media. Contact: St. Gabriel's Retreat, The Grann, Enniskillen, BT74 5PB. **T** 028 66 322 272 email frbdarcy@hotmail.com

One of Ireland's best known priests; a Christian and kindly man, the original 'Fr Trendy'; has continued to engage the younger generation as many of them have become disillusioned with the Church due to the myriad scandals.

D'ARCY, Michael; VIOLINIST
b 1968; single; *edu.* St. Malachy's College Belfast; Royal Northern College of Music, Manchester, GRNCM; MA (Hons); concert violinist performing internationally. Leader of National Symphony Orchestra 1992–95; RTE concert Orchestra 1994–2000; Leader of Camerata Ireland; Faculty, Royal Irish Academy of Music. Clubs: Royal Society of Musicians, Ulster Architectural Society, Irish Wagner Society (Hon Life Member). Contact: 100 Downshire Road, Holywood, Co Down, BT 18 9LY. **T** 086 241 5482 email info@michaeldarcy.com

D'ARCY, Raymond, Paul 'Ray'; BROADCASTER
b 1964, Curragh, Co. Kildare; single; *edu.* St. Joseph's Academy, Kildare Town; Trinity College Dublin (BA Mod Psych); Presenter, Mid Morning Show Today FM; 1988–2000: RTE young peoples programmes including The Den; moved to Today FM; has presented "You're a Star"; Presenter Rose of Tralee 2005. Recreations: tri athlete. Contact: Today FM, 123 Upper Abbey Street, Dublin1. **T** 01 804 9058 email rdarcy@todayfm.com

Ray D'Arcy

A competent broadcaster with an easy manner who has emerged unscathed from the shadows of Zig and Zag; has a huge, growing listenership, which the advertising agencies just love; at a time when most middle of the road programmes are losing listeners, the graph continues to rise for Ray; was an unexpected success at the Rose of Tralee TV special.

DAVISON Rosanna Diane; FORMER MISS WORLD
b 1984, Dublin; single; *edu.* University College Dublin (History of Art, Archaeology, Sociology); winner Miss World 2003; face of Newbridge Silverware Ireland 2003-2004. Recreations: art, sculptor, swimming, snow and water skiing, hockey, tennis, hill-walking, athletics.

> The stunningly beautiful daughter of Chris de Burgh (*qv*) - he wrote 'Into The Light' to celebrate her birth - became an international household name when she donned the Miss World tiara in 2003, the first Irish gal ever to do so; beat off competition from 106 other Miss World wanabees; more than just a pretty face, a straightforward, intelligent, unspoiled and extremely popular young woman.

DE BLACAM, Shane; ARCHITECT
b 1945; *m* Una Craddock; 1*d*; *edu.* Blackrock College Dublin; University College Dublin (BArch); University of Pennsylvania; MRIAI; Joint Partner/Director de Blacam and Meagher Architects. Worked in Philadephia with Louis Kahn; lecturer in Architecture UCD, 1972-1988; established the practice with John Meagher (*qv*) 1976; former council member Royal Institute of Architects in Ireland; architectural advisor to the Arts Council. Buildings: Herbert Mews Development Dublin 1980; The Atrium Trinity College Dublin 1984-86; Dublin Liberties 1 Castle Street 2000; Loos Bar (co-designed) 2001; wooden Building Temple Bar; ESAT Building 1 Grand Canal Quay Dublin; Education Building Cluain Mhuire Galway 2002; the Cork Institute of Technology O'Donovan Rossa Library 2003; Network Management Centre Dundrum (ESAT). Awards: 4 silver medals from the RIAI; 1st& 2ndTaoiseach's House Competition 1979; 1st& 2nd Parish Church Competitions 1976; Premiated at the International Vauxhall Cross Developments, London 1983; Europa Nostra Award for the TCD Atrium1988; the RIAI Gold Medal for the Cork I.T.O'Donovan Rossa Library 2003. Recreations: hunting, gardening, dining with friends, good conversation. Contact: de Blacam & Meagher, 29 Raglan Road, Dublin 4. **T** 01 668 1555 **F** 01 6681075 email info@debm.ie

> A quietly thrusting designer for so many important buildings in Ireland; in his practice, he and his partner John Meagher (*qv*) have been involved in all the major landmark architectural projects in Ireland over the past two decades.

de BRÍ, Orla; SCULPTOR
b 1963, Dublin; *m* Finn de Brí; 1*s* 1*d*; *edu.* Our Lady of Mercy College, Beaumont, Dublin; Grafton academy of Design; sculptor for the past eleven years, working from own studio in Co. Meath; twelve public sculptures throughout Ireland; in many corporate collections including Aer Rianta, Bank of Ireland, Dublin City University; in private collections in Ireland, USA, France, Portugal and the UK; recently completed a major public commission on the Cashel (Co. Tipperary) bypass consisting of five 20ft bronze figures; solo show Solomon Gallery 2006. Recreations: yoga, reading, gardening. Contact: The Solomon, Gallery, Powercourt Townhouse, South William Street, Dublin 2. **T** 01 679 4237 **F** 01-671 5262 email odebri@esatclear.ie www.orladebri.com

> Vivacious, friendly and extremely talented brings a commercial focus to her creativity.

Orla de Brí

De BROMHEAD, Jerome Andrew; COMPOSER
b 1945, Waterford; *m* Dolores; 3*s*; *edu.* Glenstal Abbey, Murroe, Co. Limerick; Trinity College Dublin, MA; Composer; joined Radio Telefis Éireann as a presentation director 1969; music producer 1979-94; active as a composer since 1969 producing a body of work in most genres including two symphonies. Clubs: Royal Dublin Society; member Aosdána. Recreations: reading. Contact: Martello Cottage, Strand Road, Killiney, Co. Dublin. **T** 01 282 5948

> This Waterford-born composer has made a name for himself on the modern music scene in Europe, with major works being performed on mainland Europe; technically brilliant he brings many disciplines to bear upon his work.

DE BRÚN, Bairbre; PUBLIC REPRESENTATIVE
b Dublin, 1954; single; *edu.* University College Dublin (BA hons); Queen's University Belfast (PGSE); member of the European Parliament (Sinn Féin) for Ulster, 2004 to date; joined Sinn Féin 1984; emerged politically as a leader of the H Block committee in the early 1980s; elected to Northern Ireland Assembly 1998; Teacher of French and Irish in Northern Ireland's first Gael Scoil 1991-97; a leading member of the Sinn Féin negotiations team leading to the 1998 Belfast Agreement (aka the

Bairbre De Brún

Good Friday Agreement); Minister for Health, Social Services and Public Safety 1999-'02; member European Parliament 2004 to date; member of the Regional Development Committee, European Parliament. Recreations: hill-walking, theatre, cinema. Contact: Sinn Féin Offices, Parliament Buildings, Stormont Estate, Belfast BT4 3XX. **T** 028 9052 1675 email bdebrún@europarl.eu.int

One of the Sinn Féin negotiating team that helped broker the Good Friday Agreement in 1998, the Dublin-born politician was a useful link with successive Irish governments during difficulties in the peace negotiations. Unionist detractors didn't like or admire her, but had to agree that she had been more than capable and effective; a very keen brain, a fluent Irish and French speaker, keeps a low profile socially; one of the intellects in her party she is trusted by the inner cohort and feared by everybody else.

DE BRUIN, née SMITH, Michelle; BARRISTER/ OLYMPIC GOLD MEDALLIST
b 1969; *m* Erik de Bruin; 1*d*; *edu.* Colaiste Chilliain, Clondalkin, University of Houston, Texas, USA; Kings Inns; called to the Bar 2005; Barrister at Law; former Olympic Athlete; winner of two Gold and one Silver Medal – European Championships, Vienna, Austria, 1995; three Gold Medals and one Bronze – Olympic Games – Atlanta, USA, 1996 (400 Ind. Medley; 400 Freestyle, 200 Ind. Medley, Bronze, 200 Butterfly); two Gold Medals, and two Silver Medals, European Championships, Seville, Spain, 1997; suspended for four years by the International Swimming Federation (FINA) in 1998; Patron, Irish Guide Dogs for the Blind; Patron Voice. Clubs: Honorary life Member, Mount Juliet Golf and Country Club. Recreations: current affairs, journalism, history, gardening & DIY. Contact: The Law Library, Four Courts, Dublin 7 **T** 01 817 5000 **F** 01 817 5150

Ireland's golden girl flew high during the Atlanta Olympics only to crash spectacularly in the post Games controversy; showed her mettle by regrouping and qualifying a barrister.

DE BURGH, née DAVISON, Christopher, John 'Chris'; SINGER/ SONGWRITER
b 1948, Argentina; *m* Diane Morley; 2*s* 1*d*; *edu.* Marlborough (UK); Trinity College Dublin MA; debut album *Far Beyond These Castle Walls* released 1975; has released 38 albums, most recent: *The Road to Freedom* 2004; *The Chris de Burgh Collection* 2005, *The Ultimate Collection* 2005; *Live in Dortmund 2004*; the single 'Into the Light', No 1 in UK and US; 'Lady in Red', No 1 in the charts in US and UK, still one of the most requested songs at weddings; 'Patricia The Stripper', most requested at stag parties; *Flying Colours* album No1, USA and UK; has toured extensively worldwide. Awards: over two hundred Platinum Gold and Silver disks; Berliner Award (Germany), Bambi Award (Germany), Midem International Trophy (France), ASCAP Award (America), IRMA Award (Ireland). Recreations: swimming, scuba diving, golf, wine, antique furniture. Contact: Kenny Thompson Management Ltd. UK, 754 Fulham Road, London SW6 FS1T. **T** 0044 207 171 731 7074 **F** 0044 207 171 736 8605 email: ktmuk@btconnect.com

Known as a very sharp businessman; achieved world wide recognition as an entertainer; still hugely popular in some countries, especially Germany; following the nanny scandal, his career appears to have stalled in this country anyway; in recent times better known as father of Miss World Rosanna Davison (*qv*)

DE ROSSA, Prionsias: MEMBER EUROPEAN PARLIMENT
b 1940, Dublin; *m* Monica Kelly; 2*s* 1*d*; *edu.* Marlborough St. National Schools, Dublin; Kevin Street College of Technology Dublin (Radio Officers course interrupted); Member of European Parliament. interned The Curragh Prison Camp 1956–59; worked in familybusiness Patrick Ross & Sons; contested seats for Dáil Éireann 1981 & 1997; elected TD Dublin North West (Workers Party) 1982, (topped the polls 1987 & 1989); elected to Dublin City Council 1984; elected President the Workers Party 1988; elected MEP 1989; formed Democratic Left Party; Minister for Social Affairs 1995-97; on merger of Democratic Left with Labour Party, became Party President 1999; MEP, 1999 to date; member of Committee, European Parliament, Employment and Social Affairs and Committee on Petitions; sits with Labour Party/Party of European Socialists (PES). Contact: 14th.Floor, Liberty Hall, Dublin 1 **T** 01 678 9740 email pderossa@europarl.eu.int web www.derossa.com

Liked as a person and often admired as a politician; a great survivor who turned political adversity to good fortune; a witty and incisive speaker on the floor of the house, whether Dublin or Strasbourg.

De PAOR, Tomás, Proinsias; ARCHITECT

b 1967; *m* Judith Devlin; 1*s*; *edu.* Rice College, Ennis, Co Clare; Coláiste Laictin Naofa, Inis Oirr, Co na Gaillimhe; Coláiste Na bhFiann, Rosmuc, Co na Gaillimhe; Dublin Institute of Technology; University College Dublin (Bachelor of Architecture 1991), Cert. Professional Practice, 1994; Fellow Royal Institute of architects of Ireland 2003; Director de Paor Architects to date. Awards: The Irish Pavilion 7th International Venice Biennale 2000; New Trends of Architecture 2001; Young Architect of the Year 2003. Recreations: swimming, board games. Contact: 17 Kildare Street, Dublin 2. **T** 01 6610404 **F** 01 6394803 email office@depaor.com

> One of the younger and innovative architects whose talents are seen in his many influential insertions to the Dublin streetscape.

Tom De Paor

De VALERA, Síle; PUBLIC REPRESENTATIVE

b 1954, Dublin; single; *edu.* Loreto Convent, Foxrock, Co. Dublin; University College Dublin (BA); H.Dip Ed; Dip. Career Guidance; Dip. Psychology Sc; Minister of State, Department Education and Science (special responsibility for adult education, youth affairs and educational disadvantage). Worked as career guidance councilor; elected Fianna Fáil Dáil Eireann (Dublin Mid County) 1977–81; member European Parliament 1979–84; FF Dáil Deputy (Clare) 1987 to date; resigned Party Whip 1993; FF front bench spokesperson on Arts, Culture and Heritage 1995-97; vice-president FF 1997 and 2001; Minister for Arts, Heritage, Gaeltacht and the Islands, 1997–2002 (introduced the broadcasting bill 1999, extended the Sec. 35 tax break for the film industry1999); Minister of State, Department Education and Science, 2002 to date. Contact: 9 Chapel Lane, Ennis, Co Clare. **T** 065-6840208 **F** 065-6840695

> Grand-daughter of Dev; on her election in 1977 was the youngest TD in the Dáil; in September 1979 made a strong Republican speech at the Liam Lynch commemoration in Fermoy, Co. Cork which was seen as a direct challenge to the leadership of then Taoiseach Jack Lynch, who resigned some months later; resigned the FF party whip in 1993 in protest against the Government's removal of the obligatory stop over in Shannon; with her flawless FF pedigree has had a pedestrian political career and will not contest her seat in 2007.

de VERE WHITE, John, Frederick; AUCTIONEER

b 1949; *m* Miriam Kenny; 2*s* 2*d*; *edu.* St Gerard's School, Bray; Glenstal Abbey, Murroe, Co. Limerick; worked with James Adam & Sons, 1970; established Fitzgerald & Partners with Alexis FitzGerald and Denis Bergin, c. 1973; established De Vere White & Smyth with Barry Smyth, 1982 to date; set up de Vere's Art Auctions with Barry Smyth; member MIAVI 1988 to date. Clubs: Donnybrook Tennis Club, Dooks Golf Club, Kerry. Recreations: art, wine, food, sport; Contact: 35, Kildare Street, Dublin 2. **T** 01 676 8300. **F** 01 678 8305.email info@deveresart.com web www.deversart.com

> 'Buzzer' is a lively engaging personality who has a very trenchant way of speaking on the topics which enthuse him; has become a force to be reckoned with in the world of Fine Art, causing the longer established houses to pull up their socks; kindly and generous, he is a walking dynamo; liked by colleagues and competitors, he exudes bonhomie to all.

DEANE, Raymond; COMPOSER, AUTHOR, POLITICAL ACTIVIST

b 1953, Achill, Co. Mayo; *m* Renate Braun; *edu.* Belvedere College, Dublin; College of Music Dublin; University College Dublin (B.Mus), NUI Maynooth (D.Mus); freelance Composer/Author; Chair of Ireland Palestine Solidarity Campaign; broadcasts and performs all over the world; works commissioned for some of the world's best known ensembles/soloists; artistic director of RTÉ first two Living Music Festivals, 2002 and 2004. Publ. novel *Death of a Medium* (Odell & Adair 1992); CDs of compositions; Orchestral Music (Naxos/Marco Polo); *Seachanges - Chamber Music* (Black Box). Recreations: chess, cinema, literature. Contact: 1, Haigh Terrace, Dún Laoghaire, Co. Dublin. **T** 01 284 129 email rmdeane@eircom.net

> A brilliant star in the music firmament, he drives forward the modern music agenda and is well known through his recordings on Naxos.

DEANE, Seamus; ACADEMIC

b 1940 Derry; *m* Marion Treacy; 3*s* 1*d*; *edu.* St. Columb's College, Derry; Queens University, Belfast

(BA, MA); Cambridge University, PhD; Donald and Marilyn Keough Professor of Irish Studies, University of Notre Dame, South Bend, Indiana. Visiting Fulbright lecturer, Reed College, Oregon, U.S.A. 1966-67; visiting Fulbright lecturer, University of California, Berkeley 1967-69; lecturer, University College Dublin 1968-77; visiting professor, Indiana, 1977-78; Professor of English, University College Dublin 1980-93; Keough Professor of Irish Studies, University of Notre Dame, Indiana 1993 to date; visiting professorships Washington, Minnesota 1987, 1988, 1989. Awards: AE Award for Literature 1973, Ireland/America Award for Literature 1988, Guardian Fiction Prize 1997, Irish Times Irish Fiction Award 1998, Irish Times International Fiction Award 1988; Recent publ. *The Field Day Anthology of Irish Writing* – three volumes (1991) (Ed.); *Reading in the Dark,* Booker Prize, Best Novel nominee (1996); *Strange Country* (Clarendon Lectures, Oxford), (1997); *The Irish, A Short History* (2003); *Future Crossing, Literature between Philosophy and Cultural Studies* (2001); *Foreign Affections, Essays on Edmond Burke* (2004); *Wizard* (2006). Clubs: Royal Irish Academy. Member Aosdána; a former director, Field Day Company. Contact: Keough Institute for Irish Studies, 422 Flanner Hall, Notre Dame IN 46556 ; **T** 011 574 681 3555 **F** +001 574 631 3620 email irishstu@nd.edu

A brilliant writer and academic editor; his *Field Day* anthology, although criticised for poor representation of women, is a *magnum opus* by anybody's standards; an authoritative figure in Irish and world literature.

DELANEY, John; CHIEF EXECUTIVE FOOTBALL ASSOCIATION OF IRELAND
b 1967, Waterford; *m* Emer; 1*s* 1*d*; *edu.* Tipperary; Hon Treasurer and head of Security F.A.I; Waterford United's delegate on the FAI Board of Management 1999 – 2001; sold his substantial Blues stake 2001; sold his QC Logistics 2003; appointed Chief Executive F.A.I 2004. Recreations: GAA, soccer, golf. Contact: FAI, 80, Merrion Square, Dublin 2. **T** 01 676 6864 **F** 01 661 0931 email info@fai.ie web www.fai.ie

John Delaney

Son of legendary Joe Delaney, the former Waterford United Secretary and Carraig on Suir accountant likes things done yesterday; has achieved huge change in his first two years at Merrion Square, finally making it a professionally run outfit; however there are still lots of long knives out there, especially since his appointment of Steve Staunton as Irish team manager.

DELANEY, John Gerald; CHAIRMAN AND CEO TRADEXCHANGE
b 1969, single; *edu.* Salesian College, Ballinakill, Co. Laois; Cork RTC; Dublin City University; University College Dublin Business School; FCCA (Fellow & Chartered Association of Certified Accountants), M.Sc (Investment and Treasury); MBA; Chairman and CEO, Tradexchange Ltd; Irish Life; AIB Investment Managers; Oppenheim International Finance; CEO Trade Exchange Network ltd; Founder www.tradesports.com as featured on CNN, CNBC, *FT, NY Times, LA Times, Forbes, Business Week,* Reuters, Bloomberg. Recreations: mountaineering, cycling, travel. Contact: Tradexchange Ltd.10B Parkwest Business Park, Dublin 12. **T** 01 620 0300 **F** 01 620 0301 email john@tradesports.com

DELANEY, Patrick 'Pat'; DIRECTOR BUSINESS SECTORS AND REGIONS IBEC
b 1953, Dublin; *m* Nuala; *edu.* De La Salle College, Dun Laoire, Co. Dublin; Irish Public Administration; BA; Public Policy Making; Director of Small Firms Association. Worked initially in the printing industry; Confederation of Irish Industry 1981–93; merged with Federated Irish Employers to become IBEC; Deputy Director Small Firms Association 1993–98; Director Small Firms Association 1998–06; director business sectors and regions IBEC 2006 todate; member National Competitiveness Council; SFA representative to Social Partnership; former member Pensions Board. *Publ:* Policy documents SFA; Recreations: passionate Dublin GAA supporter, National Hunt Racing, keen gardener, walking. Contact: 84 -86 Lower Baggot Street, Dublin 2 **T** 01 605 1611 **F** 01 661 2861 email Patrick.delaney@ibec.ie

Sharp, good communicator and highly respected in the business community; has elevated the SFA above it's parent IBEC by orchestrating the real issues of concern for business people; has carved out a niche for SFA as a progressive and constructive, rather than a knocking, lobbying organization.

DEMPSEY, Noel; PUBLIC REPRESENTATIVE
b 1953, Trim, Co Meath; *m* Bernadette Rattigan; 2*s* 1*d*; *edu.* St. Michael's CBS, Trim; UCD, BA H

Dip. Ed; diploma Career Guidance, St. Patrick's College Maynooth; diploma in Leadership, St. Patrick's College, Maynooth; Minister for Communications, Marine and Natural Resources. Former teacher and guidance counsellor; elected Fianna Fáil Dail Deputy for Meath, 1987; former Government Chief Whip; Minister of State in Departments of An Taoiseach and Defence; Minister for Environment and Local Government 1997-2002; Minister for Education and Science 2002-04; Minister for Communications, Marine and Natural Resources 2004 to date. Clubs: Co. Meath Golf Club, Trim Golf Club. Recreations: reading, golf, all kinds of sport. Contact: Newtown, Trim, Co. Meath **T** 046 943 1146 **F** 046 943 6643

Noel Dempsey

> Transparently honest and obstinate, one of the stormy petrels of Irish politics, some of
> the ideas he generated which were rejected (e.g. abolition of electoral dual mandate) are
> now in force; his imposition of a plastic bag tax, much criticized, has helped the
> environment; has been involved in negotiating every 'Programme for Government'
> since 1992 (except the Rainbow Coalition!)

DEMPSEY, Matthew, Austin; 'Matt' FARMER/CHIEF EXECUTIVE

b 1948, Dublin; *m* Mary O'Reilly; 3*s* 6*d*; *edu.* Clongowes Wood College, Co. Kildare; University College Dublin, B.Agr.Sc. (1st.hons); Editor, *Irish Farmers Journal*; Chief Executive Agricultural Trust; Publisher *Farmers Journal and Irish Field*; Producer RTÉ; farming Co.Kildare; Chairman of Research Institute; Editor *IFJ*; Chief Executive Ag. Trust. Clubs: Chairman RDS, Chairman Kildare Hunt Club. Recreations: farming, reading, economics. Contact: *Irish Farmers Journal*, Bluebell, Inchicore, Dublin 12. **T** 01 419 9500 web www.farmersjournal.ie

> A leading figure in Irish agriculture for over the past quarter of a century; a good
> communicator, a clear thinker, one of the most informed people on the agri scene;
> politically close to Fine Gael.

DENHAM, Susan née Gageby; JUDGE OF THE SUPREME COURT

b 1945, Dublin; *m* Dr. Brian Denham; 3*s* 1*d*; *edu.* Alexandra College Dublin; Dublin University; Trinity College Dublin, BA (Mod), LIB, LIM; Supreme Court Judge. called to Bar 1971; practice at Bar specializing in judicial review; Senior Counsel 1987; Judge, High Court 1991; Judge, Supreme Court 1993 to date; Chairperson Working Group on a Courts Commission 1995–98; member, Interim Board of The Courts Service 1998–99; member of Court Service Board, 1999–2001; Chairperson, Courts Service 2001–04; Chairperson, Committee on Court Practice and Procedure; Pro Chancellor Dublin University 1996. Recreations: gardening, horses, walking, reading. Contact: The Supreme Court, The Four Courts, Dublin 7. **T** 01 888 6533

> A quietly efficient advocate for modernising the court services; her judgements are
> seen as careful and precise, based on logic and modern precepts.

DENT, Donna; ACTOR

b 1965, Gloucester, England; *m* Joe Gallagher; 1*s*; *edu.* St. Brigid's Holy Faith Killester; The College of Music; has worked as an actress for fifteen years, leading roles include: Mrs Linde in Ibsen's *A Doll's House* (The Abbey:Theatre), Dolly in the world premiere *Dolly West's Kitchen*; Catherine Sloper in "*The Heiress,* (The Gate Theatre); Stella in *A Streetcar Named Desire,* Sonya in *Uncle Vanya*, Rosalind in *As You Like It*; favourite TV piece: Constance in *Bachelors Walk*. Awards: Irish Times Award, Best Supporting Actress; Sunday Independent/Ford KA Award, Best Actress; Sunday Tribune Best Actress 1998. Recreations: writing, drawing, painting, reading, wildlife. Contact: 48, Clonliffe Avenue, Dublin 3. **M** 086 820 8837

> Has had a remarkable career, largely through the Gate Theatre Dublin; her work in
> 2005 in the Harold Pinter season places her very high in the current 'must cast'
> category for theatres.

DERVAN, Michael; MUSIC CRITIC/MUSIC WRITER

b 1952, Dublin; *partner* Margaret O'Reilly; music critic, *The Irish Times*. Founded and edited his first magazine 1964; as student gave world premières of works by Gerald Barry and Derek Bell, as well as Irish première of Stockhausen's *Tierkreis;* music critic of *In Dublin* magazine 1979; was involved in the launch of the music magazine, *Soundpost*, and later editor 1981; edited *Music Ireland* magazine 1985 – 1991; music critic *Sunday Tribune* and the *Guardian* and *Independent* newspapers in London 1984-85, the periodicals *Classical Music, Opera Now, Radio Times British Music Worldwide, Soundings, Nordic*

Sounds and *Opera News* (magazine of the Metropolitan Opera, New York). Has also broadcast on BBC (Radio 3, World Service and Radio Ulster), RTÉ Radio 1, and Lyric FM, where *Countdown*1999 100-programme survey of the music of the 20th century was broadcast; 2001 *King Arthur,* a six-part series on the life and work of the pianist Arthur Rubinstein; has also written about computers, audio equipment and food; has lectured on contemporary music at the DIT Conservatory of Music and Drama; Music Critic of *The Irish Times* 1986 to date; Awards: 1988 won the first AT Cross Critic of the Year Award. Recreations: film, cooking, books, travel, new music, historical recordings. Contact: *The Irish Times,* 10-16 D'Olier Street, Dublin 2. **T** 01 6792 022 email mdervan@irish-times.ie

A critic of great intensity, integrity and passion for his subject; often highly controversial in his reviews but never shirks from telling it like it is.

DESMOND, Denis; CONCERT PROMOTOR

b 1953; *m* Caroline Downey (*qv*); 2*s* 1*d*; *edu.* Presentation Brothers, Cork; University College Cork, B.Eng; formed MCD in the early 1980s; promoter, Thin Lizzy concert at Slane Castle 1981; has promoted Féile Weekends (Thurles), concerts at the Point (Dublin), U2 Croke Park (Dublin), and Botanic Gardens (Belfast), the Verve concert at Slane Castle (Co. Meath); founded Solid Record Label, no Solid-Grapevine; owner Olympia, Gaiety Theatres, SFX Hall; Bought 65 % stake in Scottish promoter DF Concerts 2001; bought the Mean Fiddler Group UK from Vince Power 2003-04; Opened Spirit nightclub, one of the biggest nightclubs in New York 2003; co-owner with Graham Beere, Abrakababra fast food chain. Contact: MCD, 7 Park Road, Dun Laoghaire, Co. Dublin. **T** 01 284 1747.

The low-profile Cork businessman who has brought globally acclaimed artists to Irish venues; a modern day, extremely commercial impresario who has diversified into other business areas in recent years; has extended his empire to the UK and the US.

DESMOND, Dermot; FINANCIER

b 1950, Cork; *m* Pat Brett; 3*s* 1*d*; *edu.* Good Counsel College, New Ross; Scoil Mhuire Marino, Dublin; joined Citibank (Dublin); worked with the Investment Bank of Ireland, World Bank/United Nations; consultant with Coopers and Lybrand; established National City Brokers 1981 and sold to Nat West Group in 1994; Chairman and Founder of IIU (International Investment & Underwriting Limited), established in 1994; Chairman, Baltimore Technologies Limited, Intuition Publishing Limited, Pembroke Capital Limited; Owner, London City Airport; Intuition Publishing Limited; Betdaq; Daon; Espatial. Part Owner, Sandy Lane Hotel, Barbados; Chronicle Bookmakers; Celtic Football Club, plc; Vivas Healthcare; Rietumu Bank, Latvia; Titanic Quarter Development, Belfast. Substantial investments in numerous other companies. Previous high profile investments; Baltimore Technologies plc, Esat Digifone. Trustee of Chester Beatty Library; Chairman of Royal College of Surgeons International Development Board; Chairman of the Charity, RESPECT. Golf Clubs: K Club, Valderrama, Queenswood, Sunningdale, Portmarnock. Contact: IIU, IFSC House, Custom House Quay, Dublin 1 Tel: 6054444 Fax: 6054455

Dermot Desmond

The elegant Cork-born risk taker supreme was architect of the IFSC with the late C.J. Haughey; the building he now occupies nearly brought an end to his financial career, rescued by some fortuitous lettings - one to Barings Bank! - since then has moved onwards and meteorically upwards, has diversified into many areas including software, property, currency dealings, gambling, hotels, Glasgow Celtic Football team and recently bought a third share in Latvian bank; most of his leisure time spent on the golf courses of the world where he takes the game very seriously; tries to be low profile, but consistently fails due to the frequency of the transactions he engages in; not media friendly.

DILGER, David; CHIEF EXECUTIVE, GREENCORE GROUP

b 1956, *m* Katherine Boylan; *edu.* Clongowes Wood College, Co. Kildare; Trinity College Dublin, BA; Chartered Accountant; joined Stokes Kennedy Crowley, Manager, 1983; Woodchester Investments, 1983-88; Chief Executive, Food Industries plc, now Greencore Group plc, 1988 to date; board member, IBEC. Recreations: golf, rugby, skiing. Contact: Greencore Group plc. St. Stephen's Green House, Earlsfort Terrace, Dublin 2. **T** 01 605 1000. **F** 01 605 1100

A clinical accountant, not likely to be deemed one of the lads; had a meteoric rise through the corporate world; however received a set back with the collapse of the

Goodman Group in the late '80's; succeeded to the top job at Greencore following the forced resignation of Chris Comerford due to the 'Greencore Affair'.

DILLON CARRIGAN, Anne, née AUDIAT; CONSULTANT, SOTHEBYS AUCTION HOUSE
b 1947; *m* 1st William Dillon (decd); 1*s* 1d; *m* 2nd John Carrigan (decd); *edu.* Institute St. Dominique à Morte Fontaine; Universitè de Paris (Law); ran Hibernian Antiques; co-owner with husband of Dillon Antiques; currently consultant Sothebys Auction House in Ireland. Clubs: Kildare Street Club, Milltown Golf Club. Recreations: bridge, reading golf, all the arts. Contact: 16, Molesworth Street, Dublin 1 **T** 01 671 1786 email anne.dillon@sothebys.com

A gracious and charming representative of a great London auction house; calm and tranquil personality with great determination; a considerable force on the Irish Antiques and Fine Art world.

DILLON OSB, Rt. Rev. Christopher; LORD ABBOT, GLENSTAL ABBEY
b 1948; single; *edu.* Ampleforth College, UK; University College Dublin; Corpus Christi, Cambridge; Collegio Sant Anselmo, Rome; Profession 1971; ordination 1977. Classics Master, Glenstal School, 1977-89; Junior House Master, 1989-90; Formation Team in Nigeria, 1990-92; Prior of Glenstal Abbey, Lord Abbot Glenstal Abbey, 1992 to date; Recreations: tennis, swimming, gardening, chess. Contact: Glenstal Abbey, Murroe, Co Limerick. **T** 061 386103

From a distinguished academic and political family; his charm and intelligence keeps his Abbey in good stead; allows his monks great freedom to develop their own role as members of an enclosed foundation, whilst remaining every inch a Lord Abbott in a great and grand Benedictine tradition.

DILLON, John Myles; REGIUS PROFESSOR OF GREEK, TRINTY COLLEGE DUBLIN
b 1939, *m* Jean Montgomery; 1d; *edu.* St. Gerard's School, Co. Wicklow; Downside (UK); Oriel College, Oxford, BA, MA; University of California, Berkeley, PhD. Assistant Professor of Classics, University of California, Berkeley, 1969-72; Professor of Classics and Chairman of University of California, Berkeley, 1977-80; Regius Professor of Greek, Trinity College Dublin, 1989 to date; publ. *The Middle Platonists*, London 1977 (2nd ed. 1996); *A Classical Lexicon to James Joyce* (with Brendan O'Hehir), Berkeley 1977; *Proclus Commentary on Plato's Parmenides* (with Glenn Morrow), Princeton, 1987; *The Golden Chain* (Collected Essays) Aldershot 1991; *The Great Tradition* (more Collected Essays), Aldershot 1977; *The Heirs of Plato*, Oxford 2003; *Salt and Olives: Morality and Custom in Ancient Greece,* Edinburgh 2004; member Royal Irish Academy (Council, 1987-94, 1997-2001; Senior Vice-President, 2001; Academy Gold Medal in the Humanities, 2005); Fellow, Trinity College Dublin, 1982 to date; member International Society for Neoplatonic Studies, Secretary for Europe, 1985 to date; President, International Plato Society, 2004-7; Director, Irish Institute of Hellenic Studies in Athens, 2003 to date; recipient Gildersleeve Prize of the American Journal of Philology, 1989. Recreations: tennis, golf, walking and chess. Contact: Trinity College, Dublin.
T 01 608 1150/1208

An internationally acclaimed academic immersed in the Greek and Platonic tradition; his sense of time is an evolution of Platonic philosophy.

DINEEN, Patrick J; DIRECTOR, SEDGWICK DINEEN GROUP
b 1937; *m* Colette Healy; 2 *s* 1d; *edu.* Presentation College Cork; Harvard Business School, Boston (1986); formed Sedgwick Dineen Group 1965; currently Director, Sedgwick Dineen Group; Irish Pensions Trust Ltd; former director The Industrial Development Authority; former chairman: Bord na Mona, Bord Gais, Irish Steel; Director Gulliver Info Res Services Limited, FEXCO (Foreign Exchange Company of Ireland); capped twenty five times for Ireland (1962-73); Clubs: United Services Club, Killiney Golf Club, The Old Head Golf Links, Cork Golf Club, Royal Cork Club. Recreations: cricket, golf, tennis. Contact: 55, South Mall, Cork. **T** 021 427 1449 **F** 021 427 7674

Former Irish cricket international built a successful insurance business in his native city before being taken over by a global insurance giant; closely identified with Fine Gael; has served on a number of state boards hitting the headlines with his high profile rift with the Bord na Mona Chief Executive Eddie O'Connor.

DOBSON, Bryan; PRESENTER/REPORTER RTE

b 1960, Dublin; *m* Crea Gogan; 2*d*; *edu.* Newpark Comprehensive School, Blackrock, Co. Dublin; College of Commerce, Rathmines, Dublin; News Presenter/Reporter. News reporter, Radio Nova, Dublin 1981-83; current affairs reporter/presenter, BBC Radio Ulster, Belfast, Northern Ireland 1983-87; business correspondent RTE News, Dublin, 1987–91; presenter/reporter RTE Television News 1991 to date. Clubs: Kildare Street and University Club, Dublin; Recreations: sailing, hill walking, reading history. Contact: RTE, Montrose, Dublin 4. **T** 01 454 6089 email dobsonb@rte.ie

Always elegant and polite; great line in neckties; managed to weather the storms with RTE management over his involvement in public speaking training courses; expects him to remain the authoritative male face of RTE news for a long time.

DOHERTY, Kenneth, 'Ken'; SNOOKER PLAYER

b 1969, Dublin; *m* Sarah; *edu.* Westland Row, CBS; Snooker Player Irish Under 16 Champion 1983-84; Irish Under 19 Champion 1985-86; Irish Amateur Senior Champion 1987-89; World Junior Champion (Iceland 1989); World Amateur (Singapore 1989); World Professional Champion (England 1997); Rothmans Grand Prix 2000; Malta Grand Prix 2000; 5 - Regal Welsh 2001; Thailand Masters 2001; Currently ranked 7th Main Tour; Guinness Book of Records – holder speed snooker potting six colours yellow to black in 23.4 seconds; joined BBC as a commentator on snooker. Awards: Westland Row Past Pupils Award; Ballygowan Sports Personality Award 1997; Recreations: soccer (a huge Manchester United fan and enjoyed one of his proudest moments when he paraded the world trophy around Old Trafford in front of 55,000 fans), opera, visiting art galleries, golf, tennis, reading, movies. Contact: 110 Sport Management Ltd, First Floor, Pavilion 1, Castlecraig Business Park, Players Road, Stirling FK7 7SH, Scotland.

'Crafty Ken' became the first player from the Republic of Ireland to win the world title, and the first person to have taken the world professional and amateur titles (he captured the latter in 1989; Clean cut, very friendly and popular, totally focussed on his sport; changed the public perception of snooker in this country and also raised the profile of the sport to appeal to a mass market.

DOHERTY, Moya; MANAGING DIRECTOR ABHANN PRODUCTIONS/ TYRONE PRODUCTIONS/ RIVER PRODUCTIONS

b 1958, Co. Donegal; *m* John Mc Colgan (*qv*) 2*s*; *edu.* Manor House Clontarf, Dublin; Producer Training Course RTE; D. Litt (hc) University of Ulster; Managing Director Abhann/ Tyrone Productions; joined Team Educational Theatre Company; Presenter/Reporter GMTV, London; Producer/Presenter Arts/ Features RTE; co-founded Abhann Productions 1995; Riverdance, Hammersmith Apollo, London 1995; Riverdance Radio City Music Hall, New York 1996; 5,000th performance of Riverview, Edinburh, San Francisco 2002; Riverview continues to tour globally; Director Radio Ireland 1996; sold out to Scottish Radio Holdings 2001. Awards: Jacob's Award for TV Programme on child sexual abuse, RTE; Ernst & Young Entrepreneur of the Year Award 1999. Recreations: reading, hillwalking, cooking, theatre. Contact: 23, Mary Street Little, Dublin 7. **T** 01 889 4900 **F** 01 889 4992 email: info@riverdance.com

Spirited, able and passionate about her company, her warm and approachable manner disguises a hard nosed commercially driven business woman; deemed, to be the business brain behind Riverdance which has been parlayed into a major global success and provided the seed capitol for the diversification of their major business interests, especially in property in Ireland, UK, US and Australia.

Moya Doherty

DOHERTY, Patrick, 'Pat'; PROPERTY DEVELOPER

b 1942, *m* Doreen Rayner; 4*s* 1*d*; *edu.* (National) School, Buncrana, Co. Donegal; worked in construction in the UK; Chairman of Harcourt Developments Ltd; Harcourt Developments - a property development, investment and management company with several million square metres of property of all use-classes around the world; owner of shopping centres, office blocks, industrial estates, prime residential property and hotels in Ireland, UK, Caribbean. Recreations: horse racing, shooting, Donegal. Contact: Harcourt House, 18-19 Harcourt Street, Dublin 2. **T** 01 475 3928 **F** 01 475 3943 email: info@harcourthouse.com web www.harcourtdevelopments.com

Gregarious, gracious and the pioneer of Irish property developers; long before the Celtic Tiger bonanza, was well established though shrewd investments and the selection of sustainable developments in good locations in the UK and Ireland; has maintained a low profile in an industry now dominated by high profile operators.

DONLEAVY, James, Patrick; AUTHOR

b 1926, *m* 1st Valerie Heron (m.diss),1*s* 1*d*; *m* 2nd Mary Wilson Price (m.diss),1*s* 1*d*; *edu.* Fordham Prep School, New York; Roosevelt High School, Yonkers, New York; Naval Acad. Prep School, Port Deposit, Maryland; Trinity College, Dublin; Author, Playwright, Painter; WW11 USN 1944–'46; Publ: novels: *The Ginger Man* 1955, *A Singular Man* 1963, *The Beastly Beatitudes of Balthazar B* 1968, The *Onion Eaters* 1971, *A Fairy Tale of New York* 1973, *The Destinies of Darcy Dancer, Gentleman* 1977, 1979 *Schultz* 1979, *Leila* 1983, *Wrong Information Being Given Out at Princeton* 1998; Short stories and sketches: *Meet my Maker the Mad Molecule* 1964, *An Author and His Image, Novella* 1997, *The Saddest Summer of Samuel S* 1966, *The Unexpurgated Code: A Complete Manual of Survival and Manner* 1975, *De Alfonce Tennis, The Superlative Game of Eccentric Champions, Its History, Accoutrements, Rules, Conduct and Regimen,* 1984, *J.P.Donleavy's Ireland in All Her Sins and in Some of Her Graces* 1986, *A Singular Country* 1989, *The History of the Ginger Man* 1993, *The Lady Who Liked Clean Rest Rooms* (The Plays of J.P.Donleavy) 1995, *Are You Listening Rabbi Low* 1987, *That Darcy, That Dancer, An Autobiography* 1990, *An Author and his Image and Other Pieces* 1995, *That Gentleman* 1997, *A Letter Marked Personal* 2006. Recreations: farming, De Alfonce Tennis, Dry Stone Walling. Contact: Levington Park, Mullingar, Co. Westmeath.

The writer of several iconic novels of young maleness in a new Ireland, he is laconic and laid back in his approach to life; living in county Westmeath he's drawn a wide circle of friends to him and remains as observant and sharp as ever; A great figure of sartorial and literary elegance, he is a name with which to conjure up old and new images.

DONLON, Seán ; UNIVERSITY CHANCELLOR

b 1941, Athboy Co. Meath; *m* Paula (née Doyle); separated; 1*s* 1*d*; *edu.* Athboy, Drogheda, Cavan National Schools; St.Finian's College Mullingar; St. Patrick's College Maynooth; University College Dublin, BA; Chancellor and Chairperson University of Limerick. Joined the Department of Finance; transferred to Dept of Foreign Affairs; First Secretary Irish Embassy, Bonn 1964-69; Consul General, Boston 1969-71; Assistant Secretary, Dept of Foreign Affairs Dublin 1971-78; Irish Ambassador to United States of America 1978-81; Secretary, Dept.of Foreign Affairs, Dublin1981-87; Vice President GPA 1987–94; Special Advisor to Taoiseach John Bruton 1994-97; Chancellor, University of Limerick 2003 to date. Recreations: poker, music, reading. Contact: University of Limerick, Plassey House, Limerick. **T** 061 202 700 **F** 061 2023 0316 web www.ul.ie

A shrewd public servant, as Ireland's Ambassador to Washington successfully resisted the government's attempts to remove him; as advisor to John Bruton he had a number of successes in the peace arena, but couldn't compensate for the laissez faire approach of his boss; made a successful transition to the Commercial sector with GPA; now steers the fortunes of the University of Limerick; a great party giver at his home in Killaloe.

DONNELLY, Annette; MANAGING DIRECTOR SONY BMG

b 1972, Co. Galway; *m* Mark Buckley; *edu.* St Joseph's College, Summerhill, Co. Roscommon; University College Galway; University College Dublin; B. Comm.; M. Acc; ACA ; Managing Director Sony BMG Ireland; qualified and worked in practice with Deloitte and Touche 1993-1997; joined Sony Music Ireland 1999; General Manager Sony Music Ireland 2003; appointed Managing Director of Sony Music Ireland 2004; following merger of Sony Music and BMG became Managing Director of the newly merged company in Ireland. Recreations: avid music fan, lover of outdoor adventure sports, travel, swimming, reading, Pilates; Contact: Sony Music BMG Ireland, Embassy House, Ballsbridge, Dublin 4; **T** 01 6433400 **F** 01 6473702 email Annette.Donnelly@sonybmg.com

One of the bright new business women in Ireland, becoming Managing Director of a major Irish Music company in a cut throat industry at the age of 32; Also the first woman to head up one of the major record companies in Ireland; has put a highly motivated team on board and loves her work attending music gigs three and four nights a week.

Annette Donnelly

DONNELLY, Carolyn Mary; FASHION DESIGNER

b 1954, *m* John Spain; 2*s* 1*d*; *edu.* L.S.U. Convent, Banagher, Co Offaly; Grafton Academy of Dress Design; Grafton Academy Diploma in Dress Design; opened Ritzy 1980; started Quin & Donnelly label with Liz Quin (*qv*) 1985; won Designer of the Year Award twice; collection sells in UK through House of Fraser stores and selected outlets; in Ireland Quin & Donnelly is available in the Brown

Carolyn Donnelly

Thomas stores and selected outlets around the country; future plans include development of new markets in Denmark, Norway, Sweden and France. Recreations: walking, golf, tennis, photography and gardening. Contact: Sonole Designs Ltd, Unit 16, Finglas Business Centre, Dublin 11. **T** 01 826 8560 **F** 01 826 8561 email sonole1@eircom.net

One of the talented designing duo of the popular Quin and Donnelly label which offers much sought after, latest designer looks at extremely competitive prices.

DONNELLY, Joseph 'Joe'; BOOKMAKER
b 1947, *m* Marie O'Neill(*qv*); 3s 1d; *edu.* Christian Brothers School, Cork; Rockwell College, Tipperary. Joined family on-course bookmaking business; Director RESAM (private property investment company); former chairman, Leopardstown Racecourse; former member, Irish Horseracing Authority; former member of IMMA board; member, International Council of the Tate Gallery (London); member Glucksman Gallery board, University College Cork. Contact: J. Donnelly ltd, 15 Hume Street, Dublin 2 **T** 01 676 8200

Very low profile Corkman who was one of the early property developers in the '80's; recognized as one of the leading experts and collectors of contemporary art; a one time familiar face on the racetracks of Ireland and the UK with his bookies pitch; hit the headlines in the late '80s with the collapse of the Power Corporation, when he suffered a major financial set back; bounced back into the property world with shrewd investments and hit the headlines again with the development of his unique private residence / art gallery in Killiney, Co. Dublin.

DONNELLY, Marie née O'Neill; CHAIRMAN IRISH HOSPICE FOUNDATION
b 1950, *m* Joseph Donnelly (*qv*); 3s 1d; *edu.* Presentation Convent, Youghal; founder member Irish Hospice Foundation 1986; assisted with Hospice national fundraising campaign, board member 1989, Chairman 1997-2000; an indefatigable fundraiser for the Hospice Foundation, launched and edited *The Whoseday Book* 1999, national and international sales exceeded £2 million; launched Art Pack - a unique deck of playing cards created by 54 visual artists (raised close to 1m); 'Peter & The Wolf' narrated by Gavin Friday, illustrated by Bono and his daughters Jordan & Eve translated into several languages and sold worldwide raising funds to support the IHF and hospice worldwide already raised over €2m; former chairman IMMA; former board member, Douglas Hyde Gallery, Chester Beatty Gallery; member, International Council of the Tate Gallery, London; member ARTANGEL, London. Recreations: reading, film, art, theatre. Contact: J. Donnelly ltd, 15 Hume Street, Dublin 2. **T** 01 676 8200

An Irish style icon; has brought a commercially innovative approach to fundraising for the Irish Hospice Foundation; appears to have recovered from the controversial IMMA contretemps with then director Declan Mc Gonigal.

John Donnelly

DONNELLY, John Paul; GROUP CHIEF EXECUTIVE, OGILVY GROUP, IRELAND
b 1963, separated; 2s 1d; *edu.* Gonzaga College, Ranelagh, Dublin 6; UCD Smurfit Business School, B.Comm, MBA, Diploma in Advertising; began career in Peter Owens Advertising 1985; Young & Rubicon, New York, Account Supervisor 1987–1990; Account Director, Mc Connells Advertising, Dublin (left to do MBA) 1990–1992; Managing Director, Dimensions 1994–1999; Ogilvy & Mather Advertising (Merger of Wilson Hartnell & Bell Advertising) 1999- 2003; Group Chief, Ogilvy Group, Ireland 2003 to date (includes WHPR, Ogilvyone, Mindshare, Ogilvy & Mather, and other investments); publ: variety of articles for Marketing publications, Marketing, Irish Marketing Journal, MIQ (Marketing Institute). Clubs: UCD RFC, Fitzwilliam LTC, Milltown Golf Club, Kildare & University, Board member of Crafts Council of Ireland, Royal Victoria Eye & Ear Hospital and Smurfit Business School (Also President of Alumni 2003 to date). Recreations: marathon running (4 marathons – Boston, Paris, Dublin), Former Manager of Irish Universities Rugby Unions. Contact: 5/6 Ely Place, Dublin 2. **M** 087 255 0659 **F** 01 669 0019 email jp.donnelly@ogilvy.com

Internationally experienced, an excellent, strategic operator; a solid performer with none of the flamboyancy usually found in the advertising world.

DONOGHUE, Denis; WRITER, CRITIC, ACADEMIC
b 1928, *m* Frances Ruttledge; *3s 5d; edu.* Christian Brothers School Newry; University College Dublin, BA, MA PhD; Cambridge University MA (ex officio); Henry James Professor of English and American Letters at New York University; Administrative Officer, Department of Finance; Assistant Lecturer in English, University College Dublin, College Lecturer, Professor of Modern English and American Literature; University Lecturer in English, Cambridge University, and Fellow of King's College, Cambridge; Henry James Professor of English and American Letters at New York University, University Professor; has taught semesters at several universities, including Princeton, UCLA; taught Harvard Summer School, Edinburgh Summer School; lecturerships in prestigious international universities; First Director of the Yeats International Summer School, Sligo; Fellow, Royal Society of Literature (London), ACLS Fellowship (University of Pennsylvania). National Humanities Center, Woodrow Wilson Center for International Scholars, Washington DC; Fellow of the American Academy of Arts and Sciences; awarded Hon Litt D (National University of Ireland) and Royal Irish Academy of Music; Publ. include, *The Third Voice, Modern British and American Verse Drama* (1959), *Jonathan Swift: A Critical Introduction* (1969), *Emily Dickinson* (1969), *Yeats* (1971), *Thieves of Fire* (1974), Editor, *Seven American Poets* (1975), *The Sovereign Ghost: Studies in Imagination* (1976), *The Arts Without Mystery* (1983), *We Irish* (1986), *Editor, Selected Essays of R.P. Blackmur* (1986), *Reading America: Essays on American Literature* (1987), *Warrenpoint* (1990), *Being Modern Together* (1991), *The Pure Good of Theory* (1992), *The Old Moderns: Essays on Literature and Theory* (1994), *Walter Pater: Lover of Strange Souls* (1995), *The Practice of Reading* Yale, 1998, (winner of the Robert Penn Warren-Cleanth Brooks Prize in Literature Criticism, 1998); *Words Alone, The Poet TS Elliot;* 2000. *The Practice of Reading* (2002); essays and reviews; Contact: Glucksman Ireland House, 1,Washington Mews, New York, NY 10003. **T** 011 212 998 3950 **F** 011 212 995 4373 email ireland.house@nyu.edu

The Master of the velvet word, he is a magisterial figure in Irish modern writing; an enthralling speaker, lecturer, academic and writer he has helped make Irish literature a major subject in American universities.

DONOVAN, Maeve; CHIEF EXECUTIVE, IRISH TIMES
b 1956, Dublin; *m* Michael Donovan; *2s; edu.* Trinity College Dublin M.BS; Chief Executive *Irish Times*; ICC Bank; joined *Irish Times* advertising sales dept 1987; appointed head of marketing 1989; appointed marketing manager 1994; appointed Director *Irish Times* board 1997; appointed commercial Director 1999; appointed Chief Executive *Irish Times* 2002. Contact: Irish Times, 10-16, D'Olier Street, Dublin 2. **T** 01 675 8000 email mdonovan@irishtimes-times.ie web www.ireland.com

Very personable with a sharp intellect; a commercially driven businesswoman; extraordinary capacity for hard work; low key and very private enjoys her leisure time with her family in rural Kildare; spearheaded *Irish Times'* success in winning recruitment and property advertising.; brought in huge revenues over recent years; a major influence on the modernization of the IT printing presses.

DOOLEY, Patrick 'Pat'; CHAIRMAN DAN DOOLEY LTD
b 1954, Limerick; *m* Theresa Morrissey; *1s 2d; edu.* St. Munchen's College Limerick; CBS Hospital, Co. Limerick; worked for a time as a barman in Killiney Court Hotel and Kiely's in Donnybrook, Dublin; returned to Limerick and joined motor company established by his father, Dan Dooley Ltd., currently chairman of one of the largest motor companies in the South West, main Ford Dealers, car rental, car leasing and sale; former member, OTMI; member, ERDF 1994-99, member Killarney Golf Club. Recreations: golf, travel. Contact: Dan Dooley Ltd., Knocklong, Co. Limerick **T** 062 53103.

Great company and very popular on both sides of the Atlantic, a shrewd and innovative businessman who is an acknowledged expert on his business sector.

DOORLEY, Thomas Christopher FitzGerald 'Tom'; WINE AND FOOD CRITIC
b 1959, Dublin; *m* Johanna KcKeever; *3d; edu.* Belvedere College, Dublin; Trinity College Dublin, BA Mod, H.Dip. Ed; Assistant Master and House Tutor, St. Columbas College, Rathfarnham, Dublin 1981-85; Features Writer, *Irish Independent* 1985-89; Copy Writer, O'Connor O'Sullivan Advertising 1989-91; Wine and Food Critic, *Sunday Tribune* 1991–2003; Restaurant Critic *Irish Times* 2004 to date; Wine columnist *The Field* (UK) 1996 to date; wine columnist *Business & Finance; The Dubliner Magazine*; publications include regular contributions *Decanter, Checkout*; books: *Tom Doorley Uncorked* (On Stream 1996), *Best of*

Tom Doorley

Wine in Ireland (A.A. Farmer1998), Muck & Merlot, (O'Brien Press) 2004, L'Ecrivain: *Not Just A Cookbook* (2004); TV: co-presenter, *Movable Feast,* RTE, 1996-'98; presenter, *The Big Stew,* RTE 1999; *The Afternoon Show,* RTE; *The Restaurant,* RTE; Radio: 2004 –'05 presenter *Food Talk* (RTE Radio). Clubs: Kildare Street and University Club, Old Columban Society, Circle of Wine Writers (UK). Recreations: reading, gardening, (at 13, youngest ever Council member, of Royal Horticultural Society of Ireland). Contact: Carrigeen Hill, Conna, via Mallow, Co Cork. **T** 058 56248 email: tdoorley@irish-times.ie

> A fine critic who doesn't wear his laurels lightly; remains a reliable guide and seeks out and tests unknown or unusual eating places; gives a fair and accurate account of eating out in Ireland.

DORGAN, Seán; CEO INDUSTRIAL DEVELOPMENT AUTHORITY
b 1951, Cork; *m* Mary Lennon; 4*s*; *edu.* St. Brendan's College, Killarney, Co. Kerry 1963-68; University College Dublin; B.Comm; M.Econ.Sc.; Chief Executive Officer IDA; former secretary General Dept of Industry and Commerce; former secretary General, Dept. of Tourism and Trade; chief executive officer Institute of Chartered Accountants in Ireland; member of the Culliton Review; member board of the IDA, National Economic Council and other government boards and committees including Forfás; Chief Executive IDA Ireland 1999 - to date. Clubs: Recreations: Contacts; Wilton Park House, Wilton Place, Dublin 2. **T** 01 603 4184 web: www.idaireland.com

> A true professional who brought a great breath of experience to the IDA; has changed the focus of industrial policy to a knowledge based economy where Ireland continues to punch above its weight.

DOUGLAS, Barry; CONCERT PIANIST
b 1960, *edu.* Methody (Methodist College Belfast); Royal College of Music; Concert Pianist; recordings with BMG/RCA include: Tschaikovsky Concerto 1, Brahms Concerto 1, Liszt Concertos, Mussorgsky Pictures at an Exhibition, Beethoven Hammerklavier Sonata; appeared in Madam Soursatzka – starring Shirley McLaine; worked with Berlin Philharmonic, Leipzig, Gewandhaus, orchestras of Philadelphia, Chicago, and Los Angeles in the United States; the NHK and Tokyo Symphonies in Japan, the Israel Philharmonic and all the major London orchestras; the DSO Berlin, the Bayerischer Rundfunk, the Maggio Musicale in Florence, the Helsinki and Stockholm Philharmonics, the Orchestre Philarmonique de Radio France, the London Symphony Orchestra, the Cincinnati and Toronto Symphony Orchestras, San Francisco Symphony Orchestra, Frankfurt RSO, RAI Turin and Dresden Staatskapelle. Awards: 1985 Gold Medal at Tchaikovsky International Piano Competition, RCM Dip. (Performance), ARCM, LRAM; Queens University Belfast, D. Mus. (hc), 1986. Recreations: driving, food, wine, reading. Contact: IMG Artists, Media House, 3 Burlington Lane, London, W4 2TH. **T** 0044 181 233 5800. **F** 0044 181 233 5801.

> A fine pianist with a great sense of performing style.

DOUGLAS, Claire Charlotte; RESTAURATEUR
b 1948, London; *m* Richard Douglas (decd, m.diss); 2*s* 1*d*; *edu.* Bagstaer Boarding School, Copenhagen, Denmark 1964; Technical College, Croyden, UK 1965; Institute Française , Rambuille, Paris, 1966; School of Journalism at Aarchus University, Aarchus, Bachelors Degree Journalism, 1969–72; scholarship to study Journalism, Boston, USA, 1973; studied Spanish in Mexico City, 1974. Trainee Hotel Manager, Hilton Hotel, Copenhagen 1967. Owner of Locks Restaurant, 1 Windsor Terrace, Portobello, Dublin 8. London Correspondent, *Jylands Posten*, Demark 1976-79; freelance for Danish Radio 1976-79; publ. articles *Jyllands Posten*, Aarhus, Denmark; started Locks Restaurant, 1980; started (and then sold) Cafe Klara, Dawson Street, Dublin 2. Recreations: literature, art, architecture, history, film, theatre, design. 32, Bloomfield, Avenue, Portobello, Dublin 8. **T** 01 454 3391 **F** 01 453 8352

> Excellent hostess who has made Lock's one of the most enduringly good eateries in Dublin despite an onslaught of competition in recent years; bright, interested in everything, great company.

DOWNER; Roger George Hamill; PRESIDENT & VICE CHANCELLOR, UNIVERSITY OF LIMERICK;
b 1942, *m* Jean; 1*s* 2*d*; *edu.* Methodist College Belfast, Queens University Belfast BSc, MSc, DSc;

University of Western Ontario PhD, BSc; (Queens University Belfast), M.Sc; (Queens University Belfast), PhD; (University of Western Ontario), DSc; (Queens University Belfast), LL.D (L.C); Queens University Belfast, D.Sc (L.C); University of Waterloo, Fellow of the Royal Society of Canada, Member of Royal Irish Academy; Professor of Biology & Chemistry, University of Waterloo (1970–1996), Vice President, (1996-1998); President & Vice Chancellor, University of Limerick (1998 to Present). Clubs: Hon Member Garryowen RFC, Hon Member Castletroy Golf Club, Hon Member Limerick Rotary Club, Vice Chair, Hunt Museum, Chair, Birr Scientific & Heritage Foundation, Chair National Self –Portrait Collection, Board Shannon Development. Recreations: reading, walking & sports. Contact: Office of President, University of Limerick, Limerick, Ireland. **T** 061 202020 **F** 061 330027 email roger.downer@ul.ie

A low profile, quiet academic; displays a different style of leadership to his predecessor Ed Walsh (*qv*).

DOWNEY, Caroline Elizabeth; PROMOTER/FUNDRAISER
b 1961, Dublin; *m* Denis Desmond; 2*s* 1*d*; *edu.* Junior School (Australia), Matric (South Africa); Promoter /Fundraiser; Model; Television Producer of the Super Models Show, Childcare Concert and the Irish Music Awards; promoter of these events; fundraiser for 18 years, raised over €25 million to date; board member ISPCC/Childline, Tooth Fairy Foundation, Christina Noble Foundation, Dublin Theatre Festival. Recreations: travel, music, rugby. Contact: MCD, 7 Park Road, Dun Laoghaire, Dublin. **T** 01 **F** 01 282 6817 email Caroline@mcd.ie web www.mcd.ie

Has brought a new energy and sharp commercial edge to charity fundraising in Ireland; a tireless worker for the ISPCC for many years, has now raised almost €30 million for charities; very involved with husband Denis Desmond (*qv*) in MCD Productions; has overseen the refurbishment of the Gaiety Theatre and the Olympia Theatre; great company with endless energy.

Caroline Downey

DOWNEY, Gerard Anthony 'Gerry'; MASTER BARBER
b 1943, Dublin; *m* Marie; 1*s*; *edu.* St. Mary's National School, Haddington Road, Dublin 4; Marian College Ballsbridge, Dublin 4; Master Barber; apprenticed Flannagan's Barbers, Merrion Row, Dublin; joined Whelan's, Cork Street, Dublin, 1962 -65; Brown Thomas Barber Shop, Grafton Street, Dublin, 1965 – 68; Peter Mark Uni Sex Hairdressers, Terenure, Dublin 1968 – 69; Founder, Executive Barbers, Dublin 1969-71; opened own barbershop Burlington Hotel, Leeson Street, Dublin 1972–79; opened own barbershop Berkeley Court Hotel, Ballsbridge, Dublin, 1979 to date; Awards: Gold Medal, International Hairdressing competition, Paris, 1971. Clubs: Edmonston Golf Club. Recreations: golf, fishing, travel, eating out. Contact: Berkeley Court Hotel, Landsdowne Road, Ballsbridge, Dublin 4. **T** 01 660 1714

The upper echelons of Dublin's corporate world have their locks tended (and increasingly tinted) by this hugely experienced barber; probably knows more about the board rooms of the Capitol than most; utterly discreet, a sympathetic listener with a lively personality.

DOWNEY, Jim; GROUP FINANCE DIRECTOR UTV plc
b 1946, Belfast; *m* Gillian Mary; 3*d*; *edu.* Belfast High School, Belfast; Chartered Association of Certified Accountants; Group Finance Director UTV plc; held a number of senior posts as financial controller Viridian Group plc; Financial Controller UTV 1998; Company Secretary, UTV1999; joined UTV Board as Finance Director 2000. Recreations: gardening, walking, stamp collecting, bird watching, rugby, cricket. Contact: UTV plc, Havelock House, Ormeau Road, Belfast BT7 1EB. **T** 028 90 328122 **F** 028 90 246695

A solid financial operator; much of UTV's success in recent years is down to his judicial management.

DOWNEY, Liam; PROFESSOR EMERITUS, NUI MAYNOOTH, UCD
b 1937; *m* June; 2*s* 2*d*; edu. North Monastery Cork; University College Dublin B. Sc; Reading University, Ph.D; Professor Emeritus. Agricultural Research Institute (research milk and dairy products) 1960-74; National Science Council 1974-79; Chief Executive, An Foras Forbartha (The National Institute for Physical Planning Construction Research); Director, An Chomhairle Oiliuna

Talmhaiochta (ACOT) – The Council for Development in Agriculture 1983-88; Director, Eradication of Animal Diseases Board (ERAD) 1988-92; Director, Teagasc, The Agriculture and *Food* Development Authority 1994-2002; Publ. wide range of research publications and Food *Quality and Nutrition* 1977; member Royal Society of Antiquaries of Ireland (RSAI), Friends of the Library, (Trinity College); awarded Doctor of Science (D.Sc) by UCD in recognition of international contribution of published research in milk and dairy products. Emeritus professor of Agri UCD NUI Maynooth; Agri Business Consultant. Recreations: archaeology, history and hurling. Contact: University College Dublin Faculty of Agriculture, Belfield Campus, Dublin 4 **T** 01 716 71941 **F** 01 716 1118 email Agri-Food@ucd.ie

> An excellent media former, highly intellectual and fitness fanatic, the hardworking former public servant is one of Ireland's strategic thinkers; deeply involved at EU level in the Foresight Studies on the future of the Agri food and rural economy; a keen Cork GAA supporter.

DOYLE, Anne Aideen; BROADCASTER
b 1952, Co. Wexford; *partner* Dan McGrattan ; *edu.* Loreto Abbey, Gorey, Co Wexford; UCD, BA H.Dip in Education; Senior Newscaster RTE; Dublin Corporation Libraries; Dept. of Foreign Affairs; RTE; Recreations: travel, history, reading and folklore. Contact: RTE, Montrose, Dublin 4 **T** 01 208 31111, 086 8183946 email doylea@rte.ie

> Great company, the original anchor woman who set the standards for radio and TV newscasting; at the coal face of newsbreaking for over a quarter of a century; still number one despite competition from other sources.

DOYLE, Avril née Belton; PUBLIC REPRESENTATIVE; PRESIDENT OF THE EQUESTRIAN FEDERATION OF IRELAND
b 1949, Dublin; *m* Fred Doyle; 3*d*; *edu.* Holy Child Convent, Killiney; University College Dublin, BSc Biochemistry; MEP. Elected to Wexford County Council and Wexford Corporation, 1974; first woman Mayor of Wexford 1976; elected Fine Gael Deputy for Wexford, 1982,1989 and 1992-97; Senator and Fine Gael Leader in the Senate, 1989-92; Minister of State at the Department of Finance, 1985-87; Minister of State at the Departments of the Taoiseach, Finance and Transport, Energy and Communications 1994-97; member of the Senate 1997-99; President, Equestrian Federation of Ireland; MEP Leinster 1999-2004, MEP of The East 2004 to date. Recreations: all sports, particularly equestrian. Contact: European Parliament Offices, 43 Molesworth Street, Dublin 2. **T** 01 605 7900. **F** 01 605 7999

> Brought up with strong Fine Gael roots, father and grandfather were both members of the Oireachtas, grandfather, Paddy Belton also served as Lord Mayor of Dublin; has had a career of fluctuating fortunes; narrowly beaten by Mary Bannotti for the Fine Gael nomination for the Presidency in 1997; retained her seat at the European Parliament in 2004 despite an almost internecine war with colleague Mairead McGuinness (*qv*).

DOYLE, Conor; DIRECTOR DOYLE GROUP
b 1945, Cork; *m* Mareta Cosgrave; 2*s*; *edu.* Christian Brother School, Cork; St Gerard's Bray; Glenstal Abbey; University College Dublin; BA; Kings Inns BL. Barrister At Law; Director Doyle Group; joined family business (shipping agents, warehousing, stevedoring) 1970; Vice-Chairman Cork and Limerick Savings Bank 1989-90; Chairman Cork Harbour Commissioners 1990-92; President, Cork Chamber of Commerce,1997-90; Chairman National Sculpture Factory 2002 to date; Honorary Consul of Finland, Cork. Clubs: Kinsale YC, Royal Cork YC, Royal Irish Yacht Club, Kildare Street and University Club. Recreations: tennis, skiing, yachting. Contact: D.F. Doyle & Co. Ltd., Victoria House, 1 Victoria Road, Cork. **T** 021 4311199 email dconordoyle@eircom.net

> Member of old Cork family with long established links in commerce and sailing; former Commodore, Kinsale Yacht Club and Chairman of International Dragon Association.

DOYLE, Robert Martin; CELEBRITY PHOTOGRAPHER
b 1955, Wicklow; single; 1*d*; *edu.* St. Ignatius Jesuit College, London; co-owner OSD Photo Agency, Dublin; leading celebrity and fashion photographer supplying national and international newspapers

Robert Doyle

and celebrity magazines. Publ. with business partner produced UNICEF Ireland book 'For the Children, a celebration of the Family' which featured exclusive pictures of Irelands most famous families. Recreations: spending time with his daughter, Georgia; getting away from it all on his Harley Davidson. Contact: Greenhill House, Greenhill Road, Wicklow. **T** 086 252 3397 email: rdoylewicklow@eircom.net

> One of Ireland's most popular and prolific photographers; travels the world with UNICEF Ireland high-lighting their many projects.

DOYLE, Roger; COMPOSER

b 1949, Dublin; *m* Mary; 1*s*; *edu.* St. Paul's College, Raheny, Co. Dublin; Sutton Park School, Co. Dublin; Operating Theatre produced a one woman multimedia show *'Angel/Babel'* with actress Olwen Fouere 1999; *Under The Green Time*, a collaboration with the Netherlands Wind Ensemble 2000; began work on *Passades,* 2002; awarded the Programme Music Prize, Bourges International Electroacoustic Music Competition, with a piece from Babel *'Spirit Levels'*, France, 1997; member Aosdana. Recreations: cappuccinos in Greystones. Contact: web www.rogerdoyle.com

> Quiet and friendly, is well liked and admired by other musicians; an eclectic personality who has made a very considerable impact on modern Irish Music by his understanding of technology and its impact on composition.

DOYLE, Tamarisk 'Tamso'; PR MANAGER, HORSE RACING IRELAND

b 1977, single; *edu.* Newbridge College; Alexandra College, Milltown, Dublin 6; UCD Bachelor of Arts Degree in History of Art & Archaeology; DIT Aungier St, Masters in Public Relations; Amateur Jockey licence, certificate in film history and cinematography, acting certificate from Gaiety School of Acting; " During University I did 6 years part time work as the 1st lady spotter at Goffs Bloodstock sales. Following my MA in PR I worked a year in Slattery PR before the job as PR Manager in HRI came up. I now promote something I really love, Irish Horse racing, and I have been here for 3 1/2 years. Recreations: "I love eating out and trying new restaurants and wines. My favourite spots are the Charthouse in Dingle, Rathsallagh House, Peploes on the Green. I'm partial to a bit of boogying too. Going racing, visiting Art Galleries and reading, snow and water skiing, walking, boating, shopping & fashion" Contact: Horse Racing Ireland, Kill, Co Kildare. **T** 045 842 841 **F** 045 842 881 email tdoyle@hri.ie

> From a Kildare family steeped in bloodstock tradition; vivacious, enthusiastic, hardworking and bringing much needed innovative flair to Irish racing.

DOYLE, Vincent 'Vinnie'; EDITOR EMERITUS IRISH INDEPENDENT

b 1938, Dublin; *m* Gertrude Leech; 3*s*, *edu.* St Vincent's College, Glasnevin. Joined the *Irish Press* as a copyboy 1959; film critic and feature writer 1961-63; joined the *Sunday Independent* colour magazine 1963-64; freelance journalist UK1964-67; journalist *Evening Herald* 1967-70; assistant editor1970–73; night editor, *Irish Independent* 1973–76; editor, *Evening Herald* 1976-81; editor *Irish Independent* 1981–2005; editor Emeritus 2005 to date; Recreations: the media. Contact: Independent Newspapers, 27-32 Talbot Street, Dublin 1. **T** 01 705 53 33 email vdoyle@unison.independent.ie

> The last and longest serving of the quintessential, traditional newspaper editors; liked and loathed but always respected within media circles; his contribution to Irish journalism earned him a honorary doctorate from NUI and the ESB Special Recognition Award 2005.

DOYLE, William; CHIEF EXECUTIVE, NEWBRIDGE SILVERWARE

b 1958, Dublin; *m* Monica; 3*s* 1*d*; *edu.* 1971-76 Newbridge College, Newbridge, Co. Kildare; Trinity College Dublin, BBS (Batchelor in Business Studies); Chief Executive, The Newbridge Silverware Company. Commenced career in the family silverware company 1976 and worked through the company to become Chief Executive. voted Irish Marketing Institute, Marketer of the Year 2004; Bank of Scotland Best in Business Award 2005; Golden Spider Award ESAT/BT Best Commerical Web Site 2003. Clubs: Rathsallagh Golf Club; Curragh Golf Club. Recreations: skiing, rugby, golf, reading, art (Contemporary); Contact: The Newbridge Silverware Company, Cutlery Road, Newbridge, Co. Kildare **T** 045 431401 **F** 045 432759 email wdoyle@newbridgecutlery.ie

William Doyle

One of the most innovative businessmen in the country which put him among the finalists in the Ernst and Young Entrepreneur of the Year Award 2005; has grown his family's company from a mid size traditional cutlery company to a major, commercially successful lifestyle, silverware business with a significant export business.

DREW, Joseph Ronald "Ronnie"; ENTERTAINER

b 1934, *m* Deirdre McCartan; 1*s* 1*d*; *edu.* Christian Brothers School, Dun Laoghaire; worked as an electrician, draper's assistant, dishwasher, telephone operator (Telecom) and English teacher in Spain; started musical career as a boy soprano; studied guitar and became interested in folk music and flamenco; Ronnie Drew Group, formed 1963 (following a chance meeting in O'Donoghues pub); group later called the Dubliners, comprising John Skeahan, Barney McKenna, Sean Cannon and the late Luke Kelly; a popular group which toured and recorded extensively; recordings included *Celebration* 1987, released to celebrate 25th anniversary of group; left Dubliners 1995; subsequent recordings include, Dirty Rotten Shame, Sony Records (with songs written by Christy Moore, Donal McDonald, Keith Donald, Elvis Costelloe, Bono, Simon Carmody, Shane McGowan); has recorded music and poetry with Jah Wobble; guested on records with Giles Servat, Antonio Breschi; appeared in one-man show 'Ronnie I hardly Knew You' (director, Derek Chapman) to widespread acclaim; a gravel voiced Dub, the people's choice. Recreations: Contact: Dara Records, Unit 4 Great Ship Street, Dublin 8. **T** 01 478 1891 **F** 01 478 2143 email: shop-at-dolphin-dara.ie web: www.dolphin-dara.ie

Charming, raconteur extraordinaire; a living legend, internationally acclaimed as the lead singer in The Dubliners; a consummate performer with a huge personal following.

DRUMM, Brendan; PROFESSOR, CHIEF EXECUTIVE OFFICER, HEALTH SERVICE EXECUTIVE

b 1958, Manorhamilton, Co. Leitrim; *edu.* Summerhill College Sligo; University College Galway; MB, B.Ch; BAO 1979; Chief Executive Officer, Health Service Executive. Postgraduate clinical training at the Hospital for Sick Children in Toronto 1981; was subsequently appointed consultant Paediatric Gastroenterologist and assistant professor at the University of Toronto; appointed consultant paediatrician at Regional Hospital Limerick 1989–91; appointed professor and head of Department of Paediatrics at University College Dublin and consultant Paediatric Gastroenterologist at Our Lady's Hospital for Sick Children in Crumlin 1991-2005; CEO Health Service Executive 2005 to date; Publ. reviewer of 20 publications, a member of the editorial board of three publications and has had almost 100 manuscripts, book chapters and reviews published; Clubs: Recreations: Contact: HEA, Oak House, Limetree Avenue, Millennium Park, Naas, Co. Kildare. **T** 045 8804400 **F** 1890 200893 email info@hse.ie web www.hse.ie

Assumed what some people deem "the poison chalice of chief executives in the State sector" after Professor Halligan publicly turned it down; played hard ball before accepting the appointment, guaranteeing his chair in UCD on retirement and also the support services he considered necessary to ensure he discharged the most influential and highly paid position in the health service; friendly disposition, a good communicator will have his work cut out to deliver the health service the public is now clamoring for.

David Drumm

DRUMM, David; CEO, ANGLO IRISH BANK

b 1967, Skerries, Co.Dublin; *m* Lorraine; 2*d*; *edu.* De La Salle CBS Skerries; CEO Anglo Irish Bank; trained as a chartered accountant; qualified with Deloitte Touche; accountant with Deloittes 1984–88; Equity Enterprise (a venture capital company) 1988–93; senior manager Audit and Corporate Finance, Bastow Charlton Accountants 1993; joined Anglo Irish Bank as an assistant manager 1993; promoted to manager 1995; moved to Boston to set up Anglo Irish operation there 1997; returned to HQ to head up bank's lending operation 2002; appointed CEO Anglo Irish Bank plc. 2005; Clubs: Skerries Golf Club. Recreations: golf, fitness, hard rock music, reading biographies and American history. Contact: 18 -21, Anglo Irish Bank, St. Stephen's Green, Dublin 2. **T** 01 616200 **F** 01 616 2488 email angloirishbank.ie web www.angleirishbank.ie

The 'dark horse' who parachuted to the top job without even being a member of the main board; an accountant who applied for branch manager post at Anglo and was appointed assistant manager for much less money; wouldn't have the charisma of his flamboyant predecessor but an extremely effective administrator; disentangling himself from Seanie's legacy and making his own mark will be one of the most interesting aspects of Drumm's tenure; consensus is that Anglo is in safe hands; doubling the bank's profits between now and the end of the decade will constitute a job well done.

DRURY, Fintan; DIRECTOR PLATINUM ONE
b 1950 Dublin; *m* Brenda; 2*s* 2*d*; *edu.* Blackrock College Dublin; University College Dublin, MA (Politics); Company Director. Joined RTÉ journalist, news and current affairs; Drury Communications 1989-99; Drury Sports Management 1991; consultant to the European Golf Tour 1995 to date; American Express World Golf Championship, and Ryder Cup 2002 to date; board member Anglo Irish Bank Corporation 2002 to date; Chairman Paddy Power plc. 2003 to date; acquired Beacon Conference and Incentive, merged both companies to form Platinum One 2004; Chairman RTÉ Authority 2005-'06, resigned Jan. 2006 due to conflict of interest over government's stated intention to demand freedom to air Ryder Cup coverage in September 2006; FIFA license to act as player agent in professional football. Recreations; reading,family, golf, tennis, Manchester City; Contact:Platinum One, The Court Yard, Carmen Hall Road, Sandyford Dublin 18 **T** 2062900 **F** 206 2999 email info@platinumone.ie

The former journalist first parlayed his contacts into a successful PR company before cashing it in to concentrate on sports management where his clients include Manchester United's Liam Miller and Brian Kerr to rugby international Gordon D'Arcy; now sits on the board of a number of top companies; in 2005 got the much sought after, influential chair of the RTE Authority only to resign from that position some months later due to conflict of interest over the Ryder Cup TV rights.

DRURY, Paul; EDITOR, IRISH DAILY MAIL
b 1957, Dublin; *m* Áine Ní Fhéinne; 2*s* 1*d*; *edu.* Wesley College, Dublin; College of Commerce, Dublin. Editor *The Evening Herald* 1994-99; editor *Irish Daily Star* 1994; editor *Ireland on Sunday* 2000 – '06; editor Irish Daily Mail 2006 – todate; Clubs: United Arts Club, Dublin, Royal Dublin Society. Recreations: walking, gardening. Contact: *Ireland On Sunday* 3rd Floor, Embassy House, Ballsbridge, Dublin 4 **T** 01 637 5600 **F** 01 637 5940 email pauldrury@ireland.com

The fluent Irish speaker is an extraordinarily hard worker with an uncanny feel for a news story; having honed his trade side by side with the 'master' Vinnie Doyle (*qv*); was always tipped to make his own mark in Irish journalism; after a shaky start at IOS caused his old 'friends' at the Indo Group to sit up and take notice, not to mention the open war fare that has ensued following the launch of an Irish edition of *The Daily Mail* which he presides over.

DUFFY, Brian; CHAIRMAN, DIAGEO IRELAND
b 1952, Belfast; Jeanette; 2*s* 1*d*; *edu.* St. Malachy's College, Belfast; Queen's University Belfast; B.Sc (Econ); FCA; Global Brand Director/Chairman Diageo Ireland; managing director Diageo Ireland, managing director Guinness Group Ireland 1999 to date; president Desnoes and Geddes Jamaica; managing director Guinness Northern Ireland; Clubs: Clandeboye Golf Club, Royal Portrush Golf Club, The Kildare Hotel and Country Club. Recreations: reading, music, golf, scuba diving. Contact: St. James Gate, Dublin 8 **T** 01 643 5035 **F** 01 408 4803 email brian.duffy@diageo.com

The Belfast-born company director was central to the decision to close Park Royal brewery in London and to centralize all beer production to St James Gate in Dublin thereby guaranteeing the Guinness and Dublin remain synonymous as one of Ireland's most recognizable international brands.

DUFFY, Joseph Augustine; BISHOP OF CLOGHER
b 1934; single; *edu.* St. Macartan's College, Monaghan; St. Patrick's College Maynooth 1951-54, 1958–60, Pontifical University 1954–58, BA, MA, BD; Teacher at St. Macartan's College 1960–72; Enniskillen, Co Fermanagh 1972–79; Bishop of Clogher 1979 to date. Publ. *Lough Derg Today, Patrick In His Own Words*. Clubs: Clogher Historical Society. Recreations: local history, Irish language, travel. Contact: Oifig na Easpais, Monaghan. **T** 047 81019 **F** 047 84773 email cloghdiocoffmon@eircom.net

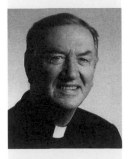

Joseph Duffy

A popular man with a soft approach but not a radical thinker; like all bishops dislikes having his authority questioned.

Joe Duffy

DUFFY, Joe; BROADCASTER

b 1956, *m* June Meehan; 2*s* 1*d*; *edu.* St. John's College, Ballyfermot, Dublin; VEC Ballyfermot; qualified as social worker and family therapist; President TCD Students Union & USI 1979-84; Probation and Welfare Service 1974-88; broadcaster RTÉ 1988 to date; presenter Liveline RTÉ Radio 1; Clubs: St. Mary's Youth Club Ballyfermot, Dublin. Recreations: broadcasting, parenting, swimming, walking; reading, painting (not hall, stairs and landing!) Contact: 395, Clontarf Road, Dublin 3. **T** 01 833 4713 email joe@rte.ie

A consummate broadcaster with an innate feel for his topics and his listeners; a real man of the people; bad press on his programme is enough to send shivers down the spine of even the most hardened politicians; no topic is taboo and there are no sacred cows; doesn't tolerate the usual talk show wafflers; on a given day could well be the most influential person in the country; received a €600,000 a year offer from Newstalk 106.FM which he turned down.

DUFFY, Kevin; CHAIRMAN, LABOUR COURT

b 1949, Dublin; *m* Therese; 1*s* 2*d*; *edu.* Pearse College, Clogher Road, Dublin; College of Technology, Bolton Street, Dublin; Kings Inns Dublin, Barrister at Law; trade union official 1973-88; assistant general secretary ICTU 1988-97; deputy chairman Labour Court 1997-2003; chairman Labour Court 2003 to date; Contact: The Labour Court, Tom Johnson House, Haddington Road, Dublin 4 **T** 01 613 6602 **F** 01 613 6667 email kevin-duffy@envcrp.ie

DUFFY, Patrick 'Paddy'; PUBLIC RELATIONS, ADVISOR, LOBBYIST

b 1943, Kells, Co. Meath; *m* Margaret; 1*s* 2*d*; *edu.* Christian Brothers St. Joseph's Baldoyle; Coláiste Chiaráin, Bray; St. Mary's Teacher Training College Marino; UCD; The Lateran University, Rome; University of Touraine; University of Bonn; N.T., B.A., H Dip in Ed. European Linguist; managing director The Right Word; school principal & college lecturer; press secretary in the Department of Finance; special adviser to and speech writer for An Taoiseach; managing director of the Right Word Company; Publ. thousands of political speeches, news releases, media profiles and written contributions. Over a dozen musicals, many songs and poems. Clubs: ALAA Sports; James Joyce Centre. Recreations: politics, business, education, Irish literature, music, art, languages, writing music, poetry, reading, gardening, An Ghaeilge, Peil Ghaelach. Contact: Harcourt House, 19 Harcourt Street, Dublin 2. **T** 01 475 3928 **F** 01 475 3943 email paddy@therightword.ie

Friendly, hardworking, great fun, a razor sharp intellect and intellectual to boot, the multilingual public relations executive is extremely well connected politically; following his resignation as the Taoiseach's Chef de Cabinet, founded his own extremely successful company which boasts a blue chip, international client list.

DUGGAN, Noel; CHAIRMAN NOEL C. DUGGAN LTD, MILL STREET HORSES LTD

b 1933, Millstreet, Co. Cork; *m* Maureen Corkery; 2*s* 2*d*; *edu.* Millstreet National School; executive chairman of Noel C. Duggan; took over small family hardware business 1946; built it into one of the major hardware, builders providers and structural steel building providers in the South West; Chairman and Managing Director, Mill Street Horses Ltd., a company involved in breeding, training and marketing the Irish Sport Horse internationally; developed Mill Street Horse Village; Managing Director, Millstreet International Horse Show. Recreations: all sports, family and business. Contact: Noel C. Duggan Ltd., Main Street, Millstreet, Co. Cork. **T** 029 70039. **F** 029 70305.

'Build it and they will come' might well have been this North Cork businessman's motto; he did and they did; created a state of the art arena in his native Millstreet which has hosted everything from Eurovision to professional boxing and international rock concerts; has built Millstreet International Horse Show into a major show on the circuit; ambitious for his part of Munster; good company and a great raconteur.

DUKES, Alan; DIRECTOR INSTITUTE EUROPEAN AFFAIRS

b 1945, Dublin; *m* Fionnuala Corcoran; 2*d*; *edu.* Colaiste Mhuire, Parnell Square, Dublin; University College Dublin, BA, MA; Director Institute European Affairs. Chief economist NFA 1969–73;

director EU office IFA Brussels 1973–77; advisor to EU Commissioner Richard Burke 1977–80; TD Kildare South (FG)1981–2002; Minister Agriculture 1981-82; Minister for Finance 1982–86; Minister for Justice 1986–87; Leader Fine Gael 1987–90. Contact: 8 North Great Georges Street, Dublin 1. **T** 01 874 6756 **F** 01 878 6880 email: info@iiea.com

One of the brightest deputies in Dáil Éireann for over twenty years; excellent media performer but showed political naivety at times; famous for the Tallaght Strategy which gave conditional support to the Haughey led Fianna Fáil Government to restore the nation's finances; joined a select group of TDs who became Ministers on their first day in the Dáil (incl. Kevin Boland and Martin O'Donoghue); the poor showing of Austin Curry in the 1990 presidential election led him to lose the leadership of FG to John Bruton.

Alan Dukes

DUNGAN, Myles; BROADCASTER

b 1954, *m* Isolde O'Doherty; 2*s* 2*d*; *edu.* UCD, MA 1977 (History), Higher DipEd; Presenter 'Rattlebag', RTE 2000 to date; presenter Five Seven Live 1988–2000; continuity announcer RTE Radio 1977-82; reporter RTE Radio/TV Sports Presenter 1982-88; presenter 'Today At Five' and 'Five Seven Live' (RTE Radio) 1988 to date. *Publ. A Good Walk Spoiled; Irish Voices From the Great War; Preferred Lies; They Should Grow Not Old; The Theft of the Irish Crown Jewels; Snuff* (novel with Jim Lusby). Clubs: Headfort Golf Club, Kells, Total Fitness, Sandyford. Recreations: cycling, jogging, golf, walking, soccer (Arsenal), music, reading, film and theatre; 'Have seen Everest, still want to see the Grand Canyon and Ireland winning the World Cup (and Arsenal winning the Champions League). Contact: R.T.E. Radio Center, Donnybrook, Dublin 4. **T** 01 208 3111

Originally considered an unusual choice for the Rattle Bag Slot, he has grown in confidence and stature; has a terrific capacity to draw all kinds of aesthetic and emotionally responsive answers from his interviewees; has overall been a very considerable success and an asset to radio in particular as his vocal timbre suits the medium.

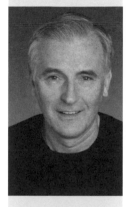

Myles Dungan

DUNICAN, Paddy; SECRETARY MANAGER OF KILBEGGAN RACES & AUCTIONEERS

b 1962, Mullingar, Co.Westmeath; single; *edu.* Mercy Secondary School Kilbeggan; Athlone Institute of Auctioneering; Farming; Race Course Management, Auctioneering; Business. Clubs: Chairman Kilbeggan Community Group; Sponsorship co-ordinator National Ploughing Championships; Mook Shaw Society; Tullamore Show; Chamber of Commerce. Recreations: horse racing, GAA, farming, sport in general, charity work. Contact: Main Street, Kilbeggan Co Westmeath. **T** 0506 33333 **F** 0506 33334 email info@paddydunican.com.

Gregarious and recognized as a first class operator; always manages to get huge crowds to his track which he has significantly upgraded in recent years.

DUNNE, Aidan; ART CRITIC

b 1955, *m* Helen Rock; *edu.* Crescent College, Limerick; Templeogue College, Dublin; National College of Art & Design (Dip Painting ANCAD); Art Critic *In Dublin* 1978-83; Art Critic *Sunday Press* 1983-87; Art Critic *Sunday Tribune* 1987; Art Critic *The Irish Times* to date; Publ. monographs on Barrie Cooke, Michael Mulcahy, Anne Madden; numerous catalogue essays. Contact: Irish Times, 10 – 16 D'Olier Street, Dublin 2. **T** 01 675 8000 **F** 01 677 9181

A pleasant and unassuming man, his early years marked him out as the artists' critic, with a sense of style and insightful writing; his move to the *Irish Times* seems to be a treading of water despite an increase in column inches; a return to acuity and sharper insights may be anticipated.

DUNNE, Ben; DIRECTOR WESTPOINT HEALTH AND FITNESS LEISURE CENTRE

b 1949, Cork; *m* Mary Goodwin; 3*s* 1*d*; *edu.* Presentation Brothers College, Cork; joined family business founded by father, Ben Dunne; Managing Director, Dunnes Stores until 1993; sold his interest in the business to the remainder of sister Margaret Heffernan (*qv*) and the rest of the Dunne family; 1995 to date established Westpoint Leisure Centres and has built up an impressive property portfolio. Clubs: Kildare Hotel and Country Club, Portmarnock Golf Club, Luttrellstown Golf Club. Recreations: golf, GAA. Contact: Westpoint Health and Fitness Leisure Centre, Blanchardstown Town Centre, Dublin 15. **T** 01 822 1103

Ben Dunne

The son of the legendary Ben Dunne, Ben Jnr. looked as if, like so many other Pres boys, he would follow in his father's footsteps and take the reins of the biggest drapery and grocery business in the country; in that business milieu he was considered the toughest dealer in the country; also made a fortune on overnight cash deposits; his Florida adventure started a series of events that fundamentally changed his life and the lives of many others; it was indirectly the precursor of the Tribunals that followed; well known for his largesse to the lateCharlie Haughey who coined the immortal line 'Thanks Big Fella'; a golf fanatic, the cognoscenti have discovered that since he took control of his own money from Dunnes Stores he is far more careful about how he spends it; departed the family business in the mid '90's with around €100 millon in his pocket and embarked upon the establishment of a leisure chain - Westpoint Health and Fitness Centres, as well as investing in property; still finds time for a punt on the golf course!

DUNNE, Felim Joseph; ARCHITECT

b 1959, Dublin; *m* Katy McGuiness; 1*s* 3*d*; *edu* De la Salle College, Churchtown, Dublin; School of Architecture, University College Dublin B. Arch (NUI); member Royal Institute of the Architects of Ireland; Architect; Director, Burdon Craig Dunne Henry Architects; Joined firm of (the late) Sir James Stirling RA, London; worked on projects such as New Science Library, University of California, The Stafe Music School, Theatre Academy, Stuttgart; Dublin projects include the Tropical Fruit Store, Sir John Rogerson's Quay, Design Yard Temple Bar, U2 Studio, Hanover Quay; 2003 BCDH won the national open competition for Landmark Tower, Britain Quay, Dublin Docklands (scheduled for completion 2008); Publ. *Architecture d'Aujourdhui* (France); *National Art Collections Fund* (UK); *Baumeister* (Germany); *Wallpaper* (UK); *Domus* (Italy); *D'Side* (Irl); *Architecture Ireland; Reflecting City* (Irl); *Building Design* (UK); *Architectural Review* (UK); *Architectural Digest* (US); *Architect's Journal* (UK). Recreations: worshipped at the altar of Le Corbusier and pilgrim to the sites of his miraculous works across the globe, inelegant horseman, early morning pier walker, enthusiastic consumer of good food and fine wines, great guest. Contact: BCDH Architects, 89 Booterstown Avenue, Blackrock, Co.Dublin. **T** 01 215 8500 **F** 01 215 8501 email felim.dunne@bcdh.com

John Bentley Dunne

DUNNE, John Bentley; DESIGNER/MANAGING DIRECTOR

b 1947, single; *edu.* St. Joseph's Secondary School, Cahir, Co Tipperary; Grafton Academy of Dress Design, Dublin; Designer, John Bentley Label, supplier women's outerwear garments to the retail trade all over Ireland, Scotland and England 1970 to date. Awards: won two of the three major awards when in the Grafton Academy, including the most promising student 1996; Dress of the Year Award 1982/83; Dress of the Year Award 1983/84; Coat of the Year Award 1984/85; Dress of the Year Award 1986/87; *Late Late Show* Fashion Award. Recreations: restoring an 18th century house & garden for the last 20 years. Contact; Marchwilton Limited, Collon House, Collon, Co Louth. **T** 041 982 6187 **F** 041 982 6741 email marchwiltonltd@eircom.net

His fashion labels are always in touch with the latest trends from Paris and Milan.

DUNNE, Sean; PROPERTY DEVELOPER/CONSTRUCTION

b 1954, Tullow, Co. Carlow; *m* 1st Jennifer Coyle (m diss); 2*s* 1*d*; *m* 2nd Gayle Killilea; 1*s*; *edu.* Tullow National School, Co. Carlow; Bolton Street College of Technology; Dip Quantity Surveying; Property Developer; Chairman/Managing Director Mountbrook Homes. One of the country's top property developers; co-developer with Sean Mulryan White Water Shopping Complex, Newbridge, Co. Kildare, the largest shopping complex in the country outside Dublin; fought off all competition to win the Jury's Hotel site in Ballsbridge, 2005; Clubs: Kildare Hotel and Country, Landsdowne Rugby Club. Recreations: golf, GAA, travel. Contact: Mountbrook Homes, 67 Merrion Square Dublin 2. **T** 01 6110300 **F** 01 6110311 email info@mountbrookhomes.ie

Spent his early years in the UK as a surveyor; returned in the late '80's and acquired the 70 acres St Helens, Booterstown site with Paul Coulson (*qv*) and Davies directors David Shubottom (*qv*) and Kyran Mc Loughlin (*qv*); litigation and national headlines followed, which left 'The Dunner' with practically nothing; quickly re established himself by acquiring several building sites particularly in the Newbridge/Celbridge area; closely connected to Fianna Fáil, built former FF minister Charlie Mc Creevy's new home at Blundellsland, Sallins; has extensive property interests in his own right and jointly with Sean Mulryan's (*qv*) Ballymore Homes; July 2004 hit the headlines again with his exotic second marriage in Italy to gossip columnist Gayle Killelea and the week long Mediterranean cruise and endless parties on board the Christina, once owned by Onassis; August 2005 hit national headlines yet again, bidding €275 million for the five and a half acre Jurys/Doyle site in Ballsbridge as well as becoming a major shareholder in Jury's plc; a tough, shrewd operator, he is thoroughly enjoying his new profile.

DUNNE, Veronica; SINGER/ MUSIC TEACHER
b 1927, *m* Peter McCarthy (decd); 1*s* 1*d*; *edu.* Sacred Heart Convent, Mount Sackville, Dublin; studied singing in Rome for four years; joined Royal Opera House, Covent Garden, London .singing major roles; Sandwith Welsh National Opera Company; English National Opera Company; Three Choirs Festival; toured internationally; numerous recordings with EMI; taught many of the important younger singers; board member of the National Concert Hall for many years; works as a teacher and international judge in singing competitions; awarded the Concorso Lirice; member Friends of the Vocal Arts.. Principal teacher Vocal and Dramatic Studies, College of Music, Dublin. Contact: Royal Irish Academy of Music, 36, Westland Row, Dublin, 2. **T** 01 676 4412 **F** 01 662 2798.

Powerful voice in the world of Irish music; a straight talking woman; excellent ear for a voice of promise; great charm masks determination and grit.

DUNPHY, Eamon Martin; JOURNALIST/AUTHOR
b 1945, Dublin, *m.* (separated); 1*s* 1*d*; *partner* Jane Gogan (*qv*); *edu.* St. Patrick's National School Drumcondra, Sandymount High School; editor/presenter of the Breakfast Show Newstalk,106 fm 2005 - 2006; joined RTE Radio 1 September 2006; *Publ: Only a Game?, A Strange Kind of Glory* (biography of Sir Matt Busby), *Unforgettable Fire* (biography of U2), *Keane* (biography of Roy Keane); journalist for various newspapers, Radio /TV. Contact: Radio One, RTE, Donnybrook, Dublin 4. **T** 01 208 3111 **F** 01 208 3080

The highest paid journalist in Ireland always gives value for money frequently dividing the nation with his opinionated reportage; a seasoned performer knows exactly what buttons to push to generate a controversy; extremely hard worker, great company.

DURCAN, Paul Francis; POET
b 1944; Dublin; separated. 2*d*; *edu.*Gonzaga College S.J., University College Dublin, BA (Archaeology & Medieval History); Ireland Chair of Poetry 2004-2007; Professor of Poetry; Awards: Patrick Kavanagh Award 1974; Whitbread Poetry Prize 1990; Publications: *Christmas Day* 1996, *Greetings Of Our Friends In Brazil* 1999; *Cries Of An Irish Caveman* 2001, *The Art Of Life* 2004, *Paul Durcan's Diary* 2003. Clubs: Ringsend Solo Club, Aosdána. Recreations: family, friends and travel. Contact: 14 Cambridge Avenue, Ringsend, Dublin 4. **T** 01 668 2276 **F** 01 668 2276

Liked, admired and sometimes feared, the power of the bard to call your name remains potent even in a modern Ireland; his sonorous tones, declaim in a low key way, his outlook on life, art, love; serious, worthy and full of good intent.

DURKAN, Mark John; PARTY LEADER, MEMBER OF PARLIAMENT, MEMBER OF NORTHERN IRELAND ASSEMBLY
b 1960, Derry; *m* Jackie; 1*d*; *edu.* St.Columb's College, Derry; Queen's University Belfast; MP and MLA; Leader of SDLP. Assistant to John Hume 1984; Member Derry City Council 1993-2000; Chairperson SDLP Party 1990-85; Multi-Party Talks Negotiator SDLP 1996-98; MLA (SDLP) Foyle 1998; Minister of Finance and Personnel 1999-2001; appointed leader SDLP 2001; Deputy First Minister Northern Ireland 2001-2002; MP (SDLP) Foyle 2005 to date. Contact: Northern Ireland Assembly, Parliament Buildings, Stormont Estate, Belfast BT4 3XX. **T** 028 9052 1649. **F** 028 9052 1329. Contact: 7B, Messines Terrace, Racecourse Road, Derry BT48 7OZ. **T** 028 71 360700 **F** 028 71 360808 email m.durkan@sdlp.ie

A nice man who was unlucky to follow John Hume as leader; against the odds he kept his MPs seat in Foyle and as an MLA member; performed well as Minister for Finance & Personnel in Stormont and has kept his grass roots student connections which stood to him at the recent elections; takes his duties as a public representative seriously and is a careful and conscientious politician; all things being equal he should have a meaningful and productive political future.

Mark Durkan

DWYER, Michael; FOUNDER & CHIEF EXECUTIVE PIGSBACK.COM
b 1965, Dundalk, Co Louth; *m* Karen Scanlan; *3d*; *edu.* Christian Brothers School, Dundalk; NIHE
(now DCU) marketing and languages; Chief Executive, Pigsback.com. W&R Jacob/Danone 1986-96;
Group Marketing Director, Green Isle Foods 1996-2000; Founder and Chief Executive
PIGSBACK.com March 2000, officially launched in UK Oct. 2005; Clubs: Naas Golf Club, Monread
Gym Naas, Co. Kildare; Recreations: horse racing, family, marathon running, golf. Contact Pigsback,
3016, Lake Drive, City West, Dublin 24. **T** 01 243 1900 email info @pigsback.com

The former marketing guru has successfully transferred his skills into the volatile IT
area with the establishment of Pigsback.com; building on the success of the company
in Ireland launched in the UK in 2005.

DWYER, Michael; JOURNALIST
b 1951, Tralee, Co. Kerry; single; *edu.* CBS Tralee, Co. Kerry; St Brendan's College, Killarney, Co.
Kerry; Trinity College Dublin; Administrator, Federation of Irish Film Societies 1978-82; Film Critic
In Dublin 1980-83; Co-founder Dublin Film Festival, 1985; Programme Director, Dublin Film
Festival, 1985-91; Film Critic, *The Irish Times*, 1988 to date; member NUJ; International Federation of
Film Critics; Awards: Arts Journalist of the Year, National Media Awards 1991. Recreations: cats,
media, books, politics, contemporary music, food, travel. Contact: *Irish Times* 10-16 D'Olier Street,
Dublin 2. **T** 01 679 2022 **F** 01 677 9181

Has set the standard for all movie critics in this country; still continues to be the film
fountain of knowledge; well regarded in movie mogul circles as a serious player; writes
well and doesn't bring personal baggage to his reportage and reviews.

EAMES, Most Rev and Rt. Hon. Robert, Henry, 'Robin'; ARCHIBISHOP, PRIMATE AND LIFE PEER
b 1937, Belfast; *m* Ann Christine Daly; 2*s*; *edu*. Belfast Royal Academy; Methodist College Belfast; Queen's University, Belfast; Trinity College Dublin; LL.D.(hc), Ph. D(Law), LL.D. DD; Archbishop of Armagh, Primate of All Ireland, Member of the House of Lords (Life Peer UK). University Tutor; Deacon St. Clement's Belfast 1960-63; Ordained 1963; Curate Dromore Cathedral 1964; Rector Gilnahirk, Rector Dundela Belfast 1966-75; Bishop of Derry & Raphoe 1975-80; Bishop of Down & Dromore 1980-86; Archbishop of Armagh, Senior Primate of the Anglican Communion 1986 – 31 December 2006. *Publ. Quiet Revolution* 1970; *Through Lent* 1973; *Chains To Be Broken* 1992; numerous articles in legal, ecclesiastical, university journals. Clubs: The Atheneum, London, University & Kildare Street, Dublin. Recreations: reading, travel, supporting rugby in Ireland, sailing. Contact: See House, Cathedral Close, Armagh BT61 7EE. **T** 00 44 37 522 851
F 00 44 37 52 7823 email larchbishop@armagh.anglican.org

As the Senior Primate in the Anglican community he is widely regarded as a moderating influence; his fire fighting skills are best seen in the Synods of his own Dioceses and Metropolitan Province, as well as the committees of Anglicanism; regarded as a politically astute and adroit, if cautious, successor to St. Patrick; has announced his decision to retire on 31 December 2006.

EARLEY, Dermot; MAJOR GENERAL, DEPUTY CHIEF OF STAFF OF THE DEFENCE FORCES
b 1948, Castlebar, Co Mayo; *m* Mary Egan; 3*s* 3*d*; *edu*. St Nathy's College, Ballaghaderreen, Co. Roscommon; The Military Academy, Curragh, Co. Kildare; St. Mary's College, Strawberry Hill, Twickenham; University of Limerick; The Royal College of Defence Studies, London; MA (Peace and Development Studies); Specialist Diploma Physical Education 9 S.Dip. Ed. Army Officer; joined the Defence Forces 1965; commissioned officer 1967; served in the Curragh, Defence Forces HQ and in the Eastern Brigade; overseas tours of duty in Lebanon (UNIFIL), Middle East (UNTSO– 4WDOF); Deputy Military Advisor to the Sec.Gen.UN HQ New York 1987–91; promoted Lt. Col. 1995; promoted Colonel 2001; promoted Brigadier General 2004; Major General 2004; *Publ.* Short articles and papers on conflict resolution for a number of international publicationns biography *The Earley Years* with John Scally (1994); played gaelic football for Roscommon for 23 years; won minor under 21 National League 1979; Railway Cup 1967 and 1969; 5 Connacht senior medals; 2 All Star awards 1974 and 1979. Clubs: Sarsfields GAA Club, Newbridge, Co. Kildare (Chairman 2005); Curragh Golf Club; Military Heritage of Ireland Trust. Recreations: sports particularly gaelic games, current affairs, reading. Contact: Defence Forces Headquarters, Parkgate Street, Dublin 8. **T** 01 804 2290 **F** 01 804 2272 email earley@eircom.net

Robin Eames

One of the all time great Gaelic footballers who never won an All Ireland Senior medal; following his long playing career became involved in GAA management in Kildare and Roscommon; he and his son Dermot Jnr are unique in being the only father and son who have won GAA All Star Awards; the popular Roscommon man has had a meteoric rise through the ranks of the army; is now well positioned to be the next Chief of Staff.

EGAN, Barry Peter; JOURNALIST
b 1967, Dublin; separated; *edu*. De La Salle, Churchtown, Dublin 14; chief feature writer, *Sunday Independent*. Joined *New Musical Express*, London 1987; joined *Sunday Independent* 1991; editor Arts Section (Culture Vultures); edited several magazines for *Sunday Independent*; work published in magazines in Australia, America, Spain, Italy, France, Japan and UK. Publ. *Redheads* (forward to coffee table book), published in Germany and the US 1999. Clubs: Lillies, Renards, David Lloyd, Riverview. Recreations: tennis, restaurants, art, cinema, swimming, Paul Weller, Gucci, yoga, sex. Contact: Sunday Independent, 27–30 Talbot Street, Dublin 1. **T** 01 705 55645 email egan_b@hotmail.com.

Titian haired reporter for the rich and famous; hardworking and dedicated to his job which he seems to hugely enjoy.

EGAN, Dr. Dermot Patrick; BOARD MEMBER, NATIONAL CONCERT HALL
b 1934, Co Carlow; *m* Noreen; 4*s*; *edu*. St. Enda's College Galway, University College Dublin; Columbia University, New York, USA; BA; H. Dip.Ed. MA (Psychology); Former Chairman, National Concert Hall. Director National Concert Hall, Dublin2006 -todate; *Publ. Joint Publication: Leaders* &

Innovators in Irish Management. Contact: The National Concert Hall, Earlsfort Terrace, Dublin 2 **T** 01 417 0077 **F** 01 417 0078 email info@nch.ie .www.nch.ie/

The sartorial, golf loving, former banker (Allied Irish Bank) continues as a director of the board he used to preside over.

Desmond Egan

EGAN, Desmond; WRITER/POET
b 1936, Athlone; *m* Vivienne Abbot Egan; 2*d*; *edu.* St. Finians College, Mullingar, Co Westmeath, NUI Maynooth BA; University College Dublin MA, H.Dip.Ed; D. Litt Washburn University, 1998; full time writer since 1987; Published 15 books of poetry, one of prose and two translations of Greek plays; 18 Collections of his translated poetry published in France, Germany, Romania, Spain, Italy, Russia, Japan, Czech Republic, Bulgaria, Hungary, China and Poland. Awards: received the National Poetry Foundation of USA Award 1983 and, among others, the Bologna Literary Award in Italy 1998. Contact: Great Connell, Co Kildare. email viv1@iol.ie

A poet of inner turmoil and angst; writes with painful internal imagery and gives it flesh and sinew; quite introverted as a writer, he keeps his pen sharp with self revelatory poetic forms.

Felim Egan

EGAN, Felim; ARTIST
b 1952, Belfast; *m* Janet Pierce; 3 step children; *edu.* St. Columb's College, Derry; St. Joseph's High, Strabane; Art Foundation, College of Art Belfast,1970; Portsmouth Polytechnic, BA Hons 1971-74; Slade School of Fine Art, University College, London HDFA 1974-76, British School Rome1980-81; Artist; currently working in Dublin and Tavira, Portugal. Recreations: photography, gardening, 2 dogs, travel. Contact: 17, Strand Road, Sandymount, Dublin 4. **T** 01 269 1957 **F** 01 260 5750 email info@felimegan.ie web www.felimegan.ie

EGAN, Kian John Francis; MUSICIAN
b 1980, Sligo; single; *edu.* Summerhill College, Sligo; Singer/Songwriter Westlife; Albums include; *Westlife* 1999; *World Of Our Own* 2001; *Unbreakable* 2002; *Turnaround* 2003; *Allow Us To Be Frank* 2004; *Face To Face* 2005; has performed with Mariah Carey and Diana Ross. Westlife have sold over 35 million albums making them a global group. Recreations: soccer, basketball, surfing, piano, guitar. Contact: Sony BMG, Embassy House, Herbert Park, Ballsbridge, Dublin 4. **T** 01 647 3400 web www.westlife.org

The blond, blue eyed Sligo man is still considered the heartthrob of Westlife despite the fact he has had a long relationship with Jody Albert of Holly Oaks; an all rounder, won his first talent competition reciting poem Whispers, aged 4; gregarious and utterly charming plans a career in music management post Westlife.

EMPEY, Sir Reg; LEADER OF THE ULSTER UNIONIST PARTY; MEMBER THE NORTHERN IRELAND ASSEMBLY
b 1947, *m* Stella; 1*s* 1*d*; *edu.* Hillcrest Primary School, Belfast; The Royal School Armagh; Queen's University Belfast; leader of the Ulster Unionist Party 2005 to date. Retailer and businessman; the Vanguard Movement 1970s; Goodyear International Corporation 1970-86; House of Fraser/Switzer & Co. McMahon & Co; established own retail clothing business 1986; member of Belfast City Council 1985 to date; Lord Mayor 1989; Board Member Laganside Corporation 1992; Lord Mayor Belfast 1993; member Standing Advisory Committee of Human Rights NI 1994-96; negotiating team The Belfast (Good Friday) Agreement 1998; Minster for Trade and Employment 1999; knighted New Year's Honours List, Knight Bachelor; elected leader the Ulster Unionist Party 2005. Clubs: Member, Orange Order; The Royal Black Preceptory; Walkway Community Group. Contact: The Ulster Unionist Party, Cunningham House, 429 Holywood Road, Belfast BT4 2LN. **T** 0044 048 9076 5500 **F** 0044 048 9076 9419 email uup@uup.org. web www.uup.org or 179, Albertbridge Road, Belfast BT 5 49Z. **T** 028 9046 3900 **F** 028 9046 970.
email enquiries@eastbelfastunionistparty.plus.com

Practical, sincere and well-respected in political and business circles; post-Good Friday Agreement he did much to build bridges between north and south to develop meaningful trade opportunities.

ENGLISH, Alan Declan; SPORTS EDITOR, THE SUNDAY TIMES
b 1965, Limerick; *m* Anne; 1*s* 2*d*; *edu.* Ardscoil RTS Limerick, University of Limerick, London
College of Printing, BA European Studies; sports editor, *The Sunday Times*. Reporter, *Limerick Leader*
1988–91; chief sports writer, *Western Morning News* 1991–93; assistant Irish editor, *The Sunday Times*
1994–1998, deputy sports editor, *The Sunday Times* 1998–2005. Clubs: Malden Golf Club,
Tottenham Hotspur Football Club. Recreations: golf, football, rugby, horseracing, collecting sports
books, newspapers, history of journalism, music, film. Contact: *The Sunday Times*, Bishops Square,
Redmond's Hill, Dublin 2. **T** 01 479 2555 **F** 01 479 2554 email alanenglish@sunday-times.ie

Alan English

> Highly rated sports editor, his section of the Irish edition of the *Sunday Times* is
> considered the best in the paper.

ENGLISH, Nicholas 'Nicky'; BANKER/ HURLING LEGEND
b 1962, Tipperary; *m* Ann; 1*s*; edu. CBS, Abbey Street, Tipperary; BA; H. Dip (Hons); Chief Manager,
Marketing/ Sales Allied Irish Bank Investment Management. Joined AIBIM, marketing/sales 1989;
has expanded his emphasis to new institutional and corporate business, has direct responsibility for
the AIBIM sales teams in different regions of Ireland, 1994 to date. Legendary hurler - honours
include: 2 All Ireland Senior Hurling medals; 1 All Ireland Minor Hurling medal; 1 All Ireland Under
21 Hurling medal; 5 Munster Senior Hurling medals; 2 Railway Cup medals; Awards: 6 All Star
Awards, Texaco Hurler of the Year 1989. Manager Tipperary Senior Team (won 3 All Irelands);
Clubs: Recreations: all sport, travel. Contact: AIB Invest Management, Percy Place, Dublin 2.
T 01 661 7077 email nicky.j.english@aib.ie

> Bright warm personality and an experienced business executive; hurling legend who
> had speed, elegance and skill in abundance on the playing field.

ENNIS, Barbara; SCHOOL PRINCIPAL
b 1960, Dublin; widow; 1*s*.1*d.* edu. Mount Anville Secondary School, Goatstown, Dublin; University
College Dublin; BA (Hons), H. Dip Ed; (Hons); M.Ed.(Hons); Principal Rathdown School,
Glenageary, Co. Dublin. Alexandra College, Teacher 1984 -00; Deputy Principal, Alexandra College
2000-02; Principal, Rathdown School, Glenageary, Co Dublin 2002 to date; Recreations: reading,
cinema, theatre, family and friends. Contact: Tudor House, Rathdown School, Glenageary, Co.
Dublin. **T** 01 285 3133 **F** 01 284 0738 email principal@rathdownehost.ie

> Experienced, progressive educationalist who has stamped her own mark on this private
> south Co. Dublin school in a very short time.

ENRIGHT, Leo Joseph; JOURNALIST, SPACE TRAVEL AND ASTRONOMY
b 1955, Dublin; *m* Lorraine Benson; 1*s*; *edu.* St. Fintan's High School Dublin, University College
Dublin; MacAlester College, Minnesota USA; Dublin correspondent BBC. Reporter *Meath Chronicle*
1976-77; Principal commentator Spaceflight Irish Radio and TV 1972; Radio Telefís Éireann 1977-
89: presenter news features 1977-80; correspondent, Middle East 1980-81, North America 1982-83;
head of news 1983-85; London correspondent 1986-89; BBC Dublin correspondent1989 to date.
Fellow, British Interplanetary Society 1976, World Press Institute 1981; member the National Union
of Journalists; Awards: National Radio Award Investigative Reporter of the Year, 1978; Publ.
Encyclopaedia of Space Travel and Astronomy 1979. Clubs: United Arts Club, Dublin. Recreations:
tennis, walking, swimming. Contact: C/o BBC 36 Molesworth Place, Dublin 2. **T** 01 662 5500

> A veteran correspondent who has worked all over the world; award winning
> investigative journalist; for many synonymous with NASA and space travel; for years
> he demystified the world of space travel and astronomy.

ENRIGHT, Olwyn; PUBLIC REPRESENTATIVE
b 1974, Birr, Co. Offaly; *m* Joe Mc Hugh; *edu.* St. Brendan's Community School, Birr; University
College Dublin, BCL; Law Society of Ireland; Solicitor; University College Galway; Dip Community
Development Practice; Public Representative; Fine Gael spokesperson Education and Science;
member Offaly County Council 1999-2004; elected to Dail Eireann TD Laois/Offaly (Fine Gael)
2002; member Midland Regional Authority; former chairperson Birr Vintage week. Contact: Leinster
House, Dublin. **T** 01 618 4217 **F** 01 618 4351 email olwyn.enright@finegael.ie
web www.olwynenright.com

The first female to represent Laois/Offaly is the daughter of former Fine Gael Deputy Tom Enright who was first elected to the Dáil in 1969 and was re-elected at every election until 1992; married to FG Senator Joe Mc Hugh, a serious, focused and impressive deputy.

ERWIN, Karen née Gageby; SOLICITOR

b 1951, Dublin; *m* John Erwin; 2*s*; *edu.* Alexandra School & College Dublin; MA TCD Solicitor, Diploma in Mediation Studies; Founder & Managing director Erwin Mediation Services (EMS); chairperson Equality Authority; director Irish Heart Foundation. A&L Goodbody Litigation Partner 1972–1994; The Irish Times Group General Counsel, Executive Director 1994–2002; past president of the International Women's Forum, Ireland; chairperson of the interim board of IAASA (the body that will oversee the Accountancy and Auditing profession in Ireland); fellow and chair of the Board of Management of St. Columba's College, Dublin; board member Mediators Institute of Ireland; council member of Irish Commercial Mediator's Association; accredited mediator ADR Group (is on their mediation panel); accredited mediator of the Centre for Effective Dispute Resolution (CEDR). Contact: Montana House, Whitechurch, Dublin 16. **T** 01 493 0268 **F** 01 493 0595 email karenerwin@erwinmediation.ie web www.erwin-mediation.ie

This highly experienced solicitor, first woman partner in A&L Goodbody at age 28 and first woman executive director *Irish Times* brings a singular combination of commercial experience, legal background, business expertise and mediation certifications to her mediation company.

Dave Evans 'Edge'

EVANS, Dave Howell 'Edge'; U2 GUITARIST

b 1961, Barking, Essex, UK; *m* 1st Aisling O'Sullivan (m.diss); 3*d*; *m* 2nd Morleigh Steinberg; 1*s* 1*d*; *edu.* Mount Temple, Malahide, Co. Dublin; Guitarist U2, after thirty still the biggest band in the world; 14 Albums; 10 sold out world tours; Best rock album, 'Sometimes You Can't Make It On Your Own', Grammy 2006; Song of the Year; Album of the Year 'How to Dismantle an Atomic Bomb' Grammy 2006; Best Rock Performance 'Sometimes You Can't Make It On Your Own', Grammy 2006; Contact: Principle Management, 30-32 Sir John Rogersons Quay, Dublin 2. **T** 01 677 7 330 **F** 01 677 7276 web www.u2.com

The all round nice guy, totally unfazed by global celebrity.

FAHEY, Frank; PUBLIC REPRESENTATIVE

b 1951; Dublin; *m* Ethelle Griffin; *2s 2d; edu.* St. Mary's College, Galway; Our Lady's College, Gort; University College, Galway; BA; H.Dip. Ed; Minister of State, Department of Justice and Equality and Law Reform; formerly secondary school teacher; first elected to the Dáil (FF) Galway West 1982; Fianna Fáil Deputy spokesperson on Youth Affairs and Sport 1982–87; Minister of State, Department of Education with special responsibility for Youth and Sport and also at the Department of Tourism, Transport and Communications with special responsibility for Sports Tourism1987–92; Minister of State, Department of Health and Children with special responsibility for Children 1997–2000; Minister, Marine and Natural Resources January 2000–June 2002; Minister of State, Department of Enterprise, Trade and Employment with responsibility for Labour Affairs 2002-04; Minister of State Department of Justice and Equality and Law Reform 2004 to date; Lost his Dáil seat 1992, regained it 1997; Senator Labour Panel, 1992–97; Former Member, Galway County Council, Galway County Vocational Education Committee; Western Health Board; Galway Regional Development Organisation. Contact: Ballybane Industrial Estate, Galway. **T** 091 771 020 **F** 091 771 040

> Has had more 'half cars' than most; despite a wide breath of experience with the exception of his ministerial stint at the Department of Marine, the full car continues to elude him; owns an impressive, extremely controversial property portfolio.

FAHEY, William 'Willie'; ACCOUNTANT

b 1955, Clonmel, Co. Tipperary; *m* Kate; *4s; edu.* Patrician High School, Fethard, Co. Tipperary; Pallaskenry Agricultural College, Co. Limerick; National College of Industrial Relations, Ranelagh, Dublin 6; Portobello College, Portobello, Dublin, BABS; Grad CIPD; CEO IFAC Accountants. Statistical analyst An Foras Taluntas 1975–79; head analysis unit IFAC Accountants 1979–98; area manager IFAC Accountants 1998–2004; chief executive officer IFAC Accountants 2004 to date. Clubs: Cashel Lions (President 2000–05); Kill, Co. Kildare GAA 1986–98, 2004/05, 2005/06, Treasurer 1992-1998. Recreations: vintage machinery, gardening, hobby farming, GAA, travel, reading, collecting egg cups. Contact: Fussough, Cashel, Co. Tipperary. **M** 087 222 8062 **F** 052 41466 email williefahey@ifac.ie

William Fahey

> Low profile, diligent business executive who retains his deep interest in rural matters.

FAITHFULL, Marianne Evelyn Gabriel; ACTOR/MUSICIAN

b 1946, London; *m* 1st John Dunbar (m.diss), *1s: m* 2nd Ben Brierly (m. diss); *m* 3rd Giorio della Tretzo 1988–91; *edu.* London convent school; Actor/Musician; chart toppers include 'As Tears Go By' 1964; 'Dreamin' My Dreams' 1977; 31 Albums from 1965 to 2005; 7 movies from 1967 to 2005; Publ. *Faithful* (autobiography) 1994. Recreations: swimming, walking. Contact: William Morris Agency (UK), 52/53 Poland Street, London W1F 7LX . **T** 00 44 020 7534 6900 web www.wma.com

> Without Mick Jagger, would there ever have been a Marianne Faithfull? With a recording career that spans over four decades, she has continually reinvented her musical persona, experimenting in vastly different musical genres and collaborating with such varied artists as David Bowie, The Chieftains, Tom Waits, Lenny Kaye and Pink Floyd; Ranked #25 on VH1's 100 Greatest Women of Rock N Roll, now a grandmother of two, has lived in Ireland for several years where she claims to find serenity and inspiration.

FALLON, Brian; HOTELIER

b 1965, Dublin; *m* Maree Cosgrove; *2s 2d; edu.* Newbridge College, Co. Kildare; School of Hotel and Catering RTC Galway; degree hotel management; Hotelier, Restaurateur. Worked in Germany, America and Australia; owned and ran The Red House Hotel, Newbridge family business for the past 20 years; Director, Lemongrass Restaurants; owner Berney's Bar and Grill, Kilcullen, Co. Kildare; co-owner Fallon & Byrne, Dublin. Clubs: Keadeen Health Club, Manchester United Fan Club, Red Bulls Soccer. Recreations: flying, sailing, bad golf! Contact: Silver Birches, Ladytown, Newbridge, Co. Kildare. **T** 045 431657 **F** 045 431878 email fal@redhouse.ie

> Has built up an impressive business in the Kildare area; lively and inventive hotel personality who is not afraid to take new directions in his business; his recently opened Fallon & Byrne Food Hall and Brasserie in Dublin already has a huge following.

Brian Fallon

FALLON, Peter; POET, EDITOR, PUBLISHER

*b.*1951; *edu.* Trinity College Dublin; BA Mod Hons; founded The Gallery Press, Loughcrew 1970; to date published more than 400 books of poems and plays by Ireland's finest established and emerging writers; has given more than 200 readings at Universities and colleges in the US including Harvard, Yale, Princeton, Berkeley, Chapel Hill North Carolina, Emory University; has read all around the world; with Derek Mahon edited the best selling anthology *The Penguin Book of Contemporary Irish Poetry* 1990; a contributor to the *Field Day Anthology of Irish Writing, 550 A.D. to the present*; poems include *The Speaking Stones* 1978, *Winter Work* 1983, *The News and Weather* 1987, *Eye to Eye* 1992, *The Deerfield Series* 1997, *Strength of Heart* 1997, an expanded edition 1998, *News of the World* included in *The Irish Times Book of the Year* 1998, *Ars Longa* published in Romanian Translation 2003, *Tarry Flynn* (based on the novel by Patrick Kavanagh) 2004; produced in the US *The Georgics of Virgil* by Oxford University Press World Classic Series; a Poetry Book Society Recommended Translation 1995; The Gallery Press celebrated its 35 years in publishing 2005; Poet in Residence Deerfield Academy, Mass. U.S. 1996-97; Inaugural Heimbold Professor of Irish Studies, Villanova University Pa. U.S. 2000; Awards: The O'Shaughnessy Poetry Award from the Irish American Cultural Institute 1993, received Honorary Doctorate; Aosdána 2003. Contact: Aosdána, 70, Merrion Square, Dublin 2. **T** 01 618 0200 **F** 01 676 1302 or The Gallery Press, Longcrew, Old Castle, Co. Meath.

As poet and publisher this brilliant animateur of the literary arts is without equal; A pleasant, unassuming man, he proudly keeps the banner of Irish writing aloft, both by personal experience and as a publisher.

FANNING, Aengus; EDITOR SUNDAY INDEPENDENT

b 1947, Kerry; *m* Mary O'Brien (decd); *3s*; fiancée Ann Harris (*qv*) ; *edu.* Christian Brothers School, Tralee; University College Cork; worked as a reporter, *The Midland Tribune* (Birr), a newspaper founded by his great grandfather in 1882; joined the Independent Group, Reporter, 1969; Group agriculture correspondent 1973-82; news analysis editor, *Irish Independent* 1982-84; Editor, *Sunday Independent* 1984 to date; Awards: Agriculture Journalist of the Year, 1978; Recreations: playing the clarinet, classical music, reading, jazz, opera, theatre, cricket, swimming. Contact: Sunday Independent, Talbot Street, Dublin 1. **T** 01 705 5333 **F** 01 705 5779 email afanning@unison.independent.ie

The gregarious Tralee-born journalist is now the longest serving newspaper editor in the country; reinvented the *Sunday Independent* and pushed circulation up to record levels; a jazz and cricket devotee and a competent clarinet player.

FANNING, Dave; BROADCASTER

b 1955, Dublin; *m* Ursula Courtney; *2s 1d*; *edu.* Blackrock College; University College Dublin; BA (English, Philosophy), H.Dip. Ed; Broadcaster. Worked as a teacher; editor, *Scene Magazine* 1977; Broadcaster, Radio Dublin 1977; Big D Pirate Radio 1978; joined R.T.E. Radio 2FM 1978; presenter, The Dave Fanning Show 1979 to date; rock correspondent, *The Irish Times* 1987-93; TV programmes include Jobsuss 1984, Visual Eyes 1986, Rock Steady (Channel 4) 1990, Friday Night at the Dome (Channel 4), The Arts Express (RTE.); The Movie Show 1993–2000 (RTE); include 2tv, Music Express, The Music Zone, What Movie?!, The Last Broadcast; joined Virgin Radio (London) 1993-95; 2 TV, RTE Television and Radio music programme 1995-2001; committee member, Mercury Music Prize (UK); Awards: Jacobs Award1980; voted No 1 DJ by *Hotpress* for 21 years. Recreations: movies, music. Contact: R.T.E., Donnybrook, Dublin 4. **T** 01 208 3111 email dave@2fm.ie

Dave Fanning

His relaxed style, humour, enthusiasm and knowledge of the music and entertainment industry have marked him out as one of Ireland's top presenters and DJs; to many musicians, he has been their conduit to success, while genuine music fans just love him; his career bears much resemblance to the development of the rock music industry; the Peter Pan of rock is easy going, shy and very popular; has an amazing knowledge and love of music, and has built up a reputation to the extent that bands such as U2 will give him the first airplay of new releases.

FANNING, John; CHAIRMAN, Mc CONNELLS ADVERTISING

b 1944, Dublin; *m* Kaye Owens; *1s 1d*; *edu.* Oatlands Christian Brothers School, Mount Merrion, Dublin; University College Dublin, B.Comm; chairman Mc Connells Advertising. Research Executive, Gallup Poll 1965-69; Research Executive, Grey Advertising 1969-71; Advertising Sales,

I.P.A.(Dublin) 1971-72; Accounts Executive, Mc Connells Advertising 1972-81; Managing Director 1982–2000; Chairman Mc Connells Advertising 2000 to date; past chairman, Marketing Society and Marketing Institute; Director Irish Times; member Commission on the Newspaper Industry 1996 to date Contact: McConnells Advertising, McConnell House, Charlemont Place, Dublin 2.
T 01 478 1544

> One of the most experienced and progressive executives in the rapidly changing world of advertising who has retained a cutting edge for his agency.

FARRELL, Brian; BROADCASTER
b 1929, Manchester; *m* Marie-Therèse Dillon; *4s 3d*; *edu.* Colaiste Mhuire, Christian Brothers School, Dublin; Salesian Fathers, Ballinakill; University College Dublin, BA, MA; Harvard University; Associate Professor, Government and Political Science, University College Dublin 1985-94; Broadcaster/Journalist 1958 to date; Presenter of every current affairs series on RTE, Seven Days, The Political Programme, Frontline, Today Tonight and Prime Time; Anchorman for RTE election coverage 1973-2002; Presenter/Reporter RTE for major national events; Awards: two Jacobs Awards for public affairs broadcasting, frequent visiting Lecturer UK and US universities; Publ. include: *The Founding of Dáil Éireann,* 1971*; Chairman of Chief?- The Role of the Taoiseach in Irish Politics* 1971; *Seán Lemass* (biography) 1983; *Child Poverty in Ireland* 2000; numerous articles for newspapers and political journals, contributing editor to four books on the Irish political and social system; chairman, Art Council 1998–2000; Director-General, Institute of European Affairs, Dublin 1994-96; vice-chairman IEA 1996 to date; member National Council of the Alzheimer Society of Ireland. Recreations: reading. Contact: R.T.E., Donnybrook, Dublin 4. **T** 01 208 3111.

> A charming man with a wonderful sense of humour; a forensic inquisitor, though always a gentleman, who set the tone for all major current affairs coverage for almost forty years; widely respected he is always polite and respectful but asks the question until gets the answer; covered most major events at home and abroad, and has presented the results programmes for ten Irish general elections.

FARRELL, Monsignor, Dermot P; PRESIDENT, MAYNOOTH COLLEGE
b 1954, Westmeath; single; *edu.* St Finian's College, Mullingar, Co. Westmeath; Maynooth College, Co. Kildare; Gregorian University, Rome; B, Sc; D.D; Vice President Maynooth College 1993-96; President Maynooth College 1996 to date; Contact: Maynooth College, Co. Kildare **T** 01 708 3958 **F** 01 708 3959 email presoff@may.ie

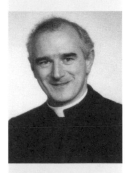

Dermot Farrell

> The Maynooth President takes a clinical approach to issues of an academic or clerical nature; extremely businesslike in his approach to the running of the College which manifested itself in his appointment to the board of insurance giant Allianz.

FARRELL, Elaine Maria; EXECUTIVE SECRETARY, IRISH FARMERS ASSOCIATION.
b 1970, Cork; single; *edu.* Loretto Abbey, Rathfarnham, Dublin; University College Dublin; B.Ag.Sc; Executive Secretary, Irish Farmers Association; directly involved in top-level negotiations and all matters relating to the sugar beet industry; lobbying and negotiating at national and EU level; member, Board of Enterprise Ireland. Clubs: Fitzwilliam Lawn Tennis Club, Dublin, Doneraile Golf Club, Co. Cork. Recreations: politics, horse racing. Contact: IFA, Irish Farm Centre, Bluebell, Dublin 12. **T** 01 450 0266 **F** 01 455 1043 email elainefarrell@ifa.ie

Elaine Farrell

> Established an international reputation with her negotiating skills during the EU sugar beet reform discussions 2005; the elegant Castletownroche native is well known in racing circles coming from a successful family agribusiness background.

FARRELL, Yvonne Catherine; DIRECTOR, GRAFTON ARCHITECTS
b Co Offaly; *m* Michael de Courcy (decd); *1s*; *edu.* Sacred Heart, Roscrea, Co Tipperary; School of Architecture, University College Dublin; B. Arch NUI; Fellow of the Royal Institute of the Architects of Ireland; Director, Grafton Architects. In private practice since 1977; studio lecturer in School of Architecture University College Dublin 1977 to date; visiting lecturer schools of Architecture abroad including Milan, Stockholm, Oslo, Nanjing, Mendrisio; Publ. *Profile: Grafton Architects,* Gandon Editions 1999; *University Builders* Martin Pearce, Wiley Academy 2001; *La Biennale Di Venezia, Next, 8th International Architecture Exhibition* 2002, *Phaidon Atlas of Contemporary World Architecture.*

Recreations: friends, ideas, being outside. Contact: Grafton Architects, 12 Dame Court, Dublin 2. **T** 01 671 3365 **F** 01 671 3178 email info@graftonarchitects.ie

With partner Shelly Mc Namara (*qv*) has run one of the most interesting and intellectual architectural practices in the country for almost thirty years; a gifted teacher she is an internationally respected lecturer.

FAY, Tara; WEDDING/EVENT PLANNER

b 1969, Dublin; *m* Seamus Mc Crosain; 1*s*; *edu* Loreto College, St. Stephen Green, Dublin; Buckinghamshire College, Brunel University; Dublin Institute of Technology, Mountjoy Square and Aungier Street, BA (Hons); European Business Studies, Graduate of the Marketing Institute of Ireland, diploma in Legal Studies; wedding planner; 1997 set up Xena Productions Ltd - the first wedding and party planning company in Ireland. Clubs: David Lloyd Riverview. Recreations: reading, yoga, swimming, weddings. Contact: Xena Productions Ltd, PO Box 8253, Dublin 4. **T** 01 269 8405 **F** 01 269 1762 email tarafay@xena-productions.com

Unflappable and ice-cool under pressure, is the original and still queen of the wedding planners; A savvy businesswoman and a real beauty, she now organizes events all over the country and internationally.

FEENEY, Geraldine; PUBLIC REPRESENTATIVE

b Tullamore, Co.Offaly; widow; 2*s* 2*d*; *edu.* Tullamore; University College Galway; Member of Seanad Éireann (Senator); elected to Seanad Éireann (Member of Oireachtas Joint Committee, Health & Children) 2002; chairperson Fianna Fáil Social and Family Affairs Policy Committee; member of Committee of 15, Fianna Fáil National Executive; Member of The Medical Council; chairperson of the Ethics Committee; former member of the Forum of Peace and Reconciliation; member Fianna Fáil Women's and Equality Forum. Contact: Ard Caoin, Sligo. **T** 01 618 3905 **F** 01 618 4791 email geraldine.feeney@oireachtas.ie

The Sligo-based senator is energetic, highly ambitious and surprised many with her election to the Seanad in 2002; the first non medical person to chair the Ethics Committee of the Medical Council; close to Finance Minister Brian Cowen and his wife Mary due to her being a native of Tullamore.

Geraldine Feeney

FEENEY, Kevin Timothy; SENIOR COUNSEL

b 1951, Dublin; *m* Geraldine Davy; 3*s* 1*d*; *edu.* Gonzaga College S.J. Dublin; University College Dublin; Kings Inns; BA (History, Politics); Barrister at Law. Called to the Bar 1973; Senior Counsel 1991 to date; called English Bar 1981; called to the Northern Ireland Bar 1988; Clubs: Donnybrook Tennis Club, Fitzwilliam Lawn Tennis Club, Portmarnock Golf Club. Recreations: playing and watching sport, reading, theatre. Contact: 1 Arran Square, Arran Square, Dublin 7 **T** 01 872 4606 **F** 01 872 4620 email kfeeneysc@eircom.net

Low profile and quiet, one of the busiest Silks in the Law Library; has featured in many major cases in recent years; known for his painstaking research into his briefs.

FEGAN, Michelle; ARCHITECT

b 1966, partner Gary Lysaght (*qv*); 2*s*; *edu.* Holy Family Post Primary School, Newbridge, Co. Kildare; Dublin Institute of Technology B.Arch Sc (TCD);1st.Class Hons Dip. Arch (DIT) 1st.Class Hons. Newenham Mulligan 1991; O.M.Ungers Architects, Frankfurt, Germany 1993; Hoger Hare RKW Architects Berlin, Germany 1994; Ahrends Burton Koralek Architects 1997; private practice with Paul and Gary Lysaght, FKL architects 1998 to date; member Royal Institute of Architects of Ireland 1997; Chartered Member of the Royal Institute of British Architects (RIBA) 2003-05; Tutor, Dublin Institute of Technology 1997-99; University College Dublin 1999-2003; Assessor AAI Awards 1996; Assessor RIAI Travelling Scholarship 2000; Guest Critic UCD 1997, 1998, 2000. Guest Critic DIT 1996-97; Architecture Association of Ireland Committee 1996-98; projects include Silicon & Software Systems 2001; Final County Council Library and Area Office Baldoyle 2003; practising Architecture Exhibition 2004; Brick House 2004; Awards: AAI Awards 1992, 2003, 2004; RIAI Awards 2004, 2005; Short-listed Kildare Civic Offices 2000, Monaghan Civic Office 2002; First Prize Martin Valley Sculptor Retreat, 40 under 40 2005; Exhibitions include: *20/20 Chair Exhibition* 1993; *Tales From Two Cities,* 1994; AAI Awards: 1996; 2001, 2004; RIAI Architecture Awards: 2003, 2004, 2005; 40 under 40 2005. Contact: Unit 10, Greenmount Industrial Estate, Harold's Cross,

Dublin 12. **T** 01 4736350 **F** 01 4736250 email design@fklarchitects.com web:www fklarchitects.com

> An intellectual architect who sees all the forms to be drawn and composed, then turned into physical fact; of a generation of brilliant architects who as women may have had a greater struggle than male colleagues… but she got there.

FEHILLY, Mark Michael Patrick; MUSICIAN
b 1979, Sligo; *p* Kevin Mc Daid; *edu.* Summerhill College, Sligo; Singer/Songwriter, Westlife; joined Westlife 1998; Albums include; *Westlife* 1999; *World Of Our Own* 2001; *Unbreakable* 2002; *Turnaround* 2003; *Allow Us To Be Frank* 2004; *Face To Face* 2005; Has performed with Mariah Carey and Diana Ross; Record breaking 13 No 1s; Recreations: music, friends. Contact: Sony BMG (Irl), Embassy House, Herbert Park, Ballsbridge, Dublin 4. **T** 01 647 3400 web www.westlife.com

> This unpop pop star is totally unassuming, extremely generous to his family and friends, his distinctive rich, soulful voice features prominently on most Westside releases; developing as a good R&B music and writer; a shrewd businessman has extensive investments in the Sligo area.

FENN, Jim; CEO FM 104
b Cork; *m* Loreto; 1*s* 2*d*; *edu.* Franciscan College, Gormanstown, Co .Meath; University College Dublin; B.Comm; Smurfit Graduate School, UCD; MBA; Chief Executive FM104; Corporate Finance Manager, Farrell Grant Sparks, Dublin; Financial Director FM104; Chief Executive FM 104. Clubs: Killiney Golf Club, Ballybunion Golf Club, Old Belvedere RFC. Recreations: golf, reading, family. Contact: FM104, 3rd Floor, Hume House, Ballsbridge, Dublin 4. **T** 01 500 6600 **F** 01 668 8401 email timf@fm.104

> Surprisingly amusing, a colourful character; easy going, affable and popular.

FENNELLY, Niall; Hon. Mr Justice; SUPREME COURT JUDGE
b 1942, *m* Maedbáine Milmo; 3*s* 1*d*; *edu.* Clongowes Woods College, Co. Kildare; University College Dublin, M.A; King Inns; Barrister at Law; High Court Judge. Trade advisor Córas Trachtala 1963-66; called to the Bar 1966; called to the Inner Bar (Senior Counsel) 1978; chairman Legal Aid Board 1983-90; chairman, General Council of Bar 1990-91; High Court Judge 2002 to date; Bencher Honourable Society of Kings Inns. Clubs: Kildare Street & University Dublin. Recreations: travel, art, horse racing. Contact: The High Court, Dublin 8. **T** 01 888 6529 email nfennelly@court.ie

> A friendly, quiet and somewhat reserved man; his amiability masks a shrewd and sagacious mind; his CTT experience means he can see through complex commercial arguments and come to a decision; a determined and honourable upholder of the law with a gimlet eye for legal niceties

FENNER, Rolf; PRINCIPAL ST KILIANS DEUTCH SCHOOL
b 1952, *m* Caroline M Searle; 2*s*; *edu.* Gymnasium Siegeufraye, Wupperkel, Germany; Ruhr Universitat Bochum, Germany; Ludwig Maximilions Universitat Munich, Germany; German State Examinations for teachers I and II; Secondary School in Wupperkel 1998-99; principal St Kilian's German School Dublin 1999 to date. Contact: St. Kilian's German School Dublin, Roebuck Road, Clonskeagh, Dublin 14. **T** 01 2883323 **F** 01 2882138 email principal@kilians.com web www.kilians.com

> His school is one of the most highly regarded in Dublin with applications from children all over south county Dublin; academically excellent he demands the highest standards from both staff and students.

FERRAN, Denise; ARTIST/ART HISTORIAN
b 1940, Saintfield, co. Down; *m* Brian Ferran; 1*s* (decd),1*d*; *edu.* Mount Lourdes, Grammar School, Enniskillen; St. Mary's University College, Belfast; Queens University, Belfast; Courtauld Institute, London University; University of Ulster; Trinity College, Dublin; Art Teacher's Diploma; Diploma, Advanced Studies in Education; BA (Hons), Art History, MFA Ph .D; Visual Artist/Art Historian; Former Head of Education, Ulster Museum, Belfast; solo and group exhibitions in Ireland and United States; Represented in many public collections in Northern

Denise Ferran

Ireland, including the Arts Council of N. Ireland; Haverty Trust; Fermanagh County Museum; UTV; Department of the Environment; Ulster Bank; First Trust Bank; Northern Bank; Bank of Ireland. Awards: Ulster Academy Silver Medal awarded by John Hewitt 1974; Ulster Academy Watercolour Prize awarded by Tom Carr 1991; British Council Travel Award to lecture in the USA 1991; Associate of Royal Ulster Academy, 1995; Fulbright Fellowship to USA, 2001; member Northern Ireland Committee of the UK Heritage Lottery Fund 1996-2001, Northern Ireland Schools Examination Council enacting new curricula in Art Education 1975– 95; Publ. *William John Leech: An Irish Painter Abroad* 1996; Frequent contributor to exhibition catalogues and Irish journals, including *Irish Arts Review, The Encyclopedia of Ireland.* Recreations: gardening, interior design, travel, visiting art galleries and museums. Contact: Goorey Rocks, Malin, Inishowen, Co. Donegal. **T** 074 93 70934 email drdeniseferran@aol.com

> A feisty artist who is also the expert on William John Leech; not afraid of controversy, she remains dedicated to her art and the pursuit of artistic truth wherever that is to be found; great company and a loyal friend she loves good company and great "craic"; landscape, particularly north Donegal, is her great inspiration.

Martin Ferris

FERRIS, Martin; PUBLIC REPRESENTATIVE
b 1959, Co. Kerry; *m* Marie Hoare; 3*s* 3*d*; *edu.* Barrow N.S. Co. Kerry; The Spa School, Co.Kerry; CBS School Tralee, Co. Kerry, Tralee Vocational School; Dáil Deputy, Kerry North (Sinn Fein) 2002; active republican 1970; jailed for his beliefs 1980s; elected Kerry Co.Council and Tralee UDC 1999; TD; Sinn Fein Party spokesperson on Agriculture and Rural Development 2002 to date; Joint Oireachtas Committee on Communications, Marine and Natural Resources; Joint Committee, Agriculture and Food; Member Sinn Fòin, Árd Comhairle; part of Sinn Fòin negotiating team; travelled extensively for the peace process. Contact: Dáil Éireann, Kildare Street, Dublin 2. **T** 066 712 9545/ 01 618 4248 **F** 066 712 9572 email mferris@oireachtas.ie

> As a Kerryman, has a strong and emphatic interest in rural development; outspoken in highlighting the need for a co-ordinated strategy to re-build rural communities which, due to a lack of government strategy and the ongoing withdrawal of essential services, have become depopulated over the last decade.

FEWER, Nicholas Jude; ARCHITECT
b 1948, Waterford; *m* Maria; 1*s*; *edu.* De La Salle College,Waterford; Bolton Street College of Technology, Dublin, Dip. Arch. B. Arch.Sc; Partner Fewer Harrington Lawlor & Partners; chairman Tall Ships Committee 2005; chairman South East Regional Airport Waterford; developed an architectural practice in Dublin and Waterford comprising 56 people, to include planners and architects; served as president of Waterford Chamber of Commerce; chaired strategy Waterford –Vision 2011; chairman of South East Regional Airport Waterford; chairman of Tall Ships Race 2005; Clubs: Dunmore East Sailing Club. Recreations: travel, blue water cruising. Contact: Wyse House, Adelphi Quay, Waterford. **T** 051 876 991

> The successful Waterford architect came to national prominence in 2005 through his chairmanship of the Tall Ships Race which brought a huge economic, social and cultural benefit to the south east region.

FIACC, Padraic; POET
b 1924, Belfast; widower; *edu.* Seminary of New York, St. Joseph's Harlem High, Hell's Kitchen; poet; R.E. Prize, Poetry Ireland Award, Northern Ireland Arts Council Award, Irish Arts Council Award; Publ: *Woe to the Boy, By the Black Stream, Odour of Blood, Missa Teribilis, Semper Vacare, Selecting Poems, Ruined Pages, Nights in the Bad Place.* Recreations: poetry, reading, classical music, radio broadcasts. Contact: Haypark Residential Home, Ormeau Road, Belfast.

> An important and widely regarded poet with a sense of doom and hell fire, but also has an optimistic range of writings; all kinds of strains run through his work which enlivens the response of his fellow poets in Northern Ireland.

Padraic Fiacc

FILAN, Shane; MUSICIAN
b 1979, Sligo; *m* Gillian Walsh; 1*d*; *edu.* Summerhill College, Sligo; Musician; lead singer Westlife; appeared in school productions of Grease and Oliver Twist playing Danny and the Artful Dodger; trophies for Show Jumping, Irish Dancing and Kick Boxing; Albums include; *Westlife* 1999; *World Of*

Our Own 2001; *Unbreakable* 2002; *Turnaround* 2003; *Allow Us To Be Frank* 2004; *Face To Face* 2005; has performed with Mariah Carey and Diana Ross; 'Most Fanciable Male,' Smash Hits Poll Winners Party UK 2000; Record breaking 13 No 1's; Has sold over 35 million albums globally. Recreations: horses, cars, family. Contact: Song BMG, (Irl), Ballsbridge, Dublin 4 Embassy House, Herbert Park, Ballsbridge, Dublin 4. **T** 01 647 3400 web www.westlife.com.

> A bright, astute, savvy entertainer; reckoned to have the best voice in the band; has known Westlifers Kian Egan (*qv*) and Mark Feehily (*qv*) since childhood; married long time sweetheart, Gillian, Egan's cousin; solid, down to earth, one of a family of seven, handles his huge fame with great ease; never lost the plot at any stage; stays close to extended family and friends; pundits predict an equally successful solo career post-Westlife.

FINAN, Mary Frances; CHAIRPERSON, RTE AUTHORITY

b 1944, Roscommon; *m* Dr. Geoffrey Mac Kechnie (decd); 1*d*; *edu.* St. Louis High School, Rathmines, Dublin 6; UCD, BA (English & French); Marketing Management Programme at Harvard Business School; joined Wilson Hartnell Public Relations 1972; Appointed Managing Director 1980; Managing Director 1983; Chairman 2003 to date; Chairperson RTE Authority 2006 – todate; Director, Canada Life (Ireland), ICS Building Society, Opera Ireland, The Gate Theatre, The Irish Chamber Orchestra, The Cheshire Foundation, The Tyrone Guthrie Centre, Annaghmakerrig, Dublin City University Educational Trust; Chairman, Economic and Social Research Institute (ERSI); member, Council of the Dublin Docklands Development Authority (DDDA); first woman president of the Dublin Chamber of Commerce. Recreations: opera, theatre, music, reading, travel, running. Contact: 45 Leeson Park, Dublin 6. **T** 01 660 8485 **F** 01 669 0039 email mary.finan@ogilvy.com

> Appointment as Chairperson RTE Authority was controversial but the super fit doyenne of PR in Ireland is widely respected; steely determination lurks behind the genial smile; specializes in strategic advice for her long time roster of blue chip clients who are guaranteed a low profile; no wonder they swear by her.

FINGLETON, Michael; BANKER

b 1938, Roscommon; *m* Eileen Mc Carroll; 2*s* 2*d*; *edu.* St Nathy's College, Ballaghdereen, Co. Mayo; UCD B.Comm; King's Inns; called to the Bar 1975; chief executive Irish Nationwide Building Society; paymaster Caritas and Concern, Nigeria; ACEC (subsidiary of Westinghouse Corp) Mgt & corp accountant; general manager Irish Industrial Benefits; changed company's name to Irish Nationwide 1975; Chairman Irish Buildings Societies Association. Clubs: Woodbrook Golf Club; The Kildare Hotel and Country Club, Las Brisas Golf Club, Nueva Andalucia, Spain. Recreations: golf, GAA, reading. Contact: Nationwide House, Grand Parade, Dublin 6. **T** 01 609 6000 web www.irish-nationwide.com

Michael Fingleton

> His folksy approachable manner and gregarious personality hide a formidable intellect, steely determination, shrewd legal and financial brain as well as a wide knowledge of the financial and banking world nationally and internationally; keeps his friends close and his enemies closer; classmates at the bar included Dick Spring (*qv*), Michael Mc Dowell(*qv*) and Adrian Hardiman (*qv*); as a lender to most of the prime movers in the property world, has been one of the chief architects of the Celtic Tiger economy; 'Fingers' has created more multi millionaires/billionaires in the property/construction world in Ireland than anyone else.

FINLAY GEOGHEGAN, Mary; JUDGE OF THE HIGH COURT

b. Dublin; *m* Mr Justice Geoghegan; 1*s* 2*d*; *edu.* Sacred Heart Convent, Monkstown, Co. Dublin; University College Dublin, BA; Auditor, Literary and Historical Society 1970-71; Incorporated Law Society of Ireland; solicitor; College of Europe, Bruges, Dip. European Law; King's Inns, Barrister-at-Law; solicitor McCann Fitzgerald 1973-79; partner 1975-79; called to the Bar 1980; called to the Inner Bar 1988; Bencher of Honourable Society of King's Inns 1996; appointed judge of the High Court; member, Board of Management Children's Hospital, Temple Street, Clubs: Belmullet Golf Club Fitzwilliam L.T.C. Contact: Four Courts, 145-151 Church Street, Dublin 1. **T** 01 817 4556

> A rather shy woman with a good sense of humour; steeped in tradition of the Law Library and The Bench; daughter of the former Chief Justice Tom Finlay, and married to a Supreme Court Judge Hon Mr Hugh Geoghegan, is an extremely able lawyer who has distinguished herself at the Bar and the Bench.

Joe Finnegan

FINNEGAN, Joseph Anthony 'Joe'; HEAD OF PROGRAMMES, RADIO STATION
b 1966, Birmingham, UK; *m* Claire; 2*s* 1*d*; *edu.* St .Colman's College, Claremorris, Co. Mayo; Hotel & Catering College, Killybegs, Co. Donegal; (City & Guilds 1+2); Head of Programmes Presenter, Shannonside Radio; Head of Programmes, Shannonside 1989 to date; Presenter of the Joe Finnegan Show 1989 to date; Clubs: Roscommon Golf Club. Recreations: all sports, reading, TV coverage of news, current affairs. Contact: Master Tech Business Park, Athlone Road, Longford. **T** 043 49336 **F** 043 48171 email joe@shannonside.ie

The very popular Shannonside broadcaster, a founder member of the Midland Radio Consortium, struck gold when the station was sold to Radio Kerry in a multi million Euro deal.

FINNEGAN, Joseph; The Hon Mr Justice; PRESIDENT, THE HIGH COURT
b 1942, *m* Kay; 1*s* 3*d*; edu. St. Mary's College, Dundalk, Co. Louth; University College Dublin B.C.L., LL.B. Law School; Incorporated Law Society of Ireland, Solicitor 1966-78; Assistant Secretary, Incorporated Law Society of Ireland; Kings Inns Dublin Barrister at Law 1978-90; Senior Counsel 1990-99; appointed Judge of the High Court 1999; President 2001 to date. Clubs: Blackrock College RFC, Bray Golf Club, El Saler Golf Club. Recreations: theatre, music, rugby, National Hunt Racing. Contacts: Four Courts, Dublin 7. **T** 01 888 6529 email josephfinnegan@courts.ie

An able and kindly lawyer who has had to face into very difficult judgments notably the Shell /Rossport Case; has a good sense of humour and he must occasionally need it on the Bench; runs a good and strict administrative High Court Barque.

FINN, Ann; HEAD OF PERSONAL SHOPPING AND MADE TO MEASURE MENS' WEAR, BROWN THOMAS GROUP
b, Dublin; single; *edu.* Holy Faith Convent, Glasnevin, Dublin; Head of Personal Shopping and Made to Measure Men's Wear; worked in various retailers; manager ladies lingerie Switzers, Dublin 1995; Manager Ladies Fashion and accessories Brown Thomas; Mens' Shop manager 2000-05; Head of Personal Shopping and Made to Measure Mens' Wear Brown Thomas Group 2005 to date; Clubs: Glasnevin Lawn Tennis Club. Recreations: cinema, theatre, reading, gardening, walking, currently learning French. Contact: Brown Thomas plc, Grafton Street, Dublin. **T** 01 605 6666 email afinn@brownthomas.ie

The more elegant captains and kings of Irish industry have her number on speed dial; utterly reliable with impeccable taste, knows the devil is in the detail, no problem too trivial for her; guarantees no two 'boys' will look alike; no wonder all the mothers, wives and partners love her.

FINUCANE, Cornelius Aengus; PRIEST/ CEO CONCERN
b 1932, Limerick; single; *edu.* Model National School, Limerick CBS Sexton St. Limerick; BA,(philosophy)University College Dublin 1953; theological studies Holy Ghost College, Kimmage, Dublin 1955-60; ordained Priest Holy Ghost Fathers 1958; posted to Diocese of Onitsha, Nigeria 1960; secondary school teacher, hospital and prison chaplain, Parish Priest Nigeria 1960-67; Diploma in Development Studies University of Wales, Swansea 1967-68; Parish Priest Biafra 1968; worked with Concern (founded 1968) at Uli Airport and with Refugees from Biafra in Libreville, Gabon 1968-71; H. Dip. Ed 1971-72; taught in Templogue College; Concern Field Director, Bangladesh 1972-78; Research MA "Poverty in Different Cultural Settings in Africa and Asia", University College Swansea 1978-79; headed a UNHCR study of "the Quality of Life in South East Asian Refugee Camps" and set up Concern Refugee Programme in Thailand 1979-80; set up Concern programme in Uganda in response to Karamjoa famine 1980-81; Chief Executive, Concern 1981-97; retired as CEO of Concern worldwide 1997 and appointed Honorary President of Concern Worldwide to date; 1994 LL.D.(hc) National Council of Education awards; LL.D.(hc) University of Limerick 1999; Granted Freedom of the City of Limerick 2005. Recreations: reading, history rugby. Contact 46, Seabury Apts, Sydney Parade Ave, Sandymount, Dublin 4. **T** 01 269 7627 **T** 01 260 2975 email aengusfinucane@eircom.net aengus.finucane@concern.net

One of the pioneers and longest serving leaders of an NGO in Ireland, with his brother Jack (*qv*) they brought Ireland to the top of the international league for corporation contributions for charitable causes whether man-made or natural disasters; despite his arduous role still always an extremely friendly and gregarious personality who enjoys good company.

FINUCANE, Jack Aquinas; PRIEST/CONCERN DIRECTOR
b 1937; single; *edu.* Presentation Convent, Sexton Street Limerick; CBS Sexton Street, Limerick; Holy Ghost Novitiate, Kilshane, Tipperary 1955; Ordained Priest 1963; Ghost Mission, Nigeria and Biafra 1964-70; Teacher, Rockwell College, Tipperary 1970-71; M.A. Studies University, San Francisco 1972-73; priest and director of Concern. Played minor hurling and football for Limerick 1955; Harty Cup Final with CBS Limerick 1955; co-ordinator Concern Bangladesh 1973-74; director Concern programme Ethiopia 1974-77; Dip. Development Studies Bath University 1977-78; director Concern Bangladesh programme 1978-84; director Concern Ethiopia programme; regional director for the Horn and Central Africa (Congo, Uganda, Rwanda, Ethiopia, Eritrea, Somalia, North Sudan, South Sudan, Kenya 1984-90; Regional Director (Angola, Sierra Leona, Liberia, Kurdistan, East Timor) 1990-2002; directed 16 major emergencies in Asia and Africa 1964-2005; retired 2002; special assignments with Concern in Bangladesh, Zimbabwe, Sudan, Ethiopia and Sri Lanka 2002-05; Freeman City of Limerick, 2005; Clubs: Newlands Golf Club. Recreations: golf, walking, reading. Contact: 2 Ashurst Apts, Mount Merrion Avenue, Blackrock, Co. Dublin. **T** 01 278 16 55 email jackfinnucane@eircom.net

Jack Finnucane

As a member of the middle class missionary order with his brother Aengus (*qv*) went, saw, and set about providing practical aid in the Third World; for the past forty years they have put into action the great Christian charges to help your neighbour, feed the hungry, clothe the naked and house the homeless.

FINUCANE, Marian; BROADCASTER
b 1950, Dublin; *m* John Clarke; 1*s* 1*d* (decd); *edu.* Scoil Chaitríona, Dublin; College of Technology, Bolton Street; Broadcaster/ Presneter The Marian Finucane Show; worked as an architect before joining RTE 1974; announcer, RTE 1974-76; presenter of numerous programmes on books, women's issues, social and political affairs 1976-80; Editor, Status 1980-81; freelance broadcaster 1981 to date; television presenter, Consumer Choice (RTE), Crimeline (RTE); Radio Presenter, The Marian Finucane Show; Director, Montrose Services Ltd., Montrose Productions Ltd; Founded Friends In Ireland who funded an Aids Hospice and Orphanage, South Africa 2002; Awards: Jacobs Award 1980, Prix Italia 1980 (for documentary on abortion), Radio Journalist of the Year Award 1988; People of the Year Award 2005. D. Litt (hc) NUI Galway. Recreations: talking, reading, walking, horses. Contact: RTE, Donnybrook, Dublin 4. **T** 01 208 3111 web www.rte.ie

The Queen of the airwaves for over twenty years has settled into her new weekend slot well, though her departure from her weekday slot is still bemoaned by her legion of female listeners throughout the country; a superb broadcaster with a positive approach to problems; has turned her attention to the plight of orphans with HIV Aids in South Africa and has opened a Hospice there.

FITZGERALD, Aidan Gerard; HAIRDRESSER
b 1956, Limerick; *m* Karen Whelan; 1*s* 1*d*; *edu.* Marian College, Ballsbridge, Dublin; managing director, hairdressing salon owner; opened first salon (aged 19) 1975; launched a series of videos for schools and training on Cutting and Colouring for the industry 1978-86; president of the Irish Hairdressers Federation 1988-'89; invited to Russia to demonstrate hairdressing skills 1990; London Earls Court World Hairdressing Congress 1997 & 2003; demonstrations on techniques and trends in hairdressing Iceland, 2003; Awards: first five star rating in Ireland from The Good Salon Guide 2003, award for 21 years of excellence from the industry 2003; *Publ.* various videos, *The Aidan Fitzgerald Cut and Colour Technique with Wella Ireland.* Clubs: The Irish Jaguar & Daimler Car Club, The Irish Veteran and Vintage Car Club. Recreations: antiques, bric a brac, gardening, cars, family, good health, fashion. Contact: 12, Main Street, Blackrock, Dublin 18. **T** 01 288 6479 **F** 01 278 413

Award winning cutting edge hair stylist who opted to operate from the suburbs; has a top class, loyal clientele; appears regularly on television on fashion based programmes; works as consultant for L'Oreal with seminars for their top accounts.

FITZGERALD, Dargan; CHARTERED ACCOUNTANT
b 1958, Dublin; *m* Jean Fitzgerald; 4*s*; *edu* .St. Conleth's College, Ballsbridge, Dublin 4; Trinity College Dublin; Mc Master University, Canada, BA(Mod), MA; FCA; Partner, Ernst and Young Partner, Financial Services - Leader of Insurance Audit Practice; KPMG, Dublin 1981-99; Ernst and Young Dublin 2000 to date. Clubs: David Lloyd Riverview. Recreations: swimming, tennis, football. Contact: Ernst & Young Building, Harcourt Centre, Harcourt Street, Dublin 2. **T** 01 221 2425 **F** 01 475 0595 email dargan.fitzgerald@ie.ey.com

One of the country's leading accountants, highly respected in the Financial Services world.

Desmond Fitzgerald

FITZGERALD, Desmond John Villiers Knight of Glin (The Black Knight); FINE ARTS SPECIALIST; ACADEMIC
b 1937; *m* 1st Lulu (Louise de la Flaise (m diss); *m* 2nd Olda Anne Willes; 3 *d*; *edu.* Stowe (UK); University of British Columbia, BA; Harvard University, MA; Fine Art Specialist /Author/Academic. Assistant and deputy keeper, Furniture and Woodwork department, Victoria and Albert Museum (London), 1965-75; Irish agent for Christies, 1975–2003; consultant for Christies 2003 to date; president, Irish Georgian Society chairman and director, Irish Georgian Foundation; director, Great Houses, Castles and Gardens of Ireland; trustee, Castletown Foundation; director, Irish Architectural Archive, 1972 to date; committee member, Great Gardens of Ireland Restoration Programme, 1977 to date; member, Royal Institute of Architects of Ireland, Fellow, Society of Antiquaries; member, Board of Governors and Guardians The National Gallery of Ireland 2004 to date; *Publ.* include numerous articles on Irish art and architecture for international journals, as well as *Ireland Observed* (with Maurice Craig) 1975, *Lost Demenses* (with Edward Malins) 1976, *The Painters of Ireland* (with Anne Crookshank) 1978, *The Watercolours of Ireland* (with Anne Crookshank) 2002, *Ireland's Painters* (with Anne Crookshank) 2004, contributor to *Vanishing Country Houses of Ireland.* Clubs: Whites, London, Beefsteak, London, Dilettante, London, Kildare Street & University Club, Dublin Recreations: art, history. Contact: Glin Castle, Glin, Co. Limerick. **T** 068 34173 **F** 068 34616

Never far from controversy, this able, astute and tempestuous hereditary knight is full of energy and drive; he restored the family home of Glin Castle, and re-made the splendid garden, as well as representing Christies and sitting on many boards and committees; with his colleague Anne Crookshank (*qv*) has assembled a mass of information on the history of the arts in Ireland.

FITZGERALD, John; BOARD MEMBER, AFFORDABLE HOMES PARTNERSHIP
b 1947, Galbally, Co. Limerick.; widower; 4*d*; *edu.* Abbey CBS, Tipperary; Night school, Dublin; trained to be an accountant; Dublin City Manager; Revenue Commissioners; Cork City Finance Officer Cork Corporation; Finance Officer Dublin Gas; Finance Officer Dublin City Corporation; Assistant City and County Manager; Dublin South County; Dublin City Manager 1996 – June 2006; founding member the Task Force Working group that established both the City and County Development Boards 2000; Chair of the Greater Dublin Area Authorities 2000- 06; board member, Government New Affordable Homes Partnership 2005 – todate; Recreations: tennis, walking. Contact: Dublin City Council, Wood Quay, Dublin 8. **T** 01 672 2222 email john.fitzgerald@dublincity.ie

One of the most successful Dublin City Managers ever; occupied the most powerful Local Authority position in the state; had responsibility for over 6,500 employees who work to serve over half a million people in the city; tipped to head up Dublin Transport Implementation Body.

FITZGERALD, Liam; CEO UNITED DRUG plc
b 1965, Dublin; *edu.* University College Dublin; B.Comm 1986; M. Business Studies 1987; Chief Executive Officer, United Drug plc; joined Smurfit Graduate programme 1987; worked in various sections of Smurfits 1987 -1990; joined Dimension Marketing Limited 1990–93; marketing executive Jefferson Smurfit Group plc 1993–96; joined United Drug plc 1996; appointed chief executive 2000- to date; appointed non executive director C & C Group 2004 to date; chairman, Government initiated Private Sector Forum to promote the development of trading and investment in developing countries; former chairman of the Marketing Society of Ireland; Smurfit Business School Outstanding Alumnus of the Year 2006.Clubs: Recreations: Contact: United Drug plc, United Drug House, Magna Drive, Magna Business Park, City West Road, Dublin 24. **T** 01 463 2300 **F** 01 4596893 email info@united-drug.com web www.united-drug.ie

One of the youngest CEO's of a leading plc when appointed to the top job in United Drug at the beginning of the millennium, taking over from Gerry Liston (*qv*); over the past five years has justified his board's confidence in appointing such a young man to the helm of one of the leading pharmaceutical companies in the country; his corporate expertise is also being utilised through other non-executive directorships; low profile, well liked and respected with a very engaging personality.

FITZGERALD, Louis; MANAGING DIRECTOR, LOUIS FITZGERALD GROUP
b 1945, Cappawhite, Co. Tipperary; *m* Helen; 2*s* 2*d*; edu. Cappawhite NS, Co. Tipperary; Doon Christian Brothers School, Co. Limerick; Managing Director, Louis Fitzgerald Group. Bought his first bar on Townsend Street, Dublin 1968 (€11,450); controls more than 20 pubs most of which are in Dublin, including Kehoes South Anne Street off Grafton Street, The Quays pubs in Galway and Temple Bar, Palmerstown House, Palmerstown, the Poitin Stil, Rathcoole Grand Central, O'Connell Street, Dublin; Bought Joels landmark restaurant, Naas Road, West Dublin (developing 189-bedroom hotel, currently under construction) 2004; bought The Stags Head, off Dame Street, Dublin 2005; acquired the Arlington Hotel, Dublin from Cyril Mulligan and Tom Quinn for €37 million, 2005 (the hotel's main turnover is believed to be generated from its bar and nightclubs). Operate 300 acres of land Dublin/Kildare area mostly for development; member of the consortium bidding for Sunderland F.C. Clubs: Beechpark Golf Club, Rathcoole, Co. Dublin; President Commercials Hurling Club, Rathcoole, ; Recreations: sport, GAA, racing, golf. Contact: Palmerstown House, Palmerstown, Dublin 20. **T** 01 626 2379 **F** 01 626 2382

Publican supreme and his wife Helen have worked in the licensed trade for over forty years building up one of the biggest pub groups in the country; well respected within a highly competitive industry; owns significant amounts of development land; now expanding into the hotel industry and an investor in Sunderland FC.

FITZGERALD, Mark; CHAIRMAN AND GROUP CHIEF EXECUTIVE SHERRY FITZGERALD GROUP
b 1957, Dublin; *m* Derval O'Higgins; solicitor; 1*s* 4*d*; edu. Gonzaga College, Dublin; FitzGerald and Partners, Auctioneers in 1975; associate director 1981; director 1982; founding director Sherry FitzGerald 1982; managing director Sherry Fitzgerald 1986; chairman and Group Chief Executive, Sherry FitzGerald Group – the largest property advisory company in Ireland 1998 to date; Fellow, Irish Auctioneers & Valuers Institute; national director of Elections for Fine Gael 1997; former chairman B.I.M. 1996-97. Clubs: St. Stephens Green Club, Fitzwilliam Lawn Tennis Club; Recreations: family, politics, walking, west of Ireland; Contact: Sherry FitzGerald, Ormonde House 12 -13 Lower Leeson Street, Dublin 2. **T** 01 661 6198 **F** 01 661 9909 web www.sherryfitz.ie

Mark FitzGerald

Pleasant and highly respected, the son of former Taoiseach Garret FitzGerald who chose a business path rather than emulate his father; has developed Sherry FitzGerald into one of the largest residential estate agents in the country; took his company public and in recent years took it back private.

FITZGERALD, Oliver M; PROFESSOR/PHYSICIAN/RHEUMATOLOGIST
b 1954, Dublin; *m* Louise Barnes; 3*s* 1*d*; edu. Gonzaga College, Dublin; University College Dublin; MB BCh. BAO MD.,FRCPI.,FRCP (UK); Newman Clinical Research Professor/ Consultant Rheumatologist 1990 to date; consultant Rheumatologist, St. Vincent's University Hospital 2000-03; chairman, Medical Board St Vincent's University Hospital 2001-03; president Irish Society for Rheumatology (International reputation/expertise in research related to Psoriatic Arthritis); *Publ.* 110 publications in peer-reviewed journals. Recreations: tennis, running. Contact: Dept. Rheumatology, St. Vincent's University Hospital, Dublin 4. **T** 01 269 5033

Internationally recognized rheumatologist specialising in psoriatic arthritis.

FITZGERALD, Rick; FOUNDER/MANAGING DIRECTOR, THE ORAN GROUP
b 1961, Cork; *m* Maeve O'Connor; 2*s* 1*d*; edu. Presentation Brothers College, Mardyke, Cork; University College Cork; B. Dental Surgery; founder/ managing director The Oran Group; Developer/owner The Raddison Hotel, Little Island, Cork; The Radisson Hotel, Limerick; Quality Inn, Youghal, Co. Cork; involved in property development with The Fleming Group and Pierce Construction in UK; acquired Snowie Group (waste management) Scotland 2005; Clubs: UCC Rugby, Cork Golf Club, Waterville Golf Club. Recreations: golf, rugby, GAA. Contact: Oran Group Ltd. Fitzgerald House. 74-76 Grand Parade, Cork. **T** 021 427 9009 email info@orangroup.com web www.orangroup.com

The former Cork dentist is a major mover in the Munster property scene and with the acquisition of a waste management company in Scotland looks set to 'clean up' on both sides of the Irish Sea.

Susan Fitzgerald

FITZGERALD, Susan; ACTOR

b 1950; *m* Michael Colgan (*qv*); *separated*; 1s 2d; *edu.* Evington Hall, Leicestershire; Trinity College Dublin, BA; Actor; Recent work includes: *May* in *Footfalls* in the Gate's acclaimed Beckett Festival in New York and London; filmed *Footfalls* for the Beckett on Film project; work for the Abbey Theatre includes: *Six Characters in Search of an Author, A Midsummer Nights Dream, Hedda Gabler* and *The Duty Master;* Most recently at the Gate she appeared as: *Lady Bracknell* in *The Importance of Being Earnest*; *Mrs. Bennett* in *Pride and Prejudice* (Spoleto Festival in Charleston) and *Jane Eyre,* all directed by Alan Stanford; with Lia Williams in *The Eccentricities of a Nightingale,* directed by Dominic Cooke; Martin Crimp's adaptation of *The Misanthrope;* recent film and television work includes numerous appearances as Nora Clancy, *Fair City*; many one off dramas, the mini-series *Rebel Heart* (BBC); *Bachelor's Walk* (Accomplice/RTE); *Proof* (Subotica/RTE); *The Big Bow Wow* (RTE); *The Trouble With* Sex. Radio roles include: *Emma Brown, Nights in the Gardens of Spain* and *Hotel du Lac* for RTE; *The Goat* directed by Michael Caven at the Project Arts Centre for Landmark productions 2005; *Teja Verdes*, Bespoke Productions 2005; also at the Project Arts Centre. *The Shooting Gallery* directed by Jimmy Fay at Andrew's Lane Theatre 2005/06. Awards: Best Actress of the Year Award, Sunday Independent/Ka, 1998. Recreations; theatre, film, anthropology, alternative medicine. Contact: Lisa Richards Agency, 46 Upper Baggot Street, Dublin 2. **T** 01 660 3534 **F** 01 660 3545 email info@lisarichads.ie

Multi-talented, natural poise, stage intelligence, a great comic actor with perfect timing and nuance; any production in which she plays is always lifted upwards by her star quality and bell-like diction.

FITZGERALD, Thomas Peter; DEPUTY COMMISSIONER, GARDA SIOCHANA

b 1943, *m* Eilis; 2d; *edu.* Leaving Certificate; BA, Public Management (1st Class Hons) Diploma in Industrial Security; joined Garda 1964; Superintendent 1988; Chief Superintendent 1992; Assistant Commissioner 1994; Deputy Commissioner 1998; Overseas Service with United Nations – Namibia; Police expert " El Salvador" 1991; Chief of Operations – Cambodia 1992/93; Commissioner in Bosnia 1996–97; Inspector General – Kosovo 2003; Police Expert– Iraq 2003; Head of Mission to Beirut 2005;. Clubs: Chairman Coiste Siamsa (Sport in An Garda Siochana), President Garda Rowing Club, Member, Stackstown Golf Club, Member Westwood Club. Recreations: sport, walking, Special Olympics. Contact: Garda Head Quarters, Phoenix Park, Dublin 8. **T** 01 666 2078 **F** 01 666 2084 email dcpfitz@iol.ie

One of the members of the Garda Siochana who has developed an international reputation through his overseas postings which should make him a front runner for the top job.

FITZGIBBON, Frank; EDITOR, SUNDAY TIMES (IRELAND)

b 1957, Dublin; *m* Isabel Charleton; 2d; *edu.* St.Mary's College, Rathmines, Dublin; College of Marketing Dublin; B.Sc.,(Management) 1979; Editor *Sunday Times* (Ireland); *Business & Finance* 1979-81; RTÉ 1 Success 1981-85; Editor, *Irish Business* 1985-89; Founder *The Sunday Business Post* 1989-91; Media Consultant 1991-94; Emerging Markets plc. 1994-98; Editor 'Business and Money' *Sunday Times* 1998 to date; Editor, *Sunday Times* (Ireland) 2005 to date. Recreations: rock music, Liverpool FC, travel, autobiographies, fiction, food. Contact: 4th.Floor, Bishop's Square, Redmond's Hill, Dublin 2. **T** 01 472 9444 **F** 01 479 2421 email frank.fitzgibbon@sunday-times.ie

A welcome choice in the business and advertising world as new editor of *The Sunday Times* (Ireland); an able and astute observer of the power of capital and capitalism; understands the world in which money is made and spent and generally moved around; a sociable man within his own peer group.

FITZPATRICK, Ivor; SOLICITOR/ PROPERTY DEVELOPER

b 1953, Dublin; *m* Susan R. Stapleton; *edu.* Trinity College (LL.B), Incorporated Law Society of Ireland; Solicitor since 1979 (Practice Areas: Commercial Law, Corporate Law, Litigation, Property Law, Banking & Finance); Managing Partner, Ivor Fitzpatrick and Company Solicitors; co-owner with Pino Harris, MV Christina, the luxury yacht once owned by Aristotle Onassis; partner with Paddy Mc

Killen in property development projects in Dublin (South Anne Street) and Vietnam. Clubs: Recreations: Contact: 44 – 45, St. Stephens Green, Dublin 2 **T** 01 678 7000 **F** 01 678 7004 email info@ivorfitzpatrick.ie

> The Dublin-based, boyish-looking solicitor possesses a razor sharp intellect and has plenty of commercial *nous*; came to national prominence through his close friendship with CJ Haughey and the Haughey family; presides over one of Ireland's top legal practices which he built up in conjunction with his wife Susan Stapleton, a leading partner in the firm; he has carved another niche as a formidable property developer in Ireland and abroad.

FITZPATRICK Lisa Frances née Breen; FASHION STYLIST
b 1972, Dublin; *m* Paul Fitzpatrick (*qv*); 1*s*.1*d*; edu. St. John of God, Dublin; MD The Lounge, Foxrock Village, Dublin; Fashion Stylist; joined Magnum Clothing wholesale/retail/manufactured ladies fashions for 10 years; opened ladies fashion boutique in Foxrock Village, Dublin, sold 2004; owner The Lounge Hair Salon, Foxrock Village, Dublin 2003 to date; fashion stylist, focusing on private clients and corporate businesses 2004 to date; Ireland AM, TV 3 Fashion advisor. Clubs: Renards, Lillys. Recreations: golf, yoga, fitness, reading. Contact: The Lounge, 1d Brighton Road, Foxrock Village, Dublin 18. **T** 01 289 1198 / 9 email lisa@thcmorgan.com

Lisa Fitzpatrick

> The boundless energy of this beautiful blonde is unbelievable; works around the clock and when not working can be found fundraising for several charities; hosted a party for husband Paul's (*qv*) new extension to his Beacon Court Hotel four days after the birth of her son; a veritable wonder woman who is carving out an impressive career as fashion/social observer on television.

FITZPATRICK, Paul; MANAGING DIRECTOR
b 1961, Dublin; *m* Lisa Breen (*qv*); 1*s* 1*d*; *edu.* Blackrock College, Co. Dublin, UNLV, (USA); Managing Director The Paul Fitzpatrick Design Collection; Managing Director, Fitzpatrick's Cork Hotel 1987-90; Joint MD, Fitzpatrick Hotel Group 1990-91,; MD Fitzpatrick Hotel Group 1993–2001; MD the Paul Fitzpatrick Design Collection, own design led hotel group 2001 to date; the Morgan Hotel, Temple Bar, Dublin, 2001; the Beacon Hotel, Sandyford, Co. Dublin, 2005. Clubs: Young Presidents Organisation, Irish Hotel Federation, Temple Bar Association. Recreations: Harley Davison's, flying helicopters, golf, travel. Contact: The Morgan Hotel, 10, Fleet Street, Temple Bar, Dublin 1. **T** 01- 6793939 email paul@themorgan.com

Paul Fitzpatrick

> Extremely bright, cut from the same cloth as his late, legendary, hotelier father Paddy Fitz.; has already made his mark with his own hotel group; currently seeking new similar properties in major European cities to expand the company; also focusing on property development.

FITZPATRICK, Peter; GROUP FINANCE DIRECTOR, IRISH LIFE & PERMANENT plc
b 1952, Belfast; *m* Maria; 2*s*; *edu.* St. Malachy's College, Antrim Road, Belfast; Queens University of Belfast, BA in Modern History; Fellow of the Institute of Chartered Accountants (FCA) in England and Wales; Fellow of the Irish Institute; graduated 1975. Coopers & Lybrand (Now PWC) Manchester 1975-80; Coopers & Lybrand (Now PWC) Dublin to date; appointed partner in firm in 1986; group finance director in Irish Life & Permanent Plc (formerly Irish Permanent Plc) 1992 to date; non executive director of Jury's Doyle Plc, chairman of the Banking Industry Group – Institute of Chartered Accountants in Ireland; chairman of the Banking Industry Group; member of the Ethics Committee. Clubs: Malahide Golf Club, Portmarnock Golf Club. Recreations: sea fishing, shooting, golf. Contact: Irish Life Centre, Lower Abbey Street, Dublin 1. **T** 01 704 1680 **F** 01 7041908. email peter.fitzpatrick@irishlife

> A well respected accountant in Dublin business and banking circles who hit national prominence as the author of the Goodman reconstruction proposals following that company's filing for examinership; quiet and shy, exceedingly bright.

FITZPATRICK, Sean P 'Seanie'; NON EXECUTIVE CHAIRMAN, ANGLO IRISH BANK CORPORATION PLC
b 1948, Bray, Co Wicklow; *m* Triona O'Toole, 2*s* 1*d*; *edu.* Presentation College Bray; University College Dublin; B.Comm; Non Executive Chairman, Anglo Irish Bank; Chartered Accountant; joined

Sean Fitzpatrick

Anglo Irish Bank, 1978; appointed to main board 1985; appointed CEO 1986-2004; appointed non executive chairman 2005; Fellow, Chartered Accountants in Ireland, Institute of Bankers, Institute of Taxation. Member, Council Institute, Chartered Accountants, Ireland; non executive director, Dublin Docklands Development Authority, Aer Lingus, Greencore plc. Clubs: Druids Glen Golf Club, Greystones Golf Club, Fitzwilliam LTC, Hibernian United Services Club. Recreations: golf. Contact: Anglo Irish Bank, Stephen's Court, 18-21 St. Stephens Green, Dublin 2. **T** 01 616 2000 email angloirishbank.com web www.angloirishbank.com

Has left a great legacy to Irish banking as he moved upstairs to the chairman's office with shares worth over €50 million; his long relationship with Anglo has driven it from modest beginnings to its current status; built up an extensive organization of well qualified people and delegated accordingly; his standing in the business world is evidenced by his list of directorships; the beneficiary, over the past ten years, of the greatest boom in property in the history of the State; now building up a personal portfolio of investment properties here and abroad; avid follower of sport - has finally more time for the golf course.

FLANNERY, Frank; DIRECTOR OF ELECTIONS FOR FINE GAEL
b 1944, Galway; *m* Marguerite MacCurtin; *edu.* St Clement's College Limerick; University College Galway BA.; University College Dublin M.B.A.; Irish Management Institute, Dip. Applied Finance; President of Union of Students in Ireland 1971-1972; Director of Elections for Fine Gael; joined Rehab Group 1973 as executive assistant to the general manager; General Manager, chief executive 1981 to 2006; member RTE Authority 1990-1993; chairman of Cablelink 1986-1990; member of National Rehabilitation Board 1983-1997; member of St. Luke's and St. Anne's Hospitals Board 1995-1998; founder Rehab Lotteries and U.K. Charity Lotteries; Advisor Fine Gael 2005 – todate; Clubs: RIAC, Fitzwilliam LTC, Loughrea Golf Club, Galway Bay Golf Club, South County Golf Club, Killimordaly GAA. Recreations: sport, politics, current affairs. Contact: 20 Quinn's Road, Shankill, Co Dublin; **T** 01 282 0432 **F** 01 205 7215 email frankflannery@rehab.ie

One of the original 'National Handlers' who was closely involved with Garret Fitzgerald during his time as leader of Fine Gael; has served on several State boards then FG in office; has used his considerable marketing skills to build Rehab into a major international disability organization; now Director of Elections for Fine Gael in the run up to the General Election 2007.

FLAVIN, James; CHIEF EXECUTIVE DCC PLC
b 1942, Dublin; *m* Mary Ryan; 1*s* 3*d*; *edu.* Blackrock College, Dublin; University College Dublin, B.Comm, DPA; Chartered Accountant, FCA; Head of Venture Capital AIB 1971-76; Founder DCC (IT, Energy, Healthcare, Food and Beverages, Enviromental)1976; Deputy Chairman/Chief Executive to date; DCC agreed to acquire 76% of Pilton, Derbshire for €8.5 million a holding company (with sales of €72 million and pre tax profits of €6.1 million) for NCV Distribution Ltd 2005; Brett Fuels, N.E. of England for €3.3 million 2005; Chairman Flogas plc., Printech International plc., Reflex Investments plc. Fannin Ltd; former Director Fyffes plc 2003, (subject to a court dispute over insider dealing); Member International Development Board, Royal College of Surgeons Ireland. Clubs: RAC, Greystones Golf Club, Stephens Green Club, Royal Irish Yacht Club. Recreations: golf, sailing. Contact: DCC House, Brewery Road, Stillorgan, Co. Dublin **T** 01 279 9400 **F** 01 283 1017 email: info@dcc.ie www.dcc.ie

Tough, highly regarded; survived his spat with Dermot Desmond in the Pernod affair; saw off the formidable Mc Cann family in the long running Fyffes legal battle; a known survivor who has built up a good organization; DCC continues to prosper under his management.

FLANAGAN, Thomas Patrick; VISUAL ARTIST- FILM MAKER
b 1981, Galway; single; *edu.* 2001 Limerick School of Art & Design; National Diploma in Fine Art-Sculpture (1.1 distinction); Limerick School of Art & Design BA (1.1 distinction) 2002; Cregal Art Award for Highest Studio Grade Achieved Fine Art Degree 2002; Artist/Film Maker; series of art shorts and feature films; current Masters in Artists Film, Video and Photography, Kent Institute of Art & Design, University of Kent, UK; regular exhibitor film festivals and exhibitions in Ireland and UK; core member of ENSO artist-led initiative in Galway for contemporary art events and platforms

for younger artists. Recreations: photography, visual arts, walking the landscape. Contact: 7 Lios na Rí, Oranmore, Galway. **M** 087 920 2432 email flanagantom@eircom.net

A bright and able young realiser of filmic images who has yet to make his mark upon the wider world; has enough drive, energy and vision to make something more of his talent in film and visual arts organisations.

FLEMING, Alec; COUNTY MANAGER, CLARE COUNTY COUNCIL
b 1954, Newcastle on Tyne; *m* Mary; 3*s*; *edu.* St. Flanans College, Ennis, Co. Clare; Public Administration, IPA (NCEA); county manager, Clare County Council; county secretary, Tipperary S.R. Co. Council 1991-96; assistant county manager, Mayo County Council 1996-2002; co. manager, Clare, Co. Council 2002 to date. Contact: Clare County Council, 1, Bindon Court, Ennis, Co. Clare. **T** 065 684 6209 **T** 065 682 0882 email afleming@clarecoco.ie

Alec Fleming

Low profile local administrator who brings a wide breath of experience from his postings in local authorities throughout the country.

FLEMING, John; BISHOP OF KILLALA
b 1948, Limerick; single; *edu.* St. Munchin's Limerick; St. Patrick's College, Maynooth, Co. Kildare; doctorate in Canon Law; Bishop of Killala; Publ: *The Pope in Limerick* (1980); *Ardpatrick, Co. Limerick* Leinster Leader, Naas (1979); *St. John's Cathedral, Limerick,* Four Courts Press (1987); *St. Munchins College Limerick, 1976 -1996* (with Sean O Grady) Limerick Leader Press (1996); *Gille of Limerick, Architect of a Medieval Church,* Four Courts Press (2001); Recreations: gardening, reading; Contact: Bishop's House, Ballina, Co. Mayo. **T** 096 21518 **F** 096 70344 email deocilala@eircom.net

Came from Rome with a very impressive CV; has settled well into his new diocese where he is very popular.

FLOOD, Ann Marie; MANAGING DIRECTOR, a|wear
b 1960, Dublin; single; *edu.* St. Mary's Presentation Boarding School, Mount Mellick, Co. Laois; state registered Nurse, Jervis Street Hospital; MD, a|wear ;studied fashion in New York and Sydney; fashion director, a|wear ltd; joined Brown Thomas group as fashion director 1998;. appointed MD a|wear 2004; judges annual Irish Young Designer of the Year. Recreations: fashion, shopping, travel, cinema, theatre, pilates, hill walking. Contact: a|wear, Creation House, Grafton Street, Dublin 2. **T** 01 671 7200 **F** 01 671 1251 email amflood@awear.ie

The former nurse is now one of the most influential players in the world of high street fashion in Ireland; top class operator and expert retailer who has an uncanny feel for her market; currently has 24 stores in Ireland, 9 of which are in Dublin and has extended the successful formula to the UK.

FLOOD, Pamela; TV PRESENTER
b 1971, Dublin; single; *edu.* Loreto College, Crumlin, Dublin; Rathmines VEC, Dublin; Presenter Off The Rails; Senior Presenter RTE; Continuity Announcer RTE 1998-2001; Presenter Travel Channel London, Jan 01–Dec 01; Presenter, 'Off The Rails' 2001 to date. Recreations: music, cinema, running. Contact: Stage 7, RTE, Donnybrook, Dublin 4. **T** 01 208 3111 email pamela.flood@rte.ie

The former model has been a huge hit as a presenter on Off The Rails, RTE fashion show; extremely popular, a hard working professional.

FLYNN Beverly; PUBLIC REPRESENTATIVE
b 1966, Tuam, Co. Galway; *m* John Cooper (m diss); *p* T.J. Gaughan; 1*d*; *edu.* St.Josephs School, Castlebar; University College Dublin, B.Comm; Public Representative, Independent TD (Mayo); financial services manager National Irish Bank; elected Dáil Éireann, Mayo Constituency, Fianna Fáil, 1997; resigned from Fianna Fáil 1999; expelled from Party 2001; re-elected 2002 Independent TD; rejoined Fianna Fáil 2002; changed name from Cooper Flynn to Flynn 2003; expelled from Party 2004; Cumann that continued to support Flynn disbanded by Party HQ 2004. Recreations: reading, travel. Contact: Dáil Éireann, Kildare Street, Dublin 2. **T** 01 618 3333 **F** 01 6184118 email: *info@oireachtas.ie*

Much loved daughter and anointed successor to Padraig Flynn (*qv*) who publicly declared her " a class act", this highly independent, articulate Mayo deputy is a chip off the old block; her popularity in Mayo is in inverse ratio to her popularity with the Dublin media; her swashbuckling style should ensure her re-election to Dáil Éireann if the fall out from the RTE Supreme Court loss does not render her ineligible; chief justice Ronan Keane rubbed salt into the wound by quoting from a recent judgment in England which held that defamation law "affords little or no protection to those who have, or deserve to have, no reputation deserving of legal protection"; she is always proud of her family and being of the great people of Mayo. "If you could bottle it you'd sell it," according to one FF TD.

FLYNN, Pádraig; FORMER EUROPEAN COMMISSIONER

b 1939, Castlebar, Co Mayo; *m* Dorothy; 4*d*; *edu.* St. Gerard's School, Castlebar, Co. Mayo; St. Patrick's Training College, Dublin; NT; first elected to Dáil Éireann, Fianna Fáil, Mayo 1977; returned at each election until 1993; appointed Minister Trade, Commerce, Tourism 1982; Minister for Environment 1987; sacked from Cabinet 1991; reinstated and appointed Minister for Justice 1992; appointed Ireland's European Commissioner (Social Affairs Portfolio) 1993; reappointed (same portfolio as before) 1995-99; made comments concerning Tom Gilmartin in 'Late Late Show' 1999 which opened a Pandora's box; Recreations: painting, walking. Contact: European Parliament Office, Molesworth Street, Dublin 2 **T** 01 605 7900 **F** 01 605 7999

The brash and arrogant persona disguises a razor sharp intellect and an amazing capacity for hard work; lasting legacy to the people of Mayo is the "Castlebar" periforique; his top drawer performance in Brussels unravelled overnight following his remarks on the 'Late Late Show' concerning the problems of running three households ("you should try it some time") and his lament for Tom Gilmartin and his wife, resulting in the latter's appearance at The Mahon Tribunal.

FLYNN, T Philip; CEO, DIGITAL HUB DEVELOPMENT AGENCY

b 1952; *m* Nicola (Ryan); 2*s* 1*d*; *edu.* Summerhill College Sligo; Trinity College Dublin, MSc (Mgmt); Digital Equipment Corporation (acquired by Compaq/Hewlett Packard 1997); Worldwide Director, Commercialisation; Partnerships & Alliances, Visio Corporation (acquired by Microsoft) 2000; V.P of International (EMEA & APAC). Clubs: Powerscourt Golf Club. Recreations: Musician, Chairperson, Dublin Simon Community, Director I.M.R.O (Irish Music Rights Organisation). Contact: 17 Priory Avenue, Blackrock, Co Dublin. **T** 01 480 6200 **F** 01 480 6201 email pflynn@thedigitalhub.com

FOLEY, Carmel; MEMBER, GARDA OMBUDSMAN COMMISSION

b 1959, Co. Mayo; single; *edu.* St. Joseph's Summerhill, Athlone, Co. Westmeath; Institute Public Administration; Irish Management Institute; Certificate in Public Administration; M.Sc. (Mgmt); Member, Garda Ombudsman Commission 2006 – todate; Director Consumer Affairs 1998 – 2006; Department of Foreign Affairs (diplomatic service including postings to Washington and Luxembourg) 1978-89; chief executive, Council for the Status of Women 1989-93; chief executive, Employment Equality Agency 1993- 98; nominated for appointment to new position as member of Garda Ombudsman Commission, 2005; Recreations: travel, languages, theatre. Contact: Department of Justice, Equality and Law Reform, 94 St. Stephens Green,Dublin 2. **T** 01 6028202 **F** 01 6615461

A former pupil of Senator Mary O'Rourke has inherited many of her formidable characteristics; the former diplomat turned trenchant defender of the public's rights was always excellent for a quick sound byte on consumer affairs before joining the Garda Ombudsman Commission replacing the Garda Complaints Board at a critical post Morris Tribunal time.

Carmel Foley

FOLEY, Sharon Ruth; MANAGING ONE 2 ONE SOLUTIONS

b 1969, Galway; *m* Patrick O'Farrell; 1*d*; *edu.* Colaiste Mhuire Athy; Kevin Street 1991; Trinity College Dublin, B.Sc Human Nutrition; Trinity College Dublin MSc, Nutrition Research 1995; University College Galway, MA in Health Promotion 1999; Currently: course in Change Management; Director Crisis Pregnancy Agency 2002 to date. Dept of Health & Children - Eastern Health Board, Senior Dietitian 1991-97; Director of Health Promotion NEHB 1997-2001; Director of Health Promotion ECAHB 2001-02; Director Crisis Pregnancy Agency 2002 – '06. One 2 One Solutions 2006 – todate. Clubs: Network Dublin, Dunamaise Theatre, Portlaoise. Recreations:

walking, minding my 3 year old!, entertaining, travel. Contact: Heathlands, Ballycarroll, Portlaois, Co. Laois. **T** 057 8646842 email sharonfoley@121solutions.ie web www.121solutions.ie

> A dynamic lady who brought much needed energy to the important and increasingly high profile Crisis Pregnancy Agency before going on to set up her own business which provides strategic guidance, facilitation and expertise to those engaged in project and programme development.

FOLEY-NOLAN, Cliodhna Mary; DIRECTOR HEALTH AGENCY

b 1957, Dublin; *m* Dr. Derek O'Connell;1*s* 1*d*; *edu.* St. Leo's College, Carlow, 1974-80; University College Cork 1984–85; University College Dublin; MB BCh BAO FFPHM Dobs; DCH; MPH; Director of Human Health & Nutrition, Safefood, the Food Safety Promotion Board; Hospital Medicine1980-84; Public Health Medicine, Specialist Training 1984 to date; Director of Community Care 1989 –95; Specialist Public Health 1989-95; Specialist Public Health Medicine 1995-2004; member Board of Food Safety Authority of Ireland; Publ. Scientific and Public Health Medicine Journals. Clubs: Sundays Well, Tennis Club, Cork; Royal Cork Yacht Club, Cork. Recreations: walking, reading, tennis, family holidays. Contact: 7, Eastgate Avenue, Littleisland, Cork. **T** 021 230 4100 email cfoley@safefoodonline.com

Cliodhna Foley-Nolan

FORDE, Aaron; CEO CONNACHT GOLD CO-OP

m Geraldine; 1*s*.3*d*; *edu.* St.Patrick's College Cavan; UCC B.Sc. (Food Business) Dip Dy.Sc; CEO Connacht Gold Co-Op; Main Board Director, Thomas McDonough, Irish Dairy Board, MD Adams Food Ingredients; Kerry Group Operations Manager; Clubs: RDS. Contact: Connacht Gold Co-op, Tubbercurry, Co. Sligo. **T** 071 918 6500

FOX, Ian; BROADCASTER, MUSIC CRITIC, LECTURER

b 1941, Dublin; single; *edu.* High School, Dublin; College of Commerce, Rathmines, Dublin; Dip. B. Studies; broadcaster, music critic; lecturer; advertising and marketing; Unilever, McConnell's Advertising, Saatchi & Saatchi etc; Chief Executive Institute of Advertising Practitioners in Ireland 1994–2000; former member of Board of Advertising Standards Authority for Ireland; former Chairman of Marketing Society; former member of Board of the European Association of Advertising Agencies; in parallel: RTE broadcaster since 1969; presenter *Top Score* quiz 1969-1992 (on TV 1975-77); wrote and presented *Bloomenlied* (Nordring International Radio Prize 1981); plus many other radio and TV programmes for RTE and BBC; presenter *The Lyric Collection*, RTE Lyric FM 2005; music critic since 1986; *Sunday Tribune* to 2005; Correspondent *Opera Magazine*, London; Opera Canada; Programme-note writer for over 30 years, currently for the RTE National Symphony Orchestra, the National Concert Hall, Celebrity Concerts; frequent lecturer on music around the country; council member, Royal Dublin Society; former Board Member/ Council Member Wexford Festival Opera, has presented annual lectures on the operas for the last 30 years at Wexford Opera Festival; board member AXA Dublin International Piano Competition. Recreations: music, gardening, cooking. Contact: The Institute of Advertising Practitioners in Ireland. Contact: 18 Lombard Street West, SCR, Dublin 8. **T** 01 416 4466 **F** 01 454 9505 email ianfox@clubi.ie

Ian Fox

> A cheerful and sociable arts figure in Dublin and Wexford, a lucky man who gets to do what he likes best - music, opera, music and opera; a clear exponent of musical theatre with a purposeful sense of how and why it works; all explained in his writings, broadcasts and personal appearances in a lucid and calm way.

FOX, Robbie; PUBLICIAN AND RESTAURATEUR

b 1957, Dublin; *m* Martina Meredith; 2*d*; *edu.* O'Connells Christian Brothers School, North Circular Road, Dublin; apprentice bartender, The Towers Bar, Ballymun, 1973; transferred to Hunters Bar and Restaurant, South Frederick Street, Dublin 2. Food & Beverage Manager 1976; opened the Pink Elephant Nightclub 1978-1986; opened Judge Roy Beans, highly successful Tex Mex restaurant 1986-1988; opened Lillies Bordello, Grafton Street 1992-1994; opened Renards Bar and Nightclub 1995 to date; opened Browns Barn City West 2000 to date; member, Restaurant Owners Association, Licenced Vintners Association, Dublin Nightclub Owners Association. Clubs: Powerscourt Golf Club. Recreations: politics, business, sport, travel. Contact: Renards, South Frederick Street, Dublin 2. **T** 01 677 5876

> Extremely popular, still King of the Night in Dublin, his one and only Renard's attracts

the domestic and visiting A-list to its private members bar most weekends; extremely hardworking, will be found at his club every night; an articulate front man on licensing matters for night club owners

FOYLE, Mark Alexander; HOTELIER

b 1977; single; *edu.* Clongowes Wood College, Clane, Co Kildare; Shannon College of Hotel Management, Clare; Dip Hotel Management, Sailing Instructor; Night and Banqueting Manager Forte, Regents Park, London; Manager Foyles Hotel, Clifden; General Manager Rosleague Manor to date; Clubs: Connemara All Blacks, Clifden GAA. Recreations: golf, cycling, sailing, swimming. Contact: Rosleague Manor Hotel, Letterfrack, Co Galway. **T** 095 41101 **F** 095 41168 email info@rosleague.com

The third generation of this west of Ireland family to offer superb hospitality and cuisine in the 'gem' of a hotel in Letterfrack.

FRENCH, Arthur; ESTATE AGENT

b 1949, Claremorris, Co. Mayo; *m* Bernie (decd); 2*s* 2*d*; *edu.* St. Colman's College, Claremorris, Co. Mayo. Joined GWI Ltd, Collooney, Co. Sligo; founder French Estates, Leixlip, Co. Kildare 1976; Principal French Estates 1976 to date; Clubs: The K Club, Straffan, Co. Kildare, Leixlip GAA Club; Recreations; golf, GAA. Contact: French Estates, Main Street, Leixlip, Co. Kildare. **T** 01 624 2320

The extrovert Mayoman is a great follower of GAA; played senior football for Mayo and Kildare; celebrity auctioneer who can get blood out of a turnip at charity auctions: accomplished golfer; close golfing friend of President Bill Clinton; well known estate agent in West Co. Dublin; has expanded his interest to property investment and development; presently best known for the K Club – a luxury development of apartments and houses.

Gavin Friday

FRIDAY, Gavin Fionán Hanvey; COMPOSER, SINGER, SONGWRITER, PAINTER

b 1959, *m* Renee O'Reilly; *edu.* St. Kevin's College CBS Ballygal, Dublin; founder, lead singer, Virgin Prunes; founder member, Avant Garde punk ensemble 1978-85; currently solo performer, composer and painter, recordings include numerous albums with Virgin Prunes, including *If I Die,* other recordings *Each Man Kills the Thing He Loves* 1989, *Shag Tobacco* 1995; film scores/soundtracks include: *In The Name of the Father* 1994, Angel Baby 1997, *The Boxer* 1998; *Disco Pigs* 2001; *In America* 2003; contributed to movie soundtracks in *Shortcuts,* William Shakespeare, *Romeo and Juliet;* solo Art Exhibition, Hendrick Gallery, Dublin 1988; has been writing in collaboration with Maurice Seezer since 1986; Publ. *The Light And The Dark* 1991; appeared in,*Breakfast on Pluto* 2004; member, I.M.R.O, Musicians Union (UK); Awards: Golden Globe nomination – Best Original Singer in Motion Picture, 1994; Ivor Novello Nomination – Best Song in Film 1995; Hotpress Award – best Irish Solo Performer 1996; Australian Academy Awards – Best Song in Movie 1997; Contact: ALK Management, 7, Seapoint Terrace, Irishtown, Dublin 4. **T** 01 667 7607 **F** 01 667 7608.

A multi talented rock and roller who has it all; energetic performer, writer of music, award winning movie scores, books; is also a talented artist whose drawing, painting, and silk screen work is much sought after, especially on eBay.

FRIEL, Brian; PLAYWRIGHT

*b*1929 *m* Anne Morrison; 1*s* 4*d edu.* St.Columb's College, Derry; St. Patrick's College, Maynooth; BA; St. Jospeh's College Belfast; Playwright; Teacher, Derry 1950-60; first plays broadcast on BBC; *A Sort Of Freedom* 1958; *A Doubtful Paradise* 1963; Other work includes: *The Enemy Within; The Blind Mind; Philadelphia Here I Come: Loves of Cass Maguire; Lovers; Crystal and Fox; The Monday Scheme; The Gentle Island; The Freedom of the City; Volunteers: Faith Healer; Translations; The Communication Cord; Making History; Aristrocrats; Dancing At Lughnasa; Molly Sweeney; Giver Me Your Answer Do*; Short stories: *The Saucer of Larks; The Gold In The Sea*; co-founder with Stephen Rea, Field Day Theatre Company 1980; member of Seanad Eireann 1987; Honorary Senior Fellow, University College Dublin; Member, Royal Society for Literature; member American Academy of Letters; numerous honorary doctorates. Recreations: fishing. Contact: Aosdána, 70 Merrion Square Dublin 2. **T** 01 661 81840 **F** 01 676 1302

One of the major contemporary writers in English internationally; his works particularly *Translations, Aristocrats* and *Dancing At Lughnasa* remain iconic works in theatre and are seminal in the teaching of drama and theatre studies worldwide; a quietly passionate and contemplative man who lives for his writing.

FRIEL, Hugh; KERRY FOODS CHIEF EXECUTIVE OFFICER
b 1944, Donegal; *m* 2*s* 2*d*; *edu.* St Eunan's College, Letterkenny; University College Galway, B.Com; Chief Executive Kerry Group plc; worked with Aer Lingus, New York; Mobil Oil Corp. London; Erin Foods, Ireland; Financial Controller North Kerry Milks Ltd (Kerry Co Op) 1972; deputy managing director Kerry Group plc 1986-2002; M.D/CEO Kerry Group plc. 2002 to date. Recreations: GAA, golf, travel. Contact: The Kerry Group, Princes Street, Tralee, Co.Kerry. **T** 066 718 2000 web www.kerrygroup.com

Following many years as Denis Brosnan's deputy, the Donegal born accountant has settled into the hot seat rapidly to Ireland's No 1 International food company, employing c.22,000 worldwide; hardworking, low profile; member of the government's enterprise strategy group (O'Driscoll Industiral Report); shrewd executive who retains his interest in Donegal GAA fortunes

FULLER, Ann; ADMINISTRATOR, AXA INTERNATIONAL PIANO COMPETITION
b 1938, Dublin; *m* Warren Fuller (decd); *edu.* Convent of Sacred Heart, Leeson Street, Dublin; Trinity College Dublin, MA; Administrator AXA International Piano Competition; cultural officer, US Embassy Dublin 1965-1970; theatre promoter, West End Theatre (UK) 1970-1971; editor, World Health Organisation 1972-1974; co-founder, with John O'Conor (*qv*), Dublin International Piano Competition 1987; chairman, Cultural Relations Committee, Department of Foreign Affairs; board member, National Concert Hall, Ireland; United States Commission for Education Exchange; World Federation of International Music Competition, Geneva; Governor, Royal Irish Academy of Music; Administrator AXA International Piano Competition; Recreations: reading, bridge, music, theatre, walking dogs. Contact: AXA Insurance, Dublin Road, Bray, Co.Wicklow. **T** 01 272 1524 **F** 01 282 1519 email pianos@dublin.ie

An able and skilled administrator, doesn't suffer fools gladly, if at all; a force of nature; has steered the Dublin International Piano competition through several changes of identity with great éclat and panache.

FURNESS; Victor Anthony; CHAIRMAN, NEW ROSS TOWN COUNCIL
b 1950; *m* Mary; 2*s* 1*d*; *edu* CBS, Good Counsel College, New Ross; Chairman New Ross Town Council; store manager/motor mechanic; member Town Council (16 years); Clubs: Golf Club, Chess Club; Recreations: all sports, chess. Contact: 20, Lacken Valley New Ross, Co. Wexford. **T** 053 912 3000 email victorfurness@newrosstc.ie

GAFFNEY, Lucy; COMPANY DIRECTOR

b 1960, Dublin; *m* Gerard Maguire; 2*d*; *edu.* Loreto Convent, Foxrock, Co. Dublin; College of Marketing and Design, Dublin; Company Director; Joined Bell Advertising, accounts director; advertising/ promotions manager, Irish Press Group mid-1980s; marketing director 98FM 1989- 95; set up The Ideas Company 1995; marketing director, Esat Telecom 1997; managing director Esat Clear 1998-2000; CEO East Telecom Group plc. 2000-03; board member Digicel Jamaica, Digicel Carribbean. Special Olympics; chairperson and non executive director of Servicecast 2003 to date; chairperson 98fm; chairperson Spin FM; member Teaxo Strategic Board, board member First Active plc; Campus and Stadium Ireland Development Ltd; chairperson NAPR (anti racisim Committee) 2005; Recreations: children, cooking, reading. Contact: First Active House, Central Park, Leopardstown, Dublin 18. **T** 01 207 5000 **F** 01 207 4900 email ifo@firstactive.com

An active and engaging personality who continues to surprise the Digi industry by taking her own line on her career and related activities; forthright and straight talking she gets things done; multi-tasking hardly covers all she does in the commercial world and pro bono.

GAFFNEY, Dr. Maureen; PSYCHOLOGIST

b 1946, Midleton, Co. Cork; *m* Dr. John Harris; 1*s* 1*d*; *edu.* St. Mary's High School, Midleton, Co. Cork; University College Cork; BA (Hons); University of Chicago, Divisional Masters in Behavioural Sciences; Trinity College Dublin, Ph.D; Psychologist; independent consultant specialising in leadership development and emotional intelligence in the workplace; chairman of the National Economic and Social Forum; chairman of the Council of the Insurance Ombudsman of Ireland; member of the Board of the Health Service Executive; Law Reform commissioner for 10 years; director of the Doctoral Programme in Clinical Psychology, Trinity College Dublin; executive member of the International Women's' Forum 2002; participant in the first Harvard University, Kennedy School of Government Programme for Women Leaders; *Publ. The Way We Live Now* 1996; co-author of *Women in Corporate Governance in Ireland* 2004 Recreations: reading, cooking, hill walking, current affairs. Contact: Strathmerton, 70 Highfield Road, Rathgar, Dublin 6. **T** 01 497 9210/497 9201.**F** 01 814 6361 email maureen.gaffney@nest.ie

Internationally trained with vast experience; well-respected, an ambitious and sagacious professional whose expertise is recognized by her many state and private board appointments.

GAGEBY, Patrick; SENIOR COUNSEL

b 1953, Rathgar, Dublin; single; *edu.* Trinity College Dublin, BA. Mod; Kings Inns; called to the Bar 1976; called to the Inner Bar 1995; practices and is an expert counsel in criminal law on the Dublin circuit; also in the areas of Administrative and Judicial Review Law; Clubs: Recreations: coarse fishing, Mayo. Contact: P.O. Box 4460, 148, Church Street, Dublin 7. **T** 01 817 5047

Despite being the brother to Supreme Court judge Susan Denham (*qv*), and son of a former distinguished editor of a national daily, he has ploughed his own furrow and seeks no favours from anybody. Has a substantial and important practice on the Criminal Bar.

GALLAGHER, Bernadette 'Bernie' née Doyle; DIRECTOR JURYS HOTEL GROUP PLC

b 1959, Dublin; *m* John Gallagher; 1*s* 2*d*; *edu.* Holy Child Convent, Killiney, Co. Dublin; University College Dublin; BA Economics/ Politics; Director Jury's Doyle Hotels; Director Crownway Investments; joined family owned hotel group Doyle Hotels 1979; worked in marketing 1980; appointed to the board; CEO Doyle Hotel Group 1990-1999; Doyle Hotel Group acquired by Jury Hotel Group for £185 million, appointed to the board Jurys Hotel Group plc 1999; director Crownway Investments, family investment holding company; director Smurfit Business School, UCD; director Failte Ireland; member Institute of Directors; former member University College Dublin Council; Recreations: art, horse riding, skiing, reading, travel. Contact: Jurys Hotel Group, 146, Pembroke Road, Ballsbridge, Dublin 4. **T** 01 607 0070 www.jurysdoyle.com

The velvet gloved blonde is the 'Iron Lady' of the Doyle sisters; committed to keeping the name of her late father (PV Doyle) alive and still very influenced by him; she saw off her brother David from the company, twice; with her husband John (*qv*) (who did all the dealings on her behalf) persevered to gain control of Jury Doyle for her family; extremely capable and now in a key role going forward.

GALLAGHER, Charles Hubert; COMPANY CHAIRMAN

b 1959, UK; *m* Patricia McCaffrey; 1*s* 3*d*; *edu.* Jesus College, Cambridge; M.A; M.Sc; chairman Abbey Group plc. Director Abbey Group 1986; executive chairman Abbey Group 1993 to date; director Matthew Homes ltd, Gallagher Holdings, M&J Engineers Plant Hire; Charles Wilson Engineering Co.Ltd, Abbey Developments Ltd, Kingscroft; Clubs: Hibernian & Stephens Green Club, Dublin. Recreations: countryside, politics, family, Sligo. Contact: Abbey Plc.1. Setanta Place, Dublin 2. **T** 01 670 3033 **F** 01 670 3010 email info@abbeyplc.ie

> This scion of the famous Gallagher building family, educated in England, still retains a strong connection and affection for Ireland, particularly the area of Cashel in Sligo where the family originates; charming and urbane with a keen business sense; the Gallagher companies, particularly Abbey, are regarded in the UK as being efficient with smaller workforce and commercially extremely successful; they own a large landbank in North Dublin and Meath as well as in Prague; they build 800 houses a year averaging €227,000 each; as a sometime Tory Candidate Charles Gallagher retains a strong interest in politics.

GALLAGHER, Dermot; SECRETARY GENERAL, DEPT. OF FOREIGN AFFAIRS

b 1945, Leitrim; *m* Maeve; 1*s* 1*d*; *edu.* Presentation Brothers College, Carrrick on Shannon, Co Leitrim; University College Dublin; BA, MA; Secretary General, Dept. of Foreign Affairs July 2001 to date. Ambassador to the United States of America, also served in San Francisco, the United Nations, New York, London, Brussels and as Ambassador to Nigeria 1991–98; second Secretary General, Dept. of Foreign Affairs with responsibility for Northern Ireland and Anglo-Irish Policy 1997-2001; Secretary General, Dept. of Taoiseach 2000–01; Clubs: Kildare Street and University Club. Recreations: all sport, especially Gaelic football, hurling, rugby, tennis, soccer, reading, theatre, travel, history, good company, conversation. Contact: Dept. of Foreign Affairs, 79-80, St. Stephens Green, Dublin 2. **T** 01 408 2133 **F** 01 478 5948 email secretarygeneral@dfa.ie

> A very unmandarin mandarin; excellent intellect and very learned, good company; One of the most experienced civil servants to represent his country as ambassador; highly respected in diplomatic circles internationally and still has excellent contacts in the major capitals; played an important but understated role in the peace process in Northern Ireland and through his myriad contacts in the United States; promotes Ireland as an industrial base to the key Fortune 500 CEOs very successfully.

GALLAGHER, John; BUSINESSMAN

b 1962, Dublin; *m* Bernadette Doyle (*qv* Gallagher Bernadette); 1*s* 2*d*; *edu.* Castleknock College, Dublin; University College Dublin; B.A. History and Politics; businessman; chairman Crownway Investments. Founded Magnum Group specialising in security 1981; acquired Thorn Security 1994; disposed of interests in Magnum 1998; Celtic Utilities 1997-2001; Celtic Anglia Water Company 1998; chairman of Vordel Limited; chairman Chubb Limited; chairman Community Foundation for Ireland. Clubs: Fitzwilliam LTC. Recreations: skiing, art, travel. Contact: Crownway Investments, Millennium Tower, Charlotte Quay Dock, Ringsend Road, Dublin 4. **T** 01 663 0124

> The son of legendary orthopaedic surgeon Joe, blossomed into an extremely successful businessman following his marriage to heiress Bernie Doyle; played a pivotal role in the Jury Doyle saga, acting as a go between for many of Dublin's major property developers, though was rebuffed by Liam Carroll who informed him he (Carroll) would only deal with the principals; rather aloof, popular in his own circle.

GALLAGHER, John; SENIOR COUNSEL

b Charlestown, Co.Mayo; *m* 1st June (decd); 2*d*; *m* 2nd Maeve (née Fallon, ne Stokes); 2*s* 1*d*; Kings Inns; Senior Counsel; FCI Arb; practises on the Dublin Circuit in administrative and local government as well as construction law; specialises in resolution and arbitration disputes, environmental and planning; member Bar of England and Wales; Contact: 1 Arran Square, Arran Quay, Dublin 7 **T** 01 817 8963 or 01 872 5908 email johngallaghersc@eircom.net

> This quiet barrister who worked on the planning tribunal and successfully secured what the public regard as outlandish information, and an understanding of how the few got away with it for so long.

GALLAGHER, Paul Martin Joseph; SENIOR COUNSEL

b 1955, Dublin; *m* Blathna Ruane; 3*s*; *edu.* Castleknock College, Dublin; University College Dublin; Kings Inns; University of Cambridge; BA, BCL, PL, LLM; Barrister at Law, Senior Council. Called to the Bar 1979; Senior Council 1991; vice chairman of the Bar Council, 1995-6; chairman of the Irish Sport anti-doping disciplinary panel 1994; Bencher of the Kings Inns 2005. Recreations: sports, reading. Contact: 2 Wellington Road, Dublin 4. **T** 01 660 6195 **F** 01 667 1512 email pshand@paulgallagher.ie

> Regarded by many as the leading Senior Counsel in the country; a razor-sharp mind mixed with pragmatism and a voracious appetite for work.

GALLAGHER, Pat 'The Cope'; PUBLIC REPRESENTATIVE

b 1948, Burtonport, Co. Donegal; *m* Anne; *edu.* Dungloe High School, Co. Donegal: St. Enda's College, Galway: University College Galway; B.Comm. Hons; Public Represenatative; former fish processor and fish exporter; first elected to Dáil Éireann 1981; relected each subsequent election until 1997; member of the European Parliament 1997; minister of State at the Dept. of Environment, Heritage and Local Government 2002-04; elected MEP for Connacht/Ulster 1994– 02; minister of State for Marine & Galetacht 1987– 94; member Donegal County Council 1979– 91; former Chairman 1985–86; member, Donegal Vocational Education Committee 1986– 99; member, Board of Management of the Tourism College Killybegs 1985– 99; former treasurer, Union for Europe of the Nations Group; member of the following European Parliament committees: Fisheries 1994-2002: Economic & Monetary 1994–99: Industry & Energy 1999–2002; chairperson of Rosses Community School, Dungloe. Recreations: family. Contact: Main Street, Dungloe, Co. Donegal. **T** 075 21176 or 01 888 2570 **F** 074 9521133 web www.patthecope.com

> A grandson of the pioneer of the Irish Cooperative movement, Paddy The Cope; lured back from European politics to win back an extra seat for Fainna Fáil in Donegal South West 2002 and was rewarded with a junior ministry; a great Gaelgoir, formidable and politically astute who has a knack of resolving any problems pertinent to his area.

GALVIN, Barry St. John; SOLICITOR

b 1946, Cork; *m* Eimear; 2*s* 1*d*; *edu.* Presentation Brothers College, Cork; University College Cork; BCL; Kings Inns (awarded Brooke's Prize); called to the Bar 1966; qualified as a solicitor; joined family practice in Cork; appointed State Solicitor for Cork, 1983; appointed Chief Legal Officer, Criminal Assets Bureau, 1996-2001; returned to private practice in Cork 2001 to date. Clubs: Royal Munster Yacht Club; Recreations: motorcycle scrambling, sailing, golf. Contact: Barry C. Galvin and Son, 91, South Mall, Cork. **T** 021 427 1962 **F** 021 427 2835

> From an old Cork legal family; his clinical style added to his courage and gung ho approach to crime and criminals, ensured that he successfully attacked the assets of Ireland's drug barons in the 1990s as chief legal officer of the Criminal Assets Bureau; has now returned to a quieter life in private practice.

GALVIN, Ian; CHAIRMAN, MOSAIC IRELAND plc

b 1963, Tramore, Co. Waterford; single; *edu.* De La Salle College, Waterford; Trinity College Dublin; B.Sc. Business Management (hons); chairman Mosaic Ireland plc; joined the family drapery business; headhunted by Brown Thomas Group 1984-96; Whistles, Harry Street, Dublin 1996-97; Karen Millen 1997-2003; joint MD Helen Mc Alinden 2000 to date; started The Late Late Show Fashion Awards; chairman, Late Late Fashion Show jury for many years. Recreations: keeping in touch with the simple things; keeping my peace of mind and health intact, travel, reading. Contact: Glendenning House, 6–8, Wicklow Street, Dublin 2. **T** 01 679 0355 email iangalvin@eircom.net

> Extremely bright, well respected in the international fashion world this Tramore man has defined popular fashion in Ireland for over two decades; pre-Celtic Tiger introduced Irish women to Armani, Versace, Dolce & Gabbana, Pucci et al; Has an uncanny knack for 'dressing' his clients; now as chairman of Mosaic Ireland has five Karen Millen outlets, five Whistles outlets, ten Coast outlets (with a combined, annual turnover of €160 million) and three Helen McAlinden outlets; has possibly the best directional fashion sense in the country, knows how to adapt international trends and provide his clients with all the latest key looks at affordable prices.

GALVIN, John; MANAGING DIRECTOR GALVINS WINE AND SPIRITS
b 1977, Cork; single; *edu.* University College Cork; B.Comm/Accountancy; joined
investment bank Boston 1997-98; Managing Director Galvins Wine and Spirits, wholesaler,
distributor, off-licence operator; returned to buy part of the family off-licence business
1998; has since bought out the entire company including associated wholesale business;
launched Galvins Carry Out (signing up independent retailers which it supplies with
product through its wholesale and distribution arm) 2004; signed up 15 Carry Out shops
2003– 04; signed up 25 new Carry Out shops in Limerick, Tipperary, Dublin, Limerick,
Kildare, Roscommon and Wexford 2004–05; plans to have 100 outlets by 2008;
Recreations: watersports, cycling, adventure sports. Contact: Head Office, Bessboro Road,
Blackrock, Cork. **T** 021 431 6098

John Galvin

> Son of Barry Galvin who opened Cork's first off licence on Bandon Road, near The
> Lough in 1968, has aggressively grown the business since he bought it in 1998;
> extremely ambitious and possessing the charm that endeared his father to so many,
> plans to continue rolling out his Galvin Carry Out chain at a furious rate; expect to
> hear much more about him nationally.

GALWAY, Sir James; MUSICIAN
b 1939, Belfast; *m* 1st (m. diss); 1*s* 2*d*; *m* 2nd Anna Christine Renggli (m.diss); 1*s* 1*d*; *m* 3rd
Jeanne Cinnante; *edu.* St. Paul's School, Belfast; Mountcollyer Secondary Modern School,
Belfast; Royal College of Music, Guildhall School of Music, London, Paris Conservatory; Musician,
Flautist. Began career at Sadlers Wells Opera, then BBC Symphony Orchestra, London Symphony
Orchestra, Royal Philharmonic (principal flute); appointed principal flute of Berlin Philharmonic
1969; launched solo career 1975; has toured extensively in the U.S.A. both in recital and with all
major U.S. orchestras, also a regular visitor to Japan as well as all major European festivals; recordings
include over fifty best selling RCA Victor albums; has premiered specially commissioned works with
leading European orchestras; appointed Principal Guest Conductor of the London Mozart Players
1999-2000; has played at both White House and Buckingham Palace; recordings have been awarded
numerous prizes including the Grand Prix du Disque; record awards from both Billboard and Cash
Box magazines (U.S.); platinum and gold albums; recipient, many honorary doctorates; OBE 1979;
Knighted 2001; President's Merit Award 8th Grammy *Salute to Classical Music* 2004; Publ. Author
and editor, *Performance Editions of Flute Works for G.Schirmer;* Current *Boehm Twelve Grand Studies OP
15-* the 1848 editions with a Master Class; new series on Deutsche Grammophone and RCA Victor
Red Seal Label 2004; Publ. *An Autobiography* 1978; Recreations: music, walking, swimming, theatre,
film, TV, chess, backgammon, conversation. Contact: IMG Media House, 3 Burlington Lane, London,
W4 2TH. **T** 0044 181 2335801 **F** 0044 181 233 5849.

> He has never forgotten his homeplace and regularly returns there to play and enthral
> his audiences; he is also always willing and glad to help with the development of young
> musicians; A very nice man with a keen sense of humour, he's a star and doesn't need
> reminding.

GANLY, Declan; CHAIRMAN/ CEO GANLY GROUP
b 1968, Watford, UK; *m* Delia; 2*s* 2*d*; *edu.* Colaiste Seosaimh, Glenamaddy, Co. Donegal; Chairman
and CEO Ganley Group; both published by Foreign Policy Research Institute; founded the Ganley
Group 1990; founded and built Kipelova Forestry Enterprises; founder Rivada Networks, pioneering
the application of mobile, wireless, broadband technologies in public safety/ defense arenas; and
Capital Route Private Hire Ltd, offering luxury chauffeur driven car services in a number of European
cities; President and co-founder of Cable Bulgaria; founder and 90% shareholder, Capital Route, an
innovative ground transportation provider which will serve the business communities in 26 European
cities; organized and chaired Forum on Public Safety in Europe and North America involving
government, law enforcement and defense leaders from Europe, United States and Canada, 2005.
Publ. *'Europe's Direction', 'Europe's Constitutional Treaty',* Awards: Irish Junior Chamber Outstanding
Young Person of the Year, 2001; board member, Irish Chamber Orchestra; member, Experts Working
Group on Telecommunications, Royal Institute International Affairs, Club de Madrid; Irish
Government's Information Society Commission Futures Group 2002 {and to its E-health working
group 2003}; member Galway Chamber of Commerce and Industry Council; Forum 2000. Clubs:
Naval and Military Club (The In and Out Club) St. James Square, London. Recreations: European
politics, clay pigeon shooting, Irish Army Reserve 54th Artillery, music (Irish traditional, classical,
jazz). Contact: Moyne Park Desmene, Co. Galway. **T** 093 43900 **F** 093 43887
email info@ganleygroup.com web wwwganleygroup.com

A serial entrepreneur and impressive public speaker, he has launched successful companies in a variety of unusual environments; has extensive experience in emerging markets; acted as a Foreign Economic Affairs Advisor to the new Latvian Government; currently holds a number of natural resource interests in the Balkans and is a significant shareholder in two Canadian publicly listed companies in the oil gas and mining sectors; profiled by CNN as one of Irelands leading Young Entrepreneurs.

GANNON, Gerard 'Gerry'; PROPERTY DEVELOPER

b 1951, Castlerea, Co. Roscommon; *m* Margaret Mc Dermott; 1*s* 3*d*; *edu.* Christian Brothers College, Castlerea, Co. Roscommon; CEO Gannon Homes; emigrated to Bermingham; returned to Dublin in the 1970s; set up Gannon Homes; during the 1980s and '90s, acquired an impressive landbank throughout north Co. Dublin emerging as one of the shrewdest property developers in the country; acquired The Bullman, Kinsale, Co. Cork, 2004; acquired the Kildare Hotel and Country Club with Sir Michael Smurfit (*qv*) 2005. Clubs: Kildare Hotel and Country Club, Straffan, Co. Kildare. Recreations: family, reading, golf, skiing. Contact: Gannon Homes, Kinvara House, 52, Northumberland Road, Ballsbridge, Dublin 4. **T** 01 608 0500 **F** 01 608 0525 email info@gannonhomes.ie web www.gannonhomes.ie

One of the biggest holders of building land in north county Dublin; 'the man with the hat' is a highly respected, successful but low key operator; hit the national headlines when he acquired the Kildare Hotel and Country Club with Sir Michael Smurfit (*qv*) from Madison Dearborne Inc; is already implementing welcome refurbishment and change at the home of the Ryder Cup 2006; one of the brightest and shrewdest dealers in land in the country and has also built up an impressive personal international property portfolio; low profile with his wife Margaret, is one of the most popular among the property developers.

GARNIER, Katherine née McCrea; FRONT OF HOUSE, RESTAURANT PATRICK GUILBAUD

b 1958, Ballinasloe, Co.Galway; widow; 1*d*; edu.Convent of the Sacred Heart, Mount Anville, Dublin; Front of House, Restaurant Patrick Guilbaud, Merrion Street, Dublin 2. Owner of La Patisserie Française, Grafton Street, Dublin 1983-86; Front of House, Restaurant Patrick Guilbaud, Dublin 1986 to date; Recreations: ballet, opera, classical music, food, wine, travel. Contact: Restaurant Patrick Guilbaud, Upper Merrion Street, Dublin 2. **T** 01 676 4192 **F** 01 661 0052 email restaurantpatarickguilbaud@eircom.net

She sees all and knows all, at least in the upper echelons of Irish dining out; always gracious, she exudes calm; tactful and discreet, a good humoured presence with a touch of steel in there somewhere.

GARVEY, Donal; DIRECTOR GENERAL CENTRAL STATISTICS OFFICE

b 1947, Cork; *m* 1st (m.diss); 3*s* 1*d*; 2nd Eithne; *edu.* Coláiste Padraig, Millstreet, Co. Cork; University College Cork, B.Sc, M.Sc; Trinity College Dublin M.Sc (Mgmt); director general, Central Statistics Office. Joined Central Statistics Office as statistician,1968; successively senior staistician, director, director general; Clubs: Cork Mountaineering Club; Recreations: International Bridge for Ireland, hill walking. Contact: Central Statistics Office, Skehard Road, Cork. **T** 021 453 5113 **F** 021 453 5117 email donal.garvey@cso.ie

Low profile North Cork man is presiding over the CSO at a time when its output is being questioned by many economists; has the capacity and the intellect to restore the integrity of its output.

Donal Garvey

GAVIN, Patrick Francis 'Frankie'; MUSICIAN

b 1956, Corrandulla, Co. Galway; *m* Tracy Harris; 2*s* 1*d*; *edu.* Franciscan Brothers Corrandulla, Co. Galway; Musician, Fiddle Player. Began playing the tin whistle 1960; made his first professional TV appearance 1963; placed first in the All Ireland Fiddle Competition and in the All Ireland Flute Competition under 18 competition (both on the same day) 1973; won All Ireland Flute competition 1974; Leader De Dannan 1980 to date; recorded with the late Sir Yehudi Menuhin and Stephane Grappelli; album with Keith Richards; recorded on *Voodoo Lounge* with the Rolling Stones; Discography: *Ireland's Harvest* 2002, with Joe Derrane; *Fierce Traditional* 2001; *Shamrocks and Holly* 2000; *Irelande* 1997; *Frankie Goes To Town* 1989; *Omós do Joe Cooley with Paul Brock* 1986; *Up And Away* 1983; *Traditional Music of Ireland* 1977; 15 albums with De Danann;

performed for state visit of Prince Charles and on numerous other state occasions; Patron, Irish Music (Traditional) School Galway; Award: AIB Musician of the Year; Bank of Ireland Arts Award. Recreations: gardening, fishing, hiking, collecting music and songs, meeting people with a sense of humour.Contact: Green Fiddle Agency, 649, Watson Avenue, Saint Paul, MN 5510 **T** 001 651-291-2678 e-mail gfa@greenfiddleagency.com web www.frankiegavin.com

A gifted traditional musician, whose playing is technically complex and unabashedly brilliant; has a gift for absorbing and switching between styles.

GEOGHEGAN, The Hon. Mr Justice Hugh; SUPREME COURT JUDGE
b 1938, Dublin; *m* Mary Finlay (*qv* Finlay Geoghegan, Mary)); 1*s* 2*d*;.*edu.* Clongowes Wood College, Co. Kildare; Kings Inns; Barrister at Law; Judge of the Supreme Court. Called to the Bar 1962; called to the Inner Bar (Senior Counsel) 1977; practised on the Midland Circuit and Dublin; member of the English Bar (Middle Temple) and the Bar of Northern Ireland; Public Service Arbitrator 1982-92; judge of the High Court 1992; judge of the Supreme Court 2000 to date; Clubs: Kildare Street and University Club, Dublin; Fitzwilliam Lawn Tennis Club, Dublin; Royal Dublin Society; Recreations: history, genealogy. Contact: The Supreme Court, Four Courts, Dublin 7. **T** 01 888 6554 email hgeoghegan@courts.ie

Broad experience; has discharged his judgements in a clear and concise way.

GEOGHEGAN, Niall John; MANAGING DIRECTOR JURYS HOTEL GROUP
b Dublin; *m* Margaret; 1*s* 3*d*; *edu.* St Mary's College, Rathmines; Rinn College, Rinn, Co Waterford; University College Dublin; IMD, Lausanne, Switzerland; B Comm, MBA (IMD); marketing director Jurys Doyle Hotel Group plc; Irish International Advertising; Thorn EMI; Guinness Ireland; marketing director, Jurys Doyle Hotel Group plc - 2006; managing director Jury's plc 2006 – todate. Clubs: Milltown Golf Club, David Lloyd Fitness. Recreations: golf, sport. Contact: Jury's Doyle Hotels plc, Head Office, Pembroke Road, 146, Ballsbridge, Dublin 4. **T** 01 607 0050 web www.jurysdoyle.com.

Was a down to earth, effective marketing executive with none of the flamboyance of many of his marketing contemporaries; having taken over from Pat Mc Cann as MD his management skills will be well tested.

GERAGHTY, Barry John; JOCKEY
b 1979, Co. Meath; *p* Paula Heaphy; 1*d*; *edu.* St. Michaels' Trim, Co Meath; Jockey; Twice Irish Champion National Hunt Jockey; 9 Cheltenham Festival winners including two Queen Mother Champion closes on Moscow Flyer; one Cheltenham Gold Cup on Lackin King; Aintree Grand National on Monty's Pass 2003; Cheltenham Gold Cup on Kicking King 2005; close to 700 winner ridden to date. Clubs: Meath Ward Union Hunt; Recreations: walking, running, golf, squash, hunting. Contact: Pelletstown House, Drumree, Co. Meath. **T** 01 823 7630 **M** 087 235 9435

Very successful champion jockey and one of the most popular on the race tracks in Ireland and the UK; remembered for his famous remark "pressure is only for tyres"

GIBBONS, JJ; ART DEALER AND WRITER
b 1976, Clara, Co. Offaly; single; *edu.* Ms Wiggins (C of I) School; Franciscan Preparatory, Clara, Co. Offaly; Institute of Education, Dublin; NUI Maynooth, BA Hons (History and Philosophy); London College of Music, Diploma (Verse Speaking); Pontifical University, Maynooth; Downside Abbey, UK; Glenstal Abbey; University of Limerick; Trinity College Dublin (2005 to date); Art Dealer and Writer; Housemaster and History Master CCR 1999-01; James Adam and Sons, Fine Art 2001-02; Jorgensen Fine Art , 2002 to date; contributions to magazines and learned journals; Clubs: The United Arts Club; The Irish Georgian Society; Friends of the National Collections; Recreations: Music and Gardening Contact: Jorgensen Fine Art, 29, Molesworth Street, Dublin 2. **T** 01 661 9758/9 **F** 01 66 19760 email jjgibbons@eircom.net

JJ Gibbons

A young art dealer who is also a connoisseur of social life in Dublin; has scored some successes in the sales rooms when others didn't notice what he'd seen; dresses to impress mostly from Fraser in Hospital, Limerick.

GIBBONS, PJ; PUBLISHER

b 1972, Co Mayo; single; *edu.* Sancta Maria College, Louisburgh, Co Mayo; Institute of Journalism, Dublin; University College Dublin, Media and Drama; H Dip Media Studies; H Dip Theatre Studies; Publisher/Editor *Social and Personal.* Reporter *Irish Press* 1993-94; features writer *Sunday Independent* 1995-97; deputy news editor, Midwest Radio 1997-98; fashion editor *Irish Examiner* 1999 to date; editor and publisher *Social and Personal* 2004 to date; *Publ. Secret Lotto Lives* (Mentor Press, 1997). Recreations: travel, golf, music. Contact: *Social and Personal*, 19 Nassau St, Dublin 2. **T** 01 633 3993 **F** 01 633 4352 email editor@socialandpersonal.ie

> A young publisher in a hurry; took over the *Social & Personal* mantle from its previous owner and is taking it to a newer, younger audience in a very competitive environment

GILLIGAN, Jack; DUBLIN CITY ARTS OFFICER;

b 1949, Riverstown, Co. Sligo; single; *edu.* Summerhill College, Sligo; Colaiste Mhuire, Ballymote, Co. Sligo; Dublin City Arts Officer; secretary to The Dublin Arts Report working group; member Dublin City Council, 2004 Arts and Cultural Strategy; Dublin City Council's 'Arts Service Plan 2006-2009. Initiated *Dublin Writers Festival,* 1998; initiated Opera in The Open; recommended setting up the *Thom Mc Ginty Performance Workshop* for professional performers; pioneered Temporary Public Art by Dublin City Council; initiated major free arts training programmes in Dublin; promoted founding *Dublin Fringe Festival*; promoted idea of a municipal arts centre, The LAB, Foley Street, opened in 2005; promoted need for artists accommodation in the city, The Red Stables Studio Complex, St Anne's Park, 2005. Earlier work includes initiating community employment arts programme in Dublin city; co-ordinator community tours county Dublin by professional arts productions; representative *Nationwide* - new band competition, member adjudication panel televised final; co-ordinator 'Memory Makers' arts project for older people; co-ordinator community variety festival; co-producer and scriptwriter amateur comedy shows; editor *The Raven* community magazine; producer books programme on community radio; member: Public Art Advisory Group, Dublin City Council; Breast Check Public Art Advisory Committee, Arts and Cultural Strategy Group, Dublin City Council, Arts Advisory Committee, Larkin Centre for Unemployed, Public Art Advisory Committee, Dublin Docklands Authority, Irish Times Living Dublin Awards Cultural Adjudication Panel; Recreations: the arts, especially theatre and opera, travel, eating out. Contact: The LAB, Foley Street, Dublin 1. **T** 01 222 7849 email jack.gilligan@dublincity.ie

> A sociable and gregarious public official, who has developed the city arts office, founded the city literary festival and finally achieved his dream of a dedicated space for the art of dance in Dublin; is development of a community arts and music programme is regarded as the best of its kind.

Eamonn Gilmore

GILMORE, Eamon; PUBLIC REPRESENTATIVE

b 1955, Galway; *m* Carol Hanley; *2s 1d*; *edu.* Garbally College, Ballinasloe, Co Galway; University College, Galway; Psychology Graduate; Public Representative, Labour TD for Dun Laoghaire, 1989 to date; Minister of State for the Marine, 1994-97; councillor, Dun Laoghaire, Rathdown Co. Council 1985-03; member National Executive of the Labour Party; Labour Party Spokesperson on the Environment and Local Government; member, Parliamentary Assembly of the Council of Europe; former Trade Union Branch Secretary ITGWU (now SIPTU) 1979–89; former President USI, 1976–78. Contact: Dáil Éireann, Dublin 2. **T** 01 618 3566 **F** 01 618 4574 email eamon.gilmore@oireachtas.ie

> Former Trade Union official with SIPTU and student leader still affectionately known as the 'Student Prince', bright, articulate with a sharp political mind; one of Dáil Éireann's most ambitious politicians.

GILMORE, Brendan; FINANCIAL CONSULTANT

b 1948, Dublin; *m* Anne; *2d*; *edu.* St. Joseph's Marino, Dublin; Accountant; financial consultant; partner Pascal Taggart in 1970s; Accountant, Financial Advisor; former financial advisor to Sir Antony J **F** O' Reilly (*qv*); extensive hotel and property interests; co-founder Fitzwilliam Hotel Group, 1989; acquired and re-developed Portmarnock Hotel and Golf Links, 1989; acquired and re-developed Royal Dublin Hotel, 1989; acquired and re-developed Metropole Hotel, Cork; acquired Mespil Estate, Dublin, 1992; sold hotel interests to partner Michael Holland 2005; (*qv*); currently developing an innovative project on Wave Energy; director, Mc Inerneys plc. Clubs: Elm Park Golf Club, Dublin. Recreations: golf. Contact: 66, Fitzwilliam Square, Dublin 2. **T** 01 703 7300

Well respected corporate advisor with an astute financial brain; extremely low profile, highly trusted by his high net worth clients in banking, business and general financial communities.

GILSENAN, Alan John; FILM MAKER/DIRECTOR/WRITER
b 1962, Dublin; *m* Catherine Nunes;1*d*; *edu.* St.Conleth's College, Ballsbridge, Dublin; Trinity College Dublin; BA (hons), English & Sociology; Film Maker & Film Director. Director/Yellow Asylum Films; feature films: *Timbuktu, All Soul's Day*; documentaries: *The Road to God Knows Where, The Ghost of Roger Casement, The Green Fields of France, God Bless America; The Asylum*; Theatre: *The Book of Evidence, What Happened to Bridgie Cleary, On the Outside, The Patriot Game, Small Craft Warnings*; Film Drama: *Eh Joe, Zulu 9, Six Nuns Die in Convent Inferno*; Chairman, Irish Film Institute, Board Member Bord Scannán na hÉireann/Irish Film Board, International Dance Festival Ireland; Clubs: Crusaders Athletic Club; Recreations: athletics, boxing, music. Contact: 28, South Frederick Street, Dublin 2. **T** 01 679 0421 email agilsenan@eircom.net

A masterly maker of images, on screen or stage; composes through his lens or as a stage director as if he was a painter; greatly admired by his colleagues and regarded as a very nice man who doesn't show temperament in his working life.

GLEESON, Dermot; BANK CHAIRMAN / BARRISTER
b 1949, Cork; *m* Darine McCloskey; 5 children; *edu.* St. Michael's College, Ballsbridge, Dublin 4; University College Dublin; BA., LL.M.; Kings Inns; Barrister at Law. Junior Counsel 1970; Senior Counsel 1979; practised on the Cork circuit; joined Allied Irish Bank Board 2000; chairman of the Board 2003 to date; member, Adjunct Law Faculty of University College Dublin; chairman, Irish Council for Bioethics; director, The Gate Theatre, Dublin; director, Barettstown Gang Camp ltd; former Attorney General and member, the Council of State; former chairman, Review Body on Higher Remuneration in the Public Sector. Clubs: Fitzwillian LTC, St. Stephen's Green Club. Recreations: family, boating, Kerry. Contact: Allied Irish Bank Head Office, Ballsbridge, Dublin 4. **T** 01 600 3111 web www.aib.ie

One of Ireland's most successful Silks; has come to national prominence in recent times through his chairmanship of Ireland's largest banking group AIB; razor sharp intellect, determined, fair minded; served as AG for John Bruton's Rainbow government in the mid 90's; has built up an impressive property portfolio; the Cork born barrister keeps a very low profile; a loyal friend and devoted family man.

GLEESON, Eileen; CHAIRMAN, WEBER SHANDWICK FCC LTD
b 1960, Dublin; *m* Gerry Hegarty; 2*s*; *edu.* Dominican College, Sion Hill, Dublin; College of Commerce, Rathmines, Dublin; Chairman, Weber Shanwick FCC ltd; Public Relations of Ireland Ltd 1979-89; formed Financial and Corporate Communications Ltd 1989; sold to Weber Shandwick 2000; managing director Weber Shandwick 2000–03; special advisor to President McAleese, 1997-2004; chairman Weber Shandwick, 2003 to date; member, Public Relations Institute of Ireland; N.U.J; IWF Ireland; non-executive director, Ulster Bank Group, Institute of Directors in Ireland, UNICEF Ireland; former director of numerous State bodies, former chairperson, Public Relations Consultants Association; Awards: Weber Shandwick FCC has been recipient of 13 awards for excellence in Communications. Recreations: current affairs, reading, relaxing with family.Contact: 2 – 4, Clanwilliam Terrace, Dublin 2. **T** 01 676 0168 **F** 01 676 5241 email fcc@webershandwick.com

Extremely able and a hard worker, a graduate of the Bill O'Herlihy (*qv*) school of PR has built up a credible reputation in corporate Ireland and has been rewarded by a seat on the board of many private and semi state organizations; held a high profile position as special advisor to President Mc Aleese (*qv*) during her first term.

GLEESON, Kate; FASHION BOUTIQUE OWNER
b 1962; separated; 1*s* 1*d*; *edu.* Sion Hill, Blackrock, Dublin; IDA Business 'Start Your Own Business' 1 year course; Commercial and Bookkeepers College; Proprietor, Diffusion Boutique, Clontarf, Dublin, 1991 to date. Employee, Stokes Kennedy Crowley, 1979-82; Marian Gale Boutique,1982-88; buyer and manager Firenze Boutique Dublin, 1988–90;

Kate Gleeson

started own "personal wardrobe" – personal shopper & styling 1990; opened Diffusion 1991; won Irish Permanent Business Woman of the Year 1996. Clubs: Renards: Recreations: walking, spending time with my children, learning French Contact: Diffusions, 47, Clontarf Road, Dublin 3. **M** 086 252 7622 **F** 01 853 1220 email katediffusion@eircom.net

Long established fashionista and successful business woman who has a very loyal, discerning clientele.

Peter Gleeson

GLEESON, Peter Joseph; CHAIRMAN AND MANAGING DIRECTOR

b 1946, Dublin; *m* Derville; 1*s*; *edu*. Belvedere College, Dublin; Textile College, Leicester, UK 1966-67; chairman and managing director, Castle Hosiery Ltd.; chairman Hyderabad Investment Company; chairman Gleeson Properties Development Co. Ltd., director, Board of Friends of the Royal Hospital Donnybrook, Dublin. Main board director Jefferson Smurfit Group plc.1981-2002; honorary fellowship Marketing Institute of Ireland 1989; Clubs: The Kildare Hotel & Golf Club; Milltown Golf Club; Rosslare Golf Club; Dunmore Demesne Golf Club; Fitzwilliam LTC.; Old Belvedere RFC; Lansdowne RFC; Recreations: golf, travel; Contact: Castle House, 2001 City West Business Campus, Naas Road, Co. Dublin. **T** 01 466 0363 **F** 01 466 0375 email p.j.gleeson@castleknitwear.com

A pleasant man who inherited his father's business and in recent years successfully diversified into the property world; a major beneficiary of the sale of Jefferson Smurfit Corporation to Madison Dearborne; stepped down from the Smurfit board following privatization though still retaining a significant shareholding.

GLYNN, John; HOTELIER

b 1954,Williamstown, Co. Galway; *m* Jill; 4 children; *edu*. Mungret College Limerick; chief executive, City West Hotel; worked in Shannon College of Hotel Management, Shannon, Co. Clare; joined Doyle Hotels assistant manager 1979; Managing Director, Clayton Hotel, Galway; joined Shelbourne Hotel as Personnel Manager 1981–82; rejoined Doyle Hotels as General Manager Burlington Hotel 1982–86; group General Manager Doyle Hotel Group 1986-99; joined Mansfield owned City West Hotel as chief executive 1999; chief executive City West Hotel 1999 - 2006; director Clayton Hotels 2006 – todate; director, Dublin Tourism; member, executive board Convention Bureau of Ireland. Clubs: Citywest Golf Club. Recreations: GAA, (Galway football/hurling), rugby, soccer, horse racing. Contact: Clayton Hotel, Ballybrit, Galway. **T** 087 250 9305 web www.claytonhotel.com

A tough performer who knows his business inside out; the naysayers said he wouldn't get City West off the ground, did he ever prove them wrong?; more than delivered for Jim Mansfield (*qv*), managed, one way or another, to hold most major events at City West, attracting all major convention business and awards ceremonies to the hotel; many wonder about the future of the hotel without him; now he faces the challenge of doing it all over again, this time in the Clayton Hotel, Galway (opening December 2006) and this time as an investor himself.

Cathal Goan

GOAN, Cathal; DIRECTOR GENERAL, RTÉ

b 1954, Belfast; *m* Maighread Ní Dhomhnaill;1*s* 1*d*; *edu*. St. Malachy's College, Antrim Road, Belfast; University College Dublin; BA (Celtic Studies); Director General Radio Telefís Éireann. Archivist RTÉ 1979; radio producer, features & current affairs 1983-88; Today Tonight producer/director 1988; editor Cúrsaí 1984; editor Irish Language Programmes 1990; 1st Ceannasaí, Telifís na Gaeilge (TG4) 1994; director, Television (RTÉ), subsequently MD 2000–03; director General RTÉ 2003 to date; Chairman, Irish Traditional Music Archive, Dublin. Recreations: music, particularly Irish traditional music, reading, history, radio, television. Contact: RTÉ, Donnybrook, Dublin 4. **T** 01 208 4531 **F** 01 208 4532 email dg@rte.ie web www.rte.ie

With a wide range of experience across the organization, has restored profitability to RTE; articulate and personable but continues to face challenges in the highly competitive broadcasting industry.

GODSIL, Arthur; HEADMASTER ST. ANDREW'S COLLEGE, DUBLIN

b 1953, Dublin; *m* Dorothy, 1*s* 1*d*; *edu*. The High School Dublin; Trinity College Dublin, College of New Jersey; MA, Med; Headmaster, St. Andrew's College. Teacher The High School, Dublin 1976–77; teacher St Andrew's College, Dublin 1977-90; headmaster St Andrew's College 1990 to date; Clubs: Rathfarnham Golf Club, Old Wesley RFC, Academy of International School Heads, Irish School heads association; Recreations: rugby, travel, reading, cooking, sport in general; Contact: St Andrew's College, Booterstown Avenue, Blackrock, Co. Dublin. **T** 01 288 2785 **F** 01 283 1627 email information@st-andrews.ie/ bsargeant@st-andrews.ie

A good leader and an excellent principal; runs a school with 1200 pupils (motto "*Ardens sed virans*" burning but flourishing) which is a popular and liberal school with good arts,culture and civics participation as well as good sports support; ambitious for the school, he makes it perform well.

GOGGIN, Brian J; GROUP CHIEF EXECUTIVE, BANK OF IRELAND
b 1952, Dublin; *m* Finula; 1*s* 1*d*; *edu.* Oatlands College, Stillorgan, Co. Dublin, Trinity College Dublin, Fellow Chartered Association of Certified Accountants (FCCA), M.Sc Management TCD; Group Chief Executive, Bank of Ireland. Joined Bank of Ireland 1969; vice president Corporate Banking (New York) 1977-82; Manager Corporate Banking (Dublin) 1982-85; managing director Bank of Ireland Home Mortgages (Britain) 1986-90; Director International Banking (Dublin) 1991–94; General Manager Area East, Retail Ireland 1994– 96; CEO Wholesale Financial Services Division, 1996; appointed to Court of Directors, 2000; Chief Executive Officer Asset Management Services Division 2003–04; Group Chief Executive Officer 2004 to date; President Irish Chapter Irish US Council 2004 to date. Clubs: Charlesland Golf Club, Faithlegg Golf Club. Recreations: golf, walking, DIY. Contact: BOI, Headquarters, Lower Baggot Street, Dublin 2. **T** 01 632 2530 email brian.goggin@boinail.com web www.boi.ie

Career banker who emerged into the top position following the resignation of Michael Soden; personable, bright, energetic, ambitious; destined to leave his mark on Irish banking.

GOOD, Rev. Harold OBE; RETIRED METHODIST CHURCH MINISTER
b 1937, Derry; *m*; 5 children; Retired Methodist Minister/ Peace Broker; edu. Theological College, Belfast and Indianapolis, United States; Former Presient of the Methodist Church in Ireland/ Peace Broker; first Ministry Shankill Road, Belfast 1968 –'73; Chaplin Crumlin Road Prison 1968 –'73; Director Corrymeela Community Center for Reconciliation 1973 – '79; served various parts of Belfast and Co. Down 1979 – 2001; elected president of the Methodist Church 2001; MBE; OBE; member, Northern Ireland Human Rights Commission 1999 – '04; became member of inter church group which met Bertie Ahern to discuss their concerns about a proposed EU directive that would have prevented Chuch run schools and hospitals from from discriminating in favour of their ethos; retired from full time ministry in 2002; with Fr Alex Reid and General John de Chastelan witnessed all IRA weaponry put beyond use 2005. Contact: The Methodist Church, Grand Parade, Belfast, BT5 5PB **T** 0044 028 90651693

The Derry born, former president of the Methodist Church and grandfather of 12 has served congregations not only in Northern Ireland but the Irish Republic and the US; highly respected by all sides, especially the Unionists, as a peacebroker; witnessing the decommissioning process on a minute-by-minute basis gave him clear and incontrovertible evidence "that beyond any shadow of doubt the arms of the IRA have now been decommissioned".

GOOD; Rt Rev, Kenneth Raymond; BISHOP OF DERRY AND RAPHOE;
b 1952; *m* Mary Louise; 2*s* 1*d*; *edu.* Midleton College; Dublin University, Nottingham University, University College Cork, BA (Hons), M.Ed. Diploma in Pastoral Studies, Higher Diploma in Education; ordained Deacon 1977; ordained Priest 1978; Curate Willowfield Parish, Belfast 1977–79; chaplain and head of R.E. Ashton Comprehensive School Cork 1979–84; Rector Dunganstown Unlon cleo Glendalough 1984– 90; Rector Shankill Parish, Lurgan 1990– 02; Archdeacon of Dromore 1997–02; Bishop of Derry and Raphoe 2002 todate. Recreations: golf, opera. Contact: The See House, 112, Culmore Road, Londonderry. BT 48 8 JF. **T** 048 7126 2440 **F** 048 7137 2100 email bishop@derry.anglican.org web www.derry.anglican.org

An unknown quantity until the rows about the gay bishop of New Hampshire, where the evangelical spirit of Derry and Raphoe came to the fore, not entirely reflecting great Christian merit on this diocese.

Kenneth Good

GOODMAN, Larry; BEEF BARON

b 1939, Dundalk, Co. Louth; *m* Kitty Brennan; 2*s*; *edu.* Marist College Dundalk; began career as trader in hides and other animal by-products; became involved in the meat processing industry; by mid 1980's Europe's biggest meat processor and exporter; Irish government's plan for the development of the Irish meat industry, launched by the late C.J. Haughey, was built around the Goodman International Group 1987; Goodman Companies went into examinership 1992; company rose from the ashes through the 1990s; currently Europe's largest beef processor; investor with Mr James Sheehan (*qv*) in Blackrock Hospital, Galway Medical Clinic, Doughiska, Co. Galway and Hermitage Medical Clinic, Lucan, Co. Dublin. Clubs: Kildare Hotel and Golf Club. Co. Kildare. Recreations: GAA, opera, golf. Contact: Food Industries, Ardee, Co. Louth. **T** 042 933 5793

The shy, quiet spoken Louth man is one of the toughest businessmen in Ireland; apart from his undoubted trading skills, is also a shrewd property investor and holds an impressive property portfolio at home and abroad; part of the Louth Golden Triangle which includes Neill Mc Cann (*qv*), Martin Naughton (*qv*), and Brendan Mc Donald; one of the first Irish businessmen to own his own jet and helicopter; developed close friendship with the late Charles J. Haughey who recalled the Dail in the summer of 1992 to pass the examinership legislation, to save the Goodman group of companies; Goodman's group also came under scrutiny from the beef tribunal, chaired by the late Liam Hamilton; keep-fit fanatic; the beef baron is also one of Ireland's largest farmers and heads the list of the Single Farm Payments for the next 8 years (2005 - 13) receiving over half a million euro per annum from the EU coffers; sponsors the Louth Co. GAA team; almost lost everything in the early Nineties including all the properties; has since repurchased many of the same properties including Setanta building on Nassau Street which is leased to the Government.

GORDAN, John Joseph; SENIOR COUNSEL

b 1951; single; *edu.* CBS Tipperary; Mungret College, Limerick; University College Dublin, BCL; Kings Inns, Barister-at-Law; Senior Counsel; called to the Bar 1974; called to the Inner Bar 1985; called to the Bar Middle Temple (London) 1986; called to the Bar New South Wales (Australia) 1993; Clubs: RIAC Club, Dublin; St. Stephen's Green Club. Recreations: travel, opera and all things Italian. Contact: 2 Arran Square, Arran Quay, Dublin 7. **T** 01 872 6544 **F** 01 872 6524

Expert in defamation, intellectual property law issues and other commercial matters; considered and forensic approach; is a bon viveur who enjoys fine wine, opera and all things Italian.

GORMAN, Richard; PAINTER / PRINT MAKER

b 1946, Dublin; single; *edu.* St. Andrew's College, Dublin; Trinity College Dublin; B.B.S; Dun Laoghaire School of Art & Design; Dip. Fine Art; Painter and Print Maker 1983 to date; exhibited all over the world with more than 90 solo, group and invited/curated exhibitions; work represented in major collections: The Arts Council of Ireland, Ulster Museum Belfast, Irish Museum of Modern Art, Allied Irish Bank, Deutsche Bank Ireland, Guinness Peat Aviation, St. Patrick's Hospital Dublin, Nissan Ireland, University College Dublin, Butler Gallery, City Gallery Limerick; elected full Member RHA Dublin 2005. Contact: Shiosai Studio, Coliemore Road, Dalkey, Co. Dublin. email richardgorman@indigo.ie

His unsual sense of colour and form give his art its particular charge; colour and elegance of shape make for entrancing viewing and his use of his own handmade paper is quite Japanese in its restraint; the mixture of Italian sensibilità and eastern influences make him an important artist.

GORMAN, TOMMY; NORTHERN EDITOR, RTE

b 1956, Sligo; *m* Ceara Roche; 1*s* 1*d*; *edu.* Summerhill College, Sligo; Rathmines College of Journalism, Dublin; had to made a choice between sitting Finals and taking job in June 1977; in September the choice was repeats or cover Sligo Rovers v Red Star Belgrade in Yugoslavia (no choice); Belfast-based, Northern Editor, RTE. Joined start up weekly newspaper, Ballina-based *Western Journal*, on invitation of co-founder, John Healy, June 1977: managing editor of *Western Journal* and sister paper *Sligo Journal*, 1979-80: north western correspondent RTE, covering news and current affairs in Derry, Donegal, Leitrim, Sligo, Cavan and Monaghan regions, 1980-89: Brussels-based RTE Europe Correspondent, later Europe Editor, covering EU and European affairs, including collapse of communism, Ireland's relationship with the European union, reform of Common

Agricultural Policy, Belgian child abduction scandals etc. 1989-2001: Belfast-based Northern Editor RTE, involved in news and current affairs coverage on Northern affairs 2001 to date. Former member, government-appointed Brennan Commission on Health Reforms; Awards: European of the Year 2002; Freeman of Sligo 2003. Clubs: Sligo Rovers, supporter of Coolera/Strandhill and St. Mary's GAA clubs. Recreations: sport, particularly GAA, soccer, current affairs (particularly health issues). Contact: RTE, Fanum House, Great Victoria Street, Belfast BT27. **T** 048 028 9032 6441 **F** 048 028 9033 2222 email gormant@ rte.ie

> An extremely brave and gutsy man in both his professional and personal life; very well respected journalist who has successfully demystified the machinations of political life in Northern Ireland.

GOULDING, William Lingard Walter; BARONET, HEAD MASTER
b 1940; single; *edu.* Winchester, Winchester, Hants; Trinity College Dublin; formerly with Conzinc Rio Tinto; manager Rionore Kilkenny and Dublin, racing driver, 1974-76; assistant master, Headfort Preparatory School, Co. Meath, 1977– 00; Headmaster, Headfort School, Co. Meath. Contact: Dargle Cottage, Enniskerry, Co. Wicklow.

> This cricket mad baronet continues a degree of eccentricity inherited from his father - without the financial acumen; much liked and respected as a sometime headmaster of Headfort Preparatory School, he still plays and teaches cricket.

GRAHAM, Rev. Laurence Arthur Moore; SUPERINTENDENT MINISTER OF CORK METHODIST CIRCUIT & PART TIME CHAPLIN UCC
b 1968, Lisburn, Co. Antrim; *m* Karen; 1*s* 1*d*; *edu.* Dolracka School, Ballymoney, Co. Antrim; Belfast Royal Academy; University of Reading; Queen's University; B Sc (Hons) Agriculture, BD (Hons); Superintendent Minister of Cork Methodist Circuit; part-time chaplin at UCC; co-ordinator of overseas work teams for Methodist Church; served with the Methodist Church as an agricultural missionary in Haiti and Antigua 1990-92; lay pastoral assistant in Cregagh Methodist Church, Belfast 1992–94; studied in Edgehill College, Belfast (part of Queen's University)1994–97; Minister of the Cavan & Longford Circuit 1997–2002; superintendent minister of Cork Methodist Circuit; part-time chaplin at UCC 2002 to date; Clubs: Douglas Golf Club; Caravan Club; Mardyke Arena Swimming Pool; Recreations: golf, walking, swimming, reading, photography, also on-going interest in Haiti. Contact: Epworth, Woolhara Park, Douglas, Douglas Road, Cork. **T** 021 429 2503 email laurence.graham@irishmethodist.org

> Gregarious and engaging with his international experience is a superb Superintendent Methodist Minister for Cork and extremely popular chaplain in University College Cork.

GRAHAM, Ian Maklin CARDIOLOGIST & PROFESSOR
b 1945; *m* Phillipa; 4*s* 1*d*; *edu.* Whitgift School, London; Trinity College Dublin; F.R.C.P.I., F.C.C.P; Director of Research St. Vincent's Hospital, Dublin; Director of Research, Irish Heart Foundation; past president Irish Heart Foundation; Consultant Cardiologist, Adelaide & Meath Hospitals; project leader, three European Concert Action Projects; founder Irish National Cardiac Surgery Register; founder & president Irish Hyperlipidaemia Association; consultant Cardiologist ,Adelaide & Meath Hospital; incorporating the National Children's Hospital Tallaght, Dublin 24; Associated Professor of Cardiology, Trinity College Dublin; Professor of Epidemiology & Public Health, Royal College of Surgeons in Ireland; *Publ.* over 100 publications in the field of cardiovascular risk prediction (at least three of these publications have the highest citation index internationally). Clubs: Fitzwilliam Lawn Tennis Club. Recreations: outdoor pursuits, hiking, rock climbing, English literature, wine. Contact: Charlemont Clinic, Charlemont Mall, Dublin 2. **T** 01 418 8461 **T** 01 475 3355 email ian.graham@amnch.ie web www.charlemontclinic.com

> Internationally recognized researcher in cardio-vascular disease; low profile, this learned professor ensures that Ireland remains at the cutting edge of medical research and development.

Fiona Gratzer

GRATZER, née Mc Court, Fiona; MANAGING DIRECTOR, UNISLIM LTD
b 1966, Newry, Co. Down; *m* Uwe Gratzer; 1*s* 1*d*; edu. Our Lady's School, Clermont, Rathnew, Co. Wicklow; University College Dublin; BA (History and Politics); College of Marketing and Design;

Post Graduate Diploma in Marketing; Managing Director Unislim; beauty columnist; runs Unislim, a healthy lifestyle and slimming company with over 180 leaders running a network of 500 weekly classes throughout Ireland; joined the family business 1990; has extended the Unislim brand into healthy food products, and on-line slimming service and slimming on your mobile phone; writes a weekly health and beauty newspaper column. Recreations: adventure sports, mountain biking, good music, good food, time with friends, reading for work and pleasure. Contact: 45, Downshire Road, Newry, Co. Down. BT 341EE **T** 283 026 3703 **F** 283 026 7293 fiona.gratzer@unislim.com web www.unislim.com

Extremely bright, attractive and focused businesswoman; has taken the company, started by her mother, Agnes Mc Court, and extended the brand into the area of health food; has embraced IT and now operates an online service.

GRAY, Danuta; CHIEF EXECUTIVE O2 IRELAND

b 1959, Sheffield, UK; *m* Andrew Caminow; 2*s*; *edu.* University of Leeds, UK; B.Sc Bio Physics; Chief Executive O2 Ireland. Joined BT 1984; account director for BT Global Communications, commercial sector 1990-92; sales manager and deputy general manager of BT Global Communications 1992-94; general manager of BT Mobile, Leeds 1994-99; senior vice president, BT Wireless's Businesses in Europe 1999–2001; chief executive O2 Ireland 2001 to date; non-executive director Irish Life and Permanent 2004 to date; board member Business in the Community 2002–05, member, St Patrick's Festival Board, member, Council Irish Management Institute. Recreations: skiing, family. Contact: 28/29 Sir John Rogersons Quay, Dublin 2. **T** 01 609 5000 email danuta.gray@O2.com web www.O2.com

The very able English born businesswoman brought remarkable background experience when she arrived in Ireland to head up O2 in 2001; in a highly competitive sector has demonstrated superb business acumen; bright, no-nonsense whose talents has been recognised in one of Dublin's most prestigious boardrooms; has shown excellent judgment in some of her sponsorship initiatives nationally.

GREENE, Judy; POTTER/RETAILER

b 1952; *m* Paul Fox; 2*d*; *edu.* L.S.U. College, Southampton; Teaching Dip in Art and Pottery; Potter/ Retailer. Teacher, Southampton 1974; art teacher and founder, Sewing Centre, Botswana, Africa, 1974-76; English teacher, ceramics student, Berne, Switzerland 1977; teacher, Crawford School of Art, Cork, 1977-78; founder/manager, Cape Clear Pottery, 1978-82; Diploma in Clay, Denver, Colorado, 1981; founder/manager, Judy Greene Pottery, Galway 1982 to date; President, Galway Chamber of Commerce, 1998-99; deputy President, 1997-98; member Network Galway, Crafts Potters Society; Awards: ACC/Evening Press Award 1994; featured in Up and Running RTE 1993, Start Me Up RTE 1996, The Last Resource, RTE 1999, Design in Ireland, US Cable TV 1999. Recreations: gardening, reading, swimming. Contact: Judy Greene, Pottery Workshop, 13 Cross Street, Galway. **T** 091 561 753 **F** 091 770 008 email info@judygreenepottery.co

She has made the world of utility ceramics usable and decorative as well as turning utility into an applicable art form of domestic use; much collected by the cognescenti.

GREEVY, Bernadette; FOUNDER/DIRECTOR ANNA LIVIA OPERA INTERNATIONAL OPERA FESTIVAL.

*b*1939, Dublin; *m* Peter Tattan (decd); 1*s*; *edu.* Holy Faith, Clontarf, Dublin; Guildhall College of Music, London; performance degree in Singing and Piano Accompaniment; Mahler singer and operatic roles include Carmen, Eboli, Don Carlos; Delilah, Samons et Delila; Orfeo, Lucrectia, Rape of Lucretia; Dido, Dido & Aeneas; Werther by Massenet, Ariodante by Handel; has performed in Teatro Colon, Buenos Aires; recordings include works by Handel, Berlioz, Elgar, Mahler, Duparc, Haydn and Bach; 2000 became the founder/artistic director of the Anna Livia International Opera Festival; awards include; Harriet Cohen International Music Award for outstanding artistry; Order of Merit of Malta; honorary doctorates of Music National University of Ireland and Trinity College Dublin; the Holy See conferred the honour of "Pro Ecclesia at Pontifice"; annual Bernadette Greevy Master classes in the Irish Museum of Modern Art, Dublin; first artist in residence at the DIT faculty of Applied Arts; member of the inaugural board National Concert Hall and 3rd.Board; Clubs: United Arts Club, Dublin; Hibernian Stephens Green Club, Dublin; Recreations: reading, walking, concerts, theatre, opera, sports. Contact: 'Melrose', 672, Howth Road, Dublin 5. **T** & **F** 01 831 3131 email.operaanna@eircom.net

Bernadette Greevy

Hardworking, punctilious and ambitious for her art form, she espouses the art of singing with conviction and has an enviable record of achievement. Always glamorous, with a swift turn of phrase

GREENSLADE, Roy; PROFESSOR OF JOURNALISM
b 1946, London; *m* Noreen McElhone; *edu.* Dagenham County High School, University of Sussex BA (hons) Politics, Honorary Doctorate, Brighton University; Professor of Journalism, City University, London; media commentator, *The Guardian*; Reporter, *Barking Advertiser* 1962-66; sub–editor, *Lancashire Evening Telegraph* 1966-67; sub-editor *Daily Mail* 1967-69; sub-editor *The Sun* 1969-71; sub-editor *Daily Mirror* 1971; production editor, *Daily Express* 1980; features editor *Daily Star* 1980-81; assistant editor *The Sun*,1981-86; managing editor, *Sunday Times* 1987-89; editor, *Daily Mirror* 1990-91; consultant editor, *Sunday Times* and *Today* 1991; freelance writer 1992-95; media commentator *The Guardian* 1995 to date; Professor of Journalism, City University London 2003 to date; Publ. *Goodbye to the Working Class* 1975; *Maxwell's Fall* 1992; *Press Gang* 2003; *How Newspapers Make Profits From Propaganda.* Clubs: Groucho, London; RSA London. Recreations: tennis, Irish politics; Contact: Ballyarr House, Ramelton, Co. Donegal. **T** 074 915 1175 **F** 074 915 1552 email roy.greenslade@pavilion.co.uk

A skilled and often liberal writer, whose views on many topics, especially Irish ones, are read with great interest by politicians and spooks alike.

GREGORY, Tony; PUBLIC REPRESENTATIVE
b 1947, Dublin; single; *edu.* O'Connell's CBS, North Richmond Street, Dublin 1; University College Dublin; B.A. H.Dip.Ed; Public Representative Independent TD Dublin Central; elected to Dublin City Council, 1979; re-elected for 25 years; elected to Dáil Éireann, 1982; re-elected to date; 24 years as an Independent TD; currently Chief Whip of the Dáil Technical Group; held the balance of power in 1982 and negotiated a major programme of renewal for the inner city; obtained the highest 1st preference % vote in the local elections in the country during the 1990s. Clubs: Westpoint Gym. Recreations: swimming, wildlife. Contact: Dáil Éireann, Kildare Street, Dublin 2. **T** 01 618 3488 **M** 087 8126348 **F** 01 618 4195 email tony.gregory@oireachtas.ie

Elected to Dáil Éireann nearly a quarter of a century ago and still one of the biggest vote getters; first TD to enter Dail Eireann without wearing a tie, in contravention of the established dress code; guaranteed his name in political history with the deal he brokered with Charles J. Haughey in 1982, thereby ensuring the election of Haughey as Taoiseach that year; hard working deputy renowned for his delivery for his constituents in inner city Dublin.

GRIBBIN, Annie Patricia; Make-Up Artist/Tutor
b 1959, Coleraine; single; 1*d*; *edu.* Loreto Convent, Coleraine; Scoil Iosa, Malahide; Loriam Beauty School, Dublin; Christian Cheveaux, Paris; Confederation of Beauty Therapy; Cidesco; Itec; International, Make-Up Artistry; Banking 1979; International Make-Up Award 1984; opened first make-up shop 1989; launched own brand Face 2 Face 1995; managing director of Make-Up Forever Ireland. Clubs: Ski Club of Ireland, David Lloyd, Riverview. Recreations: skiing, yoga, singing, theatre, art, swimming, biking, ISPCC, walking. Contact: Raglan Hallmews, 57 Raglan Lane, Dublin 4. **M** 087 258 6145 **F** 01 679 9876 email info@face2.ie

Annie Gribbin

The creative and talented Northerner was one of the pioneering make up artists in Ireland and went on to launch her own make up brand.

GRIFFIN, Eamon; MANAGING DIRECTOR, INTACTA PRINT Ltd
b 1951, Waterford; *m* Irene; 2*s* 1*d*; *edu.* Mount Sion Waterford; managing director Intacta Print ltd; apprentice printer with Croakers in Waterford; qualified printer; formed Intacta Print Ltd with late father Jimmy Griffin 1975; employs 45 in a state of art printing and finishing facility with its own in-house design studio; Director, Waterford and Tramore Racecourse; Chairman, The Friends of St. Patricks Hospital (geriatric hospice); Recreations: golf, horse racing, gardening Contact: Intacta Print, South Parade, Waterford. **T** 051 872276 **F** 051 878993 email info@intactaprint.ie www. intactaprint.ie

A shrewd and successful businessman who continues to reinvest in his company; has kept up with the latest in technological advances in print and design and driven his company from strength to strength; a dedicated fund raiser for St. Patrick's Hospital, Waterford; has helped organize many events including the Mayors Ball.

David Guest

GUEST, David; HEAD, ABN AMRO BANK (IRELAND)
b 1962, Dublin; *m* Nicola Balbirnie; 1*s* 2*d*; *edu.* Belvedere College, Dublin, Trinity College Dublin, University College Dublin, Bachelor of Business Studies, Bachelor of Arts; Head of ABN AMRO Bank (Ireland); Investment Bank of Ireland, YEOMAN International Group; Managing Director, ABN AMRO International Financial Services Company 1996 – '04; Country Executive, ABN AMRO Ireland 2004; Clubs; Kildare Hotel and Country Club, Claremont L.T.C.; Recreations: golf, tennis, theatre; Contact: ABN AMRO House IFSC Dublin 1. **T** 01 609 3800 emaildavid.f.guest@ie.abnamro.com web www.abnamro.ie

Highly respected international banker; since becoming head of one of Europe's oldest banks, has focused on margin savings and gains for his clients.

GUILBAUD, Charles John; RESTAURATEUR
b 1977, Manchester, UK; single; *edu.* King's Hospital, Palmersotwn, Co. Dublin; Trinity College Dublin; opened Venu Brasserie on Annes Lane, Dublin 2006; Custom House Administration & Corporate Services Ltd 2000–05. Clubs: Luttrellstown Castle Golf Club; Royal Dublin Golf Club; Recreations: golf, football, snooker, most sports, film, food & wine; Contact: Venu Brasserie, Annes Lane, Dublin 2. **T** 016706755

Following in father Patrick's (*qv*) very impressive footsteps, much is expected from his new eatery which has already established itself as HQ for the younger 'in' set; known as a good worker, energetic and with interesting ideas, should have no problems continuing to pack them in every night.

GUILBAUD, Patrick; RESTAURATEUR
b 1952, France; *m* Sally Lloyd Owen; 1*s* 1*d*; *edu.* Ecole Lemercier, Rue Lemercier, Paris 17; Ecole Sud Aviation, Pont De LeVallois, LeVallois; Proprietor, Restaurant Patrick Guilbaud; worked in family restaurant, Caen; British Embassy, Paris; Midland Hotel Manchester; Prop: Le Rabelais, Alderley Edge, Cheshire; Proprietor, Restaurant Patrick Guilbaud 1981 to date; Clubs: Luttrellstown Golf Club. Recreations: golf, cooking, drinking, skiing. Contact: 21, Upper Merrion Street, Dublin 2. **T** 01 676 4192 **F** 01 661 0052 email restaurantpatrickguilbaud@eircom.net

Brought Michelin starred cuisine to Dublin and in the process has educated a generation of Irish foodies; responsible for smartening up and improving not only menus but also surroundings at restaurants all over Dublin; charming and a wonderful host though some find his Gallic manners and great personal style off-putting.

GUINNESS, Hon. Desmond Walter; FARMER, WRITER; (Retired)
b 1931, UK; *m* 1st Princess Marie-Gabrielle Von Ulrach, 'Mariga'; (*decd. m.diss.*); 1*s* 1*d*; *m* 2nd Penelope Cuthbertson,' Penny'; 1*s* 1*d*; *edu.* Gordonstoun, Scotland; Christ Church, Oxford; MA; founded Irish Georgian Society 1958, succeeded by Knight of Glin (*qv*); Publ. *Georgian Dublin, Irish Houses and Castles; The White House, An Architectural History; Mr Jefferson Architect, Palladio and Newport Preserved* (with Julius Sadler,); *Dublin – A Grand Tour*, with Jacqueline O'Brien; *Great Irish Houses and Castles* with Jacqueline O'Brien (Weidenfeld & Nicolson, London & Harry Abrahams, New York, (1992 & 1994); honorary member, Royal Hibernian Academy of Arts. Clubs: Kildare Street Club, Dublin, Royal Automobile Club Dublin. Contact: Leixlip Castle, Co.Kildare. **T** 01 624 4430

This scion of a brewing family, son of Lord Moyne and Diana Mitford, founded the Georgian Society with his late wife Mariga; he pursues every avenue of support for the dwindling stock of Georgian heritage with great charm and aplomb as well as having considerable success; a great ambassador for Ireland abroad where he is royally treated.

GUIRY, Michael Dominic Richard; ACADEMIC AND MARINE BIOLOGIST
b 1949; *m* Gwendoline Mary Kilty; 1*s* 1*d*; *edu.* Dominican College, Newbridge, co. Kildare; University College Cork; B.Sc., M.Sc.; University of London, Ph.D., D.Sc.; Professor of Botany/Marine

Biologist; research fellow, Polytechnic of North London, U.K., 1972-75; post-doctoral fellow, University of Portsmouth, U.K., 1976-78; lecturer, University College Galway, 1979-90; visiting research fellow, University of Melbourne Australia, 1987-88; James Professor in Pure & Applied Science, St. Francis Xavier University, Canada, 1989; Personal Professor, University College Galway, 1991-96; Professor of Botany, National University of Ireland Galway, 1996 to date; director, Martin Ryan Marine Science Institute, National University of Ireland, Galway, 1997 to date; publ. *Seaweed Resources in Europe - Uses and Potential* (co-author 1991) *Check-list and Atlas of the Seaweeds of Britain and Ireland* (2004), and over 200 scientific articles, books and reviews; editor, *Phycologia,* Journal of the International Psychological Society 1990-92; member, Royal Irish Academy (1991; Vice-President, 1995-97); President, International Psychological Society (1996-97); President, British Psychological Society, 2005-07. Recreations: photography, seaweed, book collecting. Contact: National University of Ireland, Galway. **T** 091 49 2339 **F** 091 525 005 web http://www.algaebase.org; http://www.seaweed.ie.

> An important academic who makes his biology research relevant to the commercial world of mare culture; a prodigious worker and publisher of important papers relating to the development of the underexploited world of marine flora.

GUNNE, Patrick Joseph Fintan; MANAGING DIRECTOR CB RICHARD ELLIS
b 1972, Dublin; *m* Eimear Fitzpatrick; 1*s* 1*d*; *edu.* Castleknock College, Dublin; DIT, Dip Property Econ; Trinity College Dublin; BA Sc. Surveying; worked in UK, CB Richard Ellis, UK, 1995–97; Associate of Royal Institute of Chartered Surveyors Managing Director CB Richard Ellis Gunne 1997 to date; Clubs: Irish Auctioneers and Valuers Association, Rotary Club; Recreations: travel, swimming, time with family Contact: CB Richard Ellis Gunne, 1 Burlington Road, Dublin 4. **T** 01 618 5500 **F** 01 668 8850 email pat.gunne@cbre.com

Pat Gunne

> The son of the legendary Fintan is astute and extremely personable; following the untimely death of his father, returned to Ireland to head up the company; successfully merged and grew the commercial side of the company with CB Richard Ellis; bought out the residential side of the business 2005 and sold it 2006.

GUNNE O'CONNOR, Marianne; LITERARY AGENT
b Monaghan, "forty something"; *edu.* University College Dublin; BA, English/Spanish, H.Dip Ed; Literary Agent; own fashion business; first person to sell Dolce & Gabbana outside of Italy; sales director Lainey Keogh (*qv*); international PR; currently Literary agent; authors include: Patrick Mc Cabe, Cecilia Ahern (*qv*), Chris Binchy, Gabriel Byrne, Morag Prunty, Noel Harrison, John Lynch; Recreations: reading, pitching my authors' books, travel, being alone, walking, daydreaming, long chats, music. Contact: Morrisson Chambers, Suite 17, 32 Nassau Street, Dublin 2. **T** 01 677 9100 **F** 01 677 9101 email mgoclitagency@eircom.net

> Extremely able and articulate; known to broker the very best deal for her authors; hit the headlines with the multi million euro deal she got for Cecilia Ahern's first novels

HALL, William Walmsley: PROFESSOR AND UNIVERSITY VICE PRESIDENT
b 1949, Belfast; *m* Sonia; 3d; *edu.* Queen's University Belfast; Ph.D; Cornell University M.D; vice president for international affairs, University College Dublin; director, National Virus Reference Laboratory; consultant microbiologist St.Vincent's University Hospital Dublin; assistant and associate professor of Medicine Cornell University.; professor and head of laboratory for Medical Virology Rockefeller University; Professor and head of medical microbiology University College Dublin,1996 to date; fellow American Academy of Microbiology 1995; advisory board of Human Virology, University of Maryland 2004; adjunct professor of Microbiology Rockefeller University, New York; president of the International Retrovirology Association 2001-03; Fellow, American Academy of Microbiology; currently serves on the editorial boards of *Journal of Neurovirology, AIDS Research and Human Retroviruses, Neuropathology, Journal of the Acquired Immunodeficiency Syndrome* (JAIDS).
Contact: Vice President's Office UCD Belfield, Dublin 4. **T** 01 716 1618 **F** 01 716 1170
email william.hall@ucd.ie
web www.ucd.ie

Recognized internationally as the leader in his field and consulted by governments all over the world; was responsible for the funding and development of the Centre for Research in Infectious Diseases (CRID) in University College Dublin, whose construction was completed in August 2003.

HALLIGAN, Ursula Catherine; POLITICAL EDITOR, TV3
b 1960, Dublin; single; *edu.* Our Lady's Secondary School, Templeogue, Dublin 6; University College Dublin, Belfield, Dublin 4; BA History & Geography (Hons); MA Politics; Political Editor TV 3. Worked with *The Sunday Times; Magill Magazine;* RTE's Primetime and *The Sunday Tribune;* joined TV3 News as the station's first political correspondent, 1999-2001; appointed political editor 2003; Awards: AT Cross National Print Journalist of the Year, 1993; ESB National TV Journalist of the Year 2000; ESB National Business and Finance Journalist of the Year 2001; short-listed for ESB National Political/Current Affairs category 2004; *Publ.* Essays contributed to; *Media in Ireland: Issues In Broadcasting* (edited by Damien Kiberd 2002). *"Are You Being Served?" Commercial Versus Public Broadcasting* "; *Labour Party Annual Party Magazine,* 2005; *"TV Times"* ; *An Easter People; Essays in Honour of Sister Stanislaus Kennedy* (edited by John Scally 2005); *"Why Are There So Few Women In Irish Politics".* Recreations; reading, writing, walking, travelling abroad. Contact: Political Correspondent's Room, Leinster House, Kildare Street, Dublin 2. **M** 087 231 2150 **F** 01 611 0716
email ursula.halligan@TV3.IE web www.tv3.ie

Tenacious, hard-hitting political journalist who asks the hard questions and demands answers; her style is a bit theatrical, often making herself the focus of the interview; known and respected, even feared, in the corridors of power.

HAMILTON, Hugo; WRITER
b 1953, Dublin; *m* Maryrose Doorley; 1s 2d; *edu.* Colaiste Mhuire, Dublin; Writer; *Publ. The Sailor in the Wardrobe; The Speckled People; Sad Bastard; Headbanger; The Last Shot; The Love Test; Dublin Where The Palm Trees Grow; Surrogate City;* Awards: Rooney Prize for Literature (endowed by the Rooney family of Pittsburgh) 1992; member of Aosdána. Contact: Aosdána, 70, Merrion Square, Dublin 2. **T** 01 618 0200

A powerful author, speaker and writer of extraordinary sensitivity; his description of growing up in an almost alien world of Ireland in the 1950s, as described in *The Speckled People,* is a masterful evocation of dual cultures, reflecting dual identities.

James Hamilton

HAMILTON, James; BARRISTER/DIRECTOR OF PUBLIC PROSECUTIONS
b 1949, Dublin; *m* Noreen Keogh; 1s 2d; *edu.* Hibernian Marine School, Clontarf 1960–65, High School Dublin, 1965–66; Trinity College Dublin, deputy president Union of Students in Ireland 1969-70; B.A. (Mod) History and Political Science 1971; Kings Inn, Dublin; Barrister at Law, 1973; director of Public Prosecutions. Practice at Irish Bar 1973-81; legal advisor in office of the Attorney General 1981-99; head of office 1995-99; member of the Constitution Review Group 1995-96; member of the Council of Europe Commission for Democracy through Law (Venice Commission) 1998-2002; director of Public Prosecutions 1999 to date. Recreations: gardening, music (especially opera), history. Contact: 14-16 Upper Merrion Street, Dublin 2. **T** 01 678 9222
email jameshamilton@indigo.ie

Low-profile barrister who has continued to ensure that the role of the DPP remains cloaked in secrecy as is its entitlement; however the general public is more demanding of greater transparency

HANAFIN, Mary; PUBLIC REPRESENTATIVE

b 1959, Thurles; *m* Eamon Leahy S.C. (decd); *edu.* Presentation Convent, Thurles; St Patrick's College Maynooth; BA, H. Dip Ed; Dublin Institute of Technology, Diploma Legal Studies; Public Representative, Minister for Education: Fianna Fáil TD Dún Laoghaire. First elected 1997; re-elected 2002 topping the poll in Dun Laoghaire; appointed Minister of State at the Dept. of the Taoiseach (with special responsibility as Government Chief Whip and for the Information Society) and as Minister of State at the Dept. of Defence 2002-04; appointed Minister for Education 2004 to date; former member of Joint Committees on Heritage and the Irish Language; Justice, Equality and Womens Rights; Education and Science; candidate, Dublin South East General Election 1989; elected National Treasurer of Fianna Fáil, 1993; member, Fianna Fáil National Executive since 1980; member, Dublin City Council 1985-91; member, Senate of the National University of Ireland; vice president CENYC - European Youth Council; member Dublin Institute of Technology board; member City of Dublin Youth Services board; organiser, co-operative North Youth Exchanges; chairperson College of Catering, Cathal Brugha Street, Dublin; member Blackrock Historical Society; secretary Board of Visitors of the National Museum; Ball de Bhord Ghael Linn; member Board for the Employment of the Blind; director National Building Agency. Contact: Department of Education and Science, Marlborough House, Marlborough Street, Dublin 1. **T** 01 87 88 495 **F** 01 87 88 300 email mary.hanafin@education.gov.ie web www.maryhanafin.ie

Daughter of the legendary Des Hanafin, has top class Fianna Fáil pedigree; hard working, highly intelligent and always has a good command of her brief; will continue to perform well in any ministry in pursuit of her ultimate goal to be Ireland's first female Taoiseach.

HANAHOE, Anthony J 'Tony'; SOLICITOR

b 1945, Dublin; *m* Mary Swan; *2s 1d*; *edu.* St. Joseph's Marino, Dublin; Trinity College, Dublin; Law Society of Ireland; LLB; solicitor; captain Dublin Gaelig football All Ireland winning teams 1976 and 1977; appointed chairman DISC 1996 to date; appointed to Taoiseach's New Stadium Commission, 1998; Clubs: St Vincents Gaelig Football Club. Recreations: Kerry. Contact: Michael Hanahoe Solicitors and Co., Sunlight Chambers, 21 Parliament St, Dublin 2. **T** 01 677 2353

Former Dublin All Ireland winning captain of the famous Dublin football team of the 1970s; along with his St. Vincent's club mate, manager, Kevin Heffernan had a major influence in the professional approach taken by that team; well-known, successful solicitor in Dublin legal circles; cuts a dash with his sartorial elegance and penchant for pink socks.

HANLEY, CLARE; CATERER

b 1965, Rooskey, Co. Roscommon; *m* John Barry; *2s*; *edu.* Loreto Abbey, Dalkey; European Marketing Diploma, Belgium; Ballymaloe Cookery School, Co. Cork; Caterer; worked worked in PR; started Clare Hanley Catering Company 1992 to date. Recreations: travel, good food and wine. Contact: The Honorable Society of Kings Inns, Henrietta Street, Dublin 1. **T** 01 87 0410 **M** 01 86 829 0050 web www.dublincastle.ie/catering

Daughter of the legendary, late Peter Hanley from Rooskey; has craved out a niche market as the country's leading outdoor/home caterer; impeccable standards combined with superb cuisine and service ensures her presence at all the best parties and weddings; great charm, totally organized, never hassled, a true treasure.

HANLEY, James; ARTIST

b 1965, Dublin; *m* Órla Dukes; *edu.* Terenure College, Dublin; University College Dublin; BA 1987 (Hons, History of Art, English); National College of Art and Design Dublin, BA 1991 (1st class Hons; Fine Art, Painting); Artist, Portrait Painter; secretary of the RHA 2001 to date; full member RHA; exhibited extensively in Ireland and abroad; has had seven solo exhibitions; has work in most major public, corporate and private collections; his portraits include the official state portrait of Bertie Ahern TD, An Taoiseach; Ronnie Delaney for the National Gallery of Ireland; Maureen Potter for the Gaiety Theatre; Army Chief of Staff, Lt.General Colm E.Mangan;p time lecturer and tutor, National Gallery of Ireland; Publ. *Natural Disasters* Solo Exhibition Catalogue 1992; *Dark Rooms*: black and white drawings 1994; *White Lies*: solo exhibition catalogue 1995; *Grand Tourists* Solo Exhibition Catalogue 1997; *James Hanley, a decade of works on paper* 2005; editor, RHA Annual Exhibition Catalogue; Recreations: collecting art, film, travel, photography, music, theatre, architecture, conservation. Contact: The Solomon Gallery, Powerscourt Town House, South William Street, Dublin 2. **T** 01 679 4237 **F** 01 671 5262 email jameshanlyrha@eircom.net web www.solomongallery.com

A powerful and energetic painter who works on a very large scale; quiet, shy and apparently unassuming, he knows his own worth as an artist; a future president of the RHA he enjoys great esteem from his fellow artists and the public.

HANLON; Andrew; BROADCASTER, TV3 HEAD OF NEWS;
b 1966, Co. Wicklow; *m* Liz Allen (*qv*); 2*d* 1*s*; *edu.* Presentation Convent, Bray, Co. Wicklow; TV3 Director of News and Information Programming 1998 to date; managing director, founder and editor of Independent Network News (INN) 1997–98; head of News Classic Hits 98 FM 1989-97; broadcast journalist, RTE Radio 1987–89; television continuity announcer RTE 1 1986-88; judge, People of the Year Awards. Recreations: horse riding, hunting, point to point, walking, music, movies, current affairs. Contact: TV 3 TV3, Westgate Business Park, Ballymount, Dublin 24. **T** 01 419 3333 **F** 01 419 3300 email andrew.hanlon@tv3.ie

Highly experienced newsman who has brought gravitas to TV3's news service; low profile journalist, responsible for setting up the Independent Network news throughout the country.

HAREN, Patrick Hugh; ELECTRICAL ENGINEER
b 1950, Wolverhampton; *m* Anne; 2*s*; *edu.* Queens University of Belfast (QUB), BSc Electrical Engineering (1st class Hons) 1971, PRD, QUB (Electromagnetic Field Theory) 1976, MBA (Hons) University College Dublin; 1989-92 director, New Business Investment, Electricity Supply Board (ESB); Chairman, ESB International Ltd, Chairman, ESB Financial Services Ltd; manager, Business Ventures, ESB 1988–89; regional accountant, ESB 1987–88; manager, Strategic Planning, ESB, 1985-87; engineering management positions, ESB 1978-84; Research Fellow, CERN, Geneva 1976–77; Recreations: skiing, hill walking, languages (French, German). Contact: Viridian Group PLC, Danesfort, 120 Malone Road, Belfast BT95HT. **T** 028 90 689 101 **F** 028 90 689 263 email patrick.haven@viridiangroup.co.uk

The former ESB executive is now in direct competition with his former employer; Viridian has a generating station at Huntstown, Co. Dublin selling into the Irish market and his parent company is the biggest electricity supplier in Northern Ireland where the ESB has a new plant at Coolkeeragh, Co. Derry.

HARDIMAN, Hon. Mr Justice Adrian; SUPREME COURT JUDGE
b 1951, Dublin; *m* Judge Yvonne Murphy (*qv*); 3*s*; *edu.* Belvedere College, Dublin; University College Dublin, BA; Kings Inns, BL; Supreme Court Judge; called to the bar 1974; called to the Inner Bar 1989; appointed to the Supreme Court 2000 to date. Recreations: reading, walking, visiting sites of historic interest. Contact: The Supreme Court, The Four Courts, Dublin 7. **T** 01 888 6569 **F** 01 873 2332 web www.courts.ie

Probably one of the most outstanding advocates of his generation, reflected in his appointment to the Supreme Court directly from the bar; had a particular interest in vindicating the rights of individuals against what he perceived as the undue power of the media; his relative youth brings a new vigour to the Supreme Court; was one of the brightest of a generation at UCD, where he was president of the students' union and auditor of the L&H debating society; a frequent media contributor before his elevation to the bench; was also a founding member of the Progressive Democrats and represented Des O'Malley at the Beef Tribunal; a splendid racounteur.

HARDING, Michael; WRITER
b 1953; *m* Cathy Carman; 1*d*; *edu.* St. Patrick's College, Cavan, NUI Maynooth, Co. Kildare BA, BD,HDE; Writer; numerous awards for Theatre as Actor including; 1990 Stewart Parker Award, 1993 Writer in Association to Abbey Theatre, 1999 Writer in Residence, Trinity College Dublin; publ. author of two novels, fifteen Plays, six for National Theatre, The Abbey; Contact: Timpaun,

Lough Allen, Co. Leitrim. **M** 086 859 1116 **T** 071 964 6224 email harding@esatclear.ie

Insightful, able and straightforward he brings his former priestly life to bear on his writing.

HARNEY, Mary; PUBLIC REPRESENTATIVE
b 1953 Ballinasloe, Co. Galway; *m* Brian Geoghegan; *edu.* Newcastle National School, Co. Dublin; Convent of Mercy, Inchicore; Colaiste Bríd, Clondalkin; Trinity College Dublin. BA; Public Representative, Former Tánaiste (Deputy Prime Minister). Minister for health and Children, T.D. Dublin Mid West, Leader, Progressive Democrats; First woman auditor, Trinity College Dublin Historical Society; appointed to the Seanad 1977-81; elected deputy for Dublin South West 1981 to date; member Dublin County Council 1979-91; lost Fianna Fail Whip for voting in favour of the Anglo-Irish Agreement, 1985; co-founder (with Desmond O'Malley and Michael McDowell) of Progressive Democrats Party 1985; following 1989 general election, the Progressive Democrats formed a coalition government with Fianna Fail; Minister of State, Department of the Environment, 1989-92; following 1992 election, she returned to opposition, (party's spokesperson on Enterprise and Employment); formed a coalition government with Fianna Fail following the 1997 election; appointed Tánaiste, 1997-06; appointed Minister for Enterprise, Trade and Employment, 1997-2004; appointed Minister for Health and Children 2004 to date. Recreations: travel, current affairs, swimming. Contact: Department of Health and Children, Hawkins House, Hawkins Street, Dublin 1. **T** 01 635 4000 **F** 01 635 4001 email Mary.Harney@health.gov.ie web site www.maryharney.ie

Mary Harney

A co-founder of her party, the Progressive Democrats, with Desmond O'Malley and Michael McDowell (*qv*); became the first woman to lead a political party in Ireland; the youngest member of the Oireachtas when appointed as one of then Taoiseach, Jack Lynch's 11 nominees to Seanad Éireann 1977; first woman auditor of the Trinity College Historical Society; one of the best orators in Irish politics who has great facility for engaging her audience with unscripted, witty and intelligent speeches; single-minded in pursuit of her political vision which can occasionally land her in hot water; has made some important decisions particularly in the areas of environment and health; her anti pollution measures, through the introduction of smokeless fuel in Dublin, rid the city of chronic smog; in addition was actively involved with the introduction of the minimum wage in Ireland; strong and demanding minister, who sets very high standards for all around her; warm, friendly, engaging and entertaining company; even her most ardent supporters would agree that she faces her greatest challenge with her current portfolio, once described as the Angola of ministries by one of her predecessors, Brian Cowan (*qv*); astonished her close friends and colleagues by announcing her retirement as Tanaiste and Head of the PDs out of the blue September 2006.

HARRINGTON, Jessica Jane née Fowler; RACE HORSE TRAINER
b 1947; *m* John Harrington; 1*s* 3*d*; *edu.* Hatherop Castle, Cirencester, UK; Race Horse Trainer; Three Event Rider, represented Ireland, 1966, 1967, 1979-86; obtained permit to train 1987, full licence, 1991; has won numerous races including, Galway1997 Grand Annual (Cheltenham) 1999, winners trained include Oh So Grumpy, Dance Beat, Space Trucker, Mac Joy, Moscow Flyer - winner of 23 of his 37 starts to date including the Arkle Trophy at Cheltenham, 2002; the Queen Mother Champion Chase 2003 plus The Tingle Creek Chase at Sandown on two successive occasions; Moscow Flyer has amassed over €1.3 million in prize money alone and is regarded as one of the greatest National Hunt horses of the last 30 years; *Publ. Moscow Flyer*, Highdown Books, 2005. Recreations: golf, gardening, travel, Three Day Eventing. Contact: Commonstown Stud, Moone, Co. Kildare. **T** 0507 24153. **F** 0507 24292

The former Olympic Three Day eventer is an all round equestrienne; gregarious, intelligent and highly articulate she is now one of the most successful Irish trainers; known for meticulous attention to detail at her Co. Kildare racing establishment; extremely popular in a highly competitive industry.

HARRINGTON, Padraig; PROFESSIONAL GOLFER
b 1971, Dublin;. *m* Caroline; 1*s*; *edu.* Colaiste Eanna, Dublin; Dublin Business College, Aungier Street, Dublin (accountancy degree); Professional Golfer. Played amateur golf, throughout his childhood; turned professional in September 1995; won his first tournament, the Peugeot Open de Espana1996; finished 5th in the British Open at Troon 1997; after a run of consistent performances

Padraig Harrington

was selected to play for Europe in the Ryder Cup, 1999; gained his second European tour win at the Brazil Sao Paulo 500 Years Open, 2000 (after a multitude of close calls including being runner-up nine times); teamed up with Paul McGinley to win the World Cup for Ireland for the first time in 39 years in 1997; appears with increasing frequency in the U.S. at the majors and World Golf Championships events, and as a sponsor's invitee; won his first professional event in the U.S. at the Target World Challenge, a non-PGA Tour event hosted by Tiger Woods 2002; in both 2003 and 2004 was the runner up in the prestigious Players Championship and in the latter year he won enough money on the PGA Tour as a non-member to earn an invitation to the end of season Tour Championship; took membership of the PGA Tour, 2005; won his first PGA Tour official money event at the Honda Classic where he beat Vijay Singh and Joe Ogilvie in a sudden death playoff, 2005; member, European Ryder Cup Team, who took victory at Oakland Hills, Detroit, 2004; member, European Ryder Cup Team Kildare Hotel and Country Club 2006; set up Padraig Harrington Charitable Foundation 2005 (raised €225,000 from first event Golf Show at City West, Dublin). Ranked 17th in the PGA World rankings 2005. Clubs: Recreations: all sports especially snooker and tennis. Contact: Adrian Mitchell, IMG, Mc Cormack House, Burlington Lane, House, Chiswick, London W4 2TH London T 0044 208 233 5300 email amitchell@imgworld.com web www.imgworld.com web www.padraigharrington.com

HARRINGTON, Lord William Henry Leicester Stanhope 'Bill'; PEER, LANDOWNER.
b 1922; m 1st Eileen Foley (m.diss); 1s.2d; m 2nd Anne Chute (m.diss); 1s 2d; m 3rd Priscilla Cubitt; 1s 1d; edu. Eton College; Peer, Landowner Lord Harrington (11th Earl GB cr.1742); captain RAC (WW II); Irish Citizen 1965; Clubs: Kildare Street and University Club, Dublin. Recreations: racing. Contact: The Glen, Ballingarry, Co. Limerick T 061 399 162 F 051 399 122

"Bill" Harrington is a sporting peer who moved to Ireland and established a well known racing stud farm; closely involved with all aspects of equestrianism in county Limerick; family retain large ground rents in salubrious south west London; he remains firmly rooted in his Irish interests and the London estates are managed by his son Viscount Petersham; his family doings are often a matter for media comment especially given his granddaughter's marriage to a member of the British Royal Family, she also has strong Irish links.

Ann Harris

HARRIS, Ann née O'Sullivan; DEPUTY EDITOR, SUNDAY INDEPENDENT
b 1947, Cork; m Eoghan Harris (qv) (m.diss); fiancé Aengus Fanning (qv); 2d; edu. Ard Foyle, Blackrock, Co. Cork; University College Cork; BA; Deputy Editor, Sunday Independent; journalist with The Irish Press; Young Journalist of the Year Award; presenter Radio Telefis Eireann, Work and Money; Positively Healthy; fashion writer, Irish Independent, 1980-84; editor, Image 1984-85; deputy editor, Sunday Independent, 1985 to date; Recreations; reading, politics. Contact: Sunday Independent, 27–30, Talbot Street, Dublin 1. T 01 705 5333 email aharris@independent.unison.ie

Daughter of a Cork school teacher; is articulate, opinionated, extraordinarily hardworking and productive; extremely savvy, is considered the prime mover in the Sunday Independent's success; an impressive radio and TV performer - could easily have pursued a successful career in either; demanding, doesn't suffer fools gladly.

HARRIS, Eoghan; JOURNALIST, SCREENWRITER
b 1943, Cork; m Ann O'Sullivan (qv, Harris, Ann); (m.diss); 2d; edu. Douglas National School; University College Cork, BA.; Journalist/ Screenwriter. Producer RTE, 1986-90; Theorist, Workers Party, 1986-90; media advisor, Mary Robinson Election Committee, 1990; media advisor, Fine Gael, 1990-91; Awards: Jacobs Award, 1970, 1975; Silver Bear Award, (Berlin) for film documentary; columnist Sunday Times, 1993 to date; publications include Irish Industrial Revolution (1975), The Necessity of Social Democracy (1989); Souper Sullivan (play, 1985); Recreations: reading, politics, West Cork. Contact: Sunday Independent, 27–30, Talbot Street, Dublin 1. T 01 705 5000

Brilliant intellect; politically has served many masters in recent decades; now spends most of his time in West Cork;

HARRIS, Robert 'Pino'; MOTOR VEHICLE IMPORTER
b 1938, Dublin; m Denise Craigie; edu. Halstan Street N.S, Stoney Batter, Dublin; motor vehicle

importer; Left school to join father in his scrap metal business; built up a blue chip motor importing company, Hino, Mitsubishi; owns an impressive property and investment portfolio; major investor with Ivor Fitzpatrick (*qv*) in the MV *Christina,* the legendary yacht originally owned by Aristotle Onassis; Owner Harris Commercial Vechicles. Contact: J Harris Assemblers, Naas Road, Dublin. **T** 01 450 1900 email pino.harris@hino.ie

> One of the shrewdest businessmen in the country; said to personally know precisely where literally every nut and bolt in his empire is to be found; a wheeler/dealer who built up one of the biggest motor vehicle importing companies in Europe; has pulled off some amazing business deals including majority shareholder of Aristotle Onassis' MV Christina with Ivor Fitzpatrick (*qv*) which has huge tax benefits; hit the headlines when he purchased Carysfort College from the government and almost immediately resold it to UCD for a profit of millions.

David Harvey

HARVEY, David Gerard 'Dave'; CHAIRMAN & CEO CITY CHANNEL
b 1961, Dublin; m Siobhán McKenna; 3s; *edu.* Blackrock College. Dublin; Trinity College Dublin; B.B.S; M.A; Chairman & Chief Executive ,City Channel Ltd. Formerly a newsreader and announcer with RTÉ; established "Crimeline" programme RTÉ 1990s; founder shareholder 106.8 Radio Station; established City Channel 2005; remains a director of a number of television production companies; director, Irish Internet Advisory Board; chairman, People in Need Trust (TV's telethon). Clubs: Portmarnock Golf Club, Woodenbridge Golf Club, Fitzwilliam LTC, Dublin. Recreations: golf, reading, music, modern history. Contact: Heathfield House, Monkstown Road, Monkstown, Co. Dublin. **T** 01 260 0123 **F** 01 260 00723 email dharvey@city.ie

> Energetic, articulate and extremely media savvy; recently launched City Channel; is much acclaimed for media training politicians and high profile corporate clients; closely associated with Fianna Fáil.

HARVEY, Polly Jean 'PJ'; SINGER/ SONGWRITER
b 1969, Corscombe, Dorset, UK; Singer /Songwriter; with band PJ Harvey 1991-93; solo artist and collaborator 1993 todate; contributed to records by Pascal Comelade, Nick Cave, Tricky, Sparklehorse, Giant Sand, John Parish; Awards: Best Songwriter and Best New Female Singer Rolling Stone Magazine 1992; nomination, Mercury Music Prize 1993; nomination, Mercury Prize 1995; nomination, Mercury Music Prize 1996; Grammys and Brit Awards; winner Mercury Music Prize 2001; Publ. songs, albums and 4-track demos, issued 19 recorded works 1991 to date; Contact: c/o Principle Management 30-32 Sir John Rogerson's Quay, Dublin. **T** 01 6777330 **F** 01 6777276

HASLETT, Lindsay James; WARDEN, ST. COLUMBA'S COLLEGE
b 1956; *m* Marie Denise; 2d; *edu.* Foyle College, Springtown, Derry, 1967-1974; Lancaster University 1974-78; Trinity College Dublin 1978-79; University of Ulster 1979-82; Queen's University Belfast 1982-83; BA (Hons) D. Phil (French Literature) 1986, PGCE (Distinction-Belfast) 1983; Warden, St. Columba's College. Head of Modern Languages 1986-96 and housemaster, School House 1989-96, Rendcomb College, Cirencester, Glos; deputy headmaster Wiubech Grammar School, Cambs. 1996-2001; Warden at St Columba's College, Dublin 16; Clubs: East India Club, St James Square, London WI, HMC, Independent Schoolheads' Association (ISA); Recreations: Northern Ireland, current affairs, rugby, cricket, football, theatre, education; Contact: Gartan House, St Columba's College, Whitechurch, Dublin 16. **T** 01 4906791 **F** 01 4936655 email warden@stcolumbas.ie

> A progressive educationalist who has transformed this long established Co. Dublin College into one of the top rated academic schools.

HASTINGS, George William 'Billy' CBE; CHAIRMAN HASTINGS HOTEL GROUP
b 1928, Belfast; m Joy Hamilton; 1s 2d; *edu.* Royal Belfast Institute; inherited family public house business; opened first hotel in Ballymena 1964; Hastings Hotels now has seven hotels and two pub/restaurants; Hastings Hotels has a 50% interest in the Merrion Hotel, Dublin with Martin Naughton (*qv*) and Lochlann Quinn (*qv*); Landmark Ltd; former directorships include Director, Queens University Business and Industrial Services, Bank of Ireland (N.I.), Northern Ireland Tourist Board, former Chairman, Northern Ireland Venture Capital; Awards: O.B.E. for services to the community; D. Litt, (hc) University of Ulster 1984; Hon. Fellow, Irish Hotel Catering Institute, Justice of the Peace, Paul Harris Fellow, International Rotary. Contact: Hastings Hotel Group Ltd., Midland

Building, Whitla Street, Belfast BT15 1NH. **T** 028 9075 1066 **F** 028 9074 8152

One of Northern Ireland's leading businessmen for over half a century; is a significant player in the hospitality industry on this island; despite advancing years he continues to maintain a hands on approach to all his investments.

HAUGHEY, Seán F; PUBLIC REPRESENTATIVE

b 1961 Dublin; *m* Orla O'Brien; 3*s* 1*d*; *edu.* St. Paul's College, Raheny, Dublin 5; Trinity College Dublin, BA (Mod) Joint Hons Degree Economics & Politics; member of Dublin City Council 1985–2003; Lord Mayor of Dublin 1989–90; member of Seanad Eireann 1987–92; member of Dáil Éireann 1992 to date; Chairman, Joint Oireachtas Committee on Environment and Local Government 2004 to date. Contact: Chapelfield Lodge, Baskin Lane, Kinsealy, Dublin 17. **T** 01 845 0111 **F** 01 845 1444 email: sean.haughey@oireachtas.ie

The son and grandson of former Taoisigh and a former Lord Mayor of Dublin; low profile, hardworking TD; commands loyalty from his constituents but the charisma or national profile of his legendary father C.J. Haughey elude him.

HAUGHTON, Beth; FASHION RETAILER

b 1965, Cork; *m* Harold Lynch; 1*s* 2*d*; *edu.* Midleton College, Midleton, Co Cork; jewellery designer; opened restaurant 1993; Designer Store 1994, launched internet company in September 2005; currently designing shoe collection with Italian fashion company; Clubs: Oakgrove Leisure Centre, Blackrock Tennis Club. Recreations: media, food and wine, fashion, travel, interior decorating, living life to the full. Contact: Barrycourt House, East Douglas Village, Douglas, Cork. **T** 021 489 1155 **F** 021 489 1269 email bethstore@hotmail.com email hartefw@oceanfree.net

Bright, vivacious and stylish brings her joie de vivre to her eponymous store in Cork, a mecca for fashionistas from all over Munster and beyond.

HAVERTY, Anne; WRITER

b 1959, Holycross, Co. Tipperary; *m* Antony Cronin; *edu.* Sacred Heart school, Thurles, Co. Tipperary; Trinity College, Dublin; BA; HDipEd; Writer; Publ. *Constance Marhivicz; An Independent Life* (biography, 1989); *One Day as a Tiger* (novel, 1997); , *The Beauty of the Moon* (poems, 1999); *The Far Side of a Kiss* (novel, 2000); *The free and Easy* (novel, 2006). Contact: Aosdana, 70, Merrion Square, Dublin 2. **T** 01 618 0200 **F** 01 676 1302 email annehaverty@ireland.com

Regarded as an important new voice in Irish fiction; she brings her experience as a poet into play in the evocation of time and place, very fin de siecle; a writer, biographer and film writer, her range of skills has increased exponentially since her biography of Constance Markievicz.

HAYES, Brian George; SENATOR

b 1969; *m* Genevieve Deering; 1*s* 1*d*; edu. Garbally College, Ballinasloe, Co. Galway; St. Patrick's College, Maynooth; BA: Trinity College Dublin; H.Dip Ed; Senator. First elected to Dail Eireann 1997–2002; lost his seat in General Election 2002; Fine Gael Leader in Seanad Éireann (Dublin South West FG); spokesperson on Northern Ireland; Clubs: St. Anns Golf Club: St. Judes GAA Club; Recreations: history; Contacts: Seanad Éireann, Kildare Street, Dublin 2. **T** 01 618 3567 **F** 01 618 4563 email brian.hayes@oireachtas.ie web www.brianhayes.ie

Once seen as the bright, young star and a possible future leader of Fine Gael, he suffered a major set back to his political ambitions when he lost his seat in the 2002 general election; still retains his enthusiasm and diligence as senator but will struggle to come into the reckoning for a ministerial position if Fine Gael are to be in government in the future.

HAYES, Liam Patrick; DIRECTOR

b 1962, Navan, Co. Meath; *m* Anne O'Boyle; 2*s* 1*d*; *edu.* St. Patrick's Classical School, Navan, Co. Meath; Director; *The Meath Chronicle*, Navan; Journalist and Sports Editor, *Sunday Press*; Editor/co-founder, *Ireland on Sunday*; Editor/cofounder Dublin Dublin; former manager Carlow GAA Football Team. *Publ. Out of our Skins* (biographical); *Heroes*; Awards: Sports Journalist of the Year, 1986; All

Ireland Football Final (winner, Meath, 1987 & 1988), All Ireland Football Final (winner, Meath 1987 & 1988); All Ireland Football Final Man of the Year,1987. Recreations: reading, film, golf, running. Contact: Carlow GAA Grounds Oakpark Carlow.

HEALY, Andrew; CHIEF EXECUTIVE, NATIONAL IRISH BANK
b 1967, Dublin; *m*; 2*s* 1*d*; *edu.* Chief Executive National Irish Bank. Joined Ulster Bank 1987; moved to Belfast to head up retail banking in N.I.1996; Chief Executive National Irish Bank 2005 to date; Clubs: Recreations: Contact: National Bank of Ireland, 3rd Floor International House 3 Harbourmaster Place I.F.S.C. Dublin. **T** 01 670 1477

HEALY, Jack; CORK CITY ARCHITECT
b 1945, Cork; *m* Aileen; 1*d*; *edu.* Presentation Brothers College, Western Road Cork; Cork School of Art; Brookes University, Oxford; degree in Architecture; Cork City Architect; private practice 1972–76; Cork City Council 1976 to date; Awards: " Europa Nostra Medal" for Architecture, 1982; Independent Arts Award for Architecture, 1983; *Publ. "Architecture Ireland"* (special issue, Cork) 2005. Recreations: music, piano, guitar, art, photography, sculpture. Contact: Millview House, Templehill, Carrigrohane, Co. Cork. **T** 021 4874702 email: jwhealy@eircom.ie

> A civilized and cultivated architect who does much to beautify and consolidate the built heritage of Cork City of which he is justly proud.

HEALY; John Anthony; RESTAURANT MANAGER, FOUR SEASONS HOTEL;
b 1965; single; *edu.* Scoil Mhuire, Clane, Co Kildare; Dublin College of Catering, Cathal Brugha Street, Dublin 2; Diploma in Hotel Management & Business Studies; Restaurant Manager, Seasons Restaurant, Four Seasons Hotel, Dublin; Mezzo Restaurant, London, 1995-99; Hyatt Hotels London. New York; Four Seasons Hotel Dublin 2000-05; Presenter, *'The Restaurant'* TV Show (RTE 2003, 2004, 2005). Clubs: Naas Golf Club; Recreations: travel, shopping, dining out. Contact: 229 The Four Seasons Hotel, Simmonscourt Road, Ballsbridge, Dublin 4. **T** 01 667 8027 email john_healy2005@hotmail.com

John Healy

> One of the most professional restaurant managers in the country; manages his staff, clients and kitchen like the conductor of a symphony orchestra and with as much élan; internationally trained, totally professional, sartorially elegant and gregarious; definitely one of the reasons 'Seasons' restaurant is among the best in the country.

HEALY, Liam P; DEPUTY CHAIRMAN, (EMERITUS), INDEPENDENT NEWS & MEDIA
b 1929, Co. Mayo; *m.* Eithne Corrigan; 1*s* 2*d*; *edu.* St.Nathy's College Ballaghadereen, Co. Roscommon; Fellow Chartered Accountant of Ireland (FCA); Deputy Chairman INM; non-executive board member APN. Joined Independent Newspapers plc 1963; finance director Independent Newspapers plc 1971; managing director Independent Newspapers plc 1979-81; acting chief executive APN 1988–89; board member APN 1988 to date; Group Chief Executive Independent News & Media plc 1991-2000; deputy chairman 1992-94; chairman Independent News & Media plc 1995-2002; deputy Chairman Emeritus 2002 to date; board member, News & Media New Zealand. Clubs: Royal St.George Yacht Club Dun Laoghaire, Co. Dublin, Hibernian & Stephens Green Club, Dublin. Recreations: walking, music, theatre. Contact; Independent News & Media plc, Independent House, 2023, Bianconi Avenue, Citywest Business Campus, Naas Road, Dublin 24. **T** 01 466 3200 **F** 01 466 3222 email mail@inplc.com

> The undoubted architect of the success of Independent News and Media nationally and internationally; his low key, avuncular manner disguises one of the sharpest intellects and operators in the industry; a workaholic who is widely respected and popular everywhere.

HEALY, Fr. Sean; DIRECTOR, CORI
b Blackrock, Cork; single; *edu.* Fordham University New York; MA; PhD; Ran Parish, Kaduna, Nigeria; Justice and Development Advisor, 6 Northern Dioceses of Nigeria, 1976–81; Justice Office CORI 1983 to date; *Publ:* written and edited, with Sr Brigid Reynolds, S.M. more than a dozen books on values and public policy; actively involved with the Social Partnership talks since their inception in

the late '80s; Contact: Conference of Religious in Ireland, Bloomfield Avenue, Dublin 4. **T** 01 667 7322 email secrecariat@cori.ie

Has been a major voice for the underprivileged in Irish society for the last twenty years; the Cork-born clergyman had achieved much in Africa and is now changing the political mindset in Ireland to become more conscious of society and community issues rather than the bottom line; his attendance at the Fianna Fáil Think Tank in Owenahincha was a watershed in the current government's economic and social policy; many interpreted it as the beginning of the end of Charlie McCreevy's (*qv*) reign as finance minister before his appointment as EU Commissioner.

Tom Healy

HEALY, Tom; CEO, IRISH STOCK EXCHANGE

b 1950. Kinnegad, Co.Westmeath; *m* Marie; 1*s* 3*d*; *edu*. St. Finnian's College, Mullingar, Co.Westmeath; Trinity College Dublin; BA (Mod) Economics; Chief Executive Irish Stock Exchange. Civil Service 1970-75; Industrial Development Authority 1975-80; Irish Export Board 1980-87; Irish Stock Exchange Chief Executive 1987 to date; Clubs: National Yacht Club, Blackrock Rugby Club. Recreations: watching sports. Contact: 24, Anglesea Street, Dublin 2. **T** 01 617 4200 web www.ise.ie

The Kinnegad native had wide experience in the PR and Communications area of a number of Irish semi-state companies prior to his appoinment as CEO of the Irish Stock Exchange; politically astute, has presided over a time of unprecedented growth and change in the ISEQ.

HEANEY, Seamus Justin; NOBEL PRIZE WINNING POET

b 1939, Castle Dawson, Co. Derry; *m* Marie Devlin; 2*s* 1*d*; edu St. Columb's College, Derry; Queens University, Belfast, BA: Nobel Prize winning Poet. Secondary School Teacher 1962-63; Lecturer, St. Joseph's College of Education, Belfast 1963-66; first book, *Eleven Poems* published1965; won the Eric Gregory Award with *Death of a Naturalist*,1966; lecturer in English, Queens University, Belfast 1966-72; visiting lecturer University of California, Berkeley 1970-71; freelance writer and broadcaster; head of English Department Carysfort College, Dublin 1976-82; named Boylston Professor of Rhetoric and Oratory, Harvard 1984; Professor of Poetry at Oxford University 1989–94; appointed Ralph Waldo Emerson Poet in Residence at Harvard 1997; member, Aosdána, Honorary Fellow of Royal Irish Academy; recipient of several honorary degrees; *Publ. Eleven Poems* 1965; *Death of a Naturalist* 1966; *The Island People* 1968; *Door Into The Dark* 1969; *The Last Mummer* 1969; *A Lough Neagh Sequence* 1969; *A Boy Driving His Father To Confession* 1970, *Catherine's Poem* 1970, *Night Drive* 1970, *Chaplet* 1971, *Land* 1971, *Servant Boy* 1971, *January God* 1971, *Wintering Out* !972, *Bog Poems* 1975, *Two Decades of Irish Writing* (ed. D. Dunn, 1975); *North* 1975, *Stations* 1975, *Four Poems* 1976, *Glanmore Sonnets* 1976, *Robert Lowell: A Memorial Address* 1976; *Richard Murphy, Poet of Two Traditions* (ed. M. Harman 1978); *After Summer* 1978, *Christmas Eve* 1978, *A Family Album* 1978, *Field Work* 1979, *Gravities* 1979, *Uglomino* 1979, *Anthology: Arvon Foundation Poetry Competition* (ed. with T. Hughes 1980); *The Making Of Music; Preoccupations Selected Prose 1968-1978* (1980), *Changes* 1980, *Selected Poems* 1980, *Toome* 1980, *Holly* 1981, *Sweeney Praises The Trees; James Joyce and Modern Literature* (ed. W.J. McCormack and A. Stead, 1981); *Contemporary Irish Art* (ed. R. Knowles 1982), *Chekov on* Sakhalin 1982; ed.*The Rattlebag* (with T. Hughes 1982); *The Name of the Hare* 1982, *Sweeney and The Saint* 1982, *Verses For a Fordham Commencement* 1982, *Remembering Malibu* 1983, *A Hazel Stick for Catherine Ann* 1983, *Sweeney Astray* 1983, *An Open Letter* 1983, *Among Schoolchildren* 1983, *Hailstones* 1984, *Station Island* 1984, from *The Republic of Conscience* 1985; *Clearances* 1986, *Towards A Collaboration* 1986, *The Haw Lantern* 1987, *The Government of The Tongue* 1988, *An Upstairs Outlook* (with M. Longley 1989), *The Redress of Poetry* 1990, , 1990 *New Selected Poems 1966-87* (1990); *The Tree Clock* 1991, *Seeing Things* 1991, *The Cure At Troy* (from Sophocles' play Philoctetes, 1991); *Sweeney's Flight* 1992, *The May Anthology Of Oxford And Cambridge Poetry* (ed. 1993), *Joy or Night* 1993, *The Midnight Verdict* (from B. Merriman and Ovid 1993); *The Redress of Poetry* 1995, *Crediting Poetry: The Nobel Lecture* 1996, *The Spirit Level* 1996 - Whitbread Award 1997; *Opened Ground: Selected Poems 1966-96* (1998), translation: *Beowulf* (1999) - Whitbread Award in January 2000; *Electric Light* 2001, *Finders Keepers: Selected Prose* 2002, *The Burial At Thebes* (A Version of Sophocles's "Antigone") 2004; 1995 Nobel Prize in Literature. Recreations: reading, walking, the countryside. Contact: Aosdána, 70, Merrion Square, Dublin 2. **T** 01 618 0200 **F** 01 676 1302

The Co. Derry born, Nobel Prize winning poet is keyed and pitched unlike any significant poet now at work in the language; charismatic, quietly spoken, accessible and unpretentious, enjoys a global following.

HEASLIP, F B ' Danno'; AUCTIONEER
b 1938, Galway; *m* Mary Murphy; *2s 2d; edu.* St Joseph's College, Galway; Crescent College, Limerick; Trainee, Norwich Union (UK) 1959-61; Principal in F.B. Heaslip Ltd., Estate Agents, Auctioneers and Valuers (Galway), 1961 to date; Fellow, The Irish Auctioneers and Valuers Institute; Clubs: Galwegians RFC President 1991; 2005/2006; (played with London Irish and Galwegians and Connaught Clubs) Recreations: rugby, golf, racing. Contact: Heaslips, Estate Agents, Auctioneers and Valuers, 27 Woodquay, Galway. **T** 091 565 261 **F** 091 565 863.

> The successful West of Ireland auctioneer is well known nationally; a strong Progressive Democrat supporter.

HEATHRINGTON, Rick; CHIEF EXECUTIVE TV 3
b West Indies; *m* June; *edu.* University of Toronto School of Management Studies; managing director and C.E.O. TV3; began his business career with an international financial firm in Winnipeg; was transferred to Vancouver and Toronto in his capacity as National Advertising Manager; Glen Warren Broadcast Sales and CFTO-TV (Toronto) 1974–84; Global Executive Vice-president and General Manager of Alexander Pearson Dawson Inc.(APD) 1985–92; director, Marketing Global Television, 1992; general manager/director of marketing 1994; former director, Rainbow Stage, a non-profit professional theatre company; the Zoological Society of Manitoba; the Broadcaster's Association of Manitoba; and Western Association of Broadcasters; past-director, television bureau of Canada; past ex-officio director Canadian Association of Broadcasters; has served on numerous industry-related committees; serves as director on a number of companies; TV3 Television Network Ltd; CanWest Entertainment International Inc.; CanWest Ireland Sales Ltd. Recreations: golf, sailing, the arts. Contact: TV 3, Ballymount Industrial Estate, Clondalkin, Dublin 22 **T** 01 419 3333 email rick.heathrington@tv3.ie web www.tv3.ie

> Was moved to Ireland by CanWest Global Communications Corp. of Winnipeg Canada; respected internationally as a professional operator in his industry but demands results and doesn't suffer incompetence; has significantly increased the value of the company since he took over at the helm as was obvious when it was sold to Doughty Hanson 2006.

HEAVEY, Aidan; CHIEF EXECUTIVE TULLOW OIL PLC
b 1953, Castlerea; *m* Lorraine McCourt; *edu.* National School, Castlerea; Clongowes Wood College, Co Kildare; University College Dublin, B.Comm; Chief Executive tullow Oil; worked in several accountancy firms, 1974-84, before founding Tullow Oil; chief executive, Tullow Oil, 1984 to date, one of the few successful exploration companies based in Ireland; regarded internationally as having an exceptionally strong technical team; operates only outside of the country, mainly in Indian sub continent, Africa and Europe; member, Institute of Chartered Accountants. awards, winner, Ernst and Young Entrepreneur of the Year 2005. Recreations: tennis, golf Contact: Tullow Oil plc, Airfield House, Airfield Park, Donnybrook, Dublin 4. **T** 01 260 2611 **F** 01 260 2672.

HEAVEY; Patrick Garrett; DENTAL SURGEON;
b 1955, Dublin; *m* Maebh; *3s; edu.* St. Michael's College, Ailesbury Road, Dublin 4; Blackrock College; University College Dublin; Trinity College Dublin; BA; B. Dent. Sc., Dip. Clip Dent; general practice since 1980; President Irish Dental Association 1994; Vice Chairman Board of Dublin Dental Hospital 2000–04; Chairman Fitness Practice Committee Dental Council 1998–2003; President Dental Council 2003–05; Clubs: Royal Irish Yacht Club, Dun Laoghaire Golf Club; Woodenbridge Golf Clubs: Recreations: golf, hill walking. Contact: 2, Mountpleasant, Sandycove, Co. Dublin. **T** 01 280 1684 **F** 01 284 2344 email pgheavey@undigo.ie

Pat Heavey

HEDERMAN, Wendy E A; SOLICITOR
b 1967, Dublin; *m* Brendan Cassidy; *1s 3d; edu.* Convent of the Sacred Heart, Mount Anville, Dublin; Trinity College Dublin LLB; Université Libre de Bruxelles, Belgium, Masters in European Law; Law Society of Ireland; Solicitor; Certified Diploma in Accounting and Finance (C. Dip. A.F.) from the ACCA; joined Mason Hayes & Curran Solicitors 1990; seconded to European Law Firm in Brussels 1993; appointed Senior Associate in Mason Hayes & Curran 1998; Partner Mason Hayes and Curran 1999; general legal counsel Etel Telecom 2000–03; founder Wendy Hederman Co. specialising in information technology, telecommunications law, intellectual property, European Law, competition law and regulatory law 2004 to date; elected member Dublin City Council 2004 to date; chairman of the EU and International Affairs Committee, Law Society of Ireland; tutor in Intellectual Property

and in European Law, Law Society of Ireland; *Publ.* include contributions to *Appointing Commercial Agents in Europe*, Irish Chapter, (Wiley 1993), *Intellectual Property Laws of Europe* Irish Chapter (1994); *Telecommunications Law in Ireland* (co-author) by Mason Hayes & Curran (1999); Chairman, Society of Young Solicitors, Ireland 1998-99; member EU and International Affairs Committee, Law Society of Ireland (former Vice Chairman); member, Society for Computers and Law; member, Licensing Executives Society; member, Association International des Jeunes Avocats; member Network (the organisation for Women in Business); Clubs: Fitzwilliam LTC, Dublin. Recreations: walking with my children, tennis, politics. Contact: The Stables, Waterloo Lane, Dublin 4. **T** 01 660 7218 email wendy.hederman@iol.ie

Highly qualified and well respected professional in the legal and political arena; with a successful legal career well established now looks set to embark on a political one come the next general election; daughter of the formidable Carmencita who was a legendary councillor and Lord Mayor of Dublin.

HEFFERNAN, Anne; EXECUTIVE, DUNNES STORES

b 1968, Dublin; *m* 1st Charles O'Brien; *m.diss*, 2*d*; *m* 2nd 1*s* ; *edu.* Teresian School, Donnybrook, Dublin; Royal College of Surgeons, Dublin; MB BAO BCH; University College Dublin; MBA; joined Dunnes Stores, the family owned food, furniture and drapery business. Clubs: David Lloyd Fitness, Riverview, Dublin. Recreations: reading, family, fitness. Contact: Dunnes Stores, Beaux House, Beaux Lane, Dublin 2. **T** 01 611 2100 www.dunnesstores.com

The only daughter of Andrew and Margaret Heffernan (*qv*) is a chip off the old block, a 'superwoman' like her mother and a respected medical doctor like her father; despite qualifying one of the top of her year in Royal College of Surgeons and showing great promise as a young doctor in St Vincent's University Hospital, she abandoned medicine for a career in the family business; hardworking, down to earth, tipped as the most likely to step into her mother's shoes.

HEFFERNAN, Kevin 'Heffo'; FOOTBALL LEGEND

b 1930, Dublin; captained Dublin to All Ireland victory in 1958; was in the winning National League winning teams of 1953, 1955, and 1958; won seven Railway Cup medals with Leinster; played for Dublin at minor, junior and senior levels in both hurling and football; helped his club, St Vincent's, to win the County Championship in both sports; will always be associated with the great Dublin football teams of the 1970s which he coached to All-Ireland successes in 1974, 1976 ,1977 ,1983 and to National League titles in 1976 and 1978. The era was dominated by Dublin's great rivalry with County Kerry former county's ecstatic fans dubbed "Heffo's Army"; the only non-player to be nominated Texaco Footballer of the Year 1974; personnel manager, Electricity Supply Board (ESB);became Chairman of the Labour Court; named left corner forward on the GAA Gaelic football "Team of the Millennium." Recreations: all sport, golf. Contact: ESB Head Office, 27, Lower Fitzwilliam Street, Dublin 2. **T** 01 850 372 372

The former ESB employee became a national figure though his GAA involvements; one of the all time greats of Gaelic football; a member of the team of the century; Heffo will be best remembered by the people on the Hill - Hill 16 in Croke Park - as the manager of the highly successful Dubs of the 1970's; along with Mick O'Dwyer (*qv*) he was one of the pioneers of modern GAA management; also served as chairman of the Labour Court after his retirement as head of Personnel at the ESB; also a former Chairman of Bord na gCon.

HEFFERNAN, Margaret neé Dunne; DIRECTOR, DUNNES STORES

b 1942, Cork; *m* Dr Andrew Heffernan; 3*s* 1*d*; *edu.* Ursuline Convent, Blackrock, Co. Cork; started at the bottom in the family business Dunnes Stores in Patrick Street, Cork, 1956; quickly worked her way through every area of the company; appointed director, 1964; managing director 1993 to date; has presided over the expansion of the company to Northern Ireland, the UK and Spain; Clubs: Kildare Hotel and Country Club: Recreations: horse racing, family; Contact: Dunnes Stores, Beaux House, Beaux Lane, Dublin 2. **T** 01 611 2100 www.dunnesstores.com

Margaret Heffernan

Has given a lifetime to the family business – Dunnes Stores, Ireland's largest retail chain; definitely a chip off the old block, her father was the legendary Ben Dunne, the architect of low cost food and clothing in Ireland from the '50s; is renowned as a formidable business person who drives a hard bargain in all her dealings; founder of People in Need charity which has raised millions since its inception; has personally contributed anonymously to many worth causes; still works longer and harder than someone half her age; extremely low profile; no nonsense; loyal friend; spends her down time with her children and grandchildren on whom she dotes.

HEFFERNAN, Michael; DIRECTOR, DUNNES STORES

b 1970, Dublin; *m* Maureen Dolan; 2*d*; *edu.* Teresian School, Dublin 4; St. Michael's College, Ailesbury Road, Dublin; Loyola University, Los Angeles; Joined fashion section of family company; Received major tranche of shares from his mother Margaret Heffernan (*qv*). Recreations: friends, family; Contact: Dunnes Stores, Beaux House, Beaux Lane, Dublin 2. **T** 01 611 2100 www.dunnesstores.com

Low profile, shy, charming and extremely popular; deemed to be the brains behind Dunnes Stores' huge success in hip, stylish, low cost fashion; with his beautiful, former model wife, Maureen, cuts a dash in Dublin, Marbella, Manhattan and Barbados

HEGARTY, Adrian; GROUP CHIEF EXECUTIVE, FRIENDS FIRST HOLDINGS LTD

b 1947; *m* Anne Ellard; 2*s* 4*d*; *edu.* University College Dublin; B.Comm; Fordham University, New York; MBA; Wharton, University of Pennsylvania; Advanced Management Program; joined Bank of Ireland 1967; Vice President, Corporate Banking, Bank of Ireland, New York 1973-79; chief corporate accounts manager, Bank of Ireland, Dublin, 1983-85; head of marketing, Bank of Ireland, 1985-87; regional manager, Athlone 1987-90; operations director, Bank of Ireland Finance, 1990-96; managing director, Premier Banking and Direct Insurance Services Ltd, 1996 to date; Group Chief Executive, Friends First Holdings Ltd; Fellow, Institute of Bankers; board member, Institute of Directors; board member Interamerican, Greece. Recreations: horse racing, theatre, reading, cinema. Contact: Friends First, Cherrywood Business Park, Loughlinstown, Dublin 18. **T** 01 661 0600 **F** 01 661 6665

HEGARTY, Diarmuid Arthur; COLLEGE CHAIRMAN

b 1948, Dublin; *m* Susan; 2*s* 2*d*; *edu.* Blackrock College, Dublin.1968, B.Comm (1st hons) UCD; College Chairman; Training Contract, (tax consultancy) 1969-73; Coopers & Lybrand Tax Manager; Taxation Consultant Deloitte & Touche 1974-75; established tuition college then known as Business & Accounting, now Griffith College 1975; MD Griffith College,1975-92; Chairman Griffith College Dublin 1992 to date; Board Member Griffith College Karachi 1999 to date; ACA Institute of Chartered Accountants in Ireland 1972; FCA Institute of Chartered Accountants in Ireland 1982; member, Council Institute of Chartered Accountants in Ireland 1981-88; chairman, Accounting Review Committee ICA 1981-84; Advisor to the Irish Government 1996-98; Strategic Management Initiative Financial Management Working Group 1999 to date; member Baggot Street Hospital Board, 2000 to date; member Blackrock College Financial Advisory Group; member Higher Education and Training Awards Council 2001; advisor Pakistani Government, education and investment in the IT Sector 2001; honorary consul, Pakistan in Cork 2001; Clubs: Royal Irish Yacht Club, Dún Laoghaire; Donabate Golf Club; Recreations: sailing, skiing, golf, boxing. Contact: Griffith College Dublin, South Circular Road, Dublin 8 . **T** 01 415 04 00 **F** 01 454 9607 email chairman@ged.ie

HEGARTY, Nóirín Mary; EDITOR, THE SUNDAY TRIBUNE

b 1966; *m* Frank Hopkins; 1*s* 2*d*; *edu.* Loretto High School, Beaufort, Rathfarnham, Dublin; College of Commerce(now DIT) Dublin, Certificate in Journalism; Editor, *The Sunday Tribune*. Freelance news reporter/features writer *Evening Press* and *Irish Press*; court reporter *The Irish Times*; staff journalist Independent Newspapers, assistant director (writing) *Evening Herald*, Deputy Editor, *Evening Herald*; Chairperson, Adjudication Committee ESB/REHAB People of the Year 2000 to date; Member Adjudication Committee Media Awards 2004 to date. Recreations: travel, current affairs, walking; Contact: *Sunday Tribune*, 15, Lower Baggot Street, Dublin 2. **T** 01 631 4300 email nhegarty@tribune.ie

Focussed, hardworking and ambitious, following a sometime turbulent stint as deputy editor of the *Evening Herald*, her appointment, as editor, to the more tranquil *Sunday*

Tribune would have seemed to flag a more tranquil career path; the national exposure derived from the late Liam Lawlor reportage was hostile and damaging.

HEGARTY, Tom; ARCHITECT
b 1964; *m* Julie; 1*s* 1*d*; *edu.* Presentation Brothers College, Cork; Mackintosh School of Architects, Glasgow; B Arch, MRIA; Architect; Architect, Billy Willson Association, Cork 1990-94; architect, O'Riordan Staehli Architects 1994-2005; director Reddy, O'Riordan Staehli - to date; *Publ:* Editor, *O'Riordan Staehli Architects, The First 30 Years of the Company;* articles in architecture journals. Clubs: Royal Cork Yacht Club, Baltimore Sailing Club, Llen River Cruising Club; Recreations: skiing, sport; Contact: Reddy O' Riordan Staehli Architects, Schoolhouse Studio, Douglas, Cork. **T** 021 436 2922 **F** 021 436 3048 email tom.hegarty@orsa.ie

HEGARTY, Dr. John; PROVOST, TRINITY COLLEGE DUBLIN
b 1948, Claremorris, Co. Mayo; *m* Neasa Ní Chinnéide; 2*s*; *edu.* locally, St.Patrick's College Maynooth; University College Galway; Ph.D; Post Doctoral Fellow University of Wisconsin-Madison, Wisconsin; Provost Trinity College; University of Wisconsin and research fellow Bell Laboratories New Jersey1975-86; Professor of Laser Physics Trinity College Dublin 1986-2001; head of department of Physics 1992-95; co-founded the national research programmes Optronics Ireland 1995; co-founded Eblana Photonics 2001; adjunct professor University of Georgia (USA) 1990-95; visiting professor in the University of Tokyo and Sony Corporation Japan 1995; dean of research Trinity College Dublin responsible for securing IRL£50 million in research funding1995-2000; 43rd Provost of Trinity College Dublin 2001 to date; member Royal Irish Academy; The American Physical Society, The American Optical Society, The Institute of Electronic and Electrical Engineers; Fellow of Trinity College, Fellow of the Institute of Physics; served on the Board of Science Foundation Ireland, The Higher Education Authority, *Publ.*140+ peer reviewed papers in scientific journals in the area of Laser physics. Recreations: sailing and walking. Contact: Provost's Office, Trinity College Dublin, Dublin 2. **T** 01 618 1558 email provost@tcd.ie web www.tcd.ie

A very distinguished scholar in the field of Laser Physics, he and his scholar wife Neasa have much to contribute to the onward development of the University of Dubin. A pleasant and unassuming person with many gifts of intellect, charm and a capacity to manage an old university for the 21st.century.

HEMPHILL, Lord, Peter Patrick Fitzroy Martyn; PEER, TURF CLUB MEMBER
b 1928; *m* Olivia Anne Ruttledge; 1*s* 2*d*; *edu.* Downside, BNC Oxford (MA) Irish Resident Peer, and Turf Club Member, 5th.Baron Hemphill (UK cr.1906); Chairman Galway Race Committee 1990 to date; member Turf Club, former Senior Steward, member, Irish National Hunt Steeplechase Committee; former Senior Steward of the Turf Club; Cross of Order of Merit, Order of Malta. Clubs: White's, London, Irish Cruising Club, RIAC, Dublin. Contact: Dunkellin, Kiltulla, Co.Galway. **T** 091 848 002 **F** 091 848 174

A popular member of the Irish Horsey world; wonderful raconteur; a descendent of one of the Tribes of Galway, remains a power behind the scenes in Irish Turf Club matters and the National Hunt.

HENDERSON, Rt, Rev, Richard Crosbie Aitken; BISHOP OF TUAM, KILLALA, ACHONRY
b 1957; *m* Anita Julia; 1*s* 2*d*; *edu.* Westminster School; Magdalene College, Oxford; St. John's College, Nottingham; BA; D.Phil; Diploma in Pastoral Studies; Bishop of Tuam, Killala and Achonry; Curate of Chinnor 1986-89; Incumbent of Abbeystrewery Union (Cork, Cloyne & Ross) 1989-95; Canon of Ross Cathedral & St.Finbarr's Cathedral 1993-95; Incumbent of Ross Union & Dean of Ross 1995-98; Chancellor of St.Finbarr's Cathedral Cork 1995-98; elected Bishop of Tuam, Killala & Achonry by electoral college 1997; Recreations: woodwork, clockhanging; Contact: Bishop's House, Knockglass, Co. Mayo. **T** 096 313 17 **F** 096 31775 email bishop@tuam.anglican.org

A polite and charming churchman who has to keep the faith in a huge geographical area from North Mayo, the Western seaboard and as far as North Limerick; has seen a small increase in his flock,which has to be encouraging.

HENEGHAN, Nigel David; PUBLIC RELATIONS DIRECTOR
b 1961, Dublin; *m* Penny Alexander; 3*d*; *edu.* St Michael's College, Ailesbury Road, Dublin 4; Public Relations Director; worked in PR from 1980 in Dublin, London and Dubai; joint founding director of

Heneghan PR in 1990, became Managing Director 1998 to date; professor of Public Relations Institute in 2000-2001; Fellow of Public Relations Institute of Ireland 2005; Clubs: Portmarnock Golf Club; Recreations: golf, music, travel, politics. Contact: 54 Pembroke Road, Dublin 4. **T** 01 660 7395 **F** 01 660 7588 email nigel@hpr.ie

> Extremely convivial and well respected in the PR world; followed in his father's formidable footsteps; has established himself in his own right.

HENNESSY, Michael; PRINCIPAL, PRESENTATION BROTHERS COLLEGE, CORK
b. 1951; *m* Patricia; 2*s*; *edu*. Colaiste Chriost Ri, Cork; University College Cork; BSc, H Dip Ed, MA; Principal, Presentation Brothers College, Mardyke, Cork 1973 to date; Clubs: Rowing UCC, Lee Rowing Club; Recreations: reading, football, rugby, rowing; Contact: Cushewdall, Old Blackrock Road, Cork. **T** 021 496 6794 **F** 021 496 6794 email mhennessy@pbc-cork.ie

> Has continued the tradition of academic excellence in one of Cork's most famous schools.

HENRY, Patrick, 'Pat'; FITNESS CONSULTANT
b 1949, Dublin; *m* Maire Hickey; 2*s*; *edu*. St. Lawrence O'Toole School, Dublin; College of Retail Management /Business Degree in Body Composition, Agora Hills Body Composition and Training Academy, California; AABS, California; Owner-Director Pat Henry Fitness & Wellness Programme 1973 to date. Master Trainer; MIHCA Yoga-Philosophy Ireland; MBT Austria; MBT Head Coach; Yoga Teacher, Yoga Therapist; lectured on Yoga Philosophy all over the world; manager of Gironda GM Hollywood; started Pat Henry wellness in house programming 2000; director IABS Academy of Personal Training; director Wellness Planning;Awards: AABS best trainer in Europe 2004; Clubs: Body Building and Surfing,USA; Recreations: walking, clay shooting, bodybuilding, wave surfing; Contact: Pat Henry Fitness Centre, 14 Pembroke Street, Dublin 2. **T** 01 661 5195 email pathenry@wellness.com

Pat Henry

> A top international trainer whose clients have included Daniel Day Lewis (*The Boxer*); Ellen Barkin, Michael Flately, Sylvvester Styllone etc; extremely supportive, dedicated and inspirational.

HERATY, Anne; CHIEF EXECUTIVE, CPL RESOURCES plc
b 1960, Longford; *m* Paul Carroll; 1*s* 1*d*; edu. Secondary School Newtownforbes; University College Dublin; B.A. (Econ); Chief Executive of CPL Resources plc; sales executive with Xerox; joined Grafton Recruitment 1987-89; formed partnership with Keith O'Malley in CPL; bought out CPL 1989; chief executive, Cpl Resources 1989 to date (company provides recruitment and outsourcing services across a range of disciplines and sectors offering specialist labour market knowledge and expertise in each sector); chairperson, Expert Group on Future Skills Needs; member Further Education and Training Awards Council; non-executive director Bord na Mona; Awards: Veuve Clicquot Business Woman of the Year 2005. Contact: CPL Resources plc, 83, Merrion Square, Dublin 2. **T** 01 614 6000 web www.cpl.ie

> Regarded as one of the best operators in the country; her company's shares have been the best performers of any indigenous company on the Irish Stock Market 2004–06; widely respected as astute, professional business woman; articulate, low profile, hardworker, focused on growing her already extremely successful company in the UK and Europe.

HENRY O'CONNOR, Thelma Edith; BAR AND RESTAURANT OWNER
b 1954, Dublin; *m* John O'Connor; 1*d*; edu. Sacred Heart, Monkstown, Holy Child, Killiney, Rosslyn House Finishing School, Weybridge, Surrey, England; Owner-Manager IN (Gastrobar) Dalkey Village, Co. Dublin and TONIC (Gastrobar) Blackrock, Co. Dublin. Beauty therapist, Betty Whelan School of Beauty Fitness Institute of Ireland, Grafton Academy of Design; beauty therapist, Elizabeth Arden, London, owner of fitness clubs in Dublin venues, previously owned Laces Restaurant, Dalkey and Rumm's D4, Dublin; owner-manager IN (Gastrobar) Dalkey Village, Co. Dublin 2000 to date; owner-manager TONIC (Gastrobar) Blackrock, Co. Dublin 2003 to date; Awards: Black & White New Bar of the Year Award; Clubs: Royal Dublin Society, National Yacht Club, Irish Restaurant Society; Recreations: ashtanga yoga, hill-walking, travel, dancing, fashion, property, interior design,

good food, family and friends. Contact: Tonic Bar 1–5 Temple Road, Blackrock, Co. Dublin.
T 01 288 7671 **F** 01 288 7150

Has her finger on the pulse of what the public wants and gives it to them;

HERBST, Michael Eamonn; MANAGING DIRECTOR HERBST GROUP
b 1941, Berlin; *m* 1st Monica Kuhl (m. diss); 1*s* 2*d*; *m* 2nd Wendy McCullough; 1*s* 1*d*; *edu*. Berlin;
Founder, Managing Director Herbst Group 1965 to date - Group comprises Herbst Computer
Systems and Software, Herbst Grain, Herbst Grain Peat and Energy, Warehousing; HT Farm
Machinery. Founder/owner Polo Wicklow, Ireland's only all weather polo grounds, polo school and
polo horse training centre; committee member, Basda (British Software Association), Hurlingham
Polo Association; President, All Ireland Polo Club; member Farm Machinery Association, Chamber
of Commerce (Wicklow), Irish Grain and Feed Association; Recreations: polo, theatre Contact:
Herbst Group, Kilpoole Hill, Wicklow. **T** 0404 67164 email herbst@herbst.ie

A charming, able and efficient businessman; keen polo player whose Wicklow based
company has quietly and effectively become a major player.

HESSION, Paul Martin; HAIRDRESSER
b 1969, Dublin; separated; 1*s* 1*d*; *edu*. St Kevins, CBS, Dublin; Artistic Director, Hession
Hairdressing; Awards: IMAGE Award 2005; Salon of the Year 2004; Irish Hairdressing Federation
Best Employee award 2005; Clubs: Westwood Gym, Clontarf; Recreations: sailing, music, fashion,
architecture. Contact: Hession Hairdressing, 108 Upper Drumcondra Road, Drumcondra, Dublin.
T 01 837 6265

Following in the footsteps of his legendary father Frank, he too is an award winning
hair stylist; known for his artistic approach to his craft, extremely pleasant and
professional.

HEWSON, Alison 'Ali' née Stewart; PATRON, CHERNOBYL CHILDRENS PROJECT / ACTIVIST
b 1961, Dublin; *m* Paul David Hewson 'Bono' (*qv*); 2*s* 2*d*; *edu*. Mount Temple Comprehensive School,
Dublin; University College Dublin; B. Social Science (politics, sociology); Patron Chernobyl
Children's Project / Activist; with friend Adi Roche (*qv*) spearheaded the Children's Project in
Chernobyl, Belarus 1991 to date; a hands-on campaigner who drove trucks, lobbied rock and rollers,
did whatever it took to get funds for the children; with husband Bono, co-created with designer
Rogan, Edun, a collection of earthy but chic duds, which are created from organic materials and are
made in family-run factories in South America and Africa with fair-labour practices, 2005;
Recreations; music, art, fashion, family. Contact: Chernobyl Children's Project, Ballycurreen
Industrial Estate, Kinsale Road, Cork. **T** 021 431 2999 **F** 021 431 3170 email alihewson@adiccp.org

An unlikely rock chic, more mother earth, this quiet campaigner for trade in Africa and
anti-nuke causes in Belarus, knows what she wants and where and how to get it;
charming but steely, doesn't suffer fools gladly if at all; extremely low profile, outside
of her immediate circle regarded as a bit of a loner.

HEWSON, Paul David, 'Bono'; SINGER, SONGWRITER, ACTIVIST
b 1960, Dublin; *m* Alison Stewart (*qv*, Hewson, Alison); 2*s* 2*d*; edu. Mount Temple Comprehensive
School, Dublin; lead vocalist with U2, biggest band in the world; band formed in Dublin 1978; signed
with Island Records 1980; consistent winner of Hot Press Readers Poll since 1980; U2 have toured
throughout the world to critical and audience acclaim, topping international charts with single and
album releases; albums include *Boy* (1980), *October* (1981), *War* (1983), *Unforgettable Fire* (1984),
The Joshua Tree (1987) *Rattle and Hum* (1988), *Achtung Baby* (1991), *Zooropa* (1993); *The Joshua Tree*
was the fastest selling album in record history; band have won numerous Grammy Awards; nominated
"Best Band", *Rolling Stone* Magazine Readers Poll (US); have been described in *Time* magazine as
"Rock's Hottest Ticket" (1987); film *U2 Rattle and Hum* premiered worldwide 1988; producer, *Miss
Sarajevo* 1998; producer, *The Million Dollar Hotel* 2000; actor, *The Million Dollar Hotel*, 2000; *Across
The Universe*, 2006; *Publ. The Million Dollar Hotel*; U2 have performed frequently for charities such as
Live Aid, Self Aid, Amnesty International (UK); Awards: nominated for Nobel Peace Prize 2003;
Chevalier dans l'Ordre de la Legion d'Honneur (Knight in the Order of the Legion of Honor) 2003;
one of the people of the year featured on the cover of *Time* Magazine, December 2005. Contact:
Principle Management Ltd., 30 Sir John Rogerson's Quay, Dublin 2. **T** 01 677 7330 web www.u2.com

Known as the new Mother Teresa, now as well known as an activist for debt relief in the Third World as the lead singer in the world's biggest band U2; respected in the corridors of power all over the world with enviable access to heads of state just about everywhere; as at home in the Vatican, the White House, No 10 Downing Street as he is in Killiney; despite his great wealth, remains unspoiled if ultra mouthy.

HIGGINS, Martin; CEO, FOOD SAFETY PROMOTION BOARD

b 1955, Dublin; *m* Mary; 3*d*; *edu.* St. David's Christian Brothers School Artane; Institute of Public Adminstration, Lansdowne Road, Dublin; Cert in Health Economics, Aberdeen University; Certified Diploma in Accounting & Finance C.Dip.Af ACCA; professional qualification in Accountancy (CPFA); Chartered Institute in Public Finance & Accounting; CEO, Food Safety Promotion Board; Director Corporate Services-Food Safety Authority,1993-99; Principal Officer, Dept.of Health & Children 1994-99; Chief Executive Safefood, Food Safety Promotion Board 1999 to date. Recreations: community theatre, fishing; Contacts: 25 Parklands Rise, Maynooth, Co. Kildare. **T** 087 720 5708; email mhiggins@safefoodonline.com

Faces a Herculean task in controlling, directing and implementing the crucial food safety policies over the next few years; his impact on the health of the public cannot be underestimated.

HICKEY, Gerry; PROGRAMME MANAGER/ SPECIAL ADVISOR TO AN TAOISEACH

b 1943, Mallow, Co. Cork; *m*; 1*s* 1*d*; *edu.* Patrician Academy, Mallow, Co. Cork; Capuchin College, Rochestown, Cork; University College Cork; B.A.; Capuchin Noviate Donegal; joined Civil Service, mostly in Dept Finance,1968–94; general manager Irish Continental Line 1994–97; Programme Manager/ Special Advisor to Taoiseach 1997 to date; Recreations: reading, history, South of France. Contact: Dept. of the Taoiseach, Upper Merrion Street, Dublin 2. **T** 01 662 4888 **F** 01 6764048 email gerry.hickey@taoiseach.gov.ie web www.taoiseach@gov.ie

The 'eminence rouge' of the Taoiseach's department, known as the Sir Humphrey of Irish politics; his influence in FF politicians and policies is akin to the powerful bishops of old; low profile, a man for all seasons for Bertie.

HICKEY, James J.; SOLICITOR

b 1953, Dublin; *m* Fiona Macanna; 1*s* 1*d*; *edu.* Gonzaga College, Dublin; Trinity College Dublin; MA (DUB) LLB; qualified as a solicitor 1977; solicitor; Partner Matheson Ormsby Prentice Solicitors in charge of the Media and Entertainment Law Group 1992 to date - areas of practice include, film and television financing and production, copyright law and music. Chairman Project Arts Centre 1982–88; chairman of National Theatre Society Limited (Abbey and Peacock Theatres) 1993– 2001; chairman Broadcasting, Sub-committee of Screen Producers Ireland (film and TV producers representative organisation); member European Film Academy; member Irish Government appointed Film Industry Review Group which published the Kilkenny Report (August 1999); Member European GATS Film Industry Steering Group 2000–03; Clubs: Kildare Street and University Club. Recreations: theatre, cinema. Contact: Matheson Ormsby Prentice, 30 Herbert Street, Dublin 2. **T** 01 619 9000. **F** 01 619 9010 email james.hickey@mop.ie web www.mop.ie

From an old Dublin legal family, was the first to specialise in entertainment law making him an obvious choice as a rare successful Chairman of the Abbey Theatre.

HICKEY, Patrick 'Pat'; PROPERTY CONSULTANT/VALUER, PRESIDENT OLYMPIC COUNCIL OF IRELAND

b 1945, Dublin; *m* Sylviane Dufour-Bourreau; 3*s* 1d; *edu.* St Vincent's School, Glasnevin, Certified Valuer; FLIA; company director, managing director, Pat Hickey Financial Services, incorporating insurance, auctioneering and consultancy; member, International Olympic Committee 1995 to date; secretary general European Olympic Committee 2001 to date; President Olympic Council of Ireland 1989 to date, responsible for directing the Council and its thirty member sports federation in selecting and entering teams for the Winter and Summer Olympics; awarded third degree Judo Black Belt by International Judo Federation 1979; member Life Insurance Association, Institute of Professional Auctioneers and Valuers; member International Real Estate Federation; Recreations: travel, history, music, and sports. Contact: Olympic Council of Ireland, Olympic House, Harbour Road, Howth, Co. Dublin. **T** 01 866 0555 **F** 01 866 0130 email patrick@olympicsport.ie www.olympicsport.ie

This Northsider has seen off numerous ambushes on his position as President of the IOC; totally committed to the Olympic ideal, he has side-stepped many landmines in highly political arena of Olympic sports; highly respected among the international Olympic fraternity as a skilful politician.

HIGGINS, Anthony 'Tony'; PHOTOGRAPHER
b 1939, Co. Kildare; *m* Kathy Gara; *edu.* National School Celbridge, Co. Kildare; Technical College, Denmark Street, Dublin; Photographer; trained as a carpenter, moved into photography 1962; worked in Con Connor's Studio, St. Stephens Green, Dublin; opened own studio 1967; Recreations; carpentry, travel; Contact: The Studio, 33, Avenue Road, Dublin 8. **T** 01 454 3513 **F** 01 473 3114

One of the country's top photographers; well known for his artistic and intelligent fashion photography which has been featured in all the top glossies in Ireland and internationally; highly repected, also runs a successful commercial practice.

HIGGINS, Karen; FASHION BUYER
b 1967, Dublin; *m* John Redmond (*qv*); *edu.* Assumption Secondary School, Walkinstown, Dublin; Fashion Buyer Brown Thomas. Joined Brown Thomas 1984 to date; buying division for Fashion, concentrating on the contemporary side of the market, from designers Prada and Dolce & Gabbana to young contemporary lines like Seven and Juicy Couture, 1987 to date; senior buyer women's fashion BT2 2006 – todate; Recreations: travel, music, art. Contact: Brown Thomas Buying Office, Cavendish House, Lemon Street, Dublin 2. **T** 01 605 6646 **F** 01 605 6751 email khiggins@brownthomas.ie

Has an incredible eye for emerging trends; travels the world sourcing the latest fashions; extremely stylish fashionista; great sense of humour, superb cook and black belt shopper.

HILDITCH, David; MEMBER, THE NORTHERN IRELAND ASSEMBLY
b 1963, Larne, Co. Antrim; *m* Wilma; 2*s*; *edu.* Carrickfergus Grammar School, East Antrim Institute of Further and Higher Education; member Northern Ireland Assembly. Worked in building and construction industry 1980-87; Royal Mail (currently on career break) 1987 to date; MLA (DUP) East Antrim 1998, member Culture, Arts & Leisure Committee 1999 to date; Public Accounts Committee 2000; Carrickfergus Borough Council 1991; Mayor Carrickfergus 1997-8; Deputy Mayor Carrickfergus 1995-6; Chairman Carrickfergus District Policing Partnership; member NE Group Building Control; Ulster Tourist Development Association; Antrim Coast and Glens Tourist Organisation, DUP Assistant Whip, Deputy Whip; DUP Spokesman for Culture, Arts, Leisure, Higher and Further Education Training and Development; awards, RUC Bravery Award 1997; Contact: Constituency Office, 22a High Street, Carrickfergus, Co. Antrim BT38 7AA. **T** 028 9332 9980 **F** 028 9332 9979 (Northern Ireland Assembly, Parliament Buildings, Stormont Estate, Belfast BT4 3XX) email david.hilditch@niassembly.gov.uk

The proverbial Unionist man on the street always concerned for strategic local developments particularly the port of Larne.

HILL, Melissa; AUTHOR
b 1974, Co Tipperary; *m* Kevin Hill; *edu.* Scoil Chriost Ri, Cahir, Co Tipperary; internationally published bestselling author; *Publ. Something You Should Know* 2003; *Not What You Think* 2004; *Never Say Never* 2005; *Wishful Thinking* 2005; Recreations hill-walking, hiking, travel, tennis animal welfare. Contact: Poolbeg Press, 123 Grange Hill, Baldoyle, Dublin 13. **T** 01 806 3825 email www.melissahill.com

Based in Co. Wicklow her books are published in the Ireland, UK, Canada, New Zealand, South Africa, Australia, Egypt, Hong Kong, Sri Lanka, Singapore, Fiji, Cyprus, Finland, Scandinavia, Germany, Spain, France and Italy.

HILLERY, Brian; CHAIRMAN, INDEPENDENT NEWS AND MEDIA plc
b 1935, Co. Clare; *m* Miriam Davy; 4*s* 1*d*; *edu.* St Flannan's College, Ennis; University College Dublin; University of Georgia, USA; Oxford University; B.Comm; MBA; Ph.D; Chairman Independent News and Media plc. ACC Bank, 1959–65; Citibank 1966–67; University College Dublin, lecturer in Business in Administration 1967–74; professor of Industrial Relations and Human   Resource

Management, University College Dublin, 1974–98; executive director European Bank For Reconstruction And Development, London 1994–97; member Seanad Eireann,1977–89; member Dail Eireann 1989–92; member Seanad Eireann 1992–94; chairman UniCredito Italiano Bank (Ireland) plc 1999 to date; chairman, Providence Resources plc 1997 to date; member National Pensions Reserve Fund Commission 2004 to date; member Government Review Body on Higher Remuneration in the Public Sector 2000 to date; chairman Independent News and Media plc 2004 to date; Clubs: Fitzwilliam LTC, Milltown GC, Lahinch GC; Recreations: golf, reading, GAA, rugby. Contact: Independent News & Media PLC, Independent House, 2023 Bianconi Avenue, Citywest Business Campus, Naas Road, Dublin 24. **T** 01 466 3200 **F** 01 466 3220

> Warm, friendly and laid back the retired UCD Professor is a nephew of former President of Ireland Patrick Hillery and has made a seamless transition onto the boardroom circuit; he brings a balanced approach and a wealth of experience to any discussion.

HILLERY, John Anthony; MEDICAL DOCTOR/ PSYCHIATRIST
b 1957, Dublin; *m* Carolyn; 3*s* 1*d*; *edu.* Blackrock College, Dublin, Royal College of Surgeons in Ireland; MB.BAO.,LRCPI & SI. FRC. Psych; President, Irish Medical Council and Consultant Psychiatrist; Consultant Psychiatrist Stewards Hospital Services Ltd, St. John of God Hospitaller Order, Kildare Services for people with intellectual disability and Tallaght Mental Health Services 1997 to date; vice President Irish Medical Council 1999-2004; President Irish Medical Council & honorary lecturer Centre for Disability Studies University College Dublin 2004 to date. Member of Management Committee International Association of Medical regulatory Authorities; The European Association of Mental Health and Mental Handicap; Clubs: Lahinch Golf Club; Portmarnock Golf Club; Dún Laoghaire Motor Yacht Club; Recreations: golf, sport generally, music, poetry. Contact: Stewarts Hospital, Dublin 20. **T** 01 623 4444 **F** 01 623 5919 email president@mcirl.ie web www.stewartshospital.com

> Son of the former President of Ireland Dr Paddy Hillery, he followed his parents into the medical profession, specialising in psychiatry; extremely bright, personable and laid back, has a keen interest in party politics but is unlikely to pursue a political career; his inherent political skills will be tested to the full in his current position as President of the Irish Medical Council.

HINFELAAR, Maria Gertrude; DIRECTOR, LIMERICK INSTITUTE OF TECHNOLOGY
b 1959, The Netherlands; *m* Graham Park; *edu.*Grammar School, Alphe a.d. Rija, The Netherlands; University Leiden; University of Leicester, England; School of Education Leicester University, England; Maastricht University, Dept. Marketing, The Netherlands; BA (English Language); MA Modern English, American Literature; Post. Grad. Cert Ed. Teaching English as a native language; Ph.D International Retailing; Publ. *Key Success, Factors in International Retailing;* Director Limerick Institute of Technology; Dir. of CHN Retail Business School, The Netherlands 2001–04; Assistant Director of CHN Retail Business School, The Netherlands; Senior lecturer in Business, English and International Retailing CHN University 1993–98. Recreations: reading, cycling. Contact: Limerick Institute of technology, Moyish Park, Limerick. **T** 061 208868 **F** 061 208256 emailmariah.hinfelaar@lit.ie

HOBBS, Eddie; FINANCIAL ADVISOR/TV PRESENTER
b 1955, Cork; *m* Mary; 4 children; *edu.* The Lough National School; Colaiste Chriost Rí, Cork; Financial Advisor and TV Presenter; Joined Eagle Star Insurance 1979; appointed Inspector Eagle Star 1982; promoted to Eagle Star head office, Dublin 1984; joined Tony Taylor Financial Planning 1983; appointed member Consumer Association of Ireland 1993; appointed MD Taylor Asset Management (owning 25% of the company) 1995; TV presenter, *Show Me the Money* (TV Financial DIY series) 2004; TV presenter *Rip Off Ireland* (4 part TV consumer series) 2005; managing director, Financial Development and Marketing (FDM) 2005; non-executive director 3Q (software company, owns 18% of company); director, Foresight Financial; member, National Consumer Association; Publ. *"Short Hands, Long Pockets: The Informed Guide to Debt and Spending";* Recreations: sailing. Contact: Summerhill House, The Curragh, Co. Kildare. **T** 045 442051 email ehobbs@indigo.ie web www.eddiehobbs.com

> Hit the national headlines as a director of Tony Taylor's investment company; fast talking Leesider who sexed up consumer affairs and became an overnight guru following political outburst against his TV series *Rip Off Ireland* during the summer of

2005; his unique presentation style combined with his lilting Cork accent, one liners, banal banter and irreverent manner made him ratings topper during the silly season.

HOCTOR, Máire; PUBLIC REPRESENTATIVE

b 1963, Nenagh, Co.Tipperary; single; edu. St. Mary's Convent of Mercy, Primary and Secondary School, Nenagh, Co. Tipperary; St. Patrick's College, Maynooth, Co. Kildare; BA, H. Dip Ed; Fianna Fail T.D. for Tipperary North. Elected Urban District Council, Nenagh 1994, 1995-96 & 1999-2000; vice chair Tipperary North Riding County Council 2000-01; current vice chair Tipperary NR VEC; vice chair Mid West Regional Authority; director North Tipperary County Enterprise Board; member of the Economic, Social and Cultural Strategic Policy Committee North Tipperary County Council; chair Nenagh Community Reparation Project; vice chair Nenagh Tourism Marketing Committee; director Nenagh Community Network; director An Teach an Leinn, Nenagh; board of Management Gairmscoil an Aonaigh; St. Joseph's Communtiy College, Newport; chair Tipperary Gold Memorial Committee; PRO 2000 Jubilee Committee; FF Member of Dáil Éireann, Tipperary North 2002 to date. Contact: 3a, Ormond Court, Ormond Street, Nenagh, Co. Tipperary. T 067 32943 or 01 618 4204 F 067 50470 or 01 618 4230 email maire.hoctor@oireachtas.ie web www.mairehoctor.com

First elected to the 29th Dail, a local and national poll topper, reflecting her popularity and community based skills; given that she's in an area that needs a minister in a party that's crying out for impressive, younger women, if her party are in government next time round, she must be in with a good shout for at least a half car.

HOGAN, Gerard; SENIOR COUNSEL

single; edu. University College Dublin; BCL LLM (NUI) LLM (Penn), MA, Ph.D. (Dubl.), LLD (NUI) FTCD (1992); Senior Counsel; A practising barrister and a member of the Governing Council of UNIDROIT; Chairman of the Law Reporting Council of Ireland; former member of the Constitution Review Group, Competition and Mergers Review Group and the Offences Against the State Acts Review Group; member of the Committee on Court Practice and Procedure; former member of the Competition Authority's Advisory Panel; Judge of the OECD's Nuclear Energy Tribunal; author of several books and numerous articles on topics including Irish constitutional law, administrative law, conflict of laws and European Community law; has also appeared in and argued many important cases in the High Court, Supreme Court, European Court of Justice and the European Court of Human Rights; Publ. co-author (with Professor Gerry Whyte) of the 4th edition of Kellys', The Irish Constitution (Dublin, 2004). Contact: The Distillery Building, 149/151, Church Street, Dublin 7. T 01 817 4399 email ghogan@lawlibrary.ie

His boyish appearance belies a top class performer in Court where he is held in high esteem by M'Luds; a prominent Progressive Democrat activist, he is a regular TV and radio commentator on constitutional matters on which he is considered perhaps the country's leading expert.

HOGAN, Thomas Francis 'Frank'; COMPANY DIRECTOR

b 1945, Cashel, Co Tipperary; m Fran Nulty; 2s; edu. Rockwell College; Company Director; worked for a time on family farm; started Frank Hogan Ltd, 1973; director Hogan Oil; director Hogan Convenience Stores; former chairman Garryowen Rugby Club (former inter-provincial player); Clubs: Castletroy Golf Club, Lahinch Golf Club. Recreations: rugby, golf. Contact: Frank Hogan Ltd., Dublin Road, Limerick. T 061 416 000 F 061 416 043 email sales@frankhogan.ie web www.frankhogan.ie

Popular and succcessful businessman who has built up one of the largest motor businesses in the South West; authorised dealers for Mercedez Benz, Volkswagon, Audi and Mazda cars and commercial vehicles.

HOGAN, Phil; PUBLIC REPRESENTATIVE

b 1960, Kilkenny; separated; edu. St. Joseph's College, Freshford, Co Kilkenny; St. Kierans College, Kilkenny; University College Cork, BA, H.Dip Ed; Fine Gael Spokesperson on Enterprise, Trade and Employment; Dail member of Carlow-Kilkenny, 1989 to date; Seanad Eireann 1987–89; Chairman of Fine Gael Parliamentary party 1995 –2001; Front Bench spokesman 1992 to date; Minister of State 1994/95; Fine Gael Director of Organisation. Clubs: GAA, Castlecomer Golf Club. Recreations: Sport.Contact: 1 High Street, Kilkenny. T 056 777 1490. F 056 777 1491 email Philip.Hogan@oireachtas.ie

A grand nephew of the legendary Kilkenny hurler Lori Meagher of Tulluroan; forced to resign as junior minister at the Department of Finance during the Rainbow Coalition (1994-97) due to a leak from his office; hardworking with well recognised organizational skills and has a sharp political repartee; in the event of a Fine Gael led government definitely ministerial potential.

HOLLAND, Michael J; MANAGING DIRECTOR, FITZWILLIAM HOTEL GROUP
b 1954, Dublin; *m* Carol Swift; 1*s*; *edu.* C.U.S., Leeson Street, Dublin; Managing Director, New City Investments, 1985-87; director, Aviette – acquired H.Williams Supermarket Group 1987-89; co-founder Fitzwilliam Hotel Group 1989; acquired and re-developed Portmarnock Hotel and Golf Links 1989; acquired and re-developed Royal Dublin Hotel 1989; acquired and re-developed Metropole Hotel, Cork; acquired Mespil Estate, Dublin 1992; developed Leeside Leisure Centre, Cork 1992; director, Irish Welcome Tours and Best Western Hotel 1994; developed Fitzwilliam Hotel, St Stephen's Green 1997; New City Estates opens London Office 1998; Fitzwilliam Hotels opens; member Dublin Chamber of Commerce, Irish Property and Facility Managers Association, Dublin City Business Association. Clubs: Royal St. George Yacht Club, National Yacht Club. Recreations: sailing, reading, travel. Contact: Fitzwilliam Hotel Group, 66, Fitzwilliam Square, Dublin 2. **T** 01 478 7000 **F** 01 661 5422

Very low profile, bought out his partner Brendan Gilmore's business interests in the last year; very committed to his hotel and property interests but still finds time to be a keen sailor.

HOLLAND, Ron; YACHT DESIGNER
b 1947; partner Catherine Walsh; 4*d*; gained extensive sailing experience and worked as an apprentice boat builder, Auckland, New Zealand; sailed to USA 1967; trained as yacht designer in California and Florida; Yacht Designer; designed, built and raced the winner of the 1973 Quarter Tonne Cup in Cowes; moved to Ireland 1973; during the '70s and '80s designed many of the top international race boats; in the '80s, changed focus towards designing high performance, large, luxury yachts. Racing boats include: Eygthenes, Shamrocks, Silver Apple, Big Apple, Swan 441s, Imp, Swan 39s, Morning Cloud, Regardless, Swan 371s, Swan 42s, Kialoa, Kiwi Magic (America's Cup Challenger), Lion New Zealand, NCB Ireland; large yachts include: Whirlwind XII (103 ft), Avalon (109 ft), Sensation (110 ft), Cyclos III (110 ft), Royal Eagle II (90 ft), Juliet (141 ft), Shanakee (108 ft), Thalia (160 ft), Globana (118 ft), Charlatan (110 ft), Affinity (150 ft), Felicita West (210 ft), Mirabella V (245 ft); Ethereal (190 ft). Books published include: *Splendour Under Sail* (1989). Awarded Showboats International 'Best Sailing Yacht' for Shanakee, Monaco 1992, Showboats International 'Best Sailing Yacht' for Juliet, Monaco 1994, International Superyachts Best Sailing Yacht for Juliet, Fort Lauderdale, 1994; Showboats International 'Most Innovative Sailing Yacht' for Mirabella V, Monaco 2005, Showboats International 'Best Interior' for Santa Maria, Monaco 2005. Listed in *Who's Who* in New Zealand. Clubs: Royal New Zealand Yacht Squadron, New York Yacht Club, Royal Ocean Racing Club, Kinsale Yacht Club. Recreations: sailing, music, reading, photography. Contact: 28 Lr. O'Connell Street, Kinsale, Co. Cork. **T** 021 477 4866 **F** 021 477 4808 emailinfo@ronhollanddesign.com www.ronhollanddesign.com

Recognised internationally as one of the top yacht designers.

HOLLYWOOD, Grainne; MANAGING DIRECTOR, PALMER MC CORMACK
b 1963, Newry; single; *edu.* Sacred Heart Grammar School, Newry, Co. Down; Reading University BSc (hons); TTRICS.ASCS; Managing Director, Palmer Mc Cormack; Lambert Smith Hampton-Belfast; Woolwich Building Society, London; Treasury Holdings, Dublin; Dublin Docklands Development Authority, Director of Property; MD Palmer Mc Cormack 2005; Recreations: skiing, horse riding, travel, partying! Contact: Canada House, 55, St Stephens Green Dublin 2. **T** 01 418 5800 email ghollywood@pmcc.ie

Highly motivated, respected throughout the macho property world.

HOLMAN LEE, Celia; PRINCIPAL MODEL AGENCY
b 1950, Limerick; *m* Gerard Lee; 1*s* 1*d*; *edu.* Presentation Convent, Limerick; Principal, Holman Lee Model Agency; became model agent 1975; contributor to RTÉ *Off the Rails*; weekly fashion slot on TV3/Ireland AM; Recreations; work, training young girls to become catwalk models, Contact; Nampara House, Ballysheedy, Co. Limerick. **T** 061 412726 **F** 061 419041 email holmanlee@eircom.net

Celia Holman Lee

The glamorous former model has maintained a national profile from a provincial base for many years the Holman Lee Agency is the longest running model agency in Ireland; hugely involved in the Jim Kemmy Fashion Awards in the Limerick School of Art; a hardworking, good humoured director of fashion, always willing to help a good cause in the area

HOOPER, Br, Denis Paul; MONK/PRINCIPAL

b 1954; single; *edu.* St Mary's College, Rathmines, Dublin 6; St Patrick's College, Maynooth; BA Theology, H Dip; Principal Glenstal Abbey. Clubs: St Mary's RFC; Recreation: playing guitar, reading. Contact: Glenstal Abbey, Murroe, Co Limerick. **T** 061 386103 **F** 061 386380 email denis@glenstal.ie

An important and innovative educator of the classically educated student of Glenstal; belongs to a strong liberal tradition of his Order.

HOOPER, Richard; COMPANY DIRECTOR

b 1936, Dublin; *m* Kathleen Maxwell; 4 *d*; *edu.* Catholic University School, Dublin; University College Dublin; BE, MBA; Company Director/Chairman Jurys Doyle Hotel Group plc. Manager Unidare 1958-66; former executive director The Investment Bank of Ireland; former chairman IBI Corporate Finance Ltd; Chairman, Jurys Doyle Hotel Group plc 2005 to date; Clubs: Royal St. George Yacht Club. Recreations: sailing. Contact: Jurys Doyle Hotel Group, Head Office, 146 Pembroke Road, Dublin 4. **T** 01 6070070

The former corporate banker was thrust into the public eye as chairman of Jurys Doyle Plc prior to being taken private by the Doyle sisters; presided over the initial sell off of the Jurys Ballsbridge site to Sean Dunne (*qv*); has a sharp intellect and is a hard-nosed commercial businessman whose mettle was fully tested as a result.

HORAN, Tony; CHARTERED ARCHITECT

b 1935; *m* Christel; 2*s* 1*d*; *edu.* St Mary's College, Crosby, Lancashire; Manchester University, BA, FRIAI, RIBA, MIDI; Chartered Architect; founding partner Horan Keogan Ryan; Worked in the atelier of Erno Goldfinger, London early 1960s, associate, Stephenson Gibney & Associates 1967; founded own practice - restructured as Horan Keogan Ryan 1992; awards, RIAI Triennial Medal for Housing and 8 other RIAI and RIBA awards; practice won 3 other major awards; member RIAI Gold Medal Jury, Board of Architectural Education, external examiner Trinity College Dublin. Architect, inter alia: Review and Fitzwilliam LTC indoor tennis facilities, Monkstown Valley, 84-86, Grafton Street, Dublin; private sector housing Ireland and Britain (more recently, Rath Lodge, Ashbourne, Shelbourne Hotel (with partner), housing Kill Co. Kildare); practice (partner Jerry Ryan and collaborators) responsible for West Smithfield urban regeneration, new Bray Town Centre, Microsoft European Head Quarters, Sandyford etc; *Publ.* Paper on *Housing For Special Needs National Housing Conference*; articles, *Irish Architect; Architect Review;* Recreations; travel, travel literature, well written European " Whodunits", gardening (graphic better than actual). Contacts: 5, School House Lane, Dublin 2. **T** 01 6636400 **F** 01 6636401 email thoran@hkr.ie web www.hkr.ie

A major, important and innovative, urban city architect.

HORGAN, Cornelius George Mark 'Con'; CHAIRMAN, ABBEY TRAVEL GROUP

b 1940, Dublin; *m* Allyson Usher; 1*s* 5*d*; *edu.* University College Dublin; Dip Pub Adm.; Chairman Abbey Travel Group; Joined Aer Lingus 1958-62; district sales manager Ireland, Iberia Airlines 1962-69; joint managing director Ryan Hotels plc 1968-78; founder, chief executive & chairman Abbey Travel 1978 to date; founder, chairman Tower Hotel Groups 1978-2005; sold Tower Hotel Group 2005; Prop. Castlerosse Hotel, Golf and Leisure Club, Killarney, Co. Kerry 2005; Clubs: The Royal Dublin Golf Club, Killarney Golf and Fishing Club, Faithlegg Golf Club (Honorary Life Member). Recreations: golf, grand opera. Contact: 34 Lower Abbey Street, Dublin 1. **T** 01 873 0199 **F** 01 873 0194 email chorgan@abbeytravel.ie web www.abbeytravel.ie

One of the pioneers of the travel industry in Ireland; built up a successful company through shrewd management; popular in a cut throat industry.

HORGAN, Conor; PHOTOGRAPHER/FILM MAKER
b 1962, Dublin; single; *edu.* Newpark Comprehensive School, Blackrock; editorial & fashion photographer since 1984, including *Vogue, Harpers & Queen, G.Q*; directed over 70 TV commercials and pop videos 1992–2003, including award winning campaigns for AIB & The National Lottery; wrote & directed *"The Last Time"* (13 minutes) 2002, which went on to win several awards, including the Jameson Best Irish Short Film & VIP Best Director Award, Cork Film Festival 2002; has written scripts for RTE and other production companies; devised and directed "Happiness" a 27 minute film, asked 300 people all around Ireland what makes them happy - film funded by the Arts Council 2005; Clubs; member, NUJ, SIPTU (Film Directors Sector), Screen Directors Guild of Ireland, Irish Film Institute, director of AIDS, AID, CTD (An Irish Aids/HIV Charity (1989 – 1995); exhibitions: *Conor Horgan Portraits,* The Gallery of Photography October 1994; Recreations: music, film, people, staring out the window, reading, eating, changing the world. Contact: Conor@indigo.ie

> Multi-talented award winning fasion photographer, many top models insist on having him behind the lens; successfully diversified into TV commercial direction and short documentaries.

HOULIHAN, Michael P.; SOLICITOR & COMPANY DIRECTOR
b 1941; *m* Joan Mulhern; 1*s* 2*d*; edu. Ennis C.B.S., Cistercian College, Roscrea; University College Dublin; Law Society of Ireland; Solicitor; after qualifying as solicitor, returned to family practice, Ignatius M. Houlihan & Sons, Ennis, 1963 (now Michael Houlihan & Partners), founding director Rural ReSettlement Ireland Ltd; founding director Glor Music Ltd; director Ennis Civic Trust and Kilkee Civic Trust; director Cèifin Institute Ltd; member Advisory Board, Ireland Funds; member Irish Board of The Ireland Funds Ltd; member governing authority of the University of Limerick; member University of Limerick Foundation; former director and chairman Shannon Free Airport Development Company Ltd. 1990-95; former president Law Society of Ireland 1982-83; Co. Clare Law Association; Ennis Chamber of Commerce; Cistercian College Roscrea P.P.U; member County Clare Law Association, Law Society of Ireland, International Bar Association, American Bar Association. Recreations: music, opera, travel, art collections, community development. Contact: Michael Houlihan & Partners, 9/10/11 Bindon Street, Ennis, Co. Clare. **T** 065 684600 **F** 065 682 1870 email info@mhp.ie

> A well respected Clare personality who is very committed to life along the Western seaboard; former president of the Law Society; currently running one of the largest legal practices in Munster.

HOULIHAN, William 'Billy'; CORK COUNTY ARCHITECT
b 1946; *m* Irene; 1*s* 3*d*; *edu.* Blackrock College, Dublin, School of Art, Cork, School of Architecture, Oxford, MRIBA, FRIAI; Cork County Architect; joined Cork County Council 1974; appointed Senior Executive Cork County 1980; appointed County Architect 2001; Awards: People of the Year Award 1986, National Planning Award 1999; Recreations; golf, horseracing. Contact: **M** 086 851 5876 email billy.houlian@corkcoco.ie

> Has a major impact on one of the largest counties in Ireland in terms of planning and the built heritage of Co. Cork.

HOWLIN, Brendan; PUBLIC REPRESENTATIVE
b 1956, Wexford town; single; *edu.* CBS Wexford; St. Patrick's Drumcondra, Dublin; N.T.; Public Representative; elected Labour Party member of Wexford Borough Council 1981; contested the November General Election 1982; Senator (nominated by the Taoiseach) 1982-87; elected to Wexford County Council 1985; elected to Dáil Éireann as Labour TD for Wexford 1987; Minister Health and Environment 1993-97; deputy leader under Ruairí Quinn; challenged Pat Rabbitte (*qv*) for the leadership after Quinn resigned but lost out; had previously challenged Ruairi Quinn (*qv*) as well. Labour spokesperson Enterprise, Trade & Employment 2002 todate. Contact: Whiterock Hill, Wexford Town **T** 053 24036 **T** 01 618 3538 website: http://www.brendanhowlin.ie

> Impressive performer, hardworker, tipped by some as the next leader of Labour (sooner rather than later). Following the resignation of Albert Reynolds (*qv*) in 1993 he attempted to create a new coalition arrangement with then Fianna Fáil leader Bertie Ahern (*qv*) but they failed in this endeavour; has been critical of the Fine Gael / Labour pre-election pact for the next general election.

HUGHES, Alan Joseph; TV PRESENTER,
b Dublin; single; TV Presenter Ireland AM; worked in RTE; joined TV 3 1999; presenter Ireland AM 2002 to date; one of the most well known presenters on IRELAND AM TV3; easy style of presentation, won many fans on Ireland AM; described as the presenter the country likes to wake up with; Recreations: travel, loves to discover different countries and traditions. Contact: TV 3 Ballymount Industrial Estate, Clondalkin, Dublin 22. **T** 01 419 3333 email alan.hughes@tv3.com web www.tv3.com

His easy, undemanding style makes him ideal breakfast fare; despite his early morning commitments, still manages to be a night owl socialite; loves stage work and panto and produces and stars in the annual Panto at Liberty Hall Theatre Dublin.

Bill Hughes

HUGHES, Bill; INDEPENDENT PRODUCER/ DIRECTOR
b 1955, Athy, Co. Kildare; partner; *edu.* CBS Athy, Co. Kildare; St Mary's Knockbeg College, Carlow; UCD; London Academy Muisc & Dramatic Art; Birmingham College, Speech Training & Drama; Gold medalist Drama – Shakespearian studies; ALAM, Post Grad Hons; BA Theatre studies Birminghan; Director Mind The Gap Films, Dublin; Buyer books dept. Rackhams (House of Frazer) Birmingham 1977–80; buyer Willis Books, Ireland 1980–82; asst producer RTE 1982–85; producer Green Apple 1985-89; produced MT USA (first music video show in Europe); producer Partner Radius TV Productions; has produced over 1000 hours of music, arts, entertainment and documentary programming for RTE, ITV, BBC, PBS (US), SBS (Australia), TV4 (Sweden), SABC3 (South Africa) and CBC (Canada); produced *The Write Stuff on* ITV, featuring bestselling authors, hosted by Anne Robinson; rock music series "New Music From Ireland" for the BBC, it won the Music Critics Award for Best Producer in 1990 and '91; two series of the live rock concert show '7 Bands on the Up'; two series of the Nashville based country music video show MC USA; produced and directed five chart topping videos for *Boyzone*; formed *The Irish Tenors* 1998, produced all three of their million selling TV Specials for America, including *Live On Ellis Island*; produced PBS music specials for Ronan Tynan *The Impossible Dream, The Songs of Mama Cass, Brian Kennedy – Live in Belfast;* documentaries: *North of Naples, South of Rome* (for PBS, RTE and The Travel Channel); *The Love That Dare Not Speak It's Name; Fintan* 2002; *Anne Madden* (and her 50 year marriage to Louis le Brocquy) 2006; judge, *Popstars;* regular panelist, *You're a Star, The Afternoon Show, The View, The Sunday Show* and *Ryan's Hit List;* Awards: 1990 Critics Award for "DEF 2" BBC; nominated for Golden Rose for *Happy Birthday Oscar Wilde* 2005; Jigs and Reels, 2006. Clubs: founder member, The Groucho Club, London; Recreations: keen art collector, cooking, fund raising for Aids Ireland charities. Contact: 30, Riverbank House, Islandbridge, Dublin 8 **T** 01 670 8304 email bill@mind the gapfilms.com

One of the brightest producers in these islands, has achieved success nationally and internationally with his documentary specials; visionary, hardworking, multi-talented, knows how to enjoy life while still being a prolific producer; known as "Hatchet Hughes" for his role as the no-nonsense judge on *You're A Star*, the programme that brought him out from behind the camera; extremely popular and much in demand as a dinner guest.

HUGHES, Darren John; GROUP EDITOR, DROGHEDA INDEPENDENT
b 1968, Dublin; *partner* Elaine Grennan; 1s 1d; *edu.* Ardscoil La Salle, Raheny, Dublin; College of Commerce, Rathmines, Dublin Institute of Adult Education;; Cert. Journalism, Dip. Social Studies; higher diploma in Journalism; group editor Drogheda Independent Group; sports correspondent *Daily Express* 1987-89; sports sub-editor *Irish Independent* 1989-94; lecturer, Ballyfermot Senior College 1993-97; assistant chief sports sub-editor *Irish Independent* 1994-1998; deputy sports editor, *Irish Independent* 1998-2002; group editor Drogheda Independent Group 2002 to date; Clubs: Turvey Golf Club, Donabate, Clontarf Athletic FC, Archaeological Society, Louth; Recreations: soccer, martial arts, music, gardening, history, travel; Contact: 9 Shop Street, Drogheda, Co Louth. **T** 041 987 6800 **F** 041 983 4271 email dhughes@drogheda-independent.ie

Editor of a major journal which plays a vital role for the communities in the economic corridor between Dublin and Belfast.

HUGHES, Derek Gavin; EXECUTIVE CHAIRMAN HUGHES & HUGHES Ltd
b 1957, Dublin; *m* Dara Magner; 1s 1d; *edu.* Blackrock College, Dublin; Trinity College Dublin; MA

MMII; Executive Chairman Hughes and Hughes Ltd; founder Hughes and Hughes Booksellers; co-founder Insomnia Coffee Company, sold 2006; finalist Ernst & Young Entrepreneur of the Year Award 2004; selected as one of the top 500 Entrepreneurs in the European Union 1995; member, Advisory Board Trinity College Business School, Dublin. Clubs: Royal Irish Yacht Club, Dun Laoghire, Balinroe Golf Club. Recreations: reading, walking, golf, sailing, rugby. Contact: Unit 15, The Pavilions shopping Center, Swords, Co. Dublin. **T** 01 807 9291 **F** 01 807 9298 email dgh@indigo.ie web wwwhughesbooks.com

> Has hugely expanded the family book business he took over from his father Bobby; extremely bright, low profile, founded the successful chain of Insomnia coffee shops.

HUGHES, Neil; CHARTERED ACCOUNTANT

b 1972, Dublin; single; *edu.* Christain Brothers School Enniscorthy; Dublin City University; BA Accounting & Finance, ACA; Managing Partner Hughes Blake Accountants; founded Hughes & Associates Chartered Accountants 1997; merged with Burke Burns Blake to form Hughes Blake 2004; Publ. *Examinership in Practice, A Vehicle for Corporate Recovery* (2004); Clubs: Treasurer, Glasnevin Basketball Club; Recreations: basketball, guitar; Contact: 72 Upper Leeson Street, Dublin 4. **T** 01 669 9999 **F** 01 669 9777 email neil.hughes@hughesblake .ie

> Principal in one of the fastest growing accounting and insolvency practitioner firms in Ireland; focused and ambitious, despite his success at a very young age, still has a major masterplan for his practice.

HUGHES, Oliver; CHIEF EXECUTIVE, PORTERHOUSE BREWING COMPANY

b 1959, Bray, Co. Wicklow; *m* Helen; 1*s* 1*d*; *edu.* Ireland; University of Hertfordshire, UK; B.L; Kings Inns; chief executive, Porterhouse Brewing Company. Practised as a barrister 1979–89; founded Porterhouse Brewing Company with cousin Liam LaHart 1989; now operates six bars in Dublin and one in London; purchased Lillies Bordello and Judge Roy Bean, 2004; hotel; award winning brewery; Clubs: Lillies. Recreations: football, tennis, current affairs and researching and launching novel beers. Contact: Lillies Bordello, Adam Court, Grafton Street, Dublin 2. **T** 01 679 9204.

> The former barrister has grown the Porterhouse Brewing Company from humble beginnings on the seafront in Bray, Co. Wicklow to a major compant that includes pubs, property and the jewel in the crown, the legendary Lillies Bordello; astute, hardworking, ambitious; expect much bigger things in the future.

Oliver Hughes

HUGHES, Paul; HOTELIER;

b 1939, Dublin; *m* June Cahill; 4*s*; *edu.* Marist Fathers, CUS, Leeson Street; St Michael's College, Dublin; Christian Brothers School, Oatlands, Dublin; Proprietor/Manager Abbey Glen Castle, Clifden plc; Hotel trainee, Russell Hotel and hotels in Rome, Berne and Biarritz; assistant manager, Royal Hibernian Hotel and Moira Hotel, Dublin; founder, Old Dublin Restaurant; proprietor/manager Abbey Glen Castle, Clifden plc; director Manor House Hotels Ltd; president Clifden Chamber of Commerce 1995 & 1996; chairman Clifden and West Connemara Tourism Council; member Irish Hotels Federation; Restaurant Owners Association; Galway County Tourism Committee 1995 & 1996. Clubs: Connemara Golf Club, Clifden Boat Club, David Lloyd Riverview Club, Dublin Recreations: work, golf, music. Contact: Abbey Glen Castle Hotel, Clifden, Co. Galway. **T** 095 21201 **F** 095 21797

> Synonmous with Cliften and the West of Ireland, a great ambassador for tourism in the area; extrovert, a great showman who is indefatuigable in his promotion of his hotel, the area and the country.

HUNT, Fionnula; VIOLONIST

b 1957, Belfast; *m* Raymond Blake; *edu.* St. Dominc's High School, Falls Road, Belfast, Hochschule Fur Musik und DarstellendeKunst in Wien (Vienna); Performance degree 1st Class Hons; Violonist;

Director Laureate – Irish Chamber Orchestra; member of the Bavarian State Opera Orchestra, Munich; Leader Music (artistic director, ICO) and artistic director Killaloe International Music Festival 1984– 85; co-Leader RTE Symphony Orchestra 1986–89; Guest Leader Ulster Orchestra, London Symphony Orchestra, Scottish Chamber Orchestra, BBC Scottish Symphony; Halle Orchestra, Bournemoth Symphony Orchestra, Opera de Lyon, World Orchestra for Peace 1995–2002; Publ. Recordings: *Irish Fantasy* (Fionnula & Una Hunt 1991); *Silver Apples of the Moon* (Irish Chamber Orchestra) 1997; *Strings Astray* (Contemporary Irish Music (I.C.O); *Tchaikovsky* (Serenade, Souvenir de Florence – ICO) 1998; *Tangos and Dances* (RTE Concert Orchestra) 2001. Clubs: Kildare Street and University Club. Recreations: wine appreciation, reading, travel. Contact: 23, Oaklands park, Sandymount, Dublin 4 **T** 01 668 4251 **F** 01 668 4251 email rfblake@iol.ie

A gifted and hard working musician who brought the Irish Chamber Orchestra to its present eminence; terrific company, enjoys fine wine and good food.

Fionnula Hunt

HUNTER, Ruth; SOLICITOR

b; m; edu Trinity College Dublin, BCL, University of Cambridge, England, Master of Laws; Solicitor; Solicitor; Partner, Entertainment Law Group; focuses on the area of film and television production including the negotiation and drafting of financing agreements, distribution agreements, equity and tax based financing arrangements (including Section 481 financing), talent agreements (including film rights agreements), writers agreements, actors, directors, designers and composers agreements. She also provides advice in relation to errors and omissions, insurance and music copyright clearance as well as theatre and public performance contracts, music contracts and general intellectual property issues including trademarks; advises on sports law covering all commercial sports agreements (including employment agreements) and intellectual property rights in sport as well as related sponsorship arrangements; films Ruth worked on*: "I Went Down" ,"Nora", "About Adam", "Angela's Ashes","Reign of Fire", "On the Nose" ;* member, the Audiovisual Federation and the Irish Business, Employers Confederation (IBEC). Contact: Matheson Ormsby Prentice, 30 Herbert Street, Dublin 2. **T** 01 644 2228 **F** 01 619 9010 email ruth.hunter@mop.ie web www.mop.ie

HURLEY, John; GOVERNOR, CENTRAL BANK

b 1945, Mallow, Co. Cork; *m* Marie; 1*s*; *edu.* The Patrician College, Mallow, Co. Cork; Governor Central Bank; occupied three Secretary General positions; was appointed by the government to his current post as Secretary General, Department of Finance 2000; prior to that he was Secretary General, Public Service Management and Development, in the Department of Finance, and Secretary General, Department of Health; member, Board of the Central Bank, the Advisory Committee of the National Treasury Management Agency, the Council and Executive Committee of the Economic and Social Research Institute; member Implementation Group of Secretaries General (established by the government to oversee the Strategic Management Initiative); has also been chairman of the Top Level Appointments Committee (which makes recommendations to the government and to ministers on appointments to Secretary General and Assistant Secretary level posts in Government Departments); former board member European Institute of Public Administration, Maastricht, the Louvain Institute for Ireland in Europe and the National Centre for Partnership; former member Executive Board of the World Health Organisation, Geneva; former chairman IFRA; former chairman Consultative Committee on the new Financial Management System for the Civil Service and the Human Resources Subgroup established under the Strategic Management Initiative. Recreations: sport, especially Cork hurling. Contact: Central Bank & Financial Services Authority of Ireland, PO Box 559, Dame Street, Dublin 2. **T** 01 434 4000 **F** 01 671 6561 web www.centralbank.ie

In typical, traditional civil service mode, low profile, extremely bright and a very safe pair of hands as Governor of the Irish Central Bank; retains a keen interest in GAA matters and remains an avid supporter of the Cork Hurling team.

HUXLEY, George Leonard; UNIVERSITY PROFESSOR

b 1932; *m* Davina Best; 3*d*; *edu.* Blundell's, Magdalene College Oxford (BA); Professor of Classics, Trinity College Dublin. Military Service RE. 1951; Fellow All Souls College, Oxford 1955-61; assistant director British School, Athens, Greece 1956-58; visiting lecturer Harvard University 1958-59 and 1961-62; professor of Greek, Queen's University Belfast 1962-83; temporary assistant lecturer St. Patrick's College Maynooth 1984-85; honorary research Fellow Trinity College Dublin 1984-89; Director Gennadius Library American School of Classical Studies, Athens 1986-89;

honorary Professor of Greek, Trinity College Dublin 1989 to date. Executive NI Civil Rights Association 1971-72; secretary for Polite Literature and Antiquities Royal Irish Academy, Dublin 1979-86; senior vice president RIA 1984-85 and 1999-2000; honorary librarian RIA 1990-94; special envoy RIA 1994-97; vice president RIA 1997-98; Irish Advisory Board Institute of Irish Studies University of Liverpool 1996; chairman organising committee 8th.international congress of Classical Studies Dublin 1984; keynote speaker XVI International Congress Classical Archaeology Boston 2003; senior vice president Fédération Internationale des Sociétés d'Études Classiques 1984-89; Irish member Standing Committee for the Humanities Euro Science Foundation Strasbourg 1978-86; member managing committee American School of Classical Studies Athens 1990; Int KommThesaurus Linguae Latinae (Munich) 1999-2001; visiting professor of History University of California, San Diego 1990; Hon. President Classical Association of Ireland 1999; Cromer Greek Prize 1963; Litt.D (hc) Dublin University, D Litt (hc) Belfast; Member Academia Europea 1963; FSA, MRIA; *Publ Acheans and Hittites* 1960; *Early Sparta* 1962; *The Early Ionians* 1966; *Greek Epic Poetry from Eumelos to Panyassis* 1969; *Kythera Excavations and Studies* (ed with JN Coldstream 1972); *Pindar's Vision of the Past* 1975; *On Aristotle and Greek Society* 1979; *Homer and the Travellers* 1988; various articles on Hellenic and Byzantine subject. Clubs Atheneum, London; Recreations: siderodeomophilia; Contact: School of Classics, Trinity College Dublin 2. **T** 01 896 1000 web www.tcd.ie

HYDE, Tim; BLOODSTOCK BREEDER
b 1941; *m* Patricia Roe;1*s* 4*d*; *edu.* Christian Brothers College, Cashel; owner/manager, Camas Park Stud; director Doncaster Bloodstock Sales; Sean Barrett Bloodstock Insurance, Tipperary Racecourse; member Irish National Hunt Steeplechase Committee, Turf Club; Recreations: hunting, winter sports, golf. Contact: Camas Park Stud, Cashel, Co. Tipperary. **T** 062 61010 **F** 062 61576.

Member of prominent Tipperary racing family, former leading National Hunt rider; one of the top thoroughbred bloodstock breeders in the country.

HYLAND, Aine; FORMER VICE PRESIDENT/ PROFESSOR OF EDUCATION, UNIVERSITY COLLEGE CORK
b 1942; *m* W.J. Hyland (decd); 3*d*; *edu.* Convent of Mercy, Ballymahon, Co. Longford, 1953-59; University College Dublin, BA; Trinity College Dublin, H.Dip., M.Ed., PhD; Vice President/Professor of Education, University College Cork; Executive officer, Department of Education,1959-73; part time Tutor, Education Department, Trinity College Dublin, 1975-80; senior lecturer, Education and Admissions Officer, Carysfort College 1980-88; senior lecturer in Education, University College Dublin, 1988-93; professor of Education, University College Cork, 1993 to date; appointed vice president UCC to 2006; Publ. *Irish Educational Documents*, Vols. 1-3 (editor), author of over 40 articles and papers on education – history, policy, curriculum and assessment; member Educational Studies Association of Ireland, Irish Peace Institute, Conference on Pluralism in Education, Educate Together (Republic of Ireland); patron, Northern Ireland Council for Integrated Education, chairperson of Points Commission. Contact: University College Cork, Cork. **T** 021 427 6 871 web www.ucc.ie

The highly qualified academic is an influential figure in Irish education; she is a friendly, highly respected, articulate educationalist.

HYNES, Garry; THEATRE DIRECTOR
b 1953; single; *edu.* St Louis Convent, Monaghan; Dominican College, Galway; University College Galway, BA; Artistic Director, Druid Theatre, Galway, 1975-90 & 1994 to date. Freelance director, Royal Shakespeare Company 1988-89; artistic director Abbey Theatre 1990-94. Awards: Director of the Year (1983 and 1985), Time Out London Award for Direction (1988); first woman in the history of the Tonys to win a Best Director Award; recipient of many other theatre awards including Edinburgh Fringe First, Time Out, Harvey's Irish Theatre award and a special tribute award for her services to Irish theatre from Irish Times/ESB Theatre Awards 2005; received three L.L.D (Honoris Causa) both for service to the Irish Theatre, the first from the National Council for Educational Awards (1988), the second from the National University of Ireland (1998), Galway and third from the University of Dublin (2004); Recreations: reading, food and poker. Contact: Druid Theatre Co., Chapel Lane, Galway. **T** 091 568 660 **F** 091 563 109 email info@druidtheatre.com web www.druidtheater.com

Acclaimed internationally as one of the great directors of her time and has been recognized with top theatrical awards; first woman to win a best director Tony award; despite her success abroad still firmly rooted in the west of Ireland where her Druid Theatre continues to be a centre of excellence.

INCHIQUIN, Lord Sir Conor Myles John O'Brien; IRISH PEER, COMPANY DIRECTOR
b 1943; *m* Helen O'Farrell; *2d*; *edu*. Eton College, Windsor; managing director Dromoland Development Company, Co. Clare; 18th Baron (cr1543 and a baronet); Late Capt. 14/20th King's Hussars 1983 to date; managing director Dromoland Development Company Ltd (The Dromoland Experience) 1992 to date; chairman Swift International Developments Ltd; Clubs: Kildare Street and University Club, Dublin. Contact: Thomond House, Dromoland, Newmarket on Fergus, Co. Clare. **T** 061 368 304 **F** 061 368 285 email chiefob@iol.ie

Head of the O'Brien Clan, the lineal descendent of Brian Boru; still lives on part of the family estate in Co. Clare; pleasant and well respected locally.

IOAKIMIDES, Michael; MANAGING DIRECTOR, DIAGEO IRELAND
b 1965, Naples, Italy; *m* Jane; *1s 1d*; *edu*. Kalamaki Senior High School, Athens, Greece; Imperial College, London University; Harvard Business School; Master Degree in Chemical Engineering and Chemical Technology; Master in Business Administration; Managing Director, Diageo Ireland; business analyst, Booz Allen and Hamilton1988-90; qualified case leader, The Boston Consulting Group1992-95; senior strategy manager, United Distillers 1995-96; strategy director, United Distillers 1996-98; marketing director, UDV, Italy 1998-99; managing director, Diageo Italy Hub 1999-2002; marketing director, Diageo Ireland 2002-03; marketing and commercial director, Diageo Ireland 2003-04; managing director, Diageo Ireland 2004 to date. Clubs: Hibernian Golf Society, Kildare Hotel and Country Club, Carrickmines Tennis Club. Recreations: golf, skiing, tennis, swimming, family. Contact: Diageo Ireland, St. James's Gate, Dublin 8. **T** 01 453 6700 **F** 01 408 4865

Brought a wealth of experience in international, blue chip companies to St. James Gate; popular, hardworking, an enthusiastic sportsman, has continued to provide support for the company's most recognizable sponsorship – the Guinness All Ireland Hurling Championship.

Jonathan Irwin

IRWIN, Jonathan; FOUNDER, CEO, JACK AND JILL FOUNDATION
b 1941, Malvern, UK; *m* 1st Mikaela Rawlinson (*m diss*); *4s* (1 *decd*) *m* 2nd Mary Ann O'Brien; *3s*; *2d*; (2 *decd*); *edu*. Eton College, UK; founder/CEO, Jack and Jill Foundation; Tim Vigors & Co (Bloodstock Agent) 1960-74; British Bloodstock Agency (IRL) Ltd 1975-89; Goffs Bloodstock Sales 1981-90; CEO, Phoenix Park Race Course 1985-91; International Racecourse Ltd 1993-2004; Dublin International Sports Council 1997 to date; founder, chairman and chief fundraiser The Jack and Jill Foundation; member of the Kilannin Commission, member of the Collins Commission; council member Irish Thorougbred Breeders 1971-98; non executive director British Bloodstock Agency (IRL), founding member Irish Equine Center, Johnstown, Co. Kildare; chairman and editor, Tourism Committee, Dublin Chamber of Commerce, *Vision 2110* project; only person to be awarded Association Irish Thoroughbred Breeders Personality of the Year on two occasions; Hon. Life member Hong Kong Owners Association; director, partner and marketing consultant, Lily O'Brien's Chocolates; chairman of Venues Committee, board of the Special Olympics Committee; ESB Rehab Person of the Year 2004; Clubs: Landsdowne RFC; Irish Turf Club; Annabels, London. Recreations: reading, politics, people. Contact: Jack and Jill Children's Foundation, Johnstown, Naas, Co. Kildare. **T** 045 894538 **F** 045 894558 email jonathan@jackandjill.ie

Following a glittering career in international bloodstock sales and race course management, tragic family circumstances inspired him to co-found (with his wife Mary Ann O'Brien (*qv*) The Jack and Jill Foundation, a charity that cares for the families of physically and mentally challenged babies; eloquent, charismatic, great company and bon viveur to boot.

JACKSON, Shane; ARTIST- SCULPTOR

b 1972, Dublin; single; *edu.* De Montfort University Leicester, UK (BA, Visual Arts); Erasmus Rotterdam Art College; The Slade, London (bronze casting course); Newry Training Centre. Co. Down, N.I. Welding Approval Test Certificate; The Slade, London; (life drawing course); Institute of Art and Design, University of Central England, Birmingham (Foundation in Art and Design); Grennan Mill Crafts School, Thomastown Co. Kilkenny, VEC (Distinction); artist-sculptor; established 'votan designs' 2000; Exhibitions: *Fresh Air,* The Quenington Sculpture Trust, Gloucestershire 2005; Westmeath Arts, Killyon Manor, Hill of Down, Co Meath 2003. Recreations: bowls, fly fishing, tennis, skiing, shooting, cooking (Ballymaloe course). Contact: **T** 046 954 6978 **F** 046 954 65 34 **M** 087 668 7533 email info@votandesign.com

> A sculptor in metal whose sense of form allied to figurative idioms is a delight; collected by the discerning art patron.

JENNINGS, Jarlath; MANAGING DIRECTOR, MC CONNELLS

b 1958; *m* Marian; 1*s*; *edu.* St. Augustines College Dungarvan; Waterford Institute of Technology; College of Marketing; University of Dublin Trinity College; The Marketing Institute; Certificate in Business Studies; Diploma in Management; BSc in Management; MA Marketing Institute; Graduateship and Fellowship; Kodak Graduate Trainee; Nielsen Research; CPC Knorr (Now Unilever Foods); brand manager McConnells; chairman McConnells PR; chairman McConnells Direct; managing director McConnells Advertising. Recreations: photography, music, working and hurling. Contact: 2 Glenmurray Park, Terenure, Dublin 12 **T** 01 450 7322 email jarlath.jennings@mcconnells.ie

JENNINGS, Thomas James; CHAIRMAN AND CEO ROTARY GROUP

b 1954; *m* Jane Margaret; 2*s* 1*d*; *edu.* Sullivan Upper, Hollywood, Co. Down; Queens University, Belfast; C.Bls. BSc., C.Eng. F.I. Mech. E.FRSA; chairman Rotary Group Ltd; chairman CUSP Ltd; graduate engineer, Rotary Group Ltd; various positions leading to managing director and chairman. Recreations: country sports. Contact: 62, Ballyrogan Road, Newtownards, Co. Down BT 23 4ST email tj.jennings@rotarygroup.com

JEWELL, Dermot; CEO, CONSUMER'S ASSOCIATION OF IRELAND

b 1951, Dublin; *m* Bernadette; 1*s* 2*d*; *edu.* Synge Street CBS; DIT Diploma; Trinity College Dublin, BSc Management Law; associate member Chartered Institute of Arbitration in Ireland; chief executive, The Consumers Association of Ireland; accounts clerk Irish Farmers Association /FBD 1970-73; assistant financial controller GEC Distributors Irl. Ltd 1973-79; payroll manager, The Rohan Group Leinster; office manager Ballyfermot Estate 1979-86; office/finance manager M&M Ceiling Systems 1986-93; director of M&M 1990; one year contract to resolve credit control problems and establish Control Accounts systems, Legal & General 1993-94; CEO Consumers' Association of Ireland 1994 to date; member, Dept of Justice Customer Liaison Panel; Dept of An Taoiseach Quality Customer Service Working Group; Food Safety Authority of Ireland Consultative Group; Bord Bia Quality Assurance Branch; Dept of Justice Auctioneering Review Group; member of ComReg Consumer Advisory Panel; general assembly member of BEUC, European Consumers' Organisation; ANEC European Association for Co-ordination of Consumer Representation in Standardisation; investor Compensation Company Ltd.; Financial Services Ombudsman Council, Dept of Finance; chairperson Bord Bia Quality Assurance Certification Committee and Irish Food Quality Certification Governing Board; Ireland's representative, European Commission Consumer Consultative Group through DG Sanco; contracted by DG Sanco to provide training of management modules to staff of European consumer organisations (three courses annually); Publ. contributor to consumer journals, programmes and print /broadcast media; Recreations: guitar music, reading, travel, walking. Contact: **T** 01 497 8600 **F** 01 497 8608 email cai@consumerassociation.ie

Dermot Jewell

> The public face of the Consumer Association of Ireland for many years; his organisation's constant lobbying for many years finally led to the establishment of the office of the Director of Consumer Affairs Carmel Foley (*qv*); with his fellow officer Michael Kilcullen retains a high public profile on behalf of Irish consumers.

JOHNSON, Jennifer; AUTHOR/ DRAMATIST

b 1930; *m* 1st Ian Smyth; 2*s* 2*d*; 2nd David Gilliland; *edu.* Park House School, Dublin; Trinity College Dublin; D.Litt Ulster 1984 (hc); Trinity College Dublin 1992; QUB 1974; FRSL 1979; Author /Dramatist; member, Aosdána; Plays: *Indian Summer,* performed Belfast 1983; *The Porch,* Dublin

1986; *Shadows on Our Skin,* 1978 (dramatized for TV 1979); Publ. *The Captains and The Kings* 1971; *The Gates* 1973; *How Many Miles to Babylon* 1993; *The Old Jest* 1979 (filmed as *The Drawing* 1988); *The Nightingale and Not the Lark* 1980; *The Christmas Tree* 1981; *The Railway Station Man* 1984; *The Fool's Sanctuary* 1987; *The Invisible Worm* 1991; *The Illusionist* 1995; (contrib.) *Finbar's Hotel* 1997; *Two Moons* 1998; *The Gingerbread Woman* 2000 (not a novel). Recreations: theatre, cinema, gardening, travel.

> Daughter of a journalist and actress – the late (William) Denis Johnson OBE and Sheelagh Richards; a lively, attractive personality with great drive and energy; she combines the best of what the modern Irish writer, out of a Protestant and artistic sensibility, has to offer.

JONES, Barry John; CONSULTANT SURGEON
b 1958, Dublin; *m* Aisling; 3*s* 1*d*; *edu.* St. Fintan's High School, Sutton, Dublin; University College Dublin Medical School; FRCS; King Inns; MB. BAO. FRCSI; Master of Surgery NUI; Barrister at Law, Kings Inns; consultant surgeon; consultant urologist Our Lady of Lourdes Hospital, Drogheda and Aut Even Hospital Kilkenny; *Publ.* books; *Oncological Applications of High Energy Shock Waves*; *Medical Legal Reporting In Surgical Trauma*; Articles published in: *American Journal of Urology*; *British Journal of Urology; European Journal of Urology;* surgical training in Ireland and UK; legal training Dublin; consultant surgeon 1993 to date. Clubs: County Louth Golf Club, Hermitage Golf Club, Kilkenny Golf Club, Castleknock Tennis Club, Wanderers Rugby Football Club (medical officer); Recreations: golf, cycling, tennis, dining out with wife and friends; Contact: Suite 4, Charlemont Clinic, Charlemont Mall, Dublin 2. **T** 01 418 8411 **F** 01 4783424. email barryjones@eircom.net web www.charlemontclinic.ie

> The barrister/consultant surgeon has published many legal/medical papers and articles; with practices in Dublin, Kilkenny and Drogheda is a well respected and extremely popular surgeon.

JONES, Kenneth; ORGAN BUILDER
b 1936, Longford; *m* 1st (*m.dis*); 2*d*; m 2nd Barbara Benedict; *edu.* Wesley College Dublin; Trinity College Dublin, MA, BAI; Engineer with Nigerian Railways 1957; formed organ-building company, Nigeria 1964; returned to Ireland 1973; established Kenneth Jones Pipe Organs Ltd., Bray, Kenneth Jones and Associates; in the past 30 years prestigious commissions completed include those in Christ Church Cathedral Dublin; the Cathedral of the Madeleine Salt Lake City USA; the National Concert Hall Dublin; St. Peter's Church Eaton Square London; Trinity College Melbourne University; Tewkesbury Abbey England; Christ Church Cathedral Vancouver Canada; Youth Concert Hall Beijing China; Rugby School England; St. Macartan's Cathedral Monaghan; Christ Church Cathedral Waterford; St. Peter's Cathedral Belfast. Recreations: country life, music, photography, architecture, house design. Contact: Church Terrace, Bray, Co. Wicklow; **T** 01 2867662. **F** 01 2867664.

JONES, Geraldine; JOINT MD, DOLMEN SECURITIES
b 1960; *m* Joseph Dempsey; *edu.* Mercy Convent Roscommon; University College Dublin; B.SS, FCA; audit manager, Ernst & Young until 1988; director of listing, Irish Stock Exchange 1988-2001; joint MD Dolmen Securities 2001 to date. Recreations: football, reading, jazz; Contacts: Dolmen House, 4, Earlsfort Terrace, Dublin 2. **T** 01 633 3800 **F** 01 677 7044 email geraldine.jones@dsl.com

JONES, Martin; ARCHITECT
b 1950, Dublin; *m* Mary Keating; 2*s* 3*d*; *edu.* Terenure College, Dublin; School of Architecture; Dublin Institute of Technology, Bolton Street, Dublin; Dip Arch, RIAI; fellow, RIAI 2005; managing director (joint) Burke Kennedy Doyle Architects. Clubs: Fitzwilliam Lawn Tennis Club. Recreations: architecture, tennis, swimming, spending time with family and friends; Contact: 6/7 Harcourt Terrace, Dublin 2; **T** 01 618 2400 **F** 01 676 7385 email m.jones@bkd.ie

> Award winning and highly respected architect; as a partner in one of the country's top architectural practice has presided over some of the projects that have changed the face of the country, most recently The Dundrum Town Centre shopping mall.

JORDAN, Neil; FILM MAKER, WRITER
b 1952, Sligo; *m* 1st Vivienne Shields (*m.diss*); 2*d*; m 2nd Brenda Wran; 2*s*; *edu.* St. Pauls School

Raheny; University College Dublin; recipient of Irish Arts Bursary 1976; The Guardian Fiction Prize 1977; publications include *Night in Tunisia and Other Stories; The Past; The Dream of a Beast; Sunrise with Sea Monster*; film credits include: *The Company of Wolves* (director); *Angel* (director and screen writer); *High Spirits* (director); *Mona Lisa; We're No Angels* (director); *The Miracle* (director); *The Crying Game* 1992; *Interview with a Vampire* 1995; *Michael Collins* 1997; *The Butcher Boy* 1998; *In Dreams* 1999; *The End of the Affair* 1999; *Not I* 2000; *The Good Thief* 2002; *Breakfast on Pluto* 2006; *Borgia* 2006; *Me And My Monster*, preproduction 2007. Contact: ICM Ltd, 76, Irishtown Road, Dublin, 4 **T** 01 667 6455 email info@neiljordan.com web www.neiljordan.com

An intellectual movie maker with a real sense of telling a story; has a tremendous sense of the visual interlocking with the narrative which gives his work it's compelling charge of power and authority; intellectually curious and constantly seeking, his is a very literate art form in an otherwise non intellectual world of movie making; has great gifts to which his audience has already been exposed and much more is expected of him in the very challenging world of movie making; is greatly valued as a friend, a colleague and as an important film personality.

JORGENSEN, Ib; ART GALLERY OWNER

b 1935, Denmark; *m* Patricia Murray; (*m. diss*); 2*d*; *m* Sonia Rogers; (*m. diss*); *edu.* Morgan School, Denmark; Castleknock, Co. Dublin; Grafton Academy of Dress Design; worked with Nicholas O'Dwyer (Dublin) before opening own salon 1956; designs for international clientele, theatre and airlines; Ireland's leading couturier, with an expanding market in the ready to wear (boutique) range; closed couture salon in 1996; opened Jorgensen Fine Art Gallery dealing in Irish and European art 1990. Recreations; gardening, tennis, theatre, the Arts. Contact: Jorgensen Fine Art, 29 Molesworth Street, Dublin 2. **T** 01 661 9755 **F** 01 661 9760

A suave intelligent, articulate art dealer who possesses steely determination in the promotion of all that he regards as "best taste" in the arts; brings his skills, particularly with the eagle eye of a former couture designer, to bear on all aspects of his working life; every thing he does brings with it an austere Scandinavian Authority; is a good friend to many and despite his sometimes apparently austere countenance he is a lively party goer and a considerable figure in the upper echelons of Irish and British Society.

JOYCE, Brian; CHAIRMAN, EBS BUILDING SOCIETY; CHAIRMAN, MATER PRIVATE HOSPITAL

b 1940; *m* Peggy; 1*s* 1*d*; *edu.* St. Mary's College, Galway; University College Galway; BA, B Comm, H Dip in Ed, FCMA; chairman EBS Building Society; chairman Mater Private Hospital; formerly managing director of Irish Dairy Board; professional non Executive Director since 1989; chairman, EBS Building Society; chairman Mater Private Hospital. Recreations: football, reading, walking, politics, business. Contact: 27, Mespil Road, Dublin 4. **T** 01 667 1199 **F** 01 6671116 email: brianjoyce@eircom.net

Well-respected figure for many years in the Irish agri sector; currently holds two influential and well remunerated chairmanships in the financial services and health care sectors.

JUNCOSA, Enrique; DIRECTOR, IRISH MUSEUM OF MODERN ART

b 1961, Palma de Mallorca, Spain; single; *edu.* studied electronic music, Phonos Studio, Barcelona; University of Barcelona, (Degree, English Literature); Director, Irish Museum of Modern Art Dublin; art consultant/ exhibition organizer, Pomeroy Purdy Gallery, London 1989; deputy director, Valencian Institute of Modern Art (IVAM), Valencia 1998-2000; deputy director, Reina Sofia National Museum of Modern Art, Madrid 2000-02; adviser, Collection of the European Investment Bank, Luxembourg 2003; director, Irish Museum of Modern Art Dublin 2003 to date; trustee of the board, Pilar and Joan Miró Foundation, Palma de Mallorca 1992 to date; art critic, *El País*; curator of numerous international exhibitions; Publ. Poetry, *Amanecer Zulú, Calle Mayor* 1986; *Las Frutas* 1990; *Pastoral Con Cebras* 1990; *Libro del Océano* 1991; *Pesces de Colores* 1996; *Poemas Africanos* 1997; *Libro del Océano y Otros Poemas* 1998; *La Dádiva* 2002; *Apartamento Mínimal y Otros Poemas* 2002; *Las Espirales Naranja* 2002; essays: *Index and Metaphor, in Abstraction, Gesture, Scripture*, various authors 1999; *Caravel, Una Revista de Vanguaria Norteamericana Publicada en Mallorca En Los Años 30* 2000; *Ecrits sur Barceló*

Enrique Juncosa

2002. Contact: Irish Museum of Modern Art, Royal Hospital, Kilmainham, Dublin 8. **T** 01 612990 email catherine.punch@imma.ie

> Great-nephew of the famous Spanish Modernist painter Joan Miró, he is also a noted poet and has brought all that Iberian sensibility to IMMA; much more is expected of him in the near future; a quietly charming man.

KANE, Denis Patrick; CEO/DIRECTOR, DRUIDS GLEN RESORT;
b 1950; Dublin; *m* Vicky; 3*s* 1*d*; *edu.* CBS Westland Row, Dublin; Dublin College Hotel
Administration; Westminster College London; Hotel d'Ecole Glion, Switzerland; Degree in Hotel
Administration, Institute Personnel Management, Institute of Training & Development; hotel
administration London, Paris, Luasanne, New York, Edmonton, Canada; Failte Ireland; Hermitage
Golf Club; Clubs; Druids Golf Club; Recreations; All Sports in Croke Park, Landsdowne Road and
Parnell Park; Contact: Druids Glen Golf Resort, Newtownmountkennedy, Co Wicklow
T 01 287 3600 **F** 01 287 3699 email dkane@druidsales.ie

> Member of a well known GAA family, impeccable hospitality and hotel background
> made him an ideal choice to head up the newly established Druids Glen Golf and
> Country Club; a great ambassador for Irish golf overseas; bright, switched on, his easy
> manner makes him one of the most popular and well respected executives in Irish golf.

KANE, Michael Francis; ARTIST
b Wicklow; *m* 1st Ruth Brandt (*decd.*); 1*s*; 2nd Shelly McNamara (*qv*);
edu. local school, Wicklow; National College of Art, Dublin; Graphic
Studio Dublin; numerous exhibitions in Ireland and abroad 1960 to
date. member Independent Artists; co-founder Project Arts Centre;
member of Aosdána; Publ. *Michael Kane, His Life and Art* Henry J.
Sharpe 1983; *Michael Kane* Rubicon Gallery, Dublin; Cut Space
Gallery, London 2002; *Tracings* 2002; Irish Arts Review 2004;
numerous national newspapers and periodicals; two books of poems;
Structure Magazine 1972-78; studios in Dublin and Milan.
Recreations: the erotic in all its forms. Contact: 8a, Clyde Lane,
Ballsbridge, Dublin 4. **T** 01 660 3131

> A thoughtful practitioner of his art, a determined artist who
> has often had to stand on the sidelines and, like so many of his
> generation, had to be brave and challenge the order of things.

KAVANAGH, Brian Thomas; CEO HORSE RACING IRELAND
b 1964, Dublin; *m* Diane Dwan; 1*s* 2*d*; *edu.* CBC Monkstown, County
Dublin; B. Commerce, University College Dublin; FCA (Fellow of the
Institute of Chartered Accountants); financial controller Irish Turf
Club 1989-94; manager Curragh Racecourse 1995-99; chief executive Irish Turf Club 2000-01; chief
executive Horse Racing Ireland 2001 to date. Clubs; Curragh Golf Club. Recreations; all sports,
reading, travel. Contact: Horseracing Ireland, Thorough Bred County House, Kill Co Kildare.
T 045 842 800 **F** 045 842 880 email bkavanagh@horseracingireland.ie

Michael Kane

> Highly respected professional who is very popular in the industry; has brought a new
> professionalism to horse racing in Ireland.

KAVANAGH, Denise; PROTOCOL OFFICER AND P.A. DEPARTMENT OF AN TAOISEACH
b Kingston on Thames, UK; *m* David O'Neill; *edu.* Holy Child, Dun Laoighre; Dip. Marketing; Dip.
Public Relations & Marketing; joined Civil Service, (clerical staff), 1977, worked in various
Departments; assistant press officer Foreign Affairs, European Presidency Ireland 1990; joined
Fianna Fail (press officer /event manager) 1990 - 97; resumed position in Civil Service Department of
the Taoiseach, 1997- todate; loaned to Special Olympics, VIP and Media Relations, 2003;
Recreations: art, theatre, travel, charity work, reading, dogs. Contact: Department of the Taoiseach,
Government Buildings, Merrion Street, Dublin 2. **T** 01 619 4075 **F** 01 619 4257
emaildenise.kavanagh@taoiseach.gov.ie

> The petite, professional and personable blonde's velvet glove and easy manner masks
> an iron will as she manages the Taoiseach's hectic schedule delivering him from one
> event to the next all over the country, almost miraculously, 99% of the time, on time;
> extremely well organized and popular, despite her non stop schedule, still manages to
> have time for everyone.

KAVANAGH, Gary; HAIRDRESSER
b 1944; single; *edu.* Comprehensive, London; creative director at Peter Mark. Clubs: Iveagh Health

and Fitness. Recreations: swimming, keeping fit; Contact: 55 Rothe Abbey, Kilmainham, Dublin 8; **T** 087 652755 email AK_ONE8@hotmail.com

The Peter Pan of Irish hairdressing, continues to be one of the top creative stylists, adored by models and clients alike; great personality, extremely hard worker; articulate and excellent media performer, has been a pivotal part of spreading the hairdressing gospel according to Peter Mark all over the country.

John Kavanagh

KAVANAGH, John; ACTOR

b 1946, Dublin; *m* Anne McIvor; 1*s* 2*d*; *edu.* Our Lady's National School, Milltown, Dublin; Dundrum Technical School, Dublin; Caffrey's College, Dublin; actor; member, The Abbey Theatre 1966-67; has appeared in musicals such as *Pirates of Penzance; HMS Pinafore; Tom Foolery; Jacques Brel; Guys and Dolls; Les Miserables* 1977 to date; has appeared on Broadway; film roles include: *The Black Dahlia; Alexander; Cal; Into the West; The Butcher Boy; Braveheart; Circle of Friends; Dancing at Lughnasa; Sweeney Todd; This is My Father;* television roles: *Dr. Finlay; Bad Company; Ballroom of Romance; Sharpe; Shadow of a Gunman; Lovejoy; Children of the North; Vicious Circle;* most recent performances: Mitch in *A Streetcar Named Desire* at the Gate Theatre, Dublin; Astrov in Brian Friel's new version of *Uncle Vanya;* Awards: Dublin Theatre Festival award; a Drama Desk nomination for his portrayal of Joxer in the Gate Theatre production of *Juno and the Paycock.* Contact: Terri Hayden, The Agency, 47 Adelaide Road, Dublin 2. **T** 01 661 8535 **F** 01 676 0052

A very fine character actor whose portrayals in O'Casey plays are hallmarks of excellence; witty and lugubrious in the same moment.

KAVANAGH, Mark; PROPERTY DEVELOPER

b 1945, Dublin; *m* 1st Linda Hitzeman *(decd.)*; 1*s* 2*d*; *m* 2nd Kathleen Shugue; 2*s* 1*d*; *edu.* St. Gerard's, Bray, Co. Wicklow; Downside (UK); property developer; trainee surveyor with Jones Lang Wootton 1967-69; general manager Screenprint Ltd 1969-71; established Catering Ireland (restaurants including Captain America) 1971; joint managing director, Hardwicke Ltd 1978-79; chairman 1977 to date; chairman, chief executive, Hardwicke American Properties Inc. 1982 to date; director, American Exploration Company 1982 to date; former chairman, Custom House Docks Development Company Ltd; member, Urban Land Institute (Washington DC); New York Real Estate Board. Recreations: golf, skiing, shooting, tennis, travel. Contact: Hardwicks Ltd., 14 Wellington Road, Dublin 4 **T** 01 668 3791. **F** 01 668 0265.

A golden boy in the middle of a golden age of property development; he has retained his boyish enthusiasm for property developments of all kinds in Dublin, London and the US.

KEAN, Clodagh née Hopkins; SOLICITOR/CHARITY FUNDRAISER

b 1961, Ballina; *m* Gerald Kean *(qv)*; separated; 1*d*; *edu.* Laurel Hill, Limerick; University College Dublin; BCL; Incorporated Law Society; solicitor; solicitor, Kean's solicitors 1992-2005; started own practice Hopkins Kean Solicitors 2005; fund raiser ISPCC. Clubs: Kildare Hotel and Country Club, Co. Kildare; Woodbrook Golf Club. Recreations: golf, travel, family and friends. Contact: 69, Mespil Road, Dublin 4 **T** 01 660 1626

The bright, beautiful blonde solicitor is well known in social circles and is an indefatigable fund raiser for the ISPCC; a single handicap golfer, she is a much sought after team player on the circuit; devoted mother and daughter who has retained her friendly and warm personality, despite almost hysterical media intrusion into her private life.

KEAN, Gerald Ronan; SOLCITIOR

b 1957, Cork; *m* Clodagh Hopkins *(qv* Kean Clodagh); separated; 1*d*; *edu.* Coláiste Chriost Rí, Turner's Cross, Cork; De La Salle, Wicklow Town; University College Dublin; BCL; member Irish Law Society. LLd (hc) American College, Merrion Square, Dublin; managing partner Kean's Solicitors; principal of Kean's and founder of the firm; New York Bar late 80s; Honorary Chilean Consul to Ireland 1998-2003; trustee/director of Marie Keating Breast Cancer Charity; Publ. various articles in different journals and publications. Clubs: Kildare Hotel and Country Club, Straffan, Co. Kildare. Recreations: supporter Manchester United, golf, spending time with daughter Kirsten.

Contact: Lr Pembroke Street, Dublin 2 **T** 01 676 9955 **F** 01 676 9975 email info@keans.ie

High profile solicitor who services a celebrity client list; passionate Manchester United fan; engaging raconteur.

Gerald Kean

KEANE, Esmonde; SENIOR COUNSEL
b 1964, Dublin; *m* Susan Gilvarry; 2*s* 1*d*; *edu.* Gonzaga College, Dublin; Glenstal Abbey, Murroe, Co. Limerick; University College Dublin; BCL; B.L.; barrister, senior counsel;
New York Bar to 1987; Irish Bar 1987 to date. Clubs: Ballaghaderreen Golf Club; Recreations: mountaineering; Contact: Law Library, Distillery Building 145-151 Church Street, Dublin 7
T 01 817 4338 **F** 01 8174843 email ekeane@lawlibrary.ie

A skillful younger senior counsel whose style has often misled county authorities into thinking they were dealing with a boy sent on a man's mission; skilled performer with the skills of a forensic surgeon.

KEANE, Frank; MD MOTOR IMPORT Ltd / FRANK KEANE HOLDINGS
b 1933; *m* Ursula Hinds; 2*s* 1*d*; edu. Christian Brothers, Gorey, Wexford and CBC Monkstown; entered motor trade with Smithfield Motors Ltd. 1952; with P.R. Reilly May 1953; joined Mount Merrion Motors May 1962; Three Rock Garage January 1966; awarded BMW franchise and formed Motor Import Ltd. 1967; expanded in 1974 with Pioneer HiFi products; sold back BMW distributorship 2003; opened state of art retail BMW/Mini showrooms on the Naas Road, Dublin 2004; awarded Mitsubishi Motor Cars and Trucks Franchise 1984; combined companies under Frank Keane Holding banner. Clubs: Powerscourt Golf Club. Recreations: golf, rugby. Contact: Frank Keane Motors, Naas Road, Dublin 12. **T** 01 240 5666

His presience in acquiring the BMW franchise in the '60's made him one of the most influential operators in the motor industry in Ireland; selling back the distributorship nearly four decades later made him an even wealthier man; high energy, likeable, hardworking, has now embarked on the second stage of his career.

KEANE, Lorraine; TV CORRESPONDENT
b Dublin; *m* Peter Devlin; 1*d; edu.* City & Guilds Public Administration and Current Affairs; AA Roadwatch, Ireland 1990-98; entertainment correspondent TV3 1998 to date; Contact:
TV3,Westgate Business Park, Ballymount, Dublin 24 **T** 01 419 3333 **F** 01 419 3300.
email entertainment@tv3.ie and lorraine.keane@tv3.ie

Has established a niche for entertainment and fashion gossip through her slots on TV3's news bulletins; the vivacious presenter is an energetic networker on the Dublin social scene.

KEANE, Michael, J; PUBLIC RELATIONS DIRECTOR
b 1946; *m* Jenny; 2*s* 1*d; edu.* CBS, Athy, Co Kildare; College of Commerce, Rathmines, Dublin; Journalism graduate; Northern editor for *The Irish Press* 1972-78; deputy editor and news editor for *The Sunday Press*; assistant editor for *The Irish Press* and then editor 1988-95; director Fleishman Hillard, International Communications 1995-2005; established own consultancy Insight Consultants, 2006 to date. Recreations: music, theatre, sport, current affairs, travel, gardening; Contact: Insight Consultants, Suite 12 Beacon Court, Sandyford, Dublin 18 **T** 01 293 9977 **F** 293 9952
M 086 82444500 email michaelk@insightcoinsultants.ie web www.insightconsultants.ie

Having enjoyed a career in journalism as one of the most respected editors in the country, he carried the same esteem and work ethic to his new career as a PR consultant; down to earth, loyal to his clients and friends, many of whom are senior politicians and captains of industry.

KEARNEY, Richard Marius; UNIVERSITY PROFESSOR
b 1954, Cork; *m* Anne Bernard; 2*d; edu.* Glenstal Abbey, Murroe, Co. Limerick; University College Dublin, BA; Magill University, Montreal, Canada, MA; University of Paris X (Ph.D); professor, Charles Seelig Chair of Philosophy, Boston College. Lecturer 1981-90; rotating head of Philosophy Department University College Dublin 1993-98; EU Erasmus Exchange Professor at L'Institut

Catholique de Paris, Louvain and Lisbon University 1994-99; extern examiner, University of Warwick 1993-97; visiting professor University of Paris, Sorbonne 1997; visiting professor University of Nice-Sophia Antipolis 1999; visiting professor Boston College 1986-2001; professor, (Personal Chair) 1990-2001; professor of philosophy, Boston College 2001 to date; chair, Film School, University College Dublin 1992-2004; former member Irish Arts Council, Irish Higher Education Authority: Publ. 20 books authored; 15 books co-authored; 15 translated into many languages; other works include series editor, editorial member, and audio visual productions; currently writing three screenplays. Recreations: swimming, yoga, hiking, fishing: Contact: 22, Tennyson Road, West Newton, MA 02465, USA. **T** 00 1 617 552 8182 email kearney@bc.edu

A brilliant mind and a charming personality; a popular university tutor, much sought after as a commentator on philosophical questions, as well as on all aspects of contemporary culture.

KEARNS, Raymond; PRESIDENT, PORTOBELLO COLLEGE DUBLIN
b Ballaghdreen, Co. Roscommon; *m* Bríd; 4*s* 1*d*; *edu.* Cross NS; St. Nathys Ballaghdreen, Co. Roscommon; The Docks School, North Wall, Dublin; University College Dublin; University of Pittsburgh, Boston College; Fordham University; BA; H.Dip; MA (New Mathematics); President Portobello College, Dublin; director Institute of Education. Worked in CIE; senior mathematics master, Gonzaga College, Dublin 1962-78; started the Institute of Education, Leeson Street, Dublin 1969; founded Portobello College 1989; director Institute of Education 1969 to date; president Portobello College, Dublin 1989 to date. Clubs: Castle Golf Club; Fitzwilliam LTC. Recreations: swimming, walking, reading. Contact: Portobello College, South Richmond Street Dublin 2, Ireland **T** 01 475 5811 **F** 01 475 5817 email kearnsr@portobello.ie web www.portobello.ie

An educational innovator and visionary; challenged the system by providing private support tuition; has provided many with the opportunity to gain university admission, thereby fuelling the Celtic Tiger with a well educated work force; following the success of the Institution, founded Portobello College which attracts a national and international student body for internationally accredited third level degree courses; an engaging personality, gregarious, warm and friendly.

KEATING, Brendan; CHIEF EXECUTIVE OFFICER, PORT OF CORK
b 1955; *m* Aileen; 2*s* 2*d*; *edu.* Rockwell College, Co. Tipperary; University College Cork; B.Comm; chief executive, Port of Cork; county secretary, Meath County Council; assistant city manager, Cork City Council; city manager, Limerick City Council; chief executive, Port of Cork. Recreations: reading, sport, rugby, hurling. Contact: Port of Cork, Custom House Quay, Cork **T** 021 4273125 email bkeating@portofcork.ie

KEAVENEY, Cecelia; PUBLIC REPRESENTATIVE
b 1968, Derry; single; *edu.* Cardonagh Community School; University of Ulster, Jordanstown; B.Mus.(hons); M.Phil, PGCE Music, LTCL (performers); public representative TD (FF Donegal North East); teacher of piano, University of Ulster 1989-91; head of music, St. Joseph's High School, Coleraine, Derry 1992; music director The Ibginedion Education Centre, Benin City, Nigeria 1992-93; licensed teacher, Thomas Beckett School, Northampton, UK 1993-94; music teacher, St. Mary's Secondary School, Creggan, Derry 1995-96; elected Donegal County Council 1995; elected to Dáil Éireann (FF Donegal North East) 1996; re-elected 1997; member of Joint Oireachtas Committees on Health and Children, Education and Science, Procedure and Privileges; member British-Irish Interparliamentary Body; alternate member Forum for Peace and Reconciliation 2002 to date; member, North West Region, Cross Border Group; Fisheries and Coastal Protection; Coiste Magilligan Car Ferry; member, Guildhall Chamber Orchestra Derry; University of Ulster Choir, Chamber Choir and Orchestra; Moville Donegal North East Ógra; Moville Fianna Fáil Cumann; North Inishowen Comhairle Ceantair; member, Joint Oireachtas Committee on Art, Sport & Tourism; Community, Rural and Gaeltacht; member of UUJ; All Ireland Intervarsities Equestrian winning team; Ulster Camogie Championship Team. Recreations: racing, equestrian sports, concerts, music, performing music, camogie, swimming, canoeing; Contact: Loreto, Moville, Co. Donegal **T** 074 938 2177 **F** 074 938 2832 email cecelia.keaveney@oireachtas.ie

KEAVENEY, Mark; FOUNDING PARTNER PETER MARK HAIRDRESSING
b 1940, Kells, Co. Meath; single; *edu.* Christian Brothers Kells, Co. Meath; joint managing director Peter Mark Hairdressing. Started hairdressing career training with legendary Michele of Brussels;

established the first Peter Mark salon with his brother Peter (*qv*) at 87 Grafton Street, Dublin 1961; opened current company flagship salon at 74 Grafton Street, Dublin 1967; now over 70 Peter Mark Hairdressing salons and three training academies operating throughout the 32 counties; president, Irish Hairdressing Federation 1981-82. Awards: Meath Man of the Year 1982; Best Dressed Man of the Year 1983; Clubs: K Club, David Lloyd Racquet and Fitness Club; RIAC; Recreations: golf, swimming, football. Contact: Peter Mark Head Office, 15 Ely Place, Dublin 2 **T** 01 661 4888 **F** 01 661 3673

> While his brother Peter (*qv*) kept an eye on growing the business, Mark was always up on international, artistic trends and very often well ahead of the latest catwalk fashions; enjoys long distance travel; is also a keen golfer, switches off on the better courses around the world.

KEAVENEY, Peter; FOUNDING PARTNER PETER MARK HAIRDRESSING
b 1942, Co. Meath; *m* Mary; 2*s* 1*d*; *edu.* Christian Brothers, Kells, Co. Meath; joint managing director Peter Mark Hairdressing. Trained with celebrated London hairdresser Freddie French; established the first Peter Mark salon with his brother Mark (*qv*) at 87 Grafton Street, Dublin 1961; opened current company flagship salon at 74 Grafton Street, Dublin 1967; now over 70 Peter Mark Hairdressing salons and three training academies operating throughout the 32 counties. Awards: Meath Man of the Year 1982. Clubs: K Club, Edmonstown Golf Club, RIAC. Recreations: golf, football; Contact: Peter Mark Head Office, 15 Ely Place, Dublin 2 . **T** 01 661 4888 **F** 01 661 3673

> With his brother Mark (*qv*) pioneered excellent hairstyling at affordable prices throughout the country; after almost 40 years the company is still on top, popular with men and women; shrewd, hardworking businessman, never got bogged down in the rock and roll of hairdressing which afflicts many of his contemporaries.

KEENA, Colm Patrick; JOURNALIST
b 1960, Dublin; *p* Felicity Clear; 2*s* 1*d*; *edu.* Colaiste Mhuire, Parnell Square, Dublin; Trinity College, Dublin, BA (mod); NIHE, Dip Journalism; public affairs correspondent, *The Irish Times*. Irish Press Group 1987-95; *The Irish Times* 1995 to date; *Publ. Biography of Gerry Adams; Haughey's Millions; The Ansbacher Conspiracy.* Awards: Sunday Tribune/Hennessy Award 1993; Financial Journalist of the Year Award; Institute of Chartered Accountants 1999. Recreations: reading, mostly novels and biographies. Contact: Irish Times, d'Olier Street, Dublin 2 **T** 01 677 2022 ckeena@irish-times.ie

> Award winning and well-respected investigative journalist who continues to break serious news stories.

KEENAN, Brendan, Michael; GROUP BUSINESS EDITOR, INDEPENDENT NEWSPAPERS
b 1946, Belfast; *m* Maureen; 2*s*; *edu.* St. McNissi's College, Garron Tower, Co. Antrim; Queen's University Belfast; B.Sc (Econ), Dip.Ed; group business editor, Independent Newspapers 1993 to date. Business editor Irish Independent 1986-93; Ireland correspondent, Financial Times 1983-86; reporter/presenter, RTE 1976-81; economics correspondent, RTE News Features 1981-83; deputy political correspondent, *Belfast Telegraph* 1973-76; reporter, *Belfast Telegraph* 1969-73. Clubs: United Arts Club. Recreations: golf, fishing. Contact: Independent Newspapers, Independent House, 27 – 32 Talbot Street, Dublin 1. **T** 01 705 5000 email bkeenan@unison.independent.ie

> Respected as one of the most solid business/economics journalists in the country.

Brendan Keenan

KEENAN, Mark; PROPERTY EDITOR (THE SUNDAY TIMES)
b 1969, Dublin; 1*s; edu.* St Benildus College, Kilmacud; Rathmines College of Commerce, Certificate in Journalism; *Irish Independent* 1991-97; *Sunday Tribune*, started Sunday Property Supplement 1997-2000; *Sunday Times*, started Irish *Sunday Times* Property Supplement; freelance news & features, *The Irish Times, Sunday Tribune*, trade press 1989-91. Recreations; fly fishing.

> Has expanded the property pages of the *Sunday Times* to include excellent coverage of the Irish property market; though with so many Irish developers making headlines in London, throughout the UK and internationally, when it comes to property, there is now a keen interest in all things Irish in Wapping too.

KEHER, Eddie; HURLING LEGEND

b 1941, Kilkenny; *m* Kay Phelan; 2*s* 3*d*; *edu.* Inistioge National School; St Kieran's College, Kilkenny; career banker with Allied Irish Banks Dublin branches 1959-71; Kilkenny, Carlow and Callan 1971-99. Clubs: Callan Golf Club. Recreations: all sports especially GAA, golf.

The former hurling legend won six All Ireland medals with Kilkenny in the 1960s and 70s, captaining the victorious team in 1969; he won five successive All Star Awards along with nine Railway Cup medals with Leinster; the former AIB bank manager is one of nature's gentlemen, as well as one of the most approachable sports personalities in the country; much sought after for radio and TV due to his popularity and his acknowledged hurling prowess; a founder member of the 'No Name' club (a non alcoholic social club for young people), he currently works as development manager for that organization

KELLEHER, John Patrick; FILM CENSOR

b 1944; *m* Dara de Brí; 1*s* 1*d*; *edu.* Clongowes Wood College, Co. Kildare; University College Dublin B.C.L; University of Louisville M.A; Kings Inns, Barrister at Law; producer/director RTÉ 1970 -77; assistant controller of programmes RTÉ 1 1977-80; controller of programmes RTÉ 1 Television 1980-83; managing director, The Sunday Tribune 1983; independent film & TV producer 1984-2003; official film censor 2003 to date; produced six feature films (including *Eat the Peach*), seven TV drama series (including *Strumpet City*) and many documentaries (including *Even The Olives Are Bleeding*). Clubs: Fitzwilliam LTC, Dublin; Groucho Club, London; Recreations; cinema, reading, gym, watching sunsets on Mizen Head Peninsula, West Cork. Contact: 16 Harcourt Terrace, Dublin 2 **T** 01 799 6100; email johnparickkelleher@gmail.com

A highly regarded TV executive who heralded a new approach to current affairs; following a successful career in movie production, inherited the mantle of film censor from his good friend and long serving predecessor, Sheamus Smith.

KELLY, Andrew, Joseph; CERTIFIED PUBLIC ACCOUNTANT

b 1955, Bandon, Co. Cork; *m* Martina; 3*d*; *edu.* St. Finbarr's Seminary, Farranferris, Cork City; University College Galway; Dublin Institute of Technology; Bachelor of Commerce, Diploma Legal Studies, certified public accountant; chief executive, National Blood Transfusion Service; retired Commandant Irish Defence Forces; senior personnel officer University College Dublin; Irish Blood Transfusion Service. Clubs: Slade Valley Golf Club; Recreations; golf, basketball, hill walking, reading. Contact: National Blood Centre, James' Street, Dublin 8 **T** 01 432 2862 **F** 01 432 2932 email andy.kelly@ibts.ie

Low profile executive; has stabilized the Irish Blood Transfusion Service after many years of internal and external turmoil.

KELLY, Jen; FASHION DESIGNER

b 1960, Derry; *p* Garrett Fitzgerald; *edu.* St Peter's CBS, Derry; College of Marketing and Design, Parnell Sq; NCAD, Dublin; Dip (Hon) 1984; original costume designer for Riverdance The Show; responsible for creating the sexy iconic image that transformed modern Irish dance; handmade shoe collection; currently restoring a fine 18th century house of couture at 50, North Great George's Street, Dublin 1. Recreations: travel, sport. Contact: 50, North Great George's Street, Dublin 1 **T** 01 874 5983 email jen@jenkellydesign.com

Has successfully shown fashion collections in New York, London and Japan; multi-talented, is a stickler for detail; designs the most beautiful garments and is adored by his loyal clients.

KELLY, Mary; DIRECTOR GENERAL, ENVIRONMENTAL PROTECTION AGENCY

b 1956, Co Carlow; *m*; 1*s* 1*d*; *edu.* St. Leo's College, Dublin Road, Carlow; Trinity College Dublin; Dublin City University, BA (mod), PhD, MBA; director general Environmental Protection Agency. Worked in the areas of quality control and production before joining IBEC 1994; assistant director with responsibility for environmental policy IBEC; appointed director general of EPA in May2002. Recreations: Tennis, Swimming, Horse riding, golf, reading and theatre. Contact: Johnstown Castle Estate, Co Wexford. **T** 053 60630 email: m.kelly@epa.ie

Heads up the influential EPA, one of the first state bodies to be decentralized. it is emerging as a major force in Irish planning, and industrial development.

KELLY, Mark Daniel Patrick; PUBLISHER

b 1973, Dublin; single; *edu.* St Conleths College, Dublin; Stowe School, Bucks, UK; Royal Holloway, University of London; BA,(History Economics Politics); post graduate diploma in printing and publishing; publisher and chairman, Madison Publications Ltd; director, Image Publications Ltd; director, Checkout Publications Ltd; director, Prometheus Holdings; director Larves Financial Services & director Larves Properties; previously employed by The World of Hibernia Inc, Cadogan Publications Inc, and Euromoney PLC. Recreations: fencing, tennis, travel, current affairs. Contact: Madison Publications Ltd, Adelaide Hall, 3 Adelaide Street, Dun Laoghaire, Co. Dublin **T** 01 236 5880 **F** 01 230 0325 email mark.kelly@hospitalilty-ireland.com

Mark Kelly

Son of international publisher Kevin Kelly; has made his own way very successfully in publishing in the US, UK and Ireland.

KELLY, Patrick 'Paddy'; PROPERTY DEVELOPER/BUSINESSMAN/PUBLICAN

b 1943, Portlaois, Co. Laois; *m* Maureen; 3s 1d; *edu.* Christian Brothers College, Port Laois; own property development company; established Redquartz as family holding company controlling a vast array of investments in property and hotels at home and internationally. Contact: Redquartz Limited, 128, Lr. Baggot Street, Dublin 2. **T** 01 6391222 **F** 01 639 1444 email info@redquartz.com web www.redquartz.com

'Posh' Paddy is extrovert, sociable and an exotic traveller; has experienced many downturns and been the victim of a few property recessions in his time; boasts he has been close to bankruptcy on three occasions; is now one of the most astute property players in the market; has built up an extensive portfolio of investment properties in association with his long standing partners John Flynn and Alan McCormack; currently involved in one of the biggest residential/commercial developments in Florida; major development in Bray, Co. Wicklow; owner Clarion Hotels.

KELLY, Patrick 'Paddy'; PROPERTY DEVELOPER, KELLAND HOMES

b 1946, Suncroft, Co. Kildare; *m* Mary; 1s 4d; *edu.* Suncroft NS, Co. Kildare; property developer, MD Kelland Homes. Emigrated to London in the 1960s; returned to Ireland in the late '70s and set up Kelland Homes; one of Ireland's leading constructors of 'starter homes' in the Tallagh and Clondalkin areas; bought the Forte Resort Village in Sardinia; joint investment property company 'Markland' with Sean Mulryan investing in land and property in the UK and Eastern Europe. Clubs: Kildare Hotel and Country Club. Recreations: golf. Contact: Kelland Homes, Ballymount House, Ballymount Road Kingswood, Dublin 24. **T** 01 459 3146 **F** 01 459 1650

'Kelland' Paddy has, over the past 15 years, built up a very extensive house building business in the Clondalkin and Tallagh area; recently retired to one of Dublin's leafiest Georgian Squares from his rural South County Dublin estate; enjoys life quietly; a long term friend of Sean Mulryan (*qv*).

KELLY, Paul; ARCHITECT

b 1964, Dublin; *m* Deirdre Whelan; *edu.* Clonkeen College, Dublin; National College of Art and Design; Dublin Institute of Technology; Dip Arch, DIT (Hons), B.Arch SC. Trinity College Dublin (Hons); architect. Joined Corrigan Soundy Kiladiti Architects (UK) 1989; McGarry NiEanaigh Architects 1990; tutor, Dublin Institute of Technology 1993-2000; Council of the Royal Institute of Architects of Ireland 1996, 2004, 2005; O'Mahony Pike Architects 1998; editorial board of Architecture Ireland 2000 to date; tutor University College Dublin 2003; deputy commissioner for Ireland's Pavilion at the Venice Biennale 2004; board member of Temple Bar Gallery and Studios 2005; private practice with Michelle Fagan and Gary Lysaght, FKL architects 1999 to date; Contact: Unit 10, Greenmount Ind. Estate, Harold's Cross, Dublin 12; **T** 01 473 6250 **F** 01 473 6250 email design@fklarchitects.com Web fklarchitects.com

A lively and engaging architect who is much admired by his colleagues and possible rivals.

KELLY, Seán / Ó CEALLAIGH, Seán; EXECUTIVE CHAIRMAN IRISH INSTITUTE OF SPORT
FORMER PRESIDENT GAA (UACHTARÁIN CUMANN LÚTHCHLEAS GAEL)
*b*1952, Kilcummin, Co. Kerry; *m* Juliet McNiece; *2s 2d*; *edu.* Kilcummin N.S.; St. Brendan's College,
Killarney; St. Patrick's Training College; University College Dublin; B.A. (Hons); H. Dip.Ed.;
president GAA. Teacher, Cromcastle Primary school, North Dublin; teacher St. Brendan's College,
Killarney 1975; highlight of his playing career – winning a County Junior Championship, East Kerry
Senior Championship and County Division 3 League title 1973; won two County Intermediate
Hurling titles with St. Patrick's, East Kerry; selector when St. Brendan's College won the Hogan Cup
1992; chairman East Kerry Bord Na nOg 1975; chairman Kilcummin GAA Club 1976-77; chairman
East Kerry Divisional Board 1978-86; vice chairman Kerry County Board with responsibility for
hurling 1982-86; chairman Kerry County Board 1987-97; vice chairman Munster Council 1995-97;
chairman Munster Council 1998-2000; Uachtaran C.L.G, 2003 - 2006. Appointed Executive
Chairman, Irish Institute of Sport 2006 – todate. Awards: People of The Year 2005. Clubs: St.
Patrick's GAA Club. Recreations: reading, golf. Contact: Irish Sports Council, Top Floor, Block A
Westend Office Park Blanchardstown, Dublin 15, Ireland **T** 01 860 8800
email info@irishsportscouncil.ie .ie web www.irishsportscouncil.ie

> Was the first man in recent times to be elected as President of the GAA at the first
> attempt, and the first Kerryman to hold the position; noted for his courageous and
> stylish leadership of the GAA through times of great transition; skilful diplomacy and
> team work, not to mention a long list of outstanding achievements, were the hallmarks
> of Sean Kelly's tenure; his leadership during the negotiations leading to the
> amendment of the GAA's Rule 42 have assured his place in Irish sporting history; (the
> amendment of the rule, which in principle will allow rugby and soccer internationals to
> be played at Croke Park during the redevelopment of Lansdowne Road, was always felt
> to be the outcome which Sean personally favoured); his political skill in allowing
> debate to take place, in preventing division within the association and in linking the
> GAA's grass roots to the decision-making process paved the way for a successful and
> historic change; would be snapped up as a political candidate by any party.

KELLY, Simon; PROPERTY DEVELOPER, BUSINESSMAN, PUBLICAN
b 1972, Dublin; single; company director/property developer. Joined family property business
Redquartz Ltd; set up the Sanovitae gym chain which now has seven outlets with fellow developer
Alan McCormack and Irish canoeist and kayaker Karl Dunne; director of Coolbrook Developments -
a joint venture between the Kellys (father Paddy) and John Flynn; director, Alson Woods International
Limited; Vara Nominees Ltd; Sunstreak Properties Ltd; KF Internet Software Limited; Houston
Hospitality; Redquartz Boundary; with family and other investors involved in supermarkets Spar,
Mace; opened first of a new chain, Fresh, in Smithfield, Dublin 2006; other business interests include
the Mango franchise for Ireland; Choice Hotels; the winter Olympic village near Turin in Italy and the
Thomas Read chain of pubs in Dublin. Kelly, his father Paddy, and other members of the family are
also joint venture partners for the planned redevelopment of the Dublin retailer, Arnotts. Recreations:
triathlons.Contact: Redquartz Limited, 128, Lr. Baggot Street, Dublin 2. **T** 01 6391222
F 01 639 1444 email info@redquartz.com web www.redquartz.com

> Son of 'Posh' Paddy Kelly (*qv*) has brought a new energy to the family holding
> company; a chip off the old block.

KEIGHERY, Rody Joseph; AUCTIONEER AND VALUER
b 1963, Tramore, Co. Waterford; *m* Anne; *1s*; *edu.* De La Salle College Waterford; proprietor of
Keigherys Antiques & City Auction Rooms, Waterford; MD & owner with his wife Anne; joined the
family business; appointed MD 1980; now owner of the largest antique shop in the South East; owns
& runs the City Auction Rooms in Waterford. Recreations: Waterford Castle Golf Club. Contact:
27a, William Street, Waterford **T** 051 873692 **F** 051 873692 email rody@cityauctionrooms.com

> Took over the family antiques business and auction rooms started by his father in
> 1950; has vastly expanded it over the years, building large, modern auction rooms in
> the 1980s and presiding over the largest antique shop in the South East; travels
> extensively sourcing antiques and collectables.

KENNEDY, Brian Edward; SINGER, WRITER, TV PRESENTER
b 1966, Belfast; single; *edu.* St. Paul's Secondary School for Boys, Belfast;
singer. First solo album *The Great War of Words* 1990; performed with Van Morrison around the

world for six years; sang on five Morrison albums; sang for President Clinton five times; lead singer for 290 performances with Riverdance New York City; presented *On Song* BBC TV, 13 programmes; film soundtracks include *When A Man Loves A Woman*; *Publ.* nine albums; two novels; a section of his essay *Being Irish in 2002* appeared on the Leaving Cert syllabus. Awards: D.Litt (*hc*) Queens University, Belfast, 2006. Recreations: art, books, film, theatre, wine tasting, champagne glass holding. Contact: www.briankennedy.co.uk.

Has the voice of an angel; internationally acclaimed, but has yet to find his true performance metier; a nice man, open and charming; well liked; his genuine singing talent will bring him far.

KENNEDY, Caroline Anne Marie; PUBLIC RELATIONS CONSULTANT
b 1964; *m* Tom McGurk; *edu.* Brigidine Convent, Abbeyleix, Co Laois; Dublin City University: BA, Communications Studies, (Hons); placement, Graduate European Orientation Programme (C.I.I.); public relations consultant. Public relations manager, National Youth Council 1986-87; public relations manager, Co-Operation Ireland 1987-89; producer, Century Radio1989-91; owner/managing director, Kennedy PR 1991 to date. Recreations: travel, cinema, media. Contact: 2 Castle Street, Dublin 2. **T** 01 4762000 **F** 01 4762001 email ckennedy@kennedypr.ie

Caroline Kennedy

Extremely bright and savvy, the ideal person to head up a company that handles mainly luxury goods accounts; innovative with a great sense of style, extremely hardworking; great company, lights up a room with her infectious laugh.

KENNEDY, Danny; MEMBER, NORTHERN IRELAND ASSEMBLY
b 1959; *m* Karen McCrum; 2*s* 1*d*; *edu.* Newry High School; member Northern Ireland Assembly 1978-98; councillor Newry & Mourne District Council 1985 to date; chair 1994-95; member Newry & Mourne District Partnership Board, Peace & Reconciliation 1996 to date; member UUP 1974; MLA (UUP) Newry & Armagh 1998; member NI Tourist Board 1996-98; chairman Education Committee Newry & Mourne; director Bessbrook Development Co.; member of governing board Bessbrook Primary School. Recreations: family, church activities, sports (as a spectator), reading. Contact: Northern Ireland Assembly, Parliament Buildings, Stormont Estate, Belfast BT4 3XX **T** 028 9052 1336. **F** 028 9052 1757 email danny.kennedy@niassembly.gov.uk; advice centre, 107 Main St. Markethill, Co. Armagh, BT60 1PH **T** 028 3755 2831.**F** 028 3755 28

KENNEDY, Geraldine; EDITOR, IRISH TIMES
b 1951, Tramore, Co. Waterford; *m* David J. Hegarty; 2*d*; *edu.* S.H.M. Convent Ferrybank, Waterford; College of Commerce, Rathmines, Dublin (Journalism); Scandinavian International Management Institute 2000, Diploma in Leadership & Media Innovation; editor, *The Irish Times*. Political correspondent and public affairs correspondent *Sunday Tribune* 1980-82; political correspondent *Sunday Press* 1982-87; elected to Dáil Éireann (PD TD, Dún Laoghaire), party spokesperson Foreign Affairs and Northern Ireland 1987; with *Irish Independent* journalist Bruce Arnold successfully sued the State for invasion of privacy in the unlawful tapping of their telephones 1987; political editor, duty editor, political correspondent, political affairs correspondent for the Irish Times; editor *The Irish Times* 2002 to date; Publ. *The Irish Times/Nealon Parliamentary Guide* 2002. Recreations: cooking, family; Contact: The Irish Times, d'Olier St, Dublin 2 **T** 01 679 2022 **F** 01 671 9407 email gkennedy@irish-times.ie

Geraldine Kennedy

A tough and normally shrewd political personality; drawn to rows as a moth to light; not afraid, inclined to go where angels won't; regarded as a good friend and a worse enemy; made waves in the paper on being appointed editor; liked, loathed, feared admired, you pays your money and makes your choice.

KENNEDY, Henry Gerard, 'Harry'; CONSULTANT, FORENSIC PSYCHIATRIST
b 1957, Dublin; *m*; *edu.* Terenure College Dublin; University College Dublin; Mater Misericordiae Hospital Dublin BSc.; MB, BCh, BAO 1980; MD 1996 ; FRC Psych 2001; FRCIP 2003; clinical director National Forensic Mental Health Services, Central Mental Hospital Dundrum Dublin; clinical senior lecturer in forensic psychiatry Trinity College Dublin; medical SHO Royal Northern Hospital London 1981-82; medical SHO Brompton Hospital London 1982-83; medical registrar Hammersmith Hospital and Royal Postgraduate Medical School, London 1983-85; psychiatric registrar Maudsley Hospital London 1985-89; senior registrar and lecturer forensic psychiatry Maudsley and Broadmoor Hospitals 1989-92; consultant/clinical director forensic psychiatry North London Forensic Service 1992-2000; Chase Farm Hospital and Royal Free Hospital London; clinical

director Dundrum Central Mental Hospital Dublin 2000 to date; Publ. over 30 publications on aspects of forensic mental health. Recreations: music. Contact: Central Mental Hospital, Dundrum, Dublin 14 **T** 01 298 9266 **F** 01 298 9268 email harry.kennedy@mailD.hse.ie

Louise Kennedy

KENNEDY, Louise; DESIGNER

b 1960; single; *edu.* St. Annes, Mount Merrion Ave. Dublin; College of Marketing & Design Dublin; Grafton Academy of Design Dublin; fashion designer (under her own label) 1984 to date; designer of inauguration ensemble for Mary Robinson (first female President of Ireland) 1989; selected to join British Designer Group and exhibit at London Designer Show 1990; opened flagship retail outlets in Dublin and London; launched Crystal Collection in conjunction with Tipperary Crystal 1999; Awards: winner of numerous fashion awards; Tipperary Person of the Year 1992; first female designer to receive Outstanding Achievements in Fashion from Irish Clothing Industry 1994; Veuve Clicquot Irish Business Woman of the Year 2003; The Ireland Fund of Great Britain Bird and Bell Award 2004. Recreations: Contact: 56, Merrion Square, Dublin 2.

With a passion for fashion and heart for art no wonder her collections are eagerly awaited by some of the best dressed ladies in Ireland, the UK and US; elegant and quintessentially stylish in all her endeavours has been extremely successful with her range of crystal, particularly her chandeliers which now hang in some of the most hallowed halls and salons; poised, astute and great fun.

KENNELLY, Timothy Brendan; ACADEMIC AND POET

b 1936, Ballylongford, Co. Kerry; *div.*; 1*d*; *edu.* St. Ita's Secondary School, Tarbert, Co. Kerry; Trinity College Dublin; Leeds University England (BA.,MA.,PR.D., D.Litt., SFTCD); Professor of Modern Literature, TCD; writer, poet, academic; *Publ.* over 40 books including novels, plays, poetry, criticism. Recreations: reading, walking, visiting cities in different parts of the world, and writing "nearly every day"; Contact: Trinity College, Dublin 2 **T** 01 608 2301

A writer of extraordinary power and depth; has a considerable feel for the poetry of other cultures and languages; whilst not quite sepulchral in timbre, certainly not for a lighthearted read.

KENNY, Alan: DIRECTOR, NORTEL, IRELAND

b 1960; *m* Eleri; 4 children; *edu.* University College Galway; BA (Sociology, Economics); director Nortel Ireland; head of HR; joined Nortel, worked in a variety of financial roles 1983; moved to marketing and customer services late 1980's; transferred to human resources 1991; head of HR for Ireland 2001; director Nortel Ireland 2003 to date. Contact: Nortel Networks Galway, Mervue Business Park, Galway **T** 091 75 7671

KENNY, Conor; JOINT MANAGING DIRECTOR, CLANCOURT GROUP

b 1975, Dublin; *m* Martina; 2*s*; *edu.* Teresian School, Dublin; St. Michael's College, Dublin; University College Dublin; Trinity College Dublin; B.Comm; post graduate certificate Project Management; joint chief executive, Clancourt Group (large, privately owned commercial property development company involved in office retail investment and development, founded by his father Charlie). Clubs: Foxrock Golf Club, Westport Golf. Recreations: golf, rugby, tennis, squash. Contact: Clancourt Group Holdings, 5, Harcourt Road, Dublin 2 **T** 01 479 0030

The son of Charlie Kenny, founder of Clancourt, has been well trained to take over from his formidable father; bright, hardworking, low profile; brings a new energy to the Kenny empire.

Desmond Kenny

KENNY, Desmond Gerard; BOOKSELLER;

b 1950, Galway; *m* Anne Gilmartin; 1*s* 3*d*; *edu.* Coláiste Íognáid, Gaillimh; University College Galway; Sorbonne, Paris; BA (Hons), Maitries-et-Lettres; bookseller, Kenny's Bookshops and Art Galleries; instigator Kenny's Irish Book Parcel Service with customers in over 45 countries; second bookshop in the world to have website; editor *Galway Echo* 1982-2005; columnist *Galway Advertiser; Aer Arann Express IT Magazine*; past president Galway Lions Club; past captain and manager Our Lady's Boy's Club Annual Camp. Clubs; Galway Lions Club. Recreations; reading, sport, social work. Contact: Kennys Book Shop, High Street, Galway **T** 091 709 367 **F** 091 709351 email desi@kennys.ie

Internationally acclaimed bookseller synonymous with Galway and the West of Ireland with a global reach through long established mail order service and pioneering web site. One of the largest catalogues in the country specializing in antiquarian books

KENNY, Enda: PUBLIC REPRESENTATIVE

b 1951, Castlebar, Co. Mayo; *m* Fionnula O'Kelly; 1*s* 2*d*; *edu.* St. Gerald's College, Castlebar; St Patrick's Teacher Training College Drumcondra, Dublin; University College Galway; national school teacher; H. Dip Education; president and leader Fianna Gael; TD elected aged 24; leader of Fine Gael 2002; became a young Minister of State under Garret FitzGerald, when he was appointed Junior Minister at the Department of Education and Labour; in opposition, he has held a number of front bench portfolios including Education, Western Development, Youth Affairs and Sport; minister for Tourism and Trade 1994-97; served on many Oireachtas committees including Education and Science, Health and Children; chaired the Singapore rounds of the World Trade Organisation talks 1996; headed the EU Council of Trade Ministers during Ireland's Presidency of the Union; fluent Irish speaker; member of the Committee on the Irish Language. Recreations: Bruce Springsteen fan, hill walking (climbed Mount Kilimanjaro in aid of three Mayo charities in 2003), golf, cycling. Contact: Leinster House, Kildare Street, Dublin 2 **T** 01 618 3105 **F** 01 618 4502 email enda.kenny@finegael.ie web www.endakenny.finegael.ie

Enda Kenny

Son of a former Fine Gael TD and Parliamentary Secretary, Henry Kenny who was a famous Mayo footballer; Enda entered Dail Eireann in a by-election in 1975 following the death of his father; the youthful looking former teacher crossed Party lines when he married one of Charlie's Angels (CHJ's PAs) Fionnula Kelly, considered a huge political asset; sincere, intelligent, hardworking, a fluent Irish speaker, a great mimic with a true blue Fine Gael pedigree; a former minister for Tourism, always punching but yet to achieve a KO; he will need all the breaks if he is to become a future Taoiseach.

KENNY, Thomas 'Tom'; ART DEALER

b 1944, Galway; *m* Maureen Shiel; 1*s* 3*d*; *edu.* Colaiste Iognaid; University College Galway; BSc; chairman, Kenny's Bookshop and Art Galleries Ltd Galway; joined the family book store business; worked in retailing, cataloguing, exporting, publishing, antiquarian maps; concentrated on the visual arts, organising exhibitions, promoting and selling original work by Irish artists in Ireland and abroad since 1979; Publ. *Webb, a profile of the artist, Kenneth Webb*; *Faces In a Bookshop – Irish Literary Portraits*; weekly newspaper column on Galway history and folklore; member, Irish Executive, The Ireland Fund. Recreations: Galway, good pub talk, reading, theatre. Contact: Kennys Book Shops and Art Galleries Ltd., High Street, Galway. **T** 091 562 739 **F** 091 568 544.

A very knowledgable man who is internationally known and trusted; has established a highly respected and very interesting gallery where in addition to his stable of artists also regularly showcases new talent.

KENNY, Paul; PENSIONS OMBUDSMAN

b 1946, Dublin; *m* Ann Keating; 1*s* 2*d*; *edu.* O'Connell Schools, Dublin; Gormanston College, Co. Meath; University College Dublin; B.Comm; pensions Ombudsman. Irish Pensions Trust 1968-99; head of retirement research, Mercer 1999-2003; appointed Ombudsman 2003 to date. Recreations; gardening, wine, reading, travel. Contact: 36, Upper Mount Street, Dublin 2. **T** 01 647 1650 **F** 01 676 9577 email info@ pensionsombudsman.ie web www.pensionombudsman.ie

Brings a wealth of experience to the influential position of Ombudsman; popular and highly respected in the insurance industry; low profile unlike his older brother Pat (*qv* Kenny Pat) of *Late Late Show* fame; his office investigates and decides on complaints from individuals regarding their occupational pension or PRSAs.

KENNY, Pat; BROADCASTER/ TV SHOW HOST

b 1949, Dublin; *m* Kathy Walshe; 2*d*; *edu.* O'Connell School, Dublin; University College Dublin; Georgia Institute of Technology, U.S.; broadcaster/ TV host. Lecuter College of Technology, Bolton Street, Dublin 1970-72; joined RTE presenter/reporter 1972; presenter: *Public Account, Today*

Tonight; currently presenter *Today with Pat Kenny* (Radio 1), *The Late Late Show* (RTE 1). Clubs: Fitzwilliam LTC., Woodbrook Golf Club. Recreations: golf, walking, history. Contact: RTE, Donnybrook, Dublin 4. **T** 01 208 311 / 1850 715 900 **F** 01 208 2634 email todaypk@rte.ie web www.rte.ie/radio1/todaywithpatkenny/

The boy wonder who became the eminence grise of RTE radio and television; the chemical engineer feels totally at home in the world of technology and hard news rather than light entertainment; inherited the Maestro's mantle in winning RTE's flagship programme and has acquitted himself extremely well; continues to present a compelling, well balanced radio programme on weekdays where he retains a very loyal listenership.

Lainey Keogh

KEOGH, Lainey; INTERNATIONAL KNITWEAR DESIGNER
b 1957, Dublin; single; *edu.* Loreto Convent, Balbriggan, Dublin; Kevin Street College of Technology, Dip. Medical Sciences; worked in medical sciences; began to work with yarn 1983; started designing her own collections. Awards: recognised for work by International Wool 1987; Secretariat International Festival du Lin 1989; British Fashion Council 1994; Cable Ace Award Costume Design for the film *Two Nudes Bathing* (directed John Boorman) 1995; developed fabrics for Dior Culture Studio 1998; Prix de Coeur (France) 1998; People of the Year Award (Ireland) 1987; featured in just about every international glossy magazine, most recently *W* November 2005. Recreations: sky, walking, countryside, looking. Contact: 42 Dawson Street, Dublin 2. **T** 01 679 3299 **F** 01 679 4975

Darling of the international fashion/style meisters; a creative, award winning genius whose sensual, luxurious wool/cashmere collections are collectors' items already; her knitwear designs are stocked in the world's leading emporiums and much sought after.

KEOGH, Paul John; ARCHITECT
b 1953, Dublin; *m* Rachael Chidlow; 2*d*; *edu*. CBS Synge Street; School of Architecture University College Dublin; Royal College of Art, London; BARCH, MA RCA, FRIAI; James Stirling & Partners 1977-80; Office of Public Works 1980-84; De Blacham & Meagher 1977. Clubs: Architectural Association of Ireland, Westport Golf Club. Recreations: travel, cooking, swimming, photography and reading. Contact: 1, Johnson Place, Dublin 2 **T** 01 679 1551 **F** 01 679 3476 email PKA@INDIGO.IE

Modern and forward-looking in his work, his designs may yet reach to the sky; one of those rare enough architects who draws, and therefore finds the solution in the use of the Line.

KEOGH, Patrick James; CHIEF EXECUTIVE, BORD IASCAIGH MHARA
b 1950; *m* Siobhan Curtin; 3*s* 1*d*; *edu*. Knockbeg College, Carlow; University College Dublin, B Ag.Sc., MA (Econ.); research assistant ESRI 1973-75; economist, Pigs & Bacon Commission 1975-78; market research executive Board Iascaigh Mhara (BIM) 1979-86; division manager 1986-96; deputy chief executive 1989; chief executive 1997 to date; Publ. include reports on the agriculture and fisheries sector member, numerous professional bodies. Awards: Walne Memorial Medal from the Shellfish Association for Great Britain 1998. Recreations: cycling, walking, reading. Contact: BIM, PO Box 12 Crofton Road, Dun Laoghaire, Co. Dublin. **T** 01 284 1544 **F** 01 284 1134

KEOHANE, Tony; CHIEF EXECUTIVE OFFICER TESCO, IRELAND
b 1953, Cork; *m* Mary Conaty; 1*s* 2*d*; *edu* Coláiste Mhuire, Cork; Cork; joined Woolworths, trainee manager, (north of England and Scotland); joined Quinnsworth (store manager), 1978; appointed regional manager Quinnsworth, 1981 - 87; appointed Stores Director, Quinnsworth 1987; joined Quinnsworth Board,1995; joined the Board of Tesco, Operations Support Office Director, following the acquisition of Quinnsworth 1997 - 99; appointed Retail Director, Tesco U.K 1999 - 01 (Birmingham/Manchester area); appointed Director of Property, Supply Chain & Distribution for Tesco Ireland, 2001 - 06;. appointed CEO Tesco Ireland February, 2006 - todate; joint chairman, ECR Ireland, board member, Repak. Contact: PO Box 3, Gresham House, Marine Road, Dun Laoghaire, Co. Dublin. **T** 01 280 8441 **F** 01 280 0136 email tony.keohane@tesco.ie web www.tesco.ie

Hard nosed, skilled retailer with extensive experience in the UK and Ireland now heading up Ireland's largest food retailer; during the transitional period from Quinnsworth to Tesco was very much at the centre of management change, playing a leading role in the integration of Tesco into Ireland and the development of the Tesco Ireland business since then.

KERINS, Angela; CHIEF EXECUTIVE DESIGNATE (Jan 2007) REHAB GROUP; DIRECTOR OF PUBLIC AFFAIRS AND CARE SERVICES; REHABCARE CEO.
b Waterford; m Comdt. Seán Kerins; 1s 1d; edu. Presentation Convent, Cashel, Co.Tipperary; Basildon and Thurrock College of Nursing; Basildon and Thurrock College of Midwifery; state registered nurse (SRN); state certified midwife (SCM); numerous certificates and diplomas; LL.D.,(hc), National University of Ireland, (UCD) in recognition of her work in the disability sector; Chief Executive Rehab 2006 – todate; director of public affairs; group development Rehab Group; chairperson, Disability Legislation Consultation Group; chairperson National Disability Authority; member of Foreign Affairs/NGO Joint Committee on Human Rights; member, National Executive IBEC Board, member Broadcasting Commission of Ireland; chairperson National Co-Ordinating Committee European Year of People with Disabilities in Ireland; patron Special Olympics World Summer Games 2003; board member, Dental Hospital; Not For Profit Business Association; European Platform for Rehabilitation; Rehab Lotteries; The Chaseley Trust, Newgrove Housing Ltd., Rehab Care (UK Gandon Enterprises Ltd); Polio Fellowship of Ireland; The Rehab Council Ltd; National Learning Network Ltd; Momentum Scotland; member Advisory Committee ComReg; permanent representative to Economic & Social Council of the UN; served on other State Boards; FÁS International; National Council for the Elderly; National Council Rehabilitation Board and a number of review and other advisory bodies; Publ; contributed to many journals and publications in the sector. Clubs; RIAC, 02 Club. Recreations: public affairs, travel, cinema, leisure activities, sports, family. Contact: Rehab Group, Strand Road, Sandymount, Dublin 4 **T** 01 205 7200 **F** 01 2057381 email angela.kerins@rehab.ie

> The ambitious, politically astute Waterford-born nurse is a well-known net worker in national disability and political circles; through her chairmanship of the National Disability Authority she has raised public and political awareness of the ability of this sector in society; now as Chief Executive of Rehab. definitely one to watch.

KERR, Brian; FORMER IRISH TEAM FOOTBALL MANAGER
b 1953, Dublin; m Anne; 4d; edu. St. Michael's C.B.S. Inchicore, Dublin; James's St. C.B.S.; College of Technology, Kevin Street, Dublin; former football manager Ireland. Laboratory technician University College Dublin 1970-97; football manager Crumlin Utd. 1968-78; manager Shamrock Rovers Youths 1974-75; manager Shelbourne B 1978; manager St. Patrick's Athletic 1986-97; manager Ireland U16s, U18s, U20's 1997-2002; manager Republic of Ireland soccer team 2002-2005; Awards include Irish Soccer Writer's Personality of the Year 1996; Opel FAI Merit Award 1996; Philips Sports Manager of the Year 1997, 1998; People of the Year Award 1998; Texaco Soccer Award 1998/1999. Recreations: music, sport. Contact: Platinum One, The Court Yard, Carmen Hall Road, Sandyford Dublin 18 **T** 2062900 **F** 206 2999 email info@platinumone.ie

> Has an innate ability for spotting young talented players and bringing them on; was hailed as the best ever manager of the Irish team until they failed to qualify for the World Cup 2006, when the suits in Merrion Square blew the final whistle on this stage of his career; expected to make a come-back in club football; being mentioned as potential manager of South African national soccer squad.

KETT, Senator Tony; PUBLIC REPRESENTATIVE/ADMINISTRATOR
b 1951, Ballinasloe, Co. Galway; m Noreen Kilkenny;1s 2d; edu. St. Joseph's College, Garbally Park, Ballinasloe; College of Commerce, Rathmines, Dublin; Senator/ Administrator, Central Remedial Clinic, Dublin; member Joint Committees on Tourism, Sport and Recreation: on Justice, Equality and Womens' Rights; member Dublin City Council (co-opted to fill the vacancy following the retirement of Bertie Ahern) 1988 to date. Contact: 54 Whitethorn Road, Dublin 5 **T** 0905 78147

> An extremely well connected politician, said to be one of four people who can enter the Taoiseach's office unannounced; an extremely hard worker for his leader and Fianna Fáil.

Marian Keyes

KEYES, Marian; NOVELIST
b 1963, West of Ireland; *m* Tony Baines; *edu* University College Dublin; BCL; novelist.
Moved to London 1985; worked as a waitress; worked in accounts office London; signed
with Poolbeg Press 1993; *Watermelon* 1995; moved back to Dublin 1999; *Publ.* eight novels
to date; *Further Under The Duvet*, a compilation short stories and articles 2004; *Sushi for
Beginners; Angels; Rachel's Holiday; Lulu Sullivan is Getting Married; Last Chance Saloon; The
Other Side of the Story* 2005. Recreations: shoes, handbags, chocolate. Contact: Poolbeg
Press ltd, Marketing and Publicity, 123 Grange Hill, Baldoyle, Dublin 13 **T** 01 832 1477
F 01 832 1430 email poolbeg@poolbeg.com web www.poolbeg.com

Prolific, best selling author, her books are published in 35 countries worldwide and
have been translated into several different languages, including Hebrew and
Japanese.

KIBERD, Declan Liam; PROFESSOR
b 1951, Dublin; *m* Elizabeth Moriarty; 1*s* 2*d*; *edu.* St. Paul's College, Raheny, Dublin; Trinity
College Dublin; Oxford University; BA (mod); MA; D.Phil (Oxon); Professor of Anglo Irish
Literature University College Dublin. Lecturer in English, University of Kent at Canterbury
1976-77; lecturer in Irish, Trinity College Dublin 1977-79; lecturer/professor UCD 1979 to date;
visiting professor at Minnesota; Yale; California; Cambridge; Duke Wake Forest; Sao Paola;
Sorbonne; New South Wales; Awards, *Irish Times* Literature Prize 1997; Oscar Wilde Award 1997;
American Committee of Irish Studies Award 1997, 2002; Truman Capote Prize for Criticism 2002.
Recreations: cricket, history of rock, folk music, children's literature. Contact: 34 Haddon Road,
Dublin 3 **T** 01 833 8826 **F** 01 7161174

Fifth generation Dubliner, the award winning, internationally acclaimed academic is a
prolific media commentator; brother of Damien, founder/editor *Sunday Business Post*;
possesses a razor sharp wit and a keen intellect.

KIELTY, Patrick 'Paddy'; COMEDIAN, DIRECTOR, GREEN INC. PRODUCTIONS
b 1971, Belfast; single; *edu.* St. Patrick's Grammar, Downpatrick; Queen's University Belfast, B.A.
(Hons), Psychology; host, co-founder, Empire Comedy Club, Belfast 1992-96; BBC Comic Relief
1995; PK Tonight, BBC Belfast 1995-96; Last Chance Lottery, Channel Four 1997; BBC National
Lottery Big Ticket, BBC1 1998; co-founded Green Inc. Productions, one of the fastest growing
independent production companies in the British Isles 1996; Productions include: *Alan Tyler's Big
Night In* (Channel 4); *Stand Up For Sudan* (BBC); *Everything You Know is Wrong* (ITV); *Almost Live*
(BBC); also presented *Fame Academy; Comic Relief* 2003; *The Big Hair Do* 2003; *The British Comedy
Awards* 2003; *Tickled Pink* 2005; *Celebrity Love Island* 2005; *Celebrity Love Island* 2006. Recreations:
football, water-skiing. Contact: Green Inc. Productions, 47A Botanic Avenue, Belfast BT7 1Jl,
Northern Ireland. **T** 0044 1232 573000. **F** 0044 1232 579957.

Seems to have lost momentum as a serious comic recently, favouring presenting reality
TV series instead, where he comes across as rather bland; however great things still
expected of him on the box.

Benedict Keily

KIELY; Benedict Thomas; WRITER;
b 1919, Co Tyrone; *m* Frances Daly; 3*d* 1*s*; *edu.* Christian Brothers School, Omagh, Co Tyrone;
University College Dublin, (1st Class Honours English & History BA Hons); journalist *The
Catholic Standard*; leader writer *The Irish Independent*; literary editor *The Irish Press*; writer in
residence in four universities; ten novels including *The Cards of the Gambler, The Captain with the
Whiskers, Nothing Happens in Carmincross*; four short story collections including *A Journey to the
Seven Streams, A Ball of Malt, Madame Butterfly*; one work of non-fiction; two volumes of
memoirs. Recreations: literature, travel, trying to stay alive; Contact: 119, Morehampton Road,
Donnybrook Dublin. **T** 01 269 7823.

Almost the last in a long line of storyteller/bards; his storytelling skills built brick by
brick are the hallmark of this great Irish writer, who is adored by his fans and friends; a
writer with no enemies, this great author enjoys good company, good food and wine
and a good sing-song; a very nice man.

KIERANS, John William 'Jumbo'; EDITOR, IRISH DAILY MIRROR
b 1962; *m* Karen; 1*s* 1*d*; *edu*. St. Joseph's CBS, Drogheda, Co Louth; reporter *Drogheda Independent*;
Local News Drogheda; *Sunday World*; *The Star*, Dublin; *Daily Star*, London; news editor *Irish Mirror*;
deputy editor *Irish Mirror*; editor *Irish Mirror*. Clubs: Seapoint Golf Club, Termonfeckin, Co Louth.
Recreations: walking, golf, GAA, soccer, National Hunt Racing. Contact: Irish Mirror, Park House,
191-197 North Circular Road, Dublin 7 **T** 01 8688602 email News@mailMirror.ie

A fearless investigative journalist, now one of the top tabloid editors in the country.

KIERNAN, Buddy; FARMER, BUSINESSMAN
b 1931, Ballinamore, Co. Leitrim; *m* Teresa Sweeney; 4*s*; *edu*. National School, Ballinamore, Co. Laois;
Newbridge College, Co. Kildare; founder, Kiernan Group – pig farm units on 2,000 acres in Counties
Cavan, Longford, Westmeath, Sligo and Tipperary; owner of HKM Milling Limited, Granard, Co.
Longford; former chairman, Cavan County Council; former chairman, Fine Gael Trustees.
Recreations: politics, sport. Contact. Aughnakilmore, Kilnaleck, Co. Cavan **T** 049 36772.

One of the longest established pig producers in Ireland; grew his business empire
across the border and midland counties to remain the largest operator in the country;
now semi retired from the business, still dabbles in party politics having been a major
figure in the FG organization for over half a century in the Cavan Monaghan
constituency.

KILCULLEN, Justin Michael; DIRECTOR, TROCAIRE
b 1951, Dublin; *m* Róisín O Boyle; 2*s* 1*d*; *edu*. Oatlands College, Mount Merrion, Dublin; University
College Dublin; B. Arch (1975); director Trócaire; architect; worked on social housing programmes in
Tanzania, Cambodia, Belfast 1976-81; project officer Trócaire 1981-88; country representative
Trócaire, Laos 1988-92; director, Trócaire 1993 to date; vice-president CONCORD, the
Confederation of European Development Non-Governmental Organizations; consultor to the
Pontifical Council, Cor Unum; honorary member of the Royal Institute of Architects in Ireland;
Awards: Sir Robert Matthew Medal of the International Union of Architects 2002. Recreations:
architecture, photography, cinema, theatre, tennis, jogging. Contact: Trócaire, Maynooth, Co. Kildare
T 01 629 3333 **F** 01 629 0661

Having spent over 30 years with Trocaire, experienced his busiest and most demanding
year ever in 2005 raising funds for the Tsunami and Katrina disasters; the response of
the Irish public highlighted, once again, the remarkable gifting capacity of the Irish;
well known media commentator on Third World issues.

KILDUFF, Tony; CHAIRMAN, ELGIN CAPITAL LTD
b 1949, Belmont, Co. Offaly; *m* Rosalind; separated; 3*s*; *edu*. Christian Brothers Schools, Banagher;
University College Dublin; B. Comm; chairman of Elgin Capital Ltd; joined Coats Viyella PLC
(financial management) in the UK, Canada, Australia and Belgium 1971-79; established Kindle, a
company specialising in software for the overseas operations of international banks 1979; Kindle held
customer installations in 56 countries when it was sold in 1992; chairman Reflex plc; established
Elgin Capital, a company investing in property, technology and general business projects in Ireland,
the UK & Europe 1994 to date; investor in the e-learning, software, aviation and childcare industries
1994 to date; controls Cheval Properties, which manages the Belfry Funds, a British commercial
property portfolio which has been heavily backed by private clients of AIB. Cheval manages
properties in Britain worth more than stg£650 million (€940 million); chairman, Cappagh Hospital
Trust since its inception in 1988; director, Cappagh Hospital since its board of management was
established in 1996; chairman of the Program Board, the Royal Hibernian Academy of Arts 1999 to
date; vice-president IBEC 1994-98; former member, IBEC 1993-98; (former chair Human Resources
Policy Committee and the Economics and Taxation Policy Committee). Clubs: Kildare Hotel and
Country Club. Recreations: golf, skiing.

One Ireland's first IT pioneers who became a multi millionaire with the sale of Kindle
in the pre Celtic Tiger days; the sale enabled him to wisely invest in a prime residence
on Dublin's top residential road which had a 20-fold increase in value in 14 years;
pleasant, engaging personality, highly articulate, low profile, sartorially elegant.

KILKENNY, Osmond J 'Ossie'; ACCOUNTANT/ ENTREPRENEUR.
b 1948, Dundrum, Co. Dublin; *m* Anna; 1*s* 1*d*; *edu.* Gormanston College, Co. Meath; University College Dublin; B.Comm; accountant/entrepreneur; fellow of the Institute of Chartered Accountants; senior partner, OJ Kilkenny & Co, an accountancy firm with offices in Dublin and London; specialises in the entertainment industry; clients include Van Morrison (*qv*), Oasis, The Chemical Brothers, Bryan Adams and Bjork; founder shareholder and director of TV3; chairman of the technology company Nua Ltd; board member, The Mill (a London post-production unit); Instant Video Technologies, based in San Francisco; was also on the board of Special Olympics International; Dublin Rape Crisis Centre; chairman, Bord Scannan na Eireann, the Irish Film Board 1999-2005; chairperson, Irish Sports Council 2005 to date. Recreations: tennis, WWII sea planes. Contact: email admin@ojk.ie

Definitely not a classic 'suit'; came to national prominence through his involvement with U2 and Paul McGuinness (*qv*); charming and gregarious, despite his rock and roll involvement, this non drinking, non smoking vegetarian is a low profile, very successful entrepreneur/accountant who has built up a significant practice in Ireland and the UK; has been engaged in supporting many worthwhile Third World charitable organizations and is very supportive of young artists; known as a very loyal friend.

Tony Killeen

KILLEEN, John Anthony; PUBLIC REPRESENTATION
b 1952, Co Clare; *m* Elizabeth Lily O'Keeffe; 5*s*; *edu.* St. Flannans College, Ennis, Co Clare; Mary Immaculate College, Limerick; public representative; Minister of State at the Department of Enterprise, Trade and Employment with special responsibility for Labour Affairs; former teacher; first elected to Dail Eireann (FF TD, Clare) 1992; chairman of the Joint Oireachtas Committee on Education and Science 2002-04; member Committee on Procedure and Privileges; former chair of the Oireachtas Committee on Members' Interests in Dáil Éireann; member of the British-Irish Parliamentary Body; member of Clare County Council 1985-97 (chairman 1989-91, vice chairman 1987-89); chairman Co. Clare VEC (1991-94); former national chairman of Fianna Fail Councillor's Association; former member of management boards of Killaloe and Shannon Community Schools and Limerick R.T.C.; founder member Shannon Status Committee and chairman 1989-91. Recreations: all sports, Gaelic, rugby, football. Contact: Kilnaboy, Corofin, Co Clare/ 5 St. Anthony's Terrace, Ennis, Co Clare. **T** 065 681 5000 /065 684 1555 **F** 065 084 1514/065 684 1515 email tony.kileen@entemp.ie

Achieved national notoriety in 1993 when he resigned the Fianna Fail Whip over the controversial Shannon stop over; a former national school teacher he is an astute, articulate politician, which is a decided advantage in the marginal Clare constituency.

KILLIAN, Owen; CHIEF EXECUTIVE OFFICER, IRISH AGRICULTURAL WHOLESALE SOCIETY (IAWS) GROUP INTERNATIONAL
b 1951, South Roscommon; *m*; 2*s* 1*d*; *edu.* St. Aloysius College, Athlone, Co. Westmeath; University College Dublin; B.Ag.Sc.; chief executive officer, IAWS; joined IAWS 1977; held a number of key operational roles in the group prior; appointed chief operations officer 1997; appointed executive director 1999; assumed full responsibility for the IAWS food businesses 2001; appointed chief executive officer 2004. Recreations: GAA, rugby, horseracing. Contact: 151 Thomas Street, Dublin 8.

The diminutive Roscommon man boxes way above his weight in the competitive corporate world of the Celtic Tiger era; warm friendly personality, possesses a very sharp commercial intellect; however he will have his work cut out to maintain the momentum generated by his predecessor Phillip Lynch (*qv*).

KILROY, Claire; WRITER
b 1973, Dublin; single; Holy Faith Convent, Clontarf, Dublin; Trinity College Dublin; BA (English); M Phil Creative Writing; writer; Publ. *All Summer* 2003; *Tenderwire* 2006. Contact: C/o Faber & Faber, 3 Queen Square, London WC1N 3AU. **T** 0044 20 7465 0045 **F** 0044 20 7465 0034 email bomi.odufunade@faber.co.uk

Establishing herself on the best-seller list in both the UK and Ireland.

KING, Adele 'Twink'; ENTERTAINER
b 1951; *m* David Agnew (*qv* Agnew David); separated; 2*d*; *edu.* Loreto, Beaufort, Rathfarnham; St.

Louis Convent, Rathmines; St. Ann's School Milltown; Young Dublin Singers vocalist; founder Maxi, Dick n' Twink; lead female vocalist, Big 8 Showband (Las Vegas) 1970-75; radio and television performer/presenter (UK, Ireland and Turkey); star in annual Christmas pantomimes; written and co-produced, *Sleeping Beauty Sort of* (Point Theatre); *Robinson Crusoe* and *Robin Hood Prince of Thieves* (Olympia Theatre); drama: *Country in Our Hands* (Andrews Lane); *Not I* (Gate); *Sive*; special guest on the Perry Como Show (US); Awards: Jacobs and Montreux Awards for television; currently studying Turkish language and culture at Trinity College Dublin. Recreations: computers, sports, gym, tennis, squash, pets, needlework, scientific documentaries. Contact: Carol Hanna, 57 Meadow Bank, Bushy Park Road, Dublin 6. **T** 01 490 9339

> One of the stalwarts of popular Irish entertainement; larger than life personality, extremely talented, true professional, dedicated mother.

KINSELLA, Helena Gail; OWNER, JENNY VANDER;

b 19/1; *m* Aidan Kinsella; 1*s* 2*d*; *edu.* Cross and Passion College, Kilcullen, Co Kildare; Accountancy and Business College, Aungier Street; owner Jenny Vander 1993 to date; interior design; actively involved in local school and community. Clubs: Ladies Art Group. Contact: Ballymore Eustace, Co. Kildare **T** 045 864 264.

> A true pioneer of vintage fashion in Dublin, her exquisite stock is sought out internationally.

KITT, Michael Pascal, 'Micheál'; SENATOR

b 1950, Galway; *m* Catherine; 3*s* 1*d*; *edu.* St. Jarlaths College, Tuam, Co. Galway; University College Dublin; University College Galway; St. Patrick's College of Education, Drumcondra, Dublin; BA., H.Dip Ed; primary school teacher; Dáil Deputy 1975-77; member Galway County Council 1977-91; senator 1977-81; Dáil Deputy 1981-02; Minister of State 1991; senator 2002 to date. Clubs: Caltra GAA Mountbellew Golf Club, Mountbellew Agricultural Show Society, CB Trotters Soccer Club. Recreations: attending GAA matches. hurling, football, soccer, golf, reading, walking, swimming. Contact: Seanad Éireann, Dublin 2 **T** 01 618 3473 **F** 01 618 4555 www.michael.kitt@oireachtas.ie

Michael Kitt

> His election in 1975 to Dáil Éireann was a by election held as a result of the death of his father Michael, former Parliamentary Secretary; on the same day Máire Geogeghan Quinn was also elected following the death of her father, Johnny; had a turbulent political career but has emerged as a political marathon runner and has always held on to an Oireachtas position in the Upper or Lower Houses; friendly and popular public representative.

KITT, Proinsias Joseph; MANAGING PARTNER, KITT NOONE & CO

b 1959; *m* Anne McManus; 2*s* 1*d*; *edu.* St. Jarlath's College, Tuam, Co. Galway; National University of Ireland, Galway; B.Comm; fellow, Institute of Chartered Accountants; joined Coopers & Lybrand (Price Waterhouse Coopers) 1980-87; founded Kitt Noone & Co., Chartered Accountants with Terence Noon 1987; currently managing partner; committee member, General Practice Committee of Chartered Accountants; member (past president) Past Pupils Union of St. Jarlath's College; member Galway Football Supporters Club; member, numerous charitable organisations; Awards, Galway Person of the Year 1999. Recreations: GAA, golf, swimming, national politics. Contact: Kitt Noone & Co, Lock House, Dominick Street, Galway. **T** 091 586 146 **F** 091 586 161

> Member of the well known Galway political family; built up a very successful accountancy practice in his native city where he has strong public recognition; an integral part of the traditional culture of the City of the Tribes.

KITT, Tom; PUBLIC REPRESENTATIVE

b 1952; Galway; *m* Jacinta; 3*s* 1*d*; *edu.* St Jarlath's College, Tuam, Co. Galway; St Patrick's College, Drumcondra, Dublin; primary school teacher; public representative; Minister of State, Department Foreign Affairs; TD Dublin South Fianna Fáil; elected to Dublin County Council 1979; elected to Dail Eireann 1987; served government as Minister of State for European Affairs, Arts and Culture, Women's Affairs; Minister for Labour Affairs, Consumer Affairs, Minister for Trade; twice Minister for Overseas Development and Human Rights; Government Chief Whip; Minister of State at the Department of the Taoiseach and Defence. Recreations: GAA, soccer, rugby, athletics (ran ten marathons), jogging, golf, music, theatre. Contact: Pembroke House, 2 Glenville Terrace, Main Street,

Dundrum, Dublin 14. **T** 01 298 2304 **F** 01 298 2460 email tomkitt@tomkittd.ie

The very popular, friendly politician is one of the most acceptable faces of Fianna Fáil in the greater Dublin area; widely experienced, has earned respect with his performance in various junior ministries and should be a front runner for a full Cabinet position in any future Fianna Fáil led administration.

KNUTTLE, Graham; ARTIST

b 1954, Dublin; single; 1*d*; *edu.* Dun Laoghaire Art College, Co. Dublin; artist. Contact: Noel Kelly, CMS Marketing, Rivermount House, Unit 2B Calmount Business Park, Ballymount, Dublin 12. **T** 01 626 5346 **F** 01 4197068 email jan@cms marketing.com

His art has made him very rich indeed; his images are well known, a part of abstract and conceptual art; his figures appear in an urban landscape of which he is a part; paints from the gut; likes to paint the human predicament as he sees it; works and plays hard.

KÜRTEN, Jessica; INTERNATIONAL SHOW JUMPER

b 1969, Culybackey, Co. Antrim; *m* Eckard Kürten; *edu.* Culybackey National School, Co. Antrim; Ballymena High School, Co. Antrim; University of Limerick; B.Sc. Equine Studies; From an early age was trained as a showjumper by her parents, George and Rosemary Chesney; parents were also owners of her first international horse, Diamond Exchange. Recreations: movies, pop music, dining with husband and friends. Contact: Equestrian Federation of Ireland, Kildare Paddocks, Kill, Co. Kildare. **T** 045 886678 **F** 045 878430 email efi@horsesport.ie

The number two showjumper in the world, a two-time Olympian and a member of the 2001 European Championship gold medal-winning Irish team; in 1999 was the third Irishwoman to win the prestigious Queen Elizabeth Cup; as a member of the Irish team in the 2000 Dublin Horse Show, she helped them to an unprecedented eight Nations Cup wins for the 1999-2000 season; has wiped the eye of the selecting panels so often they still don't learn; her sterling qualities are recognized by the owners of the horses she rides to international glory; she's there for the long haul and was the only Irish rider to be invited to compete in the $1 million Las Vegas Invitational October 2005, where she won $66,000; currently ranked second in the world; still refuses to ride for Ireland as long as Cian O'Connor is on the team.

LALLY, Michael Joseph 'Mick'; ACTOR

b 1945; *m* Peige Ni Chonghaile; 2*s* 1*d*; *edu*. Trian Lar National School; St. Mary's College, Galway; University College Galway; BA, ATO, TTG; Actor; teacher of Irish, VEC 1969-75; actor with Taibhdhearc na Gaillimhe before becoming a founder member of Druid Theatre Company 1975; credits: *Who's Afraid of Virginia Woolf; The Glass Menagerie; Treats; Playboy of the Western World* (Ireland and US)*; Waiting for Godot; Wild Harvest;* moved to Dublin; has appeared in all major theatres; returned to Druid for it's 21st birthday 1996; appeared in *The Loves of Cass Maguire* and *A Skull in Connemara* (part of the *Leenane Trilogy*), (Druid Theatre, Olympia Theatre, Royal Court Theatre London, and a tour of Ireland); *The Dead School* with Macnas Galway; The DruidSynge Cycle (toured); TV credits: *Glenroe; Tales from the Poorhouse* (in English and Irish); film: *The Year of the French; Ballroom of Romance; Fools of Fortune; Circle of Friends; I Could Read the Sky; Alexander.* Awards: Jacobs Award 1979; Entertainment Personality of the Year 1984-85; Rehabilitation Institute, Mayo Person of the Year 1985; Dublin Mayo People Association 1989; Actor of the Festival, Dublin Theatre Festival; various awards from provincial newspapers; P.A.T.S. Award (Performing Artists Trust Society) 1991. Recreations: reading, listening to traditional music. Contact: Teri Hayden, The Agency, 47, Adelaide Road, Dublin 2. **T** 01 661 8535 email info@tagency.ie

One of the country's finest actors; perhaps forever remembered as Miley in Glenroe despite the fact he has many awards under his belt since then; a native Irish speaker, low profile, always turns in a top class performance.

Mick Lally

LANIGAN, Philip; SPORTS EDITOR, SUNDAY TRIBUNE

b 1974, Dublin; *m* Mary Mc Cabe; 2*s*; *edu*. Colaiste Phadraig, Lucan; Dublin City University, BA in Journalism; Sports Editor, *Sunday Tribune*; work placement at college with *The Sunday World* before gaining full time employment with the title sports newspaper; sports correspondent (mainly GAA) with the *Irish Sun*; joined the *Sunday Tribune* 2001. Clubs: Lucan Sarsfields GAA Club; member, Lucan Sarsfields hurling team. Recreations: reading. Contact: 115, Meadow Bank Hill, Ratoath, Co Meath. **T** 01 802 7611 email: planigan@tribune.ie

Has livened up the sports section of the *Tribune* and established it as one of the better Sunday reads.

LAPPIN, William 'Arthur' THEATRE AND FILM PRODUCER

b 1951, Co.Meath; *m* Kathryn Lennon; 4*s* 1*d*; *edu*. Clongowes Wood College; Royal College of Surgeons; Theatre and Film producer; Bank of Ireland 1970-78; drama and dance Officer, The Arts Council 1978-85; theatre and film producer 1985 to date; ran Groundwork Theatre production company with Ben Barnes 1986-94; currently managing director, Hells Kitchen, film production company; production credits include *My Left Foot* (line producer); *The Field* (line producer); *In the Name of the Father* (co-producer with Jim Sheridan (*qv*); *Some Mothers Son* (co-producer with Jim Sheridan); *The Boxer* (co-producer with Jim Sheridan); *Agnes Brown* (co-producer with Jim Sheridan); *Borstal Boy* (co-producer with Jim Sheridan) 2000; producer *On The Edge* 2001; executive producer *Bloody Sunday* 2001; executive producer *Laws of Attraction* 2002; co-producer (with Jim Sheridan*) In America* 2002; executive producer *Omagh* 2004; executive producer, *Get Rich Or Die Tryin'* 2005; former chairperson National Training Committee (now Screen Training Ireland); chairman, The Ark (children's cultural centre); member Minister Síle de Valera's think tank on the film industry. Clubs: Headfort Golf Club, Fitzwilliam LTC; Recreations: family, golf and tennis. Contact: Hells Kitchen, 21, Mespil Road, Dublin 4 **T** 01 667 5599

Low profile, internationally acclaimed film producer; prolific, hard working, has an impressive body of award winning work to his name.

Arthur Lappin

LAVAN, The Hon. Mr. Justice Vivan H; JUDGE OF THE HIGH COURT

b 1944, Dublin; *m* Una McCullough; 2*s* 2*d*; *edu*. Terenure College, Dublin; University College Dublin; Kings Inns; called to the Bar (Ireland) 1969; (England) 1975; co-founder of the Free Legal Advice Centres 1969; treasurer of the General Council of the Bar of Ireland 1976-80; member, Council of the Kings Inns 1976-80; director of the Legal Aid Board 1979; chairman of the Mining Board of Ireland 1982; honorary member of the American Bar Association 1983; associate of the Chartered Institute of Arbitrators 1981; Government appointee on the Panel of Conciliators and on the Panel of Arbitrators maintained by the International Centre for Investment Disputes, Washington, DC 1988; appointed a Judge of the High Court 1989. Clubs: Fitzwilliam LTC, National Yacht Club. Contact: The High Court, Dublin 1. **T** 01 637 7600 **F** 01 637 7601.

Appointed to the High Court in his early 40s by the C.J. Haughey led government; has been actively involved in Law Reform and his experience in arbitration is standing him in good stead on the Bench.

LAWLOR, Eamon; RADIO PRESENTER LYRIC FM

b 1951; *m* Maria Murray; 1*s*; *edu.* Rockwell College; University College Dublin BA, MA; joined RTE News 1974; European correspondent 1979-89; newscaster/ interviewer RTE News 1989-96; presenter/interviewer Prime Time, RTE TV 1996-99; presenter Lyric FM 1999 to date; visiting lecturer, International Academy of Broadcasting, Montreux. Recreations: music, reading, walking. Contact: RTE, Donnybrook, Dublin 4. **T** 01 208 3111.

Once the informed face of news and current affairs on national television; since he switched to radio has been responsible for the considerable success of Lyric FM which has built up a loyal following.

Le BROCQUY, Louis; ARTIST

b 1916, Dublin; *m* 1st Jean Stoney (*m dis.*); 1*d*; *m* 2nd Anne Madden (Simpson); 2*s*; *edu.* St Gerard's School, Bray; Painter; left family business 1938; self-taught artist, studied museum collections in London, Paris, Geneva, Madrid, Prado Collection; founder member, Irish Exhibition of Living Art 1943; visiting tutor, Central School of Arts and Royal College of Art, London 1947-58; Awards: LLD (hc) Trinity College Dublin 1962; Chevalier Legion d'Honneur 1975; LLD (hc) University College Dublin 1988; Saoi, Aosdána 1993; Officier des Arts et des Lettres 1998; Glen Dimplex Prize, Sustained Contribution to Arts 1998; LLD (hc) Dublin City University 1999; Chevalier, Royal Order of Belgium 2002; museum exhibitions include Venice Biennale (Premio Pre-alpino) 1956; Municipal Gallery Dublin 1966, 1978 & 1992; Ulster Museum 1967 and 1987; Fondation Maeght, St. Paul de Vence 1973; Musee d'Art Moderne, Paris 1976; New York State Museum 1980; Palais des Beaux Arts, Charleroi 1982; Festival Centre, Adelaide, National Gallery of Victoria & Museum of Contemporary Art, Brisbane 1988; Museé Picasso, Antibes 1989; Museum of Modern Art, Kamakura, Itami Museum of Modern Art, Osaka, City Museum of Contemporary Art, Hiroshima 1991; Irish Museum of Modern Art, Dublin 1996; Municipal Gallery of Art Ljubljana 1998; Presentation Portrait National Gallery of Ireland, Bono 2002; Honorary Member Royal Hibernian Academy of Arts Dublin. Contact: Taylor Galleries, 1 Kildare Street, Dublin 2. **T** 01 676 6055

A magisterial figure in the arts, charming and urbane; Ireland's millionaire painter, in his own lifetime; keeps his painterly capacity intact through hard work and determination; of great charm and keen intellect, he still remains a tranquil centre of cerebral force and vision in Irish and European Art.

LE BROCQUY, Melanie; SCULPTOR

b 1919; widow; 2*s* 2 *d*; *edu.* two years at the French Convent, Holyhead, Wales; Loretto Abbey, Rathfarnham, Dublin; New Hall, Chelmsford, Essex England; The National College of Art, Dublin; The École des Beaux Arts, Geneva; The Royal Hibernian Academy School, Dublin; Sculptor; exhibited at the Royal Hibernian Academy 1932-39, 1941, also 1974 and 1982 to 2005; Jaylor Scholarship 1938, 1939; California Gold Medal of the RDS 1939; solo exhibitions; retrospective, Taylor Galleries, Dublin 1986; Bell Gallery, Belfast 1989; Austin Desmond Art Gallery, London 1990; Taylor Galleries Dublin 1991; Bell Gallery, Belfast 1992; retrospective exhibition Royal Hibernian Academy 1999; Taylor Scholarship 1938, 1939; California Gold Medal of the RDS 1939; honorary member, Royal Hibernian Academy (HRHA) 1981 - todate; member, Aosdana 1981 to date; work has been purchased by the Arts Council, the Corporation of Dublin, Allied Irish Bank, Aer Rianta; represented at the Hugh Lane Municipal Gallery, the National Self Portrait Collection Limerick; the Technical College Wexford; Trinity College Dublin; Magdalen College Oxford, The Irish Embassy Washington; St. Patrick's Cathedral Dublin as well as many private collections in Ireland, America and Canada. Recreations: reading (novels, biographies, auto-biographies, poetry), theatre, cinema, visiting exhibitions of sculpture and painting at home and abroad, gardening; my friends – keeping in touch; above all my family. Contact: 29 Waltham Terrace Blackrock, Co. Dublin. **T** 01 288 9875

Melanie Le Brocquy

A sculptor of great charm and delicacy; her small bronze figures are huge in their implications; a quiet but forceful personality.

LEE, George Damien; ECONOMICS EDITOR RTE

b 1962, Dublin; *m* Mary Kitson; 1*s* 1*d*; *edu.* Coláiste Enna, Ballyroan; University College Dublin, BA Econ; London School of Economics, MSc.; Economics Editor RTE; lecturer in economics, University College Galway 1986-'87; economist, Central Bank 1987-'89; treasury economist ESB 1989-'90; economics correspondent, *Sunday Business Post* 1990-91; senior economist, RIADA Stockbrokers 1991-'92; current affairs economist, RTE 1992-'95; economics correspondent 1995-'97; economics editor 1997 to date; Published, *Breaking the Bank* an account of the exposure of the NIB banking scandal; member, NUJ; academic awards include scholarship in economics, UCD 1983 and 1984; post graduate scholarship in economics, ANCO 1985; Roseberry Studentship from London School of Economics 1985-'86; Awards: Barrington Medal for Economics, Statistical and Social Inquiry Survey of Ireland 1999; Journalist of the Year 1998. Contact: RTE, Donnybrook, Dublin 4. **T** 01 208 3111

> Held in respect and ridicule by different factions of the Captains of Industry; some claim he is a genius economist while others say he is a naysaying scaremonger who never 'got' the whole Celtic Tiger phenomenon; rumours were that his talents were being sought for a long time and that he would head to the commercial world but now looks as if he will see it to retirement in RTE.

LEE, Most Rev. William Francis; BISHOP OF DIOCESE OF WATERFORD & LISMORE

b 1941; single; *edu.* Rockwell College, Cashel, Co. Tipperary; St Patrick's College Maynooth; Gregorian University Rome; BA BD, L.Ph, DCL; ordained priest 19th June 1966; bursar 1971-87; president 1987-93; St. Patrick's College, Thurles; Bishop of Waterford & Lismore 1993 to date; secretary Irish Episcopal Conference 1998 to present; Contact: Bishop's House, John's Hill, Waterford; **T** 051 874463 **F** 051 852 703 email waterfordlismore@eircom.net

> A low key church figure who has seen his rural diocese from the sea to the Commeraghs expand into the modern Ireland, packed, full of non believers and a modern consumer society.

LENIHAN, Brian; PUBLIC REPRESENTATIVE

b 1959, Dublin; *m* Patricia Ryan; 1*s* 1*d*; *edu.* Belvedere College, S.J, Dublin; Trinity College Dublin; Cambridge University; Kings Inns; B.A. (Mod) Legal Science, H.B, Barrister at Law; Public Representative; Minister of State at the Department of Health and Children; appointed Minister of State with responsibility for Children at the Departments of Health and Children; Justice, Equality and Law Reform; Education and Science (special responsibility for children) in June 2002 to date; lecturer in law Trinity College Dublin; 1982-'96; Barrister at Law 1984 to date; Senior Counsel 1997 to date. Contact: Department of Health and Children, Hawkins House, Hawkins Street, Dublin 2 **T** 01 671 8142 **F** 01 671 8985 email Brian.Lenihan@oireachtas.ie

Brian Lenihan

> A quietly spoken man, extremely astute, razor sharp intellect; has a great capacity for hard work; with his brother Conor (*qv*), carrying on the Lenihan tradition in Dáil Éireann; kindly, like his late father, he eschews personal publicity – just gets on with it; deemed by the cognoscenti a talent much too great to be wasted in a half car.

LENIHAN, Conor Patrick; PUBLIC REPRESENTATIVE

b 1963, Dublin; *m* Denise; 2*s* 1*d*; *edu.* Belvedere College S.J.; University College Dublin; Dublin City University; INSEAD, France; B.A. (Hons) Economics, History, Politics; postgraduate diploma in journalism; Young Managers Programme (INSEAD); Public Representative, Minister of State, Dept Foreign Affairs with responsibility for Overseas Development and Human Rights; *Publ. Triumph of Peace*, pub by the University of Limerick's Economic & Social Review 1998; regular opinion pieces in magazines, newspapers, etc; journalist; press officer; broadcaster; radio manager; senior executive ESAT Digifone; elected TD Dublin South West 1997; re-elected 2002; Minister of State, Dept Foreign Affairs with responsibility for Overseas Development and Human Rights 2002 to date. Clubs: Tallaght Athlethic Club, Templeogue Tennis Club. Recreations: swimming, gardening, reading. Contact: Department of Foreign Affairs, Iveagh House, Dublin 2. **T** 01 408 2031 **F** 01 408 2025 email conor.lenihan@dfa.ie

Conor Lenihan

> This third generation member of the Lenihan family to enter public service, is known for gaffes; seems to shoot from the lip too often; charming and personable, has his father's ebullience; a hard worker, popular in his constituency.

LENNON, Charlie; MANAGEMENT CONSULTANT AND MUSICAL DIRECTOR
b 1938; *m* Sile; 2*s* 1*d*; *edu*; Liverpool University; B.Sc (Physics, Maths), B.Sc (Hons Physics) PhD Nuclear Physics; Musical Director; corporate planning Aer Lingus 1969-74; director management consultancy SKL /KPMG 1974- '84; partner CHL Consulting 1984-92; partner CHL Software 1984-92; managing director CHL Software 1986-98; operational research, North Holland 1975 & 1978; *Island Wedding,* orchestral work, RTE CD 145; *Musical Memoirs,* book of compositions World Music Publications; his dance musical *Waves* was screened by PBS (US) in 2005 and attracted an audience of 50 million viewers. Clubs: Comhaltas Ceoltaire Eireann. Recreations: music composition, performance. Contact: Ard Mhuire, Baily, Howth, Dublin. email Charlie@musican.com

Lauded and respected internationally for his inspired orchestral work.

LEONARD, Hugh; (John Keyes Byrne); PLAYWRIGHT
b 1926, Dublin; *m* Paula Jacquet; (*decd.*); 1*d*; *edu.* Presentation College, Dun Laoghaire; Playwright; worked in the offices of the Land Commission 1945-54; *Publ. The Big Birthday Suit* (Dublin, The Abbey Theatre) 1956; *A Leap in the Dark* (The Abbey Theatre) 1957; *Stephen D* (Adaptation of *Portrait of the Artist as a Young Man* and *Stephen Hero,* by James Joyce, Dublin Theatre Festival) 1962; published as *Stephen D* (London and New York, Evans) 1964; *The Poker Session* (London, Evans) 1964; *Mick and Mick* (London, Samuel French) 1966; *The Late Arrival of Incoming Aircraft* (London, Evans/French) 1968; *The Patrick Pearse Motel* (London, Samuel French) 1971; *The Au Pair Man* (New York, Samuel French) 1974; *Da* (Newark, Delaware, *Proscenium*) 1975; revised edition New York, Atheneum/London, Samuel French) 1974; *Time Was* (Samuel French) 1980; *A Life* (Samuel French, 1980/Atheneum, 1981); *Suburb of Babylon* three one act plays - *A Time of Wolves and Tigers, Nothing Personal,* and *The Last of the Mohicans* (Samuel French) 1983; *Pizazz: A View from the Obelisk, Roman Fever, Pizazz* three one act plays (Samuel French) 1986; *Selected Plays of Hugh Leonard* (ed. S.F. Gallagher. Gerards Cross, Buckinghamshire, Gerard Smythe) 1992; and *Moving* (Samuel French) 1994. His essays include Leonard's *Last Book* (Enniskerry, Co Wicklow, Egotist) 1978; and *A Peculiar People and Other Foibles* (Tansy Books) 1979. His autobiography is in two volumes, *Home Before Night* (London, Andre Deutsch) 1979; and *Out After Dark* (Andre Deutsch) 1989, both re-issued by Methuen (London) 2002; and he has published one novel, *Parnell and the Englishwoman* (London, Andre Deutsch, 1992); Awards: conferred with Honorary Doctorate of Humane Letters, Rhode Island College; Honorary Doctorate of Literature, TCD. Recreations: vintage films, France (canals and by-roads). Contact: Sunday Independent, 27-30 Talbot Street, Dublin 1 **T** 01 705 5333

His newspaper columns and impressive literary output hint that Hugh Leonard, real and imaginary, is an avuncular raconteur.

Sammy Leslie

LESLIE, Samantha 'Sammy' J; HOTELIER/ ESTATE OWNER
b 1966; divorced; *edu.* St. Columba's College, Rathfarnham, Dublin; L'Ecole Les Roches, Switzerland; Dip Hotel Management, Int. Instructor BHS; returned to Ireland and began work on Castle Leslie Estate, Glaslough, Co Monaghan. Recreations: horses, travel, fundraising, wine and food, restoration of historical buildings. Contact: Castle Leslie Estate, Glaslough, Co Monaghan. **T** 047 88100 email info@castleleslie.com web www.castlelesie.com

Her lineage goes back to Atilla The Hun; has worked so hard to refurbish Castle Leslie, turning it into a world class estate with an excellent equestrian center; also opened a top class cookery school; founded Castle Leslie Fine Foods now distributed to leading purveyors of gourmet food in Ireland, UK and US; hit the international headlines when Paul McCartney chose it as the venue for his marriage to Heather Mills, 2002.

LEVIS, Brian Robert; SCHOOL PRINCIPAL
b 1948; *m* Lynda; 2*d*; *edu.* Midleton College, Midleton, Co Cork; Trinity College Dublin; MA, H Dip Ed; Principal of St Patrick's Cathedral Grammar School; mathematics teacher, Newpark Comprehensive School, Blackrock, Co Dublin; principal, St Patrick's Cathedral Grammar School 1992 to date. Clubs: Carrickmines Golf Club (captain 2005); Three Rock Rovers Hockey Club. Recreations: golf, sport, reading, travel, music, DIY. Contact: 8 Aranleigh Vale, Rathfarnham, Dublin 14. **T** 01 493 5490 **F** 01 454 9632 email levispatricksgrammar@eircom.net

A skilled school principal who has to deal with making an old and venerable institution relevant to modern teaching methods.

LEWIS, Richard Patrick; FASHION DESIGNER
b 1945, Dublin; *p* Jim Greeley; *edu.* CBS Drimnagh Castle; Grafton Academy; Dip Dress Design; Fashion Designer; began couture fashion on South Frederick Street 1977 to date; received Satzenbrau fashion Oscar 1988 for best collection and 1991 for outstanding contribution to the Irish fashion industry. Recreations: travel, history, decorating, art; Contact: 22. South Frederick Street, Dublin 2. **T** 01 679 7016 **F** 01 635 9834 email richardlewis@eircom.net

His trade mark is timeless elegance; extremely sympathetic to the female form so little wonder at a time when anything goes in fashion he continues to attract new clients in addition to his army of existing loyal ones.

Richard Lewis

LEYDEN, Terry Francis; PUBLIC REPRESENTATIVE
b 1943, Roscommon; *m* Mary; 1*s* 3*d*; *edu.* Convent of Mercy National School, Roscommon; CBS Roscommon; Vocational School, Roscommon Town; N.U.I. Galway, Diploma in Politics, Sociology and Economics, Senator, elected to Roscommon County Council 1974; elected to Dáil Éireann (Roscommon/South Leitrim) 1977-'81; Roscommon/East Galway 1981-'82; Minister of State Dept. of Post, Telegraphs & Transport 1982; Front Bench spokesperson Post & Telegraphs 1983-'87; Minister of State, Dept of Health 1987-'89; Minister for Trade and Marketing 1989-'92; member, Council of Europe, Strasburg 1992; member of Seanad Éireann 1992-'93; member of Western Heath Board 1992-2002; (chairman in 2001); elected to Seanad Eireann 2002; election monitor in Bosnia 1998; subsequently set up Kosovo Refugee Aid 1999; Convener of the Friends of Palestine Group in the Oireachtas. Clubs: Fuerty & Roscommon. Recreations: current affairs, reading, travel, walking, farming and socialising with friends and family. Contact: Castlecoote, Roscommon. **T** 090 662 6422 **F** 090 662 5422 email tleyden@oireachtas.ie

The personable Senator has survived the crucible of political infighting in his Roscommon constituency; over time he had to fight off his own party candidate, the late Sean Doherty and the 'hospital candidate', Independent TD, the late Tom Fox to maintain a national profile as TD, junior minister or senator; the Leyden dynasty will continue with his daughter, a member of Roscommon Co. Council.

LILLINGSTON, Alan; BLOODSTOCK BREEDER;
b 1935; *m* Lady Vivienne Nevill; 2*s* 2*d*; *edu.* Eton College, Windsor; Trinity College Cambridge; MA; Bloodstock Breeder; runs successful stud in Co. Limerick; principal winners include One in a Million, Ragtime, Balymacad, Piney Ridge, Deep Run, Gay Lemur, Tamarisk, Dr. Massini, Family Crest; Sound Print and Brave Music both won the Hong Kong Derby; member, Turf Club, INHS Committee, Bord Na gCoppal – Irish Horse Board; awarded Team Gold Medal, European Championships, Three Day Event, Germany 1979; rode winner of Champion Hurdle, Cheltenham 1963; steward, Turf Club 1989-'90; senior steward, INHS Committee 1994-'95; Irish Horse Authority 1994-'95. Recreations: golf. Contact: Mount Coote Stud, Co. Limerick. **T** 063 98111 **F** 063 98057

Able and astute breeder and winner who is not hampered by his undoubted charm, skill and social connections; a half brother to the Earl of Harrington and son in law to the Marquess of Abergavenny, he is among the most successful breeders in the country.

LINEHAN, Conor; PIANIST- COMPOSER
b 1971, Dublin; single; *edu.* Gormanston College, Co. Meath; Trinity College Dublin; BA (mod) Music, English; studied with Peter Feuchtwanger; Pianist, Composer; finalist Guardian Piano Competition 1997; tutors in the Royal Irish Academy of Music Dublin; composed the score for *The Colleen Bawn*, Abbey Theatre Dublin; regular soloist and interpreter with LyricFM. Contact: The Royal Irish Academy of Music, Westland Row, Dublin 2. **T** 01 676 4412

A musician of great skill and power who's day is yet to come; the concert circuit is a mean street, but he retains his skill and good humour and plays every note as it comes; a man for the future.

LINEHAN, Rosaleen; ACTOR
b 1937, Dublin; *m* Fergus Linehan; 3*s* 1*d*; *edu.* Loreto College, St. Stephen's Green; University College Dublin, B.Econ; Actor; worked in review with Des Keogh for a number of years; performance credits include *A Long Days Journey into Night*; *Bailegaugaire* (Royal Court, London); *The Cripple of Innismaan*

(Geffon Play-House, L.A.); *Dancing at Lughnasa* (Dublin, London, Broadway) and the *Beckett Festival in the Barbican* 1999; *The Plough and The Stars* with Donal Mc Cann (Gaiety Dublin); *Tartuffe* (Broadway) 2003; *Des and Roise on The Luas* (Gaiety Dublin) 2005; films include *The Butcher Boy; Hilo Country; Matchmaker; All About Adam; Ulysses;* has written the scores for 12 reviews and two musicals; member, Actors Equity Ireland and USA, Screen Actors Guild, USA. Contact: Aude Powell, Suite 8A, 169 Queensgate, London, SW7 5HE. **T** 0044 171 581 3388.

> Ireland's favourite comedienne also has an impressive body of serious work on radio, TV, stage and screen to her credit; forever linked to Des Keogh, her comedy partner; they can always be guaranteed to fill the house.

LISTON, Jerry; CHAIRMAN IRISH AVIATION AUTHORITY

b 1940, Dublin*; m* Noreen Wall; 3*d; edu.* Gonzaga College, Dublin; University College Dublin; BA, MBA; Kings Inns, Barrister at Law; Chairman, Irish Aviation Authority; group product manager, P.J. Carroll & Co 1962-68; marketing manager, W.R. Grace 1968-70; general manager Ireland, Warner Lambert 1970- 74; chief executive, United Drug plc. 1974-2000; executive chairman Smurfit School of Business, University College Dublin, 2000 - 05; Chairman, Irish Aviation Authority 2006 – todate; Publ. MBA Thesis, *Determination of Advertising Budgets*; member, I.M.I. (past president and past chairman); marketing society (past chairman); fellow of Marketing Institute; life fellow, Irish Management Institute. Clubs: Milltown Golf Club, Fitzwilliam LTC, Royal St. George Yacht Club, Connemara Golf Club. Recreations: reading, golf, family. Contact: Irish Aviation Authority, Aviation House, Hawkins Street, Dublin 2. **T** 01 6718 655 **F** 01 679 2934 email info@iaa.ie web www.iaa.ie

> From a well known Dublin legal family, Liston has been prominent in Irish business circles for over a quarter of a century; has had a lifetime interest in the IMI and in more recent years The Smurfit Business School at UCD; extremely ambitious, his career reflects the achievement of that ambition.

LLOYD WEBER, Lord Andrew; COMPOSER/ PRODUCER

b 1948, London, UK; *m* 1st Sarah Hugill; (*m diss*); 1*s* 1*d; m* 2nd Sarah Brightman; (*m diss*); *m* 3rd Madeline Gurdon; 2*s* 1*d; edu.* Wetherby School, London; Westminster School, London (Queen's Scholar); Magdalen College, Oxford; (did not graduate); Composer/Producer; collaborated with Tim Rice on *Joseph and his Amazing Technicolour Dreamcoat* 1968; *Jesus Christ Superstar* 1970; *Evita* 1976; set up *The Really Useful Group* 1977; involved in theatre, film, television, video and concert productions, merchandising, magazine publishing, records and music publishing; solo career: *Cats* 1981; *Starlight Express* 1984; *Phantom of the Opera* 1986; *The Likes of Us; Aspects of Love; Sunset Boulevard* 1992; *Whistle Down the Wind* 1996; *Tell Me On A Sunday* 1979, reworked *Song and Dance* 1985; readapted *Tell Me On A Sunday* 2003; *The Beautiful Game* 2000; *The Woman in White* 2004; Films include *Jesus Christ Superstar* 1973; *Evita* 1996; *Phantom of the Opera* 2004. He composed the film scores of *Gumshoe* and *The Odessa File,* and a setting of the *Latin Requiem Mass Requiem* for which he won a Grammy for Best Contemporary Composition; he has also produced in the West End and on Broadway not only his own work but the Olivier award-winning plays *La Bête* and *Daisy Pulls It Off;* in summer 2002 in London he presented the groundbreaking A R Rahman musical *Bombay Dreams;* the first person to have three musicals running on both Broadway and The West End simultaneously.

> Awards include seven *Tonys*, three *Grammys,* six *Oliviers,* a *Golden Globe,* an *Oscar, an International Emmy, the Praemium Imperiale* and *the Richard Rodgers Award for Excellence in Musical Theatre;* knighted 1992; created honorary life peer 1997. Recreations: racing, equestrian sports. Contact: The Really Useful Group, 22, Tower Street, London 9TW WC2H. **T** 0044 0207 240 0880 **F** 0044 0207 204 1240 email querymaster@reallyuseful.co.uk www.reallyuseful.com

> Now domiciled in Co. Tipperary where he continues to compose and his wife breeds thoroughbred bloodstock; a musical genius in both classical and popular genres, is recognized as one of the all time great composers of popular musicals; has broken box office records all over the world with his major productions; when his name is on a theatre marquee the tills are alive to the sound of money in the bank.

LOGAN, Emily; OMBUDSMAN FOR CHILDREN

b 1963, Dublin; *edu.* Manor House School, Raheny, Dublin; UCL London, M Sc. Pyschology; RSCN (Paediatric Nurse); RGN (General Nurse); University College Dublin MBA; Dip. Medical Paediatric Nursing; Ombudsman for Children; 11 Years in the UK; director of nursing Our Lady's National Children's Hospital, Crumlin Hospital for four years; director of nursing

Emily Logan

Tallaght Hospital for two years. Clubs: Westwood Gym. Recreations: skiing, walking, music; Contact: Office of the Ombudsman for Children, Millennium House, 52-56 Great Strand Street, Dublin 1. **T** 01 865 6800 email oco@oco.ie

> Her extensive experience in child care in Ireland and the UK equips her well for a most demanding role as Ireland's first Children's Ombudsman; well rounded in all areas of childcare, is extremely highly respected by her peers.

LOGAN, Malachy; JOURNALIST
b 1956, Dublin; *m* Mary; 2*s* 1*d*; *edu*. Marian College, Ballsbridge; sports editor, *Irish Times*; sub-editor *Irish Times*; deputy chief sub-editor *Irish Times*; sports editor *Irish Times* to date. Clubs: Kilmacud Crokes GAA, Enniscorthy Golf Club. Recreations: GAA, golf. Contact: The Irish Times, d'Olier Street, Dublin 2 **T** 01 679 2022 email mlogan@irish-times.ie

> Produces some of the best sports pages in the country employing talented writers who make the section compulsive reading.

LOGUE, Brendan Francis; REGISTRAR, CREDIT UNIONS
b 1944, Dublin: *m* Mary; 3*s*; *edu*. Oatlands College, Mount Merrion, Co. Dublin; College of Commerce (DIT); Chartered Institute of Management Accountants 1968-81; Registrar Credit Unions; financial controller, Wavin Ireland Ltd 1981-'84; secretary/financial controller Smith Groups 1984-'89; reconstruction consultant, FOIR Teo 1989-'03; manager financial services, IDA Ireland; registrar of Credit Unions, IFSRA 2003 to date. Recreations: family, environmental issues, ham radio, DIY, Irish economics. Contacts: Whitecross, Julianstown, Co. Meath. **T** 01 4104 980 **F** 01 410 4990 email Brendan.logue@IFRSA.ie

Brendan Logue

LOONEY, Fiona; JOURNALIST/SCRIPTWRITER
b 1966, Dublin; *m* Stephen Lindsey; 1*s* 2*d*; edu. St Paul's Secondary School, Greenhills, Dublin; College of Commerce, Rathmines; Journalist/ Script Writer/Playwright; Feature writer, *Hot Press* 1985-88; *Evening Herald* 1988-89; editor *In Dublin* 1989-90; freelance features, *Irish Independent*, *Sunday Tribune* 1990-2001; presenter BBC Greater London Radio 1995-2000; *Sunday Tribune* staff 2001 - '06; *Gerry Ryan Show* 1990-2005; scriptwriter on *Monica Moody Show,* Radio 1; *Amelia Golightly* 2FM; *Golf Widows* Radio 1; *Dustin's Fowl Play* Warner Home Video; stage, *Dandelions,* Landmark Productions 2005; book, *Misadventures of Motherhood* 2005. Clubs: St Jude's GAA Club. Recreations: sports, music, running, sunbathing, cooking. Contact: Irish Mail On Sunday, 3rd Floor, Embassy House, Ballsbridge, Dublin 4. **T** 01 637 5600 **F** 01 637 5940 email fiona.looney@ireland.com

Fiona Looney

> Talented and extremely popular journalist / scriptwriter who writes some hilarious columns and sketches; her first full length production Dandelions sold out for an extended run in Dublin; equally funny on radio where she is a frequent commentator on the challenges of contemporary life.

LOUGHREY; Dan; HEAD OF GROUP CORPORATE COMMUNICATIONS, BANK OF IRELAND
b 1954; *m* Josephine; 1*s* 1*d*; *edu*. St. Jarlath's College, Tuam, Co. Galway; University College Dublin; Bachelor of Arts; Revenue Commissioners 1972-92; Aer Lingus Corporate Affairs director 1992-2003; Bank of Ireland 2004 to date. Recreations: travel, reading, theatre. Contact: Bank of Ireland, Head Office, Baggot Street, Dublin 2. **T** 01 604 3833 email dan.loughrey@boimail.com

> A consummate professional who proved his mettle with the Revenue Commissioners and Aer Lingus before joining Bank of Ireland; focused and accessible, always the best possible for his employers.

LUKE, Eric; PHOTOGRAPHER
b 1954, Dublin; *m* Yvonne Lynch; 1*s* 2*d*; *edu*. Presentation College, Glasthule, Co Dublin; Photographer; spent 17 years as staff photographer with the Irish Press Group; staff photographer with *The Irish Times* to date; Awards: Winner of World Press Photo Award in news section 1997. Recreations: fly fishing, hill walking. Contact: Irish Times, D'Olier Street, Dublin 2. **T** 01 679 2022 email ericluke@eircom.net

> Award winning photographer whose beautifully constructed images are a major selling point for the Irish Times.

Gerry Lundberg

LUNDBERG, Gerald 'Gerry'; PUBLICIST
b 1945, Dublin; single; *edu.* O'Connell Christian Brothers School, Dublin; publicist. Advertising clerk, *The Irish Times* 1963-64; worked at various jobs before becoming assistant to Brendan Smith, Dublin Theatre Festival 1974-84 and again 2000-06; has worked with most Dublin Theatres, including The Abbey Theatre, Riverdance, *I, Keano*, Dublin Fringe Festival; films include; *My Left Foot; The Field; In the Name of the Father; Michael Collins; The Boxer; Dancing at Lughnasa; Evelyn; Laws of Attraction; Reign of Fire; Tara Road; In America;* also restaurants, galleries (ROSC), various artists, most theatre organisations; member, National Union of Journalists; Public Relations Institute; Irish Actors Equity. Recreations: work, travel, swimming, backgammon. Contact: Gerry Lundberg Public Relations, 27 Dawson Street, Dublin 2. **T** 01 679 8476 email glundpr@iol.ie

Ireland's top theatre and movie publicist is not only a legend in his own lifetime, he is a walking encyclopaedia on anything to do with movies and the theatre; bright, articulate and particularly media friendly, lacks the hauteur so often associated with luvvies in this industry.

LYNCH, Frank; NAVAL OFFICER
b 1949, Galway; *m* Janette; 1*s* 1*d*; *edu.* Coláiste Chríost Rí, Cork; Naval College Cork; Britannia Royal Naval College UK (BRNC); Commander Naval Services; Defence Forces Military College (Curragh, Co Kildare); Dublin City University; Naval Watchkeeping Certificate; Command and Staff Course; B.Sc Information Technology (Computing); MSc Management of Operations; Flag Officer Commodore Naval Service; joined Naval Service October 1968; BRNC April 1969-April 1970, September 1971-May 1972; commissioned November 1970; Lt Commander November 1978; 1st Command LE FOLA (two yrs) August 1978; Command LE EMER (two yrs) September 1982; Command Staff Cse September 1984-June 1985; Commander January 1991; Command Le Eithne (two yrs) April 1993; United Nations Service 5th Lebanon May 1997; Captain (NS) September 1999; Commodore (NS) July 2002; Assumed Command Naval Service July 2002. Clubs: Douglas Golf Club. Recreations: current affairs, golf, swimming. Contact: Naval HQ, Naval Base, Haulbowline, Cobh, Co Cork. **T** 021 486 4801 **F** 021 486 4807 email frank.lynch@defenceforces.ie

LYNCH, John; EXECUTIVE CHAIRMAN, CIE
b 1942, Dublin; single; *edu.* Drimnagh Castle Christian Brothers School; Kevin Street Technical School; Bolton Street Technical College HNC (Mech. Eng); University College Dublin, B.Comm, MBA; Trinity College Dublin, PhD; Executive Chairman CIE; managing director Pye Ireland 1975-'77; director business policy, CIE 1977-'84; chief executive, Irish Productivity Centre 1984-'88; chief executive, Bord Gais 1988-'91; chairman, FÁS 1988-'91; director general, FÁS, 1991-2000; executive chairman CIE 2000 to date; visiting professor of Business Policy, University of Maine; Boston College; Memorial University, Newfoundland; Publ. include *Legal Aspects of Marketing; Strategy in Irish Business; Understanding Business in Ireland;* founder member, The Irish Hospice Foundation; past president, Institute of Industrial Engineers (1988-90). Recreations: football. Contact: CIE, Tara House, Tara Street, Dublin 2. **T** 01 703 4994

The former academic has extensive experience of the semi state sector; this experience will be fully tested in his current position in CIE as he endeavors to modernize the semi state body into a commercial transport company at a time of increasing competition from the private sector and increasing political pressure for an efficient, cost competitive system.

LYNCH, Kathleen; PUBLIC REPRESENTATIVE
b 1953, Cork; *m* Bernard Lynch; 4 *c*; *edu.* Blackpool National School Cork; Public Representative, Member of Dáil Éireann, Labour Party (Cork North Central); elected to Cork Corporation 1985; elected to Dáil Éireann, Member Democratic Left 1994; lost seat in General Election 1997; re-elected Labour party 2002; member of group which drew up Regional Submission for E.U. Structural Funds; member of Constitutional Review Committee; board member Southern Health Board; Cork City Development Board; Cork Opera House Board. Contact: Farrancleary House, 5, Assumption Road, Blackpool, Cork **T** 021 439 9930 **T** 01 618 4034 (Dáil) **F** 021 430 4293 email kathleen.lynch@oireachtas.ie web http://www.labour.ie/www.labour.ie

An articulate Dail deputy who is a great advocate of the needs and requirements of her working class constituents.

LYNCH, Philip; CHIEF EXECUTIVE ONE51
b 1946, Innishannon, Co. Cork; *m* Eileen Crowley; 1*s* 3*d*; *edu*. Hamilton High School; Copswood College; Waterford RTC; Chief Executive One51; retired chairman IAWS 2005; group managing director IAWS 1983-2003; former executive, Odlum Group & R&H Hall; Doctor of Law LLB (*hc*) 1997; chairman Educate Through Sport Foundation T/A; The First Tee of Ireland; a non-executive director of FBD Holdings plc; C&C Group plc; Cillryan's Bakery Ltd; Odlum Group Ltd.; A. Heistand Holding AG; John Thompson & Sons Ltd; Techrec Limited; Coillte Teoranta; former chairman Bord Bia, the Irish Food Board. Clubs: Turf Club, Curragh Golf Club, Las Brisas Golf Club, Nueva Andalucia, Spain. Recreations: golf, GAA. Contact: One51, 151 Thomas Street, Dublin 8. **T** 01 6121200 **F** 01 6121321

> The West Cork businessman was the darling of the stock exchange as he headed up the IAWS Group plc; has now set out on a new business mission with his attempt to transform IAWS CoOps Society into a business entity specialising primarily in the waste and energy areas; suffered a major set back with the rejection of the take over attempt of South Western Services (Bandon based Co-Op).

LYONS, Eoin; JOURNALIST
b 1976, Dublin; single; *edu*. Terenure College Dublin; School of Design Bolton Street (Graphic Design); Journalist *Irish Times*; graphic design business for three years; journalist, The Irish Times 2002 to date; interiors and fashion stylist; *Publ. The Irish Times; IMAGE* Magazine; *House & Garden* (UK). Recreations: collecting 20th century Irish art, contemporary music scene in Dublin, travel with design in mind, recently to see New England Shaker Design, Milan/Paris for furniture fairs, all aesthetic interests thanks to my architect father. Contact: Irish Times, D'Olier Street, Dublin 2. **T** 01 679 2022 **F** 01 289 6992 email elyons@irish-times.ie

> A quiet but observant journalist who loves and lives for design and interiors; highly stylish he likes anything to do with modernism and modern living.

LYSAGHT, Gary; ARCHITECT
b 1965; *p* Michelle Fagan (*qv*); 2*s*; *edu*. CBS Thurles, Co Tipperary; Dublin Institute of Technology; Trinity College Dublin; Dip Arch. (Hons), B Arch. (Hons); MRIAI; Architect: Patrick Power Design Associates 1990; Jourdain Muller PAS, Frankfurt, Germany 1993; Hoger Hare RKW Architects, Berlin, Germany 1996; Derek Tynan Architects 1997; Urban Projects 1998; private practice with Paul Kelly and Gary Lysaght, FKL architects 1999 to date; Awards include AAI Awards 2003, 2004; RIAI Awards 2004, 2005; short-listed Kildare Civic Offices 2000; short listed Monaghan Civic Offices 2002; First Prize Martin Valley Sculptor Retreat, 40 under 40 2005. Contact: FKL Architects, Unit 10, Greenmount Ind. Estate, Harold's Cross, Dublin 12. **T** 01 473 6350 **F** 01 473 6250 email design@fklarchitects.com web www.fklarchitects.com

Mc ALEESE, Mary née Leneghan; PRESIDENT OF IRELAND
b 1951, Belfast; *m* Martin Mc Aleese; 1*s* 2*d*; *edu*. St. Dominic's High School, Falls Road, Belfast; The Queen's University Belfast LLB (Hons); The Inn of Court of Northern Ireland; Trinity College Dublin; MA; The Institute of Linguists, Diploma in Spanish; Barrister-at-Law of the Inn of Court of Northern Ireland; Barrister-at-Law of the Honourable Society of King's Inns, Dublin; President of Ireland; appointed Reid Professor of Criminal Law, Criminology and Penology in Trinity College Dublin 1975-79 and 1981-87; joined RTE as current affairs journalist and presenter 1979-81; continued as part-time presenter until 1985; director of the Institute of Professional Legal Studies at the Queen's University of Belfast 1987-97; Pro Vice Chancellor of the Queen's University of Belfast 1994-97; elected President of Ireland 1997-2004; 2004-11; member, Institute of Linguists (London); fellow, Royal Society of Arts, LL.D (hc) NUI; University of Nottingham; Victoria University of Technology, Australia; St. Mary's University, Halifax; Queen's University Belfast; Honorary Bencher (King's Inns); Honorary Fellow Institute of Engineers of Ireland; Trinity College Dublin; Royal College of Surgeons; College of Anaesthetists; Liverpool John Moore's University; member, European Bar Association; International Bar Association (Northern Ireland Rapporteur); Inns of Court Northern Ireland; King's Inns Dublin; re-elected President of Ireland 2004 to date; made history when she met Queen Elizabeth in Belfast December 2005, the first time both women have met on the island of Ireland. Recreations: skiing, knitting. Contact: Áras an Uachtarán, The Phoenix Park. Dublin 8. **T** 01 677 2815 **F** 01 671 0529 web www.president.ie

President Mary McAleese

Able, astute, warm and sincere, her former roles as a university professor, lecturer, and broadcaster stand her in good stead; the second woman to be elected to the highest office in the land, the polar opposite to her immediate predecessor, Mary Robinson (*qv*); she has a natural capacity to engage with ordinary people; her address to the nation following the 9/11/01 New York calamity defined the grief of her fellow countrymen; her northern roots show through and sometimes to the disadvantage of the office; in the main she and her husband Martin have been careful in their development of all-Ireland links; their obviously happy marriage shines through though they have kept their private lives very private, keeping their children away from public notice; she suffers from her second term not being contested, (she herself would have favoured an election) and to date seems to be keeping a lower profile than before.

McALINDEN, Cormac Damien; EXECUTIVE CHAIRMAN THE LITHOGRAPHIC GROUP
b 1948; *m* Geraldine Collins; 2*s* 1*d*; *edu*. Francisan College, Gormanston; University College Dublin, BA, B.Comm; Executive Chairman The Lithographic Group; worked in Chemical Bank, New York; Wells Fargo Bank, San Francisco; returned to Ireland to run Lithographic Universal Limited, Bray, printing business; launched Lithoset Limited, Mac Publishing Limited, Core Director Marketing Limited; merged with Smurfit Web to become the largest commercial web offset printers in Europe 2003; currently executive chairman of The Lithographic Group. Recreations; sailing, golf, rugby, socialising. Contact: The Lithographic Group, Bray Business Park, Bray, Co. Wicklow. **T** 01 282 9001 **F** 01 276 1893.

Has transformed his company to a major European player in the now not so new technologies; saw the openings and went for them; a very shrewd and hard working businessman who also plays hard.

Mc ARDLE, Brendan Martin; JOURNALIST/BROADCASTER
b 1974; single; *edu*. Our Lady Secondary, Castleblaney, Co. Monaghan; Northern Ireland Hotel & Catering College, Portrush, Co. Antrim; College of Business and Finance, Belfast; M. Diploma Hotel Catering; Inst. Mgmt. Degree Hotel Catering; Journalist/Broadcaster; advertising, sales and marketing manager, *The Irish Field* 2004 to date; marketing manager Punchestown Racecourse 2003-04; marketing manager Leopardstown 2002-03; marketing manager Navan Racecourse 2002; compere, county finals Rose of Tralee; equestrian journalist RTÉ, 1NN, BBC. Recreations: horse riding, swimming, reading. Contact: Irish Field, Farm Centre, Bluebell, Dublin 12. **M** 087 685 9993 email brendanmcardle@irishfield.ie.

Gregarious, talented; excellent TV and radio equestrian sports commentator; lively and interested in all things equestrian, has made a name for himself with racing interests and related developments.

Mc CAFFREY, John Anthony; MEDICAL CONSULTANT, ONCOLOGIST
b 1965; *m* Una Molloy; 2*s* 1*d*; *edu.* Blackrock College, Dublin; University College Dublin MB B.Ch. BAO; FRCPI; Consultant Medical Oncologist (Mater Misericordiae University Hospital, Mater Private Hospital); Cavan General Hospital 1999 to date; post graduate oncology training, St. Vincent's Hospital; fellowship at Memorial Sloan Kettering Cancer Centre, New York 1993-95; attending physician and associate professor, MSKCC 1995-99; member, American Society of Clinical Oncology; European Society of Medical Oncology; American Urological Association; American Medical Association; president, Irish Society of Medical Oncology 2005; secretary ISMO 2002-05; *Publ.* more than 200 original reports, reviews, abstracts, book chapter in medical literature. Clubs: Roganstown Golf Club (abject novice!). Recreations: opera Ireland enthusiast, film. Contact: Mater Private Clinic, Eccles Street, Dublin 7. **T** 01 885 8569/843 2244 **F** 01 885 8404 email mccaffrey@ireland.com web www materprivate.ie

> Internationally trained oncologist, at the cutting edge of his speciality; was held in the highest esteem at Memorial Sloan Kettering, the world famous cancer clinic; a low key, kind gentleman whose patients all sing his praises.

Mc CAFFERY, Michael; OPERA / THEATRE DIRECTOR, DESIGNER, WRITER
b 1955, Newcastle, UK; single; *edu.* St. Cuthbert's Grammer School, Newcastle upon Tyne 1976- 74; Magdalene College, Cambridge 1975-78; BA (Hons); Opera, Theatre Director; associate director, Old Vic Company, London; associate director, Glyndbourne Festival Opera and Beyreuth Festival; lecturer in Performance Studies at the University of Manchester; former artistic director Dublin Grand Opera/Opera Ireland; freelance work includes productions for Glyndebourne, Beyreuth, Vienna Volksoper, Opera Comique de Paris, Opera National du Rhin Strasbourg, Wexford Festival Opera, RTÉ Television, Garsington Opera, Opera de Nice, Halle Handel Festival, National Theatre Tokyo; designs many of his own productions; as a writer his work has been performed by RTÉ, Lyric FM, BBC Radio 4, at the Edinburgh Festival, Chichester Festival and at several UK Theatres; *Publ. Directing a Play,* Phaidon 1989. Clubs: Wagner Society; Georgian Society; Recreations: gardening, architectural heritage and conservation, theatre, history, European literature. Contact: Fortfield, Colpe, Donnaghcarney, Co.Meath. **T** 041 988 7819 email michaelmccaffery@eircom.net;

> A man of method and precision, brings an incisive eye and intelligence to his work; passionately in love with opera, music and theatre; has strict views on the way which they should be presented; keen to make opera more readily accessible to as wide an audience as possible; now mostly works in mainland Europe, North America and Japan.

Mc CANN, Carl Patrick; CHAIRMAN FYFFES plc;
b 1953; *m* Marion Dempsey; 3*s* 1*d*; *edu.* St Mary's College, Dundalk; St Vincent's College, Castleknock, Dublin; Trinity College Dublin, B.BS; Chairman, Fyffes plc; member, Institute of Chartered Accountants; joined Fyffes plc 1980; currently chairman, Fyffes plc. Clubs: Fitwilliam LTC, Donnybrook Tennis Club. Recreations: tennis, running. Contact: Fyffes plc, 1 Beresford Street, Dublin 7. **T** 01 887 2741

> Inherited the mantle from his father Niall (*qv*); low profile, astute businessman; shell shocked by the loss of the 'insider trading' case brought against Jim Flavin (*qv*) and the financial implications for his shareholders.

Mc CANN, Colum; AUTHOR/SCREENWRITER
b 1965, Dublin; *m* Allison Hawke; 2*s* 1*d*; *edu.* Clonkeen College, Deansgrange, Dublin; College of Commerce, Rathmines, Dublin (Journalism) 1982; University of Texas 1992; Author/Screenwriter; *Publ.* novels and short stories: *Fishing the Sloe-Black River; Songdogs; This Side of Brightness; Everything in this Country Must; Dancer* and (forthcoming) *Zoli;* screenwriter, Academy Award nomination for short film *Everything in this Country Must.* Contact: c/o The Wylie Agency, 250, West 57th Street, Suite 2114 , New York, NY 10017. **T** 001 212 246 0069 email mccann158@aol.com

> A brilliant evoker of atmosphere, often of an impending tragic one.

Mc CANN, David; CHIEF EXECUTIVE FYFFES Plc
b 1958; *m* Adrienne O'Connor; 3*s* 1*d*; *edu.* University College Dublin; Blackhall Place; BCL; Chief

Executive Fyffes plc; solicitor; Daniel O'Connell & Sons (Dundalk); partner, Ivor Fitzpatrick & Co. (Dublin); joined family firm Fyffes plc; currently chief executive; member, Law Society of Ireland. Clubs: Fitzwilliam L.T.C. Recreations: golf, tennis. Contact: Fyffes plc, 1 Beresford Street, Dublin 7. **T** 01 887 2741.

> Has to face the impact of legal costs of the Jim Flavin (*qv*) debacle and onwards how to restore confidence in the company's overall standing given the revelations during the court case as to how big business works.

John Mc Cann

Mc CANN, John; GROUP CHIEF EXECUTIVE, UTV plc

b 1953, Belfast; *m* Mairead; 1*s* 3*d*; *edu* St. Malachy's Belfast; Queens University Belfast; B.Sc. (Econ), FCA; group chief executive UTV plc; financial controller/company secretary, Ulster Television 1983; general manager 1989; appointed to the Board 1992; appointed managing director (now group chief executive) 1999 to date. Contact: UTV, Ormeau Road, Belfast, BT7 1EB. **T** 048 9032 8122 email jmccann@utvplc.com

> Under his stewardship UTV is expanding into other communications areas while the ITV franchise for Northern Ireland continues to be highly profitable and visibly generating a lot of cross border advertising revenue.

Mc CANN, Neil; FORMER CHAIRMAN FYFFES plc

b 1924, Dundalk; *m* Mary Hughes; 5*s* 1*d*; *edu*. Marist College, Dundalk; Castleknock College, Dublin; Former Chairman Fyffes plc; founder, Fruit Importers of Ireland, acquired Fyffes (UK) 1987, now Fyffes plc; formerly chief executive, former chairman, Fyffes plc. Clubs: Fitzwilliam LTC, Dundalk RFC. Recreations: golf, tennis. Contact: Fyffes plc, 1 Bereford Street, Dublin 7. **T** 01 809 5555

> The octogenarian founder of Fruit Importers of Ireland steered his company over the sometimes turbulent waters to become the highly successful and profitable Fyffes plc; from the same area that produced equally successful, billionaire entrepreneurs Larry Goodman (*qv*) and Martin Naughton (*qv*); the family suffered as much a blow to their armour proper as to their pocket by losing the high profile, long running, insider trading case to Jim Flavin (*qv*) of DCC.

Mc CANN, Patrick Anthony 'Pat'; FORMER CEO JURYS DOYLE HOTEL GROUP

b 1951 Ballymote, Co Sligo; *m* Ann; 1*s* 2*d*; *edu*. Colaiste Mhuire, Ballymote, Co Sligo; HND Business Studies, University of North London; Dip Marketing, Dip Accounts and Finance, Institute of Certified Accountants; Former Chief Executive Jury's Doyle Hotels; Ryan Hotel plc, held various positions up to general manager 1969-89; Goring Hotels, London 1973-74; Jury's Hotel Group plc, general manager 1989-92; group general manager 1992-94; group operations director 1994-98; chief executive designate 1998-2000; chief executive Jury's Doyle Hotel Group plc 2000 – '06. Recreations: walking, reading, gardening, sport. Contact: 146 Pembroke Road, Ballsbridge, Dublin 4. **T** 01 607 0010 **F** 01 660 5728 email pat_mccann@jurysdoyle.com

> A solid performer who inherited a very healthy operation from his predecessor Peter Malone (*qv*); an accidental beneficiary of the 2005 Jurys Doyle sell off circus as his shareholding has rocketed to almost the same extent as Ballsbridge real estate prices; announced his plans to set down in favour of his protégé Niall Geoghegan (*qv*) at the end of 2006; in addition to his own consultancy, should be in line for some plum directorships.

Mac CANN, Peter Michael; HOTELIER

b 1961; *m* Dorothy; 2*s*; *edu*. Clongowes Wood College, Co. Kildare; hotelier; trained in hotel management with Fitzpatrick Hotels, Killiney and Shannon, Co Clare 1980-84; Hotelier/ General Manager, Merrion Hotel;Trustee Forte (UK) 1984-90; food and beverage manager, Conrad Hotel, Dublin 1990-94; general manager Sheen Falls Lodge, Kenmare 1994-96; general manager Merrion Hotel, Dublin 1996 to date. Clubs: Milltown Golf Club, Headfort Golf Club, Landsdowne RFC; Recreation: golf, fine wine, travel; Contact: Merrion Hotel, Upper Merrion Square, Dublin. **T** 01 603 0656 **F** 01 603 0657 email generalmanager@merrionhotel.com

> A superb and gracious hotelier who brings his own impressive éclat to a great hotel.

Mc CARTAN, Eamonn Gerard; PROFESSOR/CHIEF EXECUTIVE SPORTS COUNCIL
NORTHERN .IRELAND
b 1953; *m* Marian McFadden; 1*s*; *edu.* St.Joseph's Teacher Training College Belfast (B. Ed), Queen's
University, Belfast (Dip. Advance Study in Education, Dip. Management Studies, MBA);Chief
Executive Sports Council for Northern Ireland 1976-78; PE Teacher St. Mary's GS Belfast; Sydney
1978-79; Christian Brothers Secondary School Belfast 1979-80; St. Mary's GS Belfast 1980-81;
assistant manager Andersontown Leisure Centre Belfast 1981-83; PA to assistant director of Leisure
Services Belfast City Council 1983-84; assistant director PE Queen's University Belfast 1984-94;
chief Executive Sports Council for NI 1994 to date; visiting professor School of Leisure and Tourism,
University of Ulster; board member Chest Heart and Stroke Association; Youth Sport Tst; Phoenix
Tst; Odyessy Tst; co chair Community Relations Council; board member Co-operation Ireland;
Odyssey Co.; Washington Ireland Young Leaders 1991 MCIM; MIPD 1991. Clubs: Malone Golf
Club. Recreations: skiing, golf, basketball, gardening, current/political affairs. Contact: The Sports
Council for Northern Ireland, House of Sport, Upper Malone Road, Belfast BT9 5LA.
T 028 9036 1222 **F** 028 9068 2757 **M** 078 60 33 1475

> In a culture of sports he runs a good ship and enables all kinds of cross community
> developments, seen and unseen.

Mc CARTHY, Brian; CHAIRMAN, FEXCO
b 1944, Cork; *m* Mary Nagle; 2*s* 3*d*; *edu.* Presentation College, Cork; AIB Bank 1963-81; set up
FEXCO - a financial services company employing over1,400 globally administering Prize Bonds,
Gulliver Info. Res. services, VAT refund scheme, bureau de change, stockbroking, Western Union
agent, multicurrency card management services, data processing 1981; member, University College
Cork Foundation; Awards: Excellence in Marketing, Sean Lemass Award 1987. Recreations: reading,
classical music, boating, fishing. Contact: FEXCO Financial Services Centre, Iveragh Road,
Killorglin, Co. Kerry. **T** 066 976 1258 **F** 066 976 201

Mc CARTHY, Dermot; SECRETARY GENERAL, IRISH GOVERNMENT AND DEPARTMENT
OF TAOISEACH.
b 1953, Dublin; *m* Rosemary; 1*s*; *edu.* Christian Brothers School, Synge Street, Dublin; University
College Dublin; joined the Civil Service; worked his way to the most powerful position in
Government; Recreations: GAA. Contact: Dept. Taoiseach, Upper Merrion Street, Dublin 2.
T 01 619 4036 **F** 01 6194267 email govsec@taoiseach.gov.ie web www.taoiseach.gov.ie

> Ireland's most powerful civil servant, low profile, keen intellect, politically astute;
> highly respected in the corridors of power; his laid back approach disguises a very
> hardworking public servant; has continued the influential role of his predecessors in
> the emerging N I political scenario and domestic social and economic policy;
> personable, good company.

Mc CARTHY, Dr. Thomas; CHIEF EXECUTIVE, IRISH MANAGEMENT INSTITUTE
b 1959, Cork; *m* Mary Morgan; 3*s*; *edu.* University College Cork; Queens University at Kingston,
Canada; BA MA PhD; CEO Irish Management Institute; CEO, Irish Management Institute 2004 to
date; professor of economics & executive dean of DCU Business School 2002-04; dean of research &
graduate studies NUI Maynooth 1999-2002; dean of postgraduate studies NUI Maynooth 1996-99;
senior lecturer/lecturer economics, SPCM/NUI Maynooth1990-2002; college lecturer economics,
University College, Cork 1987-90; member of the Higher Education Authority 2000-05; member
Advisory Science Council 2005-08; member Irish Research Council for the Humanities & Social
Sciences 2000-06; Publ. *Ireland: EU Transfers and Demographic Dividends,* European Economy
(Reports and Studies: Generational Accounting in Europe), No 6, pp. 101-115, 1999 [published
2000] (with H. Bonin); *Regional Income Differential and the Issue of Regional Equalization in Ireland,*
Journal of the Statistical and Social Inquiry Society of Ireland, (with G.E. Boyle & J. Walsh), Vol.
XXVIII, Part 1, pp. 155-211, One Hundred and Fifty-Second Session 1998/1999; *A Simple Measure of
ß-Convergence,* Oxford Bulletin of Economics & Statistics, (with G. E. Boyle) 1997; *On and Off The
Frontier: Growth Empirics Where Taxes Affect Growth,* Economic and Social Review, (with G. E. Boyle)
1996; *Third World Debt: Towards an Equitable Solution,* Gill & Macmillan, Dublin (with M. McCarthy)
1994. Clubs: Royal Cork Yacht Club. Recreations: sailing. Contact: Irish Management Institute,
Sandyford Road, Dublin 16. **T** 01 207 8501 **F** 01 295 5150 email tom.mccarthy@imi.ie

> A very bright addition to the portfolio of public professionals who develop all kinds of
> multi cultural and cross cutting educational strategies; has a considerable future ahead

of him in the third level sector but whether some other group or company doesn't lure him away, possibly to Brussels, remains to be seen.

MacCARTHY, James Martin Anthony "Jimmy"; SINGER/SONGWRITER
b 1953, Cork; single; *edu.* Christian Brother's, Cork; trainee trainer with Vincent O'Brien 1968-70; apprentice jockey with Billy O'Gorman 1970-72; with Fergy Sutherland 1973-74; Blarney Riding School, Joe O'Reilly 1974-75; professional musician 1975 to date; albums include: *The Song of the Singing Horseman (*Mulligan Records) 1999; *The Dreamer* (Sony Records) 1994; *Warmer for the Spark* (Dara Records); compositions include *Ride On; No Frontiers; Katie; Bright Blue Rose; Ancient Rain;* writer member, I.M.R.O., also board of directors; Awards, Smithwicks /Hot Press Song Writer of the Year 1995. Recreations: horse riding, health and holistic healing, Alexander Technique, I Ching. Contact: Pat Egan Management, Merchants Court, 24 Merchants Quay, Dublin 2. **T** 01 679 8572

The Watergrasshill born, brilliant songwriter, has written for many of the great balladeers; is equally well known for singing his own compositions.

Mc CARTHY, Justine Mary; JOURNALIST
b 1959, Co. Cork; *m* Denis Murnaghan; 1*s*; *edu.* Ursuline Convent, Blackrock, Cork; College of Commerce, Rathmines; Cert. Journalist; *Aspect* current affairs magazine 1980-82; freelance 1982-84; chief features writer and columnist, *Irish Independent* 1984 - '06; Deputy Editor, Village Magazine 2006 – todate; also published articles in the *Observer*, the *Guardian, Washington Post*; Publ. *Mary McAleese, The Outsider,* Blackwater Press 1999; essay in *Quench Not The Spirit*, Columba 2005. Recreations: reading, watching rugby, theatre, visiting Kerry. Contact: 56, Wellington Road, Dublin 4. **T** 01 669 7622 email jmccarthy@the villagemagazine.ie

A very considerable intelligence in the world of journalism; has had her battles with all kinds of censorship; a writer of enormous integrity and determination, who writes with passion and style and whose immense talent should finally be set free with her departure from the *Irish Independent*.

Mc CARTHY, Thomas; POET
b 1954, Cappoquin, Co. Waterford; *m* Catherine Coakley; 1*s* 1*d*; *edu.* St. Ann's High School, Cappoquin, Co. Waterford; University College Cork; BA; H. Dip.Ed.; University of Iowa; Poet; assistant director Cork 2005, 2003-05; Awards, Patrick Kavanagh Award 1977; O'Shaughnessy Prize 1991; Annual Literary Award, Ireland Funds 1984; member, Aosdána; Publ. *First Convention, Poems* 1978; *The Sorrow Garden, Poems* 1981; *The Lost Province, Poems* 1996; *Merchant Prince, Poems* 2005. Clubs: Royal Society of Arts (fellow), London. Recreations: wine collecting, with special interest in Leoville Barton. Contact: Carrigbrack, Lover's Walk, Montenotte, Cork. **T** 021 450 3738 email tommcarthy@cork2005.ie

An important Cork writer who has added to the lustre of his work by his inclusion of many significant writers during Cork's reign as City of Culture 2005.

Mc CLARTY, David; MEMBER, NORTHERN IRELAND ASSEMBLY
b 1951*; edu.* Coleraine Academical Inst., Magee College, Londonderry; Member, Northern Ireland Assembly; fire insurance underwriter 1973-84; insurance consultant 1984-98; elected Coleraine Borough Council, 1993,1997 and 2001; Mayor of Coleraine 1993-95; MLA (UUP) E.Londonderry 1998; Freeman City of London 1994; chairman Board of Governors Christie Memorial School; member Board of Governors Coleraine Academical Inst. Clubs: Ballywillan Drama, Coleraine British Legion, Royal Artilliery Association (honorary life member). Recreations: sport, reading, music, amateur dramatics, theatre. Contact: Northern Ireland Assembly, Parliament Buildings, Stormont Estate, Belfast BT4 3XX / 22, Slievebanna, Coleraine, Co. Londonderry, BT51 3JG. **T** 028 9052 0210 **F** 028 9052 0309 **M** 077 71 605 617 email david.mcclarty@niassembly.gov.uk.

A tough and determined upholder of Unionism; a good and admired local Councillor; keeps his eye on many of the new social developments in his area and within the Province.

Mc CLEAN, Donn Patrick; JOURNALIST
b 1970; *m* Rachel; 1*d*; *edu.* CBS, Dundalk, Co Louth; Dublin City University; University College

Dublin; BA (Hons) in International Marketing and Japanese (DCU); H Dip Marketing Practice (UCD); marketing manager, Betdaq; general manager, Irish Thoroughbred Marketing; main features writer, racing, *Sunday Independent*; director of Evening School, LSB College; lecturer in marketing, UCD. Recreations: racing, soccer, writing, reading. Contact: 6 Old Chapel Wood, Caragh, Co Kildare. **T** 045 903038 email donnmcclean@eircom.net

His unique qualifications are reflected in his varied career todate; his wide experience equips him well to take a different approach to journalism and marketing.

Mc CLOSKEY, Malachy; CHAIRMAN BOYNE VALLEY GROUP

b 1939, Drogheda, Co. Louth; *m* Ann Greene; 6*s*; *edu.* Christian Brothers School, Drogheda; St. Patrick's College, Armagh; Founder and Managing Director, Boyne Valley Foods Ltd.; chairman Boyne Valley Group 1977 to date; Boyne Valley includes Boyne Valley Foods Ltd, Irish Cereals Ltd, Lifeforce Foods Ltd, Lakeshore Foods Ltd, Kileen Steel Wools, Irish Breeze Ltd, publisher of Peter Harbison's scholarly *High Crosses*; Awards, Supreme Arts Award for Treasures of the National Library; Special Recognition Award at the Ernst & Young Entrepreneur of the Year Awards. Recreations; trees, restoration, 17th century Ireland, long distance adventure holidays. Contact: Boyne Valley Foods Ltd., Planatin Road, Drogheda, Co. Louth. **T** 041 987 0300 **F** 041 987 0339.

A nice man who looks to the past to explain the future; innovative, successful entrepreneur who is brilliant in his business; very much a man for his region, supporter of many charities; which with all the new developments and the Dublin Belfast economic corridor makes him a great asset.

Mc CLOSKEY, Phelim; CHAIRMAN, CHIEF EXECUTIVE MOSNEY IRISH HOLIDAYS PLC

b 1945, Drogheda, Co. Louth; *m* Betty McKevitt; 1*s* 2*d*; *edu.* Marist College, Dundalk; Shannon College Hotel Management, Dip Hotel Mgmt; Movenpick Organisation, Geneva; director, Mosney Irish holidays plc; food and beverage manager, Doyle Hotel Group 1971-73; catering manager, Shelbourne Hotel 1973-76; involved in business activities in Drogheda, including boutique, garage, nightclub and E1 Molino Hotel, Julianstown 1973-87; acquired Mosney Holiday Centre; chairman/chief executive, Mosney Irish Holidays plc 1982 to date; director, various private companies; has instigated major re-development plans for the holiday camp; agreed with Government to provide Mosney as an accommodation center 2000. Recreations: environment, nature, sports activities. Contact: Mosney Irish Holidays plc, Mosney, Co. Meath. **T** 041 982 9200

One of the well-known Drogheda business family; has developed his own interests in the fast growing leisure/tourism area.

Mc COLGAN, John; DIRECTOR, ABHANN PRODUCTION

b 1945, Dublin; *m* 1st Virginia Cole; (*m. diss*); 1*s* 1*d*; *m* 2nd Moya Doherty (*qv* Doherty, Moya); 2*s*; *edu.* St. Joseph's School, Fairview; D. Litt; NUI Maynooth; Director Abhann Productions; turned down an acting scholarship to the Abbey Theatre to join RTE as a vision mixer; former Controller of Programmes, TV AM (London); former head of Light Entertainment, RTE; currently director, Abhann (*Riverdance The Show*); currently director, Tyrone Productions; chairman Today FM; has produced and directed television documentaries, including a tribute to *Eamon Kelly; The Man from the Mountains*; a tribute to *Maureen Potter, Super Trouper;* played a key role in the development of *Riverdance The Show,* directed the video which is now best ever selling video in the world; *Riverdance* has received numerous award worldwide; directed *The Shaughraun*, at The Abbey Theatre, Dublin; awards, Jacob's Television Award, Ernst & Young Entrepreneur of the Year. Recreations: walking, reading, music. Contact: Abhann Productions Ltd, 23 Little Mary Street, Dublin 7. **T** 01 475 3100 **F** 01 889 4991 web www.riverdance.com

John Mc Colgan

Bright, inventive and able, doesn't hide his light under a bushel; has great business acumen and capacity to consider all kinds of theatrical developments; set to launch new musical, based on the life of Queen Maeve, on Broadway 2007 and to relocate to the US from 2007 –'09; will remain one of the great entertainment entrepreneurs far into the future.

MAC CONGHAILL, Fiach; DIRECTOR THE ABBEY THEATRE

b 1954; *m* Bríd Ní Neachtain; 2*d*; *edu.* Coláiste Eoin; Trinity College Dublin, BA (Mod) Politics, Sociology; artistic director Project Arts Centre 1992-99; cultural director, Expo 2000; programme manager, Irish College Paris; Arts advisor to John O'Donoghue, Master for Arts, Sports & Tourism 2002-05; theatre & film producer (2000-05), includes *STUDS* by Paul Mercier. Recreations: Islands, Football, (Queens Park Rangers), visual Arts. Contact: Abbey Theatre, 26, Lower Abbey Street, Dublin 1. **T** 01 887 2200 **F** 01 872 9177 email info@abbeytheater.ie web www.abbeytheater.ie

> Son of Muiris and Máire and nephew of Ciarán (*qv*), is steeped in the Arts; bright and lively personality, of great charm and intelligence; is able to get along with people, even those who profoundly disagree with him on almost everything; inventive and imaginative; if anybody can make the new processes for the Abbey work he can.

John Mc Cormack

Mc CORMACK, John Anthony; CHAIRMAN, THE SALES INSTITUTE OF IRELAND
b 1960, Dublin; *m* Margaret; 1*s* 2*d*; *edu.* Christian Brothers, James Street, Dublin; Kevin Street College of Technology Dublin; College of Commerce Rathmines, Dublin; ACCA Appian Way, Dublin; FSII; MMII Grad.; C.Dip ACCA; business development director, Kainos Software Ltd; engineer with Storage Technology Products; systems engineer Cara 1983-88; sales, Cara Computers 1988; senior sales positions ICL, Compaq, Kainos. Chairman The Sales Institute of Ireland 2005-06. Clubs: Hibernian Golf Club (captain 2004); Terenure College RFC (coach U11 team); Ballyboden St Endas GAA Club (coach U10 team). Recreations: golf, mini rugby, junior GAA. Contact: 6-7 St. Stephen's Green, Dublin 2. **T** 01 636 9000 **F** 01 636 9001 email j.mccormack@kainos.com

> Charming, ambitious, hardworking, highly respected in the IT sales sector;

Mc COUBREY, Irene 'Maxi'; BROADCASTER
b 1950, Dublin; single; *edu.* Holy Faith Convent, The Coombe, Dublin; College of Commerce, Rathmines, Dublin; qualified as a journalist; broadcaster; member Young Dublin Singers; Maxi, Dick & Twink; Sheeba; 2FM; broadcaster BBC (UK); broadcaster Radio One; UNICEF ambassador; session singer, Motown Studios Detroit, USA; presenter & singer, Thames Television UK; Eurovision representative for Ireland 1973-81; Eurostar judge; Publ. *RTÉ Guide*. Clubs: Ice Bar, Four Seasons, Dublin. Time, Naas. Recreations: theatre, literature, travel, health, mind and body. Contact: Lasata, 46, Priory Drive, Blackrock, Co. Dublin. **T** 01 288 9446 **F** 01 288 9446 email maxi@indigo.ie /maxi@rte.ie

> A bubbly personality with endless chat and banter on her radio programme; has a good personality for that kind of work and is a good and respected broadcaster.

Mc COY, Danny; DIRECTOR ECONOMIC POLICY, IBEC
b 1967, Tuam, Co. Galway; *m* Ailish O'Dwyer; 2*s* 1*d*; *edu.* Universit y College Galway; B.Comm (Hons 2.1); University College Dublin; M. Econ. Sc. (Hons); director Economic Policy IBEC; senior research officer Economic and Social Research Institute 2000-05; senior economist Central Bank of Ireland 1996-2000; Centre for Economic and Social Research research associate on the Global Environment (CSERGE) 1993-96; University College London lecturer 1992-96; research assistant Economic and Social Research Institute 1990-92; business school lecturer Dublin City University 1988-90; teaching posts held: Trinity College Dublin 1997-2005; University of London, Imperial College at Wye, (external) 1993-2005; University of Oxford 1995-1996; University College London 1992-96; London Guildhall University 1992-95; Dublin City University 1987-92; other posts held: Council of the Statistical and Social Inquiry Society of Ireland; National Economic and Social Council; Awards, Barrington Medal from the Statistical and Social Inquiry Society of Ireland 1992; ESRI Research Fellow 1992-96. Recreations: running (occasional), TV, radio particularly current affairs. Contact: IBEC Head Office, Confederation House, 84/86 Lower Baggot Street, Dublin 2. **T** 01 605 1500 **F** 01 638 1500 email danny.mccoy@ibec.ie. web www.ibec.ie

> A sharp shooter economist with an impressive pedigree; his social street cred. will be a major advantage in his latest role at IBEC.

Mc CRACKEN, The Hon. Mr Justice Brian Moore; RETIRED SUPREME COURT JUDGE
b 1934 Cork; *m*; 1*s* 1*d*; *edu.* The High School, Dublin; Trinity College Dublin; Kings Inns; BA; LLB; Barrister at Law; Retired Judge of the Supreme Court; called to the Bar 1957; called to the Inner Bar 1975; practice in Chancery Law and Commercial Law 1995; appointed judge of the High Court 1995; chairman of the Tribunal of Payments to Politicians 1997; judge of the Supreme Court 2002 - 06. Contact: The Supreme Court, Morgan Place, Dublin 7. **T** 01 872 5555

Distinguished himself with his quietly and lethally forensic handling of the Sworn Enquiry (Tribunal of Enquiry (Dunnes Payments)); the stark facts of public and Golden Circle corruption became all too clear; the public were aghast as the trail led to the Cayman Islands, exposing the Ansbacher payments, and the Golden Circle who availed of secretive tax evading processes; submitted his report seven months later; this led in turn to the Moriarty Tribunal; likely to chair a major committee in the near future.

Mc CREERY, Dr, Mary; CONSULTANT NURTITIONIST AND DIETICIAN

b 1958, Dublin; *div.*; 2*s* 1*d*; *edu.* Loretto Convent, Foxrock; Institute of Technology, Kevin St. Dublin; Human Nutrition & Dietetics Trinity College Dublin, Diploma in Counselling and Psychotherapy; Ph.D. Sports Nutrition; consultant clinical nutritionist and dietician; Olympic Council nutritionist 1982-88; Blackrock Clinic 1985 to date; weight loss, eating disorders and other diet/nutrition issues expert; Publ. medical journals and newspapers. Clubs: Riverview Sports Club. Recreations: gym, gardening, skiing, psychotherapy, dining out. Contact: Suite 26, Blackrock Clinic, Blackrock, Co. Dublin. **T** 01 278 3080 email drmccreery@eircom.net

One of the country's leading nutritionists and dieticians; no nonsense approach to both; astute, good company.

Mc CREEVY, Charles 'Charlie'; EUROPEAN COMMISSIONER

b 1949, Sallins, Co. Kildare; *m* 1st Kitty O'Connor; (*m diss*); 1*s* 3*d*; *m* 2nd Noleen Halligan; 3*s*; *edu.* Christian Brothers School, Naas; Franciscan College, Gormanstown, Co. Meath; University College Dublin, BComm; chartered accountant; partner in Tynan Dillon & Company (retired); elected Deputy for Kildare 1977; elected to Kildare County Council 1979-85; Minister for Social Welfare, February 1992-January 1993; Minister for Tourism & Trade, January 1993-December 1994; frontbench spokesperson on Finance, January 1995-June 1997; Minister for Finance June 1997-2004; member of various Oireachtas committees; member, ECOFIN, 1997-2004; president ECOFIN Council Jan-June 2004; appointed European Commissioner for Internal Market and Services 2004 to date. Clubs: Naas Golf Club, Kildare Hotel and Country Club. Recreations: an enthusiastic follower of all sports, particularly horse racing, GAA. Contact: European Commission, B – 1049, Brussels, Belgium. email Charlie.Mc-Creevy@cec.eu.int v

Will always be regarded as the ultimate guru and architect of the Celtic Tiger and the most innovative Minister for Finance in the history of the state; the last of his legacies to be realised was the SSIA 2006 which will unload €12 billion into peoples' pockets for diverse purposes; a victim of his own success, rubbed many political interests the wrong way; now using his gung ho approach in Europe, where they are beginning to sit up and take notice of the Co. Kidare Commissioner; a one-off, brilliant, strong willed, great company; a tee total party animal; accomplished golfer.

Charlie Mc Creevy

Mc CULLOUGH, Denis John; SENIOR COUNSEL

b 1948, Dublin; *m* Ellie Kettle; 2*s* 1*d*; *edu.* Ring College, Co. Waterford; De La Salle College, Churchtown; University College Dublin; BA; Kings Inns; called to the Bar 1971; called to the Inner Bar 1985; called to the Bar, New South Wales 1993; elected to the Bar Council 1998; elected Bencher of the Honourable Society of Kings Inns 1998. Clubs: Kildare Street and University Club, Royal Irish Yacht Club, De La Salle Palmerstown RFC. Recreations: reading, fishing, travel and drinking wine. Contact: Law Library, Four Courts, Dublin 7. **T** 01 872 0622. **F** 01 872 0455

His participation in a long running Public Enquiry has given him an exposure he probably wouldn't want but he has revealed himself as methodical and lethal in cross examination with forensic analytical skills; he's one of those barristers everyone wants to have on their side.

Mc CULLOUGH, HUGH; CHIEF EXECUTIVE, GLENCAR MINING plc

b 1950, Dublin; *edu.* De La Salle, Churchtown, Dublin; University College Dublin; B.Sc (geology) Hons; Kings Inns, Barrister at Law; chief executive, Glencar Mining plc; joined Minarex exploration company 1972; appointed managing director Glencar 1982; began exploration at Teberebie, Ghana; appointed by the Minister for Natural Resources to serve on the National Minerals Policy Review Group 1994; delivered its report in June 1995; Wassa goldmine, Ghana goes into production 1999;

began exploration Uganda 2000; Wassa mine sold 2003; exploration began Mali 2003; surveys and drilling asheba, Ghana 2005; member: Institute of Geologists of Ireland; Federation of European Geologists. Contact: Glencar Mining plc, 71 Lower Baggot Street, Dublin 2. **T** 01 661 9974 **F** 01 661 1205 email hmc@glencarmining.ie web www.glencarmining.ie

> The Dublin born geologist brings a lot of hands-on global experience to the Irish mining company; very low profile, hardworking business executive who sticks to the knitting.

Mc DONAGH, Bobby; CIVIL SERVANT

b 1954, Washington DC; *m* Mary Garvey; 4*d*; *edu.* Gonzaga College, Ranelagh, Dublin; Balliol College, Oxford, UK; *Publ. Original Sin in a Brave New World*; *The Paradox of Europe* (an account of the negotiation of the treaty of Amsterdam), published Institute for European Affairs, Dublin; Contact: DFA, Iveagh House, 80, St. Stephen's Green, Dublin 2. **T** 01 478 0822 web www.foreignaffairs.gov.ie

> Son of a former ambassador, possesses a brilliant mind, his diplomatic skills are highly personal and deeply charming; astute and able, his various postings have been important for the government as he brings a deep intellect and a clever format of dispatches to home of great relevance.

MC DONAGH, Enda Michael; THEOLOGIAN

b 1930; single; *edu.* St. Jarlath's College, Tuam, Co. Galway; St Patrick's College, Maynooth, Co. Kildare. B.Sc.,(hons); NUI Licence in Philosophy (Angelicum University Rome. Ph.D; (Pontifical University Maynooth); Ph.D in Canon Law, Ludwigs, Munich; Chair, Governing Body, University College Cork; Emeritus professor of theology; professor of moral theology Maynooth 1958-75; visiting scholar, University of Tubingen, Germany 1967-68; Rowantree visiting fellow, University of Cambridge 1977-78; Ferguson lecturer, University of Manchester 1978; Huisking professor of moral theology, University of Notre Dame, Indiana, USA 1978-81; Paul McKeever professor of moral theology, University of St. Johns, New York 1991-93; Faith and Justice chair professor, University of St. Paul, Ottawa, Canada 1997; *Publ;* 20+ books; recent publications: *Vulnerable to the Holy* 2004; *Religion and Politics* (ed) 2003; *The Reality of HIV/Aids* joint author 2003. Recreations: art, literature, developing world, theology. Contact: Maynooth College, Maynooth, Co. Kildare. **T** & **F** 01 708 3645 email enda.m.mcdonagh@nuim.ie

> Terrific company with an engaging personality, he brings great authority to and an understanding of the Canon Laws of his church and the humane philosophy which should accompany it.

Enda Mc Donagh

Mc DONALD, Frank; JOURNALIST

b 1950, Dublin; single; *edu.* Kelly's Private School, Cabra Road; St Vincent's Christian Brothers School, Glasnevin; University College Dublin BA; environment editor, *Irish Times.* Editor student magazine, University College Dublin 1970-72; deputy president SRC, University College Dublin 1970-71; New York correspondent Irish Press 1972-73; sub-editor Irish Press 1973-77; reporter 1977-78; reporter *Irish Times* 1979-85; environment editor 1986 to date; Awards, Award for Outstanding Work in Irish Journalism 1979; Lord Mayor's Millennium Medal 1988; Chartered Institute of Transport Journalist of the Year 1998; Publ. *The Destruction of Dublin* (Gill & McMillan) 1985; *Saving the City* (Tomar) 1989; *Ireland's Earthen Houses* (A&A Farmer, joint author) 1997; *The Ecological Footprint of Cities* (International Institute for Urban Environment, joint editor) 1998; *The Construction of Dublin* 2000; *Chaos At The Crossroads* 2005 (with James Nix); member, National Union of Journalists. Contact: The Irish Times, D'Olier Street, Dublin 2. **T** 01 679 2022.

> An important writer on environmental and planning issues; considered by many to be rather pompous and self opinionated which undermines his message in some quarters; he proved so right in so many of the major pieces he wrote on the capacity of the system to breed corruption; cares deeply about the how and why of Government's local and national decisions which affect our environment.

Mc DONALD, Mary Lou; PUBLIC REPRESENTATIVE

b 1969, Dublin; *m* Martin Lanigan; 1*d*; *edu.* Notre Dame des Mission, Churchtown, Dublin; Trinity College Dublin; University of Limerick; Dublin City University; studied english litertaure, Public Representative; European integration; human resouce management; MEP for Dublin Region (Sinn

Fein); member Sinn Fein Ard Chomhairle; consultant, Irish Productivity Center; researcher Institute for European Affairs; trainer in the trade union sponsored Partnership Unit of the Educational and Training Services Trust; lecturer; business consultant; joined Fianna Fail; moved to Sinn Fein as a researcher and candidate for local, national and European elections; member of the European Parliament 2004 to date: represents the Dublin region; chaired the Sinn Fein Press Conference in Jury's Hotel Dublin when MEP, MLA Gerry Adams announced the ending of the IRA War July 2005; chaired a major EU homelessness event in the European Parliament 2005; publicly addressed such issues as pro Aids funding initiatives 2005; opposed the onward development of GM food as a step down and not up the ladder; backed the NCWI's welfare increase initiatives in Northern Ireland; supports the increased funding for EU awareness whilst opposing, on behalf of her party, the holding of the proposed EU Referendum in Ireland, pointing to the Dutch Decision to vote No; member Employment & Social Affairs Committee EUP. Contact: 44, Parnell Square, Dublin 1. **T** 01 872 2609 **F** 01 878 3595 email mlmcdonald@europarl.eu.int sfadmin@eircom net

> Mary Lou is ambitious and would like a Dáil seat, well on the way to becoming a Sinn Fein minister in Government; will need to learn to answer less strategically and more openly when questioned in the public media, as will be case when the electoral difficulties SF pose for FF increase in the future.

Mc DONNELL, Colm; MANAGEMENT CONSULTANT, DELOITTE

b 1972; *m* Gillian Gormley; *edu.* St. Conleth's College, Dublin; Institute of Chartered Accountants Professional Exams, ACA; Member of Institute of Chartered Accountants of Ireland; Management Consultant Deloitte; recruited from school directly to Deloitte where he has worked for the last 14 years; trained as an accountant in audit and moved to consultancy 1996; divides his time between financial management consulting and working with clients on business risk and control assignments. Clubs: Fitzwilliam LTC, RIAC, Old Belvedere RFC; past committee member of the junior fundraising arm of the Irish Hospice Foundation. Recreations: tennis, rugby, horse riding, reading. Contact: 99 Tritonville Road, Sandymount, Dublin 4. **M** 087 813 8198 **F** 01 417 2502 email cmcdonnell@deloitte.ie

> Divides his time between financial management consulting and working with clients on business risk and control assignments.

Mc DONNELL Jane Catherine; PUBLISHER

b 1962, Dublin; *m* Donald Hickey; *2s 1d*; *edu.* Notre Dames des Missions, Churchtown, Dublin; Trinity College, Dublin; BA Hons Mod Natural Science; Managing Director, Gloss Publications; Carlton Magazines 1988-89; *W* (UK) 1987-88; British *Vogue* 1984-87; editor *IMAGE* 1989-99; managing director/ group editorial director Image Publications 1999-2005; founding editor *IMAGE Interiors* 1990-2005; launched *Himself* 1997; *IMAGE Health* 2001; *IMAGE Business* 2005; co founded Gloss Publications (with sister Sarah *qv*) 2005 to date. Publisher, *The Gloss*, 2006 todate; Clubs: Blackrock Tennis Club. Recreations: books, architecture and design; playing tennis. Contact: Gloss Publishing, Dun Laoghaire Enterprise Centre, The Old Firestation, George's Place, Dun Laoghaire, Co. Dublin. **T** 01 230 4868 web www.gloss.com

> A personable, ambitious and hardworking publisher; the epitome of style and sophistication, with her sister Sarah (qv Mc Donnell, Sarah) she brought both to IMAGE magazine which she expanded and built into Ireland's leading glossy.

Mc DONNELL John James; CHARTERED ACCOUNTANT

b 1962, Dublin; *m* Sarah Lappin; *edu.* St. Fintan's High School, Sutton, Dublin; University College Dublin (B. Comm), FCA; Partner, PriceWaterhouseCoopers; joined PWC 1984; partner responsible for technical & IFRS services and banking and capital markets to date; partner for financial institutions; publ; various articles for newspapers and business magazines. Clubs: Westwood Gym, Clontarf. Recreations: reading, walking, wine, running. Contact: 11, Leinster Avenue, North Strand, Dublin 3. **T** 01 836 6156 **W** 01 704 8559 **F** 01 704 8721 email john.mcdonnell@pwc.com

> Has achieved a very senior position in one of the country's leading accountancy practices; his area of specialization has come into focus with the recent bank scandals and the emerging influence of the Financial Regulatory Authority.

Mc DONNELL, Sarah; DIRECTOR, GLOSS PUBLICATIONS;
b 1972; *m* Mark Taylor; 1*d*; *edu.* Notre Dame des Missions, Churchtown, Dublin; Trinity College
Dublin, BA Hons (English and French); Director, GLOSS Publications; editor *IMAGE* magazine
1999-05; director Gloss Publications 2005 to date; editor *The Gloss*, 2006 – todate; Recreations:
travel, fashion, cooking, gardens. Contact: Gloss Publications, Dun Laoghaire Enterprise Centre, The
Old Firestation, George's Place, Dun Laoghaire, Co. Dublin.
T 01 230 4868 web www.gloss.com

> A highly accomplished editor who stays very grounded in the airy fairy world of
> fashionistas; brings a wealth of experience and talent to her new magazine *The Gloss*.

MC DONAGH, Pat; FOUNDER / CHIEF EXECUTIVE SUPERMACS
b 1953,Galway; *m* Una; 4 children; Founder and Chief Executive Supermacs; schoolteacher; founded
Supermacs, Ireland's largest and fastest-growing indigenous fast food group 1978; founded Claddagh
Food Pubs in the US 2001; Supermacs Fresh Express, petrol station food outlets 2004; plans 25 by
end 2006. Recreations; GAA. Contact: Supermac's Head Office, Ballybrit Business Park, Ballybrit,
Galway. **T** 091 753511 **F** 091 752767 email info@supermacs.ie

> The former school teacher started out in a chip van at Galway races in the late 1970s;
> extremely hardworking, astute and savvy; opened first outlet in 1978 in Ballinasloe,
> Co. Galway; now has 60 outlets nationwide; about to expand into Northern Ireland;
> founded Claddagh Food Pubs in the US; expects to have 20 outlets end 2006;
> vociferous in his opposition to the compensation culture, became a pivotal figure in
> demand for change in legislation to criminalize fraudulent claimants; sponsors the
> Galway Hurling team, takes keen hands-on role in local clubs.

Mc DONOGH, Thomas; CHAIRMAN, CHIEF EXECUTIVE MCDONAGH GROUP OF
COMPANIES
b 1935, Galway; *m* Patrizia Giachin; 1*s*; *edu.* St Ignatius College, Galway; Clongowes Wood College;
University College Dublin; Chairman and Chief Executive, McDonogh Group of Companies,
involved in fertilisers, animal feed stuffs, builders merchants, etc.; among the top 200 companies in
the State; a director of 20 other companies, including Galway Harbour Company; active on many
other local and national bodies. Recreations: walking, skiing, football, travel, reading, horseracing.
Contact: McDonogh Group, Merchants Road, Galway. **T** 091 566111 **F** 091 567774.

> Synonymous with Galway Races, a well known racehorse owner and one of the West
> of Ireland's most impressive and successful businessmen; donates generously to the
> arts having given The Druid Theatre their present home; urbane, delightful company.

MACDOUGALD, Suzanne, Mary; ART GALLERY OWNER
b 1945, Bournemouth UK; *m* Kamran Fazel (*m.diss*); 1*s*; *edu.* Alexandra College Dublin; Owner,
Solomon Gallery; model & TV presenter 1960s-1970s; owner Lad Lane Gallery Dublin 1974-81;
The Solomon Gallery Dublin 1981 to date. Clubs: Kildare Street & University Club, Dublin.
Recreations: reading, gardening, cooking, travel, collecting fine art, entertaining. Contact:
Solomon Gallery, Powerscourt Centre, South William Street, Dublin 2. **T** 01 6794237
F 01 671 5262 email suzanne@solomongallery.com web www.solomongallery.com

> A classy act in the world of the commercial art gallery; former model, has transformed
> the image of gallery owners with style, panache and flair, all hiding the iron fist in a
> designer glove; has tremendous drive and energy; is generally regarded as properly
> ambitious for the Arts in Ireland.

Suzanne McDougald

Mc DOWELL, Michael; PUBLIC REPRESENTATIVE
b 1951, Dublin; *m* Niamh Brennan (*qv*); 3*s*; *edu.* Pembroke School, Baggot Street, Dublin; Gonzaga
College, Dublin; University College, Dublin; BA; Kings Inns, BL; Public Representative; Tanaiste;
Minister for Justice, Equality, Law Reform; called to the Bar 1974; called to the Inner Bar 1987;
barrister in practice 1974 to date; co-founder with Desmond O'Malley and Mary Harney of the
Progressive Democrats 1985; chairman of the Party and spokesperson on finance 1985-97; elected
Progressive Democrat deputy for Dublin South East 1987-89 and 1992-97; council member of Kings
Inns 1984 to date; chairman of the Working Group on Company Law Enforcement and Compliance
1998; chairman of the Advisory Group on Single Financial Regulator 1999; Attorney General 1999-

2002; Minister for Justice, Equality and Law Reform 2002 to date; president Progressive Democrats 2002 -06; Tanaiste 2006 – todate;. Clubs: Kildare Street and University Club. Contact: Constituency Office, The Triangle, Ranelagh, Dublin 6. **T** 01 498 8084 **F** 01 498 8087 email info@michaelmcdowell.ie web http://www.michaelmcdowell.ie

> The outspoken, highly articulate Justice Minister has brought all his adversarial skills from the Law Library to Leinster House; a vehement opponent of the unacceptable activities of subversives, is finding it difficult to match actions with words; finds it hard to let sleeping political dogs lie; following the shock resignation of Mary Harney (*qv*), now unexpectedly, Tanaiste; the dynamics between him and An Taoiseach will be closely scrutinized; however he knows he has a steep mountain to climb to rally and grow his party before next year's General Election; his Rottweiler image is not in keeping with his charming off-duty personality.

Mc ENIFF, Sean; CHAIRMAN TYRCONNELL GROUP

b 1936, Ardfarna, Co. Donegal; *m* Eilis Diver; 6*s* 2*d*; *edu.* National School, Ardfarna, Bundoran; St Macartan's College, Monaghan; Chairman Tyrconnell Group; worked in the family hotel (Bundoran); opened small restaurant and souvenir shop 1959; opened three supermarkets, Bundoran, Ballyshannon & Monaghan 1962; opened amusement arcade, sold supermarkets 1972; purchased Great Northern Hotel with brother, Brian 1977; sold share in Great Northern and purchased Mount Errigal Hotel, Letterkenny 1984; set up All Ireland Holidays 1990; built the Allingham Hotel 1992; started Tyrconnell Holiday Homes & Blazing Saddles Complex 1995; opened The Camden Court Hotel and Leisure Centre, Dublin 1998; invested in McLoughlin Components, Ballyshannon after the closure of Donegal Rubber; with brother Brian purchased Ard Ri Hotel, Waterford and Skylon Hotel, Dublin 2002; opened the Grand Canal Hotel, Dublin 2004; opened the Ardmore Hotel, Dublin 2005; member, Bundoran UDC 1998; member, Donegal County Council 1960 to date; chairman, North West Health Board 1967 to date; former chairman VEC 1997-98; elected to the Board of North West Tourism 1977 to date; chairman 1986 to date; director, Bord Failte 1993-98; Awards: AIB County Tourism Award 1995; Donegal Person of the Year 1996. Recreations: golf, football, walking. Contact: Dinglei Coush, West End Bundoran, Co. Donegal. **T** 071 984 2277 **F** 071 984 2278

> Gregarious, astute businessman, the long serving politician from Bundoran has emerged as one of Ireland's leading hoteliers with his brother Brian; has been the major figure in North Western tourism for the last quarter of a century.

Mac ENTEE, Máire; POET, WRITER

b 1922, Dublin; *m* Conor Cruise O'Brien (*qv*);1*s* 1*d*; *edu.* University College Dublin; Kings Inns Dublin; Barrister at Law; Poet and Writer. Called to the Bar 1944; on Scholarship to France 1945; Department of Foreign Affairs, serving in France, Spain and United Nations (was the first woman administrative officer by public competition)1947-62; became member of Aosdána 1996; resigned in protest at the alleged anti-Semitic views of another Aosdána member 1997; awards, honorary degree from the National University of Ireland; O'Shaughnessy Award for Poetry 1988. *Publ. Dhá Sceál Artúraíochta* (1946), *Heart Full of Thought* (1959), *Margadh na Saoire* (1956), *Codladh an Ghaiscígh* (1973), *An Galar Dubhach* (1980), *The Same Age As The State* (2003); continues to be published extensively in journals, works of reference and all major international journals of poetry. Contact: Aosdána, 70, Merrion Square, Dublin 2. **T** 01 618 0200 **F** 01 676 1302

> A formidable poetic talent in this daughter of the quintessential Irish establishment; her father Seán MacEntee was a founder of Fianna Fáil and a government minister for many years, her mother Margaret Brown, was sister to three priests, Monsignor de Brún, President of UCG and chairman of the Arts Council as well as a distinguished scholar, another was a Parish priest in Wicklow and the third was a the Master General of the Dominican Order and a Cardinal; as the man she proposed to marry was already married and of some public interest, the scandal was enormous in Ireland; she and her husband Conor Cruise O'Brien (*qv*)remain, despite the constraints of age, major figures on the cultural and political scene; she was once described as speaking the glorious Irish of Elizabethan Ireland as if English had not arrived on our shores.

MC EVADDY, Des; COMPANY DIRECTOR

b 1954, Swinford, Co. Mayo; *p* Mary Coffee; 1*s* 1*d*; *edu.* Swinford NS; Garbally Park, Ballinasloe; University College Dublin; BL; Kings Inns LLB; Barrister At Law; chief executive Omega Air; started Omega Air in the late 1970s; has grown company to become a major provider to US State departments; also owns impressive property/ land portfolio. Recreations: history, reading, flying, family. Contact: Omega Air, Dublin Airport, Collinstown Cross, Cloghran, Co. Dublin. **T** 01 837 6622 **F** 01 837 6678 email omega@iol.ie

The gregarious multimillionaire high flyer retains many Mayo mannerisms which disguise a sharp, commercial intellect; the ultimate party animal never loses sight of his main business priorities; despite presiding over a global aviation business and a diverse range of business interest in Ireland, from commercial radio to property development, he still finds time to socialise with 'The Boys'; enjoys his Harley, Ferrari and other boys toys.

MC EVADDY, Ulick; COMPANY DIRECTOR
b 1952, Swinford, Co. Mayo; *m* Mary O'Dowd, née Cranley; 1*s* 1*d*; *edu.* Garbally Park, Ballinasloe; served with Irish Defence Forces 1970-81; left the army to join brother Des in Omega Air 1981; Omega Air, specialists in manufacturing and leasing with many international interests such as Sino Swearingen (W. Virginia) where executive jets are manufactured and the experimental programmes for aircraft tankers for aviation re-fuelling are conducted (San Antonio). Clubs: Royal United Services Institute of Defence Studies, United Services Club, RDS. Recreations: reading, horse riding, helicopter flying. Contact: Omega Air, Dublin Airport, Collinstown Cross, Cloghran, Co. Dublin. **T** 01 837 6622 **F** 01 837 6678 email omega@iol.ie

The debonair former army officer is the public face of the Mc Evaddy Brothers; this extremely articulate Mayo man from a strong FG background has displayed political astuteness, developing strong personal friendships across party lines; a long term proponent of the necessity for a second, separate terminal at Dublin airport where with brother Des (*qv*) has 150 acres in North Dublin suitable for a new runway.

MC EVOY, Eleanor; SINGER / SONGWRITER
b 1967, Cabra, Dublin; *m* Mick O'Gorman (also her musical partner); 1*d*; *edu.* B.Mus.; singer and songwriter; violinist with RTÉ Orchestra for four years; first album *Not Quite Love* with her iconic song 'A Woman's Heart' sold 250,000 copies 1992; album *Snapshots* 1999; *Yola* on her own label 2001: *Early Hours* 2004; voted best contemporary Irish album by the readers of *Irish Music* magazine 2004-05 poll; *Eleanor McEvoy's Music* 2005. Contact: Entertainment Architects, 117 Strand Road, Sandymount Dublin 4. **T** 01 260 2560 **F** 01 261 1879 **M** 087 247 5791 web eleanormcevoy.net

The Dublin born singer/songwriter is a multi-talented musician; has carved out a very successful recording and live performance career; her easy going style ensures she engages fully with her audiences.

Mc FADDEN, Niall; CHAIRMAN, IRISH ESTATES/ CEO BOUNDARY EQUITY HOLDINGS
b 1966, Dublin; *m* Leisa Bennett; *edu.* Gonzaga College, Dublin; University College Dublin; B.Comm; ACA; Chairman, Irish Estates; Morgan Stanley, London; Goodman International 1991-94; joined Tedcastles 1994-98; Hibernia 1998- 02; CFO Hertal 2002-03; CEO, Boundary Equity Holdings 2003 to date; 2004 to date Redquartz Boundary (with property developer Paddy Kelly); acquired Vector Dec. 2004; acquired Irish Estates 2004; merged Vector into Irish Estates 2004; floated Irish Estates Dublin and London 2005. Contact: Ulysses House, Foley Street, Dublin 1. **T** 01 871 5400 **F** 01 871 5415 web www.irishestates.ie

A huge capacity for hard work, this former Morgan Stanley deal maker has a tremendous ability to compliment people; seen in the deals he has worked on with Barry O'Callaghan (*qv*)(Hertal/Riverdeep), Shane Reihill (Hibernia), Richard Nesbitt (Arnotts), Paddy and Simon Kelly (*qv*)(Redquartz Boundary); known to crunch numbers into the wee hours; genuinely believes he can pull off any deal.

Mc GANN, Garry; CEO SMURFIT KAPPA GROUP PLC
b 1950; *m* Moira O'Donoghue; 3*d*; *edu.* BA 1973; ACCA 1981; M.Sc.Mgt 1987; CEO, Smurfit Kappa Group; auditor, controller and auditor general 1968-76; financial controller, LM Ericsson Ltd. 1977-88; financial controller, Gilbeys 1988-94; chief executive 1992-94; group CEO, Aer Lingus Group plc 1994-98; CEO, Smurfit Kappa Group 1998 to date; Chairman Dublin Airport Authority; Clubs: Kildare Hotel and Country Club, Athlone Golf Club, RIAC, Hibernian United Services Club, Fitzwilliam LTC. Recreations: golf, music, theatre. Contact: Smurfit Kappa Group Ltd., Beech Hill,

Clonskeagh, Dublin 4. **T** 01 202 7000 **F** 01 269 4481 email info@smurfitkapp.com web www.smurfitkapp.com

A low key chief executive who has lived in the shadow of major companies and who also heads up the Dublin Airport Authority facing enormous challenges; lives quietly and modestly, not a household name, although he's likely to be in the future, as the airport world expands and changes.

Mc GARRY, Patrick 'Patsy' Thomas; JOURNALIST
b 1952; single; *edu.* St Nathy's College, Ballaghaderreen, Co Roscommon 1965-77; National University of Ireland, Galway 1971-76; BA English, history, geography, philosophy 1974; H Dip Education 1976; Journalist; head of news Sunshine Radio (pirate) 1983-87; freelancer for *Sunday World, Star, Magill, Irish Press* to 1989; set up newsroom in first independent radio station in the Republic, Capital Radio (now FM104) 1989-90; freelancer, *The Irish Press, Irish Independent, Sunday Independent, Marian Finucane Show* RTE 1990-95; began with *The Irish Times* Feb 1994; religious affairs correspondent *The Irish Times* 1997 to date. Clubs: Drama Society, auditor Literary and Debating Society 1973/74, Student Amnesty 1973-74. Recreations: theatre, politics, current affairs, GAA, international soccer, rugby. Contact: 12 Longford Terrace, Monkstown, Co Dublin. **M** 086 605 5952 email patsy@ireland.com

Highly respected journalist whose beat in religion has in recent times has become red hot news; amiable, motivated and totally professional.

MC GEADY, Andrew Colum; HEADMASTER/SCHOOL PRINICIPAL
b 1948; *m* Marita; 2s; *edu.* St. Eunan's College, Letterkenny, Co. Donegal; University College Dublin; B. Comm 1966-69; H. Dip. Ed; Trinity College Dublin; Dip. Comp Ed; M. Sc. Ed.Mgt; Headmaster, Castleknock College, Dublin; Teacher, housemaster, The Kings Hospital, Palmerstown, Co. Dublin; education officer NCCA; lecturer education, Methodolgy, Maynooth College, Co. Kildare; Publ. *Business Matters; In Business; Eagrú Gnó; Business Matters.* Contact: Castleknock College, Castleknock, Co. Dublin. **T** 01 821 4367 email amcgeady@ireland.com

A superb educator, has continued the long tradition of excellent all round education at this exclusive boys college; a high achiever who demands much of his staff and students, who mostly stand out as go-getters in their various careers.

Mc GEARY; Kieran Christopher; CEO, BEAT 102-103
b 1972, Waterford City; *m* Georgina; 2s 1d; *edu.* De La Salle College, Waterford; Luton College of Higher Education, Bedfordshire; Falmouth College of Art, Falmouth, Cornwall; HND Business & Finance (media & communications); Post Grad. Diploma in broadcast journalism; CEO, BEAT 102-103; worked extensively in the UK for the BBC as well as the commercial sector; launched Beat 102-103, Ireland's first regional radio station covering the South East; director, Waterford Chamber of Commerce; Garter Lane Arts Centre; vice chairman Independent Broadcasters of Ireland (IBI). Recreations: broadcasting, reading, Wolverhampton Wanderers, eating out. Contact: Broadcast Centre, Ardkeen, Waterford. **T** 051 849102 **F** 051 849103 email kieran@bear102/103.com

Popular and hardworking, brought much needed commercial and radio experience to Beat 102-103; respected among his national commercial broadcast executive peers.

Mc GEE, Harry; JOURNALIST
b 1965; partner Fiona Breslin; *edu.* Colaiste Iognaid, Galway; Colaiste na hOllscoile, Galway; King's Inn; BA, LLB, B-L; Journalist; *Connacht Tribune* 1989-92; *The Sunday Press* 1992-95; RTE 1995-98; *The Sunday Tribune* 1998-2000; editor of *Magill* 2000-01; *The Sunday Tribune* 2001-03; *The Irish Examiner* 2003 to date. Clubs: Mountaineering Council of Ireland. Recreations: mountaineering, rock climbing, GAA, Irish language; Contact: 5 Slade Row, Palatine Square, Dublin 7. **T** 01 679 3319 **F** 01 676 4483 email harrymcgee@eircom.net

The political editor of the *Examiner* brings a wide range of journalistic experience from newspapers and magazines; a good reputation for breaking stories and is a frequent radio contributor; a nice writing style, hardworker, good company.

Mc GINLEY, Dr. Aideen OBE; CIVIL SERVANT N.I.

b 1954, Derry; *m; 2s 1d*; edu. Salford University; BSc Hon Environmental Science 1975; UU MSc Social Policy Administration and Planning 1983; permanent secretary, Department of Culture, Arts and Leisure; honorary degree, University of Ulster 1998; honorary member of RSUA 2004; OBE 2000; planning officer, Donegal County Council; chief executive, Fermanagh District Council; director of development, Fermanagh District Council; community services officer, Strabane District Council; community services officer, Fermanagh District Council; permanent secretary, Department of Culture, Arts and Leisure 1999 to date; chair of the Cultural Forum; the NI 2012 Committee; member of the NI Committee of the British Council; NI Chief Executives' Forum; governor of St Michael's College, Enniskillen; formerly chair of the NI Millennium Company; trustee of the Northern Ireland Voluntary Trust; The Omagh Fund; director of Artspark NI; director of the NI Verbal Arts Centre; member of the NI Advisory Group of the Bank of Ireland; the UK Creative Industries Task Force; founding member in Northern Ireland and UK Member of the National Lottery Charities Board, now the Big Lottery Fund; the University for Industry UK Board and the Rural Development Council for Northern Ireland 2001; former chair of the BBC NI Appeals Advisory Committee; former director of the NI Tourism, Hospitality and Training Council; member of the PSEP EU Monitoring Committee; the Consultative Forum for Peace and Reconciliation; the NICVA Millennium Debate Group; the JCC Negotiating Council; former chairman and member of the Local Government Training Group; member of the Ministerial Steering Group who produced Strategy 2010, a review of the Northern Ireland economy; former chairman of Erne East ABSAG Group; chairman of Fermanagh Local Action Group – a local rural development partnership body; company secretary of Fermanagh Rural Community Initiative; chairman of the Western Regional Energy Agency Network; director of Fermanagh Enterprise and the Shannon Erne Waterways Promotions Ltd; member of the Community Development Review Group 1993; the Seven Year Review Committee for the University of Ulster 1997; represented the Society of Local Authority Chief Executives on the Voluntary Activity Unit Review of Community Services 1999; founder member of Playboard NI; Strabane's Citizens Advice Bureau; Strabane Workers Educational Association; participated in the PSTC Leadership Challenge Programme; the United States Information Agency; Distinguished Visitor Programme on Sustainable Economic Development; involved in distributing appeals airtime for charities and Children in Need monies within NI and the UK; in a voluntary capacity involved in a number of local community charitable initiatives including; work with Habitat for Humanity leading a NI team of 17 women to Thailand 2004; Publ. a number of papers and spoken in the United States, Europe, Africa, Australia and Japan on a variety of subjects in the field of leadership, local development, integrated strategic planning, future search and whole systems thinking and social and civic entrepreneurship. Recreations: Habitat for Humanity Build, knitting, reading, wellbeing, yoga, gardening. Contact: Permanent Secretary, Department of Culture, Arts & Leisure, Interpoint, 20-24 York Street, Belfast BT15 1AQ. **T** 028 90 258820 **F** 028 90 258831 email perm.sec@dcalni.gov.uk

As Permanent Secretary of the Department of Culture, Arts and Leisure in Northern Ireland is responsible for Cultural and Linguistic Diversity, Arts, Sports, Museums, Libraries, Ordnance Survey, Public Records Office, Inland Waterways and Fisheries; has worked in local government for 25 years and was formerly chief executive of Fermanagh District Council and previously director of development; much liked by her successive political masters, being efficient, pleasant and with no political side to her; believes in the ethics of responsibility as a public servant to the community in which she serves.

MC GINLEY, Paul; PROFESSIONAL GOLFER

b 1966, Dublin; *m* Alison; 1*s* 2*d*; *edu.* Dublin Institute of Technology; (Marketing Degree); University of Diego; International Business; professional golfer (21st in the world rankings); turned professional 1991; Tour Victories: Hohe Brucke Open 1996; Oki Pro-Am 1997; The Celtic Manor Resort Wales Open 2001; Smurfit Irish PGA Championship 2003; Volvo Masters 2005. Recreations: Formula One, music, football. Contact: Andrew 'Chubby' Chandler, International Sports Management Ltd, Cherry Tree Farm, Cherry Tree Lane, Rostherne, Cheshire, WA14 3RZ England. **T** 0044 1565 832 100 **F** 0044 1565 832 200 email ism@golfism.net web www.paulmcginley.net

Paul Mc Ginley

Extremely popular, one of Ireland's highest earning golf professionals, though his first love, until he was 19, was Gaelic football; a veteran Ryder Cup player, will go down in the annals of Ryder Cup history as the man who brought Sam Ryder's golden chalice back to Europe at The De Vere Belfry in 2002; his ten foot putt on the 18th green ensured a half in his last day singles match with Jim Furyk and sparked the joyous celebrations led by Captain Sam Torrance that went long into that memorable Sunday night; all Irish eyes will be on him to deliver another superb performance when Europe attempts to retain the Ryder Cup at the K Club in September 2006.

MACGONIGAL, Ciarán; ARTS CONSULTANT

b 1945, Dublin; single; *edu.* Ring College,Co.Waterford; Willow Park, Dublin, Catholic University School Dublin; University College Dublin; University of Florence; National College of Art, Dublin: Arts Consultant; Director MacGonigal Fine Arts 1981 – '83; Director Grafton Gallery 1983-'91;Director RHA Gallagher Gallery 1992-'98; Executive Director, The Hunt Museum Limerick 1998-'01; Strategic Co-ordinator Arts & Culture policy and Arts Report, Dublin City Council 2001-'03; (published 2004); Member Bank of Ireland Millennial Scholarship Awards Committee 2000 –'05; Fine Art Consultant and Cultural Strategist 2003 to date; Consultant to James Adam & Co. Dublin 2005 to date; Chairman, Art Advisory Committee, DublinCorporation 1980-'87 and 1988-'91; Board Member National Gallery of Ireland 1989-'98; Member of Design Committee An Post 1983-'04; Arts Council 1993-'98; Member of Hamilton Committee for Art Export Legislation 1985-'87; Member Millennial Celebration Committee for Dublin 1988; Government Bi-centenaire Committee to mark French Revolution. 1990-'98; Haverty Trust for acquisition of works of art for the State; Advisor, board member and chair SFX City Theatre; Dublin Member executive Board National College of Art & Design 2003-'06; Chair Independent Audit Review Group NCAD 2003-'06; *Publ:* Over 100 monographs ,essays and catalogues on art and artists; contributor to international lexicons; weekly columnist The Irish Times from 1988- '93 (The Opulent Eye); *The Church Silver of the Dioceses of Limerick and Limerick & Killaloe;* 2000 with the OPW; Recreations: L'art de l'escrime, equestrian sports, gardening, food and wine, the art of politics, opera, dance, theatre, collecting art, reading detective novels.Clubs: Royal Overseas (London) Contact: Ballymahon, Longwood, Co. Meath. **M** 086 3950 131 email cmacgonigal@ireland.com

Sartorially elegant, son of one of Ireland's greatest painters Maurice Mc Gonigal; gregarious, bon viveur, great raconteur; one of Ireland's leading art experts; keen observer of the transformation of contemporary Irish society; knowledgeable on a broad range of places and personalities, always in demand as a dinner guest.

Mc GONAGLE, Declan George; UNIVERSITY PROFESSOR

b 1952; *m* Mary Bernadette Carlin (Moira); 2*s*; *edu.* St. Columb's College Derry; College of Art Belfast (BA, Higher Dip Painting); Director of Irish Cultural Studies University of Ulster, Coleraine NI; lecturer in Fine Art Regenal Technical College 1976-78; organiser Orchard Gallery Derry 1978-84; director of exhibitions ICA London 1984-86; Visual Arts organiser Derry 1986-90; director Irish Museum of Modern Art, Dublin 1990- 2003; Awards, Sunday Tribune Visual Arts Award 1987; Publ. *An Outbreak of Frankness (*An Assessment, The Future Directions Of Community Art and the City Arts Centre Dublin (ed**).** Contact: Cromore Road, Coleraine, Co. Derry BT52 15A. **T** 048 7034 4141 **F** 048 9036 6872 email webmaster @ ulst.ac.uk web www. ulst.ac.uk

A likeable personality but with real steel in his backbone; saw down the challenge to his directorship and unseated the chairperson of his board in IMMA in the public eye and enormous and devastating rows damaging to all; having won his point he then left office; suffered some collateral damage, but re emerged as a powerful figure in cultural studies in Northern Ireland which is, one suspects, his natural bailiwick.

Mc GOVERN, Barry; ACTOR

b 1948; *m* Medb Ruane; 1*s* 1 ss; 1*d*; *edu.* Castleknock College, Dublin; University College Dublin; BA (NUI) 1970, Litt. D (Hons); Trinity College Dublin 1998; Actor; trained at Abbey School of Acting 1968-69; member, RTE Players 1971-74; member, Abbey Theatre Company 1978-81; member Arts Council 1984-88; artistic director of Opera Theatre Co 1989-91; composed music for many plays and co wrote lyrics and music for two musicals with Bryan Murray; Awards, Harvey's Theatre award for best actor for one-man Beckett show *I'll Go On,* produced by Gate Theatre 1985 (it has since traveled around the world); took major part in Gate Theatre's Beckett Festivals in Dublin 1991; New York 1996; London 1999; Playing Vladimir in *Waiting for Godot,* Clov in *Endgame;* films include *Joe Versus The Volcano; Far and Away; Brave Heart; The General; Waiting for Godo;* has recorded on CD the complete Beckett novels *Molloy, Malone Dies* and *The Unnameable;* board member, Pavilion Theatre, Dun Laoghaire. Clubs; Theatrical Cavaliers, Cricket Club. Recreations: music, rugby, football, James Joyce, cricket, Gilbert & Sullivan, Samuel Beckett. Contact: 31, Royal Terrace West, Dun Laoghaire, Co Dublin. **T** 01 280 6619

A highly intelligent and motivated actor who is unparalleled in his roles in the works of Samuel Beckett; a richly ironic stage presence; internationally acclaimed.

Barry Mc Govern

Mc GOWAN, Anthony Paul; CHARTERED ACCOUNTANT

b 1949, Dublin; separated; 1*s* 1*d*; *edu.* Franciscan College, Gormanston, Co. Meath 1962-67; Trinity College Dublin 1967-'71; BBS; Harvard Business School, Summer Executive Courses; fellow of the Institute of Chartered Accountants in Ireland; Tax Partner KPMG; trainee accountant 1971-74; corporate finance executive 1974-82; tax partner 1982 to date; Financial Services tax specialist 1998 to date; chairman KPMG Global Funds Network 1991-95; member Global Steering Group KPMG Bank Tax Network 1995-2001; chairman KPMG Ireland Tax Practice 1997-04; member of Council, Dublin Funds Industry Association (past president); ten years as member of Taoiseach's working group on the development of the funds industry in Ireland; Government appointee to EU Arbitration Panel on Transfer Pricing; member of the Irish Financial Services Industry (FSI) Tax Committee; seconded to Telecom Eireann as first head of treasury 1981-83. Clubs: Kildare Street & University Club, Dublin; Mount Wolseley Golf & Country Club, Carlow; Balbriggan Golf Club, Co. Dublin; Shillelagh District & Hunt Club. Recreations: golf, horse riding, cinema, politics, wine. Contact: 65a Upper Leeson Street, Dublin 4. **M** 087 744 1225 **F** 01 412 1225 email paul.mcgowan@kpmg.ie

> Another one of the brightest and best professionals in the Dublin accountancy scene, selected to advise the Taoiseach on developing the global funds management industry in Ireland.

Mc GRATTAN, Daniel 'Dan'; PUBLICAN/RESTRAUTEUR

b 1947, Dublin; *m* Anne (*decd*); 1*s* 1*d*; *p* Ann Doyle (*qv*); *edu.* Christian Brothers Synge Street, Dublin; Cathal Brugha College of Catering, Dublin; initially involved in the music business with Noel Pearson, Tribune Records 1980s; managed Billy Brown, Danny Doyle, The Dubliners; opened Trotters Restaurant, Fairview, Dublin 1980s; opened Mc Grattans Restaurant, Fitzwilliam Lane 1990; major refurbishment Bosey's Bistro and Wilde's Bar opened at Fitzwilliam Lane, Dublin 2006; has placed business for tender 2006. Recreations: music, GAA (The Dubs), racing, reading. Contact: 76, Fitzwilliam Lane, Dublin 2. **T** 01 881 8808

> Extremely popular, kind and hardworking restaureur whose eaterie provides a home from home for many of the politicians from Leinster House; has built up a very loyal clientele from both sides of the Atlantic; has decided to sell business to enjoy other pursuits.

McGUCKIAN, Alistair; BUSINESSMAN

b 1936; *m* Margery O'Donoghue; 2*s* 2*d*; *edu.* St. Mc Nissi's, Co. Antrim; Greenmount Agricultural College; National Dip Agr.; Founder/Chairman Masstock (Ireland) Ltd 1970 to date; recipient Honorary Doctorate of Laws (NUI) 1988; Honorary Doctorate, Agricultural Science (Queen's University Belfast) 1988; fellow, Royal Agricultural Societies and British Royal Agricultural Society; member, Powerscourt Golf Club, Fitzwilliam LTC; composer of musical composition *A Terrible Beauty* which he rewrote to become a full opera *The Ha'penny Bridge* which opened in Dublin's Point Theatre 2005. Recreations: piano, music, golf. Contact: Masstock (Ireland) Ltd. Crescent Hall, Mount Street Crescent, Dublin 2. **T** 01 662 8555.

> Having developed a very successful animal production system – the Masstock system, he transferred the technology to the Middle East in the 1980s; a renaissance man who has now channelled his resources both artistic and financial into his operatic production, *The Ha' Penny Bridge* which defied the critics and enjoyed an extended sold out season; still ambitious to make it on Broadway.

Mc GUCKIAN, John Brendan; CHAIRMAN ULSTER TELEVISION

b 1939; *m* Carmel Mc Gowan; 2*s* 2*d*; *edu.* St McNissi's College, Garrontower; Queen's University of Belfast, BSc; Chairman Ulster Television; chairman, Cloughmills Mfg Co. 1967; Ulster TV plc 1991; director, Munster & Leinster Bank 1972; Allied Irish Bank plc 1976 to date; Harbour GP Ltd. 1978 to date; Aer Lingus plc 1979-84; Unidare plc 1987 to date; chairman, Irish Continental Group plc 1988 to date; member, Derry Development Committee 1968-71; Laganside Corporation 1988-92; chairman, International Fund for Ireland 1990-93; Northern Ireland Industrial Development Board 1991 to date; Pro Chancellor, Queen's University, Belfast 1990 to date; chairman, Tedcastle Ltd 1996 to date. Contact: UTV Havelock House, Ormeau Road, Belfast, BT7 1EB. **T** 028 232 3281 22

> Successful businessman, one of the longest serving board directors on the island of Ireland; an active player in building cross border relations through his involvement in the International Fund for Ireland.

Mc GUCKIAN, Medbh Therese; POET

b 1950, Belfast; *m* John; *3s 1d*; *edu.* Dominican Convent, Fortwilliam; Queen's University Belfast; BA (English); MA; Dip Ed; Tutor In Creative Writing, Seamus Heaney Centre, Queen's University Belfast; writer in residence at several universities; international festivals and congresses, various literary programmes; *Publ.* 10 collections of poetry, Gallery Press, Co. Meath. Recreations: yoga, reading, walking. Contact: Queen's University, Belfast. **T** 028 90 245 133

> One of the major poetic voices to emerge from Northern Ireland, much published and translated, her themes are personal and to do with her feminism – nature, flowers, the house, pregnancy and birth.

Mc GUCKIAN, Rosheen; HEAD of G.E. MONEY, IRELAND

b N. Ireland; *m* Joey Mason; *1s 1d*; *edu.* St Gerards, Bray; Trinity College, B.A; DCU Masters; DCY Ph. D; DIT PG Dipl; head of GE Money, Ireland; PR director, GE Consumer Finance, Europe; head of change and communications, ESB Power Generator; director, Drury Communications. Contact: GE Money, 31-36 Golden lane, Dublin 8. **T** 01 405 2762 **F** 01 405 2880 email rosheen.mcguckian@ge.com

> Daughter of Alistair (*qv*) very talented, hard worker, high achiever, who from a background in public relations/ communications made a dramatic move to very successfully head up a significant financial institution.

Mc GUIRE, Cyril; CHAIRMAN, CEO, TRINTECH GROUP plc

b 1960; *m* Julie Cleary; *edu.* University College Dublin; B. Comm; MBS; chairman, chief executive officer and co-founder of Trintech Group plc; worked as an investment manager with the Industrial Credit Corporation plc; established Trintech, a leading provider of secure payment infrastructure solutions globally 1987; member, Marketing Institute of Ireland; member, Board of Directors of The Michael Smurfit Graduate School of Business; a regular speaker at various IT and software industry events and investment banking conferences; Awards: Entrepreneur of the Year for Technology, Ernst & Young, 1999; Company of the Year Award Irish Software Association. Recreations: sports, particularly rugby and golf. Contact: Trintech Group Plc, Trintech Building, South County Business Park, Leopardstown, Dublin 18. **T** 01 207 4000 **F** 01 207 4005 email: info@trintech.com web www.trintech.com

> Innovative and dynamic, recognised as a major player in global IT; invited to participate in the Government Trade Advisory Forum, chaired by the Minister for Trade & Industry which advises Government on national and international trade matters.

Mc GUINNESS, Alban; MEMBER, NORTHERN IRELAND ASSEMBLY

b 1950; *m* Carmel McWilliam; *3s 5d*; *edu.* St. Malachy's College, Belfast; University of Ulster (BA); Queen's University Belfast; Member of the Northern Ireland Assembly; Barrister at Law, NI Bar 1976; Member Belfast City Council 1985, 1989,1993,1997; Lord Mayor of Belfast 1997-98; General Election Candidate 1997-2001; MLA (SDLP) 1998; chair SDLP; chair Regional Development Committee; member EU Committee of the Regions 2002; governor Linen Hall Library. Recreations: walking, reading, theatre. Contact: 228, Antrim Road, Belfast BT15 4AN. Northern Ireland, Assembly, Parliament Buildings, Stormont Estate, Belfast BT4 3XX. **T** 028 9022 0520 **F** 028 9022 0522

Mc GUINNESS, Catherine; SUPREME COURT JUDGE / PRESIDENT OF THE LAW REFORM COMMISSION.

b 1934, Belfast; *m* Prionsias MacAonghusa (*decd*); *2s 1d*; *edu.* Dunmurray PE School, N.I.; Alexandra College and School; Trinity College Dublin; BA(mod); M.A; Kings Inns, BL; Supreme Court Judge and President of The Law Reform Commission; teacher; freelance writer 1957-61; parliamentary officer, Labour Party 1961-67; member Adoption Board 1970-77; Barrister at Law 1977-89; called to the Inner Bar, Senior Counsel 1989; member, Seanad Éireann 1979-87; chairperson National Social Sciences Board 1973-82; board member National College of Art & Design 1987; Employment Equality Agency 1988; member, Council of State 1988-91; chairperson Family Lawyers Association; VHI Board 1975-79; NESC 1982-83; member, General Synod of the Church of Ireland; Commission on the Status of Women; fellow International Academy of Matrimonial Lawyers; president the Law Reform Commission 2005. Recreations: choral singing. Contact: The Law Reform Commission, IPC House, 35-39 Shelbourne Road, Ballsbridge, Dublin 4.

T 01 6377600 **F** 01 6377601 email info@lawreform.ie web www.lawreform.ie

A quietly humorous person with a twinkle which disguises her strong beliefs and active brain; a formidable member of the Bench and an important social thinker and activist over many years.

Mc GUINNESS, Frank; DRAMATIST
b 1953, Buncrana, Co. Donegal; single; *edu.* Carndonagh College; University College Dublin; BA; M. Phil; Dramatist; Lecturer, Modern English, St. Patrick's College, Maynooth, Co. Kildare; previously lectured in the University of Ulster and University College Dublin; *Publ. The Factory Girls* (Abbey Theatre, Dublin) 1982; *Baglady* (Abbey Theatre) 1985; *Observe the Sons of Ulster Marching Towards the Somme* (Abbey Theatre) 1985, (Hampstead Theatre, London) 1986; *Innocence* (Gate Theatre, Dublin) 1986; *Cathaginians* (Abbey Theatre) 1988, (Hampstead) 1989; *Mary and Lizzie* (RSC) 1989; *The Bread Man* (Gate Theatre) 1991; *Someone Who'll Watch Over Me* (Hampstead, West End and Broadway) 1992; *The Bird Sanctuary* (Abbey Theatre) 1984; *Mutabilitie* (RNT) 1997; *Gates of Gold* (Gate Theatre) 2002; Translations: *Rosmersholm* by Henrik Ibsen (RNT) 1987; *Peer Gynt* by Henrik Ibsen (Gate) 1988, (RSC and world tour) 1994; *Hedda Gabler* by Henrik Ibsen (Roundabout Theatre, Broadway) 1994; *A Doll's House* by Henrik Ibsen (Playhouse Theatre, Broadway) 1997; *Three Sisters* by Anton Chekhov (Gate and Royal Court) 1990; *Uncle Vanya* by Anton Chekhov (Field Day Production) 1995; *Yerma* by Federico García Lorca (Abbey Theatre) 1987; *The Threepenny Opera* by Bertolt Brecht (Gate) 1987; *The Caucasian Chalk Circle* by Bertolt Brecht (RNT) 1997; *Electra* by Sophocles (Donmar and Broadway); *The Storm* by Alexander Ostrovsky (Almeida); screenplays: *Dancing at Lughnasa* (adaptation of play by Brian Friel; *Booterstown; Poems* 1994; Awards: numerous awards including *London Evening Standard* Award. Member, Aosdána. Contact: Aosdána, 70, Merrion Square, Dublin 2. **T** 01 618 0200 **F** 01 676 1302

A charming and shy man, who delights in company; a wonderful writer and inner visionary of the Irish condition, with great outbursts of stage energy and direction.

Mairéad Mc Guiness

Mc GUINNESS, Mariéad; MEMBER EUROPEAN PARLIMENT
b 1958, Drogheda, Co. Louth; *m* Tom Duff; 2*s* 2*d*; *edu.* Convent of Mercy National School Ardee; Ardee Community School; University College Dublin: B. Ag. Econ; Member, European Parliament; radio production RTÉ; researcher, *Late Late Show; Ear to the Ground* RTÉ Television 1993-04; editor *Farming Independent* 1997-2004; chairperson Guild of Agricultural Journalists (two terms); chair, Consumer Liaison Panel Dept. of Agriculture & Food 2004-09; East Constituency European Parliament 2004 to date; serves on many of the European Parliament's commitees: Agriculture and Rural Development Committee, Budget Committee, Petitions Committee, Delegation to the EU-Romania Joint Parliamentary Committee. Contact: Mentrim, Drumconrath, Navan, Co. Meath. **T** 041 685 4633 **F** 041 685 4634 email mmcguinness@europarl.eu.int web http://www.maireadmcguinness.ie

Ambitious and focused; made the dramatic transition from agri journalism to European politics as MEP for FG almost seamlessly; more than stood her corner in a closely fought competition where her biggest battle was with her own Party colleague Avril Doyle, who was also elected; the darling of the media is savvy, bright and vivacious and now faces a new challenge, does she stay in Europe or return to fly the FG flag in the next general election?

Mc GUINNESS, Martin; PUBLIC REPRESENTATIVE
b 1950, Bogside, Derry; *m* Bernie; 3*s* 2*d*; *edu.* Christian Brothers, Derry; Public Representative/Member of Parliament and Member of the Northern Ireland Assembly; Sinn Fein chief negotiator; MP (Sinn Féin) for Mid Ulster 1997 to date; second in command of Provisional IRA in Derry 1972; part of the delegation met with William Whitelaw, Secretary of State for Northern Ireland July 1972; served as chief negotiator for Sinn Féin 1990 to date; member Northern Ireland Assembly 1998 to date (Sinn Fein Mid Ulster); Minister for Education (prorogued 2002 to date) 1998-2001; contested Foyle for Sinn Féin 1983, 1992. Recreations: fishing, reading (favourite *Trout & Salmon* "which transports me to the lakes, rivers and mountains where I feel most at peace"). Contact: 32, Burn Road, Cookstown, Co. Tyrone BT80 9DN. **T** 048 3026 **F** 048 8676 6734

Some say "the Godfather of Godfathers"; pursued tactical and strategic processes and provided the militant cover for Gerry Adams' drift towards constitutional politics; by participating in regional government as Minister for Education he has proved his worth as a tactician and as an effective team player in parliamentary and cabinet terms; was regarded as a very successful and able Minister by the departmental Permanent Secretariat; depending on whom one asks, is loathed, feared or admired in almost equal measure; lives a stable, happy and domestic private life; a strong minded republican who won't be going away; a possible future minister and Tánaiste in a Dublin based Government in the not too distant future€

MC GUINNESS, Paul; FOUNDER PRINCIPLE MANAGEMENT /MANAGER U 2

b 1951, Rintelm, Hannover, Germany; *m* Kathy Gilfillan; 1*s* 1*d*; *edu*. Clongowes Wood College, Co Kildare; Trinity College Dublin ("no degree"); Founder Principle Management/ Manager U2; LL.D, National University of Ireland (UCD) (*hc*); holds numerous directorships including TV3 and Ardmore Studios; successful investments include; Ardmore Studios, McGuinness Whelan Music Publishing Limited; *Riverdance The Show*; The Mill; TV3; Principle Management clients include U2, PJ Harvey, Art Of Noise, Paddy Casey, Mytown; member, Irish US Alliance; former member, Arts Council of Ireland for 12 years; board member, Digital Media Development Ltd and of the School of Film and Drama at University College Dublin; The Millennium Committee; the Content Advisory Group of the Information Society Commission. Clubs: Stephens Green Club, Dublin, Groucho Club, London. Contact: Principle Management, 30/32, Sir John Rogerson's Quay, Dublin 2. **T** 01 677 7330

Well known and regarded throughout the world in both the film and music industries; gregarious, great company; main shareholder and founder of Principle Management Limited, one of the world's leading artiste management companies who have managed U2 from the start of their successful career.

Mc HUGH, Anna May née Brennan; MANAGING DIRECTOR, NATIONAL PLOUGHING ASSOCIATION

b 1934, Clonpierce, Ballylinan, Co. Carlow; *m* John McHugh; 1*s* 1*d*; *edu*. St. Bridget's, Athy, Co. Kildare, Domestic followed by Commercial course, three years in all; Managing Director and Secretary of the National Ploughing Association; secretary to founder of NPA 1951; secretary NPA 1956; MD NPA 1973; member of Local Enterprise Board; staff nominee to board KFM Radio; Awards: National Person of the Year Award 1998; Laois Millennium Person of the Year 2000. Clubs: Local Show Society, Local Drama Club, Irish Country Womens' Association, Community Association. Recreations: camogie (played for local clubs, county, province), organising events, activities, farming. Contact: Altona, Fallaghmore, Athy, Co. Laois. **T** 059 862 5125 **F** 059 862 5172 emailfurrow@eircom.net

Has made a name for herself as Queen of the Plough, running Ireland's largest outdoor exhibition – The National Ploughing Championships; forthright and direct she devotes her very considerable energies to the rural Ireland she so admires.

Mc HUGH, Fiona; DIRECTOR FALLON & BYRNE

b 1967, Dublin; *m* Paul Byrne; 1*d*; *edu*. Loreto College, St Stephen's Green, Dublin; University College Dublin; BA English and Philosophy; Director, Fallon & Byrne Food Specialists; Reuters European Parliament Correspondent 1992-94; The Economist Group, European Politics 1994-96; financial reporter, Dublin, Bloomberg 1996-97; business correspondent, *The Sunday Times* 1997-99; editor *The Sunday Times* 2000-05; director Fallon & Byrne Food Specialty Emporium. Recreations: food, fiction, travel. Contact: Fallon & Byrne, 11-17 Exchequer Street, Dublin 2. **T** 01 472 1000 email fiona@fallonandbyrne.com web www.fallonandbyrne.com

The highly respected journalist and former *Sunday Times* editor decided to follow her dream and switched from one of the plum career jobs in Irish journalism to join husband Paul Byrne (*qv*) and Brian Fallon (*qv*) to invest in Ireland's first serious food hall, wine cellar and restaurants under one roof in central Dublin; extremely bright, personable and energetic has brought the same enthusiasm to this project as she brought to the *ST* which flourished under her stewardship.

Mc HUGH, Kevin; FISHERMAN

b 1947; *m* Vera Ryan; 3*s* 1*d*; *edu*. National School, Castlebar, Co. Mayo; apprenticed to BIM; qualified at Skipper Level; Fisherman; owner Veronica (300 feet and 5200 gross tonnage) and Atlantic Dawn (485 feet and 15000 Gross Tonnage); company also owns fish processing factories in Norway, Killybegs and Morocco; former owner Cope House Hotel, Killybegs and Bayview House Hotel,

Killybegs. Contact: Atlantic Dawn Ltd., Elmwood Terrace, Killybegs, Co. Donegal. **T** 074 973 1644 **F** 074 973 1646 email info@atlantic-dawn.com web; www.atlantic-dawn.com

Very astute businessman who has grown his fishing business to a global scale; well connected politically, is highly respected in business and financial circles.

Mc KEE, William, Scott 'Will'; CHAIRMAN, AMTEC MEDICAL LTD
b 1945, Moy, Co. Tyrone; *m* Mary; 3*s* 1*d*; *edu*. Portadown College; University of Ulster, Jordanstown; Harvard Business School; MSc Business & Management; OPM Program at Harvard Business School; Chairman AMTEC Medical Ltd: early business career involved export marketing within the textile industry; since then has owned and managed food, LPG, pottery, dairy, packaging, construction, retailing and property corporations; led a successful buy-in to a major distribution business which ultimately resulted in a joint venture company associated with the Jefferson Smurfit Group 1983; business background includes service as a main board director of leading companies, Belleek Pottery, Mivan, Leckpatrick Holdings, Paul Costelloe, LEDU; Awards: special certificate from His Royal Highness Prince Philip, in recognition of his outstanding personal achievement in business education and training; currently chairman or director of a number of leading international companies including the Electricity Supply Board, Northern Bank; chairman of a private sector initiative for Invest Northern Ireland in support of the Accelerating Entrepreneurship campaign. Recreations: sailing, reading, rugby. Contact: 111, Ballymore Road, Tandragee, County Armagh BT62 2JY.
T 0044 7711 453 433 **F** 280 9446 0300 email wmckee@amtec-medical.com

A very successful NI businessman, who now sits on Ireland's largest semi state board; very close to Unionist Leader Sir Reg Empey; friendly and outgoing with a broad range of interests.

Mc KENNA, Felix; CHIEF SUPERINTENDENT, CRIMINAL ASSETS BUREAU.
b 1946, Monaghan; *m* Nuala; *edu*. Christian Brothers College, Monaghan; Chief Superintendent, Criminal Assets Bureau; joined An Garda Siochana 1965; moved through the CID side of the business; appointed chief superintendent 2000 to date; appointed head of Criminal Assets Bureau 2000 to date. Clubs: Westman's Town Golf Club. Recreations: golf. Contact: Garda Head Quarters, Phoenix Park, Dublin. **T** 01 666 0000 web www.angarda.ie

An experienced, affable, committed policeman; extremely high achiever at CAB focusing in on the drug barons and other criminal activity.

Mc KENNA, Mary; MANAGING DIRECTOR, TOUR AMERICA
b 1963, Portlaois, Co. Laois; single; *edu*. St. Joseph Cluny, Killiney, Dublin; started in the airline business 1983; studied at night in University College Dublin, marketing, communications, business studies; took pilots licence; worked as duty manger Club Air Dublin airport 1987-89; worked in American Holidays 1989-95; started Tour America 1995; managing director Tour America 1995 to date. Clubs: Old Conna Golf Club; Hermes Hockey Club. Recreations: photography, working out. Contact: 62 Middle Abbey Street, Dublin. **T** 01 817 3527 DL **T** 01 817 3500 email www.touramerica.ie

A consummate businesswoman, has built up an extremely successful travel/tour operator company in a relatively short time; a workaholic uses innovative marketing to attract new clients; was the first to specialize in the lucrative cruise market with over 10,000 cruise holidays sold in 2005; specializes in New York and Las Vegas; delivers a first class service.

Mary Mc Kenna

Mc KEON, Eamonn; CHIEF EXECUTIVE OFFICER, IRISH TOURIST INDUSTRY
b 1947, Sligo; *m* Carol O'Connor; 1*s* 2*d*; *edu*. Summerhill College, Sligo; Chief Executive Irish Tourist Industry Confederation; executive, Bord Fáilte 1966-69; Great Southern Hotel Group 1969-76; executive vice president, CIE Tours North America 1976-81; group hotels manager Great Southern Hotels Group 1981; chief executive Great Southern Hotels 1983-04; chief executive Irish Tourist Industry Confederation 2004 to date. Clubs: Dún Laoghire Golf Club. Recreations: golf, travel. Contact: 17 Longford Terrace, Monkstown, Co. Dublin. **T** 01 284 4222 **F** 01 280 4218 email itic@eircom.net web www itic.ie

After a lifetime in the hotel industry mostly with the Great Southern Hotel Group is now heading up the Irish Tourist Industry where he is deemed a safe pair of hands.

Mc KEON, Belinda; WRITER

b 1979, Cloonuny, Longford; single; *edu.* piano to certificate level; Trinity College Dublin (BA) 1998; University College Dublin (M.Litt) 2004; Masters of Fine Art (writing) Columbia University, New York, USA 2005-07; writer, short stories, fiction; Arts journalism (freelance) *The Irish Times* 2000-05; theatre criticism workshop facilitator Everyman Theatre Cork 2006; script reader Dublin Fringe Festival 2005; RTÉ Arts programmes (*The View* etc); Irish University Review, Dublin Review; Awards: Guardian Student Media Awards 2000; ESB National Media Awards; Costello & Littledale Prize for English Literature, Trinity College Dublin 1998; Bank of Ireland Millennial Scholarship for Creative Writing; member, TCD Players (Drama Group) and Literary Society; Publ. short stories, journalism, reviews/critical overview of the arts, The Irish Times; Contact; Cloonuny, Longford. **M** 087 634 9209 email belindamckeon@ireland.com

> A gifted young writer with an eye for the colour of sound, in speech and in nature; a considerable observer of the artist's dilemma; will go far!

Mc KEON, Mary Bernadette; HOTELIER

b 1958, Dublin; single; *edu.* Marist Convent, Carrig-on-Shannon, Co. Leitrim; Dublin College of Catering, Cathal Brugh Street, Dublin; hotel & catering management qualifications: Chief Operating Officer Monogram Hotels; international career: Marriott Hotels USA, four years; Regency Hotels USA, two years; Great Southern Hotels Ireland, 14 Years; general manager Galway Great Southern & group operations manager, based in HQ Dublin; currently COO Monogram Hotels; director Failte Ireland. Clubs: Sandymount Health & Leisure Club, Skal Club Galway (past president). Recreations: travel, music, yoga. Contact: Monogram Hotels, g Hotel, Wellpark, Galway, Co. Galway. **T** 091 865200 **F** 091 865 203 web www.ghotel.ie email mmckeon@monogramhotels.ie

Mary Mc Keon

Mc LAUGHLIN, Dermot; CHIEF EXECUTIVE, TEMPLE BAR PROPERTIES

b 1961; *m* Ursula Kennedy; *edu.* BA (early and modern Irish) M. Sc (Mgt) (Organisational Behaviour); Chief Xxecutive, Temple Bar Properties; formerly assistant director the Arts Council; director Irish Traditional Music Archive; Rough Magic Theatre Company; chairman Dublin International Dance Festival and The Theatre Shop; musician, broadcaster, writer; presented *The Raw Bar,* RTÉ 1 2004-05; Contact: 12, East Essex St. Temple Bar, Dublin 2. **T** 01 677 2255 **F** 01 677 2525 email dmclaughlin@templebar.ie

> Left the safety of the Arts Council for Temple Bar at a time when the shift in the tectonic plates of inner city living shifted again; there is much to do and not a lot of time in which to do it; brings his own sense of humour to the difficulties of the Quartier Culturel in Dublin.

Mc LAVERTY, Bernard Kieran; WRITER

b 1942, Belfast; *m* Madeline McGuckin; 1*s* 2*d*; *edu.* St. Malachy's College, Belfast; Queen's University Belfast (BA hons); Dip Ed; writer; moved to Scotland 1975; has been a medical laboratory technican, a mature student, a teacher of English, and writer in residence, University of Aberdeen; after living for a time in Edinburgh and the Isle of Islay now lives in Glasgow; currently visiting writer, Liverpool's John Moores University, and visting professor, Strathclyde University, Glasgow; many awards from the Arts Councils of Ireland, Northern Ireland and Scotland; has published four collections of short stories and is currently working on a fifth; four novels; Publ. *Secrets and other Stories* (Blackstaff Press) 1977; *Lamb* (a novel) 1980; *A Time To Dance and other Stories* 1982; *Cal* 1983; *The Great Profundo and other Stories* 1987; *Walking the Dog and other Stories* 1994; *Grace Notes* 1997; *The Anatomy School* (a novel) 2001; *Matters of Life and Death* 2006; screenplays; *Cal* (enigma) 1984; *Lamb* (flickers) 1985 ; *Bye Child* 2003; *Matters of Life and Death* 2006; *The Cone Gatherers* (with Saltire Films); drama documentary *Hostages* (Granada) 1992, HBO USA 1993; adaptation for television *The Real Charlotte* Granada/Gandon 1989. Contact: John Moore's University, Liverpool, Egerton Court, 2, Rodney Street, Liverpool, L3 5UX. **T** 0044 151 231 2121 web wwwljmu.ac.uk

> Despite his great success Bernard MacLaverty has no airs or graces - he is an interesting, courteous and hard working man and a sublimely talented writer some of whose stories are iconic in status such as *Lamb* and *Cal*

Mc LEAN, Peter; CONSULTANT UROLOGIST

b 1934; *m* Nuala; 1*s* 1*d*; *edu.* St. Eunan's College, Letterkenny, Co. Donegal; Royal College of

Peter Mc Lean

Surgeons in Ireland; M.S. Urol., F.R.C.S.I., F.R.C.S.Ed., F.R.C.S.Eng., F.A.C.S.; honorary fellow R.C.S. Glasgow; honorary fellow Academy of Medicine, Malaysia & Singapore; honorary fellow College of Medicine South Africa; graduated medical school 1958 with honours; general surgical training for three year period at The Charitable Infirmary, Jervis Street; completed full programme of post-graduate training at Mayo Clinic, Rochester, Minnesota; received Edward J. Noble Award for outstanding performance during years of training; Consultant Urologist; appointed consultant urologist/kidney transplant surgeon Charitable Infirmary Jervis Street 1968; appointed consultant urologist to Richmond Hospital 1976; played leading role in the initiation and promotion of kidney transplantation in the Republic of Ireland; elected Council of the Royal College of Surgeons in Ireland 1978; chairman, Academic Board; chairman, Admissions Board; elected vice president 1994; president 1996-98; nominated, Royal College of Surgeons in Ireland representative to International Federation of Surgical Colleges; elected vice president 2003; member Senate of Surgery of Great Britain and Ireland which involved the reforms in surgical education and examinations in Great Britain and Ireland 1994-98; Publ: 50 scientific publications in a variety of national and international medical journals. Clubs: invited member of British Urological Society "The Punch Club", Royal St. George Yacht Club, Dun Laoghaire. Recreations: Connemara pony beeder, walking, relaxing in holiday home in Co Donegal, love of nature and literature. Contact: 14 Ailesbury Road, Dublin 4. **T** 01 269 5361 **F** 01 2695244 email pmclean@eircom.net

Internationally experienced and acclaimed consultant urologist; was appropriate person appointed by Board of Beaumont Hospital to deal with Beaumont Hospital disciplinary matters.

Mc LELLAN, Andrew Thomas; ARTS MANAGER
b 1972, Belfast; partner; *edu.* Methodist College Belfast; Pembroke College, University of Oxford; MA(Music)Oxon; Trinity College Dublin; B.Th (Theology); University College Dublin, H Dip Arts Administration; Chief Executive Opera Theatre Company; producer Fabulous Beast Company 2000; manager Opera Theatre Company 2000-02; artistic administrator 2002-03; chief executive officer Opera Theatre Company 2003 to date; Recreations: reading, theatre, film, opera, classical music; Contact: Opera Theatre Company, Temple Bar Music Centre, Dublin 2. **T** 01 679 4962 **F** 01 679 4963 email amclellan@opera.ie

Heads up a small but important opera company and makes it work for the industry.

Mc LELLAND, Dr. William Morris; CEO, BLOOD TRANSFUSION SERVICE, N.I.
b 1945; *m* Margaret Christine Robinson; 1*s* 2*d*; *edu.* Portadown College, Queen's University, Belfast; MB BCh, BAO; FRC Path.; Chief Executive Blood Transfusion Service Northern Ireland; chief executive N.I. Blood Transfusion Service 1980 to date; honorary lecturer Haematology, Queen's University Belfast 2001; contact: Northern Ireland Blood Transfusion Service, Belfast City Hospital, Lisburn Road, Belfast BT9 7TS. **T** 028 9032 1414

Leads a vital service in Northern Ireland with distinction and is a good strategist for the entire area within the region of the Province.

Mc LOUGHLIN, Kyran; STOCKBROKER/ PROPERTY DEVELOPER
b 1944, Galway; *m* 1st Susan Warner (*m. diss*); 1*s* 1*d*; *p* Renagh Mc Donald; 1*d*; *edu.* Blackrock College, Dublin; University College Dublin; Stockbroker/Property Developer; joined Davy Stockbrokers; appointed chief executive Davys; resigned joint chief executive and director "for personal reasons" 1999; chairman, Elan Plc. Clubs: Blackrock RFC, Milltown Golf Club. Recreations: golf. Contact: Davy House, 49, Dawson Street, Dublin 2. **T** 01 679 7788 **F** 01 671 2704 web www.davy.ie

One of the country's most successful stockbrokers with a meteoric rise through the ranks to the top slot in Ireland's largest stockbroking firm; has now diversified into property and has a substantial portfolio at home and abroad; sharp commercial brain, also chairs controversial pharmaceutical company Elan.

McMANUS, Brigid Mary; SECRETARY GENERAL DEPARTMENT OF EDUCATION AND SCIENCE
b 1958, Drogheda, Co Louth; *m* Noel Doyle; 1*s*; *edu.* Manor House Secondary School, Raheny,

Dublin 5; University College Dublin; Ecole Nationale D'Administration, Paris 1990–91; BA (Hons), History and Economics; International Diploma in Public Administration; Secretary General, Department of Education and Science; Civil servant in various departments of Finance and Arts, Heritage, Gaeltacht and the Islands - previous positions include assistant secretary general, dealing with tax policy in Dept of Finance 2000–02. Contact: Dept. of Education and Science, Marlborough Street, Dublin 1. **T** 01 8892107 **F** 01 8747013 email secgen@education.gov.ie web www.education.ie

> As principal officer in the Dept of Arts and as advisor to Minister Sile deValera, her fire brigade skills were remarkable even by the standards of the public service; her sense of duty and obligation to the public welfare and interest are outstanding; as an Assistant Secretary in Finance has showed great tactical skill and as Secretary General in Dept of Education and Science, her powers of analysis and delivery will be needed in an over-large and politically sensitive spending department of State; she may yet rank along such greats in the public service as Noel Dorr (*qv*) and TK Whitaker (*qv*).

Mc MANUS, John P; BUSINESSMAN, RACEHORSE OWNER; GAMBLER

b 1953, Co. Limerick; *m* Noreen; 3*s* 2*d*; *edu.* Christian Brothers School Limerick; Businessman/Racehorse Owner/Gambler; started life as a cattle drover for his father; poker player, punter extraordinaire; race horse owner; Clubs: Kildare Hotel and Country Club, Co. Kildare. Recreations: GAA, racing, reading. Contact: Martinstown Stud Farm, Kilmallock, Co. Limerick. **T** 063 88234

> The 'Sundance Kid' is a legend in his own lifetime; one of the shrewdest businessmen anywhere; like Midas everything he touches turns to gold - horses, investments, property all over the world; very low profile, charming, great company; extraordinary loyal to his friends; his JP Mc Manus Pro Am Golf Classic attracts all the top international players who love to spend time as his guest in Ireland; the millions it generates plus much more is distributed to charities throughout the Limerick area.

Mc MANUS, Liz née O'Driscoll; PUBLIC REPRESENTATIVE

b 1947 (Montreal); *m* Dr. John McManus; 3 *s* 1*d*; *edu.* Holy Child Convent, Killiney; University College Dublin: B. Arch; Public Representative; practised as an architect, Derry, Galway, Dublin, Wicklow 1969-73; homemaker 1973-92; writer/columnist 1981 to date; elected Democratic Left (now Labour) Dáil Deputy for Wicklow 1992 to date; Minister for Housing and Urban Renewal (Rainbow Coalition) 1994-97; Spokesperson on Agriculture and Food, Equality and Law Reform, Health 1993; Publ. *Acts of Subversion* (novel) - nominated for Aer Lingus/Irish Times Award; awards: Irish P.E.N. Award (short stories) 1984, Hennessy Literary Award and Listowel Award 1989; chairperson Taskforce on the Needs of the Travelling Community 1992-94; elected deputy leader of the Labour Party 2002; currently Labour's spokesperson on Health; Recreations: writing, reading, hill walking. Contact: Dáil Eireann, LeinsterHouse, Kildare Street, Dublin2. **T** 01 618 340901 **F** 01 618 4307 email liz.odonnell@oireachtas.ie web www.lizodonnell.ie

> Daughter of late Dr. Tim O'Driscoll, one of the State's most prominent public servants, former ambassador and Head of Board Failte; novel nominated for Aer Lingus / Irish Times Award, short stories received Irish P.E.N. Award, 1984, Hennessy Award and Listowel Award, 1989.

Liz Mc Manus

Mc MANUS, Padraig; CHIEF EXECUTIVE, E.S.B.

b 1951 Kildare; *m* Marie O'Brien; 1*s* 1*d*; *edu.* Naas C.B.S; University College Dublin, B. Eng (Electrical); Fellow Institute of Engineers; Chief Executive ESB; ESB International Business 1973-81; Charles T. Main (Middle East) 1981-83; returned to ESB and held various positions 1983 to date; became MD ESBI and commercial director ESB implementing the PACT Agreement; appointed chief executive and director ESB (Electricity Supply Board) 2002; board member Irish Management Institute, Business in the Community, Advisory Board of Ireland Aid. Clubs: Naas GAA, Naas Golf Club; Recreations: golf, gaelig games; Contact: ESB Head Office, 22, Lower Fitzwilliam Square, Dublin 2. **T** 01 702 6319 **F** 01 661 5382 email padraig.mcmanus@esb.ie web www.esb.ie

> The Naas resident took over as chief executive of the ESB, Ireland's largest semi-state company in 2002; has delivered increased profits each year through cost efficiency and revenue growth; highly intelligent, personable engineer he is an avid Kildare GAA supporter; played minor hurling and football for his county and won a Dublin Co.

Under 21 medal with UCD. He was actively involved in developing the state of the art GAA centre and pitches in his native town.

Mac MENAMIN, Cecily; DIRECTOR BROWN THOMAS GROUP plc
b 1941, Dublin; *m* Joseph Mac Menamin; *2d*; *edu.* Convent of the Holy Child, Killiney, Dublin; Ling Physical Training College, Dublin; Director, Brown Thomas Group plc; fashion buyer Brown Thomas 1964-70; director Brown Thomas Group plc 1976 to date; awards: Satzenbrau Buyer of the Year Award 1991; member UK Fashion Council; Recreations: cooking, gardening, travel reading. Contact: Brown Thomas Group plc, Grafton Street, Dublin 2. **T** 01 605 6666

A smart stylish and inventive leader of Dublin fashion; with great flair and an undoubted eye, many a smart fashionista owes her start to her impeccable taste and quite a few men in the fashion business owe a debt to her for developing their eye as to the good, the smart and the terrific.

Mc NAMARA, Bernard; PROPERTY DEVELOPER;
b 1951, Co. Clare; *m* Moira; *3s 2d*; *edu.* St. Flannan's College, Ennis; College of Commerce Rathmines, Dublin; Chief Executive Officer Michael Mc Namara Ltd; built up the construction company started by his father into one of the biggest and most successful in Ireland; extensive interests in Boston, Mass. US; member Irish US Alliance. Clubs: Kildare Hotel and Country Club. Recreations: golf, GAA. Contact: Michael McNamara & Co Building Contractors, Grattan Bridge House, 3 Upper Ormond Quay, Dublin 7. **T** 01 872 5311 **F** 01 873 3084 email: info@mcnamaraconstruction.com web www.mcnamaraconstruction.com

The low-key man from Clare, one time FF councillor remains loyal to the Party where he is extremely well connected; has evolved from being a builder to an acquirer of extensive property investments; currently developing the School for the Blind, Merrion Road, Dublin site with Jerry O'Reilly (*qv*) with whom he has several joint ventures – hotels Raddison SAS, Galway; the landmark Shelbourne Hotel, Dublin; Superquinn Supermarkets et al; acquired the Great Southern Hotel Parknasilla, 2006; remains close to his Clare roots, his corproate logo colours are also the Clare GAA teams colours which he sponsors.

Shelley Mc Namara

Mc NAMARA; Shelley; DIRECTOR, GRAFTON ARCHITECTS
b 1952, Co Clare; *m* Michael Kane; *edu.* Convent of Mercy, Spanish Point, Co Clare, School of Architecture, University College Dublin, Bachelor of Architecture, Fellow of Royal Institute of Architects of Ireland (RIAI); Director Grafton Architects. In private practice since 1977; studio tutor in School of Architecture UCD since 1977; visiting tutor/lecturer to other European Schools of Architecture including Milan, Stockholm, Oslo & Mendrislo; member, Aosdana, 2006. *Publ. Profile: Grafton Architects* (Gandon Editions 1999), *University Builders, Martin Pearce, Wiley Academy* 2001; *La Biennale Venezia, Next, 8th International Arch Exhibition* 2002, *Phaidon Atlas of Contemporary World Architecture*; Recreations: art, music, literature, "the ordinary, the humourous, the profound"; Contact: Grafton Architects, 12 Dame Court, Dublin 2. **T** 01 671 3365 **F** 01 671378 email admin@graftonarchitects.ie

An important architect designer with an interest as a drawing architect in the built environment; greatly respected and liked by her professional colleagues; good company and highly sociable although not very visible in the social whirl.

Mc NICHOLAS, Walter Thomas; MEDICAL DOCTOR AND DIRECTOR
b 1951; *m* Nuala; *1s 3d*; *edu.* Blackrock College, Dublin; University College Dublin; MB. BCh. BAO; NUI; MD (by thesis); NUI 1982; FRCPI 1980; FRCP(Canada); FCCP; 1986 director Pulmonary & Sleep Disorders Unit St. Vincent's University Hospital Dublin 1986; consultant respiratory physician: St. Vincent's University Hospital Dublin, National Maternity Hospital Dublin, St. Luke's National Cancer Hospital Dublin; Director, Respiratory Education Centre, St. Vincent's University Hospital, Dublin 1985 to date; Medicine residencies: University of Alberta and University of Toronto, Canada 1975-79; Respiratory Medicine Residency, University of Toronto 1979-81; Medical Research Council (Canada) Fellowship, University of Toronto 1981-82; Sleep Research Laboratory; lecturer in Medicine University College Dublin 1983-84; president-elect (2002-3), president (2003-4), past-president (2004-5) European Respiratory Society; member steering committee Structure Committee and Executive 1994-96; president Irish Thoracic Society 1995-97; president Royal Academy of

Medicine in Ireland 1992-95; chairman British Sleep Society 2000-01; Chair nominations Committee (American Thoracic Society) Respiratory Neurobiology and Sleep (RNS) Assembly 1999-2000; member programme committee RNS Assembly; member Nominations Committee RNS Assembly 1998-99; EU Commission Member Concerted Action on Methodology for the Analysis of Sleep Wakefulness; *Publ.* 132 Papers in peer reviewed journals and book chapters; Clubs: Fitzwilliam LTC, Dúnlaoghaire Golf Club; Elm Park (tennis member); Recreations: tennis, golf, music, photography; Contact: St. Vincent's University Hospital, Elm Park, Dublin 4. **T** 01 260 1118 or 01 269 4533 ext 3702 **F** 01 269 7949 email walter.mcnicholas@ucd.ie

Walter Mc Nicholas

> Leading expert on sleep apnoea, an increasingly common sleep disorder; one of the
> founding members of the respiratory medicine department at St Vincent's Hospital

Mc REDMOND, Desmond Francis ; DIRECTOR, EIRCOM Plc
b 1962, Dublin; *m* Penny; 1*s* 2*d*; edu. Gonzaga College, Dublin 6; University College, Dublin; MA; Commercial Director Eircom plc; chief executive WH Smith Inc; managing director WH Smith Travel; operations director Waterstones; Contact: 17, Spencer Villas, Glenageary, Co. Dublin. **T** 01 701 5973 email dmcredmond @eircom.ie

Mc SHARRY, Marc; SENATOR
b 1973, Dublin; *m* Marie; 1*s*; Castleknock College, Castleknock; Senator; Irish Permanent, Customer Advisor 1992–1995; General Manager Baltinglass Meats Ltd, Co Wicklow 1995–2000; CEO Sligo Chamber of Commerce 2000 to date; member Oireachtas (FF) 2002 to date; Recreations: amateur drama, reading, rugby (spectator) and most sports. Contact: Seanad Éireann, Leinster House, Kildare Street, Dublin 2. **T** 01 618 4221 **F** 01 618 4357 email mmacsharry@oireachtas.ie

> Bright, articulate, one of the new generation of modern, young FF politicians; son of
> the former European Commissioner Ray Mc Sharry, is carving out a niche as a Fianna
> Fail Senator.

Mc VERRY, Rev Peter S.J; PRIEST, SOCIAL ACTIVIST
b 1944, Belfast; single; *edu.* Abbey Primary SchooL, Newry, Co. Down; Clongowes Wood College, Co.Kildare; entered Jesuit Order 1962; University College Dublin (B.Sc Chemistry); Philosophy Milltown Park College; Priest/Social Activist; Teacher Belvedere College; ordained Priest 1975; opened hostel for young, homeless boys 1979; founded Arrupe Society 1983; conferred honorary fellowship Royal College of Surgeons in Ireland 2004; *Publ. The Meaning Is In The Shadows*; articles and contributions to the print and broadcast media; Contact: Pedro Arrupe Community, 21 Mc Donagh Terrace, Dublin 9. **T** 01 842 8419 or Jesuit Faith and Justice Centre, 26, Upper Sherrard Street, Dublin 1. **T** 01 874 0814

> His life was changed in 1974 when he and two confrères went to live in a tenement in
> Summerhill in Dublin's North Inner City; his outrage and shock at the living
> conditions of the people led him to found a hostel for homeless youngsters and 1983
> he founded the Arrupe Society named after Pedro Arrupe the great Jesuit and "Man
> for others" providing care and accommodation for homeless boys between the ages of
> 15-18 years; working the ground for over 30 years he has challenged the State to
> provide for the most helpless and weak in society, stressing social justice with dignity
> and respect; as a defender of the poor and homeless he states his case with clarity and
> conviction; a turbulent priest who continues his mission of rescue and support for the
> undertow with a sense of authority and not without charm in so doing.

Mc WILLIAMS, David; ECONOMIST, JOURNALIST, BROADCASTER, COMMENTATOR
b 1968, Dublin; *m* Sian; 1*s* 1*d*; *edu.* Blackrock College, Dublin; Trinity College Dublin; College of Europe Bruges, Belgium; Economist, Broadcaster, Journalist, Commentator; currently hosts *"The Big Bite"* on RTE, Columnist *Irish Independent, Sunday Business Post*; regular appearances as an economist on CNN, CNBC and the BBC; presented a current affairs programme 'Agenda' on TV3; economist at the Central Bank (helped draft the Irish submission to the Maastricht Treaty; advised the authorities during the 1992-93 exchange rate crisis) 1990-93; headed the number 1 rated European Economics Department for UBS - Europe's largest bank, analysing, advising and investing in all major European economies and markets; was the first economist to predict the 1990s boom in Ireland; in-depth report on Ireland, its economy and its prospects 1994; head of emerging markets research, Banque Nationale de Paris (mainly focused on Russia, Israel and the former Yugoslavia) 1996-98; global strategist

Rockwest Capital, New York based hedge fund 1999-2002; Publ. *The Popes Children, The New Irish Elite* 2005; Contact: Iconic Media Ltd, 20 Upper Merrion Street, Dublin 2. **T** 01 676 4573 email info@davidmcwilliams.ie web www.davidmcwilliams.ie

Ambitious, charming and clever, brings a new dimension to media savvy; master of the sound byte but did not, however, conjure up the phrase Celtic Tiger, which is so often attributed to him (it was coined by British economist Kevin Gardiner).

MACKEY, David Edward; CHIEF EXECUTIVE ELLIOT & COMPANY
b 1949; Co Donegal; *m* Marian O'Donovan; 2*s* 1*d*; *edu.* St. Eunan's College Letterkenny, Co. Donegal; Institute of Public Administration, Landsdowne Road, Dublin 4; LL.D. (*hc*) National University of Ireland 2004; Chief Executive Elliott & Co; Irish Local Government Service 1967-89 during which time positions included: director Donegal Regional Development Organisation, assistant county manager South Tipperary County Council, and county manager Cavan County Council; six years as Group general manager The Quinn Group 1989-95, followed by four years as Group chief executive 1995-99; property development business in partnership, The Elliot Family, Cavan 1999; chief executive P. Elliot & Co Ltd; non executive director of EirGrid Plc; chairman Croke Park Executive Committee; chairman Central Fisheries Board; Director Cavan County Enterprise Fund Company; Clubs: Stephen's Green Hibernian Club, Dublin 2. Recreations: philately, music, gardening, avid collector; Contact: Drumaughra House, Drumaughra, Cavan, Co Cavan. **T** 049 433 1066 **F** 049 4331537 email d.mackey@pelliott.com

The low profile, focussed, quietly spoken property developer is closely identified with Fianna Fail in his native Cavan.

MACRI, Joe; CHIEF EXECUTIVE, MICROSOFT, IRELAND
b 1963, Sydney, Australia; *m*; 1*s* 1*d*; *edu.* B.Sc. (Computer Science); MBA Warwick University UK; Chief Executive Microsoft Ireland; worked in a number of IT firms in his native Australia before moving to the UK; joined Microsoft UK 1996; held various management positions; marketing manager Microsoft Irl 1999– 2001; country manager Microsoft Ireland 2001–05; chief executive Microsoft Ireland 2005 to date; chairman, Small Business Forum (government appointee) 2005 to date; Recreations: sailing, golf. Contact: Carmen Hall Road, Sandyford Indisutiral Estate, Dublin 18. **T** 01 295 3826 www.microsoft.com

The popular Australian brought a wealth of experience to the Irish Microsoft division and has successfully expanded the company since he arrived here; his expertise has also been tapped by the Government who appointed him Chair of the Small Business Forum.

MADDEN, Anne; ARTIST
b 1932, London; *m* Louis le Brocquy (*qv*); 2 *s*; *edu.* Wychwood School Oxford; Chelsea School of Arts and Crafts, London; 2004 LL.D.(hc) University College, Dublin; Artist; of Irish and Anglo-Chilean origin; her work hangs in major international public and private collections, including Contemporary Art Society (London), Gulbenkian Foundation (Portugal), Ulster Museum, J.H. Hirshhorn Foundation (Washington D,C.), Neuberger Museum (New York); Foundation Maeght (St. Paul, France), Musée d'Art Moderne de la Ville de Paris, Musée Picasso (Antibes); Musée d'Art Moderne et d'Art Contemporain (Nice); Crawford Municipal Gallery (Cork); Hugh Lane Municipal Gallery of Modern Art (Dublin); Irish Museum of Modern Art (Dublin); represented Ireland at the Paris Biennale, 1965, has exhibited with Leicester Galleries, London, the Dawson, Taylor and Kerlin Galleries (Dublin), Gimpel Weitzenhoffer Gallery (New York) 1970, Ulster Museum 1974, Gallery Maeght (Barcelona), Armstrong Gallery (New York), Galerie Jeanne Bucher (Paris), Foundation Maeght, 1983; New Arts Centre (London) 1970-90; major Retrospective at the RHA Gallagher Gallery (Dublin) 1991; Galerie Maeght, Paris 1996, Imaginaire Irlandais, Hugh Lane Municipal Gallery of Modern Art, Dublin 1997; Butler Gallery, Kilkenny, 1998; Chateau de Carros 1998; New Art Centre, Roach Court, England 2005; Centre Culturel Irlandais, Paris 2005; Publ. *Louis le Brocquy: Seeing His Way* (Gill & Macmillan 1993); Documentary: *Anne Madden Painter and Muse* (Mind the Gap Films), 2005; member Aosdána; Contact: Taylor Galleries, 16, Kildare Street, Dublin 2. **T** 01 676 6055

Anne Madden

A lively and attractive driven arts personality; her own work very much in the French contemporary métier, delicate, assured of touch and full of light and energy; doesn't tolerate fools easily.

MADDEN, Elizabeth Ann 'Liz'; MUSICIAN

b 1971, Dublin; single; *edu.* St. Paul's Secondary School, Greenhills, Dublin 12; London School of
Music; Diploma; Singer/Songwriter with the Irish duo Rua, director of RuaMusic Publishing Ltd;
started her song-writing career at a young age and had recorded and produced many original
compositions before joining the Irish duo RUA; as a member of RUA, has co-written and recorded
three albums, *Rua, Dream-Teller* and *Whisper*; has performed worldwide. 2006 sees Rua in preparation
for their next album; voice teacher; currently writing a set of children's books. Recreations: music,
horseriding, history, film, theatre. Contact: Sandyridge, Red Bog, Blessington, Co. Wicklow.
T 087 637 4034 email liz@ruaworld.com web www.ruaworld.com

> One of the stunning duo, a supremely talented composer/musician; with Rua partner
> Gloria Mulhall (*qv*) has established an international reputation for their Celtic
> /traditional music a cross between Puccini and Enya (*qv*).

MAGEE, Jimmy; SPORTS COMMENTATOR RTE

b 1935, New York; *m* Marie (decd); 2*s* 3*d*; *edu.* Monksland, Caryford, Co. Louth; Bush Vocational
College, Carlingford; University of Life; Sports Commentator RTE; Pharmaceutical clerk, Dundalk;
Greenore Railway; transferred to British Rail, Dublin; freelanced with UTV and in the US; joined
RTE 1956; presenter 'Sunday Sport' 1973 to date; 44th year to commentate Sunday radio live 2005;
has covered: 12 Olympic Games, 11 World Cup Football series; columnist *Sunday World* 1973 to date
(never missed a week); *Publ. I Remember It Well* (autobiography); seven songs, numerous quiz books,
Recreations: all sport, especially GAA, soccer, golf, racing, athletics, boxing. Contact: RTE,
Montrose, Donnybrook, Dublin 4. **T** 01 208 3111 **F** 01 208 3080 web www.rte.ie

> The 'Memory Man' is a legend in is own lifetime; not only has he covered every
> conceivable sport since 1956, is a walking encyclopedia on the results, dates and
> sportsmen and women involved; became part of the news himself when his horse (co-
> owned with family) Redundant Pal won 14 races; extraordinarily hardworking, totally
> committed, extremely generous with his vast store of knowledge; a tireless worker for
> charity; a thoroughly decent man.

MAGEE, Most Rev John; BISHOP OF CLOYNE

b 1936, Newry; single; *edu.* The Abbey, CBS Newry; St. Colman's College, Newry; University College
Cork; Lateran University, Rome; BA; STL; Bishop of Cloyne. Ordained 1962; principal Obadu
Training College, Nigeria 1962-65; principal Ezillo School, Nigeria 1965-68; Procurator General of
St Patrick's Missionary Society 1968-69; Official for the Congregation for the Propagation of the
Faith 1969-75; private secretary to the Pope 1975-82; Master of Pontifical Ceremonies 1982-87;
Apostolic Administrator of Limerick 1994-96; Bishop of Cloyne 1987 to date. Contact: Cork, Cloyne
and Ross Diocesan Centre, Cobh Street, Cork. **T** 021 427 2262

> Remote, low profile, the Northern Ireland native spent many years in the upper
> echelons of the Vatican prior to taking up his appointment as Bishop of Cloyne; many
> ecclestical observers expected him to return to Vatican City by now, the Red Hat still
> eludes him.

MAGNIER, John; RACEHORSE BREEDER/ PROPERTY DEVELOPER

b 1948, Fermoy, Co. Cork; *m* Susan O'Brien; 3*s* 2*d*; *edu.* Glenstall Abbey, Murroe, Co. Limerick;
Master of Coolmore Stud Farm with satellite farms in Versailles, Kentucky and Australia; appointed
by Taoiseach Charles J. Haughey to Seanad Éireann; together with business associate J. P. McManus
(*qv*) built up a 28.89 per cent shareholding in Manchester United F.C.; May 2005 sold to Malcolm
Glazer; his business interests now span healthcare, hotels, technology and property internationally.
Clubs: Kildare Hotel and Country Club; The Green Monkey, Sandy Lane, Barbados Turnberry Island,
Miami; Valderama, Spain, La Zagaleta, Nueve Andalucia, Spain; Sunningdale Golf Club, UK;
Contact: Coolmore, Fethard, Co. Tipperary. **T** 052 31298 **F** 052 31382 web www.coolmore.com

> A combination of Magnier's brilliant analysis of bloodlines, and the exquisite training
> skills of his father-in-law Vincent O'Brien, made him the stuff of legend; together with
> the late Robert Sangster, he built up a multi-million dollar bloodstock business and
> became the most powerful breeder in the world; has swerved around publicity like a
> steeplechaser side-stepping an adjacent faller; hit the international headlines when a
> personal friendship with Man. Utd manager Alex Ferguson was tested in a dispute over
> bloodstock rights to the co-owned horse Rock of Gibraltar; his business interests include

John Magnier

a major property portfolio in UK, Spain, US; investor in Sandy Lane Hotel with JP Mc Manus (*qv*) and Dermot Desmond (*qv*), technology, leisure, nursing homes and currency speculation; an extremely loyal and generous friend and a formidable adversary.

MAGUIRE, Conor J; BARRISTER

b 1946, Co. Mayo; *m* Louisa MacAllister; 2*s* 2*d*; *edu*. National School, Claremorris, Co. Mayo; Clongowes Wood College, Co. Kildare; University College Dublin BCL; Kings Inns, BL; Barrister, Senior Council. Called to the Bar 1971; Senior Counsel, Western Circuit; called to the Inner Bar 1984 and to the Middle Temple, London; wide general practice; chairman Broadcasting Commission of Ireland (formerly Independent Radio Television Commission); Clubs: Galway County Club; Recreations: theatre, travel, cooking, wine, current affairs; Contact: The Law Library, PO Box 2424, Four Courts, Dublin 7. **T** 01 872 0622 **F** 01 872 0455

An amiable and socially inclined barrister who has steered the Broadcasting Commission with care and due diligence; a High Court Seat in accordance with a long standing family tradition cannot be far off now.

MAHER, Alice; VISUAL ARTIST

b 1956; *m* Dermot Seymour; *edu*. University of Limerick; Crawford College of Art; University of Ulster; MA Fine Arts: San Francisco art Institute; Visual Artist; represented Ireland at Sao Paolo Biennale 1994; nominated for Glen Dimplex Award 1996; exhibitions include: 'Familiar' Douglas Hyde Gallery, Dublin 1995; Swimmers, Le Credac, Paris 1996; 'Coma Berenices' Hugh Lane Municipal Gallery, Dublin 1999; Books covers include *Are you Somebody?* (Nuala O Faolain) *Greetings to Our Friends in Brazil* (Paul Durcan); collaborated with composer Trevor Knight on the performance of The Sky Chair 1998; Member of Aosdána; Contact: Aosdána, 70, Merrion Square, Dublin 2. **T** 01 618 0200 **F** 01 676 1302

No Irish overseas exhibition is complete without the presence of work by this artist; she is regarded as practical, pragmatic and tough but with lots of charm; has been prominent in representing women's imagery, in exhibitions, in a modern non-threatening way; is a skilled craftsperson in her discipline; curators have a healthy respect of her working practice

Anne Marie Maher

MAHER, Anne Marie; CEO THE PENSIONS BOARD

b 1945, Co Waterford; *m* Patrick Maher; *edu*. Ursuline Convent, St. Marys, Waterford; University College Dublin; BCL; CEO The Pensions Board; Phoenix Assurance Co Ltd (London), 1965–66; New Ireland Assurance Co 1966–69; Irish Life Assurance Co 1967–69; Irish Life Assurance PLC 1970– 96; The Pensions Board 1996 to date; chairman Irish Association of Pension Funds 1993–95; current Board Memberships: Irish Accounting and Auditing Supervisory Authority (IAASA), Health Insurance Authority (HIA), Professional Oversight Board for Accountancy (UK), FTSE Policy Group (UK), Pensions Policy Institute (UK), EU Committee of European Insurance and Occupational Pensions Supervisors (CEIOPS); Publ. many papers and articles on Regulation, Insurance, Pensions, Public Policy. Recreations: farming (own farm at Nire Vale Ballymacarbry, Clonmel), reading, travel. Contact: 4 Greenfield Crescent, Dublin 4. **T** 01 613 1900 **F** 01 631 8602 email amaher@pensionsboard.ie

An elegant, very experienced and highly intelligent business executive who applies her legal background to very good effect in her current position; has led the drive to highlight the serious deficit in Irish employment where over half the population has no pension plan in place; still retains her close connection with her homestead through her involvement in the family farm in Co. Waterford.

MALLAGHAN, Lee Michael; GOLF ESTATE DIRECTOR

b Dungannon, Co. Tyrone; *m* Mary Harte; 2*s*.2*d*; Clubs: Carton House Golf Club; Recreations: GAA: Contact: Carton House, Maynooth, Co. Kildare **T** 01 505 2000 **F** 01 628 6555 web www.cartonhouse.ie

Having sold his interests in Powerscreen acquired one of the finest Georgian estates in Ireland and has developed two championship golf courses which, in 2005, hosted the prestigious Irish Open; the beautifully refurbished mansion reopened 2006 under the management of Paddy Kelly's (*qv*) Clarion hotel group.

MALLIN, Liavan; FOUNDER, CHAIRPERSON, SHOP DIRECT
b 1964, Dublin; *m*; 1*d*; *edu.* graduated from Dublin City University, 1985; Irish Management Institute;
BSc (Computer Applications); applied finance; Entrepreneur; Founder, chairperson and CEO of
ShopDirect; founder and chairperson of Onemade.com; founder Celtic Hampers, which became the
largest mail order company in Ireland; sold Celtic Hampers; member Board of Trustees, Dublin City
University 1998 to date; has worked with the Dublin City University Educational Trust to improve
teaching, sports and social facilities at the University; director Irish Special Olympics 2003 to date;
Contact: Dublin City University, Dublin 9 **T** 01 700 5000 **F** 01 836 0830.

> An extremely successful entrepreneur who established several companies.

MALONE, Declan; EDITOR, THE KERRYMAN
b 1963, Dingle, Co. Kerry; single; edu. CBS Dingle; Trinity College Dublin; Dublin City University;
BA (Sociology & Philosophy); Grad Dip in Journalism, DCU; Editor *The Kerryman*; previously sub-
editor, chief sub-editor and deputy editor; Clubs: Dingle Sailing Club; Recreations: watersports.
Contact: The Kerryman, Clash, Tralee, Co. Kerry. **T** 066 714 5546 **F** 066 714 5572
email dmalone@kerryman.ie

> The home grown editor of one of Ireland's most successful and long established
> provincial newspapers is a very influential figure in 'The Kingdom.'

MALONE, Miriam, JUDGE, PRESIDENT, THE DISTRICT COURT
b Dublin; *m*; 2 children; *edu.* University College Dublin 1972- 75; Kings Inns ,1973 – 76; called to the
Bar 1976; Judge, President of the District Court; appointed a Judge of the District Court 1997;
President of the District Court, 2005 to date; Contact: District Court, Four Courts Dublin 7.
T 01 872 5555 web www.courts.ie

> As the first woman to preside over the District Court she has to organise the affairs of
> the court in its various jurisdictions, which includes 45 court areas and 55 judges
> covering more than 550,000 cases each year; her previous background in
> contemporary crime and civil cases will give her role a new relevance in a high tech
> world of crime and punishment.

MALONE, Peter Gerard; COMPANY DIRECTOR
b 1945, Dundalk, Co. Louth; *m* Mary Breslin; 3*d*; *edu.* St.Mary's College Dundalk,
Shannon College of Hotel Management, Shannon Airport Co. Clare (1st class hons); Fellow Irish
Hotel and Catering Institute; Company Chairman and Director of numerous bodies and boards;
Manager Jury's Hotel Cork; manager Jury's Hotel Dublin; managing director Jury's Doyle Hotel
Group1989-00; Currently chairman of the following: Hibernian Group plc., National Roads
Authority; CBRE Gunn Property Group; Business Tourism Forum; and director of: Jury's Doyle
Hotel Group plc., Ulster Bank Ltd; member, Government Review Body on Higher Remuneration
in the Public Sector, former member Minimum Wage Review Group, former president Irish Hotels
Federation, former chairman Bord na Móna plc; director CPL Recruitment plc, Brain Research of
Ireland. Recreations: walking, horseracing, GAA, rugby, soccer, reading and lots of travel. Contact:
13, Stillorgan Grove, Blackrock, Co. Dublin. **M** 087 239 5399 **F** 01 288 3286
email pmalone1@eircom.net

Peter Malone

> The Dundalk-born, former Jurys Hotel's chief, has built up an impressive string of
> directorships since his retirement from Jurys; highly respected in corporate circles as
> an effective and accommodating chairman; warm and extremely personable, was
> responsible for developing Jurys into a major player in the hotel industry and for
> pioneering the budget hotel concept with the development of Jurys Inns in Ireland and
> throughout the UK.

MALONEY, Barry J; VENTURE CAPITALIST
b 1959; *m* Aileen; 3*d*; *edu.* Newbridge College, Co. Kildare; University College Dublin; B.Comm.
(Economics); International Advanced Management Programme, IMD, Switzerland; Venture
Capitalist; European pricing manager, Director of Software Business Europe and vice president of the
Component and Peripheral Business Unit Europe, Digital Equipment; vice president of first Business
Development and then Channel Operations, Xerox Corporation, Palo Alto, San Franscisco; CEO

Barry Maloney

Esat Digiphone1996–2001; non executive chairman Esat Digiphone 2001–05; general partner, Benchmark Capital, board member Alphyra, Globoforce, InnerWorkings, Newbay, Nexagent, Openet Telecom, Saw-You, Clever Communication, Setanta; member Institute of Directors, Irish US Alliance. Clubs: Wanderers RFC, Westport Golf Club, Hibernian Golf Club. Recreations: rugby, soccer, golf, music. Contact: email bmaloney@benchmark.com

One of the pioneers of the Telecoms revolution in Ireland in the 1990s; recognized as the brains behind the success of ESAT digiphone; well respected and connected; had a very public falling out with Denis O'Brien (*qv*) with his evidence to the Moriarty Tribunal; has since moved on very successfully.

MALONEY, Paul; CHIEF EXECUTIVE DUBLIN DOCKLANDS DEVELOPMENT AUTHORITY
b 1956, *m*; 3 children; *edu*. University College Galway; Trinity College Dublin; BE; M.Sc; chartered member Institute of Engineers 1989; Chief Executive Dublin Docklands Development Authority; joined the Irish Army Engineering Corps; served as a captain in the Engineering Corps; served as a lieutenant with the United Nations in Lebanon; project manager with Department of Environment on IT projects; joined Dublin City Council 1998–2006; chief executive Dublin Docklands Development Authority 2005 to date; Recreations: gym, golf, five aside soccer. Contact: Dublin Docklands Authority, Custom House Quay, Docklands, Dublin 1. **T** 01 818 3300 **F** 01 818 3399 email info@dublindocklands.ie

The army training will stand him in good stead with his hands-on management style as chief executive of D.D.D.A; he presides over the semi body at an exciting time with the development of the new conference center and the relocation of the Abbey Theatre to the Docklands.

MANAHAN, Anna Maria ACTOR
b 1924, Co. Waterford; *m* Colm O'Kelly (decd); *edu*. Convent of Mercy, Waterford; Actor; trained under Ria Mooney, Gaiety School of Acting; Actor; worked with all major companies; highlights include *The Rose Tattoo, Bloomsday, Lovers* (London & Broadway, Tony nomination), *The Plough and the Stars, Live Like Pigs, The Leenane Trilogy* (also London & Sydney), *The Loves of Cass Maguire, The Shaughran*; TV and films include: *The Riordains, Leave it to Mrs O'Brien, The Irish RM, The Bill, Lovejoy, Blind Justice, A Man of No Importance*, John B. Keane wrote *Big Maggie* for her; founder member of Play Circle (Playwrights Work Shop), member ADA (Association of Drama Adjudicators); lecturer in Drama; recipient Tony Award Nomination, 1977; Eire Society of Boston Gold Medal, 1984; Tony Award for role of 'Mags' in *Beauty Queen of Leenane* 1998; 2002, Freedom of the City of Waterford 2003 LL.D (hc) University of Limerick; Recreations; reading, music and cooking. Contact: Maureen McGlynn, First Call, 29-30, Dawson Street, Dublin 2. **T** 01 679 8401

Generally regarded as Ireland's greatest actress; but for a tattoo and a condom and a pint of Guinness, Manahan's performance in "The Rose Tattoo," combined with the notoriety of the case, were the beginning of a career during which she would come to be regarded as an incomparable interpreter of the words of Sean O'Casey, J. M. Synge, James Joyce, Christy Brown, Brian Friel (*qv*) and other Irish writers; more than 40 years later Manahan won the 1998 Tony Award for her performance in "The Beauty Queen of Leenane" by Martin Mc Donagh.

MANNION, Dermot; CHIEF EXECUTIVE, AER LINGUS
b 1958, Sligo; *m* Anna Mulholland; 3s 1d; *edu*. St. John's Primary School; Summerhill College, Sligo; Trinity College Dublin; B.BS; Chartered Accountant; Fellow, Institute of Chartered Accountants; Chief Executive Aer Lingus plc; articled clerk Arthur Young accountants, Dublin (now part of Ernst and Young); joined Ulster Investment Bank 1985-87; joined Emirates Airlines, London 1987; appointed Treasury Manager Emirates in Dubai; appointed financial director 1995–2000; appointed president Group Support Services, 2000–05; appointed chief executive Aer Lingus plc 2005 to date; Recreations: soccer (especially Sligo Rovers); Contact: Aer Lingus Head Office, Dublin Airport, Co. Dublin. **T** 0818 0365022 web www.aerlingus.com

Personable and sartorially elegant, the Sligo born airline chief takes over at the helm of the national carrier with a a superb track record at Emirates and as a director of Sri Lankan Airlines, was centrally involved in its turnaround; he also completed a multi-billion pound aircraft acquisition programme for Emirates; his international

experience will be critical in chartering a profitable and successful future for Aer
Lingus as it privatises in a highly competitive sector.

MANSERGH, Martin George; SENATOR; MEMBER, COUNCIL OF STATE;
b 1946; *m* Elizabeth Young; 1*s* 4*d*; *edu.* Kings School Canterbury, UK; Christ Church, Oxford; M.A.
D. Phil; Senator (elected to agricultural panel, Seanad Éireann, nominated by the Irish
Thoroughbred Breeders Association); co-owner of family farm Co. Tipperary; joined civil service,
Department of Foreign Affairs 1974-80; principal officer Dept of An Taoiseach 1981; head of
research Fianna Fáil 1981-87; special advisor to Taoisigh (Charles J. Haughey, Albert Reynolds,
Bertie Ahern) 1982, 1987-94, 1997-2002; intermediary in contacts with Sinn Fein prior to IRA
Ceasefire; member N.I. Talks Delegation; member IFA; *Irish Times* columnist; awards: co winner
Tipperary Peace Prize with Fr. Alex Reid and Rev Roy Magee, 1994; Commander's Cross of the
Republic of Austria, 2003; Grand Prix de la Francophonie en Irlande, 2005; member of the Council
of Alexandra College, Dublin; member, of the Council of State 2004 to date; FF Finance
spokesperson in the Upper House; *Publ. The Spirit of the Nation, edited speeches of Charles J.
Haughey,1957-86* (Mercier Press); *The Legacy of History For Making Peace In Ireland* (Mercier Press,
2003); numerous articles; Clubs: Co. Tipperary Lawn Tennis Club; Contact: Friarsfield House,
Tipperary **T** 062 57226 **F** 062 31028 email mmansergh@oireachtas.ie

> The highly intellectual, Oxford educated philosopher has a keen political brain
> which has been used to good effect by successive Taoisigh; don't be fooled by his his
> slow public delivery; might be perceived as the typical Anglo-Irish landed gentry but
> he is very much in touch with the real Ireland and the FF grass roots as evidenced by
> his election to Seanad Eireann in 2002; warm and engaging personality, has made a
> major contribution to the peace process in Ireland over the past 25 years.

MANSFIELD, JAMES 'Jim'; HOTELIER/ PROPERTY DEVELOPER
b 1940, Brittas, Co Dublin; *m* Anne; 3*s*; *edu.* Brittas National School, Co. Dublin; Hotelier/
Property Developer; left school and became lorry driver; bought his first lorry aged 19 from Pino
Harris Snr; dealt in scrap from Harris snr, father of Pino Harris (*qv*); bought and sold lorries;
machinery, cranes, diggers etc based in Rathcoole; went to Atlanta, Georgia, U.S. where he started
auctioning lorries, diggers JCBs etc; contracted Mc Cormack Mc Naughton to supply him;
expanded to plant hire equipment in the United States; returned to Ireland and started buying up
land around Rathcoole, City West; late 1980's - early 1990's in the aftermath of the Falkland war,
flew all around the Falklands and estimated the value of heavy duty equipment which he bought;
possesses a dual UK/Irish passsport; opened a warehouse in Liverpool for equipment; Thatcher put
a barring order; with Noel Smyth sued the British government and won; owner Weston Private
Airport, Co. Dublin; owner City West Hotel, Country Club and Conference Centre, owner
Palmerstown Stud and PGA National Golf Course, Co. Dublin. Recreations: GAA, car racing.
Contact: City West Hotel, Saggart, Co. Dublin. **T** 01 401 0500 web www.citywesthotel.ie

> The controversial property developer has built a very successful hotel business with
> the City West development which is now the largest Dublin based hotel for major
> sporting, political and sporting events; he parlayed his vast fortune from trading in
> used vehicles and equipment from the Falklands invasion; currently constructing the
> largest conference center in the country at his Saggart base which seems not to have
> suffered from not having advance planning approval.

MARA, Patrick 'PJ' PUBLIC AFFAIRS CONSULTANT
b 1942, Dublin; *m* Breda Brogan (decd);1*s*; *edu.* Coláiste Mhuire, Dublin; Public Relations
Consultant. Proprietor, Beeline Clothing Company, sold subsequently to Pennys; member
National Executive, Fianna Fail; member Seanad Eireann 1982; press secretary Fianna Fáil
Party, government press secretary 1987-92; director of Elections FF 1997; director of
Referendum Nice Treaty FF 2002; director of Elections FF 2002; headed up committee for
selection of new FF candidates for general election 2007; joined GPA as media consultant
1992; other clients include Denis O'Brien, Elan, Allied Irish Banks. Contact: 19, Wellington
Road, Ballsbridge, Dublin 4. **M** 086 259 2520.

> A true original; charismatic, laid back manner hides his, ironically, now far more
> powerful position within Fianna Fail than when he was employed full time by the
> Party; also has a blue chip client list which includes Ireland's wealthiest entrepreneurs

PJ Mara

MARREN, Enda; SOLICITOR

b 1934, Co. Mayo; *m* Nuala Craig; *2s 1d*; *edu.* Rockwell College, Co. Tipperary; University College Dublin; Incorporated Law Society of Ireland; B.A; LL.B; Solicitor; founded Martin E. Marren & Company Solicitors 1958; senior partner 1958–96; former member Law Reform Commission 1975–80; former director National Film Studios Ardmore, Co. Wicklow; former trustee and vice chairman, National Executive, Fine Gael. Clubs: Stephen's Green and Hibernian United Services Club. Recreations: art, politics, golf. Contact: 10 Northumberland Road, Dublin 4. **T** 01 668 6266 **F** 01 668 6351

> The charming, wily Mayoman is the eminence grise of Fine Gael; one of the original National Handlers with Bill O Herlihy (*qv*), Frank Flannery (*qv*) and Pat Heneghan, he is universally popular in all political circles.

MARREN, Paul Vincent; SOLICITOR

b 1961, Dublin; *m* Isabel Foley; *1s 1d*; *edu.* Rockwell College, Co. Tipperary; Trinity College Dublin; BA(Mod) History; College of Commerce, DLS; Law Society, Cert. Applied European Law; Solicitor; qualified 1989; Solicitor; joined family law firm assistant solicitor, Martin E. Marren & Co. 1989-96; Senior Partner 1996 to date; member Law Society of Ireland, Dublin Solicitor's Bar Association (Secretary & Corporate Affairs 1996-99); Dublin Solicitor's Bar Association, past president Society of Young Solicitors; European Young Bar Association (corporate affairs); vice president Dublin Lions Club: Recreations: kayaking, reading, fishing, golf, tennis, hill walking, local history. Contact: 10 Northumberland Road, Dublin 4. **T** 01 668 6266 **F** 01 668 6351

> A chip off the old block and son of the legendary Enda (*qv*) now runs the family legal practice with strong political and Western connections.

MARRINAN QUINN, Paulyn; OMBUDSMAN, DEFENCE FORCES

b 1946, Dublin; *m* Brendan Quinn (separated); *2s* (one decd); *1d*, *edu.* Trinity College Dublin; B.A; B.L: Kings Inns; Senior Counsel; F.C.I.Arb. Ombudsman, Defence Forces; Mediator. Called to the Irish Bar 1979; called the English Bar (Middle Temple) 1982; called the Northern Ireland Bar 1992; admitted to the Inner Bar 2000; Ombudsman Defence Forces 2005; appointed founding Insurance Ombudsman of Ireland 1992-98 (established an InsuranceOmbudsman Scheme to resolve disputes arising between policy holders and their insurance companies by way of adjudication, mediation or conciliation. The "Five Year Review" document (1992-1997), Annual Reports 1993-97 and "Digest of Cases 1992-1998" set out the main activities and achievements of the office); founding presiding officer of SICA/FICA InternationalOrganisation to promote high standards in the training, education and practice of International Commercial Arbitration, Alternative Dispute Resolution/Mediation practices 1998; estab. Private Ombudman Schemes; founder/coordinator Conflict and Dispute Resolution Studies, Trinity College 2000; founder Mediation Forum-Ireland 2004; founder-member Irish Women Lawyers Assoc. 2000; founder-member (2002) & vice-chair (2003 to date) Irish Commercial Mediation Assoc; member executive board and audit committee, Trocaire 2003 to date; patron Millenium Development Campaign, Edgehill Theological College, Belfast 2000 to date; XIV Gilmartin Lecture - Royal Col. Surg. Col. Anaests 1998; developed Comm.Glencree Centre for Reconciliation 1996-2000; chair Women's Political Assoc. 1991; appointed Irish Delegate to OECD; devised and presented 'Cases That Changed Peoples' Lives – Case Stated' (a series about court cases which set and affirmed legal precedents and rights), RTÉ Radio 1 2005 and also produced/presented series 'Generations'(Channel Four 1986); Publ.(inter alia) *Beyond ReasonableDoubt* (short stories) - BBC. *Morning Story* 1986; *Role of Women in the Economy* 1988; *Insurance Ombudsman of Ireland DIGEST OF CASES* 1992 -98; *Grasping the nettle and meeting the challenge of Coordinating Financial Regulatory Reform and Consumer Redress Schemes; Irish Insurance Law Reform,* Volume 3, No. 4, Round Hall Sweet and Maxwell 1999; *Administrative Justice in the 21st Century,* Hart Publishing, Oxford 1999; column 'Paulyn's Law' - *IT* Mag 1979-83; Clubs:University Club; Recreations: theatre, music, writing, walking, tennis, swimming. Contact: Law Library, Four Courts, Dublin 7. **T** 01 817 5229 **F** 01 284 7960 email pm@mediationforumireland.com

> Extremely bright, charming and stylish, the former insurance ombudsman brings a wealth of experience to her new position after a sojourn in the Law Library; her legal background and clinical approach to resolving issues will ensure a balanced discharge of her new duties and hopefully will have a longer term than was the case in the insurance sector.

MARSHALL, HARRY; INTERNATIONAL SHOWJUMPER
b 1954, Ballyclare, Co. Antrim; *m* Dawn; 1*s* 1*d*; International Showjumper; played soccer at schoolboy international level; was Ireland's first national showjumping champion; competed Ireland 2005 at European Showjumping Championships, Italy; former winner, Grand Prix, Gijion, Spain, 2003; Recreations: F1 motor racing, soccer. Contact: Huntingtown Farm, Balllyclare, Co. Antrim.
T 780 257 8808

> Extremely talented and highly principled member of the Irish Showjumping team; hit the national headlines over his unwillingness to participate in a team with Cian O'Connor following the Olympic Gold medal scandal.

MARTIN, Christopher Nicholas 'Chris'; MANAGING DIRECTOR, MUSGRAVE GROUP plc
b 1960, London; *m* Joanne; 1*s* 1*d*; *edu.* Wrekin College Shropshire, UK, Newcastle University BA (Hons) Economics and Accounting; member of the Institute of Accountants, England and Wales, Managing Director Musgrave Group plc; trained with Coopers & Lybrand; Pizza Hut 1991-7; Storehouse PLC 1997-2000; Mothercare PlC 2000-02; Musgrave Group PLC 2003 to date; Clubs: Fellow of Royal Society of Arts, Trustee of House of St Barnabas; member of Rabobank Advisory Board; Contact: Musgrave Group PLC, Airport Road, Ballycureen, Cork. **T** 021 452 2237
F 021 452 2290 email chrism@musgrave.ie

> A keen cricket supporter, and a charming articulate man; a very impressive track record in retailing in the UK; was a surprise appointment at Musgrave Group, but is making a significant impression amongst the professional managers in Cork; he perceives the Musgrave Group as a multinational operation with significant interest in Northern Ireland UK, Spain, and of course Ireland.

Chris Martin

MARTIN, His Grace, Most Rev. Dr. Diarmuid; ARCHBISHOP OF DUBLIN
b 1945, Dublin; single; *edu.* Oblates, Dublin, De La Salle Ballyfermot Dublin; Marian College Dublin; University College Dublin; Clonliffe College, Dublin; College of St. Thomas Acquinas Rome (Angelicum); Archbishop of Dublin; ordained priest 1969; Curate St. Brigid's Parish, Cabinteely, Dublin 1973-74; Roman Curial posts 1976-86; Under Secretary (1986) and Secretary (1994) Pontifical Council for Justice & Peace, The Vatican; appointed titular Bishop of Glendalough 1999; appointed titular Archbishop of Glendalough 2001; Vatican Representative to the United Nations, Geneva (for Special Agencies, Debt Relief, Anti Racialism, World Trade Organisation) 2001; appointed Co-Adjudator Archbishop of Dublin with right of succession 2003; Archbishop of Dublin, Metropolitan and Primate of Ireland 2004 to date; Contact; Archbishops House, Drumcondra Road, Dublin 9. **T** 01 836 0723 **F** 01 836 0793
email communications@dublindiocese.ie

> Highly intellectual, an excellent media performer; appointment to the Dublin archdiocese coincided with a turbulent time in the Catholic church in Ireland involving the child sex abuse disclosures; very well connected in the Vatican, already insiders ask if his future lies in Ireland wearing the 'Red Hat' or a return, in the near future, to the higher echelons of the Vatican.

MARTIN, Micheál; PUBLIC REPRESENTATIVE
b 1960, Cork; *m* Mary O'Shea; 2*s* 2*d*; *edu.* Coláiste Chriost Rí, Turners Cross; University College Cork; BA; H.Dip Ed; MA Political History; Public Representative; Minister for Enterprise Trade and Employment 2004 to date. Minister for Health and Children 2000–04; Minister for Education 1997–2000; Fianna Fáil Front Bench spokesperson on Education and the Gaeltacht 1995-1997; former chairman of the Oireachtas All Party Committee on the Irish Language; former member of the Dáil Committee on Crime; member of the Dáil Committee on Finance and General Affairs; first elected to Cork Corporation in 1985; Lord Mayor of Cork 1992-1993; former member of the Governing Body, UCC and of the Governing Body RTC; former member of the ASTI; member of the Fianna Fáil National Executive since 1988; former national chairman of Ogra Fianna Fáil; member of the Commission on the Aims and Structures of Fianna Fáil; Awards: Winner of the Cork Examiner Political Speaker of the Year Award 1987; Contact: Lios Laoi, 16 Silver Manor, Ballinlough, Cork.
T 021 432 0088 web www.michealmartin.ie

> The son of Paddy Martin, former international boxer, this highly ambitious, personable Corkman was deemed the most likely to succeed, in time, to the ultimate job, when he was became Minister for Education in 1997; the former school teacher got off to a

Micheál Martin

flying start; however his sojourn in Hawkins House, as Minister for Health, reversed his fortunes; his transfer to Enterprise, Trade and Employment in 2004 may have opened a new opportunity for him; definitely leadership material now.

MAUGHAN, Gemma Attilia née Saccenda; COMPANY DIRECTOR GOWAN GROUP
b 1940, Italy; m 1st Con Smith (decd); 4*d*; *m* 2nd Michael Maughan, (*qv*); *edu*. L'Ecole Hotelierre de la Société Suisse des Hoteliers, Lausanne; director of Gowan Group and subsidiary companies; appointed director of family controlled distribution group and joined main board of Gowan Group Ltd 1977; Awards: 1992 Officier de L'Ordre National de Mérite (France); Clubs: RIAC. Recreations: art, travel, gardening, walking. Contact: Gowan Group, 1 Herbert Avenue, Dublin 4. **T** 01 260 1677 **F** 01 260 1672

Quiet and self effacing, she is regarded as shrewd and sagacious; supports charities and very involved with her family and the family business of her late husband.

MAUGHAN, Matthew Michael; CHAIRMAN, GOWAN GROUP LTD
b 1938; *m* Gemma Smith (*qv* Maughan, Gemma); 4 stepdaughters; *edu*. Clongowes Wood College, College of Commerce, Rathmines; Domas Advertising 1957-65; acquired and managed Wilson Hartnell & Co which became Ogilvy & Mather Group Ltd 1965, currently president; appointed chairman of Gowan Group, Ltd, 1993 to date; member Publicity Club of Ireland (president 1993-96); fellow I.A.P.I; member Marketing Institute; fellow Institute of Directors I.M.I; Clubs: Milltown Golf Club, Fitzwilliam LTC, Royal Irish Yacht Club, R.I.A.C., R.D.S; awards: Ogilvy Eagle by Ogilvy & Mather Worldwide Board, 1988; Recreations: art, antiques, gardening, golf, reading. Contact: Gowan Group, 1 Herbert Avenue, Merrion Road, Dublin 4. **T** 01 260 1677 **F** 01 260 1672 web www.gowan.ie

The former advertising supreme retains his corporate interests through his chairmanship of the Gowan Group, major auto distribution business; sartorially elegant, bon viveur, excellent company.

MAURER, Brian Joseph; CARDIOLOGIST
b 1941, Clare; *m* Kathleen Flynn; 1*s* 2*d*; *edu*. St. Flannan's College, Ennis, Co. Clare; University College Dublin; Royal Post Graduate Medical School London and University of Alabama (post grad); M.B.,FRCPI., FACC.,FESC; Cardiologist & Medical Director Irish Heart Foundation; director Department of Cardiology, St. Vincent's University Hospital Dublin 1987 to date; consultant cardiologist 1974 to date; former president Irish Heart Foundation and Irish Cardiac Society; chairman Voluntary Hospitals Consultants Irish Medical Association 1976–82; current medical director Irish Heart Foundation 2005 to date; medical director Irish Cardiac Society 1988–91; chairman Ministerial Task Force on Sudden Cardiac Death 2004-05; *Publ:* papers on cardiovascular disease in numerous scientific and medical journals 1966 to date; director St Vincents Healthcare Group. Clubs: Stephens Green. Dún Laoghaire, Lahinch and Portmarnock Golf Clubs, Royal St.George Yacht Club; Recreations: golf, sailing, history, archaeology. Contact: Suite 12, Blackrock Clinic, Blackrock, Co. Dublin. **T** 01 206 4213

Leading cardiologist for the past twenty five years; extremely popular with his patients; excellent, low handicap golfer.

MAXWELL, Elizabeth, May; SCHOOL PRINCIPAL
b 1947; *m* Harry Barr; *edu*. Collegiate School, Celbridge, Co Kildare; Trinity College Dublin; BA Geography, English and Irish; H Dip Ed; In Service Cert. in School Leadership, ISDC of Secretariat of Secondary Schools; TEFL Cert from Linguerame, London; Principal, Mount Anville School, Dublin. Geography teacher Mount Anville 1970-90; vice-principal 1990-98; deputy principal 1998-99; principal 1999 to date; Clubs: Royal Horticultural Society of Ireland; Geographical Society of Ireland; Recreations: hill walking, travel, gardening, photography, Third World issues. Contact: Mount Annville School, Goatstown, Dublin 14. **T** 01 298 8887 **F** 01 283 2373 email emaxwell@mountanville.net

A brilliant principal and a brilliant teacher, although sadly her duties as a principal may take her away from teaching; much admired by her own pupils and by her peers.

MAYES, Right Rev. Michael Hugh Gunton; BISHOP OF LIMERICK AND KILLALOE
b 1941, Belfast; *m* Elizabeth; 1*s* 2*d*; *edu.* Royal School, Armagh; Trinity Collge Dublin; BA; London
University, BD; Bishop of Limerick & Killaloe. Ordained 1964; curate St.Mark's, Portadown 1964-
67; curate St. Columba's, Portadown 1967-68; missionary Japan 1968-74; Missionary Society area
secretary Ireland 1974-75; Rector St.Michael's Union Cork 1975-86; Rector Moviddy Union Cork
1986-88; Rector Glanmire, Little Island and Carrigtwohill, Cork 1988-93; Archdeacon of Cork
1986-93; Bishop of Kilmore, Elphin and Ardagh 1993-2000; Bishop of Limerick and Killaloe 2000 to
date; Recreations: languages, theology, music, photography, golf, "causing any idiot-proof computer to
suffer a nervous collapse within a day" Contact: Bishop's House, North Circular Road, Limerick.
T 061 451 532 **F** 061 451 100 email Bishop@limerick.anglcan.org

> An effective preacher; surprisingly became controversial in his determination to
> support a pluralist Christian approach to the ordination of gay clergy; his surprising
> support for the installation of gay US Bishop gave his rural diocese an unexpected
> profile.

MEADE, Joe; FINANCIAL SERVICES OMBUDSMAN
b 1950, Co Clare; *m* Mary; 2*s* 1d; *edu.* Ennistymon Christian Brothers School, Co. Clare; University
College Dublin; B. Comm; Ombudsman Financial Services. Comptroller and Auditor General's
Office 1967–93; European Court of Auditors 1993–95, 1995–2000; Sec. General Comptroller &
Auditor Generals Office 1995–2000; Data Protection Commissioner 2000–05; Clubs: Naomh
Mearnóg GAA Club Portmarnock; Recreations: hill walking, traditional music, hurling; Contact: 32,
Upper Merrion Street, Dublin 2. **T** 01 662 0899 **F** 01 662 0890 email
enquiries@financialombudsman.ie

> The popular Clareman brings a wide range of experience of the public service at home
> and in Europe to his new position; despite being away from his native county for many
> years continues to be steeped in the traditions of West Clare.

MEALY, Alphonsus 'Fonsie'; JOINT MANAGING DIRECTOR, MEALYS, FINE ART
AUCTIONEERS
b 1949, Castlecomer, Co. Kilenny; *m* Eileen O'Malley; 1*s* 3*d*; *edu.* Castlecomer National School;
Rockwell College; Joint Managing Director Mealys, Fine Art Auctioneers. Porter in family
auctioneering firm 1968; manager Mealys, Fine Art & Rare Book Auctioneering Specialists 1975-
81; managing director 1981 to date; lectures on fine art and rare books; contributor to television
programmes and journals; property valuer; member of Fine Art Committee Irish Auctioneers
Valuers Institute; member of board of management & council of Royal Dublin Society; fellow of
Irish Auctioneers and Valuers Institute F.I.A.V.I; past president Kilkenny Rotary Club; Clubs: RDS;
Recreations: President Kilkenny Rugby Club, badminton, squash, walking, acting, book collection,
charity work, local history. Contact: Mealy's, Chatsworth Street, Castlecomer, Co. Kilkenny.
T 056 444 1229 **F** 056 444 1627 email fonsie@mealys.com www.mealys.com

Fonsie Mealy

> A very able and astute businessman who develops any and all avenues when he sees an
> opening. Admired by his professional peers he has made his a niche market centre and
> continues with that to date.

MEAGHER, John; ARCHITECT
b 1947, Dublin; single; *edu.* Pembroke School, Dublin; St. Michael's College; Blackrock College;
School of Architecture, Dublin Institute of Technology; Dip Arch; Helsinki University of Technology;
School of Architecture, Otaniemi, Finland; Architect. Studio master, University College Dublin 1975-
83; Architect; worked in Germany and the US; set up practice with Shane de Blacam in Dublin - de
Blacam and Meagher Architects 1976; projects of de Blacam and Meagher include: The Dining Hall,
Atrium (RIAI Gold Medal for Conservation and Europa Nostra Medal); the Samuel Beckett Centre of
Performing Arts (Trinity College Dublin); The Michael Smurfit Graduate School of Business
(University College Dublin); new Library, IT and Catering School at Cork Institute of Technology;
School of Art, Galway - Mayo Institute of Technology, Galway; Chapel of Reconciliation, Knock, Co.
Mayo; restoration of Lyons House and Demesne, Co. Kildare (Europa Nostra Medal); headquarters
for Esat Telecom, Dublin, 1 Castle Street, Dublin 8 (RIAI Silver Medal 2004), The Wooden Building,
Temple Bar, Dublin 2 (RIAI Silver Medal 2005). Well known for private houses in Ireland, Spain
(Balearic Islands) and Portugal; invited lecturer at: School of Art (Glasgow), Edinburgh University,
Architectural Association of Ireland, North London Polytechnic, University of London, Portsmouth
Polytechnic, Designs on Europe Symposium, Humberside Polytechnic, University of Aberdeen,

University of Dundee, Arts Council of Northern Ireland, Belfast RIBA; president Architectural Association of Ireland 1977-80; member Art Advisory Board Hugh Lane Municipal Gallery of Modern Art 1983-90; ROSC committee member 1975-83; trustee Dublin Graphic Studio 1989-92; board member Irish Museum of Modern Art at Royal Hospital Kilmainham 1989-95; board member Black Church Print Studio, Dublin, 1995–2001; *Irish Arts Review*, editorial board 1986–2000; MRIAI, MSDI, FRIAI; Contact: de Blacam and Meagher, 4, St Catherine's Lane West, Dublin 8. **T** 01 453 4240 **F** 01 473 7959

One of the Golden Boys of Irish Architecture in the late 1970s and early '80s, he has retained his iconic status; admired by his peers and looked up to by the next generation, he is also a serial party goer; great company and a good and loyal friend.

MEE, Paula; CONSULTANT DIETICIAN
b 1963, Limerick; separated; 1*s*; *edu.* Taylor's Hill, Galway; University College Galway (B.Sc.H.Dip. Ed); Leeds Metropolitan University (Dip Dietetics M.SC.); Southampton University (Dip Allergy); British Dietetic Association's Sports Dietitian Course; Consultant Dietitian. Established own Food and Dietician Consultancy, Fruition 2004; previously Nutrition Manager for Superquinn and senior nutritionist National Dairy Council; also practised as a dietician in a number of hospitals in Northern Ireland; currently a member of the Board Consumer Foods in Bord Bia; member Consultative Council of the Food Authority of Ireland; one of the presenters of RTÉ's TV Health Squad Programmes; regular appearances on TV and Radio programmes dealing with health and dietetic issues; Contact: Fruition, 30 Hampton Crescent, St. Helen's Wood, Booterstown Avenue, Blackrock, Co .Dublin. **T** 01 210 4763 or Dublin Nutrition Clinic 19-26, Lower Pembroke Street, Dublin 2. **T** 01 639 8852 email paulamee@eircom.net

Now has a national profile from her Health Squad TV series; down to earth, no nonsense approach to diet and nutrition; doesn't lecture or hector instead her easy manner makes her advice so much easier to take.

Paula Mee

MILLER, Rt. Rev. Harold Creeth; BISHOP Of DOWN & DROMORE
b 1950, Belfast; *m* Elizabeth Adelaide; 2*s* 2*d*; *edu.* Belfast High School; Trinity College Dublin 1969-73; University of Nottingham 1973-75; St. John's Theological College 1973-6; BA, MA (TCD); BA (Hons) (Nottingham) D.P.S. (St. Johns Nottingham); Bishop of Down and Dromore. Curate assistant, Carrickfergus (St Nicholes) 1976-9; director of Extension Studies (St. John's Nottingham) 1979-84; Chaplain, Queen's University, Belfast 1984-9; Rector, Carrigrohane, Co Cork 1989-96; St. Patrick's Cathedral Dublin 1996-7; Publ. *Anglican Worship Today* (1980); *Finding a Personal Rule of Life* (1984); *Whose Office?; Daily Prayer for the People of God* (1982); *New Ways in Worship*(1986); *Making an Occasion of It* (1994); *The Desire of Our Soul* (2004); *Build Your Church, Lord* (2005); Clubs: member of Belfast High School; Member of MEWSA; Recreations: music, travel, phillumeny. Contact: 32, Knockdene Park South, Belfast BT57AB. **T** 028 9023 7602 **F** 028 90211 902 email bishop@down.anglican.org

A thoughtful and involved prelate who makes the word of his Saviour relevant to modern times and needs.

MILTON, Jim; PUBLIC RELATIONS CONSULTANT
b 1945, Dublin; *m* Carmel Barron; 2*s* 2*d*; *edu.* St. James' CBS, Dublin; Public Relations Consultant; editor *Business & Finance Magazine* 1970–73; Director Murray Consultants, Dublin, 1974 to date. Founding director with Joe Murray of Murray Consultants; founding chairman of Public Relations Consultants Association (Ireland); Recreations: mountain walking, flying, gliding, cycling. Contact: 79, Terenure Road West, Dublin 6. **T** 01 490 5890 **F** 01 492 4383 email: jmilton@eircom.net

'The Silver Fox' is now one of the elder statesmen in the public relations business in Ireland; the former editor of *Business and Finance* has established himself as the chief firefighter for the corporate A team; in this anything goes, media frenzied climate, fuelled by the 'red tops', his persuasive skills and long established contacts guarantee his clients a much sought after low profile.

MINIHAN, John; PUBLIC REPRESENTATIVE
b 1957, Cork; *m* Patricia; 2*s*; *edu.* Coláiste Chríost Rí, Turners Cross, Cork; Farrenferris, Cork; Cadet

School, Military College, 1975; Senator, Cork S Central; Spokesperson Education. First stationed in the Eastern Command, holding various appointments in Dublin, Gormonstown, Dundalk, Castleblaney and Cavan; served overseas with the United Nations on three occasions; participated in 21 Military Pilgrimages to Lourdes, working closely with head chaplains in the organisation and administration of these events; adjutant Collins Barracks, Cork 1992; received the Papal award "Pro Eglesia et Pontifice" 1995; retired army 1996 with the rank of captain; chairman Progressive Democrats 2002-03; party policy coordinator for Education and Defence 2003 to date; coordinator of the Friends of Science Group; selected to run for the PDs in Cork at next general election; clubs: Douglas Tennis Club; Nemo Rangers GAA; Recreations: tennis, all sport. Contact: Leinster House 2000, Dail Eireann, Kildare Street, Dublin 2. **T** 01 618 4347 **F** 01 618 4651 email jminihan@oireachtas.ie or minihan@indigo.ie web

Articulate, regular commentator on political affairs; would expect to feature in cabinet if he is elected for the PDs at the next election; professional, well known and liked, a definite asset to the PDs.

MISKIMMON, Annilese; OPERA/ARTISTIC DIRECTOR

b 1975, Bangor, Co. Down; single; *edu.* Glenlola Collegiate School, Belfast; Christ's College, Cambridge; Arts Management, post-graduate degree, City University at the Barbican; GCSE (7A's and 2B's); A-levels (3A's); English Literature M.A. Cantab. 2.1; Post-Grad Degree Arts Management City University; Artistic Director Opera Theatre Company; Glyndebourne's cnsultant asociate drector; recent work includes new productions of *L'elisir d'amore* (Holland Park), *Boheme* (OTC/English Touring Opera), *Semele* (British Youth Opera), *Vera of Las Vegas* (OTC), *The Queen who didn't come to Tea* by Alexander McCall Smith (Scottish Chamber Orchestra), *Ca Ira* (Rogers Waters of Pink Floyd) in Rome, *Apollo and Hyacinth* (Mozart) for Classical Opera Company/OTC (Irish, UK and European tour); future plans include *Fidelio* for OTC, her second show for Holland Park Opera, Carmen in New Zealand; previous directing work includes *La Pietra del Paragone* and *Pasquale* (Stanley Hall); *Cenerentola* (OTC); *Goehr's Arianna, Bach's Endimione* (Cambridge Classical Opera); *Weill's Protagonist and Royal Palace* (BBC Symphony /Andrew Davis); *La Vida breve* for the BBC Proms; *Vanessa* (Barber) and John Cage *Songbooks* (Slatkin /BBC SO); Bernstein's *On the Town* (BBC Concert/Paul Daniel); *Figaro* (Beijing Music Conservatory /WNO/British Council). Her WNO Traviata was the subject of an HTV documentary series; work with young professionals includes that with singers at the National Opera Studio and Irish Vocal Masterclasses and tutoring at Bristol Old Vic Theatre School. Audience development includes work at Covent Garden, WNO, Glyndebourne and Le Chatelet, including day schools and projects with young people and adults as director of Glyndcbourne Education's 'Opera Experience'. Chatelet, Paris; has directed Vick's *Pelleas* for Glyndebourne, and was associate director to Deborah Warner on Rattle's *Fidelio* for Glyndebourne /Le Chatelet. Other work includes revivals for Opera Bordeaux, Opera Bologna,Opera La Monnaie in Brussels,Toronto, San Francisco, Oslo and Oper Frankfurt. The conductors she has worked with include Mark Elder, Charles MacKerras, Paolo Carignani, Vladimir Jurowski, Louis Langree, Nicholas McGegan, and John Eliot Gardiner. Contact: Opera Theatre Company, Temple Bar Music Centre, Curved Street, Dublin 2. **T** 01 679 4962 **F** 01 679 4963 email artisticdirector@opera.ie web www.opera.ie

Annilese Miskimmon

MITCHELL, Olivia; PUBLIC REPRESENTATIVE

b 1947, Birr, Co Offaly; *m* James Mitchell; 2s 1d; *edu.* Eccles Street Dominican Convent; Trinity College Dublin; BA (Economics and Politics), H.Dip Ed; Public Representative; taught economics in Mount Anville Girls secondary school; First elected to the Dáil in 1997; FG Front Bench Spokesperson on Transport in October, 2004 – todate; FG Spokesperson on Health and Children, 2002- 04; FG Front Bench Spokesperson on Housing and Local Government from 2001 – '02; Junior Spokesperson on Traffic (Dublin and National) from 2000 to 01; spokesperson on Local Development, National Drugs Strategy & Dublin Traffic 1997-00; served on Dublin /Dun Laoighaire-Rathdown County Council, 1985-03; Cathaoirleach of Dun Laoghaire Rathdown Council from 1996 -97; member of the Regional Authority, the Eastern Health Board, Dublin Healthy Cities Project and was Dublin representative on the World Health Organisation multi-city action plan; member of the Dublin Transportation Office Advisory Committee; appointed as a Fine Gael representative to the Forum for Peace and Reconciliation; member of the Co-ordinating Committee of the European Sustainable Cities and Town Campaign. Contact: Leinster House, Kildare Street, Dublin 2. **T** 01 295 3033 (H) 01 618 3088 (O) **F** 01 618 4579 email olivia.mitchell@oireachtas.ie web www.finegael.ie

Olivia Mitchell

The striking FG Dail deputy has gained good national coverage through her hard work and grasp of her brief along with her ability to articulate issues in the current high profile, politically sensitive health sector

MOHAN, HUGH I; SENIOR COUNSEL, CHAIRMAN OF THE BAR COUNCIL
b Monaghan; *m* Sinead; 2d; *edu* Kings Inns BCL; called to the Bar 1985; called to the Inner Bar (Senior Counsel) 2000; Senior Counsel and Chairman Bar Council; practises on the Dublin and Eastern Circuits in commercial & chancery, criminal and general common law, tort and personal injury; specialises in arbitration and dispute resolution. Contact: The Distillery Buildings, 145/151 Church St. Dublin 7. **T** 01 817 4563

> A very distinguished Silk who is greatly respected by the Bench and by his colleagues; if he wants it, the High Court beckons - to the loss of the Bar which enjoys his opinions and assistance.

MOHLICH, Sonja Philipinna; FASHION STYLIST
b 1968, Antwerp; *partner* Alan Bruton (*qv*); *edu.* Ghent University, Belgium 1992, Exeter University, England 1994; BA Communication Studies, MA International Public Relations; Cert in English from University of Cambridge 1988; Cert in French from Sorbonne, Paris, France 1989; Cert in German, University of Vienna 1991; also speaks Dutch; Fashion Stylist; fashion columnist for *Sunday Independent*; Impulse Roadshow and Simply Be; worked on fashion catalogues for Dunnes Stores, Ramsay, Gaeltarra Knitwear, Roches Stores, Clerys, Brookfield; compiled wardrobes of TV weather presenters, continuity and newsreaders on TG4; regular contributor on RTE's 'Off the Rails'; fashion and beauty editor for *RTE Guide* to date; Clubs: Shelbourne Club; Recreations: films, reading, fashion. Contact: Apt 5, 46 North Great Georges Street, Dublin 1. **M** 087 260 1405

> One of the country's leading fashion stylists; possesses a great sense of personal style; well informed, extremely bright and ambitious; is a hard worker who enjoys life.

MOLLOY, Matt; MUSICIAN
b 1947, Ballaghadereen, Co. Roscommon; *m* Geraldine; 2s 2d; *edu.* Ballaghdereen Tech. Co. Roscommon; Bolton Street Institute of Technology; Aircraft Engineering qualification; Musician; joined Aer Lingus 1964–75; became professional musician 1975; Bothy Band 1975–79; Planxty 1979–80; Chieftains 1980 to date. Solo Discography: *Matt Molloy – Mulligan* 1976; *The Heathery Breeze* 1981; *Shanachie* 1993; *Stony Steps* 1987; *Green Linnet* 1992; *Shadows on Stone* Caroline Records 1997; has released several highly acclaimed solo albums and has worked with other accomplished musicians including Paul Brady, Tommy Peoples, Micheál Ó Súilleabháin, Dónal Lunny and the Irish Chamber Orchestra; has been involved in over seventy albums, working and performing with James Galway, Van Morrison, Mike Oldfield, Carlos Nunez,Mick Jagger and the Rolling Stones, Sinead O'Connor, Mark Knopfler, Tom Jones, Marianne Faithful. Clubs: Burren Sub Aqua Club, Westport Sailing Club; Recreations: scuba diving, sailing, music; Contact: Matt Molloy's Bar, Westport, Co. Mayo. **T** 098 26655 web mattmolloy.com

> A multi talented musician, performer, recording and Grammy Award winning artist; the man from Ballaghadereen is an integral member of the Chieftains as well as an accomplished solo performer; internationally acclaimed; is also the owner of the eponymous Westport Bar, a mecca for all Irish traditional music lovers.

MOLLOY, Thomas Patrick; JOURNALIST
b 1968, London; *m* Roslyn; 1s 2d; *edu.* The High School Dublin, Rathgar, Dublin; Trinity College Dublin; Cambridge University, England; B.A; M. Phil (international relations); editor *Kilkenny People*. Reporter for DPA in Washington, London and Hamburg, 1991- 96; covered Irish affairs for Bloomberg News in Dublin1997–2003; editor *Kilkenny People* 2003 to date; Clubs: National Press Club, Washington D.C.; Recreations: hill walking, shooting, newspapers. Contact: *The Kilkenny People*, 34, High Street, Kilkenny. **T** 056 772 1015 **F** 056 772 1414 email editor@kilkennypeople.ie

> Brings a wealth of international experience to his current position in the Kilkenny People which is a major player among the Provicials.

Tom Molloy

MOLONEY, John; GROUP CHIEF EXECUTIVE, GLANBIA Plc
b 1955, Sligo; *m* ; 2s; *edu.* Summerhill College, Sligo; UCD, B.Ag.Sc; University College Galway; MBA; Group chief rxecutive Glanbia plc. Assistant Ag. inspector, Dept. of Agriculture 1980-87; Waterford Co Op, head of Ag trading division 1987–94; head of dairying 1994-2001; appointed to the board 1997; Group managing director 2001 to date; board member Irish Dairy Board, Repak; council member Irish Business and Employers Confederation (IBEC), Irish Management Institute.

Recreations: golf, GAA. Contact: Glanbia House, Kilkenny, Co Kilkenny. **T** 056 777 2200 **F** 056 7772222 www.glanbia.com

> The Sligo born, agricultural scientist has turned around the fortunes of Glanbia in recent years; personable, bright, hardworking, he is well on his way to developing his company into a major player in the international food arena

MOLONEY, Paddy; MUSICIAN / COMPOSER

b 1938, Dublin; *m* Rita; 2*s* 1*d*; *edu.* St. Joseph's Marino, Dublin; D.Mus (*h.c.*) Trinity College, Dublin; Musician, Composer, Chief of The Chieftains; founded The Chieftains 1962; discography (Chieftains): *Santiago* 1996; *The Long Black* Veil (w/ Sting, Mick Jagger, Sinead O'Connor, Van Morrison, Mark Knopfler, Ry Cooder, Marianne Faithfull, Tom Jones, and The Rolling Stones) 1995; *The Celtic Harp* 1993; *The Magic of the Chieftains* 1992; *An Irish Evening: Live at the Grand Opera House, Belfast* (w/ Roger Daltry, Nanci Griffith) 1992; *Best of the Chieftains* 1992; *Another Country* (w/ various Nashville guests) 1992; *Reel Music: The Film Scores* 1991; *The Bells of Dublin* (w/ many guests)1991; *Collection* 1989; *Chieftains Celebration* (w/ Van Morrison, Nanci Griffith) 1989; *The Tailor of Gloucester* (narrated by Meryl Streep) 1988; *Irish Heartbeat* (w/ Van Morrison) 1988; *Celtic Wedding* 1987; *The Chieftains in China* 1985; *Ballad of the Irish Horse* 1986; *The Grey Fox* (soundtrack) 1984; *Year of the French* (soundtrack) 1982; *Publ. Paddy Moloney on the Chieftains; The Chieftains*, an autobiography. Recreations: gardening, walking. Contact: Grabow Associates, 4219 Creekmeadow Drive Dallas, TX 75287-6806. **T** 001 972 250 1162 or 001 888 290 1162 **F** 001 972 250 1165 email grabow@grabow.biz web www.grabow.biz

> An inspired and gifted genius; a household name all over the world in traditional music circles; can summon up a Who's Who of top Hollywood actors and iconic rock 'n rollers to collaborate with him and his band; wonderful raconteur, laid back, great company; fantastic dancer!

MOLONY, Ronan; CHAIRMAN, MC CANN FITZGERALD SOLICITORS

b 1959; *m* Christine Lavelle; 2*s* 1*d*; *edu.* Blackrock College, Dublin; University College Dublin; Incorporated Law Society; B.C.L., A.I.T.I.; Chairman Mc Cann Fitzgerald Solicitors; apprentice solicitor McCann FitzGerald 1980; solicitor, 1983; partner 1984; chairman 1997 to date; member Incorporated Law Society of Ireland; associate Institute of Taxation in Ireland; director Volkswagen Investments Limited and Bank of Montreal, Ireland; Clubs: Royal St. George Yacht Club, Royal Irish Yacht Club; Recreations: sailing, skiing; Contact McCann FitzGerald, 2 Harbourmaster Place, Custom House Dock, Dublin. **T** 01 607 1204 email Ronan.Molony@mccannfitzgerald.ie web www.mccanfitzgerald.ie

> Widely experienced in the area of financial transactions generally, presides over one of the larger legal practices in Ireland with 200 lawyers and offices in London and Brussels (and through the North South Legal Alliance, with L'Estrange & Brett in Belfast); has written and lectured extensively.

MONTAGUE, John; WRITER/POET

b 1929, Brooklyn, NY; *m* Elizabeth Wassell; 2*d*; *edu.* St. Patrick's College, Armagh, University College Dublin; Writer and Poet; 1st Ireland Professor of Poetry; publ. include: *The Rough Field, The Dead Kingdom, Selected Poems* (Penguin), *Collected Poems* (1995), 2 Volumes of short stories, a novella, a collection of essays, translations from the French, a memoir called *Company*, edited the *Faber Book of Irish Verse* and most recent collection of poems *Drunken Sailor* (2004); publishers include the Gallery Press, Duckworth, and Lilliput; Recreations: a quiet drink; Contact: Letter, Schull, Co. Cork. **T** 028 37228 email lizajohn@eircom.net

> A well known and prolific writer whose works have been much used by successive governments and much quoted by them at various ministerial conferences and even at the UN by Jack Lynch.

John Montague

MOONEY, Martin; ARTIST

b 1960; Belfast; *m* Trudie Mooney; 2*d*; *edu.* St. Mary's CBS Grammar School, Glen Road Belfast; Ulster Polytechnic Foundation Course; Brighton College of Art, BA (Hons) Fine Art; Slade School of Fine Art, University College London, 1st Class (Hons) in Fine Art (Painting); post-graduate in Fine Art University College London; Artist; Commissions: completed ten large panels for the Merrion

Martin Mooney

Hotel Dublin 1997; appointed official artist for HRH the Prince of Wales' royal tour of the Baltic States 2001; Awards: 1983 Emily Lucy Boyle Travel Scholarship, Brighton Faculty of Art; 1985 Richard Ford Award, The Royal Academy London; 1987 George Campbell Memorial Grant, Arts Council of Ireland, Arts Council of Northern Ireland and the Spanish Cultural Institute, Dublin; 1992 The Adam Salesrooms choice of artist for future appreciation award, Royal Hibernian Academy, Dublin. Contact; Old Fort Stewart, Ramelton, Donegal. **T** 074 915 1497.

A skilled artist in the representation of the real world, which is rendered with great facility; much collected, he remains a quiet and reserved personality.

MOONEY, Paschal Canice; SENATOR / BROADCASTER

b 1947, Dublin; *m* Sheila Baldrey; 3*s* 2*d*; *edu.* Presentation Brothers, Carrick on Shannon, Co Leitrim; Vocational School; Camden Institute of Education; assoc. member Institute of Employment Agency Consultants; Senator/ Broadcaster; Employment Agency Consultant; music & book Publisher; co-author *Women in Parliament* Wolfhound 2001; 1991 Leitrim Man of the Year; numerous articles for newspapers, magazines and periodicals; Recreations: country music, films, historical & political reading WW1 & WW2. Contact: Carrick Road, Drumshanbo, Co Leitrim. **T** 01 618 3483 **F** 01 618 4171 email paschal.mooney@oireachtas.ie

Son of the famous Joe Mooney, of 'An Tostal' fame, from Drumshambo, has worn many hats since his 1987 election to Seanad Eireann; a well known broadcaster in the world of country and western and sport; his engaging personality assures his popularity with TDs and county councillors throughout the country;

MOORE, Arthur; RACEHORSE TRAINER

b 1949, Dublin; *m* Mary Jones; 2*s* 1*d*; *edu.* Headfort, Preparatory School, Co. Meath; Downside Abbey, UK; National Hunt trainer 1971 to date; Racehorse Trainer; Leading Trainer 1992, 1993 season; rode Irish Grand National winner 1971; trained Irish Grand National winner Feathered Gale 1996; trained 6 winners at Cheltenham N. H. Festival, incl. 2 Queen Mother Chases; 3 Leopardstown Chases; Galway Plate; for review; Recreations: golf, swimming, reading; Contact Dereens, Naas, Co.Kildare. **T** 045 876 292 **F** 045 899247 email arthurmoore@eircom.net

Son of the legendary trainer Dan Moore, has more than emulated him; one of the most highly respected trainers in the country; extremely hard working and committed; great company.

MOORE, Christy; SINGER/SONGWRITER

b 1945, Newbridge, Co. Kildare; *m* Val; 3 children; *edu.* St. Conleths and St Marys Primary School, Newbridge, Co. Kildare; Singer/Songwriter; involved in music from childhood; joined the bank; transferred to Milltown Malbay 1964; met up with Willie Clancy and Micho Russell; during the bank strike went to London 1966; with Dominick Behan recorded first album *Paddy on the Road* 1962; *Prosperous* 1972; formed Planxty 1972; left Planxty for solo career 1975; formed Moving Hearts, 1980; retired from public perf 1998; Publ. *Whatever Tickles Your Fancy*; *The Iron Behind the Velvet*; *Christy Moore*; *H Block*; *The Time Has Come; Ride on; Ordinary Man; The Spirit of Freedom; Unfinished Revolution; Voyage; Smoke and Strong Whiskey; King Puck; Graffiti Tongue; Traveller; This is the Day;* With Planxty: *Planxty; The Well Below the Valley; Cold Blow and the Rainy Night; After the Break; The Woman I Loved So Well; Words and Music;* Planxty reformed 2005 for a number of sold out concerts at Vicar Street, Dublin. *Publ. One Voice.* (autobiography) 2000. Contact: web www.christymoore.com

Passionate about his music, a consummate performer and latter day philosopher; an icon of Irish folk music; considered by many the greatest singer of Irish folk music of the 20th century;

MORAN, Pat Joseph; PARTNER IT RISK & SECURITY

b 1967, Dublin; *m* Alison; 1*s* 1*d*; *edu.* O'Connells School, Dublin; Trinity College Dublin; BSc Computer Science; Partner IT Risk and Security, Ely Group. AIB Group 1987-96; Andersen 1996-2002; Ernst & Young 2002-5; Partner Ely Group 2005 to date; Clubs: Royal Dublin Golf Club; Recreations: Golf; Contact: ELY, Harcourt Street, Dublin 2. **T** 01 221 2769.

MORAN, Paul; J; ADVERTISING EXECUTIVE
b 1965, Dublin; single; *edu.* Templeogue College; Dublin Institute Technology; Diploma in Media
Studies; Diploma in Advertising Management; Managing Director Owens DDB; previously in media
departments of 'Young Advertising' 1983–90; O'Connor O'Sullivan Advertising; Bell Advertising;
joined Owens DDB in 1990; Clubs: Glasgow Celtic, Dublin GAA; Recreations: reading, cycling, Irish
music, Irish culture; Contact: 38 Fitzwilliam Place, Dublin 2. **T** 01 661 0161 **F** 01 662 1208
email paul.mediaworks@owensddb.com

Paul Moran

MORAN, Tom; HOTELIER
b 1950, Limerick; *m* Sheila; 5*s* 2*d*; Managing Director Moran Hotel Group; 25 years as manager, then
owner of pubs; 9 years in the hotel business; Managing Director Moran Hotel Group 1996 - to date;
Recreations: travel, hurling, GAA, golf, Contact: Red Cow Moran Hotel, Dublin. **T** 01 4593650
F 01 4591588 email tmoran@moranhotels.com

> The former Limerick publican was the first to shell out a million for a Dublin bar, The
> Red Cow Inn, 1988; converted it into one of the most profitable 4* hotels in Ireland;
> subsequently sold most of his impressive licenced premises portfolio to concentrate on
> the hotel business; bought The Silver Springs Moran Hotel, Cork from Fitzpatrick
> Hotels,1999; The Crown Moran Hotel, London opened 2003; Chiswick Moran Hotel,
> London, 2006; further acquisition of sites for development as new hotels in the UK
> and Ireland; sponsored Limerick GAA teams for many years.

MORIARTY, The Hon. Mr Justice Michael, CHAIRMAN MORIARTY TRIBUNAL
b 1946; *m* Mary Irvine; 1*s* 2*d*; *edu.* Blackrock College, Dublin; University College Dublin; Kings Inns;
BCL; called to the Bar 1968; called to the Inner Bar 1982; Chairman, Moriarty Tribunal; appointed
chairman of the Employment Tribunal 1986; appointed Circuit Court Judge 1987; appointed to the
High Court 1996; chairman Moriarty Tribunal, established to investigate payments to politicians
1997; Clubs: Fitzwilliam LTC, Pembroke Cricket Club. Recreations: music, cricket, books. Contact:
State Apartments, Dublin Castle, Dublin 2. **T** 01 670 5666 **F** 01 670 5490
web www.moriarty-tribunal.ie

> Now the longest sitting Tribunal chairman, he was appointed by the Oireachtas to
> investigate payments made to the late former Taoiseach Charles J. Haughey and former
> minister Michael Lowry; he brings a reputation of being extremely bright, clinical and
> fair-minded in the discharge of his judicial duties.

MORRICE, Jane; PUBLIC REPRESENTATIVE
b 1954, Belfast, Northern Ireland; *m* Paul Robinson; 1*s*; *edu.* Ashleigh House School, Belfast;
University of Ulster; BA (West European Studies); Public Representative; began her career as a
journalist in Brussels in 1980, specialising in international economic affairs and EU relations with the
Third World; joined BBC Northern Ireland as a reporter covering current affairs for radio and
television, 1987; became the BBC Business and Labour Relations Correspondent,1989–92;
appointed head of the European Commission office in Northern Ireland, representing the EC
1992–97; entered politics when she joined the Northern Ireland Women's Coalition Party as a
founder member, 1996; elected to the NI Assembly 1998; appointed Deputy Speaker 2000; member
Board of Governors of the Integrated Education Fund and of the European speakers' panel - Team
Europe; is involved with the North Down Victims Support Group; director Laganside Corporation
(which was established to regenerate the waterfront area of Belfast) 1998 to date. Recreations:
European affairs, women's issues, economic development, public speaking, debating,
communications, foreign languages - French (fluent), Spanish and German (basic). Contact: Northern
Ireland Assembly, Parliament Buildings, Belfast BT4 3XX. **T** 00 44 028 9052 1333
web www.niassembly.gov.uk

> A bright, hard working, well intentioned, forward looking politician; has been involved
> in the negotiations concerned with the implementation of the Good Friday Agreement,
> including the creation of the Executive and the North/South arrangements; was a
> member of the Standing Orders Committee which set the initial rules governing
> Assembly procedures post devolution; her positivity stands her in good stead.

MORRIS, The Hon. Mr. Justice Frederick; CHAIRMAN MORRIS TRIBUNAL
b 1929; *m* Valerie Farrell; 2*d*; *edu.* Glenstal Abbey; University College Dublin; Kings Inns; Middle

Temple, London; Chairman Morris Tribunal; called to the Bar 1952; called to the English Bar 1969; called to the Inner Bar 1973; appointed Judge of the High Court 1990; president of the High Court 1998-2002; served on Bar Council for ten years; served on the High Court Rules Committee for seventeen years; member of the Personal Injuries Compensation Tribunal for ten years; chairman Morris Tribunal 2002 to date; Awards: 1963 Freedom of City of Waterford; 1999 elected Honorary Bencher of Middle Temple, London; Clubs: Royal Irish Yacht Club, Milltown G.C, Blainroe Golf Club, U.C.D. Rugby Football Club; Recreations: sailing, golf, tennis. Contact: The Morris Tribunal, Belfield Office Park, Beechhill, Clonskeagh, Dublin 4. **T** 01 260 1111 **F** 01 2601122 email info@morristribunal.ie web www.morristribunal.ie

An elegant, charming, polite and gracious man who has in his two major Morris Tribunal reports to date shown tenacity and courage; he has revolutionised the way in which the man in the street views the actions of An Garda Siochána, particularly in Donegal; an unexpected revolutionary!

MORRIS, James; CHAIRMAN TV 3

b Dublin; *m*; *edu.* Ampleforth School, Yorkshire, England; Trinity College Dublin; BA H.Dip Ed.; chairman TV 3. Went to London, started as a runner in a Soho cutting room; three years later returned to Dublin as a trained film editor; set up his own editing company in 1976; with two partners moved the post-production business to Windmill Lane in Dublins dockland; set up Windmill Lane Recording Studios 1978 (the company pioneered the introduction of 1 inch C Format post-production techniques particularly in the field of commercials and pop promos in Ireland); led a consortium including Paul McGuinness (*qv*) and Ossie Kilkenny (*qv*) that was awarded the licence to operate Irelands first commercial TV station 1989; licence was withdrawn in 1991; Supreme Court gave it back in 1994; UTV pulled out of a revised consortium,1996; CanWest came on board, 1997; contract was signed with the IRTC 1997; chairman Windmill Lane Pictures; chairman The Mill, Europes largest film and video Special Effects company based in London; co-chairman, Mill Film with Ridley Scott; director of Shepperton Studios. Contact: TV 3, Ballymount Industrial Estate, Clondalkin, Dublin 22. **T** 01 419 3333 email james.morris@tv3.com web www.tve.ie

Scion of an old Galway family, son of British army Lieutenant Colonel, the late Tony Morris, from Co. Galway, the early promise does not appear to have been delivered on in his later career; amiable, pleasant, an excellent ideas man for his time.

Melanie Morris

MORRIS, Melanie Rose Josephine; EDITOR, IMAGE

b 1966, Dublin; single; *edu.* Our Lady's School, Rathnew, Co. Wicklow; U.C.D B.Comm; Journalist/Publisher/Editor *d'side* magazine; contributor *Irish Times, Sunday Business Post, The Examiner*; previously PR manager with Lynne Franks PR + Freud Communications, London; Publ. *AA Guide to Dublin, Virgin Guide to Dublin*; publisher, editor *dSide*; director Ashville Media 2002–05; Editor *Image* magazine 2005 to date. Clubs: Odessa Club; Recreations: fashion, music, contemporary art, architecture, design, travel Contact: IMAGE, 22, Crofton Road, Dun Laoghire, Co. Dublin. **T** 01 280 8415 web www.image.ie

Daughter of Mr Justice Morris (*qv*) and his elegant wife Valerie; dynamic, energetic, enthusiastic, stylish; well respected in the publishing world for her funky take on contemporary life.

MORRISSEY, James; PUBLIC RELATIONS CONSULTANT

b 1952, Kiltimach, Co. Mayo; *m* Heather; 2*s*; *edu.* Garbally Park, Ballinasloe; University College Dublin; B.Comm; Public Relations Consultant; previously financial journalist *Irish Independent*; deputy editor *Evening Herald*; founder/director *Sunday Business Post*; *Publ*: *Inishbofin – A History* (1987), *Hot Whiskey* (1989), *On the Verge of Want* (2001), *A History of the Fastnet Lighthouse* (2004); Directorships: Fleishman – Hillard, Newstalk 106; Clubs: Royal Irish Yacht Club; Recreations: sailing, walking, swimming, writing. Contact: 15 Fitzwilliam Quay, Dublin 4. **T** 01 618 8444 **F** 01 660 2123 email morrissj @fleishmancurope.com

The wily Co. Mayo, former journalist has excellent connections throughout the business and political worlds; knows the value of contacts and communications; laid back, good company; despite his impressive success in the commercial world, does he still hark after his news hound days?

MORRISSON, George Ivan 'Van'; SINGER

b 1945, Belfast; *m* Janet Minto (m.diss); 1*d*; *p* Michelle Rocca; 1*d*; *edu.* Sandy Row, Belfast; Singer; received his musical education by way of his father's extensive jazz and blues collection, as well as from his mother who worked as a professional singer; Singer, known for his singular style that combines jazz, folk, rhythm and blues and rock (also plays a variety of instruments, including the guitar, harmonica, keyboards, and saxophone); founder member of Irish group, Them 1966–68 (he penned 'Gloria' their seminal hit, 1966); embarked on successful solo career 1968 to date; career spans over four decades; has influenced many popular musical artists;inducted into the Rock and Roll Hall of Fame and the Songwriters Hall of Fame 1993; ranked number 25 on American cable music channel VH1's list of the 100 Greatest Artists of Rock and Roll, 2000; Recent discography: *Magic Time* 2005; *What's Wrong With This Picture* 2003; *Down The Road* 2002; *Van The Skiffle Sessions* 2000; *Morrission Back On Top* 1999; *The Philosophers' Stone* 1998; *Healing Game* 1996; *Tell Me Something* 1996. Contact: Grabow Associates, 4219 Creekmeadow Drive Dallas, TX 75287-6806. **T** 001 972 250 1162 or 001 888 290 1162 **F** 001 972 250 1165 email grabow@grabow.biz web www.grabow.biz web www.vanmorrison.co.uk

An idiosyncratic icon, the Belfast Soul singer is an especially private person who wants little to do with the obsessions of the common fan; 'The Man' is all about his music and has no need for the trappings of fame; many of his songs over the past decade have confronted his disdain for the illusions of success; an equal part of his catalogue consists of lengthy, loosely connected, spiritually inspired musical journeys that show the influence of Celtic tradition, jazz, and stream-of-consciousness narrative; appears to have found contement in recent years with his Dublin-born partner Michelle Rocca.

MORTELL, Mark Charles; BUSINESS COMMUNICATIONS CONSULTANT

b 1961, Dublin; *m* Aisling; 2*d*; *edu.* Blackrock College, Dublin, Presentation College Bray, Co. Wicklow; Dublin City University; B.Bus.Stud; Director Fleishman Hilliard; brand manager Guinness Ireland 1984-87; marketing manger Confectionary MARS Ireland 1987-89; marketing director Ballygowan Spring Water 1989-93; head of marketing Bank of Ireland Lifetime 1983-97; managing director Dimension Advertising 1997-99; commercial director Aer Lingus 1999-02; director Fleishman Hilliard 2002 to date; chairman Bord Fáilte 1997-2000; chairman OTMI 1995-97; FG Councillor (Bray Urban District Council) 1983-89. Clubs: Fitzwilliam LTC, Foxrock Golf Club, Bective Rangers F.C., Carrickmines Equestrian Club; Recreations: horse riding, golf, current affairs, wine, cooking. Contact: Fleishman Hilliard,15 Fitzwilliam Quay, Dublin 4. **T** 01 618 8444 **F** 01 660 2123 01 email mortellm@fleishmaneurope.com

Extremely bright and switched on, one of Ireland's top marketing consultants; consults with a stable of blue chip clients; offers a wealth of experience from an extremely impressive career.

Mark Mortell

MOUNTJOY, Dr Jim; CHAIRMAN, PROSPECTUS CONSULTANCY GROUP

b Cork; *m* Deirdre; *edu.* University College Cork; B.E; M. Eng.Sc; PhD; Chairman, Prospectus Consultancy Group; chief executive Euristix; spent six years as an executive engineer with Dept Post and Telegraphs (Eircom), including two years with Eurocontrol, the European Upper Airspace Air Traffic Control Body; co-founder & managing director Baltimore Technologies 1984; founded Euristix 1990; appointed vice-president Network Management, Marconi Communications Ltd 1999; sold Eurostix to Fore Systems 1999 (for $80 million, a value that increased to US$175 million in two months when Fore Systems was acquired by Marconi); chairman Prospectus Consultancy Group; director Science Foundation Ireland; chairman ICT Ireland, the R & D Advisory Committee; member Advisory Board of a number of Irish-based venture capital companies. Contact: Science Foundation Ireland, Wilton Park House, Wilton Place, Dublin. **T** 01 607 000 **F** 01 607 3201 email jim.mountjoy-at-sfi.ie web: www.sfi.ie

The Corkman is well-known and respected figure in the international software industry; best known for co-founding Eurostix; became a market leader with a customer list including such blue chip companies as Cisco, Tellabs, Motorola, Alcatel, IBM and HP.

MOYLAN, Pat; ARTISTIC DIRECTOR/ INDEPENDENT PRODUCER/ THEATRE OWNER

b Portlaoise; *m* Hugh McCusker; *edu.* Presentation Convent, Portlaoise; Teachers Dip. (Speech and Drama) Trinty College, London; Artisitic director Andrew's Lane Theatre, Dublin; producer: *Stones*

Pat Moylan

In His Pockets, Dublin, London West End, Broadway, New York; *I Keano; Alone It Stands; Thoroughly Modern Millie,* London West End; Recreations: reading, knitting, travel. Contact: Andrews Lane Theatre, Andrews Lane, Dublin 2. **T** 01 269 8941 **F** 01 679 7552 email pat@andrewslane.com

One of Ireland's most successful independent producers and theatre owners; has enjoyed international acclaim with several productions: extremely bright, great company, ambitious and extremely hard working; the least luvvie luvvy.

MOYNES, Adrian; MANAGING DIRECTOR, RTÉ RADIO
b 1953; *m* Rosaleen; 3*s* 1*d*; *edu.* St. Patrick's College, Armagh; Balliol College, Oxford; M.A.(English); managing director RTE Radio; lecturer in further education, 1974-79; radio producer RTÉ 1979-84; television producer/director RTÉ 1984-92; young peoples' programmes RTÉ Television 1992-93; head of schedule planning RTÉ Television 1993-97; special assistant to the director general RTÉ 1997-2002; managing director RTÉ Radio 2002 to date; Recreations: travel, the Arts. Contact: RTÉ Radio, Donnybrook, Dublin 4 **T** 01 208 4521 **F** 01 208 4523 email adrian.moynes@rte.ie

In a difficult climate has certainly breathed much needed, new life into the national radio station; is well able to navigate ego alley at Montrose.

John Mulcahy

MULCAHY, John F; INTERNATIONAL DIRECTOR AND MANAGING DIRECTOR JONES, LANG LaSALLE
b 1949, Dublin; *m* 1st (m. diss); 1*s* 1*d*; *m* 2nd Margaret Clandillon (*qv*); 3*s*; *edu.* Oatlands College, Mount Merrion; DIT environmental economics; International Director and Managing Director Jones Lang LaSalle; joined Jones Lang Wootton 1970; equity partner 1974; property partner 1976; international manager director Jones Lang LaSalle 1999; elected member Royal Institution of Chartered Surveyors in Ireland and of the Asset Valuation Standards Committee (Ireland, UK and Europe); Clubs: Fitzwilliam LTC, Stephen's Green Club, Mount Juliet Golf Club; Recreations; golf, running; Contact: Jones Lang LaSalle, 10-11 Molesworth Street, Dublin 2. **T** 01 673 1600 **F** 01 679 5147 web

Long established and respected in the commercial property world; involved in many of the bigger deals but has strong competition now.

MULCAHY, John Denis; PUBLISHER
b 1932, Perth, Western Australia; *m* Nuala O'Farrell; 6*s* 2*d*; *edu.* Clongowes Wood College, Co. Kildare; Trinity College, Dublin; Publisher; worked in the investigative and financial area in Canada; contributor to Montreal *Financial Times*; director Smiths Holdings Ltd 1960–67; editor/publisher *Hibernia* 1968–80; editor *Sunday Tribune* 1980–81; publisher *Phoenix Magazine* 1983 to date; editor *The Irish Arts Review* 2003 to date; Clubs: United Arts Club; RDS; Recreations: reading, walking; Contact: 44, Lower Baggott Street, Dublin 2. **T** 01 661 1062 **F** 01 662 4532 email jdm@indigo.ie

An irrepressible publisher and bon vivant; energetic, enthusiastic, curious; quirky sense of humour, his *Phoenix* magazine keeps the better news rooms and boardrooms on their toes; his most recent venture *The Irish Arts Review* is hailed as a triumph.

MULCAHY, Michael; BARRISTER-AT-LAW, PUBLIC REPRESENTATIVE
b 1960, Dublin; *m* Veronica Gates; *edu.* St. Conleth's College, Clyde Road, Dublin 4; University College Dublin; Trinity College Dublin; Kings Inns; public Representative/ practising barrister at the Dublin Bar 1985 to date; TD (Dublin South Central) 2002 to date. Member Dublin Corporation's housing committee 1985–2003; member Seanad Éireann (Fianna Fail spokesperson on Justice) 1994–97; chairman Dublin Regional Authority 1999–2000; Lord Mayor Dublin 2001-02; elected to Dáil Éireann 2002; appointed convener of the Oireachtas Joint Committee on European Affairs; chairperson of Fianna Fáil foreign affairs policy committee; member of the board Hugh Lane Municipal Gallery of Modern Art, Dublin; awarded the Knights Cross of the Order of Merit of the Republic of Poland; Clubs: St Judes GAA Club, Dublin; president Walkinstown United F.C; president Crumlin Community Youth Band; Contact: Dáil Éireann, Leinster House, Kildare Street, Dublin 2. **T** 01 618 3000 **F** 1 618 4779 web www.michaelmulcahy.ie,

Son of the legendary John 'Phoenix' Mulcahy (*qv*), the former Lord Mayor of Dublin was finally elected to the Dáil in 2002 after four failed attempts; the vociferous deputy still maintains a presence in the Law Library as a practising barrister on the eastern circuit;

MULCAHY, Nicholas; PUBLISHER

b 1958, Dublin; m Ann O'Neill (qv); 2s 2d; edu. St. Conleth's College, Ballsbridge, Dublin; Trinity College; Dublin BA (Mod); Publisher/Editor *Business Plus Magazine*; deputy editor *Phoenix Magazine* 1983-89; news editor *Sunday Business Post* 1989-97; editor *Business Plus Magazine* 1998 to date; Recreations: reading (history and fiction), gardening, cycling. Contact: Business Plus, 30, Morehampton Road, Dublin 4. **T** 01 660 8400 **F** 01 660 4540.

Son of John "Phoenix" Mulcahy (qv) , ink has coursed through his veins since birth; an excellent writer, now publishes a savvy business magazine that has upped the standards at the other business journals.

MULCAHY, Orna; PROPERTY EDITOR, IRISH TIMES

b 1962, Cork; m David Cox; 1s 2d; edu. Holy Faith Convent, Haddington Road, Dublin; Alexandra College Dublin; University College Dublin; B.A (History & English); Property Editor *The Irish Times* Journalist: *Harper & Queen* 1983-87; *Portfolio*, Sidney, Australia 1987-88; freelance journalist, Dublin 1988-90; *Sunday Business Post* 1990-93; columnist: IMAGE Magazine 1990-2002; *Irish Times* Property Section 1993 to date; property editor *Irish Times* 2004 to date; Recreations: reading, walking, family, travel, shopping, antiques. Contact: *The Irish Times*, D'Olier Street, Dublin 2. **T** 01 679 2022 email omulcahy@irish-times.ie

Vivacious, dynamic and hardworking, brings much of her magazine background to the property pages of the Irish Times producing great 'lifestyle' pages in addition to the nitty gritty of the property world.

Orna Mulcahy

MULDOON, Paul; POET

b 1951, Co. Armagh; m Jean Hanff Korelitz; edu. The Moy; Queens University, Belfast; Poet; worked as a radio and television producer with the BBC for thirteen years; has taught at a number of British and American universities including Cambridge University, Columbia University, the University of California at Berkeley, and the University of Massachusetts; currently Howard G.B. Clark '21 Professor in the Humanities at Princeton University and professor of poetry at the University of Oxford; awarded a Guggenheim Fellowship 1990; Sir Geoffrey Faber Memorial Award 1991; T. S. Eliot Award for *The Annals of Chile*,1994; American Academy of Arts and Letters Award in Literature 1996; *Irish Times* Irish Literature Prize for *New Selected Poems*, 1996; Pulitzer Prize 2003; *Publ. Moy Sand and Gravel* 2002; *Poems 1968-98* (Farrar Straus & Giroux, 2001); *Birds* 1999; *Hay* 1998; *Hopewell Haiku* 1997; *The Noctuary of Narcissus Batt* 1997; *Kerry Slides* 1996; *New Selected Poems 1968-94* (1996); *The Annals of Chile* 1994; *Madoc: A Mystery* 1991; *Meeting the British* 1987; has written libretti for the operas *Bandanna* 1999; *Shining Brow* 1993; *Six Honest Serving Men* (play) 1995; edited *The Faber Book of Beasts* 1997; *The Essential Byron* 1989; *The Faber Book of Contemporary Irish Poetry* 1986; Contact: Aosdana, 70 Merrion Square, Dublin 2. **T** 01 618 0200

The once precocious young poet is now the most playful, allusive and inventive poet currently writing; internationally acclaimed, his poems clearly come from the same rural Irish territory as Seamus Heaney's (qv) one of his biggest enthusiasts.

MULHERN, Eimear née Haughey; CHAIRMAN, RJ GOFF, BLOODSTOCK SALES

b 1955, Dublin. m John Mulhern; edu. Santa Sabina, Sutton, Co. Dublin; Chairman, Goffs, Bloodstock Sales; has had an interest in horses from an early age; started Abbeville Stud at her late father - former Taoiseach Charles J. Haughey's - Kinsealy Estate, North Co. Dublin many years ago; with husband John Mulhern also runs Meadow Court Stud, Co. Kildare; appointed chairman, Irish Thoroughbred Breeders Association 1998; chairman RJ Goff, January 2005 todate; director RJ Goff, 2005 todate; Recreations: racing, travel. Contact: RJ Goff and Co Ltd, Kill, Co. Kildare. **T** 045 886600 email sales@goffs.ie web www.goffs.ie

It's just possible that being The Boss's only and much loved daughter hampered rather than helped her; extremely bright and able; has been a successful and highly respected breeder for many years; charming, pragmatic, intensely loyal, extremely popular just about everywhere; her appointment to Goffs at a time when the company was floundering was inspired; following an extremely energetic marketing campaign nationally and internationally the inauguration of both Goffs Shelbourne Hotel Million; the Sportsman's Sale proved a phenomenal success in September 2005; overall figures represent an increase of 70% on 2004 returns; the aggregate reached €54, 999,900; the average was €76, 072, an increase of 89%; the Median reached €42,000, an increase of 100%; the first running of the Shelbourne Goffs Million at the Curragh, September 2006, was an overwhelming success; the future looks bright for bloodstock sales in Ireland with Mulhern at the helm at Goffs.

Larry Mullen Jnr

MULLEN, Larry Jnr; MUSICIAN/ DRUMMER, U2
b 1961, Artane, Co. Dublin; *p* Anne Acheson; 2s 1d; *edu*. Mount Temple Comprehensive School, Dublin; Musician/Drummer, U2; began drumming in 1971, taking classes with Ireland's best-known drummer, Joe Bonnie; placed a notice at the infamous Mount Temple Comprehensive School in the fall of 1976, looking to start a band! - although everyone knows the band as U2, Larry claims that the band's name is really "The Larry Mullen Band"; with schoolmates, Bono (Paul Hewson) (*qv*), Edge (Dave Evans) (*qv*) and Adam Clayton (*qv*) now part of the world's biggest rock band; Discography: *Boy* 1980; *October* 1981; *War* 1983; *Under a Blood Red Sky* 1983; *The Unforgettable Fire* 1984; *Wide Awake in America* 1985; *The Joshua Tree* 1987; *Rattle & Hum* 1988; *Achtung Baby* 1991; *Zooropa* 1993; *Pop* 1997; *All That You Can't Leave Behind* 2000; *Vertigo* 2005; has also recorded with artists Nanci Griffith, Emmylou Harris, B.B. King, Daniel Lanois, and others; also worked with fellow band mate Adam Clayton (*qv*) on the theme to the film *Mission: Impossible*, 1996; they also teamed up with Mike Mills and Michael Stipe from REM to form the group Automatic Baby for Bill Clinton's inauguration, 1993 at MTV's inaugural ball; wrote "Put 'em under pressure" for Irish Soccer Squad 1990; Best rock album, 'Sometimes You Can't Make It On Your Own', Grammy 2006; Song of the Year; Album of the Year 'How to Dismantle an Atomic Bomb' Grammy 2006; Best Rock Performance 'Sometimes You Can't Make It On Your Own', Grammy 2006; Band of the Year Grammy 2006 Recreations: art, dos, Harley Davidsons, soccer, rugby, Elvis Presley. Contact: Principal Management, 30/32, Sir John Rogerson's Quay, Dublin 2. **T** 01 677 7330 web www.U2.com

His sister, Cecilia, bought him his first drum-kit in 1973 for £17; the quiet one in U2 is down to earth and low-profile; his drumming is what gives the most popular band in the world its lift and thrust; spirit and instinct are what guides his drumming style; his award-winning career has been plagued with a battle with tendonitis, which has been helped by specially designed drumsticks

MULLIGAN, John Gerard; EDITOR
b 1971, Dundalk, Co. Louth; *m*; 2s; *edu*. Dundalk Christian Brothers School; University of Ulster, Coleraine; BA (Hons) (Humanities Combined, European Studies and Media Studies); Editor, Dundalk Argus; news reporter *Dundalk Argus* 1994; GAA correspondent 1999; sports editor 1999; appointed editor May 2004; Contact: The Argus, Partnership Court, Park Street, Dundalk, Co. Louth. **T** 042 9334632 **F** 042 9331643 email johnmulligan@argus.ie

Respected as a hardworking and innovative editor.

MULLIN, Enda; GENERAL MANAGER, THE WESTIN HOTEL; AREA MANAGER STARWOOD HOTELS AND RESORTS
b 1955, Donegal; *m* Susan Josephine; 1s 1d; *edu*. St. Tiernach's Secondary School, Clones, Co Monaghan; GMIT, Galway, BA (Hons), Hotel and Catering Management; General manager The Westin Hotel, Dublin and Area Manager, Starwood Hotels and Resorts; food and beverage manager New Mandeville Hotel, London 1978–80; food and beverage manager Shelbourne Hotel, Dublin 1980–83; food and beverage director Sun City, South Africa 1983-85; general manager Sun International Hotels South Africa 1985-92; regional director Sun International Hotels South Africa 1992-95; general manager Shangri La Hotels, Malaysia 1995–99; general manager Caledonian Hotel, Edinburgh 1999–2001; general manager Westin Hotel/Starwood Hotels and Resorts, Dublin, 2001; area manager Starwood Hotels and Resorts 2001 to date; Clubs: Leopardstown Tennis Club, Donegal Golf Club, Murvagh Recreations: sports, cinema, reading, golf. Contact: Westin Hotel, College Green, Dublin 2. **T** 01 645 1000 **F** 01 645 1201 email ENDA.MULLEN@WESTIN.com

Sophisticated; finger on the pulse of 5 star properties; oversaw the new Sheraton in IrelandFota Island Golf and Spa Resort in Cork which was officially opened September 2006.

MULLINS, William Peter 'Willie'; RACE HORSE TRAINER
b 1956, Dublin; *m* Jacqueline; 1*s*; *edu.* Cistercian College, Roscrea; Racehorse Trainer; champion amateur jockey; chairman, Irish Race Horse Trainers Association; president European Trainers Federation; director Waterford/Tramore Race Course; champion trainer; Clubs: Mount Juliet Golf Club, Gowran Golf Club; Recreations: golf . Contact: Closutton, Bagnelstown, Co. Carlow. Contact: **T & F** 059 972 1786 email wpmullins@eircom.net

Gregarious, extremely popular trainer known by his patrons for his attention to detail which has produced multiple winners of all the major races at home and abroad; great ambassador for his sport.

MULVIHILL, Liam DIRECTOR GENERAL, GAA
b 1946, Longford; *m* Máire Ní Shiochrú; 2*s* 1*d*; *edu.* St. Mel's College, Longford; St. Patrick's College Drumcondra, Dublin; University College Dublin; St. Patrick's College Maynooth, Co.Kildare; N.T; B.A, I I.Dip. Ed; Director General GAA; primary teacher, Department of Education 1966-71; schools inspector, Department of Education 1971-79; Director General GAA 1979 to date; Awards: LL.D (*hc*) Maynooth 2001; served two terms RTÉ Authority; board member, Campus Stadium Ireland. Contact: Croke Park, St. Joseph's Avenue, off Clonliffe Road, Dublin 3. **T** 01 819 2323 **F** 01 819 2324 email info@gaa.ie web www.gaa.ie

The Longford-born, former schools inspector is the most powerful man in Irish sport; quiet, unassuming personality disguises a brilliant intellect; has guided the GAA over the last quarter of a century; among his legacies are the magnificent, modern Croke Park complex, the envy of all sporting organizations in Ireland and one of the finest in Europe; his daughter Daráine overcame serious illness to become one of the People of the Year for her bravery and was appointed to the Council of State in 2004

MULRYAN, Sean Martin; COMPANY CHAIRMAN
b 1954, Oran, Co. Roscommon; *m* Bernadine; 4*s* 2*d*; *edu.* Roscommon Secondary School; ANCO, Galway, Ltd; Chairman, Ballymore Homes; stonemason; purchased land in Blackrock, 1986, with Michael Bailey (*qv*) built Merrion Park Developments; other house building developments include Tallaght, Swords and Rathfarnham; Galway Bay Golf and Country Club; major developer of London Docklands and Westminster; one of main sponsors of London Olympics 2012 successful bid; partner with James Sheehan (*qv*) and Larry Goodman (*qv*) in Dublin's newest medical clinic in Liffey Valley; founder, chairman, managing director Ballymore Properties Ltd 1981 to date; Clubs: Kildare Hotel and Country Club, Rathsallagh Golf Club, Marks, London. Recreations: horse racing and breeding, art, golf, travel. Contact: Ballymore Properties, 35-38 St Stephen's Green, Dublin 2. **T** 01 662 2300 **F** 01 662 2302 web www.ballymoreproperties.ie

The Roscommon-born, former brickie is now the greatest entrepreneur in modern Ireland as well as one of the wealthiest; solid, low profile, extremely hardworking and extraordinarily loyal to his friends, maintains strong contacts with his home county through his sponsorship of the Roscommon GAA teams; the biggest residential builder in the London area, focussing mainly in the East End, sponsored bid for the 2012 London Olympics; this will provide him with even further opportunities, ensuring that he remains No. 1 in the building and construction sector; also an emerging presence in property development in Bratislava, Poland and the United States; determined to grow his empire internationally; based on his track record, he is more than likely to achieve that ambition; a regular presence at race meetings reflects his passion for the sport of kings; is now one of the biggest and most successful National Hunt owners in France.

MUMBA, Samantha 'Sam'; SINGER
b 1983, Dublin; single; *edu.* Glasnevin; Billy Barry School, Dublin; panto Gaiety with Twink 1997; signed by Louis Walsh (*qv*) 1998; *Hot Mikado* (1998); Albums: *Gotta tell You* (No. 1 in US and Ireland; No. 3 in UK); *Body II Body*; founded dance school Samsara, 2005; face of Newbridge Silverware jewelry; face of Dunnes Stores Per Amore lingerie; Films: *The Time Machine* (2002); *Spin the Bottle* (2003); *Boy Eats Girl* (2005); *Johnny Woz* (2006); Recreations: shopping, dance, travel, entertaining friends, interior décor. Contact: www.samanthamumba.com

A confident, savvy and thoroughly pleasant young woman; her songs - which she co-writes - are a supremely confident collection of pop-inflected R&B nuggets that finally prove Europe can match the super-slick Brittany, Brandy et al; as a budding business woman is well able to maximize her marketing potential.

MURRAY, Eugene Martin; CEO IRISH HOSPICE FOUNDATION

b 1950, Limerick; *m* Avril Burgess; 3*s*; *edu.* Clongowes Wood College; Trinity College Dubin; BBS; M.Litt (Econ); CEO Irish Hospice Foundation; producer/director RTE 1980–1986; head of current affairs television/ editor Today Tonight 1986–1990; RTE director of business planning 1990–2000; director of Digital Media, RTE 2000–2003; chairman of the governing body Dun Laoghaire Institute of Art Design and Technology; Clubs: Delgany Golf Club, Greystones Lawn Tennis Club; Recreations: current affairs, travel, golf. Contact: Irish Hospice Foundation, Morrison Chambers (4th floor), 32, Nassau Street, Dublin 2. **T** 01 679 3188 **F** 01 673 0040 email info@hospice-foundation.ie web wwwhospice-foundation.ie

The quietly spoken Shannon sider is a brother of the Chief Justice John Murray (*qv*); after a distinguished career in RTE took over the running of the Irish Hospice Foundation; also sits on the board of the National Cancer Hospital, St Lukes, Dublin.

MURRAY, The Hon Mr. Justice John; CHIEF JUSTICE OF IRELAND

b 1943, Limerick; *m* Gabrielle Walsh; 1*s* 1*d*; *edu.* Crescent College, Limerick; Rockwell College, Co. Tipperary; University College Dublin; King's Inns; called to the Bar 1967; called to the Inner Bar 1981; Chief Justice of ireland; Attorney General Aug-Dec 1981, 1987-89; 1989–91; appointed Judge of the European Court of Justice 1991–99, the fourth Irish member of the Court which is the supreme judicial body in Europe; Professor of Law, invite, Université de Louvain since 1997; recipient, Doctor of Laws, (*hc*) University of Limerick, 1993; appointed to the Supreme Court 1999–04; appointed Chief Justice 2004; Contact: The Four Courts, Dublin 7 **T** 01 888 6569 **F** 01 873 2332 email SupremeCourt@courts.ie web www.courts.ie

Very sharp intellect with a concise legal brain; had a very distinguished career in private practice, (dealing with commercial, civil, and constitutional law), as Attorney General and at the European Court of Justice; was a popular appointment as Chief Justice; enjoys life and has an excellent sense of humour.

MURRAY, Peter; DIRECTOR, THE CRAWFORD ART GALLERY, CORK

b 1956, Dublin; *m* Sarah; *edu.* St.Paul's College, Raheny, Dublin; University College Dublin BA; Trinity College Dublin; MLitt; Director, The Crawford Art Gallery Cork; lecturer in Art History, National College of Art and Design 1981-84; curator (now director) Crawford Municipal Art Gallery, Cork (now Crawford Gallery) 1984 to date; member Association of Irish Art Historians; College Art Association AAM, IMA FNCI; Recreations: painting, drawing, restoring old buildings. Contact: Crawford Municipal Gallery, Emmett Place, Cork. **T** 021 427 3377 **F** 021 480 5043 email crawfordinfo@eircom.net

A most effective director. Has transformed the Crawford into a designated national cultural institution. Has a keen sense of what it takes to make his gallery the epicentre of what mattes in the arts, old and new in Ireland. Spans the worlds of classic art and cutting edge modernism.

MURRAY, Niamh; LYRIC SOPRANO

b 1963, Nigeria; single; *edu.* Carysfort College Dublin (B.Ed); associate of London College of Music; RIAM; Licentiate Speech and Drama, Leinster School of Music; Royal Northern College of Music, Manchester; international studies with Brigitte Fassbaender, Ugo Benelli and Thomas Helmsley; Italian government scholarship facilitated further study with Maestro Carlo Bergonzi in Sienna. Lyric Soprano; most frequent requested artiste to appear at the National Concert Hall; performed extensively in opera, operetta, oratorio and stage musical; grand opera appearances include Turandot, Orfeo; opera roles include Marguerite (Faust), Micaela (Carmen); highly regarded throughout the world, appearing to great critical acclaim including BBC's *Songs of Praise* productions in 1997; guest soloist at the televised Pioneer Centenary Mass in 1999; leading lady in Jury's Irish Cabaret; regular guest presenter on Lyric FM; Awards: John Count McCormack and Margaret Burke Sheridan gold medals; *Publ.* CDs *A Fairer Paradise, When Irish Eyes Are Smiling, Wedding Memories From Ireland.* Contact: Agent, Anne Boylan, Pilot View Lodge, Harbour Road, Dalkey, Co. Dublin. **T** 01 280 5982

Charming and beautiful, the talented soprano's musical talents span a broad spectrum; has performed all over the world.

MURLESS, Charles Richard; COMPANY DIRECTOR

b 1959, Co. Kildare; *m* Rhona Blake (*qv*); 2*s* 1*d*; *edu.* Headfort School, Kells, Co Meath; Cheltenham College, Cheltenham, Gloucestershire, England; Company Director; Goffs Bloodstock Sales Ltd; International Racecourse Management & IRM (UK) 1991–94; chief executive Punchestown Group 1994–2002; company director sportsticketing.com, 2002 to date; director RTA Technologies; Clubs: Turf Club Rooms; Recreations: horseracing. Contact: 18, Wellington Road, Ballsbridge, Dublin 4. **T** 01 668 9503 email charliemurless@mail.com

Charlie Murless

> Sartorially elegant, made his name in the bloodstock industry at Goff's Orby sales and subsequently as general manager of Punchestown; has encyclopedic knowledge of the racing industry; pursues successful business career; his magnetic personality makes him wonderful company and, with his beautiful and accomplished wife Rhona Blake (*qv*), a much sought after dinner party guest

MURPHY, Geordan Edward Andrew; PROFESSIONAL RUGBY UNION PLAYER

b 1978, Naas, Co. Kildare; *p* Lucie Silvas; *edu.* Newbridge College, Newbridge, Co. Kildare; De Montfort University, Leicester, UK; Professional Rugby Union Player; gained his first U18 cap for Ireland 1997; joined Leicester Tigers 1997; after representing Ireland A and an Ireland XV, selected to play for Ireland against United States 2000; selected for the Barbarians tour of the UK and Ireland 2001; Tigers top try scorer in all competitions 2001/02 season; scored a try for Ireland against Samoa in November 2001, and two more against Wales in Dublin in that season's Six Nations, but was then injured in the game against England; toured with Ireland 2002, adding 2 more caps to his tally; missed the start of Tigers 2002/03 campaign after undergoing surgery; returned to fitness in time to participate in the autumn internationals, and his form in the 2003 Six Nations earned him the accolade of Irish Player of the Season, given by the Irish rugby writers; broke his leg in warm-up game against Scotland at Murrayfield prior to the 2003 Rugby Union World Cup and did not compete; was selected for the British and Irish Lions tour to New Zealand 2005; played mostly in the midweek team but was selected at full back for the third and final test. Clubs: Leicester Tigers UK; Recreations: golf. Contact: IRFU, Landsdown Road, Ballsbridge, Dublin 4. **T** 01 647 3800 web www.irishrugby.ie

> Very personable, which enhaces his corporate earning potential; one of the new crop of Irish rugby professionals; has impacted on the world rugby stage as a member of the Lions Squad 2005

MURPHY, Loughlin Gerard 'Locky' MOTOR TRADE/ BUSINESSMAN

b 1968, Tullamore, Co. Offaly; separated; *edu.* Edenderry Secondary School, Co Offaly; Managing Director Carroll and Kinsella (Churchtown)/ Property Developer; qualified carpenter; joined Windsor Motors 1991; Opel dealership Edenderry 1993; managing director Carroll and Kinsella, Churchtown, Dublin, 1993 to date; Clubs: Edenderry Golf Club, Rhode GAA, Co. Offaly; St. Judes, GAA Club, Dublin; Recreations: GAA,golf, racing, rugby. Contact: Carroll and Kinsella, Churchtown Road, Churchtown, Dublin 14. **T** 01 298 3166

> The Tullamore born Managing Director of Carroll and Kinsella in Churchtown, is an influential figure in the Dublin motor trade; has helped build up Carroll and Kinsella into a major player in the auto industry; a shrewd businessman, property developer and racehorse owner, he is charismatic and extremely popular in Dublin social circles and always on demand for charity ball committees.

MURPHY; Martin Thomas; MANAGING DIRECTOR, HEWLETT PACKARD IRELAND

b 1962; *m* Anna; 2 *s* 1*d*; *edu.* St. Mary's College Dundalk; CUS, Leeson Street, Dublin; Priority College Dublin (Mathematics BA), B.Eng BAI, Masters in Science M.Sc. Managing Director, Hewlett Packard Ireland; research Scientist, Philips, Netherlands 1986–87; with Hewlett Packard 1987 to date; head of consulting & services 1992–95, sales director 1995–99, managing director 1999 to date; Clubs: Druids Glen Golf Club; Recreations: skiing, reading, flying. Contact: Hewlett Packard Ireland, Liffey Park, Leixlip, Co. Kildare. **T** 01 615 8276 email mmurphy@hp.com web www.hp.com

> Internationally experienced IT engineer who continues to expand HP in Ireland; one of the country's biggest employers (over 4000); highly respected with the organization which manifests itself in the corporations continued reinvestment in this country.

Moira Murphy

MURPHY, Moira; MARKETING DIRECTOR BROWN THOMAS GROUP
b 1973, Kealkill, Bantry, Co. Cork; *m* David Wilson; *edu.* Ard Scoil Phobal, Bantry, Co. Cork; University College Dublin; Smufit Business School; BBLS; H.Dip. MP; Marketing Director, Brown Thomas Group; brand manager/marketing manager Unilver Ireland 1996–2000; marketing Director Brown Thomas Group 2000 to date; Recreations: music, playing the piano, reading, running, hill walking, yoga, Sudoku. Contact: 88/95, Grafton Street, Dublin 2. **T** 01 605 6666 **F** 01 605 6753 email mmurphy@brownthomas.ie web www.brownthomas.ie

Dynamic, ebullient, extremely hardworking perfectionist; wonderful sense of style as befits the marketing director of Ireland's premier luxury goods department store group.

MURPHY, Professor Michael Brendan; DEAN OF MEDICINE, UNIVERSITY COLLEGE CORK
b 1963, Cork; *m* Siobhan O'Keeffe; 1*s* 2*d*; *edu.* St. Finbarr's College, Farranferris College, Cork; University College, Cork; Royal Postgraduate Medical School, University of London; University of Chicago; MB, BCh BAO, 1976; MD, 1985; FRCPI, 1990; FACCP, 1991; Dean of Faculty of Medicine and Health, University College, Cork 2000 to date; research fellow and honorary senior registrar in clinical pharmacology, University of London 1980-84; assistant professor of medicine and pharmacology, University of Chicago 1984-92; chairman of clinical pharmacology, University College Cork 1992 to date; professor of clinical pharmacology, Mercy University Hospital, Cork - consultant in clinical pharmacology 1992 to date; principal investigator of *PROSPER* 1997-2002; *ARAMIS* 2000-02 international clinical trials; member Association of Physicians of Great Britain and Ireland; Board of Health Service Executive 2004 to date; chairman Health Research Board of Ireland 1997-2002; honorary doctorate in medicine, Central University of Venezuela 1998; chairman Council of Deans of Irish Faculties with Medical Schools 2003 to date; on board of governors American Heart Association of Metropolitan Chicago 1991-92; chairman Permanent Working Group of Hospital Doctors of the European Economic Community 1979-80; *Publ.* original articles:105; books:1 authored and 5 edited; book chapters or invited reviews: 30; Clubs: Corrigan Club, Association of Physicians of Great Britain and Ireland; Recreations: golf, classical music. Contact: Faculty of Medicine and Health, Brookfield Health Sciences Complex, College Road, Cork. **T** 021 490 1616 **F** 021-4901549 email mmurphy@medicine.ucc.ie web www.ucc.ie

An internationally respected medical academic who plays a very influential role in the restructured UCC; highly respected by his peers, well connected nationally and internationally.

MURPHY, Michael 'Mike'; COMPANY DIRECTOR
b 1941, Dublin; *m* 1st Eileen Dixon (*m diss*); 1*s* 3*d*; *m* 2nd Ann Walsh; *edu.* St. Louis National School, Rathmines; Terenure College; Company Director; apprentice draper Crowe Wilson 1959-61; clerk Castrol Ireland Ltd.1961-62; freelance actor 1961-64; radio announcer RTE 1965-70; broadcaster/ programme presenter RTE 1970-2003; director Harcourt Developments Ltd; director Park West Business Park; Awards: 1978 Jacobs Award for 'Morning Call'; 1982 Live Mike; 1983 Murphy's America; 1987 Murphy's Australia; 1990 Business Person of the Month, Irish Press, February; *Publ.* Memoirs, *Mike and Me* (1977); Recreations: golf, arts, tennis; Clubs: Royal Dublin Golf Club. Contact: Harcourt Developments, Harcourt House, 18-19 Harcourt Street, Dublin 2. **T** 01 475 3928. **F** 01 475 3943

Charismatic, laid back, great fun, one of the legendary figues of Irish radio and television; in recent years has successfully concentrated on the property world.

MURPHY, Tara; GALLERIST
b 1971, Dublin; *m* Niall Ó hOisín; 1*s* 1*d*; *edu.* St. Andrews College, Booterstown, Dublin; University College Dublin; BA (hons); Dip. Arts Administration; Director, The Solomon Gallery Dublin; assistant Solomon Gallery 1994-97; director 1997 to date; Recreations: cinema, skiing, travel, food. Contact: The Solomon Gallery, Powerscourt Townhouse, South William Street, Dublin 2. **T** 01 679 427 **F** 01 679 5262 email tara@solomongallery.com web www.solomongallery.com

A charming and intelligent Gallerist whose taste and style is admired by her peers in the business and by the buying public alike. Draws in the younger crowd who are the future of the gallery business.

MURPHY, William 'Billy'; EXECUTIVE CHAIRMAN, DRURY COMMUNICATIONS, PUBLIC RELATIONS

b 1959; *m* Kathryn Connolly; 1*s* 1*d*; *edu.* Rockwell College, Co. Tipperary; University College Dublin 1978-1982; B. Comm; H Dip Marketing Practices; Executive Chairman Drury Communications; account executive Murray Consultants 1982-85; Pembroke Public Relations 1985-88; co-founder Drury Communications 1989, managing director 1999-2004, executive chairman 2004 to date; Clubs: President UCD Rugby Club 2005-06; Connemara Golf Club, Delgany Golf Club, St Mary's Tennis Club, Phoenix Racing Club, Rockwell College Union; Recreations: family pursuits, rugby, golf, soccer, hurling, horseracing, tennis, painting, visiting galleries and exhibitions; music (rock), reading; Contact: Drury Communications Ltd, 1 Richview Office Park, Dublin 14. **T** 01 260 5000 **F** 01 260 5066 email bmurphy@drurycomm.com

> Well respected professional who grew his company into a major player in the Irish PR world; continues to drive it forward.

MURPHY, Yvonne; CIRCUIT COURT JUDGE

b 1951, Athlone, Co. Westmeath; *m* Adrian Hardiman (*qv*); 3*s*; *edu.* Ursuline Convent Sligo; Kings Inns; Barrister at Law, 1971; Circuit Court Judge; worked as civil servant, air hostess and journalist 1971–84; RTE presenter and editor 'Industrial Relations News'; special adviser to former the late Tánaiste and Labour leader Michael O'Leary; Special Criminal Court judge 2003 to date; appointed by Government to head up Commission into the Dublin Archdiocese's handling of child abuse allegations 2005 to date. Recreations: all sport, especially soccer, travel. Contact: Fourt Courts, Dublin 7. **T** 01 888 6070 **F** 01 888 6063 web www.courts.ie

> Highly articulate, keen legal brain, the Athlone-born barrister had a broad range of experience before being appointed to the Bench; though not as well known as her husband, Supreme Court Judge Adrian Hardiman, she has carved a respected reputation as a fair minded judge.

MURTAGH, Eugene 'Gene'; CHIEF EXECUTIVE, KINGSPAN plc

b 1971, Co. Cavan; *m*; 3 children; *edu.* Gormanstown College, Co. Meath; University of Limerick ; BBS; Chief Executive Kingspan plc; joined Kingspan 1994; managing director of the environmental container business; managing director of the Group's insulated panel businesses; chief operating officer; appointed to the board 1999; Group Chief Executive 2005 - todate; Contact: Carrickmacross Road, Kingscourt, Co. Cavan. **T** 042 969 8500 www.kingspan.com

> Son of the founder Eugene, astute, hardworking businessman well respected in this now global and hugely successful business.

MUSGRAVE, Olivia Mirabel; SCULPTOR

b 1958; Dublin; *m* John E. Gardiner; *edu.* Newtown School, Waterford, City & Guilds of London Art School; BA (Sculpture); Sculptor; solo exhibitions include: Christopher Hull Gallery 2000, 2002, 2004; John Martin Gallery 1998, 2004; Jorgensen Fine Art 1998, 2004; Everard Read Gallery 2002; Public Commissions/Collections include: Boots Plc, Oxford University, National Bank of Greece, The National Self Portrait Collection of Ireland, University of Limerick, Irish Guide Dogs for the Blind; selected mixed exhibitions onclude: The Discerning Eye, Mall Galleries, London 1990, 1995; Royal Academy of Arts summer exhibition 1992, 1994; "Young British Sculptors", Beaux Arts Gallery 1996; Society of Portrait Sculptors 1996-97, 2000, 2002, 2005; The Royal Hibernian Academy, Dublin, summer exhibition 1997-2005; The Boyle Arts Festival, Ireland 1997; Royal West of England Academy, Bristol 2003; Clubs: Chelsea Arts Club; Recreations: needlepoint and car boot sales; Contact: Flat 1, 163 Sussex Gardens, London W2 2RH. **T** 0044 207 4021143 email omusgrave@compuserve.com

> Has a great sense of line, scale and treatment of surface; a collector's joy.

MUSGRAVE, Trevor; CAR SALESMAN

b 1977, Dublin; single; *edu.* Castleknock College, Dublin; Car Salesman; joined family motor business; joined Des Cullen Motors 1996–todate; Clubs: Kildare Hotel and Country Club. Renards, Lillies Bordello. Recreations: helicopter piloting, shopping, horseriding, polo. Contact Des Cullen, Beacon Court, Sandyford, Dublin 18. **M** 086 875 5911

The man to call when you want that exotic motor NOW !!!! can seemingly source, with ease this year's 'Must Have' motors while other wait for three to six months; ambitious, focussed, works hard and plays harder.

MYERS, Kevin: JOURNALIST and AUTHOR
b 1947, Leicester; *m* Rachael Nolan; *edu.* Ratcliffe College, Leicestershire; UCD; BA; Columnist, *Irish Independent.* columnist *Irish Independent*; RTE in Belfast; *Observer*; NBC Radio in Belfast. Joined *Irish Times* 1980; columnist *Irish Times* 1981-2006; columnist *Irish Independent* 2006 to date; *Publ. Selected Columns* (Four Courts); *Banks of Green Willow* (Novel, ribner); some broadcasting; Recreations: military history, Irish regiments, early 20th century poetry; antiques. Contact: Broadstone, Ballymore Eustace, Co. Kildare. **T** 045 891470 **F** 045 891470 email viga@iolfree.ie

The stormy petrel of Irish journalism, he attracts loathing and admiration in equal measure; tells it like he sees it and is not for the faint hearted; his frequently jokey references and liking for the British Military enrages as much as it engages, a punchy and betimes courageous journalist.

NAGLE, Ciaran Joseph; TENOR/MANAGING DIRECTOR EDGEWOOD PRODUCTIONS
b 1970; *m* Imelda Drumm; 1*d*; *edu.* St. Gerard's School, Bray, Co. Wicklow; LSB College, Chatham
Row, Dublin 2; Dip INT Languages & Marketing; tenor/Managing Director Edgewood Productions;
member, Riverdance, Opera Ireland, The Irish Tenors; producer of gala events and theatre shows.
Clubs: RDS, Royal Health Club. Recreations: music, sport, cinema, commerce. Contact: Edgewood
Productions Ltd, Ibd Yarns, Bray, Co.Wicklow. **T** 01 286 4680 **F** 01 282 9209
email: edgewood@indigo.

> A pleasant tenor with a great presence, member of the Irish Tenors; has sung all over
> the world and on All Ireland days; also heads up a successful production company.

NAGLE, John; CHIEF EXECUTIVE, ALPHYRA GROUP plc
b 1963, Kinsale, Cork; *m* Joan; 3 children; Chief Executive, Alphyra Group plc; joined Like Jeans
Cork; salesman Technico Ireland; founder ITG 1989; changed name to Alphyra Group 2001; MBO
Alphyra 2003. Clubs: Old Head Golf Club Kinsale, Co. Cork, Kildare Hotel and Country Club,
Straffan, Co. Kildare. Recreations: golf. Contact: 4, Heather Road, Sandyford Industrial Estate,
Dublin 18. **T** 01 207 6000 web www. alphyra.ie

> A protégée of the legendary Otto Glazer, this low profile, ambitious Corkman now
> heads up one of the most successful companies in the country.

NASH, Richard; COMPANY CHAIRMAN
b 1943, Dublin; separated; 2*s* 1*d*; *edu.* Castleknock College, Dublin; Fordham University, New York;
B.Sc.; Chairman, Nash Beverages Ltd; chairman, Nash's Mineral Waters Ltd; managing director,
Nash Wines; co-founder of Ballygowan Spring Water Company Ltd, bottling the water from a natural
spring within the company's Newcastle premises; sold to Cantrell & Cochrane 1993. Clubs: Adare
Golf Club, Ballybunion Golf Club, Kildare Street and University Club. Recreations: golf, skiing, hill
walking. Contact: The Square, Newcastle West, Co Limerick. **M** 086 241 0614
email rnash@nashwines.ie

> Likable and affable, he's made a cult of Nash Water in the blue bottle, and previously
> with Ballygowan; keeps himself low key, but within the business community has
> standing and a reputation for abilty and skill.

NATHAN, Regina; OPERA SINGER
b 1960; *m* Joseph Lynch; *edu.* St. Patrick's College, Maynooth; BA; H.Dip.Ed; Trinity College London;
Dip.Singing; attended The National Opera Studio, London; Opera Singer;
has sung in the major European opera houses, New York's Carnegie Hall; special guest, opening
concert Commonwealth Games, Kuala Lumpar 1998; roles include Susanna (*Marriage of Figaro*);
Mimi (*La Boheme*); Violette (*La Traviata*); Adina (*L'Elisir d'Amore*); Gilda (*Rigalotto*); Sophie (*Der
Rosenkavalier*); Susanna (*Susanna* by Floyd); sings oratoria, symphonic works; much in demand as a
recitalist throughout Europe; recently recorded a series of Britten songs with Malcolm Martineau for
Hyperion Records; Mahler's *Symphony No 8* with Edo de Waart (BMG); Rachmaninov's *The Bells*;
Vocalise with Djong Victorim Yu Carlton Classics; *Faith of Our Fathers* with Enigma Records; Awards:
Outstanding New Entertainer, (National Entertainment Awards) 1991; Irish Life/Sunday
Independent Music Award 1991. Recreations: reading. Contact: 19 Millington Road, Burnt Oak,
Edgeware, Middlesex HA8 OPL, England. **T** 0044 181 9310 811.

> A great solo singer, she's branched out into other musical areas as singers have a
> notoriously short performing life; well marketed and directed she's still a favourite of
> the nation for concert performances.

NAUGHTON, Martin; CHAIRMAN GLEN DIMPLEX
b 1939, Dundalk; *m* Carmel McCarthy; 2*s* 1*d*; *edu.* De La Salle Dundalk; Southampton College of
Technology; NNC (Mechanical & Production Engineering); Chairman Glen Dimplex Group; student
apprentice Hawker Siddley Aircraft 1957-61; works study engineer, SPS (Shannon) 1961; chief works
study engineer, AET (Dunleer) 1961-65; services manager Callins (Shannon) 1965-67; works
manager AET (Dunleer) 1967-73; founder, managing director Glen Electric, becoming Glen Dimplex
Group 1973; bought out his business partner Lochlann Quinn (*qv*) 2005; chairman Glen Dimplex
2005 to date; LL.D (hc) UCD 1991; LL.D (hc) Trinity College Dublin 1995; LL.D (hc) Queen's

University Belfast 1998; LL.D (hc) Notre Dame University, South Bend, Indiana 1998; appointed to the Council of State 1998; endowed the Martin Naughton Chair of Business Strategy in the School of Management, Queen's University Belfast 1998; The Carmel and Martin Naughton Fellowship Program at the Keough Insitute, University of Notre Dame 1999; founded The Glen Dimplex Art Awards; chairman, InterTradeIreland, the Cross Border Body for North South Business Developments. Contact: Glen Dimplex, Ardee Road, Dunleer, Co. Louth. **T** 041 51700 **F** 041 51807

Leading member of the Louth Golden Triangle with Larry Goodman (*qv*) and Niall Mc Cann (*qv*); has developed Glen Dimplex into a global name and now employs some 8,500 people and has annual sales of €1.3 billion; arising from the success of Glen Dimplex he has diversified into a number of private investments in the area of property, hotels and tourism; known to have one of the finest private art collections in the country; the low profile, quietly spoken Co. Louth man is a significant philanthropist.

Liam Nellis

NELLIS, Liam Francis; CEO, INTERTRADE IRELAND

b 1952; *m* Catherine; 2 *s* 1*d* (foster *d*); *edu.* St. Mary's Christian Brothers Grammar School, Belfast; University of London; LL.B; University of Ulster; M.Sc. Social Policy, Planning and Administration); CEO Intertrade Ireland; Northern Ireland Civil Service 1973; established N.I.-Co 1990; Industrial Development Board 1997; CEO Inter-Trade Ireland 2000 to date; vice chairman Drake Music Project for young people;Northern Committee Sales Institute of Ireland; advisor to National Competitiveness Council Dublin. Clubs: Fortwilliam Golf Club. Recreations: golf, music, theatre, wine, food, reading, travel. Contact: Old Gasworks Business Park, Kilmorey Street. Newry, Co. Down. **T** 028 3083 4100 email liam.nellis@intertradeirealand.com

The friendly Northerner who has a wide range of recreational interests has been very successful in developing the commercial trade links in the post Good Friday Agreement era.

Margaret Nelson

NELSON, Margaret; SALES DIRECTOR, FM104

b 1960, Ennis, Co. Clare; *m* Joe Nally; 1*s* 1*d*; *edu.* Convent of Mercy, Ennis, Co. Clare; various management and sales courses and diplomas; Sales Director FM104; after a short stint in the travel industry moved into radio marketing and sales and joined FM104 in its infancy and moved up the ranks. Clubs: David Lloyd Heath and Fitness, Riverview, Clonskeagh. Recreations: reading, cooking, gym, sailing. Contact; FM104, Hume House, Ballsbridge, Dublin 4. **T** 01 668 9750 email margaretn@fm104.ie

Dynamic sales and marketing executive; utterly charming but drives a hard bargain making her company one of the more successful in the commercial radio jungle.

NEILL, Most Reverend, John Robert Winden; ARCHBISHOP OF DUBLIN AND PRIMATE OF IRELAND

b 1945, Dublin; *m* Betty Ann Cox; 3*s*; *edu.* Avoca School Blackrock, Co. Dublin 1954-58; Sandford Park School, Ranelagh, Dublin 1958-62; Trinity College Dublin; BA (Mod) 1962-66; Jesus College, Cambridge, BA (Cantab) 1966-68; Trinity College MA 1969; MA (cantab) 1971; National University of Ireland Ll.D. (*hc*) 2003; Archbishop of Dublin and Primate of Ireland; curate assistant Glenageary, Co. Dublin 1969-71; Bishop's vicar, Kilkenny 1971-74; rector of St. Bartholomews, Leeson Park, Dublin 1974-78; Dean of Waterford 1984-86; Bishop of Tuam 1986-97; Bishop Cashel 1997-02; Archbishop of Dublin 2002 to date. Recreations: travel, photography. Contact: The See House, 17, Temple Road, Dartry, Dublin 6 **T** 01 497 7849 email archbishop@dublin.anglican.org

A well defined Anglican presence, he is authoritive and exact and gives no quarter to anybody in his role as Archbishop of Dublin; he is watching his own faith community grow when others see theirs fading; gives a clear and distinct voice to the Christian Gospel as he sees it.

NEWMAN, Sarah; FORMER CHAIRMAN and FOUNDER NEEDAHOTEL.COM

b 1969, Essex, UK; *m* Patrick O'Donoghue; (*m diss*); 2 children; *p* DJ Carey (*qv*); Former Chairman and Founder needahotel.com; founded NeedaHotel.com Dublin 1994; nominated for Ernst and

Young Entrepreneur of the Year 2005; sold needahotel.com 2006. Clubs: Mount Juliet, Co. Kilkenny. Kildare Hotel and Country Club, Co. Kildare. Recreations: golf, GAA. Contact: needahotel.com, Upper Glenageary Road, Glenageary, Co. Dublin. **T** 01 275 0275 web www.needahotel.com

> One of the most impressive lady entrepreneurs in Ireland; grew her company which sources global hotel accommodation in a second to a turnover of over €100 million in 2004; sold it 2006 for over €60 million; despite her commercial success she is best known as the partner of hurling legend DJ Carey; a modern professional power player with a sharp managerial edge; could appear aloof until rapport is established; a total no nonsense approach.

NÍ BHRAINÁIN, Eithne' ENYA': COMPOSER/MUSICIAN/SINGER
b 1961, Co. Donegal; single; *edu.* Gweedore, Co Donegal; Composer/ Musician/ Singer; started singing with family group Clannad 1980-82; joined Nicky and Roma Ryan as a solo artist 1982; one of the most successful female recording artistes in the world; Awards; Oscar Nominee for Best Original Song *May It Be;* Golden Globe nominee for Best Original Song *May It Be*; Ivor Novello Winner for International Achievement; five Monte Carlo World Music Awards; Hot Press Award Best Irish Solo Artist; Academy of Achievement Of America Golden Plate Award; Billboard Music Award For Artist; Arts Awards; Japanese Grand Prix Award New Artist of the Year; Publ. Albums: *Enya* 1987; *Watermark* 1988; *Shepard Moons* 1991; *The Celts* 1992; *The Memory of Trees* 1996; *Paint The Sky With Stars* 1997; *A Day Without Rain* 2000; album and single awards: IFPI Platinum European Award *Watermark*; Grammy Award Winner *Shepard Moons*; IFPI Platinum European Award; Billboard Music Award; NARM Best Selling Album Award; Grammy Award winner *The Memory of Trees*; Grammy Award Winner *A Day Without Rain*; Japanese Grand Prix Album of the Year; Japanese Grand Prix Album of the Year *Paint the Sky with Stars*; Echo Award *Only Time*; BMI Citation of Achievement; BMI Special Citation of Achievement *Orinoco Flow*; Las Vegas Film Critic Society for Best Original Song *May It Be*; Phoenix Film Critics Award for best original Song; BFCA (Broadcast Film Critics Award) Best Song; Filmography: The 74th Annual Academy Awards 2002 TV (*May It Be* from The Lord of the Rings, *The Fellowship of the Ring); The Lord of the Rings, The Fellowship of the Ring* 2001 (*Aníron & May It Be); Enya: The Video Collection* 2001; themes from *Calmi Cuori Appassionati* 2001; *Sweet November* 2001 (*Only Time); Cry, the Beloved Country* 1995; *Perla Negra* 1994; TV series (*Shepard's Moons, Watermark* and *The Celts; Toys* 1992); *Far and Away* 1992 (*Books of Days); Sleepwalkers* 1992 (*Boadicea); L.A. Story* 1991; *Enya: Moonshadows* 1991; *Green Card* 1990; *The Celts* 1987; TV series; *The Frog Prince* 1984; *Amarantine* 2005. Contact: Warner Music, The Sky Lab, 2nd Floor, 2, Exchange Street Upper, Dublin 2. **T** 01 284 0273 web www.enya.com

> Low profile and enigmatic, the award winning Donegal beauty is an international icon and one of the all time best-selling female artists globally; her new age haunting airs are played all over the world; is also much in demand for specially commissioned major movie soundtracks.

NÍ BHRAONÁIN, Máire 'Moya Brennan'; CELTIC SINGER
b 1952, Gweedore, Co Donegal; *m* Tim Jarvis; 1*s* 1*d*; *edu.* Gweedore, Co. Donegal; Celtic singer (best known for her work with the band Clannad); released her first solo album *Maire* 1992 (Atlantic Records); *Misty Eyed Adventures* 1994; *Perfect Time* 1998; *Whisper To The Wild Water* 1999, (nominated Best New Age Album in the Grammy Awards 2001); *Two Horizons* 2003; *Óró - A Live Session* 2005; *An Irish Christmas* 2005; signed with Word Records, released *Perfect Time* 1998; since 2002 has promoted herself as Moya Brennan; under this moniker released album *Two Horizons* 2003 under her new label, Universal; Publ. *The Other Side of The Rainbow* autobiography 2000 (translated into German); also known for her work with the dance artist Chicane, for performing the singing for *Saltwater*, featured in the VisitScotland advertising campaign. Contact: email info@moyabrennan.com web www.moyabrennan.com

> The older sister of 'Enya' (*qv*), to whom she bears an uncanny resemblance, is a successful and highly respected Celtic singer; still sings with Clannad though these days most likely to perform nationally and internationally as Moya Brennan;

NÍ CHULLEANÁIN Eiléan: POET AND PROFESSOR
b 1942, Cork; *m* Macdara Woods; 1*s*; *edu.* St. Angela's College, Cork; University College Cork; BA; Oxford; MA B.Litt; Poet and Professor; associate professor of English, Trinity College Dublin 2001 to date; Dean of Faculty of Arts (Letters); Awards: Patrick Kavanagh Prize 1973; O'Shaughnessy Prize (Irish American Institute) 1992; Publ. *The Girl Who Married The Reindeer* 2002; *The Wilde*

Legacy 2003. Recreations: travel, languages. Contact: Trinity College Dublin, College Green, Dublin 2. **T** 01 608-1000

A poet who not surprisingly comes from a literary and academic family; of quiet personal charm, her own work is severe and disciplined as befits an academic whilst retaining an incisive imagery of women's experiences in history and myth.

NI DHOMHNAILL, Nuala; POET
b 1952; Lancashire UK; *m* Dogan Leflef; 1*s* 3*d*; *edu.* Laurel Hill Convent FCJ; University College Cork; BA (Hons), H Dip Ed: Poet; writer in residence, An Díseart, Dingle, Co Kerry; high point – Ireland Professorship of Poetry 2001 – 2004; *Publ. An Dealg Droighin* 1981; *Féar Suaithinseach* 1983; *Selected Poems* 1985; *Feis* 1991; *Pharoah's Daughter* 1989; *The Astrakhan Cloak* 1993; *Ceadaighnis* 1998; *The Water Horse* 2001; *The Fifty Minute Mermaid,* accepted for 2006; *Collected Essays* 2005. Clubs: member of Irish Writers Union and Poetry Ireland. Recreations; birdwatching, reading novels, collecting folklore. Contact: 2 Little Meadow, Pottery Road, Dun Laoghaire, Co Dublin. **T** 01 235 2346 **F** 01 285 7465 email nualani@eircom.net

Displays a sense of the humour of contemporary life with a sophisticated language and technique allied to a feminist sensibility; her physical voice and her poetic voice meld into one, which is no small achievement for any writer.

NÍ RIAIN, Nóirín Máire; SINGER, THEOLOGIAN
b 1951 Limerick; *m* Michael O'Suilleabhain (*qv*); separated; 2*s*; *edu*: St. Louis Convent, Dundalk, Co. Louth; University College Cork; University of Limerick; B.Mus.; H.Dip Ed; MA; Ph.D; Dip. Phil.; NUI Dip CMSM; Singer/ Theologian; artist in residence, Laois Co. Council 2000; artist in residence, Wexford County Council 2005; full time lecturer in Theology, Mary Immaculate College Limerick 2005 to date; *Publ. Gregorian Chant Experience* (O'Brien Press) 1997; *Im Bim Baboro* (Ossian Publications) 1998; *Stór Amhrán* (Ossian Publications) 1997; *Theosony – Towards a Theology of Sound* (Veritas publications) 2006; numerous articles and book contributions. Recreations: tennis, nature, walking, reading biography and non fiction, playing the piano. Contact: Mount Marian, Caherconlish, Co.Limerick. **M** 086 813 7040 **F** 061 352 118 email noirinniriain@eircom.net

Nóirín Ní Riain

As a singer and theologian she displays great insight into a medieval tradition of plain chant, whilst extending and developing the understanding of the role of women in a medieval church which is also a modern one; her own theological development aided by her experiences of the great Benedictine traditions gives her work it's power and it's own voice.

NÍ SHUILLEABHÁIN, Aoibhinn; ROSE OF TRALEE 2005/ THEORETICAL PHYSICIST
b 1983, Carnacon, Co Mayo; single; *edu.* University College Dublin; B.Sc (1st Class Hons) (theoretical physics)2004; PhD candidate in the area of fluid dynamics and biophysics 2005 to date; (currently on a year long sabbatical to fulfill Rose of Tralee duties); Rose of Tralee 2005; academic achievements include 2004 student placement at CERN (Centre European de Research Nuclear) Geneva; Awards: International Mathematical Contest in Modelling; Entrance Scholarship from UCD in 2001; sean-nós singing; national awards for short-story and poetry; scholarships from Bord Na Gaeilge. Clubs: Comhaltas Ceoltóirí Éireann, Cómhra Gaeilge, Grúpa Ceoil. Recreations: travel, fishing on Lough Carra, music, reading poetry. Contact: Rose of Tralee, Ashe Memorial Hall, Denny Street, Tralee, Co. Kerry. **T** 066 712 1322 web www.roseoftralee.com

This native Irish speaker loves singing and also plays concertina, piano and guitar; an enthusiastic singer-songwriter in Irish and English; an advanced and respected scientist, she is a wonderful role model for young women everywhere.

NICKERSON, Jacqueline, 'Jackie'; ARTIST
b 1960, Boston, USA; *m* Kevin Gurry; Artist; self taught artist, apprenticed in New York for five years to various commercial and fashion photographers; 12 years as fashion photographer and took three year sabbatical to produce *FARM*; artist; *Publ., FARM* a book of portraits of agricultural workers taken all over Southern Africa (Jonathan Cape/ Random House) distributed worldwide and published in the UK, France and Germany 2002; solo exhibitions: *FAITH,* Paul Kane Gallery, Dublin 2006; *FARM,*

Jack Shainman Gallery, New York 2005; *FARM* and Tennessee VCUQ, Doha, Oman 2005; *FARM* Galerie 213 Paris, France 2005; group exhibitions: *Blooming, Years of Ulysses,* Blue Leaf Gallery, Dublin 2004; *Pytchoses=Folds+Pleats,* Benaki Museum, Athens, Greece 2004; *Suddenly Older,* Colgate Gallery, New York 2005; *Poiesis,* Jack Shainman Gallery, New York 2006; Awards: Nominated for the Becks Futures Award (ICA) London 2003; short-listed for the John Kobel prize 2003; Highly Commended Royal Photographic Society 150 Year Awards 2003; winner Photo-Eye Best Books Award 2002. Recreations: mountains, kung fu, dogs, Japanese food. Contact: The Beach House, Coast Road, Annagassan, Co.Louth. **T** 041 683 2915 **F** 041 685 2915 email jackienickerson@lycos.com

Jackie Nickerson

International award winning photographer whose work has been exhibited all over the world; shows exquisite sensitivity for her subjects; is also much in demand as a commercial photographer internationally shooting campaigns for major cosmetic and fashion houses; her work has appeared in most international glossy magazines.

NOLAN, Fran Catherine; MANAGING DIRECTOR, REGINE ltd
b 1950; *m* George Nolan (*m diss*); 2s 1d; started in fashion 1969; established Regine Ltd 1974; established Fran & Jane, a new chain of shops 2002. Clubs: South County Golf Club, Milltown Golf Club. Recreations: golf, sailing, walking, theatre, travel, reading, "very involved as chairperson of Next Step Charity: fundraising for orphans of the Republic of Georgia". Contact: St. John's Sandycove, Co. Dublin. **T** 01 280 1754 **F** 01 408 0859 email fran@regine.ie

One of the most glamorous Irish fashionistas, is the best possible advertisement for her company and her industry; has developed and strategically placed her company Regine in the wholesale and retail sectors and has also opened her own upmarket retail boutiques 'Fran and Jane' in Dublin, Cork and Clonmel; an engaging and warm personality she has a wide circle of business and social friends.

NOLAN, Mark Martin; MANAGING DIRECTOR/HOTEL
b 1960, Dublin; *m* Maria; 1s 3d; *edu.* Gonzaga College, Dublin; GMIT, Higher Dip. Hotel Management. H.Dip, Hotel Management; one year scholarship to New York Statler; Managing Director, Dromoland Castle and Hallmark Management; six months Arabella Hotel, Frankfurt; deputy general manager Ashford Castle Hotel 1990 – 97;; general manager, Dromoland Castle 1997 todate; managing director Dromoland Castle 1998 todate; managing director, Hallmark Mgmt.2001 todate. Clubs: Dromoland Golf Club, ex captain and president; Portmarnock Golf Club; Doonbeg Golf Club; Lahinch Golf Club. Recreations: golf, boating, travel. Contact: Dromoland Castle, Newmarket on Fergus, Co. Clare. **T** 061 700 645 **F** 061 360 596 email mark.nolan@dromoland.ie

One of the country's top hoteliers with extensive experience running internationally acclaimed five-star properties; has built Dromoland Castle into the ultimate castle experience; a wonderful host, a total professional, gregarious, manages to make it all seem so easy.

NOLAN, Philip; CHIEF EXECUTIVE, EIRCOM
b 1953; *m* Josephine Monaghan; 2s; *edu.* Queens University Belfast; London Business School; BSc.; PhD; MBA; Chief Executive Eircom; lecturer in geology University of Ulster 1979-81; geologist BP 1981-87; commercial and planning roles Head Office BP Exploration1987-93; manager acquisitions and dispolsals BP Exploration 1993-95; MD (secondment from BP) Interconnector (UK) Ltd 1995; director, Transco E.Area BG plc 1996; MD Transco 1997; appointed BG Board 1998; chief executive Transco BG plc 1998-2000; CE Lattice Group plc 2000-02; CEO Eircom Ltd 2002 to date. Recreations: walking, golf, listening to music, reading, watching football. Contact: Eircom Ltd, 112-114, St. Stephens Green, Dublin 2. **T** 01 701 5917 **F** 01 679 9748 email phil.nolan@eircom.ie

Following the delisting of Eircom, the Tony O'Reilly investment group brought in Dr Philip Nolan as CEO; with an impressive academic and commercial track record, has ensured that the company has met it's mandate of ongoing profitability in recent years resulting in successful takeover 2006.

NOLAN, Ronan John; PARTNER, DELOITTE & TOUCHE;
b Dublin; *m* Fiona; 1*s* 1*d*; *edu.* Terenure College, University College Dublin; B.Sc (hons); FCA; qualified as a chartered accountant 1978; appointed partner in Deloitte & Touche 1983; elected to Council of ICAI 2004; appointed to the Board of APB (Auditing Practicing Board) 2005. Clubs: Grange Golf Club, Dublin Chess Club, The United Arts Club. Recreations: golf, chess, music, gardening, reading. Contact: 1 Brighton Vale, Monkstown, Co Dublin. **T** 01 417 2250 **F** 01 417 2300 email rnolan@deloitte.ie

Tom Noonan

NOONAN, Tom; CHIEF EXECUTIVE OFFICER, THE MAXOL GROUP
b 1951; *m* Mary; 2*s*; *edu.* Terenure College Dublin; College of Commerce Rathmines, Dublin; (Diploma Business Studies); Chief Executive The Maxol Group; seven years as industrial relations executive, FUE (Now IBEC); 25 years with Maxol; president of SIMI 1993; vice president of IBEC 2005; chairman of the Transport Working Group, UNICE, The European Business Body. Clubs: Skerries Golf Club, Skerries RFC. Recreations: golf, rugby, current affairs. Contact: 3 Custom House Plaza, IFSC, Dublin 1. **T** 01 607 6800 **F** 01 602 6850 email info@maxol.ie

Highly respected and successful businessman who is regularly seen as the voice of the retail petroleum industry in Ireland.

NORRIS, David Patrick; PUBLIC REPRESENTATIVE
b 1944, Leopoldville, Belgian Congo; single; *edu.* St Andrew's College, Clyde Road, Dublin; The High School, Dublin; Trinity College Dublin; BA 1st Class Mod, MA; Public Representative; Senator; member Foreign Affairs Committee, Transport Committee; taught in TCD English Dept 1968-94; senior lecturer in English Literature and college tutor; founder, chairman, North Georges Street Preservation Society; founder, chairman James Joyce Center, Dublin. *Publ. James Joyce Dublin* (publ. Eason); *A Beginners Guide To James Joyce* (Icon, Oxford) editor, Proceedings of The International James Joyce Symposium 1982-93, various articles in learned journals UK; Clubs: Kildare Street & University Club. Recreations: reading, music, studying the wild life of Cyprus, jazz, travel. Contact: 18, North Great Georges Street, Dublin1. **T** 01 618 3104 **F** 01 618 4155 email david.norris@oireachtas.ie

A human rights advocate; has courageously defended the right of an Irish homosexual man to be a fully recognised citizen; annoying, rebarbarative, able, loquacious, generous of spirit and of fact he represents an important facet of Irish life, that of the Independent; others talk the talk, he walks the walk, and exemplifies the role of the very best that an independent university Senator can bring to public life in Ireland.

NUGENT, Barbara; CHIEF EXECUTIVE, THE VILLAGE
b Dublin; *m* Edward Nugent; 3*s*; *edu.* Miss Merediths, Pembroke Road, Dublin; Mount Sackville Convent, Co. Dublin; College of Catering, Cathal Brugha Street, Dublin; University College Dublin; BA H.Dip.Ed; Chief Executive *The Village*; teacher, Willow Park Junior School, Dublin; advertising manager and promotions editor, *Image* magazine 1979-82; advertising manager, *The Sunday Tribune* 1982-92; chief executive *Sunday Business Post* 1992-02; chief executive *The Village* 2005 to date; board member Stephen's Green Publications; chairman Board of the National Museum of Ireland; chairman Interim board National Museum of Ireland 1997-2005. Contact: The Village, 44, Westland Row, Dublin 1. **T** 01 642 5050 **F** 01 642 5001 email barbaranugent@villagemagazine.ie www.village magazine.ie

A very able and astute businessperson who has made her mark on a range of projects from newspapers to museums; a formidable intellect and has great powers of persuasion.

NUGENT, Don; SHOPPING CENTRE DIRECTOR
b 1957, Dublin; *m* Sandra; 1*s* 1*d*; *edu.* Chanel College, Coolock, Dublin; College of Marketing; Oxford University Summer School Graduate (scholarship); Director Dundrum Town Centre; buyer, Switzers department store Dublin 1979-86; merchandising manager 1986-88; general manager 1988-90; centre director, The Square Tallaght 1990-91; director of sales & merchandising Clery & Co., Dublin 1991-96; head of homewares, Dunnes Stores 1996-2003; centre director, Dundrum Town Centre 2003 to date; member of the Marketing Institute of Ireland. Clubs: St. Sylvesters, Malahide. Recreations: gym, walking, football, reading, travel (time permitting!). Contact: 8, Millview Court,

Malahide, Co. Dublin. **T** 01 291 772 **F** 01 299 1799 **M** 086 388 1669
email dnugent@dundrum.ie web www.dundrum.ie

Bright merchandiser whose considerable talents have been tested at the new
Dundrum Town Center; converted a dream into Dublin's largest shopping mall
and despite the nay sayers and a slowish start is already becoming a major retail
Mecca.

Don Nugent

Ó BRIAIN, Colm; COLLEGE HEAD, DIRECTOR, THE NATIONAL COLLEGE OF ART AND DESIGN
b 1944, Dublin; *m* Muireann McHugh; 2*d*; *edu.* Belvedere College, Dublin; University College Dublin; BCL. LL.B. Kings Inns, BL; Director The National College Of Art and Design; producer/director RTE Television 1967-73; director/head of training, Abbey Theatre 1973-74; director The Arts Council 1975-83; general secretary The Labour Party 1983-85; director, Arts Administration Studies (course initiation and planning),University College Dublin 1986-88; executive director COTHÚ (business sponsorship in the Arts) 1988-90; special advisor, Minster for Arts and Culture 1993; sponsorship Director University College Dublin; director, The National College of Art & Design Dublin. Contact: 100, Thomas Street, Dublin 8. **T** 01 636 4200 **F** 01 636 4207 email fios@ncad.ie web www.ncad.ie

Very diversified career to date, brings a highly personal and often tempestuous style to each new post including this one; dramatic charm, intelligence and democratic in instinct and by avocation.

Aiden O'Brien

O'BRIEN, Aidan Patrick; RACEHORSE TRAINER
b 1969, Clonroche, Co Wexford; *m* Ann Marie Crowley; 2*s* 2*d*; *edu.* Clonroche NS; St Peter's College Wexford; Racehorse Trainer; obtained trainer's licence 1993; National Hunt champion trainer 1994-95; 1996; 1997/98 season; champion flat trainer 1997; first winner as trainer, Wandering Thoughts (Tralee) 1993; first pattern winner, Dancing Sunset (Royal Whip Stakes) 1994; first Group One winner, Desert King (National Stakes) 1996; first classic winner, Classic Park (Irish 1,000 Guineas) 1997; first Royal Ascot winner, Harbour Master (Coventry Stakes) 1997; other notable winners, Shatoush (Epsom Oaks) 1998; King of Kings (2,000 Guineas) 1997; Desert King (Irish Derby & Irish 2,000 Guineas) 1997; Istabraq (Champion Hurdle) 1999; Rock Of Gibraltar, set a new record of seven consecutive Group One successes; champion trainer, his domination stretched across the Irish Sea and he became the first overseas-based trainer since Vincent O'Brien (no relation) to became Britain's leading trainer, among his winners, Chaparral and Hawk Wing, (he won 23 Group One races) 2001; won Breeders' Cup juvenile event with Johannesburg in the US 2001; O'Brien retained both his English and Irish champion trainer's crowns despite the fact that his yard was hit by a coughing bug during the summer. (That he was top dog in England with just 10 wins – earning £2.8m in prize money – proves the quality of his string) 2002; UK 2000 Guineas (footstepsinthesand) and UK 1000 Guineas (Virginia Waters) 2005; Eclipse Stakes, Irish Champion Stakes (Oratorio) 2005; Grand Prix de Paris and St Ledger (Scorpion) 2005; Phoenix Stakes (George Washington) 2005; UK 2000 Guineas (2006); Ascot Gold Cup (Yeats); UK Oaks (Alexandrova) 2006; Irish Derby (Dylan Thomas) 2006; Phoenix Stakes (Holy Roman Emperor) 2006; Poule d'Essai des Poullains(Aussie Rules) 2006; Awards, Goffs Irish Racing Personality of the Year 1997. Contact: Ballydoyle Racing, Ballydoyle, Cashel, Co. Tipperary. **T** 062 62615 email bstables@iolie web www.coolmore.com/ballydoyle

Backed by the might of the worldwide Coolmore operation this absolutely prodigious trainer's brilliance is noted all over the world; extremely low profile, a stickler for attention to the tiniest detail in training, is revered by his patrons and the racing public alike.

O'BRIEN, Conor Cruise; AUTHOR
b 1917, Dublin; *m* 1st Christine Foster; 1*s* 2*d*; *m* 2nd Máire Mac Entee (*qv*); 1*s* 1*d*; *edu.* Sandford Park School, Ranelagh, Dublin; Trinity College Dublin; BA. PhD; Author; former Government minister; Dept of External Affairs, Dublin 1944; counsellor Irish Embassy Paris 1955-56; head of UN Section and member, Irish Delegation to UN 1956-60; Rep of UN Secretary General to Katanga 1961; vice chancellor, University of Ghana 1962-65; Albert Schweitzer Professor of Humanities, New York University 1996-69; TD (Labour Dublin NE) 1969-77; Minister for Posts & Telegraphs 1973-77; member of Seanad Éireann 1977-79; editor in chief *The Observer* 1979-81; Pro chancellor University of Dublin 1973 to date; visiting fellow Nuffield College 1973-75; fellow St. Catherine's College Oxford 1978-91; visiting professor and Montgomery Fellow Dartmouth College, US 1984-85; senior research fellow, National Centre for the Humanities Durham North Carolina, USA 1993; member, Royal Irish Academy; Awards; Hon D. Litt University of Bradford 1971; University of Ghana 1974; University of Edinburgh 1976; University of Nice 1978; Valiant for Truth Media Award 1979; Coleraine 1981; Queen's University Belfast 1984; FRSL 1984; *Publ. Maria Cross* (under pseudonym Donat O'Donnell) 1952; reprinted under own name 1963; *Parnell and his Party* 1957; (ed) *The Shaping*

of Modern Ireland 1959; *To Katanga and Back* 1962; *Conflicting Concepts of the UN* 1964; *Writers & Politics* 1965; T*he UN: Sacred Drama* 1967; *Murderous Angels 1968;* (ed) *Power and Consciousness* 1969; *Introducing Ireland* 1969; (ed) *Edmund Burke: Reflections and the Revolution in France* 1969; *Camus* 1969 (revised ed 1993); *A Concise History of Ireland* (with Máire Cruise O'Brien) 1972; *The Suspecting Glance* 1972; *States of Ireland* 1972; *Herod* 1978; *Neighbours* 1978-79: *The Ewart Biggs Memorial Lectures* 1980; *The Siege, The Saga of Israel and Zionism* 1986; *The Great Melody: A Thematic Biography of Edmund Burke* 1992; *Ancestral Voices, Religion and Nationalism in Ireland* 1994; columnist, *The Irish Independent; The Independent,* London. Clubs: Atheneum, London. Recreations: travel. Contact: Whitewater, Howth Summit, Co. Dublin. **T** 01 832 2474

Diplomat, politician, man of letters; a goad for the lazy and a spur for the weak; is a major writer on many topics and an important figure in all terms for a rounded and much loved/admired/feared/hated contemporary Irishman; represents the many faces of being Irish, and that is the great conundrum; might be easier to explain away the Holy Trinity as a doctrine than the dilemma of being CCOB.

O'BRIEN, Denis; CHAIRMAN, CEO ESAT DIGICEL GROUP
b 1958, Dublin; *m* Catherine Walsh; 2*s* 1*d*; *edu.* High School, Rathgar; University College Dublin; Boston College (US), MBA; Deputy Governor Bank of Ireland (2005 - 2006); joined GPA as personal assistant to Tony Ryan; currently chairman and CEO Communicorp Group, controlling 98FM Dublin, The Czech Republic and Poland; chairman, CEO Esat Telecom Group; chairman Organising Committee Special Olympics 2003; sold Esat to British Telecom 2000; set up Digicel incorporating the e-island group 2000; chairman and chief executive Digicel plc; deputy governor Bank of Ireland 2005 -2006. Contact: ESAT Telecom, The Malt House, Grand Canal Quay, Dublin 2. **T** 01 609 5000 **F** 01 609 5010

Easy to admire his buccaneering spirit, less easy, perhaps, to like; lucky with his telephonic bid and although enmeshed in controversy, he probably always will be so regarded; now at the helm of the fastest growing cell phone company in the world, rolling out operations throughout the Caribbean; has done some good, but lives in a world of the blame culture, to which he has contributed himself; disengaged from all his Irish directorships unexpectedly September 2006; announced residency in Malta, 2006.

O'BRIEN, Helen; CHAIRMAN, HELEN O'BRIEN MANAGEMENT
b 1949, Co Limerick; single; *edu* Mercy Convent, Doon, Co. Limerick; Mercy Convent, Kilmallock, Co. Limerick; High School of Commerce, Limerick, (strategic management, financial management, philosophy, communications); Chairman, Helen O'Brien Management; joined Smurfit Cartons 1979; worked in the Smurfit Print and Publishing Division, Smurfit Distributing Division and The Jefferson Smurfit Group HQ 1985-2003; set up Helen O'Brien Management 2003; member, Institute of Travel Managers; director, Rutland Centre; director, Smurfit European Open. Recreations: golf, tennis, theatre, cinema, reading, socialising. Contact: Jefferson House, Eglington Road, Dublin 4. **T** 01 269 4848 email hobmanagement@eircon.net

First woman vice president of the Jefferson Smurfit Corporation; Group Worldwide Person of the Year 1989 (JSC); no wonder she has been snowed under with blue chip clients since she started her own management business; no fuss, no hassle, when it comes to event management, is in a league of her own.

O'BRIEN, John Martin; CHIEF EXECTUIVE FOOD SAFETY AUTHORITY OF IRELAND
b 1960, Cork; *m* Colette; *edu.* St. Colman's Vocational School, Midleton, Co.Cork; University College Cork; (B. Sc); University of Surrey; (M.Sc) PhD, FRSC., FIFST., C.Chem; Chief Executive Food Safety Authority of Ireland; lecturer food chemistry, UCC; post doctoral research fellow University of Strathclyde, Glasgow; executive editor, trends in food science & technology, Cambridge; lecturer in food safety, University of Surrey, Guildford; director of food safety, Groupe Danone, Paris; director of corporate scientific affairs, Groupe Danone, Paris. Recreations: walking, Victorian political sketches, sailing. Contact: Food Safety Authority of Ireland, Abbey Court, Lower Abbey Street, Dublin 1. **T** 01 817 1352 **F** 01 817 1252 email jobrien@fsai.ie

Took over the Food Safety Authority at a time when the consumer has food safety at the top of their agenda; with an increasing amount of food imports his organization's role will be critical in defining the origins and traceability of the consumer's shopping basket.

Mary Ann O'Brien

O'BRIEN, Mary Ann; MANAGING DIRECTOR LILY O'BRIEN CHOCLOATES

b 1960, Tipperary; *m* Jonathan Irwin (*qv*); 1*s* 2*d*; (2 *decd.*); *edu.* Loreto Abbey, Rathfarnham; Ursuline College, Waterford; University Grenoble; Sorbonne; marketing manager, Phoenix Park Racecourse 1981-90; founder and managing director of Lily O'Brien's Chocolates 1991 to date. Clubs: Rathsallagh Golf Club. Recreations: golf, family, gardening, travel, wine. Contact: Lily O'Brien Chocolates Ltd., I.D.A. Park, Green Road, Newbridge, Co. Kildare. **T** 045 486 800 **F** 045 486 865 email sales@lilyobriens.ie web www.lillyobriens.ie

A savvy, switched on, hard working businesswoman who makes the huge success of her Lily O'Brien's luxury chocolate business seem like a lot of fun; exports over 60% of ever increasing output, major clients include Marks & Spencer's, Netjets and most of the top international airlines

O' BUACHALLA, Oisin; CHIEF EXECUTIVE, KENILWORTH MOTOR

b 1950, Dublin; *m* Sharon Williams (*qv* O'Buachalla Sharon; separated; 2*s* 2*d*; *edu.* Gonzaga College, Ranelagh, Dublin 6; Blackrock College, Co. Dublin; Chief Executive Kenilworth Motors; has been involved in the motor industry for over three decades; former Leeson Street nightclubs owner with Wally Pierse. Contact: 348, Harolds Cross Road, Dublin 6. **T** 01 492 3757 **F** 01 492 2241

Very low profile; astute businessman who has spent over 30 years in the motor trade making him one of the great survivors in a cyclical industry.

O'CALLAGHAN, Jim; BARRISTER

b 1968, Dublin; *m* Julie Liston; *edu.* Gonzaga College, Dublin; University College Dublin; Cambridge University; Kings Inns; BCL, LlM, M.Phil, B.L; Barrister at Law; barrister specialising in commercial law and defamation. Clubs: University College Dublin and Wanderers Rugby Clubs, The Arts Club. Recreations: played rugby for UCD, Cambridge University, Wanderers, Ireland U21 and Leinster. Contact: 145-151 Church Street, Dublin 7. **T** 01 817 4835 **F** 01 817 2779 email jocallaghan@lawlibrary.ie

Popular Silk making a name for himself in politics; Fianna Fáil candidate to contest the constituency of Dublin South East at General Election 2007.

Jim O'Callaghan

O'CALLAGHAN, Miriam; TV PRESENTER

b 1960, Foxrock, Co. Dublin; *m* 1st Tom Mc Gurk; 4*d*; (*m. diss*); *m* 2nd Stephen Carson; 4*s*; edu. St Brigid's National School, Foxrock, Co. Dublin; St Anns, Milltown, Dublin; University College Dublin; BCL; TV Presenter; worked as a solicitor in Dublin briefly; as a solicitor in 1980; moved to London and worked on ITVs *This is Your Life* 1983; later moved to BBC's flagship news programme *Newsnight* with Jeremy Paxman; returned to Ireland to present Marketplace for RTÉ 1993; juggled working with the BBC and RTÉ but ended up working for the Irish broadcaster exclusively and moved into the *Prime Time* slot in 1996; met her present partner, Steve Carson, while working for *Newsnight*; set up Mint Productions, a TV production company with husband 2000; the company has produced documentaries on the racehorse Shergar, Pádraig Pearse, Charles J. Haughey and The Frankie Byrne Story; presented a six-week chat show on RTÉ One *Saturday Night With Miriam* 2005, 2006. Contact: Mint Productions, 205 Lower Rathmines Road, Dublin 6. **T** 01 491 3333 email info@mint.ie

Extremely ambitious and ubiquitous, likes to be seen as a cross between Mrs Everywoman and mother earth; with her young husband has been churning out new series from their Mint Production company, most of which seem to be gifted with some form of controversy; word is she is being groomed to take over as host of *The Late Late Show* when Pat Kenny eventually steps down; others speculate the Áras could well be on her radar.

O'CALLAGHAN, Noel; MANAGING DIRECTOR, O'CALLAGHAN HOTEL GROUP

b 1949; *m* Miriam Ronan; 3*d*; *edu.* Cistercian College, Roscrea; qualified as an accountant; Managing Director, O'Callaghan Hotel Group; started in hotel business with Mont Clare Hotel, Dublin, re-opened hotel following extensive refurbishment 1990; acquired former Plymouth Brethren Gospel

Hall, Merrion Hall, renovated it and opened it as Davenport Hotel 1993; acquired Whites Hotel, Gibraltar 1996, refurbished and renamed it, opened as The Elliot 1998; opened Alexander Hotel, Dublin 1996; fourth Dublin property St. Stephen's Hotel, St. Stephen's Green opened 1999. Recreations: horseracing. Contact: O'Callaghan Hotel Group, 16- 20, South Cumberland Street, Dublin 2. **T** 01 607 3900 **F** 01 661 5663 web www.ocallaghanhotels.com

A hands-on executive with a meticulous eye for detail; a global partner, Inter-Continental Hotels; a successful racehorse owner and a passionate follower of the bloodstock industry.

O'CALLAGHAN, Owen Augustine; CHARTERED SURVEYOR
b 1940, Co Cork; *m* Shelagh; 1*s* 1*d*; *edu*. St. Finbarr's College, Farranferris, Co Cork; University College Cork; member of the Royal Institute of Chartered Surveyors; fellow of Chartered Institute of Building; Chairman O'Callaghan Properties; managing director O'Callaghan Properties 1969-2000; Awards; Property Developer of the Year 2004/2005 (Irish Property Awards, Property Week); Cork Person of the Year (Cork Evening Echo Award); Cork Company of the Year 2004 (Cork Chamber of Commerce, for O'Callaghan Properties). Clubs: Youghal Golf Club. Recreations: golf, show jumping. Contact: 21 Lavitts Quay, Cork, Ireland; **T** 021 475 008 **F** 021 427 5030 email owen.ocallaghan@ocallaghanproperties.com

Has been a major force in the Irish construction industry for over 20 years; the personable Cork man has developed major shopping centers in his native city, Merchants Quay and Mahon Point along with controversial Liffey Valley in Dublin; quietly spoken, low profile, hard nosed businessman who has a keen interest in the show jumping world; the former 'Farna' alumnus has a life long interest in GAA and close political associations with Fianna Fáil.

Ó CAOLÁIN, Caoimhghin; PUBLIC REPRESENTATIVE
b 1953, Monaghan; *m* Breege; 5 children; Public Representative, Member of 29th Dáil Éireann for Cavan/Monaghan (Sinn Fein); SF Parliamentary Group Leader; SF spokesperson on the Peace Process and Six Counties as well as Finance, health and Children; attacked Minister for Finance's budget in the Dáil as entirely inadequate for social welfare and housing needs and attacked Government squandering 2004; speeches in Dáil and elsewhere on the British need to commit to peace and reconciliation 2004 and 2005; main thrust of his speeches reflect his party "brief". Contact: 21, Dublin Street, Monaghan **T** 047 82917/72228 email ocaolain@oireachtas.ie

Generally considered slow and ponderous in delivery in his public utterances, but it's for the journalists he's speaking, so they get every nudge and nuance; drives the Taoiseach into deep gloom when he's on form.

Ó CEIDIGH, Padraig; CHIEF EXECUTIVE OFFICER, AER ARANN
*b*1957, Spiddal, Co. Galway; *m* Caitlin; 1*s* 3*d*; *edu*. Spiddal NS, Co. Galway; University College Galway; B. Comm 1978; Incorporated Law Society; LL.B 1988; articled with KPMG; Chief Executive Officer, Aer Arann; taught mathematics at Colaiste Iognáid, Galway 1982-93;established Irish speaking summer camps in Colaiste Chonnacht, Co. Galway; set up Foinse, the Irish language paper (weekly) 1995; set up legal practice in Galway 1993-98; purchased Aer Arann 1994 (now boasts 550 flights a week, over 25 routes and employing 450 people); Awards, Ernst & Young Irish Entrepreneur of the Year 2002; voted Best Regional Airline by the Irish Travel Agents Association 2002; Best Online Services award presented by the Air Transport Users Council of the Chambers of Commerce of Ireland 2003; represented Ireland in Monte Carlo for Entrepreneur of the Year Awards 2003; ERA Bronze Airline of the Year 2004; member, Irish Entrepreneur Of The Year Judging Panel; former member, World Entrepreneur Of The Year Judging Panel 2004-05; NIUG Alumnae Awards Greatest Influence on Business 2003; appointed to Bord Fáilte Ireland 2003. Contact: Aer Arann, Level 5, The Atrium, Dublin Airport, Co Dublin. **T** 01 844 7700 **F** 01 844 7701 email info @aerann.com web: www.aerarann.com

Padraig Ó Ceidigh

The former Connemara born school teacher has modelled himself on the Michael 'Ryanair' O'Leary (*qv*) airline concept through the development of his own Aer Arann aviation company; the native speaking Gaelgóir is known as one of the great motivators in Irish industry and has a passionate commitment to the West of Ireland and his business.

O'CONNELL, John J; ARCHITECT

b 1949, Co. Westmeath; single; *edu.* Clongowes Wood College, Co. Kildare; Bolton Street College of Technology; Dip. Arch; Architect; established own practice 1978 has been involved with a number of restoration projects including: design and erection of a new Choir Gallery, The College of St. Columba, Rathfarnham, Co. Dublin 1989; The William Walton Foundation, Ischia, Italy 1992; the North Wing, University College Cork 1994; restoration of the 19th century French Revival interiors, The Wallace Collection, Manchester Square, London 1994-96; The Royal Irish Academy, Dawson St. Dublin 1996; new gallery in the stables and the Cottage Ornée of Churchill House, Co. Kerry 2001; restoration and development Ballyfin House, Co Laois 2005 to date; member of the Royal Institute of Architects in Ireland 1977; Fellow 1993: Silver Medal, RIAI for Architectural Conservation 1989; *Publ: The Measured Drawing, in Dr.M.Craig's Book, Classic Irish Houses of the Middle Size; Reconstruction Drawings of Waterford's Courthouse* (Dr. Edward McParland author James Gandon). Clubs: Kildare Street and University Club. Recreations: collecting 18th and 19th century wallpapers/samples. Contact: 14, North Great Georges Street, Dublin 1. **T** 01 874 7154 **F** 01 872 7834

> The most distinguished restoration and conservation architect in Ireland today; of extraordinary and wide ranging taste.

O'CONNELL, Maurice Andrew; CHIEF EXECUTIVE, ALZHEIMER SOCIETY OF IRELAND

b 1948, London; *m* Barbara; 2*d*; *edu.* St. Mary's College, Rhos on Sea, Colwyn Bay North Wales, BA MA (Psych); Chief Executive, Alzheimer Society of Ireland & Chair of Alzheimer Europe; ministry in England, Youth; lectured in Milltown Institute, Pastoral, Theology; Cheshire Foundation, Director of Barrett Cheshire House; general manager REHAB Care plc; co-founder of Peter Bradley Foundation. Clubs; Dun Laoghaire Rotary Club. Recreations: travel, reading. Contact: 43 Northumberland Avenue, Dun Laoghaire, Co. Dublin. **T** 01 284 6616 **F** 01 284 6030 email moconnell@alzheimers.ie

> Leads one of the most crucial fights of modern times in managing the world of the Alzheimer victim, a disease which is the scourge of the 21st century.

O'CONNELL, Michael 'Mick'; GAELIC FOOTBALL LEGEND

b 1937, Valentia Island, Co. Kerry; *m* Rosaleen; 2*s* 1*d*; *edu.* Valentia Island NT; Caherciveen; University College Cork; Gaelic Football Legend; worked for John Mulcahy, New York; independent councillor Kerry 1980s; played in nine All-Ireland senior football finals for Kerry and was on the winning sides of 1959 (captain), 1962, 1969 and 1970; other achievements include six National Football League medals (1959, 1961, 1963, 1969, 1971 and 1972); a Railway Cup medal 1972; All-Star award at midfield 1972; named on the Gaelic Athletic Association's Gaelic football Team of the Millennium; *Publ. A Kerry Footballer*, autobiography 1974. Clubs: Valentia Island Football Club. Recreations: fishing. Contact: Valentia Island, Co. Kerry. **T** 066 947 6132

> Regarded as one of the game's most accomplished and stylish players, renowned for his spectacular high catching and unerring point-scoring from dead ball positions.

O'CONNELL, Owen; SOLICITOR

b 1955; *m* Denise Toher; 3*s*; *edu.* Presentation College, Glasthule, Dublin; University College Dublin; joined William Fry Solicitors 1979; partner since 1985; managing partner 1998-2004; specialist in commercial and corporate law. Recreations: cooking, travel. Contact: William Fry Solicitor, Fitzwilton House, Fitzwilton Place Dublin 2. **T** 01 639 5000 **F** 01 639 5333

O'CONNOR, Charles 'Charlie'; PUBLIC REPRESENTATIVE

b 1946, Dublin; separated; 3*s*; *edu.* Driminagh Castle CBS, Dublin; Irish Management Institute, Public Relations Institute of Ireland; Public Representative; member Dublin County Council 1991 to date; elected to Dáil Éireann 2002; founder chair South West Area Dublin Health Board; treasurer Irish Parliamentary Assoc.; local clubs and groups. Clubs: St Mark's GAA Club; St Jude's GAA Club; St Mary's RTC. Recreations: writing, signature collecting, sport, films, politics. Contact: Dáil Éireann, Dublin 2. **T** 01 618 4080 **F** 01 618 4187 email coconnor@oireachtas.ie

> Elected on the fourth count in a 4 seater, he was lucky as a first timer, but it isn't clear how he will fare as an analysis of the transfers to him don't give much room for comfort; skilled in lots of areas, he has made no impact since his election and time and events are not on his side, not when his constituency colleague is the leader of the Labour Party with a taste for the sound byte.

O'CONNOR, Christy Jnr; GOLF PROFESSIONAL, COURSE DESIGNER

b 1948, Galway; *m* Ann O'Boyle; 2s (1 decd.); 1d; *edu.* St Patrick's Galway; St. Enda's College, Galway; Golf Course Designer; member winning Ryder Cup team 1975 and 1989; World Cup (5); Dunhill Cup (2); Hennessy Cup; Philip Morris International Tournament; Zambian Open; Carrolls Irish Open; Sumrie Better Ball (2); Kenyan Open; Jersey Open; Irish Match Play Championship (3); Irish Dunlop; recipient of Texaco Award, Galway Person of the Year Award, Tooting Bec 1985 (for lowest round in British Open by British and Irish player); course designer of numerous golf clubs including Galway Bay Golf and Country Club; City West Golf Club; Glasson Golf Club; Rathsallagh Golf Club. Recreations: fishing, shooting. Contact: Coldwater Lakes, Saggart, Co. Dublin. **T** 01 298 0660

> The legendary and hugely popular former golf pro is much in demand internationally as a golf course designer and already has a number of respected courses to his name.

O'CONNOR, Cian; INTERNATIONAL SHOWJUMPER

b 1980, Dublin; single; *edu.* CBS Naas; Belvedere College, Dublin; International Show Jumper; having left Belvedere College, leased Copper Ally Stud in Maynooth from John Connolly; following year leased Foxlodge Wood, Ratoath, Co. Meath as a training establishment; prodigious show jumper; winner of numerous awards; represented Ireland on the Aga Khan team 2004, 2005; member of the Irish team that competed in the World Games at Jerez, Spain 2004; member of the Irish Olympics team 2004; IJM Grand Prix League National Champion title 2005. Recreations: equestrian sports, rugby. Contact: Karlswood Stables, Broadmeadow Equestrian Center, Ashbourne, Co. Meath. **T** 01 835 1633 email cian@cinaoconnor.com web www.cianoconnor.com

> Able, energetic, talented and willing, he's paid a price for his fame; the disgrace heaped on him after the Olympic debacle will haunt this young, gifted and not quite likeable horseman.

O'CONNOR, Ciarán; ASSISTANT PRINCIPAL ARCHITECT OFFICE PUBLIC WORKS

b 1954; *m* Ditte Kummer 1s 1d; *edu.* Beneavin College, De La Salle, Dublin 11; Dublin School of Architecture; Dublin Institute of Technology; Trinity College Dublin; Dip. Arch. Sc, B. Arch, FRIAI; Assistant Principal Architect, Office of Public works; worked in Germany & Canada before joining the office of Public Works where he has been responsible for some of the largest and most important conservation and landscape projects for its architectural services; active member of the RIAI Board of Architectural Education; visiting critic and external examiner to a variety of third level institutions; Awards; The Europa Nostra Medal, Madrid 1997; The RIAI Triennial Medal for Restoration 2001; The Henry Ford Foundation European Conservation Award 1996; The RIAI Regional Annual Awards 1993, 1994, 1995, 1998, 2001, 2004, 2005; All Ireland Landscape Award 1990; sustainability Award 2002, etc (in total 21 awards over 18 years). *Publ. Space for Play* 1980; *Ireland Explored* 1986; *Public Works, The Architecture of the Office of Public Works 1832-1987* 1989; *Irish Specifiers Timber Guide* 2001. Recreations: visiting critic and external examiner to a variety of third level institutions. Contact: 51, St. Stephens's Green, Dublin 2. **T** 01 647 6000 **F** 01 6476442 email CIARAN.OCONNOR@OPW.IE

Ciarán O'Connor

> A brilliant architect who works in the public service; is highly regarded and esteemed by his peers.

O' CONNOR, Eddie; MANAGING DIRECTOR AIRTRICITY

b 1947, Roscommon; *m* Hildegarde Kirby; 1s 1d; *edu.* Blackrock College; University College Dublin, B. Chem Eng, MIE; joined ESB, various management positions 1979-87; MD Bord na Mona 1987-95; Managing Director, Airtricity; director of business admin management centers Europe 1991; member IMI Marketing Institute of Ireland; fellow Institute of Engineering; was one of the founders of Future Wind Partnership; currentlysecretary of the European Wind Energy Association; chaired the association's bi-annual conference in Madrid, June 2003; announced details to construct a new wind farm 2006. Clubs: Hibernian United Services Club, Landsdown RFC; Recreations: fishing, golf reading. Contact: Airtricity House, Ravenscourt Office Park, Sandyford, Dublin 18. **T** 01 213 0400 **F** 01 213 0444 email info@airtricity.com

> Son of the former University professor Bob O'Connor, became very involved in student politics in UCD and was known as 'Red Eddie'; Is credited with the commercial turn around in fortunes of Bord na Móna but departed from the semi state during controversial circumstances during the Rainbow Government 1994-97; a long term devotee of wind energy, set up Airtricity in the late 1990s and sold out a majority

shareholding to NTR some years ago; out-spoken critic of the establishment's attitude and policy to the future of green energy in Ireland; his best known landmark is the Arklow Banks offshore wind farms.

O'CONNOR, Edmond Michael; COUNTY MANAGER SOUTH TIPPERARY

b 1946; single; *edu.* Institute of Public Administration, Diploma in Public Administration; county manager in South Tipperary County Council; local government official; appointed county manager July 2002. Recreations: sport. Contact: South Tipperary County Council, County Hall, Emmet Street, Clonmel, Co. Tipperary. **T** 052 34591 **F** 052 80422 email manager@southtipcoco.ie

Presides over the only provincial county where the administration is divided in two; faces a major challenge in attracting modern industry to replace the ongoing closure in the traditional manufacturing area; the implementation of Transport 21 will bring benefits to his area in the years ahead.

O'CONNOR, Joseph Victor 'Joe'; NOVELIST/SCREENWRITER

Joe O'Connor

b 1963, Dublin; *m* Anne-Marie Casey; 2s; *edu.* Blackrock College, Dublin 1976-1981; University College Dublin 1981-1986; Oxford University 1986-1987; University of Leeds 1988-1989; B.A. (English and history) UCD 1984; M.A. (Anglo-Irish literature) UCD 1986; one year postgraduate research at Oxford University 1986-87 (on Stephen Spender and other English writers who were combatants in the Spanish Civil War). M.A. (screenwriting), Northern School of Film, University of Leeds 1989; Novelist/Screenwriter; *Publ.* novels: *Cowboys And Indians* 1991; *Desperadoes* 1994; *The Salesman* 1998; *Inishowen* 2000; *Star of the Sea* 2002; short Stories/ novella: *True Believers* 1991; *The Comedian* 2000; criticism/ history: *Even The Olives Are Bleeding: The Life and Times of Charles Donnelly* 1992; *Sweet Liberty: Travels in Irish America* 1996; journalism: *The Secret World of the Irish Male* 1994; *The Irish Male at Home and Abroad* 1996; *The Last of the Irish Males* 2001; stageplays: *Red Roses and Petrol* (Fishamble/Pigsback Theatre) 1995; *The Weeping of Angels* (Gate Theatre) 1997; *True Believers* (Andrews Lane Theatre) 1999; editor: *Yeats Is Dead: A Novel by Fifteen Irish Writers for Amnesty* 2001. Awards: Hennessy First Fiction Award 1989; Hennessy New Irish Writer of the Year Award 1989; Time Out New Writing Award 1990; Cork Film Festival Best Script/Irish Short Film Prize 1993; Miramax Ireland Screenplay Award 1995; In Dublin Magazine Best New Stageplay of the Year 1995, for *Red Roses and Petrol;* Macaulay Fellowship of the Irish Arts Council 1996; Awards for *Star Of The Sea*: Fellowship at the Center for Scholars and Writers, New York Public Library 2005/06; *Prix Littéraire Européen Madeleine Zepter* (France) 2003, for European Novel Of The Year; *Prix Millepages en Littérature Etranger* (France) 2003; Hennessy/Sunday Tribune 'Hall of Fame' Literary Award (Ireland) 2004; Irish Post Award for Literature (Britain) 2004; Premio Acerbi (Italy) 2003; Neilsen-Bookscan Golden Book Award 2005 (Britain), for sales in excess of 500,000 copies; American Library Association Notable Book 2004; Premio Napoli (Italy) 2005; New York Times Notable Book 2003; short listed for the International IMPAC Dublin Literary Award 2004; Vintage 'Future Classic' Citation 2005; the feature film *Ailsa* (director Paddy Breathnach) for which Joseph O'Connor wrote the script (adapted from his own short story) won the Euscal Media Prize for Best Film, San Sebastian Film Festival 1996; *Star of the Sea* was translated into 32 languages; fiction, criticism, and features contributed to many publications including the *Irish Times, Sunday Independent, Sunday Tribune, Sunday Times, Sunday Telegraph, Observer, GQ, Cosmopolitan, Le Monde, Die Zeit, La Reppublica* and *Corriere dela Sera*; has contributed regular columns in the *Sunday Tribune* (Dublin) and *Esquire* (London) and has frequently reviewed literary fiction for the *Guardian* (UK). Clubs: Honorary Life Member of Amnesty International, Irish Section; founding member the Amnesty Education Trust 2000, a registered charity working with immigrants and refugees in Ireland, and promoting cross-cultural educational exchanges between the young people of Northern Ireland; member, Irish PEN. Recreations: politics, media, culture, music. Contact: c/o Carole Blake (fiction), Conrad Williams (screenwriting), Blake Friedmann Literary, Television and Film Agency, 122 Arlington Road, London NW1 7HP, UK. **T** 00 44 207 2840408 **F** 00 44 207 284 0442 email carole@blakefriedmann.co.uk (UK) dheeney@eircom.net (Ireland)

A brilliant novelist and short storyteller, has written a series of important opinion columns over many years; for a young writer he often appears prescient beyond his years.

O'CONNOR, née Fitzpatrick, Joyce; PRESIDENT, NATIONAL COLLEGE OF IRELAND

b 1947, Bray, Co. Wicklow; *m* Pat O'Connor; *edu.* Loreto Convent, Bray, Co. Wicklow; University College Dublin; B. Soc.Sc; M. Soc.Sc.; Ph.D; Harvard University (Institute for Educational Management, Programme for University Presidents and Senior Administrators); President National

College of Ireland, Dublin; research fellow, Department of Psychiatry, UCD 1968-70; lecturer, (part time) Milltown Park Institute of Theology and Philosophy 1968-72; St. Patrick's College Maynooth, part time lecturer 1970-71; senior research fellow UCD 1971-76; part time lecturer University of Limerick 1974-76; lecturer University of Limerick 1976-79; director of Social Research Centre, University of Limerick 1979-90; senior lecturer College of Humanities, University of Limerick 1987-98; associate professor of Sociology University of Limerick 1986; adjunct associate professor Worcester Polytechnic Institute USA 1986; head, dept of Languages & Applied Social Studies 1987-90; president National College of Ireland 1990 to date; honorary doctorate DIT 2003; hon fellow Chartered Institute of Personnel and Development 2002; Awards: International Council on Alcohol and Addiction Special Award 1995, Eisenhower Fellow 1989, Enterprise scholarship US Information Agency 1987; NIHE, University of Limerick 1st. Excellence in Research Award 1986; Bronze Medal International Film & TV Festival of New York (educational category) 1985; *Publ.* over 40 published books, works, also 5 books on education, contributed to wide range of books, journals, public documentation, State and Governmental Agencies; presented papers to over 300 conferences, including 150 international conferences; major contributor to public, semi state, private, voluntary sectors, voluntary and community partnerships documentation; executive director, Cement Roadstone 2004 to date; council member, Dublin Chamber of Commerce 1997 to date; board member ICS Building Society 1994 to date; OECD advisor 1994; chair WHO Expert Committee on Alcohol and Drugs in the Workplace. Contact: President's Office National College of Ireland, Mayor St. IFSC, Dublin **T** 01 4498 500 **F** 01 4972 200 email info@ncirl.ie

A woman driven by a mission who founded and fought for funding for The National College of Ireland by recruiting the best available commercial and political talent and moved the fledgling college with University status into the heart of Irish capitalism at the IFSC; one admirer said of her that she could drill holes in granite just by thinking about it, the granite would give way sooner than she; a modern giant of energy, drive and commitment.

O'CONNOR, Michael Denis; MANAGING DIRECTOR CAPPOQUIN CHICKENS
b 1930; *m* Mary Cahill; 5*s* 2*d*; *edu.* Mount Mellery, Co. Waterford; Managing Director Cappoquin Chickens to date; member, Waterford All Ireland Senior Hurling Team 1959; member, Railway Club Munster Victorious Team 1957; member Waterford All Ireland winning Minor Hurling Team 1948. Clubs: Dungarvan Golf Club. Recreations: racing. Contact: Cappoquin Chickens, Lefanta, Cappoquin Co. Waterford. **T** 058 54402 **F** 058 54669 email cappo@iol.ie web

One of the original agri entrepreneurs, the popular Waterford All Ireland hurler continues to expand his company; in addition to supplying the Irish market, exports to Holland and also manufactures a range of cooked chicken products.

O'CONNOR, Marie; ACCOUNTANT
b 1954, Dublin; *m* Peter Conlon; 1*s* 3*d*; *edu.* St. Anne's, Milltown, Dublin 6; College of Commerce, Rathmines; University College Dublin; Kings Inns (Barrister at Law); diploma, Business Studies, (1st Place and Gold Medal); fellow of Chartered Association of Certified Accountants; Partner, PriceWaterhouseCooper (financial services & investment management leader), PWC Dublin and Toronto; first woman partner in PWC Ireland 1986; non executive directorships: The Childrens Hospital, Temple Street 1985-2002; NCAD 1988-92; Irish Life 1988-95; IDA Ireland 1993-97; ESRI 2000-04; American Chamber of Commerce 2001 to date; Irish-US Council for Trade, Commerce & Industry 1978 to date; Top Level Appointment Commission 1998-02; Dublin Airport Authority 2004 to date. *Publ.* various PWC publications co-authored. Clubs: RDS, Sportsco, Institute of Directors. Recreations: travel, art, theatre, family, USA interests. Contact: Easter Snow, 31 St. Mary's Road, Ballsbridge, Dublin 4. **T** 01 662 6308/660 5867 **F** 01 704 8729 email marie.o.connor@ie.pwc.com

Marie O'Connor

One of Ireland's leading chartered accountants who broke through the glass ceiling becoming the first female partner in PWC, Ireland; continues to give public service through her involvement in a range of semi state boards; highly intelligent, impressive performer portrays a positive image for the modern professional business woman; closely associated with Fianna Fáil for many years.

O'CONNOR, Pat; FILM DIRECTOR
b 1943, Ardmore, Co. Waterford; *m* Mary Elizabeth Mastrantonia; 2*s*; *edu.* Christian Brothers Cork; UCLA, Los Angeles, California; Ryerson Institute, Toronto; Film Director; producer/director RTE

1970-81; film credits include: *Cal* (Irish Arts Best Film Award) 1984; *A Month in the Country* (Irish Arts Award and NY Film Festival Award) 1987; *Stars and Bars* 1988; *The January Man* 1989; *Fools of Fortune* (Grand Prix at Barcelona Film Festival) 1990; *Zelda* 1993; *Circle of Friends* 1994; *Inventing the Abbots* 1996; *Dancing at Lughnasa* 1997; *Sweet November* 2001; television credits include *Force of Duty*; *Ballroom of Romance* (BAFTA); *Night in Tunisia*; *One of Ourselves*. Contact: ICM, Oxford House, 76, Oxford Street, London, W1N OAX, UK. **T** 0044 171 635 6868 **F** 0044 171 323 0101.

Well liked, low profile; has a nice line in self deprecation; able, astute, possesses an uncanny eye; has a great sense of a story which he unfolds for the viewer.

O'CONNOR, Patrick; SOLICITOR, CORONER, NOTARY PUBLIC

b 1952; *m* Gillian Flannery; 3*s* 1*d*; *edu.* National School, Swinford; Glenstal Abbey, Co. Limerick; University College Dublin BCL (Hons); University College Galway, LL.B (Hons); admitted to the Roll of Solicitors in Ireland 1974; Northern Ireland 1994; England and Wales 1995; Solicitor, Coroner, Notary Public; joined established family firm P.O'Connor & Son, Swinford, Co. Mayo; appointed Notary Public for the County of Mayo 1997, and subsequently for the counties of Sligo, Roscommon and Galway; deputy coroner, Mayo East 1979; appointed coroner 1989; *Publ. Handbook for Coroners in the Republic of Ireland* 1997; *The Royal O'Connors of Connaught* 1997; *The O'Connors of Swinford, County Mayo* 1998; member, Management Committee, O'Dwyer Cheshire Home; chairman, board of management of St. Louis Community School, Kiltimagh; board of management, Scoil Mhuire and Padraig, Swinford; HOPE House Addiction Treatment Centre; Foxford Resources Limited; I.R.D. Kiltimagh Limited; Awards: Irish Quality Association, National Services Award 1995-96; Excellent Ireland Award, Small Service Companies 1999; Law Director, Law Society of Ireland; Director, International Bar Association; President Incorporated Law Society of Ireland. Clubs: Hibernian United Services Club, Irish Club, (London), Royal Irish Automobile Club, Royal Zoological Society, Law Society of Ireland, Glenstal Old Boys Society. Recreations: rugby, tennis, sailing, soccer, Gaelic football, fishing, walking, reading, "The Law". Contact: P. O'Connor & Sons, Swinford, Co. Mayo. **T** 094 925 1333 **F** 094 925 1833

A very successful provincial solicitor who became president of the Incorporated Law Society; diplomatically steered it through a number of difficult issues during his term of office; multi talented he has also found time to develop his literary skills.

O'CONNOR, Sinead; MUSICIAN / SINGER

b 1963, Dublin; *m* 1st John Reynolds; (*m diss*) 1*s*; *m* 2nd Nicholas Sommerlad; (*m diss*); 1*d* (John Waters); 1*s* (Donal Lunny); *edu.* St. Joseph's Cluny, Killiney, Co. Dublin; School of Music Dublin (voice training and piano); Musician/ Singer; was discovered at age 15 by Paul Byrne of In Tua Nua; signed a contract with Ensign Records 1985; relocated to London, she made her recorded debut on the soundtrack of the film *The Captive*, appearing with U2 guitarist the Edge 1986; Discography: *The Lion and the Cobra* 1987; *The Lion in the Cage* 1990; *I Do Not Want What I Haven't Got* 1990; *Am I Not Your Girl?* 1992; *Universal Mother* 1994; *Gospel Oak* 1997; *So Far... The Best of Sinead O Connor* 1997; *Faith and Courage* 2000; *Sean Nós Nua* 2002; *She Who Dwells in the Secret Place of the Most High Shall Abide Under The* 2003; *Shadow of the Collaborations* 2005; *Throw Down Your Arms* 2005; Contact: Eithne Mooney, Sony Music Ireland, Embassy House, Ballsbridge, Dublin 4. **T** 01 647 3404 email eithne.mooney@sonybmg.com

A brilliant and gifted musical personality who has taken more side roads to her career than is often comfortable for her fans; erratic in many personal traits, she nevertheless remains a fascinating personality; in her persona as Mother Bernadette of the dissident Irish Orthodox and Apostolic Church she breached a taboo being ordained a priest in the Roman tradition; remains an important musical personality of great fascination to the print media.

John O'Conor

O'CONOR, John; MUSICIAN, CONCERT PIANIST, PROFESSOR OF PIANO

b 1947, Dublin; *m* Mary (*qv*); 2*s*; *edu.* Belvedere College, Dublin 1965-69; University College Dublin (B.Mus) 1971 -76; Hochschule Fır Musik und Darstellende Kunst, Vienna (K.A.), LRAM (Teachers and Accompanist), LRSM (Performance), ARCM (Performers); Musician, International Concert Pianist, Professor of Piano; director, Royal Irish Academy of Music; artistic director AXA International Piano Competition; 1st Prize Beethoven International Piano Competition Vienna 1973; has played in recital and with orchestras including: Vienna Symphony, Czech Philharmonic, Royal

Philharmonic, L'Orchestre National de France, Stuttgart Chamber Orchestra, Scottish Chamber Orchestra, The Israeli Camerata, The NHK, Yomiuri, Jyushu, Kyoto, Sapporo symphonies in Japan, The KBS Symphony in Seoul, The Singapore Symphony, New Zealand Symphony, Orchestras of Cleveland, San Francisco, Dallas, Detroit, Indianapolis, Seattle, Tampa, Toronto, Montreal, Washington, the National Symphony Orchestra of Ireland; gives master classes in The Royal Academy of Music, London; Juilliard; New York; Harvard; Yale; Awards: D.Mus *(hc)* NUI 1985; Mus.D.*(hc)* TCD 2005; Officier de l'Ordere des Arts et des Lettres (French Gov); Ehrenkreuz für Wissenshaft und Kunst (Austrian Gov); *Publ.* more than 20 recordings for Telarc Label including the complete Beethoven Piano Sonatas, and the complete nocturnes of John Field. Recreations: bridge, travel, reading, golf, all types of music. Contact: 36 Garville Avenue, Rathgar, Dublin 6 **T** 01 497 7914 **F** 01 496 6894 email johnoconor@riam.ie

> The nation's favourite concert pianist; extremely hardworking; founder of the GPA now AXA International Piano competition; great nurturer of emerging talent; highly accessible and socially adroit with great charm, with his wife Mary *(qv)*, they make a charming power couple.

O'CONOR, Mary Cecelia; PSYCHOSEXUAL THERAPIST & AUTHOR

b Limerick; *m* John O'Conor *(qv)*; 2*s*; *edu.* St. Aloysius Mercy Convent, Cork; Dip.Psyt (diploma in psychotherapy, Relate); Psychosexual Therapist; production assistant RTÉ; PA Atomic Agency Vienna; became involved in the area of counselling through working with the Samaritans; trained as a couple counsellor with Marriage Relationship Counselling Service; specialised area of sex therapy 1990; own radio show, *Pillow Talk* 98FM for a year; frequent guest on radio and televisions programmes; weekly column *Evening Herald*; *Publ. Sexual Healing* (Town House) 2002; *Links* a novel (Townhouse) 2004. Clubs: Delgany Golf Club. Recreations: golf, music travel, food, wine, writing. Contact: 36, Garville Avenue, Rathgar, Dublin 6. **M** 087 223 5117 **F** 01 496 6894 email maryoconor@g.mail.com

> Has an excellent reputation as a psychosexual therapist; deals with issues in a sympathetic and matter of fact way; outgoing and vivacious, a superb hostess who entertains with great style and charm.

Mary O'Conor

Ó' CUINNEAGÁIN, Liam; CHAIRMAN, ÚDARÁS NA GAELTACHTA

b 1953, Glencolmcille, Co Donegal; *m* Ann-Collette; *edu.* St. Eunans College, Letterkenny, Co Donegal; St. Patrick's Teacher Training College, Drumcondra, Dublin 9; University College Dublin; Boston College, Tourism Programme; qualified primary school teacher; BA psychology and Irish; H Dip in education; diploma in Tourism; Chairman, Údarás Na Gaeltachta; teacher and school principal in Dublin's inner city 1972-94; director of Oideas Gael 1994 to date; chairman of Údarás na Gaeltachta 2003 to date; Awards: Donegal Person of the Year (AIB/Rehab) 1996; director, Donegal County Tourism; *Publ. www.beo.ie* (Irish language web magazine) 1989; *A Voice for the Voiceless – Irish Emigration* 2000; *Guide Book to Glencolmcille* 2005; contributor to a number of newspapers and journals. Clubs: Naomh Columba GAA Club. Recreations: foreign travel, Native American cultures of N. Montana, music, reading. Contact: Foras Cultúir Uladh, Glencolmcille, Co Donegal. **T** 074 973 0248 **F** 074 973 0348 email oideasgael@eircom.net

> Known as the new Fr Mc Dwyer of Glencomcille due to his influential role in Gaeltacht areas and through Co. Donegal; his pioneering work with Oideas Gael made him an automatic choice as chairman of Údarás, an organization which faces serious challenges with the ongoing closure of manufacturing industries along the Western seaboard.

Ó'CUIV, Éamon; PUBLIC REPRESENTATIVE

b 1950, Dublin; *m* Áine Ní Choincheannain; 3*s* 1*d*; *edu.* Oatlands College, Mount Merrion, Dublin; University College Dublin, BSc; Public Representative, Minister for Community, Rural and Gaeltacht Affairs; formerly Gaeltacht co-operative manager; appointed Minister for Community, Rural and Gaeltacht Affairs in June 2002; elected to the Dáil 1992; Minister of State, Department of Agriculture, Food and Rural Development with special responsibility for Rural Development 2001-02; Minister of State at the Department of Arts, Heritage, Gaeltacht and the Islands with responsibility for the Gaeltacht areas, the Irish Language and for Island Development 1997-2001; Party spokesperson for Rural Development and the Islands 1997-2001; Senator, Cultural and Educational Panel 1995-97; member of Forum for Peace and Reconciliation 1989-92; member, Galway County Council 1991-97 and of a number of subsidiary committees. Recreations: GAA;

Contact: Department of Community, Rural and Gaeltacht Affairs, 43-49, Mespil Road, Dublin 4.
T 01 647 3057 **F** 01 6473101 email aire@pobail.ie

> Opinion is divided on Dev Óg as he's known, being the grandson of Eamonn deValera, whom he physically resembles; hard working and efficient he defends his patch with great vigour and determination.

Ó CURREÁIN, Seán; AN COIMISINÉIR TEANGA OMBUDSMAN FOR IRISH LANGUAGE ISSUES
b 1956, Co Dhún na nGall; *m* Caitlín Nic Dhonncha; 1*d*; *edu*. Coláiste na Croise Naofa, An Falcarrach, Co Dhún na nGall; Colaiste na hOllscoile, Gaillimh; BA (Onóracha); An Choimisinéir Teanga; Iriseoir agus Craoltóir, Léiritheoir, Eagarthóir Stiúrtha agus Leascheannaire ar RTÉ Radio na Gaeltachta; Ceaptha ag Uachtarán na hÉireann mar chéad Choimisinéir Teaga 2004; An Coimisinéir Teaga is in effect the Ombudsman for Irish Language issues. Recreations: cnocadóireacht (hill walking). Contact: An Spidéal, Co na Gaillimhe. **T** 091 504 006 **F** 091 504 036 email eolas@coimisineir.ie

> Since his appointment as An Coimisineir Teanga, the former Radio na Gaeltachta manager is already making major, welcome changes; bright and extremely able, good company, much is expected in a difficult climate.

O' DEA, Willie; PUBLIC REPRESENTATIVE
b 1952, Limerick; *m* Geraldine Kennedy; *edu*. Patrician Brothers College, Ballyfin, Co. Laois; University College Dublin; Kings Inns; Institute of Certified Accountants; BCL, LLM, BL: certified accountant; Public Representative, Minister for Defense; first elected to Dáil Éireann 1982; Minister of State at the Dept. of Justice, Equality and Law Reform (with special responsibility for Equality Issues including Disability Issues) 2002-04; Minister of State at the Department of Justice and Health 1993-94; Minister of State at the Department of Justice 1992-93; former accountant. Recreations: rugby, GAA. Contact: 2 Glenview Gardens, Farranshone, Limerick. **T** 061 454 488/454 522 **F** 061 328849 email www.willieodea.ie

> Feared and admired in equal measure, he is an able and astute local politician; well able to articulate his point of view in any of the media, print or broadcast; keeps an iron grip on his own FF constituency in Limerick and is feared by his party HQ; adores the limelight.

O'DONNELL, Daniel; SINGER/ENTERTAINER
b 1961, Co. Donegal; *m* Majella; 1*ss* 1*sd; edu.* Belcruit National School; Rosses Community School; singer/entertainer; has been in the entertainment business since leaving school in 1980; one of the country's most popular and successful entertainers with 18 top selling albums and eleven videos to his credit; recipient of numerous awards. Recreations: golf. Contact: Ritz Productions, 5-6 Lombard Street, Dublin 2. **T** 01 677 7904 web www.daniel–site.com

> The Peter Pan of Irish music continues to pack them in wherever he performs in Ireland and throughout Europe; appears to have changed amazingly little in the last quarter of a century; adored by his legion of female fans, is a terrific performer, accessible and charming.

Liz O'Donnell

O'DONNELL, Elizabeth 'Liz'; PUBLIC REPRESENTATIVE/COMPANY DIRECTOR
b 1956, Limerick; *m* Michael Carson; 1*s* 1*d; edu.* Salesian College, Limerick; Law School, Trinity College Dublin; Public Representative; worked in theatre management with Noel Pearson; executive administrator, McCann Fitzgerald Solicitors; elected to City Council for Progressive Democrats 1991; elected to Dail Eireann 1992, Dublin South; spokesperson on Justice and Chief Party Whip 1993-97; following the general election, negotiated the programme for Coalition Government; appointed Minister of State at the Department of Foreign Affairs with responsibility for Overseas Development Assistance 1997; one of the Government negotiators in the Multi Party Negotiations at Stormont, culminating in the Good Friday Agreement 1998; re-elected 2002; Chief Whip Progressive Democrats 2002 - 06; deputy leader Progressive democrats 2006 - todate; member, Commission of the Houses of the

Oireachtas; member, Foreign Affairs Committee; non-executive director Communicorp Group; Minister of State to the Government 2002; member, Committee on Procedure and Privileges; the Foreign Affairs Committee; the Broadcasting Committee; member, British-Irish Inter-Parliamentary Body;member, Commission of the Houses of the Oireachtas; Awards, the Doolin Memorial Medal for her contribution to Overseas Development and Human Rights 2002. Recreations: theatre, painting, all forms of art and design. Contact: Leinster House 2000, Kildare Street, Dublin 2. **T** 01 618 3469 **F** 01 618 4307 email liz.odonnell@oireachtas.ie web www.lizodonnell.ie

> Certainly knows the value of the sound byte and the presence of broadcast media gives her all kinds of opportunities; as a junior Minister didn't allow the senior minister of the day to impede her in any way; has some interesting things to say, even if it occasionally sounded like her former master's (Mary Harney *qv*) voice, she says it with grit and determination; it's no drawback to be photogenic; with Harney's resignation as leader of the PDs Liz seems set to embrace her career again stating she would be honoured to be a minister after the general election (2007); just two problems; 1) will she be reelected; 2) will the PDs be part of the next coalition government?

O'DONNELL, Stephanie; CIVIL SERVANT

b 1954; Dublin; *m* Des Harrold; 1*s* 2*d*; *edu.* Cross and Passion College, Maryfield, Dublin 9; University College Dublin; CD. B.A, II. Dip Ed.; Civil Servant; worked in a variety of areas across the department including public sector pay and conditions, area and related industrial relations, Government accounting, the tax side in Budget and Economic Division; part of the team involved in the emergency legislation brought forward by the Minister for Finance to facilitate the DIRT enquiry; worked as a principal in the Department of Justice Equality and Law Reform for 2 years where she was responsible for the roll-out of national anti-racism awareness KNOW RACISM 2001; policy development issues relating to the Equal Status Act 2000 and chaired the Interdepartmental Working Group on the Disabled Drivers and Passengers Tax Concession Scheme. Recreations: family, listening to music, entertaining friends, interesting holidays. Contact: Room 43, Department of Finance, Merrion Row, Dublin 2. **T** 01 669 6365 email stephanie.o'donnell@finance.gov.ie

> Highly respected Public Servant; worked part time for a number of years when children were younger, and believes that parents should strive for a work life balance, with flexibility to work longer hours as necessary for urgent work demands.

O'DONOGHUE, Breege; DIRECTOR PRIMARK AND PENNEYS (ROI AND UK)

b 1944; *m* Dr James O'Dea (*decd*); 6*ss* 4*sd*; *edu.* University College Dublin (B.Comm); CCIPD; Director Primark and Penneys (UK & ROI) 1988 to date; responsible for HR (12,000 staff) advertising and security; Great Southern Hotels (including three years in Europe); director C&C Group; member; Labour Relations Commission; IBEC, Trustee, National Executive Council; member Finance & Organisation Committee; board of governors, NUI Maynooth; The Foundation, UCD; Disputes Resolution Committee; Leopardstown Committee (Racecourse); Companion of Chartered Institute of Personnel & Development; former director An Post, Aer Rianta; chairman Shannon College of Hotel Management. Clubs: Shelbourne Leisure Club. Recreations: Spanish language. Contact: Primark, Penneys Stores PO Box 644,47 Mary St. Dublin 1/Primark Stores Ltd Primark House, 41 West St. Reading Berks RG1 1TZ. **T** 01 888 0520 email bodonoghue@primark.ie

Breege O'Donoghue

> One of the most successful businesspeople in the country; hardworking, extremely able and sharp; has significantly contributed to the phenomenal success and growth of Primark/Penneys in Ireland and throughout the UK and Spain; her talent is evidenced by the wide range of directorships she holds.

O'DONOGHUE, Cliona Mairead; PROPERTY EDITOR, IRISH INDEPENDENT

b 1960, Waterford; *m* (*m diss*) *p* Ciaran Shanley; 1*s*; *edu.* Our Lady's Bower, Athlone, Co. Westmeath; Rathmines College of Commerce, Dublin; College of Marketing & Design, Dublin; qualifications in: public relations, advertising management, marketing; Property Editor, *Irish Independent*; PRO, public relations; advertising management; marketing; worked in property and other areas for the Independent since 1985; regular TV and radio work over the years as well as features and new items for several publications; producer/ presenter *Property View* for City Channel 2005 to date; property editor *Irish Independent* 1999 to date. Recreations: reading; walking; gardening; pitch & putt, meeting friends, travel. Contact: Irish Independent 30, Talbot Street, Dublin 1. **T** 01 7055732 **F** 01 7055778 email codonoghue@unison.independent.ie

Gregarious and engaging, keen intellect she broke the glass ceiling by becoming the first female national property editor; has excellent contacts and is highly respected in the still male dominated property world.

O'DONOGHUE, Hughie; ARTIST

b 1953; *m* Clare Reynolds; 2*s* 1*d*; *edu.* Manchester and Goldsmiths College, London, MA; Artist; taught for a time before becoming a full time artist; one man exhibitions worldwide include: Rubicon Gallery (Dublin); Pfefferle Gallery (Munich); Purdy Hicks Gallery (London); Galerie Helmut Pabst (Frankfurt); Haus der Kurst (Munich) 1997; Irish Museum of Modern Art and R.H.A. Gallery (Dublin) 1998; group exhibitions include; Walker Gallery (Liverpool); University of California Art Museum; Grey Art Gallery (New York); Barbican Art Gallery (London) 1998; Yale Centre (New Haven) 1999; Museum of Fine Art (Boston) 1999. Recreations: music, film, theatre. Contact: Purdy Hicks Gallery, 65 Hopton Street, Bankside, London, SE1 9G2. **T** 0044 171 401 9229.

A world class artist renowned for memorable series of vast paintings; his artistic career works on stop go basis; his works needs large spaces and their themes may occasionally repel, but mostly invite interest and curiosity.

O'DONOGHUE, John; PUBLIC REPRESENTATIVE

b 1956, Caherciveen, Co. Kerry; *m* Kate Ann Murphy; 2*s* 1*d*; *edu.* Christian Brothers Secondary School, Caherciveen, Co. Kerry; University College Cork; The Incorporated Law Society of Ireland; B.C.L., LL.B; solicitor; Minister Arts, Tourism, Sport; member, Kerry County Council 1985-91; elected Fianna Fail Deputy for Kerry South 1987; member Oireachtas Joint Committee on Secondary Legislation of European Communities 1989-91; Minister of State, Department of Finance, with responsibility for the Office of Public Works 1991-92; Special Dáil Committee on Judicial Separation, Child Care, Foreign Adoptions, Solicitors' Bill, British-Irish Parliamentary Body 1993; Front Bench spokeman Justice Equality and Law Reform 1994-97; Minister, Justice Equality and Law Reform 1997-2002; Minister Arts, Tourism Sport 2002 to date. Clubs: St. Mary's GAA Club, Caherciveen. Recreations; English literature, history, Gaelic Games, horse riding. Contact: Office, Main Street, Caherciveen, Co. Kerry. **T** 066 947 3221 **F** 066 947 3222 web www.dast.gov.ie

Has carried on the family tradition in South Kerry; first full cabinet minister from that constituency; the reticent solicitor has a sharp intellect and an even sharper tongue when he is in the heat of political battle; close to Taoiseach Bertie Ahern, should expect a move further up the ranks; an avid horse racing fan; is able to combine business and pleasure with his current portfolio.

O' DONOGHUE, Michael; HOTELIER

b 1957, Castleisland; *m*; 2*s*; *edu.* SecondarySchool, Castle Island, Co Kerry; Hotelier; trained as an electrician; managed East Avenue Hotel, Killarney; with brother-in-law, Donal Ring, now has an interest in Killarney Plaza, Co. Kerry; Killarney Towers, Co. Kerry; East AvenueHotel, Killarney, Co. Kerry; River Island Hotel, Castle Island, Co. Kerry; circa seven Holiday Inns in UK, mainly Liverpool; pub interests in UK and Chicago. Clubs: CastleIsland Gold Club, Castle Island GAA. Recreations: golf, GAA. Contact: Killarney Plaza Hotel, Kenmare Place, Killarney, Co. Kerry. **T** 064 21100 **F** 064 31755 email infor@killarneyplaza.com web www.killarneyplaza.com

With his sister Noreen and brother-in-law Donal Ring has developed the family founded hotel company making it a major force in 'The Kingdom'; also expanded to the UK; low key, a warm personality, great host; has more exciting plans for the O'Donoghue Ring Group.

O'DONOVAN, Derry; BANKER

b 1945, Ballinspittle, Co Cork; *m* Mary Mullen; 1*s* 1*d*; *edu.* Capuchin Franciscan College, Rochestown, Co. Cork; University College Cork; University College Dublin; B. Agr. Sc; Banker; Agricultural Advisory Service, Co. Roscommon 1968-70; Nitrigin Eireann Teo, Arklow 1970-73; senior business advisor Allied Irish Bank 1973 to date; non executive directorships: ESB; First Step Micro Finance; St. Luke's Hospital Dublin; former national chairman, Irish Red Cross Society; founder director, International Breast Cancer Foundation for Ireland; former national president Agricultural Science Association; former director Foras Forbartha 1978-81; member, Irish National Commission UNESCO 1978-82. *Publ. Ballinspittle and De Courcey Country.* Clubs: Agricultural Science Association, RDS, Institute of Bankers, Guild of Agricultural Journalists. Recreations:

gardening, walking, history, Gaelic games, current affairs. Contact: AIB Bank, Bank Centre, Ballsbridge, Dublin 4. **T** 01 641 2493 email derry.o'donovan@aib.ie

The personable West Corkman has been the public face of agriculture for AIB for many years; has an encyclopedic knowledge of people and places; loves the minutiae of Irish life and believes it illuminates the wider picture as indeed it does; indefatigable worker for several charities; closely associated with FF where he has been a backroom advisor for many years.

O'DRISCOLL, Brian 'BOD'; PROFESSIONAL RUGBY PLAYER

b 1979, Dublin; single; *edu.* Blackrock College Dublin; University College Dublin; diploma Sports Management; Professional Rugby Union Player; captain Lions Tour New Zealand 2005; captain Irish rugby team; first ever under 19 World Title 1998; led Blackrock Seniors to victory 1999; first appearance for Ireland against Italy 1999; British & Irish Lions Test tour of Australia 2001; captain Irish Rugby Team 2003; captain British and Irish Lions Test Tour of Australia/New Zealand 2005; signed a new deal with the IRFU to keep him in the country and at Leinster through the 2007 World Cup; *Publ. A Year In The Center* 2005; *Social & Personal* magazine's Sexiest Man 2004. Clubs: Seafield Golf and Country Club, Gorey, Co. Wexford; Recreations: Golf. Contact: Irish Rugby Football Union, 62 Lansdowne Road, Dublin 4. **T** 01 647 3800 **F** 01 647 3801 email info@irishrugby.ie

Brian O'Driscoll

The 'BOD' is charismatic, professional, gifted, tough, totally focussed on career and the O' Driscoll brand; possibly the best ever Irish center; despite the disappointment of the Lions spear tackle debacle, which took him out of the Tour within minutes of kick off, has bounced back; enjoys a very public lifestyle, not much left to the public's imagination; reputed to be earning in excess of €1 million a year.

O 'DRISCOLL, Eoin; COMPANY CHAIRMAN

b 1951, Cork; *m*; 2*s* 1*d*; *edu.* St. Therese College, Castlemarytr, Co. Cork; University College Cork; BE: M. Eng. Sc.; Managing Director Aderra Ltd; company chairman; senior vice-president Lucent Technologies; vice-president Ascend Communications; vice-president Stratus Computers; vice-president Wang Laboratories; chairman, Forfás; chairman, E.net; chairman, ICELT; chairman, Shennick net worksystems; chairman, Aderra; president, American Chamber of Commerce in Ireland; chairman, Enterprise Strategy Group established by Táinaiste 2004; member, IBEC National Executive Council; board member, Trinity Institute of Neuro Science; board member, Cork University Foundation; board member Governing Body National College of Ireland; Publ. *Ahead of the Curve, Ireland's Place in the Global Economy.* Clubs: National Yacht Club. Recreations: sailing. Contact: 162, Merrion Road, Ballsbridge, Dublin 4. **T** 01 2185304 email eod@aderra.ie

Chaired the enterprise Strategy Group known as the new 'Culliton Report' which sets out industrial policy in Ireland for the next decade; this Corkman has a sharp intellect, one of the brightest to come out of UCC, and has a very strong commercial profile based on his global business experience.

O' DRISCOLL, Fachtna; CHIEF AGRICULTURAL OFFICER CO. LIMERICK

b 1946, Co. Cork; *m* Attracta; 3*s*; *edu.* St. Fachtna's High School, Skibbereen, Co. Cork; University College Dublin; University of Wageningen, The Netherlands; B. Agr. Sc; M. Agr. Sc; Chief Agricultural Officer, Co. Limerick; head of Agricultural Advisory and Training, Co. Limerick; member, governing body of University Limerick and Limerick Institute of Technology; chairman, University of Limerick Audit Committee; science teacher, Dublin VEC; assistant inspector, Department of Agriculture; assistant college principal, Kildalton College, Piltown, Co. Kilkenny; chief agricultural officer Co. Carlow; past president, Agricultural Science Association; *Publ. The ASA Looks Forward – Towards A History of Agricultural Science in Ireland* 1992; *Number of Dairy Farmers by 2010* 1993; *The Maastricht Treaty – An Explanation* 1992; *Challenges for the Agricultural Advisory Service* 1991; *Structural Funding* 1988. Clubs: Castletroy Golf Club, Kilkee Golf Club, Local Community. Recreations: GAA, rugby, golf, reading. Contact: Teagasc, Parnell Street, Limerick. **T** 061 415922 **F** 061 310835 email f.odriscoll@limerick.teagasc.ie

One of the youngest agricultural graduates to be appointed Chief Agricultural officer in Co Carlow in the early 1980s, has been domiciled in Limerick where he is now

Fachtna O' Driscoll

Chief Agric; highly intelligent, good company, excellent strategic thinker on agri matters and runs a highly efficient service; a UCD graduate, has been an active member of the governing body of UL in his adopted city.

O' DRISCOLL, Sean O.B.E.; CHIEF EXECUTIVE, GLEN DIMPLEX

b 1957, Drimoleague, Co. Cork; *m* Rose; 1*s* 3*d*; *edu*. University College Cork; B.Comm; Chief Executive, Glen Dimplex; joined KPMG 1979; qualified as a chartered accountant 1982; partner, KPMG 1989; appointed group finance director Glen Dimplex 1990; deputy chief executive, Glen Dimplex 1995; succeeded Martin Naughton (*qv*) as group chief executive 1998; member, Enterprise Advisory Group; patron member, Irish China Organization; Awards, Special Achievement Medal, UCC 2004. Recreations: GAA, horseracing. Contact: Glen Dimplex, 41, Ailesbury Road, Ballsbridge, Dublin 4

The popular West Cork man, brother of Fachna O'Driscoll (*qv*), is one of the country's top businessmen; has overseen the expansion of the Glen Dimplex Group out of its Irish and UK base across Europe, Canada and Asia; the quiet, low profile, award winning accountant has the Midas touch in his business dealings; former UCC graduate was recognized by his alma mater for achievement in the business world; was awarded an honorary OBE by Queen Elizabeth, 2006 (presented by the British Ambassador in Dublin 11 April 2006) for his contribution to business in the UK.

Ó DUBHGHAILL, Aodán; HEAD, LYRIC FM CLASSICAL RADIO

b 1955, Átha Cliath; separated; 1*s* 2*d*; head of Lyric FM Classical Music Station; Gael Linn Teo 1974-78; Cloney Audio, Rathmines 1978-79; producer/sound engineer RTÉ Radio 1979-2003; Head of Lyric FM 2003 to date; *Publ. A Guide to Traditional Music* on LP records, CDs; producer of various CDs. Recreations: music, walking, travel. Contact: Lyric FM, Cornmarket Square, Limerick. **T** 061 207 300 **F** 061 207 390 email aodan.odubhgaill@rte.ie

Has taken on the challenge of making classical music more relevant to mainstream taste; has adapted and reformatted many of the radio's existing slots to explain and make more relevant Art music in the modern, contemporary and classical idioms.

O'DUINN, Proinnsias; CONDUCTOR

b 1941; *m* 1st (*m diss*); 1*s* 1*d*; *m* 2nd Joan Merrigan; *edu*. Christian Brothers School, Marino; College of Commerce, Rathmines; Royal Irish Academy of Music; College of Music; Conductor; principal conductor, Iceland Symphony Orchestra 1963-64; principal conductor and music director, Orquestra Sifonica Nacional del Ecuador 1965-89; permanent principal conductor, RTE Concert Orchestra 1978; music director, Our Lady's Choral Society 1979-2003; guest conductor with engagements in various concert, opera ballet and oratorio; fellowship, Irish Arts Council 1962; Awards: Jacobs Award for radio and television 1975; works include various symphonic and chamber music compositions; *Stuff and Nonsense* (musical), composed soundtrack of *Strumpet City* TV orchestra. Recreations: gardening, DIY. Contact: RTE, Donnybrook, Dublin 4. **T** 01 208 3111web www.rte.ie

Following an impressive career as permanent principal conductor, RTE Concert Orchestra for over 20 years, is now much in demand as a guest conductor.

O'DWYER, Conor; JOCKEY

b 1966, Waterford; *m* Audrey; 2*s* 1*d*; National Hunt Jockey; approximately 600 Winners, including Ladbrook Hurdle 1991; Midlands National 1992; Cheltenham Festival Winners: Cheltenham Gold Cup (Imperial Call) 1996; Smurfit Champion Hurdle (Hardy Eustace) 2004 & 2005; other big race wins: Ladbroke Hurdle (Redundant Pal) 1990; Irish Hennessy Gold Cup (Imperial Call) 1996; Midlands Grand National (Laura's Beau) 1992; Melling Chase (Opera Hat) 1998, (Native Upmanship) 2002 and 2003; Red Rum Handicap Chase (Jeffell) 1998; Top Novices Hurdle (Joe Mac) 1999. Recreations: sea fishing, golf, DIY. Contact: Gilltoon, Kilcullen, Co. Kildare **M** 087 255 5692 **F** 045 482 212 email conorodwyeracing@eirocom.net

A stylish and tenacious jockey with a roll call of impressive wins; loved by the punters and popular with his peers.

O'DWYER, Mick; GAELIC FOOTBALL LEGEND/ MANAGER

b 1930, Waterville, Co Kerry; *m* Mary Carmel Moriarty; 4*s*; *edu.* Waterville NS; Laois Gaelic Football Manager; trained as a mechanic; started his own garage and self drive car business; acquired The Villa Marie Hotel and The Strand, Waterville; sold The Strand 2004; has been synonymous with Gaelic football for over half a century; actively involved at inter-county level for over 50 years, he is widely regarded as one of Gaelic football's most inspirational figures; won four All-Ireland senior medals, two as a defender and two as an attacker 1959, 1962, 1969, 1970; seven National League medals; Texaco Sport Star of the Year 1969; managed the most famous team in the history of the game, the great Kerry side of the 1970s and 80s; under his guidance, they won eight All-Ireland titles, always displaying a sense of style and purpose which was universally admired; managed Kildare 1990-98, (leading them to an All-Ireland final in that year); took over management Laois team 2002 – 06; (led to a famous Leinster title in 2003, first in 47 years); Clubs: Waterville Golf Club. Recreations: golf, fishing; Contact: Laois Co. Board, O'Moore Park, Portlaois, Co. Laois. **T** 087 261 7839

> A total charmer and a living legend; enjoyed a glittering playing career with Kerry; one of the most legendary figures in the history of Irish sport; the most successful Gaelic football manager of all time but for some reason was never given the ultimate accolade as manager of the Irish International Rules team.

O'DWYER, Raymond Paul; COUNTY MANAGER WATERFORD

b 1958; *m* Anne; 1*s* 1*d*; *edu.* St. Colman's College, Fermoy, Co. Cork; University College Cork; B.E. (civil) 2nd.Class Hons 1979; diploma Environment Engineering, University College Cork 1992; C. Eng. M.IEI 1993; Masters, Eng. Sc. University College Cork 1994; Waterford County Manager 2004 to date; director of Services, Physical Planning and Environment South Tipperary, County Council 2001-04; senior executive engineer environmental South Tipperary County Council 1997-2001; executive engineer Waterford County Council 1983-87; assistant engineer, Waterford County Council 1982-83; temporary assistant engineer, Cork County Council 1980-82; site engineer John Sisk & Co. 1979-80. Clubs: Red Setter Club. Recreations: field sports. Contact: Civic Offices, Dungarvan, Co. Waterford. **T** 058 22023 **F** 058 45602 email Manager@waterfordcoco.ie

> One of the new professional engineers who has moved into local authority management; with the sizeable factory closures such as Waterford Crystal and Glanbia, will face major challenges attracting industry to the Déise country; the upgrading of WIT to university status along with major roll development could be the necessary catalyst for a new era of economic development in the South East.

O'FAOLAIN, Nuala Aine Brigid; WRITER

b 1942, Dublin; single; *edu.* University College Dublin; MA; Oxon, B.Phil; Writer; Lecturer, University College Dublin; television and radio producer, BBC/ The Open University; television producer, RTE; lecturer in media studies, DCU; columnist, *The Irish Times*; *Publ. Are You Somebody? Memoir & Selected Journalism* 1996; *My Everything Always, A Romance* (in preparation); columnist *Sunday Tribune* 2004 to date; Contact: The Sunday Tribune, Lower Baggot Street, Dublin 2. **T** 01 679 2022email nofaolain@tribune.ie

> A gifted and percipient writer of the human condition; a staunch feminist, she is an acute observer of unhappiness in herself and others; a great talker to her topics; needs an audience to blossom.

Ó FIANNACHTA, RT. REV. MONSIGNOR, Pádraigh Seosamh; PARISH PRIEST, DINGLE

b 1927, Ballymore, Dingle, Co. Kerry; single; *edu.* St. Brendan's College, Killarney, Co. Kerry; Pontifical College Maynooth BA., NUI UCC, MA., H. Dip Ed.; Pontifical University of Maynooth, D.Ph (*hc*); Sacred Heart University D.Litt (*hc*), D.Hum. MRIA; Parish Priest/ Professor/ Scholar; professor of Early & Middle Irish, St. Patrick's College Maynooth, Co. Kildare 1961-82; professor of Modern Irish 1982-92; Dean of Faculty of Celtic Studies NUI Maynooth; parish priest, Dingle, Co. Kerry; Canon Diocese of Kerry; assistant, Pontifical Throne with rank of Rt. Reverend Monsignor; chairperson Bord of Díseart Institute, Dingle Co Kerry dedicated to the study of Celtic Spirituality; *Publ. DIL Dictionary of Early and Middle Irish* (RIA) contrib.; translated Bible into Irish; editor & contributor to *Léachtaí Colm Cille*; *Iris leabhar Mhá Nuad*; *An Sagart*; Catalgoue of Irish Mass in Maynooth; *Táin Bó Cuailgne* from hitherto unknown Ms "de valira I.ii, Sant T.ii"; six collections of modern Irish Poetry; *Jesus in Dingle*; *Ag Siúl na Teoran*; four travelogues. Clubs: Cuman na Sagart, Member of Cymmrodorion Society, Royal Irish Academy. Recreations: Irish theology, poetry, travel, Gaelic football, languages, especially Irish dialects, publishing, art, folklore. Contact: The Presbytery,

Dingle, Co. Kerry. **T** 066 915 1208 **F** 066 915 1173 email pof@diseart.ie

A truly good man who has created in his native place a whole new centre of spirituality; a great scholar, writer, and humanist this native Kerry man has been a gift to Maynooth and now to the Kerry Diocese; great company and adored by his friends, if the Bishops are less certain of him; but this in itself is a good housekeeping seal of approval.

O' FLYNN, Michael; PROPERTY DEVELOPER

b 1957, Ovens, Co. Cork; *m* Sheila; 4 children. *edu*; Ovens NS; St. Finbarr's College, Farrenferris, Cork; Cork Regional Technical College (now CIT); Property Developer; with brother John founded O' Flynn Construction Holdings; started building residential developments in the greater Cork area in the early 1980s; his major developments include East Gate, a 35 acre retail park and 84 acre business park in Little Island which will be the largest retail park in Munster when completed; the €400 redevelopment of the former Murphy Ballincollig barracks into a new town center and shopping complex 2005; Mount Oval scheme in Rochestown is another O'Flynn development; plans to build €200 million, 600 residential units at Dunkettle Estate, Glanmire, Co. Cork. Recreations: passionate GAA, golf, racing. Contact: O'Flynn Construction Co Ltd, Melbourne House, Model Farm Road, Cork. **T** 021 434 3111 **F** 021 434 3053 email: info@oflynnconstruction.ie web www.oflynnconstruction.ie

Ó GALLCHÓIR, Pól; CEO, TG4

b 1957; *m* Gillian; 3*s* 2*d*; *edu*. Pobal Scoil Ghaoth Dobhair; University College Galway; BA; CEO TG4; journalist RTÉ Newsroom 1980-85; regional manager Radió na Gaeltachta 1985- 94; CEO Radio na Gaeltachta 1994-2000; CEO Telifís na Gaeltachta 4 2000 to date. Contact; TG4, Baile na hAbhann, Co. na Gaillimhe. **T** 091 505057 **F** 091 505021 email pol.o.gallchoir@TG4.ie

An enthusiastic and committed Gaelgoir, has broadened the appeal of TG4 to the status of an RTE 3; with the proposed restructuring of RTE in relation to TG4 faces an uphill struggle; but he is not without friends at Court notably Eamon Ó Cuiv (*qv*).

O'GARA, Ronan; PROFESSIONAL RUGBY PLAYER

b 1977, San Diego, California, USA; *m* Jessica Daly; *edu*. Presentation Brothers College, Cork; University College Cork 1998; BA; University College Cork 1999; M.B.S; Professional Rugby Player; outhalf, Cork Constitution Munster and Irish rugby team; plays for Ireland, Munster and Cork Constitution; Munster Inter provincial 1998-99; captained AIL and PBC Team for Senior and Junior teams 1995; capped Irish-Australian Tour 2001; Six Nations Championship 2005; currently writes columns on rugby for journals including *Irish Rugby*. Clubs: Cork Constitution RFC. Recreations: property, football, journalism. Contact: Cork Constitution Rugby Football Club, Cork. **T** 021 429 2563 **F** 021 429 1960 email ronan ogara@online.ie

Ambitious and highly motivated; well liked and respected in the world of sport and beyond.

Seán Óg Ó hAilpín

Ó hAILPÍN, Seán Óg; CAPTAIN CORK HURLING TEAM/BANKER

b 1977, Sydney, Australia; single; *edu*. North Monastery College, Cork; Commercial Manager, Ulster Bank, Captain, Cork Cork Hurling Club; arrived in Cork from Australia, picked up a hurley for the first time 1989; Munster double winning a senior medal in both hurling and football 1999; Hurler of the Year 2004; represented Ireland in the International Series against Australia 2004; Captain Cork All Ireland winning teams 2004, 2005. Clubs: Na Piarsaigh; Recreations: music, reading, sport. Contact: Ulster Bank, Patrick Street, Cork. **T** 021 427 0618

One of the biggest stars in Irish sport, the determined Cork Left Half-Back may not be the most stylish or graceful player with a hurl in his hand, but he is one of the most hard-working, dedicated and honest; idolised by many young people for his clean-cut image as a dedicated professional and a fluent Irish speaker; magnificent ambassador for Cork and hurling; utterly charming, has time for everyone; he's polite, poses for photos, signs autographs, takes the appreciations and observations of everyone on board; a car crash in 2001 nearly finished his glittering career before it started; unbelievably was back in action by the end of the 2002 league campaign after months of repetitive exercises designed to build up his knee muscles once again; would be electoral gold for any political party.

O'HAGAN, Dolan John; EDITOR, DUNDALK DEMOCRAT
b 1971, Rep. South Africa; *p* Mary Martin; *edu.* St. Columb's College, Derry; University of Ulster; BA (Hons) sport and leisure studies (DS); Editor, *Dundalk Democrat*; journalist *Derry Journal*; news editor, *Drogheda Independent*. Recreations: GAA, rugby, football, golf, current affairs, reading, walking. Contact: Dundalk Democrat, Crowe Street, Dundalk, Co. Louth. **M** 086 838 9495 **F** 042 933 3199 editor@dundalkdemocrat.ie

O'HALLORAN, James Michael; FINE ART AUCTIONEER & VALUER
b 1958, Dublin; *m* Helen Long; 1*s* 2*d*; *edu.* Blackrock College, Dublin; College of Commerce Rathmines, Dublin; University College Dublin; BA; Trinity College Dublin; Diploma in Art History; FIAVI; Managing Director, James Adam and Sons, Fine Art Auctioneers and Valuers, Dublin; salesroom assistant James Adam & Sons, trained under Brian Coyle 1981; qualified member of Irish Auctioneers and Valuers Institute 1986; managing director of Adams 1998; qualified as member of IAVI 1987; fellow IAVI; chairman of the IAVI Fine Art Committee; president, Irish Auctioneers and Valuers Institute which represents over 1800 property professionals including Fine Art practitioners 2005-06; lecturer on Irish Art at IAVI Fine Art courses; UCD Continuing Learning and at University of Limerick. Clubs: Kilkee Golf Club, Co. Clare. Recreations: family, art history, travel, politics; sporting interests include golf, sea kayaking, cycling, walking. Contact: James Adam & Sons, 26 St. Stephen's Green Dublin 2. **T** 01 676 0261 email j.ohalloran@adams.ie web www.adams.ie

> His suave and laid back manner disguises a keen commercial brain; as auctioneer is able to coax the most reluctant bidder to adventurous heights; as MD has consistently delivered superb performances and increased the turn over and profit margins for this oldest established Irish auction house.

O'HARA, James R 'Jim'; GENERAL MANAGER, INTEL IRELAND
b 1951; vice president, technology and manufacturing group general manager, Ireland Operations; Fab 10/14 plant manager Intel Corp; joined Brunswick Digital (17 years); held several general management positions in Ireland and the United States; joined Intel 1991; appointed general manager Intel Ireland 2002; member, governing board for the Irish Business and Employers Confederation; chair, the information communications and technology sector; director, American Chamber of Commerce in Ireland; LL.D (*hc*) NUI Maynooth 2006. Contact: Intel Corporation, Leixlip, Co. Kildare. **T** 01 606 7000 web www.intel.com

> One of the key, most powerful and highly respected technology chiefs in Ireland; is unusual in having landed one of the top tech jobs in the country without the benefit of a third level qualification; presides over $7 billion investment (2006), 4700 direct and indirect employees, 3.7 million sq feet in buildings.

O'HARE, Daniel Oliver 'Danny'; UNIVERSITY PRESIDENT EMERITUS
b 1942, Dundalk; *m* Sheelagh; 3*s* 1*d*; *edu.* CBS Dundalk; University College Galway BSc.,1964 MSc 1963; University of St. Andrews (Scotland) Ph.D.; honorary doctorates TCD., NUI; QUB, University of Ulster; President Emeritus Dublin City University; chairman Food Safety Authority of Ireland; member e. voting commission; non executive director Calor; chairman Independent Hospitals Association of Ireland; non executive director of Framework Solutions; board member Respect; Daughters of Charity of outreach Moldova; assistant professor Michigan State University 1968-70; founding director Letterkenny Institute of Technology 1971-74; director Waterford I.T. 1974-77; Director NIHE Dublin 1977-89; founding president DCU 1989-99; *Publ.* contributions to journals, newspapers, *Irish Times*. Recreations: golf, reading, music, travel. Contact: 10, Deerpark Drive, Castleknock, Dublin 15. **M** 087 234 0313 email ohared@yahoo.com

> A very gifted university President whose talents have not been lost to the public service; keen on the arts and their humanising influence, he has been responsible for some amazing projects and is young enough to continue the good work; a likeable person who is in fact deeply shy and it must be a struggle to work in the public interface, but he gets on with it, to considerable effect.

Daniel O'Hare

O'HARE, Rita; SINN FEIN DIRECTOR OF PUBLICITY
b 1944, Glen Road, Belfast; *m* Gerry O'Hare; (*m. diss*); 2*s* 1*d*; Sinn Fein Director of Publicity; involved with the Republican movement/ Civil Rights campaign 1969; jailed for her activity in the struggle 1971; released from prison, shot and badly wounded by the British Army 1971; moved with her

family to Dublin 1972; a founding member of the Women's Department, to mobilize the political voice of Irish women 1980; continues to maintain her role as an instrumental influence on the development of the Department and the party's policies on women's issues; editor of An Pholblacht/Republican News 1985-91; Sinn Fein's Director of Publicity 1991-96; elected member of the Ard Chomhairle (National Executive) of Sinn Fein; Sinn Fein's representative to the Irish government putting forth the party's position on all manner of issues during the negotiations 1996-98; Sinn Fein's Representative to the United States 1998-05: barred from getting a US visa Feb 2005; bar lifted, accompanied Martin Mc Guinness to New York to announce end of armed struggle July 27 2005. Recreations: family. Contact: Sinn Fein, 44 Parnell Square, Dublin 1. **T** 01 872 6100 **F** 01 872 6839 web www.sinnfein.ie

The Belfast born Protestant has served Sinn Fein in several capacities; as editor of the magazine *Iris*, published groundbreaking material, raising the issues of social and political problems associated with the Nationalist struggle for self-determination; as part of the Sinn Fein delegation to the Forum for Peace and Reconciliation played a key leadership role in formulating and promoting the party's strategies in the current peace process.

Bill O'Herlihy

O'HERLIHY, William Newman 'Bill'; PUBLIC RELATIONS CONSULTANT/ BROADCASTER
b 1938, Cork; *m* Hilary Patterson; 2*d*; *edu.* St Finbarrs College, Farranferris, Cork; Chief ExecutiveO'Herlihy Communications 1973 to date; chairman, Mediawise 1980-96; producer presenter *The Distant Drum*, ground breaking TV series on the Irish Diaspora; reporter/ columnist Cork Examiner Group 1956-67; reporter/presenter *Newsbeat, 7 Days* RTE TV 1965-71; presenter RTE Sport 1971 to date; anchor *Primetime* presentations of Olympic Games, soccer and rugby World Cup finals; European Championships; World and European Track and Field Championships; The Premiership and Irish Internationals; Awards: Jacobs TV Award 1990; Sports Journalist of the Year 2002. Clubs: Foxrock Golf Club, Stephens Green Hibernian Club, member Public Relations Consultants Association; former council member Public Relations Institute of Ireland. Recreations: golf, politics, good wine. Contact: O'Herlihy Communications, 40 Eastmoreland Lane, Dublin 4. **T** 01 660 2744 **F** 01 660 2745 email bilandhil@yahoo.com

The genial Corkman is synonymous with sport throughout the country; his encyclopedic knowledge of sport, especially soccer, easy manner and lilting Leeside accent makes him a firm favourite with all sports lovers; is a highly respected public relations executive with close links to Fine Gael.

O'HIGGINS, Professor, Niall, John; PROFESSOR OF SURGERY/CONSULTANT SURGEON
b 1942; Dublin; *m* Dr. R.E. Healy; 2*s* 2*d*; *edu.* Cresent College Limerick; Clongowes Wood College Co. Kildare; University College Dublin; MB, Bch, BAO (Hons) 1967; M.Ch 1974; FRCSI 1970; FRCS Eng 1970; FRCS Edin 1970; Professor of Surgery/Consultant Surgeon; trained in Royal Postgraduate Medical School, London; president, World Federation of Surgical Oncology Societies; president, European Society of Surgical Oncology; president, Federation of European Cancer Societies; established first breast cancer service/ clinic in Ireland; advocate for improved care for patients with breast cancer; author of documents for development of cancer services in Ireland, European Union and internationally; invited expert at over 50 international cancer conferences. Clubs: Fitzwilliam Lawn Tennis Club. Recreations: reading, cycling. Contact: The Jurrett, 18 Park Drive, Ranelagh, Dublin 6. **T** 01 497 8780 email niall.ohiggins@ncd.ie

One of the country's most respected cancer specialists; was one of the architects of the National Cancer Strategy which led to the establishment of Breast Check; a renowned medical academic, has carried the torch for the Irish healthcare sector at many international conferences; extremely articulate and totally committed to his profession.

O'HIGGINS, Paul Peter; SENIOR COUNSEL
b 1954; Dublin; *m* Finola Flanagan; 2*s* 1*d*; *edu.* Gonzaga College Dublin; University College Dublin; BA Hons; Kings Inns; Senior Counsel; called to the Bar 1977; called to the English Bar (Middle Temple) 1982; called to the Inner Bar 1992. Clubs: Kildare Street & University Club, National Yacht Club, Donnybrook Lawn Tennis Club. Recreations; sailing, rugby, reading, music. Contact: The Law Library, Bar Council Administration Office, Four Courts, Dublin 7. **T** 01 4979763 **F** 01 817 5150 email pohiggins@lawlibrary.ie

A brilliant lawyer and one of the leading advocates at the Bar. Excellent company, witty, intelligent with a delicious sense of humour.

O'KANE, Frank; CEO, MERCURY ENGINEERING GROUP
b Strabane, Co. Tyrone; *m* Rosaleen; 2*s* 2*d*; *edu*. St Columb's College, Derry; electrical engineering; CEO, Mercury Engineering Group; for the past 35 years he has engaged in the establishment and development of the Mercury Engineering Group of companies. LLD (*hc*) UCD; Clubs: Kildare Golf and Country Club Hotel, Powerscourt Golf Club, Luttrellstown Golf Club. Recreations: hill walking, mountain climbing, horse racing, golf. Contact: Mercury House, Sandyford Industrial Estate, Dublin 18 **T** 01 216 3000 **F** 01 295 3995 email ann.gibney@mercury.ie web www.mercury.ie

The Strabane born electrical engineer has created one of the largest engineering company in Europe; extremely shrewd, hardworking and charismatic, has grown his company from its Dublin origins to a major international force.

Frank O'Kane

O'KELLY, Patricia, Florence; BLOODSTOCK BREEDER
b 1931; single; *edu*. St. Helen's School; Bloodstock Breeder; director, Irish National Stud; Goffs Bloodstock Sales; took on the running of Kilcarn Stud, a small commercial stud farm from her father. Clubs: Kildare Street Club, RIAC. Recreations: country life, gardening, skiing. Contact: Kilcarn Stud, Navan, Co. Meath. **T** 046 902 1732 **F** 046 902 2622.

One of the most respected and successful breeders in the country, regularly getting the top price at major sales.

O'KEEFE, Batt; PUBLIC REPRESENTATIVE
b 1945, Cullen, Mallow, Co Cork; *m* Mary Murphy;1*s* 3*d*; *edu*. St. Brendan's College, Killarney, Co. Kerry; University College Cork; BA. H Dip.Ed; Public Representative/ lecturer in Cork Institute of Technology; Dáil Deputy 1987- 89 and 1992 to date; Senator, Labour panel 1989-92; candidate 1989 general election; chairman Oireachtas Committee on Health and Children 1997-2002; member, Cork County Council 1985 to date; Cork Vocational Education Sports Advisory Committee; chairman, Southern Health Board; Cork footballer, holder of Munster medals at under-21, junior and senior levels; Cork intermediate Handball Champion 1980. Clubs: Gaelic Athletic Association, Cork Handball Board, vice chairman management committee Ballincollig Community Centre. Contact: Department of the Environment, Heritage and Local Government, Custom House, Dublin 1. **T** 01 888 2257. **F** 01 878 8642; email batto'keeffe@environ.ie

The Co. Cork politician enjoyed a great reputation as a sportsman; a hard working Fianna Fáil deputy who is extremely popular in his constituency.

O'KEEFE, James Declan; MEDICAL CONSULTANT
b 1957, Cork; separated; 1*s*; *edu*; St. Colman's College, Fermoy, Co Cork; University College Cork; MB BCH BAO FCA RCSI DPM CARCSI; Consultant, Pain Medicine; *Publ*. Peer reviewed journals in pain medicine. Contact: St. Vincent's University Hospital, Elm Park, Dublin 4. **T** 01 269 5033

Internationally recognized pain management consultant, the first to set up practice in Ireland; highly regarded by his peers internationally.

O'KEEFE, Mark, Patrick; SALON OWNER (BROWN SUGAR)
b 1973, Dublin; *m* Paula Callan (*qv* O'Keeffe, Paula)); *edu*. St. Mary's College, Rathmines; Salon Owner, Brown sugar; full time hairdresser since 1992; managed two salons' for Peter Mark including Stephen's Green; worked on high profile shows including Supermodel show and Eurovision. Clubs: Renards, Lillies, Spy. Recreations: gym, fly fishing. Contact: 50 South William Street, Dublin 2. **T** 01 616 9967 **F** 01 616 9995

O'KEEFE, Paula; MAKE UP ARTIST;
b 1972, Dublin; *m* Mark O'Keefe (*qv*); *edu*. Mercy College Dublin; Make Up Artist/Salon Owner (Brown Sugar, Dublin); creative director make up and hair; freelance make up artist 1991-97; Mac Pro senior artist Ireland 1997-2005; director, Brown Sugar with Mark O'Keefe (*qv*) 2005 to date. Clubs: Lillies, Reynards, Spy. Recreations: cooking for friends, travel, gym, reading, eating out. Contact:

Brown Sugar, 50 South William Street, Dublin 2. **T** 01 616 9967 **F** 01 616 9995
email PAULACALLANOK.@EIRCOM.NET

O'LEARY, Jane; MUSICIAN AND COMPOSER
b 1946, Hartford, Connecticut, USA; *m* Patrick M. O'Leary; 1*s* 1*d*; *edu*. Wethersfield High School, Ct.
USA; Vassar College; BA; Princeton University; Ph.D. (Musical Composition); Musician and
cComposer; moved to Ireland and lives with her family in Galway 1972; founded Concorde Musical
Ensemble and founded Music for Galway; member of The Arts Council 1998-2003; former member
of the Board of the National Concert Hall; composer/ artist in residence, Royal Irish Academy of
Music, Dublin 2002-2003; founder member of Aosdána; her work has been performed by the RTÉ
Vanbrugh Quartet; the Paul Klee String Quartet (Venice); Con Tempo String Quartet; The Irish
Chamber Orchestra; the Philharmonic Orchestra of Bacau, Romania; pianists John O'Conor, Rolf
Hind and Robert Taub; Publ. CDs with Capstone (Celtic Connections); Black Box (e-motion John
Feeley) CMC, NIC, CN and Galway Arts Festival (Containers) Black Box label, Irish Composers
Series; guest composer with *Voices of Change* in Dallas; the Irish Festival at the Kennedy Centre;
L'Imaginaire Irlandais in France; *Donne in Musica* in Fiuggi, Italy; Tampere Biennale, Finland 2003
From the Sea Grey Shores performed by the RTÉ National Symphony at the Lincoln Center New York;
works include five orchestral compositions; 15 Ensemble; seven solo; three vocal and choral. Contact:
1 Avondale Road, Highfield Park, Galway. **T** 091 522 867 email patjaneoleary@eircom.net
web; www.cmc.ie/composers/http://homepage.eircom.net/~concorde

An able and astute musical director who has guarded her patch with great zeal; a
mover and shaker in West of Ireland musical circles.

O'LEARY, Margaret, Veronica; ACCOUNTANT AND FINANCIAL CONTROLLER
b 1945; *m* Thomas O'Leary (*decd*); 1*s* 2*d*; *edu*. F.C.J. Bunclody Co. Wexford; St. Mary's College
Mountmellick Co Laois; R.C.S.I, Cathal Brugha Street; Accountancy & Business College, L.S.B.
College; Irish Taxation Institute; registered General Nurse/ management accountant; diplomas in
photography, navigation and interior design; Managing Director and Company Secretary Crane Hire
Ltd; director Dublin City Crane Hire Ltd; director Oakpark Ltd; built up business with late husband
Tom and his brother Dermot 1968; runs business with brother-in-law Dermot and son Jarlath. Clubs:
Association of Irish Racehorse owners, Royal Irish Automobile Club, Dun Laoghaire Motor Yacht
Club. Recreations: horse racing, GAA, family, friends, food, wine. Contact: Crane Hire Ltd, Marina
House, Clarence Street, Dun Laoghaire, Co Dublin. **T** 01 663 7423 **F** 01 230 3859 email
margaret@connect.ie

Margaret O'Leary

An able businesswoman, highly successful in the macho world of construction; bright,
friendly and extremely highly regarded.

O'LEARY, Mari; MANAGING DIRECTOR O'LEARY PR & MARKETING
b 1960; *m* Michael Hogan; separated; 3*s*; *edu*. Our Lady's Grove, Clonskeagh, Dublin; Public
Relations Institute of Ireland Diploma; Managing Director, O'Leary PR and marketing;
modelled in Ireland & internationally 1978-88; founder, Communicado PR 1988; founder,
O'Leary PR & Marketing 1994; presented *Head to Toe* RTE 1990. Clubs: Carlisle Fitness Club.
Recreations: sports, music, travel. Contact: 50, James Place East, Dublin 2 **T** 01 678 9888
F 01 676 5570 email marioleary@olearypr.ie

O'LEARY, Michael; CEO RYANAIR
b 1961, Dublin; *m* Anita Farrell; 1*s*; *edu*. Clongowes Wood College, Co. Kildare; Trinity College
Dublin; BBS; Chief Executive Officer Ryanair; joined Stokes Kennedy Crowley dealing in tax;
moved into property buying and selling newsagents; joined Ryanair COO 1991; chief executive
1993 to date. Recreations: farming, sport, reading, restoring his heritage property and driving
his 'taxi'. Contact Ryanair, Dublin Airport, Co. Dublin. **T** 01 812 1212 **F** 01 812 1213
web www.ryanair.com

Mari O'Leary

A legend in his own lifetime, enables masses worldwide to travel cheaply; a CEO who
lives for the photo opportunity when he's not otherwise engaged with running his
airline; famously gets on with his Ryanair founder, Tony Ryan (*qv*) and is cut from the
same fabric; tough, pragmatic and dogmatic; has revolutionised the thinking of the
travel industry and manifestly doesn't suffer fools gladly – ie not at all; broadly
contemptuous of all politicians; also has a hands-on approach to managing his estate at

Gigginstown, where he spends much of his spare time breeding thoroughbred horses and rearing Aberdeen Angus cattle.

O'LEARY, Olivia; JOURNALIST/BROADCASTER
b 1949, Co Carlow; *m* Paul Tansey (*qv*); 1*d*; *edu.* Stileo's, Carlow; Universtity College Dublin, BA 1969; Journalist, Broadcaster; *Nationalist & Leinster Times* 1969-72; RTE News 1972-76 in Dublin/London, Belfast: *Politics Programme* RTE 1976-78; political and parliamentary sketch writer *Irish Times* 1978-83; BBC News Night 1984-86; Yorkshire Television *First Tuesday* 1986-93; RTE *Today Tonight* and *Prime Time* 1980-94; BBC Radio 4 *Between Ourselves* 1998 to date; *Five Seven Live*, political column to date; *Publ. Mary Robinson – The Authorised Biography* with Helen Burke, (Hodder and Stoughton) 1998; *Politicians and Other Animals*, (O'Brien Press) 2004. Clubs; Monkstown LTC, vice chairperson of Barnardos. Recreations: piano, Barrow Valley. Contact: Radio Center, RTE, Montrose, Donnybrook, Dublin 4. **T** 01 208 3111 **F** 01 2083080 web www.rte.ie

Intelligent, perceptive and sensitive; an insightful and authoritative deliverer of the voice of reason; biography of Charles J Haughey eagery awaited.

Olivia O'Leary

O'LOAN, Nuala Patricia; POLICE OMBUDSMAN FOR NORTHERN IRELAND
b 1951 Bishop's Stortford, Hert; *m* Declan O'Loan; 5*s*; *edu.* Convent of the Holy Child, Harrogate; College of Law, London; Kings College London; LL.B; Police Ombudsman for Northern Ireland; Supreme Court of England & Wales 1976; lecturer in law Ulster Poly 1976-80; lecturer in law University of Ulster 1984-92; Jean Monnet chair in European law 1992-99; senior lecturer 1992-2000; police ombudsman for NI 2000 todate; special commissioner for Racial Equality 2004 to date; chairman NI Consumer Council for Electricity 1997-2000; member Energy and Transport Gp General Consumer Council (convenor 1994-96) 1991-96; UK Domestic Coal Consumer Council 1992-95; ministerial work on Green Economy 1993-95; N Health and Social Services Board (convenor for complaints 1996-97) 1993-97; police authority for NI 1997-99; expert member European Commission Consumers Consultative Council 1994-95; lay visitor to RUC stations 1991-97; Publ. author of more than 45 publications on consumer law, policing and other issues. Recreations: reading, music. Contact: Police Ombudsman for Northern Ireland, New Cathedral Buildings, St. Anne's Squre,11 Church St. Belfast BT1 1PG. **T** 028 9082 8600 **F** 028 9082 8615. email info@policeombudsman.org.website www.policeombudsman.org

Nuala O'Loan

A brave, tough, able and courageous person who has to face down the police and the politicians on a regular not to say weekly basis; stands up for what is right in a dangerous and unenviable post.

O'MAGAN, Dolan John; EDITOR, THE DUNDALK DEMOCRAT
b 1971 Republic of South Africa; *m* Mary Martin, partner; *edu*; St. Columb's College, Buncrana Road, Derry City; University of Ulster, Jordanstown, Belfast, Co Antrim; BA (Hons) Sport & Leisure Studies (DIS); journalist *Derry Journal*; news editor *Drogheda Independent*. Recreations; GAA, rugby, football, golf, current affairs, reading & walking. Contact: The Dundalk Democrat, Crowe Street, Dundalk, Co. Louth. **M** 086 8389495 **F** 042 9331399 email editor@dundalkdemocrat.ie

O'MAHONY, Synan John; FASHION DESIGNER
b 1970; single; *edu.* St. Nessan's Limerick; Fashion Designer; began working with other designers 1996; designed for presenter Eurovision Song Contest 1997; continues to design for celebrity clients such as Mary Harney (wedding gown), Georgina Ahern (wedding gown), and TV personality Claire Byrne (wedding gown). Recreations: oil painting, cooking. Contact.4 Brookfield Estate, Kimmage Cross Roads, Dublin 12. **M** 086 823 90 45

Indefatigable, multi talented designer; no slouch in the publicity stakes either.

O'MAHONY, Liam; CHIEF EXECUTIVE CRH PLC
b 1947, Tipperary; *m*; 2*s*; *edu.* University College, Cork, B.Eng; Trinity College Dublin, MBA; Kings Inns, BL, (awarded Brooke Scholarship) FIEI; worked as civil engineer in design and project management; joined CRH as development manager 1971; held managerial positions in CRH in Ireland and US: member CRH Board 1992; chief executive, Oldcastle Inc (US) 1994; chief executive Designate CRH plc, 1999; chief executive 2000 to date; member Irish Management Institute Council; Harvard Business School European advisory board. Contact: CRH plc, Belgard Castle, Dublin 22. **T** 01 404 1000. web www.crh.com

The Tipperary born engineer continues to drive the development of CRH as a major global player in it's sector; the quiet spoken, low profile businessman has an edge of steel but is popular with his colleagues and highly respected in the business community; continues to be a keen GAA supporter

O' MAHONY, Seamus; ACCOUNTANT/PROPERTY DEVELOPER
b 1961, Kilbrittain, Co. Cork; *m* Carmel; 2*s* 1*d*; *edu.* Farrenferris College, Cork; University College Cork; B.Comm; Chartered Accountant (ACA); principal O'Mahony Crowley Accountants, Bandon, Co. Cork; developer with John Fleming (*qv*) Lodge Hotel and Spa, Inchydoney, Co. Cork and Radisson SAS Hotel, Limerick; developer with Rick Fitzgerald (*qv*) Radissson SAS Hotel, Little Island, Cork; investor Snowie Group Waste Management Company UK which also has a considerable property portfolio. Clubs: Bandon Golf Club. Recreations: golf, GAA, racing. Contact: O'Mahony Crowley Accountants, 35, South Main Street, Bandon, Co. Cork. **T** 023 44055

The quiet spoken, low profile West Cork accountant has made many shrewd commercial investments over the past 20 years; among the Cork business elite he runs a very successful family accountancy practice; deeply involved in the local community and an avid GAA fan, particularly of his local Kilbrittain team.

O' MALLEY, Fiona; PUBLIC REPRESENTATIVE
b Limerick; single; *edu.* Laurel Hill, Limerick; Trinity College Dublin; BA (History of Western European Art & Architecture); City University, London; masters degree in Museum and Gallery Management; Public Representative (PD Dun Laoghaire); Progressive Democrats spokesperson on Arts and Culture, also the party's Energy Spokesperson; elected to Dun Laoghaire Rathdown County Council in 1999, representing the Stillorgan Ward; elected to Dail Eireann 2002; was an active member of the Council until September 2003, when she resigned her seat because of the abolition of the dual mandate. Contact: Leinster House, Dail Eireann, Kildare Street, Dublin 2 **T** 01 618 3373 **F** 01 618 4334 email fomalley@oireachtas.ie

An impressive performer, a chip off the old block, resembles her father Des O'Malley, co founder of the PDs in so many ways; an extremely hard worker and brave politician; can expect to move up the ladder quickly.

Mary O'Malley

O'MALLEY, Mary, WRITER
b 1954, Connemara; separated; 1*s* 1*d*; *edu.* University College Galway, BA (Hons); Full Time Lecturer NUIG, Writer; former member Council Poetry Ireland; Galway Arts Centre board of directors; writer in residence in the Irish Cultural Centre Paris, Mayo County Council, Derry Verbal Arts Centre, Open House Music Festival Belfast, Manhattanville College, New York. Recreations: acting in areas of environmental protection, issues of community and social justice, traditional music, sailing, walking, cats, educations and teaching skills, travel. Contact: 31 Friars Hill Galway. **T** 086 312 3197 email OMALGAL@iol.ie

The Connemara born academic is widely experienced and respected; has an active interest in human and civil rights law.

O'MALLEY, Timothy; PUBLIC REPRESENTATIVE
b 1944, Limerick; *m* Margaret Kelly; 2*s* 2*d*; *edu.* Crescent College, Limerick; University College Dublin; B.Sc. Pharm; MPSI; FPSI; Public Representative; Minister of State at the Department of Health, with Special Responsibility for Mental Health, Disability Services and Food; pharmacist for over 30 years; elected TD (PD Limerick East) 2002 to date; appointed Minister of State at the Department of Health, with Special Responsibility for Mental Health, Disability Services and Food Safety 19th ofJune 2002 to date; former councillor, Limerick County Council; former president of the Irish Pharmaceutical Union; awarded fellowship by the Pharmaceutical Society of Ireland, for services rendered to the profession. Clubs: Limerick Golf Club, Old Crescent RFC, Ballybunion Golf Club, Mungret GAA. Recreations: golf, rugby, GAA. Contact: Constituency Office Dooradoyle. Limerick **T** 061 308540 **F** 061 228718 email tim_o'malley@health.irlgov.ie

Political pedigree – cousin of the legendary FF Education minister the late Donagh O'Malley and also cousin of PD founder Des O'Malley; has campaigned tirelessly on health issues since qualifying as a pharmacist over 30 years ago.

O'MARA WALSH, Eileen; MANAGING DIRECTOR, O'MARA TRAVEL GROUP

b 1941, Limerick; single; 1*s*; *edu.* Laurel Hill, Limerick; Muckross Park, Dublin; Institut Catholique, Paris; Grosvenor House Hotel, London; established own travel group, O'Mara Travel 1978 to date; general sales agent, Club Mediterranee 1978 to date; former director, Aer Lingus plc; chair, Medieval Trust 1988 to date; former director Great Southern Hotels (chairwoman 1984-91); former director Heritage Island Ltd; Chairwoman, Forbairt 1993-98; director OTMI (Overseas Tourism Marketing Initiative) 1994 to date; director, ERDF management board (Shannon) 1996 to date; director, Opera Ireland 1998 to date; former chair, ITIC (Irish Tourist Industry Confederation); member, Dublin Chamber of Commerce, Institute of Directors. Clubs: International Womens Foundation; governor, St. Patrick's Hospital; serving on the Tourism Policy Review Implementation Group. Recreations: visual arts, opera, theatre, film buff, nineteenth century English novelists, country pursuits, politics and current affairs. Contact: O'Mara Travel, Marina House, 11 – 13 Clarence Street, Dublin. **T** 01 236 6800 **F** 01 2366880 email eomarawalsh@omara-travel.com web. www.omara-travel.com

> A highly regarded, pioneering figure in the travel industry; her ability has been recognized by the wide range of board appointments companies she has held in the private and semi state sectors.

O'MEARA, Kathleen; PUBLIC REPRESENTATIVE

b 1960, Roscrea, Co.Tipperary; *m* Kevin Dolan; 1*s* 1*d*; *edu.* Sacred Heart Convent, Roscrea; University College, Galway; NIHE (Dublin); BA; Dip Journalism; Public Representative, Member of Seanad Éireann; former RTÉ journalist; elected to North Tipperary County Council & Nenagh Town Council 1999; elected to Seanad Éireann 1997; appointed spokesperson on Labour, Agriculture and Food, Justice, Equality and Law Reform along with Social, Community and Family Affairs; member of the all party Oireactas committee on the Constitution; re-elected 2002; The Committee of Selection of Seanad Éireann 2002 to date; Joint Committee on Communications, Marine and Natural Resources 2002 to date; Labour spokesperson on Children; Chief Whip in Seanad Eireann. Contact: Full Time Office 76 Silver Street, Nenagh, Co. Tipperary. **T** 067 34190 (O) Seanad Eireann 01 618 3573 email kathleen.omeara@oireachtas.ie

> The farmer's daughter from North Tipperary is one of triplet girls; former special advisor to Jnr Minister Eithne Fitzgerald in the 1994-97 Rainbow Coalition Government; in the marginal North Tipperary constituency she continues to challenge to recover the Labour Dáil seat held by John Ryan.

Ó MUIRCHEARTAIGH, Iognáid Gearóid (Iggy); PRESIDENT, UNIVERSITY COLLEGE GALWAY

b 1943, Dublin; *m* Rosaleen Reynolds; 3*d*; *edu.* Coláiste Mhuire, Dublin; University College Dublin BA, MA, (Mathematical Science); University of Glasgow, Scotland Ph.D., (Statistics); President National University of Ireland Galway; statutory lecturer (Statistics) UCG 1970; associate professor 1985; registrar & deputy president 1998; Fulbright scholar, Stanford University; National Academy of Sciences senior research associate-ship; US Naval Postgraduate School, Monterey, California; visiting professor at US Naval Postgraduate School, University of Connecticut; University of Alberta and Glasgow; honorary degrees from University of Massachusetts 2003; University of Connecticut 2004; vice-chancellor of the NUI, Chair of Universities Ireland; incoming chair of Conference of Heads of Irish Universities (CHIU); *Publ.* more than 70 papers in international journals, including *Journal of the Royal Statistical Society, Technometrics, The Lancet, European Respirator Journal* and *Journal of Physical Oceanography.* Clubs: Galway Golf Club, Galway Lawn Tennis Club. Recreations: sports, tennis and golf. Contact: President's Office, The Quadrangle, National University Ireland, Galway, University Road, Galway. **T** 091 492 110 **F** 091 524176

Iognáid Ó Muircheartaigh

> Has proved to be a success in Galway and is very able, astute and worldly wise, traits not always found in a university president.

Ó MUIRCHEARTAIGH, Micheál; BROADCASTER

b 1930, Dingle; *m* Helena; 3*s* 5*d*; *edu.* Presentation Convent, Dingle; CBS, Dingle; Coláiste Iosagán, Ballyvourney, Co. Cork; St. Patrick's Training College Drumcondra, Dublin; University College Dublin; NT; BA; H.Dip. Ed; Broadcaster; started career as a teacher; commentated on Minor GAA games in Irish; first came to prominence after his commentary on the All Ireland Senior Football Championship final at the New York Polo Grounds 1947; joined RTE Sport full time 1980; succeeded the legendary Micheal O Hehir as the station's premier radio commentator; *Publ. From Dun Síon to Croke Park* (autobiography) 2004; Awards: D. Litt (*hc*) University College Galway. Recreations: golf, greyhound racing. Contact: RTE Radio Center, Montrose, Donnybrook, Dublin 4 **T** 01 208 3111 **F** 208 3080 web www.rte.ie

As a veteran broadcaster for over 50 years his voice is intricately linked with games of Gaelic football and hurling; hard to imagine a summer Sunday without his distinctive West Kerry accent, unmistakably that of a Gaelgeóir, filling the air waves with vivid accounts of the day's GAA action; developed his own inimitable style of commentary; a true lover of Gaelic games and a first class ambassador for the sport; it is reflected in the enthusiasm he brings to matches; his unusual turn of phrase has made him a much loved broadcaster and often imitated character.

Sean Ó Neachtain

Ó NEACHTAIN, Sean; PUBLIC REPRESENTATIVE
b 1947, Galway; *m* Cris; 5*s* 1*d*; *edu.* St Joseph's College "The Bish", Nuns Island, Galway; University College Galway; B.A. (Hons) H.Dip. Ed.; Member European Parliament (North and West Constituency); secondary schoolteacher; member of Galway County Council 1991-02; member of the Western Regional Authority 1994-02; member of the Border, Midland and Western Regional Assembly 1998-2002; member of Údarás na Gaeltachta 1979-04; chairman 1991-96; member of the European Parliament 2002 to date; member Committee of the Regions 1994-02; vice-president 1994-95; president of the European Alliance Group 1998-02. Clubs: Galway Golf Club. Recreations: sports in general especially golf and hurling, interest in local history. Contact: 42, Prospect Hill, Galway. **T** 091 560020 **F** 091 560023 email seanoneachtain@eircom.net web www.oneachtain.com

Beat the system and trounced the opposition both within the party system and made the cut; popular as this vote showed, he has yet to make a mark in European terms, but he'll get there; may have to return to fight in a general election, may not wish to but might be drafted and be a Minister.

O'NEILL, Anne; SOLICITOR
b 1960, Dublin; *m* Nicolas Mulcahy (*qv*); 2*s* 1*d*; *edu.* Alexandra College, Milltown, Dublin; Trinity College Dublin; Kings Inns Dublin Law Society, Blackhall Place, Dublin; BA Mod (LEG.SC); Barrister at Law; family law solicitor, head of Family Law Department Mc Keever Rowan, IFSC; called to Irish Bar 1986; general practice on the Dublin Circuit 1986-92; qualified as a solicitor 1994; has been active in litigation primarily in the area of family law 1994 to date; director of the Investor Compensation Company Ltd since its foundation 1998; presided over the creation of the Funding Schemes; member of the Hepatitis C Compensation Tribunal 2003 to date; Publ. *Irish Times* articles on family law. Clubs: David Loyd Riverview, Dublin. Recreations: keeping up to date with current affairs, socializing, reading, modern music, travel, wine tasting. Contact: McKeever Rowan, 5 Harbourmaster Place, IFSC, Dublin 1. **T** 01 670 2990 **F** 01 670 2988 email aoneill@mckr.ie

Very smart, larger than life, wonderful singer, works hard, plays hard; extremely popular and very well respected in family law, practical and compassionate.

O'NEILL, Julie; SECRETARY GENERAL, DEPARTMENT OF TRANSPORT
b 1955, Wexford; *edu.* Loreto College Wexford; University College Dublin; Trinity College Dublin, B Comm (Hons); University College Dublin, M.Sc (Public Sector Analysis); Secretary General Department of Transport June 2002 to date; sec general, Department of Marine and Natural Resources October 2001-June 2002; assistant secretary, Department of Tourism, Sport Recreation 1997-01; head of the Office of the Tanaiste 1993-97; career civil servant since 1972 in various departments including office of the Revenue Commissioners, Dept of Public Service, Dept of Finance, Dept of Social Welfare. Recreations; yoga, Pilates, sailing, hill walking, photography and travel. Contact: Transport House, 44 Kildare Street, Dublin 2. **T** 01 604 1348 **F** 01 6041349 email: julieoneill@transport.ie

The Wexford born senior civil servant was one of the first women to break through the glass ceiling and achieve Secretary General status; formidable and highly respected as an effective and efficient administrator, has one of the most administrative jobs in the Irish Civil Service; faces her biggest challenge in modernizing Ireland's infrastructure to meet the needs of the public and to reduce commuting times, especially in the greater Dublin area; the recent launch of Transport 21 sets out her vision for the future.

O'NEILL, Lawrence Daniel; EXECUTIVE CHAIRMAN, FASTNET BROADBAND LTD
b 1946, Granite City, Illinois, USA; *m* Marnie Inskip O'Neill; 2*s* 3*d*; *edu.* St Aloysius College, B'kara,

Malta; University of Missouri, Columbia, Missouri, USA; University of Maryland USA, BA 1971; Georgetown University, USA; BA Economics; Juris Doctor; Executive Chairman, Fasnet Broadband ltd; *Publ. Development of Telecommunication Competition in the Americas* 1978; *The Telecommunications Revolution* 1981; *The Five Top Technologies* 1984 – 1995; *Media Privacy* 1995; executive chairman, Fastnet Broadband Ltd; attorney, company director; cryptologist (linguist, National Security Agency; foreign service officer US Info. Agency, New Delhi, India 1970-73; US Consumer Product Safety Commission 1973-74; White House (office of telecom policy) 1974-81; Washington counsel, Fenwick, Stone, Davis & West 1981-85; partner, Winstone Strawn 1985-88; sec. general, SITA Paris 1988-91; Counsel Equant Amsterdam 1991-99; chairman, Stenter 1994-98; chairman QoS Networks 1999-2001. Clubs: Royal Irish Yacht Club. Recreations: sailing, golf, history, reading. Contact: 7, Longford Terrace, Monkstown, Co. Dublin. **T** 01 663 8173 **F** 01 230 3744 email doneill@fastnetbroadband.com

O'REGAN, Fiona; ADVERTISING MEDIA DIRECTOR
b 1972, Co. Cork; single; *edu.* Mercy Heights, Skibbereen, Co Cork; University College Cork; BA; Dublin Institute Technology; BA (French/Spanish); Diploma in Advertising; Advertising Media Director; TV buyer O'Connor O'Sullivan Advertising 1996; account manager Media Works 1997; appointed to board of Owens DDB/Media Works 2003. Clubs: Mount Pleasant Badminton Club. Recreations: badminton, tennis, swimming. Contact: Mediaworks, 38, Fitzwilliam Place, Dublin 2. **T** 01 661 0161 **F** 01 662 1208 email fiona.mediaworks@owensddb.com

Fiona O'Regan

O' REGAN, Gerard 'Gerry'; EDITOR, THE IRISH INDEPENDENT
b 1949, Tralee. Co. Kerry; *m* Sheila Moriarty; 2*s* 1*d*; *edu.* Tralee CBS; Editor, Irish Independent;reporter, *Tuam Herald, Leinster Express* 1978; news reporter, *Irish Independent*; subsequently assistant editor, features editor, news analysis editor, night editor, deputy editor *Irish Independent* 1995; editor *The Star* 1995-99; editor *Evening Herald* 1999-2005; editor *Irish Independent* 2005 to date. Recreations: reading, music, travel, walking and the media. Contact: The Irish Independent, 27 – 32 Talbot Street, Dublin 1. **T** 01 705 5333 email goregan@unison.independent.ie

> The Tralee born editor of the largest circulation daily newspaper in Ireland stamped his own mark very firmly from the get go; brought a new broom and a breath of fresh air with him; a tough, professional operator has very specific ideas about what he wants his paper to contain and how it looks; hardworking, well connected, the quintessential newspaperman's man.

O'REILLY, Sir Anthony John Francis 'Tony': CHIEF EXECUTIVE, INDEPENDENT NEWS & MEDIA plc: CHAIRMAN, EIRCOM, WATERFORD WEDGEWOOD plc, MATHESON ORMSBY PRENTICE.
b 1936, Dublin; *m* 1st Susan Cameron (*m diss*); 3*s* 3*d*; *m* 2nd Chryssanthie Goulandris; *edu.* Belvedere College Dublin; University College Dublin; Incorporated Law Society of Ireland; Bachelor of Civil Law (Hons) Solicitor; University of Bradford, PhD (Agri Marketing); Chief Executive Independent News and Media plc; chairman, Eircom, Waterford Wedgewood plc, Matheson Ormsby Prentice; industrial consultant, Weston Evans (UK) 1958-60; executive, Suttons Ltd, Cork 1960-62; chief executive officer, Bord Bainne 1962-66; managing director, Irish Sugar Company and Erin Foods 1966-69; managing director, H.J Heinz Company (UK) 1969 and progressed through the organisation to become chairman & chief executive officer of the Heinz Corporation 1979-98; former director, Mobil Oil, Bankers Trust, The Washington Post, The General Electric Company, The New York Stock Exchange; honorary doctorates from Wheeling College (US), Rollins College (US), Trinity College (Dublin), Indiana State University (US), Allegheny College (US), Boston College (US), De Paul University (US), University College Dublin, Queens University (Belfast), Carnegie Mellon University (US), Westminster College (US), Rhodes University (South Africa); recipient, Medal of the American-Irish Historical Society; life fellow, Irish Management Institute; honorary officer in the Order of Australia; council member, Rockefeller University, New York; Pro-chancellor, Trinity College Dublin; founder and world-wide chairman of the Ireland Funds; knighted by the Queen 2001, as a Knight Bachelor; outstanding sportsman (29 Irish Rugby Caps and 10 Lions Tests). Recreations: reading, rugby, horse racing, tennis. Contact: Independent News & Media PLC, Independent House, 2023 Bianconi Avenue, Citywest Business Campus, Naas Road, Dublin 24, Ireland. **T** 01 466 3200.

Tony O'Reilly

> One of the pioneering entrepreneurs who emerged in Ireland in the 1960s and '70s; the former Golden Boy of the international rugby world has become a globally successful

businessman in his professional career with Heinz and with his portfolio of varied global business interests; in a career that has spanned half a century has achieved many firsts on and off the pitch; cofounder of the Ireland Funds which operates in 14 countries and has raised over US$250 million for projects promoting peace, culture, community and education across the island of Ireland – North and South; sartorially elegant, a legendary raconteur.

O'REILLY, Lady Chryssanthie 'Chryss' Née Goulandris; CHAIRPERSON, THE IRISH NATIONAL STUD

b New York City; *m* Sir Anthony O'Reilly (*qv*); *edu.* The Chapin School, New York City; The Sorbonne, Paris, (History of Art and Design); Chairperson, The Irish National Stud. private investor; director of Waterford Wedgwood plc; chairperson of the Irish National Stud; a private investor and horse breeder, plays an active role in numerous charities and public interest organisations; runs leading stud farms in France and Ireland; throughout the last 20 years, she has been among the most successful bloodstock breeders in Europe; chairperson, The Irish National Stud, Ireland Fund of France, The O'Reilly Foundation; member, The American Ireland Fund; member, Board of Trustees of the Wedgwood Museum. Recreations: art, design. Contact: The Irish National Stud, Tully, Kildare, Ireland. **T** 045 521251 **F** 045 522129

A member of the well known Greek shipping family, has parlayed her passion for horses into a extremely successful breeding and racing business in Ireland and Europe; known as a connoisseur and collector of Fine Art.

O' REILLY, Emily; OMBUDSMAN AND INFORMATION COMMISSIONER

b 1957, Tullamore, Co. Offaly; *m* Stephen Ryan; 1*s* 4*d*; *edu.* University College Dublin; Trinity College Dublin; recipient, Nieman Fellowship in Journalism at Harvard University, Cambridge, U.S.; Ombudsman, Information Commissioner; education correspondent *Sunday Tribune*; political correspondent of the *Irish Press*; political columnist *Sunday Times*; political editor *Sunday Business Post*; Northern editor of the *Sunday Tribune*; editor of *Magill* magazine; broadcaster with RTÉ and Today FM; Publ. *Veronica Guerin: The Life and Death of a Crime Reporter; Master Minds of the Right Candidate*; appointed Ombudsman 2003 to date; appointed Information Commissioner 2003 todate; member, Standards in Public Office Commission. Contact: 18 Lr. Leeson Street, Dublin 2. **T** 01 678 5222 **F** 01 661 0570 email: ombudsman@ombudsman.irlgov.ie

Tough, assertive and a surprise as the choice for the post; has proved very successful and used her capacity to eyeball public figures to make a mark and to make a difference; smart, sassy, streetwise and very able; fearless, she's a terror to the lazy official; gets answers and asks many of the questions in public.

Gavin O'Reilly

O'REILLY, Gavin; GROUP CHIEF OPERATING OFFICER, INDEPENDENT NEWS AND MEDIA PLC;

b 1966, Dublin; *m* Alison Doody; separated; 2*d*; *edu* Clongowes Wood College, Co. Kildare; Georgetown University Business School; B.Sc; BA; (Hons); Group Chief Operating Officer, Independent News and Media plc; business development manager, Doyle Dale Burnbach 1985-87; institutional sales executive, First Pacific Securities 1988-89; joined Independent News and Media 1993; held various roles in the group; appointed to the board of Independent News and Media plc 1997; group COO, 2001 to date; president of the World Association of Newspapers; chairman, National Newspapers of Ireland; chairman, Dromoland Castle Hotels; other board appointments include: APN News and Media NZ, Ashford Castle Hotel, Norkom Tecnologies and various charitable foundations including The Ireland Funds, The O'Reilly Foundation and The Hole in the Wall Gang at Barretstown Castle. Contact: Independent News & Media plc, Independent House, 2003, Bianconi Avenue, Co. Dublin. **T** 01 466 3200

To those whom much is given, much is expected might well be the mantra for this able young executive, son of Sir Anthony O'Reilly (*qv*); known as Baby Doc or Baby Jesus among his Indo colleagues, has an easy manner, gregarious, ambitious, very hands on and has a voracious appetite for work; is already making his own mark on the Group.

O'REILLY, Jerry; PROPERTY DEVELOPER

b 1946, Beaufort, Co Kerry; *m* Anne Mc Donogh; 2 *d*; *edu.* Intermediate School Killorglin, Co. Kerry;

University College Cork; University College Dublin; B.Ag.Sc; M. Ag. Sc; Managing Director, O'Reilly Associates Ltd (business consultancy, property development). Clubs: Woodbrook Golf Club, Killarney Golf Club. Recreations: golf, skiing, swimming. Contact: 1 Northbrook Road, Dublin 6. **T** 01 496 2955 **F** 01 496 3000 email info@oraltd.com

> One of the most successful property developers in the country; the Beaufort born agricultural scientist learned his business from the ultimate guru John Murphy, the legendary London based property tycoon; extremely bright, low profile, unpretentious; has extensive interests in commercial property, hotels and the leisure industry with business partner Bernard Mc Namara (*qv*); with David Courtney paid €35.9 million for a State owned Ballsbridge site (equating to a staggering €95 million an acre) a new record in May, 2006. is passionate about his native county earning him the title 'Kerry Jerry'.

O'REILLY, John; CEO PADDY POWERS BOOKIES GROUP

b 1950; *m* Joan; 2 children; *edu*. Willow Park, Blackrock Co. Dublin; Blackrock College, Dublin; UCD, B.Comm; chartered accountant; Chief Executive Paddy Power Group; joined Craig Gardner (now PwC); financial controller H Williams; joined Paddy Power Group 1988; CEO Paddy Power Group 2002 to date. Recreations: golf, crosswords, Sudoku, the odd game of online poker. Contact: Paddy Power Head Office, Airton House, Airton Road, Tallaght, Dublin 24. **T** 01 404 5900 **F** 01 404 5901 email paddy power.com web www.paddypower.com

> His strategy for the company has developed a strong reputation as "The Punter Friendly Bookmaker" and has become renowned for its unique 'Money Back Specials"; was quick to recognize the new appeal of poker; continues to roll out new shop outlets.

O'REILLY, Liam; CEO, FINANCIAL REGULATOR (IFSRA)

b 1947, Newbridge, Co. Kildare; *m* Alice Kinsella; 1*s* 1*d*; *edu*; Diploma in Public Administration UCD; B.Comm, UCD 1970; M.Sc. Economics & Statistics TCD 1974; Ph.D Ecometrics/Time Series Analysis, TCD 1982; CEO Financial Regulator (IFSRA); joined the Central Bank 1967; worked in economic departments; worked at managerial level in various departments, financial control, international relations, financial markets, payments and settlements; appointed assistant director general with responsibility for the supervision of financial institutions 1998. Recreations: golf; walking. Contact: PO Box 9138, College Green, Dublin 2. **T** 01 434 4462 **F** 01 410 4899

> Coming to the end of his term of office which coincided with a number of scandals in the Irish Financial Services (NIB; FX affair in AIB); has emerged as a safe pair of hands in troubled times.

O'REILLY; Most Rev. Philip Leo; BISHOP OF KILMORE

b 1944, Cavan; single; *edu*; St. Patrick's College, Cavan 1957-62; NUI Maynooth 1962-65; Pontifical University, Maynooth 1965-69; Gregorian University, Rome 1976-81; B.Sc, H. Dip. Ed., B.D. S.T.L S.T.D; Bishop of Kilmore; teaching staff, St. Patrick's College, Cavan 1969-76; postgraduate studies, Rome 1976-81; chaplain Bailieborough Community School 1981-88; missions Nigeria 1988-95; parish priest, Castletara Kilmore 1995-97; coadjutor Bishop Kilmore 1997-98; Bishop of Kilmore 1998 to date; *Publ. Word and Sign in the Acts of The Apostles: A Study in Lucan Theology*; *Analecta Gregoriana, Rome* 1986. Clubs: Cavan Golf Club; Slieve Russell Golf Club. Recreations: golf, walking, reading; languages. Contact: Bishop's House, Cullies, Cavan. **T** 049 433 1496 **F** 049 436 1796 email bishop@kilmorediocese.ie

> The head of a small rural border diocese, he's been effective and is highly regarded as a Pastor; slightly old fashioned in his attitudes, he remains an advocate of the Truth; has good people skills, of the sort not usually found in Bishops in modern times.

O'REILLY, Tony; CHIEF EXECUTIVE, PROVIDENCE RESOURCES plc

b 1966, Dublin; *m* Robin Rafford (*m diss*); 2*s* 1*d*; *edu*. Clongowes Wood College, Co. Kildare; Brown University, Rhode Island, U.S.A.; Chief Executive Providence Resources plc; mergers & acquisitions, Dillon Read; Coopers & Lybrand; advising natural resource companies; director, Planning and Corporate, ARCON; appointed chief executive 1996-01; appointed non-executive chairman 2001-05 (company merged with Lundin Mining); served as deputy chief executive of Wedgwood, a division of Waterford Wedgwood plc from 2001-02; chief executive 2002-05; has been a director of Providence

Tony O'Reilly

since its foundation on demerger from ARCON 1997; director, Lundin Mining, (one of the world's biggest zinc producers); director, Independent News and Media plc; trustee, The O'Reilly Foundation. Recreations: tennis, rugby, skiing. Contact: Providence Resources PLC. 60, Merrion Road, Ballsbridge, Dublin 4. **T** 01 667 5740 **F** 01 667 5743 email providence@eircom.net

The son of the legendary Sir Anthony (*qv*) and brother of Gavin (*qv*) whose business career has been in a range of O'Reilly related companies; personable, a sharp businessman who is also involved in a number of charitable foundations.

O'RIORDAN, Dolores; SINGER/SONGWRITER

b 1972, Limerick; *m* Don Burton; 2*s* 1*d*; edu. Laurel Hill Convent, Limerick; Singer/Songwriter; joined the Cranberries as lead vocalist 1990; signed with Island Record; released first album *Everybody Else is Doing It, So Why Can't We* 1993; *Linger* from the album was the first big breakthrough, climbing to No. 8 in the US charts; Discography: *20th Century Masters, The Millennium Collection, The Best Of The Cranberries* 2005; *Everybody Else Is Doing It, So Why Can't We?* (The Complete Sessions 1991-93) 1993;*No Need To Argue* (The Complete Sessions 1994-95) 1994; *Stars: The Best Of 1992-2002* 2002; *To The Faithful Departed* (The Complete Sessions 1996-97) 1996; *Treasure Box* (The Complete Sessions 1991-99) 2002;*Wake Up And Smell The Coffee* 2001. Contact: Lindsay Holmes, L.H.P. The Rise, 6 Cullenswood Park, Ranelagh, Dublin 6. **T** 01 497 0313

A much loved musician and singer; her popular appeal makes her a much sought after talent; keeps her lifestyle and especially her family low key and quiet, concentrating on her work.

O'RORKE, Andrew; SOLICITOR

b 1950, Dublin; *m* Margaret; 1*s* 1*d*; *edu*. Colaiste Mhuire, Parnell Square, Dublin; University College Dublin; BCL; Law Society of Ireland; Solicitor; managing partner Hayes & Co; solicitor, Hayes 1973; partner Hayes 1976; managing partner 2000 - 06; *Publ.* articles on defamation, retail law and competition law. Clubs: Kildare Street. & University Club, South County Golf Club. Recreations: politics, marathons, sport, theatre. Contact: Lavery House, Earlsfort Terrace, Dublin 2. **T** 01 662 4747 email aororke@hayes.solicitors.ie

Renowned in the area of defamation defence law; hardworking, pragmatic and extremely able; close to Fianna Fáil.

O'ROURKE, Mary; PUBLIC REPRESENTATIVE

b 1937, Athlone; *m* Enda O'Rourke (*decd*); 2*s*; *edu*. St Peters Convent, Athlone; Loreto Convent, Bray; St Patrick's College, Maynooth; Public Representative; Senator; former school teacher Summerhill Convent, Athlone; elected FF deputy Longford Westmeath 1982; Minister for Education 1987-89; Minister for Health 1991-92; Minister for Trade and Marketing 1992-93; Minister for Labour 1993-94; deputy leader FF 1995-97; Minister Public Enterprise 1997-02; lost her seat General Election 2002; leader, and member Seanad Eireann 2001 to date. Recreations: reading, walking. Contact: Aisling, Arcadia, Athlone, Co Westmeath **T** 0902 72313 or Seanad Éireann, Kildare Street, Dublin 2. **T** 01 618 3860

Still rankling from losing her seat to Donie Cassidy in the last election, now approaching her 70th birthday 'Aunty Mary' continues to seek restoration of her place in the Dáil and plans to stand for election in 2007; an unlikely poster girl for a party now pitching it's appeal to young voters; never one to miss a worthwhile soundbyte – especially from the bath; will possibly be best remembered for telling then Minister Padraig Flynn to "fuck off back across the Shannon" or thanking her constituency helpers for "working like Blacks"; known for her integrity.

O'ROURKE, Patrick; FORMER PRESIDENT, ICMSA

b 1955, Longford; *m* Joanne; 3*s*; Former President ICSMA; worked as banker in London; dairy farmer, Co. Longford; president Irish Milk Suppliers Association; formerly Deputy President for four years; member An Bord Bia, National Dairy Council, Irish Dairy Board, Forum for Europe; founder member Longford Leader Programme. Contact: Moatfarrell, Co. Longford./ICMSA, John Feely House, Dublin Road, Limerick. **T** 061 314532 **F** 061 315737 email info@icmsa.ie

The Longford dairy farmer enjoyed a good media profile during his term as head of Ireland's second largest farming organisation; the former banker was a good media performer who developed close and productive relations with all of the social partners.

Ó SEIREADÁIN, Cuan Barra; MUSICIAN

b Dublin, 1982; single; *edu.* The High School, Rathgar, Dublin; Royal Irish Academy of Music, Dublin; Musikhochshulle, Stuttgart (Masters- Künstlerische Ausbilddung); Musician French Horn; Opera Theatre Company 2002; Aushilfe, Staatsoper Stuttgart, 2003 to date; solo horn Junge Oper, Stuttgart 2003 to date; member of National Youth Orchestra of Ireland and Senior Orchestra 1993-02; Feis Ceol Guinness Brass Bursary 2004; Raymond Kavanagh Bursary and Royal Irish Academy of Music Senior Brass Bursary 1999; Feis Ceoil Senior Horn winner 1998; Feis Ceoil Junior Horn & Brass Rose Bowl 1995; Bank of Ireland Millennial Scholarship for Music 2005; member, European Youth Parliament 2001. Recreations: athletics (former member of Dundrum South Dublin Athletics Team). Contact: 45, Hermitage Drive, Rathfarnham, Dublin 16. email cuanbarra@gmail.com

A lively and engaging personality who will make his mark as a solo horn player in a great orchestra; a credit to his Irish tutors and the onward development they afforded him.

O'SHEA, John; DIRECTOR GOAL

b 1944; *m* Judy Gallagher; 2s 2d; *edu.* CBS Schools, Charleville, Westport; O'Connells Monkstown; University College Dublin; Founder, Director GOAL: salesman for coal and oil company 1962-67; sports journalist with Irish Press Group 1967-94; founded GOAL Third World relief and development agency 1977; full time director, GOAL 1994 to date; publications include *The Book of the Dubs*; recipient, Dublin (Under 21) Gaelic football medal, Schools Basketball International, former Inter Provincial Tennis Player; Awards include: People of the Year 1987 and 1992; The Ballygowan Outstanding Achievement Award 1988; Publicity Club of Ireland Communications Award 1990; MIR Award 1992; Citizen of the Year Dun Laoghaire 1992; Association of Tennis Professionals Humanitarian of the Year 1993; Late Late Show Tribute 1995; Texaco Outstanding Achievement Award 1995; Tipperary International Peace Award 2004; Ernst & Young Social Entrepreneur of the Year 2005; current Veteran Tennis International, former interprovincial tennis player; honorary life member Sandycove LTC, Blackrock Rugby Club and Westport Golf Club; member, Monkstown Tennis Club, Fitzwilliam Tennis Club and Woodbrook Golf Club. Recreations: practically all sporting activities, golf, tennis, Tip Rugby; played soccer, Gaelic, rugby, basketball, racketball and was a middle distance runner in youth. Contact: GOAL, 9 Northumberland Avenue, Dun Laoghaire, Co. Dublin. P.O. Box 19, Dun Laoghaire, Co. Dublin. **T** 01 280 9779 web www.goal.ie

Internationally respected as a tireless humanitarian who has achieved more than many major NGOS; an aggressive advocate for the downtrodden, and campaigns tirelessly against rampant corruption; since its inception GOAL has spent in excess of €350 million on humanitarian programmes in over 40 countries; over 1,300 volunteers have worked in the developing world on GOAL's behalf and the organisation has responded to every major humanitarian disaster since 1977.

O'SHEA, Liam; MANAGING DIRECTOR, CLARE FM

b 1949, Cloughjordan, Co. Tipperary; *m* Judy 2s 2d; *edu.* Borrisokane Community College, Co. Tipperary; College of Technology, Kevin Street, Dublin; City & Guilds; Diploma in Communications; Managing Director Clare FM; Dept. of Post & Telegraphs 1969-72; RTE 1972-86; Channel 3 TV Saudi Arabia 1986-98; Clare FM Radio 1998 to date; member of boards of Clare FM, IRS and former member of Boards of IBI and INN; worked overseas in television in Middle East; very involved with world wide media, Saudi Arabia, during Gulf War of 1990-91; Clubs: Kilruane Mc Donaghs GAA Club, Co Tipperary; played hurling for Tipperary, captained club; three in a row County Championships; selector on All Ireland Club Championship win 1985/86; team manager 2001-03; won promotion to senior ranks. Recreations: GAA, soccer, rugby, walking. Contact: Knocknacree, Cloughjordan, Co Tipperary. **M** 087 223 4938 **F** 065 682 8888 email LIAMOSHEA@CLAREFM.IE

Brings the right mix to local radio with global media experience along with being anchored fully in the 'Real Ireland' through his involvement with the GAA; at a time of turbulence in the Clare provincial newspaper market, he has an opportunity with Clare FM to establish his local radio as an authentic voice for the people of his county.

Ó SNODAIGH, Rossa; MUSICIAN/COMPOSER

b 1971, Dublin; *edu.* Coláiste Eoin, Booterstown, Co.Dublin; Musician/ Composer; formed the band *KILA* as a teenager; band has played in Ireland, Sweden, France, Belgium, Germany, Austria, Switzerland, Spain, Japan, New Zealand, Australia, Canada; *Publ. Éist* 1990; *Grovvin'* 1991; *Kila* 1992; *Mind the Gap* 1995; *Tóg é go bóg é* 1997; *Album* 2000; presenter Nuachas an Dúchas, Radio na Life 2003; composed scores for *Gold on the Streets,* TnaG; *Hidden Treasures,* RTÉ; has composed for and worked with Michael Scott; The Machine; The Galloglass Theatre Company; Irish Modern Dance Theatre; Amharclann de hÍde; Awards: Kilkenny Cream of Irish Awards 1999. Recreations: writing a book, poetry, reading, clowning. Contact: Kila, c/o Music Centre Temple Bar, Dublin 2. **T** 01 670 9202

A gifted musician who, like Harpo, has great and important moments of musicality; finds new ways to make music sounds and make them sound musical; not a player of discords, he is multi talented and has many admirers.

O'SULLIVAN, Adhamhnan Domhnall; JOURNALIST

b 1941; *m* Jacqueline; 1*s* 1*d*; *edu.* CBS Monkstown Park; Sports Editor, Sunday Independent; 1959-88: sub editor, Evening Press; sports news editor, Irish Press Group; sports editor, Sunday Press; sports editor, Sunday Independent - 2006. Clubs: Dún Laoghaire Golf Club, Blackrock Bowling & Tennis Club. Recreations: sport. Contact: Sunday Independent, 27-32 Talbot St. Dublin 1. **T** 01 705 5680 **F** 01 705 5719 email aosullivan@unison.independent.ie

Highly experienced and respected sports editor; who produced some of the best sports pages in the country each weekend; an extremely pleasant man, well known for identifying and encouraging young talent.

Adhamhnan O'Sullivan

O'SULLIVAN, Chantal; ANTIQUE DEALER

b 1961, Dublin; single; *edu.* Our Lady's School Templeogue, Dublin; The High School, Rathgar, Dublin; Owner, O'Sullivan Antiques Dublin and New York; operations manager department store, Sydney, Australia 1979-81; worked in antiques business 1981; opened own business in Dublin 1990; opened own antique shop New York City 1996; board member US Chapter Irish Georgian Society; board Member RHA. Clubs: Milltown Golf Club. Recreations: golf, music, contemporary art, skiing. Contact: 42-44, Francis Street, Dublin 8. **T** 01 454 1143 **F** 01 454 1156 email info@osullivanantiques.com

Well known and connected internationally as a supplier of top class antique furniture with an enviable blue chip client list; respected by her peers on both sides of the Atlantic, in a difficult business; bright, articulate, stylish woman.

O'SULLIVAN, Michael Gerard; VICE PRESIDENT, UNIVERSITY COLLEGE CORK

b 1958, Cork; *m* Dr Eleanor O'Sullivan; 4*s*; *edu.* Douglas Community School; University College Cork; B. Comm, FCA; Vice President for Planning, Communications & Development University College Cork; trainee accountant Coopers & Lybrand Cork; qualified accountant Coopers & Lybrand London; financial controller KeyMed Ltd. Essex; asst. director Administration National Microelectronics Research Centre; vice president for Planning, Communications & Development University College Cork; chairman of Mardyke Arena Ltd; director of Cork University Foundation; director of the Cork Business Innovation Centre; member, Board Cork Chamber of Commerce; fellow of the Institute of Chartered Accountants Ireland; member, Board Institute of Electronics Communications and Information Technology (Belfast); member University College Cork Governing Body. Clubs: Monkstown Golf Club, St. Michael's Tennis Club. Recreations: current affairs, reading, golf, hurling, football, theatre. Contact: East Wing, University College, Western Road, Cork. **T** 021 4903600 **F** 021 4903611 email vpmosull@ucc.ie

Extremely influential figure who works very closely with President Wrixon (*qv*); a great ambassador for UCC, travels the world raising the profile of the university; his successful networking helps to top up the coffers; well liked and respected for his down to earth manner.

O'SULLIVAN, Turlough; DIRECTOR GENERAL IRISH BUSINESS AND EMPLOYERS CONFEDERATION (IBEC)

b 1949, Co. Dublin; *p*; 3*s*; *edu.* Mercy Convent Ballymahon, Co. Longford; St. Saran's Ferbane;

Patrician College, Fethard, Co. Tipperary; University College Dublin; BA; Director General Irish Business and Employers Confederation (IBEC); ESB; Cement Roadstone Holdings; Semperit; Federated Union of Employers (subsequently IBEC). Clubs: Edmondstown Golf Club; David Lloyd Fitness Centre. Recreations: golf, reading, music, current affairs. Contact: IBEC, Confederation House, 84/86 Lower Baggot Street, Dublin 2. **T** 01 6051555 **F** 01 6381555 email Turlough.osullivan@ibec.ie

> Dynamic and unflappable; a major player in the Irish Social Partnership which has served the national economy very well; however real challenges lie ahead as people demand more money to meet modern lifestyle requirements.

O'SUILLEABHAIN, Michael; MUSICIAN

b 1950; *m* Noirin Ni Riain (*qv*); separated; 2*s*; *edu.* University College Cork, B.Mus., MA, L.T.C.L.; Queens University Belfast, Ph.D.; Musician; assistant lecturer, University College Cork, Music Department 1975; college lecturer 1978; visiting professor, Boston College (U.S.) 1990-91; senior lecturer, University College Cork 1991; acting head 1992; Professor of Music, University of Limerick 1994 to date; discography includes *Michael O'Suilleabhain, solo performances on piano, harpsichord, clavicord, pedal organ and Moog synthesiser* (Gael Linn 1976) released 1992; *Cry of the Mountains* (Gael Linn) 1981; *The Dolphins Way* (Venture Virgin) 1987; *Casadh/Turning* (Venture Virgin) 1990; *A River of Sound,* (Lumen); *Between Worlds* (Virgin) 1995; *Becoming* (Virgin) 1998; publications include *Buntings Ancient Music of Ireland* (with Dr. Donal O'Sullivan); *The Bodhran* and numerous articles in journals; chairman, Irish Traditional Music Archive; founder/chairman, Clare Music Education Centre; member, Board of Directors, Irish Chamber Orchestra, Daghdha Dance Company, University Concert Hall, Limerick; established Irish Traditional Music and Dance Archive UCC, University of Limerick and Boston College; presented/ scripted TV series *A River of Sound; The Changing Course of Irish Music* (BBC). Contact: Irish World Music Centre, Foundation Building, University of Limerick, Limerick. **T** 061 202 590 **F** 061 202 589

> A brilliant musician, composer and musical director; his apparent soft charm hides a deeply ambitious musician who knows which strings to pull and more importantly when; like playing music, timing is all for him; now in position to do something about Irish Music and Irish Art Music at home and abroad, so how he fares will be of great and deep interest to the many in his musical and administrative constituency.

O'SULLIVAN, Sean; CHIEF EXECUTIVE CORK CO-OP MARTS LTD

b 1962, Kiskeam, Co Cork; *m* Mary O'Neill; 3*s*; *edu.* Mill Street Community School; University of Limerick; Bachelor of Business Studies; ACMA; Chief Executive Cork Co-Op Marts Ltd; financial accountant, Ballyclough Co-Op Creamery Ltd. 1986-90; group management accountant Dairy Gold Co-Op Society Ltd. 1990-91; financial manager, Logitech Ireland Ltd. 1991-94; financial controller, Cork Co-Op Marts Ltd. 1995-96; chief executive 1996 to date. Contact: Cork Co-Op Marts Ltd., Cork Farm Centre, Wilton, Cork. **T** 021 545733 **F** 021 545325.

> A sound, friendly, commercially savvy businessman, the Kiskeam native brought a solid range of professional experiences to his current position; has steered the Cork based group through a period of unprecedented change and has used its resources to full effect with new business concepts; in the process of a major rationalization programme which will gear it up going forward.

O'SULLIVAN, Sonia; ATHLETE

b 1969, Cobh, Co. Cork; *p* Nick Bideau; 2*d*; *edu.* St. Mary's Convent, Cobh; Cobh Vocational School; Villanova University, USA, Accountancy; Professional Athlete; her performance highlights include World Cross Country 8k & 4k Champion; European 5,000m and 10,000m; World Cub 5,000m and World Best 2 miles 1998; Dublin Marathon 2000; Dublin Mini Marathon 2005. Recreations; reading, music. Contact: KIM, 201 High Street, Hampton Hill, Middlesex, TW12 1NL, **T** 0044 181 941 9732

> The golden girl from Cobh is a regular marathon runner now having won in Dublin on her first outing in the distance; extremely intelligent, well organized, a gifted, focused, natural athlete.

O'TOOLE, Annrai; CHIEF EXECUTIVE, CAPE CLEAR SOFTWARE

b 1965, Dublin; single; 1*s*; *edu.* St. Joseph's CBS, Fairview; Trinity College Dublin, BA, BAI, M. Sc;

research assistant and lecturer, Trinity College Dublin; co founder/ chief executive Cape Clear Software; co founder, Cape Clear Software 1999 todate. Recreations; the fine things in life. Contact: Cape Clear Software Ltd. Donnybrook Road, Donnybrook, Dublin 4. **T** 01 241 9900 **F** 01 241 9901 emailannrai.otoole@capeclear.com web www.capeclear.com

One of Ireland's bright tekkie pioneers.

O'TOOLE, Paul Anthony; CEO TOURISM IRELAND
b 1959, London; *m* Pat (Patricia); 1*s* 2*d*; *edu.* St. Kevins Community College, Dunlavin Co. Wicklow; Griffith College, Dublin; Smurfit Graduate School of Business, UCD; A.C.C.A (Chartered Association of Certified Accountants); M.B.S; CEO Tourism Ireland; finance department, Dublin Corporation 1978-90; Bord Fáilte, including periods as general manager of central marketing & general manager of corporate services 1990-2000; CEO Tourism Ireland 2001 to date. Clubs: Dunlavin GAA Club, County Wicklow. Recreations: sport generally, cinema, reading. Contact: Tourism Ireland, Bishops Square, Redmond's Hill, Dublin 2. **T** 01 476 3451 **F** 01 476 3666 email potoole@tourismireland.com

The first chief executive of Tourism Ireland, a body set up as part of the Belfast Agreement of Good Friday 1998 to promote the island of Ireland as a tourist destination in all overseas markets; has his work cut out for him as traditional tourism to the Republic has totally changed in recent years.

OLIVER, Patricia Carmel; PUBLISHER, SECRETARY BEIT FOUNDATION
b 1941, Dublin; *m* Jeremiah; 2*s* 1*d*; *edu.* Presentation Convent, Warrenmount, Dublin; Company Secretary, The Alfred Beit Foundation; director of education, An Taisce; publisher The Hannon Press; editor Cassell Collier Macmillan; freelance journalist; publisher Zircorn Publishing Ltd 1970-80; publisher The Hannon Press 1990 to date; secretary, The Alfred Beit Foundation 1983 to date; director of education, An Taisce The National Trust for Ireland 1995 to date; board member National Roads Authority 1992-2000; chairwoman An Taisce 1990-94; board member and vice chair National College of Art & Design 2003 to date; Irish representative Foundation of Environmental Education 1993 to date; *Publ.* editor *Life and Environment* 1970s; editor *Living Heritage* 1980; editor *Taisce Journal* 1990s; editor *Who's Who, What's What and Where in Ireland* 1973. Recreations: reading, gardening, writing, cricket. Contact: River Lodge, Ballivor, Co. Meath. **T** 046 954 6089 email trisholiver@iol.ie

An extremely competent administrator and a very skilled strategist; a Dubliner through and through, she brings great common good sense to all debates; is much admired, liked and most significantly trusted by those with whom she works.

OSBORNE, James Reginald; CONSULTANT
b 1949; *m* Heather; 1*s* 1*d*; *edu.* Campbell College, Belfast; Trinity College Dublin, BA Mod; Consultant; solicitor, A & L Goodbody Solicitors 1973-94 (opened NY office); managing partner 1982-94; consultant to A & L Goodbody and director of numerous public and private companies 1994 to date; chairman, Blackstar Com; Clubs: Royal Irish Yacht Club, Fitzwilliam Lawn Tennis Club, Institute of Directors, Law Society of Ireland. Recreations: National Hunt racing, sailing, golf, squash. Contact: 1, Earlsford Centre, Hatch Street, Dublin 2. **T** 01 661 3311

Having weathered the Punchestown storm continues to be a well respected businessman much in demand on blue chip boards; well informed and good company.

ORDE, KB, Sir Hugh Stephen Roden OBE; CHIEF CONSTABLE NORTHERN IRELAND
b 1958, London, UK; *m* Kathleen, Helen 'Kath' Carabine; 1*s*; *edu.* University of Kent; BA; Chief Constable, Police Service, Northern Ireland; joined the Police Metropolitan Area (London South Central) 1977; promoted to Sergeant, Brixton 1982; police staff coll 1983; inspector Greenwich 1984-90; chief inspector SW London 1990; chief inspector Hounslow 1991-93; supt Territorial Support Group 1993-95; detective chief superintendent Major Crimes SW Area 1995-98; Cdr Crime S London 1998; deputy assistant comm. 1999-2002; Chief Constable Police Service NI 2002 to date; OBE 2002; 2005 Knight Bachelor Queen's Birthday Honours. Recreations: marathon running, wine, gardening. Contact: PSNI, 65, Knock Road, Belfast BT5 6LE.
T 028 9056 1613 **F** 028 9056 9056 email comsec@psni.police.uk web www.psni.police.uk

Hugh Orde

A policeman's ideal; tough, pragmatic and able; honest and conscientious; may not be the match for his political foes in Northern Ireland, but he must be doing something right, both sides dislike him.

ORMONDE, Donal; CONSULTANT RADIOLOGIST
b 1943; *m* Greta Eduarda (*qv* Ormonde, Greta Eduarda); 3*s* 1*d*; *edu*. St. Augustine's College, Dungarvan, Co.Waterford; University College Dublin, MB.,B.Ch.BAO. 1961-68; Royal College of Surgeons in Ireland FFR.,RCSI.,D.M.R.D.,(Lond) 1970-74; Consultant Radiologist Waterford Regional Hospital (radiologist in administrative charge); consultant radiologist W.R.H. 1975; elected to Dáil Éireann (FF) 1982; nominated to Seanad Éireann 1989; vice chairman, Comhairle na nOspidéal 2002 to date. Clubs: Waterford Rotary, Waterford Castle Golf Club, Callan Golf Club. Recreations: GAA, golf. Contact: Cregg House, Carrick on Suir, Co.Tipperary. **M** 087 259 0946 **F** 051 848571 email Ormonded@sehb.ie

The former Fianna Fail TD has developed the radiology department in Waterford hospital to become a leader in provincial Ireland.

ORMONDE, Greta Eduarda; CONSULTANT ANAESTHETIST
b 1943, Belgium; *m* Donal Ormonde (*qv*); 3*s* 1*d*; *edu*. Muckross Park, Donnybrook, Dublin 4; University College Dublin, MB BCH, BAO, PFARCSI; Consultant Anaesthetist; Santa Rosa Medical Centre, San Antonio, USA; Johns Hopkins Hospital, Baltimore, Maryland, USA; Presbyterian Hospital, Pittsburg, USA; Mater Hospital, Dublin; Waterford Regional Hospital. Recreations: gardening, horses (stud horse trials, racing). Contact: Cregg House, Carrick on Suir, Co Tipperary. **T** 051 645 900 **F** 051 645 901 email GretaO@Eircom.Net

Internationally trained, highly respected anesthetist;

OWENS, Sharon; AUTHOR
b 1968, Omagh, Co. Tyrone; *m* Dermot Owens; 1*d; edu.* Loreto Convent Omagh 1979-86; University of Ulster 1988-92, BA Hons (Design and Illustration); Writer and Mother; *Publ. The Tea House on Mulberry Street* 2003; *The Ballroom on Magnolia Street* 2004; *The Tavern on Maple Street* 2005. Recreations: painting, drawing, reading novels, 1980s pop music, trying to cook. Contact: Poolbeg Press, 123 Grange Hill, Baldoyle, Dublin 13. **T** 01 806 3825 email poolbeg@poolbeg.com web www sharonowens.co.uk

A talented and successful author; rights to *The Tea House on Mulberry Street* were sold to 13 countries in 13 months; it entered *New York Times* Bestseller List at no 27 and is currently in negotiations for film rights.

Sharon Owens

OXX, John; RACEHORSE TRAINER
b 1950, Tullamore. Co. Offaly; *m* Catriona O'Sullivan; 1*s* 2*d; edu.* Clongowes Wood College; University College Dublin; MVB, MRCVS; Racehorse Trainer; assistant trainer to father, John Oxx Snr; obtained trainers license 1979; trainer number of Group 1 winners in Ireland, UK, US, France and Italy; most successful horses include Ridgewood Pearl and Timarida; has won Irish classics: Irish St. Ledger 1987; Irish 1000 Guineas 1989; Irish Oaks 1997/1998; Epson/Irish Derbys 2000; Irish Derby 2003; 20 other Group 1 winners including Prix de l'Arc (Sindar) 2000; Irish Champion Stakes 2004; King George VI Cup 2005; Prince of Wales 2005; member, Racing Apprentice Center of Education; member, Leopardstown Racecourse; Awards: Leading Trainer 1995; Texaco Sports Star of the Year Award for Racing 1995; Bisquit Cognac & Independent Newspapers Racing Award 1995; Ascot Gold Cup 1999; Trainer of the Year HWPA (UK) 2000; Sports Celebrity Award For Racing (jointly with Johnny Murtagh); Phillips Sports Manager of the Year 2000; Jurys/ Irish Independent Sports Award 2000. Contact: Creeve, Curraghbeg, Co. Kildare. **T** 045 521 310

The Tullamore born veterinary surgeon who started out as assistant trainer to his father, is one of the top trainers in the country having won several classics and numerous Group One races; known for his attention to detail.

PAISLEY, The Rt. Hon. Rev Dr, PC MP MLA, Ian Richard Kyle; PUBLIC REPRESENTATIVE
b 1926, County Armagh; *m* Eileen Cassels; 2*s* 3*d*; *edu.* Sixmilebridge, The Model School, Ballymena Co. Antrim; Democratic Member of Parliament for Antrim North; Member of the Northern Ireland Assembly, Antrim North; Democratic Unionist Leader, Northern Ireland; leader Democratic Unionist Party (founder) 1971 to date; ordained to the Presbyterian Ministry 1946; co-founded the Free Presbyterian Church of Ulster 1951; jailed 1966 and 1969 for political demonstrations; Member of Parliament 1970 to date; Member Northern Ireland Parliament (Bannside) 1970-72; Member of the European Parliament 1979 to date; Member Northern Irish Assembly 1973-74; Member Northern Ireland Convention 1975-76; Member of the Northern Ireland Forum 1996-98; Member Northern Ireland Assembly 2003 to date; member Her Majesty's Privy Council 2005 to date. Contact: 256, Ravenhill Road, Belfast BT6 8GJ. **T** 048 9045 4255 **F** 048 045 9045 7783 Democratic Unionist Party Head Quarters, 91, Dundela Avenue, Belfast BT4 3BU. **T** 048 9047 1155 **F** 048 9033 3147. web www.dup.org.uk or www dup2win.com

His evangelical oratory has stood him in good stead over the years; of immense physical presence, does not hesitate to invoke the Lord's willingness to help him out in any or all of his difficulties; terrifies his enemies and has confounded them so often by turning up trumps electoral and otherwise; leader of his Party and the Leader of present day unionism in Northern Ireland, a force to be reckoned with; and has outmanoeuvred his DUP colleagues and if they are battle weary he is not; overall a good and able local politician and MP for his constituency.

Dr Ian Paisley

Paisley, Ian (Junior); PUBLIC REPRESENTATIVE
b 1956, Belfast; *edu.* Greenwood Primary School; Strandtown Primary School; Shaftesbury House College; Methodist College, Belfast; Queens University, Belfast; B.A. (Hons.); M.S.Sc. (Irish Politics); Politician; Democratic Unionist Party (DUP) MLA; began work as a political researcher and parliamentary aide to his father, Ian Paisley (*qv*) then leader of the Democratic Unionist Party (DUP); elected to the Northern Ireland Forum for the constituency of North Antrim as a member of the DUP 1996-98; returned again 1998 to date; with the formation of the new Northern Ireland Policing Board (NIPB) was one of the three members of the DUP to take their seats on the board 2001 to date. Contact: Democratic Unionist Party Head Quarters 91, Dundela Avenue, Belfast, BT4 3BU. **T** 048 9047 1155 **F** 048 9033 3147 web www.dup.org.uk or www dup2win.com

Able enough within the narrow confines of his father's constituency, but doesn't seem to be of the contradictory personality of his father; stuck in the groove of DUP politics and religion without the capacity to go beyond very narrow parameters of activity and practice; may blossom in time; no real sign of that to date, but remains a force within the younger set of the DUP.

PARKER, Lynne Elizabeth; THEATRE DIRECTOR
b 1961; *edu.* Strathearn Grammer, Belfast; Trinity College Dublin, BA; Co-founder and Artistic Director, Rough Magic Theatre Company 1984 to date; work for Rough Magic includes *Top Girls, Decadence, The Country Wife, Nightshade, Serious Money, Aunt Dan and Lemon, The Tempest, Lady Windermere's Fan, Digging for Fire, Love and a Bottle, I Can't Get Started, New Morning, Danti Dan, Down into Blue, The Dogs, Hidden Charges, Halloween Night, The Way of the World, Pentecost, Northern Star, The School for Scandal and the Whisperers; other theatre credits include, The House of Bernarda Alba (Charabanc), Shadow of a Gunman (Gate), The Clearing (The Bush), Doctors Dilemma (Abbey), Playboy of the Western World(Almeida), Silver Tassie (Almeida), Playhouse Creatures (Old Vic), The Importance of Being Earnest (West Yorkshire Playhouse), Love Me?! (The Car Show – The Corn Exchange);* awards include, Harvey's Theatre Award 1998, Time Out Award 1992, Bank of Ireland/Arts Show, Dublin Theatre Festival – Best Irish Production 1995. Contact: Rough Magic Ltd., 5/6, South Great George's Street, Dublin 2. **T** 01 671 9278 **F** 01 671 9301

A gifted director who can inspire others and who has a different vision to, say that of Druid Theatre Company led by Gary Hynes (*qv*); she's been working a long time in the Theatre and is well liked and respected by her peers.

PARKHILL, Kenneth; BLOODSTOCK BREEDER
b 1953; *m* Lulu; 2*s*; *edu.* Newtown School, Waterford; University College Dublin; Veterinary Surgeon;

took over successful Boyne Bank Stud 1995; concentrates on thoroughbred horses; principal winners include Corbiere, Mole Board, Morley Street, Deep Dawn, Granville Again, Sound of Islay, Atria. Contact: Boyne Bank Stud, Trim, Co. Meath. **T** 046 31442

> The Co. Meath Vet. took over Boyne Bank Stud from his father Marshall Parkhill and continues to breed excellent thoroughbreds.

PARLON, Tom; PUBLIC REPRESENTATIVE

b 1953, Coolderry, Co.Offaly; *m* Martha Loughnane; 2*s* 3*d*; *edu*. Christian Brothers School, Roscrea, Co. Tipperary; Gurteen Agricultural College, Co. Tipperary; Public Representative; Minister of State Department of Finance; farmer; contractor; deputy president IFA 1991-1993; treasurer IFA from January 1994-2001; president IFA 1997-2001; director of Bord Bia; director of FBD Insurance Company; awards: Stephen Cullinane Scholarship; 1998 Offaly Person of the Year; Elected T.D Laois-Offaly 2002; Minister of State, Finance 2002 to date; President Progressive Democrats 2006 – todate. Clubs: Coolderry GAA, Offaly Supporters Club. Recreations: GAA, horse racing, all sports. Contact: Constituency Office: 35, Main Street, Birr, Co Offaly. **T** 0509 23737 **F** 0509 23739 email info@tomparlon.ie web http://www.tomparlon.ie

> The former IFA leader made a seamless transition into party politics and received a half car one week after entering the Dáil; one of the more effective farm leaders who bridged the gap between town and country and is now famous for his slogan on decentralization 'welcome to Parlon Country'; bright with a friendly personality, has improved his TV performance since becoming a PD; seemed to think he was leadership material when Mary Harney stepped down (2006); instead settled for President of the Party; a good constituency operator but will he retain his seat after the next election?

PARSONS, Anna Julier 'Julie'; WRITER

b 1951, Dublin; *m* John Caden; 1*d*; *edu*. The Hall School, Monkstown, Dublin; University College Dublin; B.Soc..Sc; M.Soc.Sc; Writer; Radio Producer, RTE, 1984-90; TV Producer 1990-97; Writer 1997 to date; author of *Mary, Mary* (Town House & Country House), - the novel has been published in fifteen countries and the film rights sold to Paul McGuinness for a six figure sum,1998; *The Courtship Gift* (Town House & Country House) 1999; member, Crime Writers' Association. Recreations: family, garden, food, drink, sailing, gossip, story telling. Contact: Town House & Country House, Trinity House, Charleston Road, Ranelagh, Dublin 6. **T** 01 497 2399 **F** 01 498 0927.

> A gifted writer with a quiet inner voice, which coincides with her own speaking voice, that makes for a plaintive threnody in the telling of the tale; a quietly determined writer whose calmness of externals just masks a vibrating inner visceral writer's reaction to events as they unfold.

PATTERSON, Brian; CHAIRMAN, IRISH TIMES.

b 1944, Cork; *m* Jennifer Beaven; 2*s*; *edu*. Newtown School, Waterford; St. Andrew's College, Dublin; University College Dublin, BA; Chairman, Irish Times; head of management services A. Guinness Son & Co 1972-76, personnel manager 1976-'79; distribution manager 1979-81; personnel director 1981-82; director general Irish Management Institute 1982-87; director of corporate & management development Waterford Wedgewood plc, 1987-88; assistant chief executive Waterford Crystal 1988-92; chief operating officer 1992-95; chief executive officer Wedgwood 1995-2001; member Institute of Personnel and Development (Fellow); Irish Management Institute (Fellow); British Institute of Management (Fellow); Irish Institute of Industrial Engineers (Past President); Eisenhower Exchange Fellowship 1983; member of the boards of Waterford Wedgwood plc; Waterford Wedgwood UK plc; Waterford Crystal, Rosenthal AG; Central Bank of Ireland; Chairman of the National Competitiveness Council of Ireland; Council Member, Irish Management Institute; former chairman IMI; advisory group for Stoke-On-Trent Common Purpose; trustee of the New Victoria Theatre and Staffordshire University; chairman, IFSRA; chairman Irish Times; treasurer North of Ireland Centre for Trauma and Transformation; mentor to a number of chief executives through Change Partnership Ireland; member National College of Ireland; Recreations: music, history, art. Contact: Irish Times, D'Olier Street, Dublin 2. **T** 01 679 2022 **F** 01 671 9407

> The widely experienced business executive has a portfolio of business, consulting and teaching interests since retiring from Wedgewood; dapper with a pleasant and affable personality which disguises a steely and ruthless business style.

PEARCE, Colman; ORCHESTRAL CONDUCTOR
b 1938, Dublin; divorced; 1*d*; *edu.* Christian Brothers School, Synge Street, Dublin; University College Dublin, B.Mus, LTCL; Musik Akademie, Vienna; Orchestral Conductor; Music Scriptwriter, RTE 1961, acting assistant, Director of Music 1962, Orchestral Conductor 1965-77; co-principal conductor, RTE Symphony Orchestra 1978-80; principal conductor 1981-83; principal conductor and musical director, Mississippi Symphony Orchestra 1987-99; creative works include Robinson the Cat premiered in Jackson (Miss.) 1998, also choral and orchestral pieces; recordings include works by Boydell, Stanford, Buckley, Wilson, Dean, Corcoran, Bodley. *Publ. Music in Ireland.* Recreations: reading, arts in general, collecting paintings, movies, theatre. Contact: RTE, Montrose, Donnybrook, Dublin 4. **T** 01 208 3111

> An assured musical presence; forceful as a conductor with strong exercised
> idiosyncratic styles he is very much the star of the event wherever that may be.

PEARSON, Noel Philip; FILM/THEATRE PRODUCER
b 1943, Dublin; *m* Eileen; separated; 1*s* 1*d*; *partner* Rosemary Roche; *edu.* Marian College, Dublin; Belcamp College Dublin; Film / Theatre Producer; president's Medal New York University; Film/Theatre Producer; Two Tony Awards - *Dancing at Lughnasa, An Inspector Calls;* numerous nominations for *My Left Foot* including Oscar nomination, Donatello (Italian Oscar), BAFTA. Movies include *My Left Foot* 1995; *The Field* 1990; *Frankie Starlight* 1995; *Gold in the Streets* 1997; *Dancing at Lughnasa* 1998; *Tara Road* 2005; Broadway productions include: *Brothers* 1983; *Dancing at Lughnasa* 1991, swept the boards at the 1992 Tonys winning Tony for Best Play and five additional Tonys; that production won 19 major awards in all; *Someone Who'll Watch Over Me* 1992; *Wonderful Tennessee* 1993; *An Inspector Calls* 1994; *Translations* 1995; *Tara Road* 2005; NUI University College Dublin (Services to Theatre & Film) D.Litt (*hc*); Dublin University, Trinity College Dublin, D. Litt (*hc*); Stode Hill, Mass. USA, D.Litt (*hc*); Recreations: reading, politics. Contact: Old Rectory, Glenealy, Co Wicklow. **T** 0404 44664

> Gregarious, shrewd operator and deal maker, eternal optimist; has had his ups and
> downs but emerged with five Oscar nominations from My Left Foot (the movie won
> three Oscars) and a multi million dollar movie deal; well known and respected
> throughout Ireland and in Hollywood, Broadway and London; raconteur
> extraordinaire, totally irreverent; loyal to his friends.

Shih-Fu Peng

PENG, SHIH-FU; ARCHITECT
b 1966, Honalulu, USA; *m* Roisín Heneghan; *edu.* Punahou School, Honalulu, USA; Harvard University M. Arch; Cornell University B.Arch; Director/Architect; Contact: 31-37 Clarendon Street. Dublin 2. **T** 01 671 4077 **F** 01 4791151 email speng@hparc.com

> A deeply interesting and interested architect whose sense of rhythm and line may be
> thought of as deriving from calligraphy; a forceful, modern presence in the world of
> architecture.

PETTIT, John; M.D. PETTIT'S GROCERY CHAIN
b 1975, Wexford; *edu.* Clongowes Wood College, Co. Kildare; University College Dublin; B.Comm. M. Comm; Managing Director Pettit's & Associates Companies; Director, Pettits; The Stillorgan Park Hotel, Dublin; Wexford Talbot Hotel/Carlow Talbot Hotel; board member Pettits & Associated Companies 2003 to date; previously worked with Orbis.com; Recreations: running, reading, films. Contact: JJ Pettit & Sons, Wexford. **T** 053 240 55

> The next generation takes the helm of this significant provincial group, now a company
> with three hotels, a chain of five shops, and staff of more than 1,000 employees; with a
> turnover of more than €120 million he plans to grow the company along the same lines
> as his father.

PHELAN, Sue; RACECOURSE MANAGER
b 1970, Dublin; single; *edu.* Teresian School Donnybrook, Dublin 4; Pembroke School, Ballsbridge, Dublin 4; University College Dublin; B. Agr. Sc; Gurteen Agricultural College, Co. Tipperary; National College of Ireland; Dip. Management & Employee Relations; Dip. Project Management, University College Cork 2006; Manager Waterford and Tramore Racecourse; sales representative Waterford Foods, East Waterford,1993; branch manager Glanbia, Dunmore East, 1995; manager

Waterford and Tramore Racecourse 1999 to date; director Association of Irish Racecourses; Clubs: Gold Coast Golf Club, Kilotteran Riding Club; Recreations: National Hunt Racing, golf, skiing, horse riding, travel, gardening, cooking, Red Setters Contact: Tramore Race Course, Tramore, Co. Waterford. **T** 051 381425 email racing@tramore.ie

One of the few women racetrack managers in Ireland, has transformed the Tramore track over the last six years, raising the national profile of the Co. Waterford track; extremely friendly and hardworking; popular with the racing fraternity and punters alike; now focusing on plans to relocate the track to a new beachside site.

PHILIPS, Dalton Timothy; CEO, BROWN THOMAS GROUP Ltd
b 1968 Dublin; *m* Penny Nesbitt; 1*s* 1*d*; *edu.* Stowe School, Buckinghamshire, England, University College, Dublin; BA (Hons); Harvard Business School MBA; CEO, Brown Thomas Group Ltd; Irish Trade Board, Milan 1991-92; Jardine Matheson Group, Hong Kong 1993–97; Walmart International 1998–2005; CEO, Brown Thomas Group Ltd 2005 to date; Recreations. running, rugby, wine and cuisine, church affairs, family. Contact: Brown Thomas, Grafton Street, Dublin 2. **T** 01 605 6629 **F** 01 605 6753 email dphilips@brownthomas.ie

Dalton Philips

A member of the famous Wicklow Phillips, Ballyfree Foods family; built on his business background at the Harvard Business School, his career experience covers a wide range of blue chip international commercial activities; charming, sartorially elegant and stylish, brings élan to the luxury department store group;

PHILLIPS, Jonathan; NORTHERN IRELAND OFFICE DIRECTORATE
b 1952; *m* Amanda Rosemary Broomhead; 2*s*; *edu.* Queen Mary's Grammar School, Walsall; St. John's College, Cambridge; Institute of Education, University of London MA; PhD; PGCE; Northern Ireland Office Directorate; political director Northern Ireland Office. DTI 1977; seconded to economics directorate CBI 1982-83; secretary to committee of inquiry into regulatory arrangements at Lloyds 1986-97; assistant secretary DTI 1987-89; under-secretary and head Executive agencies directorates Dept of Transport 1993-96, director of investigations and enforcement DTI 1996-98; director of finances & resource management DTI 1998-2000; director general resources & services 2000-2002; operating strategy director Sea Systems BAE Systems 2000–02; political director Northern Ireland Office 2002 to date. Recreations: music, walking. Contact: Northern Ireland Office, 11 Millbank, London SW1P 4PN. **T** 0044 020 7210 6447 email jonathan.phillips@nio.x.gsi.gov.uk

Is thought to have a forensic mind, which is useful in his present post in Northern Ireland; good with systems he is also good with the establishment and would be a terror to those who transgress the rules of good governance and best practice; a very experienced public service administrator whose career will bring him to Whitehall or a Brussels directorate at the very least.

PIERSE, Ged T; NON EXECUTIVE CHAIRMAN, PIERSE CONSTRUCTION
b 1943, Listowel; Paula Morgan; 4*d*; *edu.* B.E.(civil); joined Clancy Construction UK; Mc Inerneys plc; founder Pierse Construction 1978, one of the country's most successful construction companies; investor Carton House Hotel; sponsor Pierse Hurdle Leopardstown; sponsor Draíocht; sponsor Dun Laoighaire to Dingle race; member Dublin City University Educational Trust; director Fairyhouse Race Course. Clubs: National Yacht Club, Dublin. Recreations: all sport especially off shore sailing, racing. Contact: Pierse Construction, Birmayne House, Mullhuddert, Dublin 15. **T** 01 811 5 200 **F** 01 811 5 290 email info@ pierse.ie web www.pierse.ie

A promoter and director of many of the new landmark commercial and residential developments that have reshaped the Irish landscape; an avid sportsman, a competitive offshore sailor with the National Yacht Club in Dun Laoghaire and a prominent sponsor and promoter of Irish thoroughbred horseracing.

PIGGOTT, Tracy; SPORTS PRESENTER
b 1965, UK,; single; *edu.* King School Ely, UK; Sports Presenter RTE; worked in US; came to Ireland, worked for Tommy Stack, assistant trainer,1985; joined RTE 1989; sports presenter RTE 1989 to date; member Irish Sports Council. Recreations: cycling, running. Contact: RTE, Montrose, Donnybrook, Dublin 4. **T** 01 208 3111

Daughter of the legendary jockey, the housewives' choice, Lester Piggot, has become a household name herself as one of RTE's top sports presenters; widely respected for her sense of style as an interviewer and also for her fashion sense; set up her own registered charity Playing For Life, 2005.

PIKE, James; ARCHITECT
b 1939 London; *m* Marie Gallen; 3*s* 1*d*: *edu*. Cheltenham College; The Polytechnic School of Architecture Regent, Street, London; Diploma in Architecture: F.R.I.A.I; R.I.B.A; chairman/director O'Mahony Pike Architects; moved to Dublin, set up Delany, McVeigh & Pike with Paddy Delany and Eoin McVeigh 1964; set up new practice O'Mahony Pike with John O'Mahony 1992; chairman of Public Affairs and Housing Task Force 1974; chairman of Joint Urban Design Task Force 1998- 05; member and/or chairman Joint Housing Conference Committee 1974 to date; *Publ.* Chapters in *Dublin City in Crisis* 1975; *Replace and Restrain* 1988; *The New Housing* 2002; Comhar Pamphlet – *Living Over The Shop* 2005; numerous articles, magazines etc. Clubs: Fitzwilliam LTC, Carrickmines Croquet & Lawn Tennis Club, Woodbrook Golf Club. Recreations: tennis, golf, classical music, theatre, film, watercolour painting, reading. Contact: 5, St' Ann's Terrace, Northbrook Lane, Dublin 6. **T** 01 202 7400 email jpike@omp.ie

Coming out of a good commercial architectural practice, became a leader in social regeneration in an urban context.

PILSWORTH, Michael John, 'Mick' CHAIRMAN, MOTIVE TV
b 1951; *m* Stella Frances Hore (*m.diss.*); 1*s* 1*d*; *edu*. King Edward VI Grammar School, Retford, University of Manchester (BA.,MA); Chairman Motive TV; research assistant Institute of Advanced Studies Manchester 1972-73; lecturer in adult education University of Manchester 1976-78; research fellow 1973-75; Research Associate Centre for TV Research University of Leeds 1979; programme development Executive London Weekend TV 1983-84; gp Development Controller, TVS Entertainment plc. 1987-88; head of programme planning and development 1985-86; chief executive MGMM Communications Ltd 1988-89; MD Alomo Productions Ltd. 1990-93; director 1990; MD 1993; SelectTV plc; chief executive Chrysalis TV Group 1993; director Chrysalis plc 1993-2002; MD Martini Media 2002 to date; chairman Motive TV 2005 to date; member RTS; Publ. *Broadcasting in the Third World;* 1977 Recreations: swimming, tennis, cinema, reading. Contact: 21, College Grove, Castleknock, Dublin 15. **T** 01 821 9212

His international experience in the constantly changing and evolving world of communications will ensure the British born widely experienced, executive remains at the cutting edge of commercial television technology.

PONSONBY, Faith née Brandon; EQUESTRIAN COACH, TUTOR
b 1952, Dublin; *m* Peter Ponsonby; 3*d*; *edu*. The Hall School, Monkstown, Co. Dublin; Trinity College Dublin; MA., H.Dip Ed (Hons); BHSI (sm)Regd, EFI Tutor Equestrian Coach Tutor; teacher St..Columba's College, Rathfarnham, Co. Dublin, St. Andrew's College, Booterstown, Co. Dublin, Thomastown Vocational School, Equestrianism; established Irish Centre for Equestrian Studies; EFI judge at International Horse Trials; runs Equestrian Business; on British & Irish Show Judges panel; judges at Royal International and Royal Welsh Shows in UK; Clubs: RDS, Member of Council. Recreations: equestrian, all sports, reading, cooking, gardening, travel. Contact: Kilcooley Abbey, Thurles, Co. Tipperary. **T** 056 88 3 4222 **F** 056 883 4433 email Kilcooley@indigo.ie

A charming forceful figure, tough, pragmatic and able, she adores the art of the side saddle and all arts associated with the horse; fearless ,with the good sense and good temper inherited from both her parents, she won't take a fence literally and metaphorically without knowing the ground.

POWELL, Charles; PRESIDENT, EQUESTRIAN FEDERATION OF IRELAND
b 1946, Nenagh; *m* Deborah; 3 children; President, Equestrian Federation Of Ireland; Chairman Equestrian Committee RDS; chairman Selectors for Carriage Driving Ireland; member INHS (Irish National Hunt Steeplechase) Committee; former chairman of Carriage Driving Ireland; former vice-chairman of the Irish Draught Horse. Contact: Equestrian Federation of Ireland, Kildare Paddocks, Kill, Co. Kildare. **T** 045 886 678 **F** 045 878 430 email president@horsesport.ie web www.horsesport.ie

The fall-out from various scandals in the equestrian world, and the way in which teams have been selected has been deeply troubling; it isn't clear which direction his presidency will lead the Federation over the next period, but it will be viewed with great interest and no small lack of detached observers from the outside, and not just Ireland.

POWELL, Leo Brendan: NEWSPAPER PUBLISHING
b 1957, Dublin; *m* Eileen Kilgallon; 2*s* 1*d*; *edu.* Patrician Academy, Mallow, Co Cork; Irish Management Institute: NCBS (Distinction); Managing Editor *The Irish Field*; director Goffs Bloodstock Sales Ltd 1988-2003; manager Tattersalls (Ireland) Ltd, to 1988; Clubs: Royal Dublin Society; Curragh Golf Club; Naas Lawn tennis Club. Recreations: racing, bloodstock breeding, music, theatre, books; Contact: Irish Farm Centre, Bluebell, Dublin 12. **T** 01 4051100 **F** 01 455 4008 email leopowell@irishfield.ie

Leo Powell

A leading figure in the equine world, has filled many roles with great distinction; former member of the Tote Committee, long serving member of the Council of Irish Thoroughbred Breeders Association, former director Goffs, former director of Naas Race Company plc; thoughtful, generous and extremely popular in a very competitive world.

POWER, Brenda; JOURNALIST/BROADCASTER
b South Kilkenny; *m* Mel Crystal; 2*s* 3*d*; *edu.* Sacred Heart of Mary Convent, Ferrybank, Waterford; Rathmines College of Commerce, Diploma in Journalism; Kings Inn;, Barrister at Law; Journalist; Columnist Sunday Times; reporter and columnist *Irish Press*; feature writer and columnist *Sunday Press, Sunday Tribune* 1993; *Sunday Times* 2003 to date; Radio Columns on 5-7 live Radio 1 2000; stood in for Marian Finucane & Joe Duffy 2002–2003; presented own radio programmes 2004-2005; presenter/reporter on '*Would You Believe*' 2003–2004; presenter *Crimecall* services on RTE 1 2004-2005; Recreations: reading, cinema, cooking. Contact: 13, Brighton Avenue, Rathgar, Dublin 6. **T** 01 4977024 email brendap@eircom.net

The South Kilkenny native has built up multi media experience; her legal training has enhanced her communications skills; her weekly column allows her to comment on current, topical issues on which she reflects traditional rural values.

POWER, Ethel; CHIEF EXECUTIVE, TIPPERARY FM
b 1969; partner; *edu.* St. Brigid's College, Callan, Co Kilkenny, Trinity College Dublin, College of Marketing & Design; B.Sc Management and Advanced Diploma in Marketing Techniques, MA; Chief Executive, Tipp Fm; commercial director of Dublin Zoo 2001-04 (transformed it from loss making to very profitable and progressive zoo); head of Communications at Ryanair – rolling out new routes throughout Europe & doing PR during time of huge growth 1998-00; National Youth Officer for Fine Gael 1995-98; development manager for Offaly Tourism 1993-95; Recreations: yoga, cooking, wine, travel, nature. Contact: Mangan, Nine-Mile-House, Carrick-On-Suir, Co Tipperary. **T** 052 25447 email ceo@tippfm.com

Highly regarded nationally as an innovative businesswoman; excellent communications skills; an ideal chief executive to grow this already popular and successful local radio station.

POWER, Niall Joseph; PRESENTER BEAT TALK, BEAT 102 103
b 1978, Waterford City; single; *edu.* Waterpark College, Park Road, Waterford; Dublin Institute of Technology, Aungier Street, Dublin 2; Broadcaster; presenter 'Beat Talk', 'Beat 102 103'; 98fm Dublin Producer The Chris Barry Show 1997–03; co-presenter The Afternoon Show; 'Beat 102 103' 2003 to date; Recreations: swimming, horse racing, djing, music; Contact: The Broadcast Center, Ardkeen, Waterford. **T** 051 846172 **F** 051 849103 email niall.power@beat102103.com

With wide experience in easy listening/pop broadcasting, a valuable addition to talented Waterford team.

Niall Power

POWER, Séan; PUBLIC REPRESENTATIVE
b 1960, Naas, Co. Kildare; *m* Deirdre Malone; 3*s*; *edu.* Christian Brothers School, Naas, Co. Kildare;

Public Representative, TD (FF) Kildare South, Minister of State at the Department of Health and Children; bookmaker; first elected Kildare 1989; re-elected to date; assistant chief whip 1993; member Joint Committees on European Affairs, Environment and Local Government. Contact: Castlekealy, Caragh, Naas, Co Kildare. **T** 045 432289 **F** 045 435380

> Bright, articulate and ambitious son of the legendary Kildare Minister Paddy Power, is a solid and effective junior minister; in the marginal constituency of Kildare South where high profile former FG leader lost his seat in the last election, he maintains close contact with his constituents.

PRASIFKA, William J 'Bill'; CHAIRMAN, COMPETITION AUTHORITY

b 1959, Los Angeles; edu. Columbia University School of Law; Chairman of the Competition Authority; former member, Irish Competition Authority; Irish member, Irish Competition Authority, 1996 –'99; Commissioner for Aviation Regulation, 1999 – '05; private practice, first in New York and then in Dublin, William Fry and Co. (advising in the areas of Irish, European and American competition law). Contact: Parnell House, Parnell Square, Dublin 1. **T** 01 804 5400 email info@tca.ie web www.tca.ie

> Has to follow in the footsteps of his predecessor John Fingleton, who was an extremely strong competition advocate; the former Irish Commissioner for Aviation Regulation, a position that brought him into conflict with the likes of the Dublin Airport Authority (DAA) and Ryanair, will have to start delivering on the 'promise' of the last five years where the difficulty of delivery should not be underestimated; we have had the rhetoric of the virtues of competition and now need brave moves, as well as hard cases to be fought and - most importantly – won; apart from liberalizing infrastructure and freeing the channels of commerce, will have to tackle issues such as cartels, the studies conducted by the Competition Authority and the relationship with government.

PRATT, Hilary; JOINT OWNER AND DIRECTOR AVOCA HANDWEAVERS LTD

b 1938, Scotland; m Donald Pratt; 3s 2d; edu. St. Leonard's School, St Andrews, Fife, Scotland; Trinity College Dublin, B.A.(Hist); Joint Owner and Director, Avoca Handweavers Ltd; secondary school teacher,1960-73; co-founder/owner/manager Avoca Handweavers 1974 to date; founder member and past chair Women's Political Association; board member European Women's Foundation; founder member Dalkey School Project; board member Dublin Rape Crisis Centre; past board member Kilkenny Design Workshops, National College of Art & Design, Craft Council of Ireland. Recreations: hill walking, reading historical biography, running political workshop for women in Eastern Europe. Contact: Avoca Handweavers, Kilmacanogue. Bray, Co. Wicklow. **T** 01 286 7466. **F** 01 286 2367.

> An efficient and able director of Ireland's premier craft design and retail group; a very successful family business; she has good sound taste and a keen eye; responsible for many developments within the family firm; a cool charm which is none the less real.

PRATT, Maurice Alan; MANAGING DIRECTOR CANTRELL & COCHRANE

b 1955, Dublin; m Pauline Farrell; 5s; edu. St Benildus College, Kilmacud, Co. Dublin; College of Commerce, Rathmines, Marketing Diploma; Managing Director Cantrell and Cochrane; media executive Hunter Advertising Ltd 1973-74; media manager/account director Des O'Meara and Partners 1974-82; marketing manager Power Supermarkets, 1982-87, marketing director 1987; managing director 1996; managing director Tesco Ireland Ltd, 1997–2002; managing director Cantrell and Cochrane 2002 to date; council member Dublin Chamber of Commerce, Irish Management Institute; non-executive director Eircom Group plc, Repak Limited, Uniphat plc.; fellow Marketing Institute of Ireland; past president Irish Business and Employers Confederation (IBEC). Clubs: David Lloyd Riverview, (President 1993-98), Foxrock Golf Club. Recreations: tennis, cycling, golf, soccer, travel. Contact: Cantrell and Corchrane Group plc, Kylemore Park, Dublin 10. **T** 01 616 1100   **F** 01 616 1163

> The 'housewife's choice' and lover of Machiavelli, is one of the best known executives in the country following his years of commercials for Quinnsworth and Tesco; has well made his mark at C & C in a short time; extremely popular, hardworking, well informed businessman.

Maurice Pratt

PRENDERVILLE, Patrick Joseph 'Paddy'; EDITOR
b 1946, Bury, Greater Manchester, England; separated; 1s 1d; edu. Clongowes Wood College; Middlesex

University; B.A. English, History; Dip. Industrial Relations and Trade Union Studies; Editor, *The Phoenix*; assistant editor, *Hibernia Magazine* 1978-80; foreign editor *Sunday Tribune* 1980-82; newsroom journalist *The Sunday Tribune* 1983-84; editor *The Phoenix* 1984 to date; chairman of Dublin 1981 Committee to commemorate 20th Anniversary of the Hunger Strike, 2001. Recreations: politics, football, cinema, music, Kerry. Contacts: 44, Lower Baggot Street, Dublin 2. **T** 01 661 1062 **F** 01 662 4332 web www.phoenix-magazine.ie

> For someone who edits a magazine considered compulsive reading in better boardrooms, clubs and dinner party circles, he manages to retain an extremely low profile; totally switched on to every nuance of what's happening in the country, more often than not provides the 'real' story that eludes the mainstream media.

PRENDERGAST, Patrick Joseph; RACEHORSE TRAINER

b 1974; *m* Grainne Kelly; 1*d*; *edu.* Clongowes Wood, Clane, Kildare; Racehorse Trainer; apprenticeship Eire, UK and USA, licensed trainer; former assistant trainer to Sir Michael Stoute (leading Ruckie in Ireland); Recreations; music, rugby, farming; Contact: Melitta Lodge, The Curragh, Kildare Town. **T** 045 521401 **F** 045 521875 email PRENDERGASTPJ@EIRCOM.NET

> A member of one of Ireland's most distinguished racing families with his international training is well equipped to carry on a great tradition.

PRESTON, Caroline Mary; SOLICITOR

b 1955, Dublin; *m* Punch Preston; 1*s* 1*d*; *edu.* secondary school, England; Trinity College Dublin, (History and Political Science) 1977; Law Society of Ireland, qualified solicitor 1981; Solicitor; joined A & L Goodbody 1981; Partner 1986; appointed head of litigation 1997; (specialised practice in Commercial Litigation); Governor of St. Patrick's Hospital, member of the Foundation Irish Chapter of the International Woman's Forum, joint master of the Westmeath Foxhounds; appointed Charities Solicitor to the Attorney General 1994; Recreations; fishing, wide open spaces and adventure travel; Contact: A & L Goodbody, 1, Earlsfort Centre, Hatch Street, Dublin 2. **T** 01 649 2000 **F** 01 661 3278 email cpreston@algoodbody.ie web www.algoodbody.ie

> One of the first female legal partners of a major legal practice; a lively, thrusting and energetic solicitor; is as vigorous in her legal practice as she is as Master of the Westmeath Foxhounds.

PRIOR, Sharon; PR CONSULTANT/CO DIRECTOR

b 1962, Dublin; *m* Paul Nolan; 2*d*; *edu.* St Dominic's College, Cabra, Dublin 7; University College Dublin; BA Spanish and Psychology; PR Consultant. Journalist 1982-84; Kennys PR (now Grayling) 1984-88; PR & sponsorship manager Tennents Ireland 1988-94; Prior Communications founded 1994; Clubs: Riverview; Recreations: tennis, music, drama, cooking, reading, travel; Contact: 28, Marlborough Road, Donnybrook, Dublin 4. **M** 086 251 1588 email sharon.priorcom@marketingnetwork.ie

> A solid public relations practitioner; low profile but highly respected in a constantly changing industry.

Sharon Prior

PROUD, Malcolm; MUSICIAN / LECTURER

b 1952, Dublin; *m* Susan Carolan; 2*s* 1*d*; *edu.* St Andrew's College, Dublin; Trinity College Dublin; Royal Conservatory of Music, Copenhagaen; Sweelinck Conservatory, Amsterdam; LRAM (Performer); B. Mus; Final Diploma – Conservatory Amsterdam; Musician/Lecturer; *Publ.* CDs Bach, Brandenburg Concerto No 5 (Virgin), Bach, Goldberg Variations (Maya) Bach, Violin & Harpsichord Sonatas (Maya), Purcell, Harpsichord Music (Meridian); musician and lecturer Waterford Institute of Technology; Organist St. Canice's Cathedral, Kilkenny; international performer on harpsichord and organ; concerts throughout Ireland, Great Britain, Continental Europe, USA, Canada, Japan; Clubs: Camerata, Kilkenny, Irish Baroque Orchestra; Recreations: bird watching, hill walking, poetry; Contact: St. Canice's Cottage, St. Canice's Cathedral, Kilkenny. **T** 056 776 1497 email proudmus@eircom.net

> A widely acclaimed organist who has settled at the historic St. Canice's Cathedral, Kilkenny; an international performer, he is actively involved in social activities in his adopted Marble City.

Deirdre Purcell

PURCELL, Deirdre; WRITER

b 1945, Dublin; *m* Kevin Healy; 2*s*; *edu.* Schoil Mhuire, Marlborough Street, Dublin; Gortnor Abbey, Crossmolina, Co. Mayo; Loyola University, Chicago; Writer; Civil Service Commission 1962-63; Aer Lingus 1963-65; actor, Abbey Theatre 1965-68; RTE Radio Continuity, Newsreader, News Journalist 1974-83; journalist *Sunday Tribune* 1983-90; novelist 1990-97; screenwriter/novelist 1997 to date; *Publ. A Place of Stones* (Dublin, Townhouse/London, Macmillan, 1991); *Falling for a Dancer* (Town House/Macmillan, 1993), which was filmed, starring Liam Cunningham; *Francey* (Macmillan 1994); *Full Circle* (Town House 1995); *Sky* (Town House 1995/Macmillan 1996); *Love Like Hate Adore* (Town House, 1997), which was shortlisted for the Orange Prize; *Entertaining Ambrose* (TownHouse, 2000); and *Marble Gardens* (Dublin, New Island Books, 2002); *Children of Eve* (HH Ireland, 2005); *Tell Me Your Secret*, HH Ireland 2006), contributions to various short story and feature compendiums; board member Abbey Theatre 1991–2002; awards, AT Cross Woman Journalist of the Year 1984; Benson and Hedges Journalist of the Year.1987; short-listed Orange Prize for Fiction (Love Like Hate Adore, 1998). Recreations: theatre, music, art, media; Contact: Hodder Headline Publishers, 8 Castlecourt, Castleknock, Dublin 15. **T** 01 824 6288 **F** 01 824 6289 email ciara.considine@hhireland.ie web http://www.hhireland.ie

Multi-talented novelist who has made a significant contribution to the cultural fabric of life in Ireland; focused and hardworking deserves her huge success.

PURCELL, Gerard; COMPANY DIRECTOR

b 1964; *m* Aisling Gleeson; 1*s*, 3*ss*; *edu.* St.Michael's College, Dublin, Villanova University, PA, USA, Richmond University London. B.A (Business Studies); Company Dircetor; Clubs: Kildare Golf and Country Club. Recreations: golf, art, horseracing, wine. Contact: 14 Herbert Street, Dublin 2. **T** 01 644 9494 **F** 01 644 9495 email pbl@inet.ie

Charming businessman who recovered from earlier financial problems to build a successful property business in Ireland and the UK.

Prem Puri

PURI, Prem; PAEDIATRIC SURGEON

b 1944; *m* Veena Puri; 2*s*.1*d*; Paediatric Surgeon, Newman Clinical Research Professor, University College Dublin; Director of Research, Childrens' Research Centre, Our Lady's Hospital for Sick Children, Dublin & Consultant Paediatric Surgeon OLHFSC, and the National Childrens' Hospital Dublin; vice-president World Federation of Association of Paediatric Surgeons; chairman Scientific Office of the European Association of Paediatric Surgeons; secretary International Board of Paediatric Surgical; visiting professor to universities including Harvard, Columbia, Indianapolis, Michigan; has addressed to date some 121 scientific meetings; and has made over 390 presentations at international seminars (including 92 British Association of Paediatric Surgeons, 41 American Paediatric Surgical Association, 44 American Academy of Paediatrics, and 72 Paediatric Surgical Research Society); Editor Chief Paediatric Surgery International; awarded people of the year award 1984 jointly with Professor Barry O'Donnell for the discovery of endoscopic treatment for vesicoureteric reflux; Franco Soave Medal 1996 re Hirschprung's disease, Gandhi Medal in 2001 for contribution to Paediatric Medicine; Asian Society Paediatric Urology Medal 2004; *Publ.* 8 books/monographs, 71 chapters in textbooks, 32 articles in peer reviewed journals; Contact: Childrens' Research Centre, Our Lady's Hospital for Sick Children, Crumlin, Dublin 12.
T 01 409 6420 **F** 01 455 0201 email prem.puri@ucd.ie web www.olhsc.ie

Regarded as the best pediatric surgeon ever to come out of Ireland; heads up a major research facility in Our Lady's Hospital for Sick Children, Crumlin, Dublin; has an international reputation in urological surgery.

PYE, Patrick Terence; ARTIST

b 1929; *m* Nóirín; 2*d*; *edu.* St. Columba's College, Rathfarnham, Co.Dublin; National College of Art, Dublin; Teacher's Certificate; Artist; began painting 1947; full time 1974; numerous commissions for churches in Ireland, notably Glenstal Abbey, St. Michael's, Dún Laoghaire, St.Mary's Oratory Maynooth, and Bank of Ireland H.Q. Dublin; member Royal Hibernian Academy of Arts; D.Phil(*h.c*); *Publ. Apples & Angels* (Veritas 1981); *The Time Gatherers* (on El Greco) Four Courts Press 1991; pamphlet: '*Has Art Any Meaning?*' Dolmen Press 1963; Recreations: the mystery of Life and painting is enough, accepts William Blake's valuation of imagination in the process of art and Coleridge's distinction between fantasy and imagination. Contact: Jorgensen Fine Art, 29, Molesworth Street, Dublin 2 . **T** 01-6619750

QUEALLY, Peter; CHAIRMAN, THE QUEALLY GROUP

b Waterford; *m* Eileen; 3*s* 4*d*; *edu.* National School, Kill, Co. Waterford; Chairman, The Queally Group; founded The Queally Group with brother John; Recreations: GAA; racing. Contact: The Maudlins, Naas Co Kildare. **T** 045 87 1111 **F** 045 87 1120 email info@queallygroup.com web www.queallygroup.com

> Founder of the now national and multinational private company including Dawn Meats one of the top meat companies in the world.

QUINLAN, Derek; CHAIRMAN, QUINLAN PRIVATE ASSET MANAGEMENT

b Dublin; *m* 1st Perdita (*m. diss*); 5*d*; *m* 2nd Siobhan; 3*s*; *edu.* Blackrock College, Dublin; Chairman Private Quinlan Asset Management; started his career in the Revenue Commissioners; Tax Inspector; founded Quinlan Private, Ireland's first independent client advisory group, 1989; bought The Savoy Group, UK May 2004 (€750 million); sold the Savoy Hotel and Simpsons- in- the- Strand, 2005; established Maybourne Hotel Group, (a super luxury hotel group) January 2005; chairman Maybourne Hotel Group; property developer, tax advisor, accountant, wealth manager; over 150 assets in portfolio (consisting of office blocks, car parks, shopping centers, hotels throughout Europe and North America); acquired a range of commercial property assets located in Hungary and the Czech Republic, 2006; Clubs: Fitzwiliam LTC; Marks Club, London. Contact: 8, Raglan Road, Ballsbridge, Dublin. **T** 01 631 5400

> Identified a market and has captured the confidence of Ireland's new money; has successfully put together a number of very high profile multi million and billion dollar deals in Ireland, UK, Europe and most recently in the US; low profile and charming; has now reached the stage where he doesn't have to seek the deals anymore, they come to him from all over the world; the Celtic cubs are happy to pay him substantial fees to be included in his deals from which they have done extremely well to date.

QUIGLEY, Eamonn Martin; MEDICAL PROFESSOR

b 1952, Ballineen, Co. Cork; *m* Dr. Una O'Sullivan; 1*s* 1*d*; *edu.* Glenstal Abbey, Murroe, Co. Limerick; University College Cork Medical School; MB Bch BAO(NUI).MD(NUI) FRCP, Glasgow, Edinburgh, London FRCPI.,FACP.,FACG; Medical Professor; head of the Medical School, University College Cork; professor of Medicine and Human Physiology, UCC; medical intern, Cork; SHO/Registrar, Glasgow; research fellow Mayo Clinic, Rochester, Minnesota; lecturer University of Manchester; assistant associate and professor University of Nebraska USA; president World Organization of Gastroenterology; secretary American College of Gastroenterology; former editor in Chief Journal of Gastroenterology; *Publ.* three books, over 400 articles in Medical Literature, numerous CDs and other educational material. Recreations: literature, music, walking. Contact: 3, Woodlands, Carragh, Kinsale, Co. Cork. **T** 021 477 7827 email e.quigley@ucc.ie web www.ucc.ie

> His recent appoint is a manifestation of the high standing and reputation he holds in the global medical world; his wide international experience was a major coup for University College Cork when he returned from the US as the head of the medical school in 1998; enjoys nothing more than relaxing walks around the Kinsale area.

QUIN, Elizabeth, Dorothy; CLOTHING DESIGNER

b 1955, Dublin; *m.* Felim O'Leary; separated; 1*s* 1*d*; *edu.* Grafton Academy Fashion Design, Diploma in Dress Design. Clothes Designer; Started Quin & Donnelly in 1980; sold clothing in our own retail outlet called Ritzy; also wholesaled the line from 1985; won designer of the Year award twice; Collection sells in UK through House of Fraser stores and selected outlets. In Ireland Quin & Donnelly is available in all Brown Thomas stores and selected outlets. Future plans include development of new markets in Denmark, Holland, Norway, Sweden, Finland and France; Recreations: interior design, gardening, sailing. Contact: Unit 16, Finglas Business Centre, Dublin 11. **T** 01 806 8560 **F** 01 806 8561 email sonole1@eircom.net

> A talented and stylish fashion designer who with her partner Caroline Donnelly (*qv*) has established a well known and very successful label *Quin and Donnelly*; producing two collections a year, the pieces are eagerly awaited and quickly snapped up by savvy fashionistas; stocked by 22 House of Frazer Stores throughout the UK; best selling fashion designers in Ireland.

QUINLIVAN, Ailish; VICE PRESIDENT, FINANCE, UNIVERSITY OF LIMERICK
b 1970, Limerick; *edu.* Waterford Regional Technical College; Institute of Chartered Accountants in
Ireland; ACA; Vice President, Finance, University College Limerick; trained in Coopers and Lybrand;
vice-president Finance, University of Limerick. Worked with Coopers and Lybrand in Waterford
Regional Technical College (2 years) and Limerick (4 years); Further Education department New
South Wales, Australia; joined Price Waterhouse Coopers, Risk Management; worked in 13 countries
1996 - 2004; appointed University of Limerick's first female vice-president (Finance) 2005. Contact:
University of Limerick, Pleassy, Co.Limerick. **T** 061 202 700 **F** 061 330 316 web www.ul.ie

> With her international experience, brings serious financial clout to this university
> which continues to go from strength to strength and needs a sound financial base to
> grow apace.

QUINN, Conor; CHAIRMAN QMP PUBLICIS Ltd.
*b*1943, Dublin; *m* Hilary; 2*s* 2*d*; *edu.* Blackrock College; University College Dublin (Economics);
Chairman QMP Publicis Ltd. Clubs: Blackrock Rugby Club, Elm Park Golf Club; Recreations: golf,
reading, rugby, travel; Contact: Sir John Rogerson Quay, Dublin 2 **T** 01 694 6400 **F** 01 649 6401
email Conor.Quinn@quipPublicis.ie web www.qmppublicis.ie

> A member of the well known Quinn family and brother of former Labour leader Ruairi
> (*qv*) and Lochlann (*qv*) heads up a high energy, innovative, important and fully
> integrated advertising and marketing company which he co-founded in 1973; now with
> billings of €30 million, boasts an A to Z of blue chip clients.

QUINN, Feargal; BUSINESSMAN
b 1936, Dublin; *m* Denise; 3*s* 2*d*; *edu.* Newbridge College, Co Kildare; University College
Dublin, B.Comm; Businessman; founded Superquinn (Dundalk) 1960; chairman of An Post
1979–89; elected to Seanad Eireann 1993, 1997, 2002; chairman of IMI (1985–87); chairman
St. Patrick's Festival (1999–03), chairman NCCA Committee on Leaving Cert. Applied
(1993–98); chairman of Paris Based CIES (1998-2000); LLD (*hc*) NCEA 1987; LLD (*hc*)
Dublin University1988; *Publ. Crowning the Customer*; Recreations: golf. Contact: Superquinn,
Support Office, Sutton Cross, Dublin 13. **T** 01 816 7163 **F** 01 816 7162
email himself@feargalquinn.ie

> One of the pioneering entrepreneurs of the '60's in Ireland; a trend setter in food
> retailer; didn't hide his light under a bushel.

Feargal Quinn

QUINN, Lochlann; BUSINESSMAN
b 1940, Dublin; *m* Brenda; 4*s* 2*d*; *edu.* Blackrock College, Dublin; University College Dublin,
B.Comm; Businessman; qualified as an accountant 1966; joined Arthur Andersen London; opened
Arthur Andersen Dublin office 1969, manager, partner1980; joined Martin Naughton in Glen
Dimplex 1980; chief executive Glen Dimplex 2004; a former director of AIB Bank (1995-96),
chairman AIB (1997-03); chairman of the Irish Museum of Modern Art (1990- 00); board member
Michael Smurfit Graduate Business School, UCD; chairman National Gallery of Ireland; private
business interests include, Merrion Hotel (Dublin), Patrick Guilbaud Restaurant, Dublin, commercial
properties in Dublin, London and Brussels, and a vineyard, Chateau de Fieuzal in Bordeaux. Clubs:
Elm Park Golf Club, Fitzwilliam LTC. Recreations: cars, art, wine, golf. Contact: National Gallery of
Ireland, Merrion Square West, Dublin 2. **T** 01 661 5133 **F** 01 661 5372
email info@ngi.ie web www.ngi.ie www.wine-journal.com/fieuzal.

> An extremely bright, savvy and gregarious businessman who made making a vast
> fortune look like lots of fun; deemed to be the brains at Glen Dimplex, he has
> diversified and expanded his portfolio of companies since he sold his share holding in
> that company to Martin Naughton (*qv*).

QUINN, Ruairi Colm; PUBLIC REPRESENTATIVE. ARCHITECT, PLANNER
b 1946, Dublin; *m* 1st Nicola Underwood (*m. diss.*); 2nd.Liz Allman; 2*s* 1*d*; *edu* Blackrock College,
1969 UCD, Architecture, B. Arch; 1971 Athens Center for Ekistics, Diploma in Ekistics; Public
Representative, Dáil Deputy (Lab) for Dublin South East; Architect, Planner; Labour Spokesperson
for European Affairs. Leader of the Labour Party Nov 1997–02; vice-president and treasurer Party of
European Socialists 1998 to present; deputy leader of the Labour Party 1990- 97; director of elections

Mary Robinson Presidential Campaign 1990; Minister for Finance 1994–97; Minister for Enterprise & Employment 1993–94; Minister for Public Service 1986-87; Minister for Labour 1984-87; Minister of State for the Environment 1982-83; member Dáil Éireann 1977-81 & 1982 to date; Member of Seanad Éireann 1976 and 1981; Member of Dublin City Council 1974–77; leader Civic Alliance & Labour Group 1991-93; principal of EU's Council of Social Affairs (Jan–Jun 1985); president of ECOFIN (Council of EU Finance Ministers) Jul-Dec 1996; chairperson European Movement of Ireland; executive minister Institute of European Affairs; chairperson Holocaust Educational Trust; Principal of Ruairi Quinn & Partners 2003 to date; chairperson Development Council; Faculty of Engineering & Architecture, University College Dublin 2003; Partner Burke-Kennedy, Doyle & Partners; Housing Architect's Department, Dublin City Council; Lecturer in Architecture, Housing and Urban Design. *Publ.* numerous articles; *Straight Left, A Political Memoir* 2005; Recreations: hill walking, cycling, cooking, gardening, reading. Contact: Leinster House, Dublin 2. **T** 618 3434; **F** 01 618 5153 email ruairi.quinn@ orieachtas.ie

> An excellent politician who brought a wealth of experience to the Labour Party; a breath of fresh air in Leinster House where he always added colour to the mostly hum drum debate; respected as an architect and follower of the arts, his autobiography reflected his rather quirky sense of humour; still an important political deal maker.

QUINN, Sean; EXECUTIVE CHAIRMAN, THE QUINN GROUP

Sean Quinn

b 1947, Co. Fermanagh; *m* Patricia; 4*s* 1*d*; *edu.* Garvery National School; Executive Chairman, The Quinn Group; began by selling gravel from his family's small farm in Co Fermanagh in the early 1970s; starting with one truck, the business evolved into Ireland's second-largest cement-making company by the mid-1980s, and from there became the Fermanagh-based Quinn Group, with 20 related companies; bought nine Dublin pubs and a string of Irish hotels in the mid-1990s, and their value has increased sixfold in the Irish property boom (has since sold some of these); while running these businesses, he hit problems with insurance and glass recycling - so he set up successful companies in those sectors, too; largely through the success of its insurance company Quinn-direct, the group's pre-tax profit surged to £103m last year on £448m sales; bought the Hilton and Ibis Karlin hotels in Prague in January for £100m, the largest property deal seen in the Czech Republic; now has nine hotels, including Nottingham's Holiday Inn and Crowne Plaza in Cambridge; is also building one of Europe's largest glass plants in Cheshire. National University of Ireland, Maynooth, LL.D (*hc*) 2004; Contact: Quinn Group Ltd., Derrylin, Co. Fermanagh. **T** 0801 3657 48866. **F** 0801 3657 48894.

> Easily one of Ireland's top entrepreneurs; Ireland's fourth euro billionaire and wealthiest individual but the first self-made man to achieve the status; heads one of Ireland's richest business empires, between Fermanagh and Cavan employs 2,000 people; when he was conferred with an honorary Doctor of Laws degree, some thought a doctorate in business administration might have been more apt; has divested himself of some of his Irish properties and is expanding overseas; bought the Belfry Golf Club UK; has expanded into the leisure business in high profile hotels in Eastern Europe; currently negotiating property deals in Russia; despite his tough and uncompromising profile, to those who know him, he is extremely sociable and lives a simple life style.

QUINN, Shaun; CHIEF EXECUTIVE, FAILTE IRELAND

b 1962; *m;* 1*s* 1*d*; *edu.* Royal & Prior Raphoe Co Donegal; University College Dublin; Michael Smurfit Graduate School of Business; B.Agr.Sc (Econ) MBA; Chief Exec`utive Officer Failte Ireland; chief executive CERT 1998–2003; head of marketing Bord Bia 1995-98; Strategic Planning Director, Bord Bia 1994-96; chief executive officer Failte Ireland 2003 to date Clubs: Hollywood Lakes Golf Club. Contact: Fáilte Ireland, Baggot Street Bridge, Dublin 2. **T** 01 602 4000 **F** 01 602 4027 web www.failteireland.ie

> His strategic planning skills will be much needed in developing a coherent and holistic plan for a constantly changing Irish tourism industry.

QUINN, Patricia; CONSULTANT

b 1959, Dublin; *p* John Banville; 2*d*; *edu.* Loreto College, North Great George's Street; Mount Temple Comprehensive; Trinity College Dublin BA; MBA, IMI; Consultant; worked in rare book conservation at Trinity College Dublin and Cambridge University; specialist officer, responsible for music and opera development, The Arts Council 1984-92; cultural director Temple Bar Properties

1992-6; director Arts Council 1996-2004; a founder member and former co-chair of the International Federation of Arts Councils and Culture Agencies; currently consulting in the public, private and third sectors, specializing in corporate social responsibility and cultural planning; member of the task force for cultural tourism; active member of the Leadership Initiative, an independent cross-sectoral project promoting diversity in leadership in Ireland. Clubs: Kildare Street and University Club, Dublin. Recreations: friendships, music, horses, Irish history, French culture. Contact: 46 Stephen's Place, Dublin 2. **T** 01 678 9311 **M** 087 648 8441 **F** 01 662 9711 email patriciaquinn@ireland.com

Served on the government-appointed policy committee for public art, the newspaper commission, the forum on broadcasting; responsible during her seven-year term for the production and implementation of two successive national arts strategies, attracting a very significant increase in public funding and policy recognition for the arts.

QUINN, Maura; EXECUTIVE DIRECTOR, UNICEF IRELAND
b 1960, Roscommon; *m* John O'Shea; 2*s*; *edu.* Loreto Convent, Mullingar; Convent of Mercy, Roscommon; University College Dublin; College of Marketing; Marketing graduate; Executive Director UNICEF Ireland; senior management positions in private and public sectors. Recreations: travel, international affairs, politics, cinema. Contact: UNICEF Ireland, 25, Great Strand Street, Dublin 1. **T** 01 878 3000 **F** 01 878 6655 email Info@unicef.ie web www.unicef.ie

In the highly competitive charity world more than holds her own; is helped by a committee of high profile people from business and the movie world.

QUIRK, The Hon, Mr. Justice John Michael Thornton; JUDGE OF THE HIGH COURT
b 1944; *m* Mary Cruise; 3*s* 1*d*; *edu.* Willow Park School; Blackrock College, Dublin; Trinity College Dublin; Kings Inn's; Judge Of The High Court; called to the Bar 1974; called to the Inner Bar, Middle Temple (England)1981; called to the Inner Bar 1984; appointed Judge of the High Court 1997; Clubs: Blackrock R.F.C. (Captain 1969); Blainroe Golf Club, (Captain, 1991); Recreations: all sport, especially golf, rugby. Contact: Four Courts, Morgan Place, Dublin 7. **T** 01 872 5555 web www.courts.ie

A keen sportsman, rugby capped for Ireland 1962-68; keen on social issues and social justice for the individual; may yet be appointed to the European Court.

RABBITTE, Patrick 'Pat'; PUBLIC REPRESENTATIVE
b 1949, Co Mayo; *m* Derry Mc Dermott; *3d*; *edu.* St. Coleman's College, Claremorris, Co Mayo; University College Galway; B.A, H.D.E., LL.B; Public Representative, Leader of the Labour Party, TD Dublin South West; president of the Union of Students in Ireland (USI) 1972-74; National Secretary ITGWU,1974-89; chairperson Dublin County Council 1993; elected to Dáil Éireann for Dublin South West 1989; Minister for Commerce, Science and Technology 1994–97; leader of the Labour Party 2002 to date; Contact: 56 Monastery Drive, Dublin 22. **T** 01 618 3772 **F** 01 618 4032 email pat.rabbitte@oireachtas.ie web www.labour.ie

Can deliver lethal and telling denunciations to a packed house with the flourish; shares the oratorical honours in Dáil with his left wing colleague Joe Higgins (*qv*) and his right wing parliamentary nemesis former Tánaiste Mary Harney (*qv*); as a Workers Party TD made a name for himself, and in an earlier but not inconsistent life as a Trade Unionist (Union Official and then National Secretary ITGWU) began his more public life; now at the centre of the possibility of change (in government), more leftist than Labour; can still get trapped in his own verbosity as when he couldn't or wouldn't deal with a Q& A answer on the national airways about which way he would face on a possible Labour Presidential Candidate; that did him some damage, whether lasting remains to be seen; meantime the Mullingar Accord (a policy and voting pact with Fine Gael, the other opposition party) may deliver it's calf for him and his party; for his political survival if not that of his own now amalgamated parties (Labour & The Workers Party) it has to bring him and them to power, or face the outreaches of political purgatory best described as "having seen the vision, nay the promised land…all promised now deferred but not imminent" ; his quick sound bytes can make him seem less than he is…tough, pragmatic and determined to be in government, his jovial manner disguises the foregoing.

RAPPLE, Colm; JOURNALIST/ CONSULTANT
b 1940, Dublin; *m* Nuala O' Toole-King; *1s 1d*; *edu.* St. Joseph's Marino, Dublin; University College Dublin; B.A, MBA; Freelance Writer and Consultant; Cunard Lines 1958-64; sub-editor Business Page Reporter 1969; business correspondent, group business editor *Irish Independent* 1971-85; business editor, Irish Press Newspapers 1985-95; freelance journalist & columnist, *Sunday Business Post* 1995; presenter, Money Talks, RTE Radio 1; columnist *Irish Examiner*; *Publ. Family Finance Annual*; thousands of articles on economics, business, finance; Recreations: reading, theatre, running a small holding in Mayo. Contact: 26, Millview Lawns, Malahide, Co. Dublin **T** 01 845 1929 **F** 01 845 1929

The voice of reason in demystifying economics and family finances to the man in the street.

REA, Stephen; ACTOR
b 1947, Belfast; *m* Dolores Price; (*m diss*); *2s*; *edu.* Belfast High School; Queen's University Belfast; BA (English & French); Actor; began career Abbey Theatre Dublin; played many leading roles in English National Theatre (*The Shaughran, Playboy of the Western World, Comedians*); The Royal Court Theatre (*Endgame, Freedom of the City*); Hampstead Theatre, (*Buried Child, Ecstasy, Someone Who'll Watch Over Me* - also on Broadway); founded Field Day Theatre with Brian Friel 1980; appeared in or directed all productions; Films: *The Crying Game* (Academy Award Nomination); *Angel, Michael Collins, Butcher Boy, The End of the Affair, Interview with a Vampire, Breakfast on Pluto, Vendetta*; honorary doctorates from Queen's University Belfast, University of Ulster, Staffordshire University; Ambassador for UNICEF Ireland; Patron of Cystinosis Ireland. Contact: c/o ICM,76 Oxford St. London W1D 1BST. **T** 00 44 207 636 6565

Stephen Rea

A deeply committed actor who conveys the historic brooding menace of Irish history; long involved in the creation of Field Day Theatre company and it's off shoots of literature; he continues to fascinate whilst being deeply private as a person but one who is known to be passionate on those issues for which he cares deeply.

REDLICH, Patricia; PSYCHOLOGIST/JOURNALIST
b 1940, Dublin; *m; 1s; edu.* Kings Inns Street, Dublin; College of Commerce Rathmines; Goethe University, Frankfurt, Germany; Ruhr University, Bochum, Germany; M.Sc Pyschology; Psychologist/ Agony Aunt; senior clinical psychologist Eastern health Board; freelance journalist; features Writer *Sunday Independent*; Clubs: Dungaravan Golf Club, Co. Waterford, National Yacht Club, Dun

Patricia Redlich

Laoghaire. Recreations: golf, swimming, gardening, reading. Contact: Old Parish, Dungarvan, Co. Waterford. email patriciaredlich@dearpatricia.com web www.patriciaredlich.com

A popular agony aunt who has great skills of analysis and compassion; writes well on her topic and seems to have a great empathy with the dilemmas of modern life and living.

REDMOND, Mary Patricia; EMPLOYMENT LAW CONSULTANT ARTHUR COX/DIRECTOR BANK OF IRELAND
b 1950; *m* Dr. Patrick Usher; 1*s* 3 *stepd*; *edu.* Loreto College, St. Stephen's Green, Dublin 2; University College Dublin; Christ's College, Cambridge; BCL, LLm (NUI), PHD (Cambridge University), Solicitor, Incorporated Law Society of Ireland; Fellow of Christ's College Cambridge and since 2004 Honorary Fellow; Employment Law Consultant, Arthur Cox; council member of Institute of Directors UK; fellow of the Royal Society of Arts; former director of Jefferson Smurfit plc and of Campbell Bewley Group; founder of two national Charities: the Irish Hospice Foundation (1986) and the Wheel (1998); former member of several statutory bodies; employment law consultant, Arthur Cox; director, Bank of Ireland. *Publ. Dismissal Law* (Buttersworths London 1999), *The Emergence of Women in the Solicitor's Profession; Portrait of a Profession* (2002, Dublin); Clubs: Noe Gascogne Cricket Club Recreations: family, painting, gardening, the simpler side of French country. Contact: Palmyra, Whitechurch, Dublin 16. **T** 01 493 2763 email mredmond@iol.ie

A woman of so many talents it's hard to see them all in an overview; brings glamour and hard work as well as dedication to the various strands of her professional concern; her very skill of advocacy and being articulate could make her appear remote, which is probably not the case for the causes for which she campaigns.

REDMOND, John; CREATIVE DIRECTOR, BROWN THOMAS GROUP
b 1963, Carlow; *m* Karen Higgins (*qv*); *edu.* Christian brothers College, Carlow; College of Marketing & Design, Dublin; Diploma in Retail Business Studies; Creative Director Brown Thomas Group; display manager Brown Thomas, Grafton Street, Dublin 1983; display manager Brown Thomas Group and BT2; creative director Brown Thomas Group; Recreations: gardening, music, travel. Contact: Brown Thomas Group, 88-95 Grafton Street, Dublin 2. **T** 01 605 6666 **F** 01 606 6763 email jredmond@brownthomas.ie web www.brownthomas.ie

Creative and ultra stylish his handprint is to be found all over the Brown Thomas stores; always ahead of the curve on trends is an excellent advertisement for his craft; totally focused, inspired, very hardworking and lots of fun.

REED, Leslie Philip; CHIEF EXECUTIVE CRAFTS COUNCIL OF IRELAND
b 1950; *m* Inga White; 3*s*; *edu.* Dartford Grammar School (UK); Loughborough College of Art & Design (UK), BA; Chief Exeutive Crafts Council of Ireland; head of the Ceramics Department, Crawford College of Art & Design 1977-89; director of Training, Crafts Council of Ireland 1989-96; chief executive Craft Council of Ireland 1996 to date; chairman Kilkenny School Project Association; Recreations: gardening, stone carving; Contact: Crafts Council of Ireland, Castle Yard, Kilkenny. **T** 056 61804 **F** 056 633 3754 web www.ccoi.ie

As head of the Crafts Council he ploughs an often difficult road in an age of consumerism; plays an effective enough role in the world of crafts but out of the loop despite the appeal of decentralisation; crafts sales need a buying population, and that's his conundrum - a craft based industry versus the manufacturing skills, and how to sell them; considered able if somewhat pragmatic.

REID, Fr. Alex; RC PRIEST AND PEACE BROKER
b 1943, Tipperary; single; Redemptorist priest; formerly based in Clonard Monastery, Belfast; one of the key players in the Irish peace process; worked for over 30 years in Belfast; first became involved in mediation work in the 1970's helping to broker a ceasefire between the Provisional and Official IRA. In 1980 he involved himself in attempts to end the hunger strike in the Maze prison. Image went around the world in 1988 when he was photographed administering the Last Rites to a British Army corporal murdered at a republican funeral in Belfast's Millstreet cemetery to 1988; dialogue gained added impetus when Adams became Sinn Fein President in 1983; 1986 he was talking to Charles

Haughey about his hope that the republican movements would give up violence; 1987 organized first round of talks between Gerry Adams and John Hume; led to the Hume-Adams document which set out how republican violence could be brought to an end; more recently living in Dublin and has become involved in trying to promote peace in the Basque region of Spain; Contact: St. Alphonsus Monastery, 63, Falls Road, Belfast. BT12 4PD. **T** 0232 325 668

> Played a significant role in the peace process leading to a window on decommissioning; passionate and articulate he also found himself in hot water like another Belfast person President McAleese (*qv*) in an unfortunate public linking of Ulster Protestantism and the Nazis; a blip on the screen for this pursuer of truth and peace.

REIHILL, Ann née McCoy; PUBLISHER

b 1936, Dublin; *m* 1st Patrick Dillon Malone (decd); 2*s* 1*d*; *m* 2nd John Rehill (*qv*); separated; *edu.* Loreto Convent, Dalkey and Balbriggan, UCD (1963–66) Psychology and Philosophy; Publisher, *Irish Arts Review*; Group Director & Co–Publisher *Image* Publications; chairman Hugh Lane, The City Gallery; Clubs: The Royal Irish Yacht Club, Fitzwilliam Lawn Tennis Club, Powerscourt Golf Club; Recreations: art, travel, reading, golf. Contact: IMAGE, 22, Crofton Road, Dun Laoghire, Co.Dublin Dublin. **T** 01 280 8415 email annreihill@ireland.com

> A successful, attractive businesswoman and publisher; great style; entertains beautifully.

Ann Reihill

REIHILL, John Philip; COMPANY CHAIRMAN

b 1933 Dublin; *m* 1st Eimear Collins (decd); 3*s* 3*d*; *m* Ann Dillon Malone, née Mc Coy; separated; 1*ss* 1*sd*; *edu.* Castleknock College, trained in Business Studies, England and US; chairman, Tedcastle Holdings; Clubs: Milltown Golf Club, Powerscourt Golf Club, Valderrama Golf Club, Royal Irish Yacht Club, Fitzwilliam Lawn Tennis Club, Stephens Green Hibernian Club, Carrickmines Tennis Club. Recreations: walking, golf, tennis, reading, art. Contact: Deepwell, Blackrock, Co. Dublin. **T** 01 288 8 352 **F** 01 283 1041

> A highly successful businessman who in his 70's reinvented his role in the family business; popular and highly respected; his pragmatic approach to all his business dealings continues to earn him the respect of his peers, no mean feat in a tough world.

REYNOLDS, Albert Martin; BUSINESSMAN, FORMER TAOISEACH

b 1932, Rooskey, Co. Roscommon; *m* Kathleen Coen; 2*s* 5*d*; *edu.* Summerhill College, Sligo; Businessman, Former Taoiseach and former politician;; elected to Dáil Éireann (FF) for Longford-Roscommon 1977; Minister Post & Telegraphs 1979-81; Minister for Energy 1982; Minister Industry & Commerce 1987-88; Minster, Finance 1988–91; Taoiseach /Prime Minister of Ireland 1992–94; retired from Dail Éireann,1997; and now a full time businessman; brokered ceasefire in Northern Ireland by signing Downing Street Declaration with UK PM John Major 1993; Recreations: racing, travel, current affairs, politics, reading. Contact: 18 Ailesbury Road, Ballsbridge, Dublin 4. **T** 01 260 3450 **F** 01 260 3434

> Straight talking, what you see is what you get; took many brave moves to secure the Downing Street Declaration (DSD) 1993; as minister for Post and Telegraphs tackled the then virtually non-existent telecommunications infrastructure; four imaginative budgets laid the stepping stones for the now booming economy; continues to actively comment on political developments within Northern Ireland.

REYNOLDS, Cathy Anne; DIRECTOR, KENNEDY PR

b 1971, Longford; *m* Niall Maloney; *edu.* La Sainte Union Convent, Banagher, Co. Offaly; University College Dublin, BA Economics & Politics (2.1 Hons); MBS Masters Business Studies (International Business) Smurfit Graduate School of Business; Director Kennedy PR; Jefferson Smurfit Group plc– sales, production, managerial roles; GJW Government Relations Ltd, London, director Communications Ireland; LVMH – Manager, Louis Vuitton Dublin; Louis Kennedy – fashion manager; account director Kennedy PR Public Relations, Dublin. Clubs: David Lloyd Health & Fitness Club Dublin. Recreations: current affairs, fashion, politics, gym, reading, travel. Contact: Kennedy PR., 2, Castle Street, Dublin 2. **T** 01 476 2000 **F** 01 476 2001 email: creynolds@kennedypr.ie

Cathy Reynolds

Sophisticated, hardworking, well informed PR practitioner; daughter of former Taoiseach Albert (*qv*) and his wife Kathleen, possesses the charm and joie de vivre that is the family's trademark.

REYNOLDS, John; CLUB OWNER

b 1966, Longford; single; *edu.* Castleknock College; Trinity College Dublin BBS; Nigh Club owner/hotel owner; managed Ministry of Sound Club (London); opened POD (Dublin) 1993, was co-manager, with Louis Walsh, of Boyzone; opened The Chocolate Bar, adjoining POD and Red Box; director The Home Clubs, designed by Ron McCullach, in Sydney (Australia), New York and London; joint owner with Eoin Foyle and Jay Bourke, Bellinter House, Co. Navan 2005. Recreations: music, interior design and football. Contact: POD, Harcourt Street, Dublin 2. **T** 01 478 0166 web www.pod.ie

A quiet and shy man who runs nightclubs which seems a contradiction; his newest joint venture in a Palladian Co. Meath mansion awaits completion and it may mark his move into other industries; keeps his nose clean and no scandal attaches to what could be a socially difficult area of entertainment; his private circle of friends admire and like him.

REYNOLDS, Philip; MANAGING DIRECTOR C & D FOODS

b 1964, Longford; *m* Anne Farrell; 2*s* 1*d*; *edu.* Cistercian College Roscrea; IMI Sandyford; joined family pet food manufacturing company, C & D Foods Ltd, 1982; production controller 1984-86, sales manager 1986-88, marketing director 1988-90, managing director 1999 to date; C & D Foods Ltd. Clubs: Lions Club, Mullingar, Mullingar Golf Club, Showjumping Association of Ireland; Recreations; racing, golf. Contact: C & D Foods Ltd., Edgworthstown, Co. Longford. **T** 043 71067 **F** 043 71388.

The eldest son of Albert Reynolds (*qv*) has proved an extremely able businessman, diversifying and expanding the family pet food business; articulate, gregarious could easily have been elected in his father's seat and enjoyed a successful political career; preferred to stick to the knitting and steer clear of politics to concentrate on business; coped extraordinarily well with major fire tragedy at C&D plant in Edgworthtown gaining praise and respect from both employees and clients alike.

REYNOLDS, Sonia; PR CONSULTANT and SPECIAL EVENTS MANAGER

b 1967, Lurgan, Co. Armagh; *m* Barry Lyons (*qv*); 1*s* 2*d*; *edu.* St. Michael's Grammar School, Lurgan, Co. Armagh. ; PR Consultant and Special Events Manager; Model (Fashion); Director, Dublin Fashion Week. Clubs: Odessa Club, Dublin. Recreations: travel, food and cooking, entertaining. Contact: 20 Garville Road, Rathgar, Dublin 6. **M** 087 221 9674 email sonia@soniareynolds.com

The beautiful redhead, former model has built up a successful fashion PR business; founded the now biannual Dublin Fashion Week; a great details person; hard working, enjoys life.

RICE, Rodney; JOURNALIST/BROADCASTER

b 1944, Antrim; *m* Margaret; 2*s* 1*d*; *edu.* The Royal Belfast Academical Institution; Trinity College Dublin, BA (Mod); Journalist/Broadcaster; 37 Years in television and radio; currently presenter of Saturday View & presenter/producer of Worlds Apart, RTE Radio One; Publ. *European Political Union* (with Paul Gillespie); Recreations: soccer, GAA, travel, politics, development. Contact: 14 Milltown Grove, Dublin 14. **T** 01 298 7174 email: ricer@rte.ie web www.rte.ie

A caring and incisive broadcaster full of Northern forthrightness; an unbiased political commentator with an encyclopedic knowledge of is chosen field.

ROBINSON, Iris; PUBLIC REPRESENTATIVE

b 1949, Belfast; *edu.* Knockbreda Intermediate School; Castlereagh Technical College; Public Representative, MP (DUP) Strangford; elected to Castlereagh Borough Council 1989 to date; served as Mayor of the Borough 1992 and 1995; elected to Northern Ireland Forum for Strangford constituency 1996-98; gained a seat in the new Northern Ireland Assembly 1998 to date; deputy leader DUP; returned MP for Strangford 2001 and in doing so joined her husband Peter Robinson (*qv*); memberships: Chairman (C.B.C) Staff and Office Accommodation - Ballybeen Square Regeneration Board; Director (C.B.C) Tullycarnet Community Enterprises Ltd; member Dundonald International Icebowl Board (C.B.C); member Central Services Committee (C.B.C); Recreations: fundraising for M.S., interior design. Contact: 2b James Street, Newtownards, BT23 4DY. **T** 028 9182 7701 **F** 028 9182 7703 email info@dup.org.uk web www.dup.org.uk

> A hard-working politician who is highly esteemed among her peers and in her local constituency; a good sense of humour stands her well.

ROCHA, John; DESIGNER

b 1953, Hong Kong; *m* 1st Eily Doolan (*m diss*); *m* 2nd Odette Gleeson; 1*s* 2*d*; *edu.* St. Luke's College, Hong Kong; state registered psychiatric nurse Banstead Hospital; Croydon College of Art & Design, Dip. Fashion Design; Designer; studied design in London; opened the first of his own shops in Ireland in 1985; in 1987 moved to Italy to work under licence for Reflections Milan, producing collections including Dries van Noten and Martine Sitbon; continued to produce his own collections; returned to Dublin 1989; continued to expand and promote the John Rocha Collections; shows twice yearly in London; launched menswear collection 1993; launched contemporary crystal range with Waterford Glass 1997; opened London Store (Sloane Avenue), 1998, stocking mainline collection, Rocha Jeans, crystal and home accessories; designed Virgin Atlantic uniform 1999; interior design for the Morrison Hotel, Dublin; Awards: 1994 British Designer of the Year; 1994 Honorary Doctor, University of Ulster; Clubs: The Groucho Club (London). Recreations: fly fishing, football, travel. Contact: John Rocha Studio, Hume Street, Dublin 2. **T** 01 662 9225 email john@johnrocha.ie web www.johnrocha.ie

John Rocha

> Internationally acclaimed designer whose fashion reputation is built on immaculate tailoring, creative knitwear plus his hand-painted and embroidered pieces; made a name quickly for himself as a designer of glassware for Waterford Crystal; passionate about design in general and his own work in particular, is one of Debenhams (UK) best selling designers.

ROCHE, Adi; VOLUNTEER AID WORKER

b 1995?, Clonmel, Co.Tippeary; *m* Seán Dunne; *edu.* Presentation Convent, Clonmel, Co. Tipperary; Volunteer and Aid Worker; began working on humanitarian projects 1977; Board of Directors, International Peace Bureau, Geneva 1990; founder and international executive director Chernobyl Children's Project 1991; unsuccessful candidate for the Irish Presidency 1997; Awards: 1998 Frantsysk Skryana Order, and the Liquidators Medal, Belarus; 1996 European Person of the Year and Irish Person of the Year; 2002 Cork Person of the Year and the Paul Harris Fellowship Award; 2002 LL.D., NUI (*hc*); University of Alberta Canada LL.D (*hc*); 2005 Humanitarian Award; Meteor Music Awards; 2005 Jim Larkin Peace and Justice Award (Labour Party); board member, Radiological Protection Institute of Ireland. *Publ. The Children of Chernobyl* 1996. Recreations: walking, music, reading. Contact: Chernobyl Children's Project International, Ballycurreen Industrial Estate, Kinsale Road, Cork. **T** 021 431 2999 **F** 021 431 3170 email mcgregorn@chernobyl.ireland.com web www.chernobyl.ireland.com

> Her drive and personal conviction helped her to set up the now well-respected Children of Chernobyl charity; a pleasant woman who emerged from her attempt to contest the presidency of Ireland badly bruised; returned to what she does best: humanitarian endeavour.

ROCHE, Donal; SOLICITOR AND COMPANY DIRECTOR

b 1953, Dublin; *m* Mary O'Flynn; 1*s* 3*d*; *edu.* Blackrock College, Dublin; Trinity College Dublin; MA. Legal Science (Hons) 1975; Kings Inns 1976; Incorporated Law Society 1980; Solicitor and Company Director; director Eircom Plc; director McInerney Holdings Plc; chairman Appian Wealth Management Ltd; chairman Murray Consultants Ltd; chairman DPS Ltd; director Rockhill Investments; Career: Gerrard Scallon & O'Brien Solicitors 1978-82; Matheson Ormsby Prentice 1982–2003; head of Corporate Law Division Matheson Ormsby Prentice 1990-2003; managing partner Matheson Ormsby Prentice 1994-2003. Clubs: Royal St. George Yacht Club, St. Stephen's Green Club, Kildare Hotel and country club. Club. Recreations: skiing, fishing, shooting, golf, yachting. Contact: 5 Upper Mount Street, Dublin 2. **T** 01 662 3987 **F** 01 661 9871 email donal.roche@appianwealth.ie

A member of the Roche (*Roadstone*) family, is witty, intelligent and congenial company; a gifted corporate lawyer, and one of the senior legal personnel in the capital; has advised captains and kings of industry, and state, on matters of crucial importance and at critical times; an important player currently on the Board of Eircom as it goes mobile and begins to attract the attention of Europe's telecom giants.

Dick Roche

ROCHE, Dick; PUBLIC REPRESENTATIVE

b 1947, Wexford; *m* Eleanor Griffin; 3*s* 1*d*; *edu.* Wexford Christian Brothers School; University College Dublin; B. Comm.; DPA; MPA; Public Representative, Minister for the Environment, Heritage and Local Government, TD Wicklow; University Lecturer; TD Wicklow 1987–92; Senator 1992–97; Minister of State at the Dept. of the Taoiseach and at the Dep. of Foreign Affairs (with special responsibility for European Affairs) 2002–04; former member of the Joint Committee on Public Enterprise and Transport; former member of the Committee on Procedure and Privileges; former chairman of the Oireachtas Joint Committee on State sponsored bodies and served on the Special Committee on Company Law; elected to Greystones Town Commission 1984 (Chairman 1987–88); elected to Wicklow County Council and Wicklow Vocational Education Committee 1985; appointed to Eastern Health Board 1987; appointed Minister for the Environment, Heritage and Local Government 2004 to date; past member of the International Ombudsman Institute and the Irish Council of the European Movement; past board member of the Institute of Public Administration; past chairman of Irish Commission for Justice and Peace; awards: 1979 United Nations Fellowship in Human Rights; Contact: 2 Herbert Terrace, Herbert Road, Bray, Co Wicklow. **T** 01 286 3211 **F** 01 286 7666 web www.dickroche.com

One of the most visible ministers in the Fianna Fail/PD government; an excellent media performer who he bats constantly in the highly fraught area of the Environment; ambitious, hardworking should move up the ladder in the next reshuffle.

ROCHE, Michael F; MANAGING DIRECTOR SUNDAY TRIBUNE

b 1955, Dublin; *m* 1st Tina Roche (*m diss*); 1*s*; *m* 2nd Carina; 1*s* 1*d*; *edu.* Terenure College, Dublin; Managing Director *Sunday Tribune* plc; financial journalist 1977-86; managing director Drogheda Independent Company Ltd, 1987 89; managing director People Newspaper Ltd, 1989-98; managing editor *Independent* Newspaper 1988–2005; managing director *Sunday Tribune* 2005 to date. Clubs: Grange Golf Club, Lahinch Golf Club, Rosslare Golf Club, Terenure College RFC. Recreations: golf, rugby. Contact: Sunday Tribune,15, Lower Baggot Street, Dublin 2. **T** 01 631 4300 **F** 01 661 5302

Outgoing and gregarious, a shrewd operator who is particularly well connected in his company; after much budget slashing appears to have turned the tide at the Trib and could well be heading for richer pastures in the not too distant future.

ROCHFORD, Niall John; HOTELIER

b 1969; *m* Stella; 1*s* 1*d*; *edu.* Abbey Christian Brothers School, Tipperary Town, Dublin College of Catering, Cathal Brugha St. Dublin, Diploma Hotel Management; Diploma Business Studies; General Manager Ashford Castle Hotel; deputy general manager, Dromoland Castle 1998-2002; general manager Ashford Castle Hotel 2002 to date; Recreations: all sports, food, wine, hotels; Contact: Ashford Castle, Cong, Co. Mayo **T** 094 954 6003 email naillrochford@ashfordh.ie

Personable and warm, with a career in the luxury hotel business is breathing new life into one of Ireland's most beautiful castles; well respected in the hotel industry where he is regarded as a top class operator.

ROGERS, Michael Joseph; CEO THE SALES INSTITUTE OF IRELAND

b 1942, Dublin; *m* Hilary; 3*s* 1*d*; *edu.* Drimnagh Castle CBS; DIT Kevin Street, Dublin 2; CEO The Sales Institute of Ireland. Sales and marketing director, Cara Group 1991-97; managing director Bull Cara Group 1997–00; managing director Bic Systems Ltd 2002–03; fellow Irish Computer Society (FICS); fellow Sales Institute of Ireland (FSSI); member Marketing Institute of Ireland MMII; member Institute of Directors (MIOD); Clubs: Newlands Golf Club, Hibernian Golf Club. Recreations: fly fishing for salmon, shooting, aviation, golf, horse racing. Contact: Sales Institute of Ireland, 68, Merrion Square, Dublin 2. **T** 01 662 6904 **F** 01 662 6978 email mjrogers@salesinstitute.ie

One of the pioneers of the computer revolution in Ireland, a charismatic, amiable businessman; with a diverse range of business interests; brings an energy to all of his endeavours; extremely loyal to his friends.

ROGERS, Sonia, née Pilkington; BLOODSTOCK BREEDER

b 1937; *m* 1st Capt. Tim Rogers, MC.(decd.); 2*s*; *m*. 2nd Ib Jorgensen (*qv*) (*m diss*); *edu*. Tudor Hall, Oxford; Owner/Manager Airlie Group of Studs - Airlie, Grangewilliam, Simmonstown, Kilmacredock; Winners: Bachelor Duke (Irish Two Thousand Guineas), Margarula (Irish Oaks), Petrushka (Irish Oaks, Yorkshire Oaks and Prix De l'Opera) and in 2004 Group One winner, Chelsea Rose (Moyglare Stud Stakes); has horses in training in UK and Ireland; member, Irish Turf Club; director, Goff's Bloodstock Sales; Steward of the Turf Club Dec 2005. Recreations: racing, visual arts, travel, gardening. Contact: Airlie Stud, Grangewilliam, Maynooth, Co. Kildare. **T** 01 628 6336 **F** 01 628 6674 email info@airliestud.com web www.airliestud.com

Daughter of the formidable Mrs Burke of Stackallen House and Sir Arthur Pilkington; internationally acknowledged bloodstock breeder; famous bred horses include Petrushka, Margarula, Bachelor Duke, and Cinnamon Rose; gregarious, charming and great company; does not suffer fools gladly.

ROHAN, Kenneth Charles 'Ken'; CHAIRMAN/CEO ROHAN HOLDINGS LTD

b 1944; Cork; *m* Brenda Mac Manus; 2*s* 1*d*; St. Gerard's College, Bray, Castleknock College, Dublin; Chairman & Chief Executive Rohan Holdings Ltd (Property Development & Investment Company); member, board of National Gallery of Ireland 1998 -03. Contact: 5, Mount Street Crescent, Dublin 2. **T** 01 662 4455

Extremely successful businessman who has diversified his interest in recent years; would not be closely associated with the new property boys, the plasterers, brickies or blockies; very reserved, very private, maintains a low profile in this country; an astute investor in fine art, has transformed his home into one of the greatest private homes in Ireland.

ROLFE, Angela Susan ARCHITECT

b 1952, England; *m* Nigel Rolfe; 2*s* 1*d*; *edu*. Farnham Girls Grammar School, Farnham, Surrey; Bath University 1970-74; B.Sc (Hons); University College Dublin; B. Arch.(hons); IMI Certificate Programme in project management 1998; MSc Urban Design, University of Ulster, 2003-05; Senior Architect Office of Public Works, Dublin; adjudicator Bord Fáilte Tidy Towns Competition 1977; visual arts organiser Project Arts Centre 1978; assistant architect Stephenson Associates 1978-79; contracts manager Inside Limited 1979-80; architect Office of Public Works1980-86; Herbert Newman Architects, New Haven, Connecticut, USA 1983; senior architect Office of Public Works, Dublin OPW 1996 to date; projects to date include: decentralised & centralised Government Offices, Sligo,1980-83; Dublin Castle restoration projects,1981-89; Government Buildings,1990; RIAI Silver Medal for Conservation 1987-92; fit out of government jet, Dept of Industry & Commerce & offices for the State 1991, 1992; Irish Marine Emergency Service1993; Mespil Road offices for Depts of Equality, Law Reform, Arts Culture and Gaeltactht; Johnstown Castle, Co.Wexford 1994; Chester Beatty Library 1994-95; various in-house projects and consultative committees including the Percent for Art Schemes; universal accessibility auditor The Centre for Universal Accessibility in the Built Environment, University of Ulster, 2002; chair of the Draft Development Plan Work Group, co-ordinating submissions 2004; *Publ. The Department of Industry and Commerce Kildare Street, Dublin,* 1992; Contact: Office of Public Works, 51, St. Stephens Green, Dublin 2. **T** 01 647 6000 **F** 01 661 0747 email angela.rolfe@opw.ie web www.opw.ie

Angela Rolfe

RONAN, Dr Louis; CHAIRMAN/CHIEF EXECUTIVE ENFER SCIENTIFIC

b 1955, Clonmel; *m* Kate Mc Auliffe; 1*s* 1*d*; *edu*. St Gerard's College, Bray, Co. Wicklow; Clongowes Wood College, Co. Kildare; University College Dublin; B.Sc; M. Sc; Ph.D; chemist; Chairman, Chief Executive Enfer Scientific; joined family rendering business; started Enfer Scientific early 1990's; Clubs: RIAC, Dublin. Recreations: racing, shooting, squash, GAA, rugby. Contact: Unit 4, Boxer House, Newbridge Industrial Estate, Newbridge, Co. Kildare. **T** 045 435821 **T** 045 434607 email info@enferscientific.com web www.enferscientific.com

Charismatic, low-profile and hugely publicity shy, his company was the first biotechnology company worldwide to develop a rapid test screening system for BSE;

despite his enormous success stays close to his roots; sponsors Tipperary GAA team; was the victim of a scurrilous campaign when he attempted to set up an incinerator in Co. Tipperary; now planning to build a crematorium.

ROONEY, Marie; DEPUTY DIRECTOR, GATE THEATRE
b 1951, Dublin; single; *edu.* St. Marys Holy Faith Convent, Glasnevin, Dublin; marketing, Irish Management Institute, Dublin; Deputy Director, Gate Theatre; deputy Director responsible for theatre management, public affairs, PR/Media campaigns, marketing, event management, overseeing theatre building development; marketing and PR manager Gate Theatre; previously assistant to Hilton Edwards (founder Gate Theatre); public relations officer Perstorp AB, Sweden; founding deputy chair ILE –Ireland Literature Exchange 1995–01; joined the board of Second Age Theatre Company, 2005; member of Beckett Centenary Festival Committee 2006; *Publ.* editorial advisor on *Tom Lawlor at The Gate Dublin* (Design Inc 1997). Recreations: sailing, photography, music, languages. Contact: Gate Theatre, Cavendish Row, Dublin 1. **T** 01 874 4368 **F** 01 874 5373 email marie.rooney@gate-theatre.ie

Bright and enthusiastic, part of the fabric of the Gate Theatre and responsible for much of its success, is extraordinary hardworking and focused; always has a smile and a welcome for everyone at the bijoux theater, extremely popular.

ROSNEY, Bride; RTE DIRECTOR OF COMMUNICATIONS
b 1949, Caherciveen, Co. Kerry; *partner* Peter MacMenamin; *edu.* Dominican College, Dublin 7; University College Dublin, B.Sc, H.Dip.Ed,; Trinity College Dublin, Dip. Cmp. Ed., M.Sc.; RTE Director of Communications; teacher, Second Level Education (various posts) 1971-75 & 1980–90; Third Level 1975–79; special adviser to President Mary Robinson and subsequently High Commissioner Robinson, UNHCHR 1990–98; executive director Bill O'Herlihy Communications 1999–01. *Publ.* various educational publications 1976–88. Recreations: reading, theatre, travel, media. Contact: 127, Grace Park Manor, Dublin 9. **M** 087 244 0490 email bride.rosney@rte.ie web www.rte.ie

This school teacher turned presidential and United Nations High Commissioner advisor; has settled in well as head of Corporate Affairs in RTE; the bright, articulate, Kerry native will require her formidable country cunning to avoid the many political minefields that make up RTE.

ROSS, Seamus; CHAIRMAN/CHIEF EXECUTIVE MENOLLY HOMES
b 1951, Longford; *m* Moira Whelan; 3*s* 3*d*; Chairman/Chief executive Menolly Homes; extensive building and property interests; director with Michael Smurfit (*qv*) C and G Hotels; owner dylan Hotel, Dublin; Dunboyne Castle, Co. Meath; hotel at Farmleigh, Castleknock, Dublin. Clubs: Kildare Hotel and Country Club. Recreations: golf, GAA, horseracing. Contact: 4, The Mall, Main Street, Lucan, Co. Dublin. **T** 01 626 2690 **F** 01 628 2699 email info@menolly.ie web www.menolly.ie

Extremely hard-working, tough businessman who believes in selling volume at attractive prices; could claim to be the biggest house builder in Ireland; successful bloodstock owner; new sponsor of the Meath GAA team.

ROSS, Shane; PUBLIC REPRESENTATIVE, JOURNALIST
b 1949, Dublin; *m* Ruth Buchanan; 1*s* 1*d*; *edu.* Rugby School, England; Trinity College Dublin, BA (Mod) History & Politics; Public Representative, Independent Senator/Journalist; ex-chairman, two Stockbroking companies; ex-chairman Kleinworth European Privatisation Investment Trust; ex Stock Exchange correspondent *Irish Times*; independent Senator (Trinity College Dublin) to date; Business Editor *Sunday Independent* to date. Clubs: Kildare Street & University. Recreations: tennis, food, France; travel, skiing, gardens, dogs. Contact: Seanad Eireann, Leinster House, Dublin 2. **T** 01 618 3014 **F** 01 618 4192 email shane.ross@oireachtas.ie

Provocative, outspoken TCD Senator has carved out a more influential role as business editor of *the Sunday Independent* than in the Upper House; has an in-depth knowledge of corporate Ireland from his stockbroking days and knows all the right buttons to push; a passionate advocate of many important issues like the abolition of tolls on the M 50; may not be a regular guest in the private dining room of the bigger banks but is an informed contributor on their activities in print and on the airwaves.

Shane Ross

ROSSE, Rt Hon Earl of , Sir William Brendan Parsons; BARONET, LAND, HERITAGE HOUSE, AND GARDENS OWNER
b 1936, *m* Alison Margaret Cooke-Hurle; 2*s* 1*d*; *edu.* Aiglon College, Switzerland; Grenoble University; Christ Church Oxford; BA; MA; Baronet; became 7th.Earl of Rosse (cr.1806) in 1979; Baronet (cr.1677); Baron Oxmantown (cr.1792) all in the peerage and baronetage of Ireland; second lieut Irish Guards 1955-57; UN Official 1963-80, served successively Ghana, Dahomey, Mid-West Africa, Algeria, as first UN Volunteer Field Director, Iran, UN Disaster Relief Co-ordinator Bangladesh; Government of Ireland member, Advisory Council on Development Co-operation 1984-89; director, Personal Service Overseas 1986-90; founder and director, Birr Scientific & Heritage Foundation 1985 to date; director, Historic Irish Tourist Houses and Gardens Association 1980-91; director, Lorne House Trust 1993 to date; director, The Tree Register 1989 to date; Lord of the Manor Womersly and Woodhall, Yorks; Newtown, Parsonstown, and Roscomroe, Ireland. FRAS., Hon. FIEI. Contact; Birr Castle, Co. Offaly. **T** 0509 20023 web www.birrcastle.com

With his charming and talented wife Alison has provided a safe future for the family home at Birr; has sustained and improved on the architectural and arboreal developments by his late parents, Michael, Lord Rosse and Anne Messel, Lady Rosse; has found a new role in modern Ireland for an historic title and all that goes with it; thoroughly modern in approach to keeping the immensely important scientific heritage of his family with the Birr Telescope; has managed to keep the regional development authorities on side and thereby gives the Shannon midlands region an important cultural tourism site

ROTHWELL, Eamon; CHIEF EXECUTIVE IRISH FERRIES
b 1956, Dublin; *m*; 3 children; *edu.* University College Dublin; B. Comm, M.A. (marketing); Chief Executive Irish Continental Ferries; journalist *Irish Business magazine*; Bord Failte 1978–82; Allied Irish Investment Bank 1982–1986; head of Equities National City Brokers (NCB) 1986–1991; Irish Continental Ferries 1992 to date. Clubs: Recreations: Contact: Irish Continental Ferries, P.O. Box 19, Alexandra Road, Dublin 1. **T** 01 855 2222 **F** 01 855 2272 email info@irishferries.com web www.irishferries.com

Former merchant banker, hard-nosed businessman has headed up Irish Continental Ferries where, other than receiving new vessels had kept a very low profile until 2005, when he attempted to replace his local crew with a low paid, Eastern European staff; led to a winter of serious discontent 2005 and became a household name for all the wrong reasons.

RUSSELL, Joseph James; GENERAL MANAGER, DOONBEG GOLF CLUB
b 1966; *m* Patricia; 1*s* 2*d*; *edu.* Christian Brothers School, Templemore, Co Tipperary; various Industry certificates and awards; General Manager, Doonbeg Golf Club; early 1990's commenced management career in the hotel industry in London; returned to Ireland 1997; general manager Jury's Hotel and Towers in Ballsbridge; general manager of Berkeley Court 1999-03; general manager, Doonbeg Lodge & Golf Club Development 2003 to date; Clubs; Club Managers Association of Europe, Part of " The Power of Focus" Concept (self development), Clubs, Templemore Golf Club, Doonbeg Golf Club: Recreations: all sports, GAA, golf, swimming, reading, listening to good music, family activities of various sorts. Contact: Doonbeg Golf Club, Doonbeg, Co Clare. **T** 065 905 5610 **F** 065 9055247 email Joe_Russell@doonbeggolfclub.com web www.doonbeggolfclub.com

The well regarded hotelier turned his back on 5 star Dublin hotels to head the magnificent new development in West Clare where already he has made his mark; the adjoining golf course is one of the most challenging on the Irish circuit.

RYALL, Christine; REPRESENTATIVE, CHRISTIES AUCTIONEERS AND VALUERS IRELAND
b 1945, Germany; *m* Patrick Ryall; *edu.* Germany; Royal Society of Arts and College of Commerce Bristol; Sorbonne, Paris; Institute of Languages Stuttgart, Germany; Representative in Ireland for Christies Auctioneers and Valuers; correspondent for Foreign Economic Affairs, Berlin 1962-68; sales & marketing British Airways, Berlin & Northern Ireland 1968-86; representative for Phillips International Fine Art Auctioneers in Ireland; representative in Ireland for Christies; member of Committee of the Friends of St. Patrick's Hospital. Recreations: cooking, tennis, wine tasting, reading. Contact: Christies Auctioneers & Valuers, The Old Rectory, Moone, Athy, Co. Kildare. **T** 059 862 4130 **F** 059 862 4280 web www.christies.com

A savvy, soignée representative for a great and important London Fine Art auction house; is greatly liked and admired by her working colleagues in the industry; brings great pzazz to the fine art scene.

RYAN, Arthur; CHAIRMAN/CEO PENNEYS, PRIMARK

b 1935, Dublin; *m* 1st (*m diss*); 3s 1d; *m* 2nd Alma Carroll; 1d; *edu.* Christian Brothers School, Synge Street, Dublin; worked in Swan and Edgar, London (tie buyer); returned to Ireland joined Dunnes Stores; joined Penneys late 1950's; now 35 stores in Ireland; opened first UK store, Derby, 1974 (now 90 UK stores); 2 stores in Spain; expects to open 35 new stores by March 2007; bought Littlewoods, UK 2005 – 46 stores coming on stream as Primark 2006; Recreations: work ! (enjoys watching sport on television). Contact: Primark/Penneys Stores, PO Box 644, 47, Mary Street, Dublin 1. **T** 01 872 7788 web www.primark.co.uk

Voted The Most Influential Man in British High Street Retailing by Drapers Record, 2005, is considered a genius by his international peers and hugely respected by his staff; a charming, low profile, extraordinary hard working, down to earth executive, eschews all of the frippery associated with the fashion industry; originally spotted by Garfield Weston while dressing a window in Dunnes Stores, Dublin in the 1950's; the rest is fashion retail history.

RYAN, Brendan; PUBLIC REPRESENTATIVE

b 1964, Athy; *m* Clare O'Connell; 1s 2d; *edu.* Christian Brothers School, Athy; Divine Word Seminary, Roscommon, University College Dublin; BE. Chemical Engineering; Public Representative; Senator, Leader Labour Group Seanad Eireann; political career began as a campaigner for the homeless through the Simon Community; Senator 1981–93 and 1997 to date; previously a member of Oireachtas Joint Committees on Development Co-operation and European Affairs, and Committee on Seanad Reform; current member of JC on Foreign Affairs and Seanad Committee on Procedure and Privileges; current president, Cork Simon Community; *Publ. Keeping us in the Dark* (Gill & MacMillan, 1995), contributions to a number of other books. Recreations: music, politics, reading, sport. Contact: Seanad Éireann, Kildare Street, Dublin 2. **T** 021 450 2213/ 01 618 3417 **F** 01 618 4192 email brendan.ryan@oireachtas.ie/brryan@indigo

The Kildare born, Labour Senator has a national reputation for articulating the issues of the disadvantaged; his star has waned in recent years as economic prosperity spread throughout the country.

RYAN, Eoin; PUBLIC REPRESENTATIVE

b 1953, Dublin; *m* Sheila McKeever; 1s 2d; *edu.* Willow Park School, Dublin; St. Mary's College Rathmines, Dublin; Kildalton Agricultural College, Co. Killkenny; Public Representative; Member European Parliament; commercial career in health food shops and restaurant; consultancy work for Europe; member of Dublin Corporation/ Dublin City Council 1989-00; member of Seanad Éireann (Taoiseach's nominee) 1989-92; member of Dáil Eireann Dublin South East 1992-04; member of the European Parliament (Fianna Fáil) 2004 to date; Union for a Europe of Nations Group (UEN); member of Economic and Monetary Affairs Committee European Parliament; Recreations: walking, swimming, music. Contact: (Office) ASP 04F353. **T** 00 32-2-284.5612 (Brussels) **T** 00 33-3-88.17.5612 (Strasbourg) **F** 0032-2-284.9612 (Brussels) **F** 00 33-3-88.17.9612 (Strasbourg) email eryan@europarl.eu.int web eoinryan.ie

The third generation of his family in politics; gracious, polite and civilised like his father and grandfather before him; briefly a Minister of State, the party did not particularly smile on him, may do so again if he chooses to return to frontline politics at home; still a solid vote winner.

RYAN Gerry; RADIO/TELEVISION PRESENTER

b 1956, Dublin; *m* Morah Brennan; 2s 3d; *edu.* St. Paul's School, Raheny; Trinity College Dublin; Incorporated Law Society; Radio/TV Presenter; Solicitor's apprentice Malone and Potter Solicitors, Dublin; joined RTE 1979, hosting mini chat show for Radio 2; Gerry Ryan Show (morning chat show) 1988 to date; presenter of the popular television show: Secrets and School Around the Corner, Ryan Confidential, Gerry Ryan's Hit List. Awards: Jacobs Award for the Gerry Ryan Show Radio 1991; Sunday Independent/Irish Life Radio Arts Award 1989; Recreations: reading, cinema, television, helicopter, flying. Contact: RTE, Donnybrook, Dublin 4. **T** 01 208 3111 web www.rte.ie

One of RTE's greatest assets; charismatic, professional, unpretentious and hardworking but obviously enjoys every minute of it; appeals to a huge cross-section of men and women of all ages with his down to earth approach to life; good sense of humour; doesn't preach or pontificate.

RYAN, Jerry; ARCHITECT AND MANAGING DIRECTOR
b 1958; *m* Veronica Ryan; 3*d*; *edu* CBS Nenagh; UCD School of Architecture, B Arch, MRIAT, RIBA; Architect; set up HKR Architects 1992; built it from a staff of 1 to 130 today with projected turnover of €20 million this year; designed Smithfield Market; New Bray Town Centre; Belfield Office Campus; David LIoyd Tennis Centre; opened practice in London (25 staff); plans for a further expansion this year. Clubs: Tulfarris Golf Club. Recreations: family, work, socialising, people. Contact: HKR 5, School House Lane, Dublin 2. **T** 01 663 6400 **F** 01 663 6401

RYAN, Margaret Cecily; MARKETING CONSULTANT
b 1961, Birr, Co. Offaly; *p* Brian Kennedy; *edu.* University of Limerick; BA, European Studies; Managing Director, Margaret Ryan Marketing; sales & marketing director Ryan Hotels Plc, established own company 1999; managing director Magaret Ryan Marketing 1999 to date. Recreations: walking, travel. Contact: 6, Bannaville, Ranelagh, Dublin 6. **T** 01 496 2932 email mryanmarketing@eircom.net

Bright, well connected, hardworking marketing guru with international experience which is reflected in her blue chip clientele.

RYAN, Matthew; JEWELLER
b 1944, Thurles, Co. Tipperary; single; *edu.* Christian Brothers Thurles; Jeweller; trained as a jeweller with Kneisel; Jeweller; joined the family jewellery business; specialises in equestrian jewellery and racing trophies; Racing Steward; Clubs: Aspinalls, London, Royal Dublin Society, South Tipperary Racing. Recreations: horse riding, racing, driving. Contact: Liberty Square, Thurles, Co. Tipperary. **T** 0504 21161

Utterly gregarious, most sought after dinner and weekend house guest; great style, mingles internationally with consummate ease; a talented, innovative jeweller; boasts an A list worldwide clientele.

RYAN, Michael James; VICE PRESIDENT & GENERAL MANAGER BOMBARDIER, BELFAST
b 1959, Belfast; *m* Mary; 2*s* 1*d*; *edu.* St. Mary's Grammar School, Belfast; Queen's University, Belfast, hons degree in Aeronautical Engineering; Vice-President & General Manager Bombardier, Belfast; various management positions in Bombardier including general manager Advanced Composites Unit 1989; general manager Fabrications: 1999 transferred to Montreal as GM Procurement, Bombardier, Aerospace; vice-president and general manager Bombardier Aerospace, Northern Ireland 2000 to date; awarded CBE 2005; member board Maydown Precision Engineering; member Aerospace Committee, Dept. Trade and Industry; SBAC council member; board ,member Center for Competitiveness; Fellow Royal Aeronautical Society; member Institution Mechanical Engineers; Recreations: gym, music, reading, wine. Contact: Bombardier Aerospace, Airport Road, Belfast BT3 9DZ. **T** 028 90 733 552 **F** 028 90 733 143 email diane.willis@aero.bombardier.com

RYAN, Nicky; MUSIC PRODUCER / MANAGER, ENYA
b Dublin; *m* Roma (*qv*); 2*d*; Music Producer/ Manager ENYA; producer albums: *Enya* (1987); *Shepherd Moons* (1991), *The Celts* (1992), *The Memory of Trees* (1996); *Paint The Sky With Stars* (1997); awards: Oscar Nominee For Best Original song "*May It Be*"; Golden Globe Nominee For Best Original song " *May It Be*"; Ivor Novello Winner For International Achievement; 5 Monte Carlo World Music Awards; Grammy Winner for Production - *A Day Without Rain*; Hot Press Music Critics Awards; Contact: Warner Music, The Sky Lab, 2nd Floor, 2, Exchange Street Upper, Dublin 2. **T** 01 881 4500

RYAN, Roma; LYRICIST / CO- MANAGER, ENYA
b Dublin; *m* Nicky Ryan (*qv*); 2*d*; Lyricist/ Co Manager ENYA; awards, Oscar Nominee For Best Original song *"May It Be"*; Golden Globe Nominee For Best Original song " *May It Be"*; Ivor

Roma Ryan

Novello Winner For International Achievement; Albums: *Enya* (1987); *Shepherd Moons* (1991), *The Celts* (1992), *The Memory of Trees* (1996), *Paint The Sky With Stars* (1997), Album and singles Awards: *Watermark* – IFPI Platinum European Award; *Shepherd Moons* – Grammy Award Winner; IFPI Platinum European Award; billboard Music Award; NARM Best Selling Album Award; *The Memory of Trees* – Grammy Award Winner; *A Day Without Rain* – Grammy Award Winner; Japanese Grand Prix Album of the Year; *Paint the Sky with Stars* - Japanese Grand Prix Album of the Year; *Only Time* – Echo Award; BMI Citation of Achievement; *Orinoco Flow* – BMI Special Citation of Achievement; *May It Be* – Las Vegas Film Critic Society for best Original Song; Phoenix Film Critics Award for best original song; BFCA (Broadcast Film Critics Award) Best Song; Filmography: The 74th Annual Academy Awards (2002) (song "May It Be" from *The Lord of the Rings; The Fellowship of the Ring; The Lord of the Rings: The Fellowship of the Ring* (2001) (songs *Aníron & May It Be*; *Enya: The Video Collection* (2001); themes from *Calmi Cuori Appassionati* (2001); *Sweet November* (2001, song 'Only Time'); *Cry, the Beloved Country* (1995); TV Series *"Perla Negra"* (1994, songs from *Shepard's Moons, Watermark* and *The Celts*); *Toys* (1992); *Far and Away* (1992, song 'Books of Days'); *Sleepwalkers* (1992, song 'Boadicea'); *L.A. Story* (1991); *Enya: Moonshadows* (1991); *Green Card* (1990); TV Series *The Celts* (1987); TV Series *The Frog Prince* (1984): Contact: Warner Music, The Sky Lab, 2nd Floor, 2, Exchange Street Upper, Dublin 2. **T** 01 881 4500

Primary lyricist for Enya (*qv*) who has stated that the importance of Roma's and Nicky's contributions are such that without them, "Enya" would not exist; invented new language 'Loxian' for Enya's album Amarantine 2005.

RYAN, Ronan; CO-OWNER, TOWN BAR AND GRILL, DUBLIN
b 1970, Limerick; *m*; separated; 1*s*; *edu*. CBC Thurles, trained as chef; City &Guilds 7061/2; Co-Owner Town Bar and Grill Dublin; previously manager Mermaid Café; Co-owner Town Bar and Grill 2004 to date; co owner Town Bar and Grill, Sandyford, Co. Dublin, 2007. Recreations: all things Italiano, vino, Formula One Motor Racing. Contact: Town Bar and Grill, 21, Kildare Street, Dublin 2. **T** 01 6624800 **F** 01 663 3857 email ronanryan@mac.com

The energetic co owner of Town bar and Grill Dublin hit the ground running and made his new eatery the 'in' place in Dublin during its first year in business; savvy and switched on, extremely hard worker, adored by his blue chip clientele; his new eatery in Sandyford, Co. Dublin will open in February 2007.

Ronan Ryan

RYAN, Thomas Gerard Francis; CHAIRMAN/CHIEF EXECUTIVE RYAN INTERNATIONAL CORPORATION.
b 1969, Co. Tipperary; single; *edu*. St Josephs College, Tipperary: Chairman/Chief Executive Ryan International Corporation; joined Bill O' Herlihy Public Relations 1990–92; set up own lobbying and public relations company 1992; formed Ryan International Corporation 1993; Frazcer Group Aviation (US) 1994; formed Ryans Irish Cream Liqueur 1995; director Denver Properties; director Ireland United States Council for Commerce & Industry. Clubs: Metropolitan club, New York. Recreations: sailing, motor boat racing, rugby. Contact: Ryan International Corporation, Ryan House, 13, Herbert Street, Dublin 2. **T** 01 642 4900 **F** 01 642 5633 : email tgfryan@eircom.net

Low-profile businessman who has diversified into property; continues to operate successfully in the US and Europe; extremely well connected internationally.

Tom Ryan

RYAN, Dr. Thomas Anthony 'Tony' CHAIRMAN, IRELANDIA INVESTMENTS
b 1936, Co. Tipperary; *m* Mairead; separated; 3*s*; *edu*. Christian Brothers School, Thurles, Co. Tipperary; Chairman, Irlandia Investments; held senior management positions Aer Lingus, Shannon Airport, Chicago, station manager New York; founder GPA Group plc, 1975; went out of business 1992; chairman of GPA 1985–93; founder Ryanair 1985; major donor The Martin Ryan Institute - marine science research NUI Galway 1992; served as a director Ryanair Holdings 1996 to date; director Ryanair Limited 1995 to date; chairman Ryanair Holdings (Aug-Dec 1996); chairman Ryanair Ltd (Jan 1996-Dec 1996); executive chairman General Electric Capital Corporation ("GECC") 1993-96; made $55 million from sale of AerFi aircraft leasing company 2002; conferred with honorary doctorates by Trinity College, Limerick University and NUI; founding chairman of the Hunt Museum, Limerick; has served as a governor of the National Gallery of Ireland; funded a chair in aviation technology, University of Limerick; helped found and sponsor an international piano competition, the GPA International Piano Competition; Awards: Chambers of Commerce of Ireland Air Transport Users Council first and only Life Achievement Award 2005. Recreations: farming, horse breeding, collecting art, antiques. Contact: 9, Merrion Square, Dublin 2. **T** 01 661 2843

Tough minded, hard nosed and hugely successfully businessman; legacy can be seen in Shannon where a whole cluster of industries employing well over a thousand people has formed around the airport directly as a result of his commitment to the area; upwards of 40 aviation related companies operating out of the IFSC grew out of GPA; upper echelons of that industry worldwide is dotted with GPA alumni; greatest quality probably his ability to pick outstanding people; has nurtured multi-millionaires Michael O'Leary (*qv*) and Denis O'Brien (*qv*); many lesser entrepreneurs would not have survived the collapse of GPA following the aborted IPO 1993; bounced back from the edge of personal financial ruin with Ryanair providing the lift-off; revolutionized the airline industry with low cost fares; brought celebrity chef Richard Corrigan to his two restaurants at Lyons Desmene, Co. Kildare, 2006.

Tony Ryan

RYAN, Thomas; ARTIST
b 1929, Limerick; *m* Mary Theresa Joyce; 4*s* 2*d*; *edu.* Christian Brothers Schools, Sexton St, Limerick; Limerick School of Art; National College of Art, Dublin; Painter; designer of coins, medals and stamps; art master for a period Limerick School of Art; instructor in the School of Painting, National College of Art, Dublin; president Royal Hibernian Academy of Arts 1982-92; member board of governors & guardians National Gallery of Ireland 1982-92 (*ex officio*); honorary member *jure dignatis* Royal Academy of Arts, London; Royal Scottish Academy, Edinburgh, Scotland; NCAD (National College of Art) stamp design advisory committee An Post; president United Arts Club Dublin; founder member European Council of Academies of Art (Madrid); Water Colour Society of Ireland; Friends of the National Collections of Ireland; Knight of the Order of St. Lazarus of Jerusalem (KLJ); Knight Commander of the Equestrian Order of the Holy Sepulchre of Jerusalem (KCHS); D.Litt.(*hc*) University of Limerick; former council member The British Institution, London, The British School in Rome; works represented in: Houses of the Oireachtas, Dublin, University of Limerick, The Hunt Museum Limerick and many other national and international collections; signs work Thomas Ryan (*itals*); Contact: Robertstown Lodge, Robertstown, Ashbourne, Co. Meath. **T** 01 8350198

Passionately in love with the art of painting and drawing; eschews modernism in all its forms; with great brio and panache his vision might be thought to be greater than his delivery; is in every sense a great salon painter of the great and the good in a formal 19th century way.

SARGENT, Trevor Harold; PUBLIC REPRESENTATIVE
b 1960, Dublin; *m* Heidi Bedell; *edu.* The High School, Harcourt Street, Dublin 2; Coláiste Oideachais, Eaglais na hÉireann (C.I.C.E), Coláiste na Tríonóide, BÁC (TCD); B.A (Mod); Public Representative, T.D. Dublin North; Leader Green Party. Teacher Dunmanway, Co Cork 1981; Principal of St. George's National School Balbriggan, Co Dublin 1983; founder director of SONAIRTE (ecological visitor centre), Laytown, Co Meath 1988; elected to Dublin County Council 1991; elected to Dáil Éireann for Dublin North 1993; leader of the Green Party in Ireland 2001 to date; also spokesperson Agriculture, Food, Northern Ireland; Gaeltacht; *Publ. 'The Bible and Politics'* (lecture for Hibernian Bible Society) and several newspapers and articles in books and periodicals; Clubs: Birdwatch Ireland, Organic Farming Organisations, Amnesty International, An Taisce, Friends of the Earth, Fingal Cycling Club. Recreations: organic growing, teaching Irish, singing, playing guitar, reiki, cycling, walking, bird watching, spirituality. Contact: 37, Tara Cove, Bailebrigín, Co B.Á.C. **T** 01 890 0360 **F** 01 8900361 email trevor.sargent@oireachtas.ie

The former primary school principal is an articulate, hard-working Dáil deputy; he has clearly stamped the Green Party's mark on the political landscape but finds difficulty in aligning it with the Rainbow coalition's jigsaw; with a more flexible approach to politics he could well find himself feature in a future government.

SAUNDERS, John; PUBLIC RELATIONS CONSULTANT
b 1958, Dublin; *m* Jean; 1*s* 2*d*; *edu.* Belvedere College S.J. Dublin; Omnicom University, Babson College, USA; Regional Director Europe, Fleishman Hilliard; former presenter RTÉ; founded Fleishman-Hilliard Saunders 1990 - Fleishman Hilliard is now Ireland's largest PR firm; Regional Director Europe Fleishman-Hilliard and Member of Global Management Committee 2004 to date; President ICCO(Global Industry Body for PR Profession) 2006-07; former chairman Public Relations Consultants Association of Ireland; occasional contributor *'Newstalk'*; sports presenter, Setanta TV; regular speaker on international P.R. issues at global events and conferences Iceland, India, Iran, Hong Kong and Turkey. Clubs: Fitzwilliam LTC; Hon. Life Member Everton Supporters Club, Dublin. Recreations: enjoys most sports. Contact: Fleishman–Hilliard, Fitzwilliam Quay, Dublin 4. **T** 01 618 8444 **F** 01 660 2244 email hudsons@fleishmaneurope.com

The gregarious former Century Radio sports broadcaster has emerged as a major player in the world of international public relations with his appointment as regional director of Fleishman Hilliard Europe; always personable he has built up a powerful range of contacts in the international business, political and sporting worlds; was responsible for the unprecedented success of the Budweiser Irish Derby for over twenty years; innovative, creative, accessible businessman who still enjoys life and remembers his friends.

Patricia Scanlan

SCANLAN, Patricia; WRITER
b 1956, Dublin; single; *edu.* St Pappins NS; Dominican College, Eccles Street, Dublin; Writer. librarian, Dublin Public Libraries 1975-92; first published in 1990; retired from Dublin Public Libraries 1992; full time writer 2002 to date; novels include *City Girl, Apt. 3B, City Woman, Foreign Affairs, Promises Promises, Mirror Mirror, City Lives, Second Chance, Finishing Touches, Francesca's Party;* series editor and contributing author to the Open Door series; editorial consultant with Hodder Headline Ireland; teaches creative writing to transition year students in Dominican College, Griffith Avenue, Dublin. Recreations: silk painting, reading. Contact: Declan Heeney. email dheeney@eircom.net

Prolific, successful author and first of the home grown chick lit novelists; enjoys huge world wide sales.

SCANLON, Michael; SECRETARY GENERAL, DEPARTMENT OF HEALTH AND CHILDREN
b 1956, Dublin; *m* ; 2 children; *edu.* Templeogue College, Dublin; Secretary General Department of Health and Children; executive officer civil service 1973; Dept of Public Service 1979-93; secretary to the Gleeson Report on Public Sector Pay 1993; secretary to the Buckley Report on Public Sector Pay and Conditions 1998; assistant secretary General Dept of Finance 2000-05; secretary General Dept of Health and Children 2005 to date. Contact: Hawkins House, Hawkins Street Dublin 2. **T** 01 635 4000 **F** 01 635 4001 email info@doh.ie web www.doh.ie

Came into his current position in controversial circumstances due to the removal of his predecessor; coming from Dept of Enterprise, Trade and Employment, his mettle will be well tested in this largest spending department with a budget of almost €13 billion, which has serious political consequences for the government.

SCHMIDT, Bruno; MD, PROBUS AND CAR LUXURY TOURING

b 1968, Bruges, Belgium; *m* Sandra Estelle; 3*s* 2*d*; *edu.* Bruges College of Hotel Management; degree with distinction in Hotel Management; Managing Director ProBus & Car Luxury Touring; hotel management Park Hotel Kenmare; Michelin star chef, Park Hotel Kenmare. Recreations: walking, football, motorcars. Contact: Hibernia House, Cappanacush East, Kenmare, Co. Kerry. Contact: **T** 064 42500 email BrunoSchmidt@probusandcar.com web www.probuscar.com

The Belgian born, youngest 2 star Michelin chef in Ireland spotted a gap in the luxury transport service and made a dramatic and extremely successful career change; a stickler for detail which shows in every area of his business, he now owns Ireland's leading luxury transport service.

SCOTT–LENNON née FITZPATRICK, Eithne Mary; DIRECTOR, FITZPATRICK'S CASTLE HOTEL

b 1956, Dublin; *m* James Scott Lennon; 4*s*; *edu.* Holy Child Killiney, Dublin; trained in hotel management in Lausanne, Switzerland; Managing Director, Fitzpatrick's Castle, Dublin; trained, Radisson Hotels, USA; sales & marketing director, Fitzpatrick Castle Hotel 1978; managing director 2003 to date; Government Board appointments: Failte Ireland – National Tourism Authority; Dun Laoghaire Harbour Company; member, Leopardstown Racing Committee. Clubs: Killiney Golf Club, Blainroe Golf Club, Royal Irish Yacht Club, Leopardstown Racing. Recreations: golf, reading, walking, rugby, sailing. Contact: Fitzpatrick Castle Hotel, Killiney, Co. Dublin. **T** 01 230 5400 email scott-lennon@iol.ie web www.fitzpatrickcastle.com

Eithne Scott-Lennon

The only daughter of the late, legendary hotelier, Paddy Fitzpatrick, grew up with the hotel industry in her veins so no surprise that she successfully carved out a niche for herself in the male dominated hotel sector; a chip off the old block, a tough task master but well able to delegate.

SCOTT, John Gabriel; ARTISTIC DIRECTOR/DANCER

b Dublin; single; *edu.* Christian Brothers School, Monkstown, Dublin; University College Dublin; BA; Artistic Director Irish Modern Dance Theatre; performed and studied with Dublin City Ballet, Irish Theatre Ballet, in France, Denmark, New York, Foundation Royaumont France; founded Irish Modern Dance Theatre 1991; his work *'Intimate Gold'* was a finalist in the Rencontres Internationales de Seine, Saint Denis, Bagnolet Competition 2000; represented Ireland at the European Centre for Choreography; board member, the International Dance Festival of Ireland; Association of Professional Dancers in Ireland; National Youth Theatre for the Deaf. Recreations: opera. Contact: Apt 2, 31 Castle Street, Dublin 2. **M** 086 839 8244 **F** 01 878 7784 email imdt@iol.iejohnscottireland@iol.ie

A brilliant and rising star of the stage, his masterly portrayal of ambivalent characters is an outstanding feat of artistic restraint; in stage terms a long run is predicted for him.

SCOTT, Michael Francis; THEATRE DIRECTOR/WRITER/COMPOSER

b 1956. Dublin; single; *edu.* Monkstown Park School, Dublin; University College Dublin; BA; Theatre and Opera Director, Composer; started theatre career in college; several student productions; transferred to professional theatre; awarded Arts Council Bursary 1979; studied in France; worked in theatre in Holland, Germany, Iceland; former programme manager Dublin Theatre Festival; manager Tivoli Theatre Dublin; artistic director SFX City Theatre 1999 to date; productions include *'Bent'*, *'The Normal Heart'*, *'Ella'*, *'Ghosts'* which toured to the US; adapted wrote and directed *'These Three Days'*; *'Agamemnon'*; *'Fragments of Isabella'* (Avignon, Cardiff, London); *'Torchlight and Laserbeams'* with author Christopher Nolan (Dublin, Edinburgh); adapted *'The Hostage'* with Niall Tobín; worked with John B.Keane in several landmark productions; Yeats Operas described as the best of the decade by David Nowlan; *'Songs of Leaving'* National Folk Theatre 1989; *'La Chunga'*, Lyric Belfast 2000; *'The Matchmaker'* National Tour, Edinburgh Theatre Festival, New York 2002-05; *'Tobar na Scealta'*, *'Síamsa Tíre'*, Tralee, Co.Kerry to mark the Centenary of the Kerryman Newspaper 2004; *'Sisters'* by Declan Hasssett with Anna Manahan, toured to Edinburgh Festival, and Festival of World Theatre,

Michael Scott

Colorado Springs 2005; Recreations: gardening, new computers, work. Contact: The SFX City Theatre, Upper Sherrard Street, Dublin 1. **M** 086 1686798 email director@sfx.ie

An inventive and engaging personality with a great interest in physical theatre as well as in running a theatre; ambitious for the theatre at home and abroad.

Michael Scott

SCOTT, Michael Peter; AUTHOR, SCRIPTWRITER, PRODUCER

b 1959, Dublin; *m* Anna; 1*s* 1*d*; edu. St Aidan's Christian Brothers School, Whitehall, Dublin; Author, Scriptwriter and Producer; Dublin City of Culture Writer in Residence 1991; conducted Masters of Professional Writing Course, University of Southern California; headed up drama department Tyrone Productions; scripted for The Special Olympics; The Irish Film and Television Awards 2003-04; *Publ.* over 100 titles to date in 22 countries in 15 languages; writes for children and adults; titles include: *Irish Folk & Fairy Tales, Irish Myth and Legends, Irish Ghosts and Hauntings;* also writes under the pen name Anna Dillon, titles include *Seasons* 1988; *Another Season* 1989; *Season's End* 1990; *Lies* 1998; *The Affair* 2004; *Consequences* 2005; horror novels include: *Image, Reflection, Imp, Hallows, October Moon, House of the Dead, Silverhand, Silverlight, Whom the Gods Love, The Merchant Prince.* Recreations: sailing, cycling, writing (though not all at the same time!). Contact: Poolbeg Press, 123 Grange Hill, Baldoyle, Dublin 13. **T** 01 806 3825 email poolbeg@poolbeg.com web www.dillonscott.com

Extremely popular and prolific; in both of his personas reaches gothic conclusions.

SCULLY; Gerard Joseph 'Ger'; TULLAMORE TRIBUNE EDITOR

b 1970, Roscrea, Co. Tipperary; single; *edu.* Roscrea CBS; Journalism Course, College of Commerce, Rathmines; Editor *Tullamore Tribune*; *Publ. Tullamore Tribune* 1994 – to date. Contact: Tullamore Tribune, Church Street, Tullamore, Co. Offaly. **T** 0506 21152 email tulltrib@eircom.net

As a local editor he avidly follows all political, social and sporting issues which impact upon his readership and serves the area extremely well; not afraid to publish a dissident view.

Gráinne Seoige

SEOIGE, Gráinne; BROADCASTER

b 1973, Castlebar, Co. Mayo; *m* Stephen Cullinane; 1*s*; *edu.* Coláiste Chroí Mhuire, An Spidéal, Co. na Gaillimhe; University College Galway; B.A. (English, Sociology, Political Science); H Dip. Cumarsáid Feidhmeach, Teilifís agus Raidió (applied Communications, Television and Radio); Broadcaster; Léitheoir Nuachta agus Iriseoir Físe, Teilifís na Gaeilge (News Anchor and video journalist) Oct 1996–98; News Anchor Sept 1998–04, TV3; News Anchor, Sky News Ireland, May 2004 - 06; joined RTE to host own afternoon chat show October 2006 – todate; patron, The National Breast Cancer Research Institute (NBCRI). Contact: RTE, Donnybrook, Dublin 4. **T** 01 208 3111 email grainne.seoige@rte.ie web www.rte.ie

Has brought a western island éclat to Irish news; was seen all over the world on Sky News and could have had an international career, however many feel RTE is her spiritual home.

SEOIGE, Síle; BROADCASTER

b 1979, Castlebar, Co. Mayo; *m* Glen Mulcahy; *edu.* Meán-Scoil Mhuire gan Smál, Spiddal, Co. Galway; Freelance Television and Radio Presenter; television and radio presenter RTE, TG4, Today FM. Presenter: *"You're a Star"* Series 4, RTE 1 Oct 2005 to date, *"Up for the Match"*(Sports/Entertainment RTE 1) 2004 & 2005; co-presenter on *"St. Patrick's Day Parade"* RTE 1 March 2005; presenter on *"Coisceim"* 4 part series for Seachtain na Gaeilge RTE 1 Jan 2005; reporter for *"Seachtain-the Week"* a weekly bi-lingual programme RTE 1 Oct 2004 to date; radio presenter Today FM Dec 2004 to date; reporter/presenter *'Nationwide'* RTE 1 June-Aug 2004; radio presenter Beat 102-103 2004; main presenter/researcher TG4's live wrap around kids show *CULA 4* - TG4, 2001-03; co-presenter with Craig Doyle, *"ESAT BT Young Scientist of the Year 2002"* RTE 2002; presenter *"Sport na gColáisti"* TG4 Nov 2000; weather presenter/researcher/continuity announcer TG4 1999-01; presenter/researcher *"The Kitchen Sink"* (entertainment prog.) NTL 1999-00; presenter/researcher *"Hollywood Anocht"* (movie show) TG4 1998- 99. Recreations: singing, going to the movies, taking long walks in the country, meeting my friends for coffee! Contact: c/o RTE Hynes Building, 19-29 St Augustine Street, Galway. **T** 091 505057 **F** 091 505005 email info@sileseoige.com web www.sileseoige.com

The younger Seoige, sister of Grainne (*qv*) to impact successfully on national television; has a great voice and presence; could equally pursue a career in entertainment.

SEXTON, Mae; PUBLIC REPRESENTATIVE
b 1955, Longford; *m* Tommy Sexton; 1*s* 1*d*; *edu.* Convent of Mercy, Longford; National University Ireland, Maynooth; Dip. Business Studies; Public Representative; TD Longford/Roscommon; 2002 elected to the 29th Dail as the first Progressive Democrats TD in Longford/Roscommon, having failed to be elected on two previous occasions; member, Oireachtas Committee on Europe; Progressive Democrats Spokesperson for Regional Development. Contact: Constituency Office, Dublin Street, Longford. **T** 043 41142 email maesexton@eircom.net

> Daughter of a Longford baker who was a Fianna Fáil councilor for thirty years; very personable, hardworking public representative who has the pulse of the people and has a very strong interest in the health sector

Síle Seoige

SHANLEY, Professor Diarmuid 'Derry'; PROFESSOR OF DENTISTRY
b 1942, Cork; *m* Orna; 1*s* 4*d*; *edu.* Synge Street CBS Dublin; National University of Ireland (Bachelor of Dental Surgery) 1966; Professor of Dentistry; research associate Temple University, Philadelphia 1967-68; Indiana University (Master of Science in Dentistry) 1970; fellow, Dental Surgery of the Royal College of Surgeons Edinburgh 1972; MA (Jure Officii) Trinity College, University of Dublin; fellow, Faculty of Dentistry (Ad Eundem) Royal College of Surgeons in Ireland; Fellow TCD 1992; general dental practice, Coleraine, Northern Ireland 1967; research associate Temple University Philadelphia 1967-68; teaching associate Indiana University of Dentistry 1968-78; lecturer Liverpool University School of Dentistry 1970-73; senior lecturer/consultant and head of Periodontology, Dublin Dental Hospital and Trinity College Dublin 1973-87; visiting professor Arab Medical University, Benghazi 1979; director School of Dental Science, TCD 1980-86; acting head of Restorative Dentistry, TCD 1984-86; Dean of Dental Affairs, School of Dental Science, TCD and Dublin Dental Hospital 1986-2000; secretary general Association of Dental Education in Europe 1987–92; Professor of Oral Health, Trinity College, University of Dublin 1989 to date; Dean of the Faculty of Health Science Trinity College, University of Dublin; consultant Dental Surgeon, St. Columcille's Hospital; consultant Dental Surgeon, St. James's Hospital 2002 to date; chairman of the Board, Dublin Dental Hospital 1990-2000; chairman Project Committee of New Dublin Dental Hospital Building 1992-98; awarded honorary doctorate (D. Odont Oslo *hc*) for "work done in the field of dental education" 2000; conferred with University of Columbia William J Gies Foundation Award for the Advancement of Dentistry 2001; received American Dental Education Association Presidential Citation "for contribution to international dental education" 2002; Percy T. Phillips Visiting Professor Columbia University, New York 2003; associate editor *European Journal of Dental Education*; editorial board member *International Journal of Medical Education*. Publ. *Efficacy of Treatment Procedures in Periodontics* (Quintessence Publishers Berlin)1980; Recreations: angling; a lakeside renovated schoolhouse with a boat; music, wine. Contact: School of Medicine, Chemistry Building, Trinity College Dublin 1. **T** 01 608 1476 **F** 01 671 3956 email dshanley@tcd.ie

> Herculean as an academic and practitioner; hardworking, focussed and prolific, he is internationally renowned and lauded for innovations in the teaching of dentistry and oral health education; external examiner for several universities; he has been chairman and president of a myriad of associations dealing with aspects of dental education; he sits on and chairs several committees, is a consultant to the World Health Organisation, has published a dazzling array of learned articles in over 60 publications on health sciences and European dental education; penned the EU Guidelines on Clinical Competence in Dental Education; produced several videos for students and dentists, one of which was distributed to every registered dentist in the UK by the UK government, and won First Prize at the Annual Medical Film Festival in Mauriac, France, 1993; is still very accessible and finds time to spend with his family fishing and boating at his lakeside retreat.

SHANNON, Margaret; REGIONAL MANAGER, IRELAND, KLM ROYAL DUTCH AIRLINES
b 1959, Dublin; separated; 1*s*; *edu.* Dominican Convent, Sion Hill, Blackrock, Co. Dublin; College of Management Studies, Rathmines, Dublin 6; Dip and Grad Marketing; Regional Manager, Ireland, KLM Royal Dutch Airlines; travel consultant Joe Walsh Tours 1976-79; sales executive Blue Skies (Aer Lingus Holidays) 1979-86; Ryanair start-up sales manger Ireland 1986-88; regional manager

KLM 1998 to date; Clubs: Royal Irish Yacht Club; Recreations: walking, skiing, golf, wine. Contact: 19, Longford Terrace, Monkstown, Co. Dublin. **T** 01 663 6911 **F** 01 663 6910 email margaret.shannon@klm.com

Runs an extremely successful operation, the envy of many other airlines and recognized by the powers that be in Amsterdam as the key to their success here; a no-nonsense, hardworking executive who has coped well with mergers and takeovers in the ever changing landscape of her industry; a gregarious, interesting woman of great style, who when the deal is done, knows well how to celebrate.

Sharon Shannon

SHANNON, Sharon; MUSICIAN
b 1969, Ruan, Co. Clare; single; edu. Ruan NS; University College Cork; Professional Musician, Accordion Player; founder member of the group Arcady; began solo musical career 1989; joined The Waterboys; released own album with some of the top names in Irish music, Donal Lunny, Adam Clayton, Mary Crusty, Eoin O'Neill et al, 1991; subsequently released six more albums including *The Diamond Mountain Sessions* which went triple platinum in Ireland; has toured all over the world and played for President Clinton at the White House; Latest album *The Sharon Shannon Collection 1990–2005* (double platinum sales by December 2005); Clubs: R.S.P.C.A, R.S.P.C.C. Recreations: dogs, gardening. Contact: The Daisy Label, RMG Chart, Carriglea, Naas Rd., Dublin 12 **T** 01 429 8600 **F** 01 429 8602 email Hannah@daisydiscs.com

Made the accordion sexy and easy on the ear; growing up in Ruan (near Corofin) was continually exposed to folk traditional music, her parents were set dancers and all four of the children played instruments, starting with tin whistles; started the accordion aged 11, also performs on fiddle and melodeon; played through school and afterwards; first big recognition was in her teens, when she played in Jim Sheridan's (*qv*) production of Brendan Behan's "The Hostage" for the Druid Theatre Company; she says "you just play 'til the tunes stop chasing you"

SHEEHAN, James; ENGINEER **/**ORTHOPAEDIC SURGEON/ENTREPRENEUR
b 1939, Tralee, Co. Kerry; m Rosemary Sheehan; 2s 2d; edu. St. Mary's, Rathmines, Dublin; University College Dublin MB, B.Ch., BAO; Ph. D, 1963; Mechanical Engineering; M.Sc. Bioengineering, University of Surrey, UK; FIEI. C. Engineering; F.I.A.E.; Orthopaedic Surgeon/ Medical Entrepreneur; specialist in replacement hip and knee joints; founder of the Blackrock Clinic in Dublin; winner of the Molloy Prize in Physics; winner of the Birmington Gold Medal in Anatomy; founder member Irish American Orthopedic Association; recreations: gardening, occasional fishing. Contact: The Penthouse, Blackrock Clinic, Rock Road, Blackrock, Co. Dublin. **T** 01 288 0315 web www.blackrockclinic.ie

A warm, friendly, energetic, internationally acclaimed medical consultant, a pioneering visionary in the Irish medical world who established the Blackrock Clinic and Hospital in 1980 at a time of serious economic recession in Ireland; one of the top orthopedic surgeons in the world, due to unrivalled excellence in two disciplines, engineering and medicine; invented the artificial knee replacement; continues to push the boundaries in Irish private healthcare establishing The Galway Clinic 2004 and the Leixlip Clinic currently under construction, due for completion late 2006; highly respected in the business world from where he receives commercial support for his ventures including his latest major planned redevelopment and expansion of the Blackrock Clinic and Hospital.

SHEFFLIN, Henry; HURLER
b 1979, Waterford; single; *edu.* St. Ciaran's College, Kilkenny; Waterford Institute of Technology; Degree in Business Studies (Financial Services); Hurler/ Medical Representative Altana Pharma; centre forward Kilkenny Hurling team; won 3 All Ireland Hurling Medals 2000, 2002, 2003; All Ireland Hurling finalist 1999, 2005; won six Leinster Hurling Championship Medals 1999, 2000, 2001, 2002, 2003; won three National League Hurling Medals 2002, 2003, 2005; won All Ireland Under-21 Hurling Medal 1999; won two Inter University Fitzgibbon Cup Medals; Awards: 4 GAA All Star Awards 2000, 2002, 2003, 2004; Player of The Year 2002; Texaco Hurler of the Year 2002. Clubs: Ballyhale Shamrocks, Mountain Dew Golf Club, Kilkenny. Recreations: all sports, reading, travelling. Contact: Ballyhale, Co. Kilkenny. **T** 056 7768647 email henry.shefflin@altanapharma.ie

Great personality and an excellent role model for players all over the country, a dominant force and an inspiring player for the Kilkenny Senior hurling team in recent years; combines skill, courage and ability to be a good team player; has almost a mint of coveted GAA medals in his coffers at the tender age of 28 years.

SHEERAN, Paul; JEWELLER
b 1967, Athlone, Co. Westmeath; *m* Tracy; 2*d*; *edu.* De La Salle College, Kildare; Horologist, Diamond Grader; Managing Director Paul Sheeran Jewellers; opened first shop Nutgrove Shopping Centre, Rathfarnham, Dublin 1990; moved to Grafton Street 1994, expanded and renovated Grafton Street 2001; opened second shop Dundrum Town Centre 2005. Clubs: Carton House Golf Club, Coolmine Rugby Club. Recreations: rugby, skiing, running, cycling, swimming, casual golf, anything that involves adrenalin; Contact: 7, Johnsons Court, Grafton Street, Dublin 2. **T** 01 6351136 **F** 01 635 1141 email info@paulsheeranjewellers.ie

Paul Sheeran

In a very short period has established himself as one of the top three jewelers in Ireland; charming, affable, ambitious and hardworking, has made diamonds sexy again; a serious triathlon competitor in Europe and the US.

SHEEHY, Eugene; CHIEF EXECUTIVE, ALLIED IRISH BANK plc
b 1954, Dublin; *m* Cora; 1*s* 1*d*, *edu.* Rathgar NS; Salesian College, Pallaskenry, Co. Limerick; Trinity College Dublin; M.Sc (Mgt); Chief Executive, AIB Group plc; joined AIB 1971; came up through the ranks of branch banking holding a variety of management positions in Dame Street and Phibsboro; senior manager Bank Centre, Ballsbridge 1994-97; head Business Transformation 1997-99; general manager retail operations 1999-01; managing director AIB Bank 2001-02; chairman & CEO M & **T** Bank USA 2002-05; chief executive AIB Group plc 2005 - todate.; Clubs: Éire Óg GAA, Carlow; Recreations: GAA. Contact: AIB, Bank Center, Ballsbridge, Dublin 4. **T** 01 660 0311 web www.aib.com

At 51, the youngest chief executive of Allied Irish Bank, he is the son of Maurice Sheehy, the former chief executive of CSET (Irish Sugar Company); has inherited all of his father's characteristics, hardworking, razor sharp intellect, utterly focused, personable, popular with the staff, providing Ireland's largest financial institution a much needed morale boost in the wake of the Rusnack and foreign exchange scandals era; still rooted in the real Ireland; is more comfortable in Croke Park than Lansdowne Road.

SHERIDAN, Jim; MOVIE DIRECTOR / PRODUCER/SCRIPT WRITER
b 1949, Dublin; *m* Frances Roe; 3*d; edu.* St Laurence O'Toole National School, Dublin; O'Connell Christian Brothers School, Dublin; University College Dublin, BA; Movie Director/Producer/Script Writer; joined a bank for a short while, moved into the theatre as assistant to Lelia Doolan, then artistic director of the Abbey Theatre; directed and wrote plays for the Peacock; artistic director and Chairman of the Project 1976-80; moved with family to New York 1981-89; The Children's **T** Company productions (New York); artistic director The Irish Arts Centre New York; director Oscar-winning *My Left Foot* 1989; director *The Field* 1990; script writer *Into The West* (Miramax); wrote, directed, co-produced, with Arthur Lappin (*qv*) *In The Name of the Father* 1993; co-scriptwriter (with Terry George) and co-producer (with Arthur Lappin) *Some Mother's Son*; scriptwriter, director and co-producer (with Arthur Lappin) *The Boxer* (nominated for a Golden Globe Award) 1997; co-producer (with Arthur Lappin); co-producer Agnes Brown; co-producer (with Arthur Lappin) *Borstal Boy*; co-producer (with Arthur Lappin) *On The Edge*; co producer (with Arthur Lappin) *Bloody Sunday*; co-scriptwriter (with daughter Kirsten) and director *In America* 2002; Director *Get Rich Or Die Tryin'* starring 50 Cent, 2005; Recreations: horse racing (owns champion winner Vinnie Roe), swimming, soccer. Contact: Hells Kitchen, 21 Mespil Road, Dublin 4. **T** 01 667 5599

The most successful movie industry director to come out of Ireland; respected internationally in an extremely fickle business by both 'moguls' and actors, for his integrity, intelligence and brilliant direction; extremely popular on both sides of the Atlantic, whether in the salons of top diplomats, boardrooms of the major movie companies or a saw dust on the floor snug, he just knows how to mix it up.

SHERIDAN, Kirsten; SCREENWRITER/ DIRECTOR
b 1976, Dublin; single; *edu.* Mount Temple, Malahide, Dublin; Dún Laoghaire Institute of Art, Design and Technology; New York University, Directors Course; Screenwriter /Director; credits include: *The*

Bench 1995; *Patters* 1998; *Majella Maginty* 2000; co-wrote (with Audrey O'Reilly) *Honor Bright*; co-scriptwriter (with father Jim Sheridan *qv*) *In America* 2002; Awards: Guinness Newcomer 1998; Miramax Screenplay Award 1998; won awards at Cork Film Festival, Galway Film Fleadh, Jesuit Film and Video Awards; Aspen Shorts Festival, Colorado, USA; Clemont-Ferrand Film Festival, France; Dresdent Short Film Festival, Germany; European and Mediterranean Short Film Festival Spain; nominated with father Jim(*qv*) for an Academy Award for screenplay *In America* 2003. Recreations: singing, playing the piano. Contact: Hells Kitchen, 21 Mespil Road, Dublin 4. **T** 01 667 5599

> Nominated for an Academy Award before her 30th birthday, as a young writer /director has already hit the high spots in her industry, on her own merit; shows every sign of achieving even greater accolades in the near future.

SHERIDAN, Vincent Joseph; CHIEF EXECUTIVE, VHI HEALTHCARE
b 1948, Dublin; *m* Aileen Bingham; 3s 1d; *edu*. Blackrock College, Dublin; University College Dublin; B. Comm.; Chief Executive VHI Healthcare; accountant, Reynolds Mc Carron O' Connor, Chartered Accountants 1969–73; various positions Norwich Union Life & Pensions –1973–91; group chief executive, Norwich Union Group, Ireland 1991–01; chief executive, VHI Healthcare –2001 to date; vice-president Institute of Chartered Accountants in Ireland; director, FBD Holdings ltd; director, Business 2 Arts; council member, Financial Reporting Council (UK); Clubs: Blackrock College R.F.C (former president), Castle Golf Club. Recreations: all Sport, particularly rugby and golf. Contact: 113 Lower Baggot Street, Dublin 2. **T** 01 799 7602 **F** 01 874 1950
email vincent.sheridan@vhi.ie web www.vhi.ie

> The quintessential accountant has driven the VHI to become the biggest player in the healthcare insurance sector in Ireland; faces increased competition from Bupa and Vivas which will test his mettle in the near future.

Philip Sherry

SHERRY, Philip Gerard; AUCTIONEER, CHARTERED SURVEYOR
b 1952, Dublin; *m* Mary O'Neill; 2s 1d; *edu*. Blackrock College, Dublin; University College Dublin; B.Comm; Auctioneer/Chartered surveyor; executive Jones Lang Wootton 1972; joined his father's practice Sherry & Sons 1975; Sherry & Sons merged with FitzGerald and Partners to form Sherry FitzGerald 1982; director Sherry FitzGerald holding many senior management roles 1982 to date; director, Sherry FitzGerald Group 2002 to date; managing director, Sherry FitzGerald Countrywide 1998 to date; fellow, Irish Auctioneers and Valuers Institute; fellow, Royal Institution of Chartered Surveyors and the Society of Chartered Surveyors in Ireland. Clubs: Blackrock College Past Pupils Union (1996 and 1997 President), Milltown Golf Club, Woodenbridge Golf Club, Tramore Golf Club, Royal Irish Yacht Club. Recreations: golf, skiing, walking, music, work, travel. Contact: Rinn Na Mara, Belgrave Rd., Monkstown, Co. Dublin. **T** 01 639 9200 **F** 01 639 9289 email psherry@sherryfitz.ie web www.sherryfitz.ie

> One of the oldest estate agents in the country; was perfectly poised to cash in on the property boom; has grown his once Dublin-based company nationally.

SHIPSEY, Bill; SENIOR COUNSEL
b Waterford; *m* Moira Mullaney; 3s 1d; *edu*. University College Dublin; BCL; Kings Inns; Barrister; Senior Counsel; called to the Bar 1980; called to the Inner Bar (Senior Counsel) 1994; member, Bar of Northern Ireland; Bar of England and Wales; former Chairperson of F.C.A.C. (Free Legal Advice Centres); Amnesty International (Irish Section); Irish Hospice Foundation; founder 'Art for Amnesty' an International project based in Dublin which brings together international artists of all disciplines who wish to support the work of Amnesty International; Contact: 2 Arran Square, Dublin 7. **T** 01 817 4939 (dl) 01 872 3677 **F** 01 872 3859 email bshipsey@yahoo.com

> A respected SC, who is low profile to the public eye but not in his professional practice; admired and often feared in court, he possesses a keen analytical brain and is shrewd in cross examination.

SHIPSEY, Ruth; SOLICITOR
b 1963, Waterford; *m* Brendan Dillon; 1s 2d; *edu*. Ursuline Convent, Waterford; University College Dublin; Law Society of Ireland; B.Comm; Solicitor; consultant solicitor, Hayes Solicitors; qualified as a solicitor having worked in a law firm in California 1989; joined Hayes solicitors 1991; partner, Hayes Solicitors, retired as partner 2000; consultant/director Marketing and Client Services Hayes

Solicitors 2000 to date; director, US-Irish Alliance 1998 to date; Clubs: Woodbrook Golf Club;
Blainroe Golf Club, Donnybrook Lawn Tennis Club. Recreations: golf, tennis. Contact: Lavery
House, Earlsfort Terrace, Dublin 2. **T** 01 662 4747 **F** 01 662 0677 email rshipsey@hayes-solicitors.ie
web www.hayessolicitors.ie

This extremely able Waterford-born solicitor, sister of Bill Shipsey, SC (*qv*) was very
involved with recent equality legislation and its impact on golf clubs; also involved in a
number of charities including Down Syndrome Ireland and the Irish Hospice Art Pack
Project; has organized a number of international conferences and seminars; now a
major force in the powerful Irish US - Ireland Alliance – an influential non profit
organization established to strengthen ties between the US and contemporary Ireland -
flagship project is the George J. Mitchell scholarship programme, though only six years
old the programme is already viewed as one of the most prestigious scholarship
programmes in the US.

SHORTALL, Róisín; PUBLIC REPRESENTATIVE

b 1954, Dublin; *m* Seamus O'Byrne; 3d; *edu.* Domican College, Eccles Street, Dublin; University
College Dublin; St. Mary's College of Education, Marino, Dublin; B.A; NT Dip; Public
Representative TD Labour Party, Dublin North West; teacher of the Deaf, St. Joseph's School
for the Deaf, Cabra, Dublin; Public Representative, TD Labour Party (Dublin North West);
Labour Party spokesperson on Education and Children 1997-2002; member Dublin City
Council 1991 to date; member Eastern Health Board (1997 chairperson) 1991-02; member,
Ballymun Housing Task Force; member, Finglas Vocational Educational Education Committee;
member, Finglas Area Partnership; Ballymun Local Drugs Task Force; Finglas Local Drugs Task
Force; Contact: Dáil Office, Kildare Street. Dublin 2. **T** 01 618 3593 **F** 01 618 4380 email
roisin.shortall@oireachtas.ie

Róisín Shortall

Hard working, tenacious, articulate Front Bench spokesperson whose performance
should warrant a Cabinet position in the event of Labour being part of a future
government; critical of the leadership of Ruairí Quinn and refused a position on the
party front bench after the 2002 election; resumed her front bench role as
spokesperson on transport, with Pat Rabbitte at the helm.

SHOVLIN, Patrick 'Paddy'; PROPERTY DEVELOPER

b 1963, Dublin; *m* Julie; 1s 2d; Managing Director Landmark Developments; started his career with
Shiels in Moore Street, Dublin; with Paul Gallagher opened another Shiels and two Blakes restaurants
in early 1980s; opened Thunder Road Café, Temple Bar 1994; developed the Morgan Hotel, 1996
Temple Bar, Dublin; bought a Business Park in Clondalkin; developed an office block on Harcourt
Street; currently involved in the €2 billion Landmark development of an upmarket town made up of
interlinked apartment blocks, restaurants, retail mall, hospital, medical consultants quarter, offices,
leisure and cultural activities in Sandyford, Co Dublin, 2005 to date; built the Beacon Court Hotel
2004; juggles 26 separate directorships of active companies. Recreations: motor racing, flying his
helicopter, racing. Contact: Landmark Developments, Suite 28/29 The Mall, Beacon Court,
Sandyford, Dublin 18. **T** 01 299 2100

Ambitious, charming and energetic, might appear to have had a meteoric rise in the
property world but has more than served his apprenticeship; equally successful as a
skilled racing driver; has competed around Europe for years in the European Ferrari
Challenge.

SINNOTT, Charles John; HOTEL PROPRIETOR, BUSINESSMAN

b 1947, Cork; *m* Bridget; 3s; *edu.* Terenure College Dublin; Gresham Hotel, trainee management
scheme; Palace Hotel, Madrid, Spain, trainee management scheme M.I.H.C.I. F.I.H.C.I; Hotel
Proprietor, Businessman; deputy manager Talbot Hotel Wexford; general manager Gresham Hotel
Dublin 1973-75; managing director, Trusthouse Forte (Irl) Ltd 1975-80; proprietor Connemara
Gateway Hotel 1980-04; proprietor, Connemara Coast Hotel 1985 to date; proprietor Brooks Hotel
Dublin 1997 to date; former director and chairman, Ireland West Tourism; director, Galvia Hospital
Galway, Tourism Ireland Teo. Clubs: Hibernian Stephens Green Club, Dublin, Marks Club, London.
Oughterard Golf Club, Co. Galway. Recreations: walking, football, rugby. Contact: Connemara Coast
Hotel, Furbo, Co. Galway. **T** 091 59 2108 **F** 091 59 2065 email cjksinnott@eircom.net web
www.sinnotthotels.com

Charles Sinnott

One of Ireland's best known hoteliers; has built up a very strong brand in the tourism industry as well as an extremely impressive property portfolio in Ireland and abroad; the charming, astute, Cork born hotelier demands the highest standards and, ably assisted by his Wexford born wife, delivers a premium product.

SISK, George Herbert; CHAIRMAN, SICON (JOHN SISK AND SON HOLDING CO.)
b 1941, Dublin; *m* Anne Gibney; 2*s* 2*d*; *edu.* St Mary's College, Rathmines, Dublin; University College Cork; BE (Civil); MIEI MCIOB; Chairman SICON/John Sisk and Son; joined family construction company 1965 todate; appointed to the board John Sisk and Son 1989; Clubs: Royal Irish Yacht Club, Co. Dublin; Recreations: sailing, golf. Contact: John Sisk and Son, Wilton Works, Naas Road, Clondalkin, Dublin 22, Ireland. **T** 01 4091500 **F** 01 409 1550 email info@sisk.ie web www.sisk.ie

Extremely low-profile member of the family-owned construction business which has the largest turnover of any property-related company in the state; has more than disproved the old adage of rags to rags in three generations (from 1859) by not only keeping the company very firmly in family hands but prudently steering its consolidation, expansion and diversification at home and internationally; equally successful as a yachtsman.

SLIGO, The Most Hon. The Marquess of , Browne, Jeremy Ulick; STATELY HOME OWNER, PEER
b 1939; *m* Jennifer June Cooper; 5*d*; *edu.* St. Columba's College, Rathfarnham, Dublin; Royal Agricultural College Cirencester; 11th.Marquess of Sligo, Earl of Altamont, Earl of Clanrickard, Viscount Westport, Baron Mount Eagle, Baron Mounteagle (UK) 1991 to date; Clubs: Kildare Street& University Club, Dublin. Contact: Westport House, Westport, Co. Mayo. **T** 098 277668 email info@westporthouse.ie

With his wife and daughters has made a great success of running Westport House, which was the first Heritage house to be opened to the public; took the unusual step of seeking a private bill in the Houses of the Oireachtas to set aside the entail arrangements made for the ownership of the House; has established a hotel, a zoo, and other visitor attractions; has been a brave upholder of the line taken by his famous pirate queen ancestor Grainne Mhaol "I hold what I have".

SMITH, Brendan Paul; PUBLIC REPRESENTATIVE
b 1956; *m* Anne McGarry; *edu.* St. Camillus, College, Killucan, Co Westmeath, University College Dublin, B.A. (Politics, Economics); Public Representative, TD Fianna Fáil, Cavan/Monaghan; Minister of State, Department Agriculture and Food, 2004 todate; former advisor to then Tánaiste John Wilson; elected T.D (FF) Cavan/Monaghan 1992 to date; Clubs: Templeport GAA Club, Cavan Supporters Club, GAA, Member Comhaltas Ceotoirí Eireann, Cumann Seanchais Bhreifne. Recreations: GAA, music. Contact: 3, Carrickfern, Keadue, Co. Cavan. **T** 049 436 2366 **F** 049 436 2367 email Brendanp.smith@agriculture.gov.ie web www.fiannafail.ie

The Cavan man cut his political teeth while working as a civil servant with former Tánaiste John Wilson; bright, low profile has settled in well with his new ministerial colleagues in Agriculture House; popular with deputies on all sides of the House; could be in the mix for a full car after the next General Election or could be the next Chief Whip if Fianna Fáil are victorious.

SMITH, Kate; NEWSCASTER UTV
b Belleek, Co. Fermanagh; *m* Michael Deane; 1*s*; *edu.* Mount Lourdes Grammar School, Enniskillen; Queen's University Belfast; University College Dublin; B.A. Dip Applied Soc Sc.; UTV News Anchor; Downtown Radio reporter presenter ; RTE news anchor/ journalist; UTV news anchor/journalist; Recreations: walking, skiing, tennis, home making. Contact: UTV, Havelock House, Ormeau Road, BT7 1EB. **T** 028 902 62000

Impressive, solid presenter of Northern Ireland news and current affairs.

SMITH, Most Rev. Michael; BISHOP of MEATH
b 1940, Oldcastle, Co. Meath; single; *edu.* St. Finian's College, Mullingar, Co Westmeath; Lateran University, Rome; Licentiate in Philosophy and Theology, Doctorate, Canon Law; Bishop of Meath;

ordained Rome March 1963; post-graduate studies Rome 1963-66; Bishop of Meath; attached to secretariat of Second Vatican Council 1961-65; C.C Clonmellon 1967-68; Diocesan Secretary 1968-84; chaplain St. Loman's Hospital, Mullingar 1968-74; chaplain St. Francis Private Hospital, Mullingar 1974-84; Executive National Episcopal Secretary of Irish Bishops' Conference 1970-98; Bishop of Meath 1984 to date. Contact: Bishop's House, Dublin Road, Mullingar, Co Westmeath. **T** 044 48841 **F** 044 43020 email bishop@dioceseofmeath.ie

Michael Smith

> A limited moderniser with strong Romanist leanings; a stiff and forceful Episcopal presence.

SMITHWICK, Peter Alexander; RETIRED JUDGE
b 1937, Kilkenny; *m* Deirdre Anne Cooper; 2*d*; *edu.* Castleknock College; University College Dublin; BCL; Retired Judge; solicitor 1958 – 88; judge, District Court 1988; president, District Court 2000–05; Judge, Special Criminal Court 2002-05; ex officio judge, Circuit Court 1995–05; councillor Kilkenny Borough Council 1974–79, Hereditary Freeman of Kilkenny; *Publ.* various articles *Irish Georgian Society Bulletin; Old Kilkenny Review; Butler Society Journal.* Clubs: Kildare Street and University; Royal Automobile; Casino Maltese, Valetta, Malta, Stephens Green; Knight of Malta 1962, Bailiff Grand Cross of Order of Malta 2004, President of the Irish Association of the Order of Malta 2000 to date, Grand Cross Pro Merito Melitense. Contact: The Old Rectory, Inistioge, Co Kilkenny **T** 056 775 8479

> The Kilkenny-born president of the District Court comes from the famous brewing family; prior to being appointed to the bench was active in Carlow/ Kilkenny political circles where he was director of elections for Fianna Fáil; commuted from Kilkenny to Dublin daily by train; quiet and laid back, had a reputation for being a very fair, well informed judge.

SMULLEN, Pat; CHAMPION JOCKEY
b 1977, Co. Offaly; *m* Frances Crowley (*qv*); 1*d*; *edu.* Rhode, Co. Offaly NS; Champion Jockey; winner champion apprentice jockey title twice (youngest ever winner of the title); Irish champion jockey 2005, 2003, 2002; winner of the Texaco Sports Award for Horse Racing 2004; won the Budweiser Derby riding 'Grey Swallow' 2004; partnered 'Vinnie Roe' to a remarkable fourth successive Irish St. Leger 2004 (2003, 2002, 2001), 2nd in the Melbourne Cup on Vinnie Roe 2004. Recreations: relaxing with daughter. Contact: Clifton Lodge Ballysax, The Curragh, Co. Kildare. **T** 045 442652

> The youngest ever winner of the champion Apprentice title; has gone on to even greater success at senior level, winning the Irish flat jockey championship on three occasions in five years; No 1 jockey in the Dermot Weld (*qv*) owned Rosewell House stable, is quiet, stylish, extremely hardworking, and ambitious.

SMURFIT, KBE, Sir Michael; COMPANY CHAIRMAN
b 1936, St.Helen's Lancashire, UK; *m* 1st Norma Treisman (*m.diss*); 2*s* 2*d*; *m* 2nd. Birgitta Beimark (*m diss*); 2*s*; *edu.* Clongowes Wood College, Co. Kildare; Company Chairman; Smurfit Kappa Group; trained Continental Can Corp USA; joined Jefferson Smurfit & Sons Ltd 1955; left Smurfits to form Jefferson Smurfit Packaging Ltd. Lancashire 1961; re-joined Jefferson Smurfit Group Ltd as a director 1964; appointed joint managing director Jefferson Smurfit Group plc. 1966; chairman and chief executive, Jefferson Smurfit Group plc. 1977; JSC floated on the stock exchange 1994; chairman Smurfit Stone Container Corporation1999; chairman emeritus Smurfit-Stone Container Corporation 2003 to date; director New Ireland Co. 1975–85; director, AIB plc 1978-83; chairman, Interim Telecommunications Board (which became Telecom Eireann) 1979; chairman, Racing Board 1985-90; director, CNG Travel Group plc. 2004; director, Ballymore Properties 2005 to date; Awards: Fellow International Academy of Management 1985; LL.D.(*hc*) Trinity College Dublin 1985; LL.D.(*hc*) NUI 1985; LL.D.(University of Scranton,Pennsylvania)1985; honorary Irish Consul Monaco, 1988 to date; member,Academy of Distinguished Entrepreneurs, Babson College 1989; Hon. Dr., Engineering, University of Missouri 1991; member, Advisory Council University of Notre Dame 1996; honorary fellowship, Royal College Surgeons Ireland, 1997; honorary alumnus, Notre Dame University, Indiana, 1998; Commendatore Order of Merit, Italian Republic 1988; Orden Franciso de Miranda, Venezuela 1989; Legion d'Honneur France 1990; Orden Al Merito Nacional-Columbia 1990; Cross of Merit with Silver Star of the Equestrian Order of the Holy Sepulchre of Jerusalem 1991; (Grand Cross with Gold Start same order 1996); Companion of the Royal House of O'Conor 1996; Knight Grand Cross of the Order of the Most Holy Trinity 1997; Officier de l'Orde de Saint-Charles, Monaco 1997; Knight Grand Cross of the Greek-Melikite Patriarchal Order of the

Holy Cross of Jerusalem 1998; Knight Grand Cross of The Military Hospitaller Order of St. Lazarus 1998; European Man of the Year 1994; RDS Industry Gold Medal 1995; Mater Hospital Foundation Gold Medal 1998; Special Lifetime Achievement, Ireland Fund of Great Britain 1998; Executive of the Year, Pulp and Paper Week Award 1999; Cross and Star Grand Officer The Sovereign Military Order of Malta The Order Pro Merito Melitensi 2001; Knight Commander of the Order of Francis 1 2002; Knight Commander of the Order of Our Lady of Conception of Vila Vicosa 2003; Gold Medal of St. Patrick Award, Maynooth College 2003; Business & Finance Lifetime Achievement Award 2003; Encomienda de Numero de la Orden de Isabel la Catolica 2005; Commander's Cross of the Order of Merit of the Republic of Poland 2005; Knight Commander of the Most Excellent Order of the British Empire (KBE) in HM The Queen's Birthday Honours List 2005. Clubs: Kildare Hotel & Country Club, Royal Dublin Golf Club, Woodbrook Golf Club (hon.member), Riverview Racquet and Fitness Club, Fitzwilliam Lawn Tennis Club, The Turf Club (Ireland), Walton Heath Golf Club, UK, Turnberry Isle Golf Club, Florida, Sherwood Golf Club, California, Monte Carlo Country Club, Monaco, Golf Country Club de Cannes Mougins, France, Aloha Golf Club, Nueve Andalucia, Spain. Recreations: golf, tennis, horse-riding, horse-breeding, skiing, shooting. Contact: Prince des Galles, Avenue des Citronelles, Monaco. **T** 0037 7 93 252 575

Complex, ambitious, very sharp business brain, commercially driven, one of Ireland's pioneering entrepreneurs who grew his father's local paper packaging company into one of the largest in the world; having served on many state and private boards over the years now confines himself to family involvements and Ballymore Properties; his prescience in pursuing the Ryder Cup for Ireland in the mid-nineties guaranteed a world class event at the K Club in 2006.

SMURFIT, MICHAEL JNR; DIRECTOR, KILDARE HOTEL AND COUNTRY CLUB

b 1966, Dublin; *m* Kathy Muldowney; 2*s*; *edu.* St. Michael's College, Dublin 4; Clongowes Wood College, Co. Kildare; University College Dublin; Company Director; director, Kildare Hotel and Country Club, director, JS Investments, Captain Kildare Hotel and Country Club (Ryder Cup Year) 2006. Clubs: Kildare Hotel and Country Club, Aloha Golf Club, Nueva Andalucia, Spain. Recreations: golf. Contact: Kildare Hotel and Country Club, Straffan, Co. Kildare. **T** 01 601 7200

Low profile, down to earth member of the Smurfit family; captain of the K Club during the Ryder Cup, a devoted family man and loyal friend.

SMURFIT, Sharon; COMPANY DIRECTOR / FUNDRAISER

b 1968, Dublin; *m* Jack O'Brien; separated; 2*s*; *edu.* Mount Anville Convent, Goatstown, Dublin. Company Director, Fundraiser; worked with Ladbrokes, joined Smurfit Group; owner, 'Something Original' gift store, Stillorgan Shopping Centre, Dublin, 2005 to date; Lady Captain Kildare Hotel and Country Club 2004–05. Clubs: The Kildare Hotel and Country Club, Straffan, Co. Kildare. Recreations: golf, reading, walking, gym. Contact: Something Original, Stillorgan Shopping Centre, Stillorgan, Co. Dublin. **T** 01 288 7236

Bright, energetic and hardworking; has inherited the mantle of fundraising for several charities from her parents; is currently working on funding for Ireland's first children's hospice at the Sunshine Home, Leopardstown, Co. Dublin.

Sharon Smurfit

SMURFIT, Victoria; ACTOR

b 1973, Dublin; *m* Doug Baxter; 1*d*; edu. St Columba's College, Dublin; St George's School, Ascot, Berkshire; The Bristol Old Vic Theatre School, Bristol; Actor; movies: *About a Boy* (with Hugh Grant) 2002; *The Beach* (with Leonardo De Caprio) 2000; TV: *Trial and Retribution* 2000; *The Shell Seekers* 1989; *Ballykissangel* BBC 2000; *Cold Feet* 1997–2003; Recreations: water and snow skiing, tennis, surfing. Contact: ARG, 4, Great Portland Street, WC1. **T** 0044 207 436 6400
email vasmurfit@hotmail.com

The talented, beautiful and charming daughter of Dermot Smurfit and niece of Michael (*qv*) has ploughed her own furrow and established herself as a name to be conjured with in the very problematic world of acting in Ireland, the UK and beyond; has featured in major motion pictures and award winning TV series; known for her commitment to her craft, capacity for hard work and the absence of 'luvvie' preciousness.

SMYTH, Noel; SOLICITOR

b 1951, The Claddagh, Co. Galway; *m* Ann Marie; 2*s* 2*d*; *edu.* Scoil Iosagan, Galway; St.
Brendan's CBS, Bray, Co. Wicklow; Incorporated Law Society; Solicitor/Property Developer;
apprenticed with Arthur Mc Lean; built up an impressive legal practice representing a number of
very high profile clients; took over H Williams Supermarket chain; lost the battle for Dunloe
Ewert to Liam Carroll (*qv*); extensive property portfolio in the UK and Ireland. Clubs: Kildare
Hotel and Country Club. Recreations: golf, collecting art. Contact: 22 Fitzwilliam Square,
Dublin 2 **T** 01 661 5525 **F** 01 661 3979 email noelsmyth@aulburn.com

Noel Smyth

The Galway-born solicitor gained national prominence when he represented Ben
Dunne following the Florida drugs saga 1992; went on to represent him when he broke
the Dunnes Family Trust, 1994; an extremely devout Catholic and daily communicant,
has used his helicopter to make his annual pilgrimage to Lough Derg; brought the relic
of St. Therese of Lisieux to Ireland on a tour around the country which attracted
unprecedented crowds; owns one of the finest collections of Irish art.

SMYTH, Sam; JOURNALIST

b 1945, Belfast; *m* 1st (*m diss*); 1*s* 1*d*; *m* 2nd Faela; 1*d*; *p* Angela Ryan; *edu.* Belfast CHS; Journalist;
started in career in engineering and showbusiness; director, entertainment City of Belfast 1970–72;
joined *Spotlight* magazine 1972–74; *Sunday World* 1974–86; *Irish Star* 1986–87; *Sunday Independent*
1988-92; Columnist, *The Irish Independent* 1992 to date; Presenter/Editor, ToDay fm 1999 to date
(Sunday Supplement); *Publ. Dear John, Riverdance – The Book, Thanks A Million Big Fella.* Awards: AT
Cross Journalist of The Year, 1991, ESB Journalist of the Year 1997; *In Dublin* Journalist's Journalist
1997. Recreations: reading, travel. Contact: *Irish Independent*, 27-32, Talbot Street, Dublin 1.
T 01 618 3928

The Belfast-born journalist has broken many of the biggest news stories in Ireland over
the past quarter of a century, including the Ben Dunne Florida saga which led to the
setting up of the Moriarty Tribunal, and the Greencore scandal which led to the
resignation of the then chief executive; now equally at home on radio through his
successful Sunday morning programme on ToDay fm; a great raconteur who is
comfortable in the company of gregarious politicians and top silks.

SOMERS, Dr. Michael J; CHIEF EXECUTIVE NATIONAL TREASURY MANAGEMENT
AGENCY

b 1942, Dublin; *m* ; children; *edu.* St. Mary's College, Rathmines, University College Dublin;
B.Comm; M.Econ.Sc; Ph.D; A.M.S.A.I; Chief Executive National Treasury Management Agency;
early career 1985: held various senior positions in Department of Finance and Central Bank;
secretary, Department of Defence 1985; secretary, National Debt Management Department of
Finance 1987; chief executive National Treasury Management Agency 1990 to date; director Board of
the European Investment Bank and chairman of its Audit Committee until June 2000; chairman of the
group that drafted the National Development Plan 1989-93; chairman of the European Community
Group that established the European Bank for Reconstruction and Development (EBRD); chairman,
National Development Finance Agency; director, Irish Stock Exchange; director, Abbey Theatre;
council member, Dublin Chamber of Commerce; member, Council, Financial Services Association;
chairman, Ulysses Securitisation Plc; member, National Pension Reserve Fund Commission; director,
St. Vincent's University Hospital Ltd; Awards: Chevalier, Legion d'Honneur by the President of
France; Contact: National Treasury Management Agency, Treasury Building, Grand Canal Street,
Dublin 2. **T** 01 664 0800 **F** 01 664 0890 email msomers@ntma.ie web www.ntma.ie

State housekeeper par excellence, in the last decade has been a vital part of Ireland's
economy becoming the envy of Europe; simplistic view is that he merely manages the
National Debt; however his contribution is of heroic proportions; has made a
Whitaker-esque contribution to revolutionising the management of the state's monies;
is counted as one of the architects of the financial infrastructure underpinning the
Celtic Tiger; the NTMA, under his baton, manages an awesome cash flow of €532
billion, over four times Ireland's GNP, while its total portfolio of assets and liabilities
exceeds €50 billion.

SPARKS, Gregory Gerard; ACCOUNTANT

b 1951, Dublin; *m* Catherine; 1*s* 3*d*; *edu.* Chanel College, Coolock, Dublin; University College Dublin;
B.Comm; ACA, Institute of Chartered Accountants (ICAI) 1997; Accountant: AITI; 1977–82

Industry; established practice 1982; secondment to Tánaiste's Office 1993 -97; returned to Practice 1997 to date; Clubs: St. Anne's Golf Club. Recreations: family, reading, movies. Contact: FGS, Molyneux House, Bride Street, Dublin 8. **T** 01 418 2000

His company is called in by any number of clients who, when making presentations to government, wish to test the waters of the politically possible; able and astute, has steered a wide range of clients through perceptual difficulties and that includes a wide range of arts clients.

Pat Spillane

SPILLANE, Patrick Michael 'Pat'; BROADCASTER/ COLUMNIST
b 1955, Kerry; *m* Rosarie Moloney; 1*s* 2*d*; *edu.* St. Brendan's College, Killarney; National College of Physical Education Limerick; B. Ed.; Teacher, Presenter of "The Sunday Game" RTE1, Columnist *Sunday World*, Publican; one of the all time great GAA footballers, playing on the legendary Mick O'Dwyer managed Kerry teams of the seventies and eighties; won eight All Ireland Football Medals with Kerry 1975, 1978, 1979, 1980, 1981, 1984, 1985, 1986; won a record 8 All Star GAA Football Awards; twice voted "Texaco Player of the Year"; was "Irish World Superstar" champion and represented Ireland in the "World Superstars Competition" in The Bahamas 1978; named as left half forward on the GAA/An Post "Team of the Millennium" in 1999; *Publ. Shooting From the Hip* 2000, *No Pat on The Back* (Blackwater) 2004. Clubs: chairman Templenoe GAA Club, Ring of Kerry Golf Club. Recreations: all sports. Contact: Templenoe, Kenmare, Co. Kerry. **T** 064 41183 **F** 064 41183 email rpspillane@eircom.net

His GAA footballing record is truly awesome; only four other GAA players - Ogie Moran, Paudie O'Shea (*qv*) Ger Power, Mike Sheehy - have equalled his record of eight All Ireland medals (including a four-in-a-row and a three-in-a-row); has at least 12 Munster Football Medals and 4 Railway Cup Medals; his natural skill and scoring feats on the field of play are the stuff of legend; off the field is quite a controversialist, his revealing books on football, his straight talking *Sunday World* column and now his pull no punches –and extremely successful - "*The Sunday Game*", which he presents each Sunday night during the GAA Championship season on RTE I, provoke debate, excitement, and sometimes downright hostility; whatever he does success follows.

SPRING, Dick; EXECUTIVE VICE PRESIDENT FEXCO HOLDINGS.
b 1950, Tralee; *m* Kristi; 2*s* 1*d*; *edu.* Mount St. Joseph's, Roscrea; Trinity College Dublin, BA; Kings Inns BL; Executive Vice-Chairman Fexco Holdings; member, Dáil Eireann 1981–02; leader of the Labour Party 1982-97; Tánaiste 1982-87 and 1993– 97; Minister for Justice, Environment, Energy, Foreign Affairs; International Rugby cap for Ireland; Gaelic football and hurling for Kerry. Clubs: Tralee, Ballybunnion and European Golf Clubs, International Golf Club Boston, Tralee, Rugby Football Club, Landsdowne Rugby Club. Recreations: golf, reading, swimming. Contact: Ridge Lodge, The Spa, Tralee, Co. Kerry. **F** 066 713 6701 email dsconsnlteircom.net

One of the most able Labour politicians Ireland has produced; extraordinarily keen legal brain; charismatic, brilliant communicator, highly articulate; has moved from politics to business effortlessly.

STAFFORD; Jim Joseph; PRINCIPAL, FRIEL, STAFFORD CHARTERED ACCOUNTANTS
b 1960, Dublin; *m* Grainne; 1*s* 1*d*; *edu.* Blackrock College, Dublin; College of Commerce, Rathmines, B.Sc. Mgmt; University College Dublin D.P.A; F.C.A (Fellow of Chartered Accountants); M.I.I.CM. (Member of Irish Institute of Credit Management); Principal, Friel, Stafford Chartered Accountants; Spicer & Oppenheim, New York 1987-89; Coopers & Lybrand, London 1989– 94; Friel Stafford 1994 to date; *Publ. The Practitioners Guide to Members Voluntary Liquidation; The Practitioners Guide to the Convening of Creditors Meetings; The Insolvency Practitioners' Guide to the Companies Registration Office; The Pocket Book Guide to Corporate Recovery and Insolvency;* Clubs: Blackrock Tennis Club. Recreations: tennis, golf. Contact: Friel Stafford, 44 Fitzwilliam Place, Dublin 2. **T** 01 661 4066 **F** 01 661 4145 email stafford@liquidations.ie www.liquidations.ie

STAFFORD, Victor; CHAIRMAN, STAFFORD HOLDINGS
b 1943, Wexford; *m* Mary O'Driscoll; 4*s* 1*d*; *edu.* University College Dublin; B. Comm; Stanford University, California; MBA; Chairman Stafford Holdings; started his career in the family company in

Wexford 1967; expanded and diversified into property, hotels and retailing. Contact: 4 Bracken Business Park, Bracken Rd., Sandyford, Dublin. **T** 01 291 5500

Extremely low-profile, one of Wexford's merchant princes who grew the family business from oil, fuel and stevedoring into property hotels and leisure; commercially astute; respected in the business community.

STAGG, Emmet Martin; PUBLIC REPRESENTATIVE
b 1944 Holly Mount, Co. Mayo; *m* Mary Morris; 1*s* 1*d*; *edu.* Ballinode C.B.S; Kevin Street College of Technology; Public Representative, Labour TD; Labour chief whip and spokesperson on nuclear safety; medical technician; Minister of State, Department of Transport and Energy and Communications 1994-97; Minister of State, Department of the Environment with special responsibility for Housing and Urban Renewal 1993-94; elected, Dáil Eireann in 1987; Party spokesperson on Agriculture 1987–89; Social Welfare 1989–92; member Kildare County Council 1978-93, 1999-03; chairperson, Kildare County Council 1981–82; member, Kildare County Library Committee 1985–93; member, Eastern Health Board 1978-85. Clubs: president, Celbridge Soccer Club, president, Maynooth Soccer Club, member, Straffan GAA Club. Recreations: fishing, growing vegetables, reading, shooting. Contact: Lodge Park, Straffan, Co. Kildare. **T** 01 618 3797 **F** 01 618 4538 email emmet.stagg@oireachtas.ie

Emmett Stagg

Hardworking Labour front bencher who was a very effective minister in the Rainbow Government 1994–97

STANDÚN, Rev. Pádraig; PRIEST/ WRITER
b 1946, Belcarra, Castlebar, Co. Mayo; single; edu. St. Jarlath's College, Tuam; St. Patrick's College, Maynooth, Co. Kildare; B.A; B.D. Priest/Writer; Curate Tourmakeady, Co. Mayo; Curate Inis Meán, Inis Oirr, Oileáin Árainn 1971–73; Inis Oirr 1973-75; An Cheathrú Rua 1975–87; Inis Meáin 1987–95; Tuar Mhic Éadaigh to date; *Publ. Súil le Breith,* Cló Chonamara 1983; *A.D. 2016,* Cló Chonamara 1988; *Cíocras,* Cló Iar- Chonnachta 1991; *An tAinmhí,* Cló Iar-Chonnachta 1992; *Cion Mná,* Cló Iar- Chonnachta 1993; *Na hAntraipeologicals,* Cló Iar –Chonnachta 1993; *Stigmata* Cló Iar –Chonnachta, 1994; *Lovers,* Poolbeg 1991; *Celibates,* Poolbeg, 1993; *The Anvy,* Cló Iar -Chonnachta, 1993; *Saoire,* Cló Iar -Chonnachta, 1997; *Das Vien,* Pendragon 2002; *Striogoiul Anvy,* Pandora 2003 (Romanian); *Eaglais na gCatacomaí,* C.P.C. 2004; *Sobalsaol,* Cló Iar -Chonnachta, 2005. Recreations: reading, writing, walking, drama, sport on TV. Contact: Tuar Mhic Éadaigh, Clár chlainne, Co. Mhaigheo. **T** 094 954 4037

STAPLETON, Peter Michael; CHARTERED SURVEYOR
b 1956, Dublin; *m* Sarah; 2*s* 1*d*; *edu.* St Conleths College, Dublin; Sandford Park School, Dublin; FSCS, FRICS, FIAVI; Managing Director Lisney; director, Clanmil Ireland (Housing Association); director/ member, Dublin Chamber of Commerce. Clubs: Royal Irish Yacht Club, Blainroe Golf Club. Recreations: yachting, golf. Contacts: 24 Stephen's Green, Dublin. **T** 01 638 2770 email pstapleton@lisney.com web www.lisney.com

STAUNTON, Stephen 'Steve'; MANAGER, REPUBLIC OF IRISH FOOTBALL TEAM
b 1969, Drogheda, Co. Louth; *m* Joanne; 2*s*; *edu.* Friary National School, Drogheda; De La Salle Secondary School, Drogheda; Manager, Republic of Ireland Football Team. spotted playing for Dundalk FC as a 17 yr old by Liverpool manager Kenny Dalglish, 1987; signed for Liverpool for £20,000, 1988; selected to play for the Republic of Ireland 1989; won FA Cup medal with Liverpool 1989; selected for Republic of Ireland's first World Cup team in Italia '90, youngest member of the squad; played in every match at left back as Ireland progressed to the quarter finals, when they were beaten by the host nation;sold to Aston Villa 1991; won League Cup medal at 'Villa 1994; selected to play for Republic of Ireland in World Cup USA 1994; played in each game as Ireland succumbed in the second round to the Netherlands; won another League Cup with Villa, 1996; continued to represent Republic of Ireland who failed to qualify for Euro '96 and World Cup 1998 in France; returned to Liverpool 1998; free transfer to Crystal Palace, 2000; returned to Aston Villa, 2001; captain, Republic of Ireland in World Cup 2002 in Japan and South Korea; played in every Ireland game of the tournament, with the group match against Germany proving a very special occasion as it was his 100th appearance for his country; announced his retirement from international football after a national record of 102 appearances, 2002; continued to play with Coventry City until 2005; joined Walsall 2005–06; appointed manager Republic of Ireland national team 2006. Recreations: golf. Contact: 80, Merrion Square, Dublin 2. **T** 01 676 6864 web www.fai.ie

The near neighbour of the Corrs when growing up on Ard Easmuinn Estate, Drogheda, seems to be almost universally popular; Ireland's most capped international, was also a talented GAA player playing with Clan na Gael and winning a Louth senior Football Championship 1985; played schoolboy football with St. Dominicks before signing with Dundalk FC; but with no national management experience how will all of this translate into successfully pulling a top class Irish team together?; early international results aredeeply depressing.

Amelia Stein

STEIN Amelia PHOTOGRAPHER/OPTOMETRIST

b 1958, Dublin; single; *edu.* Alexandra College, Dublin; Kevin Street, College of Technology. Dublin; Photographer and Optometrist; production photographer, art photographer and artists' photographer to many theatre companies including the Project Arts Centre, Abbey Theatre, Focus Theatre, Gate, Gaiety, Druid Theatre Company, Rough Magic and Wexford Opera Festival,1980 to date. Her portraits of artists have been widely used in Ireland and abroad; work is also exhibited by the Rubicon Gallery Dublin, and at many national and international exhibitions; L'imaginaire Irlandais, 1985; the Palm House series exhibited at the Rubicon Gallery, 'Loss and Memory' work based on the possessions of her late parents Rubicon Gallery, 2001; 2002; elected member of the Royal Hibernian Academy of Arts, Dublin, 2004; member, Aosdana 2006. *Publ.* her works are represented in all major Irish collections including the Arts Council, RHA, Office of Public Works Ireland (Farmleigh House), Contemporary Arts Society Ireland and the Gulbenkian Foundation UK; Recreations: gardening, walking cycling, classical music. Contact: 4 Camden Market, Grantham Street, Dublin 8. **T** 01 475 1275 email info@rubicongallery.ie

A brilliant photographer with an international reputation; great sense of the essence of her subjects; her compositions are works of art in themselves; she knows the quality of her own work and isn't shy about it!

STEPHENSON, Sam; ARCHITECT

b 1933, Dublin; *m* 1st Bernadette Flood; (*m. diss*); 2s 2d; *m* 2nd Caroline Sweetman; 2s; *edu.* Belvedere College, Dublin; College of Technology, Bolton Street, Dublin; FRIAI; MSIA; RHA; Principal, Sam Stephenson & Co. Ltd; a founding partner Stephenson Gibney & Associates; moved his practice to London for a period; current practice, Sam Stephenson & Co. Co. Kildare; major projects included: Bórd na Mona HQ (Dublin); ESB Head Offices, Dublin; Central Bank Dublin and part of the Civic Offices for Dublin Corporation, completed by another architectural firm; Contact: Ryevale House, Leixlip, Co. Kildare. **T** 01 624 6467

Extraordinarily bright designer; highly gregarious and the best company; has had a major and often very controversial impact on the Dublin city skyline.

STEWART, Duncan; ARCHITECT, TV PRESENTER

b 1947: Dublin; *m* Agneta Lundstrom; 1d 4s; *edu.* Colaiste Mhuire, University College Dublin (B.Arch), DIT Bolton Street (Diploma in Irish Arbitration Law, Diploma in International Arbitration Law); Ecological Architect, Television Producer and Presenter; lecturer DIT Bolton Street, early 1970s; now partner in Stewart & Sinnott Architects; director, Time Horizon Productions; director, Earth Horizon Productions; presenter and producer, *Our House* RTE I 1991-98; presenter, *Wood from the Trees* RTE 1 1997; presenter, *Engine Earth* RTE 1, UTV, and Swedish TV 1998; presenter and producer, *The State We Are In* RTE 1 1999-00; presenter and producer, *About the House* RTE 1, Discovery Home and Leisure Channel 1999 to date; presenter and producer, *Ecoeye* RTE 1 2001 to date; presenter, *The Changing Face of Dublin* RTE 1 2002; *Publ: Our Home* (Blackwater) 2002. Clubs: active member Chernobyl Children's International Project; links with many eco and wildlife associations. Recreations: cycling, swimming, was a 10K per week runner prior to accident in Chernobyl. Contact: Horizon Productions, 13 Windsor Place, Dublin 2. **T** 01 6617475 **F** 01 6620337 email info@earthhorizon.ie

As interests in the preservation of the planet and intelligent lifestyles grow, he has become a kind of national treasure on our television screens telling us "how to" participate in sustaining and managing the earth's natural resources; viewing ratings for his TV shows are on the increase and he has become the public face of the renewable energy movement; is also deeply concerned about the aftermath of Chernobyl and the issues it raises for the future about nuclear energy; had a serious accident, from which he has largely recovered, while working in Chernobyl; his next television venture is a documentary called *"True Lives"* about Chernobyl; his campaigning and concern for the earth and its future is not surprising in that he led the student sit-in protesting for the preservation of Hume Street's Georgian buildings when he was at University College Dublin.

Duncan Stewart

STEWART, Ercus; SENIOR COUNSEL, ARBITRATOR, LECTURER
b 1949, Tipperary; *m* Ria; *2s 2d*; *edu.* Colaiste Mhuire, Dublin; University College Dublin; King's Inns; Barrister-at-law; DIT, Dublin; Diploma in International Arbitration; Fellow Chartered Institute of Arbitrators; Chartered Arbitrator; Senior Counsel; called to the Bar 1970; called to the Inner Bar 1982; called to Northern Ireland Bar 1976; called to Middle Temple Bar 1982; called to New South Wales Bar 1992; *Publ:* Labour Law in Ireland 1979, *Arbitration Law* 2003, *Dismissal and Employment law* 2005. Clubs: Irish Mountain Running Association, Irish Triathlon Association, Fitzwilliam LTC, chairman, Irish Romanian Breadbasket Appeal, board member, Chernobyl Children's Project International, GOAL. Recreations: running, swimming walking, cycling, travelling. Contact: Law Library Buildings, 145 Church Street, Dublin 7. **T** 01 817 5101 **F** 01 817 5175 email es@ercus.com and estewart@lawlibrary.ie

Ireland's foremost legal expert on all aspects of labour and employment law; brother of Duncan (*qv*); his outdoor pursuits are legendary; was four times Irish Mountain running champion (Vet, over 50, 1999-03), and has completed the Iron Man Triathlon and 16 marathons.

STOKES, Christian; RESTAURANTEUR/PROPERTY DEVELOPER
b 1975, Dublin; single; *edu.* Sandford Park, Ranelagh, Dublin; Wesley College, Dublin; Dublin Business School; Managing Director Mayfair Properties; sold his interest in Bang Café and Clarendon Bar to brother Simon 2006; Clubs: Powerscourt Golf Club. Recreations: travel, fashion, interiors, golf. Contact: 11, Merrion Row, Dublin 2. **T** 01 6760898 **F** 01 6760899

Gregarious, charming and a hardworker, with his twin brother Simon (*qv*) is already on his way to creating an impressive career in the restaurant and property business; is taking a sabbatical in the US and trying the property market there 2006-07

STOKES, Jeffrey; DEVELOPER & RESTAURANTEUR
b 1949; *m* Pia Bang (*qv* Stokes, Pia Bang); *2s*; *edu.* Sandford Park, Ranelagh, Dublin; Modeling, Mens Retail, Restauranteur, Interior Design. Clubs: Pat Henry Fitness, Westwood Sandyford. Recreations: fitness, tennis, rugby. Contact: c/o Unicorn Restaurant, 11 Merrion Row, Dublin 2. **T** 01 662 4197

With his business partner Giorgio Casari (*qv*), has made The Unicorn one of the consistently hottest restaurants in the country; now has two fine sons Christian (*qv*) and Simon (*qv*) following in his footsteps.

STOKES, Niall; PUBLISHER, HOT PRESS
b 1952, Dublin; *m* Maureen Sheehy ; *2s*; *edu.* Synge Street CBS; University College Dublin; BA; Founding Publisher/Editor *Hotpress* 1978; with partner Mairin Sheehy runs Osnovina which publishes *Hot Press, Enterprise* (on-board magazine for the Dublin-Belfast rail service), *MQ* (the quarterly magazine for IMRO - the Irish Music Rights Organisation); the company published three books 2004 and has more in the pipeline; has a 25 per cent stake Hot Press Irish Music Hall of Fame facility; aggressively pursuing commercial radio projects; founded Hotpress.com; Awards: Publisher of the Year Hotpress, 2004. Recreations: music, soccer, contemporary politics. Contact: 13 Trinity Street, Dublin 2. **T** 01 241 1500 email niall@hotpress.ie web www.hotpress.ie

Has consistently rattled the cages of Irish society and broken exciting new ground in contemporary journalism; each fortnight, in his trenchant editorial column, The Message, Stokes remains uncompromising.

STOKES Pia Bang; FASHION RETAILER
b 1945, Copenhagen; *m* Jeff Stokes (*qv*); *2s*; *edu.* Alexandra College, Dublin; Managing Director Pia Bang; designer and retailer; started her own business Pia Bang to date; Pia Bang Home Interiors South Anne St. Dublin, 2005 to date. Recreations: travel, painting, gardening, family. Contact: 46, Grafton Street, Dublin 2. **T** 01 671 5065 **F** 01 671 5644

Always elegant and the best advertisement for her own business, has impeccable taste in everything she does.

Simon Stokes

STOKES, Simon; RESTAURANTEUR/PROPERTY DEVELOPER
b 1975, Dublin; *m* Conach; 1*s*; *edu.* Sandford Park/Wesley College, Dublin Business School, Business Degree; co-owner Bang Café 1999 to date; bought Clarendon Bar, Dublin 2003; revamped/re-opened Clarence Bar 2004; Clubs: Carton House Golf Club; Recreations: golf, travel; Contact: 11 Merrion Row, Dublin 2. **T** 01 676 0898 **F** 01 676 0899

The former male model is a well rounded, confident, unassuming young man; has already shown a maturity way in business way beyond his years.

SWAN, Charlie; HORSE TRAINER
b 1968, Co Tipperary; *m* 1st Tina (*m.diss*); 1*s*; *m* 2nd Carol Hyde; 1*s* 1*d*; edu; St. Columba's College, Rathfarnham, Dublin 16; Horse Trainer; Ireland's champion jump jockey for nine consecutive seasons; has ridden more National Hunt winners in Ireland than any other jockey in history; holds the Irish records for both the most winners in a season and the most in a calendar year; has twice been leading jockey at the Cheltenham Festival and has a string of big-race victories to his credit including three Champion Hurdles, the Queen Mother Champion Chase, the Irish Grand National, two Whitbread Gold Cups and four Irish Champion Hurdles. Recreations: golf, family. Contact: Modreeny, Cloughjordan, Co. Tipperary. **T** 0505 42221 / 0505 42128

Calm, charming and totally focused; rode his first winner as a baby faced fifteen year old on his father's Final Assault in a two year old maiden at Naas in March 1983; went on to create new records as a jockey; now a successful trainer with nearly 300 winners under his belt since he took out his trainer's license in 1998.

SWEENEY, Brody; FOUNDER, M.D. O'BRIEN'S SANDWICHES
b 1962, Dublin; *m* Lulu; 3*s* 1*d*; *edu.* Blackrock College, Dublin; Rockwell College, Tipperary; NIHE Glasnevin; Founder, Managing Director O'Brien's Sandwiches; Entrepreneur; opened sixteen outlets Prontoprint (1980 -88); started O'Briens Sandwich Company1988; opened four shops in Dublin 1988-92; first franchised O'Briens 1994; now has circa 300 outlets globally of which 130 in Republic of Ireland with others in such diverse locations as Thailand, Australia, Singapore, Spain and Taiwan; now employs in excess 3000 people; indicated an interest in a political career, 2005; secured the Fine Gael nomination for Dublin North East (2007 General Election); Contact:Constituency Office: Office No 3, 61 St. Assams Park, Raheny, Dublin 5. **T** 01 851 2256 **F** 01 851 2267 email info@brodysweeney.ie

While seeming an unorthodox businessman Sweeney has become one of Ireland's leading entrepreneurs; built his sandwich business out of the depressed '80's; owes much to the improving economic fortunes under the Haughey/McSharry regime which led to the emergence of the Celtic Tiger; whether its a Wrappo, Toostie, Gourmet Coffee, Juice or Smoothie, O'Briens' deliver delicious made-to-order food across 13 countries, everyday; with one of the most successful franchise companies under his belt, wants to "give something back to society" and is running for Fine Gael in Dublin North East in the General Election 2007; but will winning a seat be the doddle FG initially expected?

SWEENEY, Ciarán; CREATIVE DIRECTOR
b 1971, Drogheda; single; *edu.* Schull Community College; Summerhill College, Sligo; Sligo Technical Institute; National College of Art and Design; BA, Art and Design Education; Artist, Costume and Fabric Designer; numerous solo shows and group exhibitions; produced and directed the NCAD Graduate Fashion Show 2000 to date; Harrods launch Homeline 2005; created unique piece for Kylie Minogue; Liberty London stock Sweeney Accessories 2004; costume designer PGA European Golf Championship, The K. Club 2003; commissioned by University of Notre Dame, USA, to create hand-painted pieces for its board members on their visit to Ireland and also a piece for President Mary McAleese (*qv*) 2002; costume designer for Moya Brennan (*qv*) at The Grammy Awards, Los Angeles 2001; costume designer for TV debut The Celtic Divas 2000; piece acquired by Ulster Museum to represent Irish fashion at the turn of the millennium 1999; costume designer The Corrs World Tour

1996; *Publ. Brennan, Moya* Artwork; *An Solas Uaigneach, An Saggart, Maynooth*; Contact: Ciaran Sweeney Studio, 12 E. Newmarket Square, Dublin 8. **T** 01 411 3953 email ciaran@ciaransweeney.com; www.ciaran-sweeney.com,

Multitalented designer who has received many prestigious commissions; prolific and hard working, always working on the next project.

Ciarán Sweeney

SWEENEY, Michael; BANKER
b 1960, London; divorced; *edu.* Hamilton High School, Bandon, Co. Cork; University College Dublin; B. Comm (Hons); Chief Executive Officer Bank of Ireland Global Markets; joined Bank of Ireland 1979; joined Treasury Division 1988; Treasurer Bank of Ireland, UK Treasury London 1993; head of Trading & Investment Group (Dublin & UK) 1998; chief executive Bank of Ireland Global Markets with offices in Bristol, Belfast, London, Manchester, Glasgow and New York, 2003 to date; team of 600 and balance sheet of c. €100 billion; Recreations: all sports, philosophy, travel, marathon running, film review. Contact: Bank of Irland Global Mkts, Colvill House, Talbot Street, Dublin 1. **T** 01 609 3300 email mick.sweeney@boigm.com web www.boigm.com

Widely experienced in the rapidly changing global treasury area; the Hammie's educated executive is extremely well got in financial circles; tipped for greater things in the Bank of Ireland

TAAFFE, Tom J; RACEHORSE TRAINER

b 1963, Dublin; *m* 1st Peaches Kemp; (*m diss*) 2nd Elaine; *2s; edu.* Christian Brothers School, Naas; successful jockey until he retired in 1994, winning all the major races in Ireland over jumps and many in the UK; now training horses with good results, winning the Cheltenham Gold Cup 2005 – Kicking King the highlight. Recreations: golf. Contact: Portree, Straffan, Co Kildare. **T** 01 627 3604 **F** 01 627 4231 email PORTREESTABLES@EIRCOM.NET

Son of the legendary Pat forever associated with Arkle; has emulated his famous father, winning the ultimate blue riband of the National Hunt calendar, The Cheltenham Gold Cup.

TAGGART, Pascal; FORMER CHAIRMAN BORD NA gCON

b 1946, Antrim; *m* Helen; *2s; edu.* St. Mary's Christian Brothers School Antrim; Businessman; worked in the UK Revenue 1970-73; tax advisors Spicer and Peckler 1973; moved back to Ireland, working in the financial sector; partner Bastow Charlton 1975-85; director Doyle Hotels 1982 -88; chairman Bord na gCon 1995 – 06; established Cooney Taggart 1989; chairman Orbiscom; board member Datalex; owner *Ireland on Sunday* 1998-00; former chairman of Telco ITG; Jervis Street Shopping Centre 1995-99; Rosslough Holdings 1995-99; sold the "eight to twelve" convenience stores 1991; led a number of business consortia including the purchase of H. Williams chain of supermarkets; acquired 1.5% of Jurys Doyle Hotel Group 2005; chairman Bord na gCon. 1997 – 06.. Clubs: Castle Golf Club, Dublin, Sotogrande Golf Club, Spain. Recreations: greyhounds, GAA, golf. Contact: Cooney Taggart, 23 Fitzwilliam Square, Dublin 2. **T** 01 676 2205 **F** 01 661 9575

Irrespective of the end result or financial benefit to himself, loves to be involved in transactions, loves the thrill of the deal; respected by the wider business community.

TANSEY, Paul, Anthony; ECONOMIST

b 1949, Dublin; *m* Olivia O'Leary (*qv*); 1d; *edu.* Blackrock College; Trinity College Dublin; London School of Economics & Political Science; MA MBA; Managing Director, Tansey Website Stewart & Company; The Irish Times 1973-83; The Sunday Tribune 1983-86; economic consultant 1986 to date; director TOTE Ireland, independent member (appointed by Government) National Economic and Social Reform; member, Tourism Action Plan Implementation Group; *Publ. Making the Irish Labour Market Work* (Gill & MacMillan) 1992; *Ireland at Work* (Cork Tree Press) 1998. Clubs: Irish Economic Association, Monkstown Lawn Tennis Club, Greenvalley Riding Club. Recreations: amateur show jumping, tennis, horse racing. Contact: 10 Belgrave Road, Monkstown, Co Dublin. **T** 01 2801303 **F** 01 2802303

A quiet and charming man who exercises a great deal of influence on all kinds of thinking, not just in the sphere of economics but also of socio-political global economic strategies; delightful company, enjoys the open air life as well as more convivial pursuits.

TATTON, Oliver; CHIEF EXECUTIVE, VIVAS HEALTH

b 1964, Co. Tipperary; *m* Beatriz de sa Ferriera Villanova; 1s 3d; *edu.* CBS Cashel; University College Dublin; University of South Africa; INSEAD; B. Ch. Eng; industrial psychology; MBA; Chief Executive, Vivas Health; assistant managing director John Somers Estanhos Ltd Brazil 1988-89; product and production manager Heraus Holding, 1989-90; sales and marketing manager International Subsidiaries Director 1992-93; general manager Hanau, Germany 1993-96; chief executive Irish Trade Board and non executive director Forfás 1996-98; chief executive VHI 1998-2001; worked with Dermot Desmond companies 2001-03; chief executive Vivas Health Insurance 2003 to date. Contact: Vivas Health, Paramount Court, Corrig Road, Sandyford, Dublin 18. **T** 01 481 7800 email info@vivashealth.ie web www.vivashealth.ie

Cashel born executive had a meteoric rise in the business world when he was appointed chief executive of the Irish Trade Board at a very young age; after a varied career is back in the private health insurance sector where he is pitched in a bitter battle with his old employers VHI in the new risk equalization era; his new employers Dermot Desmond (*qv*) and AIB plc have very deep pockets.

Oliver Tatton

TAYLOR, Cliff; EDITOR, SUNDAY BUSINESS POST
b 1961, Dublin; *m* Elizabeth; 2*s*; *edu*. St. Andrew's College, Booterstown, Dublin; Trinity College Dublin, BA (Mod) Economics; Editor, Sunday Business Post; freelance journalist, including spell with RTE 1983-85; press officer, IDA 1985-87; *Irish Times*, various positions including financial editor 1987-04; *Sunday Business Post* Jan 2005. Clubs: Roganstown Golf Club. Recreations: family, golf, running, media in general. Contact: Sunday Business Post, Harcourt Street, Dublin 2 **T** 01 602 6000 email ctaylor@sbpost.ie web www.sbp.ie

As befits the editor of Ireland's leading business paper, has a broad and distinguished career in financial journalism; runs a tight ship; highly articulate, popular and well respected in the national business world.

Cliff Taylor

TAYLOR, John Noel; GALLERIST
b 1948, Dublin; *m* Mary Preece; 2*s* 1*d*; edu. De La Salle Brothers, Churchtown, Dublin; Director, The Taylor Galleries; manager The Dawson Gallery, Dublin 1964-78; director with brother Patrick, The Taylor Galleries, Dublin 1978 to date; represents many of the leading Irish and international artists including; Norah McGuinness, Louis Le Brocquy, Tony O'Malley, Maurice MacGonigal, Anne Madden, Brian Bourke, Conor Fallon, William Crozier, Melanie Le Brocquy, Patrick Scott, Camille Souter, Seán McSweeney, Janet Pierce; member, Irish Contemporary Art Galleries Association. Recreations: golf, walking. Contact; The Taylor Galleries, 16, Kildare Street, Dublin 2. **T** 01 676 6055

A national institution; is regarded as being the confidant of many and the friend of all artists; has a great eye and is the great clearing house for all kinds of artistic and arts political information in the city; has launched more careers than Helen launched ships; his gentle and laid back manner disguises an essential toughness, but a ready and willing helper for the good cause; eschews personal publicity preferring it for his gallery, artists and the general welfare of the visual arts.

TEEHAN, Rhona; RESTAURATEUR
b 1949, Dublin; single; *edu*. Beaufort, Loreto Abbey Rathfarnham, Dublin; San Jose Junior College, California; Restaurateur; croupier Playboy Club (London) 1972-74; coffee bar proprietor, St. Stephen's Green, Dublin 1976-78; restaurant and nightclub chain: Kilmartins Wine Bar 1979; Susey Street Night Club 1984; Trocadero 1983; Café Caruso 1991. Clubs: Castle Golf Club, Luttrellstown Golf Club. Recreations: golf. Contact: Trocadero, 3, St. Andrew Street, Dublin 2. **T** 01 677 5545 **F** 01 679 2385 **M** 087 256 1919

A bright, open and candid person who has had the good sense to keep her best asset, her staff, always with her; knows the restaurant business inside out; an excellent golfer, she remains an extremely popular and attractive public personality who has retained all her longstanding friendships.

TEEHAN, Virginia; DIRECTOR, THE HUNT MUSEUM
b 1962, Tipperary; *m* Dr. Cian Ó Mathúna; 2*s* 1*d*; *edu*. Coláiste Bhríde, Callann, Co. Kilkenny; Kilkenny College, Kilkenny; University College Cork (BA); University College Dublin (DAA); Trinity College Dublin; (M.Phil); Director, The Hunt Museum, Limerick: University Archivist and Director, Heritage and Visual Arts Office, University College Cork 1988-03; director The Hunt Museum Limerick 2003 to date; member of The Heritage Council 2000-05; member of the management board, Glucksman Gallery, University College Cork 2003 to date; *Publ*. with Elizabeth Heckett *A Golden Vision, The Honan Chapel* (Cork University Press) 2004: *Archives* in Buttimer, N., Rynne, C., Guerin H., *The Heritage of Ireland* (The Collins Press) 2000; *The Provision of Genealogical Services in Ireland*, The Heritage Council, (Consultant's Report Commissioned by the Heritage Council on behalf of the Minister for Arts, Heritage, Gaeltacht and the Islands) 1999; (co-author) *Standards for the Development of Archives' Services in Ireland* (The Society of Archivists) 1997. Recreations; history, history of decorative arts, cultural affairs. Contact: The Hunt Museum, Rutland Street, Limerick. **T** 061 312833 **F** 061 312832 email director@huntmuseum.com

A lively and engaging personality who did much to retrieve the information and material relating to the glories of the Honan Chapel in University College Cork; now facing into a turbulent period in the Hunt Museum.

John Teeling

TEELING, John; EXECUTIVE CHAIRMAN, DISTILLER
b 1946, Dublin; *m* Deirdre Shaw; 2*s* 1*d*; *edu*. St. Joseph's CBS Fairview, University College Dublin; B. Comm; M.Econ.Sc; Wharton School, University of Pennsylvania, MBA; Harvard Business School, Boston, DBA; Executive Chairman Cooley Distillery plc; lecturer, University College Dublin 1968-88; managing director Seafield Group plc 1979-81; chairman, 1987; Pan Andean Resources 1983 to date; Minco; Petrol Resources; African Diamonds; executive chairman Countryglen plc. 1987; executive chairman Cooley Distillery plc. 1987 to date. (Ireland's only independent distillery, producing the brand names Kilbeggan, Lockes, Millars, Connemara, The Tyrconnell and special blends Inishowen, Eblana and Sainsbury's own label); Publ. *Modern Irish Business; Business Organisation; Financial Management* (co-author). Clubs: Clontarf Rugby Club, Clontarf Cricket Club, Royal Dublin Golf Club. Recreations: golf, cricket, rugby. Contact: Cooley Distillery plc, 162 Clontarf Road, Dublin 3. **T** 01 833 2833 **F** 01 833 3505 email info@cooleywhiskey.com web www.cooleywhiskey.com

The former academic made a seamless transition into the world of business; has displayed great management skills in dealing with a number of his business acquisitions; now publicly identified with the development of the Cooley Distillery and it's portfolio of unique Irish whiskey brands.

TERRITT, Martin; DIRECTOR, E.C. REPRESENTATION, IRELAND
b 1960, Portlaoise; *m* Catherine; 1*s* 1*d*; *edu*. Kings Inns; Barrister at Law 1991; director European Commission Representation Ireland; Dept Justice 1977-91; Dept of Labour 1991-95; press officer to Minister Richard Bruton and Minister of State Pat Rabbitte, Dept of Trade and Employment 1995-97; press officer to Tánaiste Mary Harney, Dept of Trade and Employment 1997-99; member, Cabinet of EU Commissioner David Byrne 1999-04; director European Commission Representation Ireland 2005 to date. Recreations: family, reading, music and golf. Contact: European Commission Representation in Ireland, 18. Dawson Street, Dublin 2. **T** 01 634 1111 email grainne.galvin@cec.eu.int

An experienced civil servant in Dublin and Brussels prior to taking up his appointment in Dublin; with the increasing impact of various EU Directives and Regulations on Irish society his office will continue to be point of information for Irish consumers.

TELFORD, Michael Bruce; HEADMASTER
b 1952, Aldershot, England; *m* Mary; 2*s*; *edu*. St Columba's College, Rathfarnham, Dublin 16; Trinity College, Dublin; BA (Mod), PhD, H.Dip, Ed; Head Master John Scottus Senior School; founding head master John Scottus School, Dublin 1986; member, Board of Studies NCCA; chair, Ancient Greek Working Group; chair, Classical Association of Ireland. Clubs: treasurer Irish Institute of Hellenic Studies at Athens. Recreations: philosophy, Spanish, choral singing. Contact: 11 Morehampton Road, Donnybrook, Dublin 4. **T** 01 668 0828 **F** 01 667 6672 email telford@clubi.ie

Presides over an exclusive educational institution which has produced a glittering alumnae; has a committed following.

TIGHE, David; CHIEF EXECUTIVE LIVE 98FM LIMERICK
b 1969; *m* Debbie; 1*s* 2*d*; *edu*. Hinchingbrooke School, Huntingdon, Cambridgeshire, UK; The Huntingdonshire College, Diploma in Business and Professional Management; Chief Executive, Live 98FM, Limerick; Cambridge Evening News; broadcast show presenter CNFM 103, Cambridge; radio presenter Severin Sound, Cheltenham; breakfast show presenter Chiltern Radio, Luton; programme director emap Radio; CEO Live 95FM UTV. Recreations: soccer, watersports, travel, history, hurling. Contact: Live 95FM, Dock Road, Limerick. **T** 061 461 900 **F** 061 419 595 email david@live95fm.ie

Extremely bright and energetic, brings a wealth of experience from UK commercial radio to his position as chief executive of Live 95FM in Limerick.

TIMMINS, Billy Godfrey; PUBLIC REPRESENTATIVE
b 1959, Baltinglass, Co. Wicklow; *m* Madeleine Hyland; 2*s* 3*d*; *edu*. Patrician College, Ballyfin, Co Laois; University College Galway; BA (Economic and Legal Science); Dip. P.R. Marketing and Advertising, University College Galway; Public Representative (FG Wicklow); Spokesperson Defence 2004; spokesperson Agriculture and Food 2002-04; deputy spokesperson Justice and Defence 2001-02; spokesperson Housing 2000-01; Defence, Peacekeeping & Humanitarian Relief 1997-00; elected

to the Dáil 1997; re-elected to the Dáil 2002; army officer with Irish army, Galway, Donegal and Kilkenny 1997; time with United Nations in Lebanon and Cyprus. Clubs: Baltinglass GAA Club, Baltinglass Historical Society. Recreations: history, genealogy. Contact: Weaver Square, Baltinglass, Co Wicklow. **T** 01 618 3384 /059 648 1016 **F** 01 618 4604/ 059 648 2445 email Billy.Timmins@Oireachtas.ie

> The former army officer is interested in social justice and social housing; may occupy much of the middle ground where Labour takes its vote; could be in for a half car if FG form part of the next government.

TOIBÍN, Colm; AUTHOR

Colm Toibín

b 1955, Eniscorthy, Co. Wexford; single; *edu.* Christian Brothers School, Enniscorthy; St Peter's College, Wexford; University College Dublin; BA; Author; Barcelona 1975-78: taught at the Dublin School of English, followed closely the political developments in Barcelona, marched in all the main demonstrations for Catalan autonomy and for Spanish democracy; returned to Dublin 1978; wrote for *In Dublin* and *Hibernia* and later *The Sunday Tribune*; features editor *In Dublin* 1981-82; editor *Magill* 1982-85; began to travel, moving first through South America and ending in Argentina where he attended the trial of Galtieri and the other generals in Buenos Aires 1985; later traveled in the Sudan and Egypt; Publ. his best journalism from the 1980s, which includes sections on South America and Africa, is collected in *The Trial of the Generals; Walking Along the Border* with photographs by Tony O Shea 1987; *Homage to Barcelona* 1988; first novel *The South* 1990; *The Heather Blazing* 1992; drama critic, TV critic, political commentator, *Sunday Independent*; *The Story of the Night* (novel); *The Blackwater Lightship* (novel); *The Sign of the Cross: Travels in Catholic Europe* (travel guide); edited several anthologies, including *The Penguin Book of Irish Fiction*; edited *The Kilfenora Teaboy,* a book of essays on the Irish poet Paul Durcan 1995; *The Modern Library: The 200 Best Novels since 1950* in collaboration with Carmen Callil 1999; regular contributor *The London Review of Books* 1994 to date; *Love In a Dark Time: Gay Lives from Wilde to Almodovar*; became a Fellow at the Center for Scholars and Writers at New York Public Library, working mainly on the Lady Gregory papers there 2000; *Lady Gregory's Toothbrush*, a section of which appeared in *The New York Review of Books* 2002; *Lady's Gregory's Toothbrush* appeared in book form (Lilliput) 2003; featured on the top 10 best book list *NYT*; winner of *LA Times* Novel of the Year; short-listed for Man Booker; winner International IMPAC Literary Award, 2006; has given workshops and master classes at Listowel Writers Week, The Arvon Foundation, The American University at Washington D.C.; has also taught at the MFA program at the New School in Manhattan; books have been translated into 18 languages. Contact: Aosdana, 70, Merrion Square, Dublin 2. **T** 01 618 0200 **F** 01 676 1302 email aosdana@artscouncil.ie web www.colmtoibin.com

> A writer and cultural commentator of great power and delight; his novel *The Master* winner of the International IMPAC Literary Award 2006, was also nominated in 2005 for the Man Booker prize; his novel the *Blackwater Lightship* was seen as a gay novel; he has also written non fiction works including the *Sign of the Cross*; a private personality of great charm and deep sensitivity, adored by his friends and family and the legions of his readers.

TODD, Michael; RACECOURSE MANAGER

Michael Todd

b 1960, Ballymena, Co Antrim; *m* Donna; 2s 1d; *edu.* Ballyclare High School; sales director Kitchenmaster Ltd 1988-92; sales manager Allegro Chemicals Ltd 1992-96; general manager Down Royal Racecourse 1996 to date. Recreations: horse racing, motor sport. Contact: Langan House, Ballynoe Road, Antrim, Co. Down. **T** 04892 621256 **F** 04892 621433 email miketodd@downroyal.com

> Professional, enthusiastic, popular and well regarded in the industry; has attracted much needed investment and increased sponsorship since taking over the helm of the North's premier racetrack.

TREACY, Noel; PUBLIC REPRESENTATIVE

b 1952, Ballinsloe, Co. Galway; *m* Mary Cloonan; 4d; *edu.* St. Joseph's College, Garbally, Ballinsloe, Co. Galway; Public Representative, Fianna Fáil Galway East, Minister of State at the Departments of An Taoiseach and Foreign Affairs with special responsibility for European Affairs 2002-04; Minister of State at the Department of the Taoiseach and became the State's First Minister for Heritage Affairs 1988-89; Minister of State at the Department of Health 1989-91; Minister of State at the

Department of Agriculture and Food (with special responsibility for Food and Horticulture); Minister of State at the Department of Finance (with special responsibility for the Office of Public Works and the Central Development Committee) 1992-93; Minister of State at the Departments of the Taoiseach, Finance, Transport, Energy and Communications (with special responsibility for Energy) 1993-94; Member of the Environment and Sustainable Development Committee 1995-97; Minister of State at the Department of Enterprise, Trade & Employment (with special responsibility for Science, Technology and Commerce 1997-02; established County Enterprise Boards 1994; Member of Galway County Council (chairman 1986 - 87) 1985-91; Galway County Vocational Education Committee 1985-91; chairman Galway/Mayo Regional Development Organisation 1986-87; member Macra na Feirme since 1968; Macra na Tuaithe and Muintir na Tire; youth officer; Galway GAA County Board 1970-83; represented Connacht on the GAA National Youth Council 1970-83. Clubs: Irish Auctioneers and Valuers Institute, Irish Livestock Auctioneers Association. Contact: Cross Street, Athenry, Co. Galway. **T** 091 844360 **F** 091 844360

> The bright energetic and highly personable Galway politician has a wide circle of friends in the political world; despite an impeccable track record has been extremely unlucky not to have made it to the Cabinet table despite his wide experience in the junior ministry ranks; always a great ambassador for the West of Ireland he retains his strong GAA links.

John Trethowan

TRETHOWAN, John; BANKER

b 1953, Belfast; *m* Vivien; 1*s*; *edu*. Royal Belfast Academical Institution; Ulster Business School, University of Ulster, MBA, Diploma in Management Studies; Banker; career banker; 26 years in various roles with Northern Bank Ltd; seven years in senior management roles in National Irish Bank; acting CEO National Irish Bank; deputy president of Institute of Bankers in Ireland 2005-06; board member, Business in the Community Ireland; Junior Achievement Ireland. Clubs: Hibernian & Stephens Green Club. Recreations: travel, DIY, gardening. Contact: National House, 1 Airton Close, Airton Road, Dublin 24. **T** 01 438 5772 **F** 01 438 5776 email JT@NIB.IE

> Fully fledged home grown banker who brought a wide range of experience to his new position at NIB; his banking knowledge and managerial skills will be fully tested as he endeavors to restore the credibility and perception after the major scandals that beset that institution in recent years; ultimately leading to its acquisition by Danske bank.

TREVOR, Hon KBE William; AUTHOR

b 1928, Co. Cork; *m* Jane Ryan; 2*s*; *edu*. St.Columba's College, Dublin; Trinity College Dublin; Writer and Dramatist; awards, Hawthornden Prize 1964; RSL Award 1975; Whitbread Award 1976, 1983, 1994; AIB Literature Award 1976; Hon CBE 1977; Giles Cooper Award 1980/82; Hon. Litt. D.Ex TCD 1994; Cork 1986; Belfast 1990; Bennett Award (USA) 1989 -90; David Cohen British Literature Award 1999; CLitt 2000 Pen/Macmillan 1994: Irish Times Literary Award; Hon. KBE 2002; Listowel Prize for Irish Fiction 2003; Irish Funds Literary Award 2005. *Publ.* since 1956 his works have included nine television plays; five radio plays; 31 books including *The Ballroom of Romance*, also adapted for BBC TV, short stories and stories for children. Clubs: hon. member American Academy of Arts & Letters 2005, Irish Academy of Letters, Aosdána. Contact: Aosdána, 70, Merrion Square, Dublin 2. **T** 01 618 0200 **F** 01 676 1302

> A writer of loss, deracination and minority sensibilities; his delineation of the impact which politics may have on lives, their devastating impact gives his works on decline their elegiac edge.

TRIMBLE, David; NOBEL PRIZE WINNER

b 1944,Bangor, Co. Down; *m* Daphne; 2*s* 2*d*; *edu*. Bangor Grammar School 1969; Queen's University Belfast; Member of Northern Ireland Assembly to 2003; former First Minister; First Minister Northern Ireland Assembly, former Privy Councillor 1999- 01; called to the Bar of Northern Ireland; lecturer Queen's University Law Faculty 1968-90; Vanguard Movement 1971; represented Vanguard at the Northern Irish Convention 1975; joined the Official Unionist Party 1977; elected MP 1990; leader 1995 - 04; lost Westminster seat 2004; member Northern Ireland Assembly 1998; awarded the Nobel Peace Prize 1998; proposed Dominion Status for Ulster 1987; resigned as First Minister 2001; re-elected First Minister 2001; Assembly was suspended and he lost office 2000; lost his Upper Bann Seat 2004; resigned as leader of his Party. Contact: 2, Queen Street. Lurgan, Co. Armagh BT66 88Q **T** 048 3832 8088 **F** 048 3832 2343

Succeeded the hard line Sir James Molyneaux to the leadership of the Ulster Unionist Party following his march down the Gavaghy Road with Dr Ian Paisely (*qv*), who later became a bitter political enemy; having achieved the single honour of First Minister of the devolved Stormont parliament he had a turbulent period as leader of his party, being subjected to numerous leadership challenges and on-going political ambushes; amiable and pleasant man halfway between the Big House Unionism of yore and a modern day version; seen as not being Unionist enough by his own and too Unionist by the other side; he couldn't win and didn't.

TUBRIDY, Ryan Patrick; BROADCASTER

b 1973; Dublin; *m* Ann-Marie Power; separated; 2*d*; *edu.* Blackrock College; University College Dublin BA (History); winner of UCD President's Medal; radio and television broadcaster; presenter *The Tubridy Show* Radio 1 and *Tubridy Tonight* RTE1; reporter on *Pat Kenny Show* 1995-97; presenter *Morning Glory* Radio 1 1997-98; presenter *The Sunday Show* Radio 1 1998-2002; reporter 5 7 *Live* Radio 1 1998, presenter *The Full Irish* radio show 2FM (2004 Winner Meteor Award for Best Irish DJ, and Winner of PPI Award for Best Breakfast Programme) 2002-03; host *Tubridy Tonight* television show RTE 1 2004 to date; presenter *The Tubridy Show* RTE Radio 1 2005 to date. Recreations: cinema, walking Dun Laoghaire pier, old movies, fly fishing, Connemara. Contact: Tubridy Tonight, Entertainment Department, Stage 7, RTE Montrose, Dublin 4. **T** 01 208 311 **F** 01 208 2143 email ryan.tubridy@rte.ie

Ryan Tubridy

Probably the most talented new broadcaster from the RTE stable; seems to have come to the top in Montrose overnight and at a very early age; can be relied on by RTE mandarins to drive up listening and viewing figures in one of the most competitive markets on the globe; his audiences take a little time to adjust to his different style after the Gaybo and Marion Finnucane years, but within a few weeks they are won over by his freshness, modern outlook and non-adversarial personality (a new phenomenon in Donnybrook); very open and personable, exuding no airs or graces;.

TUCKER, Leigh; FASHION DESIGNER

b 1973, Dublin; partner Oran Heron; *edu.* Santa Sabina, Sutton, Dublin 13; The National College of Art and Design, Dublin; B.Des; Fashion Designer; entered into retail management after graduating; launched label leighlee Oct 2000; director/designer of Leighlee. Recreations: running, entertaining, cinema, arts. Contact: 4 Emmet Street, Dublin 1. **T** 01 408 0082 **F** 01 408 0085 email leighlee@eircom.net

Daughter of fashionistas Brian and Billie has developed a successful niche market for her design company which provides a unique collection of funky gear.

TUOMEY, John; ARCHITECT

b 1954; *m* Sheila O'Donnell; 2*s*; *edu.* St. Mary's College Dundalk; University College Dublin, B Arch, MARCH, FRIAI, RIBA; Architect; worked in London with James Stirling, in Dublin with the Office of Public Works and set up partnership with Sheila O'Donnell in 1988. Buildings include Irish Film Centre, Ranelagh School Dublin, Furniture College, Letterfrack and Glucksman Gallery, Cork. Contact: 20 A Camden Row, Dublin 2. **T** 01 475 2500 **F** 01 475 1479 email info@odonell-Tuomey.ie

The former OPW architect has developed an excellent commercial career in the private sector; his University College Cork commission for the Lew Glucksman Gallery has won international recognition and was short listed for the prestigious Sterling Award.

TURLEY, Greg; CHIEF EXECUTIVE ETRAWLER (ArgusCarHire.com)

b 1961, Dublin: *m* Audrey; 1*d*; *edu*; Terenure College, Dublin; Founder and Chief Executive ETRAWLER; joined Argus Motors (started by his father) 1981; ArgusCarHire.com first English language car hire web site to launch in Europe 1996; ArgusCarHire.com first European car hire web site to launch quotation and booking technology facility 1999; ArgusCarHire.com first European car hire web site with WAP phone interface (this did not take off due to slow implication of 3G) 2000; ArgusCarHire.com launched pioneering base technology, specifically the user interface 2003; ArgusCarHire.com was first car hire provider to launch a unique "3 clicks to confirmation" system offering consumers fast access to cheap, all-inclusive car hire deals 2004; CarTrawler.com became first worldwide car-rental company to offer its services on the iMode phone to web interface, launched in the UK and Ireland by 02 October 2005; finalist Ernst & Young Entrepreneur of the Year 2005. Clubs: Terenure Rugby Club; RAC Dawson Street, Dublin. Recreations: golf, motor racing, fishing, rugby, music. Contact: Argus Car and Van Rentals, Argus House, 59, Terenure Road, East, Dublin 6. **T** 01 490 4444 **F** 01 490 6328 email info@arguscarhire.com web arguscarhire.com

> Though only a few years old, his company is now one of the top three global car hire providers operating two divisions to consumers through ArgusCarHire.com and to business though etrawler; provides cars to 6000 destinations in 70 countries; despite several approaches to sell his company, has no plans to sell, citing huge untapped potential in the company.

TURLEY, Niall; COFOUNDER ETRAWLER (ArgusCarHire.com)
b 1968, Dublin; *m* Sinead; 1*s* 2*d*; *edu.* St. Mary's College, Dublin; Newbridge College, Newbridge, Co. Kildare; Owner/ Director ArgusCarHire.com; joined Argus Car Hire in 1991 as a customer service agent; gained experience in a number of different departments in the company and became a company director 1995; was one of the key people instrumental in launching the Argus Car Hire website 1996; (the website was the first European English language car rental web site); in Argus established the first European car rental web site with quotation technology solutions 1999; evolved into its current form Arguscarhire.com 2003 to date; awards: Golden Spider Best E-Commerce Website and Best Travel and Tourism website 2005. Clubs: Terenure RFC, South Dublin Golf Club. Recreations: active sports, rugby. Contact: Argus Car and Van Rentals, Argus House, 59, Terenure Road, East, Dublin 6 **T** 01 490 4444 **F** 01 490 6328 email info@arguscarhire.com web arguscarhire.com

> With his brother Greg (*qv*) has rapidly grown the family business and introduced cutting edge technology making it one of the most successful car hire companies in Europe.

TURNER, Martyn; POLITICAL CARTOONIST AND SATIRIST
b 1948, Wanstead, Essex; *m* Jean Caroline; 1*s*; *edu.* Bancrofts School, Woodford Green, Essex; Queen's University Belfast, BA (Hons); D.UNN (University of Ulster); D.SPC.SCI, (Queens); Political Cartoonist/Satirist; co-editor *Fortnight* magazine, Belfast 1971-76; freelance political cartoonist 1976 to date; syndicated by C&W/*New York Times*; awards: Commentator of the Year, Irish Media Awards 1998; European Political Cartoonist of the Year 2002; Publ: *The Book* political cartoons 1973-83 (Irish Times Books) 1983; *Illuminations – 101 Drawings From Early Irish History* (Boethius Press) 1986; *A Fistful of Dailers* political cartoons 1983-87 (Gill & Macmillan) 1987; *Not Viking Likely* (Irish Life Viking Adventure) 1988; *Heavy Weather* (Gill & Macmillan) 1989; *The Guy Who Won The Tour De France* political cartoons 1987-91 (Gill & Macmillan) 1991; *The Long Goodbye* a cartoon history of the career of Charles J. Haughey (Irish Times Books) 1992; *Politics Et Al* political cartoons 1991-92 (Irish Times Books) 1992; *The Odd Couple* political cartoons 1991-94 (Irish Times Books) 1994; *Pack Up Your Troubles: 25 Years of Northern Ireland Cartoons* (Blackstaff Press) 1995; *The Noble Art of Politics* political cartoons 1994-96 (Blackstaff Press) 1996; *Brace Yourself, Bridge It* political cartoons 1996-98 (Blackstaff Press) 1998; *The Golfers Guide to World History* (Blackstaff Press) 1999; *Railings* political cartoons 1998-2000 (Blackstaff Press) 2000; *Martyn Turner's Greatest Hits* (Gill & Macmillan) 2004; books edited by Martyn Turner: *Thin Black Lines* political cartoons and development education, Co-edited with Dr Colm Regan & Scott Sinclair (Development Education Center Birmingham) 1988; *Columba!* a cartoon history of South America, co-edited Dr Colm Regan (Potato Press) 1993; *Thin Black Lines Rides Again* political cartoons and development education, co-edited Dr Colm Regan, Scott Sinclair (Development Education Center, Birmingham) 1994. Clubs: The Curragh Golf Club. Recreations: golf, reading, getting out of Ireland, sleeping, Red Setters. Contact: Stephenstown, Brannockstown, BME, Co Kildare. **T** 045 876 496 email dunswood@eircom.net

> One of the best known and most talented cartoonists in these islands; appreciated and enjoyed by readers and feared and dreaded by his targets; compulsive viewing in the IT, has captured the core of major news items and personalities of the day.

TWOMEY, Denis Vincent: PRIEST/THEOLOGIAN PROFESSOR OF MORAL THEOLOGY.
b 1941, Cork; single; *edu.* Our Lady of Lourdes Primary School, Ballinlough, Cork 1945-49; Christian Brothers College, Wellington Road, Cork 1949-58; Baccalaureate in Divinity Maynooth 1969; Doctor of Sacred Theology, University of Bavaria, Regensburg, Germany 1979; Professor of Dogmatic Theology, Regional Seminary of Papua New Guinea and then the Solomon Islands 1979-

81; Professor of Dogmatic Theology Philosophisch Theologische Hochschule St.Gabriel, Mödlin, Vienna, Austria 1981-83; lecturer in Moral Theology, Pontifical University, Maynooth 1983-2004; professor of Moral Theology, Pontifical University Maynooth 2004 to date; visiting professor, University of Fribourgh, Switzerland (summer semester) 1984; founded The Patristic Symposium, Maynooth 1986; visting professor at the Studium Generale of the Brothers of the Common Life, Maria-Bronnen, Waldshut, Germany 1994 and 97; editor *Irish Theological Quarterly* 1997; general editor *ITQ Book Series* 2003; editor *The Word* 2004; Publ. *Apostolikos Thronos; The Primacy of Rome as Reflected in the Church History of Eusebius and the Historico-Apologetic Writings of Saint Athanasius the Great, Münster Westphalia; Christianity and Neoplantonism; Proceedings of the First Patristic Conference* Dublin 1981 (joint editor with Thomas Finan); *Scriptural Interpretation in the Fathers; Letter and Spirit: Proceedings of the Second Patristic Conference* Dublin 1992 (joint editor with Thomas Finan); *The End of Irish Catholicism?* 1995; *Forthcoming The Holy Trinity in the Fathers of the Church: Proceedings of the Fourth Patristic Conference;* Dublin 2005 (joint editor with Mark Humphries); *Pope Benedict XVI: The Conscience of Our Age* San Francisco (Ignatius Press) 2005; *Salvation in the Fathers of the Church: Proceedings of the Sixth Maynooth Patristic Conference held at the Institute of Byzantine Studies QUB* Dublin 2006 (joint editor with Dirk Krausmüller); *In Preparation: An Introduction to Bioethics;* many articles in learned journals and contributions to the public debate. Clubs: Fellowship of Catholic Scholars, The Patristic Symposium, Maynooth, member, Divine Word Missionaries. Recreations: music, art, literature. Contact: St. Patrick's Maynooth, Co. Kildare. **T** 01 798 3317 **F** 01 708 3441 email dv.toomey@may.ie

His work has taken on much greater theological and political significance with the Papacy of Benedict XVI; a gifted Patristic writer he is also a firm believer and that gives his work much of its dimension; may be too old now for a bishopric, but Rome will confer something on him.

UPTON, Dr, Mary Elizabeth; PUBLIC REPRESENTATIVE
b 1946, Derrylough, Kilrush, Co. Clare; single; *edu.* Colaiste Muire, Ennis, Co. Clare; University College Galway; University College Dublin; M.Sc; Ph.D; Public Representative, Labour Party TD, Dublin South Central; elected to Dail Eireann in by-election 1999; reelected in General Election 2002; Labour Party Spokesperson on Agriculture and Food 2002 to date; *Publ.* numerous scientific publications, especially in food science/microbiology; lecturer in microbiology, University College Dublin; Hon. fellow Institute of Food Science and Technology of Ireland. Recreations: current affairs, reading, bridge, cooking. Contact: 9 Fortfield Grove, Terenure, Dublin 6W/ Dail Eireann, Kildare Street, Dublin 2. **T** 01 6183756 **F** 01 618 3497 email maryupton@eircom.net

A politician by accident, the former university lecturer won her seat in the Dáil in the by-election of October 1999 caused by the death of her brother Dr. Pat Upton (for whom she had served as director of elections); highly intelligent, articulate and an excellent communicator who has used her expertise in the food science area to demystify food scares – BSE, foot and mouth and dioxins, all of which are of major consumer interest.

Mary Upton

VERVELDE, Nicko; MANAGING DIRECTOR, HEINEKEN IRELAND
b 1956, Rotterdam, Holland; *m* Clementina; 6 children; *edu.* University of Agriculture, Wageningen; managing director, Heineken Ireland; joined Heineken 1984; commercial director Heineken Rwanda 1990-92; general manager Commonwealth Brewing, Nassau, Bahamas 1995-98; director Commonwealth Brewing, Nassau, Bahamas 2002-03; appointed managing director Heineken Ireland 2003 to date. Contact: Murphy's Brewery, Leitrim Street, Cork City. **T** 021 450 3711 **F** 021 450 3011 email info@heinekenireland.ie web www.heinekenireland.ie

> The popular Dutch man has immersed himself in Ireland and Cork in particular; focussed, dynamic and sound commercial brain; continues to drive his brand forward in the Irish market place.

VON PRONDZYNSKI, Ferdinand; PRESIDENT, DUBLIN CITY UNIVERSITY
b 1954, Bevensen, Germany; *m* Heather Ingman; 2*s*; *edu.* Thomas Morus Gymnasium, Oelde, Germany; Trinity College Dublin 1978; (BA, LL.B.); Cambridge (Ph.D.) 1982; Bankkaufmann Germany; President, Dublin City University; lecturer Trinity College Dublin 1980-90; fellow, Trinity College Dublin 1987-90; professor University of Hull 1991-2000; dean of the Faculty of Social Sciences, University of Hull 1997-2000; president of Dublin City University 2000 to date; director, Skillsoft plc; member National Competitiveness Council 2002. Recreations: photography, music, literature, public policy, technology, innovation. Contact: President's Office, Dublin City University, Dublin 9. **T** 01 700 5666 **F** 01 700 5888 email president@dcu.ie

> An efficient and able university president who has brought a European vision to his university and has made a great difference to it; this in turn is reflected in the quality of the university's graduates; also enjoys life as the squire of his family home, Knockdrin Castle, outside Mullingar; an all rounder.

WALL, Finbarr; ARCHITECT

b 1947, Dublin; *m* Anne; 2s 1d; *edu*. Colaiste Mhuire, Dublin; University College Dublin; B.Arch. FRIAI; assistant principal architect, Office of Public Works; private practice 1970-75; public service 1975 to date. Clubs: Connemara Golf Club. Recreations: golf, opera. Contact: 31, Eaton Square, Terenure, Dublin 6W. **T** 01 647 6355 **F** 01 662 7097 email finbarr.wall@opw.ie

His rich career experience will ensure that standards of excellence, the hallmark of the OPW architects, will be sustained into the future; with the massive range of buildings at home and abroad, his expertise is in great demand; the Government's decentralization will add further to his work load.

WALL, Toni; PUBLIC RELATIONS EXECUTIVE

b 1965, Dublin; *m* Richard Duggan IV; *edu*. Dominican Convent, Muckross Park, Dublin; Diploma in Journalistic Writing; Diploma PR; MPRII; Managing Director, Wall 2 Wall PR & Event Management; Pembroke PR 1985; Fleishman Hillard Saunders; Toni Wall & Associates; Wall 2 Wall PR & Event Management; director, Forfás. Clubs: David Lloyd Riverview. Recreations: reading, flamenco dancing, cooking, collecting art, shoes. Contact: 12, Lower Pembroke, Street, Dublin 2. **T** 01 669 0938 **F** 01 676 8404 email info@wall2wallpr.com

The diminutive, energetic PR gal punches way above her weight in the highly competitive PR and event management world; hardworking, innovative and extremely outgoing; well connected politically, the face of Fianna Fail at the Ballybrit Suite at Galway Races for many years where she controls entry in the most pleasant and engaging way.

WALL, Vincent; DIRECTOR

b 1960, Eniscorthy, Co. Wexford; *m* Cathy Herbert; 2d; *edu* CBS Carlow; University College Dublin; Dublin City University; BA, H.Dip.Ed; Masters, Journalism; joined Bank of Ireland; teacher, St. Josephs of Cluny, Killiney; Irish Press 1986 - 87; RTE 1987-96, (newsroom, *Today Tonight , Evening Extra);*; deputy business editor, Irish Independent, 1996 -99 ; editor business and finance 1999- 03; director communication Dublin airport 03 – todate. Clubs: GAA Na Fiuanna Glasnevin. Recreations: GAA reading, hill walking. Contact; Dublin Airport, OCTB, Co. Dublin. **T** 01 814 4107 **M** 087 686 0727 **F** 01 8145050 email vincent.wall@dublinairportauthority.com web www.dublinairportauthority.com

Mary Wallace

WALLACE, Mary; PUBLIC REPRESENTATIVE

b 1959, Dublin; *m* Declan Gannon; 1s; *edu*. Loreto Convent Balbriggan, Co. Dublin; Loretto Convent, North Great Georges Street, Dublin; College of Commerce, Rathmines, Dublin; Dip Hospital and Health, Services Administration; Public Representative, TD Fianna Fáil Meath; Minister of State, Department Agriculture and Food, 2006 todate; ; former Minister of State and former Personnel Executive in Blanchardstown Hospital; senator 1987-89; appointed Minister of State at the Department of Justice, Equality and Law Reform with Special Responsibility for Equality and Disabilities 1997-02; member, Oireachtas Joint Committee on Women's Rights 1987-97; vice chairperson 1989-92; chairperson 1995-97; member ,Oireachtas Committee on the Family 1995-97; chairperson, Fianna Fáil National Women's Committee 1992-94; opposition spokesperson, People with Disabilities and Carers 1995-97; member, Meath County Council 1982-97; North Eastern Health Board 1985-89; Meath Vocational Education Committee 1991-95; Meath County Committee of Agriculture (chairperson 1986/1987) 1982-87; Blanchardstown Hospital 1977-87. Contact: Fairyhouse Road, Ratoath, Co Meath **T** 01 825 6259 **F** 01 825 6848 email mary.wallace@oireachtas.ie web www.marywallace.ie

Since her election to the Dáil in 1989 has held onto her seat in the highly competitive, marginal constituency of Meath, despite having to fight off national names like John Bruton and Noel Dempsey (*qv*); very personable but much more low profile since she was consigned to the back benches having served as a Junior Minister from 1997-02; there she achieved some progress in the area of equality and disabilities; was rewarded with a half car at Agriculture and Food 2006.

WALLACE, Nicky; FASHION DESIGNER

b 1953, Wexford; *m* Carmel Corish; separated; 1s 1d; *edu*. De La Salle Waterford; University College

Dublin; abandoned commerce degree; joined Berwins, Leeds, UK 1971; graduated with distinction Leed's College of Fashion 1975; Fashion Designer; set up design workshop, Wexford 1977; selected by Universal Studios to dress *Miami Vice* stars 1986; consultant to Irish Export Board mid 1990s; opened Dublin store, South William Street 2002 to date. Recreations: the sea, sailing, "being a boulevardier". Contact: South William Street, Dublin 2 **T** 01 616 8911 email nicky@nickywalace.ie web www.nickywallace.ie

> A cheerful man who loves all things Italian, particularly Italian fabric; designs for a wide audience and has an important male clientele; known to few, but noticed by many.

WALLACE, Dr, Patrick Francis; DIRECTOR, THE NATIONAL MUSEUM OF IRELAND
b 1948, Limerick; *m* Siobhán Cuffe; *edu.* St. Mary's Askeaton, Co. Limerick; University College Galway; BA, Ph.D; Director ,The National Museum of Ireland; archaeologist with National Museum of Ireland 1972-88; director Wood Quay excavations 1974-81; conceived and designed Viking Adventure for Irish Life 1987; director National Museum of Ireland 1988 to date; fellow Society of Antiquaries (London); member, Royal Society of Antiquaries, hon general secretary 1983-89; member Birka Reference Group (Sweden); Kempang (Norway); Discovery Panel; council member Union of Pre- and Proto-Historical Sciences; board member Dublin Medieval Trust; hon member RIAI Knight of the Danneborg (Denmark); civic honours of Limerick City Council; *Publ. The Viking Age of Dublin*, 2 Vols 1992; *Treasures of the National Museum* with Raghnaill Ó Floinn 2002; *Weights, Balances and Leadweights in Viking Dublin* (in prep); *Dublin in the Viking Age* (Yale) for publ. 2006; articles on archaeology, social and political history, obits and reviews; excavation projects; popular heritage on TV; radio programmes at home and abroad; lectures abroad, esp. *National Georgraphic* Washington D.C. Recreations: conservation of medieval tower house at Corofin, Co.Clare; theatre; Gaelic games; Europe; politics; history of Askeaton. Contact: National Museum of Ireland, Kildare Street, Dublin 2. **T** 01 677 7444 (ext 306) **F** 01 678 5404 email pfwallace@museum.ie web www.museum.ie

> An immensely successful museum director, and an important archaeologist of medieval Dublin; oversaw the development of new museum buildings in Collins Barracks and Turlough Park in Co.Mayo (folk life); rarely out of the public eye; pro excavation stances at Wood Quay, and Woodstown, Waterford and pro conservation stances at Durrow and Tara.

WALSH, Diarmuid Fitzpatrick; DIRECTOR OF OPERATIONS B&Q (NORTHERN DIVISION: N. ENGLAND/ SCOTLAND/IRELAND)
b 1956, Coleraine; *m* Freda; 1*s* 1*d*; *edu.* St Mary's CBS Grammar School, Belfast; Belfast Royal Academy; B.Sc. (Hons); University of Ulster, Jordanstown; Director Operations B&Q Northern Division N. England, Scotland, Ireland; Marks & Spencer 1977-79; Hampden Group plc 1979-99; J. Sainsbury plc 1999-01; B&Q plc 2001 to date. Clubs: Carrickfergus Golf Club. Recreations: golf, keen Manchester United fan, DIY. Contact: B&Q Plc, Portswood House, 1 Hampshire Corporate Park, Chandlers Ford, Eastleigh, Hampshire, SO53 3YX **T** 0044 0845 609 6688 web www.bandq.co.uk

> Brings a wide range of blue chip retailing experience to the development of B&Q DIY superstores, who are expanding their retailing outlets throughout the country.

WALSH, Edward; UNIVERSITY PRESIDENT EMERITUS
b 1939, Cork; *m* Stephanie Barrett; 3*s* 1*d*; *edu.* Christian Brothers College, Cork; University College Cork 1961-64; Iowa State University; B. Eng; M.Sc; PhD; President Emeritus University of Limerick; chairman Growcorp; principal Oakhampton Consultants; chairman National Allocation Advisory Group (Carbon Trading); deputy chairman Irish Chamber Orchestra; board member: International Association of University Presidents' Prosoft Training Austin, Texas; Prosoft Training Europe; Eolas Institute; member: Advisory Committee to Ict Sector on R&D; Advisory Council Transparency International; Legal Affairs Council, Gerson Lehrman Group New York; Adviser Citywest, Dublin; founding president University of Limerick 1989-98; founding chairman National Technological Park; National Council for Curriculum and Assessment; National Self Portrait Collection; Birr Historic Science Foundation; numerous foundations, universities and strategic planning in Ireland and US; LL.D. (*hc*) Trinity College Dublin 1992; LL.D. (*hc*) Queens Belfast 1995; D.Sc (*hc*) University of Ulster 1997; LL.D. (*hc*) NUI 1998; chartered engineer Institute of Engineers of Ireland; civic honours; Freeman, City of Limerick 1995; World Innovation Foundation 2001; Irish Academy of Engineering

1998; Institution of Engineers of Ireland 1995; Institution of Electrical Engineers, London 1990; member: Royal Society for the Arts, London; New York Academy of Science; Royal Irish Academy; Royal Hibernian Academy; hon member National College of Art & Design (*hc*); *Publ. Energy Conversion; Vision 2020; What Future For Business?* (O'Brien Press) 1995; author, over 50 publications in various journals. Clubs: Kildare St & University Club, Kinsale Yacht Club. Recreations: sailing, skiing, walking, gardening, registered silversmith company of goldsmiths of Dublin. Contact: Oakhampton House, Newport, Co.Tipperary. email oakhampton@eircom.net

The Cork born academic raised the profile of the newly established University of Limerick to challenge its more established peers in the university sector; a trailblazer for fundraising in the United States for his fledgling institution where he received millions of dollars from philanthropists Chuck Feeney (*qv*) and the lateLew Glucksman; an outspoken professor who had an informed opinion on many issues even those unrelated to his area of expertise; also made a statement in the sartorial elegance stakes.

Edward Walsh

WALSH, Edward S; BARRISTER AT LAW
b 1958, Kent; *m* Constance Cassidy (*qv*); 3*s* 4*d; edu.* Catholic Boys School, Hythe, Kent; Drimnagh Castle CBS Dublin; Trinity College Dublin; BA Mod (legal studies); called to the Bar 1979; called to the Inner Bar 1997; Barrister At Law; specialises in medical negligence; defamation, personal injury, planning law; practices in Dublin, Galway and Sligo; Publ. *Agriculture and the Law* (Sweet and Maxwell); director, First Law; business and property interests. Recreations: gardening, architecture, farming. Contact: The Law Library, Four Courts, Dublin 7 **T** 01 817 4613 **F** 045-435 665

The distinguished, extremely hardworking Silk has built up an enviable reputation in the law library; married to a highly successful SC (*qv* Cassidy Constance), he has, with his wife and family, not only transformed Lissadell the great Sligo mansion of myth and poetry, but proved that a private person may often achieve more in terms of preserving a cultural site than the great institutions of the State; an excellent conversationalist with an engaging personality; a doer who shows the power of positive thinking and effective action.

WALSH, Ena; HEAD OF OPERATIONS, ROYAL COLLEGE OF SURGEONS IRELAND
b 1958, Louth; *m* Niall Fenton; *edu.* Presentation Convent, Kildare, Co. Kildare; University College, Dublin 1975-79; B.Sc Biochemistry; Ph.D Biochemistry 1984; Smurfit Business School MBA 1998; Head of Operations and Business Development, Royal College of Surgeons Ireland; MD, Health and Life Sciences Consultancy, Dublin 1999-04; head of strategic marketing, Otsuka, Pharmaceuticals Co Ltd, London UK 1996-97; European project manager, Otsuka, Pharmaceuticals Co Ltd, London UK 1994-96; commercial development manager, Elan Corporation, Athlone, Ireland 1991-94; senior registrations officer, Elan Corporation plc. Athlone, Ireland 1990-91; research scientist, Fujisawa Pharmaceuticals & Co. Osaka, Japan 1984-87. Contact: 17, Anne Villa, Ranelagh, Dublin 6. **T** 01 496 3595

With its increased emphasis and marketing internationally, the Louth lady brings a superb CV laced with top notch experience with blue chip multi nationals to the Royal College Surgeons Ireland.

WALSH, Kate; PUBLIC REPRESENTATIVE
b 1947, Ballyfoyle, Mageny, Co. Laois; *m* Eugene Walsh (*decd*); *edu.* Coláiste Charibre, Dunmanway, Co. Cork; Senator; nominated to Seanad Eireann; spokesperson Social and Family Affairs 2002; unsuccessfully contested the general election for the Progressive Democrats in North Kildare; member of the Oireachtas Committee on Social and Family Affairs; elected honorary Lord Mayor of Celbridge; and with a break of six years continued in the role 1982; elected Kildare County Council Independent Community Candidate 1999; resigned County Council seat following abolition of dual mandate 2003. Recreations: for the last 30 years has been a community activist, involved in voluntary and community organisations in Celbridge and the surrounding areas. Contact: Seanad Éireann, Leinster House, Kildare Street, Dublin 2. **T** 01 618 4078/01 628 8118 **F** 01 618 3655 email kate.walsh@oireachtas.ie or kate.walsh@oireachtas.irlgov.ie

Has a long and cherished involvement with youth, senior citizens, charitable and fund-raising events and charity organizations throughout North Kildare; each year, in

November, organizes the Black and White Ball, the proceeds of which go to the aged, which has now become one of the social events of the year in North Kildare.

WALSH, Louis Vincent; MUSIC MANAGER/ TV PERSONALITY
b 1955, Kiltimach, Co. Mayo; single; *edu.* St. Nathys College, Ballaghaderreen, Co Roscommon; St. Patrick's College, Swinford, Co Mayo; Music Manager/TV Personality; boy band creator/manager/ TV celebrity; pop manager of Boyzone, 11 million albums; Westlife, 28 million albums; Girls Aloud, 2 million; G4, 1 million; Samantha Mumba, 1 million; has had 26 number 1 singles in UK charts; judge, ITV *X Factor* with Simon Cowell and Sharon Osbourne 2004, 2005, 2006, 2007. Recreations: travel, music, TV, pop art, modern and contemporary art, cars, dining out. Contact: 24 Courtney House, Appian Way, Dublin 6. **T** 01 668 0309 **F** 01 668 0721 email louiewalsh@eircom.net

Louis Walsh

Having created a number of home grown celebrities, he has emerged as a fully grown one himself through his participation in the wildly successful *X Factor* talent series the biggest show on ITV (2006); as much a household name and face as any of his boy/girl bands, continues to work all hours at the day job; low profile (mostly), acerbic yet totally charming; bright and one of the most highly respected figures in pop music in Europe.

WALSH, Nicholas Joseph; CONSULTANT DERMATOLOGIST
b 1959, Waterford; *m* Catherine; *2s 2d; edu.* De La Salle College, Waterford; University College Dublin; University of Alberta, Edmonton, Canada (post graduate) FRCP (C), diplomate of the American Board of Dermatology; consultant dermatologist; consultant dermatologist to: The Blackrock Clinic, Mount Carmel Hospital, Bon Secours Hospital Dublin; lectures at international dermatological meetings; *Publ.* 15 publications in peer reviewed journals. Clubs: Kildare Hotel and Country Club, Royal Irish Yacht Club. Recreations: horseracing, travel, farming, soccer (manager of a junior soccer team), fishing. Contact: Suite 18, Blackrock Clinic, Rock Road, Co. Dublin.
T 01 490 7710 **F** 01 406 4223

Extremely hardworking and accessible consultant; internationally trained and recognized as one of the top dermatologists in Europe; specialises in cosmetic dermatology, skin cancer surgery, paediatric dermatology.

WALSH, Most Rev, Patrick Joseph; BISHOP of DOWN and CONNOR
b 1931, Cobh, Co. Cork; single; *edu.* St. Mary's Christian Brothers Grammar School, Belfast; MA, Queen's University, Belfast; MA, Christ's College, Cambridge; S.T.L. Pontifical Lateran University, Rome; Bishop of Down and Connor; teacher, St. Mac Nissis College, Garron Tower 1958-64; chaplain, Queens University 1964-70; president, St. Malachy's College, Belfast 1970-83; Auxiliary Bishop, Down and Connor 1983-91; Bishop, Down and Connor 1991 to date. Recreations: walking, music, theatre. Contact: Lisbreen, 73 Somerton Road, Belfast BT 15 4DE **T** 028 907 76185 **F** 028 907 79377

An able and cultivated Bishop yet to make a major impact on the Irish church world; academic and serious minded, he has worthwhile, modernizing ideas.

WALSH, Ruby; CHAMPION NATIONAL HUNT JOCKEY
b 1979, Co Kildare; *m* Gillian Doran; *edu.* Christian Brothers School, Naas; Champion National Hunt Jockey; leading amateur NS jockey on two occasions; turned professional 1999; won Irish Grand National 2000; Irish, English and Welsh Grand Nationals 2005; rode a double on the first day of the Cheltenham Festival, 2006; awards, Jump Jockey of the Year at the annual HWPA (Horserace Writers and Photographers Association) awards in London 2005. Recreations: soccer, Man. Utd, travel, golf. Contact: Jennifer Walsh (agent), 39, Oak Glade, Craddockstown, Naas, Co. Kildare. **T** 045 883704 **M** 087 252 8025

One of the most successful and stylish national hunt jockeys of all time; has broken both his legs, his wrist and his hip whilst race-riding; has won all major races at home and in the UK; utterly professional, quietly spoken, a highly respected senior figure in the Weigh Room; won the Irish, Welsh and Aintree Grand Nationals and was pipped at the post to second place in the Scottish Grand National 2005.

Ted Walsh

WALSH, Ted; NATIONAL HUNT TRAINER/ TV PERSONALITY
b 1950, Co. Kildare; *m* Helen; 2*s* 2*d*; *edu.* Christian Brothers School, Naas; National Hunt Trainer/ TV personality; was a successful amateur jockey before he turned his hand to training; won the Irish amateur championship 11 times in a career in the saddle that saw him take in four victories at the Cheltenham Festival; trainer 1999; winners include Papillon 2000; 21 (Ire) wins 2001-2002; 14 (Ire) wins 2000-2001; 12 (Ire) wins 1999-2000 (stable stars: Rince Rí, Commanche Court); TV racing commentator RTE. Recreations: golf. Contact: Greenhills, Kill, Co. Kildare. **T** 045 877818 email tedwalsh@kildarehorse.ie

The former amateur champion jockey, father of the legendary Ruby,(*qv*) transferred seamlessly into an equally successful trainer; landed a dream father and son (Ruby) Grand National with Papillon in 2000; has reached national prominence through his TV sports reportage; his encyclopaedic knowledge and witty anecdotes, controversial and outspoken opinions have made him darling of the punters and the housewives choice.

WALSH, Most Rev. William; BISHOP of KILLALOE
b 1935, Roscrea, Co. Tipperary; single; *edu.* St. Flannan's College, Ennis Co. Clare; St. Patrick's College, Maynooth; B.Sc; Irish College Rome, Latern University Rome; (S.T.L; Latern); University College Galway; H.Dip Ed; Roman Catholic Bishop of Killaloe; teacher at St. Flannan's College, Ennis 1963-87; curate and administrator Cathedral Ennis 1987-94; Bishop of Killaloe 1994 to date; member of Bishops' Communication on Education and Pastoral Care; *Publ.* numerous articles in *Furrow* and other magazines, contributions to several books. Clubs: Éire Óg GAA Ennis, Ennis and Lahinch Golf Clubs. Recreations: hurling, golf, walking, reading. Contact: Westbourne, Ennis, Co. Clare. **T** 065 682 8638 **F** 065 6842538 email cildalua@iol.ie

Possibly one of the most respected Bishops in Ireland due to his forthright comments even on sensitive church issues; a lifelong GAA follower, he has been a selector for the Clare Senior hurling team and an avid supporter of Clare GAA teams; is a real man of the people, warm, friendly and extremely hardworking.

WATCHMAN, David; RACEHORSE TRAINER
b 1974, Kingswood, Co. Dublin; *m* Katie Magnier; 2*s*; *edu.* Newbridge College, Newbridge, Co. Kildare; Racehorse Trainer; has built up an impressive yard with top national and international patrons; Contact: Longfield Stud, Goold's Cross, Cashel, Co. Tipperary. **T** 0504 42234 **M** 087 257 0574

Charming and unpretentious; the extremely hardworking son in law of John Magnier (*qv*) is grounded and an exciting prospect as emerging top trainer.

WATERFORD, MOST HON. MARQUESS OF, John Hubert de la Poer Beresford; HERITAGE HOUSE & LAND OWNER
b 1933; *m* Caroline Wyndham-Quinn; 3*s* 1*d*; *edu.* Eton; Marquess 1934 to date (8th Marquess created 1789); landowner. Clubs: Whites, London; Turf Club. Recreations: polo, fast cars. Contact: Curraghmore, Portlaw, Co. Waterford **T** 051 387102 **F** 051 387481

Tyronie Waterford, with his brother, has long graced the social pages in these islands; the owner of a major heritage house and possibly the largest landowner (Waterford and Wicklow) in the Republic; the head of a once powerful political dynasty known as the Undertakers (an 18th century political term), he is hardly known outside the country sports field, but remains an important social figure within the Polo playing and landowning fraternity; driver of fast cars.

WATERS, John; WRITER
b 1955, Roscommon; single; 1*d*; *edu.* Mean Scoil Iosef Naofa, Castlerea; Writer/ columnist/ Playwright; *Publ. Jiving at the Crossroads* (Blackstaff) 1991; *Race of Angels* (Fourth Estate) 1994; *The Intelligent Person's Guide to Modern Ireland* (Duckworth) 1997; *The Politburo Has Decided That You Are Unwell* (Liffey Press) 2004; plays: *Long Black Coat* (Cleere's Theatre, Kilkenny and Project Arts Centre, Dublin) 1994; *Easter Dues* (Kilkenny Theatre) 1995; radio plays: *Holy Secrets* (BBC Radio 4)

Winner Richard Imison Award; *Career* 1996; *Adverse Possession* (BBC Radio 3) 1997; writer with *Hotpress* 1981-85; freelance with *Sunday Tribune* and *Irish Independent* 1985-87; editor *In Dublin* 1985-87; editor *Magill* 1988-90; features writer *Irish Times*; columnist *Irish Times* 1991 to date. Recreations: books, music, travel. Contact: 10-16 D'Olier Street, Dublin 2. **T** 01 6792022 email jwaters@irish-times.ie

> A talented, creative, independent minded, principled man who, if pushed, will enforce his rights, as the *Irish Times* hierarchy discovered to its chagrin; has been an important voice on the Irish media landscape since he first made his appearance on *The Late Late Show* over two decades ago; in particular he articulated the power-broking role rural life plays in the Irish State and punctured holes in the pomposity and arrogance of the Dublin 4 hegemony; these days he argues for "equal rights for single fathers", "equality for men" and "fair treatment for men".

WELD, Dermot Kenneth; RACEHORSE TRAINER

b 1948, England; *m* Mary; *2s*; *edu.* Newbridge College, Newbridge, Co Kildare; University College Dublin; Veterinary Surgeon; Racehorse Trainer; leading amateur jockey; Irish Champion Trainer (Prize Money) 9 times, winning 18 times; winner of All Irish Classics; only Non American to win a leg of US Triple Crown, Belmont Stakes 1990; only Northern Hemisphere trainer to win the Melbourne Cup 1993 and 2002; major races worldwide: 19 European Classic Winners, Irish Record, 3000 Career Victory in Dubai March 2005; freedom of city, Melbourne, Australia; recipient UCD Charter Day Medal; Person of the Year Award 2002 and 2003. Recreations: current affairs, reading, travel, Irish rugby. Contact: Rosewell House, The Curragh, Co Kildare **T** 045 441273 **F** 045 441119. email dkweld@eircom.net

Dermot Weld

> Recognized internationally as a champion trainer who began his career as a veterinary surgeon; now equally successful in the property world;

WENT, David; CEO IRISH LIFE AND PERMANENT plc

b 1947, Dublin; *m* Mary Milligan; *1s 1d*; *edu.* High School, Dublin; Trinity College Dublin; Kings Inns, Dublin; BA.(mod). LLB., BL.; Chief Executive Officer, Irish Life and Permanent plc; general manager Citibank N.A. (Dublin) 1970-75; general manager Citibank (Jeddah) 1975-76; deputy chief executive, Ulster Bank (Belfast) 1976-87; chief executive, Cootes Bank London 1987-88; chief executive Ulster Bank 1988-99; chief executive officer Irish Life & Permanent plc 1999 to date; fellow Institute of Bankers; president Irish Bankers Association 1991; chairman Northern Ireland Bankers Association 1989-91; chairman of the Trinity College Foundation; director of Allianz (Ireland) and The Irish Times Ltd. Clubs: Royal Belfast Golf Club, Royal North Yacht Club, Kildare Street and University Club, Dublin. Recreations: tennis, squash, community involvement. Contact: Irish Life and Permanent plc, Irish Life Center, Lower Abbey Street, Dublin 1 **T** 01 704 1010 email information@irishlife.ie web www.irishlife.ie

> A hard nosed banker with wide experience from his days in a number of financial institutions; hit the headlines during his short stay as chief executive of Cootes Bank, the British Royal family's bankers; returned to take up the top job at Irish Life and Permanent.

WHELAN, Bill; COMPOSER

b 1950, Limerick; *m* Denise *2s 2d*; *edu.* Crescent College, Limerick; University College Dublin; BCL; Kings Inns; Barrister at Law; Composer; joined Planxty 1979; *Publ.* wrote musical score for film commemorating the work of Seán O'Riada 1987; *The Seville Suite* 1992; *The Spirit of Mayo* 1993; *Riverdance* 1994; *Inishlacken* for Fionnuala Hunt (*qv*) and Irish Chamber Orchestra 2003; production and arranging credits include, among others, U2, Van Morrison and Kate Bush; Awards: Grammy Awards 1997; People of the Year Awards 1999; Ph.D (*hc*) DIT 1999; record producer: Andy Irvine, Patrick Street, Stockton's Wing, Davy Spillane; composed Music for *Riverdance the Show*; *Lamb*; *Some Mother's Son; Dancing at Lughnasa; At the Cinema Palace.* Grammy award for Best Musical Show Album, Riverdance 1997. Recreations: boating, fishing, walking travel. Contact: Mc Guinness-Whelan, 30-32, Sir John Rogersons Quay, Dublin 2. **T** 01 677 7330 **F** 01 677 7267 web www.billwhelan.com

> Multi talented, charming, excellent company, hit the spot internationally with his now iconic music for *Riverdance*; despite his international acclaim lives a quiet, low key life in Connemara; has restored and rebuilt Kate O'Brien's house on the water's edge overlooking Bertraghboy Bay and the Twelve Bens.

Des Whelan

WHELAN, Desmond Anthony; MANAGING DIRECTOR WLR FM
b 1957, Waterford; *edu.* Waterpark College, Waterford; WIT, Waterford; managing director
WLR FM; Executive Chairman Beat 102-103; started with WLR FM in 1978, won franchise
for Waterford city and county in 1989; founded Beat 102-103; won franchise of Ireland's first
regional station in 2003; former Chairman of Independent Radio Sales; director of People in
Need Trust; director of Waterford Spraoi Street Theatre Group. Clubs: St. Anne's Tennis Club,
Dunmore East Tennis Club, Waterford Harbour Sailing Club. Recreations: jogging, tennis,
music, talking to my kids, sailing, hurling, soccer, windsurfing, (National Champion way back in
1983). Contact: WLR FM, The Broadcast Centre, Ardkeen, Waterford, Ellsley, Johns Hill,
Waterford. **T** 051 877592 **F** 051 877420 email des@WLRfm.com

Highly regarded among the local community; successful, innovative and hardworking.

WHELAN, John; CHIEF EXECUTIVE, IRISH EXPORTERS ASSOCIATION
b 1944, *m* Margaret; 7*s* 1*d*; *edu.* Christian Brothers College Monkstown, Co. Dublin; University
College Dublin; B.Sc.; M.B.A.; Chief Executive, Irish Exporters Association; director, Institute
of International Trade of Ireland; director, Celbridge Enterprise Centre, Co. Kildare; former senior
executive Lufthansa Airmotive Ireland; former operations director Smith Group; *Publ. Irish Exporters
Essential Facts; IP Management for Exporters; Channel Partners – International; Distribution; Selling to
USA by Internet;* Contributor to the *Irish Times* and *Irish Independent* on trade issues. Clubs: Naas Golf
Club, Celbridge and Straffan Choral groups, Royal Dublin Society (life member), Kildare Street
Club. Recreations: golf, music. Contact: Irish Exporters Association, 28 Merrion Square, Dublin 2.
T 01 661 2182 **F** 01 661 2315 web www.irishexporters.ie

Widely experienced, the public face of the growing Irish export sector for many years;
due to his career experience is highly respected in the industry.

WHELAN, Noel; VICE PRESIDENT, UNIVERSITY OF LIMERICK
b 1940, Cork city; *m* Joan Gaughan; 2*s* 2*d*; *edu.* Sacred Heart Convent, Buttevant, Co. Cork; Diploma
in Public Admin (DPA) 1962; B.Comm (Hons) University College Dublin 1964; M.Econ Sc.(Hons)
University College Dublin 1965; PhD University College Dublin (thesis in the area of science policy)
1968; Vice President, University of Limerick; various positions in the Irish public service (local
authorities, State-sponsored bodies and national Government) 1960-82; vice president of the
European Investment Bank and vice chairman of its board of directors, Luxembourg 1982-88; senior
academic and management positions at the University of Limerick as professor of business and
management, dean of College of Business, and vice president (of the university) plus external
corporate involvement at chairperson and non-executive director levels 1989 to date; *Publ.* papers,
commentaries in the areas of economic development, public sector development, public finance,
investment appraisal and the economics of science and technology; also, various public analytical
papers published as part of the National Economic and Social Council (NESC) output 1978-1984.
Recreations: music, swimming, walking, photography. Contact: University of Limerick, Limerick.
T 061 202 115 **F** 061 336 559 email noel.whelan@ul.ie

The Buttevant born academic had a rapid rise through the civil service ranks emerging
as one of the youngest heads of a government department; reached national
prominence becoming head of the newly formed government department Economic
Planning and Development under Martin O' Donoghue 1977; after a period in Europe
became vice president of UL and chairman of St Vincent's Hospital, Dublin; bright,
articulate, somewhat aloof.

WHELEHAN, Frankie; MANAGING DIRECTOR, CHOICE HOTELS, IRELAND
b 1969, Dublin; *m* Josephine; 3*d*; *edu.* St. Finians College, Mullingar, Co Westmeath; Shannon College
of Hotel Management, Shannon Airport, Co Clare; Diploma in Hotel Management; MD Choice
Hotels Ireland; Founder Choice Hotels, Clarion, Quality and Comfort Inns Ireland. Clubs: Bandon
Golf Club, Parknasilla Golf Club, St Mary's GAA Club, Mullingar, Valley Rovers GAA, Innishannon,
Co. Cork. Recreations: golf, walking. Contact: Choice Hotels, Thomas Ashe House, 15 Father
Matthew Quay, Cork. **T** 021 490 8208 **F** 01 427 1489 web www.choicehotelseurope.com

Presides over a rapidly expanding low cost group of hotels around the country;
ambitious, hardworking, the result of which is already bearing very profitable fruit.

WHITE, Mary née Casey; PUBLIC REPRESENTATIVE
b 1944, Dundalk, Co. Louth; *m* Padraic White(*qv*); 1*d*; *edu.* Holy Family Convent, Newbridge, Co. Kildare; Bolton Street College of Technology (Dip Architect Tech.); University College Dublin; BA (Politics and Economics); Public Representative, Senator, Seanad Éireann (elected to Industrial and Commercial Panel); architectural technologist, Office of Public Works; architects dept, Aer Rianta; architectural technologist, National Building Agency 1974-86; co-founded Lir Chocolates with Connie Doody 1986; joint managing director to 2000; marketing director 2000 to date; member Irish Exporters Association; council member of International Trade of Ireland; member Marketing Institute of Ireland; chairwoman of the President's Award – Gaisce 1999-01; director Bord Bia 1997-05; member of council Dublin Chamber of Commerce 1996-01; member board, National College of Art & Design 1993-96; member of Higher Education Authority 1990-95; member Dublin City Enterprise Board Evaluation Committee 1993-97; member National Executive Fianna Fáil 1993-98; member of Fianna Fáil 1983 to date; Fianna Fail National Executive 1993-98; member of Joint Oireachtas Committee on Finance and the Public Sector. Contact: 6, Wyckham Park Road, Dundrum, Dublin 16. **T** 01 618 3820/ 01 618 4258 **F** 01 618 4046 email mwhite@oireachtas.ie

Mary White

In a relatively short period of time, the wife of the former IDA chief Padraic White (*qv*) has carved out a significant niche on the political landscape; is single minded, very ambitious, extremely driven and tenacious; is an extraordinarily hard working political lobbyist who has the ability to identify issues of critical importance to the electorate such as her present campaign on child care; as the cofounder of Lir Chocolates with Connie Doody her business experience and huge success has been a definite advantage in the political arena; received a national profile though her support for the Columbia Three which proved to be a major disadvantage when she attempted to fulfil her dream of becoming the FF TD in Dublin South East in 2006. perhaps an error to target a constituency not known for it's Republican tradition; but definitely one to watch!

WHITE, Padraic; CHAIRMAN, RAIL PROCUREMENT AGENCY
b 1942, Kinlough, Co Leitrim; *m* Mary White (*qv*); 1*d*; *edu.* De La Salle, Ballyshannon; University College Dublin; B.Comm; Dip. Public Administration; Chairman Railway Procurement Agency; chairman Railway Procurement Agency responsible for light rail and metro transport; chairman Irish Maritime Development Office Advisory Group (promoting Ireland as a centre for international shipping services); chairman National Drugs Strategy Team; chairman, National Crime Council of Ireland reporting to the Minister for Justice; chairman, St Luke's Hospital, Rathgar, Dublin (national specialist centre for radiotherapy treatment); member Executive Council of the Economic & Social Research Institute of Ireland; chairman West Belfast & Greater Shankill Employment Services Board; chairman West Belfast Task Force Report on Unemployment & Disadvantage; chairman Northside Partnership Ltd (North Dublin local area partnership focusing on unemployment and disadvantage); chairman Q102 Radio station, Dublin (owned by UTV plc); executive chairman Collins Mc Nicholas Recruitment & Training Group; chairman Certification Europe Ltd (certifies compliance with high level international standards in quality, health & safety, environment, information security, e-signatures); chairman Arigna Smokeless Fuel and Wind Energy companies; director Coyle Hamilton Willis insurance brokers, Dublin; director London Life & General Re-insurance Ltd, IFSC, Dublin; director Zurich Premier Series Ltd (hedge fund company); chairman Coolock Development Council Ltd; former managing director Industrial Development Authority of Ireland (IDA Ireland); *Publ.* co-author with Ray McSharry of best-seller *The Making of the Celtic Tiger – The Inside Story of Ireland's Boom Economy* (Mercier Press) 2000; *Decommissioning Requirements for Ireland's Demersal and Shellfish Fleets*, a report to Marine Minister Pat the Cope Gallagher TD July 2005. Clubs: Stephens Green Hibernian Club, Dublin; Riverview Racquet and Fitness Club, Dublin. Recreations: opera, fitness, rail based holidays, Croatia in all its aspects. Contact: 6 Wyckham Park Road, Dundrum, Dublin 16. **M** 087 256 0534 **F** 01 6766097 email whitepad@iol.ie

The Leitrim born, former IDA chief took over the mantle from the legendary Michael Killeen and steered the Agency though the depressed 1980s; instrumental in attracting foreign direct investment to Ireland in the healthcare and pharmaceuticals industries which laid the foundation for the emergence of the Celtic Tiger; IDA Ireland negotiated with industry leaders such as Microsoft, IBM Software, Lotus and Intel to establish European operations in Ireland and organised the successful campaign to establish an International Financial Services Centre in Dublin; winning of Intel for Ireland in 1989 was a particular highlight of his tenure as MD of the IDA; since leaving the semi state has built up an impressive string of board directorships in the semi state and private sectors; sartorially elegant, personable and well got in Fianna Fáil circles having been a former chairman of the national policies forum.

WHITE, Trevor; EDITOR/PUBLISHER

b 1972, Dublin; single; *edu.* St. Columba's College, Rathfarnham, Dublin; Trinity College Dublin; Diploma, Theatre Studies; Publisher/ Editor *the Dubliner*. Editor *Food and Wine Magazine* 1997 -98; Contributing Editor, *Europe's Elite 1000,* 1998- 99; Senior Editor *America's Elite 1000,* 1999; publisher/editor *the Dubliner,* 2001 – todate. Clubs: Kildare Street and University Club, Dublin. Recreations: playing pool, squash, table tennis. Contact: the Dubliner, 23 Wicklow Street, Dublin 2 **T** 01 635 9825 **F** 01 675 2158 email trevor@thedubliner.ie web www.thedubliner.ie

> Son of Peter and Alicia, former owners of the legendary Whites On The Green, has a good handle on contemporary culture, style and entertainment; once regarded as the *enfant terrible* of Irish publishing, is no longer an *enfant* but knows how to push the buttons of various sectors especially the restaurateurs, many of whom have a major problem with his annual Top 100 listings; having tried to make his mark nationally, finally achieved international notoriety when his magazine carried an off the wall, scurrilous attack on Elin Woods, wife of Tiger, on the eve of tee off for the Ryder Cup.

WHITE, Willie James; ARTS MANAGER

b 1970, Dublin; *m* Gillian Clarke; 1*s*; *edu.* Clongowes Wood College, Naas, Co. Kildare; University College Dublin; Trinity College Dublin; BA, MA, English; M.Phil Irish Theatre Studies; Artistic Director, Project Theatre; RTE Television 1998-02. Recreations: arts, travel, cycling, cookery. Contact: 39, Essex Street Temple Bar, Dublin 2. **T** 01 881 9627 **F** 01 679 2310 email willie.white@project.ie

> Polite, determined and ambitious for the arts, he likes and is liked by his colleagues; doesn't personalise issues; rather, he focuses on what can and should be done; a doer and an achiever; his considerable *sang froid* enables him to get places others might not; certainly a future Arts Council Chairman or something similar?

WHITAKER, Thomas Kenneth (TK); PUBLIC SERVANT/ECONOMIST

b 1916, Rostrevor, Co. Down; *m* 1st Nora (*decd*); 5*s* 1*d*; *m* 2nd Marie; *edu.* Christian Brothers School, Drogheda, Co. Louth; London University (external student); M.Sc (Econ); Public Servant/Economist; Irish Civil Service 1934-38; Dept. of Finance 1938; secretary general, Dept of Finance 1956-69; governor Central Bank of Ireland 1969-76; director Bank of Ireland 1975-85; Guinness board of directors 1976-84; president Economic and Social Research Institute 1970-85; chairman Dublin Institute for Advanced Studies 1980-90; chancellor National University of Ireland 1976-96; president Royal Irish Academy Dublin 1985-87; headed inquiry into the Penal System 1985; Common Fisheries Policy Review 1991; D. Econ Sc NUI (*hc*); LLD University of Dublin (*hc*); Queen's University Belfast. D.Sc (*hc*); Awards: RDS honorary life member; honorary fellow Institution of Engineers; commandeur de la Legion d'Honneur; *Publ.* economic analysis for Government 1958 resulting in first programme for economic expansion; financing by Credit Creation; economic developments and papers in relevant journals and newpapers. Recreations: angling, music. Contact: Stillorgan Road, Co. Dublin. **T** 01 269 3474

> A highly respected and major contributor to the life of the State by direct advocacy and economic philosophical rationale; a cheerful public servant who doesn't stand on his great achievements but instead a man of great personal charm and integrity.

WHYTE, Ian William; AUCTIONEER AND VALUER OF FINE ART AND COLLECTIBLES

b 1961, Dublin; *m* ; separated; 2*s*; *edu.* Managing Director, Whyte & Sons Auctioneers Ltd; dealing in collectibles since the mid 1960s when the 200-year-old family firm closed its famous glass and china showrooms; co-founder of *Stampa*, Irish National Stamp Exhibition 1972; licensed auctioneer since 1977; has run auctions containing an eclectic mix of collectibles including stamps, coins, cigarette cards, antiquarian books, historical documents and manuscripts, paper ephemera, pop and sports memorabilia and antique toys; more recently Whyte's have become a leading player in the Irish art world, with major sales held quarterly at the RDS; *Publ.* contributor and correspondent to various collector journals since 1967; publisher of reference works on collectibles and art, including forthcoming monographs on Camille Souter and John Kingerlee; sponsor of *A Buyer's Guide to Irish Art* (Ashville Media) 2001 to date. Clubs: The Albert (London and New York); Chelsea FC, London; RIAC Dublin; Irish Philatelic Society; Numismatic Society of Ireland. Recreations: collecting art and ephemera, watching sport, especially rugby and football, travel, reading. Contact: 38, Molesworth Street, Dublin 2 **T** 01 676 2888 **F** 01 676 2880 email iw@whytes.ie

Has made his firm into the three biggest players in the world of Irish art auctions from a standing start; popular, highly respected and successful, his development of the Irish art market has amazed and infuriated his business rivals; will take the art market further with his foresight and drive.

WILLIAMS, Scott; MANAGING DIRECTOR DUBLIN'S Q102
b 1957, Dublin; *m* Karen Garrett; 4*s* 1*d*; *edu.* Synge Street CBS; Trinity College Dublin; BA (Natural Science); Managing Director Dublin's Q102; Q102 Dublin 2002; Lite FM Dublin 2000; Radio Nova Dublin 1980s; RTE 1988-89; FM104 Dublin 1989-95; GWR Group PLC (UK) 1995-97; Live 95 FM Limerick 1997-2000. Recreations: reading, motoring, technology, sport. Contact: Glenageary Office Park, Co Dublin **T** 01 662 1022 **F** 01 201 3871 email scott.williams@Q102.ie

One of the most successful executives in commercial radio; affable, hardworking and extremely popular; runs a tight ship.

Scott Williams

WOODS, Angela; FASHION DESIGN CONSULTANT
b 1951, Warwickshire, UK; single; 1*d*; *edu.* Stoke Lodge School for Girls, Coventry Warwickshire, England; Birmingham College of Art & Design; Royal College of Art, London; DipAD (Hons), M.Des (RCA); Fashion Design Consultant; head of design faculty, National College of Art & Design 1996 to date; had worked in the fashion industry, traveled extensively, lecturing to major 3rd level design institutions and head of fashion and textile design at Ravensbourne College of Design and Communication in London. Clubs: member of the Institute of Designers in Ireland (IDI); active member of the IDI Education Committee. Recreations: gardening, art and design, cinema. Contact: National College of Art and Design, 100 Thomas Street, Dublin 8. **T** 01 636 4270 **F** 01 636 4277 email woodsa@ncad.ie web www.ncad.ie

For someone of her stature is extremely tenacious and gutsy; astute, clever business person; a motivational tour de force, has her finger on the fashion pulse.

WOODS, Michael; PUBLIC REPRESENTATIVE
b 1935, Bray, Co. Wicklow; *m* Margot Maher; 3*s* 2*d*; *edu.* Synge Street, C.B.S. Dublin; University College Dublin; Institute of Public Administration, Dublin; Harvard Business School, USA; B.Agr.Sc., M.Agr.Sc, Ph.D, D.Sc; Diploma and Fellowship in Public Administration; Diploma in Marketing; Public Representative, TD, FF, Dublin North East; chairman Joint Committee on Foreign Affairs and Public Representatives; *Publ.* author research in Ireland – *Key to Economic and Social Development*; numerous technical and scientific papers; numerous papers on public affairs, health, social welfare, agriculture, marine; programs economic, social development; Minister Education and Science 2000-02; Minister Marine and Natural Resources 1997-00; Opposition Spokesman Social Welfare, February 1997-97; Opposition Spokesman Equality and Law Reform 1994 -97; Minister Health 1994-94; Minister Social Welfare 1993-94; Minister Marine 1992-92; Minister Agriculture and Food 1991-92; Minister Social Welfare 1989-91; Minister Social Welfare 1987-89; Opposition Spokesman Justice 1983-87; Minister Health and Social Welfare 1982-December 1982; Minister Health and Social Welfare 1979-81; Minister of State Departments An Taoiseach and Defence, Government Chief Whip, 1979; elected to Dáil Éireann 1977 - todate; managing director, Associated Producer Groups Ltd 1974-79; managing director F11 Produce Ltd 1970-73; head of department and principal officer, Agriculture Research Institute 1960-70; lecturer ,Franciscan College of Agriculture, Multyfarnham, Co. Westmeath 1958-59. Recreations: walking, swimming, boating, reading, TV, community, work of NGOs at home and abroad. Contact: 13 Kilbarrack Grove, Raheny, Dublin 5. **T** 01 832 3357 **F** 01 832 5222 email michael.woods@oireachtas.ie

Following a brilliant academic career (the only Dáil Deputy to hold a D.Sc.) he became an internationally recognized researcher with An Foras Talúntais now Teagasc; following his selection to Dáil Éireann moved rapidly up the political ladder serving in a wide range of ministries; accessible to all sides of the House; affable and always in great demand to sing at parties.

WOODWORTH, Judy; ARTISTIC DIRECTOR, THE NATIONAL CONCERT HALL
b 1951; *m* Tim Lloyd; *edu.* Alexandra College, Dublin; Trinity College Dublin; BA (Mod) (History, Political Science); Royal Irish Academy of Music; awarded various prizes and scholarships piano and singing; Artistic Director The National Concert Hall; artists' manager Ibbs and Tillett (London)

Judith Woodworth

1975-78; artists' manager Harrison Parrott (London) 1976-86; artistic director GPA Music in Great Irish Houses 1982-99; concert promoter Celebrity Concert Series, National Concert Hall 1986 (presenting international artists such as Nigel Kennedy, Anne Sophie Mutter, Kyun-wha Chung, Alfred Brendel); director, National Concert Hall 1993 to date; appointed by Government to be first chair, Council of National Cultural Institutions; associate member, British Association of Concert Agents; governor, The Irish Times Trust 2002 to date; founder member, Irish Branch, International Women's Forum; trustee, Irish Music Industry Charity, the IRMA Trust; board member, Alexandra College, Dublin. Recreations: gardening, music (classical and opera), hill walking. Contact: 16, Idrone Terrace, Blackrock, Co. Dublin. **T** 01 288 6102 email judith.woodworth@nch.ie

A quiet, shy but hardly self effacing musical figure; very active on the Dublin social scene; gets things done, and has produced a major development plan for the NCH (2005); a force to be reckoned with.

WRIXON, Gerard Thomas; PRESIDENT, UNIVERSITY COLLEGE CORK
b 1940, Limerick; *m* Marcia; 2*s* 1*d*; *edu.* Christian Brothers Cork; University College Cork; California Institute of Technology; University of California, Berkeley; B.E., MSc (Caltech), Ph.D (University of California); President, University College Cork, due to retire December 2006; professor; director of the National Micro Electric Centre 1989-99. Clubs: Kildare Street & University Club, Kinsale Yacht Club, Royal Dublin Society. Contact: President's Office, University College Cork, Western Road, Cork. **T** 021 490 3623 **F** 021 427 5006 email president@ucc.ie web www.ucc.ie

The Kinsale resident has brought a sharp business approach to the Presidency of UCC which is now one of the largest corporate entities in the Munster region; though granted an extension to his term (2005) decided not to avail of it and surprised everyone by announcing his retirement in December 2006; was totally committed to his college becoming a global centre of academic excellence; his successor, not yet announced, will have a hard act to follow.

ZOTTO, Peter; PRESIDENT IONA TECHNOLOGIES

b 1945, New Hampshire, US; *m*; 2*s* 1*d*; *edu.* University of New Hampshire (degree Political Science and Economics); President Iona Technologies plc; worked in IT for 30 years; served in a number of senior roles in the Compaq owned Digital Equipment Corp, including sales and marketing in Switzerland; left Digital to lead up a series of start-ups, including Irish firm WBT Systems; joined Iona 2003; appointed chief operating officer October 2003; appointed president October 2004. Recreations: golf, reading. Contact: Iona House, Shelbourne Road, Dublin 4. **T** 01 637 2000 **F** 01 637 2888 web www.iona.com

With an international track record, came to Iona at a time when his experience was vital to reengineer the profits in the struggling IT company; his reputation should be enhanced with the improving sentiment for technology stocks.

ANDERSON, Jennifer; SUPERIOR COURT JUDGE DC; FORMER CHIEF OF HOMICIDE, US ATTORNEY'S OFFICE
Born, Killester, Dublin; Deputy Chief of Homicide, US Attorney General's Office. 2004 nominated by President Bush to the Superior Court in Washington D.C.; presides over local matters in the Washington DC area for its residents; has lived and worked in Washington D.C. for 14 years; having worked at night to put herself through college and working an internship in the Attorney General's office she regards her nomination by the President as epitomizing the American Dream.

BALDWIN, Alexander Rae 'Alec'; OSCAR NOMINATED ACTOR
Born, 3, April 1958, Long Island New York; father, Irish American high school history teacher, drama club director and football coach; oldest and best known of the Baldwin bothers; equally well known as a political activist; liberal Democrat; Bush opponent; best known for: Hunt For Red October, 1990, The Marrying Man, 1991; Glengary Glenross, 1994, The Shadow, 1994, The Getaway, 1994, Academy Award Nominate (Supporting role) The Cooler, 2003, Running With Scissors, 2006.

BALDWIN, Stephen; ACTOR DIRECTOR
Born, 12, May 1966, Long Island, New York; father, Irish American high school history teacher, drama club director and football coach; Bush supporter; Best known for: directed and produced Livin' It and Livin' It LA films that focuses on Christian athletes involved in extreme sports and evangelism; movies from 1988 to date includes, Born On The Fourth of July 1989, The Usual Suspects, 1995, The Flintstones in Viva Rock Vegas, 2000, Shelter Island, 2003, The Snake King 2005.

BALDWIN, William 'Billy'; ACTOR
Born, 21, February 1963, Long Island, New York; father, Irish American high school history teacher, drama club director and football coach; best known for: Flatliners,1990, Backdraft, 1991, The Squid and The Whale, 2005.

BARRETT, Dr Craig R; PRESIDENT AND CEO, INTEL CORP
Born, 29, August 1939, San Francisco, California; Before joining Intel, Barrett was immersed in the world of academia as an associate professor at Stanford University, where he received his B.S., M.S., and Ph.D. in materials science; a Fulbright Fellow at the Danish Technical University in 1972 and a NATO Postdoctoral Fellow at the National Physical Laboratory in England from 1964 - '65; co-chairman of the Business Coalition in Excellence in Education and Chairman of the Computer Systems Policy Project; As President and CEO of Intel is in charge of the world's largest producer of microprocessors; began working at Intel in 1974 as a technology development manager and began his work at the upper echelons of the corporation in 1984 as a vice president, and was elected to the board of directors, 1992; Chair, National Academy of Engineering; Board member, U.S. Semiconductor Industry Association, and the National Forest Foundation; appointed to the President's Advisory Committee for Trade Policy and Negotiations and to the American Health Information Community (AHIC).

BARTON, Mischa; ACTOR
Born, 24, January 1986, UK; 1st generation Irish, (Irish mother); best known for her role as Marissa Cooper in the TV series The O.C.; role ended in a fatal car "accident" during the third season's finale, which aired on May 18, 2006; modeled for Calvin Klein; has appeared in advertisements for Aéropostale, bebe, Accessorize, Dooney and Bourke, JC (Jeans and Clothes), and cover girl for their new worldwide ad campaign Neutrogena; commercial for Keds sneakers; Best known for: Notting Hill, 1999, Lost and Delirious, 2001, Octane, 2003, The OH in Ohio, Closing the Ring, 2007.

BIDEN, Joseph Robinette Jnr 'Joe'; SENATOR AND FOREIGN RELATIONS EXPERT.
Born, November, 20 1942, Scranton, Pennsylvania, 4th generation Irish American; Senior Senator for Delaware; in his 6th.Term as a Democratic Senator, has pioneered legislation on crime prevention, constitutional law and arms control, including being known for the Biden Crime Law; a likely candidate for the 2008 Presidential Election.

BOLAND, Dr Patrick J. FCRSI, FRCS; SURGEON
Born, 1944, Monasterevan, Ireland; Internationally acknowledged orthopaedic cancer specialist; a full-time, senior member of the Orthopedic Service, Department of Surgery, Memorial Sloan-Kettering Cancer Center; specializes in the management of malignant and benign tumors of the bones, including those of the spine and pelvis, and in soft-tissue sarcomas of the extremities; has special training in limb salvage surgery—that is the removal of the limb cancers while preserving a functional extremity; involved in extensive research activities, including on-going clinical research in sacral tumors and in the assessment of quality of life in patients with metastatic bone cancer; has also authored and co-authored chapters and scientific papers on surgery for tumors of the extremities and the spine; Fellow, American College of Surgeons; Fellow, Royal College of Surgeons in England; Fellow Royal College of Surgeons in Ireland.

BOYLE, Fr. Gregory F 'Greg' SJ; FOUNDER/ EXECUTIVE DIRECTOR, JOBS FOR A FUTURE
Born, Los Angeles, 2nd generation Irish American; Roman Catholic Priest; Social Activist; founder and executive

director of Jobs for a Future - a referral center that assists 1000 people a month in finding jobs and redirecting their lives, 1992; pastor of the Dolores Mission Church, one of the poorest parishes in LA, 1986 – '92; served as Chaplain of the Islas Marias Penal Colony in Mexico and Folsom Prison; founded the organisation with the mantra "nothing stops a bullet like a job"; expanded the centre to include Homeboy Industries; Awards: The California Peace Prize from The California Wellness Foundation; ACLU's Monroe Eason Courageous Advocate award; honorary degrees from Holy Cross and Gonzaga Universities. one of the 10 man delegation to President Clinton's Summit on Children, 1998.

BOYLE FLYNN, Lara; ACTOR
Born, 24, March, 1970; 2nd generation Irish (three Irish grandparents) best known TV roles, Twin Peaks, The Practice; movies include Men in Black and Wayne's World; overcame childhood shyness by taking Irish dancing classes in Chicago where she grew up and regularly accompanied her mother to the annual St. Patrick's Day parade; Best known for: Ferris Bueller's Day Off, 1986, Poltergeist, 1988, Dead Poet's Society, 1989, Twin Peaks (TV), Waynes World, 1992, The Practice (TV) 1997 – 2003, Men in Black 11, 2002, Las Vegas (TV) 2005.

BRADY, James; EDITOR COLUMNIST AUTHOR
Born, 1928, Brooklyn, New York; Marine Lieutenant, Korean War 1951-'52; publisher, Women's Wear Daily (in which capacity helped create W); publisher & editor, Harper's Bazaar; editor, Star, editor, New York Magazine; TV interview ABC-TV, CBS-TV; columnist: Advertising Age 1978 to date, Parade magazine 1986 to date, Forbes 2006 to date; Publ. incl. Christmas in the Hamptons, The House that Ate the Hamptons, The Coldest War (Pulitzer Prize); The Marines of Autumn; The Scariest Place in the World. 2005, The Rewrites, 2006; Awards: Emmy, Pulitzer;

BRADY, Tom; PROFESSIONAL FOOBALL STAR
Born, 3, August, 1977, San Mateo, California; 3rd generation Irish American, roots in Co. Cavan and Co. Cork; led the New England Patriots to the 3rd.Victory in the NFL Super Bowl in 4 years, ((the youngest staring quarterback ever to win the Super Bowl, 2002, 2004, 2005); named MVP (Most Valuable Player) 2002 and 2004; one of People Magazine's 50 Most Beautiful People, 2002, Sports Illustrated's Sportsman of the Year, 2005

BREEN, Maura C; SENIOR VICE PRESIDENT VERIZON
Born, Connecticut; 3rd generation Irish American, with roots in Cork; worked with American Red Cross; joined New England Telephone 1978; moved to NYNEX 1990; CEO Bell Atlantic Communications Inc; group president Verizon Long Distance; Snr vice-pres Verizon & CMO retail markets 2002 to date; a David Rockefeller Fellow alumnus, selected to be among the Academy of Women Achievers in New York;

Telephony magazine named her as one of the Top Twenty people to watch, 2000; Awards: from the St. Patrick's Home for the Aging in New York, Irish America Magazine Top 100 Business People.; member, Committee of 200 and the New York Women's Forum. Partnership.

BRENNAN, Donald, PATRICK 'DON'; FORMER MANAGING DIRECTOR MORGAN STANLEY MERCHANT BANK
Born, 1941; 3rd generation Irish American; Vice chairman, International Paper 1967 –'82; Head, Morgan Stanley, Merchant Bank Divison, 1982 – '96; Advisory Director, Morgan Stanley and Co, 1996; former director, Container Corporation of America; former deputy chairman, Waterford Wedgewood UK plc., member, Ireland America Economic Advisory Board.

BRESLIN, Jimmy, COLUMNIST, AUTHOR
Born, 17, October 1930, New York, ancestors emigrated from Donegal; syndicated columnist NY Herald Tribune, Paris Tribune, NY Daily News, Newsday, 1984-'04; host TV series, Jimmy Breslin's People, 1986; Publ: Can't anybody here play this Game? 1963, World without End, Amen, 1973, How the Good Guys Finally Won, 1975, The World According to Breslin, 1984, Table Money, 1986, He Got Hungry and Forgot His Manners,1988, Damon Runyon, 1991, American Lives: The Stories of the Men and Women Lost on September 11, (2002), The Church That Forgot Christ, 2004; delegate, Democratic National Convention 1972, 1976; Awards: recipient award for national reporting Sigma Delta Chi 1964, Meyer Berger award for local reporting 1964, Pulitzer Prize for Commentary 1986.

BRODERICK, Matthew; ACTOR
Born, 21, March 1962, New York; 2nd generation Irish; best known as title character in Ferris Bueller's Day Off and as the voice of Simba in The Lion King; also acclaimed for his role as Leo Bloom in The Producers on Broadway; won two Tony Awards, one in 1983 for his featured role in the play Brighton Beach Memoirs, and one in 1995 for his leading role in the musical How to Succeed in Business Without Really Trying; was also nominated for The Producers, but lost to co-star Nathan Lane; married to Sarah Jessica Parker, they have one son; the coupe have a home in Killybegs, Co. Donegal; Best known for: Brighton Beach Memoirs, 1983 (Broadway, Tony Award), How to Succeed in Business Without Really Trying, (Broadway, Tony Award), 1995, Ferris Bueller's Day Off , 1986, Lion King (voice of Simba) 1994, The Producers (Broadway, Tony Nomination) 2001, The Producers (movie) 2005, The Odd Couple (Broadway) 2005.

BROSNAHAN, James J ; CIVIL RIGHTS LAWYER
Born, 1931, 3rd.generation Irish; Senior Partner, San Franciso Law firm Morrison & Foerster; (Investigated the murder of Belfast Lawyer Rosemary Nelson; represented

John Walker who had converted to Islam and joined the Taliban in Afgahanistan, 2001; defended Kevin Barry Artt after he'd escaped from the Maze Prison in Northern Ireland); always carries a copy of the Constitution in his front pocket; named Trial Lawyer of the Year by the American Board of Advocates and was inducted into the State Bar of California's "Trial Lawyers Hall of Fame" 2001, received the Living the Dream Partner Award from the Lawyers' Committee for Civil Rights of the San Francisco Bay Area at the 19th Annual Dr. Martin Luther King, Jr., Luncheon, 2006.

BROSNAN, Pierce Brendan; ACTOR
Born, 16, May 1953, Drogheda, County Louth, Ireland; lived in Navan, County Meath until he moved to England, UK at an early age; Best known for: role as British secret agent James Bond; Seraphim Falls, 2006, The Topkapi Affair, 2006, Mexicali, 2005, Butterfly on a Wheel, 2007, Instant Karma, 2005, The Matador, 2005 (was nominated for a Golden Globe award for Best Actor in a Musical or Comedy, 2006), After the Sunset, 2004, Laws of Attraction, 2004, James Bond 007: Everything or Nothing, 2004, Die Another Day, 2002, Evelyn, 2002, The Tailor of Panama, 2001,Grey Owl,1999, The Match (aka The Beautiful Game (UK)1999, The Thomas Crown Affair, 1999. 1980s, The Manions of America (TV), Remington Steele (TV); Breast Cancer Advocate; naturalized American citizen, 23 September, 2004; Awards: Hon. OBE July 2003, for his "outstanding contribution to the British film industry".

BUCHANAN Pat; COLUMNIST, AUTHOR, PUNDIT, GOVERNMENT
Born, 2, November 1938, Washington DC; 3rd generation Irish American; former host Crossfire; author: best known for: Right from the Beginning, 1988, memoir, The Great Betrayal: How American Sovereignty and Social Justice Are Being Sacrificed to the Gods of the Global Economy, 1998; A Republic, Not an Empire: Reclaiming America's Destiny 1999; The Death of the West: How Dying Populations and Immigrant Invasions Imperil Our Country and Civilization, 2001; Where the Right Went Wrong: How Neoconservatives Subverted the Reagan Revolution and Hijacked the Bush Presidency, 2004.

BUCKLEY Jr, William Frank 'WFB'; AUTHOR, COMMENTATOR
Born, 24, November 1925, New York City; 3rd generation Irish American; founded the influential conservative political magazine National Review, 1955; hosted the award-winning television show Firing Line from 1966 until 1999; conservative journalist and commentator based in New York City and Sharon, Connecticut.

BURKE, Michèle; ACADEMY AWARD WINNING MAKE UP ARTIST
Born, Dalkey, Co. Dublin, Ireland; Winner of two Academy Awards for Best make Up in Quest For Fire, 1981 and Dracula; Trained in Spain and Canada; known as the 'Queen of Horror', a self-described "makeup artist who designs and creates characters and unusual beings"; best known for her work on, Cyrano De Bergerac (Academy Award Nomination), Interview With A Vampire, As Good As It Gets, 1997, Moll Flanders, Some Mother's Son,Jerry Maguire, Austin Powers, The Spy Who Shagged Me; The Cell,Mission Impossible III, Monster House, Elizabethtown, Spanglish, Minority Report, Austin Powers 2: The Spy Who Shagged Me; official Max Factor movie makeup artist;

BURNS, Brian P; CHAIRMAN AND PRESIDENT BF ENTERPRISES, INC
Born, Irish roots in County Kerry; a nationally regarded business executive and the moving force behind some 40 corporate mergers; also known for his Irish art collection, and for being the founder and chief benefactor, the John J. Burns (named for his father) Library of Rare Books at Boston College; (endowed the library with a Visiting Scholar in Irish Studies Chair,1990); named by Art & Antiques Magazine, as one of the 100 top collectors in America 1996; served as Vice Chairman of the Irish American Fulbright Commission, 1995-'98; member, The Trinity College Foundation Board in Dublin; member, Economic Advisory Board of Ireland; lifetime Trustee of The American Ireland Fund; his wife, Eileen, is a member of the Advisory Board to the National Gallery of Ireland.

Ed Burns

BURNS, Edward J 'Ed'; ACTOR, DIRECTOR, PRODUCER WRITER
Born, 29, January 1968, Woodside, New York; 1st generation Irish American; Best known for: Brothers McMullen, 1995, (Producer, Director, Jury special prize Deauville Film Festival 1995, Ind. Spirit award 1995, Nova award 1995, Grand Jury prize Sundance Film Festival 1995);

BYRNE, Gabriel; ACTOR, AUTHOR, UNICEF AMBASSADOR
Born, 12, May 1950, Dublin; star of movies such as The Usual Suspects and Millers Crossing, Vanity Fair and Assault on Precinct 13; filming the movie Wah Wah in Swaziland was moved by the plight of HIV/Aids suffers; accepted the invitation to become the UNICEF Ambassador, 2005; supporter of the Irish Arts Centre, New York and has long been active in humanitarian, charitable and cultural organizations; Best known for: Excalibur, 1981, Millers Crossing, 1990, Little Women, 1994, The Brylcreem Boys,1997, Polish Wedding, 1998, End of Days, 1999, Ghost Ship, 2002, P.S, 2004, Jindabyne, 2006.

CAHILL, Dr. Kevin; TROPICAL DISEASE
SPECIALIST
Born, the Bronx, New York; director,
Tropical Disease Center, Lenox Hill
Hospital; worked in the slums of Calcutta
studying tropical diseases alongside
Mother Teresa 1961; the first to predict famine in Somalia;
was caught in the crossfire in Beruit and Managua as well as
treating refugees in the Sudan; Chairman, Department of
International Health at the Royal College of Surgeons
Dublin; works with other organisations including the
Institute for Humanitarian Affairs and the NYPD; Director,
International Health and co operation, Lenox Hill Hospital;
Clinical director, parasitic diseases at New York Medical
School; President, Irish American Historical Society; Has
received 25 Honorary Doctorates and authored 29 books on
a wide range of topics medical, literary and historical;
patients included Pope John Paul II, President Ronald
Reagan.

CAHILL, Thomas; AUTHOR
Born,1940, New York City; 2nd generation Irish American;
Author; taught at Queens College, Fordham University, and
Seton Hall University, served as the North American
education correspondent for The Times of London, and was
for many years a regular contributor to the Los Angeles
Times Book Review. Prior to retiring recently to write full-
time, he was Director of Religious Publishing at Doubleday
for six years. He and his wife, Susan, also an author, founded
the now legendary Cahill & Company, whose Reader's
Catalog was much beloved in literary households throughout
the country; Best known for: How The Irish Saved
Civilization, Desire of The Everlasting Hills, The Gift of The
Jews, Sailing the Wine-Dark Sea.

CALLAGHAN, Jeremiah; LEGENT CLEARING, LLC, NEW
YORK, NY
Born, February 1943, New York; 1st generation Irish
American, parents from Dingle and Tralee, moved to New
York in the 1930s; Very interested in mental health issues and
Special Olympics; member, New York board, American
Ireland Fund

CALLAGHAN, Michael J; SENIOR VICE PRESIDENT,
GENERAL COUNSEL, SECRETARY YAHOO!
3rd generation Irish-American with ties to Cork on his
father's side; has distinguished himself as one of the Top 100
Lawyers in California; Associated with the law firm of
Skadden, Arps, Slate, Meagher & Flom LLP, where he put his
efforts towards business mergers; joined Electronics for
Imagine, Inc. where he was heavily involved with overall
business development; Joined Yahoo! 1999, Deputy General
Counsel and Assistant Secretary; appointed Senior Vice
President, General Counsel, and Secretary of Yahoo!
September 2003; (in charge of the worldwide legal affairs
and public policy for Yahoo!)

CAREY, Chase; PRESIDENT, CEO DIRECTV
3rd generation Irish American; CEO, COO, News
Corp.,1988 '02, notably with its subsidiary Fox
Entertainment and was instrumental in the growth of Fox
Television Stations from seven to its current 35 affiliates,
which draw nearly 300 million subscribers. Prior to his
tenure with Fox and News Corp. Carey spent six years in
senior capacities with Columbia Pictures; appointed
President and CEO, DirecTV, 2003, in charge of operations
and the overall strategic direction of the company in the
United States and South America; a trustee of Colgate
University.

CAREY, Dennis J., VICE PRESIDENT CORPORATE
OPERATIONS NORTEL
3rd generation Irish American with roots in County Kildare,
Vice President Corporate Operations, Nortel, global leader in
innovative communications and services that are enabling the
transformation of businesses around the world, 2004 –
todate; executive vice president of Motorola, president and
chief executive officer of Motorola's Integrated Electronic
Systems Sector (IESS); joined The Home Depot, executive
vice president, Business Development, Strategy and
Corporate Operations; (The Home Depot Revenue: $45.7
Billion Employees: 250,000), 1998 –'02; Consultant to Home
Depot, 2003 – '06; Prior to that he served as president and
general manager of corporate productivity and mergers at
AT&T and chairman of the board of LIN Television;
Director, CRM provider Blue Martini Software; Active in
The Home Depot's community involvement, Team Depot;
Member, Advisory Board of Habitat for Humanity and the
Board of Trustees for the National Urban League.

CAREY, Hugh Leo Carey; FORMER GOVERNOR OF NEW
YORK
Born, 11, April 1919, Brooklyn, New York; joined the U.S.
Army as an enlisted man during World War II, served in
Europe, and reached the rank of major; received his
bachelor's degree in 1942 and law degree in 1951 from St.
John's University and was admitted to the bar that same year;
ran as a Democrat, Carey, elected to the United States House
of Representatives, 1960; served seven terms; served on the
House Ways and Means Committee and led the effort to pass
the first Federal Aid to Education program; was elected
Governor of the State of New York in 1975 and resigned his
Congressional seat on December 31, 1974; served two terms;
returned to private law practice with the firm of Harris Beach
in New York City, where he still resides; he was the first
congressman from Brooklyn to oppose the Vietnam War;
along with Senator Edward Kennedy and Speaker Tip
O'Neill he led efforts to end the violence in Northern Ireland
and support peace in the region; Governor Carey endorsed
Attorney General Eliot Spitzer in April, 2006 for Governor
of New York.

CAREY, Mariah; DIVA
Born, 27, March 1970, Huntington, Long Island, New York; 1st generation Irish (Mother Irish opera singer, Patricia Hickey) singer songwriter; seventeen number one hits; best known for   Grammy Best New Artist (1990), Grammy Best Pop Vocal Performance, Female (Vision of Love,1990); Best known for Don't Forget Us 2005, We Belong Together, 2005, Against All The Odds 2000, Thank God I Found You, 2000, Heartbreaker 1999, My All, 1998, One Sweet Day, 1995.

CARROLL, Pete; FOOTBALL COACH
Born, San Francisco 1951; 3rd generation Irish; Head coach New England Patriots 1997-'99; 2001 Head Coach University of Southern California Trojans. 2002 USC had it's best season for many years; Regarded as an important University Coach.

CASHMAN, Thomas J; TRADER, SHATKIN, ARBOR & KARLOV
Self employed grain broker; 1984-'90: Vice President of Victor Grain;
1980-92 Vice President, Cashman & Co., Inc; 1980-92 – Cashco Oil Company; Irish Georgian Society, Irish Fellowship Club, Chicago Board of Trade Ampac Committee, National Feed and Grain Association, Director, Geneva Lake Association, America Soybean Association, Chicago Board of Trade.

CASSIDY, Gerald S. J 'Gerry'; FOUNDER, CHAIRMAN & CEO THE CASSIDY COMPANIES, INC.
Born, 1941; Founder of Cassidy & Associates, Founder, Chairman and CEO, The Cassidy Companies, Inc., (the largest integrated public affairs and government relations network in the world); The Cassidy Companies Inc. consists of six companies: Cassidy & Associates, Inc. (a government relations firm), Powell Tate (a public relations and financial communications firm), The Rhoads Group (a commerce-oriented government relations firm), SWR Worldwide (a public opinion research firm), Bork & Associates, Inc. (a litigation communication firm) and Murphy Pintak Gautier Hudome Agency, Inc., (an advocacy advertising and strategic consulting firm); Clients include Fortune 500 corporations, financial institutions, regional companies, start-up enterprises, states and state agencies, trade associations, other major interest groups and non-profit institutions; has gained widespread recognition for creating Washington's number one integrated government relations and public affairs firm and the city's number one firm in billings; has been profiled by such publications as Washingtonian Magazine and the New York Times, and Forbes Magazine has recognized him in its annual list of the Power 100; Chairman, Fundraising Campaign, Villanova University, Chairman, Steering Committee, Villanova University.

CLEARY, Mark; PRESIDENT, CLEMENTINA-CLEMCO HOLDINGS INC.
3rd generation Irish American; Irish roots from both his father and mother(mother's parents came from counties Cork and Longford); President, Clementina-Clemco Holdings, Inc., a family held company based in San Francisco; (The company was founded in 1941 in order to supply construction equipment for the post World War II building boom. In the late 1940s the company expanded by creating a manufacturing subsidiary and in the 50s it broke into the international market. In 1991 the company sold its rental operations and took up the ownership and management of golf courses. Celtic Golf Management is the newest addition to the Clemco family. It currently owns two golf courses in Northern California); Supporter, The American Ireland Fund and "Crossroads".

CLINTON, William Jefferson Blythe IV 'Bill'; 42ND PRESIDENT OF THE UNITED STATES
Born, 19, August 1946, Hope, Arkansas, Irish roots on maternal side (Virginia Cassidy Kelley); U.S. President, two terms 1993 to '01; founder and director of the William J. Clinton Foundation; served five terms as the Governor of Arkansas; his wife, Hillary Rodham Clinton, is presently in her first term as the junior U.S. Senator from New York; a moderate and a member of the New Democrat wing of the Democratic Party, he headed the centrist Democratic Leadership Council in 1990 and 1991; the first baby boomer president and the first Democratic president to be re-elected since Franklin D. Roosevelt in 1944; the third youngest president in history at 46, while Vice President Al Gore was 44; one of only two presidents in American history to be impeached - the vote to impeach was along party lines in the Republican-dominated House of Representatives; was acquitted by a vote of the United States Senate on February 12, 1999; remained popular with the public throughout his two terms as president, ending his presidential career with a 65% approval rating, the highest end-of-term approval rating of any president in the post-Eisenhower era; Publ: Putting People First, 1992; Between Hope and History,1996.

CLODAGH, de Sillery Phipps; INTERIOR DESIGNER
Born, 1937, Cong, Co. Mayo, Ireland; started her own couture business in Dublin aged 17; moved Spain early 1970s and became interior designer; opened Clodagh Design International New York 1983; designs incl Dentsu conference center Japan; Spa de Serville, Auckland, New Zealand; Nemacolin Woodlands Resort and Spa in Farmington, PA (nominated by Burt & Lechtman in 100 Best Spas of the World); Publ Total Design (2001); named one of world's '100 leading interior designers' by Architectural Digest; Interior Design magazine inducted her into their Hall of Fame in 1997; designed White Horses Spa, Doonbeg, Co. Clare, Ireland, opened 2006.

CLOONEY, George; ACTOR, PRODUCER, DIRECTOR, WRITER
Born, 6, May 1961, Lexington, Kentucky; 3rd generation Irish, roots in Sligo; nephew, legendary 1950's chanteuse Rosemary Clooney; Oscar nominated Director Good Night and Good Luck 2006; Oscar nominated Best Screenplay, 'Good Night and Good Luck', 2006; Oscar nominated Best Supporting Actor Syriana 2006; became the first person in Oscar history to be nominated for directing one movie and appearing in another in the same year; first major role- tv medical comedy/drama, E/R; But he first gained attention in his semi-regular supporting role in the sitcom Roseanne, playing Roseanne Barr's overbearing boss; has also appeared in a number of movies such as Return of the Killer Tomatoes (1988), From Dusk Till Dawn (1996), One Fine Day (1996), Batman & Robin (1997), Out of Sight (1998), Three Kings (1999), The Perfect Storm (2000), O Brother, Where Art Thou? (2000), Ocean's Eleven (2001), Welcome to Collinwood (2002), Intolerable Cruelty (2003), and Ocean's Twelve (2004), Good Night and Good Luck, 2005; Syriana, 2005; The Good German, 2006; Michael Clayton, 2006; Ocean's Thirteen, 2007.

Cady Coleman

COLEMAN, Catherine G 'Cady'; ASTRONAUT
Born, 16, December 1960, Charleston, South Carolina; Astronaut; Colonel, U.S. Airforce; research chemist Wright-Patterson Air Force base; selected by NASA 1992, assigned to Astronaut Office Mission Support branch, special asst Center Director, Johnson Space Director; first space flight Oct-Nov 1995, Flight STS-73, orbited Earth 256 times, traveled 6 million miles; 2nd space flight, July 1999, Flight STS-93; first woman to command a space shuttle; member, American Chemical Society, International Women's Air and Space Museum.

COLLINS, Eileen; ASTRONAUT SPACE SHUTTLE COMMANDER COLONEL USAF (RTD)
Born, 19, November, 1956, Elmira, New York, 4th generation Irish American, roots in West Cork; an American astronaut and a retired U.S. Air Force Colonel; a former military instructor and test pilot, Collins was the first female pilot and first female commander of a Space Shuttle; Collins completed her U.S. Air Force Undergraduate Pilot Training in 1979, after which she was a T-38 instructor pilot until 1982. From 1983 to 1985, Collins was an instructor pilot and aircraft commander on the C-141 Starlifter; from 1986 to 1989, she was an assistant professor of mathematics and a T-41 instructor pilot at the United States Air Force Academy; she was selected for NASA's astronaut program while attending the prestigious U.S. Air Force Test Pilot School at Edwards Air Force Base, from which she graduated in 1990; she has logged more than 6,000 hours in 30 different types of aircraft; served as pilot on STS-63 (3 - 11February, 1995)

and STS-84 (May 15-24, 1997) first woman to command a space shuttle, STS 93, Columbia, (23 -27 July1999); STS-114 Discovery, was the Return to Flight mission during which the Shuttle docked with the International Space Station and the crew tested and evaluated new procedures for flight safety and Shuttle inspection and repair techniques. After a 2-week, 5.8 million mile journey in space, the orbiter and its crew of seven astronauts returned to land at Edwards Air Force Base, California, (July 26-August 9, 2005); Collins also participated in the U.S. invasion of Grenada, evacuating medical students and their families off the island as part of Operation Urgent Fury in 1983; retired, May 1, 2006 having logged over 872 hours in space, to pursue private interests.

COLLINS, Susan; SENATOR
Born, 7, December, 1952, Caribou, Maine (the family lumber business in Maine was founded by her Irish ancestors in 1844); after graduation worked for Maine Senator William S. Cohen; in cabinet of Maine Governor John R. McKernan as Commissioner of Professional and Financial Regulation 1987-92; New England Administrator of the U.S. Small Business Administration 1992 to 1993; ran her first campaign for public office 1994 and became the first woman in Maine history to receive a major party nomination for governor; lost the general election in the fall; founding executive director of the Center for Family Business at Husson College in Bangor, Maine 1994-96; Senator Maine 1996 to date; Republican; chairman Homeland Security and Governmental Affairs Committee (HSGAC); member, Armed Services Committee, Special Committee on Aging; Congressional Leadership award (for work on juvenile diabetes); one of Irish American Magazine 'Top 100'.

CONDRON, Christopher 'Kip' M; PRESIDENT, CEO AXA FINANCIAL, INC.
Born, 1947, Scranton, Pennsylvania, 3rd generation Irish-American, family hails from Mayo, Roscommon, and Galway; member, AXA Group Management Board; former president and COO, The Mellon Financial Corporation; former chairman and CEO of the Dreyfus Corporation; member, Investment Company Institute's Board of Governors and its Executive Committee; board member, Financial Services Roundtable; director and treasurer, The American Ireland Fund; serves on the Board of Trustees, St. Sebastian's Country Day School, Needham, MA.

Chris Connor

CONNOR, Christopher M 'Chris'; CHAIRMAN CEO SHERWIN-WILLIAMS
Born, 1956, Pensacola, Florida, 4th generation Irish American with roots in Roscommon; Joined Sherwin-Williams Paint Store Group, 1983 as director of advertising, promoted successively to general manager of Diversified Brands Division, president of the Paint Stores Group, CEO 1999 to

date; chairman 2000 to date; President 2005 to date; presides over leading company, named by Forbes Mag in 2005 and 2006 as one of 100 best business to work for in US; director, National City Corporation and Diebold Inc, chairman board of trustees, Keep America Beautiful; serves as a Trustee of University Hospitals of Cleveland, The Catholic Diocese of Cleveland Foundation, Cleveland Tomorrow, The Greater Cleveland Roundtable, The Cleveland Growth Association, United Way Services of Greater Cleveland, The Musical Arts Association, Boys Hope/Girls Hope, and Walsh Jesuit High School.

COOK Richard 'Dick'; CHAIRMAN, DISNEY
Born, 1954, Bakersfield, Ca; began his career with Disney as a ride operator at Disneyland in Anaheim and moved to the Disney Studios in Burbank, 1977; worked in the company's film distribution department; entered the motion picture business at Disney in 1980 as assistant domestic sales manager for the Buena Vista Distribution Company, 1980; promoted to president of Buena Vista Pictures Distribution, 1988; assumed the additional responsibility of film marketing when he was promoted to president of Buena Vista Pictures Distribution and Marketing, 1994;, appointed chairman of The Walt Disney Studios, oversees the development, production, worldwide distribution and marketing for all live-action and animated films released under the Walt Disney Pictures, Touchstone Pictures and Hollywood Pictures banners. He is also responsible for Disney's worldwide home entertainment operations under Buena Vista Home Entertainment and Buena Vista Home Entertainment International, as well as the Studio's legal and business affairs departments,2002; USC trustee since 1998 and has served as president of the USC Alumni Association; member, Academy of Motion Picture Arts & Sciences, former president, The Chandler School, president, Flintridge Preparatory School Board of Trustees, director, Verdugo Hills Hospital, the Will Rogers Foundation, and the Foundation of Motion Picture Pioneers; awards: The Freedoms Foundation of Valley Forge awarded him the prestigious George Washington Medal of Freedom.

CORBOY, Michael R; PRESIDENT, CEO, CORBOY INVESTMENT COMPANY.
3rd generation Irish American; great grandfathers both emigrated from Ireland during the famine, sometime from 1845 –1847; President, School Board of St. Anthony's; member, Advisory Board of The Children's Education Fund and the Steering Committee for the University of Dallas; Board Member of The Aquinas Funds, Netensity, NetPliance and Zygo Corporation.

CORCORAN, Barbara; FOUNDER, CHAIRMAN, THE CORCORAN GROUP
Born, 1950, New York; 2nd Irish American, roots in Roscommon on her mother's side and Cork on her father's; known as The "Queen of New York Real Estate"; credits her

success to her mother "who managed her 10 children like a boot camp" ; launched her career from her own apartment with an initial investment of $1,000; The Corcoran Group Sales $2.2 Billion, Employees: 550; sold her company to NRT, 2001 $66 million; Corcoran's title and reputation remain the same. In addition to her phenomenal firm, she is also founder of The Corcoran Report, which provides a barometer of market conditions and emerging trends; also created the first video real estate gallery, and had the first real estate site on the web; started television production and business consulting company Barbara Corcoran Inc. 2005, pursing a career in TV and as a public speaker; author: If You Don't Have Big Breasts, Put Ribbons on Your Pigtails.

CORCORAN, Thomas A 'Tom'; PRESIDENT CORCORAN ENTERPRISES LLC
Founder, President Corcoran Enterprises LLC, 2000 – todate; Senior Advisor to The Carlyle Group,(aeropsace and defense group), 2000 – todate; former President & Chief Executive Officer, Gemini Air Cargo; former Chairman and Chief Executive Officer, Allegheny Technologies; engineering degree from Stevens Institute of Technology (honorary Ph.D. from Stevens), and also completed the General Electric Manufacturing Program where he worked from 1967 – '90 and in general and management positions; Vice President and General Manager, General Electric Aerospace. 1990 – '93; President Martin Marietta, Electronics Group 1993 – '95 President and COO, Lockheed Martin Electronics,1995 – '00; Trustee, Worcester Polytechnic Institute and Stevens Institute of Technology. Director, REMEC Corporation and L-3 Communications Corporation; Supporter of the Northern Ireland & Border Counties Trade & Investment Council; Recipient, Stevens Institute of Technology Honor Award; guest lecturer, WPI, Dartmouth College and Stanford University; member, member on the Boards of Directors, Gemini Air Cargo, Inc., L-3 Communications Corporation, REMEC, Inc., Sippican, Inc., United Industrial Corporation and Vought Aircraft Industries, Inc.; member, Wings Club; serves on the Board of Trustees of Stevens Institutes of Technology, is a Trustee Emeritus at Worcester Polytechnic Institute; active in the American Ireland Fund; member, Ireland America Economic Advisory Board.

COSTNER, Kevin Michael; ACTOR, DIRECTOR
Born, 18, January,1955, Lynwood California; 3rd generation Irish on his mother, Sharon Tedrick's, side; Oscar winning film actor and director who has often produced his own films; during his career, Costner's films have grossed over $1.3 billion dollars; best known for the epic Dances With Wolves which he directed and starred in the film and served as one of two producers; film was nominated for twelve Academy Awards and won seven, including two for him personally (Best Picture and Best Director); Robin Hood: Prince Of Thieves; the Oliver Stone-directed JFK ; The Bodyguard, all of which provided huge box office takings or critical acclaim.

CURRAN, John; FOUNDER & PRESIDENT OF CURRAN CAPITAL MANAGEMENT, NEW YORK, NY
Prior to forming Curran Capital Management was employed by Pfizer, Inc. and served as a Wall Street securities analyst specializing in pharmaceutical companies; honoured as a University of Pittsburgh Legacy Laureate at the University's 2002 Annual Honors Convocation; involved in several philanthropic initiatives; member, Cathedral of Learning Society, which honors those individuals whose lifetime of giving to the University of Pittsburgh totals $1million or more. He is on the Board of Directors of the American Ireland Fund; Phelps Hospital, NY and is Chairman, Parish Council, Church of St. Theresa's, NY. He graduated from Fordham University with a BS on pharmacy and subsequently completed both the master's and Ph.D. degrees in Pharmacy at the University of Pittsburgh in 1968 and 1971 respectively.

CURRY, Ann; TODAY SHOW PRESENTER
Born, 19, November,1956, Guam; 3rd generation Irish and 1st generation Japanese; a member of the NBC's The Today Show, 1997 to date; a contributing editor for Dateline NBC, and a substitute anchor for the Sunday Editor of NBC Nightly News; a four time winner of the Golden Mike award and won an NAACP Award for excellence in reporting; As a result of being diagnosed with breast cancer joined the Susan B.Komen Foundation for which she does fundraising and public service announcements; Established the Ann Curry Scholarship for School of journalism and Communication Broadcasting Students at her alma mater at the Oregon University School of Journalism.

CURRY, Karen; FORMER CNN BUREAU CHIEF
Has been in the news biz for over 25 years and has in the course of that has covered the Death of Diana when she was posted in London as Bureau Chief for NBC News; witnessed the TWA hijacking, the European involvement in the first gulf war, the fall of the Berlin Wall and the collapse of the Soviet Union; as Vice President and North Eastern Regional Bureau Chief, oversaw a professional staff of 4,000; Awards: the Overseas Press Club and Emmy Awards; member, Board of Visitors of Fordham University.

DALEY, Richard Michael; CHICAGO MAYOR
Born, 24, April, 1942, Chicago, Illinois, son of the late Chicago Mayor Richard J. Daley whose parents emigrated from Ireland; elected mayor in 1989 and reelected in 1991, 1995, 1999 and 2003; powerful member of the national and local Democratic Party; if he is re-elected, Mayor Daley will break his father's record as longest-serving Chicago mayor on December 25, 2010; chosen by Time Magazine, April 25, 2005 as the best mayor, out of five best mayors of large cities in the United States; oversaw overwhelming revitalization and growth; served during a

Chicago population boom, the first of its kind since 1950; married to Margaret Daley; four children: Nora, Patrick, Elizabeth and Kevin; brother to William M. Daley, former United States Secretary of Commerce under President Bill Clinton, and John P. Daley, an elected member of the Cook County Board of Commissioners.

Richard M Daley

DALEY, William M; MIDWEST CHAIRMAN J.P. MORGAN CHASE AND BANK ONE CORP
Born, 9, August 1948, Chicago, Illinois, son of the late Chicago Mayor Richard J. Daley whose parents emigrated from Ireland, brother of Richard M. Daley (*qv*); called to the bar Illinois 1975. worked with Daley and George, Chicago; vice-chairman Amalgamated Bank, Chicago 1989, President, COO 1990-'93; Partner, Mayer, Brown, Platt 1993-'97; Special Counsel to president on issues relating to NAFTA

1993; Secretary Dep. Commerce, Washington 1997-'00; Chairman Al Gore's presidential campaign 2000; President, SBD Communications 2001; Midwest Chairman, J.P. Morgan Chase and Bank One Corp 2004 - to date; Director, Boeing, Merck & Co, Loyola University Chicago; Awards: St. Ignatius Award for Excellence in the Practice of Law, 1994.

William Daley

DALY, Charles U 'Chuck'; EXECUTIVE DIRECTOR EMERITUS JFK LIBRARY
Born, 29, May 1927, Dublin, Ireland; served in the Navy during World War II and as a platoon leader in the Marine Corps during the Korean War; awarded Silver Star and Purple Heart Medals; awarded an American Political Science Association Congressional Fellowship in 1959-1960 during which time he served in the offices of Senator John F. Kennedy of Massachusetts and Representative Stewart Udall of Arizona. In 1961, Daly was recruited to serve as staff assistant to President John F. Kennedy for Congressional Liaison, a position he continued to hold under President

Lyndon Johnson until 1964. In addition to serving in the White House, Daly was Vice President for Development and Public Affairs at the University of Chicago, 1964-'69; founder and President of the Children's Foundation in Washington, D.C.1969 to '71; Vice President of Government and Community Affairs at Harvard 1971 –'76; and President of the Joyce Foundation in Chicago,1978 –'86; Irishman of the Year, Friends of the J.F. Kennedy Presidential Library and Museum, 2006; Director of Joyce Foundation; Joint Center for Political and Economic Studies, Chorus Communications, Independent New & Media; Advisory Board Member on the Council on Foundations; keeps a home in Bantry, Co. Cork.

DALY, Lee Ann; SENIOR VICE PRESIDENT, MARKETING, ESPN

Born, Indianapolis, Indiana; 3rd generation Irish American, traces her roots to County Offaly; oversees the development, direction and implementation of all branding, creative services and marketing for ESPN's media businesses, encompassing television, print, radio, the Internet and all outdoor advertising; she is also responsible for the company's synergy efforts, recently expanded to include project management for ESPN-branded business activities supported by The Walt Disney Company, including the ESPN Zones; her creativity and commitment to people extends beyond the boardroom into the homes she helps build with Habitat for Humanity and as a supporter of Alice Water's Chez Panisse Foundation.

DALY, Mary C; Dean, ST JOHN'S UNIVERSITY SCHOOL OF LAW

Born, Bronx, New York, 2nd generation Irish American, grandparents hailed from Cork and Kerry; Dean, St John's University School of Law. Associate, Rogers & Wells; assistant US attorney for Southern district New York 1975, subsequently chief of that office's civil division; joined faculty Fordham University 1983; James H. Quinn Professor, Legal Ethics, Fordham University; Reporter, New York State Bar Association Task Force on the Profession 1994-'95; Dean, St. John's University School of Law 2004 to date; Trustee, Federal Bar Council Foundation 1997-'04; Publ. New York Code of Professional Responsibility: Opinions, Commentary, and Caselaw (1997 & 2003); Rights, Liability and Ethics in International Legal Practice (1995), numerous articles in peer-reviewed journals.

DAVIES LEWIS, Maryon; CIVIC LEADER, SAN FRANCISCO, CALIFORNIA

Born, San Francisco; A Civic Leader; board member, American Ireland Fund, Board of Governors, San Francisco Symphony; Director of Santa Fe Opera, Member, Executive Board, American Himalayan Foundation, SF; Advisor, San Francisco Antique Show; Trustee of the National Parks Conservation Association and Board of International Service Agencies.

DAY - LEWIS, Daniel Michael Blake; ACTOR

Born, 29, April 1957, London, England; Irish citizen; Oscar Award winning actor My Left Foot, 1990; Best known for The Ballad of Jack and Rose, 2005, Gangs of New York, 2002, The Boxer, 1997, The Crucible 1996, In the Name of the Father, 1993, The Age of Innocence, 1993, The Last of the Mohicans, 1992, My Left Foot,1989, Stars and Bars 1988, The Unbearable Lightness of Being, 1988, A Room with a View, 1985, My Beautiful Laundrette, 1985, The Bounty, 1984, Gandhi 1982.

De NIRO, Robert; ACTOR

Born, 17, August,1943, New York City; 2nd generation Irish American; Oscar Award winning actor; first screen appearance came in a 1965 French drama filmed in New York, and De Niro had no lines (he just ate in a diner); second film was Brian De Palma's farce Greetings, in 1968; Most Notable Roles: "Vito Corleone" in The Godfather: Part II, "Travis Bickle" in Taxi Driver, "Jake La Motta" in Raging Bull. Awards: Academy Award, Best Actor in a supporting Role, 1974, Best Actor, Raging Bull, 1980. Fee for 1st movie, The Wedding Party $50; Fee for Analyze That $20,000,000; coowner of coowner of top restaurant chain NOBU.

DENNEDY FINNERAN, Michelle; CPO SUN MICROSYSTEMS INC.

Served as a litigator in both New York and Palo Alto; joined Sun, 2000 as a member of the marketing and brands legal team, where she was responsible for a variety of legal issues including intellectual property, unfair competition, e-commerce and data privacy 2000; co-founded Sun's Privacy Council, an organization dedicated to promoting a cohesive privacy practice throughout the company; Chief Privacy Officer (CPO), Sun Microsystems, Inc. (Founded in February 1982, Sun employs 35,000 people worldwide with revenues of $11.4 billion for 2003 and is ranked 153 on the Fortune 500 list); is responsible for continuing to develop and implement Sun's data privacy policies and practices, working across Sun's business groups to drive the company's continued data privacy excellence. She works with Sun's product development teams and partners to deliver privacy enabling products and services).

DILLON, Gregory Rusell 'Greg'; VICE CHAIRMAN EMERITUS HILTON HOTEL CORPORATION

Born 1923, Chicago; 3rd generation with maternal roots in Limerick; a leading lawyer who served as Conrad Hilton's legal counsel before joining the Hilton Corporation; joined board Hilton Hotel Corporation; served as many years as Vice Chairman; an internationally respected and extremely popular figure in the International hotel, gaming and hospitality industry; was largely responsible for bringing Conrad Hotels to Ireland; board member, Irish US Council for Commerce and Industry.

DISNEY, Roy Edward; CHAIRMAN SHAMROCK
HOLDINGS DIRECTOR (EMERITUS) DISNEY
Born, 10, January 1930, Burbank California; son of Disney
cofounder Roy O Disney (Co Chairman 1929 –1966 and
nephew of Walt, Co Chair 1929 –'60; (Disney founded 16,
October 1923); grandfather Elias Disney was Irish Canadian;
best known for organizing the ouster of two top Disney
executives: first, Ron Miller, 1984, and Michael Eisner, 2005;
began working for the Walt Disney Company as an assistant
director of Walt Disney and produced "True-Life Adventure"
films, 1954; continued to work as a writer, director and
producer until 1967 when he was elected to the Board of
Directors of the company; resigned as an executive, due to
disagreements with his colleagues' decisions at the time,
1977; retained a seat on the board of directors; resigned from
the board, 1984; returned to the company as vice-chairman
of the board of directors and head of the animation
department, 1985; received Disney Legends Award 1998;
announced his resignation on citing "serious differences of
opinion about the direction and style of management" in the
company, November 30, 2003; helped establish the website
SaveDisney.com; rallied by Disney, shareholders oppose
Michael Eisner's reelection as Chairman and George
Mitchell (*qv*) is appointed 3 March 2004; Reinstated to the
board as a director (emeritus) and consultant to the
company, 8 July 2005; shut down Save Disney.com 7, August
2005; well known in international sailing circles; holds
several sailing speed records including the Los Angeles to
Honolulu monohull time record, (set it on his boat
Pyewacket, July 1999 -7 days, 11 hours, 41 minutes, 27
seconds); trustee, California Institute of the Arts; spends four
months every year at his home in Kilbrittan Castle, West
Cork, Ireland.

DODD, Christopher J 'Chris'; SENATOR
Born, 27, May 1944, Connecticut, 3rd generation Irish
American; called to the bar, Connecticut 1973; Volunteer
Peace Corps, Dominican Republic, 1966-'68; Attorney
Suisman, Shapiro, Wool & Brennan, New London,
Connecticut 1973-'74, Member, 94th-96th Congresses from
2 nd Connecticut Dist 1975-'80; Senator, Connecticut, US
Senate 1980 - to date; Member, Banking, Housing and Urban
Affairs Committees, Snr Member, Health, Education, Labor
and Pensions Committee, Member, Education and Early
Childhood Development Subcommittee, Foreign Relations
Subcommittee on Western Hemisphere, Peace Corps, and
Narcotics; Served with AUS 1969-'75; Awards: **T** Edmund S.
Muskie Distinguished Public Service Award, Hubert H.
Humphrey Pub. Svc award, Outstanding US senator award,
Nathan Davis award, Head Start Senator of Decade award.

DODGE, née Moran, Lore; PHILANTHROPIST
Board Member of the Hospice Foundation of Palm Beach
County; previously involved as a Board Member of Planned
Parenthood, Palm Beach County; was Chairman of the
American Red Cross Charity Ball, the Raymond F. Kravis
Center for Performing Arts, Charity Ball and The American

Cancer Society Charity Ball; member, Palm Beach Chapter
of the Colonial Dames of America and the Daughters of the
American Revolution.

DOLAN, Peter Robert 'Bob'; CHAIRMAN, CEO, BRISTOL
MYERS SQUIBB
Born, 1956, Massachusetts, 3rd generation Irish American
with roots in Galway; Joined General Foods Corp 1980, rose
to group product manager 1986-'87, category manager 1987-
'88; Joined Bristol-Myers Co, NYC, 1988, rose to president
1993-'94; President, Mead Johnson Nutritional Group,
Evansville Ind. 1995-'96; Group President Nutritionals and
Medical Devices Bristol-Myers Squibb Co 1997; President,
Europe Worldwide Medicines, 1988; Sr Vice-Pres Strategy,
1999, CEO 2001 - to date; Chairman, September 2001 –
todate; co-author: Insider's Guide to the Top Ten Business
Schools (1982); Director, American Express Company;
Overseer, Tufts Medical School; Member, American Cancer
Society's CEO Advisory Board, Member, Steering
Committee of the National Dialogue on Cancer.

DONAGHY, Patrick 'Pat'; CO FOUNDER STRUCTURE
TONE
Born, 1941, Carrickmore, Co. Tyrone; emigrated to New
York, 1959; worked as a carpenter 1959 –'71; Co Founder
Structure Tone, New York, (with Lewis Marino), 1971; first
project was for Velcro, 1971; Broke into Fortune 500 client
base with work for IBM, Garden City, New York, 1971;
enters retail market with first project for Orbach's New York,
1977; London office opens with work for Chemical Bank,
1984; Boston office opens 1985; Washington DC office
opens 1985; Dallas office opens 1987; San Antonio office
opens, 2001; Princeton office opens, 2001; employing over
1600 people recorded sales of close to $2 billion dollars
2006; is one of Sinn Féin's largest benefactors and
fundraisers in the US

Thomas Donahoe

DONAHOE, Thomas Joseph;
PRESIDENT CEO US CHAMBER
OF COMMERCE
Born, 1938, New York City; Vice
President, Fairfield University 1967-
'69; Deputy Asst. Postmaster General
US Postal Service, Washington 1969-
'71; Asst Regional Postmaster General,
San Francisco, 1971-'73; Dist.
Manager US Postal Service, NYC
1973-'75; Asst Regional Postmaster Gen NYC, 1975-'76;
Group Vice-President, USA Chamber of Commerce, 1976-
'84; Pres, CEO American Trucking Association, Alexandria
1985-'97; Pres, CEO US Chamber of Commerce 1997- to
date; Member, President's Council on the 21st Century
Workforce, President's Advisory Committee for Trade Policy
and Negotiations; President, Center for International Private
Enterprise.

DONAHUE, Phillip John 'Phil'; BROADCASTER
Born, 21, December 1935, Cleveland, Ohio, 3rd generation
Irish American; began his career in 1957 as a production
assistant at TV and AM station KYW, Cleveland; hosted
Conversation Piece, a phone-in talk show from 1963–'67; *The
Phil Donahue Show* on WLW-D (now WDTN), Dayton, Ohio,
1967 (nationally syndicated 1969;moved the program's
operations to WNBC-TV, New York, 1985; Donahue
celebrated the 25th anniversary of his local and national
program with a special produced at the Ed Sullivan Theater
in New York City,1992; show finally ended,1996, after 27
years, the longest running tabloid TV show ever); Returned
to TV with top rated show on MSNBC, 2001; Show
cancelled 2003; Awards: Multiple Emmies, Peabody, 1980;
Author, Donahue, My Own Story, memoir, 1979,

DOWD, Maureen; AUTHOR, JOURNALIST
Born, 14, January 1952, Washington D.C., 1st.generation
Irish American, (daughter of an Irishman, born in Co. Clare,
who became a Washington Policeman and her Irish
American mother who was the historian for the Hibernians),
so a republican, but as they quip, of the Irish variety - she's
disliked by Democrats and Republicans alike; OP ED
Columnist, New York Times; Pulitzer Prize winner for her
series of articles on Monica Lewinsky, 1999; Awards: A
Woman of the Year, Glamour Magazine 1996; Damon
Runyan Award for Outstanding Contribution to Journalism,
2000; Mary Alice Davis Lectureship award from the College
of Communication at The University of Texas at Austin,
2005; Author, bestseller, Bushworld, Enter At Your Own
Risk (a series of her collected columns which will ignite
some additional controversy), 2004; Are Men Necessary?:
When Sexes Collide, 2005; bete noire of the Bush
Administration; a powerful and important writer she pulls no
punches.

DOWLING, Michael; CHIEF EXECUTIVE, NORTH
SHORE-LIJ MEDICAL CENTERS
Born, Limerick; Graduate University College, Cork; went to
US and worked as a long
shore-man on the docks; went to Fordham and got his
degree in social work and Masters;
Instructor, Harvard School of Public Health; Prior to
becoming president and CEO on
Jan. 1, 2002, served as North Shore-LIJ's executive vice
president and chief operating officer, and earlier as senior
vice president of hospital services; came to the North Shore-
LIJ Health System in July 1995 from Empire Blue Cross/Blue
Shield, where he was a senior vice president; served in the
New York State government for twelve years, including two
years as commissioner of social services; was a long-time
chief advisor to former New York Governor Mario Cuomo
on health and human services issues; earlier, was a professor
of social policy and an assistant dean of the Fordham
University Graduate School of Social Services; began his
career as a caseworker in the New York City school system.
by Gov. Cuomo to a key position in health and went on to

head up North Shore; fifth largest health care system in the
country and perhaps the best managed.

DOWLING, Vincent Gerard; ACTOR, DIRECTOR
Born, 7, September 1929, Dublin; Lifetime Associate
Director and former Artistic Director of the Ireland's
National Theatre- The Abbey Theatre, where he was a
leading actor/ director for 23 year;. Producing Director of
The Great Lakes Shakespeare Festival in Cleveland; President
for Life, Founder and first Artistic Director and President for
Life of The Miniature Theatre of Chester; has produced,
acted or directed in London, Paris, Hong Kong, The Moscow
Arts, Florence, Boston, New York, Toronto, and at The
Kennedy Center in Washington DC; has toured Ireland,
England, Scotland, Wales, and the United States; has made
countless appearances on film, TV and Radio; Awards: has
honorary doctorates from four major American Educational
Institutions; has appeared in solo performances on three state
occasions at President Reagan's White House; won an
"Emmy' for directing and producing The Playboy of the
Western World on PBS; discovered Tom Hanks , gave him his
first years of professional acting work and brought to the
American Stage - Colm Meaney (*qv*) ; David Kelly (The
Waking of Ned Devine) and Roma Downey (*qv*) (Touched by
an Angel); has lectured and spoken at schools, colleges,
universities, city halls, state houses, churches, chapels,
cathedrals, and synagogues; written plays, poems, op-ed
articles, and his recently published autobiography- Astride
The Moon.

DOWNEY, Roma; ACTOR, PRODUCER, FILM, TV STAR,
JEWELLERY DESIGNER
Born, 6, May 1960, Derry, Northern Ireland; Best Known
For, One Life To Live, (TV) 1996, A Woman Called Jackie,
1991; Star of award winning series *Touched by an Angel* 1994
– '03; Saturday Night Live, 1998, Funky Monkey, 2004,
produced and starred CBS TV movies 2004 - todate; designs
her own range of jewellery for QVC; recently commissioned
to design range of home ware for QVC; lives in Malibu Beach
with 9 year old daughter Reilly;

DUFFY, John G; CHAIRMAN, CEO KEEFE BRUYETTE &
WOODS, INC.
Born, 8, May 1949, The Bronx, New York, 1st generation
Irish American, mother from Newtongore, Leitrim, father
from Culleens, Sligo; Chairman, CEO, Keefe Bruyette
&Woods, 2001 – todate; President, Co-CEO KBW, 1992 –
'01; also executive vice president and in charge of the firm's
Investment Banking Department; instrumental in rebuilding
Keefe, Bruyette & Woods after the losses they suffered on
9/11; his son Chris who also worked for the company, was
lost on that day; prior to joining KBW he was vice president
at Standard & Poor's Corporation; member, Board of
trustees, Michael Smurfit Graduate School of Business,
University College Dublin and St, Michael's College,
Colchester, Vermont, The Ursuline School, New Rochelle,

New York, Chairman, Investment Committee of the Cardinal and Gold Fund of Cardinal Hayes High School, Bronx, NY; Publications: Triumph Over Tragedy and the Rebirth of a Business, 2002.

DUFFY, Patrick; ACTOR

Born, 17, March 1949, Townsend, Montana, 3rd generation Irish; best known as Mark Harris, The Man from Atlanta, 1976 –'78, Bobby Ewing in Dallas, 1978 – 91, Frank Lambert, Step By Step, 1991 – 1998, Family, Guy, Touched By An Angel, Justice League, The Bold and The Beautiful 2006, Broken Trail, 2006.

DUNFEY, John P; CHAIRMAN & CEO THE DUNFEY GROUP NEW HAMPSHIRE.

Born, Lowell, Massachusetts, 2nd generation Irish roots in Kerry; Chairman and CEO, The Dunfey Group, 1950-1988: Founder and CEO, Dunfey Hotels Corp; 1942-1945: Officer, U.S. Air Corp Founding Director, Citizens Advisers, Inc. CA and NH; Director, International League for Human Rights; member, Board of Governors, member Board of Trustees, Dana Farber Cancer Institute

DUNFEY, Robert J. 'Bob' Sr; FOUNDER, HONORARY DIRECTOR SUSAN L. CURTIS FOUNDATION, MAINE.

Born, Lowell, Massachusetts, 2nd generation Irish roots in Kerry; Founder, Vice-President and Director, Dunfey Hotels Corp; Director, The Dunfey Group, NH, 1950-1988: 1991 – to date, President, Founding Director/ Investor, Working Assets Management Company; Founding director, The Dunfey Group1986 – todate, Trustee, The Jackson Laboratory, Maine, 1987 – todate; Director, Key Bank of Maine,1975 – todate; Founding Treasurer and Director, New England Circle, Omni Parker House Hotel. 1974 – todate;

DUNLEAVY, Michael Joseph; HEAD COACH, LOS ANGELES CLIPPERS

Born, 21, March 1954; Brooklyn, New York; first head coaching job as coach of the Los Angeles Lakers, 1990 - led his team to the NBA Finals against the Chicago Bulls in his first season but they lost in five games; Joined Milwaukee Bucks as head coach prior to the 1992-1993 season, remained with the Bucks until the end of the 1995-1996 season in a dual role as Vice President of Basketball Operations and Head Coach; General Manager, Bucks – 1997; Head Coach, Portland Trail Blazers in 1997 2001, was named NBA Coach of the Year, 1999; joined the Clippers in 2003; was a candidate for the 2006 Coach of the Year (did not win, the award went to Avery Johnson); has lead the Clippers to the 2nd round of the playoffs; father of Mike Dunleavy Jr, the Golden State Warriors forward who signed a $44 million contract in Oct. 2005, son Baker Dunleavy plays for Villanova and youngest son James, a senior at Harvard-Westlake High School, is a nationally touted prospect.

Dominick Dunne

DUNNE, Dominick; AUTHOR

Born, 29, October 1925, Hartford Connecticut, Irish roots on his father's side; best known as a contributing editor at Vanity Fair; Author: The Winners,1982, The Two Mrs Grenvilles,1985, People Like Us 1988, An Inconvenient Woman,1990, A Season in Purgatory, 1993, Another City Not My Own: (A Novel in the Form of a Memoir), 1997, The Way We Lived Then, (The Recollections of a Well-known Name Dropper), 1999, Justice: Crimes, Trials, And Punishments, 2001. Movies: The Boys In The Band (Executive Producer), 1970,

DWYER, Jim; AUTHOR, JOURNALIST

Born, 1959, New York City, 1st generation Irish American, parents hail from Kerry and Galway; Reporter Hudson Dispatch, N.J. 1980-'82, Bergen Record, N.J., 1983-'84; Newsday 1984 –'95, (1992 part of a team that won a Pulitzer Prize for sports reporting, as a columnist won a Pulitzer Prize 1995, columnist NY Daily News 1995, reporter New York Times to date; Publ. Actual Innocence: Five Days to Execution and Other Dispatches from the Wrongly accused (with Barry Scheck and Peter Newfeld,, 2000, 102 minutes: the Untold Story of the fight to survive inside the Twin Towers, with Kevin Flynn, 2005, (National Book Award nomination), Two Seconds Under the World, an account of the 1993 bombing of the World Trade Center (with Dee Murphy, David Kocieniewski and Peg Tyre), "Subway Lives: 24 Hours in the Life of the New York Subways."

EGAN, His Eminence Cardinal Edward Michael; ROMAN CATHOLIC CARDINAL NEW YORK
Born, 12, April 1932, Oak, Park, Illinois, Irish roots thought to derive from Co. Mayo on his father's side and Co. Clare on his mother's side; ordained December 15, 1957; became private secretary to Albert Cardinal Meyer, Archbishop of Chicago and attained the office of assistant chancellor of the archdiocese; returned to the Pontifical Gregorian University where he became assistant vice-rector and repetitor of moral theology and canon law, 1960; was appointed private secretary to John Cardinal Cody, Archbishop of Chicago; appointed auxiliary bishop of the Archdiocese of New York on April 1, 1985; appointed Bishop of Bridgeport, November 5, 1988; appointed Archbishop of New York on May 11, 2000; elevated to Cardinal on February 21, 2001; member, Board of Trustees at The Catholic University of America.

EGAN, Richard John; FOUNDER CHAIRMAN EMERETUS EMC CORP; FORMER US AMBASSADOR TO IRELAND
Born, 1936, Boston; Vice-President Marketing, Cambridge Memories (now Cambex Corp), Waltham, Massachusetts 1968-'75; General Manager Intel Corp., California 1975-'77; Founder, CEO EMC Corp, Hopkinton, Massachusetts, Massachusetts most valuable technology company 1979-'88, Chairman & CEO EMC 1988-'01; Chairman Emeritus EMC 2001 - to date; US Ambassador to Ireland 2001-'03, (resigned because he found diplomacy boring); included in Forbes '400 Richest Americans' List.

EGEN, Maureen Mahon; DEPUTY CHAIRMAN & PUBLISHER HACHETTE BOOK GROUP USA
Born, Bryn Mawr, Pennsylvania with Irish roots in Sligo; held numerous positions at Doubleday & Company Inc. where she was employed for more than twenty years, these include senior editorial positions, marketing and finance positions, and Publisher and Editorial Director of the Doubleday Book Clubs (now a part of Bookspan). Editor-in-Chief, Warner Hardcover Books at which time she was responsible for editing *Scarlett* and discovering and publishing *The Bridges of Madison County*, 1990; after a number of executive editorial positions, she was named President Hachette Book Group,1998 –'06; deputy chairman and publisher Hachette Book Group 2006 - to date (Time Warner Book Group was taken over by Hachette Livre in 2006); has been the driving force behind the company's biggest successes, including books from bestselling authors Brad Meltzer, David Baldacci, James Bradley, Maria Shriver, James Patterson, Sidney Sheldon, Robert Kiyosaki, J. Randy Taraborelli, and Nelson DeMille; Member, Women's Media Group; Board Member, Center for Independence of the Disabled in New York; Awards: Time Inc President's award.

ESTEVEZ, Emilio; ACTOR DIRECTOR
Born, 12, May 12 1962, New York City, 3rd generation Irish (father *Martin Sheen* (qv)); Best known for St Elmo's Fire, The Mighty Ducks, Mission Impossible; directed episodes of the TV series, Cold Case, Close to Home, The Guardian and CSI: NY.

FARRELL, Colin J 'Coll'; ACTOR
Born, 31, May 1976, Dublin; studied acting at the Gaiety School of Drama, Dublin; began turning heads in Hollywood when he starred in Joel Schumacher's Tigerland (2000), garnered a Best Actor Award from the Boston Society of Film Critics for his portrayal of "Bozz", a roughneck Texan recruit who helps his boot-camp buddies avoid Vietnam combat; starred alongside Kevin Spacey in Thaddeus O'Sullivan's Dublin gangster movie, Ordinary Decent Criminal (2000); (Spacey who suggested him for the part after catching Farrell's riveting performance in the play, In a Little World of Our Own at the Donmar Warehouse in London) American Outlaws (2001); Phone Booth (2002), Minority Report (2002); Alexander (2003); Miami Vice (2006)

Farrell, Thomas F. II; CHAIRMAN, CEO DOMINION RESOURCES INC.
Born, 1955; practiced law with regional company; joined Dominion 1995 (Dominion is one of the US' largest producers of energy with an energy portfolio of more than 24,000 megawatts of generation. Dominion also serves 5.3 million retail energy customers in nine states); successively CEO Dominion Generation; CEO Dominion Energy 2000; exec vice pres Virginia Power; president COO Dominion 2004-5; CEO Dominion 2005 to date; director Virginia Electric and Power Company and President/COO/director Consolidated Natural Gas Company (subsidiaries of Dominion); director Institute of Nuclear Power Operations (INPO); Vice Rector, Board of Visitors, University of Virginia, 2003 -20'05; Rector, 2005 – todate.

FARROW, Maria de Lourdes Villiers 'Mia'; ACTOR
Born, 9, February 1945, Los Angeles, 1st generation American (mother, Maureen O'Sullivan, born in Boyle, Co. Roscommon); best known for relationship with director Woody Allen in the 1980s which resulted in a number of film collaborations; appeared in most of Allen's critically acclaimed films during the decade and the early 1990s, including most notably Hannah and Her Sisters (playing the title role of "Hannah"), The Purple Rose of Cairo (lead role) and 1990's Alice, again as the title character; also played Alura, mother of "Kara" (Helen Slater), in the 1984 movie Supergirl.

FEENEY, Charles F 'Chuck'; CHAIRMAN, GENERAL ATLANTIC GROUP INC – MEDALLION HOTELS.
2nd generation Irish American, with roots in Co. Fermanagh; Co founded Duty Free Shops with Robert Miller; has gifted close to $2 billion to his philanthropic foundation, The Atlantic Foundation; is a major benefactor of Trinity College Dublin, University College Dublin, was instrumental in bringing American involvement to bear on the Irish peace process; funded the establishment of the Sinn Féin Office in Washington, D.C. ; In the late 80s and early 90s,played a

crucial role in helping Irish immigrants win legal status in the United States, a cause he still fervently supports through his role on the advisory board of The Irish Lobby for Immigration Reform (ILIR).

FINEGAN, Dr. Michael; PSYCHOLOGIST
3rd generation Irish; following the Tsunami on December 26th 2005, he volunteered through Catholic Relief Services (CRS) to lesson the impact of the disaster on the survivors; an expert on police psychology, has trained officers at the Maryland State Police Department in a variety of topics including hostage negotiations; leads a team of 18 psychologists in providing counselling to officers who have experienced trauma through their work; Works in the area of adolescent suicide, mob violence and Attention Deficit Hyperactive Disorder (ADHD)

FINUCANE, Anne; PRESIDENT, NORTH EAST, BANK OF AMERICA
Born, 1952; was a Public Information officer at the office of then Mayor of the city of Boston Kevin White; rose to a senior position in the Boston ad agency Hill Holliday and ultimately to executive positions at Fleet and Bank of America; headed up charitable giving dept. for Fleet Bank; married Mike Barnicle - a world renowned columnist and radio talk show host; president, MA Womens Forum; board member, The New England Council, Ireland America Economic Advisory Board; Literacy Partners, Stonehill College, Boston Public Library, Museum of Fine Arts, Boston; previously, Director of Corporate Development, Director of Account Management, Head of Creative Services and Broadcast at Hill, Holiday, Connors and Cosmopolus, Inc; also worked with WBZ-TV.

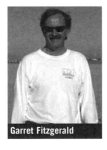
Garret Fitzgerald

FITZGERALD, Garret Adare; CARDIOLOGIST, PHARMACOLOGIST
Born, 1950, Dublin, Ireland; Intern, St. Vincent's Hospital, Dublin 1974-'76; Snr House Officer Endocrinology/Diabetes Mellitus Mater Hosp, Dublin 1976-'77; Research Fellow, Royal Postgrad. Med. School of London Clinic of Pharmacology 1977-'79; Research Fellow Dept internal medicine II U. Cologne 1979-'80; Joined Vanderbilt University School of Medicine 1980, Successively Research Fellow 1980-'91, Chief of Division Clinical Pharmacology 1988-'91, William Stokes Professor, 1989-'91; Director, Centre of Cardiovascular Science & Chairman Dept of Medicine and Experimental Therapeutics UCD/Mater Hosp 1991-'94; Professor, Medicine and Pharmacology University of Pennsylvania 1994 - to date; Has worked in the U.K Germany and Nashville; A leading expert in cox-2 inhibitors, he showed that the use of popular arthritis drugs was a time bomb waiting to happen, 1999; Awards: recipient of many

honours for his work including D.Sc (*h.c*) from University College Dublin, RDS/Irish Times Boyle Medal; most famous for being the first to predict that Vioxx and other popular drugs used to reduce the pain of arthritis could cause heart attack and stroke.

FITZPATRICK, John; CEO, FITZPATRICK HOTEL GROUP NORTH AMERICA
Born, 1958, Dublin; relocated to New York from Ireland 1991 to found and operate Fitzpatrick's Manhattan Hotel, Lexington Avenue, NYC; began his career at the family's hotels in Bunratty Co. Clare and Fitzpatrick's Killiney Castle, Co. Dublin; opened two more hotels in Manhattan, 1995 and 1998; opened of the Fitzpatrick Chicago Hotel, May 2001; sold Fitzpatrick Hotel Chicago 2006; appointed vice chairman of the hotel association on New York City, 2005; Board member, The American Ireland Fund; Board member, Ireland-US Council; has received numerous awards including the Ellis Island Medal of Honor in 2002.

FLANIGAN, Dr. Timothy; AIDS SPECIALIST
4th.generation Irish, family roots are in Newcastle Co. Down, Northern Ireland; became involved in aids treatment programmes through Tropical disease research at Case Western Reserve University, Ohio; Transferred to Brown University's medical school, where he became Professor and director of the Samuel and Esther Chester Immunology Centre at the Miriam Hospital; Has pioneered treatment for women and prison inmates; Has worked tirelessly with RISE and STARKIDS two local programmes; Was one of 10 selected from 387 nominees for an award of €95,000 for a three year grant from the Robert Wood Johnson Foundation; received an honorary Doctorate from Salve Regina University, 2004.

FLATLEY, Michael Ryan: DANCER, CHOREOGRAPHER, ENTREPRENEUR
Born, 16, July 1958, Detroit, Michigan, 1st generation, parents from Co. Mayo and Co. Carlow ; dancer with The Chieftains for tours in the 1980s; star /choreographer of Riverdance; producer/choreographer/star, Lord of The Dance; producer/Star/ Choreographer, Feet of Flames; producer/Star/ Choreographer Celtic Tiger; received the National Endowment for the Arts National Heritage Fellowship, 1988; named one of National Geographic Society's Living Treasures in 1991 for mastery of a traditional art form, the youngest person at that time ever to receive this accolade; Flatley set a Guinness Book world record for tapping speed at 28 taps per second, May 1989; when this record was broken, he set another record in February 1998, by achieving 35 foot taps per second; became the first recipient of the Irish Dancing Commission Fellowship award, December 2001; made a Fellow of the American Irish Dance Teachers' Association, 2001; Irish America Magazine named Flatley Irish American of the Year, March 2003.

FLATLEY Thomas E 'Tom'; PRESIDENT, THE FLATLEY COMPANY
Born, 1934, Co. Mayo; quit his job selling insurance and emigrated to United States, 1952; today owns America's sixth most valuable property portfolio; made more than £273m in 2003 selling the last portion of his rental properties to Aimco; a noted benefactor of Catholic causes; Director and Trustee, Boston College, Morality in Media, AmeriCares, Finance Council of the Archdiocese of Boston; Trustee for Jobs for Massachusetts; member, Ireland America Economic Advisory Board.

FLYNN, William 'Bill'; PEACE BROKER
Born, New York; 1st generation Irish-American, with roots in counties Mayo, mother's family, the 'Stamper' Connors hailed from Lackafinna, Kiltimagh and father was born in Co. Down; former Chairman, Mutual of America Insurance; Grand Marshall St. Patrick's Day Parade, New York, 1999; Chairman, The Flax Trust, America; serves on the Boards of The Alfred E. Smith Memorial Foundation, The Elie Wiesel Foundation for Humanity, Nassau County Crime Stoppers, The Ireland America Economic Advisory Board, The Forum Club. Awards: received the Outstanding Civilian Service Medal from the Department of the Army 2001, for extraordinary service as an expert consultant on the U.S. Army War College Board of Visitors; a recipient of the Ellis Island Medal of Honor, the American Cancer Society's Alfred P. Sloan Jr. Memorial Award and the Life Services for the Handicapped National Leadership Award; was to the fore of the US involvement with the Irish peace process.

FOLAN, Jon K; GALLATIN CAPITAL PARTNERS
Born, San Francisco, 2nd generation Irish-American with roots in counties Galway, Cork and Kerry; With over 30 years in the securities industry, is a partner with Gallatin Capital Partners, a money management company in San Francisco that adheres to a risk-averse investment philosophy seeking capital appreciation within the context of preserving clients' assets. Prior to this position, was senior managing director with Bear, Stearns & Co., in San Francisco. Joined Bear Stearns from Prudential Volpe Technology Group where he was a managing director and group head of corporate and venture services; has served on boards including the National Handicapped Sports Board, The American Ireland Fund and is a founding member of The Parents' Board at The University of California at Berkeley. Awards: the Award for Distinguished Leadership from The American Ireland Fund; visits Ireland frequently.

FORD, Harrison; ACTOR
Born, 13, July 1942, Chicago, 3rd generation Irish; Academy Award-nominated actor; best known for his performances as the tough, wisecracking space pilot Han Solo in the Star Wars film series, and the adventurous, tenacious archaeologist/action hero Indiana Jones of Raiders of the Lost Ark and its sequels; has also been the star of many high

grossing hit Hollywood blockbusters such as Air Force One and The Fugitive which have distanced him from his famous Star Wars and Indiana Jones roles; as of January 2006, the combined domestic box office grosses of Ford's films total approximately US$3.05 billion with worldwide grosses at approximately US $5.65 billion; is an Honorary Chair of the Indianapolis Prize, the world's leading award for animal conservation; has said "I feel Irish as a person but I feel Jewish as an actor"(maternal grandparents were Jewish immigrants from Minsk, Belarus.

FRAWLEY BAGLEY, Elizabeth; FORMER US AMBASSADOR TO PORTUGAL
Born, New York 1952, 2nd generation Irish American; Started working for Ted Kennedy (qv), 1974; held several positions in the Department of State: Congressional Liaison Officer for the Panama Canal Treaties 1977–'79; Special Assistant to Ambassador Sol Linowitz for the Camp David Accords 1979-'80; Congressional Liaison to the Conference on Security and Cooperation in Europe 1980–'81; Ambassador to Portugal 1993-'97; Senior adviser to the Secretary of State for Media Programming Acquisition and NATO Enlargement 1997-'01; Counsel, Snr Managing Director, Manatt, Phelps & Phillips, LLP and Manatt Jones Global Strategies, LLC, 2002 - to date; Member Boards of Directors, National Democratic Institute for International Affairs, the Council on Foreign Relations, the American Ireland Fund, the Council of American Ambassadors, the Association of Diplomatic Studies and Training, and Vital Voices International. She is presently serving as Deputy Director to the Democracy Task Force, as well as the Public Diplomacy Task Force, for the Council on Foreign Relations.US Advisory Commission on Public Policy 2003 to date.

FUGAZY, William Denis 'Bill'; FOUNDER NATIONAL ETHNIC COALITION OF ORGANIZATIONS (NECO)
Born, New York; 1st generation Irish American, mother hailed from Cork, father from Genoa; Fugazy Limousine and Travel; founder National Ethnic Coalition of Organizations, 1986; organization presents the Ellis Island Medal of Honor to ethnic individuals that help make America a better place. Past recipients have included such notables as Presidents Bush, Reagan, and Clinton; acting President of the Coalition of Italo-American Associations, chairman, Annual New York Yankee Homecoming Dinner, Annual New York Giants Football Luncheon and the Forum Club.

GALLAGHER, John E Snr; CHAIRMAN, ARROW INTERNATIONAL INC
Born, Cleveland, Ohio, 1st generation Irish American, parents hail from Co. Mayo; currently serves as Chief Executive Officer and Chairman of the Board of Arrow International, Inc., a privately held company which he founded. He has provided the leadership and direction which has made the company a leading supplier to the world's charitable gaming industry; headquartered in Cleveland they are the innovators in the manufacturing of charitable gaming tickets, equipment and related products; thirteen satellite facilities span the globe; the company employs in excess of 2,000 individuals; total revenue is $100 million dollars plus; founding members of the Ireland Chamber of Commerce USA (ICCUSA); former Vice Chairman of the organization. Irish America Magazine named him one of the Top 100 Businessmen in 1990, 1995, 1997, and 1998. has been honored many times for his humanitarianism, his extensive dedication to philanthropic causes as well as for his support of Ireland.

GALLAGHER, Peter; ACTOR
Born, 19, August 1955, Armonk, New York, 2nd.generation Irish American; Best known in: Sex, Lies and Videotape, The Player, American Beauty, Center Stage, The House on Haunted Hill, How to Deal, Mr Deeds, The OC, 2003-todate; Tony nomination for his role in 1986 revival of O'Neill's Long Days' Journey Into Night;

GARR, Teri; ACTOR, STAGE AND DANCE STAR. MS CAMPAIGNER
Born, 11, December 1944, Lakewood, Ohio, 3rd.generation Irish American with roots from Cork. Awarded the Shining Star for her work on behalf of those suffering from Multiple Sclerosis 2000; formerly a Ballet dancer with San Francisco Ballet; began her movie career in 1967, Swingin' Affair; Academy Award Nomination for her role in Tootsie (best supporting actress); Best known in: Friends (Phoebe's mother), Life Without Dick, 2001, Dick, 1999, Perfect Alibi, 1995, Ready To Wear,1994, Dumb and Dumber, 1994, The Player, 1992.

GARRITY RANK, Erin; CEO AND PRESIDENT OF HABITAT FOR HUMANITY'S GREATER LOS ANGELES AREA (HFH GLA)
Born, St. Louis, Missouri; 3rd generation Irish-American; first person of Samoan heritage to play in the National Basketball Association; responsible for over 1,000 employees and an area that covers over 900 square miles. She was instrumental in helping to organize 400 volunteers build the frames for six houses that were shipped from California to Louisiana in the wake of Hurricane Katrina.

GEORGE, Terry; WRITER, DIRECTOR
Born, Northern Ireland; Best known for The Waterhorse, 2007 (filming), Hotel Rwanda 2004, Hart's War, 2002, "The District", 2000; TV Series, A Bright Shining Lie, 1998, The Boxer, 1997, Some Mother's Son,1996, In the Name of the Father,1993.

GIBBONS, Michael J 'Mike'; VICE PRESIDENT ESTÉE LAUDER COMPANIES
Born, The Bronx, New York; 1st generation Irish American, father hailed from Partry, Co. Mayo; graduated from St. Francis College in Brooklyn, NY and served in the U.S. Navy; joined Estée Lauder, Inc. 1967; has been a Marketing Director for Estée Lauder, Vice President, Clinique; General Manager, Aramis; currently Executive Vice President, Estée Lauder Companies (one of the world's leading manufacturers and marketers of quality skin-care, makeup, fragrance and hair-care products); an Executive Vice President at the Estée Lauder Companies, Inc.; President of The Ireland-U.S. Council; former Chairman of the International Center, New York, (welcomes new immigrants and refugees and assists them in learning English and adapting to American culture and ways - they help people from over 90 countries through the efforts of 500 volunteers and a small paid staff, hundreds of foreign newcomers seek assistance at The Center each week); past Director, American-Ireland Fund; past director, Eugene O'Neill Theater Foundation; former co-chairman, Knights of St. Patrick; director, The Irish Repertory Theater; member, Irish Economic Advisory Board (United States); member Croquet Hall Of Fame; member, World Croquet Federation.

GLUCKSMAN BRENNAN, Loretta; CHAIRMAN AMERICAN IRELAND FUND
Born, 1939, Allentown, Pennsylvania, 3rd generation from Leitrim and Donegal; began to visit Ireland with her late husband Lewis Glucksman,1987; Chairman of the American Ireland Fund and has raised over $11 million, helping to make it the largest Irish Fundraising group in the world; The AIF encourages Peace and Reconciliation in Northern Ireland through education, culture, the arts, and community investment; She and her husband are responsible for New York University's Ireland House; Trustee, National Gallery of Ireland; Board Member, The Abbey Theatre, Dublin, College of Arts & Sciences, NY University, Co-Chair, Glucksman Ireland House, NYU; Trustee, Trinity College Foundation, National Library of Ireland; With her late husband, the late Lewis Glucksman, has funded the building of the Glucksman Gallery in University College Cork and endowed a Chair at the University of Limerick.

GRADY, Patricia; DIRECTOR, NATIONAL INSTITUTE OF NURSING RESEARCH
Born, Connecticut; 2nd generation Irish American, roots in ; the Director of the National Institute of Nursing Research (NINR), a division of the National Institutes of Health (NIH)

since 1995; is an internationally recognized researcher who has written many articles on strokes and their effects; is an editorial board member of the major stroke journals; before coming to NIH in 1988, Grady held several academic positions, including serving concurrently on the faculties of the University of Maryland School of Nursing and School of Medicine; she has been honored with a variety of awards including the NIH merit award, Public Health Service Superior Service Award, and the Centennial Achievement Medal from Georgetown University.

GREELEY, Rev. Dr. Andrew M; ROMAN CATHOLIC PRIEST, SOCIOLOGIST, BEST SELLING AUTHOR
Born, 5, February 1928, Oak Park, Illinois; Irish roots, Co. Mayo; ordained, St. Mary of the Lake Seminary in Chicago,1954; author of over 50 novels and 100 works of non-fiction; has been an outspoken critic of the George W. Bush administration and the Iraq War.

GRIFFIN, Mervyn Edward Jnr 'Merv'; CHAIRMAN THE GRIFFIN GROUP, ENTERTAINER
Born, 6, July 1925, San Mateo, California, 1st generation Irish American, (father hailed from Clare, mother from Clonmel, Co. Tipperary); Performer, Merv Griffin Show, Radio KRFC San Francisco 1945-'48; Vocalist, Freddy Martin's Orchestra 1948-'52; Contract player, star So This Is Love (Warner Bros) 1953-'55; Host, Play Your Hunch, 1958 –'62; Merv Griffin Show NBC-TV 1962-'63; Host, Word For Word, 1964 '64; Westinghouse Broadcasting Co. 1965-'69, CBS-TV 1969-'72, Syndication 1972-'76; Exec. Producer Wheel of Fortune, Jeopardy!; owner The Griffin Group, Beverley Hills 1996 to date, which owns a number of hotels including The Beverley Hilton Hotel, California and St Cleran's, Craughwell, Co. Galway; successful thoroughbred bloodstock owner; Awards: 15 Emmys.

HAMILL, Pete; AUTHOR JOURNALIST
Born, 1935, Park Slope, Brooklyn, 1st generation Irish American, parents emigrated from Northern Ireland; served in US Navy; Reporter New York Post 1960; in subsequent years, became one of the city's best known reporters, as columnist for the Post, New York Daily News, and Newsday; was editor-in-chief of both the New York Post and the New York Daily News; has written for numerous national magazines including Village Voice, Playboy, Esquire, Vanity Fair, Esquire; Contributing editor, New York Times Magazine; currently on the staff of The New Yorker; Publ. A Drinking Life: A Memoir, 1995, Snow in August, 1998, Why Sinatra Matters, 2003, Forever, 2003, Downtown : My Manhattan 2004, The Gift, 2005. Member, Writers Guild of America, PEN, the Society of Silurians, AFTRA.

HANNITY, Sean; CONSERVATIVE COMMENTATOR, FOX TV
Born, 30, December 1961, Long Island, New York; 2nd generation Irish American; co host Hannity and Colmes Fox TV (Monday – Friday) 1996 –todate, 12 million people listen every day; known for his provocative style, Hannity has become one of the most popular radio personalities in New York; host of WABC-AM's highly rated afternoon talk program, The Sean Hannity Show; has been named "Talk Show Host of the Year" and one of the "Top 100 Talk Hosts in America." by Talkers Magazine.

HANRATTY, Donald; FOUNDER, THE CAREER CONTROL GROUP
Founder, The Career Control Group, 1984; (Career Control Group has grown to be the Southwest U.S.'s largest independent career management firm); Founding Board Member, International Association of Career Management Professionals; board member, Career Partners International; Philanthropic interests include: Dallas For Children Special Olympics, Crystal Charity Ball, Stars Foundation, Catholic Foundation, Jesuit College Prep, The Family Place, The American Ireland Fund.

HARTNETT, John; SENIOR VICE PRESIDENT PALM, INC.
Born, Limerick; Senior Vice President, responsible for Palm, Inc.'s (formerly palmOne) sales and customer support for all channels, including retail, distribution, carrier, eCommerce, and Palm's retail stores; Prior to this position, he was executive VP of worldwide operations, service, support and eCommerce at Handspring Inc.;(, Palm acquired Handspring, Inc. and the new company was named palmOne, October 2003). Hartnett was a member of the merger leadership team, and Palm is estimating this year it will have revenues of $1.21 billion. The company recently opened its first European engineering center in Dublin; member, The American Ireland Fund.

HARTY, Patricia, 'Trish'; PUBLISHER
Born, Tipperary, Ireland; Editor-in-Chief and Co-Founder of Irish America Magazine, 1985; since its inception has become a powerful vehicle of expression on a range of political, economic, social and cultural themes that are of paramount importance to the Irish in the United States; has helped re-establish the Irish ethnic identity in the U.S. (40 million according to the last U.S. Census) and spotlighted political and business leaders, organizations, writers and community figures, who previously had no national vehicle for their aspirations; Among Ms. Harty's many interviews in the past 20 years are Nobel Prize-winning poet Seamus Heaney, Wall Street guru Peter Lynch, best-selling author Pat Conroy, and Hollywood legend Gregory Peck; editor of the book, "Greatest Irish-Americans of the 20th Century."; serves on the advisory board of Glucksman Ireland House, NYU's center for Irish studies.

HAYDEN, Peter E 'Pete'; FIRE DEPARTMENT NEW YORK CHIEF AND 9/11 HERO
Born, Rockaway, New York, 1st generation with roots in County Mayo and Kildare; New York City Fire Chief, 2004 – todate; As the 32nd.Chief of Department, is the highest ranking uniformed member; was Division Commander of the 1st.Division on September 11th; On his orders the command post was moved out of the north tower before it fell and led to many lives being saved; led the rescue and recovery efforts at Ground Zero leading some 1,500 fire fighters; 2002 and 2003, spoke at the dedication of the Firefighters Memorial, Donadea Park Co. Kildare..

HAYES-WHITE, Joanne; FIRE CHIEF SAN FRANCISCO
Born, San Francisco; 1st generation Irish American, father Tom is a native of Ballingarry, Co Limerick; Made history when she was appointed San Francisco's first female fire chief, 2004, the first in any city in the US; and San Francisco became the largest fire department in the world led by a woman. What makes this even more astounding is the fact that women weren't even allowed to be firefighters in the city until 1987; Joined the fire department, 1990 and quickly moved up the ranks; appointed Captain, 1998; appointed Director of Training and Assistant Deputy Chief, 2000; knows almost every one of her 1,800 firefighters by name.

HEALY, Denis J; CO CHAIRMAN, TURTLE WAX, INC
Born, 1934; Co Chairman Turtle Wax, 2005 –todate; CEO Turtle Wax, 2002 – 05, President of Turtle Wax, Inc. 1977- '02: Executive Vice President, Turtle Wax, Inc. 1971-'77; Director, Research and Development, Barr Company, IL; R&D Colgate Palmolive; R&D Mennen Company; Board Member, Catholic Charities, Chicago Symphony Association, Evanston Hospital, Irish Fellowship Club of Chicago, Junior Achievement of Chicago, Northwestern University Associates, United Republican Fund of Illinois, United Service Organization of Chicago.

HENNESSEY, John LeRoy; PRESIDENT STANFORD UNIVERSITY
Family hails from Kerry; faculty member Stanford University since 1977; Director, Stanford's Computer System Laboratory 1989-'93; Chair, Computer Science 1994-'96; Dean, School Engineering 1996-'99; Provost, 1999-'00; President 2000 - to date; Founder MIPS Computer Systems Inc; Publ. Computer Organization and Design: the Hardware/Software Interface; Computer Architecture: A Quantitative Approach. Awards: 2000 IEEE John von Neumann Medal, 2000 ASEE Benjamin Garver Lamme Award, 2001 ACM Eckert-Mauchly Award, 2001 Seymour Cray Computer Engineering Award, 2004 NEC C&C Prize for lifetime achievement in computer science and engineering, 2005 Founders Award from American Academy of Arts and Sciences, Board member, Google.

John Hennessey

HICKEY, James; COLONEL US ARMY
Born, Chicago, Illinois,1962, 1st generation irish American (James Sr. and Anne Marie Hickey emigrated from Clare, Ireland in the 1950s and live in Naperville, where they own "The Irish Way" shop); 2nd Lieutenant US army 1982; Cavalry Platoon Leader, Troop exec officer, Squadron Adjutant 3rd squadron, 7th cavalry, Schweinfurt, Germany 1982-'85; Command L Troop 3rd squadron, 11th Armoured Cavalry Regiment, Bad Hersfeld, Germany 1986; Operations Officer 1st Squadron, 11th Armoured Cavalry Regiment (ACR), Fort Irwin, California; Regimental Executive Officer 3rd ACR 1998; Commander 2nd Squadron, 3rd ACR; Brigade Snr Observer Controller Combat Manoeuver Training center Hofenfels, Germany 2001; Commander 1st Brigade, 4th Infantry Division, 2003 – todate, (leader of the division that captured Saddam Hussein in "Operation Red Dawn" 13 Dec 2003);

James Hickey

HIGGINS CLARK, Carol; ACTOR, AUTHOR
Born, New York; 4th generation with family roots in Counties Mayo and Sligo.
Daughter of Mary Higgins Clark (*qv*) her own novels about LA PI Regan Reilly are hugely popular; was the lead in the film A Cry in the Night based on her mother's book; has recorded the novels she wrote with her mother as well as her mothers novels and stories

HIGGINS CLARK, Mary; NOVELIST
Born, 24, December 1929, Bronx, New York; 3rd generation, family roots in Counties Mayo and Sligo; queen

of suspense and best selling author – her books have sold over 80 million copies in the US alone; two of her novels were made into feature films, Where Are the Children? and A Stranger Is Watching. Many of her other works, novels and short stories, were made into television films; co-author, with her daughter Carol Higgins Clark (*qv*), of three suspense novels Deck the Halls, 2000, He Sees You When You're Sleeping, 2001 and The Christmas Thief , 2004. first suspense novel Where Are The Children, 1975, most recent Two Little Girls in Blue, 2006.

HIGGINS, Colonel Patrick; COMMANDING THE TROOPS IN AFGHANISTAN
3rd.generation with roots in Loughrea, Co.Galway and Doolin Co.Clare; Grew up in Long Island, NY; Commander of the Combined/Joint Special Operations Task Force-Afghanistan(CJSOTT-A); Commands a group including the Green Berets of the 3rd.Special Forces Group (airborne) and Navy SEALS to coalition allies; Awards and decorations include; The Bronze Star; Purple Heart; and Meritorious Service Medal; Won a 3 year Army ROTC Scholarship to Hofstra University where he majored in social sciences, studying mainly history and pushed for an Irish Studies Programme and was successful with others in having courses in Irish History and literature instituted.

HIGGINS, James F; CHAIRMAN, INDIVIDUAL INVESTOR GROUP, MORGAN STANLEY DEAN WITTER & CO.
Chairman, Individual Investor Group, Morgan Stanley Dean Witter & Co. 2000-01; President and Chief operating officer, Individual Investor Group, Morgan Stanley Dean Witter & Co1990-2000; Chairman, Executive Committee, Georgetown University, Board of Regents; Director, Georgetown University; member, The American Association of the Sovereign Military Order of Malta

HILFIGER, Thomas Jacob 'Tommy'; FASHION DESIGNER
Born, Elvira, New York , March, 24 1951; 2nd generation Irish; world-famous fashion designer best known for his eponymous "Tommy Hilfiger" and "Tommy" brands; Opened his first store People's Place 1969; went bankrupt 1976; founded The Tommy Hilfiger Corporation 1984; went public 1992; sold his company 2005 to Apax Partners Corporation for $ 1. 6 billion (cash).

HILTON, Paris; CELEBUTANTE
Born, 17, February 1981, Los Angeles; 4th generation Irish American, paternal grandmother had Irish roots; grand daughter Baron Hilton, (*qv*)Chairman Hilton Hotel Corp; a famous socialite, has dabbled in modeling, acting, singing, and writing;

HILTON, William Barron; CHAIRMAN, HILTON HOTEL CORPORATION
Born, October 23, 1927, Dallas, Texas; 3rd generation Irish

American, mothers family had Irish roots; Beverly Hills based son of Conard Hilton, founder of Hilton Hotel Corporation and Mary Barron; grandfather of Paris (*qv*); active for several years in organizing and managing businesses in Los Angeles, and was also a member of the board of directors of the Statler Hotels Delaware Corporation and of the Conrad N. Hilton Foundation;a elected a vice-president of Hilton Hotels Corporation, of which his father was president, 1954; also became president of the Carte Blanche credit card firm, was owner of a $6,000,000 orange juice company, head of a business leasing jets and an investor in a Texas oil company; founded the San Diego Chargers American football team, 1954; appointedppresident, Hilton Hotel chain, 1966; was responsible for getting Hilton Hotels into the gambling business,1970; Forbes 400, which lists the 400 Richest Americans, put Barron Hilton's worth in 2005 at $1 billion; privately owns a Cessna Citation V Ultra which he uses for both corporate and personal travel; also owns and flies four gliders and a tow plane, a Stearman biplane, a Citabria aerobatic plane, a helicopter, a restored Beech Staggerwing, and three hot air balloons; was the lead sponsor of two teams that tried to fly around the world in balloons.

HUGHES, Sarah Elizabeth; ICE SKATER, OLYMPIC GOLD MEDALLIST

Born, Great Neck, New York, May, 2 1985, 2nd generation Irish American, grandfather was a Northern Irish soccer player before emigrating to Canada; winner US. Junior Championships 1998; 2nd World Championships 1999; bronze medal National Championships 2000; bronze Grand Prix Final and World Championships 2001; gold Olympics women figure skating 2002; 2nd US Championships 2003; professional skater with Smuckers Stars 2004-'05. Awards: James E. Sullivan Award 2002; Breast cancer advocate by doing a commercial for General Electric promoting breast cancer awareness and research, (mother Amy is a breast cancer survivor).

HUSTON, Anjelica; ACTOR DIRECTOR

Born, 8, July 8 1951, Los Angeles, Irish roots on her father's side; raised mainly Co. Galway; distinguished movie career since Casino Royale 1967; Academy Award, Best Supporting Actress, Prizzi's Honour, 1985; nominated for Academy Award, Best Supporting actress, The Grifters, 1990, nominated for an Academy Award for Best Supporting Actress for her work in Enemies, a Love Story,1989, received five Emmy Award nominations for her television work over the years, won a Golden Globe Award for Supporting Actress in a TV Program for Iron Jawed Angels, her first win, after eight nominations; most recent movies, These Foolish Things, 2005, Material Girls, 2006, Seraphim Falls, 2006; director, Bastard Out of Carolina, 1996, Agnes Browne, 1999, Riding the Bus with My Sister, 2005.

ISDELL, E Neville; CHAIRMAN AND CHIEF EXECUTIVE COCA COLA CORPORATION

Born 1944, Belfast, Northern Ireland; joined The Coca-Cola Company in Zambia, 1966; general manager of Coca-Cola Bottling of Johannesburg, the largest Coca-Cola bottler in Africa, 1972; was named region manager for Australia 1980; he became president of the bottling joint venture between The Coca-Cola Company and San Miguel Corporation in the Philippines, where he oversaw the turnaround and renewal of the Coca-Cola business in that key country, 1981; moved to Germany as president of the Company's Central European Division in 1985; In 1989, he was elected senior vice president of the Company and appointed president of the Northeast Europe/Africa Group (renamed the Northeast Europe/Middle East Group in 1992) and led the Company's entry into new markets in India, the Middle East, Eastern Europe and the former Soviet Union. In 1995, he was named president of the Greater Europe Group; From Mr. Isdell served as chairman and CEO of Coca-Cola Beverages Plc in Great Britain, where he oversaw that company's merger with Hellenic Bottling to form the world's second largest Coca-Cola bottler, Coca-Cola Hellenic Bottling Company (HBC). July 1998 to September '00; retired as vice chairman of Coca-Cola HBC in December 2001; international consultant to The Coca-Cola Company and headed his own investment company in Barbados. January 2002 to May '04; Chairman and Chief Executive, Coca Cola 2004 – todate; Mr Isdell is 12th chairman of the Board in the history of the Company; He is chairman of the U.S.-Russia Business Council and a member of the board of trustees of the International Business Leaders Forum, the United States Council for International Business and the Center for Strategic and International Studies; also a member of the Corporate Advisory Board of the Global Business Council on HIV/AIDS; In Atlanta, Mr. Isdell serves on the board of directors of SunTrust Banks, Inc. and the Commerce Club and as a trustee of Emory University; a lifetime trustee of Pace Academy.

KEENAN, Don; LAWYER
Born, North Carolina; 3rd generation
Irish-American, paternal great-
grandparents were from Dublin and
maternal great-grandparents hailed from
Galway and Mayo; the Atlanta-based
lawyer now heads Keenan's Kids Foundation, a children's
advocacy group founded in 1993 out of his law office; now
the most successful children's advocate lawyer in America
and a regular guest on Oprah, Good Morning America and
60 Minutes.

KELLEHER, Denis P; FOUNDER CHAIRMAN CEO, WALL
STREET ACCESS
Born, Gneeveguilla, Killarney, Co. Kerry; arrived in America
1958 to work as a messenger in Merrill Lynch; rose through
the company ranks; served as Vice President The Sequoia
Fund and founded his own company Ruane Cunniff & Co.;
founder, Wall Street Access, 1981; currently Chairman,
CEO, Wall Street Access - a diversified financial services
organization; supporter, America Ireland Fund and
established scholarships in his native Co. Kerry; Board
member, St. John's University; Grand Marshal St. Patrick's
Day Parade, New York, 2005; board member, SI Bank &
Trust, New Ireland Fund; Ellis Island Medal of Honor, 1995;
Member, Ireland America Economic Advisory Group.

KELLEHER, Herbert David 'Herb'; CO-FOUNDER,
CHAIRMAN, FORMER CEO SOUTHWEST AIRLINES
Born, 12, March, 1931, New Jersey,; called to the New York
Bar 1957, Texan Bar 1962; Clerk, New Jersey Supreme
Court 1956-'59; Assoc. Lum, Biunno & Tompkins 1959-'61;
Partner, Matthews, Nowlin, Macfarlane & Barrett, San
Antonio 1961-'69; Senior Partner, Oppenheimer, Rosenberg,
Kelleher & Wheatley 1969-'81; Founder, President,
Chairman, Southwest Airlines, Dallas, CEO 1971-2001
(third-largest airline in the world by number of passengers
carried, the most successful airline in the world and the
largest in the United States by number of passengers carried
domestically); Awards: named to Texas Hall of Fame 1988;
Airline Industry Service Award 1988; Master Entrepreneur
Award Inc. Mag. 1991.

KELLY, Dr, Daniel Fain; BRAIN SURGEON
5th generation Irish American; Director UCLA Pituitary
Tumour and Neuroendocrine Program; Affiliations:
Associate Professor, Surgery, Physician, Neurosurgery,
Stotter Chair, Pituitary Tumor and Neuroendocrine
Program, Director, Pituitary Tumor and Neuroendocrine
Program, Pituitary Tumor and Neuroendocrine Program,
Co-Director, Brain Injury/Trauma, Physician,
Comprehensive Brain Tumor Program, Associate Professor,
Pituitary Tumor and Neuroendocrine Program, Pituitary
Tumor and Neuroendocrine Program.

KELLY, Edmund F; CHAIRMAN, PRESIDENT AND CEO,
LIBERTY MUTUAL GROUP
Born, Ireland, 1946; Joined Aetna Life and Casualty
Company 1974-'92, began as actuarial student rose to
president of employee benefits; joined Liberty Mutual, 1992,
President, COO, Liberty Mutual Group, 1992 –to date;
previously, senior Operating Executive, Aetna Life and
Casualty; Board of Directors, Inroads/Central New England,
Inc; Board Member, United Way of Mass. Bay and Boston
Private Industry Council, Private Industry Council U.S.
chamber of Commerce, National Association of
Manufacturers, Board of trustees, Boston College, Fellow,
Society of Actuaries; Member, American Academy of
Actuaries, Ireland America Economic Advisory Board,
Museum of Fine Arts Corporate Advisory Board, Board of
Advisory, Boston College's Wallace E. Carroll School of
Management; Chairman, Alliance of American Insurers,
American Red Cross of Massachusetts Bay Citizens
Financial Group, Inc,Greater Boston Chamber of
Commerce; B. of Trustees AICPCU/IIA, Initiative for a
Competitive Inner City, Senior Advisory Council, New
England College of Finance, Insurance Information Institute.

KELLY, Raymond W 'Ray'; POLICE COMMISSIONER NEW
YORK
Born, Manhattan, New York, in the Irish Area off Columbus
Avenue; New York's 'Commish' became the 41st.Police
Commissioner of the New York Police Department, 2002;
the first person to hold the post for a second, separate tenure,
(previously served as the 37th. Commissioner 1992-94);
formerly Senior Managing Director, Global Corporate
Security, Bear, Stearns & Co. Inc; served as Commissioner of
the U.S. Customs Service, where he managed the agency's
20,000 employees and $20 billion in annual revenue; served
for 31 years in the NYPD; a combat veteran of Vietnam,
remained in the Marine Corps reserve for 30 years retiring as
Colonel; has worked as Director of the International Police
Monitors in Haiti; Sept 11th.inspired him to leave the
company and return to the NYPD. Awards: The Alexander
Hamilton Medal for Exceptional Service in the Customs
Department and for his work in Haiti; The Exceptionally
Meritorious Service Commendation by the President of the
United States. 2003 received the American Irish Historical
Society's Gold Medal.

KENNEDY, Edward Moore 'Ted'; SENATOR
Born, 22, February, 1932, Boston, Massachusetts; 3rd
generation with roots in Co. Wexford; Senior Democrat in
US Government; elected Senator Massachussets, 1962, and
most recently re elected 2000; brother, US President John F
Kennedy and US Attorney General Robert Kennedy;
described as The Senate's Fighting Liberal; as a member of
the most powerful Irish American families, has been able to
raise the profile of the problems in Northern Ireland and was
instrumental in persuading President Clinton to become
involved in the peace process.

KENNEDY, Patrick Joseph; CONGRESSMAN

Born 14, July, 1967, Brighton, Massachusetts; 4th generation Irish American with roots in Co. Wexford, son of Senator Ted Kennedy (*qv*); Congressman, Rhode Island, Democratic Party; elected to the Rhode Island State House,1988 at the age of 21, becoming the youngest Kennedy family member ever to win office; 1994, elected to the US Congress at 27, youngest Congressman that year; appointed to the House Appropriations Committee, and appointed to a two-year term as the chairman of the Democratic Congressional Campaign Committee, 1998; assumed his seat on the influential Appropriations Committee, 2001.

KENNEDY, Robert Francis Jr.; ENVIRONMENTAL LAWYER

Born, 17, January 1954, Mc Clean, Virginia, 4th generation Irish American, son of the late Robert Kennedy, US Attorney General and Presidential candidate, , attorney Hudson Riverkeeper organization 1984 to date; prof Environmental Law, Pace University School of Law, co-director Pace Environmental Litigation Clinic; co-founder Keeper Springs 1998; inaugural director Watershed Institute Boston College; co-host 'Ring of Fire' Air America Radio; worked on presidential campaigns, Edward M. Kennedy (*qv*) 1980, Al Gore 2000, John Kerry 2004; Publ. The Riverkeepers 1997, Crimes Against Nature 2004, blogger The Huffington Post 2005 to date; Awards: 'Heroes of the Planet' Time Magazine.

KENNEY, Edward 'Ed'; EXECUTIVE VICE PRESIDENT, EXTERNAL AFFAIRS, MUTUAL OF AMERICA

Born, 6, January, 1944, New York City, 2nd generation Irish American; Probation Officer, Yonkers Family Court, 1966 –'67; U.S. Army, Ft. Knox KY & Aberdeen Proving Grounds MD, Assigned Mental 9; Hygiene Consultation Service, 1967 –'68; Federal Bureau of Investigation, Louisville KY, Washington DC, New York NY, 1970 –'94; Mutual of America 1994 – todate.

KENNY, Tom; VOICE ACTOR

Born, 13, July 1962; Syracuse, New York, 3rd generation Irish American; though he has dozens of credits to his name, is probably most well known as the voice of SpongeBob SquarePants; first aired in 1999 on Nickelodeon, the animated series is about a fry cook who lives at the bottom of the sea. Popular with both young and old audiences, the show became one of the most highly-rated cartoons on TV; was also the narrator and various other characters on the show, and reprised his role for The SpongeBob SquarePants Movie in 2004.

KEOUGH, Donald R 'Don'; CHAIRMAN, ALLEN & COMPANY

Born, 1929, 2nd generation Irish American, paternal grandfather hailed from Co. Wexford; Known as 'the heart of Coca Cola'; Until he reached the mandatory age limit, was President and Chief Operating Officer of The Coca-Cola Company; Aged 76, made a return to the board of the company making a statement against ageism, 2005; Notre Dame Benefactor; Has donated $2.5 million to establish the Donald R. Keough Chair in Irish Studies at Notre Dame University, 1992; and the Keough Notre Dame Centre in Dublin; has also led delegations of businesspeople to Ireland and Northern Ireland; Member, Taoiseach's Ireland America Economic Advisory Board; Serves on the board of IAC/InteractiveCorp; Global Yankee Holdings; Convera Corporation,Berkshire Hathaway Inc; McDonald's Corporation; The Washington Post Company; H.J. Heinz Company and Home Depot.

KING, Michael; FORMER PRESIDENT & CEO KINGWORLD

Born, 1952, New Providence, New Jersey, 3rd generation Irish American; With brother Roger, took the company his father Charles established in 1964 (with just six dollars in his pocket, bought the syndication rights to the classic children's series, "The Little Rascals.") and grew it to the largest syndication company in the US; Began working in radio, sold advertising time for WORC-AM in Worcester, Mass.; Joined WAAF-FM, Worcester as sales manager and eventually became part owner; But the family business beckoned, sold his interest in the station to focus on building King World; assumed the presidency at a salary of $150 a week, also took a second job as a sales representative with another television syndicator; King World purchased the syndication rights for a little-known game show called "Wheel of Fortune"from Merv Griffin (*qv*)1983; Next acquired the rights to "Jeopardy" and the "Oprah Winfrey Show," giving the firm three of the top four syndicated shows in the country; The company went public, profits soared and more than 100 million Americans daily watched shows syndicated by King World; Began selling their own productions like the hit program "Inside Edition," now the longest-running and highest-rated television newsmagazine in syndication; also branched out internationally while continuing to find top shows to syndicate; In the last few years, it has added "Dr. Phil" as well as smash hits "Everybody Loves Raymond," "CSI: Crime Scene Investigation," "CSI: Miami" and "Hollywood Squares"; Sold the firm to CBS Corp., for $2.5 billion, with Michael King acting in an advisory role, 1999; No longer involved in the day-to-day activities of the premier syndication giant, King is active in a wide range of efforts from breeding horses to overseeing investment funds; He also directs some of his energies toward the sports arena. He's part of an investment group that owns the New Jersey Devils, and he sits on the board of the Stanley Cup champions; has investments in boxing; Established, The Michael King Family Foundation, which benefits numerous efforts, but particularly supports the advancement of educational programs.

KING, Peter T 'Pete'; CONGRESSMAN
Born, 5, April 1944, New York City; 3rdgeneration;
Congressman, representing Long Island, 1993 – todate;
worked with President Clinton on the Northern Ireland Peace
Accord and the Good Friday Agreement and accompanied
him on his historic visits to Northern Ireland in 1995,1998
and 2000; has also been an activist in the fight against Breast
Cancer which in the Long Island area is higher than the
national average and has been so for many years; athe highest
garnerer of votes in his area of over 73% , he is equally well
placed to be a beacon for Ireland and Breast Cancer
awareness.

KLINE, Kevin Delaney; ACTOR
Born, 24, October 1947, St. Louis, Missouri, 2nd generation
Irish (mother Peggy Delaney); Academy Award- and Tony
Award-winning American stage and film actor; best known
for Sophie's Choice, A Fish Called Wanda, The Bill Chill,
French Kiss; New York Shakespeare Festival, dubbed the
Lawrence Olivier of America.

LANE, Nathan; ACTOR
Born, 3, February 1956, Jersey City, New
Jersey, 3rd generation Irish American;
Award winning star of stage and screen;
best known for movie credits: The
Producers, 2005, Nicholas Nickleby,
2000, Isn't She Great, 2000, Stuart Little, 2000; stage
credits: distinguished career including as Max Bialystock,
alongside Matthew Broderick in "The Producers", 2001,
which made him a Broadway icon; "The Odd Couple", 2005,
"Guys and Dolls."

LANSBURY, Angela, Brigid; CBE; ACTOR
Born, 16, October 1925, London, 1st generation (mother
Belfast born actress Moyna Mac Gill); four-time Tony-
winning, three-time Oscar-nominated actress; best known for
her Academy Award nominated film debut in 1944 in
Gaslight with Ingrid Bergman and Charles Boyer; followed
by another Oscar nomination for her role as Sibyl Vane in
film adaptation of the Oscar Wilde novel The Picture of
Dorian Gray, 1945; has since enjoyed a long and varied
career, mainly as a film actress, appearing in everything from
Samson and Delilah (1949) to Disney's Bedknobs and
Broomsticks ,1971;. biggest triumph of Lansbury's career
was her smash hit success on the New York stage in the title
role of Mame in the musical of the same name; opening at
The Winter Garden Theater on May 24,1966, Mame ran for
1508 performances earning her a Tony Award for Best
Actress in a Musical; subsequent Tony awards were earned by
Lansbury for Dear World,1969 and the first Broadway
revival of Gypsy ,1974; she is a two-time winner of the Sarah
Siddons Award (1975 & 1980) for dramatic achievement in
Chicago theatre; as Jessica Fletcher in the long-running
television series, Murder, She Wrote ,1984 - 1996, she found
her biggest success and a worldwide following; .it made her
one of the highest paid actresses in the world and a record as
the most nominated lead actress without a win in the prime
time Emmy awards (with 12 nominations); in the early 1990s
Queen Elizabeth II of the United Kingdom awarded her the
CBE; she was named a Disney Legend, 1995; she received a
Screen Actors Guild Lifetime Achievement Award, 1997, and
Kennedy Center Honors in 2000; she has a home in Co.
Cork.

LEAHY, Patrick Joseph 'Pat'; SENATOR
Born, 31, March 1940, Montpelier, Vermont; Senior US
Senator Vermont (Democratic Party), 1974 –todate; was
only the second Democrat ever elected to Congress from
Vermont and was the first and only Democrat ever elected to
the US Senate from Vermont. He had served four terms as
State's Attorney of Chittenden County from 1966 to 1974
prior to being elected to the Senate.

LEAHY, William, S.J., PRESIDENT BOSTON COLLEGE
Born, 1948, Omaha, Nebraska; Ordained priest 1978;
Teaching asst. Stanford Univ 1981; Joined faculty Marquette

University, Milwaukee 1985, successively asst professor 1986-'91, Acting asst chrm 1988-'90, Assoc prof history, Exec. Vice-Pres 1991-'96; President Boston College 1996 - to date; Publ. Adapting to America: Catholics, Jesuits and Higher Education in the Twentieth Century, 1991; Founder member, Committee for Boston Irish Famine Memorial Inc.

Denis Leary

LEARY, Denis; ACTOR, WRITER, DIRECTOR, COMIC
Born, 18, August 1957, Worcester, Massachusetts, 1st generation (Irish parents John and Nora); best known for his often angry humor with an extremely libertarian viewpoint; best known as a stand up comic; has appeared in over 40 movies including The Sandlot, Monument Ave., The Match Maker, The Ref, Suicide Kings, Dawg, Wag the Dog, Demolition Man, The Thomas Crown Affair and Operation Dumbo Drop; Leary picked up an Emmy nomination for Outstanding Lead Actor in a Drama Series for his performance in "Rescue Me,2006; now the star and co creator of F/X's Rescue Me.

LYNCH, John T; PRESIDENT TRALLION TECHNOLOGIES
President Trallion Technologies, 1998-1999: President and CEO, Catholic Radio Network, LLC; Chairman and CEO, Noble Broadcast Group; Consultant, Jacor Communications, Inc. 1997; Vice Chairman, Jacor Communications, Inc.1996; Chairman, CEO, Co-Founder, Noble Broadcast Group 1978-1996; Westinghouse Broadcasting IL and Chicago Tribune; General Sales Manager, KFMB AM & FM, San Diego; Board of Trustees, for Uni of San Diego and Drake Uni; President, San Diego International Sports Council; Board Member, CEOs Roundtable; Co-Founder, Past President, Member, Nice Guys; Member, Century Club; Previously, President, The Century Club; Chairman, Major Market Radio Advisory Board; drafted by Pittsburgh Steelers, 1969

LYNCH, Peter S; FORMER VICE CHAIRMAN, FIDELITY MANAGEMENT & RESEARCH COMPANY
2nd generation Irish American Irish roots Limerick; took Fidelity Magellan from nowhere to the largest fund in the world; This is a man who created an extraordinary track record at Fidelity's Magellan Fund, a record that still inspires awe; Previously Exec Vice President, Director Fidelity Management & Research Company ,1977-'90: Portfolio Manager, Fidelity's Magellan Fund 1969: Fidelity Investments Managing Director, FMR Corp; Leader, Growth Group, Fidelity Investments; Author: One Up On Wall Street, 1990; Lieutenant, U.S. Army; Trustee, Fidelity Group of Funds; member, Advisory Board, AmeriCares; Trustee, Boston Public Library Foundation, MASS. Eye & ear Museum of Fine Arts, Boston College, JFK Foundation,

Historic Deerfield and Mass. General Hospital; Finance Council, Third Century Foundation; President, Catholic Schools Foundation; member, Board of Councilors, Order of Malta.

MAGUIRE, Mary B; FORMER VICE PRESIDENT CHASE BANK
Born, New York City, 2nd generation Irish American roots in Dublin and Kerry; Davis Consulting Group, LLC, New York, NY, Senior Consultant, 2003 –'06; EBUSINESSWARE, INC., New York, NY Partner, 2001-'02; J.P. MORGAN CHASE & CO., New York, NY Managing Director, Global Asset Management and Mutual Funds, 1998 – '01; Chase Manhattan Bank: Managing Director and Division Executive, Treasury Department ,1996-'98; Senior Vice President, Treasury Department , 1991-'96;Vice President and Division Executive, Investment Division,1989-'91; Vice President, Investment Division, 1985-'89; Vice President, Treasury Department , 1978-'85;Assistant Vice President, Investment Portfolio Division ,1973-'78; Assistant Treasurer, Investment Portfolio Division ,1971-'73; Member, ERISA Advisory Board, U.S. Department of Labor, appointed by the Secretary ofLabor; Member, First Judicial Department Disciplinary Committee, New York State Supreme Court, Appellate Division; Member, Vatican Delegation to the United Nations; Trustee, St. John's University, Member, Financial Advisory Committee, Carmelite Sisters Healthcare Network, Member, Ireland-American Economic Advisory Board (advisory to Prime Minister)

MAHONEY, John, ACTOR
Born, 20, June1940, Blackpool, England, 2nd generation Irish American,(grandfather emigrated from Cork); Trained for theatre in St. Nicholas Theatre, Chicago; Stage performances incl. The Water Engine 1977, The Hothouse, Death of a Salesman, Orphans 1985, The House of Blue Leaves 1986; films incl. The Manhattan Project 1986, Streets of Gold 1987, Tin Men 1987, Moonstruck 1987, Frantic 1988, Love Hurts 1990, Barton Fink 1991, The Hudsucker Proxy 1994, Primal Fear 1996, The Broken Hearts Club 2000; TV series: The Human Factor 1991, Frasier 1991-2004 (Best known as Marty Crane, Frazier's father); Eugene O'Neill's Long Day's Journey into Night (James Tyrone) at the Galway Arts Festival, Ireland, 1999; Awards: Theater World award 1985, Tony Award, Clarence Derwent award 1986, recipient award SAG 2000

MAHONY, His Eminence Cardinal Roger Michael;
CARDINAL, LOS ANGELES
Born, 27, February 1926, Hollywood, CA; ordained a priest in the Diocese of Fresno, May 1, 1962; was ordained titular bishop of Tamascani, and auxiliary bishop of Fresno. March 19, 1975; Governor Jerry Brown appointed Bishop Mahony the first chair of the California Agricultural Labor Relations Board, where he worked with the United Farm Workers and various growers in the state to resolve labor disputes, 1975; appointed Bishop of the Diocese of Stockton February 15, 1980; appointed Archbishop of Los Angeles, the first native Angeleno to hold the office, July 16, 1985; was made a Cardinal by Pope John Paul II in the consistory of June 28,

1991, and was appointed Cardinal Priest of *Titulus Ss. Quattuor Coronatorum.*

MALLON, Meg; U.S. OPEN GOLF WINNER
Born, 14, April, 1963, Natick, Massachusetts, 3rd Generation, family roots Galway and Tyrone; Winner: Oldsmobile LPGA Classic 1991, Mazda LPGA Championship 1991, Women's US Open 1991, Daikyo World Championship 1991, ranked 4th woman LPGA tour 1992, winner PING/Welch's Chamionship 1993, Sara Lee Classic 1993, 1996 & 1999, du Maurier Classic 2000, ADT championship 2003, US Women's Open 2004, BMO Financial Group Canadian Women's Open 2004. Member, Solheim Cup Team 8 times.

MANNING, John P. 'Jack'; PRESIDENT & CEO OF BOSTON CAPITAL CORPORATION BOSTON, MA
President & CEO of Boston Capital Corporation Boston, MA, 1974 – to date; also associated with National Housing Conference, Woodrow Wilson Council, John F. Kennedy Library, JFK Center for Performing Arts; Founding President and Chairman Emeritus, Affordable Housing Tax Credit Coalition.

MARINEAU, Philip A 'Phil'; PRESIDENT, CEO LEVI STRAUSS CORP & CO
Born, New Orleans, Louisana, 3rd generation Irish American, with roots in Co. Kerry; Joined Quaker Oats Company 1973 – '96; President, COO Dean Foods Company, 1996 –'97; President, CEO Pepsi-Cola North America 1997, (was the leader in the 1990's Pepsi surge that climaxed with Pepsi outselling Coke in 1998); President and CEO, Levi Strauss Corp & Co 2000 –'06, (retiring end 2006)

MARTIN, Stephen Glenn; Actor, Writer, Producer, Musician, Composer
Born 14, August 1945, Waco, Texas; is an American comedian, writer, producer, actor, musician, and composer; Irish, English, Scottish descent; best known for appearances in Saturday Night Live, Planes, Trains & Automobiles 1987, Cyrano de Bergerac adaptation Roxanne, 1987 (Martin co-wrote and won a Writers Guild of America award), Parenthood, 1989, My Blue Heaven, 1990, L.A. Story, 1992. The Spanish Prisoner,1997, The Out-of-Towners 1999, Bringing Down The House, 2003, Cheaper By The Dozen 2003, Shopgirl, 2005, Cheaper By The Dozen 2, 2005, The Pink Panther, 2006.

MATTHEWS, Christopher, John 'Chris'; TALK SHOW HOST, AUTHOR, COLUMNIST
Born, 17, December 1945, Nicetown, Pennsylvania; 1st generation Irish (his paternal grandmother emigrated from Northern Ireland; best known TV: Hardball with Chris

Matthews, a nightly, hour-long talk show called on the American cable television channel MSNBC, formerly on CNBC, and a syndicated NBC News-produced panel program called The Chris Matthews Show on weekends; Publications: How Politics Is Played Told By One Who Knows The Game,1989, memoir, Now, Let Me Tell You What I Really Think, 2001, memoir, American: Beyond Our Grandest Notions, 2002, memoir.

Terry McAuliffe

Mc AULIFFE, Terence 'Terry'; LEGENDARY DEMOCRATIC NATIONAL COMMITTEE HEAD Born, 1957, Syracuse, New York, ancestors hailed from Tipperary and Cork; Legendary fund-raiser for Democrats and entrepreneur (Campaign agent Jimmy Carter; finance director Democratic National Committee (DNC) and Democratic Campaign Committee; National Finance Chairman, Gephardt for President Committee; National Co-Chairman, Clinton-Gore re-election committee 1996; Chairman, Democratic National Convention Los Angeles 2000; Chairman DNC 2001-'05; also entrepreneur , in 1997 bought $100,000 worth of Global crossing stock, sold it the following year when the company went public for $100 million, has successfully started over 24 companies in fields of banking, insurance, marketing and real estate

Mc CABE, Eugene; EXECUTIVE VICE PRESIDENT, WORLDWIDE OPERATIONS AT SUN MICROSYSTEMS, INC.
Born in Ireland; Joined DEC Europe and later Compaq, where he gained an array of skills, including system product design; Joined Sun Microsystems 1999, vice president for High End Operations. He was in charge of the supply chain and operations engineering for the company's flagship Enterprise server. While in this position he created advancements in Sun's Customer Ready Systems; appointed Executive Vice President, Worldwide Operations, in charge of Sun's supply chain and its manufacturing and logistics programs; (Sun is a worldwide leader in computer networking); plays an integral role in providing cost effective product execution for Sun's global customer demands; Awards: has garnered several awards for his contributions, one of which was the inaugural Sun Leadership Award in 2002.

Mc CANN, James F 'Jim'; CHAIRMAN CEO 1-800-FLOWERS.COM
Born, 1952, New York; administrator at St. John's Home for Boys in Rockaway, New York; has served as the Company's Chairman of the Board and Chief Executive Officer since inception; has been in the floral industry since 1976 when he began building a chain of retail flower shops in the New York metropolitan area; Mr. McCann acquired the 800-FLOWERS phone number and renamed the company, 1986, followed by his launch on the Internet, 1992; Today, 1-800-FLOWERS has more than 150 franchises worldwide and generates approximately 10 percent of its sales ($30 million) on the Internet, through America Online and with a number of Internet and on-line services; a published author and award winning public speaker; is active in numerous business and community organizations, which include the national board of directors, Gateway 2000, Office Max, Inc., PETCO, Inc., the National Retail Federation, and Very Special Arts, as well as the boards of Hofstra University and Winthrop University Hospital. He also supports programs for the developmentally disabled. Named Toastmaster International's Outstanding Speaker for Commerce and Industry in 1997, McCann has discussed business and social issues before AT&T, IBM and Fortune 500 companies; Awards include: Entrepreneur of the Year award by Merrill Lynch and Inc. Magazine; Retailer of Year award from Chain Store Executive Magazine; Advocate of the Year award from Ernst & Young and the Long Island Association; Direct Marketer of the Year from Direct Marketing Day New York; has been named one of the Top Business 100 in Irish America Magazine; active in numerous business and community organizations; supports programmes for the developmentally disabled.

McCANN; Robert J; PRESIDENT, GLOBAL PRIVATE CLIENT GROUP, MERRILL LYNCH
Born, 1959; 2nd generation Irish American, father's family comes from Co. Armagh; Joined Merrill Lynch aged 23, beginning as an associate in the MBA sales and trading program; has held various positions in Merrill including head of global securities research and economics, chief operating officer of the Global Markets & Investment Banking Group; also led the firm's Global Institutional Client Division; is also a member of the firm's Executive Management and Operating Committees; had a brief stint in AXA Financial as Chairman and director of distribution and marketing; Member, executive committee of the Board of Directors for the American Ireland Fund;

Mc CARTHY, Paddy; PUBLISHER
Born, 30, December 1945, Cork City,; founder, Publisher Irish Connections, 2000; founder, publisher, Irish Examiner USA, 2006; emigrated to United States 1982; worked as a bartender on Second Avenue for six years; joined the Irish Voice in sales, 1988; moved up to the position of Advertising Director before resigning in 1986; opened an establishment, Nevada Smith's; Advertising Director, World of Hibernia Magazine, 1997 – '01.

Mc COURT, Frank; AUTHOR
Born, 19, August, 1930, Brooklyn New York; 1st generation Irish American, parents hailed from Limerick ; Mc Court was raised there; Pulitzer Prize winning author, Angela's Ashes

1997, National Book Circle Critics Award, 1996; Tis: A Memoir, 1999, memoir, Teacher Man, 2005, memoir; taught English, Stuyvesant High School, New York City, NY; awarded an honorary degree from the University of Western Ontario; with his brother Malachy (*qv*) created stage play A Couple of Blaguards, a two-man show detailing their experiences

Mc COURT, Malachy; ACTOR, AUTHOR
Born, 20, September, 1931, Brooklyn, New York; first generation Irish American, parents hailed from Limerick and Mc Court was raised there; Stage and Screen Actor; Best Known as: Gods and Generals, 2003, The Guru, 2002, Ash Wednesday, 2002, The Deli, 1997, The Devil's Own, 1997, Turbulence, 1997, She's the One, 1996, Green Card,1990, The Bonfire of the Vanities, 1990, Mr. & Mrs. Bridge, 1990, The Field, 1990, Reversal of Fortune, 1990, January Man, 1989, Brewster's Millions, 1985; A Monk Swimming, memoir, 1998, Singing My Him Song memoir, 2000, Danny Boy: The Legend of the Beloved Irish Ballad, 2002

Marianne Mc Donald

Mc DONALD, Marianne;
PROFESSOR OF CLASSICS & THEATRE, UNIVERSITY OF CALIFORNIA, SAN DIEGO
Adjunct Professor, Dept of Theater, Univ. of California1992-1994: Yearly visiting lectures, School of Classics, Trinity College, Dublin1990 – todate; Fellow, University College Dublin and Theatre; Adjunct Associate Professor, Dept. of Theater, Univ. of California1990-1992; Teaching Assistant, Dept. of classics U of Cal. 1972 – 1974; Member of RIA1994-todate; Board of Overseers, UCSD,1985 – todate; International President, Women's International Center, 1984 – todate; Founder, Board, McDonald Center1984 – todate

Mc DONNELL, John 'Jack'; FOUNDER, CHAIRMAN AND CEO, TRANSACTION NETWORK SERVICES
Born, 1941, New York, 1st generation Irish American; a pioneer in the telecommunications industry; has also been Chairman and CEO of Paylinx, Corp. and President and CEO of Digital Radio Network, Inc.; Founder and still active on the board of directors, Electronic Funds Transfer Association; (Transaction Network Services, Inc (NYSE:TNS), entered Ireland in 1994 by establishing a software development group in Dublin.); Recipient, KPMG Peat Marwick LLP's High Tech Entrepreneur Award 1997; Rensselaer Polytechnic Institute Entrepreneur of the Year Award,2002; named to the top 100 Irish American businessmen by Irish America Magazine2004;. Member, North American Advisory Board for the Prime Minister of Ireland; serves on the Board of Directors of CyberSource Corp(NASDAQ:CYBS); serves on the Board of Directors of The American Ireland Fund; With wife Jackie founded the

McDonnell Charitable Foundation which supports a Mitchell scholar and a student at the Smurfit School of Business at University College Dublin.

Mc ENROE, John Patrick Jnr; TENNIS CHAMPION/TV COMMENTATOR
Born, 16, February 1969, Wiesbaden, Germany, grew up in Douglaston, N.Y; 2nd generation Irish American; ranked Number one in the world from 1981 – 1984; winner of Wimbledon, 1981, 1983, 1984; winner of US Open, 1979, 1980, 1981, 1984; winner of the Masters, 1979, 1983 1984; won several doubles with his partner Peter Fleming; inducted into International Tennis Hall of Fame, 1999; Author: You Cannot Be Serious, 2002; sports commentator for CBS television.

Mc GOVERN, Maureen Therese; SINGER ACTOR
Born, 27, July 1949, Youngstown, Ohio, 3rd.generation Irish American; her 1973 hit "The Morning After" earned her a Grammy nomination for "Best New Artist"; has recorded 25 new albums; made dozens of film, radio and television appearances and acted in over 30 productions, including the Broadway production of "Little Women"; hit with the theme for the Poseidan Adventure and "The Towering Inferno"; appeared in the Pirates of Penzance with Linda Ronstadt, and with Sting in the 3 Penny Opera and the role of Anna in the national tour of The King and I.

Judy Mc Grath

Mc GRATH, Judith 'Judy';
CHAIRMAN, CEO MTV NETWORKS CO
Born, 1952, Scranton, PA, Irish on both sides with ancestors from Armagh and the West; Began career working at a radio station out of college; Joined Condé Nast publications; Worked as on-air prompt writer at MTV, 1981; Assumed all responsibily at MTV for programming, music, production and promotion, 1991; Named president of MTV,1993; executive producer of the feature "Joe's Apartment", 1996; Appointed President, MTV Networks, overseeing MTV, VH1, and Country Music Television, 2002. Chairman, CEO MTV Networks Company (including MTV, MTV2, VH-1, CMT, Nickelodeon, TV Land) 2004 - to date; Ranked 49th on Forbes '100 Most Powerful Women' list, 2005.

Mc GUINN, Martin G 'Marty'; CHAIRMAN CEO, MELLON FINANCIAL CORPORATION
Born, Philadelphia; Chairman, Chief Executive Officer, Mellon Financial Corporation, (a global financial services company headquartered in Pittsburgh, Pennsylvania. Mellon is one of the world's leading providers of financial services for institutions, corporations and high net worth individuals,

providing institutional asset management, mutual funds, private wealth management, asset servicing, payment solutions and investor services, and treasury services); 1999 – to date; Chairman and CEO of Mellon Bank, N.A. 1998 – to date; Director, Corporation and Mellon Bank; Vice Chairman of the Corporation and of Mellon Bank, 1990 – 1998; joined Mellon, 1981; appointed by President Bush to the National Infrastructure Advisory Council, 2002; recently concluded a one-year term as chairman of the Financial Services Roundtable; Director, Shinsei Bank (Japan).President, Federal Reserve Board's Advisory Council, 2005; serves on several nonprofit boards, including the American Ireland Fund, Carnegie Mellon University, the Carnegie Museums of Pittsburgh, the Historical Society of Western Pennsylvania, University of Pittsburgh Medical Center and the Eisenhower Exchange Fellowships; Chairman, Allegheny Conference on Community Development.

Mc KENNA, Andrew; CHAIRMAN SCHWARTZ; CHAIRMAN MC DONALDS CORPORATION
2nd generation Irish-America, has roots in counties Mayo and Monaghan; Director, AON Corporation and the Chicago Bears Football Club, Click Commerce and Skyline Corporation; has served on many civic, community and philanthropic boards; director, American Ireland Fund, Children's Memorial Hospital of Chicago, the Big Shoulders Fund of the Archdiocese of Chicago, The Ireland Economic Advisory Board and Lyric Opera of Chicago.

Mc LOUGHLIN, Kieran; VICE PRESIDENT AND DIRECTOR OF DEVELOPMENT OF THE AMERICAN IRELAND FUND AND THE IRELAND FUNDS WORLDWIDE
Born, 13, September 1966, Dublin, Ireland; focused on developing major gifts across the Funds' Global Network; oversaw the Funds' single most successful event, the 2006 New York Dinner which raised $4.1 million; served as Director Ireland of The Ireland Funds in Ireland 1999 –'05; (during this period, the Funds grew significantly and became self-funding); Prior to working with The Funds, held a series of positions with The Dublin Chamber of Commerce, The Dublin International Sports Council.

Vince Mc Mahon

Mc MAHON, Vince Kennedy Jnr; WRESTLING PROMOTER
Born, 24, August 1945, Pinehurst, North Carolina; 3rd generation Irish American, Galway roots; son of Vince Mc Mahon Founder, World Wrestling Federation; chairman, Owner, Founder and majority shareholder of World Wrestling Entertainment, Inc. (WWE);

Mc MULLEN, Michael; FORMER PRESIDENT INTERNATIONAL, THE HOME SHOPPING NETWORK
During his term at HSN, was responsible for establishing live TV shopping networks in several world markets; prior to that, McMullen spent a decade as senior international advisor to CNN , helping set up the network's international sales and marketing organization; also worked for The Coca-Cola Company as Coca-Cola's brand manager in Japan; member, Advisory Board, Eyewonder; member, Ireland America Economic Advisory.

Mc NALLY, William J 'Bill'; PRESIDENT, DIRECTOR, FORD HALL FORUM
President, Director, Ford Hall Forum; Board Member, Colonel Daniel Marr Boys and Girls Club, Board of Trustees, Boston Bar Foundation, The New England Circle Member, New England Committee, NAACP Legal Defense Fund, Inc; Attorney at Law at Bingham Dana LLP since 1986; Executive Director, the American Ireland Fund 1982-'92; Executive Director, Greater Boston Legal Services 1975-'82; Executive Director, Lawyers' Committee for Civil Rights Under Law, Chicago IL, 1970-'74; Associate, Schiff, Hardin & Waite, Chicago, IL.1968 – '70.

MEANEY, Colm; ACTOR
Born 30, May 1953, Dublin, Ireland; Trained Abbey School of Acting, Dublin; spent the next eight years in England, touring with several theatre companies; first television appearance was in Z-Cars on BBC1, 1978; Best known as Miles O'Brien in Star Trek; The Next Generation and Star Trek: Deep Space Nine; guest-starred on shows like Remington Steele and Moonlighting before embarking on a successful film career; He received a Golden Globe nomination for Best Actor for his role in *The Snapper*. Recently, he has played a minor recurring role as Cowen, leader of the Genii on the Sci-Fi Channel series Stargate Atlantis, and he guest-starred on Law & Order: Criminal Intent; Phil Hogan in Eugene O'Neill's A Moon for the Misbegotten at London's Old Vic Theatre, September 2006

MERIWETHER, John 'J.M'; LONG TERM CAPITAL MANAGEMENT
Born, 1947, Rosemoor, Chicago, 2nd generation Irish; Joined Salomon Brothers, New York, 1974; Formed the legendary Arbitrage Group at Salomon, 1977; Considered the high priest of the calculated gamble; Appointed Vice President and head of Bond Trading, Salomon; 1991 stepped aside, caught in a Treasury securities trading scandal, paid a $50,000 civil penalty and left the company; Founded Long Term Capital Management, (managing partner, managed money for 100 investors, employed 200),1994; (hailed as the most impressive hedge fund in history, the partnership included two Nobel Prize winning economists and a cadre of Wall Street's and academia's elite traders; began trading with $1,011,060,243 of investor capital); 1994 –'98 LTCM dazzled as a $100 billion money making juggernaut; 1998

LTMC collapsed, in addition to the $100 billion, the fund had entered into thousands of derivative contracts which covered an astronomical sum, more than $1 trillion worth of exposure, threatening not just the biggest banks on Wall Street but the financial system itself, the Fed. had to step in to save the system); 1999, founded JWM Partners, a Greenwich, Connecticut, hedge fund, started with about $500 million under management; (with approximately $2 billion under management in 2006 according to Meriwether's SEC registration); investor in the golf club at Waterville, Co. Kerry; bloodstock interests in Ireland.

MITCHELL, George John; CHAIRMAN DISNEY
Born, 20, August 1933, Waterville, Maine; Irish American paternal side; US Senator 1980 -95 (Democratic Party); member board Disney, Xerox, Federal Express; Chairman, Disney. 2004 – todate; Partner and Chairman of the Global Board of DLA Piper Rudnick Gray Cary, a global law firm; founder of the Mitchell Institute, in Portland, Maine; Iran-Contra Scandal Select Committee on the Iran-Contra Affair (1987); member, American Red Cross, Bilderberg Group, Council on Foreign Relations, International Crisis Group, Chairman Emeritus, Four Freedoms Medal, 2003, Presidential Medal of Freedom, 1999; major broker peace in Ireland as President Bill Clinton's envoy; Chancellor Queens University, Belfast,

MONAGHAN, Brian D; ATTORNEY, LAW OFFICES, BRIAN D. MONAGHAN, (RETIRED)
Member, Board of Directors: Uni of California; Hastings College of Law; San Diego Padres; Association of Trial Lawyers of America; Consumer Attorneys of San Diego; American Inns of Court, San Diego Chapter; American Board of Trial Advocates; California Trial Lawyers; Awards: Trial Lawyer Hall of Fame – Consumer Attorneys of SD, 2000: AIF Heritage Award, 1999; California Trial Lawyer of the Year, 1998, 1999; Steve J. Sharp Public Service Award – Association of Trial Lawyers of America,1998; Trial lawyer of the Year – San Diego Trial Lawyers Association,1979, 1984 and 1988; Outstanding Trial Lawyer Award – San Diego Trial Lawyers Association, 1978,'79, '81 '83, '84, '89, '91, '93, '98;

MOORE, Dr. George; CHAIRMAN CEO AND FOUNDER TARGUS CORPORATION
Born, 1951, Louth Ireland; Previously Chairman Performix Technologies, Ireland; Chair and Founder, Information Decision Systems; Chairman Buyers Choice Media, Inc.; The Eclectic American Catalogue Company; Chairman and Owner Erne Heritage Holdings Managing Partner, Calzada del Bosque, Inc.

MORAN, Thomas J 'Tom'; CHAIRMAN, PRESIDENT AND CEO, MUTUAL OF AMERICA
Born, Staten Island, New York; 3rd generation from Tipperary on paternal side, 2nd generation Cavan and Fermanagh on maternal side; Chairman, President and CEO, Mutual of America Insurance Corp; Chairman, Concern North America; during his 30 years of service, he has participated in Mutual of America's growth from a small retirement association to a mutual life insurance company with over $11 billion in assets; one of his first projects after becoming President and COO was to oversee the purchase and renovation of Mutual of America's headquarters building at 320 Park Avenue in New York City; upon completion, the building was recognized with numerous awards for its design and immediately became one of the prestigious addresses on Park Avenue; has written for The Peter F. Drucker Foundation's *Leader to Leader* magazine and has been quoted in *Business Week* on the subject of "What Leaders Owe."; has also presented at the World Economic Forum, where he is a regular attendee; has served in several insurance industry leadership positions including, Chairman of the Medical Information Bureau and Chairman of the Life Insurance Council of New York; currently the Chairman of Concern Worldwide (U.S.), an international humanitarian relief organization which operates in 29 of the poorest countries of the world; former Chairman of the North American Advisory Board of the Michael Smurfit Graduate School of Business at University College Dublin; serves on the Boards of Directors of the American Cancer Society, the Greater New York Council of the Boy Scouts of America, Channel Thirteen WNET, the National Committee on American Foreign Policy, the Leader to Leader Institute and the United Way of New York City; a member of the Taoiseach's Economic Advisory Board, as well as the Boards of the Irish Chamber of Commerce in the USA and the Ireland-United States Council for Commerce and Industry, Inc; Mr. Moran is the second American to ever be invited to serve as a member of the Court of Directors of Ireland's oldest corporation, the Bank of Ireland, appointed to the board of Aer Lingus, Irish Airlines, 2006.

MOYNAHAN, Dr, Paula; RECONSTRUCTIVE SURGERY EXPERT
2nd generation Irish American; a leading cosmetic surgeon and teacher of reconstructive surgery in Pakistan and China; Past President New York Society Plastic Surgeons; One of the few women to receive double board certification from the American Board of Surgery and the American Board of Plastic Surgery; Much sought after media expert; awards: Pakistan league of American Appreciation Award; member, Women's Physician delegation to the People's Republic of China's Citizen-Ambassador Programme.

MULCAHY, Anne; PRESIDENT AND CEO XEROX CORPORATION
Born, 21, October 1952, Rockville Centre, New York, 2nd Irish American, traces her roots to Counties Cavan and Mayo; One of Fortune magazine's Top 50 Women Executives in the United States; the first recipient of the Women Elevating Science and Technology Award from Working

Woman magazine; appointed chairman, Xerox Corp. 2002; appointed CEO of Xerox, 2001; appointed president and COO 2000; (Revenue: $18.7 Billion Employees: 85,600); The culmination of a 25-year career with 'The Document Company', providing high-value hardware, software, services and solutions to business managers world-wide; she credits the success of Xerox to teamwork, says, "I am surrounded by some of the most brilliant minds in technology today. This innovative and smart thinking is inspiring, helps to drive the success of the company and continues to power the strength of the Xerox brand."Xerox has sales, service, customer administration, and manufacturing operations in Ireland, including the company's European Customer Support center in Dublin and a major manufacturing facility in Dundalk.

MULVIHILL, Daniel F 'Dan'; CHAIRMAN & CEO PACIFIC SOUTHWEST REALTY SERVICES
Mortgage Bankcr1954 – todate; formed Pacific Southwest Realty Services, a commercial real estate mortgage company, 1972; previously held various positions with Percy H. Goodwin Co., starting as a farm loan officer, 1954 and then as chairman of the board in 1967; has been active on national, state and local Mortgage Bankers Associations for more than 40 years, including president of the California MBA, the San Diego MBA and treasurer of the National MBA; Board Member, Mercy Hospital Foundation, Scripps Foundation for Medicine and Science, The Hahn Chair of Real Estate Finance, University of San Diego; named 2006 Nice Guy of the Year by The Nice Guys a non profit organization San Diego.

MURPHY, Bartholomew 'Bart'; REAL ESTATE INVESTOR AND DEVELOPER IN SAN FRANCISCO, CA.
Born, California, 1st Irish American to parents from counties Kerry and Clare; grew up near Cashel, Co Tipperary; attended Saint Joseph's Christian Brothers Schools, Thurles, received his primary law degree from University College Dublin, 1981 and graduate law degree from the Honorable Society Of King's Inns, Dublin, 1983; practiced as a barrister in Dublin 1983 –'86; returned to San Francisco1986; practiced commercial and real estate law 1986 – 1998; serves on the boards of several Irish related non-profits and charities in the U.S. and Ireland; is a director and past president of the Coalition for Better Housing; member, Mayor Gavin Newsome's Transition Team on Affordable Housing Issues; Since has served as a Commissioner of the San Francisco Rent Control Board 1997 – to date.

MURPHY, James J 'Jimmy'; CHAIRMAN BRENDAN TOURS
Born, Dublin, Ireland; joined Leslie Harris Travel in Dublin, Ireland, as an office boy 1946; moved to New York, 1955; worked with Cunard Lines; joined Aer Lingus as a sales representative,1958; promoted to passenger sales manager for North America; moved to California to become the vice president , Brendan Tours, 1969; president, Brendan Tours

1975; became sole owner, 1979; joined ASTA, (American Society of Travel Agents, The Society is the world's largest and most influential travel trade association with over 20,000 members in 140 countries), 1969; between served as vice president of ASTA's Southern California Chapter 1973 –'75; national treasurer ASTA 1975 - '78; pre- and post-tour chairman for both the Manila and Rome Congresses; president of the U.S. Tour Operators Association (USTOA); sold Brendan Tours 2006.

MURPHY, Martin J Jnr 'Marty'; PUBLISHER, THE ONCOLOGIST
Irish citizen; Irish roots, Achill Island, Co. Mayo; Chairman and CEO of AlphaMed Consulting, a corporation that provides strategic support to cancer centers, advocacy groups, as well as the global pharmaceutical and biotechnology industry; is Founding Executive Editor of the international, peer-reviewed journal, *The Oncologist*, which is read by more than 21,000 physicians entrusted with cancer patient care; Founder and Executive Editor of *Stem Cells*, a scientific journal that has more than two decades of publishing excellence in this fast-paced and promising field; was also Founder and former CEO of the Hipple Cancer Research Center; was principal investigator of more than $21 million of cancer grants and research contracts, authored more than 150 peer-reviewed papers and is the editor of a score of books; is currently Chairman of the Scientific Advisory Board of ArraDx, Ltd., a biotech company developing prognostic assays as well as anti-cancer drugs in Craigavon, Northern Ireland; member, board of trustees of the American Cancer Society Foundation. has been instrumental in the creation and building of the All Ireland Cancer Fund which will finally bring Ireland to a place of distinction in the world of Cancer care; already, some amazing things are happening in Belfast and similar things are about to happen in the Republic.

MURRAY, William James 'Bill'; COMEDIAN ACTOR DIRECTOR PRODUCER WRITER POET
Born, 21, September 1950, Wilmette, Illinois, 2nd generation Irish American; graduated to Saturday Night Live (SNL) from Chicago's famed Second City comedy troupe; best known in: Garfield A Tail of Two Kitties, 2006, (voice), Lost in Translation, 2003 - nominated for Academy Award, Best Actor, 2004, The Royal Tenenbaums, 2001, Hamlet, 2000, Cradle Will Rock, 1999, Groundhog Day, 1993, What About Bob, 1991, Ghostbusters 11, 1989, Ghost Busters, 1984, Caddyshack, 1980, SNL, 1977 – '99;; co owner with brothers John, Joel and Brian Doyle- Murray of Murray Bros Caddyshack Restaurants, motto 'Eat, Drink and be Murray'.

NAUGHTON, Eileen; GOOGLE, HEAD OF ADVERTISING SALES NEW YORK

Appointed, Head of Advertising Sales, New York, Google August 2006 – todate; President Time Inc 2002 – '05, (the flagship magazine of Time Inc. and the world's largest news magazine, with a worldwide circulation of 5.4 million); Previously, served as vice president of investor relations for AOL Time Warner, 2000 - '02. In 1999, served as president of Time Inc. Interactive, where she led the evolution of online strategies for TIME Inc.'s core brands 1999 -2000; began her career at Time Inc. 1989; general manager, Fortune, 1993 - '97; served as vice president and director of finance at TIME Inc. 1997 - '99; serves on the board of directors for Volunteers of America of New York, board member, FRAXA, the Fragile X Research Foundation, dedicated to funding research aimed at treatment for Fragile X Syndrome; has been active in fundraising efforts for NYC public schools heavily impacted by September 11th; also contributes her support and aid to a number of community outreach programs, in conjunction with the New York City Mission Society, which enjoys a long-standing relationship with TIME.

NEESON, Liam; ACTOR

Born, 7, June, 1952, Ballymena Co. Antrim, Northern Ireland; film actor from 1981 (Excalibur) – todate) ; best known: Schindler's List (Academy Award Nomination best Actor, 1993); Michael Collins, 1996, Star Wars, Episode 1, 1999, Star Wars, Episode 11, 2002, Love Actually 2003, Kinsey, 2004, Seraphim Falls, 2006, Lincoln, 2007, The Chronicles of Narnia, Prince Caspian, 2008; Broadway performances include Anna Christie 1993 (Tony Award nomination) The Crucible, 2002 (Tony Award nomination; Officer of the Order of the British Empire, 1999; UNICEF ambassador..

NOONAN, Margaret 'Peggy'; AUTHOR POLITICAL ANALYST BROADCASTER

Born, 7, August 1950, Brooklyn, New York, close family roots in Donegal; Adjutant professor journalism 1978-'79; Producer CBS News, New York; Special assistant/speechwriter President Ronald Reagan 1984-'86; Speechwriter George Bush Snr 1988; Author; Columnist, Wall Street Journal 2000 - to date; Consultant, George W. Bush reelection campaign 2004; Publ. What I Saw At The Revolution: A Political Life In The Reagan Era, 1990, Life, Liberty And The Pursuit Of Happiness,1994, The Case Against Hillary Clinton, 2000; A Heart, a Cross and a Flag, 2003; Member, Manhattan Institute;

O'BRIEN, Conan; BROADCASTER
Born, 18, April 1963, Brookline, Massachusetts, 3rd.generation Irish America; NBC's Late night anchor, now in it's 12th.season O'Brien's show is a huge success; nominated for several Emmys; has won four Writers' Guild Awards; regarded as one of the 'must watch' night shows.

Conan O'Brien

O'BRIEN, Archbishop Edward F 'Ed'; ROMAN CATHOLIC ARCHDIOCESE FOR THE MILITARY SERVICES
Born, 8, April, 1939, the Bronx, New York, 2nd generation Irish American; ordained a priest for the New York archdiocese, 1965; pastor, to the United States Military Academy at West Point in New York, 1965; left his job as auxiliary bishop of New York to move into the military post; April 1997, was named coadjutor archbishop under then Military Archbishop Joseph Dimino. Appointed Military Archbishop 1997 –'70; enrolled in Army, 1970 –'73, earned the rank of Captain; studied moral theology and completed his doctoral dissertation at the Angelicum in Rome, 1976; appointed vice chancellor for the archdiocese and associate pastor of St. Patrick's Cathedral, 1976; 1976 – '96, held numerous positions within the New York archdiocese and spent some time at the Pontifical North American College in Rome; served as one of John Cardinal O'Connor's auxiliary bishops for the archdiocese; elevated as archbishop of the military, leads one of the largest ecclesiastical jurisdictions in the world, 2000 – todate.

O'BRIEN, Soledad; BROADCASTER
Born, 19, September 1966, Smithtown, Long Island, New York, 3rd. generation Irish American, father Australian/Irish; began her career as an associate producer and news writer at WBZ-TV, then the NBC affiliate in Boston; joined NBC New York 1991; joined CNN from NBC 2003; named as one of the country's most beautiful people in People en Espanol being Cuban American on her mother's side 2004; included among her many honours is being named one of the top '40 under 40' 2005; Co hosts CNNs American Mornings with Bill Hemmer.

O'BYRNE, Brian F; ACTOR;
Born, 16, May 1967, Mullagh, Co. Cavan; Trained at the Samuel Beckett Center and Trinity College, Dublin; Best known in: Before You Know You're Dead, 2007, Bug, Million Dollar Baby (directed by Clint Eastwood), 2004; The New Wood, 2005, Intermission, 2003, Easy, 2003, Disco Pigs, 2001, also appears in Law & Order; stage roles include: Shining City, Doubt; The Beauty Queen of Lenane; The Lonesome West and Frozen; Winner Tony Award, Best

Performance by a Featured Actor in a Play 'Frozen' , 2004; Tony Award nominee, Best Performance by a Leading Actor in a Play, 'Doubt', 2005; won Drama Desk Award, Outstanding Actor for his Role in John Patrick Shanley's Doubt, 2004-2005

O'CONNOR, John; MANAGING PARTNER, PRICEWATERHOUSECOOPERS

Managing Partner, PriceWaterhouseCoopers, 1973 – todate; Other Associations:
Member, Society of CPAs and American Institute of CPAs, Dana Farber Cancer Institute Board of Trustees, Suffolk University; Board of Directors, Partners for Youth with Disabilities, Inc. Massachusetts High Technology Council, Massachusetts Business Roundtable, Massachusetts Taxpayers Foundation, Boston Public Library Foundation.

O'CONNOR, Patrick J; PRESIDENT, CEO COZEN O'CONNOR

President and CEO of Cozen O'Connor; An accomplished trial lawyer (focuses his practice on litigation arising out of contracts, banking matters, estates, professional liability involving legal and accounting matters, health care and aviation-related claims); named, one of the top 100 Lawyers in Pennsylvania, a selection resulting from a poll conducted of Pennsylvania lawyers; actively involved in many legal, professional, civic and educational organizations; Fellow, American College of Trial Lawyers, American Bar Foundation; member, Supreme Court of Pennsylvania's Committee on Rules of Evidence; Board Member, Historical Society of the United States District Court for the Eastern District of Pennsylvania; International Board Member, American Ireland Fund; Mediator, United States District Court for the Eastern District of Pennsylvania; Chairman of the Board, Mellon Private Asset Management Mutual Funds; Board Member, Philadelphia Police Foundation, Board Member, Philadelphia Children's First Fund; Current member (and former Chairman), Board of Consulters for the Villanova University School of Law; Trustee, Temple University; previously served as Member and Chairman of the Board of Trustees of College Misericordia, and as a Member of the Board of Directors at Kings College. In 2002, the Villanova Law Alumni Association honored him with the Gerald Abraham Alumni Association Award for Service.

O'DONNELL, Christopher Eugene 'Chris'; ACTOR

Born, 26, June 1970; Winnetka, Illinois, best known in Men Don't Leave, 1990 (1st moive), Fried Green Tomatoes, 1991, Scent of a Woman, 1992, Mad Love, 1995, Circle of Friends, 1995, Batman and Robin, 1997, Vertical Limit, 2000, Kinsey, 2004; appeared on Broadway in Arthur Miller's "The Man Who Had All the Luck".

O'DONNELL, Kelly; NBC WHITE HOUSE CORRESPONDENT

Family roots Galway and Down; reporter WJM-TV Cleveland, Ohio; correspondent NBC 1994 to date; has covered four Olympic Games, Oklahoma City bombing, September 11th, Iraq, 2004 presidential race, was made White House correspondent 2005; Awards: Regional Emmy award, two awards Los Angeles Press Club, Ohio inducted, Radio/Television broadcasters Hall of Fame 2004, The Irish Abroad 'Top 100'

O'DONNELL, Rosie; TV PERSONALITY

Born, 21, March 1962, Queens, New York, 1st generation Irish American, (father hailed from Belfast); 1996 to 2002, stand up comedian; hosted the daytime talk show, The Rosie O'Donnell Show, 1996 –'02; ; co-host on the ABC talk show, The View, September 2006 todate; launched Rosie magazine 2000; has also starred in various film: A League of Their Own, 1992, Sleepless in Seattle, 1993, The Flintstones 1994, Tarzan, 2000. television: Gimme a Break!(cast member from 1986–'87, Stand-Up Spotlight, 1988–'91, The Rosie O'Donnell Show, 1996–'02 (also producer and executive producer), The Twilight of the Golds, 1997, Jackie's Back!,1999 (cameo), Riding the Bus with My Sister,(TV movie, 2005, (also executive producer); and stage productions; Grease, 1994, Seussical, 2001, (replacement for David Shriner), Fiddler on the Roof, 2004 (replacement for Andrea Martin in 2005); Awards: Emmy Awards for Outstanding Talk Show, The Rosie O'Donnell Show 1998 –'02; Outstanding Variety, Music or Comedy Special, 52nd Annual Tony Awards,1999.

O'DOWD, Niall; PUBLISHER

Born, 1957, Co. Tipperary, Ireland; an arts graduate of University College Dublin; worked briefly as a high school teacher in Ireland, emigrated to the United States, 1978; often described as "the authentic voice of the Irish in America, who has more knowledge of this community than almost anyone else alive"; cofounding publisher of Irish America magazine,(with Trish Harty (qv)1985 and the Irish Voice, 1987 newspaper, the two largest and most prominent Irish-American publications in the United States; was also the founder of the Irish-American Peace delegation, which helped bring about the August 1994 IRA ceasefire; is currently an analyst on Northern Ireland affairs for CNN, has appeared on Good Morning America, NBC Today, and The Charlie Rose Show on PBS; In addition he has written many opinion pieces published in the New York Times, Washington Post and for the Irish Times and Ireland on Sunday newspapers; Author: Fire in the Morning; Awards: The American Book Award for "excellence in writing." by the Before Columbus Foundation,1996.

O' HARA, Maureen; ACTOR

Born, 17, August 1920, Ranelagh, Dublin, Ireland, née Fitzsimons; dubbed by John Wayne " the greatest guy I ever knew"; joined Abbey Players Dublin 1934;had first screen test in London, 1937; won a seven year contract, first movie, My Irish Molly, 1938, Alfred Hitchcock's *Jamaica Inn, 1939*; went to United States 1939; appeared in The Hunchback of Notre Dame with Charles Laughton; Best known in: How Green Was My Valley 1941, The Black Swan, 1942, Buffalo Bill, 1944, Miracle on 34th Street, 1947, Rio Grande, 1950, The Quiet Man,1952, Malaga, 1954, Our Man in Havana, 1959, The Parent Trap, 1961, Spencer's Mountain, 1963, How Do I Love Three, 1970, Only The Lonely, 1991; for her contributions to the motion picture industry, has a star on the Hollywood Walk of Fame at 7004 Hollywood Blvd; inducted into the Western Performers Hall of Fame at the National Cowboy & Western Heritage Museum in Oklahoma City, Oklahoma, 1993; Grand Marshal of the New York City St. Patrick's Day Parade, 1999; *Tis Herself,* autobiography, 2004; Lifetime Achievement Award by the Irish Film and Television Academy in her native Dublin, Ireland, 2004.

O'LEARY, Stella; PRESIDENT, IRISH AMERICAN DEMOCRATS (IAD)
President of the Irish American Democrats, founded 1996 in response to President Clinton's peace initiatives in Irelandbased in Maryland consultant for the Clinton School of American Studies University College, Dublin;, member, Advisory Board, University of Virginia, International Center for International Studies

O'MALLEY, Sheila; PRESIDENT, COO ROCKFLEET MEDIA
President, COO Rockfleet Media,(with management responsibilities for four television stations); Board member, American Ireland Funds; President, Georgian Society; Director, Ashford Castle, Mayo; Board member, American Ballet Theater, Women's Campaign Fund, Stonehill College Massachusetts.

O'NEILL, Tom; PARTNER, SANDLER O'NEILL
Founded Sandler O'Neill along with Herb Sandler and Jimmy Dunne, 1988; from that time until the attacks on the World Trade Center, he and his partners worked hard to build one of the premier investment banks in New York City; After Mr. Sandler perished in the attacks, O'Neill and his partners marshaled Sandler O'Neill's remaining resources to rebuild the company; member, The American Ireland Fund, The Irish American Partnership, ICCUSA.

O'REILLY, Bill; BROADCASTER AUTHOR
Born, 10, September 1949, Manhattan NYC, 2nd generation Irish American; Presenter, The O'Reilly Factor, Fox TV; author, print and radio journalist, (The Radio Facto)r; began his broadcasting career in Scranton, Pennsylvania; proceeded to Dallas, Denver, Boston and Portland, Oregon as a local news reporter/anchor; returned home to New York City for a stint at WCBS-TV before moving to the national news scene

reporting for CBS and ABC News. Mr. O'Reilly continued his climb as the anchor of the syndicated program "Inside Edition," 1980 –'96; joined FOX News 1996; Author: "The O'Reilly Factor", "The No Spin Zone", "Who's Looking Out for You", have all reached the number one spot on The New York Times best seller list; , "The O'Reilly Factor for Kids," was the best selling children's non-fiction book of 2005; Awards: has won a bevy of journalism awards including two Emmys.

O'REILLY, David J; CHAIRMAN, CEO CHEVRON CORPORATION
Born, January, 1947, Dublin, Ireland; joined Chevron Research Co. Process Engineer,1968; Senior Vice-President and COO Chevron Chemical Co 1989-'91; Vice-President, Chevron Corporation 1991-'94, President, Chevron Products Co 1994-'98; Vice-Chairman board of Chevron Corp 1998-'00; Chairman, CEO 2000 - to date, (Chevron Texaco is the fifth largest oil company in the world); Member, World Economic Forum's International Business Council; National Petroleum Council, Business Roundtable, JPMorgan International Council; Director, Institute of International Economics, Eisenhower Fellowships Board of Trustees, member of the American Petroleum Institute and a director of the Institute for International Economics.

O'ROURKE, Patrick Jake 'P.J'; AUTHOR
Born, 14, November 1947, Toledo, Ohio ; a political observer and humorist with definite libertarian, sometimes conservative, and decidedly anti-leftist viewpoints; wrote articles for several publications before joining National Lampoon, 1973 – '81; went freelance 1981; Republican Party Reptile,1987, The Bachelor Home Companion,1987, Holidays in Hell,1988, Modern Manners, 1990, Parliament of Whores, 1991, Give War a Chance, 1992, All the Trouble in the World, 1994, Age and Guile Beat Youth, Innocence, and a Bad Haircut, 1995, The American Spectator's Enemies List, 1996, Eat the Rich, 1999, The CEO of the Sofa, 2001, Peace Kills: America's Fun New Imperialism, 2004.

PATAKI, George E; GOVERNOR
NEW YORK
Born, 24, June 1945, Irish roots 3rd
generation Irish American, maternal
grandmother hails from Cork; Current
Governor State of New York; has held
that office since January 1995, and as of June 2006 is the
longest-serving of the current 50 U.S governors; Mayor of
Peekskill, New York, 1981-'84; New York Assembly, 1985-
'92, New York State Senate,1993-'94, New York Governor
(First Term),1995-'99, New York Governor (Second
Term),1999-'03, New York Governor (Third Term), 2003-
'07; is frequently mentioned as a contender for the 2008
Republican Presidential Nomination.

Regis Philbin

PHILBIN, Regis Francis Xavier 'Reege';
BROADCASTER ENTERTAINER
AUTHOR
Born, 21, August 1931, Bronx, New York
City, 1st generation Irish American, roots
in the West of Ireland; Stagehand
Hollywood; NBC page The Tonight Show;
Co-host, The Joey Bishop Show 1967-'69;
Host, KABC Am L.A; WABC TV Morning
Show 1983-'88; Co-host, Live! With Regis
and Kathie Lee (Gifford), 1988-'00, Show became Live with
Regis, 2000-'01 and Live with Regis and Kelly (Ripa), 2001 -
to date; Host, Who Wants to be a Millionaire?, 1999; Who
Wants To Be A Super Millionaire, 2004; Host, America's
Got Talent, 2006 - to date; Set a Guinness World Record on
his Aug 20 2004 show for having appeared a total of 15,188
hours on television; Publ., Cooking with Regis and Kathie
Lee, co-author 1994, I'm Only One Man 1995, Who Wants
To Be Me, 2000; Singer, albums, It's Time For Regis, 1968,
When You're Smiling, 2004, The Regis Philbin Christmas
Album, 2005; Award: 2 Day Time Emmies, 2001 (2), 2006;
2001: TV Guide Personality of the Year, 2001; Winner,
Walter Camp's "Distinguished American Award" February
2003, Receives Star on Hollywood Walk of Fame, 2003,
Inducted into the National Association of Broadcasters
Broadcasting Hall of Fame 2006

PURCELL, Dennis J; SENIOR MANAGING PARTNER,
PERSEUS - SOROS MANAGEMENT LLC
Born, 1955; Appointed, senior managing partner of the $400
million Perseus-Soros BioPharmaceutical Fund, L.P. April
2000 – todate, (responsible for the overall management of the
fund, which is dedicated to making private equity
investments in the life sciences industry and is also a
significant investor in the Company); Prior to joining
Perseus-Soros served as Managing Director of Life Sciences
Investment Banking at Chase H&Q (formerly Hambrecht &
Quist) from 1994 – '00; Has been cited as one of the life
sciences sector's leaders; Honored, "Biotech Hall of Fame" by
Genetic Engineering News, June 1998; named to the
Biotechnology All-Stars list by Forbes ASAP, May 1999;
Prior to joining H&Q, was a Managing Director in the

Healthcare Group at PaineWebber, Inc.; Currently serves on
the Bioethics Committee of The Biotechnology Industry
Organization; member of the Editorial Board of
Biotechnology Investors Forum, serves on the Board of
Directors of the New York Biotechnology Association,
Auxilium Pharmaceuticals, Inc., Cengent, Inc., and Valentis,
Inc. director; Member, Biological and Molecular
Pharmacology Advisory Council at Harvard Medical School,
Ireland America Economic Advisory Board

PURCELL, Patrick; OWNER, PRESIDENT AND
PUBLISHER, BOSTON HERALD
Born New York, 1947, 2nd generation Irish-American with
roots in Killarney; President and CEO, News America
Publishing, Inc. 1993; Publisher, New York Post 1993;
President, News America/Newspapers, 1990; President and
Publisher, Boston Herald,1987; News Corporation,
Associate Publisher, Village Voice, Vice President of
Advertising Sales, New York Post,1980; New York Daily
News,1970; Other Associations: Board Director, Genesis
Fund, United Way of Mass. Bay, JFK Library Foundation;
Exec Committee, Greater Boston Chamber of Commerce;
Board of Trustees, New England Medical Center, Stonehill
College.

PURCELL, Philip J 'Phil'; FORMER CHAIRMAN CHIEF
EXECUTIVE OFFICER, DEAN WITTER AND CO
Served as chairman and chief executive officer, Dean Witter,
Discover & Co., and its predecessor companies since 1986;
On completion of the merger of Dean Witter, Discover & Co.
and Morgan Stanley Group Inc appointed chairman and
CEO; retained position until June 2005; elected, director of
AMR Corp. and American Airlines, 2000; one of the
founding members, Financial Services Forum; (served as
Chairman, of the Forum for three years); member, Executive
Board of the New York Stock Exchange; (Served six years as
a director of the Exchange and held the elected position of
Vice-Chairman during 1995 and 1996.) Member, University
of Notre Dame Board of Trustees (appointed Chairman of
the Athletic Affairs Committee, 2002)

QUICK, Thomas C; QUICK & REILLY, INC.

Retired vice chairman, Quick & Reilly/Fleet Securities, Inc; Quick & Reilly became part of Fleet, now Bank of America, 1998; Previously, President and COO of The Quick & Reilly Group, Inc. the New York Stock Exchange-listed holding company for the firm's securities businesses; President of Quick & Reilly, Inc., the leading national discount brokerage firm, 1985 -1996. Quick received a bachelor's degree in business from Fairfield University in 1977. He now serves as a trustee of Cold Spring Harbor Laboratories, St. Jude Children's Research Hospital in Memphis, TN, The National Corporate Theatre Fund and Fairfield University. He is a member of the Board of Directors of The Inner-City Scholarship Foundation and a member of its Endowment Fund. Quick is a third generation Irish-American

QUILTY, Shelly Ann; LAWYER

Born Co. Wexford, Ireland; has won back-to-back Legal Aid Society's Pro Bono Awards for outstanding services to clients. She was recently awarded the 2005 Gong for her ongoing work in helping low income New Yorkers, and in particular, cases that deal with the rights of children and young adults.

QUINN, James E; PRESIDENT, TIFFANY & CO.

Born, 24, January 1952, Brooklyn, New York, 2nd generation Irish American, grandparents hail from Westmeath, Offaly and Killorglin and Listowel; President, Tiffany & Co., the internationally renowned jeweler and specialty trader; held several financial management positions in the banking field; joined Tiffany in 1986; executive vice president and then became vice chairman, a position he held until his appointment as president. 1992 – '98; named to the company's board of directors in 1995; appointed President, 2003; (as president, oversees retail sales in Tiffany stores throughout 17 countries, with responsibility for the company's global expansion strategy, including such notable store openings as the Tiffany stores in Beijing, China and Shanghai); also executive vice president of the Tiffany& Co. Foundation, established in 2000, which supports arts preservation and environmental conservation groups; serves on the board of directors of BNY Hamilton Funds, Inc., and Mutual of America Capital Management; is also chairman of the Fifth Avenue Association, a trustee of the Museum of the City of New York, and serves as chairman of the North American Advisory Board for the University College Dublin, Smurfit School of Business; member, Ireland America Economic Advisory.

QUINN, Paul; PARTNER, PERKINS SMITH, COHEN & CROWE LLP

Co-Founder, Wilkinson, Barker, Knauer & Quinn; Private Practice 1961-'62: Rhode Island Senator Claiborne Pell's First Legislative Asst; Perkins, Smith, Cohen & Crowe, LLP; Previously involved Clinton/Gore Finance Council and Re-election Committee; Founder, Committee for a New Ireland; Established Tip O'Neill Chair for Peace and Reconciliation, University of Ulster,1995: Organizer, White House Conference on Trade and Investment in Ireland; member, Executive Board, Smurfit Graduate School of Business, University College Dublin.

QUINN, Peter; AUTHOR SPEECHWRITER

Born, 1947, Bronx, New York City, 3rd generation Irish American with roots in Tipperary and Cork; speechwriter 1979 to date, for New York Governor Hugh Carey (*qv*) 1979-'82, for Governor Mario Cuomo 1983-'85; Chief Speech Writer, Time Warner 1999; Corporate Editorial Director, AOL Time Warner - to date; Publ. Banished Children of Eve, 1994, (American Book Award winner); Hour of the Cat, 2005.

REGAN, Judith; PUBLISHER, REGAN BOOKS
Born, 1953, Massachusetts, with roots in Boyle, Co.Roscommon, (where her brother now lives); Reporter, National Enquirer 1978-'87; Consultant, Simon & Schuster 1987-'94; Taken on by Rupert Murdoch and given own subdivision at HarperCollins, with her own imprint, Regan Books 1994 - to date, (considered the most successful woman in publishing in America and the last of the red hot synergists); Host, Judith Regan Tonight, Fox News Show.

REYNOLDS, Robert L 'Bob'; VICE CHAIRMAN, CHIEF OPERATING OFFICER, FIDELITY INVESTMENTS
Born, 1954, Concord, Massachusetts; Vice chairman and COO, Fidelity Investments - the largest mutual fund company in the U.S. and a leading provider of financial services, chairman, of its Operating Committee; President, Fidelity Investments Institutional Retirement Group, responsible for Fidelity's retirement products and related services offered to corporations, not-for-profit organizations and government entities, and Fidelity's benefits outsourcing and human resources/payroll administration and processing services to corporate clients, 1996- '00; formerly president, Fidelity Institutional Retirement Services Company, and an executive vice president of Fidelity Management Trust Company, which manages pension assets for large corporations, endowments and public entities; joined Fidelity, 1984; Senior vice president of NCNB (now Bank of America) in Charlotte, North Carolina, 1977 –'84;

RILEY, Patrick James 'Pat'; BASKETBALL HEAD COACH MIAMI HEAT, AUTHOR
Born, 20, March 1945, Rome, New York,; after a career as a basketball player retired 1976; returned to NBA as a broadcaster for the Lakers, 1977; became one of the team's assistant coaches during the 1979-80 season; became head coach during the 1981-82 season, led the Lakers to four consecutive NBA Finals appearances, took the title against Philadelphia 76ers 1982, Boston Celtics 1985, Boston Celtics, 1987, Detroit Pistols, 1988, becoming the first team in 20 years to repeat as champions; NBA Coach of the Year, 1990; head Coach New York Knicks, 1991 –'95; Coach of the Year, 1993; Head Coach, Miami Heat 1995 –'04; General Manager Miami Heat 2004 –'05' Head Coach Miami Heat 2005 – todate; posted an unprecedented record of thirteen straight seasons of fifty plus wins, an iconic sports personality, considered one of the greatest NBA coaches of all time; known for his trademark Armani suits on the basketball court, is a close friend of the designers; a noted motivational speaker; author: Showtime, Inside The Lakers Breakthrough Season, 1990; The Winner Within, 1994 (paperback).

ROARTY, Michael J 'Mike'; FORMER VICE PRESIDENT, CORPORATE MARKETING AND COMMUNICATIONS ANHEUSER BUSCH
Born, 1929, Detroit, Michigan; 2nd generation Irish American with roots in Mayo and Donegal; Joined Anheuser Busch,1953; Executive Vice President-Marketing, Anheuser-Busch, Incorporated,1983-'90; .rose though the ranks in A.B. while capturing upwards of nearly 46% of the beer share in America; appointed Vice President, Corporate Marketing and Communications, 1990 - '94; appointed, Chairman, of the Company's subsidiary, Busch Media Group, Inc., 1990 –'94; Chief Executive Officer, Busch Creative Services Corporation, 1990 –'94; Consultant Anheuser Busch, 1994 – ' ; cited by Advertising Age as one of that year's 10 top newsmakers in his profession, 1986; widely respected throughout the brewing, advertising and broadcasting industries, has continually been recognized as one of the 10 most influential people in all of sports, is well-known among many of the nation's leaders and has scores of friends and associates around the globe; former President, Irish US Council for Industry and Commerce; member, Ireland America Economic Advisory Board.

ROCHE, Kevin Eamonn; ARCHITECT
Born, 1922, Michelstown, Co Cork, Ireland; educated, Rockwell College, Tipperary, University College Dublin, B. Architecture; Principal Design Associate to Eero Saarinen 1950-'61; Upon Mr. Saarinen's death, completed works in progress which included the TWA Terminal at JFK Airport, Dulles International Airport, CBS Headquarters in New York City, and the St. Louis Arch. Firm became Kevin Roche John Dinkeloo and Associates in 1966; As Design Principal his completed works include 8 museums, 38 corporate headquarters, 7 research labs, performing arts center, theatres, campus buildings for 6 universities and for the past 38 years developed the master plan for the Metropolitan Museum of Art in New York City; Projects in design or under construction in USA, Europe and Asia; Awards: 1977 Academie d'Architecture Grand Gold Medal, 1982 Pritzker Architecture Prize, 1990 American Academy of Arts & Letters Gold Medal Award for Architecture, 1993 American Institute of Architects Gold Medal Award.

ROONEY, Daniel M 'Dan'; PRESIDENT PITTSBURGH STEELERS FOOTBALL CLUB
Born, 20, July 1932, Pittsburg PA, 2nd generation Irish American, roots in Newry, Co. Down; Served more than 45 years with the Pittsburgh Steelers organization; has emerged as one of the most active executives in the National Football League; Credited for coming up with the '*Rooney Rule*', (requires NFL teams with head coaching and general manager vacancies to interview at least one minority candidate); Inducted into the Pro Football Hall of Fame, 2000; 1972 - todate, Steelers have been AFC Central Division champions 14 times, AFC champions six times and won five Super Bowls; With Sir Anthony O'Reilly (*qv*) founded The Ireland Fund 1976; serves on the Ireland Fund board; serves on the boards of many organizations, United Way, University of Pittsburgh Medical Center, American Diabetes Association to name but a few; Benefactor of the Rooney Prize for Irish Literature.

ROONEY, Patrick; PRESIDENT & CEO INVESTMENT CORPORATION OF PALM BEACH
Born, Pittsburg, PA, 2nd generation Irish American, roots in Newry, Co. Down; President, CEO, Palm Beach Kennel Club1978 – '02; President, Green Mountain Race Track, Vermont,1973-'92; President, Continental Racing Association PA,1969-'73; General Manager, Liberty Bell1964-'69; Pennsylvania National Guard; Sales Representative, CG Hussey Company, PA, 1960-'63; Shareholder and Director: Yonkers Racing Corp; Pittsburgh Steelers Football Club, Delta Electric; Investment Corp. of Palm Beach; Trustee, American College Dublin and Lynn University, Florida; Board of Governors, Inter coastal Health Systems.

ROONEY, Timothy 'Tim'; PRESIDENT YONKERS RACEWAY CORP.
Born, 1938, Pittsburg, PA, 2nd generation Irish American, roots in Newry, Co. Down; President of Yonkers Raceway, 1972 – todate (when the Rooney family purchased the Westchester County (NY) harness track); Since then, the third son of Pittsburgh Steelers founding father, Arthur J. Rooney, Sr., has seen the Raceway maintain its status as one of the premier Standardbred facilities in North America; A successful horse breeder and owner, received the 1997 Man of the Year from the Standardbred Owners Association of New York; numerous charitable endeavors have also been recognized; received the Terence Cardinal Cooke Award at the New York City CYO annual Club of Champions Dinner,1997, Police Athletic League of Yonkers honored him as Man of the Year, 1999, The Emerald Golf Society and the American Irish Association of Westchester have also honored him; a partner for 10 years with the investment banking house of Chaplin, McGuiness Company of Pittsburgh, an associate member of the New York Stock Exchange and the American Stock Exchange; Business manager, family owned Shamrock Farms, operational since 1948, it is Maryland's oldest breeding facility; President, Delta Electric, a Westchester County electrical contracting corporation, director, Pittsburgh Steelers, Vice-president, Palm Beach (FL) Kennel Club; Grand Marshall, St. Patrick's Day Parade, New York, 2006; Board Member, The American Ireland Fund. 1987 – todate; Associated with many other organizations including Irish-American Children's Research Foundation, Hospice Palm Beach and the Pittsburgh Steelers to name but a few; coowns a stud farm in Co. Kildare, Ireland.

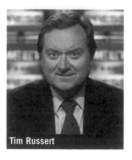
Tim Russert

RUSSERT, Timothy John Jnr 'Tim'; BROADCASTER
Born, 7, May 1950, Buffalo, New York, 4th generation Irish American, roots in Cork, a cousin of legendary hurler Christy Ring; counselor, Governor Mario Cuomo 1983-'84; chief of staff, Senator Daniel Moynihan 1977-'82; joined NBC News 1984; political analyst Today Show, NBC Nightly News; Host, Meet the Press (NBC) 1991- to date; Host, Tim Russert Show, CNBC; Snr Vice Pres/Washington Bureau Chief News NBC - to date; Publ. Big Russ and Me, 2004; Wisdom of Our Fathers: Lessons and Letters from Daughters and Sons, 2006; Awards: Emmy 2005; Golden Plate Award of the Academy of Achievement; Joan S. Barone Award, Annenberg Center's Walter Cronkite Award, John Peter Zenger Award, American Legion Journalism Award, Veterans of Foreign Wars News Media Award, Congressional Medal of Honor Society Journalism Award, Allen H. Neuharth Award for Excellence in Journalism, David Brinkley Award for Excellence in Communication, Academy for Communication's Gabriel Award.

RYAN, Arthur F; CHAIRMAN AND CEO, THE PRUDENTIAL INSURANCE COMPANY OF AMERICA
Born,1942, Brooklyn, New York, and raised on Long Island; Control Data Corporation, various positions, 1965–'72; Chase Manhattan Bank, project manager, data processing, 1972–'75; securities processing,1975–'76; head of securities processing,1976–'78; oversaw domestic wholesale operations; 1982–'84, head of bank's systems worldwide,1978–'82; executive vice president, worldwide retail-banking operations,1984–'85; vice chairman, retail banking,1985–'90; president and chief operating officer,1990–'94; Prudential Insurance Company of America, chief executive officer and chairman, 1994–'01, first outsider to be named chief executive officer (CEO) and chairman of Prudential Insurance Company of America; Prudential Financial, chief executive officer and chairman, 2001– todate; Other Directorships include Regeneron Pharmaceuticals, Inc.; Awards: National Alumni Personal Achievement Award, 75th Anniversary Alumni Services Award, and the Diamond Anniversary Award, Providence College; Member, Ireland America Economic Advisory Board

RYAN, John 0; CHAIRMAN CO FOUNDER MACROVISION CORP
Born, 1946, Tipperary Town, Ireland; moved to California 1974; co-founded Macrovision, 1983; an inventor of Macrovision's core copy protection technologies; (This technology was the first that blocked widespread copying of VHS tapes;also invented the PhaseKrypt scrambling method); holds 50 U.S. patents in television camera design, and video and audio security; his patents appear on many common household electronics, including three on DVD players alone; has succeeded in a field that is viewed as the only way to prevent pirating and file sharing, an ever-growing global problem for businesses; Macrovision is now a publicly traded, multi national company valued at over a billion dollars with over 650 employees; It has received patents for video-cassette protection technology for use in digital pay-per-view media markets; has served as Chairman of the Board of Directors since June 1991; served as Macrovision's Chief Executive Officer from June 1995 - October '01; served as Macrovision's Vice-Chairman of the Board of Directors from 1987 - June '91; Prior to founding Macrovision, was Director, Research and Development of Ampex Corporation's

broadcast camera group for six years; Before Ampex Corporation, served as a staff engineer in camera development for three years at International Video Corporation; Prior to that held various technical positions at Yorkshire T.V. Ltd. in England and Radio Telefis Eireann, Ireland, 1966; Awards: 'Silicon Valley Inventor of the Year', 1997; Spirit of Ireland Award; Author, several technical articles on the subject of television camera design; Board Member, University of Limerick Foundation; continues commitment to his home town, shown by his sponsorship of the Excel Centre heritage project through American Ireland funding, (The Excel Centre, dedicated to the development of artistic and cultural life in Tipperary Town incorporates the Ballet Ireland workshop for children; the project has brought new life into the centre of Tipperary and created a focal point for its rich cultural history); also provides annual scholarships to three secondary schools in Tipperary; The Tipperary Technology Park also benefited from seed capital assistance provided by John and his wife Pauline.

RYAN, PATRICK G 'Pat'; FOUNDER, CHAIRMAN AON CORPORATION

Born 1937; started out selling insurance policies at his father's car dealership, 1964, eventually created his own company The Ryan Group, Chief Executive, 1964 – merger with Combined International Corporation; first sold warranties and then moved to other products, taking his business to Chicago; hoped to "go national and create specialty insurance agents for every industry" (*Forbes*, August 23, 1999); Ryan Corporation went public in 1971 with $27 million in sales; merged his company with Combined International Corporation, 1982 into what came to be called Aon Corporation, 1987; ("Aon" is Gaelic for unity or oneness); Chief Executive, 1982- '05; Executive Chairman 1990 – todate; Aon is the world's second-largest insurance brokerage and consulting company, after March & McLennan; After the 2001 terrorist attacks, Ryan hired the consulting firm of Rudolph Giuliani, the former mayor of New York, to help revamp the Aon's image after the tragedy; Aon had 1,151 employees in 2 World Trade Center and lost 176; reopened an office in Lower Manhattan in June 2003; One of Chicago's most visible business and civic leaders, numerous tributes including 2001 Man of the Year for the Juvenile Diabetes Research Foundation, Greater Chicago Chapter; 1997 Crain's Chicago Business Executive of the Year Award; College of Insurance's Insurance Leader of the Year; with wife Shirley awarded 1998 Distinguished Philanthropist Award, (The Ryans founded and are active in the Pathways Center and the Pathways Awareness Foundation, dedicated to serving the needs and interests of children and young people with physical movement difficulties); Chairman, Board of Trustees of Northwestern University, life trustee, Rush University Medical Center; Director, Chicago Bears Football Club, Inc.; Chairman and CEO, Chicago 2016 Olympic Evaluation Committee .member, Ireland America Economic Advisory Board

RYAN, Pauline E; MACROVISION, INC

Born, Ireland: Has had considerable involvement in the educational sector; Former Chair, National Convention of High School Leaders; Former member, Freemont Union School District Foundation Board; involved with the PTA of both Cupertino School District and Freemont Union High School District; The John and Pauline Ryan Foundation has funded several education projects in Tipperary; member, American Ireland Fund

RYAN, Timothy James 'Tim'; CONGRESSMAN

Born, 16, July 1973 Ohio; Congressional aide U.S. House of Representatives Jim Traficant 1995; Intern Trumbull County Prosecutor's Office; Ohio State Senator 2000-'02; congressman Ohio's 17th District 2003 to date, when he took office was the youngest Democrat in the house of Representatives; Member, House Armed Services Committee, House Committee on Education and the Workforce, Co-chair House Manufacturing Caucus; member, member, Thirty Something Working Group, which is a Congressional caucus composed of all of the members of the US House of Representatives who are in their 30s or younger; was the inspiration of the 2005 movie "Steel Valley".

SCHLOSSBERG KENNEDY, Caroline Bouvier; AUTHOR
Born, 27, November 1957, New York City; 4th generation Irish American, father, John F. Kennedy's roots in Co. Wexford; interned with uncle Ted Kennedy (qv), interned at New York Daily New; worked at the Metropolitan Museum of Art, 1980; coauthored with Ellen Alderman In Our Defense - The Bill of Rights In Action, 1990; and The Right to Privacy, 1995; president of the Kennedy Library Foundation,2006, chairperson of the American Ballet Theatre; adviser to the Harvard Institute of Politics, a living memorial to her father.

SCULLEY, Arthur B; GENERAL PARTNER SCULLEY BROTHERS LLC
General Partner, Sculley Brothers LLC, (with brother John (qv) and David (qv) a private international investment and advisory firm, 1995 – todate; Joined JP Morgan 1970, spent twenty-five years at the $80 billion private bank, sixteen years in corporate finance and nine years in asset management; was head and a Managing Director; During the 1970's spent eight years in Hong Kong and Singapore helping to establish Morgan's presence in S.E. Asia; Left JP Morgan 1995 and specialized in B2B and B2B exchanges primarily in financial services; Was an early pioneer in recognizing the importance of the internet to large corporations; Institutional Investor selected him for the top twenty people revolutionizing online finance, 1997; has been co-founder and/or Chairman of several highly successful B2B companies including IntraLinks, Credit Trade ad the electronic Bermuda Stock Exchange; has become a world-recognized authority on B2B exchanges and has acted as an advisor to the governments of Ireland, New Zealand and Bermuda; Author, co-authored a best seller business book: B2B Exchanges – The Killer Application in the Business-to-Business Internet Revolution published in four languages, 1999.

SCULLEY, David; MANAGING PARTNER SCULLEY BROTHERS LLC
Former, Managing Partner, The Blackburn Group; Managing Partner, Sculley Brothers LLC, (with brothers John (qv) and Arthur (qv) 1985 - todate; Senior Vice President and Member, Board of Directors, H, J. Heinz Company; President and CEO, Heinz U.S.A; Deputy Manager, Heinz U.K; Group Products Manager, Lever Brother, New York; Director, Waterford Wedgwood, PLC; I Touch; Wolfgang Puck Worldwide; Bermuda Perfumery; Chairman, Country Gourmet Foods LLC; Board Member, The Bermuda Perfumery; actively involved with Harvard University

SCULLEY, John; PARTNER, SCULLEY BROTHERS LLC
Born,6, April 1939, New York City; joined the Pepsi-Cola division of PepsiCo, 1967; appointed company's youngest marketing vice-president, 1970; invented Pepsi Challenge (an advertising campaign initiated from Sculley's own research

that Pepsi-Cola tasted better than Coca-Cola.),1980; Joined Apple Computers, 1983 –'94, becoming CEO, 1985; signed on with Spectrum Information Technologies, a US$100 million wireless communications company, 1994; major supporter, President Bill Clinton, 1992; Partner, Sculley Brothers LL C 1995 – todate (with brothers David (qv) and Arthur (qv); Joined the board of directors, OpenPeak, 2004; named Chairman of IdenTrust (formerly Digital Signature Trust Company) 2006;

SCULLY, Sean; ARTIST
Born, 1945, Inchicore, Dublin, Ireland; Manager, Vinyl Club, Soho, London 1965; moved to New York permanently in 1975; Teacher, Princeton University; Donated eight of his works to the newly-reopened Hugh Lane Gallery, Dublin, Ireland – where they're housed in a bespoke room, now has a permanent place in his home city; is a leading representative of a new generation of abstract painters and his work is already strongly acclaimed, and has been exhibited in museums such as the Metropolitan Museum of Art, New York, 2000, the Albright-Knox Gallery, 1998-'99, Galleria de Arte Moderna, Bologna and Gallerie de Jeu de Paumme, Pais, 1996; work is heavily influenced by the American and European traditions, embodied in the figures of Mondrian and Matisse in Europe, and Pollock and Rothko in America. How to combine these different influences has remained the basic question of Scully's work, to which he gave slightly different answers throughout the decades.

SHEEHAN, Michael 'Mike'; PRESIDENT CEO HILL, HOLLIDAY
The first non-founder to hold the title of CEO at Hill, Holliday, one of the15 largest agencies in the United States; joined Hill, Holliday, from DDB Chicago, where he was Executive, creative director, 2000; Prior to that, was executive creative director of Hill, Holliday's Boston office; also worked at Leo Burnett Chicago, as well as ClarkeGoward and Ingalls Quinn & Johnson, Boston. (As a creative director and copywriter, Mike has created campaigns for many leading U.S. brands, including McDonald's, John Hancock, Dunkin' Donuts, Tyco, Fidelity Investments, Maytag, Gatorade and Budweiser); his work has received virtually every local, national, and international creative, including the Grand Clio, One Show Gold, Cannes Lion; Best of Show at Hatch, and Communication Arts; Adweek's National Creative Director of the Year, 1998; Currently Chairman, Board of Trustees. Saint Anselm College; Serves, Board of Trustees of Thayer Academy and Cardinal Cushing School, where he chairs the Capital Campaign.

SHEEHAN, Robert; LAWYER
Born, 1944, New York, Irish roots Co. Westmeath; Called to the New York Bar, 1970; joined Skadden, Arps, Slate, Meagher and Flom 1969; rose successively to partner 1978, executive partner 1994 - to date.

SHEEN, Martin; ACTOR
Born, 3, August 1940, Dayton, Ohio as Ramón Gerardo Antonio Estévez ; 1st generation, Irish American maternal side, Co. Tipperary (Mary Phelan);has appeared in over fifty movies; his first major role was on Broadway, in *The Subject Was Roses*, which he recreated in the 1968 film of the same name; best known for todate; star of The West Wing (President Bartlet; has been arrested more than 60 times for public demonstrations; The Green Party asked Sheen to run for President with Ralph Nader, 1996; Emmy Outstanding Guest Actor in a Comedy Series, *Murphy Brown*, 1994; Hollywood Walk of Fame 1500 Vine St.

SHRIVER, Maria Owings; FIRST LADY OF CALIFORNIA, JOURNALIST
Born, 6, February 1955, Chicago, Illinois; 4th generation Irish on maternal side (Eunice Kennedy Shriver); wife of Arnold Swartzeneger, Governor of California; TV : contributing anchor Dateline NBC 1989 - 04; co-anchored the *CBS* Morning News; has won Peabodyand Emmy awards; Author of five best-selling books: What's Heaven, Ten Things I Wish I'd Known Before I Went Out Into The Real World, What's Wrong with Timmy?, What's Happening to Grandpa?, and And One More Thing Before You Go; member board, Special Olympics.

SMITH KENNEDY, Jean; Former US Ambassador to Ireland
Born, 20, February 1928, Brookline, Massachusetts, 3rd generation Irish American, roots in Co. Wexford; founded the Very Special Arts, a nonprofit organization which promotes the artistic talents of mentally and physically challenged children, 1974; appointed by President Bill Clinton as the American Ambassador to Ireland, 1993 – '98, continuing a legacy of diplomacy begun by her father, Joseph Kennedy, who was Ambassador to the Court of St. James's during the Roosevelt administration; played a pivotal role in the peace process in that region for almost five years; board member, John F. Kennedy Center for the Performing Arts.

SMYTH, Edward D, 'Ted'; SENIOR VICE PRESIDENT, CORPORATE AND GOVERNMENT AFFAIRS, H.J. HEINZ COMPANY
Born, Ireland; Vice President, Corporate Affairs, 1988- '98; Press Secretary, Irish Government in Great Britain, 1985-'88; Diplomatic Service of Ireland: serving embassies and offices in Portugal, Washington, D.C, New York and London; Special Advisor, Irish Prime Minister on Media Matters and Anglo-Irish Affairs 1974-'75; delegate, Conference on Security and Cooperation, Geneva, Switzerland.

SOMMERS, Suzanne Marie (née Hamilton); LIFESTYLE GURU ACTOR
Born, 16, October 1946, San Bruno, California, 2nd generation Irish American; Best known in Serial Mom, 1994, Say It Ain't So, 2001; multiple TV appearances from 1963 – todate. Established Suzanne Summers Inc, specializing in diet, fitness, lifestyle and fashion design; Author, Suzanne Sommers Diet, Touch Me, The Poems of Suzanne Sommers; Motivational speaker.

STACK, Brian; PRESIDENT AND CEO CIE TOURS, NA INC.
Born, Dublin, Ireland; In the seventeen years that Brian Stack has been president and CE0, CIE Tours has grown into the single largest generator of tourists to Ireland; long considered the best operator of Ireland tours, Travel & Leisure magazine readers voted CIE Tours one of the top 10 tour operators in the world; vice president of the Ireland-U.S. Council for Commerce and Industry, board member, Irish the American Cultural Society, The Travelers Conservation Foundation.

SULLIVAN, Brian; NEUROSURGEON
Born, Washington, DC, 3rd generation Irish American; Dr. Neurosurgeon, Anne Arundel Medical Center at John Hopkins Hospital, Maryland;member of, and a partner in the Maryland Neurological Institute; offering new hope to patients with spinal and neck injuries; received nationwide attention for a new clinical trial involving inserting a cervical disc prosthesis into the space between the patient's neck vertebra. While traditional treatment fuses the two vertebra together, leaving part of the neck permanently immobile, the new procedure allows the patient to move his neck afterwards, and puts him on track for a speedier, more productive recovery; current interests include stereotactic radiosurgery, complex spinal surgery, and hc the aforementioned FDA trial of a cervical disc prosthesis that he is leading.

SULLIVAN, Craig G; RETIRED CHAIRMAN AND CEO, THE CLOROX COMPANY
Former, Chairman & CEO, The Clorox Company; held various Management and Senior Management positions of increasing responsibility, including Stints with Procter & Gamble, American Express; Other associations include Director, Levi Strauss & Company and Grocery Manufacturers of America; former Chairman, International Advisory Board of the Center for Corporate Community Relations at Boston College; Director, Bay Area Chapter of the Red Cross, Director for the Bay Area Council and Oakland Ballet; Member Board, Governors for The Commonwealth Club of California.

SULLIVAN, James; EXECUTIVE VICE PRESIDENT MARRIOTT INTERNATIONAL
Born 1944; has held several positions with Marriott International, Inc. (and its predecessor, Marriott Corp.), including Vice President of Mergers and Acquisitions, and his current position of Executive Vice President of Development. From 1983 to 1986, Mr. Sullivan was Chairman, President

and Chief Executive Officer of Tenly Enterprises, Inc., a privately held company operating 105 restaurants. Prior to 1983, he held senior management positions with Marriott Corp., Harrah's Entertainment, Inc., Holiday Inns, Inc., Kentucky Fried Chicken Corp. and Heublein, Inc. He also was employed as a senior auditor with Arthur Andersen & Co. and served as a director of Classic Vacation Group, Inc. until it was acquired by Expedia, Inc. in March 2002, director, Integra Life Sciences Holdings Corporation, 1992 – todate; Member, Ireland America Economic Advisory Board.

SULLIVAN, Michael John 'Mike'; FORMER US AMBASSADOR TO IRELAND

Born 22, September 1939; Omaha, Nebraska, Irish roots on both sides of his family, Beara Peninsula, Co. Cork; Governor State of Wyoming 1987 –'95, US Ambassador to Ireland 1999 – '01, partner Rothgerber, Johnson & Lyons LL.P 2001 – todate, director Allied Irish Banks 2001 – todate, Director of Kerry Group plc, Sletten Construction Inc., Cimarex Energy, Inc., First Interstate BancSystem, Inc., and a Trustee of the Catholic Diocese of Wyoming, member of the Bar, State of Wyoming.

SWANSON, Denis D; PRESIDENT STATION OPERATION FOX TV

Born, 1940, Springfield, Illinois; After a job doing everything at WMT (AM) and WMT-TV (now KGAN-TV) Cedar Rapids, Iowa, it was quickly on to WGN Chicago and then to desk and producer jobs at NBC News in Chicago and at its owned station in the Windy City, WMAQ; executive producer KABC Los Angeles 1976; WLS General manager; discovered Oprah Winfrey and brought her to Chicago; head of ABC Sports 1986 –'96; NBC New York 1996 –'02; Executive VP and COO, Viacom's 40 CBS and UPN stations 2002 '05; President Station Operation Fox TV 2005 - todate.

Anne Sweeney

SWEENEY, Anne; PRESIDENT, DISNEY-ABC TELEVISION GROUP

Born, 1957, New York, traces Irish roots Meath, Kerry, Mayo; joined Nickelodeon/Nick at Nite 1981, various exec positions incl snr vice pres program enterprises; Chairman, CEO FX Networks Inc 1993-6; joined Walt Disney Company 1996 as president Disney Channel & exec vice-pres Disney/ABC Networks 1996-'00; president ABC Cable Networks Group & Disney Channel Worldwide 2000-'04; co-chair of Disney Media Networks and president, Disney-ABC Television Group 2004 to date; inducted into the Broadcasting & Cable "Hall of Fame" 2005, 2004 Muse Award from New York Women in Film & Television; honored repeatedly by Women in Cable & Telecommunications; STAR Award from American Women in Radio and Television; inducted into the American Advertising Federation's Advertising Hall of Achievement in 1996; Women in Film's Lucy Award 2002; named "Most Powerful Woman in Entertainment" by The Hollywood Reporter, one of the "50 Most Powerful Women in Business" by Fortune and one of "The World's 100 Most Powerful Women" by Forbes.

SWEENEY, John J; LABOR LEADER

Born, 5, May 1934, The Bronx, New York; 1st generation Irish American, both parents emigrated; President of the AFL-CIO; An AFL-CIO vice president since 1980, he was elected president of the AFL-CIO at the federation's biennial convention, October 1995; most recently re-elected, 2005; with three million workers under its umbrella, judged to be the most powerful Labor leader in the United States.

TANI, Dan; ASTRONAUT
Born, 1961, Ridley Park, Pennsylvania; Irish citizen;; *m* Jane née Egan, Kinsale, Co. Cork, Ireland; 1s; Astronaut; worked at Hughes Aircraft Corporation in El Segundo, California as a design engineer in the Space and Communications group. worked for Bolt Beranek and Newman in Cambridge, Massachusetts, in the experimental psychology department; 1988, senior structures engineer, Orbital Sciences Corporation (OSC) in Dulles Virginia; promoted mission operations manager for the Transfer Orbit Stage (TOS); served as the TOS flight operations lead, working with NASA/JSC mission control in support of the deployment of the ACTS/TOS payload during the STS-51 mission in September 1993; moved to the Pegasus program at OSC as the launch operations manager - served as lead for the development of procedures and constraints for the launching of the air launched Pegasus unmanned rocket; was also responsible for defining, training, and leading the team of engineers who worked in the launch and control room. 1996 selected as an astronaut candidate by NASA Johnson Space Center; 1998 qualified for flight assignment as a mission specialist; held technical duties in the Astronaut Office Computer Support Branch, and EVA Branch; served as a Crew Support Astronaut (CSA) for Expedition-2; flew on STS-108 in 2001, has logged over 11 days in space, including over 4 EVA hours in one space walk; is currently assigned as the Expedition-11 backup flight engineer; AWARDS: Orbital Sciences Corporation Outstanding Technical Achievement Award, 1993.

THOMPSON, H. Brian; CHAIRMAN, PRESIDENT CEO UNIVERSAL TELECOMMUNICATIONS INC
Heads his own private equity investment and advisory firm, Universal Telecommunications, Inc.,; was previously chairman and CEO of Global TeleSystems Group, Inc; also served as chairman and CEO of Virginia-based LCI International, Inc. 1991 – '98, and is widely credited for leading the transformation of the money-losing, debt-laden, US$200 million long distance company into a US$2 billion national, top competitor ranked among *Fortune*'s 100 fastest-growing companies. Thompson merged LCI, with an enterprise value of more than US$5 billion, with Qwest, 1998; serves as a member of the board of directors of Bell Canada International Inc., DynCorp, ArrayComm, Inc., Axcelis Technologies, Inc., and United Auto Group, also co-chairs the Global Information Infrastructure Commission member, Ireland America Economic Advisory Board.,

TILLOTSON, John; PRESIDENT & CEO ARENA BRANDS, INC.
Irish roots, Kilkenny and Co. Limerick; previously, Account Executive, IBM; Regional Sales Manager, Farah Mfg. Co. Vice President, Sales & Marketing, General Manager, Farah Europe; Executive Vice President, Vanity Fair, Lee Co.; President and COO, Lucchese; also associated with: Board, St. Paul's Medical Center Foundation, The Jesuit College Preparatory School, Association for the Independent Living for the Mentally Challenged; Patron, Vatican Arts, Dallas Opera, executive committee member, American Ireland Fund; Grand Marshall, St. Patrick's Day Parade, Dallas, 2006.

TIMMONS, Edward; PRESIDENT, TIMMINS & ASSOCIATES, LLC
Member, The American Ireland Fund 2000 – to date; Chairman of the board, Denver Public Schools, Chairperson-elect, Executive Council, Colorado Bar Association and fellow, Colorado Bar Foundation; Chaired, Harvard Schools Committee, Director of Otten, Johnson, Robinson, Neff & Ragonetti Law Firm.

TIMONEY, John; CHIEF OF THE CITY OF MIAMI POLICE
Born, 1948, Dublin, Ireland; emigrated to New York, 1961; joined the New York Police Department, 1967 where he rose to First Deputy Commissioner; was recognized, with then Commissioner William Brattan, to be the architect of the Zero Tolerance crime policy which cleaned up the City and made it one of the safest cities in the US; was the youngest person in New York City history to hold the "four star" position of Chief of Department; he is the recipient of over 65 Department Medals, including the prestigious Medal of Valor; Police Commissioner of the Philadelphia Police Department, where he commanded a diverse police force of approximately 7,000 officers and over 900 civilian employees in the fifth largest metropolitan city in the United States, 1998 – '01; joined international security company, New York, 2002 – '03; before being appointed Police Chief Miami 2003 – todate; has been personally requested by high-ranking government officials to make a security needs assessment in Haiti, as well as to evaluate detainee facilities in Guantanamo Bay, Cuba; serves on the boards of the Police Executive Research Forum, the Penn Institute for Urban Research, Philadelphia University, and Cedars Medical Center; also Co-Chairman of the FBI's South Florida Joint Terrorism Task Force.

TIMONEY, Peter Joseph; VETERINARIAN, HEAD GLUCK EQUINE RESEARCH CENTER
Born, 1941, Dublin, Ireland; Research Associate, College of Vet. Med. University of Illinois, 1964-'66; Research officer Vet Res Laboratory, Abbotstown, Dublin, ireland 1966-'72; head Equine Diseases Section Abbotstown 1972-'79; Assoc Prof & Snr Virologist NY State Coll Vet. Med, Cornell University 1979-'81; Scientific Director Irish Equine Centre, Kildare 1981-'83; Prof virology & assoc chrm research, University Kentucky 1987-'89; Chairman, Dept Vet Science & acting dir Maxwell H. Gluck Equine Research Center, University of Kentucky 1989-'90; Chairman, Dept Vet Science, University, Kentucky 1990-'99, 2002; Director, Maxwell H. Gluck Equine Research Center 1990 - to date; O.I. E. Designated World Expert on Equine Viral Arteritis.

TOWNSEND, Stuart; Actor

Born, 15, December 1972, Howth, Dublin, Ireland; studied acting at the Gaiety School Dublin; film debut, Trojan Eddie, 1996, Best Known for About Adam, 2000, Queen of the Damned 2002, Trapped 2002, Head in the Clouds, 2004, Best Man, 2005, Chaos Theory 2006; partner, Charlize Theron.

TULLY, Daniel P 'Dan'; CHAIRMAN EMERITUS, MERRILL LYNCH & CO INC

Born, 1932, New York, 1st generation Irish American, father born in Donegal; Chief Executive Merrill Lynch 1993 – 1997; spent his entire business career at Merrill Lynch, beginning in 1955 in the accounting department; within two years he was named operations manager of the Stamford, Conn., office; his rise through the company was rapid; account executive, 1959, manager, Stamford office, 1970, vice president of the firm 1971; successive appointments placed him on the Board of the firm's principal securities subsidiary, Merrill Lynch, Pierce, Fenner & Smith, and in a wide range of management positions, leading to his being named President and Chief Operating Officer in 1985; Chief Executive Officer from 1992 – '96, Chairman, 1993 to '97; has served as vice chairman of the American Stock Exchange and the Securities Industry Association, director, New York Stock Exchange, including a term as vice chairman; member, Ireland America Economic Advisory Board; former president, Ireland United States Council for Commerce and Industry former chairman, Board of Governors of NASD; In four years at the helm, Chairman and CEO Tully steered Merrill Lynch to record earnings and completed its shift from a retail brokerage Goliath to a global investment banking powerhouse. The 65-year-old Tully, who stepped down as CEO on Dec. 27, defused the Orange County disaster, built Merrill into a top M&A player, and doubled assets under management—all of which helped triple Merrill's stock, to 82, during his tenure.

UNGARO KELLEHER , Susan; FORMER EDITOR IN CHIEF FAMILY CIRCLE

Born, 1954, Manhattan, NYC, 1st generation Irish American, both parents hailed from Castlegregory, Co. Kerry; worked for the school newspaper and radio station (William Patterson University);upon graduation, she headed for Manhattan's magazine publishing world and began working her way up Family Circle's masthead; appointed Editor in Chief 1994, responsible for maintaining a magazine that 4.5 million women want to read and buy every three week, under her leadership, Family Circle received several awards, including a National Magazine Award; she herself has been honored with such awards as the President's Award from the New Jersey Press Women's Association and the William Patterson University Legacy Award; served as Editorial Consultant for Gruner & Jahr's Rosie: The Magazine.

VAN KIRK, Francis J 'Fran'; OFFICE MANAGING PARTNER-PHILADELPHIA PRICEWATERHOUSECOOPERS
With over 30 years with PWC, one of the senior client engagement partners; serves as an advisor to client management and the firm partnership among others and his clients have included GlaxoSmithKline, VF Corporation, C&D Technologies, Hercules Incorporated, and The West Company; Member, both the American and Pennsylvania Institutes of Certified Public Accountants; serves on the boards and executive committees of the greater Philadelphia Chamber of Commerce and YMCA of Philadelphia. member, Board of The American Ireland Fund.

VAN SUSTEREN, Greta; LAWYER, JOURNALIST
Born, 11, June 1955, Appleton, Wisconsin; Irish roots on her maternal side; hosts On The Record, Fox TV, the highest rated on cable news at 10 p.m. (EST). She previously worked at CNN from 1991 – 02; first came to prominence in 1991, covering the William Kennedy Smith trial for CNN; was given a co-anchor spot alongside political analyst Roger Cossack on the legal affairs news show Burden of Proof; also hosted the primetime program The Point with Greta Van Susteren which was the second highest rated program on CNN.

VARGO, Trina Y; PRESIDENT IRISH AMERICAN ALLIANCE
Born, 6, February 1962, Kittanning, Pennsylvania; Irish roots traced to her maternal grandfather whose name was Daugherty and most likely hailed from Donegal; Founded Irish US Alliance, a non-profit, non-partisan organization dedicated to educating Americans about Ireland and to strengthening the relationship for the years to come In that capacity, she created the George J. Mitchell Scholarships which has already become recognized as one of the most prestigious scholarships for study abroad for young Americans, 1998; Foreign Policy Adviser to Senator Edward M. Kennedy (D-MA) in Washington D.C. 1987 –'98; recognized as "the leading expert on Ireland on Capitol Hill," was named one of Irish America Magazine's "Top 100 Irish Americans, 1995

VINCENT – KIERAN, A.W.B 'Billie'; PHILANTHROPIST
Born, 1926, Killarney, Co Kerry; President Ireland Fund of Monaco, Vice Chairman International Ireland Funds; Property interests throughout the United States, Hiler Aircraft Company, Inistech cap fund; served Royal Inniskilling Fusilliers; Director Independent News Media; Freeman Killarney, Ireland; Hon Fellow, Maudlin College Oxford, Pres The American Irish Foundation; Founder American Ireland Fund, 1983; Monaco, 1996, Ireland Fund Germany.

WALSH, James; CONGRESSMAN
Born, 1947 New York, 2nd generation Irish-American, roots in Tipperary; social services case worker Onondaga County; telephone company executive; former director Telecommunication Institute SUNY Institute of Technology; third district councilor City of Syracuse 1977-85; President Syracuse Common Council 1985; elected to House of Representatives for New York's 25th Congressional District 1988 to date; Republican; co-chairman House Appropriations Subcommittees (aka "the College of Cardinals"); Chairman Subcommittee on Military Construction, Veterans Affairs and Related Agencies; Chair MilQual; Chairman of the Friends of Ireland; co-chair of the U.S.-Irish Inter parliamentary Group; awards: 2002 Ellis Island Medal of Honor by the National Ethnic Coalition of Organizations; accompanied President Clinton to Northern Ireland twice and has led other delegations there; responsible for the Walsh Visa, (1998, reauthorized 2004), which as part of the peace process allows citizens from Northern Ireland and the border counties to live and work in the U.S. for three years.

WALSH, John; BROADCASTER, AUTHOR, CAMPAIGNER
Born 26, December 1945, Auburn, New York; Irish roots; TV Host, 'America's Most Wanted'; known for his anti-crime activism, particularly against those who target children; partner, hotel management company, Hollywood, Florida,1981; six year old son Adam was abducted, 27 July 1981; his severed head was found in a drainage canal more than 100 miles away from home, 12 August 1981; rest of body never recovered; soon began a campaign to help missing and exploited children; in spite of bureaucratic and legislative problems, John and wife Revé's efforts eventually led to the creation of the Missing Children Act of 1982 and the Missing Children's Assistance Act of 1984; founded the Adam Walsh Child Resource Center, a non-profit organization dedicated to legislative reform; The centers, originally located in West Palm Beach, Florida; Columbia, South Carolina; Orange County, California; and Rochester, New York; merged with the National Center for Missing and Exploited Children (NCMEC), where John Walsh serves on the Board of Directors; Host, Fox TV's America's Most Wanted, 1988 – todate; host John Walsh Show, 2002 –'04; Author, Tears of Rage",1997, "No Mercy", 1998, "Public Enemies", 2001.

WALSH, Siobhan; EXECUTIVE DIRECTOR, CONCERN WORLDWIDE USA
Born Limerick, Ireland; over the past 16 years, her work has taken her to Uganda, Rwanda, Congo, Ethiopia, Haiti, Burundi, Albania, Bangladesh, Somalia, Sri Lanka and more recently to Sudan; prior to joining Concern, she also worked as a Community worker in Ireland, caring for young girls who are victims of mental and physical abuse; is an active member of the Women's Foreign Policy Group, the National

Society of Fundraising Executives and an active member of Interaction, the US coalition for 170 international NGO's; has won a number of Awards including the European DMA Award - Direct Marketing Association Award for the creative design and innovation of a program called 'houses for life', which raised over $900,000 from companies in Ireland donating $450 to rebuild a home for families in Cambodia; has also been recognized for her passionate leadership style by Irish America Magazine, the leading publication focused on the success of the Irish in America; included in their annual listing of the top 100 people in business for her leadership and success in building the Concern Worldwide brand in America; has been recognized with the Fellowship Award from the American Ireland Fund; Her commitment to young people and the expansion of education to include programs that focus on international issues of poverty and hunger resulted in her being given a special recognition award by Cathedral High School in New York City.

WALSH, William 'Bill'; CHAIRMAN, SEQUOIA ASSOCIATES LLC, MENLO PARK, CA
Born, New York; Irish roots Mayo; Began his career, Assistant U.S. Attorney for Southern District of New York; became Counsel to New York State Commission of Investigation; worked as a Consultant for McKinsey & Co.; was Senior Vice President and CAO at Arcata Corporation; is also associated with the Board of Trustees at Fordham University; Member, Visiting Committee; Co-Chair, Harvard Law School; Order of Malta, St. Vincent de Paul Society, Scripps and the Hoover Institution.

WELCH, John Francis Jnr 'Jack'; FORMER CEO GENERAL ELECTRIC
Born, 19, November 1935, Peabody, Massachuetts, 2nd generation Irish American on both sides; CEO, General Electric, 1981-2001 increased the value of the company by more than $400 billion during his tenure; dubbed 'Neutron Jack' for eliminating employees while leaving buildings in tact; had a record $94 million salary and record $8 million a year retirement plan; remains a highly-regarded figure in business circles due to his innovative management strategies and leadership style; named 'Manager of the Century, Forbes Magazine, 1999; member, Board of NBC, trustee George Bush Presidential Library, member, Alfalfa Club 1983, member, American Philosophical Society, 2000, member, Augusta National Golf Club, member, National Academy of Engineering; Publications: At Any Cost, Straight From The Gut, The New GE: How Jack Welch Revived an American Institution, Winning by Jack and Suzy Welch, 2005; 2006, started teaching a class at MIT Sloan School of Management to a hand-picked group of dozen students who have demonstrated career interest in operational management.

WESTMAN, Tom; WINNER SURVIVOR REALITY TV SERIES
Born, 4, January 1964, Queens, New York; 3rd generation Irish American with roots in Clonbur, Co. Mayo and Waterford; winner CBS Survivor, Reality TV Series, 2005; former member FDNY; member, Uniformed Fire Officers Association, Fire Department of New York Emerald Society, Alexander Graham Bell Association for the Deaf and Hard of Hearing; supports the Thomas Elsasser Fund, (which raises funds for families of N.Y.C. firefighters who died), Disabled Sports USA; listed as one of TV Guides Sexiest Men; won million dollar contract for Caribbean Joe Clothing.

WHELAN, Wendy, BALLERINA
Born, 1968, Kentucky; joined New York City Ballet 1986, successively soloist 1989, principal dancer 1991 to date; has been called one of America's greatest dancers.

WILMOT, Helen M; VICE PRESIDENT CLINIC OPERATIONS, STANFORD HOSPITAL AND CLINICS
Born, 1963, Dublin Ireland; Vice President of Clinic Operations at Stanford Hospital and Clinics, (Palo Alto, California); Stanford Hospital has 4,000 employees and brings in $1.2 billion in annual revenues; leading the strategic initiative to build a $250 million outpatient center off-campus; Prior to Stanford, was senior vice president, strategy and development for Sensitron, Inc. (responsible for the private funding efforts and the company's business alliances); Has also worked for Concuity (formerly eHealthContracts) and Kaiser Permanente.

INDEX

A

1	ABBOTT, The Hon. Mr Justice, Henry
1	ABERCORN K.G., His Grace, Duke of, James, Hamilton
1	ABERCORN, Her Grace, Duchess of, Anastasia Alexandra, 'Sacha' née Phillips
1	ABRAHAMS, Declan
2	ACHESON, Carrie, née Barlow
2	ADAMS, Gerard, 'Gerry'
2	AGAR, David
2	AGNEW, David
3	AHERN, Bertie
3	AHERN, Cecelia
4	AHEARN, Dee
4	AHERN, Dermot Chris
4	AHERN, Michael
4	AHERN, Noel
5	AIKEN, James, 'Jim'
5	AIKEN, Peter, Kevin
5	AIKINS, Kingsley
5	AKRAM, Yasmine
6	ALDERDICE, Rt. Hon. LORD, John
6	ALLEN, Bert
6	ALLEN, Colm
7	ALLEN, née O'Connell, Darina
7	ALLEN, Elizabeth, 'Liz'
7	ALLEN, née Hill, Myrtle
7	ALLEN, Rachel Sheila née O'Neill
8	ANDREWS, Barry
8	ANDREWS, David
8	ARNOLD, Dr, Bruce, OBE
8	ARNOLD, Hugo
9	AUNGIER, Grace Mary
9	AUSTIN, Pat
9	AYLWARD, Liam, Gerard
9	AYLWARD, Seán

B

10	BACIK, Ivana, Catherine
10	BADDELEY, David, John
10	BAILEY, Michael 'Mick'
11	BAKER, Jane Catherine
11	BALLAGH, Robert
11	BALLINTINE, Sarah, Pamela
11	BALLYEDMOND, The Lord Edward Haughey
12	BANVILLE, John
12	BARDWELL, Leland
12	BARRETT, Gerry
12	BARRETT, Richard
12	BARRETT, Roy
13	BARRINGTON, Colm
13	BARRINGTON, Kathleen
13	BARRY, Frederick, John
13	BARRY, Gerald
14	BARRY, Gerald, Joseph 'Gerry'
14	BARRY, Oliver
14	BARRY, Peter
14	BARRY, Sebastian
15	BARRY, Susannah, Elizabeth
15	BARRY, Tony
15	BARTELS, Adriann, Gerben
15	BARTON, Bernard
16	BATES, Ray
16	BEGG, David

16	BEHAN, John
16	BENNETT, Mary
17	BENTON, Seán, Brian
17	BERESFORD, Marcus, Rt. Hon. Lord Decies
17	BERGIN, Joan
17	BERKERY, Michael
18	BEWICK, Pauline
18	BINCHY, Maeve
18	BINCHY, William
18	BIRD, Charlie
19	BIRTHISTLE, Lorcan Gerard
19	BLACK, Frances, Patricia
19	BLACK, Mary
19	BLACKSHAW, Basil
20	BLAKE, Rhona, Elizabeth
20	BLANEY, Orlaith
20	BLOOD, Baroness May
20	BODLEY, Seoirse
21	BOHAN, Edward 'Eddie'
21	BOLAND, Eavan, Ashling
21	BOLAND, Frank
21	BOLGER, Aisling
21	BOLGER, Dermot
22	BOLGER, James, Stephen 'Jim'
22	BOLTON, Ivan, Wesley
22	BOORMAN, John
23	BOUCHER-HAYES, Philip
23	BOUCHIER-HAYES, Timothy
23	BOURKE, Jonathan 'Jay'
23	BOWE, Mary, née Murphy
24	BOWLER, Gillian
24	BOWMAN, Dr John
24	BOYCE, Most Reverend, Philip
25	BOYD, Dermot, Gordon, Mahon
25	BOYLAN Ken, Brian, Patrick
25	BOYLE, Consolata, Mary
26	BRADSHAW, Lar
26	BRADY, Angela, Maria
26	BRADY, Conor
26	BRADY, Cyprian, Francis
27	BRADY, Francis, Brian, 'Rory'
27	BRADY, Dr, Hugh, Redmond
28	BRADY, Paul
28	BRADY, His Grace, The Most Reverend, Sean
28	BRADY, Thomas, John
28	BRAIDEN née Egan, Olive, Carmel
29	BRANDON, née Orr, Cherry, Ann
29	BRAYDEN, David, James
29	BRAZIL, Tony
30	BREATHNACH, Paddy
30	BREHENY, Martin
30	BREEN, Sean, Macarius
30	BRENNAN, Barry
30	BRENNAN, Brian
31	BRENNAN, Brian, Stephen
31	BRENNAN, Cecily
31	BRENNAN, Donald
31	BRENNAN, Eamonn, Noel
31	BRENNAN, Francis
32	BRENNAN, John Gerard
32	BRENNAN, John, Joseph
32	BRENNAN, Joseph 'Joe'
33	BRENNAN, Michael

64	COLLINS, Anthony M		79	CROWN John Paul
64	COLLINS, Finghin James		79	CROZIER, William 'Bill'
64	COLLINS, Liam		80	CRYAN, Mary Geraldine
64	COLLINS, Mary née Deasy		80	CULLEN, Martin
64	COLLINS, Sean M		80	CULLEN, Michael
65	COLLINS, Stephen		80	CULLEN, Michael
65	COLTON, Rt. Rev. William Paul		81	CULLEN, William 'Bill'
65	COMYN, Edward Frederick		81	CULLINAN, Bernadette Maria 'Bernie'
65	CONDELL, Catherine		81	CULLINANE, Stephen Joseph
65	CONNELL, His Eminence, Desmond, Cardinal		81	CUMMINS, Adrian
66	CONNELLY, Alpha Margaret		81	CURRAN, Edmund
66	CONNOLLY, Geraldine Denise		82	CURRAN, Noel, Anthony
66	CONNOLLY, Michele		82	CURRAN, Richard
66	CONSIDINE, Thomas		82	CURTIN, Donal
67	CONROY, Michael, Robert		82	CURTIS, Brendan
67	CONROY, Noel,		83	CUSACK, Evelyn
67	CONWAY, Patrick			
67	COOKE, Barrie		**D**	
67	COOMBES, Ian Francis			
68	COONEY, Garret		84	DALGARNO, Conor
68	COONEY, Marie Therèse née WHITE		84	DALY, His Eminence, Cathal Brendan
68	COONEY, Patrick		84	DALY, Frank
68	COOPER, Colm 'Gooch'		84	DALY, Francis 'Frank'
68	COOPER, Mathew Joseph 'Matt'		84	DALY, Seán
69	COOTE, John, Hugh		85	DANAHER, J. Gerard 'Gerry'
69	CONCANNON, John		85	DARDIS, John Michael
69	COPELAND, Louis		85	DAVERN, Michael
69	COPPEL, Andrew Maxwell		85	DAVIS, Julian
70	CORR, Andrea Jane		85	DAVIS, Mary
70	CORR, Caroline Georgine		86	DAWSON, Barbara
70	CORR, James Steven Ignatius 'Jim'		86	D'ARCY, Brian Fr
70	CORR, Sharon Helga		86	D'ARCY, Michael
71	CORRIGAN, Maria		86	D'ARCY, Raymond, Paul 'Ray'
71	COSGRAVE, Terence		87	DAVISON Rosanna Diane
71	COSTELLOE, Joe		87	DE BLACAM, Shane
71	COSTELLOE, Paul		87	de BRI, Orla
71	COSTIGAN John Francis		87	De BROMHEAD, Jerome Andrew
72	COUGHLAN, Mary		88	DE BRÚN, Bairbre
72	COULSON, Paul		88	DE BRUIN, née SMITH, Michelle
72	COULTER, Phil		88	DE BURGH, née DAVISON, Christopher, John 'Chris'
73	COVENEY, Simon		88	DE ROSSA, Prionsias
73	COWAN, Brian		89	De PAOR, Tomás, Proinsias
73	COWLEY, Dr. Jerry		89	De VALERA, Síle
74	COWLEY, Martin		89	de VERE WHITE, John, Frederick
74	COWMAN, Steve		89	DEANE, Raymond
74	COYLE, Brian		89	DEANE, Seamus
74	COYLE, John		90	DELANEY, John
75	CRAIG, Maurice James Waldron		90	DELANEY , John Gerald
75	CRAWFORD, Leo		90	DELANEY, Patrick 'Pat'
75	CREEDON John, Joseph		90	DEMPSEY, Noel
75	CROOKSHANK, Anne Olivia		91	DEMPSEY, Matthew, Austin 'Matt'
76	CRONIN, Anthony		91	DENHAM, Susan née Gageby
76	CROSBIE, Alan		91	DENT, Donna
76	CROSBIE, Henry 'Harry'		91	DERVAN, Michael
76	CROSBIE, Thomas Edward 'Ted'		92	DESMOND, Denis
77	CROSS, Dorothy		92	DESMOND, Dermot
77	CROWLEY, Brian		92	DILGER, David
77	CROWLEY, Caroline		93	DILLON CARRIGAN, Anne, née AUDIAT
77	CROWLEY, Carrie		93	DILLON OSB, Rt. Rev. Christopher
78	CROWLEY, Frances Majella		93	DILLON, John Myles
78	CROWLEY, Kieran James		93	DINEEN, Patrick J
78	CROWLEY, Laurence		94	DOBSON, Bryan
78	CROWLEY, Niall		94	DOHERTY, Kenneth, 'Ken'
78	CROWLEY, Peter		94	DOHERTY, Moya
79	CROWLEY, Philip		94	DOHERTY, Patrick, 'Pat'

127 FLOOD, Pamela
127 FLYNN Beverly
128 FLYNN, Pádraig
128 FLYNN, T Philip
128 FOLEY, Carmel
128 FOLEY, Sharon Ruth
129 FOLEY-NOLAN, Cliodhna Mary
129 FORDE, Aaron
129 FOX, Ian
129 FOX, Robbie
130 FOYLE, Mark Alexander
130 FRENCH, Arthur
130 FRIDAY, Gavin Fionán Hanvey
130 FRIEL, Brian
131 FRIEL, Hugh
131 FULLER, Ann
131 FURNESS Victor Anthony

G

132 GAFFNEY, Lucy
132 GAFFNEY, Dr. Maureen
132 GAGEBY, Patrick
132 GALLAGHER, Bernadette 'Bernie' née Doyle
133 GALLAGHER, Charles Hubert
133 GALLAGHER, Dermot
133 GALLAGHER, John
133 GALLAGHER, John
134 GALLAGHER, Paul Martin Joseph
134 GALLAGHER, Pat 'The Cope'
134 GALVIN, Barry St. John
134 GALVIN, Ian
135 GALVIN, John
135 GALWAY, Sir James
135 GANLY, Declan
136 GANNON, Gerard 'Gerry'
136 GARNIER, Katherine née McCrea
136 GARVEY, Donal
136 GAVIN, Patrick Francis 'Frankie'
137 GEOGHEGAN, The Hon. Mr Justice Hugh
137 GEOGHEGAN, Niall John
137 GERAGHTY, Barry John
137 GIBBONS, JJ
138 GIBBONS, PJ
138 GILLIGAN, Jack
138 GILMORE, Eamon
138 GILMORE, Brendan
139 GILSENAN, Alan John
139 GLEESON, Dermot
139 GLEESON, Eileen
139 GLEESON, Kate
140 GLEESON, Peter Joseph
140 GLYNN, John
140 GOAN, Cathal
140 GODSIL, Arthur
141 GOGGIN, Brian J
141 GOOD, Rev. Harold OBE
141 GOOD Rt Rev, Kenneth Raymond
142 GOODMAN, Larry
142 GORDAN, John Joseph
142 GORMAN, Richard
142 GORMAN, Tommy
143 GOULDING, William Lingard Walter
143 GRAHAM, Rev. Laurence Arthur Moore
143 GRAHAM, Ian Maklin

143 GRATZER, née Mc Court, Fiona
144 GRAY, Danuta
144 GREENE, Judy
144 GREEVY, Bernadette
145 GREENSLADE, Roy
145 GREGORY, Tony
145 GRIBBIN, Annie Patricia
145 GRIFFIN, Eamon
146 GUEST, David
146 GUILBAUD, Charles John
146 GUILBAUD, Patrick
146 GUINNESS, Hon. Desmond Walter
146 GUIRY, Michael Dominic Richard
147 GUNNE, Patrick Joseph Fintan
147 GUNNE O'CONNOR, Marianne

H

148 HALL, William Walmsley
148 HALLIGAN, Ursula Catherine
148 HAMILTON, Hugo
148 HAMILTON, James
149 HANAFIN, Mary
149 HANAHOE, Anthony J 'Tony'
149 HANLEY, Clare
149 HANLEY, James
150 HANLON Andrew
150 HAREN, Patrick Hugh
150 HARDIMAN, Hon. Mr Justice Adrian
150 HARDING, Michael
151 HARNEY, Mary
151 HARRINGTON, Jessica Jane née Fowler
151 HARRINGTON, Padraig
152 HARRINGTON, Lord William Henry Leicester
        Stanhope 'Bill'
152 HARRIS, Ann née O'Sullivan
152 HARRIS, Eoghan
152 HARRIS, Robert 'Pino'
153 HARVEY, David Gerard 'Dave'
153 HARVEY, Polly Jean 'PJ'
153 HASLETT, Lindsay James
153 HASTINGS, George William 'Billy' CBE
154 HAUGHEY, Seán F
154 HAUGHTON, Beth
154 HAVERTY, Anne
154 HAYES, Brian George
154 HAYES, Liam Patrick
155 HEALY, Andrew
155 HEALY, Jack
155 HEALY John Anthony
155 HEALY, Liam P
155 HEALY, Fr. Sean
156 HEALY, Tom
156 HEANEY, Seamus Justin
157 HEASLIP, F B 'Danno'
157 HEATHERINGTON, Rick
157 HEAVEY, Aidan
157 HEAVEY Patrick Garrett
157 HEDERMAN, Wendy E A
158 HEFFERNAN, Anne
158 HEFFERNAN, Kevin 'Heffo'
158 HEFFERNAN, Margaret neé Dunne
159 HEFFERNAN, Michael
159 HEGARTY, Adrian
159 HEGARTY, Diarmuid Arthur

W

Z

A

366   ANDERSON, Jennifer

B

366   BALDWIN, Alexander Rae 'Alec'
366   BALDWIN, Stephen
366   BALDWIN, William 'Billy'
366   BARRETT, Dr Craig R
366   BARTON, Mischa
366   BIDEN, Joseph Robinette Jnr 'Joe'
366   BOLAND, Dr Patrick J. FCRSI, FRCS
366   BOYLE, Fr. Gregory F 'Greg' SJ
367   BOYLE FLYNN, Lara
367   BRADY, James
367   BRADY, Tom
367   BREEN, Maura C
367   BRENNAN, Donald, Patrick 'Don'
367   BRESLIN, Jimmy,
367   BRODERICK, Matthew
36/   BROSANAN, James J
368   BROSNAN, Pierce Brendan
368   BUCHANAN, Pat
368   BUCKLEY Jr, William Frank 'WFB'
368   BURKE, Michèle
368   BURNS, Brian P
368   BURNS, Edward J 'Ed'
368   BYRNE, Gabriel

C

369   CAHILL, Dr. Kevin
369   CAHILL, Thomas
369   CALLAGHAN, Jeremiah
369   CALLAGHAN, Michael J
369   CAREY, Chase
369   CAREY, Dennis J
369   CAREY, Hugh Leo Carey
370   CAREY, Mariah
370   CARROLL, Pete
370   CASHMAN, Thomas J
370   CASSIDY, Gerald S. J 'Gerry'
370   CLEARY, Mark
370   CLINTON, William Jefferson Blythe IV 'Bill'
370   CLODAGH, de Sillery Phipps
371   CLOONEY, George
371   COLEMAN, Catherine G 'Cady'
371   COLLINS, Eileen
371   COLLINS, Susan
371   CONDRON, Christopher 'Kip' M
371   CONNOR, Christopher M 'Chris'
372   COOK, Richard 'Dick'
372   CORBOY, Michael R
372   CORCORAN, Barbara
372   CORCORAN, Thomas A 'Tom'
372   COSTNER, Kevin Michael
373   CURRAN, John
373   CURRY, Ann
373   CURRY, Karen

D

373   DALEY, Richard Michael
373   DALEY, William M

373   DALY, Charles U 'Chuck'
374   DALY, Lee Ann
374   DALY, Mary C
374   DAVIES LEWIS, Maryon
374   DAY - LEWIS, Daniel Michael Blake
374   De NIRO, Robert
374   DENNEDY FINNERAN, Michelle
374   DILLON, Gregory Rusell 'Greg'
375   DISNEY, Roy Edward
375   DODD, Christopher J 'Chris'
375   DODGE, née Moran, Lore
375   DOLAN, Peter Robert 'Bob'
375   DONAGHY, Patrick 'Pat'
375   DONAHOE, Thomas Joseph
376   DONAHUE, Phillip John 'Phil'
376   DOWD, Maureen
376   DOWLING, Michael
376   DOWLING, Vincent Gerard
376   DOWNEY, Roma
376   DUFFY, John G
377   DUFFY, Patrick
377   DUNFEY, John P
377   DUNFEY Robert J. 'Bob' Snr
377   DUNLEAVY, Michael Joseph
377   DUNNE, Dominick
377   DWYER, Jim

E

378   EGAN, His Eminence Cardinal Edward Michael
378   EGAN, Richard John
378   EGEN, Maureen Mahon
378   ESTEVEZ, Emilio

F

379   FARRELL, Colin J 'Coll'
379   FARRELL, Thomas F. II
379   FARROW, Maria de Lourdes Villiers 'Mia'
379   FEENEY, Charles F 'Chuck'
379   FINEGAN, Dr. Michael
379   FINUCANE, Anne
379   FITZGERALD, Garret Adare
380   FITZPATRICK, John
380   FLANIGAN, Dr. Timothy
380   FLATLEY, Michael Ryan
380   FLATLEY, Thomas E 'Tom'
380   FLYNN, William 'Bill'
380   FOLAN, Jon K
380   FORD, Harrison
381   FRAWLEY BAGLEY, Elizabeth
381   FUGAZY, William Denis 'Bill'

G

381   GALLAGHER, John E Snr
381   GALLAGHER, Peter
381   GARR, Teri
381   GARRITY RANK, Erin
382   GEORGE, Terry
382   GIBBONS, Michael J 'Mike'
382   GLUCKSMAN BRENNAN, Loretta
382   GRADY, Patricia
382   GREELEY, Rev. Dr. Andrew M
382   GRIFFIN, Mervyn Edward Jnr 'Merv'

H

383 HAMILL, Pete
383 HANNITY, Sean
383 HANRATTY, Donald
383 HARTNETT, John
383 HARTY, Patricia, 'Trish'
383 HAYDEN, Peter E 'Pete'
383 HAYES-WHITE, Joanne
383 HEALY, Denis J
384 HENNESSEY, John LeRoy
384 HICKEY, James
384 HIGGINS CLARK, Carol
384 HIGGINS CLARK, Mary
384 HIGGINS, Colonel Patrick
384 HIGGINS, James F
384 HILFIGER, Thomas Jacob 'Tommy'
384 HILTON, Paris
384 HILTON, William Barron
385 HUGHES, Sarah Elizabeth
385 HUSTON, Anjelica

I

385 ISDELL, E. Neville

K

386 KEENAN, Don
386 KELLEHER, Denis P
386 KELLEHER, Herbert David 'Herb'
386 KELLY, Dr, Daniel Fain
386 KELLY, Edmund F
386 KELLY, Raymond W 'Ray'
386 KENNEDY, Edward Moore 'Ted'
387 KENNEDY, Patrick Joseph
387 KENNEDY, Robert Francis Jr.
387 KENNEY, Edward 'Ed'
387 KENNY, Tom
387 KEOUGH, Donald R 'Don'
387 KING, Michael
388 KING, Peter T 'Pete'
388 KLINE, Kevin Delaney

L

388 LANE, Nathan
388 LANSBURY, Angela, Brigid
388 LEAHY, Patrick Joseph 'Pat'
388 LEAHY, William, S.J.
389 LEARY, Denis
389 LYNCH, John T
389 LYNCH, Peter S

M

390 MAGUIRE, Mary B
390 MAHONEY, John
390 MAHONY, His Eminence Cardinal Roger Michael
390 MALLON, Meg
390 MANNING, John P. 'Jack'
390 MARINEAU, Philip A 'Phil'
390 MARTIN, Stephen Glenn
390 MATTHEWS, Christopher, John 'Chris'
391 Mc AULIFFE, Terence 'Terry'

391 Mc CABE, Eugene
391 Mc CANN, James F 'Jim'
391 Mc CANN Robert J
391 Mc CARTHY, Paddy
391 Mc COURT, Frank
392 Mc COURT, Malachy
392 Mc DONALD, Marianne
392 Mc DONNELL, John 'Jack'
392 Mc ENROE, John Patrick Jnr
392 Mc GOVERN, Maureen Therese
392 Mc GRATH, Judith 'Judy'
392 Mc GUINN, Martin G 'Marty'
393 Mc KENNA, Andrew
393 Mc LOUGHLIN, Kieran
393 Mc MAHON, Vince Kennedy Jnr
393 Mc MULLEN, Michael
393 Mc NALLY, William J 'Bill'
393 MEANEY, Colm
393 MERIWETHER, John 'J.M'
394 MITCHELL, George John
394 MONAGHAN, Brian D
394 MOORE, Dr. George
394 MORAN, Thomas J 'Tom'
394 MOYNAHAN, Dr, Paula
394 MULCAHY, Anne
395 MULVIHILL, Daniel F 'Dan'
395 MURPHY, Bartholomew 'Bart'
395 MURPHY, James J 'Jimmy'
395 MURPHY, Martin J Jnr 'Marty'
395 MURRAY, William James 'Bill'

N

396 NAUGHTON, Eileen
396 NEESON, Liam
396 NOONAN, Margaret 'Peggy'

O

396 O'BRIEN, Conan
396 O'BRIEN, Archbishop Edward F 'Ed'
396 O'BRIEN, Soledad
396 O'BYRNE, Brian F
397 O'CONNOR, John
397 O'CONNOR, Patrick J
397 O'DONNELL, Christopher Eugene 'Chris'
397 O'DONNELL, Kelly
397 O'DONNELL, Rosie
397 O'DOWD, Niall
397 O'HARA, Maureen
398 O'LEARY, Stella
398 O'MALLEY, Sheila
398 O'NEILL, Tom
398 O'REILLY, Bill
398 O'REILLY, David J
398 O'ROURKE, Patrick Jake 'P.J'

P

399 PATAKI, George E
399 PHILBIN, Regis Francis Xavier 'Reege'
399 PURCELL, Dennis J
399 PURCELL, Patrick
399 PURCELL, Philip J 'Phil'

Q

400 QUICK, Thomas C
400 QUILTY, Shelly Ann
400 QUINN, James E
400 QUINN, Paul
400 QUINN, Peter

R

401 REGAN, Judith
401 REYNOLDS, Robert L 'Bob'
401 RILEY, Patrick James 'Pat'
401 ROARTY, Michael J 'Mike'
401 ROCHE, Kevin Eamonn
401 ROONEY, Daniel M 'Dan'
402 ROONEY, Patrick
402 ROONEY, Timothy 'Tim'
402 RUSSERT, Timothy John Jnr 'Tim'
402 RYAN, Arthur F
402 RYAN, John O
403 RYAN, Patrick G 'Pat'
403 RYAN, Pauline E
403 RYAN, Timothy James 'Tim'

S

404 SCHLOSSBERG KENNEDY, Caroline Bouvier
404 SCULLEY, Arthur B
404 SCULLEY, David
404 SCULLEY, John
404 SCULLY, Sean
404 SHEEHAN, Michael 'Mike'
404 SHEEHAN, Robert
405 SHEEN, Martin
405 SHRIVER, Maria Owings
405 SMITH KENNEDY, Jean
405 SMYTH, Edward D, 'Ted'
405 SOMMERS, Suzanne Marie (née Hamilton)
405 STACK, Brian
405 SULLIVAN, Brian
405 SULLIVAN, Craig G
405 SULLIVAN, James
406 SULLIVAN, Michael John 'Mike'
406 SWANSON, Denis D
406 SWEENEY, Anne
406 SWEENEY, John J

T

407 TANI, Dan
407 THOMPSON, H. Brian
407 TILLOTSON, John
407 TIMMONS, Edward
407 TIMONEY, John
407 TIMONEY, Peter Joseph
408 TOWNSEND, Stuart
408 TULLY, Daniel P 'Dan'

U

408 UNGARO KELLEHER , Susan

V

409 VAN KIRK, Francis J 'Fran'
409 VAN SUSTEREN, Greta
409 VARGO, Trina Y
409 VINCENT – KIERAN, A.W.B 'Billie'

W

409 WALSH, James
409 WALSH, John
409 WALSH, Siobhan
410 WALSH, William 'Bill'
410 WELCH, John Francis Jnr 'Jack'
410 WESTMAN, Tom
410 WHELAN, Wendy
410 WILMOT, Helen M

rrington Barry Bartels Barton Bates Begg Behan Bennett Benton Beresford Bergin Berkery Bewick Binchy Bird Birt
wman Boyce Boyd Boylan Boyle Bradshaw Brady Braiden Brandon Brayden Brazil Breathnach Breen Breheny B
nburdon Burke Burns Burnside Burrows Burton Butler Byrne Byron Caffrey Cagney Cahill Cairnduff Callaghan
vanagh Cawley Chadwick Chawke Chesneau Church Claffey Clancy Clandillion Clarke Clayton Cleary Clifford
nnell Connelly Connolly Conroy Considine Conway Cooke Coombes Cooney Cooper Coote Copeland Coppel Cor
onin Crookshank Crosbie Cross Crowley Crown Crozier Cryan Ullen Cullinan Cummins Curran Curtin Curtis Cusa
or De Rossa De Valera De Vere-White Deane Delaney Dempsey Denham Dent Dervan Desmond Dilger Dillon Carrig
yle Drew Drumm Drury Duffy Duggan Dukes Dungan Dunican Dunne Dunphy Durcan Durkan Dwyer Eames E
nelly Fenner Ferran Ferris Fewer Fiacc Filan Finan Fingleton Finlay Geoghegan Finn Finnegan Finucane Fitzgerald
rness Gaffney Gageby Gallagher Galvin Galway Ganly Gannon Garnier Garvey Gavin Geoghegan Geraghty Gibb
ay Greene Greenslade Greevy Gregory Gribin Griffin Guest Guilbaud Guinness Guiry Gunne Hall Halligan Ham
ughton Haverty Hayes Healy Heaney Heaslip Heatherington Heavey Hederman Heffernan Hegarty Hemphill Henc
gan Holland Hollywood Holman Hooper Horan Horgan Houlihan Howlin Hughes Hunt Hunter Hurley Huxley Hyc
an Keane Kearney Kearns Keating Keaveney Keena Keenan Keher Keighery Kelleher Kelly Kennedy Kennelly Kenny
sella Kitt Knuttle Kürten, Lally Lanigan Lappin Lavan Lawlor Le Brocquy Lee Lenihan Lennon Leonard Leslie Levis
nn Mac Conghaill Mac Entee Mac Menamin Maccarthy Macdougald Macgonigal Mackey Macri Madden Magee
rrinan Quinn Marshall Martin Maughan Maurer Maxwell Mayes Mc Aleese Mc Ardle Mc Caffrey Mc Cann Mc Cart
Cullough Mc Dolald Mc Donagh Mc Donald Mc Donnell Mc Donogh Mc Dowell Mc Eniff Mc Evaddy Mc Evoy Mc F
Guinness Mc Guire Mc Hugh Mc Kee Mc Kenna Mc Keon Mc Laughlin Mc Laverty Mc Lean Mc Lellanmc Lelland M
ade Meagher Mealy Mee Miller Milton Minihan Miskimmon Mitchell Mohan Mohlich Molloy Moloney Molony
lhern Mullen Mulligan Mullin Mullins Mulryan Mulvihill Mumba Murless Murphy Murray Murtagh Musgrave Mye
Shuilleabháin Nickerson Nolan Noonan Norris Nugent O'Driscoll Ó Briain Ó Caolain Ó Ceidigh Ó Curreáin
Cuinneagáin O'Dea O'Donoghue O'Driscoll O'Flynn O'Mahony O'Malley O'Brien O'Callaghan O'Connor O'Con
Hare O'Higgins O'Kane O'Kelly O'Loan O'Magan O'Mahony O'Malley O'Mara Walsh O'Meara O'Neill O'Reilly
sley Parker Parkhill Parlon Parsons Patterson Pearce Pearson Peng Pettit Phelan Philips Phillips Pierse Piggott Pike Pils
inlan Quinlivan Quinn Quirk Rabbitte Rapple Rea Redlich Redmond Reed Reid Reihill Reynolds Rice Robinson Roch
hmidt Scott Scott-Lennon Née Fitzpatrick Scully Seoige Sexton Shanley Shannon Sheehan Sheehy Sheeran Shefflin
ring Stafford Stagg Standún Stapleton Staunton Stein Stephenson Stewart Stokes Swan Sweeney Taaffe Taggart Tan
omey Turley Turner Twomey Upton Vervelde Von Prondzynski Wall Wallace Walsh Watchman Waterford Waters Weld
ams Agar Agnew Ahearn Ahern Aiken Aikins Akram Alderdice Allen Andrews Arnold Aungier Austin Aylward Bac
han Bennett Benton Beresford Bergin Berkery Bewick Binchy Bird Birthistle Black Blackshaw Blake Blaney Blood Bo
ady Braiden Brandon Brayden Brazil Breathnach Breen Breheny Brennan Breslin Brett Brighton Britton Brophy Bros
tler Byrne Byron Caffrey Cagney Cahill Cairnduff Callaghan Callan Callanan Callely Callery Campbell Canavan C
affey Clancy Clandillion Clarke Clayton Cleary Clifford Cloake Clune Coady Cody Coen Coffey Cogan Coghlan Co
ombes Cooney Cooper Coote Copeland Coppel Corrigan Cosgrave Costelloe Costigan Coughlan Coulson Coulter
yan Ullen Cullinan Cummins Curran Curtin Curtis Cusack D'arcy Dalgarno Daly Danaher Dardis Avern Davis Da
mpsey Denham Dent Dervan Desmond Dilger Dillon Carrigan Dineen Dobson Doherty Donleavy Donlon Donne
ungan Dunican Dunne Dunphy Durcan Durkan Dwyer Eames Earley Megan Empey English Ennis Enright Erwin Eva
gleton Finlay Geoghegan Finn Finnegan Finucane Fitzgerald Fitzgibbon Fitzpatrick Flanagan Flannery Flavin Flem
nly Gannon Garnier Garvey Gavin Geoghegan Geraghty Gibbons Gilligan Gilmore Gilsenan Gleeson Glynn Goan
iffin Guest Guilbaud Guinness Guiry Gunne Hall Halligan Hamilton Hanafin Hanahoe Hanley Hanlon Hardiman
atherington Heavey Hederman Heffernan Hegarty Hemphill Henderson Heneghan Hennessy, Henry Heraty Herbst H
rgan Houlihan Howlin Hughes Hunt Hunter Hurley Huxley Hyde Hyland Hynes Inchiquin Ioakimides Irwin Jackson Je
enan Keher Keighery Gallagher Kelly Kennedy Kennelly Kenny Keogh Keohane Kerins Kerr Kett Keyes Kiberd Kielty K
van Lawlor Le Brocquy Lee Lenihan Lennon Leonard Leslie Levis Lewis Leyden Lillingston Linehan Liston Lloyd We
ccarthy Macdougald Macgonigal Mackey Macri Madden Magee Magnier Maguire Maher Mallaghan Mallin Malon
xwell Mayes Mc Aleese Mc Ardle Mc Caffrey Mc Cann Mc Cartan Mc Carthy Mc Clarty Mc Clean Mc Closkey Mc C
Donnell Mc Donogh Mc Dowell Mc Eniff Mc Evaddy Mc Evoy Mc Fadden Mc Gann Mc Garry Mc Geady Mc Geary
nna Mc Keon Mc Laughlin Mc Laverty Mc Lean Mc Lellanmc Lelland Mc Loughlin Mc Manus Mc Namara Mc Nichol
nihan Miskimmon Mitchell Mohan Mohlich Molloy Moloney Molony Montague Moore Moran Moriarty Morrice M
lryan Mulvihill Mumba Murless Murphy Murray Murtagh Musgrave Myers Nagle Nash Nathan Naughton Neill Nellis
rris Nugent O'Driscoll Ó Briain Ó Caolain Ó Ceidigh Ó Curreáin Ó Dubhghaill Ó Fiannachta Ó Gallchóir Ó Hailpín
Mahony O'Malley O'Brien O'Callaghan O'Connor O'Conor O'Cuiv O'Donnell O'Donoghue O'Donovan O'Drisc
Mahony O'Malley O'Mara Walsh O'Meara O'Neill O'Reilly O'Riordan O'Rorke O'Rourke O'Shea O'Suilleabháin O
rson Peng Pettit Phelan Philips Phillips Pierse Piggott Pike Pilsworth Ponsonby Powell Power Prasifka Pratt Prendergas
dlich Redmond Reed Reid Reihill Reynolds Rice Robinson Rocha Roche Rochford Rogers Rohan Rolfe Ronan Roone
oige Sexton Shanley Shannon Sheehan Sheehy Sheeran Shefflin Sheridan Sherry Shipsey Shortall Shovlin Sinnott